D0460822

NOTABLE
SCIENTISTS
FROM 1900 TO THE PRESENT

NOTABLE

SCIENTISTS

FROM 1900 TO THE PRESENT

VOLUME
4
N-S

Brigham Narins, Editor

Contents

Introduction

E very year The Gale Group receives numerous requests from librarians for sources providing biographical information. *Notable Scientists: 1900 to the Present* has been designed specifically to fill a niche for scientific biographies. This set, which is the updated second edition of *Notable Twentieth-Century Scientists* and its accompanying volume, *Notable Twentieth-Century Scientists Supplement,* provides students, educators, librarians, researchers, and general readers with an affordable and comprehensive source of biographical information on approximately 1,600 scientists active in the twentieth century in all of the natural, physical, and applied sciences, including the traditionally studied subjects of astronomy, biology, botany, chemistry, earth science, mathematics, medicine, physics, technology, and zoology, as well as the more recently established and as yet sparsely covered fields of computer science, ecology, engineering, and environmental science. *Notable Scientists: 1900 to the Present* is international in scope, and its coverage ranges from the well-known scientific giants of the early twentieth century to contemporary scientists working on the latest advances in their fields.

Superior Coverage of Women, Minority, and Non-Western Scientists

Addressing the growing interest in and demand for biographical information on women, minority, and non-Western scientists, *Notable Scientists: 1900 to the Present* also seeks to bring to light the achievements of women scientists, Asian American, African American, Hispanic American, and Native American scientists, as well as scientists from countries outside North America and Western Europe. Due to the scarcity of published information on these scientists, information for many of the sketches on these listees has been obtained through telephone interviews and correspondence with the scientists themselves or with their universities, companies, laboratories, or families. Our hope is that in presenting these entries, we are providing a basis for future research on the lives and contributions of these important and historically marginalized segments of the scientific community.

Inclusion Criteria

A preliminary list of scientists was compiled from a wide variety of sources, including established reference works, history of science indexes, science periodicals, awards lists, and suggestions from organizations and associations. The advisory board evaluated the names and made suggestions for inclusion. Final selection of names to include was made by the editors on the basis of the following criteria:

■ Discoveries, inventions, overall contributions, influence, or impact on scientific progress in the twentieth century

■ Receipt of a major science award, including Nobel Prizes in Physics, Chemistry, and Physiology or Medicine, the Fields Medal (mathematics), Albert Lasker awards (medicine), the Tyler Prize (environmental science), the National Medal of Science, and the National Medal of Technology

■ Involvement or influence in education, organizational leadership, or public policy

■ Familiarity to the general public

■ Notable "first" achievements, including degrees earned, positions held, or organizations founded; several listees involved in the first space flights are also included

Entries Provide Easy Access to Information

Entries are arranged alphabetically by surname. The typical *Notable Scientists: 1900 to the Present* entry provides the following information:

■ **Entry head**—offers at-a-glance information: name, birth/death dates, nationality, and primary field(s) of specialization.

■ **Biographical essay**—ranges from 400 to 2500 words and provides basic biographical information, including date and place of birth, name(s) of spouse(s) and children, educational background and degrees earned, etc. The primary focus of the essay, however, is the subject's scientific endeavors and achievements, all of which are explained in prose accessible to high school students and readers who do not possess a scientific background. Headings within the essays highlight the significant events in the subject's life and career, allowing readers to easily find information they seek. Bold-faced names in the entries direct readers to other entries found in *Notable Scientists: 1900 to the Present*.

■ **Selected Writings** by the Scientist section—lists representative publications, including important papers, textbooks, research works, autobiographies, lectures, etc.

■ **Further Reading** section—provides citations of biographies, interviews, periodicals, obituaries, and other sources about the subject for readers seeking additional information.

Indexes Provide Numerous Points of Access

In addition to the complete list of scientists and the Chronology of Scientific Advancement found at the beginning of each volume, readers seeking more information can consult the four indexes at the end of Volume 5 for additional listings:

■ **Field of Specialization Index**—groups listees according to the scientific fields to which they have contributed.

■ **Gender Index**—provides lists of the women and men covered.

■ **Nationality/Ethnicity Index**—arranges listees by country of birth, citizenship, or ethnic heritage.

■ **Comprehensive Subject Index**—provides volume and page references for scientists and scientific terms used in the text. Includes cross references.

Photographs

Individuals in *Notable Scientists: 1900 to the Present* come to life in the 443 photos of the scientists.

Advisory Board

Contributors

Russell Aiuto, Ethan E. Allen, Julie Anderson, Olga K. Anderson, Denise Irene Arnold, Kenneth E. Ball, Nancy Bard, Dorothy J. Barnhouse, Jeffrey Bass, Karl Leif Bates, Madeleine D. Beckman, Matthew A. Bille, Maurice Bleifeld, Michael J. Boersma, Ervin Bonkalo, Janice Borzendowski, Barbara Boughton, Stephen Bowlsby, Barbara Branca, Barbara A. Branch, Hovey Brock, Michael Broder, Tammy J. Bronson, Valerie J. Brown, Leonard C. Bruno, Ray Bullock, Bryan H. Bunch, Margorie Burgess, Gerard Buskes, Joe Cain, Jill Carpenter, Chris Cavette, Katherine Chapin, Dennis W. Cheek, Kenneth Chiacchia, Miyoko Chu, Jacquelyn Coggin, Anne Compliment, Jane Stewart Cook, Kelly Cooper, Victor I. Cox, G. Scott Crawford, Thomas P. Crawford, Wendy Crooks-Frazier, Wilbur Cross, Michael T. Cruz, Antonella Cupillari, Karin M Deck, Lori DeMilto, Margaret DiCanio, Mindi Dickstein, Laurie DiMauro, Simon Dixon, Rowan L. Dordick, John Henry Dreyfuss, Thomas Drucker, Kala Dwarakanath, Marianne Fedunkiw, Martin R. Feldman, Eliseo Fernandez, George A. Ferrance, Jerome P. Ferrance, James R. Flanders, William Fletcher, David N. Ford, Fran Locher Freiman, Randall Frost, George L. Garrigues, Amanda de la Garza, Karyn Hede George, C. J. Giroux, Sheila Gray, Chris Hables Gray, Loretta Hall, Bridget K. Hall, Ernst P. Hamm, Betsy Hanson, Robert M. Hawthorne Jr., Carolyn Hemenway, Elizabeth Henry, Thomas A. Heppenheimer, Frank Hertle, Fran Hodgkins, Gillian S. Holmes, Dale (John) D. Hunley, Kelley Reynolds Jacquez, Roger Jaffe, Jessica Jahiel, Jeanne Spriter James, J. Sydney Jones, D. George Joseph, Mark J. Kaiser, Lee C. Katterman, Sandra Katzman, Janet Kieffer Kelley, Evelyn B. Kelly, Karen Susan Kelly, Roseann Kent, Roberta Klarreich, James Klockow, Susan Kolmer, Geeta Kothari, Jennifer Kramer, Marc Kusinitz, Steve LaRue, Roger D. Launius, Penelope Lawbaugh, Benedict A. Leerburger, Jeanne Lesinski, Linda Lewin, Paul Lewon, John E. Little, Pamela O. Long, Carol Lord, Anne Hladio Macios, Barbara Magalnick, Laura Mangan-Grenier, Gail B. C. Marsella, Liz Marshall, Renee Mastrocco, Patricia M. McAdams, William M. McBride, Mike W. McClure, Avril McDonald, Chris McGrail, Kim McGrail, Donald J. McGraw, William McPeak, Carla Mecoli-Kamp, Leslie A. Mertz, Robert Messer, Philip Metcalfe, Fei Fei Wang Metzler, George A. Milite, Tony Mitchell, Carol L. Moberg, Sally M. Moite, Patrick Moore, Paula M. Morin, Angie Mullig, J. Paul Myers, Miriam Nagel, Margo Nash, Laura Newman, David E. Newton, Joan Oleck, Donna Olshansky, Kristin Palm, Geriann P. Park, Nicholas Pease, Isleta L. Pement, Daniel Pendick, David A. Petechuk, Annette Petrusso, Tom K. Phares, Devera Pine, Karl Preuss, Rayma Prince, Pamela Proffitt, Barbara J. Proujan, Amy M. Punke, Lewis Pyenson, Jeff Raines, Mary B. Raum, Leslie Reinherz, John Rhea, Vita Richman, Jordan P. Richman, Larry Riddle, Marijke Rijsberman, Francis J. Rogers, Terrie M. Romano, Dan Rooney, Joshua Rosenbaum, Nancy Ross-Flanigan, Shari Rudavsky, Ted Rueter, Doris Runey, Kathy Sammis, Karen Sands, Neeraja Sankaran, Joel Schwarz, Philip Duhan Segal, Margaret M. Seiler, John A. Shanks, Susan Shelly, Alan R. Shepherd, Joel Simon, Michael Sims, Sankar Sitaraman, Doug Smith, Caroline B. D. Smith, Julian A. Smith, Linda Wasmer Smith, Lawrence Souder, Daniel A. Spatz, Dorothy Ann Spencer, John Spizzirri, David Sprinkle, Darwin H. Stapleton, Monica Stevens, Melissa A. Stewart, Sharon Fine Suer, Maureen L. Tan, Peter Hyde Taylor, David R. Teske, Melinda Jardon Thach, Sebastian Thaler, Brenda Tilke, Russell F. Trimble, Carol Turkington, Melissa Vaughn, Patricia M. Walsh, Cynthia Washam, Giselle Weiss, Wallace M. White, Katherine Williams, Nicholas Williamson, Philip K. Wilson, Rodolfo A Windhausen, Karen Withem, Alexandra M. Witze, Emily J. Yaghmour, Joshua Yoder, Cathleen M. Zucco.

Photo Credits

Photographs and illustrations appearing in *Notable Scientists* were received from the following sources. Every effort has been made to trace copyright, but if omissions have been made, please let us know.

Abraham, Edward, photograph. University of Oxford. Reproduced by permission. Ahlfors, Lars (pursed lips, saggy skin), Oberwolfach, Germany, 1988, photograph. Mathematisches Forschungsinstitut, Oberwolfach. Reproduced by permission. Aki, Keiiti, photograph. Reproduced by permission. Alfven, Hannes Olof Gosta, photograph. Nordisk Pressefoto/Archive Photos, Inc. Reproduced by permission. Alpher, Ralph A., photograph. Reproduced by permission. An Wang (posing next to a computer), photograph. Corbis-Bettmann. Reproduced by permission. Anderson, Carl D., photograph. AP/Wide World Photos. Reproduced by permission. Anderson, Dr. Gloria L., photograph. AP/Wide World Photos, Inc. Reproduced by permission. Anfinsen, Christian, photograph. AP/Wide World Photos, Inc. Reproduced by permission. Apgar, Virginia, photograph. The Mount Holyoke Archives and Special Collections. Reproduced by permission. Askey, Richard (standing in front of steps), Oberwolfach, Germany, 1977, photograph. Mathematisches Forschungsinstitut Oberwolfach. Reproduced by permission. Atanasoff, John, Ames, Iowa, 1983, photograph. AP/Wide World Photos, Inc. Reproduced by permission. Auger, Pierre (sitting with George P. Miller, and James A. Van Allen), photograph. UPI/Corbis-Bettmann. Reproduced by permission. Avery, Mary Ellen, photograph. Reproduced by permission. Avery, Oswald (with petri dish), photograph. AP/Wide World Photos, Inc. Reproduced by permission. Baade, Walter (smoking pipe), photograph. Corbis-Bettmann. Reproduced by permission. Babcock, Horace W. (wearing dark frame round glasses), photograph. Archive Photos, Inc. Reproduced by permission. Bakker, Dr. Robert (standing with Brontosaur bone), photograph by Francois Gohier. Photo Researchers, Inc. Reproduced by permission. Baltimore, David, 1975, photograph. AP/Wide World Photos, Inc. Reproduced by permission. Bardeen, John, photograph. AP/Wide World Photos. Reproduced by permission. Barghoorn, Else Sterren (sitting at side of desk), photograph. UPI/Corbis-Bettmann. Reproduced by permission. Beadle, George W., photograph. AP/Wide World Photos, Inc. Reproduced by permission. Bellow, Alexandra, photograph. Mathematisches Forschungsinstitut Oberwolfach. Reproduced by permission. Berners-Lee, Tim, photograph by Stephan Savoia. AP/Wide World Photos. Reproduced by permission. Bethe, Hans (at chalkboard), 1976, photograph. AP/Wide World Photos, Inc. Reproduced by permission. Bigeleisen, Dr. Jacob with T.J. Thompson, Dr. Albert Latter, Dr. Marshall Rosenbluth, and Glenn T. Seaborg, Ernest Orlando Lawrence Memorial Awards, photograph. AP/Wide World Photos. Reproduced by permission. Bird, R. Byron, photograph. University of Maryland. Reproduced by permission. Birkhoff, Garrett (tie with concentric circle design), photograph. Mathematisches Forschungsinstitut Oberwolfach. Reproduced by permission. Blobel, Gunter, Howard Hughes Medical Institute, Rockefeller University, New York, photograph. ©AFP/CORBIS. Reproduced by permission. Bloch, Konrad (seated at desk), photograph. AP/Wide World Photos, Inc. Reproduced by permission. Blodgett, Katharine Burr, photograph. General Electric Research and Development. Reproduced by permission. Blum, lenore (long, thick flowing dark hair), Berkeley, California, photograph. Mathematisches Forschungsinstitut Oberwolfach. Reproduced by permission. Blumberg, Dr. Baruch S., photograph. AP/Wide World Photos. Reproduced by permission. Bolin, Bert, 1997, photograph. AP/Wide World Photos. Reproduced by permission. Borlaug, Norman (standing in a field of wheat), photograph. AP/Wide World Photos. Reproduced by permission. Boyer, Paul, photograph. Reproduced by permission. Bragg, W.L., photograph. AP/Wide World Photos. Reproduced by permission. Brans, Carl, photograph. Reproduced by permission. Bremermann, Hans (open necked white shirt), Berekely, California, 1984, photograph. Mathematisches Forschungsinstitut Oberwolfach. Reproduced by permission. Bridges, Calvin B., photograph. National Academy of Sciences. Reproduced by permission. Bromley, D. Allan, photograph. Reproduced by permission. Bruce Ames (gesturing in front of a blackboard), photograph. AP/Wide World Photos. Reproduced by permission. Burbidge, Margaret, (head and shoulders) portrait. UPI/Corbis-Bettmann. Reproduced by permission. Burkitt, Denis (wearing tweed jacket), photograph. London Daily Express/Archive Photos, Inc. Reproduced by permission. Butenandt, Adolf, photograph. Deutche Presse/Archive Photos, Inc. Reproduced by permission. Cairns, John, portrait. AP/Wide World Photos. Reproduced by permission. Caldicott, Helen, photograph. AP/Wide World Photos. Reproduced by permission. Callender, Dr. Clive, 1987, photograph. AP/Wide World Photos. Reproduced by permission. Cannon, Annie J. (looking at photographic plates), photograph. UPI/Corbis-Bettmann. Reproduced by permission. Carothers, Wallace H., stretching rubber, photograph,. AP/Wide World Photos. Reproduced by permission. Carson, Dr. Ben (with model human brain), photograph. AP/Wide World Photos. Reproduced by permission. Carson, Rachel, 1971, photograph. AP/Wide World Photos. Reproduced by permission. Cartan, Elie Joseph (wearing shirt with pointed collar, his right side shadowed), 1920, photograph. Mathematisches Forschungsinstitut, Oberwolfach. Reproduced by permission. Cartan, Henri (with Mrs. D.J. Struik), photograph. UPI/Corbis-Bettmann. Reproduced by permission. Chadwick, James (standing next to a fireplace), photograph. AP/Wide World Photos. Reproduced by permission. Chandrasekhar, Subrahmanyan, 1983, photograph by Charlie Knoblock. AP/Wide World Photos, Inc. Reproduced by permission. Chandrasekhar, Subrahmanyan (seated), photograph. UPI/Corbis-Bettmann. Reproduced by permission. Chinn, May Edward, photograph. AP/Wide World Photos. Reproduced by permission. Chomsky, Noam (seated in chair), photograph. © Donna Coveney. Reproduced by permission. Chu Paul Ching-Wu, photograph. UPI/Bettmann. Reproduced by permission. Chu, Steven, photograph by L. A. Cicero. Stanford University News Service. Reproduced by permission. Clemence, Gerald M., (comparing illustrations of the moon), photograph. AP/Wide World Photos, Inc. Reproduced by permission. Cohen, Stanley, King Carl Gustav (Cohen receiving Nobel Prize from Gustav), photograph by Rolf Hamilton. Reuters/Archive Photos. Reproduced by permission. Cohen, Tannoudji Claude (in his laboratory), 1997, photograph. Agence France Presse/Corbis-Bettmann. Reproduced by permission. Colburn, Theo, photograph. Reproduced by permission. Commoner, Barry, (with a copy of his book "Making Peace With the Planet"), photograph. AP/Wide World Photos. Reproduced by permission. Condon, Edward U., photograph. National Academy of Sciences. Reproduced by permission. Cooley, Denton photograph. Archive Photos. Reproduced by permission. Cori, Gerty and Carl F. Cori, portrait. UPI/Bettmann Newsphotos. Reproduced by permission. Cousteau, Jacques (arms crossed in front of him), photograph. Corbis-Bettmann. Reproduced by permission. Cowings, Patricia, photograph. AP/Wide World Photos. Reproduced by permission. Cray, Seymour (jacket flung over shoulder), photograph. AP/Wide World Photos, Inc. Reproduced by permission. Crick, Francis, (sitting in front of a blackboard), photograph. The Bettmann Archive. Reproduced by permission. Crutzen, Paul, photograph. Agence France Presse/Corbis-Bettmann. Reproduced by permission. Curie, Marie, photograph. AP/Wide World Photos. Reproduced by permission. Curl, Robert (holding ˇbuckyballˇ), photograph. Reuters/Andrees A. Latif/Archive Photos, Inc. Reproduced by permission. Dale, Henry, 1954, photograph. AP/Wide World Photos. Reproduced by permission. Dallmeier, Francisco, (holding a monkey), photograph. Courtesy of Francisco Dallmeier. Reproduced by permission. Darden, Christine Mann, photograph. AP/Wide World Photos. Reproduced by permission. de Forest, Dr. Lee and Shockley, Dr. William, photograph. AP/Wide World Photos. Reproduced by permission. DeBakey, Dr. Michael, photograph by Donna Carson. AP/Wide World Photos, Inc. Reproduced by permission. Diamond, Dr. Jared, photograph. AP/Wide World Photos. Reproduced by permission. Dicke, Robert H. (wearing tweed jacket, white shirt, striped tie), photograph. UPI/Corbis-Bettmann. Reproduced by permission. Doherty, Peter, photograph. Reuters/News Limited/Archive Photos, Inc. Reproduced by permission. Dolby, Ray (holding film up to light), photograph. The Gamma Liaison Network. © Liaison Agency. Reproduced by permission. Drew, Charles Richard (with microscope), photograph. AP/Wide World Photos. Reproduced by permission. Drickamer, Harry G., photograph. Reproduced by permission. Durrell, Gerald, monkey on back, photograph. AP/Wide World Photos, Inc. Reproduced by permission. Earle, Dr. Sylvia (diving outside the Aquarius underwater habitat), 1998, Florida Keys National Marine Sanctuary, Key Largo, Florida, photograph. AP/Wide World Photos. Reproduced by permission. Eckert, J. Presper, photograph. AP/Wide World Photos, Inc. Reproduced by permission. Eddington, Arthur (holding pipe), photograph. UPI/Corbis-Bettmann. Reproduced by permission. Edison, Thomas and George Eastman (showing first Kodak color movie film), Rochester, N.Y., 1928, photograph. AP/Wide World Photos, Inc. Reproduced by permission. Ehrlich, Paul (in field), photograph. AP/Wide World Photos. Reproduced by permission. Ehrlich, Paul with Dr. Anne Ehrlich, Dr. Richard Turco and Soviet scientist Dr. Georgiy Golitsyn, Scientists Against Nuclear Arms (SANA) conference on "Britain after Nuclear War," London, photograph. AP/Wide World Photos. Reproduced by permission. Eisenhower, Dwight, Walter H. Spinks, Charles C. Finucane, Mylon Merriam, Walter S. McAfee, Franklin D. Orth, (Eisenhower, meeting with grant recipients), 1956, photograph. UPI/Corbis-Bettmann. Reproduced by permission. Elion, Gertrude (in the laboratory), photograph. UPI/Corbis-Bettmann. Reproduced by permission. Erdos, Paul (close-up of face, open-necked shirt), photograph. Mathematisches Forschungsinstitut Oberwolfach. Reproduced by permission. Ewing, Maurice (seated in his office), photograph. AP/Wide World Photos. Reproduced by permission. Fabry, Charles (with Henri Abrahams), 1924, photograph. UPI/Corbis-Bettmann. Reproduced by permission. Fairbank, William M., 1965, photograph. UPI/Corbis-Bettmann. Reproduced by permission. Falconer, Etta, photograph. Reproduced by permission. Farnsworth, Philo (holding television tube), 1929, photograph. UPI/Corbis-Bettmann. Reproduced by permission. Fasenmyer, Sister Mary, photograph. A.K. Peters Ltd. Reproduced by permission. Fauci, Dr. Anthony S., photograph. AP/Wide World Photos. Reproduced by permission. Ferguson, Lloyd, photograph. Reproduced by permission. Flanagan, James L., 1974, photograph. UPI/Corbis-Bettmann. Reproduced by permission. Flory, Paul J., photograph. AP/Wide World Photos. Reproduced by permission. Folkers, Dr. Karl, photograph by Rudy Baum. Courtesy of C&EN News. Reproduced by permission. Fossey, Dian (surrounded by gorillas, holding camera in right hand), photograph. AP/Wide World Photos. Reproduced by permission. Fred Hoyle, photograph. UPI/Corbis-Bettmann. Reproduced by permission. Fredholm, Ivar (bushy grey mustache, white hair), photograph. Mathematisches Forschungsinstitut Oberwolfach. Reproduced by permission. Frisch, Dr. Karl, photograph. AP/Wide World Photos. Reproduced by permission. Fujita, Dr. Tatsuya and Sumiko Fujita, portrait. AP/Wide World Photos. Reproduced by permission. Fuller, Solomon Carter, photograph. Reproduced by permission. Gabor, Dr. Dennis (examining spool of film or tape), 1969, photograph. AP/Wide World Photos, Inc. Reproduced by permission. Galdikas, Dr. Birute (being embraced by two orangutans), Borneo, photograph. The Gamma Liaison Network. © Liaison Agency. Reproduced by permission. Gallo, Robert, photograph. Archive Photos, Inc. Reproduced by permission. Gates, Bill, photograph. Geiger, Hans Wilhelm (seated in laboratory), photograph. Corbis-Bettmann. Reproduced by permission. Gelfond, Aleksandr O. (head and shoulders), drawing. Mathematisches Forschungsinstitut Oberwolfach. Reproduced by permission. Gell-Mann, Murray (seated at desk), 1969, photograph. AP/Wide World Photos. Reproduced by permission. Ghiroso, Albert, teaching a class, photograph. AP/Wide World Photo. Reproduced by permission. Gilbert, Walter, photograph. AP/Wide World Photos. Reproduced by permission. Gilman, Alfred (standing in laboratory), photograph. AP/Wide World Photos, Inc. Reproduced by permission. Glenn, John, Astronaut, speaking at a news conference, photograph by Pat Sullivan. AP/Wide World Photo. Reproduced by permission. Godel, Kurt (white carnation in lapel), 1951, photograph. AP/Wide World Photos, Inc. Reproduced by permission. Gold, Thomas, photograph. AP /Wide World Photos. Reproduced by permission. Goldhaber, Dr. Maurice, photograph. AP/Wide World Photos. Reproduced by permission. Gould, Stephen; Christian Alfinson; and Francisco Ayala (standing, holding papers), photograph by Ron Bennett. UPI/Corbis-Bettmann. Reproduced by permission. Gould, Stephen Jay (seated, arms crossed over), photograph. AP/Wide World Photos. Reproduced by permission. Gourdine, Meredith, (working with research experiment), photograph. AP/Wide World Photos. Reproduced by permission. Grier, Herbert E., photograph. EG&G, Inc. Reproduced by permission. Groves, Major General Leslie, photograph. AP/Wide World Photos. Reproduced by permission. Guion Buford (in space shuttle simulator), photograph. AP/Wide World Photos. Reproduced by permission. Haber, Fritz, photograph. AP/Wide World Photos, Inc. Reproduced by permission. Harris, Wesley L., photograph. AP/Wide World Photos, Inc. Reproduced by permission. Hawking, Stephen (in wheelchair), photograph. AP/Wide World Photos. Reproduced by permission. Healy, Bernadine, photograph. American Heart Association. Reproduced by permission. Hermite, Charles (reading, holding book in both hands), photograph. Corbis-Bettmann. Reproduced by permission. Hilbert, David (his left hand on piece of paper), photograph. Corbis-Bettmann. Reproduced by permission. Hinton, Dr. William A., photograph. AP/Wide World Photos. Reproduced by permission. Ho, David, photograph. Reproduced by permission. Hodgkin, Dorothy Crowfoot, photograph. Hodgkin, Dorothy, photograph. Archive Photos, Inc./Express Newspapers. Reproduced by

permission. Min-Chueh Chang, Worcester Foundation for Experimental Biology, photograph. AP/Wide World Photos, Inc. Reproduced by permission. Minsky, Marvin, photograph. AP/Wide World Photos. Reproduced by permission. Mitchell, Peter (accepting Nobel Prize), photograph. AP/Wide World Photos, Inc. Reproduced by permission. Montagnier, Luc (close-up of face, reading glasses down on nose), 1990, photograph by Gareth Watkins. Reuters/Archive Photos, Inc. Reproduced by permission. Moore, Dr. Stanford, photograph. UPI/Corbis-Bettmann. Reproduced by permission. Mordell, Louis J. (buttoning rumpled suit, white hair), Nizza, 1970, photograph. Mathematisches Forschungsinstitut Oberwolfach. Reproduced by permission. Morgan, Ann Haven, photograph. Mount Holyoke College Archives and Special Collections. Reproduced by permission. Mossbauer, Rudolf, photograph. Archive Photos, Inc. Reproduced by permission. Mott, Nevill, photograph. AP/Wide World Photos, Inc. Reproduced by permission. Moulton, Dr. Barbara, 1960, photograph. UPI/Corbis-Bettmann. Reproduced by permission. Mullis, Kary (seated, legs crossed, two cameras filming him), photograph. Archive Photos, Inc. Reproduced by permission. Mundel, Robert A. with Walter Kohn (r), Stockholm, photograph. ©AFP/ CORBIS. Reproduced by permission. Nakanishi, Koji, photograph. Camera One. Reproduced by permission. Nash, John, 1994, photograph by Robert P. Matthews. Reproduced by permission. Nathans, Daniel, teaching a class, photograph. UPI/Corbis-Bettmann. Reproduced by permission. Ne^eman, Yuval, photograph. Archive Photos, Inc. Reproduced by permission. Needham, Joseph, photograph. Needham Research Institute. Reproduced by permission. Neufeld, Elizabeth (short curly hair, wearing dark striped blouse), photograph. AP/Wide World Photos. Reproduced by permission. Neumann, Hanna (wearing polka dot dress and wool coat), photograph. Mathematisches Forschungs-institut Oberwolfach. Reproduced by permission. Nicholson, Seth Barnes (seated at his spectroscope), 1929, photograph. AP/Wide World Photos. Reproduced by permission. Noether, Emmy (standing, looking down), photograph. Mathematisches Forschungsinstitut Oberwolfach. Reproduced by permission. Noether, Max (short grey hair, greying beard, oval glasses), photograph. Mathematisches Forschungs-institut Oberwolfach. Reproduced by permission. Noyce, Robert (semiconductor in hand), 1989, photograph. AP/Wide World Photos, Inc. Reproduced by permission. O^Neill, Gerard K., photograph. Space Studies Institute. Reproduced by permission. Ochoa, Severo, photograph. AP/Wide World Photos, Inc. Reproduced by permission. Oeschger, Hans (seated at desk), photograph. AP/Wide World Photos. Reproduced by permission. Olah, George, photograph. Reuters/Fred Prouser/Archive Photos, Inc. Reproduced by permission. Oleinik, Olga (standing with Vekua at her left), 1976, photograph. Mathematisches Forschungsinstitut Oberwolfach. Reproduced by permission. Onsager, Lars (receiving Nobel Prize from King Gustaf Adolf), 1968, photograph. Archive Photo/Express News. Reproduced by permission. Osheroff, Douglas, photograph. Reuters/Bruce Young/Archive Photos, Inc. Reproduced by permission. Packard, David, 1969, photograph. AP/Wide World Photos, Inc. Reproduced by permission. Packard, David (standing in front of electronic equipment) 1958, photograph. AP/Wide World Photos. Reproduced by permission. Parker, Eugene N., photograph. © 1993 Matthew Gilson. Reproduced by permission. Patel, Kumar N., photograph. Reproduced by permission. Patrick, Jennie R. (wearing necklace and earrings), photograph. Reproduced by permission of Jennie R. Patrick. Patrick, Ruth, photograph. AP/Wide World Photos. Reproduced by permission. Paul, Wolfgang, photograph. AP/ Wide World Photos, Inc. Reproduced by permission. Pavlov, Ivan. Hulton-Deutsch Collection/Corbis-Bettmann. Reproduced by permission. Peierls, Rudolf, photograph by Norman McBeath. Reproduced by permission. Peirce, Charles S., photograph. Corbis-Bettmann. Reproduced by permission. Perl, Martin (standing in laboratory), photograph. AgenceFrance Presse/Corbis-Bettmann. Reproduced by permission. photograph. © Bettmann/CORBIS. Reproduced by permission. photograph. © Bettmann/CORBIS. Reproduced by permission. Pilbeam, David (holding fossilized bone), 1984, photograph. AP/Wide World Photos, Inc. Reproduced by permission. Plotkin, Mark J., photograph. Reproduced by permission. Ponnamperuma, Cyril, photograph. AP/Wide World Photos, Inc. Reproduced by permission. Pople, John, 1998, photograph. The Gamma Liaison Network. © Liaison Agency. Reproduced by permission. Press, Frank, photograph. Bachrach. Reproduced by permission. Progogine, Ilya, photograph. AP/Wide World Photos. Reproduced by permission. Prusiner, Dr. Stanley B. (close-up, laughing, in olive suit), 1997, photograph by Luc Novovitch. Reuters/Archive Photos, Inc. Reproduced by permission. Puck, Dr. Theodore T., 1954, photograph. AP/Wide World Photos. Reproduced by permission. Purcell, Edward, photograph. AP/Wide World Photos, Inc. Reproduced by permission. Ramanujan, Srinivasa, photograph. The Granger Collection. Reproduced by permission. Reed, Dr. Major Walter, photograph. AP/Wide World Photos. Reproduced by permission. Rice, Dr. Stuart A. (seated at desk), photograph. AP/Wide World Photos. Reproduced by permission. Rich, Dr. Alexander, 1973, photograph. AP/Wide World Photos. Reproduced by permission. Richter, Dr. Charles, photograph. AP/Wide World Photos. Reproduced by permission. Ride, Sally, photograph. AP/Wide World Photos. Reproduced by permission. Rita Levi-Montalcini, photograph. AP/Wide World Photos. Reproduced by permission. Rodbell, Dr. Martin, 1994, photograph. AP/Wide World Photos. Reproduced by permission. Roentgen, Wilhelm Konrad, photograph. Archive Photos, Inc. Reproduced by permission. Rubin, Vera (looking up at the stars and universe), photograph. © 1993 R.T. Nowitz. Photo Researchers, Inc. Reproduced by permission. Russell, Elizabeth S., 1972, photograph. AP/Wide World Photos, Inc. Reproduced by permission. Sabin, Florence Rena, photograph. The Granger Collection, New York. Reproduced by permission. Sagan, Carl, photograph. AP/Wide World Photos, Inc. Reproduced by permission. Sager, Ruth, photograph. AP/Wide World Photos, Inc. Reproduced by permission. Salam, Abdus (holding a pen), photograph. The Bettmann Archive/Newsphotos, Inc. Reproduced by permission. Salk, Jonas, Pittsburgh, Pennsylvania, 1955, photograph. A/P Wide World Photos. Reproduced by permission. Schick, Dr. Bela (center), with Mayor Robert Wagner and Catherine Schick, 1962, photograph. UPI/Corbis Images. Reproduced by permission. Schwarzschild, Dr. Martin, photograph. AP/Wide World Photos. Reproduced by permission. Simmons, Dr. Howard E. (wearing glen plaid suit), photograph. Archive Photos, Inc. Reproduced by permission. Sinclair, Clive (holding new pocket TV), photograph. UPI/Corbis-Bettmann. Reproduced by permission. Smale, Stephen, Moscow, 1966, photograph. AP/Wide World Photos, Inc. Reproduced by permission. Snyder, Solomon H., photograph. Reproduced by permission. Solomon, Susan, photograph. AP/Wide World Photos. Reproduced by permission. Spitzer, Lyman, photograph. AP/Wide World Photos, Inc. Reproduced by permission. Spitzer, Lyman, photograph. AP/Wide World Photos, Inc. Reproduced by permission. Stanley, Richard P., photograph. Reproduced by permission. Steptoe, Patrick, photograph. Archive Photos. Reproduced by permission. Stokes, Sir George Gabriel (thinning hair, bushy muttonchops), illustration. Archive Photos, Inc. Reproduced by permission. Stormer, Horst L. (smiling, disheveled hair, bushy eyebrows), Murray Hill, New Jersey, 1998, photograph by Mike Derer. AP/Wide World Photos. Reproduce by permission. Suomi, Verner (holding device in hands), photograph. AP/Wide World Photos, Inc. Reproduced by permission. 't Hooft, Gerardus, photograph. AP/Wide World Photos. Reproduced by permission. Tatum, Edward, photograph. Archive Photos, Inc. Reproduced by permission. Taussing, Helen, (helping a small girl find her heart with a stethoscope), photograph. AP/Wide World Photos. Reproduced by permission. Taussky-Todd, Olga, photograph. Reproduced by permission of the estate of Olga Taussky-Todd. Telkes, Maria, photograph. UPI/Corbis-Bettmann. Reproduced by permission. Tembaugh, Clyde W. (with homemade telescope), photograph. AP/Wide World Photos. Reproduced by permission. Thomson, Sir George, 1944, photograph. AP/Wide World Photos. Reproduced by permission. Tinbergen, Nikolaas, photograph. Mary Evans Picture Library. Reproduced by permission. Topchiev, Aleksandr (giving a speech), photograph. Archive Photos, Inc. Reproduced by permission. Torvalds, Linus, Las Vegas, Nevada, 1999, photograph. ©Reuters Newmedia Inc./CORBIS. Reproduced by permission. Tsui, Lap-Chee, photograph. Reproduced by permission of Lap-Chee Tsui. Turing, Alan, photograph. Photo Researchers, Inc. Reproduced by permission. Velez-Rodriguez, Argelia, photograph. Reproduced by permission. Veltman, Martinus J. G., 1999, photograph. AP/Wide World Photos. Reproduced by permission. Von Neumann, John, (testifying before the Atomic Energy Commission), photograph. AP/Wide World Photos. Reproduced by permission. Walker, John, photograph. Reuters/HO/Archive Photos, Inc. Reproduced by permission. Walton, Ernest T. S., photograph. AP/Wide World Photos. Reproduced by permission. Weber, Ernst, photograph. AP/Wide World Photos, Inc. Reproduced by permission. Wegener, Alfred, (head and shoulders), photograph. UPI/Corbis-Bettmann. Reproduced by permission. Weyl, Hermann (standing, from his right), 1954, photograph. AP/Wide World Photos, Inc. Reproduced by permission. Whitehead, Alfred North, photograph. AP/Wide World Photos. Reproduced by permission. Whittle, Frank, photograph. AP/Wide World Photos, Inc. Reproduced by permission. Widnall, Sheila, photograph. AP/Wide World Photos. Reproduced by permission. Wigner, Eugene, photograph. Archive Photos, Inc. Reproduced by permission. Wilmut, Ian, 1997, Washington, D.C., photograph. AP/Wide World Photos, Inc. Reproduced by permission. Wilson, Edward O., sitting at the table, with a insect sculpture in front of him, photograph by Jon Chase/Harvard. Reproduced by permission. Wilson, Robert, photograph. UPI/Corbis-Bettmann. Reproduced by permission. Wu, Chien-Shiung, photograph. UPI/Bettmann. Reproduced by permission. Wu, Chien-Shiung (sitting

Entry List

Blum, Lenore
Blumberg, Baruch Samuel
Bodmer, Walter Fred
Bohr, Aage
Bohr, Niels
Bolin, Bert
Bondar, Roberta Lynn
Bondi, Hermann
Booker, Walter M.
Borcherds, Richard Ewen
Bordet, Jules
Borel, Émile
Borlaug, Norman
Bormann, Frederick Herbert
Born, Max
Bosch, Karl
Bose, Satyendranath
Bothe, Walther
Bott, Raoul
Bovet, Daniel
Bowie, William
Boyer, Herbert W.
Boyer, Paul D.
Boykin, Otis
Brady, St. Elmo
Bragg, William Henry
Bragg, William Lawrence
Brans, Carl Henry
Branson, Herman
Brattain, Walter Houser
Braun, Karl Ferdinand
Breit, Gregory
Bremermann, Hans-Joachim
Brenner, Sydney
Breslow, Ronald C.
Bressani, Ricardo
Bridges, Calvin Blackman
Bridgman, Percy Williams
Brill, Yvonne Claeys
Brockhouse, Bertram Neville
Broecker, Wallace S.
Bromley, D. Allan
Bronk, Detlev Wulf
Brønsted, Johannes Nicolaus
Brooks, Ronald E.
Brouwer, Luitzen Egbertus Jan
Browder, Felix Earl
Brown, Herbert C.
Brown, Lester Russell
Brown, Michael S.
Brown, Rachel Fuller
Brown, Robert Hanbury
Browne, Marjorie Lee
Bucher, Walter Herman
Buchner, Eduard
Bullard, Edward
Bundy, Robert F.
Burbidge, E. Margaret
Burbidge, Geoffrey
Burger, Alfred
Burkitt, Denis Parsons
Burnet, Frank Macfarlane
Burton, Glenn W.
Bush, Vannevar

Butement, William Alan Stewart
Butenandt, Adolf

C

Cahn, John Werner
Cairns, John Jr.
Calderón, Alberto P.
Caldicott, Helen
Callender, Clive O.
Calvin, Melvin
Cambra, Jessie G.
Canady, Alexa I.
Cannon, Annie Jump
Cantor, Georg
Cardona, Manuel
Cardozo, W. Warrick
Cardús, David
Carlson, Chester
Carothers, E. Eleanor
Carothers, Wallace Hume
Carrel, Alexis
Carrier, Willis
Carruthers, George R.
Carson, Benjamin S.
Carson, Rachel
Cartan, Élie Joseph
Cartan, Henri
Cartwright, Dame Mary Lucy
Carver, George Washington
Castro, George
Cech, Thomas R.
Chadwick, James
Chain, Ernst Boris
Chamberlain, Owen
Chamberlin, Thomas Chrowder
Chance, Britton
Chandrasekhar, Subrahmanyan
Chang, Min-Chueh
Chang, Sun-Yang Alice
Chang, Te-Tzu
Chargaff, Erwin
Charnley, John
Charpak, Georges
Chase, Mary Agnes Mera
Chaudhari, Praveen
Cherenkov, Pavel A.
Chestnut, Harold
Chew, Geoffrey Foucar
Child, Charles Manning
Chinn, May Edward
Cho, Alfred Y.
Chomsky, Avram Noam
Chu, Paul Ching-Wu
Chu, Steven
Chung, Fan R. K.
Church, Alonzo
Clarke, Edith
Claude, Albert
Claude, Georges
Clay-Jolles, Tettje Clasina
Clay, Jacob
Clemence, Gerald Maurice
Cloud, Preston

Cobb, Jewel Plummer
Cobb, William Montague
Cockcroft, John D.
Cocke, John
Cohen, Joel Ephraim
Cohen, Paul
Cohen, Stanley Harold
Cohen, Stanley N.
Cohen-Tannoudji, Claude
Cohn, Mildred
Cohn, Zanvil
Coifman, Ronald R.
Colburn, Theodora E.
Colmenares, Margarita
Colwell, Rita R.
Commoner, Barry
Compton, Arthur Holly
Condon, Edward Uhler
Conway, Lynn Ann
Conwell, Esther Marly
Cooke, Lloyd M.
Cooley, Denton Arthur
Coolidge, William D.
Cooper, Leon N.
Corey, Elias James
Cori, Carl Ferdinand
Cori, Gerty T.
Cormack, Allan Macleod
Cornforth, John Warcup
Coster, Dirk
Coulomb, Jean
Courant, Richard
Cournand, André F.
Cousteau, Jacques
Cowings, Patricia S.
Cox, Elbert Frank
Cox, Geraldine V.
Cox, Gertrude Mary
Cram, Donald James
Cray, Seymour
Crick, Francis Harry Compton
Cronin, James W.
Crosby, Elizabeth Caroline
Crosthwait, David Nelson Jr.
Crutzen, Paul J.
Culler, Glen Jacob
Curie, Marie
Curie, Pierre
Curl, Robert Floyd Jr.
Cushman, David W.

D

Dale, Henry Hallett
Dalén, Nils
Dallmeier, Francisco
Dalrymple, G. Brent
Daly, Marie Maynard
Daly, Reginald Aldworth
Dam, Henrik
Daniels, Walter T.
Dansgaard, Willi
Dantzig, George Bernard
Darden, Christine

Dart, Raymond A.
Daubechies, Ingrid
Dausset, Jean
Davidson, Norman R.
Davis, Margaret B.
Davis, Marguerite
Davis, Raymond Jr.
Davisson, Clinton Joseph
DeBakey, Michael Ellis
de Broglie, Louis Victor
Debye, Peter J. W.
de Duve, Christian René
de Forest, Lee
de Gennes, Pierre-Gilles
de Sitter, Willem
Dehmelt, Hans
Deisenhofer, Johann
Delbrück, Max
Deligné, Pierre
Dennis, Jack Bonnell
d'Hérelle, Félix
Diacumakos, Elaine
Diamond, Jared M.
Diaz, Henry F.
Dicciani, Nance K.
Dick, Gladys Rowena Henry
Dicke, Robert Henry
Diels, Otto
Diener, Theodor Otto
Diggs, Irene
Dijkstra, Edsger W.
Dirac, Paul Adrien Maurice
Djerassi, Carl
Dobzhansky, Theodosius
Doherty, Peter C.
Doisy, Edward Adelbert
Dolby, Ray Milton
Dole, Vincent P.
Domagk, Gerhard
Donaldson, Simon
Douglas, Donald W.
Draper, Charles Stark
Dresselhaus, Mildred S.
Drew, Charles R.
Drickamer, Harry G.
Drucker, Daniel Charles
Dubois, Marie Eugène Francoise Thomas
Dubos, René
Dulbecco, Renato
Durand, William F.
Durrell, Gerald
du Vigneaud, Vincent
Dyson, Freeman J.

E

Eagle, Harry
Earle, Sylvia A.
Eastwood, Alice
Eccles, John Carew
Eckert, J. Presper
Eddington, Arthur Stanley
Edelman, Gerald M.
Edgerton, Harold

Edinger, Tilly
Edison, Thomas Alva
Edwards, Cecile Hoover
Edwards, Helen T.
Ehrenfest, Paul
Ehrenfest-Afanaseva, Tatiana
Ehrlich, Anne Howland
Ehrlich, Paul
Ehrlich, Paul Ralph
Eigen, Manfred
Eijkman, Christiaan
Einstein, Albert
Einstein-Maric, Mileva
Einthoven, Willem
Eisner, Thomas
El-Sayed, Mostafa Amr
Eldredge, Niles
Elion, Gertrude Belle
Elsasser, Walter M.
Elton, Charles
Emerson, Gladys Anderson
Enders, John Franklin
Engler, Adolph Gustav Heinrich
Enskog, David
Erdös, Paul
Erlang, Agner
Erlanger, Joseph
Ernst, Richard R.
Esaki, Leo
Esau, Katherine
Estes, William K.
Estrin, Thelma
Euler-Chelpin, Hans Karl Simon August
  von
Euler, Ulf von
Evans, Alice
Evans, James C.
Ewing, William Maurice

F

Faber, Sandra M.
Fabry, Charles
Fairbank, William
Falconer, Etta
Farman, Joseph C.
Farnsworth, Philo T.
Farquhar, Marilyn G.
Farr, Wanda K.
Fasenmyer, Sister Mary
Fauci, Anthony S.
Favaloro, René Geronimo
Fedoroff, Nina V.
Feigenbaum, Edward A.
Feigenbaum, Mitchell
Fell, Honor Bridget
Fenchel, Kate
Ferguson, Lloyd N.
Ferguson, Margaret Clay
Fermi, Enrico
Fersman, Aleksandr Evgenievich
Feynman, Richard P.
Fibiger, Johannes
Fieser, Louis F.

Fieser, Mary Peters
Fischer, Edmond H.
Fischer, Emil
Fischer, Ernst Otto
Fischer, Hans
Fisher, Elizabeth F.
Fisher, Ronald Aylmer
Fitch, Val Logsdon
Fitzroy, Nancy D.
Flanagan, James L
Fleming, Alexander
Fleming, John Ambrose
Flexner, Simon
Florey, Howard Walter
Flory, Paul
Flügge-Lotz, Irmgard
Fokker, Anthony H. G.
Folkers, Karl A.
Forbush, Scott Ellsworth
Ford, Henry
Forrester, Jay Wright
Forssmann, Werner
Fossey, Dian
Fowler, William A.
Fox, Sidney Walter
Fraenkel, Abraham Adolf
Fraenkel-Conrat, Heinz Ludwig
Franck, James
Frank, Il'ya
Franklin, Rosalind Elsie
Fraser-Reid, Bertram Oliver
Fréchet, Maurice
Fredholm, Ivar
Freedman, Michael H.
Freitag, Herta Therese
Frenkel, Yakov Ilyich
Friedman, Jerome
Friedmann, Aleksandr A.
Friend, Charlotte
Frisch, Karl von
Frisch, Otto Robert
Fujita, Tetsuya Theodore
Fukui, Kenichi
Fuller, (Richard) Buckminster
Fuller, Solomon

G

Gabor, Dennis
Gadgil, Madhav
Gadgil, Sulochana
Gagarin, Yuri A.
Gajdusek, D. Carleton
Galdikas, Birute
Gallo, Robert C.
Gamow, George
Gardner, Julia Anna
Garrod, Archibald
Gasser, Herbert Spencer
Gates, Bill
Gates, Sylvester James Jr.
Gaviola, Enrique
Gayle, Helene Doris
Geiger, Hans

Geiringer, Hilda
Gelfond, Aleksandr Osipovich
Gell-Mann, Murray
Geller, Margaret Joan
Gentry, Ruth
Ghiorso, Albert
Giacconi, Riccardo
Giaever, Ivar
Giauque, William F.
Gibbs, Josiah Willard
Gibbs, William Francis
Giblett, Eloise R.
Gilbert, Walter
Gilbreth, Frank
Gilbreth, Lillian
Gilman, Alfred Goodman
Glaser, Donald
Glashow, Sheldon Lee
Glenn, John Herschel, Jr.
Goddard, Robert H.
Gödel, Kurt Friedrich
Goeppert-Mayer, Maria
Goethals, George W.
Gold, Thomas
Goldberg, Adele
Goldhaber, Gertrude Scharff
Goldhaber, Maurice
Goldmark, Peter Carl
Goldreich, Peter M.
Goldring, Winifred
Goldschmidt, Richard B.
Goldschmidt, Victor
Goldstein, Avram
Goldstein, Joseph L.
Golgi, Camillo
Gomez-Pompa, Arturo
Good, Mary L.
Goodall, Jane
Gorer, Peter Alfred
Goudsmit, Samuel A.
Gould, Stephen Jay
Gourdine, Meredith Charles
Gourneau, Dwight
Govindjee
Gowers, William Timothy
Granit, Ragnar Arthur
Granville, Evelyn Boyd
Greatbatch, Wilson
Greenewalt, Crawford H.
Grier, Herbert E. Jr.
Griffith, Frederick
Grignard, François Auguste Victor
Gross, Carol
Grothendieck, Alexander
Groves, Leslie Richard
Guillaume, Charles-Edouard
Guillemin, Roger
Gullstrand, Allvar
Gutenberg, Beno
Guth, Alan
Guthrie, Mary Jane
Gutierrez, Orlando A.

H

Haagen-Smit, A. J.
Haber, Fritz
Hackerman, Norman
Hadamard, Jacques
Hahn, Otto
Haldane, John Burdon Sanderson
Hale, George Ellery
Hall, Lloyd Augustus
Hamburger, Viktor
Hamilton, Alice
Hammond, George S.
Hanafusa, Hidesaburo
Hannah, Marc R.
Hansen, James
Harden, Arthur
Hardy, Alister C.
Hardy, Godfrey Harold
Hardy, Harriet
Harmon, E'lise F.
Harris, Cyril
Harris, Wesley L.
Hartline, Haldan Keffer
Harvey, Ethel Nicholson Browne
Hassel, Odd
Hauptman, Herbert A.
Haus, Hermann A.
Hausdorff, Felix
Hawking, Stephen
Hawkins, W. Lincoln
Haworth, Walter
Hay, Elizabeth D.
Hay, Louise
Hayes, Ellen Amanda
Hazen, Elizabeth Lee
Hazlett, Olive Clio
Healy, Bernadine
Heezen, Bruce Charles
Heimlich, Henry Jay
Heinkel, Ernst
Heisenberg, Werner Karl
Hench, Philip Showalter
Henderson, Cornelius Langston
Henry, John Edward
Henry, Warren Elliott
Hermite, Charles
Herschbach, Dudley R.
Hershey, Alfred Day
Hertz, Gustav
Hertzsprung, Ejnar
Herzberg, Gerhard
Herzenberg, Caroline L.
Hess, Harry Hammond
Hess, Victor
Hess, Walter Rudolf
Hevesy, Georg von
Hewish, Antony
Hewitt, Jacqueline N.
Hewlett, William
Heymans, Corneille Jean-François
Heyrovský, Jaroslav
Hibbard, Hope
Hicks, Beatrice

Higgs, Peter Ware
Hilbert, David
Hill, Archibald V.
Hill, George William
Hill, Henry A.
Hill, Robert (Robin)
Hille, Bertil
Hinshelwood, Cyril N.
Hinton, William Augustus
Hitchings, George H.
Ho, David Da-I
Hobby, Gladys Lounsbury
Hodgkin, Alan Lloyd
Hodgkin, Dorothy Crowfoot
Hoffman, Darleane C.
Hoffmann, Roald
Hofstadter, Robert
Hogg, Helen Sawyer
Holdren, John Paul
Holley, Robert William
Hollinshead, Ariel Cahill
Holmes, Arthur
Hooft, Gerardus 't
Hopkins, Frederick Gowland
Hopper, Grace
Horn, Michael Hastings
Horstmann, Dorothy Millicent
Houdry, Eugene
Hounsfield, Godfrey
Houssay, Bernardo
Hoyle, Fred
Hrdlička, Aleš
Huang, Alice Shih-hou
Hubbard, Philip G.
Hubbert, M. King
Hubble, Edwin
Hubel, David H.
Huber, Robert
Huggins, Charles B.
Hughes, John
Hulse, Russell A.
Humason, Milton L.
Hunsaker, Jerome C.
Hutchinson, G. Evelyn
Huxley, Andrew Fielding
Huxley, Hugh Esmor
Huxley, Julian
Hyde, Ida H.
Hyman, Libbie Henrietta

I

Imes, Elmer Samuel
Ioffe, Abram F.
Isaacs, Alick
Itakura, Keiichi
Iverson, F. Kenneth

J

Jackson, Shirley Ann
Jacob, François
Janovskaja, Sof'ja Aleksandrovna
Jansky, Karl

Janzen, Dan
Jarvik, Robert K.
Jason, Robert S.
Jeffreys, Alec John
Jeffreys, Harold
Jeffries, Zay
Jemison, Mae C.
Jencks, William Platt
Jensen, Johannes Hans Daniel
Jerne, Niels K.
Jewett, Frank Baldwin
Jobs, Steven
Johannsen, Wilhelm Ludvig
Johnson, Barbara Crawford
Johnson, Clarence L.
Johnson, John B. Jr.
Johnson, Joseph Lealand
Johnson, Katherine Coleman Goble
Johnson, Marvin M.
Johnson, Virginia E.
Johnson, William Summer
Johnston, Harold S.
Joliot-Curie, Frédéric
Joliot-Curie, Irène
Jones, Fred
Jones, Mary Ellen
Jordan, Ernst Pascual
Josephson, Brian D.
Julian, Percy Lavon
Juran, Joseph M.
Just, Ernest Everett

K

Kadanoff, Leo Philip
Kamerlingh Onnes, Heike
Kan, Yuet Wai
Kandel, Eric R.
Kapitsa, Pyotr
Karle, Isabella
Karle, Jerome
Karlin, Samuel
Karp, Richard M.
Karrer, Paul
Kastler, Alfred
Kates, Robert W.
Kato, Tosio
Katz, Bernard
Katz, Donald L.
Kay, Alan C.
Keen, Linda
Keith, Arthur
Keller, Evelyn Fox
Kelsey, Frances Oldham
Kemeny, John G.
Kendall, Edward C.
Kendall, Henry W.
Kendrew, John
Kettering, Charles Franklin
Kettlewell, Bernard
Kety, Seymour S.
Khorana, Har Gobind
Khush, Gurdev S.
Kilburn, Thomas M.

Kilby, Jack St. Clair
Kimura, Motoo
King, Helen Dean
King, Louisa Boyd Yeomans
King, Reatha Clark
Kinoshita, Toichiro
Kinsey, Alfred
Kishimoto, Tadamitsu
Kistiakowsky, George B.
Kittrell, Flemmie Pansy
Klein, Christian Felix
Klug, Aaron
Knopf, Eleanora Bliss
Knudsen, William Claire
Knuth, Donald E.
Koch, Robert
Kocher, Theodor
Kodaira, Kunihiko
Koehl, Mimi A. R.
Köhler, Georges
Kohn, Walter
Kolff, Willem Johan
Kolmogorov, Andrey Nikolayevich
Kolthoff, Izaak Maurits
Konishi, Masakazu
Kontsevich, Maxim
Kornberg, Arthur
Korolyov, Sergei
Koshland, Daniel E., Jr.
Kossel, Albrecht
Kouchner, Bernard
Kountz, Samuel L.
Kouwenhoven, William Bennett
Kramer, Fred Russell
Krebs, Edwin G.
Krebs, Hans Adolf
Krieger, Cecilia
Krim, Mathilde
Krogh, August
Kroto, Harold Walter
Kuhlmann-Wilsdorf, Doris
Kuhn, Richard
Kuiper, Gerard Peter
Kuperberg, Krystyna
Kurchatov, Igor
Kurtz, Thomas Eugene
Kurzweil, Raymond
Kusch, Polycarp

L

L'Esperance, Elise Depew Strang
Ladd-Franklin, Christine
Lamb, Willis E., Jr.
Lancaster, Cleo
Lancefield, Rebecca Craighill
Land, Edwin H.
Landau, Edmund Georg Hemann
Landau, Lev Davidovich
Landsberg, Helmut E.
Landsteiner, Karl
Langevin, Paul
Langlands, Robert
Langmuir, Irving

Latimer, Lewis H.
Lattes, C. M. G.
Laub, Jakob Johann
Laue, Max von
Laughlin, Robert B.
Lauterbur, Paul C.
Laveran, Alphonse
Lawless, Theodore K.
Lawrence, Ernest Orlando
Le Beau, Désirée
Le Cadet, Georges
Leakey, Louis
Leakey, Mary Douglas Nicol
Leakey, Richard E.
Leavitt, Henrietta
Lebesgue, Henri
Leder, Philip
Lederberg, Joshua
Lederman, Leon Max
Ledley, Robert Steven
Lee, David M.
Lee, Raphael C.
Lee, Tsung-Dao
Lee, Yuan T.
Leeman, Susan E.
Leevy, Carroll Moton
Leffall, LaSalle D. Jr.
Lehmann, Inge
Lehmer, Emma Trotskaya
Lehn, Jean-Marie
Leloir, Luis F.
Lemaître, Georges
Lenard, Philipp E. A. von
Leopold, Aldo
Leopold, Estella Bergere
Leopold, Luna Bergere
Lester, William Alexander, Jr.
Levi-Civita, Tullio
Levi-Montalcini, Rita
Lévi-Strauss, Claude
Lewis, Edward B.
Lewis, Gilbert Newton
Lewis, Julian Herman
Lewis, Warren K.
Li, Ching Chun
Li, Choh Hao
Libby, Willard F.
Liepmann, Hans Wolfgang Leopold Edmund Eugene Victor
Likens, Gene Elden
Lillie, Frank Rattray
Lim, Robert K. S.
Lin, Chia-Chiao
Lindemann, Ferdinand von
Lipmann, Fritz
Lippmann, Gabriel
Lipscomb, William Nunn, Jr.
Little, Arthur D.
Litvinova, Elizabeta Fedorovna
Lizhi, Fang
Lloyd, Ruth Smith
Loeb, Jacques
Loewi, Otto
Logan, Myra A.

London, Fritz
Long, Irene D.
Lonsdale, Kathleen
Lorentz, Hendrik Antoon
Lorenz, Edward N.
Lorenz, Konrad
Lorius, Claude J.
Lovejoy, Thomas Eugene
Lovelock, James Ephraim
Lubchenco, Jane
Luria, Salvador Edward
Lwoff, André
Lynen, Feodor
Lynk, Miles Vandahurst

M

Maathai, Wangari
MacArthur, Robert H.
Macdonald, Eleanor Josephine
MacDonald, Gordon James Fraser
MacGill, Elsie Gregory
Macintyre, Sheila Scott
MacKinnon, Roderick
Macklin, Madge Thurlow
MacLane, Saunders
MacLeod, Colin Munro
Macleod, John James Rickard
MacPherson, Robert D.
Maddison, Ada Isabel
Maillart, Robert
Maiman, Theodore
Malone-Mayes, Vivienne
Maloney, Arnold Hamilton
Mandel'shtam, Leonid Isaakovich
Mandelbrot, Benoit B.
Manton, Sidnie Milana
Marchbanks, Vance H., Jr.
Marconi, Guglielmo
Marcus, Rudolph A.
Margulis, Gregori Aleksandrovitch
Margulis, Lynn
Marie-Victorin, Frère
Markov, Andrei Andreevich
Martin, A(rcher) J(ohn) P(orter)
Massevitch, Alla G.
Massey, Walter E.
Massie, Samuel P., Jr.
Masters, William Howell
Matthews, Alva T.
Matuyama, Motonori
Mauchly, John William
Maunder, Annie Russell
Maury, Antonia
Maury, Carlotta Joaquina
Maynard Smith, John
Mayr, Ernst
McAfee, Walter S.
McCarthy, John
McCarty, Maclyn
McCarty, Perry L.
McClintock, Barbara
McCollum, Elmer Verner
McConnell, Harden

McDuff, (Margaret) Dusa
McMillan, Edwin M.
McMullen, Curtis T.
Mead, George Herbert
Medawar, Peter Brian
Meitner, Lise
Mendenhall, Dorothy Reed
Meray, Hugues Charles Robert
Merrifield, R. Bruce
Merrill, Helen Abbot
Merrill, Winifred Edgerton
Meselson, Matthew
Metchnikoff, Élie
Mexia, Ynes
Meyerhof, Otto
Michel, Hartmut
Micheli-Tzanakou, Evangelia
Michelson, Albert
Midgley, Thomas, Jr.
Miller, Elizabeth C. & James Alexander
Miller, Stanley Lloyd
Millikan, Robert A.
Milne, Edward Arthur
Milnor, John
Milstein, César
Minkowski, Hermann
Minkowski, Rudolph
Minot, George Richards
Minsky, Marvin Lee
Mintz, Beatrice
Mitchell, Peter D.
Mittermeier, Russell
Mohorovičić, Andrija
Moissan, Henri
Molina, Mario
Moniz, Antonio Egas
Monod, Jacques Lucien
Montagnier, Luc
Moore, Charlotte E.
Moore, Raymond Cecil
Moore, Ruth Ella
Moore, Stanford
Morawetz, Cathleen Synge
Mordell, Louis Joel
Morgan, Ann Haven
Morgan, Arthur E.
Morgan, Garrett A.
Morgan, Thomas Hunt
Mori, Shigefumi
Morley, Edward Williams
Morrison, Philip
Moseley, Henry Gwyn Jeffreys
Mossbauer, Rudolf
Mott, Nevill Francis
Mottelson, Ben R.
Moulton Browne, Barbara
Moulton, Forest Ray
Muller, Hermann Joseph
Müller, K. Alex
Müller, Paul
Mulliken, Robert S.
Mullis, Kary
Munk, Walter
Murphy, William P.

Murray, Joseph E.

N

Nabrit, Samuel Milton
Nagata, Takesi
Nakanishi, Koji
Nambu, Yoichiro
Nash, John Forbes, Jr.
Nathans, Daniel
Natta, Giulio
Ne'eman, Yuval
Neal, Homer Alfred
Needham, Joseph
Néel, Louis-Eugène-Félix
Neher, Erwin
Nelson, Evelyn M.
Nernst, Walther
Neufeld, Elizabeth Fondal
Neumann, Hanna
Newell, Allen
Newell, Norman Dennis
Nice, Margaret Morse
Nichols, Roberta J.
Nicholson, Seth Barnes
Nicolle, Charles Jules Henri
Nier, Alfred O. C.
Nirenberg, Marshall Warren
Nishizawa, Jun-ichi
Nishizuka, Yasutomi
Noble, G. K.
Noddack, Ida Tacke
Noether, Emmy
Noether, Max
Noguchi, Hideyo
Nomura, Masayasu
Norrish, Ronald G. W.
Northrop, John Howard
Novikov, Sergei
Noyce, Robert
Nozoe, Tetsuo
Nüsslein-Volhard, Christiane

O

O'Neill, Gerard K.
Oberth, Hermann
Ocampo, Adriana C.
Ochoa, Ellen
Ochoa, Severo
Odum, Eugene Pleasants
Odum, Howard T.
Oeschger, Hans
Ogilvie, Ida H.
Olah, George A.
Olden, Kenneth
Oldham, Richard Dixon
Oleinik, Olga
Ondetti, Miguel A.
Onsager, Lars
Oort, Jan Hendrik
Oparin, Aleksandr Ivanovich
Oppenheimer, J. Robert
Osborn, Mary J.

Osheroff, Douglas D.
Osterbrock, Donald E.
Ostwald, Friedrich Wilhelm

Packard, David
Palade, George Emil
Panajiotatou, Angeliki
Panofsky, Wolfgang Kurt Hermànn
Papanicolaou, George
Pardue, Mary Lou
Parker, Arthur C.
Parker, Charles Stewart
Parker, Eugene Newman
Parsons, John T.
Patel, C. Kumar N.
Patrick, Jennie R.
Patrick, Ruth
Patterson, Claire
Patterson, Frederick Douglass
Paul, Wolfgang
Pauli, Wolfgang
Pauling, Linus
Pavlov, Ivan Petrovich
Payne-Gaposchkin, Cecilia
Peano, Giuseppe
Pearson, Karl
Peden, Irene Carswell
Pedersen, Charles John
Peebles, Phillip James Edwin
Peierls, Rudolf Ernst
Peirce, Charles S.
Pellier, Laurence Delisle
Pennington, Mary Engle
Penrose, Roger
Penry, Deborah L.
Penzias, Arno
Perey, Marguerite
Perl, Martin L.
Perrin, Jean Baptiste
Pert, Candace B.
Perutz, Max
Péter, Rozsa
Petermann, Mary Locke
Peterson, Edith R.
Pettersson, Hans
Phelps, Michael Edward
Phillips, William D.
Piasecki, Frank
Piccard, Auguste
Pierce, George Edward
Pierce, Naomi E.
Pilbeam, David Roger
Pimentel, David
Pinchot, Gifford
Pincus, Gregory Goodwin
Planck, Max
Pless, Vera
Plotkin, Mark
Pogue, William Reid
Poincaré, Jules Henri
Poindexter, Hildrus A.
Polanyi, John C.

Polubarinova-Kochina, Pelageya Yakov-
    levna
Pólya, George
Ponnamperuma, Cyril
Pople, John A.
Porter, George
Porter, Rodney
Poulsen, Valdemar
Pound, Robert Vivian
Powell, Cecil Frank
Powless, David
Prandtl, Ludwig
Pregl, Fritz
Prelog, Vladimir
Press, Frank
Pressman, Ada I.
Prichard, Diana Garcia
Prigogine, Ilya
Profet, Margie
Prokhorov, Aleksandr
Prusiner, Stanley B.
Puck, Theodore T.
Punnett, R. C.
Purcell, Edward Mills

Qöyawayma, Alfred H.
Quarterman, Lloyd Albert
Quate, Calvin F.
Quimby, Edith H.
Quinland, William Samuel

Rabi, I. I.
Rainwater, James
Ramalingaswami, Vulimiri
Raman, C. V.
Ramanujan, S. I.
Ramart-Lucas, Pauline
Ramey, Estelle R.
Ramón y Cajal, Santiago
Ramsay, William
Ramsey, Frank Plumpton
Ramsey, Norman Foster
Randoin, Lucie
Rao, C. N. R.
Ratner, Sarah
Raven, Peter Hamilton
Ray, Dixy Lee
Reber, Grote
Reddy, Raj
Reed, Walter
Rees, Mina S.
Reichmanis, Elsa
Reichstein, Tadeus
Reid, Lonnie
Reines, Frederick
Revelle, Roger
Rice, Stuart A.
Rich, Alexander (a.k.a. Alan)
Richards, Dickinson Woodruff, Jr.
Richards, Ellen Swallow

Richards, Theodore William
Richardson, Lewis Fry
Richardson, Owen W.
Richardson, Robert C.
Richet, Charles Robert
Richter, Burton
Richter, Charles F.
Rickover, Hyman G.
Ride, Sally
Rigas, Harriett B.
Risi, Joseph
Ritchie, Dennis
Robbins, Frederick
Roberts, Lawrence
Roberts, Richard J.
Robinson, Julia
Robinson, Robert
Rock, John
Rockwell, Mabel M.
Rodbell, Martin
Roddy, Leon
Roelofs, Wendell L.
Rogers, Marguerite M.
Rohrer, Heinrich
Roman, Nancy Grace
Romer, Alfred Sherwood
Romero, Juan Carlos
Röntgen, Wilhelm Conrad
Rosenbluth, Marshall N.
Ross, John
Ross, Mary G.
Ross, Ronald
Rossby, Carl-Gustaf
Rothschild, Miriam Louisa
Rous, Peyton
Rowland, F. Sherwood
Rowley, Janet D.
Rubbia, Carlo
Rubin, Vera Cooper
Rudin, Mary Ellen
Runcorn, S. K.
Ruska, Ernst
Russell, Bertrand
Russell, Elizabeth Shull
Russell, Frederick Stratten
Russell, Henry Norris
Russell, Loris Shano
Rutherford, Ernest
Ružička, Leopold
Ryle, Martin

S

Sabatier, Paul
Sabin, Albert
Sabin, Florence Rena
Sacks, Oliver Wolf
Sagan, Carl
Sager, Ruth
Sakharov, Andrei
Sakmann, Bert
Salam, Abdus
Salk, Jonas
Samuelsson, Bengt

Sanchez, David A.
Sanchez, Pedro A.
Sandage, Allan R.
Sanford-Mifflin, Katherine Koontz
Sanger, Frederick
Satcher, David
Schafer, Alice T.
Schaller, George
Schally, Andrew Victor
Scharrer, Berta
Schawlow, Arthur Leonard
Schick, Bela
Schneider, Stephen H.
Schou, Mogens
Schrieffer, J. Robert
Schrödinger, Erwin
Schultes, Richard Evans
Schwartz, Melvin
Schwarz, John Henry
Schwinger, Julian
Scott, Charlotte Angas
Seaborg, Glenn Theodore
Segrè, Emilio
Seibert, Florence B.
Seitz, Frederick
Selberg, Atle
Semenov, Nikolai N.
Serre, Jean-Pierre
Shannon, Claude
Shapiro, Irwin
Shapley, Harlow
Sharp, Phillip A.
Sharp, Robert Phillip
Shaw, Mary
Sheldrake, Rupert
Shepard, Alan B., Jr.
Shepard, Roger N.
Sherrington, Charles Scott
Shockley, Dolores Cooper
Shockley, William
Shoemaker, Eugene M.
Shokalsky, Yuly Mikhaylovich
Shtokman, Vladimir Borisovich
Shull, Clifford Glenwood
Shurney, Robert E.
Siegbahn, Kai M.
Siegbahn, Karl M. G.
Sierpiński, Waclaw
Sikorsky, Igor I.
Silbergeld, Ellen Kovner
Simmons, Howard Ensign, Jr.
Simon, Dorothy Martin
Simon, Herbert Alexander
Simpson, George Gaylord
Sinclair, Clive Marles
Singer, I. M.
Singer, Maxine
Sioui, Richard H.
Skoog, Folke Karl
Skou, Jens C.
Slater, John Clarke
Slipher, Vesto M.
Slye, Maud
Smale, Stephen

Smalley, Richard Errett
Smith, Hamilton O.
Smith, Michael
Snell, George Davis
Snyder, Solomon Halbert
Soddy, Frederick
Solberg, Halvor
Solomon, Susan
Sommerfeld, Arnold
Sommerville, Duncan McLaren Young
Sorensen, Charles E.
Sørensen, Søren Peter Lauritz
Spaeth, Mary
Sparling, Rebecca H.
Spedding, Frank Harold
Spemann, Hans
Sperry, Elmer
Sperry, Roger W.
Spitzer, Lyman, Jr.
Stahl, Franklin W.
Stanley, Richard P.
Stanley, Wendell Meredith
Stark, Johannes
Starling, Ernest H.
Starr, Chauncey
Starzl, Thomas Earl
Staudinger, Hermann
Stefanik, Milan Ratislav
Stein, William Howard
Steinberger, Jack
Steinman, David B.
Steinmetz, Charles P.
Steitz, Joan Argetsinger
Steptoe, Patrick
Stern, Otto
Stevens, Nettie Maria
Stever, H. Guyford
Steward, Frederick Campion
Stewart, Thomas Dale, Jr.
Stibitz, George R.
Stock, Alfred
Stokes, George Gabriel
Stoll, Alice M.
Stommel, Henry Melson
Størmer, Fredrik
Stott, Alicia Boole
Strassmann, Fritz
Straus, William Levi, Jr.
Strutt, John William
Strutt, Robert
Stubbe, JoAnne
Sturtevant, A. H.
Sumner, James B.
Suomi, Verner E.
Sutherland, Earl, Jr.
Sutherland, Ivan
Sutton, Walter Stanborough
Svedberg, Theodor
Swaminathan, M. S.
Synge, Richard
Szego, Gabor
Szent-Györgyi, Albert
Szilard, Leo

 T

Tamm, Igor
Tan, Jiazhen
Tapia, Richard A.
Tarski, Alfred
Tatum, Edward Lawrie
Taube, Henry
Taussig, Helen Brooke
Taussky-Todd, Olga
Taylor, Frederick Winslow
Taylor, Joseph H., Jr.
Taylor, Moddie
Taylor, Richard E.
Taylor, Stuart
Telkes, Maria
Teller, Edward
Temin, Howard
Tereshkova, Valentina
Terman, Frederick
Terzaghi, Karl
Tesla, Nikola
Tesoro, Giuliana Cavaglieri
Tharp, Marie
Theiler, Max
Theorell, Axel Hugo Teodor
Thom, René Frédéric
Thomas, E. Donnall
Thomas, Martha Jane Bergin
Thompson, D'Arcy Wentworth
Thompson, Kenneth
Thomson, George Paget
Thomson, J. J.
Thurston, William
Tien, Ping King
Tildon, J. Tyson
Timoshenko, Stephen P.
Tinbergen, Nikolaas
Ting, Samuel C. C.
Tiselius, Arne
Tishler, Max
Tizard, Henry
Todd, Alexander
Tombaugh, Clyde W.
Tomonaga, Sin-Itiro
Tonegawa, Susumu
Topchiev, Aleksandr Vasil'evich
Townes, Charles H.
Trotter, Mildred
Trump, John G.
Tsao, George T.
Tsiolkovsky, Konstantin
Tsui, Daniel Chee
Tsui, Lap-Chee
Tswett, Mikhail
Turing, Alan Mathison
Turner, Charles Henry
Tuve, Merle A.
Twort, Frederick William

U

Uhlenbeck, George
Uhlenbeck, Karen

Urey, Harold
Uvarov, Boris Petrovitch
Uyeda, Seiya

V

Vallée-Poussin, Charles Jean Gustave Nicolas de la
Vallois, Henri-Victor
Van Allen, James
Van de Graaff, Robert J.
Van de Kamp, Peter
van der Meer, Simon
van der Waals, Johannes Diderik
van der Wal, Laurel
van Straten, Florence W.
Van Vleck, John
Vane, John Robert
Varmus, Harold E.
Vassy, Arlette
Vedder, Edward Bright
Veksler, V. I.
Velez-Rodriquez, Argelia
Vernadsky, Vladimir Ivanovich
Vine, Frederick John
Virtanen, Artturi Ilmari
Vollenweider, Richard
Volterra, Vito
von Braun, Wernher
von Kármán, Theodore
von Klitzing, Klaus
von Mises, Richard
von Neumann, John
Voûte, Joan George Erardus Gijsbert
Vries, Hugo de

W

Waelsch, Salome
Wagner-Jauregg, Julius
Wahl, Arnold C.
Waksman, Selman
Wald, George
Walker, John E.
Wallach, Otto
Walton, Ernest
Wang, An
Wang, James C.
Wankel, Felix
Warburg, Otto
Washington, Warren M.
Watkins, Levi, Jr.
Watson-Watt, Robert
Watson, James D.
Weber-van Bosse, Anne Antoinette
Weber, Ernst
Weertman, Julia

Wegener, Alfred
Weidenreich, Franz
Weil, André
Weinberg, Robert A.
Weinberg, Steven
Weinberg, Wilhelm
Weiss, Mary Catherine Bishop
Weizsäcker, Carl F. Von
Weller, Thomas
Went, Frits
Werner, Alfred
West, Harold Dadford
Wetherill, George West
Wexler, Nancy
Weyl, Hermann
Wheeler, Anna Johnson Pell
Wheeler, John Archibald
Whinfield, John Rex
Whinnery, John R.
Whipple, Fred Lawrence
Whipple, George Hoyt
White, Augustus
White, Gilbert Fowler
White, Raymond L.
Whitehead, Alfred North
Whittaker, Robert Harding
Whittle, Frank
Wickenden, William E.
Widnall, Sheila E.
Wiechert, Emil
Wieland, Heinrich
Wien, Wilhelm
Wiener, Alexander
Wiener, Norbert
Wieschaus, Eric F.
Wiesel, Torsten
Wigglesworth, Vincent
Wigner, Eugene Paul
Wiles, Andrew J.
Wilkes, Maurice Vincent
Wilkins, J. Ernest, Jr.
Wilkins, Maurice Hugh Frederick
Wilkinson, Geoffrey
Williams, Anna W.
Williams, Cicely Delphin
Williams, Daniel Hale
Williams, Evan James
Williams, Frederic C.
Williams, Heather
Williams, Ozzie S.
Williamson, James S.
Willstätter, Richard
Wilmut, Ian
Wilson, C. T. R.
Wilson, Edmund Beecher
Wilson, Edward O.
Wilson, J. Tuzo

Wilson, Kenneth G.
Wilson, Robert Rathbun
Wilson, Robert Woodrow
Windaus, Adolf
Wirth, Niklaus
Witkin, Evelyn Maisel
Witten, Edward
Wittig, Georg
Wolman, Abel
Wood, Harland G.
Woodland, Joseph
Woodward, Robert B.
Woodwell, George M.
Wozniak, Stephen
Wright, Almroth Edward
Wright, Jane Cooke
Wright, Louis Tompkins
Wright, Sewall
Wright, Wilbur & Orville
Wu, Chien-Shiung
Wu, Y. C. L. Susan

X

Xide, Xie

Y

Yalow, Rosalyn Sussman
Yang, Chen Ning
Yau, Shing-Tung
Young, Grace Chisholm
Young, J. Z.
Young, Lai-Sung
Young, William Henry
Yukawa, Hideki

Z

Zadeh, Lotfi Asker
Zamecnik, Paul Charles
Zeeman, E. C.
Zeeman, Pieter
Zel'dovich, Yakov Borisovich
Zen, E-an
Zernike, Frits
Ziegler, Karl
Zinder, Norton David
Zinkernagel, Rolf M.
Zinn, Walter Henry
Zinsser, Hans
Zsigmondy, Richard
Zuse, Konrad
Zworykin, Vladimir

Chronology of Scientific Advancement

1895 Scottish physicist C.T.R. Wilson invents the cloud chamber

French physicist Jean Baptiste Perrin confirms the nature of cathode rays

1896 American agricultural chemist George Washington Carver begins work at the Tuskegee Institute

1897 English physicist J.J. Thomson discovers the electron

1898 Polish-born French radiation chemist Marie Curie and French physicist Pierre Curie discover polonium and radium

1900 German physicist Max Planck develops Planck's Constant

1901 Austrian American immunologist Karl Landsteiner discovers A, B, and O blood types

German geneticist Wilhelm Weinberg outlines the "difference method" in his first important paper on heredity

1902 English geneticist William Bateson translates Austrian botanist Gregor Mendel's work

1903 Polish-born French radiation chemist Marie Curie becomes the first woman to be awarded the Nobel Prize

German chemist Otto Diels isolates molecular structure of cholesterol

1904 English electrical engineer John Ambrose Fleming develops the Fleming Valve

Russian physiologist Ivan Petrovich Pavlov receives the Nobel Prize for digestion research

1905 German-born American physicist Albert Einstein publishes the theory of relativity

German chemist Fritz Haber publishes *Thermodynamics of Technical Gas Reactions*

German chemist Walther Nernst's research leads to the Third Law of Thermodynamics

1906 Danish physicist and chemist Johannes Nicolaus Brønsted publishes his first paper on affinity

English neurophysiologist Charles Scott Sherrington publishes *The Integrative Action of the Nervous System*

1907 Prussian-born American physicist Albert Michelson becomes the first American to receive the Nobel Prize for Physics

1908 American astrophysicist George Ellery Hale discovers magnetic fields in sunspots

1909 German bacteriologist and immunologist Paul Ehrlich discovers a cure for syphilis

American engineer and inventor Charles Franklin Kettering successfully tests the first prototypes of the electric automobile starter

1910 English American mathematician Alfred North Whitehead and English mathematician and philosopher Bertrand Russell publish the first volume of *Principia Mathematica*

American engineer and inventor Lee De Forest attempts the first live broadcast of radio

New Zealand-born English physicist Ernest Rutherford postulates the modern concept of the atom

1911 English mathematician Godfrey Harold Hardy begins his collaboration with J. E. Littlewood

Polish-born French radiation chemist Marie Curie becomes the first scientist to win a second Nobel Prize

1912 Danish physicist Niels Bohr develops a new theory of atomic structure

Austrian physicist Victor Hess discovers cosmic rays

English biochemist Frederick Gowland Hopkins publishes a groundbreaking work illustrating the nutritional importance of nutrients

German physicist Max von Laue discovers x-ray diffraction

Austrian physicist Lise Meitner becomes the first woman professor in Germany

German meteorologist and geophysicist Alfred Wegener proposes the theory of continental drift

1913 German bacteriologist and immunologist Paul Ehrlich gives an address explaining the future of chemotherapy

English physicist Henry Gwyn Jeffreys Moseley discovers atomic number of the elements

French physicist Jean Baptiste Perrin verifies German-born American physicist Albert Einstein's calculations of Brownian Motion

American astronomer and astrophysicist Henry Norris Russell publishes the Hertzsprung-Russell diagram

Russian-born American aeronautical engineer Igor I. Sikorsky designs the *Ilya Mourometz* bomber

German chemist Richard Willstätter and Arthur Stoll publish their first studies of chlorophyll

American geneticist A.H. Sturtevant develops gene mapping

1916 American chemist and physicist Irving Langmuir receives a patent for an energy-efficient, longer-lasting tungsten filament light bulb

American geneticist and embryologist Thomas Hunt Morgan publishes *A Critique of the Theory of Evolution*

German theoretical physicist Arnolde Sommerfeld reworks Danish physicist Niels Bohr's atomic theory

American anatomist Florence Rena Sabin publishes *The Origin and Development of the Lymphatic System*

1918 Daniel physical chemist Johannes Nicolaus Brønsted publishes his thirteenth paper on affinity

1919 New Zealand-born English physicist Ernest Rutherford determines that alpha particles can split atoms

1920 American astronomer Harlow Shapley convinces the scientific community that the Milky Way is much larger than originally thought and the Earth's solar system is not its center

1921 Canadian physiologist Frederick G. Banting and Canadian physiologist Charles Herbert Best discover insulin

1923 Danish physical chemist Johannes Nicolaus Brønsted redefines acids and bases

English astronomer Arthur Stanley Eddington publishes *Mathematical Theory of Relativity*

American astronomer Edwin Hubble confirms the existence of galaxies outside the Milky Way

American physicist Robert A. Millikan begins his study of cosmic rays

1924 French theoretical physicist Louis Victor de Broglie publishes findings on wave mechanics

English astronomer Arthur Stanley Eddington determines the mass-luminosity law

1925 German-born American physicist James Franck and German physicist Gustav Hertz prove Danish physicist Niels Bohr's theory of the quantum atom

Italian-born American physicist Enrico Fermi publishes a paper explaining Austro-Hungarian-born Swiss physicist Wolfgang Pauli's exclusion principle

English statistician and geneticist Ronald A. Fisher publishes *Statistical Methods for Research Workers*

1926 German-born English physicist Max Born explains the wave function

American physicist and rocker pioneer Robert H. Goddard launches the first liquid-propellant rocket

American geneticist Hermann Joseph Muller confirms that x rays greatly increase the mutation rate in Drosophila

Austrian physicist Erwin Schrödinger publishes his wave equation

1927 American physicist Arthur Holly Compton receives the Nobel Prize for x-ray research

English physiologist Henry Hallett Dale identifies the chemical mediator involved in the transmission of nerve impulses

German chemist Otto Diels develops a successful dehydrogenating process

German physicist Werner Karl Heisenberg develops the Uncertainty Principle

Belgian astronomer Georges Lemaître formulates the big bang theory

Hungarian American mathematical physicist Eugene Paul Wigner develops the law of the conservation of parity

American astronomer Edwin Hubble puts together the theory of the expanding universe, or Hubble's Law

1928 German chemist Otto Diels and German chemist Kurt Alder develop the Diels-Alder Reaction

Scottish bacteriologist Alexander Fleming discovers penicillin

Austro-Hungarian-born German physicist Hermann Oberth publishes a book explaining the basic principles of space flight

Indian physicist C. V. Raman discovers the Raman Effect

1929 American physicist Robert Van de Graaff constructs the first working model of his particle accelerator

Danish astronomer Ejnar Hertzsprung receives the Gold Medal Award for calculating the first intergalactic distance

Norwegian American chemist Lars Onsager develops the Law of Reciprocal Relations

German-born American mathematician Hermann Weyl develops a mathematical theory for the neutrino

Russian-born American physicist and engineer Vladimir Zworkin files his first patent for color television

1930 English statistician and geneticist Ronald A. Fisher publishes *The Genetical Theory of Natural Selection*

Austrian-born American mathematician Kurt Friedrich Gödel proves the incompleteness theorem

Austro-Hungarian-born Swiss physicist Wolfgang Pauli proposes the existence of the neutrino

1931 American engineer Vannevar Bush develops the differential analyzer with colleagues

American chemist Wallace Hume Carothers founds the synthetic rubber manufacturing industry with his research

South African-born American virologist Max Theiler's research leads to the production of the first yellow-fever vaccine

German biochemist Otto Warburg establishes the Kaiser Wilhelm Institute for Cell Physiology

1932 English atomic physicist John Cockcroft and Irish experimental physicist Ernest Walton split the atom

American physicist Carl David Anderson discovers the positron

English-born Indian physiologist and geneticist John Burdon Sanderson Haldane publishes *The Causes of Evolution*

American physicist Ernest Orlando Lawrence develops the cyclotron and disintegrates a lithium nucleus

1933   Canadian-born American biologist and bacteriologist Oswald Theodore Avery identifies DNA as the basis of heredity

English physicist Paul Adrien Maurice Dirac wins the Nobel Prize for his work on the wave equation

Italian-born American physicist Enrico Fermi proposes his beta decay theory

German inventor Felix Wankel successfully operates the first internal combustion, rotary engine

1934   French nuclear physicist Frédéric Joliot-Curie and French chemist and physicist Irène Joliot-Curie discover artificial radioactivity

American inventor Edwin H. Land develops a commercial method to polarize light

New Zealand-born English physicist Ernest Rutherford achieves the first fusion reaction

American chemist and physicist Harold Urey receives the Nobel Prize in Chemistry for his discovery of deuterium, or heavy hydrogen

1935   American seismologist Charles F. Richter and German American seismologist Beno Gutenberg develop the Richter(-Gutenberg) Scale

English physicist James Chadwick receives the Nobel Prize for the discovery of the neutron

1936   German experimental physicist Hans Geiger perfects the Geiger-Mueller Counter

Russian biochemist Aleksandr Ivanovich Oparin publishes his origin of life theory

English mathematician Alan Turing publishes a paper detailing a machine that would serve as a model for the first working computer

1937   Russian-born American biologist Theodosius Dobzhansky writes *Genetics and the Origin of Species*

Australian English pathologist Howard Walter Florey discovers the growth potential of polymeric chains

German-born English biochemist Hans Adolf Krebs identifies the workings of the Krebs Cycle

Hungarian American biochemist and molecular biologist Albert Szent-Györgyi receives the nobel Prize for isolating vitamin C

1938   German chemist Otto Hahn, Austrian physicist Lise Meitner, and German chemist Fritz Strassmann discover nuclear fission

American physicist Carl David Anderson discovers the meson

1939   Swiss-born American physicist Felix Bloch measures the neutron's magnetic movement

American chemist Wallace Hume Carothers founds the synthetic fiber industry with his research

French-born American microbiologist and ecologist René Dubos discovers tyrothricin

American chemist Linus Pauling develops the theory of complementarity

Russian-born American aeronautical engineer Igor I. Sikorsky flies the first single-rotor helicopter

1940   American physicist and inventor Chester Carlson receives a patent for his photocopying method

English experimental physicist George Paget Thomson forms the Maud Committee

1941   German-born English biochemist Ernst Boris Chain and Australian English pathologist Howard Walter Florey isolate penicillin

German-born American physicist Hans Bethe develops the Bethe Coupler

American biochemist Fritz Lipmann publishes "Metabolic Generation and Utilization of Phosphate Bond Energy"

1942   Hungarian American physicist and biophysicist Leo Szilard and Italian-born American physicist Enrico Fermi set up the first nuclear chain reaction

German-born American biologist Ernst Mayr proposes the theory of geographic speciation

American physicist J. Robert Oppenheimer becomes the director of the Manhattan Project

1943   German-born American molecular biologist Max Delbrück and Italian-born American molecular biologist Salvador Edward Luria publish a milestone paper regarded as the beginning of bacterial genetics

English physicist James Chadwick leads the British contingent of the Manhattan Project

French oceanographer Jacques-Yves Cousteau patents the Aqualung

Italian-born American molecular biologist Salvador Edward Luria devises the fluctuation test

1944   German American rocket engineer Wernher Von Braun fires the first fully operational V-2 rocket

Austrian-born American biochemist Erwin Chargaff discovers the genetic role of DNA

American nuclear chemist Glenn T. Seaborg successfully isolates large amounts of plutonium and develops the actinide concept

American paleontologist George Gaylord Simpson publishes *Tempo and Mode in Evolution*

Russian-born American microbiologist Selman Waksman develops streptomycin

1945   English physicist James Chadwick witnesses the first atomic bomb test

American biochemist Fritz Lipmann discovers coenzyme A

Hungarian American mathematician Johann Von Neumann publishes a report containing the first written description of the stored-program concept

American chemist Linus Pauling determines the cause of sickle-cell anemia

Austrian physicist Erwin Schrödinger publishes *What Is Life?*

1946   American geneticist Joshua Lederberg and American biochemist Edward Lawrie Tatum show that bacteria may reproduce sexually

English zoologist Julian Huxley becomes the first director-general of UNESCO

1947   French oceanographer Jacques-Yves Cousteau breaks the free diving record using his Aqualung

Hungarian-born English physicist Dennis Gabor discovers holography

American inventor Edwin H. Land demonstrates the first instant camera

American mathematician Norbert Wiener creates the study of cybernetics

1948   American physicist John Bardeen develops the transistor

American chemist Melvin Calvin begins research on photosynthesis

Russian-born American physicist George Gamow publishes "Alpha-Beta-Gamma" paper

American zoologist and sex researcher Alfred Kinsey publishes *Sexual Behavior in the Human Male*

American biochemist Wendell Meredith Stanley receives Presidential Certificate of Merit for developing an influenza vaccine

Swedish chemist Arne Tiselius receives the Nobel Prize for research in electrophoresis

1949   Hungarian-born American physicist Edward Teller begins developing the hydrogen bomb

American astronomer Fred Lawrence Whipple suggests the "dirty snowball" comet model

1950   American geneticist Barbara McClintock publishes the discovery of genetic transposition

1951

American chemist Katherine Burr Blodgett receives the Garvan Medal for women chemists

American biologist Gregory Goodwin Pincus begins work on the antifertility steroid the "pill"

Dutch-born English zoologist and ethologist Nikolaas Tinbergen publishes *The Study of Instinct*

1952

German-born American astronomer Walter Baade presents new measurements of the universe

French-born American microbiologist and ecologist René Dubos publishes a book linking tuberculosis with certain environmental conditions

American microbiologist Alfred Day Hershey conducts the "Blender Experiment" to demonstrate that DNA is the genetic material of life

Italian-born American molecular biologist Salvador Edward Luria discovers the phenomenon known as restriction and modification

American microbiologist Jonas Salk develops the first polio vaccine

English chemist Alexander Todd establishes the structure of flavin adenine dinucleotide (FAD)

1953

Russian theoretical physicist Andrei Sakharov and Russian physicist Igor Tamm develop the first Soviet hydrogen bomb

English molecular biologist Francis Crick and American molecular biologist James D. Watson develop the Watson-Crick model of DNA

English molecular biologist Rosalind Elsie Franklin provides evidence of DNA's double-helical structure

American physicist Murray Gell-Mann publishes a paper explaining the strangeness principle

American zoologist and sex researcher Alfred Kinsey publishes *Sexual Behavior in the Human Female*

French microbiologist André Lwoff proposes that "inducible lysogenic bacteria" can test cancerous and noncancerous cell activity

English biologist Peter Brian Medawar proves acquired immunological tolerance

American chemist Stanley Lloyd Miller publishes "A Production of Amino Acids under Possible Primitive Earth Conditions"

Austrian-born English crystallographer and biochemist Max Perutz develops method of isomorphous replacement

1955

English chemist Alexander Todd and English chemist and crystallographer Dorothy Crowfoot Hodgkin determine the structure of vitamin B12

American biochemist Sidney W. Fox begins identifying properties of microspheres

American microbiologist Jonas Salk's polio vaccine pronounced safe and ninety-nine percent effective

English biochemist Frederick Sanger determines the total structure of the insulin molecule

1956

American biochemist Stanley Cohen extracts NGF from a mouse tumor

American experimental physicist Leon Max Lederman helps discover the "long-lived neutral kaon"

1957

American biochemist Arthur Kornberg and Spanish biochemist Severo Ochoa use DNA polymerase to synthesize DNA molecules

1958

American physicist James Van Allen discovers Van Allen radiation belts

American geneticist George Wells Beadle receives the Nobel Prize for the One Gene, One Enzyme Theory

American population biologist Paul R. Ehrlich makes his first statement regarding the problem of overpopulation

German physicist Rudolf Mössbauer discovers recoilless gamma ray release

1959

American computer scientist Grace Hopper develops the COBOL computer language

German physicist Rudolf Mössbauer uses the Mössbauer Effect to test the theory of relativity

1960   English physicist and biochemist John Kendrew and Austrian-born English crystallographer and biochemist Max Perutz formulate the first three-dimensional structure of the protein myoglobin

American chemist Willard F. Libby receives the Nobel Prize for his development of radiocarbon dating

Russian-born American virologist Albert Sabin's oral polio vaccine is approved for manufacture in the United States

1961   French biologists François Jacob and Jacques Monod discover messenger ribonucleic acid (mRNA)

American chemist Melvin Calvin receives the Nobel Prize in Chemistry for his research on photosynthesis

American biochemist Marshall Warren Nirenberg cracks the genetic code

1962   American marine biologist Rachel Carson publishes *Silent Spring*

Russian theoretical physicist Lev Davidovich Landau receives the Nobel Prize for his research into theories of condensed matter

Hungarian-born American physicist Edward Teller becomes the first advocate of an "active defense system" to shoot down enemy missiles

New Zealand-born English biophysicist Maurice Hugh Frederick Wilkins shows the helical structure of RNA

1963   German American physicist Maria Goeppert-Mayer becomes the first woman to receive the Nobel Prize for theoretical physics

American chemist Linus Pauling becomes the only person to receive two unshared Nobel Prizes

1964   American psychobiologist Roger W. Sperry publishes the findings of his split-brain studies

1965   American geneticist A.H. Sturtevant publishes *The History of Genetics*

1967   English astrophysicist Antony Hewish and Irish astronomer Jocelyn Susan Bell Burnell discover pulsars

South African heart surgeon Christiaan Neethling Barnard performs the first human heart transplant

American primatologist Dian Fossey establishes a permanent research camp in Rwanda

1968   American physicist Luis Alvarez wins the Nobel Prize for his bubble chamber work

1969   American astronaut Neil Armstrong becomes the first man to walk on the moon

1970   Indian-born American biochemist Har Gobind Khorana synthesizes the first artificial DNA

American biologist Lynn Margulis publishes *Origins of Life*

1971   English ethologist Jane Goodall publishes *In the Shadow of Man*

1972   American evolutionary biologist Stephen Jay Gould and American paleontologist Niles Eldredge introduce the concept of punctuated equilibrium

American physicist John Bardeen develops the BCS theory of superconductivity

American inventor Edwin H. Land reveals the first instant color camera

1973   American radio engineer Karl Jansky receives the honor of having the Jansky unit adopted as the unit of measure of radiowave intensity

Austrian zoologist and ethologist Konrad Lorenz receives the Nobel Prize for his behavioral research

American biochemist and geneticist Maxine Singer warns the public of gene-splicing risks

1974   English astrophysicist Antony Hewish receives the first Nobel Prize awarded to an astrophysicist

1975   French oceanographer Jacques-Yves Cousteau sees his Cousteau Society membership reach 120,000

American zoologist Edward O. Wilson publishes *Sociobiology: The New Synthesis*

1976 American computer engineer Seymour Cray introduces the CRAY-1 supercomputer

1977 Russian-born Belgian chemist Ilya Prigogine receives the Nobel Prize in Chemistry for his work on nonequilibrium thermodynamics

1980 American biochemist Paul Berg receives the Nobel Prize for the biochemistry of nucleic acids

1981 American virologist Robert C. Gallo develops a blood test for the AIDS virus and discovers human T-cell leukemia virus

1982 American astronaut and physicist Sally Ride becomes the first American woman in space

1983 Italian-born American astrophysicist and applied mathematician Subrahmanyan Chandrasekhar receives the Nobel Prize for research on aged stars

American primatologist Dian Fossey publishes *Gorillas in the Mist*

French virologist Luc Montagnier discovers the human immunodeficiency virus (HIV)

American astronomer and exobiologist Carl Sagan publishes an article with others suggesting the possibility of a "nuclear winter"

1986 American physicist Richard P. Feynman explains why the space shuttle *Challenger* exploded

1987 Chinese American physicist Paul Ching-Wu Chu leads a team that discovers a method for higher temperature superconductivity

1988 English theoretical physicist Stephen Hawking publishes *A Brief History of Time: From the Big Bang to Black Holes*

English pharmacologist James Black receives the Nobel Prize for his heart and ulcer medication work

1989 German-born American physicist Hans Dehmelt and German physicist Wolfgang Paul share the Nobel Prize for devising ion traps

1990 American physicists Jerome Friedman, Henry W. Kendall, and Richard E. Taylor are awarded the Nobel Prize for confirming the existence of quarks

American surgeon Joseph E. Murray receives the Nobel Prize for performing the first human kidney transplant

1991 German physician and cell physiologist Bert Sakmann and German biophysicist Erwin Neher are awarded the Nobel Prize for inventing the patch clamp technique

1993 English biochemist Richard J. Roberts and American biologist Phillip A. Sharp share the Nobel Prize for their research on DNA structure American astrophysicists Russell A. Hulse and Joseph H. Taylor, Jr. receive the Nobel Prize for their work on binary pulsars

1994 American researchers Alfred G. Gilman and Martin Rodbell win the Nobel Prize for their discovery of the role of G-proteins in cellular communication

1995 American biologists Edward B. Lewis and Eric F. Wieschaus and German biologist Christiane Nusslein-Volhard are awarded the Nobel Prize for discoveries concerning the embryonic development of fruit flies

1996 American paleobiologist J. William Schopf determines that a Martian meteorite which struck Antarctica 16 million years ago did not contain evidence of life on Mars.

American medical researcher David Ho heads a research group that announces the results of a study in which nine HIV-infected men were treated with a combination of drugs that halted the progression of AIDS so that HIV was not detected in blood tests a year after treatment ended

1997 English embryologist Ian Wilmut at the Roslin Institute reports that a sheep named Dolly is the first mammal successfully cloned from adult tissue

American biologist Stanley Prusiner wins the Nobel Prize for his discovery of prions, cellular proteins capable of causing disease

 1998

American Robert B. Laughlin, German-born American Horst L. Störmer, and Chinese American Daniel C. Tsui receive the Nobel Prize in Physics for their discovery of a new form of quantum fluid with fractionally charged excitations

English theoretical chemist John A. Pople and Austrian American physicist Walter Kohn receive the Nobel Prize in Chemistry for pioneering work in computational methods in quantum chemistry. Pople developed the computational methods, and Kohn developed density-functional theory

 1999

Dutch physicists Gerardus 't Hooft and Martinus J.G. Veltman receive the Nobel Prize in Physics for elucidating the quantum structure of electroweak interactions in physics. They made particle physics theory more mathematically sound; in particular, the two showed how the theory may be used for precise calculations of physical quantities

German American medical researcher Günter Blobel receives the Nobel Prize in Physiology or Medicine for the discovery that proteins have intrinsic signals that govern their transport and localization in the cell

Samuel Milton Nabrit
1905–
American biologist

Samuel Milton Nabrit is known for his research into animal regeneration, the ability of body parts to regrow or repair themselves after injury, and for his academic career as a promoter of science instruction among young African Americans. The first black Ph.D. from Brown University, Nabrit served as chairman of the biology department and as dean of the graduate school of arts and sciences at Atlanta University, and as president of Texas Southern University.

Born in Macon, Georgia, February 21, 1905 to James M. Nabrit, a Baptist minister and teacher, and Augusta Gertrude West Nabrit, Nabrit studied at Morehouse College, where he received his bachelor's degree in 1925. Taking to heart the desire to teach inherited from his father, Nabrit returned to Morehouse College as a professor of biology from 1925–31, while he attended Brown University, working towards his advanced degrees. He obtained his M.S. in 1928 and his Ph.D. in biology in 1932.

While teaching during the school year at Morehouse, Nabrit conducted research at the Marine Biological Laboratory in Woods Hole, Massachusetts, every summer from 1927 to 1932. His specialty was the regenerative abilities of fish, particularly studying their ability to regrow tail fins. He found that the size of the fin rays on fishes' fins determined the rate of regeneration. The results of his research were published in the *Biological Bulletin.* A citation presented to Nabrit on April 30, 1982, by the Beta Kappa Chi Scientific Honor Society to which Nabrit belonged, noted that a study published by Nabrit in 1928 was still being quoted in studies of animal regeneration as late as the 1980s.

After earning his doctorate in 1932, Nabrit was appointed chairman of Atlanta University's biology department, a position he held until 1947. He continued his regenerative research at Atlanta University, focusing on fish embryo regeneration in particular. His work was described in articles appearing in such scientific publications as the *Anatomical Record, Journal of Parasitology,* and the *Journal of Experimental Zoology.* In 1947, Nabrit became dean of Atlanta University's graduate school of arts and sciences. In 1955 he was appointed president of Texas Southern University, where he served until 1966. During his tenure as president, Nabrit also served as president of the Association of Colleges and Secondary Schools and as a member of the board of directors of the American Council on Education. He also joined several committees for the Departments of State and Health and Human Services, and was appointed by President Eisenhower to a six-year term on the National Science Board in 1956. In 1966 President Johnson selected Nabrit for a term on the Atomic Energy Commission. The following year Nabrit became director of the Southern Fellowships Fund, an operating agency of the Council of Southern Universities, where he stayed until his retirement in 1981.

Nabrit was one of the founders of Upward Bound, a program designed to increase the numbers of qualified youth staying in college beyond one year. While a guest speaker at Kashmere Gardens High School, Nabrit was told that most of the scholarship winners would drop out during their first year in college. Nabrit decided to do something about this problem. In 1957, scholarship winners and other high potential students were invited to Texas Southern for the summer, essentially enrolling in the college for 11 weeks. Three nationally established specialists in reading, logical thinking and mathematics were recruited to hold classes daily, and the students were paired with volunteers who stayed with them in the dormitories and tutored them every night. The number of students remaining in college was greatly increased by the program.

In a phone interview, Nabrit recalled that when he began his academic career the "leading scientist in our field . . . produced only one or two biology students. All of his students he steered into medicine. My notion was that we needed to increase the number of young people who would be able to get the Ph.D. in biology and all the other sciences. At Brown, where I was the first Negro to graduate with a Ph.D. in biology, I made sure that the next four black Ph.D.s were all out of my lab."

Throughout his college career, Nabrit played baseball and football. The game he loved playing the most, though, and continued playing into the 1940's was bridge; he and his foursome became expert enough to advance to a national bridge championship. Nabrit married Constance T. Crocker in 1927; she passed away in 1984. They had no children. Dr. Nabrit still lives in Georgia.

SELECTED WRITINGS BY NABRIT:

Periodicals

Biological Bulletin, The Role of the Fin Rays in Tail-fins of Fishes Fundulus and Goldfish, April, 1929.

Biological Bulletin, The Role of the Basal Plate of the Tail in Regeneration of Fishes Fundulus, February, 1931.

Science Education, Human Ecology in Georgia, October, 1944.

Negro History Bulletin, The Negro in Science, January, 1957.

FURTHER READING:

Books

Sammons, Vivian O., *Blacks in Science and Technology,* Hemisphere Publishing Corp. p. 179, 1990.

Other

Sammons, Vivian O., *Blacks in Science and Technology,* Beta Kappa Chi, text of citation, April 30, 1982.

Nabrit, Samuel Milton, *Interview with Sharon F. Suer* conducted January 18, 1994.

Sketch by Sharon F. Suer

Takesi Nagata
1913–1991
Japanese geophysicist

Takesi Nagata was one of the first scientists to investigate the magnetic properties of volcanic rocks. Additional studies into what he termed thermoremanent magnetization (TRM) led to a renewal in the 1950s of the theory of continental drift and ocean floor spreading. Nagata was also an active field scientist, leading Japan's Antarctic expeditions in the mid- to late-1950s, and establishing a Japanese base there for the study of polar magnetism. His interests in space physics led to his becoming the primary geophysical investigator of lunar matter from the Apollo space missions. Additionally, Nagata was a science administrator of international stature, organizing and chairing conferences and committees worldwide for the advancement of geophysical observation.

Born in Okazaki City, in the prefecture of Aichi, on June 24, 1913, Nagata graduated from Tokyo Imperial University (later the University of Tokyo) in 1936. He then became a research associate at the Earthquake Research Institute of the university, studying the electric and magnetic properties of seismic and volcanic occurrences and focusing particularly on volcanic rocks. It was in the late 1930s that he discovered the strong magnetism of such rocks, classifying both natural remanent (NRM) and thermoremanent magnetism of lavas as they cooled. In May, 1941, Nagata accepted a position as associate professor at the Geophysical Institute of Tokyo Imperial University, his research interests broadening to include rock magnetism in general and the measurement of the NRM of sedimentary rocks in hopes of uncovering the course of early development of the Earth. He continued his research during World War II in addition to working for the Japanese navy on the military applications of magnetism.

Takes on an International Research Agenda

After the war, Nagata became more involved in organizational work, heading various geophysical and geomagnetic research groups in Japan, founding the Society of Terrestrial Magnetism and Electricity of Japan among others. In 1951 he was a research fellow at the department of terrestrial magnetism at the Carnegie Institute in Washington, D.C., a turning point in his career that pointed him in new research directions, particularly toward geomagnetism as it relates to the ionosphere and outer space. That same year he was awarded the prestigious Japan Academy prize in recognition for his work in rock magnetism, and the following year he became a full professor at the University of Tokyo.

With the advent of the International Geophysical Year from 1957 to 1958, Nagata pushed for Japan to mount an Antarctic expedition, which he led in 1956, establishing a Japanese observation base at Syowa Station. Nagata also led subsequent expeditions to the base, and later, after retirement from the University of Tokyo in 1973, he became the director general of Japan's newly created National Institute of Polar Research, responsible for overseeing the functions of Syowa Station, particularly the space launches from Antarctica to study the upper atmosphere. He also set up an additional two Japanese stations in Antarctica. Nagata's interest in space physics grew over the years: a full one-third of his four hundred professional articles deal with that subject. In the 1960s and 1970s much of his time was spent in studying lunar samples from the various Apollo missions, measuring and discovering surprisingly strong magnetism in various rocks, as well as high electrical conductivity of crystalline rock samples containing metallic iron.

From 1961, Nagata held an adjunct professorship at the University of Pittsburgh, where he continued to do research in between international meetings. But much of his time in later years was taken up with administration. He was the president of the International Association of Geomagnetism and Aeronomy (IAGA) from 1967 to 1971, as well as vice-president of the Scientific Committee on Antarctic Research (SCAR) from 1972 to 1976. Later honors included Japan's Order of Culture in 1974 and the Gold Medal from the Royal Astronomical Society of Great Britain in 1987. He was also elected a member of the National Academy of Sciences in the United States in 1959. Nagata remained active in scientific affairs until his death on June 3, 1991, at the age of seventy-seven. Two mountains were named after the renowned geophysicist: One is in the Pacific Ocean and the other in Victoria Land of Antarctica.

SELECTED WRITINGS BY NAGATA:

Books

Rock Magnetism, Maruzen, 1953.
National Report of Japanese Antarctic Research Expeditions, 1958–1960, Ministry of Education, 1960.
Physical Properties, Magnetic Properties of Apollo 11–17 Lunar Materials with Special Reference to Effects of Meteorite Impact, Volume 3, Pergamon, 1974, pp. 2827–2839.

Periodicals

American Association of Petroleum Geologists' Bulletin, Magnetism of the Earth's Crust and the Earth's Interior, Volume 49, number 3, 1965, p. 354.
Pure and Applied Geophysics, Effects of Uniaxal Compression on Remanent Magnetizations of Igneous Rocks, Volume 78, 1970, pp. 100–109.
Nankyoku Shiryo, Geomagnetic Secular Variation in the Antarctic Region during 1960–1975, Volume 74, 1982, pp. 27–44.
Antarctic Journal of the United States, Geophysical Studies on Mount Erebus, Volume 19, number 5, 1985, pp. 22–24.

FURTHER READING:

Periodicals

Fukushima, N., *Journal of Geomagnetism and Geoelectricity,* Nagata, Takesi (1913–1991), Volume 43, number 11, 1991, pp. 883–884.
Fukushima, N., *Planetary and Space Science,* Nagata, Takesi (1913–1991), October, 1991, pp. 1323–1324.
Fukushima, N., *New York Times,* Japan Will Send Antarctic Party, September 23, 1956, p. 30.
Rikitake, Tsuneji, *Earth Science Review,* Takesi Nagata: Portrait of a Scientist, Volume 9, number 1, 1973, pp. 81–86.
Yukutake, Takesi, *Kasan—Bulletin of the Volcanological Society of Japan,* To the Memory of Dr. Takesi Nagata, (Japanese language) October, 1991, pp. 389–390.

Sketch by J. Sydney Jones

Koji Nakanishi
1925–
Japanese-born American chemist

K oji Nakanishi believes in conventional values, like devotion to family and respect for authority. Yet, his career and life have been anything but conventional. In his autobiography, *A Wandering Natural Products Chemist,* Nakanishi describes himself as a "hybrid" who grew up in Europe, Egypt, and Japan and whose philosophy and behavior in life have been influenced by both Eastern and Western thought. A dedicated, world-renowned organic chemist with wide-ranging interests, Nakanishi is also an amateur magician who delights in mystifying his audience and likes "drinking in quiet bars with friends." Although he has spent the past 30 years primarily in the United States conducting research and teaching, Nakanishi has always maintained strong ties with his homeland.

In his autobiography, Nakanishi says that his wife accuses him of having too many professional interests instead of specializing. He also modestly asserts that he does not consider himself "brilliant." However, with the dedicated help of his students and colleagues, Nakanishi has made important contributions in elucidating the structures of natural bioactive compounds and their modes of action. For example, his work in the isolation and structural studies of visual pigments has led to new insights into the mechanism of vision. As a result, he has gained international respect and numerous honors, including the Imperial Prize and the Japan Academy Prize, which represent the highest honors for a Japanese scholar.

Nakanishi was born in the hills of Hong Kong on May 11, 1925, the eldest of Yuzo and Yoshiko Nakanishi's four sons. In Japanese, the characters for KO in Nakanishi's first name are identical to Hong, which means perfume. (Hong Kong means perfume harbor.) Nakanishi's father, Yuzo, worked in international banking, and the family moved to Lyon, France, soon after Nakanishi's birth. His father was then transferred to England, where Nakanishi learned English at a young age and "proper English manners." The family eventually relocated to Alexandria, Egypt, and then to Japan in 1935.

During the next 10 years, Nakanishi was to experience one of the most tumultuous times in Japanese history. A fanatic militarism was on the rise in Japan, culminating in World War II and ultimate defeat at the hands of the Allies. While he was interested in chemistry and biology, Nakanishi chose chemistry as a major without any specific plans or ambitions. After high school, he applied to Tokyo Imperial University and was the only applicant from his school not to be accepted. "The failure was devastating to both my mother and myself," he writes. Because of the country's military build-up, Nakanishi and his family knew he would be drafted unless he went to college.

Koji Nakanishi

Nakanishi eventually was accepted by Nagoya Imperial University, located between Tokyo and Kyoto. He enjoyed the university's pastoral setting and the young and bright staff. It was also here that he met his future wife, Yasuko, who was a laboratory assistant. He eventually moved in with his future wife's family after his apartment was bombed during an air raid. In his autobiography, Nakanishi recounts the numbing effects of war, describing his engagement to Yasuko as "strangely emotionless because I did not think we would live to be married."

Embarks on Career in Natural Products

Following the war, Nakanishi and his colleagues quickly emersed themselves in chemistry, trying to catch up on lost time. In 1946, he joined the research group ofFujio Egami, who was carrying on Japan's tradition of excellence in natural products chemistry. After completing his graduate work in structural studies of the red crystalline antibiotic actinomycin, Nakanishi went on to become a Garioa Fellow at Harvard. Unfortunately, because of his financial situation, he was forced to leave his wife and newly born daughter Keiko in Japan for two years. (Nakanishi also has a son, Jun.) He returned to Nagoya University in 1952 as an assistant professor of chemistry. Shortly afterward he was diagnosed with tuberculosis and required to rest for several months. Nakanishi used this time to complete his translation of *Organic Chemistry* (the original work was coauthored by his mentor at Harvard, Louis Fieser) in a three-volume set. The book, which became a best-selling chemistry book well

into the 1960s, brought financial security to Nakanishi and his family.

In 1969, after stints as a professor of chemistry at Tokyo Kyoiku and Tohoku universities in Japan, Nakanishi accepted a professorship at Columbia University in New York. "I had no pressing reason to leave Tohoku University except that, subconsciously, I was interested in trying out life abroad," writes Nakanishi. This interest would drastically change the Nakanishis' life. Although his plan was to conduct advanced research in chemistry for 10 years in the United States and then return to Japan to upgrade his home country's efforts in the field, Nakanishi has spent 30 years at Columbia. Yet, he still found time to direct the Suntory Institute for Bioorganic Research (SUNBOR) in Japan and fulfilled his dream of improving Japanese science by starting the first true international postdoctoral system in Japan in 1980.

Helping Solve the Molecular Mysteries of Life

Over his career, Nakanishi has been noted for his multidisciplinary and international collaborations. He has directed research that has characterized more than 180 natural products, including antimutagens from plants and metal-sequestering compounds from sea squirt blood. He has also worked with visual pigments and wasp toxins, an effort that has led Nakanishi and colleagues to synthesize a series of compounds structurally similar to the venom of a type of Egyptian wasp. These synthetic compounds are 33 times more powerful than the natural venom and will help in obtaining pure samples of glutamic acid receptors on the surface of nerve cells for further study.

Like wasp venom, many of the compounds Nakanishi has worked with can be found only in minuscule amounts. As a result, much of his research has focused on methods stressing isolation and purification of such compounds and on new approaches to structure elucidation. Beginning in the late 1980s, his worked has centered on investigations into the interaction of bioactive molecules with receptor molecules.

A man of many interests professionally, Nakanishi also enjoyed building miniature railroads for many years and collects paintings and sculptures of bulls and cows. "Cows are pastoral, never appear to be rushing about, and give one a peaceful feeling; I am the opposite," he writes. But his favorite hobby has been magic, which he took up as a way to entertain people at graduations, weddings, and parties. When he received the prestigious Imperial Prize, Nakanishi performed magic rope tricks for Japan's Crown Prince during the reception and dinner.

As for the future of chemistry, Nakanishi is optimistic. "Medicines and pharmacy are built completely around organic compounds," he writes in his autobiography. "In this interdisciplinary era, if we want to solve the mode of action of bioactive compounds for the purpose of uncovering the mysteries of life and to develop more active compounds, chemistry simply has to play a central role."

SELECTED WRITINGS BY NAKANISHI:

Books

A Wandering Natural Chemist. Washington, DC: American Chemical Society, 1991.

Periodicals

"Bioorganic Studies of Receptors with Philantoxin Analogs." *Pure and Applied Chemistry* 66 (1994): 671-678.

FURTHER READING:

Periodicals

"Koji Nakanishi Receives Mosher Award." *Chemical and Engineering News* (February 21, 1994): 38.

Rouhi, Maureen. "Nakanishi Wins Welch Award in Chemistry." *Chemical and Engineering News* (May 20, 1996): 9.

Wheeler, David. "Research Notes." *Chronicle of Higher Education* (September 9, 1991): A16.

Sketch by David Petechuk

Yoichiro Nambu
1921–
American physicist

Yoichiro Nambu is a theoretical physicist whose research has contributed to the understanding of elementary atomic particles. In 1982, he was awarded the National Medal of Science by President Ronald Reagan "for seminal contributions to the understanding of elementary particles and their interactions." Since 1991 he has been professor emeritus of physics at the University of Chicago.

Nambu was born in Tokyo, Japan, on January 18, 1921. Despite the tumult of World War II, he completed his studies in physics at the University of Tokyo, receiving his B.S. in 1942 and his Ph.D. in 1952. He was appointed professor of physics at Osaka City University before his doctorate was granted; his six-year appointment there began in 1950, although the latter years of this period were spent largely in the United States. In 1952 Nambu became a member of the Institute for Advanced Study in Princeton, New Jersey, and in 1954 he joined the physics department at the University of Chicago as a research associate. Nambu has remained affiliated with the University of Chicago for most of his career. In 1956 he was promoted to associate professor and in 1958, professor. From 1974 until 1977 he was the chair of the department of physics, and in 1977 he became a Henry Pratt Judson Distinguished Service Professor.

In the 1950s, when Nambu entered the field of particle physics, only a few subnuclear particles were known to exist. The existence of these particles can only be demonstrated by using powerful nuclear accelerators, and during that period it was only possible to push particles through an accelerator with 500 million electron volts of energy. By the mid-1980s, accelerators could attain energies a thousand times higher and several hundred subnuclear particles had been identified. Throughout his career, Nambu's research has been aimed not only at predicting the existence of various subnuclear particles, but at making sense of their behavior. He has advanced ideas and explanations that have helped to create a body of intellectual work known as the grand unification theories. Known also as "GUTs," these theories are an attempt to explain the fundamental forces of nature in a single framework.

Nambu's best known contribution to the GUTs is his concept of "spontaneous symmetry breaking" in particle physics. The laws of physics predict that subatomic particles should behave symmetrically, but experimental results show that they do not. Nambu proposed that while the laws of nature may predict symmetry in subatomic interactions, the stage or space-time continuum in which the interactions occur causes symmetry to break down. In the mid-1980s physicists built on Nambu's work to advance a GUT explanation that describes at least two of nature's forces, weak force and electromagnetism. This theory, now widely embraced by physicists, is known as the electroweak theory.

Nambu has been highly decorated for his contributions to the understanding of elementary particles and their interactions. He was awarded the Dannie Heineman Prize for Mathematical Physics from the American Institute of Physics in 1970. He was elected to the National Academy of Sciences in 1971. In 1976 he was awarded the J. Robert Oppenheimer Prize. In 1978 he received the Order of Culture Award of the Japanese government. The Max Planck Medal was awarded to him in 1985, and the P. A. M. Dirac Medal in 1986. Nambu holds honorary degrees from universities in the United States and Japan. He has published numerous professional articles as well as a popular book on particle physics, entitled *Quarks*. Nambu became a citizen of the United States in 1970. He is married to Chieko Hida, with whom he has had two sons.

SELECTED WRITINGS BY NAMBU:

Books

Quarks, World Scientific, 1985.

FURTHER READING:

Periodicals

University of Chicago News, Nambu Looks at Past and Future of Particle Physics, March 29, 1984, p. 7.

Sketch by Leslie Reinherz

John Forbes Nash
1928–
American algebraist and game theorist

John Forbes Nash

John Forbes Nash is considered one of America's most eminent mathematicians, having been awarded the 1994 Nobel Prize in economic science for his work in game theory, which he shared with economists John C. Harsanyi and Reinhard Selten.

A Genius of the Postwar Era

Nash was born in Bluefield, West Virginia, and came of age during the Depression. His mother, Lillian, was a Latin teacher, and his father, John Sr., an electrical engineer. The Depression did not affect the Nash family as severely as other families in West Virginia; they lived in an upper–class home down the road from the local country club. Nash and his younger sister, Martha, were both well educated. He was an avid reader, skilled at chess, and enough of an accomplished whistler to whistle complete melodies of Bach. Always curious, problem solving was his passion even as a child. One of Nash's mathematics teachers told his parents he was having trouble in class when in actuality the young prodigy was solving math problems in a different way than his teacher could formulate.

In 1945, Nash entered the Carnegie Institute of Technology (now Carnegie Mellon University), in Pittsburgh, Pennsylvania. Nash completed the requirements for a bachelor of science degree in two years, and immediately began graduate study. In 1948, Nash began his doctoral work at Princeton University, at that time the home of such renowned scholars as **Albert Einstein** and **John von Neumann**. It was in his second year at Princeton that Nash wrote his thesis paper which laid the mathematical foundations of game theory and, 45 years later, earned him the Nobel Prize.

What Is Game Theory?

Game theory was first invented by John von Neumann and Oskar Morgenstern, an economist at Princeton, who wrote of their discovery in *The Theory of Games and Economic Behavior* in 1944. Game theory became a very popular concept during the Cold War. As the nuclear arms race between the United States and the USSR escalated, a methodology which could predict the possible outcome of a worst or best case scenario was a priceless commodity. Von Neumann and Morgenstern provided a theory based on pure rivalries where the gain for one side exactly balances the loss for the other side (called a "zero–sum situation"). In his doctoral thesis, Nash focused on nonzero–sum noncooperative games involving two or more players when the players are in direct competition. He proved that under appropriate conditions, there always exists stable equilibrium strategies for the players. In such a collection of strategies, no player can increase his gain by changing his strategy while the other players' strategies remain fixed. This concept is now known as the Nash equilibrium.

In 1952 Nash became an instructor at the Massachusetts Institute of Technology and began working on a series of papers, the first of which involved real algebraic varieties. His work was important to a theorem of Artin and Mazur concerning how the number of periodic points for a smooth map can increase as a function of the number of points. Nash's work allowed Artin and Mazur to translate the problem into an algebraic one of counting solutions to polynomial equations.

Nash also tackled one of the fundamental problems in Riemannian geometry, the isometric embedding problem for Riemannian manifolds. What Nash did was to introduce an entirely new method into nonlinear analysis, which enabled him to prove the existence of isometric embeddings. Nash also developed deep and significant results about basic local existence, uniqueness, and continuity theorems for parabolic and elliptic differential equations.

Nash was diagnosed with paranoid schizophrenia at the age of 30 and spent the greater part of what could have been his most productive years in and out of mental institutions. In 1966, during a period of remission, Nash published his last paper, which was a continuation of his work on the isometric embedding theorem.

In 1994, Nash shared the Nobel Prize in Economic Science for his work in game theory. Of his achievements, **John Milnor** writes: "It is notoriously difficult to apply precise mathematical methods in the social sciences, yet the ideas in Nash's thesis are simple and rigorous, and provide a firm background, not only for economic theory but also for research in evolutionary biology, and more generally for the study of any situation in which human or nonhuman beings face competition or conflict."

SELECTED WRITINGS BY NASH:

Books

(With C. Kalisch, J. Milnor, and E. Nering) "Some Experimental *N*–Person Games." In *Decision Processes,* edited by R.M. Thrall, C.H. Coombs, and R.L. Davis. 1954.

Periodicals

"Equilibrium Points in *N*–person Games." *Proceedings of the National Academy of Sciences USA* 36 (1950): 48–49.
"The Bargaining Problem." *Econometrica* 18 (1950): 155–162.
"Real Algebraic Manifolds." *Annals of Mathematics* 56 (1952): 405–421.
"Two–Person Cooperative Games." *Econometrica* 21 (1953): 128–140.
"Results on Continuation and Uniqueness of Fluid Flow." *Bullentin of the American Mathematical Society* 60 (1954): 165–166.
"A Path Space and the Stiefel–Whitney Classes." *Proceedings of the National Academy of Sciences USA* 411 (1955): 320–321.
"The Imbedding Problem for Riemannian Manifolds." *Annals of Mathematics* 63 (1956): 20–63.
"Continuity of Solutions of Parabolic and Elliptic Equations." *American Journal of Mathematics* 80 (1958): 931–954.
"Analyticity of the Solutions of Implicit Function Problems with Analytic Data." *Annals of Mathematics* 84 (1966): 345–355.

FURTHER READING:

Books

Casti, John L. *Five Golden Rules, Great Theories of 20th–Century Mathematics—and Why They Matter.* New York: John Wiley & Sons, Inc., 1996.

Periodicals

Milnor, John. "A Nobel Prize for John Nash." *The Mathematical Intelligencer* 17, no. 3 (Summer 1995): 11–17.
Nasar, Sylvia. "The Lost Years of a Nobel Laureate." *New York Times* (November 13, 1994).
Warsh, David. "Economist Share Nobel Trio Pioneered Use of Game Theory in the Field." *The Boston Globe* (October 12, 1994): 43.

Sketch by Tammy J. Bronson

Daniel Nathans
1928–1999
American molecular biologist

Daniel Nathans was the father of modern biotechnology who received the 1978 Nobel Prize for medicine for discovering the "biochemical scissors" that led to a surge in biotechnology knowledge. His research focused on tumor-causing viruses in animals and cellular response to growth factors. He is best known for his work with restriction enzymes which are used to cut or break DNA (deoxyribonucleic acid) molecules. This technique helped scientists understand the basic structure of viruses, and opened the door for recombinant DNA research, leading to such breakthroughs as synthetic insulin, growth hormone, and genetic mapping. His work, which laid the groundwork for the worldwide effort to map the human genome, was recognized in 1978 with a shared Nobel Prize in physiology or medicine with **Werner Arber** and **Hamilton O. Smith**.

Nathans was born on October 30, 1928, in Wilmington, Delaware, the last of nine children born to Russian Jewish immigrants Samuel and Sarah Nathans. Following in the footsteps of his brothers and sisters, Nathans went to the University of Delaware, where he received a B.S. in chemistry in 1950. He went on to study medicine at Washington University in St. Louis, receiving his M.D. in 1954. It was during the summer after his first year of medical school that Nathans had his initial exposure to laboratory work and realized he was better suited to laboratory research than private practice.

After medical school, Nathans completed a one-year internship at Columbia-Presbyterian Medical Center, followed by two years (1955–57) at the National Cancer Institute studying protein synthesis. In 1956, Nathans married Joanne Gomberg, with whom he had three sons. Returning to Columbia-Presbyterian, Nathans completed his residency in 1959. That same year Nathans won a United States Public Health Service grant to do biochemical research at Rockefeller University in New York with **Fritz Lipmann** and **Norton Zinder**. It was at this point that Nathans fully committed to work in the laboratory rather than in a clinical practice. In New York, Nathans continued his work on protein synthesis and began viral research, mostly related to host-controlled variations in viruses.

In 1962, Nathans began his long relationship with Johns Hopkins University as assistant professor of microbiology and director of genetics. He became an associate professor in 1965, and a full professor in 1967. He was named director of the molecular biology and genetics department in 1972 and Boury Professor of Molecular Biology and Genetics in 1976, positions he retained for many years.

Pioneers Research in DNA

In 1962, when Nathans first arrived at Johns Hopkins, Werner Arber, at Basel University in Switzerland, predicted the existence of an enzyme capable of cutting DNA at specific sites. Deoxyribonucleic acid (DNA) is assumed to be the source of autoreproduction in many viruses. An ability to cut or cleave the DNA into specific and predictable fragments was important to greatly improving our capabilities for researching and understanding viruses. The necessity of "specific" and "predictable" fragments relates to the need of the scientist to know the fragment he or she is studying is identical to the fragment any other scientist would get following the same laboratory procedure.

In 1968, Arber got halfway to his goal, finding an enzyme (type I) capable of cleaving DNA, but in seemingly random patterns. In 1969, Hamilton O. Smith, a colleague of Nathans at Johns Hopkins, wrote to Nathans (who was in Israel at the time) to tell him he had developed a type II enzyme. This enzyme, named Hind II, was capable of cleaving DNA into specific and predictable fragments.

At this time, Nathans was working on a simian virus (SV40) which causes tumors in monkeys. SV40 was particularly impervious to then-current methods of study, so Nathans immediately saw an application of Smith's tool. Nathans, with Kathleen Danna, used Hind II to cut SV40 into eleven pieces and show its method of replication. One technique they employed in this process was radioactive labeling. The combined efforts of Arber, Smith, and Nathans over a period of more than a decade led to their receipt of the Nobel Prize in physiology or medicine in 1978. Their inter-laboratory cooperation greatly advanced the potential for consistent DNA and gene research.

Nathans continued his work with Hind II and cleared the path for much of the work that has been done since in research on DNA function and structure (such as restriction maps, used to define DNA structure). This early work has also led to the area of recombinant DNA research, which involves the process of joining two DNA fragments from separate sources into one molecule. This field of research was uncharted territory and carried some risks, including the creation of new pathogens. Nathans was among an early group of scientists who, in 1974, encouraged the publication of research guidelines and some self-imposed limits on DNA research. Despite the risks, recombinant DNA research has created supplies of previously scarce enzymes and hormones, including human-produced insulin.

In the 1980s, Nathans's research continued to be linked closely to DNA and genetics. A good portion of his scientific work during this time related to the effect of growth factors on genes and gene regulation.

Nathans was the 1993 recipient of the nation's highest scientific award, the National Medal of Science. He was a member of the American Academy of Arts and Sciences, a senior investigator at the Howard Hughes Medical Institute, a member of the American Philosophical Society, and a member of the National Academy of Sciences. He has served on the editorial board of *Proceedings of the National Academy of Sciences*, where he was a regular contributor, and from 1990 to 1993 he served on the President's Council of Advisers on Science and Technology. He also wrote dozens of articles for several scientific journals. Nathans, who taught in the microbiology department at The Johns Hopkins University for 37 years, served as department chair and stepped in as interim president from June 1995 to July 1996 when the university president unexpectedly resigned. He died of leukemia on November 16, 1999 in Baltimore at the age of 71.

SELECTED WRITINGS BY NATHANS:

Periodicals

Annual Review of Biochemistry, "Restriction Endonucleases in the Analysis and Restructuring of DNA Molecules," 1975, pp. 273–93.

Proceedings of the National Academy of Sciences, "Induction of Protooncogene c-jun by Serum Growth Factors," November 1, 1988, pp. 8464–66.

Proceedings of the National Academy of Sciences, "DNA Binding Site of the Growth Factor-inducible Protein Zif268," November 1, 1989, pp. 8737–39.

FURTHER READING:

Books

Daintith, J., S. Mitchell, and E. Tootill, editors, *A Biographical Encyclopedia of Scientists,* Volume 2, Facts on File, 1981, pp. 584–85.

Fox, D., M. Meldrum, and I. Rezak, editors, *Nobel Laureates in Medicine or Physiology: A Biographical Dictionary,* Garland, 1990, pp. 427–29.

Fox, D., M. Meldrum, and I. Rezak, editors, *McGraw-Hill Modern Scientists and Engineers,* Volume 2, McGraw-Hill, 1980, pp. 348–49.

Periodicals

Fox, D., M. Meldrum, and I. Rezak, editors, *New York Times,* October 13, 1978, p. 60.

Fox, D., M. Meldrum, and I. Rezak, editors, *Science,* December 8, 1978, pp. 1069–71.

Other

Johns Hopkins University, press release, Jan. 6, 1997.

Nathans, Daniel, "Autobiography of Daniel Nathans," The Nobel Foundation, Dec. 1, 1999, http://www.nobel.se/medicine/laureates/1978/nathans-autobio.html

Sketch by Kim McGrail

Giulio Natta
1903–1979
Italian chemist

Giulio Natta was a highly regarded Italian chemist who, during an active career spanning almost fifty years, worked closely with the Italian chemical industry to create many new processes and products. His studies of high polymers and his discovery of the hard plastic substance polypropylene ushered in the age of plastics with immense world-wide impact. For his work in this field he shared the 1963 Nobel Prize in chemistry with the German chemist **Karl Ziegler**.

Natta was born on February 26, 1903, in Imperia, Italy, a resort town located about sixty miles southwest of Genoa on the Ligurian Sea. His parents were Francesco Natta, a lawyer and judge, and Elena Crespi Natta. He received his primary and secondary education in Genoa. Having read his first chemistry book at age twelve, he quickly became fascinated by the topic. At age sixteen, Natta graduated from high school and entered the University of Genoa, intending to study mathematics. Finding this subject too abstract, he then transferred to the Milan Polytechnic Institute in 1921 and earned his doctorate in chemical engineering in 1924, at the early age of twenty-one.

Following graduation, Natta remained at the Polytechnic Institute as an instructor. He was promoted to assistant professor of general chemistry in 1925, and to full professor in 1927. Moving to the University of Pavia in 1933, Natta served as professor and director of the school's chemical institute. Next, in 1935, he became professor and chairman of the department of physical chemistry at the University of Rome, then professor and director of the institute of industrial chemistry at the Turin Polytechnic Institute in 1937. He returned to the Milan Polytechnic Institute as professor and director of the Industrial Chemical Research Center in 1938 and remained there for the rest of his career. He married Rosita Beati, a professor of literature at the University of Milan, in 1935. The couple had a daughter, Franca, and a son, Giuseppe. In his younger days, Natta was an enthusiastic skier, mountain climber, and hiker.

Natta's decision to seek a degree in chemical engineering rather than in chemistry, or some other pure science, was the earliest manifestation of the basic attitude which characterized his entire career. He was always concerned with the practical results of scientific research and believed that science should serve chiefly to meet the needs of business and industry. His research in the 1920s and early 1930s was largely devoted to x-ray and electron diffraction analyses to determine the structure of various inorganic substances. One of his early practical breakthroughs was the discovery of an effective catalyst for the synthetic production of the important chemical, methanol.

In the early 1930s Natta became interested in the chemistry of polymers, or large molecules, thus shifting his focus from inorganic to organic chemistry, the study of carbon compounds. In the late 1930s the Italian government headed by Benito Mussolini actively promoted scientific research in order to increase Italy's self-sufficiency in the production of vital materials. Natta, using his recently acquired expertise in polymer chemistry, contributed to the national effort especially in the development of new methods to produce synthetic rubber. Following the conclusion of World War II, Natta continued his research in polymer chemistry, his work being subsidized by the large Milan chemical firm, the Montecatini Company.

Discovery of High Polymers

In 1952 Natta attended a lecture at Frankfurt, Germany, given by the chemist Karl Ziegler, then the director of the Max Planck Institute for Coal Research in Mulheim. Ziegler spoke about his recently discovered Aufbau ("growth") reaction, which could be used to create large molecules from ethylene molecules, a gaseous product of the refining of petroleum. Though Ziegler had lectured frequently on his discovery, Natta was one of the first scientists other than Ziegler to grasp its potential importance for the production of high polymers (very large molecules), a venture which might have significant practical applications. Natta and representatives of the Montecatini Company soon invited Ziegler to Milan where they reached an agreement under which Montecatini would have commercial rights to exploit Ziegler's discoveries in Italy and Ziegler and Natta would exchange information on their respective research projects.

In the autumn of 1953 Ziegler and his research staff developed a catalytic process which allowed them to synthesize from ethylene a true high polymer, linear polyethylene, a plastic substance much harder and stronger than any plastic then known. Ziegler promptly patented the new substance but not the process which had produced it. Natta learned of the new discovery through representatives of the Montecatini Company who had been stationed in Ziegler's laboratory in Mulheim. Natta and his research group decided to try Ziegler's catalytic process on propylene, another gaseous product of petroleum which was much cheaper than ethylene. On March 11, 1954, they synthesized linear polypropylene, another high polymer with even more desirable chemical properties than polyethylene. The new plastic proved capable of being molded into objects stronger and more heat resistant than polyethylene. It could be spun into fiber stronger and lighter than nylon, spread into clear film, or molded into pipes as sturdy as metal ones.

Natta and his associates followed up on their discovery with a careful series of x-ray and electron diffraction experiments which demonstrated conclusively the exact nature of the polymer they had created. It was a molecular chain structure in which all of the subgroups were arranged on the same side of the chain. The substance had a high degree of crystallinity which was the cause of its strength. Natta and his colleagues soon discovered other high polymer plastics, including polystyrene. Natta did not inform Ziegler of his discovery of polypropylene until after he had filed for a patent on the new substance. Ziegler was greatly disturbed by what he considered to be Natta's failure to live up to their earlier agreement to share their research and the incident disrupted their previously close friendship to the extent that they were not on speaking terms for many years. The two scientists patched up their quarrel sufficiently to appear together at the 1963 ceremony in Stockholm at which they jointly received the Nobel Prize in chemistry.

In 1959 Natta contracted Parkinson's disease and was already seriously crippled by it at the time of the Nobel Prize award ceremony. He retired from active work in the early 1970s and died at Bergamo, Italy, on May 2, 1979, from complications following surgery for a broken femur bone. In the course of his career, Natta authored or coauthored over five hundred scientific papers and received nearly five hundred patents. He was the recipient of numerous gold medals and at least five honorary degrees for his scientific contributions.

SELECTED WRITINGS BY NATTA:

Books

Stereoregular Polymers and Stereospecific Polymerizations, 2 volumes, translated by Luisa M. Vaccaroni, Pergamon Press, 1967.
Stereochemistry, translated by Andrew Dempster, Longmans, 1972.

Periodicals

Journal of the American Chemical Society, Crystalline High Polymers of c-Olefins, March 20, 1955, pp. 1708–1710.
Scientific American, How Giant Molecules Are Made, September, 1957, pp. 98–104.
Scientific American, Precisely Constructed Polymers, August, 1961, pp. 33–41.
Science, Macromolecular Chemistry, January 15, 1965, pp. 261–272.

FURTHER READING:

Books

Carra, Sergio, and others, editors, *Giulio Natta: Present Significance of His Scientific Contribution,* Editrice di Chimica, 1982.
Magill, Frank N., editor, *The Nobel Prize Winners: Chemistry,* 3 volumes, Salem Press, 1990, pp. 757–764.
McMillan, Frank M., *The Chain Straighteners,* Macmillan, 1979.

Periodicals

McMillan, Frank M., *New York Times,* June 7, 1956, p. 43; November 6, 1963, p. 46.

Sketch by John E. Little

Yuval Ne'eman
1925–
Israeli theoretical physicist

Few scientists in the twentieth century have had a more colorful career than Yuval Ne'eman. Ne'eman had been a colonel the Israeli Army and deputy director of military intelligence before he became a physicist. His work in physics helped revolutionize our view of the structure of the universe. While continuing to work in physics, Ne'eman also became involved in his country's politics and held a seat in its chief parliamentary body and also served as a cabinet minister.

Ne'eman was born on May 14, 1925, in Tel Aviv, Palestine, the son of Gedalia and Zipora (Ben Ya'acov) Ne'eman. While Ne'eman obtained degrees in engineering from the Israel Institute of Technology (Technicon) in Haifa (he received a B.S. in 1945 and an M.S. in 1946), he was already a member of the Jewish Underground. After graduation, he worked for a time on hydrodynamical design

Yuval Ne'eman

at a pump factory, but in 1946 progress in creating the Jewish state of Israel stalled, and Ne'eman joined the Underground full time. At this time the Underground mainly engaged in smuggling Jews into Palestine and in acts of sabotage. Finally in 1947 the General Assembly of the United Nations voted to partition Palestine into Jewish and Arab states. The state of Israel officially came into being on Ne'eman's birthday in 1948, but was immediately invaded by its Arab neighbors. Ne'eman moved from the Underground into the regular armed services. Although all-out war lasted officially only about a year, the Middle East remained tense. Ne'eman continued in the Israeli Defense Forces until 1955, advancing to the rank of colonel. During this period he also married Dvora Rubinstein (1951), with whom he has two children, and obtained a Staff College Diploma at the Ecole Superieure de Guerre in Paris, France (1952). A second Arab-Israeli war broke out in 1956; by that time, Ne'eman had moved into the intelligence division, where he was deputy director.

In 1957, after Israel's victory in the war, Ne'eman asked Moshe Dayan, then Israeli Chief of Staff, for a leave to study physics. Dayan did not grant the leave, but did offer Ne'eman a less demanding post as defense attaché in London. This job allowed Ne'eman the time to take physics courses on the side. Ne'eman accepted and arrived in London at the beginning of 1958.

Kings College, where Ne'eman hoped to study relativity, was too far from the embassy for Ne'eman to travel back and forth to classes. Imperial College, however, was only a

five-minute walk. But when Ne'eman told his first advisor at Imperial that he wanted to study gravitational field theory, he learned that there was no one there working on that subject. The advisor had heard, however, that theoretical physicist **Abdus Salam** was working with field theory at Imperial College. Ne'eman applied to study with Salam, an Islamic Pakistani. Salam agreed to supervise the apparently unqualified Ne'eman because Salam felt that Islamic science owed a debt to medieval Jewish scholars. The field theory that Salam and his group at Imperial College were studying was called gauge theory, which applied to particle physics.

Beginning with the Iraqi revolution in 1958, Ne'eman was required to spend all his time on military duties for almost two years. But after complaining to a new Israeli Chief of Staff and reminding him of Dayan's promise that he would be allowed to study physics, Ne'eman was finally released from the armed services in 1960; he now could devote himself to physics completely for a few years. At that time one of the main problems in particle theory was the recent discovery of unexpected particles that seemed to fit nowhere in existing theories. Their odd decay patterns had earned them the name "strange particles." Ne'eman wanted to apply a mathematical tool called group theory to the task of classifying these strange particles. Salam, an excellent mathematician as well as a physicist, was able to direct Ne'eman to the proper mathematical resources. Within six months, in the fall of 1960, Ne'eman thought that he had the answer. Meanwhile, in the United States, at almost exactly the same time, Caltech physicist **Murray Gell-Mann** had found the same answer as Ne'eman.

At the start of the 1960s, however, observations seemed to doom the group-theoretical ideas of Ne'eman and Gell-Mann. But the whole picture changed in June, 1962, when new data indicating the existence of two new particles were presented at a large physics conference. Both Ne'eman and Gell-Mann were at the conference and both recognized that their theory had been vindicated. Ne'eman used the new data to show some friends how his group-theory predicted the existence of exactly one more strange particle. The next day Gell-Mann made the same prediction before the whole conference. At that point Ne'eman and Gell-Mann met for the first time. They had not known of each other's work before the conference. When the particle that Ne'eman and Gell-Mann had predicted was found two years later, the theory was proven. By then Ne'eman and Gell-Mann were fast friends and even collaborated on a book about their theory, which Gell-Mann had named "the eightfold way" after one of the basic tenets of Buddhism. The name was a kind of joke, since the only connection is that the mathematical group involved contains parts with eight members, called octets.

It was not clear at first how the eightfold way applied to particle classification. Scientists believed that the basis of the group used in the eightfold way should be the set of three strange particles. Ne'eman recognized that the three particles should be the basis of the whole group and proposed the existence of additional particles with fractional charges. But Ne'eman did not work out all the implications of this idea, which proved to be correct. Two years later, Gell-Mann described in some detail three previously unknown particles with fractional charges, which he named quarks, as the basis of the eightfold way.

Ne'eman received a D.I.C. from Imperial College and his Ph.D. in physics from London University in 1962, but by then he had already returned to Israel to head a research group of the Israeli Atomic Energy Commission. In 1965 he became the first head of the physics department at Tel Aviv University. From 1972 through 1975 he worked as president of the university, and he currently holds its Wolfson Extraordinary Chair of Theoretical Physics. Ne'eman has also directed the Center for Particle Theory at the University of Texas in Austin since 1968. In 1981 Ne'eman entered politics and was elected to Israel's parliament, the Knesset, taking the cabinet post of Minister of Science during 1982-84 and again in 1990-92. He has also served as Minister of Energy in the Israeli Cabinet. Ne'eman has been awarded the Israel Prize (1969), the Einstein Medal (1970), and the Wigner Medal (1982).

SELECTED WRITINGS BY NE'EMAN:

Books

(With Murray Gell-Mann) *The Eightfold Way.* 1964.
(With Yoram Kirsh) *The Particle Hunters.* Cambridge, UK: Cambridge University Press, 1986 (original Hebrew version published by Masada in Israel in 1983).
(With Elena Eizenberg) *Membranes and Other Extendons: p-branes.* Singapore: World Scientific, 1995.

FURTHER READING:

Books

Crease, Robert, and Charles C. Mann. *The Second Creation.* New York: Macmillan, 1986.

Sketch by Bryan Bunch

Homer Alfred Neal
1942–

American physicist

A physicist, physics educator, and university administrator, Homer Alfred Neal has devoted much of his career to researching high-energy physics. He has carried out extensive studies of elementary particle interactions and has also made some of the first experimental studies of spin effects in proton-proton collisions at high energies. In addition, he is concerned with methods of particle detection (including spark chamber and scintillation counter techniques), digital and analog electronics, and computer analysis.

Neal was born in Franklin, Kentucky, on June 13, 1942. The son of Homer Neal and Margaret Elizabeth Holl, he was educated at Indiana University, receiving his B.S. in physics with honors in 1961. On June 16, 1962, Neal married Donna Jean Daniels; the couple has two children, Homer Alfred, Jr. and Sharon Denise. Neal's son is also a scientist, studying laser physics and computer programming, and helping his father prepare work for publication.

Neal earned his M.S. at the University of Michigan as a John Hay Whitney fellow in 1963, and received his Ph.D. in 1966. Neal's dissertation was titled "Polarization Parameter in Elastic Proton-Proton Scattering from .75 to 2.84 GeV," a topic he has returned to in several subsequent papers for such journals as the *American Physical Review* and the Italian *Nuovo Cimento*.

After graduation, Neal became a National Science Foundation (NSF) fellow at the European Organization of Nuclear Research until 1967, and a Sloan Foundation Fellow in 1968. During 1967, he returned to Indiana University at Bloomington, as an assistant professor of physics between 1967 and 1970. He became an associate professor in 1970, professor in 1972, and dean of research and graduate development in the late 1970s. His research at Indiana consisted of extending his previous work on elastic proton-proton scattering, studying pion-proton interactions, and other phenomena of high-energy physics.

Between 1970 and 1972, Neal was chairperson of the Argonne Zero Gradient Synchrotron (ZGS) Accelerator Users Group. The ZGS was a proton accelerator developed by the Argonne National Laboratory, a physics research center founded in 1946 and operated by the University of Chicago. Neal used the ZGS to measure large-angle elastic proton-proton polarization and recoil-proton polarization. An Argonne University Association trustee from 1971 to 1974 and 1977 to 1980, Neal continued his ZGS work until its closure in 1979, studying hadron-induced reactions and elastic scattering, spin-flip amplitudes, asymmetry, and other effects of elementary particle physics. Neal then took on a substantial role as administrator and advisor to various science organizations and corporate boards. During 1976 to 1979 he served on a physics advisory panel for the NSF; he chaired a similar panel in the late 1980s. In 1977, Neal joined a U.S. Department of Energy advisory panel on high-energy physics, a position he held for four years. He was also a National Science Board member between 1980 and 1986.

In addition, Neal served on the Ogden Corporation's Board of Directors and the New York Sea Grant Institute. His Ogden Corporation work dealt with the increasing problem of urban garbage disposal. This led to his 1987 book, *Solid Waste Management and the Environment: The*

Mounting Garbage and Trash Crisis, written with J. R. Schubel. Neal surveyed the many technical, economic, environmental, and societal issues surrounding solid waste disposal, and suggested novel methods of disposal. These included the notion of making artificial ocean reefs from stable ash blocks.

Despite Neal's increasing administrative work in the 1980s, he continued his elementary particle physics research, becoming a Guggenheim Fellow at Stanford University in 1980. In 1981, after an unsuccessful bid for the presidency of City College in New York, Neal moved on to the State University of New York (SUNY) in Stony Brook as its provost. His continued studies of high-energy interactions resulted in his 1983 election as a fellow of the American Association for the Advancement of Science. In 1984 he received an honorary doctorate from Indiana University.

In 1986, Neal became department chair and professor of physics at the University of Michigan in Ann Arbor. His research during the late 1980s and early 1990s involved meson and lepton decays, studies of quarks, and experimental tests of quantum electrodynamics (QED), a theory explaining the electromagnetic forces of charged particles. Many of Neal's experiments were carried out at the Stanford Linear Accelerator Center (SLAC) in California.

During the 1990s, Neal has taken on additional administrative positions, including membership in the Superconducting Super Collider's board of overseers in 1989. In the same year he joined the Smithsonian Institution's Board of Regents. He also become a Center for Strategic and International Studies trustee in 1990.

SELECTED WRITINGS BY NEAL:

Books

Solid Waste Management and the Environment: The Mounting Garbage and Trash Crisis, Prentice-Hall, 1987.

Periodicals

American Institute of Physics Conference Proceedings, The Universities and the ZGS in the Seventies, Volume 60, 1980, pp. 269–289.

Other

Polarization Parameter in Elastic Proton-Proton Scattering from .75 to 2.84 GeV, (dissertation), University of Michigan, 1966.

FURTHER READING:

Books

Sammons, Vivian Ovelton, *Blacks in Science and Medicine,* Hemisphere Publishing, 1990, p. 180.

Periodicals

Sammons, Vivian Ovelton, *New York Times,* Search for New President of City College Is Narrowed to 3 Candidates, February 9, 1981, p. B2.

Sketch by Julian A. Smith

Joseph Needham
1900–1995
English biochemist

After distinguishing himself as a research scientist with his work on the biochemistry of embryonic development, Joseph Needham embraced an entirely different career before his 40th year and devoted himself to a life-long, comprehensive study of the development of science in China. In 1954, he produced the first volume of his monumental *Science and Civilisation in China,* a seminal work that reached 17 volumes by the time of his death, and which is continued by a team of scholars at the Needham Institute at Cambridge. Needham was undoubtedly the greatest Western sinologist or student of China of the twentieth century.

Born in London, England, on December 9, 1900, Noel Joseph Terence Montgomery Needham was the only child of Joseph Needham, a successful physician, and Alicia Adelaide Montgomery, a gifted musician. Although his parents had distinctly different styles and temperaments—his father was a practical, serious man who loved learning and possessed a fine library, and his mother was an artistic type who was also a successful songwriter—they shared strict Victorian standards of decorum. They agreed upon little else however, and with his father calling his son Noel and his mother calling him Terence, the solitary, introspective boy decided to call himself Joseph—a traditional family name that always went to the first-born son. During his early school years at Dulwich College Preparatory School, Needham had few companions except for his Parisian governess. At the beginning of World War I, he was sent to Oundle School in Northamptonshire in 1914. During the war, he served as surgeon sub-lieutenant in the Royal Navy Volunteer Reserve, assisting at the overcrowded military hospitals. In 1918 he entered Gonville and Caius College, Cambridge to study natural sciences and obtained his B.A. in 1921.

Gives Up Medical Career and Pursues Biochemistry

At this point in his life, Needham turned away from pursuing a career in medicine as a surgeon. Once he began as a postgraduate at the Cambridge Biochemical Laboratory

Joseph Needham

and studied under Sir **Frederick Gowland Hopkins**, who essentially founded modern biochemistry in England and who would win a Nobel Prize in 1929, Needham realized that surgery did not offer the intellectual challenge he desired, and that the future lay, as one colleague put it, with atoms and molecules. In 1924 he married a fellow student, Dorothy Mary Moyle, whose work on the biochemistry of muscles led to her being elected a fellow of the Royal Society in 1948. The two became the first married couple (besides Queen Victoria and Prince Albert) to be so elected. After receiving his Ph.D., Needham joined the staff of Caius College, which would remain his academic home for the rest of his life. There he would establish himself as a chemical embryologist of distinction, eventually publishing a three-volume work, *Chemical Embryology*, that offered the untraditional thesis that embryonic development is controlled chemically. Had Needham continued his work in biochemistry, he no doubt would have continued to pursue his correct idea that only structural chemistry could fully explain the complex changes that take place during the development of an organism.

Although always generally interested in the history of science, Needham found himself drawn more to that field in 1937 when he met three young Chinese biochemistry students who had come to Cambridge for study. He became especially close to one of these students, Lu Gwei-Djen, whose father was a pharmacist in China and who herself was interested in traditional Chinese science. She was to become the dominant influence in Needham's life and proved to be the catalyst in his deciding to change from

being a research scientist and become a historian of science in China. Drawn suddenly to all things Chinese, Needham learned the Chinese language as a labor of love and began a life-long collaboration with Lu Gwei-Djen who became his wife in 1989, two years after his first wife, Dorothy, died.

Travels to China and Lays Foundation for Life's Work

As Needham began to educate himself about the development of Chinese science, he found himself puzzled by what scholars later came to describe as "the Needham question." The question he posed was why modern science never developed in China the way it did in the West. As Needham learned the Chinese language, he found that although China had produced such breakthroughs as gunpowder, printing, and the magnetic compass centuries before the West, the scientific and industrial revolutions had occurred in the West and not in China. Attempting to find the answer to this question became the guiding theme of his life.

By 1942 the world was once again engulfed in a global conflict, and when England decided to send a scientific mission to China, it chose Needham as its head. As a British scientist who spoke Chinese and understood its history and culture, he was by far the most qualified. For the next six years, he traveled throughout China, immersing himself in Chinese life and learning more and more about China's approach to science and technology. In 1946, after the war, Needham went to Paris to direct the department of natural sciences at the newly established United Nations Educational, Scientific and Cultural Organization. It is Needham who is often credited with literally putting the "S" in UNESCO.

Begins Pioneering Work of Synthesis on Chinese Science

By the early 1950s, Needham finally was able to begin the work he and his close colleague, Lu Gwei-Djen, had originally conceived around 1939. When he first began to explore the issue of why modern science originated only in Europe and not in China, Needham thought he would probably produce a single small volume. However, as his work began to expand to a planned seven volumes and each volume itself was then projected as having multiple parts, the work grew so extensive that he and dozens of associates worked on it for the next five decades. The first volume of *Science and Civilisation in China* appeared in 1954, and by the time of Needham's death in 1995, 17 large volumes had been published. Twenty-five total volumes are planned, and the work is being continued by the Needham Research Institute at Cambridge.

Recognized as the Greatest Sinologist of the Twentieth Century

By spending nearly a lifetime writing and editing his monumental history of scientific development in China,

Needham became almost universally acclaimed as the foremost Western interpreter of China. The factual information alone contained in his monumental work guarantee its lasting value. Still, Needham has had his critics who argue that he emphasizes only the positive aspects of Chinese culture, while others say he tries too hard to put science in a socioeconomic context.

Indeed, Needham was from his earliest adult years a socialist who, in a provocative and controversial manner, tried to blend his science, socialism, and religion. Contradiction and paradox were often found in his life and work, as he proved to have a mind that was open to all forms of cultural experience. In the 1920s, Needham and his wife, Dorothy, considered each other's extramarital affairs unobjectionable and to be entirely consistent with their radical politics. Needham also held deep religious feelings, and while a firm Christian, he also described himself to be an "honorary Taoist." He also called himself a Marxist, humanist, and scientist. In a 1992 interview in the *Scientific American*, Needham offered a partial answer to the question that drove his life's work, saying that the bureaucratic nature of Chinese society was partly responsible for inhibiting modern science, however he also referred to the second part of his conclusion which he said did not please him. "I think the answer is going to be that modern science arose with capitalism, and I don't like that, because I have been a socialist all of my life." When Joseph Needham died on March 24, 1995 at the age of 94, his pioneering work of scientific synthesis was immediately compared to that of Gibbons and Toynbee.

SELECTED WRITINGS BY NEEDHAM:

Books

Chemical Embryology. 3 vols. Cambridge, England: The University Press, 1931.
Order and Life. Cambridge, England: The University Press, 1935.
Science and Civilisation in China. Cambridge, England: The University Press, 1954-1994.

FURTHER READING:

Books

Goldsmith, Maurice. *Joseph Needham: 20th-Century Renaissance Man.* Paris: UNESCO Publishing, 1995.
Porter, Roy, ed. *The Biographical Dictionary of Scientists.* New York: Oxford University Press, 1994, pp. 507-508.

Periodicals

Holloway, Marguerite. "Joseph Needham: The Builder of Bridges." *Scientific American* (May 1992): 56-57.

Lyall, Sarah. "Joseph Needham, China Scholar From Britain, Dies at 94." *The New York Times* (March 27, 1995): B, 10.

Sketch by Leonard C. Bruno

Louis Néel
1904–
French physicist

Louis Néel is a French physicist who explored the magnetic properties of solids. He is famous for discovering antiferromagnetism—a property possessed by some metals, alloys, and salts by which their magnetic fields line up in a way that negates their magnetism. He also explained some of the magnetic properties of ferrites (iron salt compounds), making it possible to prepare synthetic ferrites with properties that could be used in computer memories. For his fundamental work and discoveries, Néel received the 1970 Nobel Prize in physics along with the Swedish physicist **Hannes Olof Gösta Alfvén**.

Louis Eugène Félix Néel was born in Lyons, France, to Antoinette Hartmayer and Louis Néel, a director in the civil service. Néel received his secondary education at the Lycée du Parc in Lyons and the Lycée St.-Louis in Paris. He studied at the distinguished Ecole Normale Supérieure in Paris, was graduated in 1928, and continued there as a lecturer. Néel received his doctorate in 1932 from the University of Strasbourg. He studied under Pierre Weiss, a leading investigator of magnetization (a solid's capability of being magnetized). After receiving his doctorate, Néel joined the faculty of the University of Strasbourg and remained there until 1945.

Advances Heisenberg's Work

When Néel was beginning his doctoral work, German physicist **Werner Karl Heisenberg** announced his finding that large scale magnetic attraction is produced by neighboring atoms of ferromagnetic substances orienting in the same direction. Heisenberg also showed that the alignment of magnetic moments—the small amount of magnetism around each atom—became parallel at low temperatures.

In 1930, Néel, building on Heisenberg's work, suggested that there are also "antiferromagnetic" substances, with interactions that cause the magnetic moments of neighboring atoms to realign in opposing directions, resulting in zero magnetization. The realignment only occurs at a very low temperature, a temperature that has come to be known as the Néel point or Néel temperature. During World War II, Néel used his expertise to protect French warships against magnetic mines by "neutralizing" them. He gave them a magnetization opposite the normal terrestrial magnetic field.

In 1945, Néel joined the faculty of the University of Grenoble and established the Laboratory of Electrostatics and the Physics of Metals. In 1947, he also developed the concept of ferrimagnetic substances. When the temperature of antiferromagnetic substances is raised, the spontaneous magnetization slightly deforms the antiparallel arrangement of the two sets of atoms, leaving one set slightly stronger than the other, previously equal, set. The result is paramagnetism, in which the substances are slightly attracted to an external field but are essentially independent of one another. Ferrites, which are not electrical conductors, are ferrimagnetic substances. Ferrimagnetic substances share some of the properties of ferromagnetic elements (such as iron, nickel, and cobalt) and some of the properties of antiferromagnetics. They have been used to coat magnetic tape in computer memory cores and in other types of communication technology.

Néel developed a theory of magnetization that described the subdivision of ferromagnetic substances into elementary domains, regions of ferromagnetic material, with spikes and walls. He also analyzed the process of magnetic creep, the effect of time on magnetization of ferromagnetic substances. There are two classes of creep, one due to temperature changes and the other due to the redistribution of atoms in the crystal that accompanies spontaneous magnetization.

Work in Magnetics Leads to Nobel Prize

In 1956 Néel was asked to found the Center for Nuclear Studies at Grenoble. Through his involvement, Grenoble became an important center for physics research. Néel was also president of the Institut National Polytechnique de Grenoble. Between 1963 to 1983 he was French delegate to the NATO Scientific Council. In 1970 Louis Néel received the Nobel Prize in physics for his fundamental work and discoveries concerning antiferromagnetism and ferrimagnetism. That year the prize for physics was also given to Hannes Alfvén for his research into magnetohydrodynamics.

Néel received many honors besides the Nobel Prize. He was named to the French Legion of Honor and received the Gold Medal of the National Center for Scientific Research and the Holweck Medal of the Institute of Physics, London. He was also elected to the Academy of Sciences of Paris, the scientific academies of Moscow, Warsaw, Romania, and Amsterdam and to the Royal Society of London and the American Academy of Arts and Sciences.

Néel married Hélène Hourticq in 1931. The couple had a son and two daughters. Néel's pastimes include carpentry, strolling in the country, and reading mystery stories and eighteenth-century French literature.

FURTHER READING:

Books

McGraw-Hill Modern Scientists and Engineers, McGraw-Hill, 1980.
Wasson, Tyler, editor, *Nobel Prize Winners,* H. W. Wilson, 1987.

Sketch by Margo Nash

Erwin Neher
1944–
German biophysicist

Erwin Neher, along with **Bert Sakmann**, was awarded the 1991 Nobel Prize in physiology or medicine for the development of the patch clamp technique. The use of this technique enabled Neher and Sakmann to forge new paths in the study of membrane physiology and to understand the structure and functions of ion channels found in the plasma membranes of most body cells. The patch clamp technique has given physiologists a precise understanding of cellular microelectrical activity and has contributed significantly to the research and treatment of cystic fibrosis, diabetes, epilepsy, and other disorders of the cardiovascular and neuromuscular systems.

Neher was born in Landsberg, Germany, on March 20, 1944, the son of Franz Xavier Neher and Elisabeth Pfeiffer Neher. In 1965 he completed his undergraduate studies at the Institute of Technology in Munich with a major in physics. Two years later he earned his master's degree from the University of Wisconsin under a Fulbright scholarship. He then went on to complete his doctorate at the Institute of Technology in Munich, Germany, in 1970.

While the existence of ion channels that transmit electrical charges was hypothesized as early as the 1950s, no one had been able to see these channels. As a doctoral student, Neher was drawn to the question of how electrically charged ions control such biological functions as the transmission of nerve impulses, the contraction of muscles, vision, and the process of conception. He realized that in order to get answers to these questions he would have to look for the ion channels.

Collaboration with Sakmann Begins

It was in his doctoral thesis that Neher first developed the concept of the patch clamp technique as a way of discovering the ion channels. In 1974 he shared a laboratory space with Bert Sakmann at the Max Planck Institute in Göttingen. They both agreed that understanding the nature of ion channels was the most important problem in the biophysics of the cell membrane, and they set out to develop the techniques of patch clamping.

Neher briefly worked with Charles F. Stevens at the University of Washington. When Stevens moved to Yale, Neher followed him while maintaining his collaboration with Sakmann. From 1975 to 1976, Neher was a research associate in the department of physiology at Yale University, and much of the data for the paper on patch clamps came from the Yale studies.

In 1976 Neher and Sakmann published their landmark paper on the use of glass recording electrodes with microscopic tips, called micropipettes, pressed against a cell membrane. With these devices, which they called patch clamp electrodes, they were able to electrically isolate a tiny patch of the cell membrane and to study the proteins in that area. They could then see how the individual proteins acted as channels or gates for specific ions, allowing certain ions to pass through the cell membrane one at a time, while preventing others from entering. Their work with patch clamps allowed them to remove a patch of the membrane and to enter the interior of the cell. They then were able to conduct various experiments to observe the intricate mechanism of ion channels.

Refinement to Reduce Noise Improves Technique

Several years passed after they presented their findings to an audience at the Biophysical Society meeting in 1976 in which Neher and Sakmann, along with their co-workers, refined the technique of patch clamping. Creating a better seal between the micropipette and the patch of cell membrane it pressed against was one of the refinements they sought. Without a tight seal there was interference by "noise" that overshadowed the smaller electrical currents.

The problem of outside noise interference was solved by Neher in 1980 when he was able to observe on his oscilloscope a marked drop in the noise level to almost zero. From this drop he was able to infer that he had produced a seal that was one hundred times better than previously attained. While other researchers had noticed an abatement of noise at times, Neher was the first to realize the significance of the drop in noise level.

Neher found that by using a light suction with a super clean pipette, he could create a high-resistance seal of 10–100 gigohms (a gigohm is a measure of electrical resistance equal to one billion ohms). He called this seal a "gigaseal." With the gigaseal, background noise could be decreased, and a number of new ways could be used to control cells for patch clamp experimentation. Patches from the cell could now be torn away from the membrane to act as a membrane coating over the mouth of the pipette, thus allowing for more exact measurement of electrical ion movement. A strong suction could force the pipette into the cell while still maintaining a tight seal for the cell as a whole.

In 1976 Neher returned to the Max Planck Institute in Göttingen. On December 26, 1978, he married Eva-Maria Ruhr, a microbiologist. They have five children: Richard, Benjamin, Carola, Sigmund, and Margret. He became director of the membrane biophysics department at the Max Planck Institute in 1983, and in 1987 he was made an honorary professor. In 1991 Neher and Sakmann won the 1991 Nobel Prize in physiology or medicine for proving the existence of ion channels.

Researchers using the patch clamp technique were able to discover a defective ion channel that was responsible for cystic fibrosis. Because of the use of patch clamps in research, there is now a better understanding of hormone regulation and the production of insulin as it relates to diabetes. The Nobel Committee also praised the work of Neher and Sakmann for helping in research on heart disease, epilepsy, and disorders affecting the nervous and muscle systems. Patch clamp research has helped in the development of new drugs for these conditions.

SELECTED WRITINGS BY NEHER:

Books

Single Channel Recording, Plenum, 1983.
Molecular Mechanisms in Secretion, edited by N. A. Thron, [Copenhagen], 1988, pp. 262–270.

Periodicals

Scientific American, The Patch Clamp Technique, March, 1992, pp. 44–51.
Science, Ion Channels for Communication between and within Cells, April 24, 1992, pp. 498–502.

FURTHER READING:

Periodicals

Aldous, Peter, *Nature,* Patch Clamp Brings Honour, October 10, 1991, p. 487.
Altman, Lawrence K., *New York Times,* Cell Channel Finding Earns Nobel Prize, October 13, 1992, pp. C1, C3.
Brown, Phyllida, *New Scientist,* Ion Channels Bring Nobel Prize to Germany, October 12, 1991, p. 14.
Brown, Phyllida, *Chemical and Engineering News,* Ion Channels: Discoverers Win Physiology Nobel, October 14, 1991, p. 4.
Zeman, Ellen J., *Physics Today,* Neher and Sakmann Win Physiology Nobel for Cell Membrane Studies, January, 1992, pp. 17–18.

Sketch by Jordan Richman

Evelyn Nelson
1943–1987
Canadian algebraist

Though Evelyn Nelson's mathematical career was cut short by cancer, she published about 40 papers on her main research topics: algebra and theoretical computer science. She was specifically concerned with equational compactness, model theory, and formal language theory. A generous teacher and researcher, Nelson spent her career at McMaster University.

Nelson was born Evelyn Merle Roden in Hamilton, Ontario, Canada, the daughter of Russian immigrants. A gifted student, Nelson attended Westdale High School in Hamilton. With her parents' constant encouragement, she began her undergraduate education at the University of Toronto in the honours course of mathematics–physics–chemistry. Two years later, she transferred to the honours mathematics program at McMaster University in Hamilton. Soon after her transfer she married Mort Nelson, and they had two daughters together. They later divorced.

Nelson began publishing her research quite early, beginning with her master's thesis. It was published in 1967 as "A finiteness criterion for partially ordered semigroups and its application to Universal Algebra," in *Canadian Journal of Mathematics*. She completed her university education at McMaster, earning her Ph.D in 1970 with a thesis titled "The lattice of equational classes of commutative semigroups." It was also published, though in a modified form, in the *Canadian Journal of Mathematics*.

Nelson wrote over 40 papers, primarily in the general area of universal algebra. The topic of her thesis, the lattice of equational classes of semigroups, continued to be explored in her first five papers. Her other papers ranged from various aspects of equations compactness to partially ordered universal algebra subject to conditions originating in theoretical computer science.

Nelson also taught mathematics at her alma mater, McMaster, throughout her career. She first lectured as a postdoctoral fellow (1970–73), then as a research associate (1973–78). She was finally promoted to the tenure track level as an associate professor in 1978 and became a full professor in 1983. Nelson also served as chair of the computer science unit from 1982 to 1984, but could not continue in the position when computer science became a full–fledged department because of her increasing illness.

Nelson served the mathematical community and McMaster University in other ways. She edited the prestigious journal *Algebra Universalis*, and refereed articles and reviewed other scholars' work for several other journals. She also held many memberships in academic societies, among them the American Mathematical Society and the Canadian Mathematical Society. She also served on some committees for the latter. Nelson was active in the McMaster community outside of the mathematics department as well.

In 1987, Nelson died of cancer after battling the disease for many years.

SELECTED WRITINGS BY NELSON:

Periodicals

"Finiteness of semigroups of operators in Universal Algebra." *Canadian Journal of Mathematics* 19 (1967): 764–68.
"The lattice of equational classes of commutative semigroups." *Canadian Journal of Mathematics* 19 (1971): 875–95.

FURTHER READING:

Periodicals

Adamek, Jiri. "A Farewell to Evelyn Nelson." *Cahiers de topologie et géométrie différentielle catégoriques* (1988): 171–74.
Banaschewski, B. "Evelyn M. Nelson: An Appreciation." *Algebra Univeralis* 26 (1989): 259–64.

Other

"Evelyn Nelson." *Biographies of Women Mathematicians.* June 1997. http://www.agnesscott.edu/lriddle/women/nelson.htm (September 21, 2000).

Sketch by Annette Petruso

Walther Nernst
1864–1941
German chemist

Walther Nernst made a significant breakthrough with his statement of the third law of thermodynamics, which holds that it should be impossible to attain thet temperature of absolute zero in any real experiment. For this accomplishment, he was awarded the 1920 Nobel Prize for chemistry. He also made contributions to the field of physical chemistry. While still in his twenties, he devised a mathematical expression showing how electromotive force is dependent upon temperature and concentration in a galvanic, or electricity-producing, cell. He later developed a theory to explain how ionic, or charged, compounds break

Walther Nernst

down in water, a problem that had troubled chemists since the theory of ionization was proposed by **Svante A. Arrhenius**.

Born Hermann Walther Nernst in Briesen, West Prussia (now Wąbrzeżno, Poland), on June 25, 1864, he was the third child of Gustav Nernst, a judge, and Ottilie (Nerger) Nernst. He attended the gymnasium at Graudenz (now Grudziadz), Poland, where he developed an interest in poetry, literature, and drama. For a brief time, he considered becoming a poet. After graduation in 1883, Nernst attended the universities of Zurich, Berlin, Graz, and Würzburg, majoring in physics at each institution. He was awarded his Ph.D. summa cum laude in 1887 by Würzburg. His doctoral thesis dealt with the effects of magnetism and heat on electrical conductivity.

Nernst's first academic appointment came in 1887 when he was chosen as an assistant to professor **Friedrich Wilhelm Ostwald** at the University of Leipzig. Ostwald had been introduced to Nernst earlier in Graz by Svante Arrhenius. These three, Ostwald, Arrhenius, and Nernst, were to become among the most influential men involved in the founding of the new discipline of physical chemistry, the application of physical laws to chemical phenomena.

The first problem Nernst addressed at Leipzig was the diffusion of two kinds of ions across a semipermeable membrane. He wrote a mathematical equation describing the process, now known as the Nernst equation, which relates the electric potential of the ions to various properties of the cell.

In the early 1890s, Nernst accepted a teaching position appointment at the University of Göttingen in Leipzig, and soon after married Emma Lohmeyer, the daughter of a surgeon. The Nernsts had five children, three daughters and two sons. In 1894, Nernst was promoted to full professor at Göttingen. At the same time, he also received approval for the creation of a new Institute for Physical Chemistry and Electrochemistry at the university.

At Göttingen, Nernst wrote a textbook on physical chemistry, *Theoretische Chemie vom Standpunkte der Avogadroschen Regel und der Thermodynamik* (*Theoretical Chemistry from the Standpoint of Avogadro's Rule and Thermodynamics*). Published in 1893, it had an almost missionary objective: to lay out the principles and procedures of a new approach to the study of chemistry. The book became widely popular, going through a total of fifteen editions over the next thirty-three years.

Pursues Questions of Solution Chemistry

During his tenure at Göttingen, Nernst investigated a wide variety of topics in the field of solution chemistry. In 1893, for example, he developed a theory for the breakdown of ionic compounds in water, a fundamental issue in the Arrhenius theory of ionization. According to Nernst, dissociation, or the dissolving of a compound into its elements, occurs because the presence of nonconducting water molecules causes positive and negative ions in a crystal to lose contact with each other. The ions become hydrated by water molecules, making it possible for them to move about freely and to conduct an electric current through the solution. In later work, Nernst developed techniques for measuring the degree of hydration of ions in solutions. By 1903, Nernst had also devised methods for determining the pH value of a solution, an expression relating the solution's hydrogen-ion concentration (acidity or alkalinity).

In 1889, Nernst addressed another fundamental problem in solution chemistry: precipitation. He constructed a mathematical expression showing how the concentration of ions in a slightly soluble compound could result in the formation of an insoluble product. That mathematical expression is now known as the solubility product, a special case of the ionization constant for slightly soluble substances. Four years later, Nernst also developed the concept of buffer solutions—solutions made of bases, rather than acids—and showed how they could be used in various theoretical and practical situations.

Around 1905, Nernst was offered a position as professor of physical chemistry at the University of Berlin. This move was significant for both the institution and the man. Chemists at Berlin had been resistant to many of the changes going on in their field, and theoretical physicist and eventual Nobel Prize winner **Max Planck** had recommended the selection of Nernst to revitalize the Berlin chemists. The move also proved to be a stimulus to Nernst's own work. Until he left Göttingen, he had concentrated on the reworking of older, existing problems developed by his predecessors in physical chemistry. At Berlin, he began to search out, define, and explore new questions. Certainly the most important of these questions involved the thermodynamics of chemical reactions at very low temperatures.

Research Leads to the Third Law of Thermodynamics

Attempting to extend the Gibbs-Helmholtz equation and the Thomsen-Berthelot principle of maximum work to temperatures close to absolute zero—the temperature at which there is no heat—Nernst eventually concluded that it would be possible to reach absolute zero only by a series of infinite steps. In the real world, that conclusion means that an experimenter can get closer and closer to absolute zero, but can never actually reach that point. Nernst first presented his "Heat Theorem," as he called it, to the Göttingen Academy of Sciences in December of 1905. It was published a year later in the *Nachrichten von der Gesellschaft der Wissenschaften zu Göttingen.* The theory is now more widely known as the third law of thermodynamics. In 1920, Nernst was awarded the Nobel Prize in chemistry in recognition of his work on this law.

The statement of the heat theorem proved to be an enormous stimulus for Nernst's colleagues in Berlin's chemistry department. For at least a decade, the focus of nearly all research among physical chemists there was experimental confirmation of Nernst's hypothesis. In order to accomplish this objective, new equipment and new techniques had to be developed. Nernst's heat theorem was eventually integrated into the revolution taking place in physics, the development of quantum theory. At the time he first proposed the theory, Nernst had ignored any possible role of quantum mechanics. A few years later, however, that had all changed. In working on his own theory of specific heats, for example, **Albert Einstein** had quite independently come to the same conclusions as had Nernst. He later wrote that Nernst's experiments at Berlin had confirmed his own theory of specific heats. In turn, Nernst eventually realized that his heat theorem was consistent with the dramatic changes being brought about in physics by quantum theory. Even as his work on the heat theorem went forward, Nernst turned to new topics. One of these involved the formation of hydrogen chloride by photolysis, or chemical breakdown by light energy. Chemists had long known that a mixture of hydrogen and chlorine gases will explode when exposed to light. In 1918, Nernst developed an explanation for that reaction. When exposed to light, Nernst hypothesized, a molecule of chlorine (Cl_2) will absorb light energy and break down into two chlorine atoms (2Cl). A single chlorine atom will then react with a molecule of hydrogen (H_2), forming a molecule of hydrogen chloride and an atom of hydrogen (HCl + H). The atom of hydrogen will then react with a molecule of chlorine, forming a second molecule of hydrogen chloride and another atom of chlorine. The process is a chain reaction because the remaining atom of chlorine allows it to repeat.

In 1922, Nernst resigned his post at Berlin in order to become president of the Physikalisch-technische Reichsan-

stalt. He hoped to reorganize the institute and make it a leader in German science, but since the nation was suffering from severe inflation at the time, there were not enough funds to achieve this goal. As a result, Nernst returned to Berlin in 1924 to teach physics and direct the Institute of Experimental Physics there until he retired in 1934.

Makes a Fortune with Invention

In addition to his scientific research, Nernst was an avid inventor. Around the turn of the century, for example, he developed an incandescent lamp that used rare-earth oxide rather than a metal as the filament. Although he sold the lamp patent outright for a million marks, the device was never able to compete commercially with the conventional model invented by **Thomas Alva Edison**. Nernst also invented an electric piano that was never successfully marketed.

The rise of the Nazi party in 1933 brought an end to Nernst's professional career. He was personally opposed to the political and scientific policies promoted by Adolf Hitler and his followers and was not reluctant to express his views publicly. In addition, two of his daughters had married Jews, which contributed to his becoming an outcast in the severely anti-Semitic climate of Germany at that time.

Walther Nernst was one of the geniuses of early twentieth-century German chemistry, a man with a prodigious curiosity about every new development in the physical sciences. He was a close colleague of Einstein, and was a great contributor to the organization of German science—he was largely responsible for the first Solvay Conference in 1911, for example. In his free time, he was especially fond of travel, hunting, and fishing. Nernst also loved automobiles and owned one of the first to be seen in Göttingen. Little is known about his years after his retirement. Nernst died of a heart attack on November 18, 1941, at his home at Zibelle, Oberlausitz, near the German-Polish border.

SELECTED WRITINGS BY NERNST:

Books

Theoretische Chemie vom Standpunkte der Avogadros-chen Regel und der Thermodynamik, [Göttingen], 1893.

Einführung in die mathematische Behandlung der Naturwissenschaften-Kurzgefasstes Lehrbuch der Differential- und Integralrechnung mit besonderer Berücksichtigung der Chemie, [Leipzig], 1895.

Die Ziele der physikalischen Chemie, [Göttingen], 1896.

Experimental and Theoretical Applications of Thermodynamics to Chemistry, [London], 1907.

Die Theoretischen und experimentellen Grundlagen des Neuen Wärmesatzes, [Halle-Salle], 1918.

Periodicals

Nachrichten von der Gesellschaft der Wissenschaften zu Göttingen, Üeber die Berechnung chemischer Gleichgewichte aus thermischen Messungen, 1906, pp. 1–40.

FURTHER READING:

Books

Concise Dictionary of Scientific Biography, Macmillan, 1981, pp. 499–501.

Farber, Eduard, editor, *Great Chemists,* Interscience, 1961, pp. 1203–1208.

Gillispie, Charles Coulson, editor, *Dictionary of Scientific Biography,* Volume 15, Scribner, 1975, pp. 432–453.

Mendelsohn, Kurt, *The World of Walther Nernst: The Rise and Fall of German Science, 1864–1941,* Pittsburgh, 1973.

Periodicals

Einstein, Albert, *Scientific Monthly,* The Work and Personality of Walther Nernst, February, 1942, pp. 195–196.

Partington, James R., *Journal of the American Chemical Society,* The Nernst Memorial Lecture, 1953, pp. 2853–2872.

Sketch by David E. Newton

Elizabeth F. Neufeld

Elizabeth F. Neufeld
1928–
American biochemist

Elizabeth F. Neufeld is best known as an authority on human genetic diseases. Her research at the National Institutes of Health (NIH) and at University of California, Los Angeles (UCLA), provided new insights into mucopolysaccharide storage disorders (the absence of certain enzymes preventing the body from properly storing certain substances). Neufeld's research opened the way for prenatal diagnosis of such life-threatening fetal disorders as Hurler syndrome. Because of this research, she was awarded the Lasker Award in 1982 and the Wolf Prize in Medicine in 1988.

She was born Elizabeth Fondal in Paris, on September 27, 1928. Her parents, Jacques and Elvire Fondal, were Russian refugees who had settled in France after the Russian revolution. The impending occupation of France by the Germans brought the Fondal family to New York in June 1940. Her parents' experience led them to instill in Neufeld a strong commitment to the importance of education. "They believed that education was the one thing no one could take from you," she told George Milite in a 1993 interview.

Neufeld first became interested in science while a high school student, her interest sparked by her biology teacher. She attended Queens College in New York, receiving her bachelor of science degree in 1948. She worked briefly as a research assistant to Elizabeth Russell at the Jackson Memorial Laboratory in Bar Harbor, Maine. From 1949 to 1950 she studied at the University of Rochester's department of physiology. In 1951 she moved to Maryland, where she served as a research assistant to Nathan Kaplan and Sidney Colowick at the McCollum-Pratt Institute at Johns Hopkins University. In 1952 Neufeld moved again, this time to the West Coast. From 1952 to 1956 she studied under W. Z. Hassid at the University of California, Berkeley. She received her Ph.D. in comparative biochemistry from Berkeley in 1956 and remained there for her postdoctoral training. She first studied cell division in sea urchins. Later, as a junior research biochemist (working again with Hassid) she studied the biosynthesis of plant cell wall polymers—which would prove significant when she began studying Hurler syndrome and related diseases.

Neufeld began her scientific studies at a time when few women chose science as a career. The historical bias against women in science, compounded with an influx of men coming back from the Second World War and going to college, made positions for women rare; few women could be found in the science faculties of colleges and universities. Despite the "overt discrimination" Neufeld often witnessed, she decided nonetheless to pursue her interests. "Some people looked at women who wanted a career in science as a little eccentric," she told Milite, "but I enjoyed what I was doing and I decided I would persevere."

Begins Research on Hurler Syndrome

After spending several years at Berkeley, Neufeld moved on to NIH in 1963, where she began as research biochemist at the National Institute of Arthritis Metabolism and Digestive Diseases. It was during her time at NIH that Neufeld began her research on mucopolysaccharidoses (MPS), disorders in which a complex series of sugars known as mucopolysaccharides cannot be stored or metabolized properly. Hurler syndrome is a form of MPS. Other forms of MPS include Hunter's syndrome, Scheie syndrome, Sanfillipo, and Morquio. These are all inherited disorders. Defectively metabolized sugars accumulate in fetal cells of victims. The disorders can cause stunted physical and mental growth, vision and hearing problems, and a short life span.

Because some plant cell wall polymers contain uronic acids (a component of mucopolysaccharides), Neufeld, from her work with plants, could surmise how the complex sugars worked in humans. When she first began working on Hurler syndrome in 1967, she initially thought the problem might stem from faulty regulation of the sugars, but experiments showed the problem was in fact the abnormally slow rate at which the sugars were broken down.

Working with fellow scientist Joseph Fratantoni, Neufeld attempted to isolate the problem by tagging mucopolysaccharides with radioactive sulfate, as well as mixing normal cells with MPS patient cells. Fratantoni inadvertently mixed cells from a Hurler patient and a Hunter patient—and the result was a nearly normal cell culture. The two cultures had essentially "cured" each other. Additional work showed that the cells could cross-correct by transferring a corrective factor through the culture medium. The goal now was to determine the makeup of the corrective factor or factors.

Identifies Enzyme Deficiency

Through a combination of biological and molecular techniques, Neufeld was able to identify the corrective factors as a series of enzymes. Normally, the enzymes would serve as catalysts for the reactions needed for cells to metabolize the sugars. In Hurler and other MPS patients, enzyme deficiency makes this difficult. A further complication is that often the enzymes that do exist lack the proper chemical markers needed to enter cells and do their work. Neufeld's subsequent research with diseases similar to MPS, including I-Cell disease, showed how enzymes needed markers to match with cell receptors to team with the right cells.

This research paved the way for successful prenatal diagnosis of the MPS and related disorders, as well as genetic counseling. Although no cure has been found, researchers are experimenting with such techniques as gene replacement therapy and bone marrow transplants.

In 1973 Neufeld was named chief of NIH's Section of Human Biochemical Genetics, and in 1979 she was named chief of the Genetics and Biochemistry Branch of the National Institute of Arthritis, Diabetes, and Digestive and Kidney Diseases (NIADDK). She served as deputy director in NIADDK's Division of Intramural Research from 1981 to 1983.

In 1984 Neufeld went back to the University of California, this time the Los Angeles campus, as chair of the biological chemistry department, where she continues her research. In addition to MPS, she has done research on similar disorders such as Tay-Sachs disease. But her concerns go beyond research. She strongly believes that young scientists just starting out need support and encouragement from the scientific community, because these scientists can bring new and innovative perspectives to difficult questions and issues. At the same time, young scientists can learn much from the experience of established scientists. In her capacity as department chair, Neufeld encourages interaction among established scientists, young scientists, and students.

Neufeld has chaired the Scientific Advisory Board of the National MPS Society since 1988 and was president of the American Society for Biochemistry and Molecular Biology from 1992 to 1993. She was elected to both the National Academy of Sciences (USA) and the American Academy of Arts and Sciences in 1977 and named a fellow of the American Association for Advancement in Science in 1988. In 1990 she was named California Scientist of the Year.

Married to Benjamin Neufeld (a former official with the U.S. Public Health Service) since 1951, she is the mother of two children. Although her work takes up a great deal of her time, she enjoys hiking when she gets the chance, and travel "when it's for pleasure and not business."

SELECTED WRITINGS BY NEUFELD:

Books

Methods in Enzymology, Volume 8, Academic Press, 1966.

NIH: An Account of Research in its Laboratories and Clinics, edited by DeW. Stetten and W. T. Carrigan, Academic Press, 1984, pp. 330–336.

FURTHER READING:

Books

O'Neill, Lois Decker, editor, *The Women's Book of World Records and Achievements,* Anchor Press, 1979.

Other

Neufeld, Elizabeth F., *Interview with George Milite* conducted December 17, 1993.

Sketch by George A. Milite

Hanna Neumann

Hanna Neumann
1914–1971
German algebraist

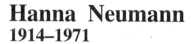

Hanna Neumann was a well-traveled mathematician who instilled a humble sense of dignity to the mathematics programs that she headed. She fled Nazi Germany to England, where she obtained a doctorate in mathematics and went on to solve many problems, including the finite basis problem for varieties generated by a finite group.

Born in Berlin on February 12, 1914, Neumann was the youngest of three children of Hermann and Katharina von Caemmerer. Her father was a historian who was killed in World War I, leaving only a war pension to support the family. To earn extra money, Neumann coached younger children in academics and evolved into an organized and studious pupil as a result. She entered the University of Berlin in 1932 and became inspired by her mathematics professor, Ludwig Bieberbach. He influenced her studies toward geometry, but it would be professors Erhard Schmidt and Issai Schur who would introduce her to analysis and algebra. Her future husband, Bernhard H. Neumann, was also a mathematics student at the university. They became secretly engaged in 1934, but due to the rise of Nazism in Germany, Bernhard (who was Jewish) moved to England, and their plans were put on hold. Neumann remained in Germany and lost her job at the Mathematical Institute as a result of her activities to protect other Jewish lecturers. Neumann was advised that because of her political stance, she should avoid the oral exam on "political knowledge," which was required for a doctorate, and switch to the *Staatsexamen* final. This exam was a written essay, and she chose as her topic the epistemological basis of numbers in Plato's later dialogues. She graduated with distinctions in mathematics and physics.

Teaches in England

To escape the Nazis, Neumann moved to England and began working in Bristol. Her natural talent for learning new languages benefitted her career by being able to read journals and books in a number of different languages. She experimented with finite plane geometries, wrote several papers, and presented them at lecture courses. Neumann also contributed an explanation of the two types of quadrangles found in finite planes: those whose diagonal points are collinear, and those that are not (the Fano configuration).

In 1938, Neumann moved to Cardiff, England, and married Bernhard in secret to protect his parents, who were still living in Germany, from any reprisals. In 1939, their first child, Irene, was born. The family was soon uprooted because of their classification as "least restricted" aliens, whom are barred from living along the coast. Moving to Oxford, Neumann resumed her doctoral studies while pregnant with her second child, Peter. The acute housing shortage grew as European refugees swamped England, forcing Neumann and her children to move into a rented caravan in 1942. It would be here, by candlelight, that she would write her doctoral thesis, submitting it in 1943. Her third child, Barbara, was born shortly after, and when the war ended the entire family was able to move back to Cardiff. Bernhard was decommissioned from the army and returned to his job at the University College in Hull, where Neumann began her teaching career as a temporary assistant lecturer of applied mathematics. Their fourth and fifth children, Walter and Daniel, were born in 1946 and 1951, respectively. She continued to work at Hull for the next twelve years, changing the curriculum toward the more pure mathematics that she herself had been trained in.

In 1955, Neumann received a D.Sc. from Oxford based on her research and papers, two of which were published in the *American Journal of Mathematics*. A highly motivated individual, she chose to work as the secretary of a local United Nations Association in her spare time. Her husband had moved to Manchester to lecture in 1948. As she continued to search for a job that would bring her and her husband closer together, the faculty of Technology of the University of Manchester finally added an honors program that would enable her wish to come true.

Breaks New Ground

Neumann was hired as senior lecturer at the University of Manchester in 1958 and set about making very abstract ideas more accessible for her students. She worked with a model building group, lectured on prime numbers and the dissection of rectangles into incongruent squares, and advised several graduate students. Neumann went beyond the confines of a teacher/student relationship and regularly invited staff and students over to her home for coffee and discussions. She mentored many individuals who would themselves go on to become successful mathematicians, including John Bowers, Jim Wiegold, and Chris Houghton.

In the following summer, Neumann toured the universities in Hungary, lecturing on her research on groups and analysis. She also attended the 12th British Mathematical Colloquium, held in 1960, and was asked to speak about wreath products (a group construction). A group theory, such as the wreath products, consists of a set of elements subject to one binary operation and meeting these three requirements: (1) It is a closed system; (2) It obeys the associative law; (3) There is an identity element, e, such that e Ө x = x for any element x in the group (Ө the binary operation).

Upon her return to England, Neumann began preparing for a joint study leave with her husband to the Courant Institute of Mathematical Sciences in New York. Her three sons accompanied them and the oldest, Peter, began to study under Gilbert Baumslag, one of the professors at Courant. During the course of the year, Peter and his parents solved the problem of the structure of the semigroup of varieties of groups, demonstrating that it is free. Neumann also presented a number of lectures and taught a graduate course on varieties of groups. During this time, Bernhard Neumann was invited to organize a research department of mathematics at the Australian National University and Hanna was offered a post as a reader.

The Next Frontier

Neumann began her new job in Australia in 1964. She overhauled the department and trained its teachers on subject matter covered in the new syllabuses. The material reflected the changes in mathematics worldwide, including more emphasis on pure mathematics and take-home assignments that promoted the use of ideas and theorems firsthand. Due to the difficulty of the subject matter, Bernhard's research students helped part-time with tutoring.

A conference on the theory of groups was organized by Neumann in 1965. The next year, she finished a monograph about group varieties. With the royalties, she was finally able to buy a good camera and revive her hobby of photography, collecting shots of flowers and trees. She also enjoyed extensive bike rides, later taking to four wheel drives with her husband in the outback.

In January of 1966, the Australian Association of Mathematics Teachers was formed and Neumann was elected to the position of vice president. She took on the responsibility of bringing together math teachers representing all areas of Australia. In 1967, she became president of the Canberra Mathematical Association and helped prepare pamphlets for teachers; her most famous one was on probability. During a sabbatical leave in 1969, Neumann wrote letters to publicize the inadequacy of Australian mathematics programs compared to the rest of the world and the need for reorganization of the content in many courses. She also visited the United States on a National Science Foundation Senior Foreign Scientist Fellowship. During her stay at Vanderbilt University in Nashville, Tennessee, Neumann and Ian Dey solved the problem on the free product of finitely many finitely generated Hopf groups.

Neumann's return to Australia was short-lived, for she accepted a lecture tour of Canada in 1971, speaking at the universities of British Columbia, Calgary, Alberta, Saskatchewan, and Manitoba. All of this travel and intense lecturing exhausted her, and she fell ill on November 12, checking into a hospital only to lapse immediately into a coma. Neumann did not regain consciousness and died two days later at age 57. After her death, a memorial fund was created from supporters all over the world to further Neumann's courageous and inspiring teaching.

FURTHER READING:

Books

Newman, M. F. "Hanna Neumann," in *Women of Mathematics: A Biobibliographic Sourcebook.* Edited by Louise S. Grinstein and Paul J. Campbell. Westport, CT: Greenwood Press, 1987, pp. 156–160.

Periodicals

Newman, M.F. and G. E. Wall. "Hanna Neumann." *Journal of the Australian Mathematical Society* 17 (1974): 1–28.

Records of the Australian Academy of Science 3, no. 2. (1975).

Other

"Hanna Neumann." *Biographies of Women Mathematicians.* June 1997. http://www.agnesscott.edu/lriddle/women/neumann.htm (September 21, 2000).

Sketch by Nicole Beatty

Allen Newell
1927–1992
American computer scientist

Allen Newell, an expert on how people think and a developer of complex information processing programs, was a pioneer in the field of artificial intelligence. From his development in the 1950s of Logic Theorist, one of the initial forays into artificial intelligence, to his presentation of the sophisticated problem-solving software system know as "SOAR" in the 1980s, Newell worked to link computer science and advances in understanding human cognition.

Newell was born in San Francisco on March 19, 1927, the son of Robert R. and Jeannette (LeValley) Newell. Robert Newell, a professor of radiology at Stanford Medical School, had a strong influence on his son. "[My father] was in many respects a complete man," Newell told Pamela McCorduck in an interview reported in *Machines Who Think*. "We used to go up and spend our summers on the High Sierra. He'd built a log cabin up in the mountains in the 1920s. And my father knew all about how to do things out in the woods—he could fish, pan for gold, the whole bit. At the same time, he was the complete intellectual. . . . My father knew literature, all the classics, and he also knew a lot of physics." Newell told McCorduck, however, that his own desire for scientific achievement had led him to focus his interests much more narrowly than had his father.

Newell served for two years on active duty in the Naval Reserve during World War II. In 1947, he married Noel Marie McKenna; they would have one son, Paul Allen Newell. After obtaining his B.S. in physics from Stanford University in 1949, Newell spent a year at Princeton University doing post-graduate work in mathematics, then went to work in 1950 as a research scientist for the RAND (Research and Development) Corporation in Santa Monica, California.

A Pioneer in the Field of Artificial Intelligence

While at RAND, Newell worked with the Air Force to simulate an early warning monitoring station with radar screens and a crew. His need to simulate the crew's reactions led to his interest in determining how people think.

Working together throughout the 1950s and into the 1960s, Newell and his colleagues **Herbert A. Simon** and Clifford Shaw were able to identify general reasoning techniques by observing the problem-solving behavior of human subjects. One of the best known of these techniques is means-end analysis, a process that analyzes the gap between a current situation and a desired end and searches for the means to close that gap.

In order to make use of computers in studying problem-solving behavior, Newell, Simon, and Shaw observed individuals as they worked through well-structured problems of logic. Subjects verbalized their reasoning as they worked through the problems. The three scientists were then able to code this reasoning in the form of a computer program. To make the program work, the scientists used a language called Information Processing Language (IPL) that they had developed previously for a computerized chess game. Their program, known as Logic Theorist, was not subject-matter specific; rather, it focused on the problem-solving process. Newell, Simon, and Shaw followed Logic Theorist with the development of General Problem Solver, a program that used means-end analysis to solve problems. Like Logic Theorist, General Problem Solver used the IPL language they had developed earlier.

During the summer of 1956, Newell and Simon were among a group of about a dozen scientists that gathered at Dartmouth College. The scientists came from a wide variety of fields, including mathematics, psychology, neurology, and electrical engineering. Though their backgrounds differed, they all had one thing in common: all were using computers in their research in an effort to simulate some aspect of human intelligence. With their Logic Theorist program, however, Newell and Simon were the only participants who could offer a working program in what would come to be known as "artificial intelligence." The Dartmouth Conference is generally viewed as the formal beginning of the field of artificial intelligence.

In 1957, Newell earned his Ph.D. in industrial administration from Carnegie Institute of Technology in Pittsburgh, Pennsylvania. In 1961 he left his position at RAND to join the faculty of Carnegie-Mellon University (formerly the Carnegie Institute of Technology), where he helped develop the School of Computer Science.

Problem-solving Software that Thinks

During the 1980s, Newell, along with his former students John Laird and Paul Rosenbloom, developed a more sophisticated software system that solved problems in a manner similar to the human mind. This system, called SOAR (State, Operator, and Result), was a general problem-solving program that learned from experience in that it was able to remember how it solved problems and to make use of that knowledge in subsequent problem-solving. SOAR, like humans, used working memory and long-term memory to solve problems. If SOAR was working toward a desired goal, it used working memory to keep track of the current situation, or "state," in the problem-solving process compared with the desired goal or "result." In order to make the decisions necessary to achieve a goal, people use information they have accumulated through experience. People use long-term memory to access information; SOAR also used long-term memory, programmed as a series of IF/THEN statements.

While the use of IF/THEN statements in a computer program wasn't a new idea, the way in which SOAR processed those statements was new. In the past, only one IF/THEN statement could control a computer program at any given time. If conflicting statements could apply to a problem, the problem-solving process would break down. SOAR, on the other hand, was designed to look at all of the programmed IF/THEN statements at once. After looking at all of the statements, SOAR would weigh them as suggestions, then decide which move, or "operator," would best advance it towards the desired result. If there were no IF/THEN statements stored in memory that applied specifically to the problem at hand, SOAR would use any available information that seemed potentially useful to try to resolve the problem. Whenever it solved one of these unexpected problems, SOAR would remember how it solved the problem, adding this information to its long-term memory. Like the human mind, SOAR was thus able both to generate original responses to new problems and to "learn" from its experiences.

In the late 1980s, Newell began an active campaign to promote the use of SOAR as the basis for a new effort to develop a unified theory of cognition. Whereas current research in artificial intelligence tended to focus on narrow and isolated aspects of cognition, Newell hoped SOAR would help cognitive psychologists devise broad theories of human cognition and advance towards an integrated understanding of all aspects of human thought.

Career Capped with National Medal of Science

Newell received the National Medal of Science from President George Bush just a month before his death from cancer on July 19, 1992. His work had already brought him a number of other honors, including the Harry Goode Memorial Award, which he received from the American Federation of Information Processing Societies in 1971, and the A. M. Turing Award, presented jointly to Newell and Simon by the Association for Computing Machinery in 1975. Newell was founding president of the American Association for Artificial Intelligence and also served as head of the Cognitive Science Society. Along with his colleague Herbert Simon and computer scientists **Marvin Minsky** and **John McCarthy**, he is considered one of the fathers of artificial intelligence.

SELECTED WRITINGS BY NEWELL:

Books

The Logic Theory Machine: A Complex Information Processing System, RAND Corp., revised edition, 1956.

GPS, A Case Study in Generality and Problem Solving, Academic Press, 1969.
Human Problem Solving, Prentice-Hall, 1972.
The Psychology of the Human Computer, L. Erlbaum Associates, 1983.
Unified Theories of Cognition, Harvard University Press, 1990.

FURTHER READING:

Books

McCorduck, Pamela, *Machines Who Think,* W.H. Freeman, 1979, pp. 122–123.
Mishkoff, Henry C., *Understanding Artificial Intelligence,* Howard W. Sams, 1985, pp. 31–35, 152.

Periodicals

Fox, John, *Nature,* Models of Mind, September 26, 1991, pp. 312–313.
Fox, John, *New York Times,* July 20, 1992, p. D8.
Waldrop, M. Mitchell, *Science,* SOAR: A Unified Theory of Cognition?, July 15, 1988, pp. 296–298.
Waldrop, M. Mitchell, *Science,* Toward a Unified Theory of Cognition, July 1, 1988, pp. 27–29.

Sketch by Daniel Rooney

Norman Dennis Newell
1909–
American paleontologist and geologist

Paleontologists spend their lives investigating the events of millions of years ago through the fossil record and stratigraphy, or the examination of the layers of the earth's crust. It is a complex record, and since the nineteenth century when such studies burgeoned, a debate has raged between uniformitarians, who argue that life has evolved over the ages in a relatively smooth progression, and the catastrophists, who counter that life forms have undergone radical changes through the millennia as a result of climatic and geologic catastrophes. Norman Dennis Newell, through painstaking research of the fossil record around the world, has added greatly to this debate, and his findings suggest a much more radical and episodic process of evolution than was thought possible. Newell has done much to popularize the understanding of rapid extinctions and introductions of life forms on earth, and has explored the changes in sea level brought about by geographic or climatic changes as one cause of such rapid alterations. In his long career as a paleontologist and geologist, Newell has surveyed parts of the earth from Texas to the Bahamas to the Pacific atolls, and as an academic, curator, and writer, he has introduced paleontology to new generations of scholars and lay people alike.

Born on January 7, 1909, in Chicago, Illinois, Newell is the son of Virgil Bingham and Nellie (Clark) Newell. His father was a dental surgeon and amateur geologist who instilled in the young Newell a lasting interest in rocks and in nature in general. Newell grew up in central Kansas, attended the University of Kansas, and earned his B.S. there in 1929 and his A.M. in 1931. He worked with the Kansas Geologic Survey during this time and performed in a jazz band to help put himself through school. While a graduate student he married his first wife, Valerie Zirkle, in 1928. After graduating from the University of Kansas, Newell attended Yale University, where he earned his Ph.D. in 1933.

Early Interest Focuses on Bivalves

Newell stayed on at Yale as a Sterling Fellow, and it was during this fellowship at the Yale Peabody Museum that he became intensely interested in bivalve mollusks (animals with two-part shells, such as clams) as indicators of evolutionary principles. He studied both living and fossil mollusks and developed a classification system that was adopted internationally. He was made an assistant professor of geology at the University of Kansas in 1934. In 1937 he was chosen as a delegate to the 17th International Geologic Congress in Moscow, and that same year accepted a position at the University of Wisconsin as an associate professor of geology, where he remained until 1945. From 1939 to 1942, he was the co-editor of the *Journal of Paleontology*. While at Wisconsin, Newell led a research team to Peru to survey for petroleum reserves. Once in Peru, he also surveyed the entire Lake Titicaca basin, the results of which led to a revised theory of the geological formation of the Andes mountains. After World War II, Newell moved on to Columbia University in New York, where he was made a full professor of geology, holding also a concurrent position as chairman and curator of invertebrate paleontology at the American Museum of Natural History.

Conducts Worldwide Geologic Surveys

The next decades were a period of intense research and rich field work for Newell, as he conducted field surveys from the South Pacific to the Bahamas. His work in the Guadalupe Mountains of western Texas from 1949 to 1952 uncovered such a rich and varied fossil record that the area was subsequently designated a national park. Working in the South Pacific at the Raroia coral atoll in 1952, Newell verified Darwin's theory of the development of coral atolls, and surveying in the Great Bahama Bank in 1950 and 1951, he demonstrated that such islands were indeed remnants of a huge barrier reef, one that was once far more extensive even than modern day Australia's Great Barrier Reef. In 1967 he was also a member of a Scripps Institute of Oceanography

expedition to Micronesia. Other field work took him to North Africa for surveys in Tunisia and Morocco. Through all of these studies, Newell was able to put together a picture of the earth's geologic and fossil record that suggests a less than gradual evolution of life forms. Indeed, the differences in fossilized life forms that Newell found embedded in rock strata indicated what he termed episodic revolutions in life, or large and radical changes over relatively brief periods of geologic time.

The author of numerous books and articles on geology and paleontology, Newell has been internationally honored for his work in these fields. In 1960 he was awarded the Mary Clark Thompson Medal from the National Academy of Sciences (of which he is a member); a medal from the University of Hiroshima in 1964; the Hayden Memorial Award in paleontology and geology from the Academy of Natural Sciences in 1965; Yale University's Verrill Medal in 1966; the Gold Medal for Distinguished Achievement in Science from the National Museum of Natural History in 1978; and the Raymond C. Moore Medal in 1980. Newell's first wife died in the early 1970s and he married Gillian Wendy Wormall Schacht in 1973. Retiring from both Columbia University and the American Museum of Natural History in 1977, Newell continued on at both institutions in an emeritus capacity. The year after his retirement he was an exchange scholar to the Soviet Union under the sponsorship of the American Academy of Sciences. In his retirement, Newell spends several days a week at the American Museum of Natural History and enjoys field expeditions and collecting minerals.

SELECTED WRITINGS BY NEWELL:

Books

The Geology of Johnson and Miami Counties, Kansas, and the Geology of Wyandotte County, Kansas, University of Kansas, 1935.

Late Paleozoic Pelecypods: Pectinacea and Mytilacca, University of Kansas, 1937.

Geology of Lake Titicaca Region, Peru and Bolivia, Geological Society of America, 1949.

The Permian Reef of the Guadalupe Mountains Region, Texas and New Mexico: A Study in Paleoecology, W. H. Freeman, 1953.

Upper Paleozoic of Peru, Geological Society of America, 1953.

Organism Communities and Bottom Facies, Great Bahama Bank, American Museum of Natural History, 1959.

Creation and Evolution: Myth or Reality?, Columbia University Press, 1982.

FURTHER READING:

Books

Contemporary Authors, Volume 104, Gale, 1982, pp. 338–339.

McGraw-Hill Modern Scientists and Engineers,
  McGraw-Hill, 1980, pp. 358–359.

Sketch by J. Sydney Jones

Margaret Morse Nice
1883–1974
American ornithologist

Margaret Morse Nice became one of America's leading ornithologists due to her insistence on the importance of studying the behavior of individual birds to better understand the nature of each species as a whole. Her detailed observations provided a major contribution to the study of birds and have had a lasting effect on the field of ornithology, despite the fact that she never held a faculty appointment or received university funding. Nice was also a wife and the mother of four children, with a traditional role in her family, and most of her contributions were made by investigating birds in her own backyard.

Nice was born Margaret Morse on December 6, 1883, in Amherst, Massachusetts, to Anson and Margaret (Ely) Morse. Her father was a professor of history at Amherst College; he was also a dedicated gardener and had a deep love of the wilderness. Her mother had studied botany at Mount Holyoke and helped inspire in her daughter a love of nature, teaching her the name of wild flowers as they walked in the woods. In her autobiography, *Research Is a Passion with Me,* Nice would later describe how in her family's two-acre orchard and garden, "we learned of nature at first hand, planting and weeding in our own small gardens." Her interest in ornithology began early: she was recording her observations of birds by the age of twelve.

Nice attended a private elementary school and the public high school in Amherst, and then in 1901 she enrolled in Mount Holyoke College, as had her mother. At first she concentrated on languages, but later switched to the natural sciences. She graduated in 1906 and the following year received a fellowship to study biology for two years at Clark University in Worcester, Massachusetts. In August of 1909, she married Leonard Blaine Nice, whom she had met there. That same year, the couple moved to Cambridge, where Leonard Nice entered Harvard Medical School. In 1913, he was appointed the head of the physiology department at the University of Oklahoma and Nice moved with him to Norman, Oklahoma.

Nice's first paper, which dealt with bobwhites, was published after more than two years of research. Mostly confined to the house during the following years as her four daughters were born and she tended to them, Nice would not publish any more ornithological research until 1920.

Frustrated by her inability to pursue her studies in this field, Nice began studying how her daughters acquired language. This work later earned her a master's degree in psychology from Clark University in 1915, and she published eighteen articles on child psychology.

Researches Territorial Behavior of Birds

In the 1920s, Nice was influenced to return to the study of birds by an older friend, Althea Sherman, an amateur ornithologist. In 1920, Nice published a description of Oklahoma bird life. Thirty-five more articles about Oklahoma birds followed, and in 1924 she published a book on the subject, *The Birds of Oklahoma.* In 1927, her husband accepted a teaching position in Columbus, Ohio, and the family moved to a house on the bank of a river which attracted a number of nesting and migratory birds, including sparrows. There, Nice studied the territorial behavior of birds by placing colored bands on them and following them for years in a way no one had before. Her studies resulted in several publications, the most important of which was her two-part *Studies in the Life History of the Song Sparrow,* published in 1937 and 1943. With the publication of these volumes, she became one of the world's leading ornithologists. *Notable American Women* quoted German evolutionary biologist **Ernst Mayr** as saying that Nice had "almost singlehandedly, initiated a new era in American ornithology."

Nice and her family moved to Chicago in 1936, where her husband had accepted an appointment at the University of Chicago Medical School. She was not able to do nearly as many field observations there, but she continued to write and study. Her knowledge of languages enabled her to expose Americans to European ornithology through translations and reviews of articles in German and other languages. During this period she became increasingly active as a conservationist, advocating the preservation of wildlife and restrictions on the use of pesticides.

Nice was president of the Wilson Ornithological Society in 1938 and 1939, the first woman to be elected president of a major American ornithological society. She was also associate editor of the journal *Bird-Banding* from 1935 to 1942 and 1946 to 1974. Mount Holyoke awarded her an honorary doctorate in 1955. In 1969, the Wilson Ornithological Society inaugurated a grant in her name to be given to self-trained amateur researchers. Nice died in Chicago on June 26, 1974, at the age of ninety.

SELECTED WRITINGS BY NICE:

Books

The Birds of Oklahoma, University of Oklahoma, 1924, revised edition, 1931.
Studies in the Life History of the Song Sparrow, two volumes, [New York], 1937 and 1943, Dover, 1964.

The Watcher at the Nest, Macmillan, 1939.
Research Is a Passion with Me, Consolidated Amethyst, 1979.

FURTHER READING:

Books

Conway, Jill K., editor, *Written by Herself,* Vintage Books, 1991.
Sicherman, Barbara, and Carol Hurd Green, editors, *Notable American Women: The Modern Period,* Belknap, 1980.

Periodicals

Trautman, Milton B., *The Auk,* In Memoriam: Margaret Morse Nice, July, 1977.

Sketch by Margo Nash

Roberta J. Nichols
1931–
American engineer

As a principal research engineer with Ford Motor Company since 1979, Roberta J. Nichols is an internationally recognized innovator in alternative fuel for transportation vehicles. She is the holder of three patents for the Flexible Fuel Vehicle (FFV), which can run on alcohol, gasoline, or any combination of these substances mixed in one fuel tank. Nichols has delivered lectures or seminars in Europe, Japan, Australia, China, and India. She has served as consultant for the Office of Technology Assessment (OTA) of the U.S. Congress, and has been a witness at numerous federal and state government hearings on the use of alcohol-fueled vehicles.

Nichols was born on November 29, 1931, in Los Angeles, California, and received her education there. She first began her career as a mathematician with Douglas Aircraft Company in 1957, working in the company's data analysis section in missiles engineering. She held a similar position at TRW's Space Technology Laboratory from 1958 to 1960 in the propulsion department.

In 1960 Nichols accepted a position as research associate of the Aerodynamics and Propulsion Laboratory with the Aerospace Corporation in El Segundo, California. During her employment with the firm, she was widowed and decided, with two children to raise, to return to school to better her career prospects. Her interest in boat and car racing propelled her to study engineering. Nichols thus completed work on her bachelor of science degree in physics at the University of California at Los Angeles in 1968. She earned a master of science degree in environmental engineering in 1975 and a Ph.D. in engineering in 1979, both at the University of Southern California. In addition to her schooling, she conducted research on Air Force-related projects, such as wind-tunnel testing of re-entry vehicles, from 1960 until 1969.

During 1969 Nichols was also named co-manager of the Chemical Kinetics Department at the Aerospace Corporation and subsequently established and operated the Air Pollution Laboratory. She conducted various studies, developing emission reductions through two-stage combustion and the use of lead-free, high-octane fuel.

In 1978, Nichols served as consultant to the State of California's Synthetic Fuels Program, where she developed engine and vehicle modifications used to create a station wagon which ran only on methanol fuel. Her work in the late 1970s also encompassed research on police vehicles and hydrogen-powered vehicles.

Earns Patents for Multi-Fuel Burning Engines

Nichols began her leadership role in Flexible Fuel Vehicles (FFV) soon after joining Ford in 1979. She has earned three patents for technologies used in engines which burn fuels of different octane, volatility, and volumetric energy content. In 1992, she was named as electric vehicle external strategy and planning manager in the Electric Vehicle Program Office of Car Product Development. While at Ford, Nichols developed ethanol-fueled engines for Ford of Brazil; designed and developed 630 methanol-fueled Escorts, which were used primarily for California government fleets; designed and developed the powertrain for the Alternate Fuel Vehicle (AFV), an auto which was displayed at the Knoxville, Tennessee, World's Fair in 1982; gave seminars in Europe, New Zealand, Australia, the Philippines, and Japan; consulted on alternative fuels in India and China; and served as Ford spokesperson to the media. Nichols also has participated on numerous advisory committees, and has been a guest lecturer at universities across the United States and Canada.

Among the honors received by Nichols are the Outstanding Engineer Merit Award, given by the Institute for the Advancement of Engineering; the Aerospace Corporation's Woman of the Year Award; and the South Coast Air Quality Management District's Clean Air Award for Advancing Air Pollution Technology. She was also the recipient of the Society of Women Engineers Achievement Award in 1988 and was nominated for the National Medal of Technology in 1989. An avid boat and auto racer, she held the women's world water speed record from 1966 to 1969. She has designed and built the boat and auto engines, including her first methanol engine, that she has driven in various competitions. Her husband, Lynn Yakal, shares her love of racing.

On being a woman pioneer in engineering, Nichols told *UCLA Magazine:* "I was the typical tomboy, and always went to welding shops and junkyards with my dad. I didn't know I wasn't supposed to like that stuff!"

FURTHER READING:

Periodicals

Michigan Woman, A Woman's Driving Passions, September/October 1988, p. 30–31.

UCLA Magazine, Roberta Nichols, Designing Superwoman, winter, 1990, p. 96.

Sketch by Karen Withem

Seth Barnes Nicholson

Seth Barnes Nicholson
1891–1963
American astronomer

Nicholson is best known for his discovery of four satellites of Jupiter, an accomplishment equaled in number only by Galileo. He also gained prominence for his documentation of sunspot cycles and for his estimations of planetary and lunar temperatures.

Seth Barnes Nicholson was born on November 12, 1891, in Springfield, Illinois, to William Franklin and Martha (Ames) Nicholson. His father, who had a master's degree in geology from Cornell University, was an elementary school teacher and principal. He worked first in Springfield, then when his son was seven years old, moved the family to a farm near Toulon, Illinois, for health reasons. Six years later he returned to teaching, eventually becoming principal of Toulon Academy, a high school in the small farming community. Nicholson had one older sister, Neva, who became a missionary in India, and two younger sisters, Carrie and Helen, who became schoolteachers in California. Although Nicholson grew up in a rural environment, he possessed a great interest in science, something his father instilled in him early in life. He later recalled that his father "was interested in science of all kinds and from him I learned the names of the stars, flowers, birds, and rocks. . . .Electricity was my favorite hobby and my father showed me how to make toy motors, telegraph instruments, and induction coils."

Discovers a Love of Astronomy

In 1908 Nicholson entered Drake University in Des Moines, Iowa, having no special interest in astronomy. At Drake however, he came under the influence of D. W. Morehouse, a professor of astronomy who had discovered a comet two years earlier. When Halley's comet appeared in 1910, Nicholson took what came to be considered some of the classic photos of that famous comet using Drake's 8-in (20-cm) telescope. It was at Drake also that Nicholson met Alma Stotts, a classmate in astronomy whom he would marry after graduation in 1913, the same year they both enrolled in the graduate department of astronomy at the University of California at Berkeley. They eventually had three children, Margaret, Donald, and Jean.

It was at Berkeley that Nicholson would do his most significant astronomical work. As a graduate student there in 1914, it was Nicholson who was chosen to remain at Lick Observatory to study a recently discovered satellite of Jupiter that had an oddly retrograde rotation. Most other staff members were making a trip to Russia, one of the few locations where an eclipse of the sun would be visible. Nicholson took his orders seriously and, to be safe, decided to make an extra-long photographic exposure using what was then the largest telescope in the world. Because of this, he was able to barely detect yet another tiny satellite heretofore unknown. Thus at the age of 23, Nicholson had discovered the ninth known moon of Jupiter. This satellite later proved to be a twin of Jupiter's eighth moon, and it provided Nicholson with a sufficiently original topic for his doctoral dissertation, in which he offered calculations of its orbit and position. After receiving his Ph.D. in 1915, Nicholson joined the staff of the Mount Wilson Observatory, which was run by the Carnegie Institution and operated primarily as a solar observatory. Ironically for Nicholson, this position determined that the bulk of his career would be spent observing the sun instead of the planets.

Studies Lunar and Planetary Temperatures and Discovers Three More of Jupiter's Moons

Nicholson remained at Mount Wilson until his retirement in 1957, and because of his long-term and detailed observations of the surface features and spectrum of the sun, he was able to conduct highly delicate and sensitive measurement studies of its temperatures. He also issued regular reports on sunspot activity and studied their effects on Earth's atmosphere, eventually compiling a continuous solar history maintained over several sunspot cycles. His skill with temperature studies was eventually applied to the moon and the planets, and in 1927, he demonstrated that the moon's temperature dropped as much as 390°F (200°C) when it was in Earth's shadow. Applying such newly discovered facts to questions of the origin and composition of the planets, Nicholson then was able to make several insightful and correct theoretical observations.

Besides his important work on the temperatures of planetary bodies, Nicholson served as an observer on several solar eclipse expeditions in the 1920s and 1930s. In 1938, Nicholson returned to observing Jupiter when, in a replay of his graduate days, most of the Mount Wilson astronomers traveled to Stockholm to attend a meeting of the International Astronomical Union. This allowed him sufficient time to not only reconfirm his 1914 discovery but, surprisingly, to discover two more satellites orbiting Jupiter. These became the tenth and eleventh of Jupiter's moons. Finally, in 1951, while intending to observe the tenth moon, he discovered Jupiter's twelfth moon. All four of the satellites found by Nicholson were very faint and extremely difficult to locate, and when he was asked about the "thrill" of such discoveries, he replied that he experienced no such feelings, since confirmation of an actual discovery took such a long time.

Throughout his career and even after his retirement, Nicholson was an engaging and highly effective lecturer, and was deeply involved with all aspects of the astronomical community on the West Coast. From 1935 to 1960, he served as president of the Astronomical Society of the Pacific, as well as editor of its *Publications* from 1940 to 1955. A regular hiker of mountain trails, he also enjoyed tennis and ping-pong. After his retirement in 1957, he continued to work for the United States Weather Bureau. The recipient of several awards and honorary degrees, Nicholson died of cancer in Los Angeles, California, on June 2, 1963.

SELECTED WRITINGS BY NICHOLSON:

Periodicals

"Discovery, Observations and Orbit of the Ninth Satellite of Jupiter." *Lick Observatory Bulletin*, 1915, Volume 8, pp. 100-103, 147-49.

"The Ninth Satellite of Jupiter." *Proceedings of the National Academy of Sciences*, 1917, Volume 3, pp. 147-49.

FURTHER READING:

Books

Asimov, Isaac. *Asimov's Biographical Encyclopedia of Science and Technology*. Doubleday & Company, 1972, p. 639.
Gillispie, Charles Coulston, ed. *Dictionary of Scientific Biography*. Charles Scribner's Sons, 1981, p. 107.
Herget, Paul. "Seth Barnes Nicholson." *Biographical Memoirs. National Academy of Sciences*. Columbia University Press, 1971, pp. 200-227.

Periodicals

"Seth Nicholson, Astronomer, Dies." *The New York Times* (July 3, 1963): 25.

Sketch by Leonard C. Bruno

Charles J. H. Nicolle
1866–1936
French bacteriologist

Charles J. H. Nicolle, the recipient of the 1928 Nobel Prize for physiology or medicine, was recognized by the Swedish Academy for his research into the cause of typhus, a severe and widespread disease during the early twentieth century. Nicolle's discovery that typhus is transmitted by the human body louse—and therefore can be readily prevented—was of great benefit to both military and civilian medicine.

Born September 21, 1866, in Rouen, France, Charles Jules Henri Nicolle was the son of physician Eugène Nicolle. Charles's father was a medical doctor at the municipal hospital, as well as a professor of natural history at the École des Sciences et des Art. Encouraged by his brother, the noted bacteriologist Maurice Nicolle, Charles took a course in bacteriology at the Institute Pasteur in Paris, studying under the renowned bacteriologists, Émile Roux and **Élie Metchnikoff**. For his doctoral dissertation, Nicolle investigated the bacterium then called Ducrey's Bacillus (also known as *Hemophilus ducreyi*), the causative agent of soft chancre, a type of venereal disease.

Charles took his medical degree in 1893 in Paris, then returned to Rouen for a staff position in a hospital. Shortly thereafter, he married Alice Avice; their two sons, Marcelle and Pierre, would eventually become physicians. Unable to develop a major biomedical research center in Rouen as he desired, Nicolle agreed in 1902 to assume the directorship of the Institute Pasteur in Tunis, Tunisia. For the remainder of his life, Nicolle lived and worked primarily in Tunis with occasional lecturing in Paris.

Investigating the Source of Typhus

Affiliated with the original Institute Pasteur (which was founded in Paris in 1888), the institute in Tunis was basically an organization in name only. Over the years to come, however, Nicolle improved a run-down antirabies vaccination unit into a leading center for the study of North African and tropical diseases. It was in Tunis where Nicolle accomplished his groundbreaking work on typhus. He became intrigued by the observation that an outbreak of typhus did not seem to take hold in hospital wards as it did among the general populace of the city. Although the contagion infected workers who admitted patients into the hospital, it did not affect other patients or attendants in the actual wards. Those who collected or laundered the dirty clothes of newly admitted patients typically came down with the disease.

Realizing that the washing, shaving, and providing of clean clothes to the new patient was possibly the key to the pattern of infection, Nicolle initiated a series of experiments in 1909 to confirm his suspicion of the arthropod-borne nature of typhus. He theorized that lice, which attached themselves to the bodies and clothes of human beings, transmitted the disease, so he began his investigation by infusing a chimpanzee with human blood infected with typhus, then transferred the chimpanzee's blood to a healthy macaque monkey. When the fever and rash of typhus was seen on the monkey, Nicolle placed twenty-nine human body lice obtained from healthy humans on the skin of the macaque. These lice were later placed on the skin of a number of healthy monkeys, which all contracted the disease.

Once Nicolle isolated the relationship between typhus and the louse, preventative measures were established to counter unsanitary conditions. Nevertheless, the trenches of World War I remained major breeding places for the louse and typhus killed an enormous number of soldiers on all sides of the conflict. The development of the insecticide DDT by **Paul Müller** in 1939 was the most effective prophylactic against typhus, nearly eradicating the disease among soldiers during World War II.

Nicolle is also responsible for other important contributions to the science of bacteriology. Stemming from his research into typhus was his recognition of a phenomenon known as "inapparent infection," a state in which a carrier of a disease exhibits no symptoms. This theoretical discovery suggested how diseases survived from one epidemic to another.

Nicolle, along with a variety of other colleagues over time, also researched African infantile leishmaniasis, which

affected humans, and a related disease in dogs. Another significant discovery concerned the role of flies in the transmission of the blinding disease trachoma. For these and other works, Nicolle received the French Commander of the Legion of Honor and was named to the French Academy of Medicine. In 1932 he became a professor in the College de France.

Besides his work in science, Nicolle was an accomplished literary figure, having published several novels. His scientific writings include five major books as well as numerous articles. Nicolle died on February 28, 1936 in Tunis.

SELECTED WRITINGS BY NICOLLE:

Books

La destinee humaine, par Charles Nicolle, Felix Alcan, 1936.
Destin des Maladies Infectieuses, Presses universitaires de France, 1939.

Periodicals

Annales de l'Institut Pasteur, Recherches expérimentales sur le typhus exanthématique, Volume 24, pp. 243–275, 1910.

Sketch by Dr. Donald J. McGraw

Alfred O. C. Nier
1911–1994
American physicist

Alfred O. C. Nier's research and discoveries were in the area of examining and defining isotopes through mass spectroscopy, particularly in the areas of uranium isotopes used in nuclear fission and the use of isotopes for geological dating methods. Nier invented the double-focusing mass spectrometer which was used in the *Viking* spacecraft's visit to Mars, bringing back the first on-site data from that planet.

Alfred Otto Carl Nier was born on May 28, 1911, in St. Paul, Minnesota. His parents were August C. and Anna J. Stoll Nier, both immigrants to the United States from Germany. Nier attended the University of Minnesota, from which he received a bachelor of science degree in 1931 and a master of science degree in 1933, both in the field of electrical engineering. He then changed his major to physics and earned his Ph.D. in that subject in 1936.

Begins Studies in Mass Spectroscopy

From his days as a graduate student, Nier's career reflected his ability to look at problems from two perspectives: that of the technologically-oriented engineer, and that of the research-oriented physicist. Much of his work involved the use of mass spectrometers to analyze the isotopic composition of elements.

The principle of mass spectroscopy was developed in the first decade of the twentieth century by **Francis W. Aston**. In a mass spectrometer, atoms are ionized and then accelerated through electrical and magnetic fields. Since these fields act with different force on ions of different mass, the spectrometer can be used to separate particles according to their masses. That separation is relatively clear-cut when mass differences are large, but becomes less clear as the masses of two particles become closer in size.

An important objective of Nier's work was to refine the mass spectrometric process so that it could distinguish smaller and smaller mass differences. One such refinement is the double-focusing mass spectrometer. In Nier's version of the double-focusing mass spectrometer, a beam of ions is accelerated first through an electrical field at an angle of ninety degrees, and then through a magnetic field at an angle of sixty degrees. Nier found that this arrangement could be used to achieve a high degree of separation of ions with similar masses at a cost much lower than that of conventional mass spectrometers.

Mass Spectrometer Used to Discover Important Isotopes

Nier's first major discovery, the radioactive isotope potassium-40, was made while he was still a graduate student in Minnesota. That discovery was of considerable importance, since potassium is one of the most abundant elements in the Earth's crust, and potassium-40 is, therefore, an important source of background radiation. In 1934, Nier and Lyman T. Aldrich were able to show how the decay of potassium-40 to argon-40 can be used to measure the age of very old objects. That technique has since become extraordinarily useful in the dating of geological objects and materials.

From 1936 to 1938, Nier worked at Harvard University under a National Research Council fellowship. While there, he used the mass spectrometer to determine the isotopic composition (the percentage of each isotope of a given mass) for a number of elements. During this work he discovered a number of new isotopes whose abundance is so low that they had never been identified previously. These included sulfur-36, calcium-46, calcium-48, and osmium-186. He also carried out studies on the relative abundance of two isotopes of carbon, carbon-12 and carbon-13, and showed that the ratio of the two is a function of the source from which the carbon is taken. This research has been put to use in recent attempts to estimate the temperature of past geological years.

Nier's most important research was his study of the isotopes of uranium. His earliest research was aimed at determining the relationship between the radioactive isotopes of this element and the isotopes of lead, some of which are formed during the decay of uranium. This work eventually provided scientists with a second method for estimating the age of rocks, a method based on the ratio of radiogenic lead (from uranium) to non-radiogenic lead.

The early uranium studies led to even more significant research during World War II. In 1938, **Otto Hahn** and **Fritz Strassmann** discovered that fission occurs when uranium is bombarded by neutrons. Physicists immediately understood the enormous potential of this discovery as a source of energy for both peaceful applications and, more relevant at the time, for the development of weapons. One practical problem of the development of nuclear fission as a source of energy was the uncertainty as to which isotope of uranium actually undergoes fission. Nier answered this question in 1940, working with J. R. Dunning, E. T. Booth, and A. V. Grosse at Columbia University, as they were able to show that it is the relatively uncommon uranium-235, rather than the more common uranium-238, that undergoes fission. During and after the war, Nier was active in the development of methods for separating these two isotopes from each other.

In 1938, at the conclusion of his postdoctoral work at Harvard, Nier returned to Minnesota. He remained there for the rest of his academic career as assistant professor, from 1938 to 1940, associate professor from 1940 to 1944, professor, from 1944 to 1956, and Regents' Professor of Physics, from 1956 until his retirement in the early 1980s. Continuing his scientific work after his retirement, Nier supervised a study of cosmic dust in the 1990s. He died on May 16, 1994 in Minneapolis.

Nier's research using mass spectrographs to measure isotopes and other atomic masses led to his invention of the first double-focusing mass spectrometer, miniature versions of which were later used on satellites observing the lower thermosphere. Nier was appointed by the National Aeronautics and Space Administration to lead the Entry Science team to study the composition and structure of the Martian atmosphere during the *Viking* spacecraft's descent to the planet's surface. On this mission, Nier's mass spectrometer provided the first on-site information known about the make-up of the atmosphere of Mars.

Nier was married twice, first to Ruth E. Andersen in 1937, and then to Ardish L. Hovland in 1969. He had one son and one daughter. His work was recognized by the American Geological Society's Arthur L. Day Medal (1956), the Goldschmidt Medal of the Geochemical Society (1984), the U.S. Atomic Energy Commission's Field and Franklin Award (1985), and the Thomson Medal of the International Mass Spectrometry Conference (1985).

FURTHER READING:

Books

McGraw-Hill Modern Scientists and Engineers. Vol. 2. New York: McGraw-Hill, 1980, pp. 361-63.

Marshall Warren Nirenberg

Periodicals

"Alfred Nier; Helped Build Atom Bomb" (obituary). *Los Angeles Times* (19 May 1994): A20.

"Alfred O. C. Nier, 82, Physicist Who Helped Develop Atomic Bomb" (obituary). *Boston Globe* (18 May 1994): 33.

Hilchey, Tim. "Alfred Nier, 82; Physicist Helped Foster A-Bomb" (obituary). *New York Times* (18 May 1994): B8.

Johnson, Walter H., Jr., and Konrad Mauersberger. "Alfred Nier" (obituary). *Physics Today* 48 (January 1995): 68-69.

Sketch by David E. Newton

Marshall Warren Nirenberg
1927–
American biochemist

Marshall Warren Nirenberg is best known for deciphering the portion of DNA (deoxyribonucleic acid) that is responsible for the synthesis of the numerous protein molecules that form the basis of living cells. His research has helped to unravel the DNA genetic code, aiding, for example, in the determination of which genes code for certain hereditary traits. For his contribution to the sciences of genetics and cell biochemistry, Nirenberg was awarded the 1968 Nobel Prize in physiology or medicine with **Robert W. Holley** and **Har Gobind Khorana**.

Nirenberg was born in New York City on April 10, 1927, and moved to Florida with his parents, Harry Edward and Minerva (Bykowsky) Nirenberg, when he was ten years old. He earned his B.S. in 1948 and his M.S. in biology in 1952 from the University of Florida. Nirenberg's interest in science extended beyond his formal studies. For two of his undergraduate years he worked as a teaching assistant in biology, and he also spent a brief period as a research assistant in the nutrition laboratory. In 1952, Nirenberg continued his graduate studies at the University of Michigan, this time in the field of biochemistry. Obtaining his Ph.D. in 1957, he wrote his dissertation on the uptake of hexose, a sugar molecule, by ascites tumor cells.

Shortly after earning his Ph.D., Nirenberg began his investigation into the inner workings of the genetic code as an American Cancer Society (ACS) fellow at the National Institutes of Health (NIH) in Bethesda, Maryland. Nirenberg continued his research at the NIH after the ACS fellowship ended in 1959, under another fellowship from the Public Health Service (PHS). In 1960, when the PHS fellowship ended, he joined the NIH staff permanently as a research scientist in biochemistry.

Nirenberg cracks the genetic code

After only a brief time conducting research at the NIH, Nirenberg made his mark in genetic research with the most important scientific breakthrough since **James D. Watson** and **Francis Crick** discovered the structure of DNA in 1953. Specifically, he discovered the process for unraveling the code of DNA. This process allows scientists to determine the genetic basis of particular hereditary traits. In August of 1961, Nirenberg announced his discovery during a routine presentation of a research paper at a meeting of the International Congress of Biochemistry in Moscow.

Nirenberg's research involved the genetic code sequences for amino acids. Amino acids are the building blocks of protein. They link together to form the numerous protein molecules present in the human body. Nirenberg discovered how to determine which sequence patterns code for which amino acids (there are about 20 known amino acids).

Nirenberg Honored with Nobel Prize

Nirenberg's discovery has led to a better understanding of genetically determined diseases and, more controversially, to further research into the controlling of hereditary traits, or genetic engineering. For his research, Nirenberg was awarded the 1968 Nobel Prize for physiology or medicine. He shared the honor with scientists Har Gobind Khorana and Robert W. Holley. After receiving the Nobel Prize, Nirenberg switched his research focus to other areas of biochemistry, including cellular control mechanisms and the cell differentiation process.

Since first being hired by the NIH in 1960, Nirenberg has served in different capacities. From 1962 until 1966 he was head of the Section for Biochemical Genetics, National Heart Institute. Since 1966 he has been serving as the chief of the Laboratory of Biochemical Genetics, National Heart, Lung and Blood Institute. Other honors bestowed upon Nirenberg, in addition to the Nobel Prize, include honorary membership in the Harvey Society, the Molecular Biology Award from the National Academy of Sciences (1962), National Medal of Science presented by President Lyndon B. Johnson (1965), and the Louisa Gross Horwitz Prize for Biochemistry (1968). Nirenberg also received numerous honorary degrees from distinguished universities, including the University of Michigan (1965), University of Chicago (1965), Yale University (1965), University of Windsor (1966), George Washington University (1972), and the Weizmann Institute in Israel (1978). Nirenberg is a member of several professional societies, including the National Academy of Sciences, the Pontifical Academy of Sciences, the American Chemical Society, the Biophysical Society, and the Society for Developmental Biology.

Nirenberg married biochemist Perola Zaltzman in 1961. While described as being a reserved man who engages in little else besides scientific research, Nirenberg has been a strong advocate of government support for scientific research, believing this to be an important factor for the advancement of science.

SELECTED WRITINGS BY NIRENBERG:

Periodicals

Scientific American, March, 1963, p. 33.

FURTHER READING:

Books

Wasson, Tyler, editor, *Nobel Prize Winners,* H. W. Wilson, 1987, pp. 767–768.

Periodicals

Wasson, Tyler, editor, *New York Times,* October 12, 1982, p. C3.

Sketch by Carla Mecoli-Kamp

Jun-ichi Nishizawa
1926–
Japanese electrical engineer

Inventor, educator, and engineer Jun-ichi Nishizawa has made significant contributions to the field of semiconductor devices, which are materials that can act as insulators or conductors; they are used in electronics and are a main component in computers. Nishizawa's inventions include the "pin" diode, which is a type of diode (a device which carries electrical current in one direction only) that is a building block in semiconductors and also used in motor drives and power supplies. He also developed the static induction transistor (SIT), which is a high-power, high-frequency device that operates as a kind of switch and is applied in AM/FM transmitters, ultrasonic generators, and high voltage power supplies. Nishizawa has twice received the Director's Award of the Japanese Science and Technology Agency for his work on semiconductors, and received the Medal of Honor with Purple Ribbon from the Japanese government in 1976 for his invention of the SIT.

Jun-ichi Nishizawa was born in Sendai, Japan on September 12, 1926, the second of five children. His father, Kyosuke Nishizawa, was the director of the Faculty of Engineering of Tohoku University. Nishizawa attended elementary and high school in Sendai before attending Tohoku University where he studied electrical engineering, receiving his bachelor of science in 1948.

In 1950, while doing postgraduate work at Tohoku University, he invented the pin diode and the "pnip" transistor, a variation on a bipolar transistor, which is a semiconductor used in almost all types of electronic circuits. Nishizawa's transistor was an improvement because it has an additional layer of high resistivity semiconductor material between the usual positive and negative semiconductor layers. During this time he also invented the SIT and the avalanche photo diode, which is a type of semiconductor that converts optical signals to electrical signals; they are highly sensitive devices with quick response speed and low noise. Avalanche photo diodes have many uses, especially in fiber-optic communications. Nishizawa also proposed the use of ion implantation in semiconductors.

Nishizawa joined the staff of the Research Institute of Electrical Communication at Tohoku University in 1953 as a research assistant; he became an assistant professor the following year. Throughout this period he conducted research which led to his invention of semiconductor injection lasers, transit time effect negative resistance diodes, which are among the most powerful sources of solid-state microwave power, and the hyperabrupt variable capacitance diode, a type of diode used in resonant circuits.

Nishizawa also continued his education, earning his doctor of engineering degree in 1960. Two years later he was made a full professor. During his tenure, he was appointed to various directorships at Tohoku University including director of the Semiconductor Research Institute, a position he has held since 1968, and director of the Research Institute of Electrical Communication, which he held in 1983 and again from 1989 to 1990. He remained active as a full professor until 1990, when he was elected president of the university. Nishizawa has written numerous technical papers on semiconductor devices, and has been granted over two hundred Japanese and fifty U.S. patents. Besides the positions held at Tohoku, he was also head of the Perfect Crystal Technology Research Project. This was an Exploratory Research Project for Advanced Technology sponsored by the Japanese Science and Technology Agency.

Nishizawa's extensive honors include the 1966 Imperial Inventions Prize, the 1985 Asahir Prize, the 1986 Honda Prize, and the 1989 Order of Cultural Merits. In addition, he was made a fellow of the Institute of Electrical and Electronics Engineers in 1969 for his technical contributions to solid state electronics, and received the Jack A. Morton Award from this organization in 1983. He was made a foreign member of the USSR Academy of Sciences (later the Russian Academy of Sciences) in 1988. Nishizawa has also been active in other technical societies including the Institute of Physics, the Institution of Electrical Engineers, and the Electrochemical Society. In 1991 he served as president of the Institute of Electronics and Communication Engineers of Japan.

In 1956, Nishizawa married Takeko Hayakawa and the first of their three children was born a year later. Besides his technical interests, he enjoys China ceramics, classical music, and French impressionist paintings.

SELECTED WRITINGS BY NISHIZAWA:

Books

Semiconductor Technologies 1982, Ohmsha Ltd, Tokyo, 1981.

Periodicals

IEEE Transactions on Electron Devices, High-Frequency High-Power Static Induction Transistor, Volume 25, March, 1978, pp. 314–322.
Journal of Applied Physics, Current Amplification in Nonhomogeneous Base Structure and Static Induction Transistor Structure, Volume 57, May, 1985, pp. 4783–4797.
IEEE Electron Device Letters, Simple Structured PMOSFET Fabricated Using Molecular Layer Doping, March, 1990, pp. 105–106.

Sketch by George A. Ferrance

Yasutomi Nishizuka
1932–
Japanese biochemist

Yasutomi Nishizuka is a celebrated biochemist who discovered protein kinase C, an enzyme which controls the biology of cells. In further studies, he and his group found that tumor-promoting agents could trigger unregulated cell growth by activating protein kinase C. In 1989, Nishizuka won the Lasker Basic Medical Research Award "for his profound contributions to the understanding of signal transduction in cells and for his discovery that carcinogens trigger cell growth by activating protein kinase C." In 1988, he received The Order of Culture from the Emperor of Japan. Nishizuka is professor and chairman of the department of biochemistry at Kobe University School of Medicine and director of the Biosignal Research Center in Kobe.

Nishizuka was born on July 12, 1932. He received his medical degree in 1957 and his Ph.D. in 1962, both from Kyoto University. For the next two years, Nishizuka was a research associate in the laboratory of Osamu Hayaishi in the department of medical chemistry at Kyoto University. While still a research associate, Nishizuka was named an NIH International Postdoctoral Research Fellow in 1964; he went to Rockefeller University in New York City, where he worked in the laboratory of **Fritz Lipmann** for two years. Nishizuka remained on the faculty of Kyoto University until 1969, when he was appointed professor and chairman of the department of biochemistry at Kobe University Medical School.

It was at Kobe University, in 1977, that Nishizuka and his group announced the discovery of protein kinase C, with characteristics which resemble an enzyme. An enzyme is an organic catalyst produced by living cells but capable of acting independently; they are proteins that can cause chemical changes in other substances without being changed themselves. At first, the role of protein kinase C in intracellular signaling was not recognized. But later Nishizuka and his colleagues showed that it could be activated by tumor-promoting agents known as phorbol esters. These substances can remain in a cell membrane, causing it to continually produce protein kinase C—which can lead to uncontrollable cell growth, the basis of many types of carcinogenesis, or cancer.

The work done by Nishizuka and his team initiated many new lines of research; scientists began looking for substances that activate protein kinase C. Nishizuka's work also revealed the overwhelming importance of protein kinase C in the maintenance of normal health in all living things above the level of unicellular microorganisms. Exploration of the enzyme continues. It is now understood that it is part of a large family of proteins with multiple subspecies exhibiting individual enzymological characteristics and distinct patterns of tissue distribution.

Among the many prizes Nishizuka has received for his work are the Award of the Japan Academy in 1986; the Cultural Merit Prize from the Japanese government in 1987; the Alfred P. Sloan Jr. Prize in 1988 from the General Motors Cancer Research Foundation; the Gairdner Foundation International Award in 1988; the Order of Culture in 1988 from the Emperor of Japan; the Albert Lasker Basic Medical Research Award in 1989, and the Kyoto Prize in 1992. In 1994, he received the Dale Medal from the British Endocrine Society. He was elected a foreign associate of the National Academy of Sciences in the United States in 1988 and a foreign member of the Royal Society of the United Kingdom in 1990. In addition to being a member of the Japan Academy, he is also a foreign associate of l'Academie des Sciences in France and a foreign honorary member of the American Academy of Arts and Sciences. The magazine *Science* noted that of the ten most cited Japanese papers of the 1980s, five were written by Nishizuka.

In June of 1992, Nishizuka was appointed director of the Biosignal Research Center at Kobe University and continues in the position. Nishizuka is married and has two daughters. The family lives in Ashiya.

SELECTED WRITINGS BY NISHIZUKA:

Periodicals

Nature, The Role of Protein Kinase C in Cell Surface Signal Transduction and Tumor Promotion, Volume 308, 1984, pp. 696–697.
Science, "Studies and Perspectives of Protein Kinase C" Volume 233, 1986, pp. 305–312.

FURTHER READING:

Periodicals

Science, Science News, Volume 258, 1992, p. 574.

Other

Nishizuka, Yasutomi, written communication to Margo Nash sent February 17, 1994.

Sketch by Margo Nash

G. K. Noble
1894–1940
American zoologist and naturalist

Zoologist and naturalist G. K. Noble was one of those rare individuals who was able to transform a childhood fascination into his life's work. As a young boy Noble was attracted to animals and nature and these early interests carried over to a career as a naturalist and zoologist with the American Museum of Natural History in New York. Noble's interest in the natural world ranged from reptiles, amphibians, birds, and fish to animal behavior based on psychological and biological factors.

Gladwyn Kingsley Noble was born in Yonkers, New York, on September 20, 1894, the son of Gilbert Clifford Noble and Elizabeth Adams. He spent his youth in Yonkers and fixed on a career as a naturalist even before graduating from Yonkers High School. His career choice led him to Harvard University, where he earned his bachelor's and master's degrees in zoology in 1916 and 1918, respectively. As a college student, Noble's initial interest was in birds, and he published his first scientific paper—on the predation of cats on nesting seagull colonies—at age 19. At Harvard he participated in two field trips, to the islands of Newfoundland and Guadeloupe, to collect bird specimens. An expedition as a general zoologist to Peru in 1916 prompted Noble's deep interest in reptiles and amphibians.

After serving in the Office of the Chief of Naval Operations during World War I, Noble began his long affiliation with American Museum of Natural History in 1919. He joined the institution as an assistant curator of herpetology, which is the study of reptiles and amphibians. Simultaneously, he began work on his doctorate in zoology at Columbia University, which he completed in 1922. Noble's thesis reclassified frogs and toads and almost immediately was hailed as a significant contribution to herpetology. Meanwhile, he became an associate curator in 1922 and then, in 1924, curator of herpetology at the museum.

Noble married Ruth Crosby, an assistant curator in the museum's education department, in 1921, and she and their two sons often accompanied him on field trips. During his relatively short career, Noble was a prolific writer and lecturer. He published nearly 200 scientific papers—many of them on amphibians—as well as the 1931 guide to amphibian animals, *The Biology of the Amphibia.* In the final decade of his life, Noble switched his zoological attention to behavioral and physiological pursuits and expanded his field of research to fish and birds. This work and his lectures and notes resulted in the posthumous publication of the book *The Nature of the Beast,* a popular account of animal psychology, edited by his wife. Noble rejected a number of job offers from universities and remained at the American Museum of Natural History for his entire career. He did, however, dedicate time to the education of others, giving biology lectures at Columbia and serving as a visiting professor at the University of Chicago and New York University.

SELECTED WRITINGS BY NOBLE:

Books

The Biology of the Amphibia, McGraw-Hill, 1931.
The Nature of the Beast, edited by Ruth Crosby Noble, Doubleday, 1945.

Sketch by Joel Schwarz

Ida Tacke Noddack
1896–1979
German chemist

Working with fellow chemist Walter Noddack (her future husband) and x-ray specialist Otto Berg, Ida Tacke discovered element 75, rhenium, in 1925, thus solving one of the mysteries of the periodic table of elements introduced by Russian chemist Dmitri Ivanovich Mendeleev in 1869. Ida Tacke Noddack's continuing study of the periodic table also led her to be the first to suggest in 1934 that physicist **Enrico Fermi** had not made a new element in an experiment with uranium as he thought, but instead had discovered nuclear fission. Her prediction was not verified until 1939.

Ida Tacke was born in Germany on February 25, 1896 and studied at the Technical University in Berlin, where she received the first prize for chemistry and metallurgy in 1919. In 1921, soon after receiving her doctorate, she set out to isolate two of the elements that Mendeleev had predicted when he proposed the Periodic System and displayed all known elements in a format now called the periodic table. Mendeleev had left blank spaces on his table for several elements that he expected to exist but that had not been identified. Two of these, elements 43 and 75, were located in Group VII under manganese.

Assuming that these elements would be similar in their properties to manganese, scientists had been searching for them in manganese ores. Tacke and Walter Noddack, who headed the chemical laboratory at the Physico-Technical Research Agency in Berlin, focused instead on the lateral neighbors of the missing elements, molybdenum, tungsten, osmium, and ruthenium. With the assistance of Otto Berg of the Werner-Siemens Laboratory, who provided expertise in analyzing the x-ray spectra of substances, Tacke and Noddack isolated element 75 in 1925 and named it rhenium,

from *Rhenus,* Latin for the Rhine, an important river in their native Germany. It took them another year to isolate a single gram of the element from 660 kilograms of molybdenite ore. They also believed they had discovered traces of element 43, which they dubbed masurium. Later research, however, did not confirm their results. Now known as technetium, element 43 has never been found in nature, although it has been produced artificially.

In 1926, Ida Tacke married Walter Noddack. They would work together in their research until Walter Noddack's death in 1960, and together would publish some one hundred scientific papers. The Noddacks were awarded the Leibig Medal of the German Chemical Society in 1934 for their discovery of rhenium.

In 1934 Ida Noddack challenged the conclusions of Enrico Fermi and his group that they had produced transuranium elements, artificial elements heavier than uranium, when they bombarded uranium atoms with subatomic particles called neutrons. Although other scientists agreed with Fermi, Noddack suggested he had split uranium atoms into isotopes of known elements rather than added to uranium atoms to produce heavier, unknown elements. She had no research to support her theory, however, and for five years her hypothesis that atomic nuclei had been split was virtually ignored. "Her suggestion was so out of line with the then-accepted ideas about the atomic nucleus that it was never seriously discussed," fellow chemist **Otto Hahn** would later comment in his autobiography. In 1939, after much research had been done by many scientists, Hahn, **Fritz Strassmann** and **Lise Meitner** discovered that Noddack had been right. They named the process nuclear fission.

The Noddacks moved from Berlin to the University of Freiburg in 1935, to the University of Strasbourg in 1943, and to the State Research Institute for Geochemistry in Bamberg in 1956. In 1960, Walter Noddack died. Ida Noddack received the High Service Cross of the German Federal Republic in 1966. During her life she received honorary membership in the Spanish Society of Physics and Chemistry and the International Society of Nutrition Research, as well as an honorary doctorate of science from the University of Hamburg. Ida Noddack retired in 1968 and moved to Bad Neuenahr, a small town on the Rhine. She died in 1979.

FURTHER READING:

Books

Hahn, Otto, *A Scientific Autobiography,* Scribner, 1966.
Weeks, Mary E., *The Discovery of the Elements,* Mack, 1954, pp. 321–322.

Periodicals

Habashi, Fathi, *Chemistry,* Ida Noddack, 75 & Element 75, reprint from February, 1971, in Element Profiles, American Chemical Society, 1972, pp. 81–82.

Starke, Kurt, *Journal of Chemical Education,* The Detours Leading to the Discovery of Nuclear Fission, December, 1979, pp. 771–775.

Sketch by M. C. Nagel

Emmy Noether
1882–1935
American mathematician

Emmy Noether

Emmy Noether was a world-renowned mathematician whose innovative approach to modern abstract algebra inspired colleagues and students who emulated her technique. Dismissed from her university position at the beginning of the Nazi era in Germany—for she was both Jewish and female—Noether emigrated to the United States, where she taught in several universities and colleges. When she died, **Albert Einstein** eulogized her in a letter to *New York Times* as "the most significant creative mathematical genius thus far produced since the higher education of women began."

Noether was born on March 23, 1882, in the small university town of Erlangen in southern Germany. Her first name was Amalie, but she was known by her middle name of Emmy. Her mother, Ida Amalia Kaufmann Noether, came from a wealthy family in Cologne. Her father, Max Noether, a professor at the University of Erlangen, was an accomplished mathematician who worked on the theory of algebraic functions. Two of her three younger brothers became scientists—Fritz was a mathematician and Alfred earned a doctorate in chemistry.

Noether's childhood was unexceptional, going to school, learning domestic skills, and taking piano lessons. Since girls were not eligible to enroll in the gymnasium (college preparatory school), she attended the Städtischen Höheren Töchterschule, where she studied arithmetic and languages. In 1900 she passed the Bavarian state examinations with evaluations of "very good" in French and English (she received only a "satisfactory" evaluation in practical classroom conduct); this certified her to teach foreign languages at female educational institutions.

Begins a Teaching Career

Instead of looking for a language teaching position, Noether decided to undertake university studies. However, since she had not graduated from a gymnasium, she first had to pass an entrance examination for which she obtained permission from her instructors. She audited courses at the University of Erlangen from 1900 to 1902. In 1903 she passed the matriculation exam, and entered the University

of Göttingen for a semester, where she encountered such notable mathematicians as **Hermann Minkowski**, Felix Klein, and **David Hilbert**. She enrolled at the University of Erlangen where women were accepted in 1904. At Erlangen, Noether studied with Paul Gordan, a mathematics professor who was also a family friend. She completed her dissertation entitled "On Complete Systems of Invariants for Ternary Biquadratic Forms," receiving her Ph.D., summa cum laude, on July 2, 1908.

Noether worked without pay at the Mathematical Institute of Erlangen from 1908 until 1915, where her university duties included research, serving as a dissertation adviser for two students, and occasionally delivering lectures for her ailing father. In addition, Noether began to work with **Ernst Otto Fischer**, an algebraist who directed her toward the broader theoretical style characteristic of Hilbert. Noether not only published her thesis on ternary biquadratics, but she was also elected to membership in the Circolo Matematico di Palermo in 1908. The following year, Noether was invited to join the German Mathematical Society (Deutsche Mathematiker Vereinigung); she addressed the society's 1909 meeting in Salzburg and its 1913 meeting in Vienna.

Formulates the Mathematics of Relativity

In 1915, Klein and Hilbert invited Noether to join them at the Mathematical Institute in Göttingen. They were working on the mathematics of the newly announced general theory of relativity, and they believed Noether's expertise would be helpful. Einstein later wrote an article for the 1955 Grolier Encyclopedia, characterizing the theory of relativity by the basic question, "how must the laws of nature be constituted so that they are valid in the same form relative to arbitrary systems of co-ordinates (postulate of the invariance of the laws of nature relative to an arbitrary transformation of space and time)?" It was precisely this type of invariance under transformation on which Noether focused her mathematical research.

In 1918, Noether proved two theorems that formed a cornerstone for general relativity. These theorems validated certain relationships suspected by physicists of the time. One, now known as Noether's theorem, established the equivalence between an invariance property and a conservation law. The other involved the relationship between an invariance and the existence of certain integrals of the equations of motion. The eminent German mathematician **Hermann Weyl** described Noether's contribution in the July 1935 *Scripta Mathematica* following her death: "For two of the most significant sides of the general theory of relativity theory she gave at that time the genuine and universal mathematical formulation."

While Noether was proving these profound and useful results, she was working without pay at Göttingen University, where women were not admitted to the faculty. Hilbert, in particular, tried to obtain a position for her but could not persuade the historians and philosophers on the faculty to vote in a woman's favor. He was able to arrange for her to teach, however, by announcing a class in mathematical physics under his name and letting her lecture in his place. By 1919, regulations were eased somewhat, and she was designated a Privatdozent (a licensed lecturer who could receive fees from students but not from the university). In 1922, Noether was given the unofficial title of associate professor, and was hired as an adjunct teacher and paid a modest salary without fringe benefits or tenure.

Noether's enthusiasm for mathematics made her an effective teacher, often conducting classroom discussions in which she and her students would jointly explore some topic. In *Emmy Noether at Byrn Mawr*, Noether's only doctoral student at Bryn Mawr, Ruth McKee, recalls, "Miss Noether urged us on, challenging us to get our nails dirty, to really dig into the underlying relationships, to consider the problems from all possible angles."

Lays the Foundations of Abstract Algebra

Brilliant mathematicians often make their greatest contributions early in their careers; Noether was one of the notable exceptions to that rule. She began producing her most powerful and creative work at about the age of 40. Her change in style started with a 1920 paper on noncommutative fields (systems in which an operation such as multiplication yields a different answer for a x b than for b x a). During the years that followed, she developed a very abstract and generalized approach to the axiomatic development of algebra. As Weyl attested, "she originated above all a new and epoch-making style of thinking in algebra."

Noether's 1921 paper on the theory of ideals in rings is considered to contain her most important results. It extended the work of Dedekind on solutions of polynomials—algebraic expressions consisting of a constant multiplied by variables raised to a positive power—and laid the foundations for modern abstract algebra. Rather than working with specific operations on sets of numbers, this branch of mathematics looks at general properties of operations. Because of its generality, abstract algebra represents a unifying thread connecting such theoretical fields as logic and number theory with applied mathematics useful in chemistry and physics.

During the winter of 1928–29, Noether was a visiting professor at the University of Moscow and the Communist Academy, and in the summer of 1930, she taught at the University of Frankfurt. Recognized for her continuing contributions in the science of mathematics, the International Mathematical Congress of 1928 chose her to be its principal speaker at one of its section meetings in Bologna. In 1932 she was chosen to address the Congress's general session in Zurich.

Noether was a part of the mathematics faculty of Göttingen University in the 1920s when its reputation for mathematical research and teaching was considered the best in the world. Still, even with the help of the esteemed mathematician Hermann Weyl, Noether was unable to secure a proper teaching position there, one that would be equivalent to her male counterparts. Weyl once commented: "I was ashamed to occupy such a preferred position beside her whom I knew to be my superior as a mathematician in many respects." Nevertheless, in 1932, on Noether's fiftieth birthday, the university's algebraists held a celebration, and her colleague Helmut Hasse dedicated a paper in her honor, which validated one of her ideas on noncommutative algebra. In that same year, she again was honored by those outside her own university, when she was named cowinner of the Alfred Ackermann-Teubner Memorial Prize for the Advancement of Mathematical Knowledge.

Teaches in Exile

The successful and congenial environment of the University of Göttingen ended in 1933, with the advent of the Nazis in Germany. Within months, anti-Semitic policies spread through the country. On April 7, 1933, Noether was formally notified that she could no longer teach at the university. She was a dedicated pacifist, and Weyl later recalled, "her courage, her frankness, her unconcern about her own fate, her conciliatory spirit were, in the midst of all the hatred and meanness, despair and sorrow surrounding us, a moral solace."

For a while, Noether continued to meet informally with students and colleagues, inviting groups to her apartment. But by summer, the Emergency Committee to Aid Displaced German Scholars was entering into an agreement with Bryn Mawr, a women's college in Pennsylvania, which offered Noether a professorship. Her first year's salary was funded by the Emergency Committee and the Rockefeller Foundation.

In the fall of 1933, Noether was supervising four graduate students at Bryn Mawr. Starting in February 1934, she also delivered weekly lectures at the Institute for Advanced Study at Princeton. She bore no malice toward Germany, and maintained friendly ties with her former colleagues. With her characteristic curiosity and good nature, she settled into her new home in America, acquiring enough English to adequately converse and teach, although she occasionally lapsed into German when concentrating on technical material.

During the summer of 1934, Noether visited Göttingen to arrange shipment of her possessions to the United States. When she returned to Bryn Mawr in the early fall, she had received a two-year renewal on her teaching grant. In the spring of 1935, Noether underwent surgery to remove a uterine tumor. The operation was a success, but four days later, she suddenly developed a very high fever and lost consciousness. She died on April 14th, apparently from a post-operative infection. Her ashes were buried near the library on the Bryn Mawr campus.

Over the course of her career, Noether supervised a dozen graduate students, wrote forty-five technical publications, and inspired countless other research results through her habit of suggesting topics of investigation to students and colleagues. After World War II, the University of Erlangen attempted to show her the honor she had deserved during her lifetime. A conference in 1958 commemorated the fiftieth anniversary of her doctorate; in 1982 the university dedicated a memorial plaque to her in its Mathematics Institute. During the same year, the 100th anniversary year of Noether's birth, the Emmy Noether Gymnasium, a coeducational school emphasizing mathematics, the natural sciences, and modern languages, opened in Erlangen.

SELECTED WRITINGS BY NOETHER:

Books

Collected Papers, Springer-Verlag, 1983.

FURTHER READING:

Books

Brewer, James W., *Emmy Noether: A Tribute to Her Life and Work,* edited by Martha K. Smith, Marcel Dekker, 1981.

Kramer, Edna E., *The Nature and Growth of Modern Mathematics,* Princeton University, 1981, pp. 656–672.

Magill, Frank N., editor, *Great Events from History II,* Books International, 1991, pp. 650–654, 716–719.

Osen, Lynn M., *Women in Mathematics,* Massachusetts Institute of Technology, 1979, pp. 141–152.

Perl, Teri, *Math Equals: Biographies of Women Mathematicians,* Addison-Wesley, 1978, pp. 172–178.

Srinivasan, Bhama and Judith D. Sally, *Emmy Noether in Bryn Mawr: Proceedings of a Symposium,* Springer-Verlag, 1983.

Periodicals

Kimberling, Clark H., *The American Mathematical Monthly,* Emmy Noether, February, 1972, pp. 136–149.

Sketch by Loretta Hall

Max Noether
1844–1921
German algebraist

Today, Max Noether's career as a mathematician is perhaps overshadowed by his more famous daughter, **Emmy Noether**. Still, at the height of his career, Noether led the German school of algebraic and geometric mathematics from the University of Erlangen. Noether's primary interests were algebra and algebraic geometry, and he is responsible for the development of algebraic function theory. His work on curves and related theorems inspired many Italian geometrists.

Noether was born in Mannheim, Germany, on September 24, 1844, the son of Hermann (an iron wholesaler) and Amalia (nee Würzburger) Noether. With his four siblings, Noether began his education in Mannheim. He contracted polio at age 14, and could not use his legs for two years. Because of this illness, Noether was handicapped for life. He continued his education at home, following the gymnasium curriculum.

In 1865, Noether began his university studies in astronomy at the Mannheim Observatory, although he did not stay there long. He entered the University of Heidelberg in 1865, studying mathematics. He also studied at the University of Gissen and the University of Göttingen, before earning his doctorate (without a dissertation) from Heidelberg in 1868. Noether was the first member of his family to earn this degree. Noether began teaching at Heidelberg as a lecturer (privatdozent) from 1870 to 1874. In 1874, Noether became an associate professor at the University of Erlangen.

The mathematical research Noether did in this early part of his career, from approximately 1869 to 1879, is arguably his most important. His 1869 paper, "Über

Max Noether

on refining his earlier publications. This work also inspired and opened up fields for other mathematicians, especially in Italy.

Some of Noether's later publications that are widely known include the 1882 publication on algebraic curves, *Zur Grundlegung der Theorie der Algebraischen Ramkurven*. In 1894 he coauthored *Bericht über der Entwicklung der algebraischen Funktionen*, with Alexander von Brill. This treatise concerned algebraic functions.

Noether was also involved with the journal *Mathematische Annalen*. In addition to publishing in it almost continuously from 1870–1921, he served as its director for a time. Noether also wrote many of the biographic obituaries for this journal and other publications. These pieces gained recognition and were known for their thoroughness and insight.

Noether's important mathematical contributions did not go unnoticed by his peers. In 1903, he became a member of the French Académie Royale des Sciences. He was also a member or honorary member of many other academic societies, among them the London Mathematical Society, the Academy of Berlin, and the Royale Accademia dei Lincei.

The last decade of his life saw Noether lose his wife and retire from teaching. When Ida Noether died 1915, Noether's daughter Emmy started to fill in for her father's lectures as necessary. Four years later, in 1919, he retired from teaching, and was given an emeritus professorship.

Noether died in Erlangen on December 13, 1921. In his obituary published in the *Proceedings of the London Mathematical Society*, the author describes the three main ways Noether contributed to his field: "By the new and fruitful ideas contained in his original researches, by the patient investigation and encouragement he gave to other writers, and by his acutely critical and detailed historical work."

Flächen, welche Scharen rationaler Kurven besitzen" ("Concerning Surfaces which have Families of Rational Curves"), began this work, containing what came to be known as Noether's fundamental theorem. In 1871, he published a proof that improved on work done by one of his inspirations as a mathematician, Antonio Cremona. In it, Noether proved the result that a plane Cremona transformation can be built up from a sequence of quadratic and linear transformations. Two years later, Noether published another theorem, perhaps his most famous result, concerning two algebraic curves and their intersection under certain so-called Noether conditions. The conditions concern the complexity of contact of curves and their common multiple points. This result could also be extended to surfaces and hypersurfaces, though Noether himself did not prove it.

After 1880, Noether's private life became more domesticated, perhaps accounting for the changes in Noether's research. Noether married Ida Amalia Kaufmann in 1880. Together they had four children, three of whom became scientists. His eldest daughter, Amalie Emmy Noether, born in 1882 and familiarly called Emmy, became a mathematician whose work built on and surpassed her father's. She had three younger brothers: Alfred, born in 1883, who became a chemist; Fritz, born in 1884, also a mathematician; and Gustav, born in 1889.

Still, Noether continued to do his original research and teaching at Erlangen, where he served as an associate professor until 1888. That year he became a full professor. From about 1879 onward, his mathematical work focused

SELECTED WRITINGS BY NOETHER:

Books

"Über Flächen, welche Scharen rationaler Kurven besitzen" ("Concerning Surfaces which have Families of Rational Curves"), 1869.
Zur Grundelgung der Theorie der Algebraischen Ramkurven, 1882.
(With Alexander von Brill) *Bericht über der Entwicklung der algebraischen Funkionen*, 1894.

FURTHER READING:

Books

Kimberling, Clark. "Emmy Noether and Her Influence," in *Emmy Noether: A Tribute to Her Life and Work*. Edited by James W. Brewer and Martha K. Smith. New York: Marcel Dekker, Inc., 1981, pp. 3–8, 20.

Kramer, Edna E. "Max Noether," in *Dictionary of Scientific Biography*. Volume X. Edited by Charles Coulston Gillispie. New York: Charles Scribner's Sons, 1970, pp. 137–39.

Periodicals

"Max Noether." *Proceedings of the London Mathematical Society*. Volume 21, 2nd Series (1921): 37–42.

Sketch by Annette Petruso

Hideyo Noguchi
1876–1928
Japanese microbiologist and pathologist

Hideyo Noguchi was a controversial microbiologist who overcame poverty, a physical handicap, and linguistic and cultural barriers to make some pioneering contributions to the field of bacteriology. Chosen by bacteriologist **Simon Flexner** to be a member of the original scientific staff at the Rockefeller Institute, Noguchi's most important achievements advanced the understanding of syphilis, trachoma, and bartonellosis. He worked tirelessly, almost day and night, on a number of scientific problems, but the energy which made his accomplishments possible also made him hasty and occasionally careless. Some of the claims he made for his research have not been substantiated; his work on yellow fever, in particular, was discredited, and Noguchi succumbed to this disease while studying it in Africa.

Hideyo Seisaku Noguchi was born in Japan in the mountain village of Inawashiro, Fukushima, on November 24, 1876. Given the childhood name Seisaku, he was the second child and only son of Sayosuke, a peasant farmer who soon deserted the family; his mother, Shika, worked in the rice fields to support her household. When very young, Noguchi fell into an open hearth fire and was severely burned, losing the use of his left fingers. He nevertheless excelled in school, and he was noticed by the superintendent, Sokae Kobayashi, who became something of a foster father to him, coordinating financial support and overseeing the rest of his education.

Kobayashi arranged for a surgeon to restore some functioning to the child's crippled hand, and it was as a result of his experience that Noguchi decided to study medicine. The surgeon retained him as an apprentice; in his office Noguchi used a microscope and first encountered spirochetes—microbes that would become a major focus of his research. In 1894, Noguchi entered the Tokyo Medical College, and in 1897 he passed the government examinations for a medical degree. He served as a lecturer at a dental college and studied the bubonic plague briefly in China before accepting a position as an assistant under bacteriologist Shibasaburo Kitasato at his Institute for Infectious Diseases. About this time, Noguchi changed his first name to Hideyo, meaning "great man of the world."

In 1899, a medical commission was sent from the United States to study tropical diseases afflicting American soldiers stationed in the Philippines. Flexner, who was a leading bacteriologist from Johns Hopkins University, was a member of this commission; he was with the group when it passed through Japan and visited Kitasato's Institute for Infectious Diseases. Noguchi met Flexner there and told him he wanted to study bacteriology in the United States. In a memorial piece originally published in *Science*, Flexner remembers that "no particular encouragement was given to this request." He only encouraged him to write; he told Noguchi he would be moving to the University of Pennsylvania and gave him his address there.

Later that same year, about six months after he had met Flexner, Noguchi simply arrived at the University of Pennsylvania. He traveled on borrowed money and, as Flexner remembers, "presented himself at the dormitories unexpectedly, and in accordance with eastern custom bearing several gifts, which the writer still possesses and cherishes." Flexner arranged for him to be appointed as a research assistant to Silas Weir Mitchell, with whom he studied the hemolysins and agglutinins of snake venoms and the protective sera against them. The work he did with Mitchell won Noguchi a year-long Carnegie fellowship at the Statens Seruminstitut in Copenhagen. Here, under Thorvald Madsen, he mastered certain quantitative and chemical methods that were related to his snake venom studies.

Works on Syphilis at the Rockefeller Institute

Flexner became the organizing director of the Rockefeller Institute in New York City when it opened in 1904, and he immediately asked Noguchi to work in his laboratory on poliomyelitis. In 1905, the two men were the first scientists in the United States to confirm Fritz Schaudinn's identification of *Treponema pallidum (T. pallidum)* as the spirochete responsible for syphilis. Noguchi's research on syphilis continued for a number of years, and the energy he devoted to this resulted in a major breakthrough. Syphilis patients had long been observed to suffer from paresis, a kind of partial paralysis. The connection had long been assumed but never proven until 1913, when Noguchi found a spiral organism in the brains of patients who had died of paresis. His work proved that general paresis and tabes dorsalis are the late stages of tertiary syphilis in the brain and spinal cord. He made the discovery early one morning, after spending the entire night inspecting 200 slides from paretic brain specimens. Flexner remembers being woken in bed and brought to the laboratory to confirm the discovery.

Despite this success, Noguchi's research during this period also resulted in some notorious failures. In 1911, he claimed he had obtained *T. pallidum* in pure culture, but no other investigator has ever duplicated his results, and the organisms have never been successfully isolated. He also developed a single diagnostic test for syphilis, which involved the injection of *T. pallidum* into the skin of patients believed to be suffering from the disease. The skin test proved unreliable, and according to Paul Franklin Clark in the *Bulletin of the History of Medicine* even a researcher who worked with Noguchi on this project was unable to duplicate his results in a different laboratory. In another study, Noguchi and Flexner reported that they had cultivated the "globoid bodies" of the virus that produces polio in monkeys, but this finding was later discredited as well, though their mistake may have been the result of the generally imperfect understanding at the time of the difference between bacteria and viruses.

On April 10, 1912, Noguchi married Mary Dardis. She was the daughter of Irish immigrants from Scranton, Pennsylvania, where her three brothers worked as coal miners. Noguchi was initially very secretive about his wife, even with his closest colleagues, and this may have been because of the interracial nature of his marriage. They had no children.

Researches the Origins of Infectious Diseases

In 1918, Noguchi turned to experiments on the etiology of obscure infectious diseases. Each required a different method of approach, and he made field expeditions to the American West as well as Central and South America. In the Peruvian Andes, he worked on carrion's disease, now called bartonellosis, and he established the existence of two different manifestations of the disease which had the same etiology. In one disease, there is an acute febrile anemia (Oroya fever), and in the other a local cutaneous eruption (verruga peruana). Noguchi also did invaluable work in trachoma, a disease of the eyes. He attributed its cause to a bacterium; his findings were later challenged and the cause identified as a virus, but today the causative organism of trachoma is considered a unique microbe which is more closely related to bacteria than to viruses. Despite this controversy, Noguchi's critical work on trachoma's secondary bacterial infection contributed to its cure. During this period, he also searched for the causes of rabies and Rocky Mountain spotted fever.

The most controversial work that Noguchi did was on yellow fever. Using evidence he had gathered during four expeditions to the southern hemisphere, Noguchi became convinced that yellow fever was caused by a spiral organism which he had isolated. He named it *Leptospira icteroides*, and he published several reports based on these field observations. He even prepared an experimental vaccine against the disease that was distributed by the Rockefeller Institute. Noguchi's research, however, was almost totally invalid. The evidence he had been examining had been taken from patients who had been misdiagnosed by local physicians; instead of suffering from yellow fever, they had hemorrhagic jaundice, also known as Weil's disease or leptospirosis. In addition, Noguchi had assumed without

conducting sufficient research that the spirochete which caused leptospirosis differed from the one he believed caused yellow fever. By 1924, other researchers had showed that the two spirochetes were identical.

In 1927, Adrian Stokes determined that a filterable virus was the cause of yellow fever. Stokes made this discovery in African patients from whom no *Leptospira* could be recovered, but he died from yellow fever before his report was published. In October of that year, Noguchi sailed for Africa to compare yellow fever there with that of South America. He wanted to test Stokes' findings for himself, and he worked for six strenuous, hectic months in a crude field laboratory with William Young, the resident British director of the Medical Research Institute. Noguchi was stricken with yellow fever just as he was about to return to New York. He died on May 21, 1928, at the age of fifty-one. Young confirmed the diagnosis of yellow fever during an autopsy and then succumbed to the disease himself a week later.

For indefatigable research into infectious diseases, Noguchi received honorary degrees from many universities and was decorated by many foreign governments. In 1915, he returned to Japan to receive the Order of the Rising Sun and an Imperial Prize from the Emperor. He received the John Scott Medal in 1920 and was the first recipient of the Kober Medal in 1925. Noguchi and his wife are buried in Woodlawn Cemetery in New York City. He is remembered in Japan as well, where, among many memorials, his portrait was issued on a postage stamp in 1950. His family home is a museum where many of his papers and memorabilia are preserved.

SELECTED WRITINGS BY NOGUCHI:

Books

Snake Venoms, Carnegie Institution of Washington, 1909.
Serum Diagnosis of Syphilis and the Butyric Acid Test for Syphilis, [Chicago], 1910.

Periodicals

Journal of Experimental Medicine, A Demonstration of *Treponema Pallidum* in the Brain in Cases of General Paralysis, Volume 17, 1913, pp. 232–238.
Journal of Experimental Medicine, The Etiology of Verruga Peruana, Volume 45, 1927, pp. 175–189.
Journal of Experimental Medicine, The Etiology of Trachoma, Volume 48, 1928, supplement 2, pp. 1–53.
The Newer Knowledge of Bacteriology and Immunology, The Spirochetes, edited by E. O. Jordan and I. S. Falk, University of Chicago Press, 1928, pp. 452–497.

FURTHER READING:

Books

Eckstein, Gustav, *Noguchi,* Harper & Brothers, 1931.

Plesset, Isabel R., *Noguchi and His Patrons,* Associated University Presses, 1980.

Periodicals

Clark, Paul Franklin, *Bulletin of the History of Medicine,* Hideyo Noguchi, 1876–1928, Volume 33, 1959, pp. 1–20.

Flexner, Simon, *Science,* Hideyo Noguchi. A Biographical Sketch, Volume 69, 1929, pages 653–660.

Flexner, Simon, *MD,* Pioneer Bacteriologist, April 1976, pp. 143–150.

Williams, Greer, *The Plague Killers,* Scribner, 1969, pp. 215–249.

Sketch by Carol L. Moberg

Masayasu Nomura
1927–

American molecular biologist

Masayasu Nomura is the American molecular biologist who demonstrated that those ribosomes present in bacteria can be reduced to their molecular components of ribonucleic acid (RNA) and proteins. Four years later he further demonstrated that they can then be reunited to regenerate themselves.

Nomura was born on April 27, 1927, in Hyogo-ken, Japan. He married Junko Hamashima on February 10, 1957; they had two children—Keiko and Toshiyasu. After receiving his Ph.D. in microbiology at the University of Tokyo in 1957, Nomura went to the United States to work as a postdoctoral fellow in Sol Spiegelman's laboratory. While at Spiegelman's lab, Nomura isolated a kind of RNA that receives information from a bacteriophage (a virus that infects bacteria) genome, then serves as a model for producing the proteins within the bacteriophage. This type of RNA later became known as messenger RNA (mRNA). He then briefly returned to Japan as an assistant professor at the Osaka University Institute of Protein Research before emigrating to the United States in 1963 to join the faculty of the University of Wisconsin's department of genetics, where he became a full professor in 1966.

Demonstrates the Reversibility of Protein Splitting in Ribosomes

By the early 1960s, the basic decoding of genetics had been clarified and the protein biosynthesis components been identified, thanks to the efforts of such scientists as Paul Zamecnik and **Marshall Warren Nirenberg**. The term "ribosome" had been introduced in 1958 to describe the tiny organs that are present in all living cells, and that synthesize proteins; furthermore, it was known that ribosomes were the sites where amino acids were assembled to form proteins, and that ribosomes were made up of two different subunits, one larger than the other, each with its own complicated structure consisting of RNA molecules and various protein molecules. But what was not known was how the molecular components were assembled into sophisticated ribosome structures, or how the assembled structures performed their functions.

Using the work of Zamecnik and Nirenberg as a springboard, Nomura discovered that by centrifuging bacterial ribosomes in heavy salt concentrations some ribosomal proteins would split off from the ribosomes, and it occurred to him that the situation might be reversible. Four years later, under very specific conditions, Nomura mixed those particles lacking protein with the split-off proteins; like magic, functionally active ribosomal particles were formed. The significance of this reconstitution proved that the necessary information for the proper construction of ribosomal particles was contained in their molecular components, rather than in some extraneous factor. It also opened the way for study of the molecular components of ribosomes. In 1968 Nomura and his colleagues actually reconstituted the small ribosome subunits from purified RNA and dissociated ribosomal proteins, and in 1970, as professor of genetics and biochemistry, he did the same with the larger ribosomal subunit. He and his team also did significant research into the ribosomal makeup of chromosomes, isolating a number of genes from *Escherichia coli* (also known as *E. coli*) cells.

During the 1960s and 1970s, Nomura also showed how certain strains of enterobacteria, called colicins, have a tendency to kill other, related bacterial strains. Some colicins kill bacteria by splitting RNA in ribosomes, while others eliminate it by causing deoxyribonucleic acid (DNA) breakdown. This discovery initiated many modern studies of colicins.

Nomura shed much light on the processes of information transfer from genes to proteins. In 1970 he was appointed co-director of the Institute for Enzyme Research at the University of Wisconsin. He was elected to the National Academy of Sciences in 1978.

SELECTED WRITINGS BY NOMURA:

Books

Ribosomes, Cold Spring Harbor Laboratory, 1974.

Ribosomes: Structure, Function and Genetics, University Park Press, 1980.

Periodicals

Journal of Molecular Biology, Characterization of RNA Synthesized in *Escherichia coli* After Bacteriophage T2 Infection, Volume 2, 1960, p. 306.

Science, Assembly of Bacterial Ribosomes, March 2, 1973, p. 864.

Journal of Molecular Biology, Ribosomal Proteins L7/L12 Localized at a Single Region of the Large Subunit by Immune Electron Microscopy, Volume 128, 1976, pp. 123–140.

FURTHER READING:

Books

McGraw-Hill Modern Scientists and Engineers, McGraw, 1980, pp. 365–366.

Sketch by Janet Kieffer Kelley

Ronald G. W. Norrish
1897–1978
English physical chemist

The English chemist Ronald G. W. Norrish spent his academic life studying reaction kinetics, a discipline in chemistry concerned with rates of chemical reactions and factors influencing those rates. Norrish received the 1967 Nobel Prize for chemistry—which he shared with a former student, **George Porter**, and German scientist **Manfred Eigen**—for his work in this realm. A pioneer researcher in flash photolysis (chemical reactions induced by intense bursts of light), Norrish developed a process allowed minute intermediate stages of a chemical reaction to be measured and described. He also contributed to chemistry an understanding of chain reactions, combustion, and polymerization (the formation of large molecules from numerous smaller ones). Over his career, Norrish was awarded the Liversidge Medal of the Chemical Society and the Davy Medal of the Royal Society, both in 1958, and the Bernard Lewis Gold Medal from the Combustion Institute in 1964. In addition, he was a member of scientific academies in eight foreign countries.

Ronald George Wreyford Norrish was born on November 9, 1897, in Cambridge, England. The son of Amy and Herbert Norrish, he attended the Perse Grammar School and won a scholarship to study natural sciences at Emmanuel College in Cambridge University. Although Norrish entered Cambridge in 1915, World War I intervened and he served in France as a lieutenant in the Royal Field Artillery. Captured by the Germans in 1918, he spent a year in a prisoner of war camp before being repatriated. Norrish then returned to his academic career at Cambridge and finished his bachelor of science degree in chemistry by 1921.

Norrish studied for his doctorate under the renowned physical chemist E. K. Rideal, who directed him to investigations of chemical kinetics and photochemistry (the effect of light upon solutions of potassium permanganate). By 1924 he had earned his Ph.D. in chemistry, staying on at the university to become a fellow of Emmanuel College and then, in 1925, a demonstrator in chemistry. The following year Norrish married Anne Smith who was a lecturer at the University of Wales. They would eventually have twin daughters together.

Norrish served for the rest of his academic and research life at Cambridge University. He became the Humphrey Owen Jones Lecturer in Physical Chemistry in 1930, then seven years later, he was named professor of physical chemistry as well as the director of the department of physical chemistry. He retained this position until 1965, when he retired.

Researches Chemical Kinetics and Polymerization

Norrish's early work at Cambridge involved the photochemistry of rather simple compounds, such as ketones, aldehydes, and nitrogen peroxide. He discovered that light breaks down these compounds in one of two directions, creating either stable molecules or unstable "free radicals," which are molecules that have unpaired electrons. As a corollary to this work, Norrish and his laboratory also began studying chemical chain reactions. Working with M. Ritchie, Norrish was able to describe the process by which hydrogen and chlorine react when initiated by light. Studies of other chain reactions led Norrish and his fellow workers to a study of hydrocarbon combustion, building on **Nikolai N. Semenov**'s work in branching chain reactions to describe the means by which methane and ethylene are combusted. They discovered that formaldehyde formation is a necessary intermediate step in such a chain reaction.

Norrish also conducted an investigation into the mechanics of polymerization, primarily in vinyl compounds. It was Norrish who coined the term 'gel effect' to describe the final slowing-down stages of polymerization as a solution undergoing the process becomes increasingly semi-fluid or viscous. With the advent of World War II, Norrish's laboratory work increasingly involved military projects, such as research into gun-flash suppression. Norrish became chairman of the Incendiary Projectiles Committee during this period and also assisted in the development of incendiary devices.

Flash-Photolysis Techniques Win the Nobel

After the war, Norrish worked with Porter to pioneer the study of flash-photolysis. This involved the measurement of very fast chemical reactions while exposing the substance to extremely strong and short blasts of light. Unstable molecules turned into free radicals, thus resulting in a dissociative reaction. Intermediate stages and products of such fast chemical reactions were then gauged by use of spectrographic analysis—the illumination by weaker flashes of light following at millisecond intervals upon the initial flash. Such analysis went a long way toward proving intermediate stages of reactions which had been, until the Norrish-Porter work, only theoretical.

Norrish and Porter continued their research together from 1949 to 1965, perfecting their technique to allow analysis of short-lived intermediate compounds down to a thousandth of a millionth of a second. They published numerous articles and opened new vistas of research in fast reactions. For such work, Norrish and Porter shared the 1967 Nobel Prize for chemistry with Eigen, who was doing similar work (although he employed a "relaxation technique," whereby small disturbances of equilibrium were induced rather than the intense ones elicited by flash-photolysis).

After his retirement in 1965, Norrish remained a senior fellow at his old college, Emmanuel. Having lived in Cambridge most of his life, Norrish felt an abiding affection for all things dealing with the university. Famous for his hospitality, Norrish held at-homes with an eclectic blend of cultural personalities in attendance. He died on June 7, 1978, in Cambridge.

SELECTED WRITINGS BY NORRISH:

Periodicals

Nature, Chemical Reactions Produced by Very High Light Intensities, Volume 164, 1949, p. 658.

Discussions of the Faraday Society, The Application of Flash Techniques to the Study of Fast Reactions, Volume 17, 1954, pp. 40–46.

Proceedings of the Royal Society, The Gas Phase Oxidation of n-Butenes, Series A272, 1963, pp. 164–191.

Chemistry in Britain, The Kinetics and Analysis of Very Fast Reactions, Volume 1, 1965, pp. 289–311.

FURTHER READING:

Books

Biographical Memoirs of Fellows of the Royal Society, Volume 27, Royal Society (London), 1981, pp. 289–311.

Periodicals

Bamford, C. H., *Nature,* R. G. W. Norrish, 1897–1978, September 7, 1978, pp. 78–79.

Eyring, Henry and Edward M. Eyring, *Science,* Nobel Prize Winners: Chemistry, November 10, 1967, pp. 746–748.

Sketch by J. Sydney Jones

John Howard Northrop
1891–1987
American biochemist

J ohn Howard Northrop, a Nobel laureate in chemistry, is best known for his work on the purification and crystallization of enzymes, which regulate important body functions like digestion and respiration. Northrop's studies on the chemical composition of enzymes enabled him to confirm the hypothesis that enzymes are proteins—a discovery that spurred much additional research on these critical catalysts of biochemical reactions. For this discovery, Northrop was awarded the Nobel Prize in chemistry in 1946. In addition to these studies, he also contributed to the development of techniques for isolating—and thus identifying—a variety of substances, including bacterial viruses and valuable antitoxins.

Northrop was born in Yonkers, New York, on July 5, 1891, to John Isaiah and Alice Belle (Rich) Northrop. The Northrops hailed from a long list of notable ancestors; well-known relations include the Reverend Jonathan Edwards, president of Princeton University in 1758. Prior to his son's birth, Isaiah Northrop was killed in a laboratory fire at Columbia University, where he taught zoology. Alice Northrop, a biology teacher at Normal (Hunter) College, influenced her son's interest in zoology and biology. John Northrop received a B.S. in 1912 from Columbia University, where he majored in biochemistry. He continued his studies in Columbia's chemistry department and was awarded an M.A. in 1913 and a Ph.D. in 1915.

Research at RIMR

In 1915 Northrop accepted a position in the laboratory of **Jacques Loeb** at the Rockefeller Institute for Medical Research (RIMR). Loeb, an experimental physiologist, headed RIMR's laboratory of general physiology. There Northrop studied the effect of environmental factors on heredity through experimentation with *Drosophila* (fruit flies). He developed a method for producing *Drosophila* free of microorganisms, which revolutionized studies that investigated factors affecting the flies' lifespan. Using these flies, Northrop and Loeb demonstrated that heat affected the life and health of the flies—not light or expenditure of energy, as previously believed.

Northrop's work in Loeb's laboratory was interrupted by the advent of World War I. At that time he became involved with research geared toward wartime concerns. Northrop developed a fermentation process for acetone that was used in the production of explosives and airplane wing coverings. As a result of these efforts, he was commissioned a captain in the U.S. Army Chemical Warfare Service. He was subsequently sent to the Commercial Solvents Corporation in Terre Haute, Indiana, to oversee the plant development of acetone production.

Although Loeb and Northrop remained close associates, Northrop was ready for independent work upon his return to the institute in 1919. At this time he studied the digestive enzymes pepsin and trypsin; these studies continued throughout the 1920s and 1930s, but Northrop was also interested in a myriad of other scientific investigations. He studied vision in the *Limulus* crab; with RIMR colleague Moses Kunitz he analyzed the chemical composition of gelatin; and he worked with Paul De Kruif on bacterial suspensions.

Shortly after Loeb's death in 1924, Northrop transferred to the institute's Princeton, New Jersey, department of animal pathology; at this time he was made a full member of the institute. The animal pathology department was opened in 1917 to study basic research in animal diseases and later expanded in 1931 to include a department of plant pathology. Inspired by the work of **James B. Sumner**, who had isolated and crystallized an enzyme called urease, Northrop continued his studies of the protein-splitting enzymes pepsin, trypsin, and chymotrypsin; he eventually isolated and crystallized all three substances. In 1929, Northrop and M. L. Anson developed the diffusion cell, a relatively simple means for isolating materials. In 1931, with Kunitz, Northrop validated the usefulness of the phase rule solubility method of studying the purity of substances, which tests for the homogeneity of dissolved solids. By applying this testing method to crystalline pepsin, chymotrypsin, and trypsin, he corroborated Sumner's controversial belief that enzymes were proteins. The research of this period was presented in *Crystalline Enzymes* (1939), written by Northrop, Kunitz, and Roger Herriott.

Northrop's investigation of bacteriophages (viruses that attack bacteria) began in the 1920s, but did not flower until the 1930s. He and associate **Wendell Stanley** applied their techniques for isolating enzymes to crystallizing the tobacco mosaic virus—isolation being the first step in determining the chemical composition of any substance. From 1936 to 1938 Northrop examined the chemical nature of bacteriophages and successfully isolated purified nucleoprotein (protein plus DNA and RNA) from cultures of *Staphylococcus aureus,* the bacteria that causes boils; this finding was one of the earliest indications that nucleoproteins are an essential part of a virus. Using his ability to isolate and crystallize substances, in 1941 Northrop produced the first crystalline antibody, for diphtheria. He would later, with W. F. Goebel, produce an antibody for pneumococcus.

With the start of World War II, Northrop was once again called on to become involved with government research undertaken at RIMR. In 1941, RIMR and the U.S. Office of Scientific Research and Development (OSRD) initiated the investigation of lethal gases used in battle. One of Northrop's biggest wartime achievements was developing the Northrop titrator and the portable, battery-operated Northrop field titrator. These devices measure the concentration of mustard gas in the air at some distance from the gassed zone. The Northrop titrator is considered an important prototype for subsequent development of the more sophisticated defensive instruments used in chemical warfare today.

Accepts Position at Berkeley

In 1949, RIMR's Princeton facility closed, prompting Northrop's move to the University of California, Berkeley. During his tenure as visiting professor, Northrop maintained his association with RIMR and was named professor emeritus in 1961. While at Berkeley, Northrop continued his work with bacteriophages. He conducted research on the life cycle of *Bacillus megatherium* cells from their normal stage to that of a phage. He also investigated the origin of bacterial viruses and found that they were mutations of normal cells.

In addition to the Nobel Prize, which he shared with Stanley and Sumner, Northrop was also awarded the W. B. Cutting Travelling Fellowship and the Stevens Prize of the College of Physicians and Surgeons of Columbia University, and he was elected to the National Academy of Sciences. Beginning in 1924, he also served on the editorial board of the *Journal of General Physiology,* an association that spanned a sixty-two year period.

Northrop retired from Berkeley in 1959 and moved to Wickenburge, Arizona, where he died on May 27, 1987. He left his wife, Louise Walker, whom he married in June, 1918, and two children, Alice Havemeyer and John.

SELECTED WRITINGS BY NORTHROP:

Books

Crystalline Enzymes, Columbia University Press, 1939.

Periodicals

Biological Review, The Chemistry of Pepsin and Trypsin, Volume 10, 1935, pp. 263.
Journal of General Physiology, Factors Controlling the Production of Lysogenic Cultures of B. megatherium, March, 1961, pp. 859–867.

FURTHER READING:

Books

Corner, George W., *A History of the Rockefeller Institute: 1901–1953,* The Rockefeller Institute Press, 1964.

Periodicals

Herriott, Roger M., *Journal of General Physiology,* A Biographical Sketch of John Howard Northrop, March, 1962 (Part 2), pp. 1–16.
Herriott, Roger M., *Journal of General Physiology,* John Howard Northrop, June, 1981, pp. 597–599.

Sketch by Renee D. Mastrocco

Sergei Novikov
1938–
Russian mathematician

Sergei Novikov, a mathematician interested in everything from topology to theoretical physics, made important contributions to several fields. He has worked on finding links between high-level mathematics and theoretical physics, but he is best known for his research on Pontryagin classes, which led to the classification of certain types of manifolds. For his work on Pontryagin classes, he was awarded both his own country's Lenin Prize and the international recognition of the Fields Medal.

Sergei Petrovich Novikov was born into a mathematical family on March 20, 1938, in Gorky, Russia. His father, Petr Sergeevich Novikov, had founded the Soviet Union's school of mathematical logic and made outstanding contributions to the field of set theory. His mother, Lyudmila Vsevolodovna Keldysh, was also a mathematician, whose research was concentrated on geometric topology, a field in which her son would later excel. (Topology is a branch of mathematics concerned with properties of geometric configurations that are not altered by changes in shape—sometimes described as the study of continuity.) Novikov entered Moscow University as an undergraduate in 1955, and very early on he showed signs of mathematical brilliance. His first paper, a short work on a part of topological theory, was published when he was only twenty-one; his second, published a year later, held the beginnings of his later research on manifolds. Novikov graduated from the faculty of mathematics and mechanics of Moscow University in 1960, and he entered the Steklov Institute of Mathematics as a doctoral student.

Breakthrough Research Leads to Top Award

Under the supervision of M. M. Postnikov, Novikov began his research at Steklov, where he would stay for five years. In 1962, he married Eleonora Tsoi (with whom he had three children); he received his Ph.D. in 1964 and his doctor of science degree in 1965. At Steklov, Novikov uncovered the crucial ideas of his manifold research. A manifold can be broadly described as a topological space containing a set of items—for example, a plane can be understood as a two-dimensional manifold of points. At the time of Novikov's research, three different categories of manifolds were discussed: differentiable, piece-wise linear (also known as combinatorial), and topological. In differentiable manifolds, those on which calculus is performed, the items in the set are connected by curves or twists. Piece-wise linear manifolds, on the other hand, are connected by straight lines. This distinction was already recognized at the time of Novikov's work. However, very little was known about topological manifolds. Did they behave more like differentiable manifolds or piece-wise linear ones? This was the question Novikov set out to answer.

He began by looking at the Pontryagin classes. On a differentiable manifold, a Pontryagin class is a structure related to the manifold which is unchanged, or invariant, when the manifold is manipulated. They can be used to describe the amount of twisting or curvature present in the manifold. However, in 1957, French mathematician **René Thom** and others had proved that, when using real or rational numbers, the Pontryagin classes are piece-wise linear invariants; in other words, they are a characteristic feature of a piece-wise linear manifold, just as they are of a differentiable manifold. Finally, in 1965, Novikov was able to show that they were also topologically invariant. This dramatic result showed that topological manifolds are, in the last analysis, most similar to piece-wise linear ones, a result which had great impact on future work in topology. An impressive aspect of this research was that Novikov was relatively isolated from other mathematicians working in this field at the time, and yet he solved a problem which had puzzled the entire mathematical community.

Moscow University, where Novikov had been teaching since 1964, recognized the importance of his work by appointing him to a full professorship in 1966. Other recognitions soon followed. In 1967, he won the Soviet Union's Lenin Prize, and in 1970, the International Mathematical Union awarded him the Fields Medal, the most prestigious honor a mathematician can receive.

After receiving the Fields Medal, Novikov turned his attention to a new topic, theoretical physics. He wanted to help form connections between the two subjects, using the research being done in modern mathematics to inform the progress of theoretical physics. His extensive research after 1971 varied between articles strictly concerned with algebraic geometry and those on modern mathematical physics. In particular, Novikov concentrated on equations involving solitons, or non-linear waves; he also worked in spectral theory and other areas. This work, much of which he did in collaboration with his students, helped further not only the fields of physics and algebraic geometry, but related areas as well. In 1975, he accepted a position as head of the mathematics department at the L.D. Landau Institute.

In 1981 Novikov received belated recognition for work he had done over ten years earlier. As part of his research on manifolds, he had studied foliations, which are decompositions of manifolds into smaller ones (called leaves). Leaves could be either open or closed, but the closed type was most mathematically interesting because at the time its existence had not been proved. Novikov, using geometric proofs, solidified the existence of closed leaves in the case of a sphere, and became the first person ever to do so. The mathematical community began using this research immediately, but it was not until 1981 that Novikov was honored for the work with the Lobachevsky International Prize of the Academy of Sciences of the Soviet Union.

In 1983, in addition to his professorship at Moscow University and his directorship of the Landau Institute, Novikov accepted the position of head of the department at the Steklov Mathematical Institute. A year later, he was appointed chair of the department of geometry and topology at Moscow University. In spite of these prestigious appointments, Novikov did not limit himself to administrative duties. The mid-1980s also saw the publication of two important mathematical texts by Novikov and his colleagues, one in mathematical physics called *Theory of Solitons: The Inverse Scattering Methods* and one in geometry, *Modern Geometry: Methods and Applications.* Throughout his career, Novikov looked for ways to link the three major areas of modern-day pure mathematics: calculus, geometry, and topology. His 1990 work, *Basic Elements of Differential Geometry and Topology,* showed not only his ability to achieve the goal of finding connections within mathematics but also his concern that future mathematicians might be capable of doing so as well.

SELECTED WRITINGS BY NOVIKOV:

Books

Modern Geometry: Methods and Applications, 2 volumes, Springer-Verlag, 1984.
Theory of Solitons: The Inverse Scattering Methods, Consultants Bureau, 1984.
Basic Elements of Differential Geometry and Topology, Kluwer Academic Publishers, 1990.

Periodicals

Journal of the Academy of Science of the USSR, Homotopic and Topological Invariance of Certain Classes of Pontryagin, Volume 162, 1965, pp. 854–57.

FURTHER READING:

Periodicals

Atiyah, M. F., *Actes, Congrès International Mathématiques,* On the Work of Sergei Novikov, Volume 1, International Mathematics Union, pp. 11–13.

Atiyah, M. F., *Russian Mathematical Surveys,* Sergei Petrovich Novikov (on His Fiftieth Birthday), Volume 43, 1988, pp. 1–10.

Sketch by Karen Sands

Robert Noyce
1927–1990
American physicist and inventor

Robert Noyce coinvented the integrated circuit, an electronic component that is considered to be among the twentieth century's most significant technological developments. The laptop computer, the ignition control in a modern automobile, the "brain" of a VCR that allows for its programming, and thousands of other computing devices all depend for their operation on the integrated circuit. Noyce was not only a brilliant inventor, credited with more than a dozen patents for semiconductor devices and processes, but a forceful businessman who founded the Fairchild Semiconductor Corporation and the Intel Corporation and who, at the time of his death, was president and CEO of Sematech.

Robert Norton Noyce was born December 12, 1927, in Burlington, Iowa, the third of four boys in the family. His parents were Ralph Noyce, a minister who worked for the Iowa Conference of Congregational Churches, and Harriet Norton Noyce. Growing up in a two-story church-owned house in Grinnell, a small town in central Iowa, Noyce was gifted in many areas, excelling in sports, music, and acting as well as academic work. He exhibited a talent for math and science while in high school and took the Grinnell College freshman physics course in his senior year. Noyce went on to receive his baccalaureate degree in physics from Grinnell, graduating Phi Beta Kappa in 1949. It was at Grinnell that he was introduced to the transistor (an electronic device that allows a small current to control a larger one in another location) by his mentor Grant Gale, head of Grinnell's physics department. Noyce was excited by the invention, seeing it as freeing electronics from the constraints of the bulky and inefficient vacuum tube. After he received his Ph.D. in physics from the Massachusetts Institute of Technology in 1954, Noyce—who had no interest in pure research—started working for Philco in Philadelphia, Pennsylvania, where the company was making semiconductors (materials whose conductivity of an electrical current puts them midway between conductors and insulators).

After three years, Noyce became convinced Philco did not have as much interest in transistors as he did. By chance in 1956 he was asked by **William Shockley**, Nobel laureate and coinventor of the transistor, to come work for him in

Robert Noyce

microchip as it became commonly known, had been born. More than one person, however, was working toward this invention at the same time. **Jack Kilby** of Texas Instruments had devised an integrated circuit the year before, but it had no commercial application. Nevertheless, both Kilby and Noyce are considered coinventors of the integrated circuit. In 1959 Noyce applied for a semiconductor integrated circuit patent using his process, which was awarded in 1961.

Both technological advances and competition in the new microchip industry increased rapidly. The number of transistors that could be put on a microchip grew from ten in 1964 to one thousand in 1969 to thirty-two thousand in 1975. (By 1993 up to 3.1 million transistors could be put on a 2.15-inch-square microprocessor chip.) The number of manufacturers eventually grew from two (Fairchild and Shockley) to dozens. During the 1960s Noyce's company was the leading producer of microchips, and by 1968 he was a millionaire. However, Noyce still felt constricted at Fairchild; he wanted more control and so—along with Gordon Moore (also a former Shockley employee)—he formed Intel in Santa Clara, California. Intel went to work making semiconductor memory, or data storage. Subsequently, Ted Hoff, an Intel scientist, invented the microprocessor and propelled Intel into the forefront of the industry. By 1982 Intel could claim to have pioneered three-quarters of the previous decade's advances in microtechnology.

Noyce's management style could be called "roll up your sleeves." He shunned fancy corporate cars, offices, and furnishings in favor of a less-structured, relaxed working environment in which everyone contributed and no one benefited from lavish perquisites. Becoming chairman of the board of Intel in 1974, he left the work of daily operations behind him, founding and later becoming chairman of the Semiconductor Industry Association. In 1980 Noyce was honored with the National Medal of Science and in 1983, the same year that Intel's sales reached one billion dollars, he was made a member of the National Inventor's Hall of Fame. He was dubbed the Mayor of Silicon Valley during the 1980s, not only for his scientific contributions but also for his role as a spokesperson for the industry. Noyce spent much of his later career working to improve the international competitiveness of American industry. Early on he recognized the strengths of foreign competitors in the electronics market and the corresponding weaknesses of domestic companies. In 1988 Noyce took charge of Sematech, a consortium of semiconductor manufacturers working together and with the United States government to increase U.S. competitiveness in the world marketplace.

Noyce was married twice. His first marriage to Elizabeth Bottomley ended in divorce (which he attributed to his intense involvement in his work); the couple had four children together. In 1975 he married Ann Bowers, who was then Intel's personnel director. Noyce enjoyed reading Hemingway, flying his own airplane, hang gliding, and scuba diving. He believed that microelectronics would continue to advance in complexity and sophistication well beyond its current state, and that the question would finally

California. Excited by the opportunity to develop state-of-the-art transistor technology, Noyce moved to Palo Alto, which is located in an area that came to be known as Silicon Valley (named for the silicon compounds used in the manufacture of computer chips). But Noyce was no happier with Shockley than he had been with Philco; both Shockley's management style and the direction of his work—which ignored transistors—were disappointing. In 1957 Noyce left with seven other Shockley engineers to form a new company, financed by Fairchild Camera and Instrument, to be called Fairchild Semiconductor. At age twenty-nine, Noyce was chosen as the new corporation's leader.

Invents the Integrated Circuit

The first important development during the early years at Fairchild was the 1958 invention, by Jean Hoerni (an ex-Shockley scientist), of a process to protect the elements on a transistor from contaminants during manufacturing. This was called the planar process, and involved laying down a layer of silicon oxide over the transistor's elements. In 1959, after prodding from one of his patent attorneys to find more applications for the planar process, Noyce took the next step of putting several electronic components, such as resistors and transistors, on the same chip and layering them over with silicon oxide. Combining components in this fashion eliminated the need to wire individual transistors to each other and made possible tremendous reductions in the size of circuit components with a corresponding increase in the speed of their operation. The integrated circuit, or lead to what use society would make of the technology. Noyce died on June 3, 1990, of a sudden heart attack.

FURTHER READING:

Books

Bonner, M., W. L. Boyd, and J. A. Allen, *Robert N. Noyce, 1927–1990,* Sematech, 1990.

Bonner, M., W. L. Boyd, and J. A. Allen, *Encyclopedia of Computer Science,* Van Nostrand, 1993, pp. 522–523.

Bonner, M., W. L. Boyd, and J. A. Allen, *Fifty Who Made the Difference,* Villard Books, 1984, pp. 270–303.

Palfreman, Jon, and Doron Swade, *The Dream Machine,* BBC Books, 1991.

Slater, Robert, *Portraits in Silicon,* MIT Press, 1987.

Sketch by Frank Hertle

Tetsuo Nozoe
1902–1996
Japanese organic chemist

Tetsuo Nozoe was an organic chemist whose work on the synthesis and structure of tropolones helped found a new field in chemistry, the study of novel aromatic compounds.

He was born on May 16, 1902, in Sendai, Japan, the middle child of eleven children born to Juichi and Toyoko Nozoe. His father practiced law in Sendai and served as a member of the House of Representatives. During Nozoe's childhood he suffered from a variety of illnesses, including typhoid fever, beriberi, and pneumonia. Because his primary schooling was frequently interrupted by poor health, his mother hired a private tutor for him. Nozoe's interest in chemistry began to develop when he entered middle school. Around this time he constructed a makeshift chemistry laboratory in a garden storage shed, assembling various pieces of glassware, chemicals, and an alcohol lamp from a local pharmacy. His parents, who wanted him to pursue a medical career, were fearful he would set fires or injure himself in his shed, though no such mishaps occurred.

In 1923 Nozoe entered Tohoku Imperial University in Sendai, where he began pre-medical studies. Soon he convinced his family he was more suited to the study of chemistry. At Tohoku he came under the tutelage of Riko Majima, one of the leading Japanese organic chemists of his day. Nozoe's thesis work on the synthesis of the thyroid hormone, thyroxine, became the subject of his first scientific

publication, which appeared in 1927 in the *Journal of the Chemical Society of Japan.* Shortly after his graduation in 1926, the Government Monopoly Bureau Research Laboratories in Formosa (now Taiwan) offered him a position as an industrial organic chemist. His journey from Sendai to Formosa took five days by train and ship.

Begins Study of Organic Compounds

By the summer of 1926, Nozoe had settled in the city of Taipei and begun research on the *taiwanhinoki*, a local tree that was economically important to the region. His work focused on identifying the organic components of the essential oils derived from the tree's leaves. In 1929 he received an appointment as an assistant professor of chemistry at the newly created Taihoku Imperial University in Taipei. His research shifted to the chemistry of another economically important plant, *Barringtonia asiatica*, a type of mangrove. In the seeds of this plant he isolated saponins, a class of chemicals that are used as soap substitutes and fish poisons. Saponins and the related sapogenins would become one of the primary subjects of research for Nozoe until the early 1940s. In 1936, he submitted a summary of his early work on the structure of organic natural products to Majima, who had recently been appointed dean of the faculty of science at the newly established Osaka University. As a result of this summary, Nozoe became the first recipient of the D.Sc. degree awarded by the university.

In 1936 Nozoe also began a new line of research, studying the components of wool wax. He was intrigued by the fact that wool wax, an animal product, contained triterpenoids, which are usually found in plants. His work on wool wax helped elucidate the physical properties of its commercially valuable components. Another research project that Nozoe pursued simultaneously was the investigation of hinokitin and hinokitiol, essential oils that he derived from several of the island's coniferous trees. In 1938 it was discovered that hinokitiol had an antibacterial effect against the tubercle bacillus.

Discovery of Tropolones

War activities from 1942 to 1945 brought a temporary end to Nozoe's organic chemistry research. In 1946 he resumed his studies of hinokitiol and experimentally demonstrated that it was a new type of aromatic compound, different from traditional benzene type aromatics, which was later named "troplone." Since Formosa had been reoccupied by the Chinese, Taihoku Imperial University was now known as National Taiwan University. Most of the Japanese faculty members left their posts and returned to Japan, but because of his importance to the chemistry department, Nozoe was not granted permission to leave until the spring of 1948.

In the fall of 1948 he took a post in the chemistry department of Tohoku Imperial University, back in Sendai. Continuing his investigation of the non-benzenoid aromatic hinokitiol, he resolved the structure and aromatic properties of its various derivatives. He also began work on the synthesis of tropolones from hinokitiol. His study of tropolones and other troponoids was to become his most important contribution to the field of organic chemistry. Many of the tropolones have fungicidal properties, and colchicine, a tropolone derivative, is useful both as a medicine and as an agent for biomedical research. Nozoe retired from Tohoku University in 1966, but continued for several decades to conduct research on non-benzenoid aromatics.

Nozoe received many awards throughout his career. He received the Majima Award for Organic Chemistry in 1944, the Asahi Cultural Award in 1952, the Japan Academy Award in 1953, the Order of Cultural Merit Medal in 1958, and the 1980 Wilhelm August von Hofman Memorial Medal. He became a foreign member of the Royal Sweden Academy of Sciences in 1972 and was also made an honorary member of the Swiss Chemical Society.

Shortly after taking his first post in Formosa, Nozoe married Kyoko Horiuchi. Together they had four children: one son, Shigeo, and three daughters, Takako, Yoko, and Yuriko. Nozoe pursued a variety of hobbies during his career, including stamp and autograph collecting. His personal autograph books included signatures, cartoons, and written commentary from many of the leading chemists of the twentieth century. He was also an accomplished photographer. During his early years in Formosa, his forays into the countryside to collect plant samples brought him in contact with the indigenous tribes of the island, and Nozoe's photographs of tribal dance and dress remain important documents of the region's anthropological history. His death, which came a month before his 94th birthday, marked the end of an era of organic chemistry.

SELECTED WRITINGS BY NOZOE:

Books

Nozoe, Tetsuo. *Seventy Years in Organic Chemistry.* American Chemical Society, 1991.

Sketch by Leslie Reinherz

Christiane Nüsslein-Volhard
1942–

German genetic researcher

Christiane Nüsslein-Volhard, winner of the 1995 Nobel Prize in physiology or medicine, is the first German woman to win in this category. She is most noted for her contribution to research in identifying genes that control the early stages of embryonic development in fruit flies. Nüsslein-Volhard and two other scientists, **Edward B. Lewis** and **Eric F. Wieschaus**, paved the way for the study of the human counterparts to genes that influence human development, including ones responsible for birth defects.

Nüsslein-Volhard was born on October 20, 1942, in Magdeburg, Germany. The daughter of Rolf Volhard, an architect, and Brigitte (Hass) Volhard, a musician and painter, Christiane decided at a young age that she wanted to be a scientist. She stood out in a family of artists and architects—two of her four siblings are architects, and all of them are amateur painters and musicians (Nüsslein-Volhard herself plays the flute and sings). If her family had any doubts about her chosen career, the earliness of her decision helped them to grow accustomed to the idea. Teachers also adjusted to her determination, and she moved easily through school.

Embarks on Scientific Career

Even though few women of her generation chose scientific careers, Nüsslein-Volhard found that being female in a male-dominated field presented little in the way of an obstacle to her studies. She received degrees in biology, physics, and chemistry from Johann-Wolfgang-Goethe-University in 1964 and a diploma in biochemistry from Eberhard-Karls University in 1968. In 1973 she earned a Ph.D. in biology and genetics from the University of Tübingen. Nüsslein-Volhard was married for a short time as a young woman and never had any children. She decided to keep her husband's last name because it was already associated with her developing scientific career.

In the late 1970s Nüsslein-Volhard finished post-doctoral fellowships in Basel, Switzerland, and Freiburg, Germany, and accepted her first independent research position at the European Molecular Biology Laboratory (EMBL) in Heidelberg, Germany. She was joined there by Eric F. Wieschaus who was also finishing his training. Because of their common interest in *Drosophila*, or fruit flies, Nüsslein-Volhard and Wieschaus decided to work together to find out how a newly fertilized fruit fly egg develops into a fully segmented embryo.

Nüsslein-Volhard and Wieschaus chose the fruit fly because of its incredibly fast embryonic development. They began to pursue a strategy for isolating genes responsible for the embryos' initial growth. This was a bold decision by two scientists just beginning their scientific careers. No one had done anything like this before, and it wasn't certain whether they would be able to actually isolate specific genes.

Unique Strategy Creates Useful Mutants

Their experiments involved feeding male fruit flies sugar water laced with deoxyribonucleic acid (DNA)-damaging chemicals. When the male fruit flies mated with females, the females often produced dead or mutated embryos. Nüsslein-Volhard and Wieschaus studied these embryos for over a year under a microscope which had two viewers, allowing them to examine an embryo at the same time. They were able to identify specific genes that basically told cells what they were going to be—part of the head or the tail, for example. Some of these genes, when mutated, resulted in damage to the formation of the embryo's body plan. Nüsslein-Volhard became known for her ability to spot the slightest deviation from the norm and know whether it was significant to the way the embryo would develop.

Nüsslein-Volhard and Wieschaus published the results of their research in the English scientific journal *Nature* in 1980. They received a great deal of attention because their studies showed that there were a limited number of genes that control development and that they could be identified. This was significant because similar genes existed in higher organisms and humans and, importantly, these genes performed similar functions during development. Nüsslein-Volhard and Wieschaus's breakthrough research could help other scientists find genes that could explain birth defects in humans. Their research could also help improve in vitro fertilization and lead to an understanding of what causes miscarriages. With this important work recognized by the scientific community, Nüsslein-Volhard began lecturing at universities in Germany and the United States. She was the Silliman Lecturer at Yale University and the Brooks Lecturer at Harvard.

Launches Controversial New Research

In 1991 she and Wieschaus received the Albert Lasker Medical Research Award, which is considered second only to the Nobel. During this time Nüsslein-Volhard had begun new research at the Max Planck Institute in Tübingen, Germany, similar to the work she did on the fruit flies. This time she wanted to understand the basic patterns of development of the zebra fish. She chose zebra fish as her subject because most of the developmental research on vertebrates in the past was on mice, frogs, or chickens, which have many technical difficulties, one of which was that one couldn't see the embryos developing. Zebra fish seemed like the perfect organism to study because they are small, they breed quickly, and the embryos develop outside of the mother's body. The most important consideration, however, was the fact that zebra fish embryos are transparent, which would allow Nüsslein-Volhard a clear view of development as it was happening.

Despite her prize-winning research on fruit flies, she received skeptical feedback on her zebra fish work. Other scientists claimed it was risky and foolish. When she submitted papers about her laboratory's work for publication, one reviewer even asked her why she was bothering. Nüsslein-Volhard was not one to be stopped by criticism or to rest on her laurels. Even though her reputation was built on her fruit fly research, her love of new challenges pushed her to take on this risky new project and set her sights to the future.

Unique Research Wins Nobel

Then on October 9, 1995, in the midst of criticism about her new research, Nüsslein-Volhard, Wieschaus, and Edward B. Lewis of the California Institute of Technology won the Nobel Prize in physiology or medicine for their work on genetic development in *Drosophila*. Lewis had been analyzing genetic mutations in fruit flies since the forties and had published his results independently from Nüsslein-Volhard and Wieschaus.

It has yet to be proven if zebra fish will actually provide any answers to the complex genetic questions Nüsslein-Volhard has raised. But her love of genetics compels her to continue. Her home country of Germany recognizes her as a national treasure, despite her controversial research. Nüsslein-Volhard herself dismisses public fear about gene research on embryos. "No one has in their grasp the genes that make humans wiser, more beautiful, or that make blue eyes," she said when she accepted the Nobel Prize. Her research, she says, has helped people "become wiser, understand biology better, understand how life functions."

SELECTED WRITINGS BY NÜSSLEIN-VOLHARD:

Periodicals

"Embryology Goes Fishing." *Nature,* May 22, 1986, pp. 380-1

"Determination of Anteroposterior Polarity in Drosophila." *Science,* December 18, 1987, pp. 1675-81

"From Egg to Organism: Studies on Embryonic Pattern Formation." *The Journal of the American Medical Association,* October 2, 1991, p. 1848

"Large-Scale Mutagenesis in the Zebrafish—In Search of Gene-Controlling Development in a Vertebrate." *Current Biology,* March 1, 1994, pp. 189-202

"Of Flies and Fishes." *Science,* October 28, 1994, p. 572

Sketch by Pamela Proffitt

O

Gerard K. O'Neill
1927–1992
American physicist

As an experimental physicist, Gerard O'Neill invented and developed the technology of storage rings that became the basis of today's high-energy particle accelerators. Not content to be only a pioneer of physics, O'Neill went on to become a visionary teacher and educator who advocated large-scale human colonization of outer space, as well as an entrepreneur who founded several corporations devoted to developing new space-based technologies.

Gerard Kitchen O'Neill was born in New York City on February 6, 1927. The only child of Edward Gerard and Dorothy Lewis (Kitchen) O'Neill, he was raised in Connecticut and upstate New York. He attended the Newburgh Free Academy in Newburgh, New York, and edited the school newspaper. During this time, he also earned money broadcasting news for a local radio program. After graduating from high school in 1944, he joined the U. S. Navy on his birthday. There he was trained as a radar technician and was sent to the Pacific theater just as the war ended. Following his discharge in 1946, he entered Swarthmore College in Pennsylvania to study physics and mathematics, graduating Phi Beta Kappa in 1950. During the war, O'Neill had realized the potentially destructive role physicists could play in society, and decided to use his knowledge of physics only to benefit human beings. Upon graduation, he received an Atomic Energy Commission fellowship and entered Cornell University in Ithaca, New York. He received his Ph.D. in physics in 1954 and accepted a faculty position at Princeton University the same year.

Pioneers High-Energy Physics with his Colliding-Beam Principle

During only his second year as an instructor in the Princeton physics department, O'Neill published a two-page letter in *Physical Review* titled "Storage-Ring Synchrotron: Device for High-Energy Physics Research." Discussing this important paper in a 1993 article, British physicist **Freeman Dyson** stated, "it laid down the path that high-energy physics has followed for the next 36 years. If you read the letter now, you can see that almost everything in it is right." However, in 1956 when his letter was written, O'Neill encountered a highly skeptical physics community. His special storage ring design for increasing the collision

Gerard K. O'Neill

energies of atomic beams from particle accelerators was simply a theory that had not been proven. Finally obtaining financial support in 1959 from the Office of Naval Research and the Atomic Energy Commission, O'Neill and his colleagues built two particle storage rings at Stanford University that used his high-vacuum technique and successfully demonstrated his colliding-beam theory. Physicists around the world concurred immediately and soon hurried to build their own. O'Neill became a full professor at Princeton in 1965.

Embraces "Humanization" of Outer Space

In 1966, when the National Aeronautics and Space Administration (NASA) opened its astronaut program to civilian scientists, O'Neill immediately applied and, following months of training and testing, was selected as a finalist. Although NASA later discontinued this program, O'Neill used the experience to reform the teaching of physics at Princeton. Seeking to replace the same traditional problems that students of classical physics had always considered, he encouraged them to apply physics to something real and relevant like the *Apollo* moon missions that were taking place in 1969. After asking his class to consider his question, "Is the surface of the planet earth really the right place for an expanding technological civilization?" O'Neill found himself as intrigued and enthusiastic about the notion of a possible human habitat in space as were his students. This led him to a prolonged study of the technical issues of building human colonies in space, such as energy, land area, size and shape, atmosphere, gravitation, and sunlight. By 1974, O'Neill wrote an article, "The Colonization of Space," that led to his most significant book, *The High Frontier: Human Colonies in Space*, published in 1977.

This lively book expanded upon his thesis that a "breakout" from Earth was inevitable, and that this future colonization, or "humanization," of space would ultimately determine the continuance of intelligent life. The book proved to be both a popular and a critical success, winning the Phi Beta Kappa Science Book of the Year Award. It has since seen six English editions and been translated into six languages. As he continually reevaluated and revised his ideas, O'Neill shifted his emphasis for colonizing space from relieving population pressure to providing Earth with a limitless supply of clean, inexpensive energy. His plans included ambitious space manufacturing programs, and he argued that several potentially profitable space-based industries could exist.

Founds the Space Studies Institute

O'Neill realized that because of political influences and budgetary constraints, NASA could not be a reliable and steady supporter of the kind of basic research he felt needed to be done. Therefore, in 1977 he sought and obtained private support for a new, non-profit corporation called the Space Studies Institute. Located at Princeton University, the Space Studies Institute supports technical research on the science and engineering of living and working in space with grants made possible by members' contributions.

In addition to providing dependable funding, the Space Studies Institute was intended to usher in a new style of space technology development. Ever the individualist, O'Neill believed fervently that small, private groups were superior to large, governmental bureaucracies in developing the tools of exploring space. He felt strongly that the settlement of space offered such potential benefits to mankind that it was too important to be left in the hands of national governments. In 1983, he founded the Geostar Corporation which, based on O'Neill's own patent, developed the first private satellite navigational system to guide travel on earth. The company, however, went out of business in 1991, despite having developed a satellite-based navigational and position locating system.

O'Neill died on April 27, 1992, of leukemia. He left behind three children, Janet Karen, Eleanor Edith, and Roger Alan, from his 1950 marriage to Sylvia Turlington. Divorced in 1966, he married Renate Steffen in 1973, with whom he founded the Space Studies Institute. O'Neill's son,

Roger, became chairman of the Institute's board of directors and is working to carry on his father's tradition. Before his death, O'Neill wrote in *Who's Who*: "To me the ideals of human freedom, of individual choice, and of concern for others have always been of the greatest importance. I hope that at the end of my life I can look back on work honestly done and on fair dealings with others."

In April 1997, a Pegasus rocket carried O'Neill's ashes into space along with those of 21 others, including *Star Trek* creator Gene Roddenberry, counter-culture guru Timothy Leary, and Harvard psychologist Krafft Ehricke. His remains should circle the earth for up to a decade before reentering the atmosphere and burning up harmlessly.

SELECTED WRITINGS BY O'NEILL:

Books

The High Frontier: Human Colonies in Space. New York: Morrow, 1977.
2081: A Hopeful View of the Human Future. New York: Simon and Schuster, 1981.
The Technology Edge: Opportunities for America in World Competition. New York: Simon and Schuster, 1983.

FURTHER READING:

Periodicals

Daniels, Lee A. "Gerard K. O'Neill, Professor, 69 (sic); Led Studies on Physics and Space." *The New York Times*. April 29, 1992, D: 24.
"Gerard K. O'Neill." *Current Biography* (1979): 290-293.
"Interview: Gerard K. O'Neill." *Omni* (July 1979): 77–79, 113-115.

Sketch by Leonard C. Bruno

Hermann Oberth
1894–1989
German physicist

Hermann Oberth is one of three scientists considered to be the founders of space flight. The other two, Russian aerospace engineer **Konstantin Tsiolkovsky** and American physicist **Robert Goddard**, may have preceded him in many discoveries, but Oberth's writings enjoyed a much wider audience, inaugurating a movement which led first to the development of the long-range military missile, the German V–2 guided missile, and then to human space flight. In recognition of his important contributions to space flight, Oberth was the first recipient of the international R. E. P. Hirsch Astronautics Prize in 1929; he also received the Diesel medal of the Association of German Inventors in 1954, the American Astronautical Society Award in 1955, and the Federal Service Cross First Class from the German Federal Republic in 1961.

Hermann Julius Oberth was born on June 25, 1894, in the German town of Hermannstadt, Transylvania; formerly a part of Austria-Hungary, the town is now known as Sibiu, Romania. His father was Dr. Julius Gotthold Oberth, and in 1896 he became the director and chief surgeon of the county hospital in Schässburg, Transylvania, where Oberth grew up. His mother was Valerie Emma (Krassner) Oberth, the daughter of a doctor who had prophesied accurately in July of 1869 that humans would land on the moon in a hundred years. In an autobiographical piece published in *Astronautics,* Oberth remembered that "at the age of eleven, I received from my mother as a gift the famous books, *From the Earth to the Moon* and *Travel to the Moon* by Jules Verne, which I . . . read at least five or six times and, finally, knew by heart." He was fascinated by space flight, and even as a child began to perform various calculations about how it could be done. Although Oberth learned infinitesimal calculus at the Schässburg secondary school, he taught himself differential calculus, and he successfully verified the magnitude of escape velocity.

In 1913, Oberth began studying medicine at the University of Munich, but he also attended lectures in physics and related subjects at the nearby technical institute. During World War I, he served in the Infantry Regiment on the eastern front. He was wounded in February of 1916, and was detailed to a reserve hospital, where he had the opportunity to continue the experiments with weightlessness which he had begun as a teenager. He experimented on himself with drugs, including scopolamine, which is still used to treat motion sickness. Although Oberth's pioneering work in the field of space medicine has received some recognition, it does not appear to have had any direct influence on later developments.

Develops Space-Flight Theory

After leaving the army, Oberth began to work more seriously on developing solutions to the problems posed by space flight. In an autobiographical piece published in *First Steps Toward Space,* Oberth recalled that in 1918 the German Ministry of Armament rejected his proposal for "a long-range rocket powered by ethyl alcohol, water, and liquid air, somewhat similar to the V–2, only bigger and not so complicated." This was also the same year that he married Mathilde Hummel; the wedding was on June 6, and the couple would have four children, two of whom would die during World War II. In 1919 Oberth resumed his schooling, this time studying physics. He began at the University of Klausenburg in his native Transylvania, but

subsequently transferred several times: first back to the University of Munich and the technical institute there, then to the University of Göttingen, and finally to the University of Heidelberg. He submitted his doctoral dissertation at Heidelberg; the thesis was on rockets and space-flight theory and it was not accepted. Denied his doctorate, Oberth taught physics and mathematics at a girls' school for teachers in Sighisoara (also known as Schassburg) from 1922 to 1923, when the University of Klausenburg granted him the title of professor. He taught for a year at his former secondary school before transferring in 1925 to the secondary school in nearby Mediasch, where he taught physics and mathematics periodically until 1938.

In 1928, Oberth published his doctoral dissertation under the title *Die Rakete zu den Planeträumen* ("The Rocket into Planetary Space"). Although filled with complicated equations, Oberth's book sold well. In it he set forth the basic principles of space flight and discussed possible solutions to a number of specific problems. He examined such matters as liquid-propellant rocket construction, the use of propellants for different stages of rockets, and the employment of successive stages that would disengage as their propellants were used up, thereby enabling the rocket to achieve the velocities necessary to escape from the earth's atmosphere. He also discussed the use of pumps to inject the propellants into a rocket's combustion chamber, reviewed procedures to prevent burnout of that chamber, speculated on the effects of space flight upon humans, and proposed the idea of a space station. In 1929, Oberth published a considerably expanded version of this book, now entitled *Wege zur Raumschiffahrt* (translated and published as *Ways to Spaceflight*); this volume was more popularly written and the highly technical material was highlighted. Both versions of the book were important for their new ideas and for the inspiration they provided to other spaceflight pioneers.

One of the most important consequences of this publication was the German Rocket Society (Verein für Raumschiffahrt), which was founded in 1927 to raise money for Oberth's rocket experiments. With Oberth as president from 1929 to 1930, the society provided considerable practical training in rocketry to several of its members, including **Wernher Braun**, who later became part of the German army's rocket center at Peenemünde and participated in developing the V–2 guided missile. As public interest in space flight increased, the German film director Fritz Lang decided to make a movie on the subject; it was called *Frau im Mond* ("Woman on the Moon"), and he employed Oberth as technical advisor. Lang and his film company also provided funds for Oberth to construct a liquid-propellant rocket which would be launched at the movie's premier, but Oberth was unable to meet the deadline. He designed and built a rocket which never flew, but it did undergo a static test on July 23, 1930, that was certified by the Government Institute for Chemistry and Technology. Soon after this, Oberth returned to his teaching duties in Romania, but the German Rocket Society continued its work, and rocket development benefitted from the increased credibility that had been bestowed on it by government certification.

Participates Less in Later Development of Rocketry

Oberth's most important contributions to rocketry were his initial theoretical work and the publicity he was able to generate during the 1920s. After 1930, he resumed liquid-propellant rocket experiments while continuing to teach at Mediasch. He succeeded in launching one rocket in 1935, but during these years he remained outside the mainstream of rocket development. In 1938 he received an appointment to the Technical Institute in Vienna to work on liquid-propellant rockets under a contract with the German Air Force, but he was not given adequate facilities or sufficient staff to do anything significant. In 1940 he was transferred to the Technical Institute of Dresden to develop a fuel pump for what turned out to be the V–2 rocket. But the system for this rocket had already been designed when he started, and Oberth left Dresden once he discovered that his work had no purpose. He went to Peenemünde, where he worked under his former assistant, Wernher von Braun, but by the time he arrived the V–2 rocket was already essentially developed. Oberth, who became a German citizen in 1941, was put to work examining patents and other technical information for possible use on rockets. After doing some analytical work with the supersonic wind tunnel at Peenemünde in 1943, he began work on an antiaircraft rocket, using a solid propellant. He was transferred to a firm that dealt in solid fuels, Westfälisch-Anhaltische Sprengstoff A.G., where he worked until the end of the war.

After World War II, he moved to Feucht in what became West Germany. In 1948, Oberth obtained a position in Switzerland as an advisor and technical writer on matters related to rocketry, and in 1950 he was hired by the Italian Navy to develop a solid-propellant rocket. The project was discontinued in 1953, and he returned to Feucht, where in 1954 he published *Menschen im Weltraum* (translated and published as *Man into Space*), in which he discussed electric spaceships and a vehicle for moving about on the moon, as well as many of the topics covered in his previous books. In 1955 Oberth published another book, *Das Mondauto* (translated and published as *The Moon Car*), in which he elaborated on his conception for a vehicle to operate on the moon.

Also in 1955, von Braun obtained for Oberth a position with the U.S. Army Ballistic Missile Agency (ABMA) at Redstone Arsenal in Huntsville, Alabama. At ABMA, Oberth was involved in advanced planning for projects in space, including electrical and thermonuclear propulsion for rockets, guidance devices, and vehicles for the moon. Von Braun believed that Oberth had inspired the roving vehicle used on the *Apollo 15* flight to the moon. The concept of inspiration is what best characterizes Oberth's other designs at Huntsville as well, for they seem to have contributed little directly to the space effort. In 1958 he returned to Feucht where he resided for the rest of his life, although he did return to the United States in July of 1969 to witness the launch of *Apollo 11* that carried the first humans to the moon.

In *The Spaceflight Revolution*, William Sims Bainsbridge writes of Oberth that "his rocket work was conducted simultaneously with the development of a theosophical system that must be described, delicately, as variant, if not deviant." As early as 1930 but increasingly during the 1950s, Oberth was publishing and expressing a number of views that many of his admirers found disconcerting. These included claims that unidentified flying objects could be space vehicles carrying intelligent people from beyond our world, and that each human cell had its own immortal soul; he also supported such movements as parapsychology and the occult. Oberth's real importance lay in his two first books, which launched the space flight movement in Germany and laid the foundations for the exploration of space after 1957. Of the three preeminent founders of space flight, Oberth alone lived to witness the results of his early ideas. He died at age ninety-five in Nuremberg, West Germany, on December 29, 1989.

SELECTED WRITINGS BY OBERTH:

Books

Die Rakete zu den Planeträumen, ("The Rocket into Planetary Space"), [Germany], 1923, reprinted, Uni-Verlag, 1960.

Wege zur Raumschiffahrt, [Germany], 1929, translation published as *Ways to Spaceflight*, The National Aeronautics and Space Administration, 1972.

Menschen im Weltraum, [Germany], 1954, translation by G. P. H. de Freville published as *Man into Space*, Harper, 1957.

Das Mondauto, [Germany], 1959, translation by Willy Ley published as *The Moon Car*, Harper, 1959.

First Steps Toward Space, My Contributions to Astronautics, edited by Frederick C. Durant and George S. James, Smithsonian Institution Press, 1974, pp. 129–140.

Periodicals

Astronautics, Hermann Oberth: From My Life, June, 1959, pp. 38–39, 100–105.

FURTHER READING:

Books

Bainbridge, William Sims, *The Spaceflight Revolution*, Wiley, 1976.

Barth, Hans, *Hermann Oberth: "Vater der Raumfahrt,"* Bechtle, 1985.

Ley, Willy, *Rockets, Missiles, and Men in Space*, Viking, 1968.

Ordway, Fred, and Wernher von Braun, with Dave Dooling, *Space Travel: A History*, Harper, 1975.

Winter, Frank H., *Rockets into Space,* Harvard University Press, 1990.

Periodicals

Winter, Frank H., *Ad Astra,* March, 1990, pp. 37–40.
Winter, Frank H., *Spaceflight,* July-August, 1977, pp. 243–256.

Other

Harwit, Martin, and Frank Winter, oral, *Interview with Hermann Oberth,* National Air and Space Museum, Smithsonian Institution, November 14–15, 1987.
Harwit, Martin, and Frank Winter, oral, *Interview with Hermann Oberth,* Von Braun, Wernher, letter to Dr. C. Stark Draper, 30 June 1971.

Sketch by J. D. Hunley

Adriana C. Ocampo
1955–

American planetary geologist

Adriana C. Ocampo is a geologist whose duties at the National Aeronautics and Space Administration (NASA) have involved coordinating aspects of the flight of the unmanned spacecraft *Mars Observer* and the long-term Jupiter mission called Project Galileo. The ongoing Project Galileo mission is the most complex flown by NASA in nearly twenty years, and Ocampo is responsible for one of the spacecraft's four remote sensing instruments. She has served her profession as national secretary of the Society of Hispanic Professional Engineers (SHPE) and later as its national vice president.

Adriana C. Ocampo was born on January 5, 1955, in Barranquilla, Colombia. When she was only a few months old, her family moved to Buenos Aires, Argentina. When she was fifteen they emigrated to the United States, settling in Pasadena, California. Although the results from aptitude tests she had taken in Argentina directed her toward a career in the fields of business or accounting, Ocampo was able to convince her school counselors in Pasadena that she was serious about taking physics and calculus. When she participated in a science program sponsored by NASA's Jet Propulsion Laboratory (JPL) during her junior year as an aerospace engineering major at Pasadena City College, her resolve and ability became apparent.

Located in Pasadena, the Jet Propulsion Laboratory (JPL) would play an important role in shaping Ocampo's education and career. She worked there part-time during her last two years of high school and continued to do so after entering Pasadena City College. It was during this time that Ocampo discovered her real scientific focus and decided to switch to geology. She also entered California State University at Los Angeles, where she received her B.S. in geology in 1983, accepting a full-time position at JPL.

The Jet Propulsion Laboratory put her skills as a planetary geologist to the test during their Viking mission to Mars when they assigned her the task of producing a photo atlas of one of the moons of Mars. Published by NASA in 1984, this volume is the only available atlas of the moon Phobos. Ocampo subsequently became science coordinator for separate sensing instruments on two major planetary missions. For the *Mars Observer* mission, NASA's first Mars venture in seventeen years, she was responsible for the thermal emission spectrometer—an instrument that would measure the heat produced by the planet, thus enabling cartographers to create more accurate maps. This mission failed, however, during 1993 when, after an eleven-month journey, the spacecraft inexplicably fell silent, spinning out of control due to a malfunction. Ocampo's instrument thus remained untested.

Ocampo, however, became involved with another assignment at JPL, overseeing the operation of the Near-Infrared Mapping Spectrometer (NIMS) mounted on NASA's Project Galileo spacecraft. As one of four remote sensing instruments mounted on the space probe, NIMS will measure reflected sunlight and heat from Jupiter's atmosphere and help scientists to determine the planet's composition, cloud structure, and temperature. Using the data gathered by Ocampo's instrument, scientists will begin to learn more about the surface chemistry and mineralogy of Jupiter's four moons. The Galileo mission was launched successfully in 1989 and entered Jupiter's orbit in December 1995. During its voyage, it has successfully returned images of the Earth, the Moon, Venus, and Jupiter and its moons. Ocampo's NIMS instrument scanned the asteroid Gaspra's surface as it flew past and revealed valuable new information—indicating that the asteroid is covered by a "soil" of pulverized rock and dust thinner than the Moon's, and that its peak temperature is about 230 degrees kelvin.

Ocampo is fluent in Spanish and English and reads French and Italian, so it is not surprising that she originated the idea of an international sharing of space information. Called the Pan American Space Conference and sponsored by the United Nations, this symposium met in Costa Rica in 1990 and in Chile in 1993 and provided a forum for scientists and engineers of North and South America to discuss cooperative efforts in space research and technology. Ocampo is married to archeologist Kevin O. Pope who shares her interest in geology and whose company does remote-sensing geological and ecological research.

SELECTED WRITINGS BY OCAMPO:

Books

Phobos: Close Encounter Imaging from the Viking Orbiters, NASA, 1984.

FURTHER READING:

Periodicals

Mellado, Carmela, *Hispanic Engineer,* Adriana Ocampo, fall, 1987, pp. 22–24.

Mellado, Carmela, *Hispanic Engineer,* The Women Leaders of the SHPE National Board of Directors, fall, 1989, pp. 22–25.

Sketch by Leonard C. Bruno

Ellen Ochoa
1958–
American electrical engineer and astronaut

Ellen Ochoa

A specialist in optics and optical recognition in robotics, Ellen Ochoa is noted both for her distinguished work in inventions and patents and for her role in American space exploration. Her optical systems innovations include a device that detects flaws and image recognition apparatus. In the late 1980s she began working with the National Aeronautics and Space Administration (NASA) as an optical specialist. After leading a project team, Ochoa was selected for NASA's space flight program. She made her first flight on the space shuttle *Discovery* in April 1993, becoming the first Hispanic woman astronaut.

The third of five children of Rosanne (Deardorff) and Joseph Ochoa, she was born May 10, 1958, in Los Angeles, California. She grew up in La Mesa, California; her father was a manager of a retail store and her mother a homemaker. Ochoa attended Grossmont High School in La Mesa and then studied physics at San Diego State University. She completed her bachelor's degree in 1980 and was named valedictorian of her graduating class; she then moved to the department of electrical engineering at Stanford University. She received her master's degree in 1981 and her doctorate in 1985, working with Joseph W. Goodman and Lambertus Hesselink. The topic of her dissertation was real-time intensity inversion using four-wave mixing in photorefractive crystals. While completing her doctoral research she developed and patented a real-time optical inspection technique for defect detection. In an interview with Marianne Fedunkiw, Ochoa said that she considers this her most important scientific achievement so far.

In 1985 she joined Sandia National Laboratories in Livermore, California, where she became a member of the technical staff in the Imaging Technology Division. Her research centered on developing optical filters for noise removal and optical methods for distortion-invariant object recognition. She was coauthor of two more patents based on her work at Sandia, one for an optical system for nonlinear median filtering of images and another for a distortion-invariant optical pattern recognition system.

Becomes an Astronaut for NASA

It was during her graduate studies that Ochoa began considering a career as an astronaut. She told Fedunkiw that friends were applying who encouraged her to join them; ironically, she was the only one from her group of friends to make it into space. Her career at NASA began in 1988 as a group leader in the Photonic Processing group of the Intelligent Systems Technology Branch, located at the NASA Ames Research Center in Moffett Field, California. She worked as the technical lead for a group of eight people researching optical-image and data-processing techniques for space-based robotics. Six months later she moved on to become chief of the Intelligent Systems Technology Branch. Then in January 1990 she was chosen for the astronaut class, becoming an astronaut in July of 1991.

Her first flight began April 8, 1993, on the orbiter *Discovery*. She was mission specialist on the STS–56 Atmospheric Research flight, which was carrying the Atmospheric Laboratory for Applications and Science, known as Atlas–2. She was responsible for their primary payload, the Spartan 201 Satellite, and she operated the robotic arm to deploy and retrieve it. This satellite made forty-eight hours of independent solar observations to measure solar output and determine how the solar wind is produced. Ochoa was the lone female member of the five-person team that made 148 orbits of the earth.

Ochoa's technical assignments have also included flight-software verification in the Shuttle Avionics Integration Laboratory (SAIL), where she was crew representative for robotics development, testing and training, as well as crew representative for flight-software and computer-hardware development. Ochoa's next flight was on the STS–66 Atmospheric Laboratory for Applications and Science–3 (ATLAS–3) flight in November 1994. ATLAS–3 continued the Spacelab flight series to study the sun's energy during an eleven-year solar cycle; the primary purpose of this is to learn how changes in the irradiance of the sun affect the Earth's environment and climate. Ochoa was Payload Commander for that mission. Ochoa was mission specialist and flight engineer on the STS-96 flight in 1999. She is currently based at the Lyndon B. Johnson Space Center in Houston, Texas.

Ochoa is a member of the Optical Society of America and the American Institute of Aeronautics and Astronautics. She has received a number of awards from NASA including the NASA Group Achievement Award for Photonics Technology in 1991 and the NASA Space Flight Medal in 1993. In 1994, she received the Women in Science and Engineering (WISE) Engineering Achievement Award. She has also been recognized many times by the Hispanic community. Ochoa was the 1990 recipient of the National Hispanic Quincentennial Commission Pride Award. She was also given *Hispanic* magazine's 1991 Hispanic Achievement Science Award, and in 1993 she won the Congressional Hispanic Caucus Medallion of Excellence Role Model Award.

Ochoa is married to Coe Fulmer Miles, a computer research engineer. They have no children. Outside of her space research, Ochoa counts music and sports as hobbies. She is an accomplished classical flautist—in 1983 she was the Student Soloist Award Winner in the Stanford Symphony Orchestra. She also has her private pilot's license and in training for space missions flies "back seat" in T–38 aircraft.

SELECTED WRITINGS BY OCHOA:

Periodicals

Optical Engineering, Detection of Multiple Views of an Object in the Presence of Clutter, Volume 27, 1988, p. 266.

Optics Letters, Real-time Enhancement of Defects in a Periodic Mask Using Photorefractive BSO, Volume 10, 1985, p. 430.

Applied Optics, Real-time Intensity Inversion Using Two-Wave and Four-Wave Mixing in Photorefractive BGO, Volume 24, 1985, p. 1826.

FURTHER READING:

Periodicals

NASA Johnson Space Center, *Missions Highlights STS–56,* May 1993.

Other

NASA Johnson Space Center, *Biographical Data—Ellen Ochoa,* August 1993. http://www.jsc.hasa.gov/bios/htmlbios/ochoa.html

Ochoa, Ellen, *Interview with Marianne Fedunkiw,* conducted March 18, 1994.

Sketch by Marianne Fedunkiw

Severo Ochoa
1905–1993
Spanish biochemist

Spanish-born biochemist Severo Ochoa spent his life engaged in research into the workings of the human body. In the 1950s, he was one of the first scientists to synthesize the newly discovered ribonucleic acid (RNA) in the laboratory. This feat marked the first time that scientists managed to combine molecules together in a chain outside a living organism, knowledge that would later prove to be an essential step in enabling scientists to create life in a test tube. For this work, Ochoa received the Nobel Prize in 1959. In addition to his laboratory work, Ochoa, who was trained as a physician in Spain, taught biochemistry and pharmacology to many generations of New York University medical students.

Severo Ochoa was born on September 24, 1905, in Luarca, a small town in the north of Spain. Named after his father, a lawyer, Ochoa was the youngest son in the family. He lived in this mountain town until the age of seven, when his parents decided to move to Málaga, Spain. The move gave young Severo access to a private school education that prepared him for entrance into Málaga College, which is comparable to an American high school. By this time, Ochoa had decided on a career in the sciences; the only question in his mind was in which field he would specialize. Because Ochoa found mathematics at Málaga College very taxing, he decided against pursuing an engineering career. Instead, he chose biology. After Ochoa received his B.A. from Málaga in 1921, he spent a year taking the prerequisite courses for medical school—physics, chemistry, biology, and geology. In 1923 he matriculated at the University of Madrid's Medical School.

Acquires a Medical Education

At Madrid, Ochoa had dreams of studying under the Spanish neurohistologist Santiago Rámon y Cajal, but these were quickly dashed when he discovered that the 70-year-old histology professor retired from teaching, although he still ran a laboratory in Madrid. Ochoa hesitated in

Severo Ochoa

approaching Cajal even at the lab, however, because he thought the older man would be too busy to be bothered by an unimportant student. Nonetheless, by the end of his second year in medical school, Ochoa had confirmed his desire to do biological research and jumped at one of his professor's offers of a job in a nearby laboratory.

The Medical School itself housed no research facilities, but Ochoa's physiology teacher ran a small research laboratory under the aegis of the Council for Scientific Research a short distance away. Working with a classmate, Ochoa first mastered the relatively routine laboratory task of isolating creatinine—a white, crystalline compound—from urine. From there, he moved to the more demanding task of studying the function and metabolism of creatine, a nitrogenous substance, in muscle. The summer after his fourth year of medical school he spent in a Glasgow laboratory, continuing work on this problem. Ochoa received his medical degree in 1929.

In an attempt to further his scientific education, Ochoa applied for a postdoctoral fellowship under **Otto Meyerhof** at the Kaiser-Wilhelm Institute in a suburb of Berlin. Although the Council for Scientific Research had offered him a fellowship to pursue these studies, Ochoa turned down their offer of support because he could afford to pay his own way. He felt the money should be given to someone more needy to himself. Ochoa enjoyed his work under Meyerhof, remaining in Germany for a year.

On July 8, 1931, he married Carmen García Cobian, a daughter of a Spanish lawyer and businessman, and moved

with his newlywed wife to England, where he had a fellowship from the University of Madrid to study at London's National Institute for Medical Research. In England, Ochoa met Sir **Henry Hallett Dale**, who a few years later won the 1936 Nobel in medicine for his discovery of the chemical transmission of nerve impulses. During his first year at the Institute, Ochoa studied the enzyme glyoxalase, and the following year he started working directly under Dale, investigating how the adrenal glands affected the chemistry of muscular contraction. In 1933, he returned to his alma mater, the University of Madrid, where he was appointed a lecturer in physiology and biochemistry.

Spanish Civil War Forces Him to Flee Native Country

Within two years, Ochoa accepted a new position. One of the heads of the department of medicine was planning to start an Institute for Medical Research with sections on biochemistry, physiology, microbiology, and experimental medicine. The institute was partially supported by the University of Madrid, which offered it space in one its new medical school buildings, and partially supported by wealthy patrons, who planned to provide a substantial budget for equipment, salaries, and supplies. The director of the new institute offered the young Ochoa the directorship of the section on physiology, which he accepted, and provided him with a staff of three. However, a few months after Ochoa began work, civil war broke out in Spain. In order to continue his work, Ochoa decided to leave the country in September 1936. He and his wife immigrated to Germany, hardly a stable country in late 1936.

When Ochoa arrived, he found that his mentor Meyerhof, who was Jewish, was under considerable political and personal pressure. The German scientist had not allowed this to interfere with his work, though Ochoa did find to his surprise that the type of research Meyerhof conducted had changed dramatically in the six years since he had seen him last. As he wrote of the laboratory in a retrospective piece for the *Annual Review of Biochemistry:* "When I left it in 1930 it was basically a physiology laboratory; one could see muscles twitching everywhere. In 1936 it was a biochemistry laboratory. Glycolysis and fermentation in muscle or yeast extracts or partial reactions of these processes catalyzed by purified enzymes, were the main subjects of study." Meyerhof's change in research emphasis influenced Ochoa's own work, even though he studied in the laboratory for less than a year before Meyerhof fled to France.

Before Meyerhof left, however, he ensured that his protege was not stranded, arranging for Ochoa to receive a six-month fellowship at the Marine Biological Laboratory in Plymouth, England. Although this fellowship lasted only half a year, Ochoa enjoyed his time there, not the least because his wife Carmen started working with him in the laboratory. Their collaboration later led to the publication of a joint paper in *Nature*. At the end of six months, though,

Ochoa had to move on, and friends at the lab found him a post as a research assistant at Oxford University. Two years later, when England entered the war, Oxford's biochemistry department shifted all its efforts to war research in which Ochoa, an alien, could not take part. So in 1940 the Ochoas picked up stakes again, this time to cross the Atlantic to work in the laboratory of **Carl Ferdinand Cori** and **Gerty T. Cori** in St. Louis. Part of the Washington University School of Medicine, the Cori lab was renowned for its cutting edge research on enzymes and work with intermediary metabolism of carbohydrates. This work involved studying the biochemical reactions in which carbohydrates produce energy for cellular operations. Ochoa worked there for a year before New York University persuaded him to move east to take a job as a research associate in medicine at the Bellevue Psychiatric Hospital, where he would for the first time have graduate and postdoctoral students working beneath him.

Appointed Chair of NYU's Pharmacology Department

In 1945, Ochoa was promoted to assistant professor of biochemistry at the medical school. Two years later when the pharmacology chair retired, Ochoa was offered the opportunity to succeed him and, lured by the promise of new laboratory space, he accepted. He remained chairperson for nine years, taking a sabbatical in 1949 to serve as a visiting professor at the University of California. His administrative work did not deter him from pursuing his research interests in biochemistry, however. In the early 1950s, he isolated one of the chemical compounds necessary for photosynthesis to occur, triphosphopyridine nucleotide, known as TPN. Ochoa continued his interest in intermediary metabolism, expanding the work of **Hans Adolf Krebs,** who posited the idea of a cycle through which food is metabolized into adenosine triphosphate, or ATP, the molecule that provides energy to the cell. The Spanish scientist discovered that one molecule of glucose when burned with oxygen produced 36 ATP molecules. When the chairman of the biochemistry department resigned in 1954, Ochoa accepted this opportunity to return to the department full-time as chair and full professor.

Once more ensconced in biochemistry research, Ochoa turned his attentions to a new field: the rapidly growing area of deoxyribonucleic acid (DNA) research. Earlier in his career, enzymes had been the hot new molecules for biochemists to study; now, after the critical work of **James Watson** and **Francis Crick** in 1953, nucleic acids were fascinating scientists in the field. Ochoa was no exception. Drawing on his earlier work with enzymes, Ochoa began investigating which enzymes played roles in the creation of nucleic acids in the body. Although most enzymes assist in breaking down materials, Ochoa knew that he was looking for an enzyme that helped combine nucleotides into the long chains that were nucleic acids. Once he isolated these molecules, he hoped, he would be able to synthesize RNA and DNA in the lab. In 1955, he found a bacterial enzyme in sewage that appeared to play just such a role. When he added this enzyme to a solution of nucleotides, he discovered that the solution became viscous, like jelly, indicating that RNA had indeed formed in the dish. The following year, **Arthur Kornberg**, who had studied with Ochoa in 1946, applied these methods to synthesize DNA.

Wins Nobel for Synthesis of RNA

In 1959, five years after he assumed the directorship of the biochemistry department, Ochoa shared the Nobel Prize for physiology or medicine with Kornberg, for their work in discovering the enzymes that help produce nucleic acids. Ochoa was particularly delighted to share the prize with his old colleague; by this time, he was no stranger to academic plaudits. The holder of several honorary degrees from both American and foreign universities, including Oxford, Ochoa was also the recipient of the Carl Neuberg Medal in biochemistry in 1951 and the Charles Leopold Mayer Prize in 1955. Ochoa served as chairperson of NYU's biochemistry department for 20 years, until the summer of 1974, just before his seventieth birthday. When he retired from this post, he rejected the department's offer to make him an emeritus professor, preferring to remain on staff as a full professor. But even that could not keep Ochoa sufficiently occupied. In 1974, he joined the Roche Institute of Molecular Biology in New Jersey.

In 1985, he returned to his native Spain as a professor of biology at the University Autonoma in Madrid to continue his lifelong fascination with biochemical research. At the age of 75, Ochoa wrote a retrospective of his life, which he titled "Pursuit of a Hobby." In the introduction to this piece, he explained his choice of title. At a party given in the forties in honor of two Nobel laureate chemists Ochoa listed his hobby in the guest register as biochemistry, although he was at the time professor of pharmacology at New York University. Sir Henry Dale, one of the party's honorees, joked, "now that he is a pharmacologist, he has biochemistry as a hobby." Ochoa concluded this tale with the statement, "In my life biochemistry has been my only and real hobby." He died in Madrid on November 1, 1993.

SELECTED WRITINGS BY OCHOA:

Books

Pullman, Maynard, ed. *An Era in Biochemistry: A Festschrift for Sarah Ratner.* New York: New York Academy of Sciences, 1983.

Periodicals

"The Pursuit of a Hobby." *Annual Review of Biochemistry.* 48 (1980): 1-30.

FURTHER READING:

Books

Moritz, Charles, ed. *Current Biography.* New York: H. W. Wilson, 1962.

Wasson, Tyler, ed. *Nobel Prize Winners.* New York: H. W. Wilson, 1987.

Periodicals

"Biochemist Severo Ochoa Dies; Won Nobel Prize" (obituary). *Washington Post* (3 November 1993): D4.
"Severo Ochoa, Biochemist, A Nobel Winner, 88, Dies" (obituary). *New York Times* (3 November 1993): D25.

Sketch by Shari Rudavsky

Eugene Pleasants Odum
1913–
American ecologist and ornithologist

Ecologist and ornithologist Eugene Pleasants Odum is renowned for his views concerning the interrelationship between man and environment, having researched the ecology of birds, wetland ecology, landscape ecology, and vertebrate populations, as well as the general principles of ecology. The author of numerous works, including the widely used textbooks *Fundamentals of Ecology* and *Ecology,* Odum was the recipient of the 1987 Crafoord Prize from the Royal Swedish Academy of Science for his investigations into ecological issues (the Crafoord Prize is regularly awarded to scientists working in disciplines not addressed by the Nobel Prize). This honor was bestowed jointly upon Eugene P. Odum and his brother, **Howard T. Odum**, also an ecologist.

A native of Lake Sunapee, New Hampshire, Odum was born September 17, 1913. He received his undergraduate education at the University of North Carolina at Chapel Hill in 1934, then obtained his doctorate degree in ecology and ornithology from the University of Illinois in 1939. During his studies, Odum was assistant zoologist at the University of Georgia from 1934 to 1936. Upon completion of his doctoral studies, he was named resident biologist at the Edmund Niles Huyck Preserve in New York, a position he held from 1938 to 1940, and again during the summer of 1941.

Odum became an instructor at the University of Georgia in 1940 and was named assistant professor in 1942, then associate professor in 1945, receiving full professorship at the university in 1954. Odum also held two adjunct positions during his career: in the summers of 1942 and 1945, he carried out research at the Mountain Lake Biological Station at the University of Virginia, and from 1957 to 1961 he was an instructor of marine ecology during the summer training program of the Marine Biological Laboratory at Woods Hole, Massachusetts. Named Callaway Professor of Ecology at the University of Georgia in 1977, Odum also served as director of the university's Institute of Ecology from 1960 until 1984, when he became director emeritus.

Authors Primary Ecology Textbook

Odum wrote the influential textbook *Fundamentals of Ecology* in 1953, when ecological science was generally regarded as a subtopic within the field of biology. In the book, Odum describes the delicate balance of life among plants, herbivores, and carnivores, and their interaction with microorganisms. These complex relationships play a crucial role in the recycling of nutrients and the continuation of each species.

By 1989, when Odum authored *Ecology and Our Endangered Life-Support Systems,* ecology had not only emerged as its own field of study, but was evolving into an integrative discipline which encompasses human life and the environment in which we live. In this volume, which was written for general readers as well as students of science, Odum declares that we have reached a "turning point in history . . . when we cannot continue to postpone the environmental and human costs of development without incurring widespread damage to our global life-support systems." Reiterating basic ecological principles, Odum then demonstrates that each life form, rather than engaging in a merely competitive struggle, is connected with the others as part of a unified, dynamic process. Species of plants, herbivores, and carnivores maintain a beneficial interdependence upon one another. Odum also explains how human economic activities have disturbed both local and global ecosystems.

Discussing ecological and human systems, Odum notes that human communities are similar to organic communities, since each pass through phases from pioneering—when resources abound—to maturity, when resources are less plentiful and their consumption must be moderated. In *Ecology and Our Endangered Life-Support Systems* Odum describes biological organization within a hierarchical framework, applying the concept to such examples as endangered species, prescribed burning, population biology, and the Gaia hypothesis, which views the Earth as an organism able to regulate its own biosphere. Also included in the volume are sketches of prominent scientists in the field of ecology.

Odum has received numerous honors for his work in ecological science. In addition to the Crafoord Prize, he was awarded the prestigious Prix de l'Institute de la Vie by the French government in 1975. Odum was honored in 1956 with the Mercer Award of the Ecological Society of America and was presented with the Tyler Ecological Award by United States president Jimmy Carter in 1977. A member of the National Academy of Science, the American Academy of Arts and Sciences, and the American Society of Limnology and Oceanography, Odum also served as president of the Ecological Society of America from 1964 to 1965.

SELECTED WRITINGS BY ODUM:

Books

Fundamentals of Ecology, Saunders College, 1953.
Ecology, Holt, 1963.
Ecology: The Link Between the Natural and the Social Sciences, Saunders College, 1975.
Basic Ecology, Saunders College, 1983.
Ecology and Our Endangered Life-Support Systems, Sinauer Associates, 1989.

Periodicals

Science, Input Management of Production Systems, January 13, 1989, pp. 177–81.
BioScience, Great Ideas in Ecology for the 1990s, July/August, 1992, pp. 542–45.

Sketch by Karen . Withem

Howard T. Odum
1924–
American ecologist

Howard T. Odum is a systems ecologist whose research encompasses biological oceanography, ecological engineering, energy analysis, biogeochemistry, and tropical meteorology. He is most noted for his concept of the self-organizing system and its relation to energy production and consumption. He has done some of his most important work with his brother, **Eugene Pleasants Odum**, who is also an ecologist, and they have been the joint recipients of two prestigious international awards: the 1987 Crafoord Prize, which in the field of ecology is equivalent to the Nobel Prize, and the 1976 Prix de l'Institute de la Vie, a comparable award from the French government.

Howard Thomas Odum was born on September 1, 1924, in Durham, North Carolina. He served with the U.S. Air Force from 1944 to 1945 as a meteorologist in the Panama Canal Zone. He completed his undergraduate education at the University of North Carolina at Chapel Hill, graduating in 1947. He then entered the doctoral program in zoology at Yale University, receiving his Ph.D. in 1951.

From 1950 to 1954, Odum was assistant professor of biology at the University of Florida, followed by two years as assistant professor of zoology at Duke University, where he continued his research at Duke Marine Laboratory. In

1956, Odum accepted a post as director and resident scientist of the Institute of Marine Sciences, University of Texas at Port Arkansas, where he also served as editor of publications. Odum left this post in 1963 to study as chief scientist on the rain forest program at the Puerto Rico Nuclear Center at Rio Piedras, staying until 1966. In that year, he was named professor of ecology at the University of North Carolina, Chapel Hill, where he remained until he began his association with the University of Florida in 1970. He has served there as Graduate Research Professor of Environmental Engineering Sciences since 1970, and as director of the Center for Wetlands since 1972.

One of the primary fields of research for Odum is how what he calls self-organizing systems use energy. He has defined self-organizing systems to include an ecosystem in nature or an economy in human society, and in an article in *Science* he has observed that "ecosystem study has generated concepts that may apply to all complex systems when appropriately generalized." Odum has questioned the traditional model for these systems, the steady-state paradigm, which proposes that growth of production is followed by growth of consumption until both factors become level in a steady state. He has argued that the organization of these systems is more dynamic, and that the production and consumption of energy actually affects the development of the system itself. The systems tend toward the maximum utilization of energy as Odum has explained in *Science:* "During the trials and errors of self-organization, species and relations are being selectively reinforced as more energy becomes available to those designs that feed products back into increased production." Odum believes that the long-range performance of such systems are maximized by what he calls "pulsing": intense, short-term consumption that does not interfere with production, such as cattle being allowed to graze for a few weeks on grass that has been allowed to grow for months.

In his analysis of these self-organizing systems, including ecosystems, Odum has examined why energy is distributed in such a way that, as he claimed in *Science,* "hierarchies are universal in physical and biological systems." In examining the transformation of energy, he has distinguished between low-quality energy, which is generally present in large quantities, and high-quality energy, which is generally available in smaller amounts. Sunlight would be an example of a lower-quality energy; plant matter would be higher-quality energy. Odum has noted the difficulty of actually calculating the passage of energy through such a system, because it is constantly being transformed from one type to another. He has proposed the concept of "emergy" to clarify this problem, defining emergy in his *Science* article as "the energy of one type required in transformation to generate a flow or storage."

Odum's career in ecology has been recognized with the prestigious Crafoord Prize and Prix de l'Institute de la Vie. He also received the George Mercer Award from the Ecological Society of America in 1957. He was honored by the International Technical Writers Association, which gave him their Award of Distinction in 1971. In 1973, he received a million-dollar grant jointly awarded by the Rockefeller Foundation and the National Science Foundation to study the feasibility of putting treated sewage in wetlands. Odum is a member of the American Society of Limnology and Oceanography, the American Meteorological Society, the Ecological Society of America, and the Geochemical Society. He is a fellow of the American Association for the Advancement of Science, and in 1979 he was appointed Erskine Fellow by the University of Canterbury in New Zealand to help that nation use its natural and human resources to produce energy.

SELECTED WRITINGS BY ODUM:

Books

Energy: Basis for Man and Nature, McGraw-Hill, 1976.
Systems Ecology, Wiley, 1983.
Cypress Swamps, University Presses of Florida, 1984.

Periodicals

Science, Self-Organization, Transformity, and Information, November 25, 1988, pp. 1132–1139.

Sketch by Karen Withem

Han Oeschger

Hans Oeschger
1927–1998
Swiss environmental physicist and climatologist

The Swiss environmental physicist and climatologist Hans Oeschger was born on April 2, 1927 in Ottenbach, Switzerland. He earned a doctor of science degree from the University of Bern in 1955, and remained there for the rest of his career as a researcher and professor, becoming professor emeritus in 1992. Oeschger died on December 25, 1998 following a long illness.

Oeschger was a pioneer in the measurement of the composition of gases such as methane and carbon dioxide in polar ice, and in the use of these measurements to track past changes in global temperature. Through his development of methods for extracting data from the sequential layers of polar ice, he demonstrated the value of the geochemical data that resides in the ice archive.

Trained as a nuclear physicist at ETH Zurich, Oeschger went on to earn his doctorate from the University of Bern under the Professor F. G. Houtermans. In 1955 he built a counter to measure background radioactivity. This counter proved key to making it possible to apply the carbon-14

dating method to geophysical problems. Houtermans and Oeschger established the first carbon-14-dating laboratory in Switzerland, and the laboratory achieved international distinction under their stewardship.

Oeschger was the first scientist to date the Pacific deep water. Oeschger's counter allowed his team to measure the activity of many naturally occurring radioisotopes, and to use the results to quantify exchange processes that have taken place on the planet.

In 1962, Oeschger began studying the tritium content of old snow (also known as firn) and ice, and using the environmental data obtained for archival purposes. Between 1964 and 1992, he made many trips to Greenland and Antarctica to study polar ice cores. The analytical methods and drilling techniques adopted by Oeschger and his collaborators allowed them to reconstruct the climate changes on Earth over the past 150,000 years.

Oeschger's studies of ice cores led to many unprecedented discoveries. His team made the first measurements of the glacial-interglacial change of atmospheric carbon dioxide. In 1979, they reported that the atmospheric concentration of carbon dioxide during the glacial period was almost 50% lower than it is today. By analyzing the changes in carbon dioxide concentration over the last 1,000 years, they were also able to show that the rapid increase over the last 200 years has been a direct effect of the burning of fossil fuels.

Oeschger and his colleagues also documented a series of abrupt climate changes in Greenland ice cores. Stable isotope measurements on lake carbonates in Switzerland confirmed that these climate changes had occurred over the entire hemisphere. Twenty-four of these events were documented as having taken place during the last glacial period, and these are now known as Dansgaard-Oeschger events. (Glaciologist Willi Dansgaard of the University of Copenhagen was, like Oeschger, a pioneer in developing techniques for dating ice, measuring temperature, and analyzing the chemical composition of the ice and trapped air bubbles.)

Oeschger was particularly concerned about the possibility that the steady increase in atmospheric carbon dioxide might lead to an increased greenhouse effect. In addition to public lectures about this problem, he contributed to the First Assessment Report of the Intergovernmental Panel on Climate Change (IPCC) as lead author. This report led to the Earth Summit in Rio de Janeiro in 1992, and to subsequent conferences.

As early as 1984, Oeschger recognized the role that ocean circulation plays in abrupt climate changes. Under the influence of small perturbations, the ocean circulation can switch from one mode of operation to another. Oeschger was also one of the first to point out that the increase of carbon dioxide due to human factors could produce such a perturbation, and contribute to changes in the ocean circulation. Although his early warnings were met with skepticism, recent studies have tended to support his ideas about global warming. Most scientists today believe that changes in the levels of atmospheric gases related to ocean circulation have contributed to the creation of the great glacial ice caps.

Among the awards that Oeschger received during his career were the Harold Urey Medal from the European Association of Geochemistry (1987); Seligman Crystal from the International Glaciological Society (1991); Marcel-Benoist Prize (1991); Tyler Prize for Environmental Achievement (1996); and the Revelle Medal of the American Geophysical Union (1997).

Oeschger was a member of the Leopoldina and the Academia Europaea, the Swiss Academy of the Technical Sciences, and the Swiss Academy of Natural Sciences. He was also a foreign member of the U.S. National Academy of Sciences. He founded the Division of Climate and Environmental Physics at the Physics Institute of the University of Bern in 1963 and remained its director until his retirement in 1992.

Sketch by Randall Frost

Ida H. Ogilvie
1874–1963
American geologist

Ida H. Ogilvie was instrumental in making careers in geology accessible to women. The founder and first chair of Barnard College's geology department, she was also a renowned field researcher, conducting explorations in Maine, New Mexico, Mexico, California, and her home state of New York. Her areas of specialization included glacial geography and petrology.

Born on February 12, 1874, in New York City, Ida Helen Ogilvie was the daughter of Clinton Ogilvie, who traced his ancestry to the Earl of Airlie in Scotland, and of Helen Slade Ogilvie, a Mayflower descendant who was related to many of the colonial founders of America. The wealthy family expected their daughter to follow the usual debutante-wife-matron progression of the Gilded Age. But Ogilvie had different plans. She received her early education at home, being taught to speak French before English and learning how to draw expertly, before going to the Brearley School. She also attended schools in Europe before entering Bryn Mawr, and it was at that women's college that she found an abiding interest in geology, studying under Florence Bascom who had just founded Bryn Mawr's program in geology. She earned an A.B. from Bryn Mawr in 1900 and then studied at the University of Chicago for two years, where she began to focus on both petrology, or the origin of rocks, and glacial geology. She published her first paper in petrology in 1902 and then went to Columbia University, where she earned her doctorate in 1903.

Founds the Geology Department at Barnard

That same year she became the first lecturer in geology at Columbia University's Barnard College. She did not want to give up teaching graduate courses at Columbia, however, so she focused on the one field in geology where a lecturer was needed, glacial geology, even though her real love was petrology. From 1903 until her retirement in 1941, Ogilvie was the chair of Barnard's geology department, responsible not only for administration, but also for instruction and research. She was honored for her work in geology by being the second woman elected to the Geological Society of America.

Additionally, she took on the responsibilities of a farm she purchased at Bedford, New York, where she raised registered Jersey cattle, as well as horses, dogs, and ponies. During World War I she turned this into a model farm, recruiting young women from across the United States into agriculture during the manpower shortage created by the hostilities. After the war, some of her recruits stayed on, and Ogilvie bought a larger farm of 660 acres in Germantown,

New York, the Hermitage, where she continued to breed her prize-winning herd.

With all of these responsibilities, Ogilvie was still able, until 1920, to do distinguished research, investigating glaciation in Canada, conducting field mapping in Maine and New York, and studying volcanic activities. Thereafter, she concentrated on instruction, becoming a noted lecturer who fretted over each presentation and who encouraged and nurtured her students. She also helped endow scholarships for young women in the sciences at Barnard, Columbia, and Bryn Mawr. After retiring from teaching in 1941, she devoted herself full time to her farm and to her hobby of knitting afghans in geologic designs. She died at the age of eighty-nine on October 13, 1963, at her farm in Germantown, having, as Elizabeth Wood reported in the *Bulletin of the Geological Society of America,* "lived a long and mostly happy life, doing the things she wanted to do."

SELECTED WRITINGS BY OGILVIE:

Periodicals

Journal of Geology, Glacial Phenomena in the Adirondacks and Champlain Valley, Volume 10, 1902, pp. 397–412.

Journal of Geology, An Analcite-Bearing Camptonite from New Mexico, Volume 10, 1902, pp. 500–507.

Journal of Geology, Geological Notes on the Vicinity of Banff, Alberta, Volume 12, 1904, pp. 408–414.

Journal of Geology, The Effect of Superglacial Debris on the Advance and Retreat of Some Canadian Glaciers, Volume 12, 1904, pp. 722–743.

New York State Museum Bulletin, Geology of the Paradox Lake Quadrangle, N.Y., number 96, 1905, pp. 461–509.

American Geologist, The High-Altitude Conoplain; A Topographic Form Illustrated in the Ortiz Mountains, Volume 36, 1905, pp. 27–34.

New York Academy of Sciences Annals, A Contribution to the Geology of Southern Maine, Volume 17, 1907, pp. 519–558.

Journal of Geology, Some Igneous Rocks from the Ortiz Mountains, New Mexico, Volume 16, 1908, pp. 230–238.

Columbia University Quarterly, The Interrelation of the Sciences in College Courses, Volume 17, number 3, 1915, pp. 241–252.

New York Academy of Sciences Annals, Field Observations on the Iowan Problem, Volume 26, 1916, pp. 432–433.

FURTHER READING:

Books

Arnold, Lois Barber, *Four Lives in Science,* Schocken Books, 1984, pp. 117-119.

Periodicals

Arnold, Lois Barber, *New York Times,* Dr. Ida Ogilvie of Barnard Dies; First Geology Chairman Was 89, October 15, 1963, p. 39.

Arnold, Lois Barber, *New York Times,* Geology Attracts Feminine Workers, November 27, 1938, p. 4.

Arnold, Lois Barber, *New York Times,* 38-Year Career at Barnard Ends, May 26, 1941, p. 17.

Wood, Elizabeth A., *Bulletin of the Geological Society of America,* Memorial to Ida Helen Ogilvie, February, 1964, pp. 35–39.

Sketch by J. Sydney Jones

George A. Olah
1927–
Hungarian-born American chemist

The recipient of the 1994 Nobel Prize for Chemistry, Olah is primarily known for his crucial work on reactive intermediates in hydrocarbons. The complex chemistry of hydrocarbons, compounds of carbon and hydrogen, includes the study of numerous reactions, which are sometimes extremely difficult to record. Reactive intermediates, or substances acting as the intermediate steps of a chemical reaction mechanism, are so short-lived and elusive that chemists used to regard them as purely hypothetical entities.

Before there was empirical evidence for the existence of reaction intermediates, chemists believed that carbon ions, or positively charged atoms, played an intermediary role in hydrocarbon reactions; the action of these intermediaries, however, was imagined to be so rapid, maybe measurable in millionths of a second, that scientists only postulated their existence. Olah, however, did not doubt the existence of reactive intermediates were real, deciding, in fact, to empirically prove their existence. In order to identify a reactive intermediate, Olah needed a substance that would somehow arrest the reaction mechanism, thus enabling the observer to capture processes which cannot be seen under normal circumstances. The substances that worked, he found, were superacids (a superacid is an extremely powerful acid—for example, more than a trillions times the strength of sulfuric acid). Olah subsequently created a superacid which could extract individual atoms from hydrocarbon compounds. What remained when a hydrocarbon compound was exposed to a superacid, Olah noticed, was an alkyl (an alkyl is a univalent group created when a hydrogen atom is removed from an open-ended hydrocarbon compound) carbon ion, which, although unstable, was

George A. Olah

measurable. The carbon ion, or *cation*, was the reaction intermediary.

Born in Budapest, Hungary, on May 22, 1927, the son of Julius Olah and Magda Krasznai, Olah received his Ph.D. from the Technical University of Budapest in 1949. That year, he married Judith Lengyel; they have two sons. Olah taught at the Technical University from 1949 to 1954, subsequently joining the Hungarian Academy of Sciences, where he served as associate director of the Central Chemical Research Institute from 1954 to 1956. When the Soviet Union crushed the Hungarian revolt in 1956, Olah and his family fled to the West. In 1957, he joined Dow Chemical in Sarnia, Ontario, where he worked as a research scientist from 1957 to 1965. From 1965 to 1977, he was professor of chemistry at Case Western University. Since 1977, he has worked as professor of chemistry and director of the Hydrocarbon Research Institute at the University of Southern California.

Discovery Finds Applications in Industry

Following his discovery, in 1962, that superacids could neutralize the extreme reactivity of cations, Olah has worked on developing new superacids to be used in both industry and fundamental research. As Olah's work has opened vast areas of research, many younger chemists have contributed to the search for new superacids. Significantly, the study of intermediate reactants has also resulted in numerous industrial applications, particularly in fuel synthesis. For example, the synthesis of high-octane gasoline is

one of the notable industrial uses of Olah's original research. In essence, Olah has created the scientific instruments for creating cleaner and more efficient fuels.

Olah's awards include the 1966 Baekeland Award, the 1989 American Chemical Society Award, the 1993 Pioneer of Chemistry Award given by the American Institute of Chemists, and the Mendeleev Medal, which he received from the Russian Academy of Sciences in 1992.

SELECTED WRITINGS BY OLAH:

Books

Superacids. New York: Wiley, 1985.
Cage Hydrocarbons. New York: Wiley, 1990.
Chemistry of Energetic Materials. San Diego: Academic Press, 1991.
Synthetic Fluorine Chemistry. New York: Wiley, 1992.
Hydrocarbon Chemistry. New York: Wiley, 1995.
Onium Ions. New York: Wiley, 1998.

FURTHER READING:

Periodicals

Baum, Rudy. "George Olah Reflects on Chemical Research." *Chemical and Engineering News* 73, no. 9 (27 February 1995):44-48.
Brown, David. "Chemical 'Intermediates' Work Honored." *Washington Post* (13 October 1994): A3.
Flam, Faye. "Snaring an Elusive Quarry–and a Prize." *Science* 226, no. 5184 (21 October 1994): 369-70.
Lipkin, Richard. "Hydrocarbon Research Garners Nobel Prize." *Science News* 146, no. 17 (22 October 1994): 261.

Sketch by Zoran Minderovic

Kenneth Olden
1938–
American cellular biologist and biochemist

Kenneth Olden has been investigating the possible links between the properties of cell-surface molecules and cancer for more than two decades. In 1991 he was named director of the National Institute of Environmental Health Sciences and the National Toxicology Program, the first African American to become director of one of the National Institutes of Health.

Olden was born in Parrottsville, Tennessee, on July 22, 1938, the son of Mack and Augusta Christmas Olden. In 1960, he received a bachelor's degree in biology from Knoxville College. He was awarded a master of science in genetics from the University of Michigan in 1964 and a doctorate in biology and biochemistry from Temple University in 1970. During the summers of 1964 and 1965, Olden worked in New York City at two academic institutions at the same time, a pattern that he has followed throughout much of his career. He was a research assistant at Columbia University's Department of Biological Chemistry and a biology instructor at the Fashion Institute of Technology, part of the State University of New York.

In September 1970, Olden went to Harvard University Medical School as a research fellow and a physiology instructor. In 1973, the fellowship ended and he continued as a physiology instructor through 1974. That year, Olden joined the Laboratory of Molecular Biology, Division of Cancer Biology and Diagnosis of the National Cancer Institute at the National Institutes of Health in Bethesda, Maryland, as a senior staff fellow. He was promoted to expert in biochemistry in 1977 and in 1978 became a research biologist in the same division. During this time Olden published two articles on cell biology which in 1980 were listed among the 100 most cited papers of 1978 and 1979: "The Role of Carbohydrates in Protein Secretion and Turnover," and "Fibronectin Adhesion Glycoprotein of Cell Surface and Blood."

Olden is now considered a leading authority on the structure and function of the extracellular matrix glycoprotein fibronectin, one of a family of proteins involved in interactions between cells and the supporting structure around cells. The interactions are important to the spread of cancer. Olden was first to demonstrate that sugar residues of glycoproteins are not required for the export or secretion of glycoproteins. He was also the first to show that metastasis of malignant cells in particular organs could be prevented by blocking the interaction between fibronectin and the glycoprotein receptor around the cell.

In 1979, Olden left NIH to become associate professor of oncology and associate director for research at the Howard University Cancer Center in Washington, D.C. In 1982 he became its deputy director and in 1984 director of research; in that year he was also named professor and in 1985 chairman of the oncology department. In 1991, Olden became director of the National Institute of Environmental Health Sciences and the National Toxicology Program. He was the first African American to become director of any of the seventeen National Institutes in the organization's 100 year history. During his tenure at NIH, Olden has devoted particular attention to the anticancer drug Swainsonine. In 1991, the drug was approved by the Treatment Division of the National Cancer Institute to be on its list of drugs for high-priority development for possible clinical trials on humans.

Olden was named by President George Bush to the National Cancer Advisory Board in January 1991 but resigned six months later due to his appointment to NIH causing a conflict of interest. He has participated widely as an invited speaker at scientific symposia and seminars and as a reviewer for programs in his field; he has authored and coauthored more than 108 publications. Olden is a member of the American Society of Cell Biology; the American Society of Biological Chemistry; the American Association of Cancer Research, for which he is on the board of directors; the Society for Biological Response Modifiers; the North Carolina Institute of Medicine; and the International Society for the Study of Comparative Oncology.

Olden lives in Durham, North Carolina, and is married to the former Sandra L. White. The couple has four children. Olden likes to play tennis, hike, bicycle, and cook.

SELECTED WRITINGS BY OLDEN:

Periodicals

Nature, Fibronectin Adhesive Glycoprotein of Cell Surface and Blood, Volume 275, 1978, pp. 179–184.

Cell, Role of Carbohydrates in Protein Secretion and Turnover: Effects of Tunicamycin on the Major Cell Surface Glycoprotein of Chick Embryo Fibroblasts, Volume 13, 1978, pp. 461–473.

Environmental Health Perspectives, Opportunities in Environmental Health Science Research, April 22, 1993, pp. 6–7.

Anticancer Research, A Preliminary Pharmacokinetic Evaluation of the Antimetastatic Immunomodulator Swainsonine; Clinical Implications, July-August 1993, pp. 841–844.

FURTHER READING:

Periodicals

Science, Ken Olden Heals NIEHS's Split Brain, March 5, 1993, pp. 1398–9.

Other

Roberts, John, *Interview with Margo Nash,* conducted March 11, 1994.

Sketch by Margo Nash

Richard Dixon Oldham
1858–1936
Irish geologist and seismologist

Richard Dixon Oldham was a geologist whose most important contributions were to the field of seismology, in the era after useful seismographs had been developed and accurate records of earthquakes had begun to be kept. He became famous for his study of the great earthquake of June 12, 1897, in Assam in northeast India; approaching the evidence with unprecedented rigor, he made several discoveries which became the foundation of modern seismology, including the identification of three types of seismic waves. Later in his career, Oldham used his knowledge of these waves and some of their irregularities to establish that the earth has a central core.

Oldham was born in Dublin, Ireland, on July 31, 1858. He was the third son of noted geologist Thomas Oldham, a professor of geology at Trinity College, Dublin, and director of the geological surveys that were being done of Ireland and India. The younger Oldham was educated in England, first at Rugby School and then at the Royal School of Mines; he joined the staff at the Geological Survey of India in 1879. His father had died in 1878, leaving behind an exhaustive study he had begun of an 1869 earthquake in Cachar, India; one of Oldham's first contributions to the group was to finish this study.

Oldham eventually occupied his father's position as superintendent of the Geological Survey of India, and among his primary concerns were investigating the earthquakes and hot springs of India, and researching the structure of the Himalaya Mountains and the plain of the Ganges River. Members of the group made geodetic observations of these various conditions and locations—that is, by measurements and mathematical calculations they determined both their proportions and their exact location on the surface of the earth. Oldham's analyses of these observations provided the material for about forty publications he wrote while he held this position.

Conducts Landmark Earthquake Study

Oldham directed and carried out most of the investigation of the great Assam earthquake of June 12, 1897. This remains one of the largest earthquakes known; though the seismographic records are not entirely compatible with modern measurements, its force has been estimated at 8.7 on the Richter scale. It destroyed an area of more than 9,000 square miles. In his search for a greater understanding of the activity of the earthquake and the physical properties of the earth itself, Oldham reviewed a wide body of evidence. He spoke with people who had seen stones bouncing "like peas on a drumhead," and he photographed boulders that had been thrown from the ground without touching the edges of

the dirt that had lain around them. He made careful examinations of cracks in buildings and a pair of damaged tombs, as well as a hill he had been told was "rent from top to bottom." As **Charles F. Richter** writes in *Elementary Seismology:* "His observations were minutely careful and his reasoning ingenious."

Oldham made a number of discoveries about the geology of India, including the location of two major faults. He also made a number of discoveries that contributed to the knowledge of geology in general. By citing evidence of fractures in the earth that were not accompanied by rock displacement, he was able to argue that the surface of the earth was more elastic than had previously been recognized. This theory was supported by other evidence; he was able to identify places where increases in the speed at which the ground was moving during the earthquake had not increased the height at which it was moving. A further consequence of his work on the elasticity of the earth was his discovery of three types of seismic waves. First predicted in theory by the mathematician Siméon Poisson, Oldham established the existence of primary or longitudinal waves, secondary or transverse waves, and surface waves. Oldham's conclusions set precedents for the field of seismology, establishing a new relationship between the changes in the earth's surface and the study of seismic waves.

Oldham left India in 1903 because of health problems. He returned to England, where he continued his research on the Isle of Wight with the distinguished seismologist John Milne. Through analysis of Milne's research on large earthquakes, Oldham was able to establish in 1906 that the earth has a central core. Earlier geologists and seismologists had suggested its existence, but Oldham's work provided the first indisputable confirmation, and his conclusions were based on his discovery of primary and secondary waves.

Oldham observed that when an earthquake occurred on one side of the earth, the primary waves it created could be recorded by a seismograph on the other side of the earth. But he also observed that the arrival of these waves was delayed. It had already been established that the earth had a crust and a mantle, but the mantle was not elastic enough to delay the primary waves in this fashion. Thus Oldham was able to hypothesize the existence of core matter within the earth which was less dense and rigid than the rocks of the mantle and so slowed the transmission of the waves. Later analyses, using Oldham's findings about the arrival and distortion of primary and secondary waves, provided significant insight for scientists into the structure of the earth. By 1914, geologists had prepared a comprehensive set of tables, including tables for a number of phases corresponding to waves that penetrate into the central core, and it was estimated that the depth of the boundary of this core was 2900 kilometers below the earth's outer surface.

In 1903, Oldham retired and became the director of the Indian Museum in Calcutta. He was awarded the Lyell Medal of the Geological Society of London in 1908 and was elected to the Royal Society in 1911. He continued to make contributions to the fields of geology and seismology through the late 1920s. He died in Llandrindod Wells, Wales, on July 15, 1936.

SELECTED WRITINGS BY OLDHAM:

Periodicals

Memoirs of the Geological Survey of India, Report on the Great Earthquake of 12th June 1897, Volume 29, 1899, pp. i-xxx.

Philosophical Transactions of the Royal Society, On the Propagation of Earthquake Motion to Great Distances, 1900, pp. 135–174.

Quarterly Journal, The Earthquake of 7th August, 1895, in Northern Italy, Volume 79, 1923, pp. 231–236.

Quarterly Journal, The Depth of the Origin of Earthquakes, Volume 82, 1926, pp. 67–92.

FURTHER READING:

Books

Bullen, K. E., *An Introduction to the Theory of Seismology,* Cambridge University Press, 1947, pp. 2, 168, 206.

Richter, Charles F., *Elementary Seismology,* W. H. Freeman, 1958, pp. 49–55.

Sketch by Kelly Otter Cooper

Olga Oleinik
1925–
Russian mathematical physicist

Olga Oleinik is a prolific writer and educator with eight books and nearly 60 graduate students to her credit. She teaches mainly in Russia at Moscow State University, but she also travels to colloquia in America, and has held classes as a visiting scholar at such institutions as the University of South Carolina. Oleinik has also contributed more than 300 papers to a variety of professional journals and is a member of the Russian Academy of Sciences. She has made important findings in the area of algebraic geometry in projective space.

Olga Arsenievna Oleinik was born in Kiev, Ukraine on July 2, 1925. Her parents, Arseniy Ivanovich and Anna Petrovna lived in an area known as Matusov. Olga's early years spanned times of great upheaval and difficulty in the Soviet Union, especially World War II. She did, however,

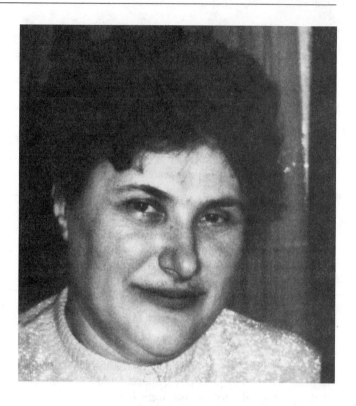

Olga Arsenievna Oleinik

earn a degree from Moscow State in 1947. She received her doctorate in 1954, and shortly thereafter began the professorship in mathematics at Moscow State University that she holds today.

In 1972 Oleinik was promoted to the head chair of differential equations in her department. Her specialty is partial differential equations. Although her classes can carry such intimidating titles as "Asymptotic Properties of Solutions of Nonlinear Parabolic and Elliptic Equations and Systems," she is generous with her ideas and more than willing to give her students the right start, according to one former student. Igor Oleinik remembers how much time his "PDE" professor was willing to give to her students despite her busy schedule. Because they were fellow Ukrainians, and Oleinik is as common a name there as Smith is in America, Igor had to put up with a little teasing from fellow class members who joked that he was really Olga Oleinik's grandson.

Oleinik's studies in mathematics cover broad areas of physics, such as the interactivity of liquids or gases in porous substances, the thermodynamics of bodies in different phases, as well as problems in elasticity and homogenization.

Oleinik is married and has one son, Dmitri. She holds an honorary doctorate from Rome University, granted in 1981, and is also an honorary member of the Royal Society of Edinburgh. She is a member of various societies throughout Europe. Her awards include the medal of the College de France and a "first degree" medal from Prague's

Charles University, as well as various prizes from Russian institutions.

SELECTED WRITINGS BY OLEINIK:

Books

Homogenization of Differential Operators and Integral Functionals, 1994.
Mathematical Problems in Elasticity and Homogenization, 1992.
Some Asymptotic Problems of the Theory of Partial Differential Equations, 1995.

FURTHER READING:

Books

Who's Who in the World, 1993–1994. Eleventh edition. New Providence, NJ: Marquis, 1992.

Other

Oleinik, Igor, in an electronic mail interview with Jennifer Kramer, conducted July 12, 1997.
"Olga Oleinik." *The Emmy Noether Lectures of the American Association for Women in Mathematics. Profiles of Women in Mathematics.* http://www.math.neu.edu/awm/noetherbrochure/Oleinik96.htm

Sketch by Jennifer Kramer

Miguel A. Ondetti
1930–
Argentine Chemist

The Argentine chemist Miguel A. Ondetti was born on May 14, 1930 in Buenos Aires. Ondetti attended a technical high school in Argentina, where he studied bookkeeping. Later as a chemistry student at the University of Buenos Aires, he worked part time as a bookkeeper for Argentina's Department of Energy. He obtained an undergraduate degree in chemistry from the University of Buenos Aires in 1955.

After earning his undergraduate degree, Ondetti accepted a one-year grant to conduct scientific research at the Squibb Institute for Medical Research in Argentina. While at the Institute, he worked on his doctoral thesis, which dealt with carbohydrates. At the end of that year, Squibb offered him a full-time position.

Wanting to broaden his experience, Ondetti turned the offer from Squibb down and instead took a position with another chemical company. That job lasted only one week, however, so Ondetti resumed his bookkeeping work at the Department of Energy. As it turned out, Squibb soon had another opening, and Ondetti rejoined Squibb in 1957. In the same year, he received his Ph.D. in Organic Chemistry from the School of Sciences at the University of Buenos Aires in 1957.

For the next three years (1957 to 1960), Ondetti divided his time between teaching (at the Catholic Institute for Teachers and the University of Buenos Aries), and research on the isolation of alkaloids as a senior research chemist at Squibb. In 1960, Ondetti found himself in the position of having to choose between accepting a scholarship from the British Council that would allow him to study in Manchester, England, and an opportunity to work at Squibb's New Brunswick, New Jersey facility. He opted to move to the United States and work for Squibb.

In New Jersey, Ondetti joined the Squibb's new peptide chemistry research group as a senior research chemist. Squibb was at that time trying to develop peptide-based drugs. Peptides were of particular interest to chemists because their many structures suggested that they might be amenable to fine tuning, possibly leading to the development of drugs with few side effects. Ondetti's first assignment was to synthesize the polypetide bradykinin. In the mid-1960s, he took up research on insulin.

The major drawback with peptide-based drugs was that they had to be administered by injection. As a result, by the early 1970s, many pharmaceutical companies, including Squibb, had decided to abandon peptide-based drug research. So Ondetti instead began looking at gastrointestinal hormones, and the synthesis of secretin, a peptide involved in the stimulation of pancreatic juice. Because secretin contains 27 amino acids, its synthesis required a collaborative effort. Although Ondetti and his collaborator Emily Sabo accomplished the synthesis, clinical trials did not justify further research on the hormone. So Ondetti next turned to sincalide, which is involved in gallbladder contraction. Although Ondetti's group realized that sincalide would have diagnostic applications, i.e., in the diagnosis of gallstones, sincalide also turned out to be useful as a therapeutic agent.

In 1973, Ondetti became the section head for research on peptides, steroids, and antibiotics. About this time, Ondetti's research became focused on the antihypertensive agent captopril, which was to be the first member of a new class of drugs known as angiotensin-converting-enzyme (ACE) inhibitors. Initially approved by the FDA for restricted use in 1982, captopril was eventually approved without restriction for the treatment of hypertension and heart failure two-and-a-half years later. In 1991, captopril was also shown to improve long-term survival after heart attacks and to reduce the chances of another heart attack.

When Ondetti retired from Squibb in 1991, he had risen to the position of Senior Vice-President of Cardiovascular and Metabolic Diseases at the Bristol-Myers Squibb Pharmaceutical Research Institute in New Jersey. That same year he was awarded the Perkin Medal for his achievements in applied chemistry, and for his role in the development of captopril. In 1999, Ondetti won the Albert Lasker Clinical Medical Research Award for having developed a new approach to drug design based on protein structure, as well as ways to use it to create, powerful oral agents (ACE inhibitors) that can be used to treat high blood pressure, heart failure, and diabetic kidney disease.

During his career, Ondetti held memberships in numerous professional societies, including American Chemical Society; American Heart Association Council on High Blood Pressure; American Society for Biological Chemists; American Society of Hypertension; and the Pharmaceutical Manufacturers Association.

Awards received by Ondetti include the Alfred Burger Award in Medicinal Chemistry, awarded by the American Chemical Society (1981); Thomas Alva Edison Patent Award, awarded by the Research and Development Council of New Jersey (1983); Ciba Award for Hypertension Research, awarded by the Council on High Blood Pressure Research-American Heart Association (1983); Chairman's Edward Robinson Squibb Award. awarded by the Board of Directors, E. R. Squibb & Sons, Incorporated (1986); Pharmaceutical Manufacturers Association and National Health Council Award for contributions to medical science (1988); Inventor of the Year Award, presented by the New Jersey Inventors Congress (1988); Perkin Medal, for outstanding work in applied chemistry awarded by the American Section, Society of Chemical Industry (1991); Warren Alpert Foundation Prize, for outstanding achievement in biomedical research, presented by Harvard Medical School (1991); American Chemical Society Award for Creative Invention (1992); and the first Herman Bloch award for scientific excellence in industry (1992).

Ondetti is the author or co-author of 100 scientific publications, including a book entitled *Peptide Synthesis* (John Wiley and Sons, New York, New York, 1966; Second Edition, 1976) that he co-authored with M. Bodanszky.

Sketch by Randall Frost

Lars Onsager
1903–1976
American chemist

Born in Norway, Lars Onsager received his early education there before coming to the United States in 1928 to do graduate work at Yale University. After receiving his Ph.D. in theoretical chemistry he stayed on at

Lars Onsager

Yale and ultimately spent nearly all of his academic career at that institution. Onsager's first important contribution to chemical theory came in 1926 when he showed how improvements could be made in the Debye-Hückel theory of electrolytic dissociation. His later (and probably more significant) work involved non-reversible systems—systems in which differences in pressure, temperature, or some other factor are an important consideration. For his contributions in this field, Onsager received a number of important awards including the Rumford Medal of the American Academy of Arts and Sciences, the Lorentz Medal of the Royal Netherlands Academy of Sciences, and the 1968 Nobel Prize in Chemistry.

Lars Onsager was born in Oslo (then known as Christiania), Norway, on November 27, 1903. His parents were Erling Onsager, a barrister before the Norwegian Supreme Court, and Ingrid Kirkeby Onsager. Onsager's early education was somewhat unorthodox as he was taught by private tutors, by his own mother, and at a somewhat unsatisfactory rural private school. Eventually he entered the Frogner School in Oslo and did so well that he skipped a grade and graduated a year early. Overall, his early schooling provided him with a broad liberal education in philosophy, literature, and the arts. He is said to have become particularly fond of Norwegian epics and continued to read and recite them to friends and family throughout his life.

In 1920, Onsager entered the Norges Tekniski Høgskole in Trondheim where he planned to major in chemical engineering. The fact that he enrolled in a technical high school suggests that he was originally interested in practical rather than theoretical studies. Onsager had not pursued his schooling very long, however, before it became apparent that he wanted to go beyond the everyday applications of science to the theoretical background on which those applications are based. Even as a freshman in high school, he told of making a careful study of the chemical journals, in order to gain background knowledge of chemical theory.

Refines Arrhenius and Debye-Hückel Theories

One of the topics that caught his attention concerned the chemistry of solutions. In 1884, **Svante Arrhenius** had proposed a theory of ionic dissociation that explained a number of observations about the conductivity of solutions and, eventually, a number of other solution phenomena. Over the next half century, chemists worked on refining and extending the Arrhenius theory.

The next great step forward in that search occurred in 1923, when Onsager was still a student at the Tekniski Høgskole. The Dutch chemist **Peter Debye** and the German chemist Erich Hückel, working at Zurich's Eidgenössische Technische Hochschule, had proposed a revision of the Arrhenius theory that explained some problems not yet resolved—primarily, whether ionic compounds are or are not completely dissociated ("ionized") in solution. After much experimentation, Arrhenius had observed that dissociation was not complete in all instances.

Debye and Hückel realized that ionic compounds, by their very nature, already existed in the ionic state *before* they ever enter a solution. They explained the apparent incomplete level of dissociation on the basis of the interactions among ions of opposite charges and water molecules in a solution. The Debye-Hückel mathematical formulation almost perfectly explained all the anomalies that remained in the Arrhenius theory.

Almost perfectly, but not quite, as Onsager soon observed. The value of the molar conductivity predicted by the Debye-Hückel theory was significantly different from that obtained from experiments. By 1925, Onsager had discovered the reason for this discrepancy. Debye and Hückel had assumed that most—but not all—of the ions in a solution move about randomly in "Brownian" movement. Onsager simply extended that principle to *all* of the ions in the solution. With this correction, he was able to write a new mathematical expression that improved upon the Debye-Hückel formulation.

Onsager had the opportunity in 1925 to present his views to Debye in person. Having arrived in Zurich after traveling through Denmark and Germany with one of his professors, Onsager is reported to have marched into Debye's office in Zurich and declared, "Professor Debye, your theory of electrolytes is incorrect." Debye was sufficiently impressed with the young Norwegian to offer him a research post in Zurich, a position that Onsager accepted and held for the next two years.

In 1928, Onsager emigrated to the United States where he became an associate in chemistry at Johns Hopkins University. The appointment proved to be disastrous: he was assigned to teach the introductory chemistry classes, a task for which he was completely unsuited. One of his associates, Robert H. Cole, is quoted in the *Biographical Memoirs of Fellows of the Royal Society:* "I won't say he was the world's worst lecturer, but he was certainly in contention." As a consequence, Onsager was not asked to return to Johns Hopkins after he had completed his first semester there.

Fortunately, a position was open at Brown University, and Onsager was asked by chemistry department chairman Charles A. Krauss to fill that position. During his 5-year tenure at Brown, Onsager was given a more appropriate teaching assignment, statistical mechanics. His pedagogical techniques apparently did not improve to any great extent, however; he still presented a challenge to students by speaking to the blackboard on topics that were well beyond the comprehension of many in the room.

Law of Reciprocal Relations Developed while at Brown

A far more important feature of the Brown years was the theoretical research that Onsager carried out in the privacy of his own office. In this research, Onsager attempted to generalize his earlier research on the motion of ions in solution when exposed to an electrical field. In order to do so, he went back to some fundamental laws of thermodynamics, including Hermann Helmholtz's "principle of least dissipation." He was eventually able to derive a very general mathematical expression about the behavior of substances in solution, an expression now known as the Law of Reciprocal Relations.

Onsager first published the law in 1929, but continued to work on it for a number of years. In 1931, he announced a more general form of the law that applied to other non-equilibrium situations in which differences in electrical or magnetic force, temperature, pressure, or some other factor exists. The Onsager formulation was so elegant and so general that some scientists now refer to it as the Fourth Law of Thermodynamics.

The Law of Reciprocal Relations was eventually recognized as an enormous advance in theoretical chemistry, earning Onsager the Nobel Prize in 1968. However, its initial announcement provoked almost no response from his colleagues. It is not that they disputed his findings, Onsager said many years later, but just that they totally ignored them. Indeed, Onsager's research had almost no impact on chemists until after World War II had ended, more than a decade after the research was originally published.

The year 1933 was a momentous one for Onsager. It began badly when Brown ended his appointment because of financial pressures brought about by the Great Depression. His situation improved later in the year, however, when he was offered an appointment as Sterling and Gibbs Fellow at

Yale. The appointment marked the beginning of an affiliation with Yale that was to continue until 1972.

Prior to assuming his new job at Yale, Onsager spent the summer in Europe. While there, he met the future Mrs. Onsager, Margarethe Arledter, the sister of the Austrian electrochemist H. Falkenhagen. The two apparently fell instantly in love, became engaged a week after meeting, and were married on September 7, 1933. The Onsagers later had three sons, Erling Frederick, Hans Tanberg, and Christian Carl, and one daughter, Inger Marie.

Onsager had no sooner assumed his post at Yale when a small problem arose: the fellowship he had been awarded was for postdoctoral studies, but Onsager had not as yet been granted a Ph.D. He had submitted an outline of his research on reciprocal relations to his alma mater, the Norges Tekniski Høgskole, but the faculty there had decided that, being incomplete, it was not worthy of a doctorate. As a result, Onsager's first task at Yale was to complete a doctoral thesis. For this thesis, he submitted to the chemistry faculty a research paper on an esoteric mathematical topic. Since the thesis was outside the experience of anyone in the chemistry or physics departments, Onsager's degree was nearly awarded by the mathematics department, whose chair understood Onsager's findings quite clearly. Only at the last moment did the chemistry department relent and agree to accept the judgment of its colleagues, awarding Onsager his Ph.D. in 1935.

Onsager continued to teach statistical mechanics at Yale, although with as little success as ever. (Instead of being called "Sadistical Mechanics," as it had been by Brown students, it was now referred to as "Advanced Norwegian" by their Yale counterparts.) As always, it was Onsager's theoretical—and usually independent—research that justified his Yale salary. In his nearly four decades there, he attacked one new problem after another, usually with astounding success. Though his output was by no means prodigious, the quality and thoroughness of his research was impeccable.

Continued Productivity with Increasing Age

During the late 1930s, Onsager worked on another of Debye's ideas, the dipole theory of dielectrics. That theory had, in general, been very successful, but could not explain the special case of liquids with high dielectric constants. By 1936, Onsager had developed a new model of dipoles that could be used to modify Debye's theory and provide accurate predictions for all cases. Onsager was apparently deeply hurt when Debye rejected his paper explaining this model for publication in the *Physikalische Zeitschrift,* which Debye edited. It would be more than a decade before the great Dutch chemist, then an American citizen, could accept Onsager's modifications of his ideas.

In the 1940s, Onsager turned his attention to the very complex issue of phase transitions in solids. He wanted to find out if the mathematical techniques of statistical mechanics could be used to derive the thermodynamic properties of such events. Although some initial progress had been made in this area, resulting in a theory known as the Ising model, Onsager produced a spectacular breakthrough on the problem. He introduced a "trick or two" (to use his words) that had not yet occurred to (and were probably unknown to) his colleagues—the use of elegant mathematical techniques of elliptical functions and quaternion algebra. His solution to this problem was widely acclaimed.

Though his status as a non-U.S. citizen enabled him to devote his time and effort to his own research during World War II, Onsager was forbidden from contributing his significant talents to the top-secret Manhattan Project, the United State's research toward creating atomic weapons. Onsager and his wife finally did become citizens as the war drew to a close in 1945.

The postwar years saw no diminution of Onsager's energy. He continued his research on low-temperature physics and devised a theoretical explanation for the superfluidity of helium II (liquid helium). The idea, originally proposed in 1949, was arrived at independently two years later by Princeton University's Richard Feynman. Onsager also worked out original theories for the statistical properties of liquid crystals and for the electrical properties of ice. In 1951 he was given a Fulbright scholarship to work at the Cavendish Laboratory in Cambridge; there, he perfected his theory of diamagnetism in metals.

During his last years at Yale, Onsager continued to receive numerous accolades for his newly appreciated discoveries. He was awarded honorary doctorates by such noble universities as Harvard (1954), Brown (1962), Chicago (1968), Cambridge (1970), and Oxford (1971), among others. He was inducted to the National Academy of Sciences in 1947. In addition to his Nobel Prize, Onsager garnered the American Academy of Arts and Sciences' Rumford Medal in 1953 and the Lorentz Medal in 1958, as well as several medals from the American Chemical Society and the President's National Medal of Science. Upon reaching retirement age in 1972, Onsager was offered the title of emeritus professor, but without an office. Disappointed by this apparent slight, Onsager decided instead to accept an appointment as Distinguished University Professor at the University of Miami's Center for Theoretical Studies. At Miami, Onsager found two new subjects to interest him, biophysics and radiation chemistry. In neither field did he have an opportunity to make any significant contributions, however, as he died on October 5, 1976, apparently the victim of a heart attack.

Given his shortcomings as a teacher, Onsager still seems to have been universally admired and liked as a person. Though modest and self-effacing, he possessed a wry sense of humor. In *Biographical Memoirs,* he is quoted as saying of research, "There's a time to soar like an eagle, and a time to burrow like a worm. It takes a pretty sharp cookie to know when to shed the feathers and . . . to begin munching the humus." In a memorial some months after

Onsager's death, Behram Kursunoglu, the director of the University of Miami's Center for Theoretical Studies, described him as a "very great man of science—with profound humanitarian and scientific qualities."

SELECTED WRITINGS BY ONSAGER:

Periodicals

Transactions of the Faraday Society, Report on a Revision of the Conductivity Theory, Volume 23, 1927, pp. 341–49.
Physical Review, Reciprocal relations in irreversible processes, pt. I, 1931, Volume 37, pp. 405–26.
Physical Review, Reciprocal relations in irreversible processes, pt. II, 1931, Volume 38, pp. 2265–79.
Physical Review, Crystal Statistics, pt. I, Volume 65, 1944, pp. 117–49.
Vortex, The Electrical Properties of Ice, Volume 23, 1962, pp. 138–41.

FURTHER READING:

Books

Biographical Memoirs of Fellows of the Royal Society, Volume 24, Royal Society (London), 1978.
Current Biography 1958, H. W. Wilson, 1958.
Nobel Lectures in Chemistry, 1963–1970, [Amsterdam], 1972.

Sketch by David E. Newton

Jan Hendrik Oort
1900–1992
Dutch astronomer

One of the fathers of modern astronomy, Jan Hendrik Oort altered commonly held perspectives of the universe as profoundly as the great classical astronomers changed ancient views of the Earth's relationship to the solar system. "Like a modern Copernicus, Oort showed that our position in nature's grand scheme was not so special," commented astronomer Seth Shostak in Oort's obituary in the *New York Times,* referring to Oort's repudiation of the belief that the Earth and Sun were near the center of the galaxy. Oort proved that the solar system is in the galactic hinterlands, thirty thousand light years away from the galaxy's center. Oort's accomplishments were many; he calculated the structure of the Milky Way, discovered the existence of dark matter, and pioneered radio astronomy. He

is best known, however, for his theory on the source of comets and an astronomical phenomenon known as the Oort cloud.

Oort was born on April 28, 1900, in Franeker, a small farming town in Friesland, one of the northern provinces of the Netherlands. His parents were Abraham Hermanus Oort, a physician, and Ruth Hannah Faber Oort. He had two brothers and two sisters. Oort's grandfather, a professor of Hebrew at the University of Leiden, was one of the principal contributors to a translation of the bible into Dutch, known as the Leiden translation. When he was three years old, his family moved to Wassenaar, near Leiden.

In 1917 Oort graduated from the gymnasium in Leiden, but instead of staying at the university where his grandfather had taught, he decided to go back north and enroll at the University of Groningen. His express intention was to study under Jacobus Kapteyn, a prominent astronomer and the first scientist to quantitatively measure and compute the position of stars in the Milky Way. Prior to the efforts of Kapteyn and others at the turn of the century, astronomers had little concrete knowledge concerning the size and mass of the galaxy. Using photographic plates of the southern sky, Kapteyn correctly ascertained that the Milky Way was convex in shape, like an eyeglass lens or a discus, with a bulge in the middle. Throughout his life, Oort cherished his studies under Kapteyn and kept a portrait of his teacher, who died in 1922, on his office wall.

Gains International Recognition

Oort's gift for astronomy was evident by 1920 when he won the Bachiene Foundation Prize for a paper he cowrote on stars of the spectral types F, G, K, and M. After graduating from Groningen in 1922, he became a research assistant for two years at the Yale University Observatory in New Haven, Connecticut. During this time, Oort studied the work of **Harlow Shapley** at Harvard, whose study of the galaxy correctly postulated that its size was much larger than Kapteyn had estimated. Oort returned to the Netherlands in 1924 and received his Ph.D. from Groningen in 1926 for his dissertation on high-velocity stars. He then became an instructor at the University of Leiden, where he was to spend the remainder of his career.

Oort quickly gained worldwide recognition in 1927 when he built on the work of Swedish astronomer Bertil Lindblad and correctly ascertained the rotation of the Milky Way. With his knowledge of high-velocity stars, Oort was able to use complex mathematical calculations to measure the relative velocities of stars as they moved in the rotating galaxy; he showed that they did not rotate as an aligned unit like a wheel, but rather the stars nearer the Milky Way's center moved faster than those further away. These calculations allowed him to estimate the center's gravitational field, from which he deduced that the mass of the galaxy is one hundred billion times that of the Sun, that the galaxy contains some one hundred billion stars, and that it measures one hundred thousand light years across and twenty thousand light years deep at the center. When Oort received the Vetlesen Prize in 1966 from Columbia University, Bengt Stromgren noted that Oort's early paper analyzing the galaxy's mass and structure was responsible for changing the astronomical community's outlook, including the once-held belief that the solar system was near the center of the galaxy. According to Oort's calculations, the solar system was thirty thousand light years away from the galactic center, around which it took three hundred million light years to make a complete orbit.

In 1935 Oort was appointed professor of astronomy at Leiden, and he continued his work at the observatory there. His studies of galaxies NGC 3115 and NGC 4494 as well as his work on the velocity of stars in the solar system convinced him that galaxies contain much more mass than can be detected either visually or by current calculations. Far ahead of his time, Oort's early recognition of dark matter, or "missing mass," in the universe continues to baffle astronomers. According to some calculations, more than ninety percent of the universe could be made up of dark matter, which also might be responsible for gravitational clustering of stars into galaxies.

Oort's work was disrupted during World War II when the Germans, who had occupied The Netherlands, forced him from his position at the observatory in 1940 because he opposed the firing of fellow professors who were Jewish. Soon the observatory was closed, and Oort and his family went into hiding in a rural area east of Leiden. Oort and his colleagues still continued their work, however, although with great difficulty.

In 1942 Oort began collaborations with J. L. L. Duyvendak, an Asian language professor who had translated Chinese texts concerning the "guest star" of July 4, 1054, the sudden appearance of which had confounded contemporary Chinese and Japanese astronomers. The star was so bright that for several months it remained visible even during daylight. By studying the light curve of this star, Oort and Nicholas Mayall hypothesized that is was a supernova. (A supernova occurs when a hugely massive star implodes or bursts inward from extreme pressure and the resulting shock wave blows the stars apart, releasing energy equal to at least fifteen million Suns.) They also identified the Crab Nebula—named by the nineteenth-century Irish astronomer William Parsons Rosse because it appeared crablike in structure in his homemade telescope—as a supernova remnant of this 1054 event.

Begins Radio Astronomy Research

Following the war, Oort was appointed director of the Leiden Observatory. In collaboration with Hendrik van de Hulst, he discovered that clouds of gas and dust surround extremely bright, hot stars and provide the material for spontaneous formation of new stars. But the two also collaborated on a much more important project that was to thrust astronomy light years ahead of previous efforts. Working with a German radar antenna that had been made into a radio telescope, the two began their pioneering efforts in radio astronomy.

Although scientists in the United States were leading the way in radio astronomy in the 1930s, World War II had halted most efforts in this area. Oort knew that radio waves would be an unparalleled tool for the study of the galaxy's structure because they are not hampered by gas and dust as is visible light. As a result, astronomers could observe the galaxy in detail not possible with normal optical telescopes. The first task was to find a wavelength that radio telescopes could be tuned into. In 1944, at the request of Oort, van de Hulst had calculated that the hydrogen atom emits radio waves at a constant wavelength of twenty-one centimeters. After several years of research, in 1951 the pair detected the twenty-one-centimeter hydrogen line, a gaseous cloud of cold hydrogen that passes through the Milky Way. Oort and van de Hulst used the newfound knowledge of a moving mass of hydrogen gas to confirm the speed of the galaxy's rotation at 225 million years. They also completed a comprehensive map of the galaxy's spiral structure at the outer region. Their efforts not only placed the Netherlands at the forefront of modern astronomy but also firmly established radio astronomy as one of the most important technological advances in astronomy in that era.

Oort's work in the fifties continued to shed light on the structure of the Milky Way. Working with Australian astronomer Frank Kerr, he discovered that the galaxy's core consists of so-called turbulent hydrogen and hypothesized that this turbulence was caused by a massive explosion some ten million years ago. Oort eventually proved that the galaxy is a rapidly whirling disk with two spiral arms moving outward from the core. In 1964 he and G. W. Rougoor discovered a corona of hydrogen encircling the galaxy and rapidly moving outward, approximately at the same speed as the galaxy's rotational velocity. Oort went on to theorize that the location of the densest part of the corona above the galaxy was forcing the galaxy upward. He estimated that the galaxy would change in shape every three billion years due to some of the gases moving inward or being "absorbed."

Postulates the Source of Comets

Oort was most widely recognized by the public, however, for his postulation of the Oort cloud, a mass of icy objects that surround the Sun from one light year away and reach almost to the nearest stars. Oort theorized that when other stars pass in close proximity to the solar system, some of these "cometary nuclei" (numbering from one hundred-ninety billion to one hundred trillion) are perturbed from the orbit by a gravitational flurry and thrust into the solar system's inner orbit where they can be seen. Although no astronomer has ever observed the Oort cloud, few doubt its existence, a testament to Oort's scientific integrity. During the course of his career, Oort headed several international astronomical groups, including serving as president of the International Astronomical Union from 1958 to 1961. In 1962, he was one of the cofounders of the European Southern Observatory, one of the preeminent optical observatories in the world.

Although Oort retired in 1970, he continued his astronomical studies, much to the chagrin of his wife, Mieke, a poet whom he had married on May 24, 1927. According to Govert Schilling in an article in *Sky & Telescope,* she politely complained, "For me, nothing seemed to change." Oort relished the outdoors, especially hiking, rowing, and skating, which he often did in the company of fellow astronomers from the Leiden Observatory. He was also fond of reading poetry. The Oorts had two sons, Coenraad and Abraham, a daughter, Marijke, and several grandchildren and great grandchildren.

Oort published more articles in the 1970s than he did the previous decade and, for several years, shared an office with his grandson, Marc, at the Leiden Observatory. Many of these articles have become landmarks in astronomical literature, especially those concerning the center of the Milky Way and on super clusters of galaxies. Oort's enthusiasm for the study of the sky was remembered by Gart Westerhout and noted in the *Sky & Telescope* article. On a visit to the Southern Hemisphere to pick a site for the Leiden Southern Station, Westerhout saw Oort "flat on his back in the wet grass, risking pneumonia" to ponder the southern sky. "His fascination, and the theories that must have formed in his mind at that time, almost physically radiated from him." Up until his death at the age of ninety-two on November 5, 1992, Oort continued to keep his family informed of the latest astronomical discoveries with cosmology lectures.

SELECTED WRITINGS BY OORT:

Books

The Stars of High Velocity, Gebroeders Hoitsema, 1926.

FURTHER READING:

Books

The Biographical Dictionary of Scientists: Astronomers, Peter Bedrick Books, 1989, pp. 119–120.
The Great Scientists, Volume 9, Grolier, 1989, pp. 110–115.
McGraw-Hill Modern Men of Science, McGraw, 1966, pp. 359–360.
Seargent, David A., *Comets: Vagabonds of Space,* Doubleday, 1982, pp. 100–102.

Periodicals

Schilling, Govert, *Sky & Telescope,* Jan Oort Remembered, April, 1993, pp. 44–45.
Wilford, John Noble, *New York Times,* Jan H. Oort, Dutch Astronomer in Forefront of Field, Dies at 92, November 12, 1993, p. 15.

Sketch by David Petechuk

Aleksandr Ivanovich Oparin
1894–1980
Russian biochemist

Aleksandr Ivanovich Oparin was a prominent biochemist in the former Soviet Union whose achievements were recognized throughout the international scientific community. He is best known for his theory that life on earth originated from inorganic matter. Although a belief that life formed through spontaneous generation was prevalent up to the nineteenth century, that theory was disputed by the development of the microscope and the experiments of French scientist Louis Pasteur. Oparin's materialistic approach to the subject was responsible for a renewed interest in how life on earth originated. His book *The Origin of Life* outlined his basic theory, which was that life originated as a result of evolution acting on molecules created in the primordial atmosphere through energy discharges. In addition to his work on the origin of life, he played a major role in the development of technical botanical biochemistry in the Soviet Union.

Oparin was born near Moscow on March 2, 1894. He was the youngest child of Ivan Dmitrievich Oparin and Aleksandra Aleksandrovna. He had a sister, Aleksandra, and a brother, Dmitrii. His secondary education was marked by his achievements in science. He studied plant physiology at Moscow State University, graduating in 1917. He was a graduate student and teaching assistant there from 1921 to 1925. He also studied at other institutes of higher learning in Germany, Austria, Italy, and France, but it is thought that he never earned a graduate degree (he was awarded a doctorate in biological sciences in 1934 by the U.S.S.R. Academy of Sciences).

Aleksei N. Bakh, Oparin's mentor during his years of graduate study, was to have great influence on Oparin's later role in the development of Soviet biochemistry. Bakh was well known internationally for his research in medical and industrial chemistry, and played an important role in the organization of the chemical industry in Russia. After the Russian Revolution in 1917, Bakh helped develop the chemical section of the National Economic Planning Council (VSNKh) and founded its Central Chemical Laboratory. Oparin studied plant chemistry with Bakh in 1918, and from 1919 through 1925, he worked under Bakh at the VSNKh and the Central Chemical Laboratory. Bakh and Oparin cofounded the Institute of Biochemistry at the Academy of Sciences of the Soviet Union in Moscow in 1935. Oparin was appointed deputy director of the institute and held that position until 1946. After Bakh's death that same year, Oparin assumed the director's position, which he held until his death.

The practical aspects of Oparin's work during his association with Bakh in the early thirties involved biochemical research for increasing production in the food industry, work that was of extreme importance to the Soviet economy. Through his study of enzymatic activity in plants, he found that it was necessary for molecules and enzymes to combine in order to create starches, sugars, and other carbohydrates and proteins. He was able to show that this biocatalysis was the basis for producing many food products in nature. He held a post from 1927 through 1934 as assistant director and head of the laboratory at the Central Institute of the Sugar Industry in Moscow, where he conducted research on tea, sugar, flour, and grains. During this same period, he also taught technical biochemistry at the D. I. Mendeleev Institute of Chemical Technology. As professor at the Moscow Technical Institute of Food Production from 1937 to 1949, he continued his research of plant processes and began the study of nutrition and vitamins.

Oparin's biochemical research on plant enzymes and their role in plant metabolism, so important for its practical application, would also be important for what was to be the focus of his career, the question of how life first appeared on earth. His first paper on this subject was presented to a meeting of the Moscow Botanical Society in 1922. This paper, which was never published, was revised and published in 1924 by the *Moscow Worker*. In it, Oparin discussed the problem of spontaneous generation, arguing that any differences between living and nonliving material could be attributed to physicochemical laws. This work went largely unnoticed, and Oparin did not seriously consider the topic again until the mid-thirties. In 1936, he published *The Origin of Life,* which modified and enlarged his earlier ideas. His ideas at this time were influenced not only by contemporary international thinking on astronomy, geochemistry, organic chemistry, and plant enzymology, but also by the dialectic philosophy espoused by Friedrich Engels, and the work of H. G. Bungenburg de Jong on colloidal coacervation. Translated into English in a 1938 edition, *The Origin of Life* was also revised and updated in 1941 and 1957. Although the later versions amended the original, the concept that life arose through a natural evolution of matter remained central, and he often described this concept metaphorically by comparing life to a constant flow of liquid in which elements within are constantly changed and renewed.

The Origin of Life Theory

Oparin's theory that the origin of life had a biochemical basis was based on his suppositions concerning the condition of the atmosphere surrounding the primeval earth and how those conditions interacted with primitive organisms. It was his idea that the primeval atmosphere (consisting of ammonia, hydrogen, methane and water) in conjunction with energy (probably in the form of sunlight, volcanic eruptions, and lightning) gave this primitive matter its metabolic ability to grow and increase. He speculated that the first organisms had appeared in ancient seas between 4.7 and 3.2 billion years ago. These living organisms would have evolved from a nonliving coagulate, or gel-like,

solution. Oparin argued that a separation process called coacervation occurred within the gel, causing nonliving matter at the multimolecular level to be chemically transformed into living matter. He further theorized that this chemical transformation was dependent upon protoenzymatic catalysts and promoters contained in the coacervates. From there, a process of natural selection began, which resulted in the formation of increasingly complex organisms and, eventually, primitive systems of life. Although others, such as de Jong and T. H. Huxley, would postulate that life arose from a kind of "sea jelly," Oparin's theory that nonliving material was a catalyst for the formation of living organisms is considered by many to be his special contribution to the issue.

His suppositions on life's origins were not merely theoretical. In laboratory experiments, he showed how molecules might combine to produce the needed protein structure for transformation. Experiments of other scientists, such as **Stanley Lloyd Miller**, **Harold Urey**, and **Cyril Ponnamperuma**, confirmed his initial experiments on the chemical structure necessary to produce life. Ponnamperuna took the work a step further when he altered Oparin's original experiments and was able to easily produce nucleotides, dinucleotides, and adenosine triphosphate, which also contribute to the formation of life. Building on Ponnamperuna's research, Oparin was able to produce droplets of gel that he called protobionts. He believed these protobionts were living organisms because of their ability to metabolize and reproduce. Although later research of scientists in both the Soviet Union and the West would develop independently of Oparin's biochemical experiments, he must be given credit for putting the question of the origin of life into the realm of modern science. It has been said that his work in this area opened the door, and scientists in the West walked through.

Biochemistry in the Service of Dialectical Materialism

Oparin was a man of his time, and his thinking was greatly influenced by Charles Darwin's theory of natural selection and the ideological climate of dialectical materialism which pervaded Soviet society during the 1930s. Although Oparin was never a Communist Party member, both his writings and his research methods reflect a bias toward dialectical materialism. However, it has been suggested that his denigration of the science of genetics and his support of Trofim Denisovich Lysenko and the Marxist-Leninist ideology which permeated and controlled Soviet genetics at that time may have resulted from political pressure and a desire to protect his career, as much as philosophical and scientific belief. Whatever the reasons, Oparin used his influence and prestige as chief administrator of the U.S.S.R. Academy of Sciences from 1948 through 1955 to implement policies that advanced Lysenko's views at the expense of the advancement of Soviet genetics. The influence of Lysenko and the Marxist-Leninist view of biology waned after Stalin's death in 1953. In 1956, as the result of a petition by 300 scientists calling for his resignation, Oparin was removed from his top position in the academy's biology division. He was replaced by Vladimir A. Engelhardt, a leading Soviet advocate of molecular biology. The 1950s saw an international explosion in the growth of molecular biology, but Oparin was severely critical of its principles. Although he considered the discoveries made by Watson and Crick concerning DNA to be important, he was skeptical of the idea of a genetic code, calling it "mechanistic reductionism." He did, however, support DNA research within his own Institute of Biochemistry during this time, and was a coauthor of papers discussing DNA and RNA in coacervate droplets.

Although Oparin's influence in Soviet science weakened in the early sixties, his international reputation, based on the origin of life theory, remained strong. This, coupled with his political reliability, led his government to send him abroad as a Soviet representative. Traveling by scientists in the Soviet Union was severely restricted in the 1950s, but Oparin was sent on official Soviet business not only to countries in the Eastern bloc and Asia, but to Europe and the United States as well. He also represented his country at international scientific and political conferences, such as the World Peace Council and the World Federation of Scientists.

His work brought him numerous honors. His awards from the Soviet Union include the A. N. Bakh Prize in 1950, the Elie Metchnikoff Gold Prize in 1960, the Lenin Prize in 1974, and the Lomonosov Gold Medal in 1979. The International Society for the Study of the Origin of Life elected him as its first president in 1970. He also was elected a member of scientific societies in Finland, Bulgaria, Czechoslovakia, East Germany, Cuba, Spain, and Italy.

Beginning in 1965 and continuing through 1980, the Soviet Union placed new emphasis on the science of genetics and molecular biology. However, Oparin's Institute of Biochemistry remained a stronghold of old-style biochemistry, and it eventually was bypassed by more progressive research institutions. Oparin died of heart disease in Moscow on April 21, 1980.

SELECTED WRITINGS BY OPARIN:

Books

The Origin of Life, translated by Sergius Morgulis, Macmillan, 1938.
The Chemical Origin of Life, translated by Ann Synge, Charles C. Thomas, Springfield, Illinois, 1964.

FURTHER READING:

Books

Graham, Loren R., *Science and Philosophy in the Soviet Union,* Knopf, 1972.

Sketch by Jane Stewart Cook

J. Robert Oppenheimer
1904–1967
American physicist

Theoretical physicist J. Robert Oppenheimer was a pioneer in the field of quantum mechanics, the study of the energy of atomic particles. His research on protons and their relation to electrons led directly to the discovery of a new particle, the positron. His later work shed light on deuterons, the nuclei of heavy hydrogen atoms. He was a charismatic teacher and effective administrator who directed the laboratory at Los Alamos, New Mexico, where the atomic bomb was developed during World War II. In the postwar years, however, Oppenheimer staunchly opposed the proliferation of nuclear weapons. This stance brought him before Congress during the McCarthy era and cost him his security clearance as a government consultant.

Julius Robert Oppenheimer was born in New York City on April 22, 1904, to a wealthy and cultured family. His father, Julius Oppenheimer, who emigrated from Germany as a young man, had a successful business importing textiles. His mother, the former Ella Friedman, was a painter and a great lover of the arts. Oppenheimer, his parents, and his younger brother, Frank, divided their time between a spacious New York apartment overlooking the Hudson River and a summer house on Long Island.

It became apparent when he was quite young that Oppenheimer had a quick mind, a vast appetite for learning, and a wide range of interests. At age eleven, he was the youngest person ever admitted to the New York Mineralogical Society, and at the age of twelve he presented a paper there. He attended the Ethical Culture School in New York, and after graduating he spent the summer in Europe. Unfortunately, he contracted dysentery there, and needed the following year to recuperate. When he was well again he took his first trip to the West, where the expanse of the Pecos Valley of New Mexico captured his imagination. His family eventually bought a ranch there, returning year after year.

Oppenheimer entered Harvard College in 1922. He studied a broad curriculum, which included several languages as well as chemistry and physics. As an undergraduate he was especially close to physicist **Percy Bridgman**, also a man of many interests, who may have shaped the way Oppenheimer combined physics with philosophy in his later career. Despite his course load, Oppenheimer graduated from Harvard *summa cum laude* in just three years, and in 1925 he left the United States for Europe to study theoretical physics.

It was in Europe during that period that the most important advances were being achieved in the study of the behavior and energy of particles that make up the atom—a discipline known as quantum mechanics. Such brilliant theoreticians as **Werner Heisenberg**, **Erwin Schrödinger**

J. Robert Oppenheimer

and **Paul Dirac** were formulating their theories about quantifying and predicting the movement and location of atomic particles. Oppenheimer initially went to the Cavendish Laboratory in Cambridge, England, and within just a few months he had submitted his first paper, which used some of the most recent theoretical advances in nuclear physics to explain aspects of molecular behavior.

Explains Molecular Activity

In 1926 Oppenheimer left the Cavendish for the University of Göttingen in Germany. He did independent research on radiation at Göttingen and also collaborated with the physicist **Max Born** in a further investigation of molecular activity. The two scientists tackled variations in the vibration, rotation, and electronic properties of molecules. Their results led to the so-called "Born-Oppenheimer method," which is in effect a quantum mechanics at the molecular rather than the atomic level. After receiving his doctorate in 1927, he left Göttingen for Leiden, Holland, and then went on to Zurich where he worked with another distinguished physicist, **Wolfgang Pauli**. Throughout this period, Oppenheimer consistently demonstrated his ability to synthesize ideas, draw connections between theories, and detect their inherent contradictions.

Oppenheimer's work in Europe had been of such quality that he was able to arrange teaching positions both at the University of California at Berkeley and at the California Institute of Technology. For the next thirteen years he taught and did research at these schools during alternating semesters. During this period, Oppenheimer evolved into an extraordinary, charismatic teacher. Although many students complained that he set an impossible pace in the classroom, he attracted a number of students and even some colleagues to theoretical physics by his quick wit and probing questions. He inspired many of his students, and some even adopted his gestures and way of speaking. Oppenheimer's social life was very much involved with his teaching; he would often discuss subjects such as astrophysics and cosmic rays or nuclear physics and electrodynamics for hours on end.

Some of his best work in particle physics was also done during these years. In 1930 he was able to demonstrate that the proton is not the antimatter equivalent of the electron (or antielectron) as had until then been supposed. One of Oppenheimer's students, **Carl Anderson**, used this work in his search for the true antielectron and found the positron. Oppenheimer's earlier work on radiation led to his contribution to the discovery that cosmic ray particles could break down into another generation of particles, a phenomenon commonly called the "cascade process." In 1935, he discovered that it was possible to accelerate deuterons, made up of a proton and a neutron, to much higher energies than neutrons alone. Deuterons, as a consequence, could be used to bombard positively charged atomic nuclei at high energies, enabling further research into atomic particles.

Leads the Manhattan Project

For years physicists had been aware of the possibility of manipulating nuclear fission. Bombarding the nuclei of certain molecules, they suspected, could result in a chain reaction that would release an extremely large amount of energy. In the United States and Nazi Germany, scientists were rushing to work on a weapon that could harness this energy—the atomic bomb. At Berkeley's Radiation Laboratory under the direction of Oppenheimer's colleague, **Ernest Orlando Lawrence**, researchers selected uranium as the chemical element most likely to lend itself to nuclear fission for military purposes. However, no coordinated effort to design and fabricate an actual atomic weapon was made.

According to Oppenheimer's colleague Victor Weisskopf, "many physicists were drawn into this work by fate and destiny rather than enthusiasm," and Oppenheimer was one of them. Early in 1942 he brought together a group of theoretical physicists—many of whom had been working in separate laboratories under the umbrella of the Manhattan Project—and became director of the new research lab at Los Alamos to develop the first nuclear weapon.

The administration of the research at Los Alamos presented its challenges, which Oppenheimer handled effectively. The intense and sustained work that was done on the Manhattan Project was due in large part to his evident sense of purpose and his ability to provide a creative, cooperative environment for scientists forced to work in secret. A design for the bomb was ready and a fissionable form of plutonium produced to fuel it by mid–1945. On the fateful morning of July 16, 1945, Oppenheimer stood silently awaiting the detonation of the test bomb nicknamed "Fat Man" at nearby Alamogordo. He wrote in his *Letters and Recollections* that, upon seeing the power it unleashed, he thought the play of the light had the "radiance of a thousand suns," but he was also reminded of a dark, foreboding line from the Hindu *Bhagavad-Gita:* "I am become death, the Shatterer of Worlds."

Oppenheimer was one of a panel of four scientists including Ernest Orlando Lawrence, **Enrico Fermi**, and **Arthur Compton** that was asked to formulate an opinion regarding the use of the atomic bomb to end the war against Japan. They were told that there was a choice between a military invasion of Japan, which was certain to cost many American lives, and a nuclear attack on a military target that would also kill many civilians. Confronted with this choice, the panel voted to use the bomb. Oppenheimer later regretted his decision, saying that the intentional slaughter of civilians had been unnecessary and wrong.

Political Controversies

After the war, Oppenheimer became more and more concerned about the devastating potential of atomic weaponry. With this concern foremost in his mind, he cowrote the "Acheson-Lilienthal Report," which opposed the nuclear arms race at its very outset, instead proposing stringent international controls on the development of nuclear arsenals. The report was rewritten and presented to the United Nations as the Baruch Plan, but the Soviet Union vetoed its adoption. In 1946 Oppenheimer became chair of the general advisory committee of the Atomic Energy Commission and continued to advocate controls on the development of nuclear power.

In October of 1947, Oppenheimer became director of the Institute for Advanced Study at Princeton University, New Jersey. Under his directorship, the institute became one of the foremost centers of research in theoretical physics, even though Oppenheimer himself did little research from this time forward. He was keenly aware of what others were doing at the institute both inside and outside theoretical physics, but much of his energy was now spent on policy issues rather than science, and many considered his scientific judgment no longer as keen as it had been.

As the 1940s drew to a close, President Truman decided that it was in the country's best interest to develop the hydrogen bomb. Oppenheimer's position was clear; he did not believe in the proliferation of nuclear weapons, and he did not hesitate to express his opinion in public. His position disturbed many of those in power in Washington. In November of 1953 William Borden, former executive director of Congress' Joint Atomic Energy Committee, sent a registered letter to J. Edgar Hoover of the FBI, stating he had considerable evidence to show that Oppenheimer was a Soviet agent. In December Oppenheimer was informed that his security clearance, which he needed to have access to classified information, was revoked on suspicion of unpatriotic activities on his part.

A Congressional hearing giving Oppenheimer the opportunity to clear himself did little to dispel the myth of his lack of patriotism. It was the era of the Cold War and the anti-communist hysteria spearheaded by Senator Joseph McCarthy. Oppenheimer's association with Communists during the 1930s, never a secret nor an obstacle to his receiving clearance when he was director of Los Alamos, was now presented as a blot on his character and a challenge to his patriotic commitment. Both his position on nuclear weapons and his arrogance and ability to argue had made him unpopular in some quarters, and there were those who wanted to see him removed from his public position. After many grueling hours of testimony, the majority of a three-man panel found that Oppenheimer was "a loyal citizen," but still denied him clearance on the basis of "defects of character."

After this very public hearing was finally over, Oppenheimer emerged somewhat aged and wounded. Yet he continued to lecture on science and express his opinions on politics. In 1963 Oppenheimer received the prestigious Enrico Fermi Award, which was something of a public vindication but did not undo all the harm done earlier.

Almost every published photograph showed Oppenheimer with a cigarette or pipe in hand, and he knew for some time that he had throat cancer. He died at home in Princeton on February 18, 1967. After his cremation, his wife Kitty spread his ashes in the sea near their vacation retreat in the Virgin Islands.

SELECTED WRITINGS BY OPPENHEIMER:

Books

Letters and Recollections, edited by Alice Kimball Smith and Charles Weiner, Harvard University Press, 1980.

Periodicals

Physical Review, On the Quantum Theory of Field Currents, May, 1928, p. 914.
Physical Review, The Disintegration of Lithium by Protons of High Energy, March, 1933, p. 380.
Physical Review, The Density of Nuclear Levels, August, 1936, p. 391.
Physical Review, On the Applicability of Quantum Theory to Mesotron Collisions, February, 1940, p. 353.

FURTHER READING:

Books

Contemporary Authors, New Revisions Series, Volume 34, Gale, 1991.
Kunetka, James W., *Oppenheimer: The Years of Risk,* Prentice-Hall, 1982.

Rabi, I. I., et al., *Oppenheimer,* Scribner, 1969.
Stern, Philip M., *The Oppenheimer Case: Security on Trial,* Harper, 1969.

Periodicals

Stern, Philip M., *Biographical Memoirs of Fellows of the Royal Society,* Volume 14, Royal Society (London), 1968, pp. 391–416.

Sketch by Barbara A. Branca

Mary J. Osborn
1927–
American biochemist

Mary J. Osborn is the first person to demonstrate the mode of action of methotrexate, a major cancer chemotherapeutic agent and folic acid antagonist (in other words, it opposes the physiological effects of folic acid). Best known for her research into the biosynthesis of a complex polysaccharide known as lipopolysaccharide—a molecule that is essential to bacterial cells—Osborn helped to identify a potential target for the development of new antibiotics and chemotherapeutic agents.

Mary Jane Osborn was born in Colorado Springs, Colorado, on September 24, 1927, and raised in west Los Angeles and Beverly Hills, California. Her father, Arthur Merten, had an eighth-grade education and was a machinist; her mother, Vivian, went to secretarial classes and also taught school. "Both parents were high achievers and their ambitions for me were considerable," Osborn told Laura Newman in an interview. Osborn noted that her background was somewhat atypical for girls growing up in the 1930s. She recalled reading a book for young girls about being a nurse when she was ten years of age. "I got very interested in being a nurse, but when I told my parents, they asked me, 'Why don't you want to be a doctor?'" Osborn credited her parents for their early support of her interest in science; from her mother and father she gained "a very naive and blind assumption that I could do whatever I wanted to do." In describing her academic progress as a girl Osborn noted, "The thing that amazes me about my primary and secondary education is that I remained interested in biology. What I remember of the teaching was pretty awful."

Osborn entered the University of California at Berkeley as a pre-med student. "By senior year I realized that there was no way in the world that I wanted to treat patients." She then pursued biochemistry courses. Osborn recalled, "I realized that I liked bench research and could do it well. I was good at planning experiments and thinking about the results and going on to the next step." She was

awarded a B.A. in physiology from the University of California at Berkeley in 1948, then went on to the University of Washington, attaining a Ph.D. in biochemistry in 1958. Osborn's thesis examined the functions of the vitamins and enzymes whose action depended on folic acid. In 1957, Osborn reported the mode of action of methotrexate, which became a major cancer chemotherapeutic agent, especially for leukemia.

In 1959, Osborn moved into a new area, the study of the structure and building blocks—or biosynthesis—of a molecule complex polysaccharide named lipopolysaccharide. Lipopolysaccharide is unique to a certain class of bacteria that includes pathogens such as salmonella, shigella, and the cholera bacillus. Abundant on the surface of these bacteria, lipopolysaccharide is responsible for major immunological reactions and for the bacteria's characteristic toxicity. Osborn's work led to a new understanding of a previously unknown mechanism of polysaccharide formation.

For her contributions to biochemistry, Osborn was accepted as a fellow of the American Academy of Arts and Sciences in 1977 and was elected to the National Academy of Sciences in 1978. Other major distinctions include having served as president of the American Society of Biological Chemists from 1981 to 1982 and as president of the Federation of American Societies for Experimental Biology from 1982 to 1983. She has been appointed to numerous scientific advisory councils, including the National Institute for General Medical Sciences, National Institutes of Health Division of Research Grants, and the National Science Board. In addition, Osborn has served as editor of several journals, including *Biochemistry, Journal of Biological Chemistry,* and the *Annual Review of Biochemistry.*

Osborn became professor of microbiology at the University of Connecticut Health Center School of Medicine in 1968 and she has been head of the department since 1980. Her interest in the development of antibiotics and chemotherapeutic agents continues on into the 1990s. She is married to a painter, Ralph, and they have no children. In her leisure time, Osborn gardens.

SELECTED WRITINGS BY OSBORN:

Periodicals

Proceedings of the National Academy of Science, Biosynthesis of Bacterial Lipopolysaccharide V. Lipid-Linked Intermediates in the Biosynthesis of the O-Antigen Groups of *Salmonella typhimurium,*, Volume 54, 1965, pp. 228–33.
Proceedings of the National Academy of Science, Isolation of a Mutant of *Salmonella typhimurium* Dependent on D-Arabinase–5-phosphate for Growth and Synthesis of 3-deoxy-D-mannoctulosonate (Ketodeoooxyoctonate), Volume 69, 1972, pp. 3756–60.
The Harvey Lectures, Biogenesis of the Outer Membrane of *Salmonella,*, Series 78, 1984, pp. 87–103.

Other

Interview with Laura Newman, conducted March 8, 1994.

Sketch by Laura Newman

Douglas D. Osheroff

Douglas D. Osheroff
1945–
American physicist

Douglas D. Osheroff, co-recipient of the 1996 Nobel Prize for Physics with his colleagues **David M. Lee** and **Robert C. Richardson**, is known for his important role in the work that led to the discovery of superfluidity in helium-3, a rare isotope of helium. A junior member of the Cornell scientific team that made the discovery (he was a doctoral student of his co-workers Lee and Richardson), Osheroff has continued work with helium-3, focusing on the two transitions occurring in the superfluid state.

Osheroff was born in Aberdeen, Washington, on August 1, 1945, the son of William Osheroff and Bessie Anne (Ondov) Osheroff. He married Phyllis S. K. Liu in 1970. After obtaining a B.S. at the California Institute of Technology in 1967, he came to Cornell University, where he collaborated in low-temperature physics research with his doctoral mentors. In 1973, Osheroff completed his doctorate. He remained at Cornell, while concurrently working at Bell Laboratories, where he stayed until 1982. At Cornell, he headed the Solid State and Low Temperature Department from 1982 to 1987. Osheroff left Cornell in 1987 to accept a full professorship at Stanford University. Chair of Stanford's Physics Department from 1993 to 1996, he was named J. G. Jackson and C. J. Wood Professor of Physics in 1992.

Notices Crucial Clue Leading to Historic Discovery

When Osheroff and his colleagues started the research that would eventually lead to discovery of helium-3 in a superfluid state, they were actually looking for the transition of frozen helium-3 to a magnetic state. As a sample of helium-3 cooled to the temperature of 2.7 millikelvins, it was Osheroff who noticed significant, and unexpected, deviations in the cooling rate of the sample. Realizing that the results of the experiments were pointing in a new direction, the scientists abandoned the magnetic state hypothesis, theorizing instead that the helium-3 may have attained a particular solid state. However, additional observation led Osheroff and his colleagues to conclude that their sample had reached the state of superfluidity. In fact, the scientists found that helium-3 can exist in two distinct states of superfluidity.

Physicists find superfluidity fascinating because substances in a superfluid state exhibit behaviors that are much different than those observed in other states. For instance, a superfluid in an open cup-like container will spontaneously overflow. While classical mechanics cannot account for such phenomena, superfluidity does not violate the principles of quantum mechanics. When, for example, a liquid is cooled to a temperature near absolute zero, it loses its inner resistance, or friction, because its atoms, which at "normal" temperature move around in a random fashion, fall into a rigid structure. The lack of inner resistance is responsible for the liquid's unusual behavior. However, more important is the light that superfluidity can shed on microscopic and macroscopic quantum physics. In addition to widening the horizons of quantum theory, superfluidity may also explain certain puzzles pertaining the genesis of the universe. For example, scientists have used superfluid helium-3 to experimentally replicate certain helium reactions that, having occurred in the first microseconds following the big bang, may account for the hypothetical cosmic strings, which, scientists believe, played an important role in the formation of galaxies.

Osheroff is a Fellow of the American Physical Society. His memberships include the National Academy of Sciences and the American Academy of Arts and Sciences. A recipient of the 1981 John D. and Catherine T. MacArthur Fellowship, Osheroff also won a Walter J. Gores Award for

Excellence in Teaching. With his colleagues Lee and Richardson, Osheroff received Britain's Institute of Physics Sir Francis Simon Memorial Prize in 1976. In recognition for their discovery, the three scientists also received the 1980 Oliver E. Buckley Solid State Physics Prize.

SELECTED WRITINGS BY OSHEROFF:

Periodicals

(With M. C. Cross) "Novel Magnetic Properties of Solid Helium-3." *Physics Today* (February 1987): 34.

FURTHER READING:

Books

Leggett, A. J. *The Problems of Physics*. Oxford: Oxford University Press, 1987.
Tilley, Donald E., and Walter Thumm. *College Physics: A Text with Applications to the Life Sciences*. Menlo Park, CA: Cummings, 1971.

Periodicals

Browne, Malcolm W. "Discoveries of Superfluid Helium, and 'Buckyballs,' Earn Nobels for 6 Scientists." *New York Times* (10 October 1996): D21.
Lounasmaa, O. V., and George Pickett. "The ^{3}He Superfluids." *Scientific American* (June 1990): 104-11.
Peterson, Ivars. "Superfluidity Earns Physics Nobel." *Science News* 150, no. 16 (19 October 1996): 247.

Other

Nobel Foundation WWW Server Posting (9 October 1996). http://www.nobel.ki.se

Sketch by Jane Stewart Cook and Zoran Minderovic

Donald E. Osterbrock
1924–
American astronomer

Donald E. Osterbrock, an admired astronomer and author of astronomy books, has been among the most significant players in the study of gas in space and the determination of its structure and composition. Because of him, twentieth-century astronomers gained a greater understanding of gas motions and the centers of galaxies. His work on radiation emitted from gas regions and the hearts of

galaxies opened these fields to a wider audience of astronomers, while his textbooks and popular books allowed students and lay audiences to share in the excitement of astronomy.

Donald Edward Osterbrock was born in Cincinnati, Ohio, on July 13, 1924, to William Carl Osterbrock and Elsie Wettlin Osterbrock. After serving in the U.S. Air Force from 1943 to 1946, he received both a Ph.B. and a B.S. degree from the University of Chicago in 1948; his M.S. degree followed the next year, and in 1952, he received his Ph.D. in astronomy. He worked as an astronomy fellow at Princeton University for a year before joining the faculty of the California Institute of Technology in 1953. Until he left that position five years later, he also served on the staff of the Mount Wilson and Palomar observatories. While at Caltech, Osterbrock began training young astronomers, among them George O. Abell, future president of the Astronomical Society of the Pacific. He worked at the University of Wisconsin at Madison from 1958 to 1973, taking time off from 1960–61 to work at the Institute for Advanced Study at Princeton. At Madison, Osterbrock became an astronomy professor in 1961, serving as department chairman in 1966–7 and 1969–72. In the early 1970s, he took on other duties, including a stint as letters editor of the *Astrophysical Journal* (1971–73) and president of Commission 34 (on interstellar matter and planetary nebulae) of the International Astronomical Union (1967–70). In 1972, Osterbrock joined the faculty of the University of California at Santa Cruz, as professor of astronomy and astrophysics at Lick Observatory, where he also served as director until 1981. He was president of the American Astronomical Society for two years, succeeding Bernard F. Burke of MIT in 1988.

In the 1950s, Osterbrock's research on middle-aged stars gave astronomers a clue to the importance of motion in the stars' outer layers. The motion, called convection, occurred when chunks of matter physically percolated out from inner layers of the star towards the surface. Before Osterbrock's work on convection, such noted astronomers as Karl Schwarzschild, Arthur Eddington, and S. Chandrasekhar thought convection was *not* an important process in stars. Osterbrock opened the path to better models of stars.

Penetrated Mysteries of Interstellar Gas

Osterbrock explored diffuse clouds of gas in regions between stars. These clouds of gas shine because of the ultraviolet light given off by stars concealed in them. The gas, affected by this ultraviolet light, "ionizes"—that is, its electrons are ejected from its atoms. Once freed, these electrons combine with other atoms, and the processes of ionization and recombination balance each other. When electrons recombine, the gas emits a spectrum. Spectra may give clues to the temperature, density, and types of elements in the gas. Some parts of spectra appear brighter than others, and comparing brightness provides clues to the physical makeup of the gas. In the late 1950s, Osterbrock and Michael J. Seaton used brightness ratios to explore small, bright regions of gas with a single central star. Osterbrock also examined dimmer and more diffuse gas regions. He made a detailed model of the Orion Nebula, showing what physical phenomena would account for the observed spectrum. The Orion Nebula work was adopted by other astronomers in their studies of other gas regions. In the mid–1970s, Osterbrock and students at Santa Cruz took advantage of the capabilities of the Lick Observatory to study the nature of spiral galaxies with bright centers—the so-called "Seyfert" galaxies. They also looked at galaxies emitting strong radio waves. Osterbrock's student Alan T. Koski found that extreme amounts of radiation in galaxy centers were coming not from stars but from the cores of the galaxies themselves. Koski's finding added fuel to the argument that the tremendous energy in galactic centers is due to disks of matter surrounding giant black holes. Into the 1980s, Osterbrock strove to collect data of uniform quality from different galaxies so they could be compared and contrasted.

Osterbrock's studies of the relative strengths of spectra helped astronomers understand both the Milky Way's center and the center of other galaxies. By the late 1980s, Osterbrock had extended his research interests to the spectra of unusually bright galactic centers. As with clouds of gas, the components of spectra in galactic centers can be analyzed to estimate their temperature and density. While most of the atoms in gas clouds have two or three electrons stripped away, the atoms in galaxy centers can have as many as six missing. Osterbrock and student Ross D. Cohen compared galaxies that emitted in the radio part of the spectrum with those that did not. They found very few differences, but suggested that those few differences could hold the key to why some galaxies give off a lot of radio emission and others do not.

Osterbrock has written several books; his two most widely praised and popular ones are *James E. Keeler, Pioneer American Astrophysicist, and the Early Development of American Astrophysics* and *Eye on the Sky: Lick Observatory's First Century.* "Osterbrock is not content to give superficial descriptions of the work of others, but always integrates their results into his own thinking and writes about it with as much depth and clarity as if it were his own," said Nancy Morrison of the University of Toledo and chair of the Astronomical Society of the Pacific Awards Committee on the occasion of Osterbrock's winning the Bruce medal. A more recent book, *Pauper & Prince,* concerned the life of George Willis Ritchey, the guiding force behind Mount Wilson Observatory's 60- and 100-inch reflecting telescopes.

Osterbrock has been highly decorated for his contributions to the fields of astronomy and astrophysics. In January 1991, he won the Henry Norris Russell Lectureship, the highest honor of the American Astronomical Society, for "lifetime achievement." The award citation called him "a leader in the investigation of the properties of gaseous nebulae." Also in 1991, Osterbrock won the Catherine Bruce Wolfe medal of the Astronomical Society of the Pacific, for his research, writing, and educational efforts.

Having a keen interest in the history of astronomy, Osterbrock served as chairman of the history committee of the Astronomical Society of the Pacific from 1982 until 1986, and as vice chairman of the history of astronomy division of the American Astronomical Society from 1985 until 1987. A Congregationalist, he married Irene L. Hansen on September 19, 1952, and has three children: Carol Ann, William Carl, and Laura Jane. At the time of his professorship at the Lick Observatory, Osterbrock resided in Santa Cruz, California.

SELECTED WRITINGS BY OSTERBROCK:

Books

Astrophysics of Gaseous Nebulae, W. H. Freeman, 1974.

James E. Keeler, Pioneer American Astrophysicist, and the Early Development of American Astrophysics, Cambridge University Press, 1984.

Eye on the Sky: Lick Observatory's First Century, University of California Press, 1988.

Pauper & Prince: Ritchey, Hale, and Big American Telescopes, University of Arizona Press, 1993.

FURTHER READING:

Periodicals

Morrison, Nancy, *Mercury: The Journal of the Astronomical Society of the Pacific,* The 1991 A.S.P. Award Winners, November/December, 1991, pp. 182–184.

Sketch by Sebastian Thaler

Friedrich Wilhelm Ostwald
1853–1932
German physical chemist

Around the turn of the twentieth century, Friedrich Wilhelm Ostwald was responsible for organizing physical chemistry into a discipline distinct from organic chemistry. He wrote a basic textbook on the subject and co-founded a journal that provided physical chemists with a forum for their theories and experimental results. For his work in the measurement of chemical reactions, electrochemistry, and the acceleration of chemical reactions by the use of catalysts, Ostwald won the 1909 Nobel Prize for chemistry. He was also a prolific writer in both the philosophy and psychology of science, and he culminated a long academic career with valuable independent research into color theory.

Ostwald was born on September 2, 1853, in Riga, Latvia (now Estonia) into a family of master artisans. His parents, Gottfried and Elisabeth (Leuckel) Ostwald, were descendants of German immigrants; his father was a master cooper who had been a painter as a young man. The humanities were emphasized in the Ostwald home, and young Friedrich Wilhelm learned to paint and play the viola and piano; he was also an avid reader. These passions stayed with him throughout his life, but at an early age he also became enthralled with chemical experimentation, creating his own fireworks when he was eleven. He studied at the Riga Realgymnasium and in 1872 enrolled at the University of Dorpat (now the State University of Tartu in Estonia), where he studied both chemistry and physics. At this time, chemists were almost exclusively concerned with research on organic molecules, but Ostwald's natural inclinations led him to a study of physical chemistry. He received his bachelor's degree in 1875 from Dorpat and stayed on to lecture and complete his master's degree in 1876 and his Ph.D. in 1878.

Explores the Nature of Chemical Affinities

Ostwald's early interests in the measurement of chemical reactions were spurred by the work of Julius Thomsen, who had measured the heat accompanying chemical reactions. Ostwald had realized that other properties could serve equally well for such measurements; his master's thesis had concerned the density of substances by volume in a watery solution, and his doctoral thesis dealt with optical refraction. The result of the laboriously repetitive experiments he performed were affinity tables for twelve acids. During this period, he became increasingly interested in the subject of chemical affinities, or the combinational reactions between various chemicals. In 1881 Ostwald was appointed professor of chemistry at the Riga Polytechnic University, where he expanded his research into chemical affinities by measuring the rate at which chemical changes take place. He confirmed his earlier measurements of volume and density with measurements of the velocity at which acids will split esters into alcohol and organic acid, and he was able to assign precise numerical values to chemical reactions and affinities.

Ostwald's name was becoming known for such discoveries, and he was soon joined in his work establishing physical chemistry by two younger scientists: **Svante Arrhenius** from Sweden and Jacobus Van't Hoff from Holland. In 1884, Arrhenius sent Ostwald his doctoral dissertation; hotly contested by many of the scientists at his university, it concerned affinity and electrical conductivity. Ostwald immediately saw the importance of Arrhenius's work, and he recognized that it included the beginning of the idea of electrolytic dissociation and thus of ionization, or the conversion of a neutral atom into a positive ion and a free electron. He did all he could to sponsor Arrhenius. In 1886, Ostwald became interested in van't Hoff's work on the similarities between solutions and gases; he was no longer working alone in physical chemistry.

In 1885 Ostwald had begun work on the *Lehrbuch der allgemeinen Chemie,* a textbook of general chemistry which he finished in 1887, the year he received an appointment at the University of Leipzig as the first professor of physical chemistry in Germany. There van't Hoff joined him as an assistant and the two soon created a center for the study of physical chemistry and founded the influential journal for the new discipline, *Zeitschrift für physikalische Chemie.* In 1889, Ostwald published a book on analytical chemistry, *Grundriss der allgemeinen Chemie,* which further distinguished physical chemistry from organic chemistry. By this time, Ostwald had begun to understand the world in terms of energy; he believed that everything could be reduced to that single concept, and this was a theme that would dominate the rest of his life and work. By 1898 Leipzig University had created a physical chemistry institute, a training and research center where much of Ostwald's later work was done.

Work on Catalysis Leads to Nobel Prize

Ostwald's research into the dynamics of chemical reactions in solutions led to the dilution law of 1888, which established a relationship between electrolytic dissociation and conductivity. Arrhenius's theory of electrolytic dissociation states that atoms will come apart (dissociate) in water, creating charged ions that have gained or lost electrons. Excited by this theory, Ostwald and his researchers turned their attention to electrochemistry, seeing it as a model for chemical reactions that are accelerated or catalyzed by weak bases or acids. This led to his most important research, which was in the area of catalysis, whereby a substance is used to speed up a chemical reaction but remains unaffected by that reaction. Though the process of catalysis had been described some sixty years earlier, Ostwald made such processes measurable and also connected them with his own work on chemical affinity. Although his theory that catalysis operates simply by having catalysts present and that catalysts do not take part in the reaction is now known to be incorrect, his work on catalysis was otherwise productive. In 1901, Ostwald's work led to the process for converting ammonia to nitric acid, which was accomplished by burning ammonia in the presence of platinum. This process was patented in 1902 and allowed mass manufacturing of the basic component of explosives. Renewed interest in catalysis also led to great strides in the chemical industry: oil, for example, is transformed into fuel and natural gas by the catalytic process. In 1909, Ostwald was awarded the Nobel Prize in chemistry for this work.

In 1905, Ostwald spent a year as an exchange professor at Harvard University in the United States, spreading the word of physical chemistry across the Atlantic. The following year he retired from his chair of physical chemistry at Leipzig, tired of administrative duties and political infighting. His working life was far from over, however. He bought an estate in a Leipzig suburb, which he dubbed 'Energie,' and there he continued a number of experimental and writing projects. Along with editing professional journals, he also worked on a history and classification of people who were considered geniuses, reprints of significant papers in chemistry and physics, and a three-volume autobiography. Some of his many interests included the philosophy and history of science, pacifism, internationalism, and the creation of a world language—he was very interested in Esperanto while he was a visiting professor at Harvard and later he wrote his own language, Ido. Ostwald also made important contributions to color theory—standardization of colors and a theory of color harmony. This was an outgrowth of his own interest in painting.

In 1880 Ostwald had married the daughter of a medical doctor in Riga, Helene von Reyher. They had three sons and two daughters. One of his sons, Wilhelm Wolfgang, would grow up to be a well-known chemist himself. Until his death from uremia in early April of 1932, Ostwald continued to work tirelessly for the causes he espoused.

SELECTED WRITINGS BY OSTWALD:

Books

Lehrbuch der allgemeinen Chemie, 2 volumes, Engleman, 1885–1887.
Grundriss der allgemeinen Chemie, Engleman, 1889.

Die wissenschaftlichen Grundlagen der analytischen Chemie, Engleman, 1894.
Grundlinien der anorganischen Chemie, Engleman, 1900.

Periodicals

Zeitschrift für physikalische Chemie, Über physico-chemische Messmethoden, Volume 17, 1895, pp. 427–445.
Verhandlungen der Gesellschaft Deutsche Naturforscher und Ärtze, Über Katalyse, Volume 73, 1901, pp. 184–201.

FURTHER READING:

Books

Concise Dictionary of Scientific Biography, Charles Scribner's Sons, 1981, pp. 522–523.
Gillespie, Charles Coulson, editor, *Dictionary of Scientific Biography,* Volume 15, Scribner, 1978, pp. 455–469.
Farber, Eduard, editor, *Great Chemists,* Interscience Publishers, 1961, pp. 1021–1030.

Periodicals

Donnan, F. G., *Journal of the Chemical Society,* Ostwald Memorial Lecture, 1933, pp. 316–332.

Sketch by J. Sydney Jones

David Packard
1912–1996
American electrical engineer

David Packard was an electrical engineer and entrepreneur who had a profound impact on politics and industry in the United States. With **William Hewlett**, he founded Hewlett-Packard in 1939, one of the nation's first high-technology companies. He served as Deputy Secretary of Defense under President Nixon, and as vice chairman of the President's Commission on Defense Management, known as the Packard Commission, under President Reagan. He also made large charitable contributions through the David and Lucile Packard Foundation.

Packard was born in Pueblo, Colorado, on September 7, 1912, the second child of Sperry and Ella (Graber) Packard. His mother was a high school teacher of German descent, and his father was a lawyer descended from New England colonialists. Packard was educated at Somerlid Grade School, where he first became interested in electrical engineering, and at Centennial High School in Pueblo. He later attended Stanford University, where he first met Hewlett. Packard played football and received his B.A. in electrical engineering in 1934. In 1935, he was hired by the General Electric company to work in the vacuum-tube engineering division at Schenectady, New York. Offered a fellowship by an engineering professor, **Frederick Terman,** he returned to Stanford and in 1939 took a master's degree in electrical engineering with a focus on radio engineering.

Co-founds Hewlett-Packard Company

In 1939, Packard and Hewlett, two of the most successful partners in the history of industry, used $538 to start their firm in Packard's garage in Palo Alto. Many of their early inventions were related to work that Hewlett had done at Stanford. One of Packard and Hewlett's first projects was production of a new kind of audio oscillator, called a "resistance-capacitance oscillator," the design of which was the subject of Hewlett's master's thesis at Stanford. The oscillator, named the 200A, produced electrical signals in the range of human hearing, from 20 to 20,000 cycles per second. The device was used primarily to measure the intensity of recorded sound. Hewlett and Packard presented the oscillator, which sold at a quarter the cost of similar instruments of its day, at a 1938 meeting of the International Radio Engineers in Portland, Oregon.

David Packard

Here, they met Walt Disney; later, the chief sound engineer at Disney Studios ordered eight of these devices for use in making the landmark film *Fantasia.*

Hewlett-Packard was incorporated a year later, and the two men flipped a coin to see whose name would go first. Packard co-founded the West Coast Electronics Foundation in 1942 and was awarded the Medal of Honor of the Electronics Industry for his involvement. Packard, who was more the businessman than Hewlett, served as president of Hewlett-Packard from 1947 to 1964, and as chairman of the board and chief executive officer from 1964 to 1968. During World War II, the company grew rapidly as the result of defense contracts; forced to reorganize and redefine their objectives after the war, Hewlett and Packard decided to focus development and marketing efforts on the engineering industry. The company specialized in instruments for measuring and testing; they were also one of the first companies to make use of semiconductors, and in 1966 they introduced their first computer.

Hewlett-Packard was a highly successful technology firm by the 1960s, but almost none of their market was outside of industry; their first successful product in the popular market was the hand-held calculator, introduced in 1968 as the HP 9100. Growth at Hewlett-Packard was the result of continuing technological innovation, but as *Fortune* magazine observed in a 1988 profile of Packard, "No single product . . . has brought the company as much distinction as its management style." An informal management style, which often involved what Hewlett remembered as "wandering around," cultivated loyalty and commitment from their work force and encouraged creative participation.

Becomes Involved in National Politics

Packard was chairman of the board of trustees of Stanford University in 1958 and 1959. Packard was also a friend of Herbert Hoover, and in keeping with Hoover's wishes, he prevented a takeover by liberal faculty of the Hoover Institution, where he sat on the advisory board. He became acquainted with Richard Nixon during this period and supported him for president in the election of 1968. In 1969, Packard was asked by the Secretary of Defense, Melvin Laird, to serve under Nixon as Deputy Secretary of Defense, a post he held until 1971. During his tenure at the Pentagon, Packard made sure he did not benefit from any changes in the value of Hewlett-Packard stock; during the three years he was in his office, the value of his stock rose over twenty million dollars, but he arranged his holdings so he never received this increase.

Another California politician to whom Packard developed strong ties was Ronald Reagan. In 1985, he was chosen by President Reagan to head the Packard Commission, which was charged with making recommendations to overhaul defense-procurement policies. This was during a period when government was spending a great deal of money on defense, and Packard was appointed in the midst of a scandal over the prices many defense contractors were charging the Pentagon. In the report his committee submitted to the president, Packard recommended strengthening the role of the chair of the Joint Chiefs of Staff and stimulating better long-term planning, as well as appointing what *U.S. News and World Report* called "a high-level civilian procurement czar to oversee the services' buying plans." After the report was released, Packard told *U.S. News and World Report:* "There's no question that, because of long-term structural problems, we've wasted tens of billions of dollars out of the more than a trillion that's been spent." The Reagan administration submitted to Congress most of the recommendations he included in his report.

Both Packard and Hewlett retired from active leadership of their company in 1978, but they returned to take the helm at Hewlett-Packard in 1990, guiding the company through difficulties caused by mismanagement and changing circumstances in the computer industry. They restructured the divisions of the company and reduced the power of the centralized bureaucracy, and Hewlett-Packard was posting a profit again within two years. Packard remained chairman of the company until 1993, when he took the title of chairman emeritus.

On April 8, 1938, Packard married Lucile Laura Salter, a Stanford classmate; the couple had four children. His wife, who died in 1987, shared many of his interests, and they founded the David and Lucile Packard Foundation to support scientific and health research, as well as a broad range of social and educational programs. The foundation made a $70 million contribution to the children's hospital at Stanford University. The Packards were also the major contributors to the construction of the Monterey Bay Aquarium, where Packard designed a machine to simulate tidal movements. He once financed a project to salvage four U.S. Navy Sparrowhawk biplanes that had gone down in 1,500 feet (450 m) of water off the Pacific coast in 1935 aboard the U.S.S. Macon. In 1988, Packard announced that he would give most of his fortune, which was estimated to amount to over two billion dollars, to the David and Lucile Packard Foundation. Their children supervise many of the foundation's programs, particularly those in archaeology and marine biology. Packard died on March 27, 1996 at Stanford University Hospital.

SELECTED WRITINGS BY PACKARD:

Periodicals

"The Real Scandal in Military Contracts." *Across the Board* (November 1988): 17-23.

FURTHER READING:

Books

Kanter, Rosabeth Moss. *The Change Masters.* New York: Simon & Schuster, 1983.
Peters, Thomas J., and Robert H. Waterman. *In Search of Excellence.* New York: Warner Books, 1982.
Schoenbaum, Elenora, ed. *Political Profiles: The Nixon/ Ford Years,* New York: Facts on File, 1979.

Periodicals

"Calling for a Pentagon Shake-Up." *U.S. News and World Report* (10 March 1986): 23-24.
Goff, T. J. "The Best in Business: 1986." *California Business Magazine.* (December 1986): 40-45.
Guzzardi, Walter, Jr. "The U.S. Business Hall of Fame." *Fortune,* (14 March 1988): 142-44.
Guzzardi, Walter, Jr. "Packard's Big Giveaway." *Time* (9 May 1988): 70.
Guzzardi, Walter, Jr. "A Pentagon Manifesto." *Newsweek* (10 March 1986).
Guzzardi, Walter, Jr. "A Quartet of High-Tech Pioneers." *Fortune* (12 October 1987): 148-49.
Guzzardi, Walter, Jr. "Silicon Valley's Troubled Olympus." *California* (February 1991): 12-13.
Barnes, Bart. "David Packard Dies at 83; Founded Hewlett-Packard" (obituary). *Washington Post* (27 March 1996): D4.

Fisher, Lawrence M. "David Packard, 83, Pioneer of Silicon Valley, Is Dead" (obituary). *New York Times* (27 March 1996): D20.

King, Peter H. "One Who Took The High Road." *Los Angeles Times* (31 March 1996): A3.

Other

Packard, David. Interview by John Henry Dreyfuss. 9 February 1994.

Sketch by John Henry Dreyfuss

George Palade

George Palade
1912–
American cell biologist

George Palade entered the science of cell biology at a time when techniques such as electron microscopy and sedimentation of discrete bits of cell structure were beginning to reveal the minute structure of the cell. He not only advanced these techniques, but also, by investigating the ultrastructure or fine structure of animal cells, identified and described the function of mitochondria as the power-house of the cell and of ribosomes as the site of protein manufacture. For his research in the function and structure of such cell components, he shared the 1974 Nobel Prize in physiology or medicine with two other cell researchers, **Albert Claude** and **Christian R. Duvé**.

George Emil Palade was born on November 19, 1912, in Jassy (Iași), in northeastern Romania. One of three children, Palade came from a professional family—his father, Emil, was a philosophy professor at the University of Jassy, while his mother, Constanta Cantemir, taught elementary school. Palade's two sisters, Adriana and Constanta, would grow up to be a professor of history and a pediatrician, respectively.

Attending school in Buzau, Palade entered the University of Bucharest in 1930 as a medical student. Ten years later he received his degree, having completed his internship as well as a thesis on the microanatomy of the porpoise kidney. Having earned his medical degree, Palade chose to focus on research instead of practicing medicine. His particular interest was histology, or the microscopic structure of plant and animal tissue. With the advent of the World War II, Palade was drafted into the army and stationed at the University of Bucharest Medical School as an assistant professor of anatomy. In 1941, he married Irina Malaxa; they eventually had two children together, a daughter, Georgia Teodora, and a son, Philip Theodore.

Proceeds with Research in United States

In 1945, after being discharged from the army, Palade obtained a research position at New York University. While there he met the eminent cell biologist Albert Claude, who had pioneered both the use of the electron microscope in cell study and techniques of cell fractionation (the separation of the constituent parts of cells by centrifugal action). The older scientist invited Palade to join the staff at the Rockefeller Institute (now Rockefeller University), and in 1946 Palade accepted a two-year fellowship as visiting investigator. In 1947 the communist-led government in Romania declared the country a people's republic and forced the abdication of King Michael. Palade, who had always planned to return home to work, now opted to remain in the United States. He became a U.S. citizen in 1952 and a full professor of cytology at Rockefeller in 1958.

At the Rockefeller Institute, Palade's first achievements came in the preparation of cell tissue for both the fractionation process and electron microscopy. In the former, collaborating with W. C. Schneider and George Hogeboom, Palade introduced as a fixative the use of gradient sucrose, and in the latter, buffered osmium tetroxide. But his accomplishments soon went beyond improvements in methodology. Claude left the institute in 1949, and in the next decade Palade and his collaborators, building on Claude's work, reported groundbreaking descriptions of the fine appearance of the cell and of its biochemical function. Concentrating on the cytoplasm—the living material in the cell outside the nucleus—Palade was first attracted to larger organelles (bodies of definite structure and function in the cytoplasm) which Claude had earlier called "secretory granules." Palade showed that these tiny sausage-shaped structures, mitochondria, are the site where energy for the cell is generated. Animal cells typically contain a thousand such mitochondria, each creating adenosine triphosphate—ATP, a high-energy phosphate molecule—through enzymic (enzyme-catalyzed) oxidation or breakdown of fat and sugar. The ATP is then released into the cytoplasm where it powers energy-requiring mechanisms such as nerve impulse conduction, muscle contraction, or protein synthesis.

Using the high-power electron microscope (a device that utilizes electrons instead of light to form images of minute objects), Palade next revealed a delicate tracery, subsequently termed the endoplasmic reticulum by his collaborator, Keith R. Porter. The endoplasmic reticulum is a series of double-layered membranes present throughout all cells except mature erythrocytes, or red blood cells. Its function is the formation and transport of fats and proteins. By far Palade's most significant work was with so-called microsomes, small bodies in the cytoplasm that Claude had earlier identified and shown to have a relatively high ribonucleic acid (RNA) content. RNA is the genetic messenger in protein synthesis. Palade observed these microsomes both as free bodies within the cytoplasm, and attached to the endoplasmic reticulum. In 1956, using a high-speed centrifuge, Palade and his colleague Philip Siekevitz were able to isolate microsomes and observe them under the electron microscope. They discovered that these microsomes were made of equal parts of RNA and protein.

Traces the Pathway of Protein Synthesis

Palade assumed that these RNA-rich microsomes were in fact the factories producing protein to sustain not only the cell but the entire organism. The microsome was renamed the ribosome, and Palade and his team went to work to investigate the pathway of protein synthesis in the cell. Palade and Siekevitz began a series of experiments on ribosomes of the liver and pancreas, employing autoradiographic tracing, a sophisticated process similar to x-ray photography in which a picture is produced by radiation. Investigating in particular exocrine cells (those that secrete externally) of the guinea pig pancreas, the team was able, by 1960, to show that ribosomes do in fact synthesize proteins that are then transported through the endoplasmic reticulum. Further research with Lucien Caro, J. D. Jamieson, C. Redman, David Sabatini, and Y. Tashiro elucidated the function of the larger ribosomes attached to the endoplasmic reticulum, establishing them as the site where amino acids assemble into polypeptides (chains of amino acids). Palade's team also traced the transportation network as well as the function of the Golgi complex, tubelike structures where proteins are sorted before final transport to the cell surface for export.

Having completed his work on protein synthesis, Palade turned his attention to cellular transport—the means by which substances move through cell membranes. Working with **Marilyn G. Farquhar**, Palade demonstrated by electron micrography (images formed using an electron microscope) that molecules and ions were engorged by sacs or vesicles that move to the surface from within the cell. These vesicles actually merge with the outer membrane for a time, and then swallow up and bring the substances inside the cell. This vesicular model was in distinct contrast to the then current pore model whereby it was thought that molecules simply entered the cell through pores in the membrane.

Following the death of his wife in 1969, Palade married Marilyn Gist Farquhar. In 1972 he left the Rockefeller Institute and became a full professor of cell biology at Yale University, continuing his research in cell morphology and function, but also turning to practical clinical uses of his discoveries. His later work is an attempt to establish links between defects in cellular protein production and various illnesses. In 1974 Palade shared the Nobel Prize in Physiology or Medicine with his former mentor, Albert Claude, and with Christian R. de Duvé, for their descriptions of the detailed microscopic structure and functions of the cell. He was also the recipient of the Passano Award in 1964, the Albert Lasker Basic Medical Research Award in 1966, the Gairdner Foundation Special Award in 1967, and the Horowitz Prize in 1970. In addition, Palade is the founding editor of the *Journal of Cell Biology*.

In 1990, Palade left Yale to become the dean for scientific affairs at the University of California, San Diego. He is also serving at the university as a professor-in-residence in cellular and molecular medicine.

SELECTED WRITINGS BY PALADE:

Periodicals

Journal of Morphology, The Nature of the Golgi Apparatus, I and II, Volume 85, 1949, pp. 35–111.

Journal of Biophysical and Biochemical Cytology, Liver Microsomes: An Integrated Morphological and Biochemical Study, Volume 2, 1956, pp. 171–200.

Journal of Biophysical and Biochemical Cytology, Pancreatic Microsomes: An Integrated Morphological and Biochemical Study, Volume 2, 1956, pp. 671–690.

Woods Hole Subcellular Particles Symposium, Functional Changes in the Structure of Cell Components, 1958, pp. 64–80.

Journal of Biophysical and Biochemical Cytology, A Cytochemical Study on the Pancreas of the Guinea Pig, 1–4, Volume 4, 1958, pp. 203–218, 309–319, 557–566; Volume 5, 1959, pp. 1–10.

Journal of Cell Biology, Functional Evidence for the Existence of a Third Cell Type in the Renal Glomerulus: Phagocytosis of the Filtration Residues by a Distinctive 'Third Cell,', Volume 13, April, 1962, pp. 55–87.

FURTHER READING:

Books

McGraw-Hill Modern Scientists and Engineers,
McGraw, 1980, pp. 388–389.
Nobel Laureates in Medicine or Physiology, Garland,
1990, pp. 442–445.
Nobel Prize Winners, H. W. Wilson, 1987, pp.
789–791.

Periodicals

New York Times, October 11, 1974, p. 22.
Science, November 8, 1974, pp. 516–520.

Sketch by J. Sydney Jones

Angeliki Panajiotatou
1875–1954
Greek physician

Angeliki Panajiotatou and her sister were the first women to graduate from the University of Athens with medical degrees. Because of discrimination against her on the basis of her sex, however, it took Panajiotatou many years to be accepted as a physician in her native country. She had to leave Greece in order to practice medicine, moving to Egypt where she became an internationally recognized authority on tropical diseases.

Panajiotatou was born in Greece in 1875. She and her sister enrolled at the University of Athens in 1896, then Panajiotatou pursued her medical studies in Germany after graduation. She returned to the University of Athens in 1905, where she was appointed lecturer on the faculty of medicine and became the subject of bitter controversy. The sight of a woman teaching medicine proved too much for the medical students. According to the *Continuum Dictionary of Women's Biography,* the students shouted at her, "Back in the kitchen, back in the kitchen!" They refused to take her classes and she was eventually forced to resign.

Panajiotatou went to Alexandria, Egypt, where she practiced as a municipal doctor and was appointed professor at Cairo University. Later, she became chief of laboratories at the Greek Hospital in Alexandria, remaining in that position for twenty years. Upon passing a competitive examination, she also became a member of the Quarantine Service of Egypt, a post she held for more than thirty years.

Panajiotatou was interested in tropical diseases such as cholera and typhus, and she experimented to find ways of controlling them. Throughout her career, she journeyed to many international conferences to present the results of her

work. The hygiene of ancient Greece was another of her interests, and her book on the subject has often been quoted by medical historians. A popular figure for many years in Alexandria's Greek community, she was often visited by artists and intellectuals who valued her interest in Greek culture.

Panajiotatou returned to Greece in 1938 and was appointed professor at the University of Athens. She died in Athens in 1954.

SELECTED WRITINGS BY PANAJIOTATOU:

Books

The Hygiene of the Ancient Greeks, Vigot Freres, 1923.

Periodicals

Grammata, Dysentery and Enteritis in Tropical Countries, Volume 27, 1932, pp. 737–783.

FURTHER READING:

Books

Uglow, Jennifer, editor, *The Continuum Dictionary of Women's Biography,* Continuum, 1989.

Periodicals

Morton, Rosalie S., *The Medical Woman's Journal,* Report of Work of Women Physicians in the Near East, August, 1936, p. 203.
Morton, Rosalie S., *Quarterly Bulletin of the Medical Women's National Association,* Volume 42, 1932.

Sketch by Margo Nash

Wolfgang K. H. Panofsky
1919–
American physicist

Wolfgang K. H. Panofsky is known for his research in the area of atomic particles, especially in pi-mesons, and for his part in designing, building, and maintaining the Stanford Linear Accelerator, a two-mile-long atomic accelerator which has been the site of many important nuclear discoveries. He has also held prominent positions with governmental science, energy, and defense agencies.

Wolfgang Kurt Hermann Panofsky was born in Berlin, Germany, on April 24, 1919. His parents were Erwin Panofsky, an eminent art historian, and the former Dorothea Mosse. His older brother, Hans, later became professor of meteorology at Pennsylvania State University. Both Panofsky children showed signs of unusual intelligence at an early age, and Wolfgang was a strong chess player by the age of eight.

Panofsky received his early education at the Johanneum Gymnasium in Hamburg, where his father had taken a job at the local university. By the early 1930s, however, the Panofskys realized that they would have to leave their homeland. Adolf Hitler's anti-semitic laws and policies made it clear that those of the Jewish faith, such as the Panofskys, were certain to lose their jobs and, very likely, their lives as well. As a result, they left Germany for the United States, where the elder Panofsky accepted an appointment at the Institute for Advanced Studies in Princeton, New Jersey. Wolfgang enrolled at Princeton University in 1934, at the age of 15, and received his B.A. in physics four years later. He then continued his graduate studies at the California Institute of Technology, earning his Ph.D. there in 1942.

Becomes Involved in Government Research

Having graduated just as World War II was getting under way, Panofsky immediately became involved in military research. From 1942 to 1943 he served as director of the Office of Scientific Research and Development Projects at the California Institute of Technology. He then became a consultant to the Manhattan Project at the Los Alamos Scientific Laboratory in New Mexico. At the war's end, he was appointed a research physicist at the University of California's Radiation Laboratory and then, in 1946, joined the university's physics department as assistant professor. In 1951, Panofsky began his long-term affiliation with Stanford University when he accepted a position as professor of physics there.

Panofsky's most notable research during his years in Berkeley involved the study of pi mesons ("pions"), first discovered by English physicist **Cecil Frank Powell** in 1947. Pions are mesons, or fundamental particles, that consist of combinations of elementary particles known as quarks, and that are subject to the strong force. Panofsky's approach was to generate pions by bombarding a target with protons from the 184-inch synchrocyclotron on the Berkeley campus. Gamma rays released during this reaction were then analyzed to determine the characteristics of the pi mesons with which they were associated. Among the discoveries resulting from this series of experiments was a new and more precise value for the mass of the pion and surprising new data about the pion's parity.

Oversees the Construction of Stanford's Linear Accelerator

At Stanford, Panofsky became involved in the university's program of research on elementary particles and the machinery needed to carry out that research. In his capacity as director of the Stanford High Energy Physics Laboratory, he was responsible for the design of the projected two-mile-long linear accelerator (linac) planned for the campus. In 1961, he obtained a grant of $114 million from the U.S. government for the construction of the machine. It was designed to lie about 25 feet underground along a line directly under interstate highway 280 connecting San Francisco and San Jose. The linac was completed five years later and opened officially on September 10, 1967. By that time, initial tests had confirmed that the accelerator was capable of generating the 20 billion electron volt beams for which it had been designed. It took its place as one of the half dozen most powerful particle accelerators in the world.

In the meantime, Panofsky had been appointed director of the newly created Stanford Linear Accelerator Center (SLAC), the facility responsible for the linac's operation. In the twenty-three years that he held this position, Panofsky oversaw the expansion and re-design of the linac necessitated by new needs and changing technology. In 1984, he was named Director Emeritus of SLAC and, in 1989, added the title of Professor Emeritus of Physics.

Panofsky's wartime work marked the beginning of a long commitment to serving the government in a number of capacities. He served, for example, as a member of the President's Science Advisory Committee from 1960 to 1964, as consultant to the Office of Science and Technology from 1965 to 1973, as a member of the steering committee for JASON, a project of the Institute for Defense Analyses, from 1965 to 1973, as a consultant to the Arms Control and Disarmament Agency from 1959 to 1980, and as a member of the Department of Energy Panel on Nuclear Warhead Dismantlement and Special Nuclear Materials Controls beginning in 1991. Panofsky was also president of the American Physical Society from 1974 to 1975 and a member of the Commission on Particles and Fields of the International Union of Pure and Applied Physics.

Panofsky was married to Adele Irene DuMond on July 21, 1942. The couple has five children, Richard Jacob, Margaret Anne, Edward Frank, Carol Eleanor, and Steven Thomas. His awards include the Ernest Orlando Lawrence Memorial Award (1961), the National Medal of Science (1969), the Franklin Institute Award (1970), and the Leo Szilard Award (1982).

SELECTED WRITINGS BY PANOFSKY:

Books

Classical Electricity and Magnetism, Addison-Wesley, 1955.
Particles and Policy, AIP Press, 1993.

FURTHER READING:

Books

McGraw-Hill Modern Scientists and Engineers, Volume 2, McGraw-Hill, 1980, pp. 390–391.

Sketch by David E. Newton

George Papanicolaou
1883–1962
American physician and anatomist

George Papanicolaou was a physician and researcher who was associated with the Cornell University school of medicine for forty-eight years. While studying microscopic slides of cells that had been cast off (exfoliated) in body fluids of laboratory animals and humans, he recognized the presence of abnormal cancer cells. The discovery led to the famous test that bears the first syllable of his last name, the Pap test. He is recognized by his colleagues as the father of modern cytology.

George Nicholas Papanicolaou was born on May 13, 1883, in Coumi, Greece, to Nicholas (a physician) and Mary Critsutas Papanicolaou. He received an M.D. degree from the University of Athens in 1904 and a Ph.D. from the University of Munich in 1910. He married Mary A. Mavroyeni on September 15, 1910. His first position was as a physiologist for an expedition of the Oceanographic Institute of Monaco for one year. In 1912, during the Balkan War, he became an officer in the Greek army medical corps. He came to the United States in 1913, working initially as a salesman, but soon securing work in his field as an anatomy assistant at Cornell University, where he eventually became a full professor in 1924. He also served on the pathology staff of New York Hospital from 1913. Papanicolaou became a United States citizen in 1927.

Finds Cancer Cells in Vaginal Fluid

In the pathology lab at Cornell, Papanicolaou began working with microscope slides of vaginal secretions of guinea pigs. He found that changes in forms of the epithelial cells (the outer layer of the skin or of an organ) correspond with the animal's estrus or menstrual cycle. Using the changes as a measuring device, he was able to study sex hormones and the menstrual cycles of other laboratory animals.

In 1923 Papanicolaou studied vaginal smears of women who had cervical cancer and found cancer cells present. Writing in the medical journal *Growth* in 1920, he outlined his theory that a microscopic smear of vaginal fluid could detect the presence of cancer cells in the uterus. At this time physicians relied on biopsy and curettage to diagnose and treat cancer and ignored the possibilities of a new test based on Papanicolaou's research.

Papanicolaou himself paid little attention to his research in this area for the next decade. At the encouragement of a colleague, Dr. Herbert F. Traut, and with the support of Dean Joseph C. Hinsey of Cornell medical college, he later continued his work in this field and was allowed to devote full time to his research. In 1943 he published conclusive findings that showed smears of vaginal fluid could indicate cervical and uterine cancer before symptoms appear. This time the medical community took notice, and the "new cancer diagnosis," the Pap smear test, won acceptance and became a routine screening technique.

During a Pap test, a scraping or smear is taken from the woman's cervix (the mouth of the uterus) or from the vagina, then is stained and examined under the microscope, where cells may appear normal, cancerous, or suspicious. It is a simple, painless, and effective means of early cancer detection.

Wins International Fame for the Pap Test

Papanicolaou soon won international acclaim for his discovery. The American Cancer Society (ACS) launched massive education campaigns for the test, and Dr. Charles Cameron, a Philadelphia surgeon (who was director of the ACS), said that this test was the most significant and practical discovery in our time. Papanicolaou spent much of his time promoting the test and trained thousands of students in the microscopic detection techniques. Once the test had been accepted, he began to apply the same principle of exfoliate cytology to cancers of the lung, stomach, and bladder.

At Cornell Papanicolaou founded the Papanicolaou Research Center and worked six and a half days a week peering at slides and looking for malignant cells. He seldom took a vacation. When associates advised him to rest, he stated that the work was so interesting and that there was so much to be done. His wife worked as his research assistant and driver.

Papanicolaou was a member of many societies and won twelve prestigious awards including the Borden award of the Association of Medical Colleges in 1940, the Lasker award of the Public Health Association in 1950, and the honor medal from the American Cancer Society in 1952. The king of Greece gave him the medal of the Cross of the Grand Commander award, and his native town of Coumi renamed their town square in his honor. He was the author of four books and over one hundred articles.

At the age of seventy-eight, Papanicolaou ended his forty-eight year association with Cornell and took over the Papanicolaou Cancer Institute in Miami. He maintained a busy schedule and was planning for the further expansion of the institute when he suffered a heart attack and died on February 19, 1962. He was buried in Clinton, New Jersey.

In 1983, the hundredth anniversary of Papanicolaou's birth, several articles appeared in scientific journals honoring him and his persistent spirit of scientific discovery. In December, 1992, the *Journal of the Florida Medical Association* issued a thirty year commemorative of his death, which states that because of his persistence, there has been a seventy-percent decrease in cervical and uterine cancer. His techniques are also being applied to other organs and systems in the use of fine needle aspiration.

SELECTED WRITINGS BY PAPANICOLAOU:

Books

The Sexual Cycle of Human Females as Revealed in Vaginal Smears, 1933.
Diagnosis of Uterine Cancer by the Vaginal Smear, 1943.
Epithelia of Women's Reproductive Organs, 1948.
Atlas of Exfoliate Cytology, 1954.

FURTHER READING:

Books

Carmichael, D. Erskine, *The Pap Smear: Life of George N. Pananicolaou,* 1973.

Periodicals

Cameron, Charles S., *Journal of the American Medical Association,* Dedication of the Papanicolaou Cancer Research Institute, 1962, pp. 556–59.
Koprowski, I., *Journal of the American Medical Women's Association,* Remembering George N. Papanicolaou, November-December, 1984, pp. 200–202.
Palatianos et al., *Journal of the Florida Medical Association,* George N. Papanicolaou, M.D., Father of Modern Cytology, December, 1992, pp. 837–38.

Sketch by Evelyn B. Kelly

Mary Lou Pardue
1933–

American biologist

Mary Lou Pardue is a biologist noted for her work in insect genetics. She was born in Lexington, Kentucky, on September 15, 1933, the daughter of Mary Allie Marshall and Louis Arthur Pardue, professor of physics and administrator at the University of Kentucky and Virginia Polytechnic Institute. She received a B.S. in biology from the College of William and Mary in 1955, an M.S. in radiation biology from the University of Tennessee in 1959, and a Ph.D. in biology from Yale University in 1970. At Yale, Pardue's mentor was Joseph G. Gall, with whom she conducted some of her most important research as well as coauthoring several significant articles. In 1972 she became an associate professor of biology at the Massachusetts Institute of Technology, where she has been a professor since 1980. She also participated in summer courses at the Cold Spring Harbor Laboratory between 1970 and 1980.

Pardue's area of specialization is the structure and function of chromosomes in eukaryotic organisms. Eukaryotic organisms are those whose deoxyribonucleic acid (DNA), which provides the information for reproduction, is contained in their cell's nuclei or centers. Pardue's work excludes lower organisms such as bacteria and viruses, which are prokaryotic organisms, having their genetic material located in the cytoplasm (the cell area surrounding the nucleus). Her studies primarily centered on the breed of fruit fly (*Drosophila*) known as *D. melanogaster;* the rapid succession of fruit fly generations—due to their short lifespans—facilitates a time-saving study of genetic developments. Also of importance to Pardue and her coworkers is the fact that the flies' gene activity is similar, and therefore applicable, to higher organisms.

In the late 1960s, Pardue and Gall developed a technique called in situ hybridization for localizing, with intact chromosomes, specific nucleotic sequences, which determine traits imparted during reproduction. These experiments were carried out using the chromosomes for *Drosophila*'s salivary glands. This method, designed to locate genes on the chromosomes, is used to identify the chromosomal regions of DNA that are complementary to specific nucleic acid molecules, or RNAs. The technique involves squashing chromosomes and fixing them on a slide; the DNAs are denatured (a process that diminishes their biological activity) by means of a mild alkaline solution to break hydrogen bonds without separating the DNA from the chromosome. Radioactive RNA is then introduced to the chromosomes under incubating heat which bonds the RNA with the DNA. Once hybridization occurs, the unbonded, single-stranded RNA is removed. Photographic emulsion is then placed on the chromosomes to detect DNA-RNA hybrids by autoradiography, which registers an image through a substance's radioactive properties.

During the mid–1970s Pardue concentrated on the heat-shock response. This refers to the effects of temperature on genetic activity. Studies of the fruit fly showed that increases in its normal environmental temperature exceeding ten degrees resulted in the suspension of some genetic activity; the studies attempted to determine what genes are affected by the heat increase. In a related area of research, insect muscle cell biology of stress response, Pardue found that stress also resulted in the suspension of some genetic activity and the associated synthesis of proteins. An understanding of this, the most basic cellular stress mechanism, is significant because of its potential application in cancer treatment; it points to a relationship between stress and the cellular processes associated with the development of that disease. An understanding of how to turn genetic activity on and off carries potential benefits in establishing new forms of cancer therapy as well as other scientific/ medical treatments.

As a result of her work, Pardue received the Esther Langer Award for Cancer Research in 1977. In 1989 the Yale Graduate School awarded her its Lucius Wilbur Cross Medal. She has also received an honorary D.Sc. from Bard College (1985).

SELECTED WRITINGS BY PARDUE:

Books

Journal of Cellular Biology, The Nucleus-limited Hsromega–1 Transcript Is a Polyadenylated RNA with a Regulated Intranuclear Turnover, Volume 125, Number 1, April, 1994, pp. 21–30.

Periodicals

Proceedings of the National Academy of Science USA, Formation and Detection of RNA-DNA Hybrid Molecules in Cytological Preparations, Volume 63, 1969, pp. 378–83.
Science, Chromosomal Localization of Mouse Satellite DNA, Volume 168, 1970, pp. 1356–58.
Cell, Analysis of Drosophila mRNA by In Situ Hybridization: Sequences Transcribed in Normal and Heatshocked Cultured Cells, Volume 4, 1975, pp. 395–404.
Molecular Cellular Biology, HeT-A, a Transposable Element Specifically Involved in 'Healing' Broken Chromosome Ends in *Drosophila Melanogaster,*, Volume 12, 1992, pp. 3910–18.

FURTHER READING:

Periodicals

Pardue, Mary Lou, *Interview with Michael Sims,* conducted January, 1994.

Sketch by Michael Sims

Arthur C. Parker
1881–1955
American anthropologist

Anthropologist Arthur C. Parker was instrumental in preserving the culture of the Seneca people through his directorship of the Rochester (New York) Municipal Museum. At the same time, he also did much to promote Native Americans as members of American society. Most remarkably, he accomplished his scientific achievements without the aid of a college degree.

Arthur Caswell Parker was born April 5, 1881, on the Cattaraugus Indian Reservation near Iroquois, New York. His father, Frederick Ely Parker, who was half Seneca, was a railroad worker and a descendent of General Ely Parker, Ulysses S. Grant's civil war military secretary. His mother, Geneva Hortense Griswold, had been a teacher on the Cattaraugus and Allegheny reservations.

Arthur spent much of his childhood on the reservation. Even after his father was transferred to White Plains, New York, in 1892, the family returned often. Because clan and tribal affiliations among the Seneca were passed down through the mother's side of the family, neither Arthur nor his father had affiliations, however they were both later adopted into the Seneca's Bear Clan. In his early twenties, Parker received the adult name *Gawasowanah,* which means Big Snowsnake.

Parker and his sister attended public schools. He graduated from high school in White Plains in 1897, and briefly attended Centenary College in Hackettstown, New Jersey, in 1899. Later that year, he went to the Williamsport (Pennsylvania) Dickinson Seminary, but left without graduating in 1903.

During his time at the seminary, Parker was exposed to anthropology through lectures given by Harvard University anthropologist Frederick Ward Putnam at the American Museum of Natural History in New York. In 1900 he worked for a short time as an anthropological assistant at the museum.

Between 1900 and 1903, Parker worked as a field anthropologist for Putnam and Harvard's Peabody Museum. His first field project was collecting the myths, stories, and oral history of the Seneca people on the Cattaraugus Reservation. In 1904, the year he took a temporary job collecting cultural materials with the New York State Library and Museum, he married his first wife, an Abenaki Indian named Beatrice Tahamont. He married his second wife, Anna Theresa Cooke, on September 17, 1914. Together, they had two daughters and a son.

Continues Anthropological Endeavors After Meeting with Franz Boas

While in New York, Parker was able to meet some of the most intriguing people who would influence the course of his professional life. Among them was Franz Boas, considered the father of American anthropology, who was at the time lecturing at Columbia College. Boas specialized in the study of the Northwest Indians. He encouraged Parker to formally pursue a degree in anthropology, but Parker eventually decided against it. His decision was made in part because he disagreed with Boas's stance on the evolutionary theories of Lewis Henry Morgan, an anthropologist who, like Parker, had been adopted by the Seneca. Although he never earned a degree, Parker would go on to write over 300 articles and numerous books.

Besides Boas, Parker also met many scholars through his acquaintance with Harriet Maxwell Converse. "Aunt Hattie" was an amateur scientist whose special interest was Iroquois culture. Like Parker and Morgan, she too had been adopted by the Seneca.

In 1905 Parker passed the civil service examination and became an archaeologist with the New York State Museum. During his nine years there, he extensively researched and published on folklore, ethnology, archaeology, museology, and race relations. While at the state museum, Parker became active in the Society of American Indians (SAI), a newly formed group that promoted cooperation among Native Americans. The SAI—and Parker—believed that Native Americans could adapt successfully to mainstream American culture without losing their cultural identity. He remained active with the group until 1920, when he became president of the New York State Indian Welfare Association. From 1919 to 1922, Parker served as secretary to the New York State Indian Commission.

In 1924 Parker became the director of the Rochester (New York) Municipal Museum, a professional affiliation he would maintain for the rest of his life. While director, he obtained federal funding for an Indian arts and crafts program. Able to pay wages to Iroquois artists and craftsmen for a variety of traditional items, Parker both created an outstanding collection for his museum and helped maintain an important part of Seneca culture.

Recognized for Establishing and Contributing to Many Native American Organizations and Publications

Parker was unafraid of new ventures. During his career he founded several organizations and publications, and even initiated American Indian day, a holiday celebrated on the second Saturday in May. Parker founded and edited the SAI's *Quarterly Journal* as well as *American Indian* magazine, *Museum Service,* and *Research Records of the Rochester Municipal Museum.* He founded both the Albany Philosophical Society and the New York State Archeological Association. Besides the SAI, he was a member of the Indian Rights Association, the New York State Indian Welfare Association, the American Association of Museums, the American Anthropological Society, the American Ethnological Society (of which he was a fellow), and the New York State Historical Society (trustee). He was also a

member of the Royal Order of Scotland and was a 33rd degree Mason.

Parker also enjoyed collecting coins (he was a member of the American Numismatic Association), collecting manuscripts and autographs, hiking, and camping. Besides his work on behalf of Native Americans, he also actively promoted the establishment of public parks and forest preserves.

Parker may never have earned a college degree, but he received several honorary degrees. The University of Rochester presented him an honorary master's degree in 1922. In 1940 Union College gave him an honorary doctorate in science, and in 1945 he received an honorary doctorate in human laws from Keuka College. In 1916 he received the Cornplanter Medal for his ethnographic research.

Arthur C. Parker died of a heart attack on New Year's Day, 1955.

SELECTED WRITINGS BY PARKER:

Books

Excavations in an Erie Indian Village, 1906.
Code of Hansome Lake, 1913.
Seneca Myths and Folk Tales, 1923.
Analytical History of the Senecas, 1925.
Rumbling Wings, 1929 (a children's book of legends).

FURTHER READING:

Books

Liberty, Margot, ed. "Arthur C. Parker—Seneca, 1881–1955." *American Indian Intellectuals, 1976 Proceedings of the American Ethnological Society.* West Publishing Co., 1978, pp. 128-138.
Saari, Peggy and Stephen Allison, eds. *Scientists: The Lives and Works of 150 Scientists.* Detroit: UXL, 1996.

Sketch by Fran Hodgkins

Charles Stewart Parker
1882–1950
American botanist

Charles Stewart Parker was a botanist whose research led to the control of stone-fruit blight, which, until the 1920s, had been responsible for hundreds of thousands of dollars in lost harvests each year. He also discovered dozens of new plants, and both a new species of sweet pea and a new subspecies rose have been named after him.

Parker was born in Corinne, Utah, on March 31, 1882. He attended Trinity College, receiving his bachelor of arts degree in 1905. Before continuing his education, he served as director of a field expedition to Mexico for a brief period, from 1908 to 1912. He then attended the State College of Washington (now Washington State University) where he earned his B.S. in 1922 and his M.S. in 1923. Parker then moved to Pennsylvania State College, where he worked toward his Ph.D. in botany. He titled his dissertation "A Taxonomic Study of the Genus *Hypholoma* in North America." He joined Howard University as an associate professor of botany in 1925 and was promoted the following year to professor. In 1936 he became head of the botany department, where he remained until his retirement in 1947.

For a year, beginning with the spring of 1922, Parker had conducted a field study of orchards in the state of Washington. In January 1925, he published an article titled "Coryneum Blight of Stone Fruits" in the *Howard Review,* where he described the life history of the blight that particularly attacked stone fruits such as cherries, plums, peaches, and apricots. He wrote: "Coryneum Blight is a fungus disease of stone fruits . . . which has been reported in many of the peach growing sections of the United States, east of the Rocky Mountains, since the first announcement of its presence on the Pacific Coast in 1900. . . . Coryneum blight attacks the twigs, leaves, blossoms and fruit of its host plants, causing a spotting, gumming and death of affected parts."

According to Parker's study, the disease attacked the twigs most often and most severely, developing small spots that could culminate in the formation a canker. He also found that infections near buds either killed the buds directly or killed the leaves and flowers afterward. The fruits that did mature often carried spots that enlarged with ripening. Parker also noted that weather patterns affected the disease. For example, he explained in his *Howard Review* article, a damp summer led to "continued spore production and new infections," while a dry summer resulted in scattered spores which "lie dormant or are protected within the stromatic tissue, gum, etc." Parker also put forth that in 1920, the blight had resulted in $250,000 of damage to the cherry crop in one region of Washington alone.

Over the course of his career, Parker discovered and described thirty-nine species of plants, wrote many papers, and described a new subgenus and section of the genus *Carex.* Additionally, Parker was a member of the Botanical Survey Party in Washington from 1921 to 1922, as well as the Mycology Society, the Botanical Society, the Phytopathological Society, and the Torrey Botanical Club. Perhaps the two greatest recognitions of his work, however, were the naming of a new species of sweet pea, *Lathyrus Parkeri,* and a new variety of rose, *Rosa Spaldingii, var. Parkeri,* after him. He died on January 10, 1950, in Seattle, at the age of sixty-eight.

SELECTED WRITINGS BY PARKER:

Periodicals

The Howard Review, Coryneum Blight of Stone Fruits, Volume 2, January 1925, pp. 3–40.

FURTHER READING:

Periodicals

Downing, Lewis K., *Crisis,* Contributions of Negro Scientists, June, 1939, pp. 167–68.
Downing, Lewis K., *Washington D.C. News,* Necessity Is Again Mother of Invention, September 16, 1938.
Downing, Lewis K., *Science,* February 3, 1950, p. 122.

Sketch by Leslie Mertz

Eugene Newman Parker
1927–
American astrophysicist

Eugene Parker's career changed the then-prevailing notion of space as a silent, still vacuum. In the space that Parker explored, stars like our Sun blow energetic streams of protons and electrons through interstellar space at a million miles per hour like a powerful wind. In Parker's universe, stars, planets, and even galaxies are surrounded by huge magnetic fields that attract or repel the elements in these solar winds. Though he first published these ideas in the 1950s, numerous space-based scientific missions in the 1990s were still trying to get precise measurements of the solar wind and its interaction with Earth's magnetic field.

Parker was the first-born child of Glenn Parker, an engineer, and Helen MacNair. He was born in Houghton, Michigan, where his mother went in June of 1927 to be with her mother for the birth and care of the newborn child. Parker's father was then in graduate school at Purdue University in West Lafayette, Indiana, pursuing a degree in aeronautical engineering. "It was a hand-to-mouth business in those years," Parker told contributor Karl Leif Bates in a November 7, 1997 interview. His father worked for a series of airplane makers, but by 1935, he had joined the Chrysler Motor Company in Detroit, Michigan, to work in automotive engineering.

"I was always terribly curious about everything and how things work," Parker said. "I remember being curious about how a railroad locomotive worked and how the signal on the tracks worked, and my father of course was well prepared to answer." Parker remembers being given a

Eugene Newman Parker

microscope as a gift when he was about six years old, and exploring the little worlds inside a drop of stagnant pond water. But the life sciences were not for him, Parker decided. "You have to remember so many darn things."

He majored in physics at Michigan State University, graduating in 1948. Then it was off to the California Institute of Technology for a Ph.D. in physics in 1951. Parker's first job was as an instructor in the mathematics department at the University of Utah in Salt Lake City, but it was not a tenure-track position, nor did it allow any time for research. In 1953 he switched departments to become a research assistant to Utah physicist **Walter M. Elsasser**, a pioneer in the field of studying Earth's magnetic field. Magnetism was not a subject that was unknown to Parker, as he had done his Ph.D. dissertation on the magnetic field lines seen in the dust surrounding the Pleiades, or Seven Sisters star cluster, in the constellation Taurus. Working with Elsasser turned out to be a key turning point in Parker's career.

Further Explains Earth's Magnetic Field with Illustrations and Math

Elsasser was advancing the notion that Earth's magnetic field resulted from a dynamo effect; the planet's spinning liquid core created an electro-magnetic current much as the windings in an electric generator do. Parker further refined that concept by showing how the azimuthal (or equatorial) fields produced by such a dynamo would be converted to the dipole (or north and south) field lines we experience so

strongly on Earth's surface. "Once I got to it, it was a matter of a month or so," Parker said of this breakthrough. "You draw a sketch of it on a piece of paper and suddenly it hits." The math to prove his concept took most of the time. "It turns out that the process seems to work quite generally in the universe," Parker added. He quickly showed that this same sort of "cyclonic effect" was at work in our Sun as well. Parker published this paper in 1955, but it was ignored for some time.

Solves Solar Wind Riddle

In 1957 Parker moved to the University of Chicago to work under physicist John Simpson, who was exploring cosmic rays. Simpson had some new instruments that would measure the radiation of interplanetary space. "That's what got me thinking about interplanetary space," he told Bates.

In 1958 Parker solved the riddle of what is now known as solar wind. Though the Sun's gravity is a massive force, some of the hot gases being accelerated by the star's magnetic fields are able to escape, roaring across our solar system as streams of charged particles. "You take the equation F = ma (force equals mass times acceleration). It follows," Parker said. "Plasma moving fast enough is simply able to escape the Sun's gravity." Though solar wind is impossible to measure from within Earth's protective atmosphere and magnetosphere, interplanetary probes launched in the 1960s provided confirmation of Parker's idea.

Combining Parker's two ideas, it is understood today that Earth's magnetosphere prevents the solar wind from penetrating the atmosphere, but that in doing so, the magnetic field is blown back in an extreme teardrop shape that extends nearly 1,000 Earth diameters on the dark side of the planet. Having exhausted his study of solar wind, Parker turned his attention to the magnetic fields of the Milky Way galaxy, and returned to the study of magnetic fields and dynamos throughout the 1970s.

In an age when many astronomers and physicists are pushing the limits of understanding further and further into space, Parker said he still prefers to stay close to home. "You can do hard physics only when you have enough detailed observations to figure out what the processes are," he said. "I like to needle my friends that they have a theory for everything that is not resolved in the telescope." In fact, he said, much of the theoretical physics being done in the 1990s will never be confirmed by measurement. In June 1995, at age 68, Parker retired from the University of Chicago.

SELECTED WRITINGS BY PARKER:

Periodicals

"Magnetic fields in the cosmos." *Scientific American* (August 1983): 44-54.

"Why do stars emit x rays?" *Physics Today* (July 1987): 36-42.

Sketch by Karl Leif Bates

John T. Parsons
1913–

American inventor

John T. Parsons is an industrialist whose inventions revolutionized machining and tooling, making American manufacturing much more precise and uniform. In addition, the changes he made in the tooling used for metalworking have greatly simplified that industry, while his work with composites and adhesively bonded structures have led directly to some of the most recent technologies used in aviation manufacturing.

John Thoren Parsons was born to Carl and Edith (Thoren) Parsons on October 11, 1913, in Detroit, Michigan. His mother was very involved in the work of the church, and his father ran his own company, the Parsons Corporation, which supplied Detroit automakers with various parts. From the age of five, Parsons liked to visit his father's company and observe the work that went on there; the experience awakened in him his lifelong fascination with machining and metalworking.

Parsons was working for his father's company by the time he was in high school, having been put on the payroll in August of 1928. In September of 1933, he entered Wayne University (now Wayne State University) in Detroit, but the financial pressures of the Great Depression forced his father to choose which of his two sons should finish college. He decided that Parsons' brother would be the one to get his degree, and part way through his second semester at Wayne University, Parsons withdrew. He never went back to college. In an interview with Susan E. Kolmer, Parsons said that not having a college degree initially hampered him in some ways, but that all in all it was a positive development for him. He believes that his mind was not forced into a predetermined way of approaching problems which might have prevented him from finding solutions no one had before. After leaving Wayne University, Parsons returned to his father's company, where he remained for the next nineteen years. During that time, he became a division manager.

The advent of World War II diversified the Parsons Corporation; by 1940 they were doing work for the U.S. Army and Air Force. Under the military contracts, the Parsons Corporation manufactured land mines, bomb fins, and bomb casings. Looking ahead to the end of the war and the specialized contracts that went with it, Parsons began searching for a product which was both useful to the military during the war but would also be in demand during peacetime as well. He settled on the idea of manufacturing helicopter and other rotor blades, initially manufacturing them out of wood, but later progressing to steel, aluminum, titanium, and finally composites, which most are still made of today.

Develops Numerical Control for Manufacturing

Under contract with the U.S. Air Force in the late 1940s, Parsons started work on the idea of manufacturing by numerical control. Since the early 1900s, machining was done mostly by hand, with the most experienced and skillful machinists able to turn out relatively uniform and precise products. However, there was always variation, sometimes quite slight and sometimes significant. In 1948, Parsons started working in earnest on a system that used a binary punched card system that was coded to tell a machine tool exactly what lines to follow, how fast to operate, and at what depth to cut. This innovation in manufacturing proved to be far more precise than any person could be in turning out parts to exact specifications; the parts produced were also far more uniform than human hands could make them. In 1952, Parsons was awarded his patents for the numerical control process.

By 1952, Parsons' father no longer had control of the company, although he retained ownership. Parsons became embroiled in a dispute with a superior who fired him, despite his contributions. The Danville Division of F. L. Jacobs Company initially employed him as a salesperson, but he was made division manager there after only three months. Parsons stayed only eleven months before being re-hired at the Parsons Corporation by the same manager who had fired him. Determined not to let such a thing happen to him again, Parsons was able to buy control of the corporation in 1954. While a division still manufactured auto parts, Parsons Corporation continued its work on rotor blades. Some of the blades the corporation manufactured were for wind tunnels, most notably the tunnel at the Arnold Engineering Development Center in Tullahoma, Tennessee.

Blades were not the only aviation-related item the Parsons Corporation produced. The company also developed a process for metal-to-metal adhesive bonding, a very sophisticated process because of the great obstacle involved in bonding different metals having different specific heats. Adhesive bonding paved the way for the modern manufacture of aircraft. During 1954 and 1955, the Parsons Corporation developed composites for aircraft using fiberglass, an improvement over titanium. The process was so complicated that over fifty patents, both foreign and domestic, were issued for it. Under the Parsons Corporation, licensees in England and France turned out rotor blades. Later the company established an aircraft division in Stockton, California for manufacturing helicopter blades and other bonded structures.

Uses Polysterene Foam to Form Casts

In 1968, Parsons sold the Parsons Corporation, which is now owned by British Petroleum, and he founded the John T. Parsons Company. The focus of the new company was process development. Using the adhesive bonding technology which he had developed, Parsons engaged in research for jet fan blades and marine propellers, such as those that drive the largest ships. This research led Parsons to pioneer the development of polystyrene foam patterns. Used mainly to package goods and in the production of drinking cups, Parsons put polystyrene foam to an entirely different use. Working with only a small number of employees, he engineered the idea of using polystyrene foam to form the casts of body dies. This process proved to be much faster and more accurate than conventional methods, resulting in much less machining needed to get a part right. The use of polystyrene foam for castings also greatly reduced the weight of castings, thus saving industry much money. In fact, this process was such a boon to Detroit automakers that the lead time needed to get a car into production dropped from five to three years.

Parsons also worked extensively on metal machining. Because metals tend to warp as they are tooled, the conventional method of machining a piece was to do one surface, then turn it to do the other surfaces. As each surface is done to perfection, the others warp, albeit a little less each time, and a part is flipped over and over again until all of the surfaces are machined to within tolerable limits. Parsons developed a means of machining metal that minimized warping so greatly that each surface needed only be machined once. With the new process, even metal as thin as three-one-thousands of an inch could be machined with minimal warping.

In 1968, Parsons received the Jacquard Medal from the Numerical Control Society for his development of numerical control. Named for the inventor of the Jacquard loom, this award previously had never been presented. In 1975, the Society of Manufacturing Engineers presented Parsons with an engineering citation that claimed his " . . . brilliant concept of numerical control ushered in the second Industrial Revolution." In an interview with Kolmer, Parsons said one of the highlights of his life was receiving the National Medal for Technology from the United States Department of Commerce in 1985. He received the medal from the hand of President Ronald Reagan in a White House ceremony held in the East Room. Parsons was inducted in the National Inventor's Hall of Fame in 1993.

Parsons considers his home and family as his hobbies, although he gives the lion's share of credit for raising their six children to his wife. Born Elizabeth Mae Shaw, she married Parsons in 1940. While still busy with John T. Parsons Company, Parsons began working on an autobiography. He devoted much of his time to that effort as well as directing the Society of Manufacturing Engineers. He was first elected as one of its directors at the age of seventy-eight.

FURTHER READING:

Books

Parsons, John T., *Interview with Susan E. Kolmer*, conducted November 29, 1993.

Sketch by Susan E. Kolmer

C. Kumar N. Patel
1938–
Indian-born American physicist and engineer

As a scientist and administrator, C. Kumar N. Patel has shown leadership qualities that have made him one of the leading spokesmen in both academic and industrial research. Considered one of the most extraordinary scientists in America, Patel holds 35 major patents, including groundbreaking contributions in gas lasers, nonlinear optics, molecular spectroscopy, pollution detection, and laser surgery. Eloquent and thoughtful, Patel has also spearheaded a shift in the university research environment, stressing the need for more industrial-sponsored research rather than government- and military-sponsored research.

Although Patel's scientific accomplishments cover a broad spectrum, he is especially noted for his work in lasers. His invention of the carbon dioxide laser resulted in numerous industrial, scientific, medical, and defense applications. The first person to carry out infrared nonlinear optics experiments, Patel literally created the field. His inventions include the spin-flip Raman laser, which was the first tunable Raman laser in any wavelength region, and a tunable laser opto-acoustic measurement technique for detection of pollutant gases in extremely small concentrations.

Patel was born in Baramati, India, on July 2, 1938, to Naran Phai and Mani Ben Patel. He has one older brother and a younger sister. Naran, Patel's father, a civil engineer employed by the government, was transferred often, and Patel was tutored at home until he was 11 years old. A good student, Patel was placed in the eighth grade with older students when he started formal schooling. He received his bachelor's degree in telecommunications from the College of Engineering in Poona, India, when he was 20 years old.

The Accidental Scientist

Upon graduation, Patel planned to enter the Indian Foreign Service but had to wait until he reached age 25 to be hired. Not one to waste his time, Patel decided to earn his Ph.D. in the interim. With financial support guaranteed by

C. Kumar N. Patel

Patel, the carbon dioxide laser has had a greater impact on society than any other laser.

Patel followed up this success by creating the field of infrared nonlinear optics in 1966 and, in 1970, invented the spin-flip Raman lasers (a class of tunable infrared lasers). In 1970 he developed a tunable laser opto-acoustic measurement technique that could detect minute concentrations of pollutant gases in the atmosphere and that became the standard for measuring small absorptions in gases. He also invented an opto-acoustic detection technique capable of measuring small optical absorptions in liquids, solids, thin films, and powders. In the area of spectroscopy, Patel's opto-acoustic spectroscopy studies of cryogenic liquids and solids have supplied important data for understanding their practical applications.

During his 32 years at Bell Laboratories, Patel held many important management positions. He was head of the Infrared Physics and Electronics Research Department, director of the Electronics Research laboratory, director of the Physical Research Laboratory, and executive director of the Research Physics and Academic Affairs division.

Time for a Change

After 30 years in industry, Patel began to ponder a career change. "I asked myself what would happen to if I stayed [at Bell] for 15 more years," Patel told Petechuk. "Although I might become vice-president for research, which would be exciting, it would also be more of the same."

Although devoted to his laboratory work, Patel had developed a strong interest in public policy issues concerning science and the relationship of pairing industry with universities. In 1992 Patel left Bell Laboratories to become vice chancellor for research at the University of California, Los Angeles (UCLA), which recruited Patel to help the university make the transition from a defense-based economy to a high-tech consumer-oriented economy.

"Because of his background, he had other ways of looking at problems [than most academicians]," Alan Fogelman, who was on the UCLA search committee, told Petechuk. "He has been every bit as good as his reputation."

Since moving to UCLA, Patel has played a pivotal role in helping universities rethink their approach to research. In 1994 he organized and chaired the first national conference on reinventing the research university. He has placed a special emphasis on recognizing the importance of coupling universities with small-to-medium size companies and how university research can contribute to the creation of jobs and wealth in society.

Patel, who married in 1961, has two children. Despite the demands on his time, he enjoys tennis and wind surfing and has taken up roller blading. He also enjoys French cooking, especially "eating his experiments."

Throughout his accomplished career, Patel has shown himself to be a man of vision with the ability to make his

his father for the first year of graduate school, Patel enrolled in Stanford University in the United States.

"After the first year, I really got interested in research," Patel told contributor David Petechuk in a December 8, 1997, interview. "It was such fun, much more than I ever imagined. I guess you could say I was an 'accidental scientist.'"

Patel's gift for independent, innovative thinking was nurtured early at Sanford, where he was given free reign to develop his own Ph.D. research agenda in electrical engineering. After receiving his Ph.D. in 1961, thoughts of the foreign service had long fallen by the wayside. Patel, who became a naturalized U.S. citizen, was to embark on a remarkable research career.

The Bell Laboratory Years

After graduation, Patel joined Bell Laboratories, which would prove to be ideal for Patel's independent way of thinking. "Bell Laboratories really valued science, technology, and independence," Patel told Petechuk. "They wanted us to be discoverers and inventors. We were given a free hand and basically told to 'just go do it.'"

However, along with the autonomy came the burden of providing results. Patel did not disappoint. In two short years, he discovered and invented efficient vibrational energy transfer between molecules, which led to experiments with carbon dioxide lasers and their use in a wide range of industrial and scientific applications. Because of ideas come to fruition. In 1996 he received the National Medal of Science, the United States equivalent to the Nobel Prize. He is fond of quoting his favorite comic book character, Pogo, who points out that "we are surrounded by insurmountable opportunities."

"What people call insurmountable obstacles are really opportunities," Patel told Petechuk. "Some things work and some don't; but you don't know unless you try."

SELECTED WRITINGS BY PATEL:

Periodicals

"Controlled Environment Processing for Semiconductors–A Factory-in-a-Bottle (A Lean Manufacturing Alternative)." *Journal of Electronics Manufacturing* 1 (1991): 45.
"Materials and Processing: Core Competencies and Strategic Resources." *AT&T Technical Journal* 69 (1990).

FURTHER READING:

Periodicals

"Insurmountable Opportunities." *Nature* (April 1, 1993): 394-395.
"Technology Transfer." *Nature* (April 1, 1993): 395.

Sketch by David Petechuk

Jennie R. Patrick
1949–

American chemical engineer

Jennie R. Patrick is the first African American woman to earn a doctorate degree in chemical engineering. A successful chemical engineer, manager, and educator who has applied her skills with a number of different companies and universities, she has also been honored with the Outstanding Women in Science and Engineering Award in 1980, and by CIBA-GEIGY Corp. in its Exceptional Black Scientist poster series in 1983.

Patrick was born January 1, 1949, in Gadsden, Alabama, one of five children of James and Elizabeth Patrick, working-class parents who emphasized knowledge as an escape from poverty. Patrick was both nurtured and challenged in a segregated elementary school and junior high, but in high school she was one of the first participants in a controversial and sometimes explosive program of

Jennie R. Patrick

racial integration, where she successfully overcame violence and unsupportive white teachers to graduate with an A-minus average in 1969.

Patrick was accepted at several prestigious universities, but chose to begin her pursuit of engineering at Tuskegee Institute, which she attended until 1970 when the chemical engineering program was eliminated. She then transferred to the University of California at Berkeley to finish her degree, receiving her B.S. in 1973 and meanwhile working as an assistant engineer for the Dow Chemical Company in 1972 and for the Stauffer Chemical Company in 1973. She continued her education at the Massachusetts Institute of Technology (MIT), receiving a Gilliland Fellowship in 1973, a DuPont Fellowship in 1974, and a Graduate Student Assistant Service award in 1977. She was also awarded a fellowship in 1975 from the American Association of University Women, and a National Fellowship Foundation Scholarship in 1976.

Conducts Research on Superheated Liquids

Her research at MIT involved the concept of superheating, where a liquid is raised above its boiling temperature but does not become a vapor. She investigated the temperature to which pure liquids and mixtures of two liquids could be superheated. Patrick finished her research and completed her doctorate in 1979. While pursuing her graduate studies, Patrick worked as an engineer with Chevron Research in 1974 and with Arthur D. Little in 1975.

After completing her doctorate, Patrick joined the Research and Development Center at General Electric (GE) in Schenectady, New York, where she held the position of research engineer. Her work there involved research on energy-efficient processes for chemical separation and purification, particularly the use of supercritical extraction. In supercritical processes, the temperature and pressure are varied so that a substance is not a liquid or a gas, but a fluid. Unique properties make these fluids useful in both separations and purification processes. She has published several papers on this work, and has received patents for some of her advancements.

Patrick remained at GE until 1983, when she accepted a position at Philip Morris as a project manager in charge of the development of a program to improve several of the company's products. Patrick transferred to the Rhom and Haas Company in 1985, as manager of fundamental chemical engineering research. In this position she interacted with all aspects of the chemical business, from engineering to marketing to manufacturing. By being exposed to the overall business she was able to direct development of new research technology within her division and promote its implementation throughout the company. In 1990, Patrick became assistant to the executive vice president of Southern Company Services, a position that emphasized her management skills in both the business and technical aspects of the company. Having earlier held adjunct professorships at Rensselaer Polytechnic Institute from 1982 to 1985 and the Georgia Institute of Technology from 1983 to 1987, Patrick decided to make teaching a bigger part of the her life. In January 1993, she left Southern Company Services and returned to Tuskegee University, as the 3M Eminent Scholar and Professor of Chemical Engineering. In addition to her teaching duties, Patrick is developing research projects in material sciences, is actively involved in leadership roles at Tuskegee, and remains firmly committed to helping minority students find success, particularly in the fields of science and engineering.

SELECTED WRITINGS BY PATRICK:

Books

Supercritical Fluid Technology, Supercritical Extraction of Dixylenol Sulfone, edited by J. M. L. Penninger and others, Elsevier, 1985, pp. 379–384.

Periodicals

Industrial and Engineering Chemistry Fundamentals, Superheat-Limit Temperature of Polar Liquids, November, 1981, pp. 315–317.
Canadian Journal of Chemical Engineering, High Pressure Phase Equilibria in the Carbon Dioxide-n-Hexadecane and Carbon Dioxide-Water Systems, February, 1988, pp. 319–325.

The Black Collegian, Let Others' Experience Be Your Roadway to Success, September/October, 1992, p. 39.

FURTHER READING:

Books

Outstanding Young Women of America, Junior Chamber of Commerce, 1979, p. 981.
Sammons, V. O., editor, *Blacks in Science and Medicine,* Hemisphere Publishing Co., 1990, p. 185.

Periodicals

Bradby, Marie, *US Black Engineer,* Professional Profile: Dr. Jennie R. Patrick, fall, 1988 pp. 30–33.
Bradby, Marie, *Ebony,* Engineering Their Way to the Top, December 1984, pp. 33–36.
Kazi-Ferrouillet, Kuumba, *NSBE Journal,* Jennie R. Patrick: Engineer Extraordinaire, February, 1986, pp. 32–35.

Sketch by Jerome P. Ferrance

Ruth Patrick
1907–
American limnologist

Ruth Patrick has pioneered techniques for studying the biodiversity of freshwater ecosystems over a career that spans sixty years. Her studies of microscopic species of algae, called diatoms, in rivers around the world have provided methods for monitoring water pollution and understanding its effects. Federal programs to monitor the status of freshwater rely on Patrick's method of growing diatoms on glass slides. Her studies of the impact of trace elements and heavy metals on freshwater ecosystems have demonstrated how to maintain a desired balance of different forms of algae. For example, she showed that addition of small amounts of manganese prevents the overgrowth of blue-green algae and permits diatoms to proliferate.

Patrick received the prestigious Tyler Ecology Award in 1975, and serves on numerous governmental advisory committees. She advanced the field of limnology, the study of freshwater biology, and in the late 1940s established the Department of Limnology at the Academy of Natural Sciences in Philadelphia. She remained its director for more than four decades. Headquarters for her research are in Philadelphia, with a field site in West Chester, Pennsylvania. An estuary field site at Benedict, Maryland, on the

Ruth Patrick

Patuxent River near Chesapeake Bay, serves for studies of pollution caused by power plants.

Patrick was born in Topeka, Kansas, on November 26, 1907. Her undergraduate education was completed at Coker College, where she received a B.S. degree in 1929. She obtained both her M.S. degree in 1931 and her Ph.D. in botany in 1934 from the University of Virginia. The roots of Patrick's long and influential career in limnology can be traced to the encouragement of her father, Frank Patrick. He gave his daughter a microscope when she was seven years old and told her, "Don't cook, don't sew; you can hire people to do that. Read and improve your mind." Patrick's doctoral thesis, which she wrote at the University of Virginia in Charlottesville, was on diatoms, whose utility derives from their preference for different water chemistries. The species of diatoms found in a particular body of water says a lot about the character of the water.

Confronted with Bias against Women Scientists

When Patrick joined the Academy of Natural Sciences in 1933, it was as a volunteer in microscopy to work with one of the best collections of diatoms in the world; she was told at the time that women scientists were not paid. For income she taught at the Pennsylvania School of Horticulture and made chick embryo slides at Temple University. In 1937 persistence paid off, and she was appointed curator of the Leidy Microscopical Society with the Academy of Natural Sciences, a post she held until 1947. She also became associate curator of the academy's microscopy

department in 1937, and continued in that capacity until 1947, when she accepted the position of curator and chairman of the limnology department at the academy. Continuing as curator, in 1973 she was offered the Francis Boyer Research Chair at the academy.

Conducts Pioneering Studies of Freshwater Ecosystems

In the late 1940s Patrick gave a paper at a scientific meeting on the diatoms of the Poconos. In the audience was William B. Hart, an oil company executive, who was so impressed with the possibilities of diatoms for monitoring pollution that he provided funds to support Patrick's research. Freed from financial constraints, Patrick undertook a comprehensive survey of the severely polluted Conestoga Creek, near Lancaster, Pennsylvania. It was the first study of its kind, and launched Patrick's career. She matched types and numbers of diatoms in the water to the type and extent of pollution, an extremely efficient procedure now used universally.

By her own account Patrick has waded into 850 different rivers around the globe in the course of her research. She participated in the American Philosophical Society's limnological expedition to Mexico in 1947 and led the Catherwood Foundation's expedition to Peru and Brazil in 1955. Patrick was an advisor to several presidential administrations and has given testimony at many hearings on environmental problems and before congressional committees on the subject of environmental legislation. She was an active participant in drafting the federal Clean Water Act.

Pens Book on Groundwater Concerns

In 1987 Patrick coauthored a book, *Groundwater Contamination in the United States,* which provides an overview of groundwater as a natural resource, and a state-by-state description of policies designed to manage growing problems of contamination and depletion. Another of her concerns is global warming, the rise in the earth's temperature attributed to the buildup of carbon dioxide and other pollutants in the atmosphere. In an interview reported in the *Philadelphia Inquirer* in 1989, Patrick said, "We're going to have to stop burning gasoline. And we're going to have to conserve more energy, develop ways to create electricity from the sun and plants, and make nuclear power both safe and acceptable."

Patrick has received many awards in addition to the Tyler prize, including the Gimbel Philadelphia Award for 1969, the Pennsylvania Award for Excellence in Science and Technology in 1970, the Eminent Ecologist Award of the Ecological Society of America in 1972, and the Governor's Medal for Excellence in Science and Technology in 1988. She holds many honorary degrees from United States colleges and universities. Patrick has authored over 130 papers, and continues to influence thinking on limnology and ecosystems. Her contributions to both science and public policy have been vast.

SELECTED WRITINGS BY PATRICK:

Books

Groundwater Contamination in the United States, University of Pennsylvania Press, 1987.

Periodicals

Environment, Managing the Risks of Hazardous Waste, April, 1991, pp. 13–35. :

FURTHER READING:

Periodicals

Detjen, Jim, *Philadelphia Inquirer,* In Tiny Plants, She Discerns Nature's Warning on Pollution, February 19, 1989.

Other

Detjen, Jim, *The Wonderful World of Dr. Ruth Patrick,* unpublished paper by Geraldine J. Gates, Wharton School, University of Pennsylvania, February 16, 1987.

Sketch by Karen Withem

Claire Patterson
1922–
American geochemist

Claire Patterson's contributions to science ranged from developing dating techniques using radioactive decay to alerting the public about the dangers of lead, although he began his career as an emission and mass spectroscopist with the Manhattan Project in 1944. Much of Patterson's professional career was spent as a research associate of environmental science at California Institute of Technology (Caltech) until his retirement in 1992. His early studies focused on using isotopes to date rocks—a process that enabled him to estimate the age of the earth. Later research on lead levels in the environment and their dangers to public health proved fundamental to the enactment of the Clean Air Act in 1970. He was elected to the National Academy of Sciences in 1987; his other honors include having a mountain and an asteroid named after him.

Claire Cameron Patterson was born in Des Moines, Iowa, on June 2, 1922, to Claire Cameron Patterson, a rural letter carrier, and his wife Vivian Ruth (Henny) Patterson. He obtained an A.B. in chemistry in 1943 from Grinnell College in Iowa, an M.S. in 1944 from the University of Iowa, and a Ph.D. in 1951 from the University of Chicago. Patterson met his wife Lorna (McCleary) Patterson while at Grinnell; the two married in 1944 and had two sons and two daughters. Lorna worked as a high school chemistry and physics teacher until her retirement.

Early in his career at Caltech, Patterson conducted studies to determine the age of various rocks. He did this by using the radioactive elements uranium and thorium to measure the rate of decay of an element's isotopes (forms of atoms) into lead. Decay is the process whereby rocks and minerals are transformed into new, more stable chemical combinations. While studying meteorites using his method, Patterson solved a problem that had mystified scientists for over 300 years—he calculated the age of the earth. Patterson determined the earth to be about 4.6 billion years old. Estimates prior to his 1953 calculations put the earth at approximately three billion years old. Subsequent research by others has not overturned Patterson's findings.

In 1973, twenty years after his historic finding, Patterson was elected to the National Academy of Science (NAS), one of the highest honors to be bestowed on a U.S. scientist or engineer. Caltech vice president and provost, geophysicist Barclay Kamb, as quoted in a California Institute of Technology press release, commented on the occasion by heralding Patterson's "thinking and imagination [as] so far ahead of the times that he has often gone misunderstood and unappreciated for years, until his colleagues finally caught up and realized he was right."

Patterson was often recognized as a scientist who did not follow the status quo. This reputation was gained in part by his inclination to challenge the findings of his peers and his disdain for what he calls "ivory-tower scientists." In a 1990 interview with the *Los Angeles Times,* Patterson asserted that science as it is practiced in United States has lost its imagination and creativity. It was this view of progress that prompted novelist Saul Bellow to pattern his disillusioned scientist in *The Dean's December* after Patterson.

Patterson's renegade stature may have originated during World War II when, as a member of the Manhattan Project, he contributed to the development of the atomic bomb by analyzing the uranium isotopes that went into the bombs. He told the *Los Angeles Times* that developing such a destructive force was "the greatest crime that science has committed yet," and that science, which "remains an abstract, beautiful refuge within the mind," is often misguided.

Discovers Dramatic Increase in Lead Levels

Continuing his work with isotopes, Patterson began studying the evolution of the earth's crust from the mantle (an area between the earth's outer crust and its inner core). During this research he discovered that millions of years ago the amount of lead stored in plankton (microscopic plant and animal life) and in ocean sediments was only 1/

10th to 1/100th the amount of lead now being introduced into the ocean by rivers. Lead, the end product of the decay of radioactive minerals, is normally one of the rarest elements in ocean water.

Interested in this dramatic increase in the ocean's lead levels, Patterson set out to measure the amount of lead present in the atmosphere, the polar ice caps, and other oceans to see if they showed similar shifts. In December of 1963, Patterson, Tsaihwa J. Chow of University of California's Scripps Institution of Oceanography, and M. Tatsumoto of the U.S. Geological Survey in Denver reported the results of a study in which they had sampled waters of the Pacific and Atlantic oceans and the Mediterranean sea. The scientists determined that nearly 500,000 tons of lead were annually entering the oceans in the Northern Hemisphere. But more startling than the amount was the fact that quantities of lead this high were apparently a new phenomenon; for centuries the rate had remained at 10,000 tons per year.

To arrive at these estimates, small amounts of a particular form of lead (an isotope called lead 208), called a tracer, were added to lead-free containers. When the container was submerged in the ocean, the water mixed with the tracer lead. Using chemicals, the scientists removed the tracer lead, and from the residue they were able to calculate the proportions of tracer lead to the lead already present in the sea water.

The three geochemists proposed that the increase in lead was the result of automobile exhaust emissions, which introduced small particles of lead oxide into the atmosphere. From the 1930s to the 1960s, the lead content of gasoline increased from near zero to about 175,000 tons a year in the United States alone. Winds carried vehicles' exhaust particles through the atmosphere to the world's rivers and oceans either as dry particles or in the form of rain. Once thought a natural, relatively benign part of the environment, lead was being consumed by humans in hundreds of times the quantities taken in by pre-industrial people, Patterson's studies revealed. These high levels of lead were contributing to damage to bones, kidneys, blood circulation, and brain cells, especially in children. Armed with Patterson's research, environmentalists and scientists successfully lobbied for passage of the Clean Air Act of 1970. Enactment of the legislation reduced lead emissions from cars and trucks by about 96 percent, but Patterson remained concerned about the quantity of lead remaining in the atmosphere, which may continue to affect public health for years to come.

Findings Lead to Changes in Laboratory Procedures

Patterson also determined that biological laboratories are highly contaminated with industrial lead. This finding had wide ramifications because it implied that previous biochemical knowledge was based on studies of biological systems that were grossly contaminated by lead. Patterson believed that knowledge of the biochemistries of natural systems unaffected by lead toxicity probably do not exist.

As a result, Patterson formulated strict and sterile laboratory procedures which since have become standard in the field. To protect his experiments from lead drifting through the air, Patterson pressurized and lined his lab with plastic. Before entering his lab, he washed his hands with distilled water and put on a lab coat and surgical cap.

Patterson, with the help of graduate students, post doctoral fellows, and research associates from all over the United States and the world, has focused on delineating the extent to which industrial lead during the past two centuries has altered natural biogeochemical cycles of lead. They have measured lead in the earth's atmosphere, hydrosphere (the water on earth and in the atmosphere), and ecosystems on both land and water. Patterson's research has demonstrated that the magnitude of global pollution can be determined only after pre-industrial chemical levels are established. To do this, Patterson analyzed lead concentrations in buried skeletal remains of pre-Colombian Southwest Native Americans. The natural level of lead in the remains was found to be about 1/1000th of the average amount of lead in twentieth-century adult Americans.

Patterson's most recent work has involved investigating the factors that encouraged humans to poison the earth's biosphere with lead. To do this, he studied the development of lead technologies and production over the past 10,000 years. In the process he utilized isotopes to determine methods of medieval metallurgy (the science of making and manipulating metals). Another alarming statistic he uncovered was that tuna packed in cans sealed with lead contains 10,000 times more lead than tuna from the pre-industrial era. This study from 1980 also found that lead pollution in United States and its effects on public health have been vastly underestimated.

Based on his study, Patterson proposed that there is a feed-back link (a self-perpetuating mechanism) between the development of engineering technologies and the emergence of social institutions that define a culture. He reports that the geometries of the brains of those who lived in cultures that used metals and alloys for utilitarian purposes appear to be different from those who used lead for artistic purposes.

Despite Patterson's criticism of some scientific institutions' methods and focus, he has received many honors. These include the J. Lawrence Smith medal given by the National Academy of Science in 1975, the V.M. Goldschmidt medal given by the Geochemical Society in 1980, and the Professional Achievement award given by the University of Chicago in 1980.

SELECTED WRITINGS BY PATTERSON:

Books

Earth Science and Meteoritics, edited by J. Geiss and E. D. Golding, Amsterdam: North Holland Publishing, 1963.

Periodicals

Science, Age of the Earth, 1955, pp. 69–75.

Nature, Concentrations of Common Lead in Some Atlantic and Mediterranean Waters and in Snow, 1963, pp. 350–352.

Science of the Total Environment, Lead in Ancient Human Bones and its Relevance to Historical Developments of Social Problems with Lead, 1987, pp. 167–200.

FURTHER READING:

Periodicals

Chemical and Engineering News, Earth's Age: 4.6 Billion Years, November 1953, pp. 4874–4878.

On Campus, News Notes, November 1992.

Newton, Edmund, *Los Angeles Times,* Lead Man, October 14, 1990.

Other

Newton, Edmund, *Clair Patterson of Caltech Elected to National Academy of Sciences,* California Institute of Technology Press Release, May 11, 1987.

Sketch by Margaret DiCanio

Frederick Douglass Patterson
1901–1988
American veterinarian

Founder of the United Negro College Fund (UNCF), Frederick Douglass Patterson was known for his visionary and pioneering efforts in promoting higher education for African American higher education. Under his guidance, the UNCF became the nation's largest independent source of monetary aid to educational institutions that were traditionally African American. Patterson also went on to establish the College Endowment Funding Plan, and he was the founder of the first African American school of veterinary medicine in the United States at Tuskegee Institute. All through his life, Patterson acted on his conviction that education was the best means to achieve African American mobility. For his lifelong efforts in promoting education, Patterson was awarded the Presidential Medal of Freedom, the nation's highest civilian honor, in 1987.

Born to William Ross Patterson and Mamie Lucille (Brooks) Patterson in Washington, D.C., on October 10, 1901, Patterson was named after the African American journalist and antislavery leader, Frederick Douglass. Patterson, who was orphaned at the age of two, was raised in Texas by his sister, Wilhelmina, who was a schoolteacher there. After attending Prairie View State College in Texas from 1915 to 1919, he attended Iowa State College in Ames, Iowa, and received his doctorate in veterinary medicine in 1923. In 1927 he earned his M.S. degree at that same school and later entered Cornell University at Ithaca, New York. He was awarded a Ph.D. in veterinary medicine from Cornell in 1932.

Begins a Teaching Career

Patterson also began teaching as an instructor in veterinary science at Virginia State College in Petersburg, Virginia, while he was still a student. Later, from 1927 to 1928, Patterson was appointed director of agriculture at Virginia State. In 1928 he was invited to join the Tuskegee Normal and Industrial Institute, an organization he remained affiliated with for the next twenty-five years. Patterson held various positions at Tuskegee, including serving as the first head of the school's new veterinary division and later as director of the School of Agriculture. From 1935 to 1953, he served as the Institute's third president, raising the school to new heights of achievement and national recognition. Tuskegee had been founded by Booker T. Washington, a black American educator, who believed that African Americans should receive vocational training. Patterson's ideas went beyond that, and he stressed the importance of both job training as well as the need to develop confident leadership skills. After he retired as president of the Tuskegee Institute in 1953, Patterson remained president emeritus until his death.

The Founding of the United Negro College Fund

In 1943, a few years after he had become president of Tuskegee, Patterson proposed that a group of African American colleges form a consortium to raise funds for their mutual benefit. Called the United Negro College Fund (UNCF), the organization had twenty-seven original members who amassed an endowment of $765,000. Thirty-five years later, the Fund had grown to include forty-two members with a combined monetary legacy of $42 million. The UNCF provided money for scholarships, staff salaries, library resources, and laboratories, and their motto, "A mind is a terrible thing to waste," became a well-known slogan. In addition to establishing the UNCF, Patterson was also instrumental in creating the College Endowment Funding Plan, which would encourage private businesses to donate funds by matching their gifts with Federal funds.

Patterson also served as president and trustee of the Phelps-Stokes Fund, which worked for the improvement of the status of blacks in Africa and the United States, the welfare of the Native American, and the improvement of low-income housing in New York City. In 1987, Patterson was honored by the White House, along with actor Danny Kaye and composer Meredith Wilson, when former President Ronald Reagan named him a recipient of the Presidential Medal of Freedom for his life's work. When Patterson died of a heart attack on April 26, 1988, at his home in New Rochelle, New York, he was survived by his wife of fifty-three years, Catherine Elizabeth (Moton), and his son, Frederick Patterson.

SELECTED WRITINGS BY PATTERSON:

Books

College Endowment Funding Plan, American Council on Education, 1976.

FURTHER READING:

Periodicals

New York Times, April 27, 1988, Section D, p. 27.
Washington Post, April 28, 1988, Section D, p. 4.

Sketch by Leonard C. Bruno

Wolfgang Paul

Wolfgang Paul
1913–1993
German physicist

Wolfgang Paul's Nobel Prize-winning research included the invention of an "ion trap" (also known as an "electrical bottle" or "Paul trap") which holds particles in place by means of two electrical plates and a ring-shaped electrode for the purpose of very precise measuring and observation. Paul was widely esteemed for his research in the fields of molecular-beam physics, mass spectroscopy, high-energy physics, and radiobiology.

Paul was born in Lorenzkirch, Saxony, Germany, on August 10, 1913. He was the fourth of six children born to Theodor and Elizabeth (Ruppel) Paul. Theodor Paul was professor of pharmaceutical chemistry at the University of Munich and a colleague of the eminent theoretical physicist **Arnold Sommerfeld**. Wolfgang developed an interest in science at an early age and, after graduating from high school, entered the Technical University of Munich in 1932. Two years later, he transferred to the Technical University of Berlin, from which he received his diploma (comparable to a master's degree) in 1937.

Paul then stayed on in Berlin to work on his doctoral degree under Hans Kopfermann, a specialist in nuclear and atomic physics. He was nearly prevented from completing his degree by his induction into the German military at the

onset of World War II. His service was cut short, however, when he was allowed to return to graduate school and excused from further military obligations. Paul was granted his Ph.D. in 1939 for a thesis on the properties of the beryllium nucleus.

After completing his doctoral studies, Paul joined his former advisor Kopfermann, who was then at the University of Kiel. The two worked together for sixteen years, moving to the University of Göttingen in 1942, where Paul was appointed assistant professor two years later. He remained at Göttingen until 1952.

Works on Mass Spectrometry and Radiobiology

Paul's earliest research interest at Kiel and Göttingen was mass spectrometry, a technique in which magnetic and electrical fields are used to separate ions of different masses from each other. The devastation caused by Germany's defeat in World War II eventually made a continuation of this line of research impossible, however. It was a difficult time for physicists, with an acute lack of equipment and severe governmental restrictions on the type of research allowed. As a consequence, Paul briefly refocused his studies to the field of radiobiology, where these limitations were not as serious.

Shortly after receiving his Ph.D., Paul married Liselotte Hirsche. The couple had four children, two sons and two daughters. Mrs. Paul died in 1977. Paul later married

Doris Walch, a professor of medieval literature at the University of Bonn.

Paul moved to the University of Bonn in 1952 to become a professor of physics. He remained there for three decades, until his retirement in 1983. It was at Bonn that Paul carried out the research for which he is best known and which won him the 1989 Nobel Prize for physics. That research involved the development of methods for focusing the path of ions, and was done with collaborating scientists **Norman Foster Ramsey** of Harvard University, and **Hans Dehmelt** of the University of Washington.

Develops Electric and Magnetic Lenses and Traps

The development of devices that can be used to divert the path of moving particles goes back to the invention of the mass spectrometer by the English physicists **J. J. Thomson** and **Francis W. Aston** in the first decade of the twentieth century. In the mass spectrometer, a beam of charged particles is deflected as it is forced to travel through a strong magnetic field. The device is used to separate particles of differing masses from each other since those particles are deflected differentially by the magnetic field.

In the 1950s, Paul began to work on modifications of the mass spectrometric principle known as electrical and magnetic lenses. In a lens of this type, electrical and magnetic fields are arranged to focus a beam of particles in much the same way that glass and plastic lenses can focus a beam of light. Paul's electrical and magnetic lenses have become valuable tools in the use of atomic and molecular beams used for the study of the structure and properties of atoms and molecules.

An electrical or magnetic lens is a device for limiting the movement of a particle beam in two directions. The logical extension of this device is to find a way of restricting movement in three dimensions, that is, of stopping the motion of an individual particle and holding it in a suspended state for some period of time. A device of this type is of enormous value to scientists since it makes possible very precise studies of the changes that take place within an individual atom or ion and the changes that occur when energy interacts with that particle.

In the late 1950s, Paul invented such a device. It consists of a ring-shaped electrode placed between two electrical plates. A particle placed within the ring is prevented from moving in any direction by the electrical field that surrounds it. The device has been described as an "electrical bottle" or a "Paul trap." With it, scientists have been able to observe transitions within an atom with far greater precision than had ever been possible before.

In the 1970s, Paul turned his attention to an even more challenging task, the trapping of uncharged particles. Since traditional mass spectrometric and beam focusing methods do not work on uncharged particles, Paul and his associates (including his two sons, Lorenz and Stephan) found variations on the Paul trap to use with such particles.

Paul later became interested in the study of elementary particles. He was responsible for the construction at Bonn of Germany's first particle accelerator, a 500 million-electron-volt electron synchrotron, and later for the installation of a more powerful 2.5 billion-electron-volt accelerator.

Paul served both as director of the nuclear physics division at CERN, the European Center for Nuclear Research in Geneva, and as executive director of DESY, Germany's national particle accelerator laboratory. From 1979 to 1989, he was president of the Humboldt Foundation. In addition to the Nobel Prize, Paul received the Robert W. Pohl Prize of the German Physical Society and the Gold Medal of the Czech Academy of Sciences. He died in Bonn on December 6, 1993.

SELECTED WRITINGS BY PAUL:

Periodicals

"A New Mass Spectometer without Magnetic Field." *Zeitschrift für Naturforschung* 89 (1953): 448-50.
"Production of Elementary Particles in the Laboratory." *Naturwissenschaften* 46 (1959): 277-83.

FURTHER READING:

Periodicals

Hall, Nina. "Perfect Timing Wins Belated Nobel for Paul." *New Scientist* 21 October (1989): 29.
Levi, Barbara Goss. "Ramsey, Dehmelt, Paul Win Nobel for Helping to Set High Standards." *Physics Today* (December 1989): 17-19.
Pool, Robert. "Basic Measurements Lead to Physics Nobel." *Science* (20 October 1989): 327-28.
Whitney, Craig H. "Dr. Wolfgang Paul, 80, Is dead; German Winner of Nobel" (obituary). *New York Times* (9 December 1993): D23.

Sketch by David E. Newton

Wolfgang Pauli
1900–1958
Swiss physicist

W olfgang Pauli's exclusion, or "Pauli," principle asserted the later-proven existence of the neutrino, a chargeless, massless particle. This discovery led to the Nobel Prize-winning theory of a fourth quantum number with only two possible values (a quantum number expresses

Wolfgang Pauli

the distinct state of a quantum system). The exclusion principle limits the number of electrons possible in the first level of energy to two, a restriction not previously seen in quantum physics.

Wolfgang Ernst Pauli was born on April 25, 1900, in Vienna, in what was then Austria-Hungary. His father was Wolfgang Joseph Pauli, a medical doctor and biochemist who later became a professor at the University of Vienna. His mother was the former Bertha Schültz, an author. R. E. Peierls reports in *Biographical Memoirs of Fellows of the Royal Society* that Pauli's parents' "background and their acquaintance with the leading authorities in many fields had a profound effect in creating the high standards and the impatience with anything but the best of its kind, which became later an important characteristic of the young Pauli."

Masters Relativity Theory at an Early Age

Pauli was a very bright student who sometimes found Vienna's schools dull and boring. He took to reading advanced treatises on modern physics during his most tedious classes, gaining familiarity with such new and revolutionary concepts as American physicist **Albert Einstein**'s general theory of relativity. In 1918, Pauli graduated from high school in Vienna and entered the University of Münich. He chose Münich because it was the home of German theoretical physicist **Arnold Sommerfeld**, then one of the greatest teachers of theoretical physics alive. Two years into his course of study, Pauli was given a special assignment by Sommerfeld: he was asked to write an entry

on the subject of relativity for the forthcoming *Encyclopedia of Mathematical Sciences*. The two-hundred-fifty-page article that Pauli produced was not only a summary of all that was known on the subject but also an analysis of the information. In a letter to Einstein, Sommerfeld described Pauli's work as "simply masterful." A year later, after the shortest time allowed by the university, Pauli was awarded his Ph.D. for a thesis on the hydrogen molecule ion.

When Pauli was a graduate student, the field of physics was in a state of disarray, stumbling towards new perspectives on the nature of matter and energy. The development of quantum mechanics and relativity theory was still encumbered by remnants of classical theory. Pauli made important contributions to the clarification of the nature of modern theory, especially with his enunciation of the exclusion principle. In addition, Pauli tackled a then-troublesome problem in which the emission of electrons during beta decay (a form of radiation) does not appear to obey the law of conservation of energy. To resolve this difficulty, Pauli hypothesized the existence of a chargeless, massless particle later given the name neutrino.

After receiving his degree, Pauli was offered a job as assistant in theoretical physics at the University of Göttingen. There he came into contact not only with English physicist **Max Born**, professor of theoretical physics, but also with Danish physicist **Niels Bohr**, who was guest lecturer at Göttingen in 1922. It was through Bohr's lectures that Pauli began to think about some of the fundamental difficulties that still remained in Bohr's quantum theory of the atom. One of these problems was the existence of various electron energy levels within an atom. Nothing in classical physics could explain the fact that electrons are distributed in various energy levels outside the nucleus, with each energy level having a maximum permitted number of electrons. Bohr had derived such a model from empirical data rather than any theoretical concept, and the fact that the model worked did not detract from questions as to *why* it worked.

Solving the Zeeman Effect Leads to the Exclusion Principle

Over the next three years, Pauli worked on this question. He continued to do so when he went to the University of Copenhagen as Bohr's assistant in 1922 and then to the University of Hamburg as assistant professor of theoretical physics in 1923. At Hamburg, he also began to think about another puzzle in atomic theory, the Zeeman effect. In 1896, the Dutch physicist **Pieter Zeeman** had found that the presence of a strong magnetic field causes the lines of an atomic spectrum to split. More than twenty years later, no one had yet devised an explanation for this phenomenon, but, early in 1925, Pauli found a possible explanation. He suggested that a fourth quantum number—in addition to the three already known—was needed to describe completely the energy state of an electron. In addition to its principle quantum number (n), its azimuthal quantum number (l), and its magnetic quantum number (m), an electron must also have a fourth quantum number, Pauli said. This fourth number could have one of two (but only two) possible values.

At the time, Pauli had no idea as to how this fourth quantum number could be interpreted in physical terms. That problem was solved three years later when Dutch physicists **Samuel Goudsmit** and **George Uhlenbeck** discovered electron spin. Goudsmit and Uhlenbeck suggested that an electron could spin in one of two directions, clockwise or counter-clockwise. Their designation of these spins as $+\frac{1}{2}$ or $-\frac{1}{2}$ corresponded precisely to the two-valuedness of the fourth quantum number that Pauli had predicted.

Proposes the Exclusion Principle

As significant as the discovery of the fourth quantum number was, it was perhaps even more important in terms of what it led to: the exclusion principle. Prompted by a 1924 paper by the English physicist E. D. Stoner, Pauli was able to develop an explanation for the fact that all electrons in an atom do not occupy the lowest energy level. The reason, he said, is that no two electrons can have exactly the same set of quantum numbers. An electron in the first energy level (n = 1) is restricted to an azimuthal quantum number of zero (because $l = n - 1$) and a magnetic quantum number of 0 (because $m = \pm l$). It can have spin quantum numbers of $+\frac{1}{2}$ or $-\frac{1}{2}$. These restrictions mean that electrons in the first energy level can have quantum numbers of $1,0,0,+\frac{1}{2}$ or $1,0,0,-\frac{1}{2}$, but no others. Therefore, since the exclusion principle says that there can be no more than one electron of each of these two kinds, only two electrons can occupy that first energy level. By a similar argument, it is possible to show how the second energy level can hold no more than eight electrons, the third level no more than eighteen, and so on. In this way, a theoretical basis is provided for the electron orbital capacities originally devised empirically by Bohr more than a decade earlier.

In 1928, Dutch American chemical physicist **Peter Debye** retired as professor of theoretical physics at the Eidgennössische Technische Hochschule (ETR, or Federal Institute of Technology) in Zürich and Pauli was appointed as his successor. Pauli was to remain at this post until his death, with two brief interruptions. The first came in the academic year 1935–36 when he was visiting professor at the Institute for Advanced Studies in Princeton, New Jersey. The second came five years later when German leader Adolf Hitler's armies had begun to sweep through Europe. Even though he lived in a neutral country, Pauli decided that it would be safer to leave Europe. He traveled back to the Institute for Advanced Studies, where he again held an appointment. Although Pauli returned to Zürich in 1946, he continued to hold a permanent appointment at the Institute and went back for short visits several times.

Pauli Proposes the Existence of the Neutrino

During his first years in Zürich, Pauli turned to another problem troubling physicists: beta decay. According to quantum theory at the time, the loss of a beta particle by a radioactive particle should be accompanied by the loss of a discrete quantity of energy. The spectrum produced by beta decay should, therefore, be characterized by a series of lines. Instead, the spectra associated with beta decay were always continuous spectra. In 1930, Pauli proposed a solution for this dilemma. He suggested that the loss of a beta particle by a nucleus was accompanied by the loss of a second particle. The characteristics of beta decay required that this particle have no electrical charge and no—or almost no—mass. At first, Pauli referred to the particle as a "neutron," a name later given to the chargeless nuclear particle discovered by English physicist **James Chadwick** in 1932. After Chadwick's discovery, American physicist **Enrico Fermi** rechristened Pauli's particle as the "neutrino," or "little neutron." A year later, Fermi had also incorporated the neutrino into an elegant and totally satisfactory mathematical theory of beta decay. Because of the characteristics of this elusive particle, the neutrino itself was not actually discovered for more than two decades after the work of Fermi and Pauli. Shortly before his return to Switzerland in 1945, Pauli was informed of his selection as the winner of the Nobel Prize in physics. After resuming his post in Zürich, he became a Swiss citizen and continued his research on elementary particles.

Pauli was married twice, first to Kate Depner, then to Franciska Bertram on April 4, 1934. There were no children from either marriage. Pauli's work was acknowledged not only by the Nobel Prize but also by the Lorentz Medal of the Royal Dutch Academy of Sciences in 1930, the Franklin Medal of the Franklin Institute in 1952, and the Max Planck Medal of the German Physical Society in 1958. Pauli died unexpectedly in Zürich on December 14, 1958.

SELECTED WRITINGS BY PAULI:

Books

Encyklopädie Mathematische Wissenschaft, Relativi-tätstheorie, [Leipzig], 1921.
Natureklarung und Psyche, Rasher, 1952.
Collected Scientific Papers, edited by R. Kronig and V. F. Weisskopf, Interscience, 1964.

Periodicals

Zeitschrift fur Physik, Über den Zusammenhang des Abschlusses der Elektron Engruppen im Atom mit der Komplex Struktur der Spektren, Volume 31, 1925, pp. 765–783.
Viert. Naturf. Ges. Zürich, Zür Älteren und Neuen Geschichte des Neutrinos, Volume 102, 1957, pp. 387–388.

FURTHER READING:

Books

Biographical Memoirs of Fellows of the Royal Society, Volume 5, Royal Society (London), 1959, pp. 175–192.

Current Biography 1946, H. W. Wilson, 1946, pp. 468–470.

Gillispie, Charles Coulson, editor, *Dictionary of Scientific Biography,* Volume 10, Scribner, 1975, pp. 422–425.

Gillispie, Charles Coulson, editor, *McGraw-Hill Modern Scientists and Engineers,* Volume 2, McGraw, 1980, pp. 398–399.

Wasson, Tyler, editor, *Nobel Prize Winners,* H. W. Wilson, 1987, pp. 795–798.

Weber, Robert L., *Pioneers of Science: Nobel Prize Winners in Physics,* American Institute of Physics, 1980, pp. 125–126.

Sketch by David E. Newton

Linus Pauling

Linus Pauling
1901–1994
American chemist

Linus Pauling is the only person ever to win two unshared Nobel Prizes. His 1954 prize for chemistry was given in recognition of his work on the nature of the chemical bond, while the 1963 Nobel Peace Prize was awarded for his efforts to bring about an end to the atmospheric testing of nuclear weapons. Pauling has made important contributions to a number of fields, including the structure of proteins and other biologically important molecules, mineralogy, the nature of mental disorders, nuclear structure, and nutrition.

Linus Carl Pauling was born in Portland, Oregon, on February 28, 1901. He was the first of three children born to Herman Henry William Pauling and Lucy Isabelle (Darling) Pauling, usually called Belle. Herman Pauling was a druggist who struggled continuously to make a decent living for his family. With his business in Portland failing, Herman moved his family to Oswego, seven miles south of Portland, in 1903. He was no more successful in Oswego, however, and moved on to Salem in 1904, to Condon (in northern Oregon) in 1905, and finally back to Portland in 1909. A year later, Herman died of a perforated ulcer, leaving Belle to care for the three young children.

Linus was a precocious child who read every book he could get his hands on. At one point, his father wrote the local paper asking for readers to suggest additional books that would keep his son occupied. Pauling's interest in science was apparently stimulated by his friend Lloyd Jeffress during grammar school. Jeffress kept a small chemistry laboratory in a corner of his bedroom where he performed simple experiments. Pauling was intrigued by these experiments and decided to become a chemical engineer.

Early Interest in Chemistry Leads to Oregon Agricultural College

During his high school years, Pauling continued to pursue his interest in chemistry. He was able to obtain much of the equipment and materials he needed for his experiments from the abandoned Oregon Iron and Steel Company in Oswego. Since his grandfather was a night watchman at a nearby plant, Linus was able to "borrow" the items he needed for his own chemical studies. Pauling would have graduated from Portland's Washington High School in 1917 except for an unexpected turn of events. He had failed to take the necessary courses in American history required for graduation and so did not receive his diploma. The school corrected this error 45 years later when it awarded Pauling his high school diploma—after he had been awarded two Nobel Prizes.

In the fall of 1917, Pauling entered Oregon Agricultural College (OAC), now Oregon State University, in Corvallis. He was eager to pursue his study of science and signed up for a full load of classes. Finances presented a serious problem, however. His mother was unable to send him any money for his expenses and, in fact, Pauling was soon forced to help her pay family bills at home. As a result, Pauling regularly had to work 40 hours or more in addition to studying and attending classes. By the end of his sophomore year, it became apparent that Pauling could not afford to stay in school. He decided to take a year off and help his mother by working in Portland. At the last minute, however, those plans changed. OAC offered him a job teaching quantitative analysis, a course he had completed as a student only a few months earlier. The $100-a-month assignment allowed him to return to OAC and continue his education.

During his last two years at OAC, Pauling learned about the work of **Gilbert Newton Lewis** and **Irving Langmuir** on the electronic structure of atoms and the way atoms combine with each other to form molecules. He became interested in the question of how the physical and chemical properties of substances are related to the structure of the atoms and molecules of which they are composed and decided to make this topic the focus of his own research. An important event during Pauling's senior year occurred when he met Ava Helen Miller, a student in one of his classes. Ava Helen and Linus were married on June 17, 1923, and later had four children: Linus, Jr., born in 1925, Peter Jeffress, born in 1931, Linda Helen, born in 1932, and Edward Crellin, born in 1937.

Pursues Studies at Cal Tech and in Europe

After graduation from OAC in 1922, Pauling entered the California Institute of Technology (Cal Tech) in Pasadena. At the time, Cal Tech was a vigorous, growing institution that served as home to some of the leading researchers in chemistry and physics in the nation. Pauling quickly became immersed in a heavy load of classes, seminars, lectures, and original research. He was assigned to work with Roscoe Gilley Dickinson on the x-ray analysis of crystal structure. As a result of this research, his first paper, "The Crystal Structure of Molybdenite," was published in the *Journal of the American Chemical Society* (*JACS*) in 1923. During his remaining years at Cal Tech, Pauling was to publish six more papers on the structure of other minerals.

Pauling was awarded his Ph.D. in chemistry *summa cum laude* in 1925 and decided to continue his studies in Europe. He planned to spend time with three leading researchers of the time, **Arnold Sommerfeld** in Munich, **Niels Bohr** in Copenhagen, and **Erwin Schrödinger** in Zurich. Sommerfeld, Bohr, and Schrödinger were all working in the new field of quantum mechanics. The science of quantum mechanics, less than a decade old at the time, was based on the revolutionary concept that particles can sometimes have wave-like properties, and waves can sometimes best be described as if they consisted of massless particles. Pauling had been introduced to quantum mechanics at OAC and was eager to see how this new way of looking at matter and energy could be applied to his own area of interest, the electronic structure of atoms and molecules. After two years in Europe, Pauling was determined to make this subject the focus of his future research. He and Ava Helen left Zurich in the summer of 1927 and returned to Cal Tech, where Pauling took up his new post as Assistant Professor of Theoretical Chemistry.

Pauling's first few years as a professor at the college were a time of transition. He continued to work on the x-ray analysis of crystals, but also began to spend more time on the quantum mechanical study of atoms and molecules. He wrote prolifically, turning out an average of ten papers a year during his first five years at Cal Tech. His reputation grew apace, and he was promoted quickly to associate professor in 1929 and then to full professor a year later. By 1931, the American Chemical Society had awarded Pauling its Langmuir Prize for "the most noteworthy work in pure science done by a man 30 years of age or less."

In the meanwhile, Pauling had spent another summer traveling through Europe in 1930, visiting the laboratories of Laurence Bragg in Manchester, Herman Mark in Ludwigshafen, and Sommerfeld in Munich. In Ludwigshafen, Pauling learned about the use of electron diffraction techniques to analyze crystalline materials. Upon his return to Cal Tech, Pauling showed one of his students, L. O. Brockway, how the technique worked and had him build an electron diffraction instrument. Over the next 25 years, Pauling, Brockway, and their colleagues used the diffraction technique to determine the molecular structure of more than 225 substances.

Work on Chemical Bond Leads to First Nobel Prize

In some ways, the 1930s mark the pinnacle of Pauling's career as a chemist. During that decade he was able to apply the principles of quantum mechanics to solve a number of important problems in chemical theory. The first major paper on this topic, "The Nature of the Chemical Bond: Applications of Results Obtained from the Quantum Mechanics and from a Theory of Paramagnetic Susceptibility to the Structure of Molecules," appeared in the April 6, 1931, issue of *JACS*. That paper was to be followed over the next two years by six more on the same topic and, in 1939, by Pauling's magnum opus, *The Nature of the Chemical Bond, and the Structure of Molecules and Crystals*. The book has been considered one of most important works in the history of chemistry, and the ideas presented in the book and the related papers are the primary basis upon which Pauling was awarded the Nobel Prize for chemistry in 1954.

Pauling's work on the chemical bond proved crucial in understanding three important problems in chemical theory: bond hybridization, bond character, and resonance. Hybridization refers to the process by which electrons undergo a change in character when they form bonds with other atoms. For example, the carbon atom is known to have two distinct kinds of bonding electrons known as 2s and 2p electrons. Traditional theory had assumed, therefore, that carbon would form two types of bonds, one type using 2s electrons and a second type using 2p electrons. Studies had shown, however, that all four bonds formed by a carbon atom are identical to each other. Pauling explained this phenomenon by illustrating that carbon's electrons change their character during bonding. All four assume a new energy configuration that is a hybrid of 2s and 2p energy levels. Pauling called this hybrid an sp^3 energy level.

In a second area, Pauling examined the relationship between two kinds of chemical bonding: ionic bonding, in which electrons are totally gained and lost by atoms, and covalent bonding, in which pairs of electrons are shared equally between atoms. Pauling was able to show that ionic and covalent bonding are only extreme states that exist in relatively few instances. More commonly, atoms bond by sharing electrons in some way that is intermediate between ionic and covalent bonding.

Pauling's third accomplishment involved the problem of the benzene molecule. Until the 1930s, the molecular structures that were being written for benzene did not adequately correspond to the properties of the substance. The German chemist Friedrich Kekulé had proposed a somewhat satisfactory model in 1865 by assuming that benzene could exist in two states and that it shifted back and forth between the two continuously. In his work on the chemical bond, Pauling suggested another answer. Quantum mechanics showed, he said, that the most stable form of the benzene molecule was neither one of Kekulé's structures, but some intermediate form. This intermediate form could be described as the superposition of the two Kekulé structures formed by the rapid interconversion of one to the other. This "rapid interconversion" was later given the name resonance.

Turns to Research on Biological Molecules

By the mid–1930s, Pauling was looking for new fields to explore. The questions he soon addressed concerned the structure of biological molecules. These molecules are complex substances that are found in living organisms and can contain thousands of atoms in each molecule rather than the relatively simple molecules that Pauling had studied previously that contained only twenty or thirty atoms. This was a surprising choice for Pauling, because earlier in his career he had mentioned that he wasn't interested in studying biological molecules. One reason for his change of heart may have been the changes taking place at Cal Tech itself. In an effort to expand the institution's mission beyond chemistry and physics, its administration had begun to build a new department of biology. Among those recruited for the department were such great names as **Thomas Hunt Morgan**, **Theodosius Dobzhansky**, Calvin Bridges, and Alfred Sterdevant. Pauling's almost daily interaction with these men opened his eyes to a potentially fascinating new field of research.

The first substance that attracted his attention was the hemoglobin molecule. Hemoglobin is the substance that transports oxygen through the bloodstream. Pauling's initial work with hemoglobin, carried out with a graduate student Charles Coryell, produced some fascinating results. Their research showed that the hemoglobin molecule undergoes significant structural change when it picks up or loses an oxygen atom. In order to continue his studies, Pauling decided he needed to know much more about the structure of hemoglobin, in particular, and proteins, in general.

Fortunately, he was already familiar with the primary technique by which this research could be done: X-ray diffraction analysis. The problem was that x-ray diffraction analysis of protein is far more difficult than it is for the crystalline minerals Pauling had earlier worked with. In fact, the only reasonably good x-ray pictures of protein available in the 1930s were those of the British crystallographer **William Astbury**. Pauling decided, therefore, to see if the principles of quantum mechanics could be applied to Astbury's photographs to obtain the molecular structures of proteins.

The earliest efforts along these lines by Pauling and Coryell in 1937 were unsuccessful. None of the molecular structures they drew based on quantum mechanical principles could account for patterns like those in Astbury's photographs. It was not until eleven years later that Pauling finally realized what the problem was. The mathematical analysis and the models it produced were correct. What was wrong was Astbury's patterns. In the pictures he had taken, protein molecules were tilted slightly from the position they would be expected to have. By the time Pauling had recognized this problem, he had already developed a molecular model for hemoglobin with which he was satisfied. The model was that of a helix, or spiral-staircase-like structure in which a chain of atoms is wrapped around a central axis. Pauling had developed the model by using a research technique on which he frequently depended: model building. He constructed atoms and groups of atoms out of pieces of paper and cardboard and then tried to fit them together in ways that would conform to quantum mechanical principles. Not surprisingly, Pauling's technique was also adopted by two contemporaries, **Francis Crick** and **James Watson**, in their solution of the DNA molecule puzzle, a problem that Pauling himself very nearly solved.

Pauling also turned his attention to other problems of biological molecules. In 1939, for example, he developed the theory of complementarity and applied it the subject of enzyme reactions. He later used the same theory to explain how genes might act as templates for the formation of enzymes. In 1945, Pauling attacked and solved an important medical problem by using chemical theory. He demonstrated that the genetic disorder known as sickle-cell anemia is caused by the change of a single amino acid in the hemoglobin molecule.

Efforts on Behalf of Peace Movement Bring Second Nobel Prize

The 1940s were a decade of significant change in Pauling's life. He had never been especially political and, in fact, had voted in only one presidential election prior to World War II. But he rather quickly began to immerse himself in political issues. One important factor in this change was the influence of his wife, Ava Helen, who had long been active in a number of social and political causes. Another factor was probably the war itself. As a result of his own wartime research on explosions, Pauling became more concerned about the potential destructiveness of future wars.

As a result, he decided while on a 1947 boat trip to Europe that he would raise the issue of world peace in every speech he made in the future, no matter what topic.

From that point on, Pauling's interests gradually shifted from scientific to political topics. He devoted more time to speaking out on political issues, and the majority of his published papers dealt with political rather than scientific topics. In 1958 he published his views on the military threat facing the world in his book *No More War!*. Pauling's views annoyed many of his scientific colleagues, fellow citizens, and many legislators. In 1952 he was denied a passport to attend an important scientific meeting in London, and in 1960 he was called before the Internal Security Committee of the United States Senate to explain his antiwar activities. Neither professional nor popular disapproval could sway Pauling's commitment to the peace movement, however, and he and Ava Helen continued to write, speak, circulate petitions, and organize conferences against the world's continuing militarism. In recognition of these efforts, Pauling was awarded the 1963 Nobel Prize for Peace.

Studies of Vitamin C Provoke Controversy

At the age of 65, when many men and women look forward to retirement, Linus Pauling had found a new field of interest: the possible therapeutic effects of vitamin C. Pauling was introduced to the potential value of vitamin C in preventing colds by biochemist Irwin Stone in 1966. He soon became intensely interested in the topic and summarized his views in a 1970 book, *Vitamin C and The Common Cold*. Before long, he became convinced that the vitamin was also helpful in preventing cancer.

Pauling's views on vitamin C have received relatively modest support in the scientific community. Many colleagues tend to feel that the evidence supporting the therapeutic effects of vitamin C is weak or nonexistent, though research on the topic continues. Other scientists are more convinced by Pauling's argument, and he is regarded by some as the founder of the science of orthomolecular medicine, a field based on the concept that substances normally present in the body (such as vitamin C) can be used to prevent disease and illness.

Pauling's long association with Cal Tech ended in 1964, at least partly because of his active work in the peace movement. He accepted an appointment at the Study of Democratic Institutions in Santa Barbara for four years and then moved on to the University of California at San Diego for two more. In 1969 he moved to Stanford University where he remained until his compulsory retirement in 1974. In that year, he and some colleagues and friends founded the Institute of Orthomolecular Medicine, later to be renamed the Linus Pauling Institute of Science and Medicine, in Palo Alto.

Pauling died of cancer at his ranch in the Big Sur area of California on August 19, 1994. He was 93 years old.

SELECTED WRITINGS BY PAULING:

Books

The Nature of the Chemical Bond, and the Structure of Molecules and Crystals, Cornell University Press, 1939.
General Chemistry, California Institute of Technology, 1941.
College Chemistry, W. H. Freeman, 1950.
No More War!, Dodd, Mead & Company, 1958.
Vitamin C and the Common Cold, W. H. Freeman, 1970.
Vitamin C, the Common Cold, and the Flu, W. H. Freeman, 1976.
Cancer and Vitamin C, Linus Pauling Institute of Science and Medicine, 1979.
How to Live Longer and Feel Better, W. H. Freeman, 1986.

Periodicals

The Science Teacher, The Social Responsibilities of Scientists and Science, May, 1966, pp. 14–18.
Daedalus, Fifty Years of Progress in Structural Chemistry and Molecular Biology, fall, 1970, pp. 988–1014.
Chemical & Engineering News, Chemistry and the World of Tomorrow, April 16, 1984, pp. 54–56.
New Scientist, Why Modern Chemistry is Quantum Chemistry, November 7, 1985, pp. 54–55.

FURTHER READING:

Books

Goodell, Rae, *The Visible Scientists,* Little, Brown, 1977.
Gray, Tony, *Champions of Peace,* Paddington Press, 1976.
Judson, Horace Freeland, *The Eighth Day of Creation,* Simon and Schuster, 1979.
Judson, Horace Freeland, *Current Biography 1949,* Linus Pauling, H. W. Wilson, 1949, pp. 473–475.
Judson, Horace Freeland, *Current Biography 1964,* Linus Pauling, H. W. Wilson, 1964, pp. 339–342.
Newton, David E., *Linus Pauling,* Facts on File, 1994.
Olby, Robert, *The Path to the Double Helix,* University of Washington Press, 1974.
Serafini, Anthony, *Linus Pauling: A Man and His Science,* Paragon House, 1989.
White, Florence Meiman, *Linus Pauling: Scientist and Crusader,* Walker & Co., 1980.

Periodicals

Campbell, Neil A., *BioScience,* Crossing the Boundaries of Science, December, 1986, pp. 737–739.

Fry, William F., Jr., *The Humanist,* What's New with You, Linus Pauling? November/December, 1974, pp. 16–19.

Goertzel, Ted G., Mildred George Goertzel, and Victor Goertzel, *Antioch Review,* Linus Pauling: The Scientist as Crusader, summer, 1980, pp. 371–382.

Goodstein, Judith R., *Social Research,* Atoms, Molecules, and Linus Pauling, autumn, 1984, pp. 691–708.

Grosser, Morton, *Saturday Evening Post,* Linus Pauling: Molecular Artist, fall, 1971, pp. 147–149.

Hogan, John, *Scientific American,* Profile: Linus C. Pauling, March, 1993, p. 36.

Hogan, John, *Omni,* Interview: Linus Pauling, December, 1986, pp. 102–110.

Hogan, John, *Mother Earth News,* The Plowboy Interview: Dr. Linus Pauling, January/February, 1978, pp. 17–22.

Pogash, Carol, *Science Digest,* The Great Gadfly, June, 1981, pp. 88–91.

Ridgway, David, *Journal of Chemical Education,* Interview with Linus Pauling, August, 1976, pp. 471–476.

Sketch by David E. Newton

Ivan Petrovich Pavlov

Ivan Petrovich Pavlov
1849–1936
Russian physiologist

Ivan Petrovich Pavlov was a Russian physiologist whose research on mammalian digestion earned him the Nobel Prize and whose research on conditioned reflexes brought him international recognition. The colloquial expression "Pavlov's dog" refers to Pavlov's famous experiments in which he taught a dog to salivate at the sound of a bell by associating the bell with feeding. This research helped spawn a physiologically oriented school of psychology that focused on the influence of conditioned reflexes on learning and behavior. Because of his contribution to the fields of psychology and physiology, Pavlov became one of Russia's most revered scientists in his day and was even tolerated by the communist Soviet regime, of which he was openly critical.

Pavlov was born in Ryazan, Central Russia, on September 26, 1849. His father, Pyotr Dmitrievich Pavlov, was a priest who rose through the ranks and eventually headed one of the most influential parishes in the area. A devoted reader and scholar, Pyotr taught his son at an early age to read all worthwhile books at least twice so that he would understand them better—a bit of fatherly advice that helped shape Pavlov's intense dedication to his work.

Pavlov's mother, Varvara Ivanova, also came from a family of clergy and had ten children after Pavlov, six of whom died in childhood.

The family expected the young Pavlov to follow the family tradition of entering the clergy. Thus, Pavlov attended Ryazan Ecclesiastical High School and the Ryazan Ecclesiastical Seminary. During his studies at the seminary, Pavlov became seriously interested in science, physiology in particular, and was greatly influenced by a radical philosopher named Dmitri Pisarev who espoused many of evolutionist Charles Darwin's theories.

In 1870 when the government decreed that divinity students could attend nonsectarian universities, Pavlov decided to leave the seminary and attend St. Petersburg University to study the natural sciences. At St. Petersburg, Élie de Zion, a professor of physiology, made a formidable impression on Pavlov. By all accounts the two scientists had a mutual admiration for one another. According to Boris Babkin in his book *Pavlov: A Biography,* Pavlov said of his early mentor, "Never can such a teacher be forgotten," and in turn Zion called Pavlov a "skilled surgical operator."

Upon graduation from St. Petersburg University in 1875, Pavlov followed Zion to the Military Medical Academy in St. Petersburg, where Zion had been appointed chair of physiology. Pavlov became an assistant in Zion's laboratory and worked toward his medical degree. But Zion was soon dismissed because he was Jewish, and Pavlov, intolerant of his mentor's dismissal, left the Medical Academy in favor of the Veterinary Institute where he spent the next two years studying digestion and circulation. In 1877 Pavlov traveled to Breslau, Germany (later Poland), to study with Rudolf Heidenhain, a specialist in digestion. After receiving his medical degree from the Military Medical Academy in 1879, Pavlov went on to earn his postdoctoral degree and was honored with a Gold Medal for his doctoral dissertation in 1883.

Upon graduation, Pavlov was one of ten students awarded a government scholarship for postgraduate studies abroad. Thus, Pavlov returned to Germany to work with Carl Ludwig on cardiovascular physiology and blood circulation; he also collaborated with Heidenhain again on further digestion research. Another mentor, Sergei Botkin, eventually asked Pavlov to direct an experimental physiological laboratory. This lab, devoted to the school of "scientific medicine," focused on the physiological and pathological relations in an organism. Under Botkin's guidance, Pavlov first developed his interest in "nervism," the pathological influence of the central nervous system on reflexes.

Awarded Nobel Prize for Digestion Research

Pavlov returned to St. Petersburg University and began his exhaustive research on digestion which eventually gained him worldwide recognition in scientific circles. Focusing on the physiology of digestion and gland secretions, Pavlov devised an ingenious experiment in which he severed a dog's gullet, forcing the food to drop out before it reached the animal's stomach. Through this sham feeding, he was able to show that the sight, smell, and swallowing of food was enough to cause secretion of the digestive acidic "juices." He demonstrated that stimulation of the vagus nerve (one of the major cranial nerves of the brain) influences secretions of the gastric glands. In 1904 Pavlov received the Nobel Prize for Medicine or Physiology for these pioneering studies on the physiology of the digestive system.

Pavlov's work on blood circulation earned him a professorship at the Military Medical Academy. In 1895 Pavlov became the chairman of the physiology department at the St. Petersburg Institute for Experimental Medicine, where he spent the greater part of his remaining career. Ironically, by the time Pavlov received the Nobel Prize, his work delineating the central nervous system's effects on digestive physiology was soon to be overshadowed by subsequent investigations by **William Bayliss** and others, who demonstrated that chemical (hormone) stimulation induces digestive secretions from the pancreas. Ever curious, Pavlov himself conducted experiments that also confirmed this discovery.

Although Pavlov's "nervism" theory was relegated to secondary importance in the study of digestion, his experiments profoundly influenced biological research. Pavlov strongly believed that a healthy laboratory animal subject free from disease and the influence of pharmaceuticals was imperative to his work. "It has become abundantly clear that the usual simple cutting of an animal, the so-called acute

test, is a source of many errors," Pavlov said, as noted by Alexander Vucinich in his book *Science in Russian Culture.* Among the laboratory techniques advanced by Pavlov were the use of aseptic surgical procedures on laboratory animals and the development of chronic, or long-lasting, experiments on the same animal. Pavlov believed in minimizing an animal's pain for both moral and scientific reasons and led the way for the humane treatment of laboratory animals.

Pavlov's Dog Becomes Conditioned

Ironically, Pavlov's most famous studies were conducted after he received the Nobel Prize. Concentrating on the neural influences of digestion, Pavlov set out to determine whether he could turn normally "unconditioned" reflexes or responses of the central nervous system into conditioned reflexes. Pavlov noticed that the laboratory dogs would sometimes salivate merely at the approach of lab assistants who often fed them. Through careful repeated experiments, Pavlov demonstrated that if a bell is rung each time a dog is given food, the dog eventually develops a "conditioned" reflex to salivate at the sound of the bell, even when food is not present. Thus, Pavlov showed that the unconditioned reflexes—gastric activity and salivation—could become conditioned responses triggered by a stimulus (the bell) not previously associated with the physiological event (eating).

Pavlov traced this phenomenon to the cerebral cortex and continued to study the brain's role in conditioned reflexes for the remainder of his life. Although this research led to a proliferation of studies of conditioned reflexes in physiology, the conditioned reflex theory became a popular subject in the fields of psychiatry, psychology, and education.

Pavlovian psychology contends that a person's behavioral development and learning are profoundly affected by conditioned nervous responses to life events, similar to the dog's learned response to the bell. This behavioral theory created a schism in the field of psychology, with Pavlovian psychologists opposing the views of Sigmund Freud, who theorized that an individual's thought processes—especially the unconscious—were the driving forces of human behavior. Eventually, Freudian psychology usurped Pavlovian psychology in popularity to become the primary approach to mental health treatment outside of Russia. But Pavlov maintained his devotion to the importance of conditioned reflexes in human behavior, believing that human language was probably the most intricate example of such conditioning. Pavlov also applied his theory to the treatment of psychiatric patients in which he placed patients in a quiet and isolated environment in order to remove any possible physiological or psychological stimuli that might negatively affect their mental health.

Pavlov Outspoken on Communist Regime

Pavlov's life spanned three distinct Russian political eras, which sometimes intruded upon his personal and professional life. He was born during the reign of Czar Nicholas I, an oppressive feudal monarch who sought to retain aristocratic rule at any price. Pavlov saw this oppressive regime give way to a new ideology of reform, known as post-Emancipation Russia, which heralded technological advancements but was mired in turmoil on both the social and political level. Shortly after the Bolshevik Revolution in 1917 which attempted to impose a socialist structure on society, Pavlov became a staunch and vocal opponent of the new and often hostile regime. Years earlier, Pavlov had shown a willingness to oppose authority when he resigned from the Medical Military Academy to protest the dismissal of his mentor, Zion, because he was Jewish.

By the time of the Bolshevik Revolution, Pavlov had achieved international recognition and was living a comfortable life. He had overcome the extreme economic hardships he faced early in his career when he had struggled to support his growing family on the meager salary of a lab assistant. In 1881 he married Seraphima Vasilievna Karchevskaya, a naval doctor's daughter and friend of Russian novelist Fyodor Dostoevsky. They eventually had four sons and a daughter.

Pavlov's legendary self-discipline and devotion to his work, however, often led him to disregard opportunities for advancement. His feud with the military academy over Zion's dismissal also hindered his career. So consumed was Pavlov with his scientific investigations that he once bought dogs for his experiments with money students had collected for him to give special lectures. Pavlov's wife had difficulty impressing upon her husband the severity of the family's needs. When she complained of his unwillingness to seek a higher position, he told her that their lack of money was nothing compared to the tragic deaths of his butterflies.

Despite these hardships, Pavlov was willing to risk his hard-earned success by opposing the new communist regime. His religious background caused him to become enraged when all clergymen's sons were expelled from the Medical Academy, and in 1924 he resigned from the Medical Academy as the chair of physiology in protest. The new Soviet government, however, was intent on accommodating a person they considered to be a shining example of Russian science, who, in addition to the Nobel Prize, had been awarded the Order of the Legion of Honor of France and the Copley Medal of the Royal Society of London. Vladimir Lenin, who emerged as the most powerful leader of the revolution, signed a decree guaranteeing Pavlov's personal freedom and his right to continue his research and even to attend church. These special privileges were in stark contrast to countless other scientists whose work was suppressed by the government. Pavlov, however, continued to speak out, once refusing extra rations of food unless all his laboratory assistants received the same privileges.

The rulers in the new Soviet republic believed that Pavlov's work with conditioned reflexes could be adapted for political purposes. For example, they hypothesized that the masses could be conditioned just as Pavlov had conditioned the dog. In a sense, they saw the opportunity to develop a type of mass mind control in which the Soviet system would appear to have complete power, even over those who were originally reluctant to follow the communist way. To appease their favorite scientist, in 1935 the government built Pavlov a spacious laboratory equipped with the latest scientific technology which the scientist called "the capitol of conditioned reflexes."

Although Pavlov was known in the last five years of his life to publicly praise the government for their efforts to foster education and science, he repeatedly denounced the Soviet "social experiment." He died of pneumonia on February 27, 1936, in Leningrad. While some of Pavlov's early research has not stood the test of time and further scientific inquiry, he remains one of the fathers of modern science whose observations provided a basis from which much scientific knowledge arose in the twentieth century.

SELECTED WRITINGS BY PAVLOV:

Books

Lectures on Conditioned Reflexes, International, 1928.
Conditioned Reflexes: An Investigation of the Physiological Activity of the Cerebral Cortex, Dover, 1960.

FURTHER READING:

Books

Babkin, Boris P., *Pavlov: A Biography,* University of Chicago Press, 1949.
Babkin, Boris P., *The Great Scientists,* Grolier Educational Corporation, 1989, pp. 186–191.
Vucinich, Alexander, *Science in Russian Culture,* Stanford University Press, 1963, pp. 301.
Wells, Harry K., *Ivan P. Pavlov: Toward a Psychology and Psychiatry,* International, 1956.

Sketch by David Petechuk

Cecilia Payne-Gaposchkin
1900–1979
American astronomer

Cecilia Payne-Gaposchkin was a pioneer in the field of astronomy and one of the most eminent female astronomers of the twentieth century. She was the first to apply the laws of atomic physics to the study of the temperature and density of stellar bodies and to conclude that hydrogen and helium, the two lightest elements, were also the two most common elements in the universe. Her revelation that hydrogen, the simplest of the known elements, was the most abundant substance in the universe has since become the basis for analysis of the cosmos. Yet she is not officially credited with the discovery, made when she was a 25-year-old doctoral candidate at Harvard, because her conservative male superiors convinced her to retract her findings on stellar hydrogen and publish a far less definitive statement. While she is perhaps best known for her later work in identifying and measuring variable stars with her husband, Sergei I. Gaposchkin, Payne-Gaposchkin helped forge a path for other women in the sciences through her staunch fight against sexual discrimination at Harvard College Observatory, where she eventually became the first woman appointed to full professor and the first woman named chairman of a department that was not specifically designated for a woman.

Cecilia Helena Payne was born on May 10, 1900, in Wendover, England, the eldest of three children born to Edward John and Emma Leonora Helena (Pertz) Payne of Coblenz, Prussia. Her father, a London barrister, died when she was four years old. Her mother, a painter and musician, introduced her to the classics, of which she remained fond throughout her life. Payne-Gaposchkin recalled that Homer's *Odyssey* was the first book her mother read to her as a child. She knew Latin by the time she was 12 years old, became fluent in French and German, and showed an early interest in botany and algebra. As a schoolgirl in London she was influenced by the works of Isaac Newton, Thomas Huxley, and Emmanuel Swedenborg.

In 1919 she won a scholarship to Newnham College at Cambridge University, where she studied botany, chemistry, and physics. During her studies there, she became fascinated with astronomy after attending a lecture on **Albert Einstein**'s theory of relativity given by Sir **Arthur Eddington**, the university's foremost astronomer. Upon completion of her studies in 1923 (at that time women were not granted degrees at Cambridge), Payne-Gaposchkin sought and obtained a Pickering Fellowship (an award for female students) from Harvard to study under **Harlow Shapley**, the newly appointed director of the Harvard Observatory. Thus, Payne-Gaposchkin embarked for the United States, hoping to find better opportunities as a woman in astronomy. Harvard Observatory in Boston, Massachusetts, became her home for the rest of her career—a "stony-hearted stepmother," she was said to have called it.

Harvard: A Stony-Hearted Stepmother

Payne-Gaposchkin's career at Harvard began in 1925, when she was given an ambiguous staff position at the Harvard Observatory. By that time she had already published six papers on her research in the field of stellar atmospheres. That same year, she was awarded the first-ever Ph.D. in astronomy at Radcliffe. Her doctoral dissertation, *Stellar Atmospheres,* was published as Monograph No. 1 of the Harvard Observatory. A pioneering work in the field, it was the first paper written on the subject and was the first

research to apply Indian physicist Meghnad Saha's recent theory of ionization (the process by which particles become electrically charged by gaining or losing electrons) to the science of measuring the temperature and chemical density of stars. However, she was discouraged in her views and was convinced to alter them by **Henry Norris Russell**, a renowned astronomer at Princeton who several years later reached her same conclusions and published them, thereby receiving credit for their origin. Despite this, Payne-Gaposchkin's research remains highly regarded today; Otto Struve, a notable astronomer of the period, was quoted in *Mercury* magazine as saying that *Stellar Atmospheres* was "undoubtedly the most brilliant Ph.D. thesis ever written in astronomy."

In 1926 when she was 26 years old, she became the youngest scientist to be listed in *American Men of Science.* But her position at Harvard Observatory remained unacknowledged and unofficial. It was not until 1938 that her work as a lecturer and researcher was recognized and she was granted the title of astronomer, which she later requested to be changed to Phillips Astronomer. From 1925 until 1938 she was considered a technical assistant to Shapley, and none of the courses she taught were listed in the Harvard catalogue until 1945. Finally, in 1956 when her colleague Donald Menzel replaced Shapley as director of the Harvard Observatory, Payne-Gaposchkin was "promoted" to professor, given an appropriate salary, and named chairman of the Department of Astronomy—the first woman to hold a position at Harvard University that was not expressly designated for a woman.

Payne-Gaposchkin's years at Harvard remained productive despite her scant recognition. She was a tireless researcher with a prodigious memory and an encyclopedic knowledge of science. She devoted a large part of her research to the study of stellar magnitudes and distances. Following her 1934 marriage to Gaposchkin, a Russian emigre astronomer, the couple pioneered research into variable stars (stars whose luminosity fluctuates), including research on the structure of the Milky Way and the nearby galaxies known as the Magellanic Clouds. Through their studies they made over two million magnitude estimates of the variable stars in the Magellanic Clouds.

From the 1920s until Payne-Gaposchkin's death on December 7, 1979, she published over 150 papers and several monographs, including "The Stars of High Luminosity" (1930), a virtual encyclopedia of astrophysics, and *Variable Stars* (1938), a standard reference book of astronomy written with her husband. She also published four books in the 1950s on the subject of stars and stellar evolution. Moreover, though she retired from her academic post at Harvard in 1966, becoming Emeritus Professor of Harvard University the following year, she continued to write and conduct research until her death. Her autobiography, writings collected after her death by her daughter, Katherine Haramundanis, was entitled *Cecilia Payne-Gaposchkin: An Autobiography and Other Recollections* and was published in 1984.

Payne-Gaposchkin was elected to the Royal Astronomical Society while she was a student at Cambridge in 1923, and the following year she was granted membership in the American Astronomical Society. She became a citizen of the United States in 1931. She and her husband had three children: Edward, born in 1935, Katherine, born in 1937, and Peter, born in 1940—a noted programmer analyst and physicist in his own right. In 1934 Payne-Gaposchkin received the Annie J. Cannon Prize for significant contributions to astronomy from the American Astronomical Society. In 1936 she was elected to membership in the American Philosophical Society. Among her honorary degrees and medals, awarded in recognition of her contributions to science, are honorary doctorates of science from Wilson College (1942), Smith College (1943), Western College (1951), Colby College (1958), and Women's Medical College of Philadelphia (1961), as well as an honorary master of arts and doctorate of science from Cambridge University, England (1952). She won the Award of Merit from Radcliffe College in 1952, the Rittenhouse Medal of the Franklin Institute in 1961, and was the first woman to receive the Henry Norris Russell Prize of the American Astronomical Society in 1976. In 1977 the minor planet 1974 CA was named Payne-Gaposchkin in her honor.

Payne-Gaposchkin is remembered as a woman of boundless enthusiasm who refused to give up her career at a time when married women with children were expected to do so; she once shocked her superiors by giving a lecture when she was five months pregnant. Jesse Greenstein, astronomer at the California Institute of Technology and friend of Payne-Gaposchkin, recalled in *The Sciences* magazine that "she was charming and humorous," a person given to quoting Shakespeare, T.S. Eliot, and Gilbert and Sullivan. Her daughter remembers her in the autobiography *Cecilia Payne-Gaposchkin* as a "world traveler, ... an inspired seamstress, an inventive knitter and a voracious reader." Quoted in *Sky and Telescope,* Payne-Gaposchkin revealed that nothing compares to "the emotional thrill of being the first person in the history of the world to see something or to understand something."

SELECTED WRITINGS BY PAYNE-GAPOSCHKIN:

Books

Stellar Atmospheres, W. Heffer & Sons, 1925.
The Stars of High Luminosity, McGraw-Hill, 1930.
Variable Stars, Harvard Observatory Monograph No. 5, 1938.
Stars in the Making, Harvard University Press, 1952.
Introduction to Astronomy, Prentice-Hall, 1954; second edition, 1970.
The Galactic Novae, Interscience, 1957.
Stars and Clusters, Harvard University Press, 1979.
Cecilia Payne-Gaposchkin: An Autobiography and Other Recollections, edited by Katherine Haramundanis, Cambridge University Press, 1984.

Periodicals

Science Monthly, Stellar Evolution, May 1926, p. 419.
Astrophysical Journal, The Classification of Stellar Spectra, 1935, pp. 107–108.
Telescope, New Stars, no. 4, 1937, pp. 100–106.
Telescope, The Topography of the Universe, no. 8, 1941, pp. 112–114.
Popular Astronomy, Interesting Variable Stars, no. 49, 1941, pp. 311–319.
Sky and Telescope, Problems of Stellar Evolution, Volume 2, no. 9, 1943, pp. 5–7.
Nature, Variable Stars and Galactic Structure, no. 170, 1952, pp. 223–5.
Journal for the History of Science, Myth and Science, Volume 3, 1972, pp. 206–211.
Astronomical Journal, Fifty Years of Novae, no. 82, 1977, pp. 665–673.
Annual Review of Astronomy and Astrophysics, The Development of Our Knowledge of Variable Stars, no. 16, 1978, pp. 1–13.

FURTHER READING:

Books

Abir-Am, P. and D. Outram, editors, *Uneasy Careers and Intimate Lives: Women in Science 1789–1979,* Rutgers University Press, 1987.
Kass-Simon, G. and Patricia Farnes, editors, *Women of Science: Righting the Record,* Indiana University Press, 1990.

Periodicals

Bartusiak, Marcia, *The Sciences,* The Stuff of Stars, September/October, 1993, pp. 34–39.
Dobson, Andrea K. and Katherine Bracher, *Mercury,* A Historical Introduction to Women in Astronomy, January/February 1992, pp. 4–15.
Lankford, John, *Isis,* Explicating an Autobiography, March 1985, pp. 80–83.
Lankford, John and Ricky L. Slavings, *Physics Today,* Gender and Science: Women in American Astronomy, 1859–1940, March 1990, pp. 58–65.
Smith, E., *Physics Today,* Cecilia Payne-Gaposchkin, June 1980, pp. 64–66.
Whitney, C., *Sky and Telescope,* Cecilia Payne-Gaposchkin: An Astronomer's Astronomer, March 1980, page 212–214.

Sketch by Mindi Dickstein

Giuseppe Peano
1858–1932
Italian mathematician

Giuseppe Peano served most of his adult life as professor of mathematics at the University of Turin. His name is probably best known today for the contributions he made to the development of symbolic logic. Indeed, many of the symbols that he introduced in his research on logic are still used in the science today. In Peano's own judgment, his most important work was in infinitesimal calculus, which he modestly described as "not . . . entirely useless." Some of Peano's most intriguing work involved the development of cases that ran counter to existing theorems, axioms, and concepts in mathematics.

Peano was born in Spinetta, near the city of Cuneo, Italy, on August 27, 1858. He was the second of five children born to Bartolomeo Peano and the former Rosa Cavallo. At the time of Peano's birth, his family lived on a farm about three miles from Cuneo, a distance that he and his brother Michele walked each day to and from school. Sometime later, the family moved to Cuneo to reduce the boys' travel time.

At the age of twelve or thirteen, Peano moved to Turin, some fifty miles south of Cuneo, to study with his uncle, Michele Cavallo. Three years later he passed the entrance examination to the Cavour School in Turin, graduating in 1876. He then enrolled at the University of Turin and began an intensive study of mathematics. On July 16, 1880, he passed his final examinations with high honors and was offered a job as assistant to Enrico D'Ovidio, professor of mathematics at Turin. A year later he began an eight-year apprenticeship with another mathematics professor, Angelo Genocchi.

Writes "Genocchi's" Textbook on Calculus

Peano's relationship with Genocchi involved one somewhat unusual feature. In 1883 the publishing firm of Bocca Brothers expressed an interest in having a new calculus text written by the famous Genocchi. They expressed this wish to Peano, who passed it on to his master in a letter of June 7, 1883. Peano noted to Genocchi that he would understand if the great man were not interested in writing the book himself and, should that be the case, Peano would complete the work for him using Genocchi's own lecture notes and listing Genocchi as author.

In fact, that was just Genocchi's wish. A little more than a year later, the book was published, written by Peano but carrying Genocchi's name as author. Until the full story was known, however, many of Genocchi's colleagues were convinced that Peano had used his master's name to advance his own reputation. As others became aware of

Peano's contribution to the book, his own fame began to rise.

Peano's first original publications in 1881 and 1882 included an important work on the integrability of functions. He showed that any first-order differential equation of the form $y' = f(x, y)$ can be solved provided only that f is continuous. Some of these early works also included examples of a type of problem of which Peano was to become particularly fond, examples that contradicted widely accepted and fundamental mathematical statements. The most famous of these, published in 1890, was his work on the space-filling curve.

Derives the Space-Filling Curve

At the time, it was commonly believed that a curve defined by a parametric function would always be limited to an arbitrarily small region. Peano showed, however, that the two continuous parametric functions $x = x(t)$ and $y = y(t)$ could be written in such a way that as t varies through a given interval, the graph of the curve covers every point within a given area. Peano's biographer Hubert Kennedy points out that Peano "was so proud of this discovery that he had one of the curves in the sequence put on the terrace of his home, in black tiles on white."

Peano's first paper on symbolic logic was an article published in 1888 in which he continued and extended the work of George Boole, the founder of the subject, and other pioneers such as Ernst Schröder, H. McColl, and **C. S. Peirce**. His magnum opus on logic was written about a year later. In it Peano suggested a number of new notations including the familiar symbol Σ to represent the members of a set. He wrote in the preface to this work that progress in mathematics was hampered by the "ambiguity of ordinary language." It would be his goal, he said, to indicate "by signs all the ideas which occur in the fundamentals of arithmetic, so that every proposition is stated with just these signs." In succeeding pages, then, we find the introduction of now familiar symbols such as $\cap$ for "and," $\cup$ for "or," $\supset$ for "one deduces that," and Π for "is prime with." Also included in this book, *Arithmetices principia, nova methodo exposita* (*The Principles of Arithmetic, Presented by a New Method*), were Peano's postulates for the natural numbers, an accomplishment that Kennedy calls "perhaps the best known of all his creations."

In 1891 Peano founded the journal *Rivista di matematica* (*Review of Mathematics*) as an outlet for his own work and that of others; he edited the journal until its demise in 1906. He also announced in 1892 the publication of a journal called *Formulario* with the ambitious goal of bringing together all known theorems in all fields of mathematics. Five editions of *Formulario* listing a total of forty-two hundred theorems were published between 1895 and 1908.

By 1900 Peano had become interested in quite another topic, the development of an international language. He saw the need for the creation of an "interlingua" through which people of all nations—especially scientists—would be able to communicate. He conceived of the new language as being the successor of the classical Latin in which pre-Renaissance scholars had corresponded, a *latino sine flexione,* or "Latin without grammar." He wrote a number of books on the subject, including *Vocabulario commune ad latino-italiano-français-english-deutsch* in 1915, and served as president of the Akademi Internasional de Lingu Universal from 1908 until 1932.

While still working as Genocchi's assistant, Peano was appointed professor of mathematics at the Turin Military Academy in 1886. Four years later he was also chosen to be extraordinary professor of infinitesimal calculus at the University of Turin. In 1895 he was promoted to ordinary professor. In 1901 he resigned his post at the Military Academy, but continued to hold his chair at the university until his death of a heart attack on April 20, 1932.

Peano had been married to Carla Crosio on July 21, 1887. She was the daughter of the painter Luigi Crosio and was particularly fond of the opera. Kennedy points out that the Peanos were regular visitors to the Royal Theater of Turin where they saw the premier performances of Puccini's *Manon Lescaut* and *La Bohème.* The couple had no children. Included among Peano's honors were election to a number of scientific societies and selection as knight of the Crown of Italy and of the Orders of Saints Maurizio and Lazzaro.

SELECTED WRITINGS BY PEANO:

Books

Calcolo differenziale e principii di calcolo integrale, pubblicato con aggiante dal Dr. Giuseppe Peano, Bocca, 1884.

Calcolo geometrico secondo l'Ausdehnungslehre di H. Grassmann, preceduto dalle operazioni della logica deduttiva, Bocca, 1888.

Arithmetices principia, nova methodo exposita, Bocca, 1889.

Gli elementi di calcolo geometrico, Candeletti, 1891.

Lezioni di analisi infinitesimale, Candeletti, 1893.

Notations de logique mathématique, Guadagnini, 1894.

Vocabulario commune ad linguas de Europa, Bocca, 1909.

Fundamento de Esperanto, Cavoretto, 1914.

Vocabulario commune ad latino-italiano-français-english-deutsch, Academia pro Interlingua, 1915.

FURTHER READING:

Books

Dictionary of Scientific Biography, Volume 10, Scribner, 1975, pp. 441–444.

Selected Works of Giuseppe Peano, translated and edited with a biographical sketch and bibliography by Hubert C. Kennedy, University of Toronto Press, 1973.

Sketch by David E. Newton

Karl Pearson
1857–1936
English statistician

Karl Pearson is considered the founder of the science of statistics. He believed that a true understanding of human evolution and heredity required mathematical methods for analysis of the data. In developing ways to analyze and represent scientific observations, he laid the groundwork for the development of the field of statistics in the twentieth century and its use in medicine, engineering, anthropology, and psychology.

Pearson was born in London, England, on March 27, 1857, to William Pearson, a lawyer, and Fanny Smith. At the age of nine, Karl attended the University College School, but was forced to withdraw at sixteen because of poor health. After a year of private tutoring, he went to Cambridge, where the distinguished King's College mathematician E. J. Routh met with him each day at 7 A.M. to study papers on advanced topics in applied mathematics. In 1875, he was awarded a scholarship to King's College, where he studied mathematics, philosophy, religion, and literature. At that time, students at King's College were required to attend divinity lectures. Pearson announced that he would not attend the lectures and threatened to leave the college; the requirement was dropped. Attendance at chapel services was also required, but Pearson sought and was granted an exception to the requirement. He later attended chapel services, explaining that it was not the services themselves, but the compulsory attendance to which he objected. He graduated with honors in mathematics in 1879.

After graduation, Pearson traveled in Germany and became interested in German history, religion, and folklore. A fellowship from King's College gave him financial independence for several years. He studied law in London, but returned to Germany several times during the 1880s. He lectured and published articles on Martin Luther, Baruch Spinoza, and the Reformation in Germany, and wrote essays and poetry on philosophy, art, science, and religion. Becoming interested in socialism, he lectured on Karl Marx on Sundays in the Soho district clubs of London, and wrote hymns for the Socialist Song Book. Pearson was given the name Carl at birth, but he began spelling it with a "K," possibly out of respect for Karl Marx.

During this period, Pearson maintained his interest in mathematics. He edited a book on elasticity as it applies to physical theories and taught mathematics, filling in for professors at Cambridge. In 1884, at age twenty-seven, Pearson became the Goldsmid Professor of Applied Mathematics and Mechanics at University College in London. In addition to his lectures in mathematics, he taught engineering students, and showed them how to solve mathematical problems using graphs.

In 1885, Pearson became interested in the role of women in society. He gave lectures on what was then called "the woman question," advocating the scientific study of questions such as whether males and females inherit equal intellectual capacity, and whether, in the future, the "best" women would choose not to bear children, leaving it to "coarser and less intellectual" women. He joined a small club which met to discuss questions of morality and sex. There he met Maria Sharpe, whom he married in 1890. They had three children, Egon, Sigrid, and Helga. Maria died in 1928, and Pearson married Margaret V. Child, a colleague at University College, the following year.

Develops Statistical Methods to Study Heredity

Pearson was greatly influenced by Francis Galton and his 1889 work on heredity, *Natural Inheritance.* Pearson saw that there often may be a connection, or correlation, between two events or situations, but in only some of these cases is the correlation due not to chance but to some significant factor. By making use of the broader concept of correlation, Pearson believed that mathematicians could discover new knowledge in biology and heredity, and also in psychology, anthropology, medicine, and sociology.

An enthusiastic young professor of zoology, W. F. R. Weldon, came to University College in 1891, further influencing Pearson's direction. Weldon was interested in Darwin's theory of natural selection and, seeing the need for more sophisticated statistical methods in his research, asked Pearson for help. The two became lunch partners. From their association came many years of productive research devoted to the development and application of statistical methods for the study of problems of heredity and evolution. Pearson's goal during this period was not the development of statistical theory for its own sake. The result of his efforts, however, was the development of the new science of statistics.

Remaining at the University College, Pearson became the Gresham College Professor of Geometry in 1891. His lectures for two courses there became the basis for a book, *The Grammar of Science,* in which he presented his view of the nature, function, and methods of science. He dealt with the investigation and representation of statistical problems by means of graphs and diagrams, and illustrated the concepts with examples from nature and the social sciences. In later lectures, he discussed probability and chance, using games such as coin tossing, roulette, and lotteries as examples. He described frequency distributions such as the normal distribution (sometimes called the bell curve because its graph resembles the shape of a bell), skewed distributions (for which the graphed design is not symmetri-

cal), and compound distributions (which might result from a mixture of the two). Such distributions represent the occurrence of variables such as traits, events, behaviors, or other incidents in a given population, or in a sample (subgroup) of a population. They can be graphed to illustrate where each subject falls within the continuum of the variable in question.

Pearson introduced the concept of the "standard deviation" as a measure of the variance within a population or sample. The standard deviation statistic refers to the average distance from the mean score for any score within the data set, and therefore suggests the average amount of variance to be found within the group for that variable. Pearson also formulated a method, known as the chi-square statistic, of measuring the likelihood that an observed relation is in fact due to chance, and used this method to determine the significance of the statistical difference between groups. He also developed the theory of correlation and the concept of regression analysis, used to predict the research results. His correlation coefficient, also known as the Pearson r, is a measure of the strength of the relationship between variables and is his best known contribution to the field of statistics.

Between 1893 and 1901 Pearson published thirty-five papers in the *Proceedings* and the *Philosophical Transactions* of the Royal Society, developing new statistical methods to deal with data from a wide range of sources. This work formed the basis for much of the later development of the field of statistics. He was elected to the Royal Society in 1896, was awarded the Darwin Medal in 1898, and, in 1903, was elected an Honorary Fellow of King's College and received the Huxley Medal of the Royal Anthropological Institute.

Establishes Journal and Compiles Statistical Tables

In 1901, Pearson helped found the journal *Biometrika* for the publication of papers in statistical theory and practice. He edited the journal until his death. His research often required extensive mathematical calculation, which was carried out under his direction by students and staff mathematicians in his biometric laboratory. Since high-speed electronic computers had not yet been invented, performing the calculations by hand was tedious and time-consuming. The laboratory staff produced tables of calculations which Pearson made available to other statisticians through *Biometrika,* and later as separate volumes. Access to these tables made it possible for others to carry out statistical research without the support of a large staff, and, again, proved to be a valuable contribution to the early development of the field of statistics.

Pearson became the Galton Professor of Eugenics in 1911, and headed a new department of applied statistics as well as the biometric laboratory and a eugenics laboratory, established to study the genetic factors affecting the physical and mental improvement or impairment of future generations. During World War I, Pearson's staff served Britain's interest by preparing charts showing employment and shipping statistics, investigating stresses in airplane propellers, and calculating gun trajectories. From 1911 to 1930, Pearson produced a four-volume biography of Francis Galton. In 1925, he founded the journal *Annals of Eugenics,* which he edited until 1933. In 1932, Pearson was the first foreigner to be awarded the Rudolf Virchow Medal by the Anthropological Society of Berlin. He retired in 1933 at age seventy-seven, and received an honorary degree from the University of London in 1934. Pearson died on April 27, 1936, in Coldharbour, Surrey.

Pearson produced more than three hundred published works in his lifetime. His research focused on statistical methods in the study of heredity and evolution but dealt with a range of topics, including albinism in people and animals, alcoholism, mental deficiency, tuberculosis, mental illness, and anatomical comparisons in humans and other primates, as well as astronomy, meteorology, stresses in dam construction, inherited traits in poppies, and variance in sparrows' eggs. Pearson was described by G. U. Yule as a poet, essayist, historian, philosopher, and statistician, whose interests seemed limited only by the chance encounters of life. Colleagues remarked on his boundless energy and enthusiasm. Although some saw him as domineering and slow to admit errors, others praised him as an inspiring lecturer and noted his care in acknowledging the contributions of the members of his lab group. For Pearson, scientists were heroes. The walls of his laboratory contained quotations from Plato, Pascal, Huxley and others, including these words from Roger Bacon: "He who knows not Mathematics cannot know any other Science, and what is more cannot discover his own Ignorance or find its proper Remedies."

SELECTED WRITINGS BY PEARSON:

Books

The Ethic of Freethought, Fisher Unwin, 1888.
The Grammar of Science, Walter Scott, 1892.
The Chances of Death and Other Studies in Evolution, Edward Arnold, 1897.
Tables for Statisticians and Biometricians, Cambridge University Press, 1914.
The Life, Letters, and Labours of Francis Galton, four volumes, Cambridge University Press, 1914, 1924, 1930.

FURTHER READING:

Books

Froggatt, P., *Modern Epidemiology: The Pearsonian Legacy,* New Lecture Series No. 54, The Queen's University, Belfast, 1970.
Haldane, J. B. S., *Karl Pearson, 1857–1957, The Centenary Celebration at University College, London, 13 May 1957,* [privately issued by Biometrika Trustees], 1958.

Pearson, E. S., *Karl Pearson, An Appreciation of Some Aspects of His Life and Work,* Cambridge University Press, 1938.

Periodicals

Camp, Burton H., *Journal of the American Statistical Association,* Karl Pearson and Mathematical Statistics, December, 1933, pp. 395–401.
Camp, Burton H., *Obituary Notices of Fellows of the Royal Society,* Karl Pearson, Volume 2, number 5, December, 1936, pp. 72–110.
Pearl, Raymond, *Journal of the American Statistical Association,* Karl Pearson, 1857–1936, December, 1936, pp. 653–664.

Sketch by C. D. Lord

Irene Carswell Peden
1925–
American electrical engineer

Irene Carswell Peden is a specialist in radio science and electromagnetic wave propagation and scattering. She built her niche as a scientist conducting geophysical studies of radio wave propagation in Antarctica, where she became the first American woman engineer/scientist to live and work in the interior of that continent. She was born September 25, 1925, in Topeka, Kansas, to Mr. and Mrs. J. H. Carswell. Her mother was a country school teacher specializing in mathematics and music education, and her father was in the automobile business.

Peden's interest in science was sparked in high school, when she enrolled in a required chemistry course. Eventually, her scientific interests were diverted to electrical engineering, the field in which she received her bachelor's degree from the University of Colorado in 1947. After graduating, she began work for the Delaware Power and Light Company and, in 1949, she joined the Stanford Research Institute's Aircraft Radio Systems Lab.

Peden earned her master's degree from Stanford University in 1958 and worked at the university's Hansen Lab. While studying for her doctorate at Stanford, Peden became an acting instructor of electrical engineering and physics. In 1962, she became the first woman to earn a Ph.D. in any engineering field at the university.

Achievements in the Antarctic

Peden achieved early recognition in her study of radio wave propagation through the Antarctic ice pack. Through her research in the 1970s at the Byrd Antarctic Research

Station, she developed new methods to characterize the deep glacial ice by studying the effect it has on radio waves directed through it. She continued this line of research by studying certain properties in the lower ionosphere over Antarctica. Not only was she responsible for developing the methodology for her experiments, she also invented mathematical models to study and interpret the data collected. In so doing, Peden and her students were the first researchers to measure many of the electrical properties of Antarctic ice and to describe important aspects of very low frequency (VLF) propagation over long paths in the polar region. Peden later turned her attention to subsurface exploration technologies, using very high frequency (VHF) radio waves to detect and locate subsurface structures and other targets. Again, she found that she was paving new scientific ground and therefore had to design methodology and models to collect and interpret her data.

For her research, Peden has received a number of awards, including the Society of Women Engineers' Achievement Award in 1973, and the U.S. Army's Outstanding Civilian Service Medal in 1987. She has also been awarded Centennial Medals from the Institute of Electrical and Electronics Engineers, the University of Colorado and the American Society for Engineering Education, which named her to its 100-member Hall of Fame. A member of the national Academy of Engineering, Peden served a two-and-a-half-year term as director of the Division of Electrical and Communications Systems at the National Science Foundation. Peden was married in 1962 to attorney Leo J. Peden and has two step-daughters, Jefri, a high school athletic director, and Jennifer, a vocational and rehabilitational counselor. Peden continues her career at the University of Washington as a researcher in the Electromagnetics and Remote Sensing Laboratory, where she is a professor of electrical engineering.

SELECTED WRITINGS BY PEDEN:

Periodicals

IEEE Transactions on Geoscience and Remote Sensing, A Scale-model Study of Down-hole VHF Dipole Arrays with Application to Subsurface Exploration, Volume 30, number 5, September, 1992, p. 845.

IEEE Transactions on Geoscience and Remote Sensing, Detection of Tunnels in Low Loss Media Illuminated by a Transient Pulse, Volume 31, number 2, March, 1993, p. 503.

Sketch by Roger Jaffe

Charles John Pedersen
1904–1989
American organic chemist

Charles John Pedersen was a chemist and researcher credited with discovering how to make simple molecules that mimic the more complex molecules produced by living cells. These molecules, called macrocyclic crown polyethers or "crown ethers," shed light on the shape and size of organic molecules in general. For this work, Pedersen shared the Nobel Prize in chemistry in 1987 with the chemists **Donald J. Cram** and **Jean-Marie Lehn**.

Pedersen was born in Pusan, Korea, on October 3, 1904. His father was a Norwegian sailor who later became a mechanical engineer. His Japanese mother came from a family of silkworm traders. At the age of eight Pedersen started school in Nagasaki, Japan, and was educated in Roman Catholic schools. He emigrated to the United States in 1922 and later received his Bachelor of Science degree from the University of Dayton. His Master of Science degree was awarded by the Massachusetts Institute of Technology in 1927.

Pedersen worked for Du Pont in Wilmington, Delaware, as a researcher from 1927 to 1946. The company recognized his value and appointed him research associate in its Elastomers Chemicals Department in 1947. Pedersen remained in that position until his retirement in 1969. As a research associate, he was authorized to pursue whatever experiment he chose, free from the normal constraints of commercial or academic researchers. His work at Du Pont led to more than sixty patents, most of them in the field of petrochemicals.

Failure Leads to Fame

In the early 1960s Pedersen was trying to find a catalyst for polymerization processes. Polymerization is the combination of molecules into a more complex structure. Although he was unsuccessful in finding the catalyst, the end result of one of his failed experiments caught his attention and he began to study it more carefully. Pedersen found that his "mistake" was itself a small polymer that had some special properties. It later was determined to be the first recognized crown ether, named after its three-dimensional crown-like structure consisting of pairs of carbon and hydrogen atoms arranged in a ring. Pedersen found that the crown ethers he was able to synthesize formed complexes with a range of salts by trapping molecules within its ring structure. Complexes formed from a crown ether have distinctive electrical properties which have been the object of many subsequent studies by scientists. Pedersen's research helped to explain the relationship between a molecule's size and shape and its reactivity. The crown ether's ability to trap molecules within its structure has also led to the design of drugs with specific actions in pharmacology, and to an understanding of the transport of ions through biological membranes in biophysics.

In 1969, two years after publication of his work on crown ethers, Pedersen retired from Du Pont. He worked briefly at the Agricultural Research Council Unit of Structural Chemistry in London before retiring altogether. Over the course of his career he published some twenty-five papers in such periodicals as the *Journal of the American Chemical Society*. His work on crown ethers was continued by many researchers, including Donald J. Cram of the University of California at Los Angeles and Jean-Marie Lehn of the Collège de France in Paris and the Louis Pasteur Institute in Strasbourg. The three scientists were named co-winners of the 1987 Nobel Prize in chemistry.

Although Pedersen did collaborate with an occasional academic, the vast majority of his work was conducted on his own in the Du Pont laboratories. He never pursued a doctorate or an academic career. Pedersen married Susan J. Ault in 1947; the couple had two daughters, Shirley and Barbara. Susan Pedersen died in 1983. Pedersen became a United States citizen in 1953. After a long struggle with blood cancer and Parkinson's disease, Pedersen himself died on October 26, 1989, at the age of eighty-five, and was buried in Salem, New Jersey.

FURTHER READING:

Books

The Annual Obituary, St. James Press, 1990.

Sketch by Evelyn B. Kelly

Phillip James Edwin Peebles
1935–
Canadian-born American cosmologist

P. J. E. Peebles was an important figure in establishing the leading theory of the origin of the universe in 1965, and since then, he has conducted influential studies that reflect on how it will end.

Phillip James Edwin Peebles often signs his professional writing simply as P. J. E. Peebles and is known in the Princeton University telephone directory as Phillip J., but his coworkers call him Jim. He was born on May 25, 1935, in Winnipeg, Manitoba, Canada, where his father, Andrew Charles Peebles, worked at the Winnipeg Grain Exchange. His mother, the former Ada Marion Green, was a homemaker. Working his way through college at the University

of Manitoba in Winnipeg, he initially had the vague idea of becoming an engineer, but discovered the joy of physics and switched his major. In 1958 he took his B.S.C. in physics and moved on to Princeton University in the United States, where he earned a Ph.D. in physics in 1962. He began teaching at Princeton in 1961 while he was finishing his doctorate and has continued working at the University ever since.

Early in his career at Princeton, Peebles encountered **Robert H. Dicke**, who started Peebles on a lifelong interest in gravity and cosmology. Peebles has often been termed an astronomer, but his main work and teaching, although concerned with the large-scale nature of the universe, has been in physics. He is an Albert Einstein Professor of Science at Princeton, a post in the physics department that he has held since 1984. Peebles is married to Alison Peebles. Jim and Alison have never found any connection between her Peebles family from Ireland and Jim's from southern England. They have three children, Lesley, Ellen, and Marion.

Shortly after he received his Ph.D., Peebles worked with Dicke in 1965 on the problem of the origin of the universe. At that time the big bang was only one of several competing theories about the evolution of the universe, and many believed that a different cosmology, known as steady state, was more likely. Peebles's calculations connected the temperature of the cosmic origin in a great expansion of space to the wavelength of the cooled radiation that would still be observable. He also determined the expected and observed density of matter in the universe, as well as the total amount of helium, two other numbers that would be important evidence for or against the big bang theory.

The best-known of Peebles's results from this period is his and Dicke's proposed cosmic background radiation, confirmed that year by **Arno Penzias** and **Robert Woodrow Wilson** at the same time as Peebles and Dicke were developing their theory. Penzias and Wilson had discovered and measured the radiation but did not know how to explain it. Someone told them about a seminar on the subject of background radiation given by Peebles. They phoned Princeton, spoke to Dicke, and soon the two pairs of scientists published separate papers in the same journal issue on the discovery and its meaning. Since then the big bang theory has become generally accepted and the steady-state theory almost totally abandoned. Peebles's 1965 value for the total amount of helium was another important calculation that also tended to establish the big bang theory.

Investigates the "Flatness" of the Universe

In 1979 Peebles, again working with Dicke, developed another idea with important implications for the history of the universe. They investigated what cosmologists call the "flatness" of the universe. Flatness refers to the curvature of space predicted by Einstein's theory of general relativity. Such curvature is directly related to the density of matter in the universe, which in turn tells the fate of the cosmos. If there is too much matter for the amount of space, not only will space be curved with a positive curvature, but all the universe will eventually stop expanding and collapse. However, if there is too little matter, space will have a negative curvature and the universe will expand forever, gradually thinning to nothingness. If the universe has just the right amount of matter, space will be flat and the expansion of the universe will gradually slow down and eventually stop. In the late 1970s, although there was not enough evidence for a definite conclusion, it appeared likely to Peebles and Dicke that space actually is flat. In turn, this led to several theories by various physicists, astronomers, and cosmologists in the 1980s that purported to explain why this happens.

More recently, Peebles has reached the somewhat unpopular conclusion that the evidence now on hand indicates that the mass density of the universe is too low to produce flatness by itself. Unless there is some other factor, which some scientists think is possible, space has a negative universe and expansion should continue indefinitely. This model is known as an "open" universe instead of a flat one.

Peebles also has worked extensively on a related problem in cosmology. If the universe originated in a big bang from a uniform past, why is it not uniform today? That is, why is matter gathered into great aggregations called galactic clusters and galaxies that have large amounts of empty space between them? One of the main tools in trying to resolve this problem has been analysis of the cosmic background radiation, the very radiation that made Peebles and Dicke famous in 1965.

Published Works and Awards

Peebles has been an important author throughout his career, presenting the main ideas of cosmology, relativity, and quantum physics to two generations of physical scientists. His classic textbook, *Physical Cosmology,* from 1972 has only been succeeded by his more recent *Principles of Physical Cosmology,* published in 1993. He has also written a textbook for quantum mechanics as well as outlining *The Large Scale Structure of the Universe* for fellow cosmologists.

Peebles has been honored with the A.C. Morrison Award of the New York Academy of Sciences (1977), the Eddington Medal of the Royal Astronomical Society (1981), the Heineman Prize of the American Astronomical Society (1982), the Robinson Prize (1992), the Bruce Medal of the Astronomical Society of the Pacific (1995), and the Lemaître Award (1995) in addition to many honorary degrees and special lectureships.

SELECTED WRITINGS BY PEEBLES:

Books

Physical Cosmology. Princeton, NJ: Princeton University Press, 1972.

The Large-Scale Structure of the Universe. Princeton, NJ: Princeton University Press, 1980.
Quantum Mechanics. Princeton, NJ: Princeton University Press, 1992.
Principles of Physical Cosmology (Princeton Series in Physics). Princeton, NJ: Princeton University Press, 1993.

FURTHER READING:

Books

Voyage Through the Universe: The Cosmos. The Editors of Time-Life Books. Richmond, VA: Time-Life Books, 1988.
Wheeler, John Archibald. *A Journey into Gravity and Spacetime.* New York: Scientific American Library, 1990.

Sketch by Bryan Bunch

Rudolf Peierls
1907–1995
German-born English theoretical physicist

As Rudolf Peierls lay on a hill in New Mexico on June 16, 1945, and watched through darkened glass as the first atomic bomb turned night into day, he was struck with awe. Although he was a Manhattan Project scientist and knew exactly what to expect, he later wrote that, "no amount of imagination could have given us a taste of the real thing." As a theoretical physicist who had made contributions to quantum mechanics, it was Peierls and his associate **Otto Frisch** who in 1940 wrote the scientific report that informed governmental leaders that an atomic bomb of extraordinary power was technically possible. Working first for the British, the German-born Peierls eventually moved to the United States and joined the American team assembled at Los Alamos to help build the first bomb.

Rudolf Ernst Peierls was born in Berlin, Germany, on June 5, 1907. His father, Heinrich Peierls, was managing director of the cable factory Allgemeine Elektrizitaets-Gesellschaft. His mother, Elisabeth Weigert, died when he was fourteen. The youngest of three children, he was educated at the Humboldt School, Oberschoenewide. Always fascinated by machinery, he decided by the time he was eighteen to become an engineer. However, since he was rather clumsy with his hands and always had poor eyesight, he was persuaded to study the next best subject, physics. Throughout his university career, Peierls was able to study

Rudolf Peierls

under, or have as classmates, some of the greatest minds of twentieth-century physics. In 1925 he began at the University of Berlin, where he attended lectures on theoretical physics given by **Max Planck** and **Hermann Walther Nernst**. After two semesters there, he moved to Munich and studied under **Arnold Sommerfeld**, who many consider the greatest teacher in theoretical physics. There Peierls became good friends with **Hans Bethe** who was a year ahead of him. In early 1928, Peierls moved again, this time going to Leipzig on the advice of Sommerfeld to study under **Werner Heisenberg**. In Leipzig, he met and became good friends with fellow student **Felix Bloch**. After a fruitful year there, he moved to Zurich, Switzerland in 1929 to join **Wolgang Pauli** at the Federal Institute of Technology. Of these teachers and classmates, only Sommerfeld did not receive a Nobel Prize.

Although this was a time of intense work and study for Peierls, he did not describe it as especially difficult or burdensome when he recalled it in his 1985 autobiography, *Bird of Passage*. He mentioned the stimulating intellectual life, theater, and cabarets of Berlin, the mountain-climbing and swimming at Leipzig, and the sailing, concerts, and cinema of Zurich as often as he recalled encountering a new theory or learning something new.

Continues Associations with Nobel Winners

After receiving his Ph.D. in 1929, Peierls remained at Zurich as Wolgang Pauli's research assistant at the Federal Institute of Technology. The following year he met his future wife, a recent Ph.D. named Eugenia Nikolaevna Kannegiser, at a physics conference in the Soviet Union held at Odessa. They married in Leningrad in 1931.

After they returned to Zurich and Peierls completed his three-year stay at the Institute, he was advised by Pauli to apply for a fellowship at the Rockefeller Foundation, which he received in 1932. Peierls decided to divide the fellowship between Rome for the winter and Cambridge for the summer. Just as he had spent time with **Niels Bohr** when visiting Copenhagen, he met **Enrico Fermi** in Rome and **Ernest Rutherford** in Cambridge, where he also became friends with **Patrick Blackett**—four more colleagues who were or would become Nobel Prize winners. Throughout these years, Peierls's own research remained in the realm of theoretical physics, divided between studying electrons in metals and relativistic field theory.

As his fellowship came to end in 1933, Peierls found himself competing with many other "non-Aryan" scientists who were leaving an increasingly uncomfortable Germany and appearing in England. Unable to obtain a teaching post and already the father of a baby girl named Gaby, he accepted a two-year grant in Manchester University. There he was reunited with his friend, Hans Bethe, and worked with four more Nobel Prize winners, **William L. Bragg**, **James Chadwick**, **Paul Dirac**, and **Eugene Wigner**. During his initial year in Manchester, Peierls and Bethe first began work in the new field of nuclear physics. In early 1935, Peierls left Manchester to accept a temporary fellowship at the Royal Society's Mond Laboratory at Cambridge, which by now had become the center of physics in England. The fellowship had been established to help refugees like Peierls whose Jewish origins made his return to Germany unthinkable.

By this time, he had also become the father of a second child, Ronald (a daughter, Catherine, would be born in 1948 and another, Joanna, in 1949). After two years there, Peierls applied for and received a chair at the University of Birmingham, a position he was to hold until 1963. By 1938, the situation in Germany had deteriorated, and Peierls's father fled to the United States. In 1939, World War II broke out.

Collaboration with Frisch Leads to Startling Atomic Discovery

The discovery of nuclear fission by German scientists **Otto Hahn** and **Fritz Strassmann** was roughly coincidental with the start of World War II. Although discovered by them, it was the Austrian physicists **Lise Meitner** and **Otto Frisch** (her nephew) who were able to explain this startling phenomenon to the world. Their laboratory work revealed that when a neutron is sent into a uranium nucleus, violent internal motions occur that cause the uranium to split into two other elements. Most importantly, the byproduct of this fission process was the release of an enormous amount of energy. Frisch named the process "fission," since it was so similar to the division of a biological cell.

Like many other physicists, Peierls became interested in fission and wrote a preliminary paper on it. He hesitated to publish, however, since it could have had possible bearings on the design of a weapon. He decided to show the paper to Otto Frisch, who had come to Birmingham, England, when it appeared the Nazis might overrun Denmark. In early 1940, Frisch made a fateful suggestion to Peierls about his paper. Up to this point, most physicists had considered using only natural uranium, but what, Frisch suggested to Peierls, do you suppose would happen if you used a quantity of pure 235 isotope of uranium? Working on this idea together, they produced in three-days time an estimate of the energy released in such a chain reaction. Their conclusions staggered them. Where every other physicist had assumed that tons of scarce uranium would be needed to make an atomic bomb, their calculations indicated that a substantial fraction of that amount, maybe as little as a pound, would result in an energy release equivalent to thousands of tons of ordinary explosive.

The possibility that the Germans may have also made this breakthrough discovery and that Hitler might have already ordered work to begin on such a bomb terrified them and pointed immediately to their next task. In his autobiography, Peierls said, "It was our duty to inform the British government of this possibility. At the same time our conclusion had to be kept secret; if the German physicists had not yet seen the point, we did not want to draw their attention to it."

Discovery Leads to the Manhattan Project

Peierls and Frisch decided to write a memorandum in two parts: one was technical and gave the arguments, and the other was nontechnical and summarized the conclusions. After passing it on to a fellow physicist, Mark Oliphant, who promised to get it to the right person, it went to Sir **Henry Tizard** and then to G. P. Thomson, the chairman of a committee charged with studying this exact problem. The committee was about to disband itself after concluding that no such weapon was technically feasible. At first Peierls and Frisch were told that they could have no more involvement with the committee since they were "enemy aliens." Reason prevailed later and their expertise was eventually requested.

Peierls was soon relieved of his teaching duties in order to work full time on the British effort to build a bomb. By 1943, after Churchill and Roosevelt had direct talks, the British and the Americans decided that it was neither wise nor economical to have duplicate efforts. In late 1943, Peierls led the British group that went to the United States, and he eventually found himself at Los Alamos in the New Mexican desert. Peierls met many old friends from Europe there. One of these friends, Klaus Fuchs, who would later prove to be a Soviet spy, was there because Peierls himself had hired him in 1941 after he had fled the Nazis. Fuchs tricked Peierls and everyone else until his capture in early 1950. At Los Alamos, Peierls worked hard, with what he called "grim determination," and found that his special knowledge of shock waves was especially useful to the Americans. The successful atomic test at Alamogordo on June 16, 1945, meant that the new weapon would soon be ready for use. The United States would soon use this fearsome new weapon twice against Japan.

Peierls remained at Los Alamos until the war was over and then returned to England. Reflecting on his role in building the bomb, Peierls was ever the realist, stating that while he could take no pride in building a weapon that resulted in the horrors of Hiroshima and Nagasaki, he felt that once nuclear fission had been discovered, it could not be undiscovered. It was inevitable, therefore, that the atomic bomb would be built, but it was unthinkable for it to be possessed first by the enemy.

Peierls remained in Birmingham until 1963 when he became Wykeham Professor of Theoretical Physics at Oxford University. From 1974 to 1977, he was Professor of Physics at the University of Washington, Seattle. His many honors include a knighthood in 1968, the Royal Medal in 1959, the Copley Medal in 1986 from the Royal Society, the Max Planck Medal from Germany in 1963, and the Enrico Fermi Award from the United States in 1980. He died in Oxford, England, on September 19, 1995, after suffering from a kidney ailment.

SELECTED WRITINGS BY PEIERLS:

Books

The Laws of Nature. Allen & Unwin, 1955.
Bird of Passage. Princeton University Press, 1985.

FURTHER READING:

Books

McGraw-Hill Modern Scientists and Engineers. New York: McGraw-Hill, 1980, pp. 403-05.
Porter, Roy, ed. *The Biographical Dictionary of Scientists.* New York: Oxford University Press, 1994, p. 542.

Periodicals

Thomas, Robert M., Jr. "Rudolph Peierls, 88, Atomic Physicist, Dies in England," *The New York Times.* September 22, 1995, B7.

Sketch by Leonard C. Bruno

Charles Sanders Peirce
1839–1914
American logician

Charles Sanders Peirce remains one of the enigmatic figures in the history of American science. He made substantial contributions to a number of fields, especially logic, but his use of unusual terminology makes it difficult to appraise much of his work. As the project of publishing his collected writings continues, it may become possible to do justice to this many–sided thinker.

Charles Sanders Peirce was born on September 10, 1839, in Cambridge, Massachusetts. His father, Benjamin Peirce, was not only a professor of mathematics at Harvard University but also perhaps the most accomplished American mathematician of his generation. Peirce's early education outside the home was at various private schools in Boston and Cambridge, and he showed an interest in puzzles and chess problems. By the age of 13, he had read Archbishop Whately's *Elements of Logic*, perhaps a hint of the interests to come. Peirce entered Harvard in 1855, and the results were not impressive. Although he succeeded in graduating four years later, it was with a class rank of 71 out of 91. Upon graduation Peirce obtained a temporary position with the United States Coast Survey, which was to be his employer for most of his working life. His contributions to geodesy were many, and his service to the Coast Survey have been recognized with a memorial.

In the early 1860s Peirce studied under Louis Agassiz at Harvard, but his work with the Coast Survey proved to have had its benefits. He had become a regular aide to the Survey in 1861, which resulted in his exemption from military service. He was an assistant to the Coast Survey from 1867 to 1891, but that did not prevent his continuing researches in other areas. In particular, not only did he observe a solar eclipse in the United States in 1869, a year later he led an expedition to Sicily to observe a solar eclipse from a position that he had selected.

Broadens the Scope of Logic

Peirce had developed a technical competence in mathematics that came in handy when he turned to logic. As an example of a result in mathematics itself, he succeeded in showing that of linear associative algebras (a subject to which his father had devoted a book), the only three that had a uniquely defined operation of division were real numbers, complex numbers, and the quaternions of Sir William Rowan Hamilton. Perhaps the most significant innovation he made in logic was the extension of Boolean algebra to include the operation of inclusion. The most widely influential treatise on the algebra of logic was produced by the German mathematician Ernst Schröder beginning in 1890, and he displayed a detailed familiarity with Peirce's

Charles Sanders Peirce

work. In fact, had Peirce made the effort to produce a systematic account of the subject before Schröder, it would be easier to measure the importance of Peirce's contributions.

One of the factors that played a role in Peirce's interest in logic and its algebraic expression was his having taken a position in 1879 at Johns Hopkins University in Baltimore. During the five years that he worked at the university, he stayed on at the Coast Survey. As Nathan Houser remarked in an article about Peirce, "during those years Peirce was a frequent commuter on the B & O Railroad between Baltimore and Washington." Peirce's first paper on the algebra of logic was published in the *American Journal of Mathematics* in 1880. The period 1880 to 1885 saw Peirce's introduction of two ideas to mathematical logic: truth–functional analysis and quantification theory. Truth–functional analysis is the ancestor of the technique used by the Austrian philosopher Ludwig Wittgenstein to serve as the basis for logic in his *Tractatus Logi-co–philosophicus*. Quantification theory was at the heart of the logical apparatus introduced by Gottlob Frege for the reduction of mathematics to logic. It is difficult to imagine two more crucial contributions at the time, although Peirce's share of the recognition suffers by virtue of the scattered nature of his contributions.

Develops an Alternative Philosophy of Science

Peirce was never one to limit his scientific investigations to a single discipline. In 1879, he determined the length of the meter based on a wavelength of light. This provided a natural alternative to the standard meter bar on deposit in Paris. Three years later, he worked on a mathematical study of the relationship between variations in gravity at different points on the Earth's surface and the shape of the Earth. Better known is his role in serving as an advocate of a philosophy of science called pragmatism. Peirce's pragmatism was heavily dependent on the idea of inference to the best explanation. In other words, what existed was determined by what was needed for successful scientific practice at the time. While neither realists nor their opponents were happy with Peirce's position, it has continued to offer an alternative. In particular, philosophers of science with an inclination to take the history of science seriously find Peirce's approach one of the few that take change in one's scientific models to heart.

In light of Peirce's contributions in so many areas of science and mathematics the puzzle remains of why he was unable to secure an academic position commensurate to his abilities. One factor may have been domestic; he married Harriet Melusina Bay in 1862 and was divorced from her in 1883, the year of his second marriage (to Juliette Froissy of Nancy, France). Peirce and his first wife had been separated since 1876, and public sentiment was on her side. More generally, however, Peirce's personality tended to go between extremes, and it was difficult for others to adjust to his mood swings. He was quick to enter into disputes (and frequently with the wrong party) and was easily influenced by others.

Peirce spent his later years in Milford, Pennsylvania, removed from the centers of intellectual life. He had been asked to resign from the Coast Survey in 1891 and for the rest of his life his income was uncertain, despite prodigious periods of writing. Even his philosophy, to which he continued to devote his best efforts, was neglected, if only as a result of his remoteness from university settings. He died in Milford on April 19, 1914, having made contributions across the intellectual map, but more to the benefit of the discipline than his own.

SELECTED WRITINGS BY PEIRCE:

Books

Collected Papers, volumes 1–6. Edited by Charles Hartshorne and Paul Weiss, 1935.
Collected Papers, volumes 7–8. Edited by Arthur W. Burks, 1958.
Writings of Charles S. Peirce, 1982–.

FURTHER READING:

Books

Brent, Joseph. *Charles Sanders Peirce: A Life*. Bloomington: Indiana University Press, 1993.

Eisele, Carolyn. "Charles Sanders Peirce," in *Dictionary of Scientific Biography*. Volume X. Edited by Charles Coulston Gillispie. New York: Charles Scribner's Sons, 1973, pp. 482–488.
Hookway, Christopher. *Peirce*. London: Routledge and Kegan Paul, 1985.
Houser, Nathan. "Peirce and the Law of Distribution," in *Perspectives on the History of Mathematical Logic*. Edited by Thomas Drucker. Boston: Birkhauser, 1991, pp. 10–32.
Mlsak, Cheryl I. *Truth and the End of Inquiry*. Oxford: Oxford University Press, 1985.
Weiss, Paul. "Charles Sanders Peirce," in *Dictionary of American Biography*. Volume 7. Edited by Dumas Malone. New York, Charles Scribner's Sons, 1962, pp. 398–403.

Sketch by Thomas Drucker

Laurence Delisle Pellier
French-born American metallurgist

Laurence Delisle Pellier is the owner of Pellier-Delisle Metallurgical Laboratory, a consulting firm in Westport, Connecticut. A metallurgist of great experience, Pellier has studied powder metallurgy, corrosion, and physical metallurgy. Additionally, Pellier holds two patents, including one granted in 1956 for gold plating surgical needles. Her other research interests include the study of construction metals for chemical plants and she is one of the pioneering researchers in applying electron microscopy to metallurgy. For her work and achievements in the field of metallurgy, Pellier received the Society of Women Engineers' (SWE) Annual Achievement Award in 1962.

Born Laurence Delisle in Paris, France, Pellier came to the United States at a young age. After receiving her B.S. in chemical engineering from the College of the City of New York, from where she graduated *cum laude* in 1939, Pellier went on to obtain an M.S. in metallurgy from Stevens Institute of Technology in 1942. Following this she began doctoral work in physical metallurgy at Columbia University.

From 1940 to 1946 Pellier was a research associate and research fellow for the International Nickel Company and General Bronze Company; in this position she studied and designed alloys using powder metallurgy. She then accepted a position as senior metallurgical engineer with Sylvania Electric Products, where she developed techniques for the application of electron microscopy to problems in physical metallurgy. She remained at Sylvania until 1951, when she joined the American Cyanamid Company as a metallurgist. It was here that she studied corrosion, metals for construction of chemical plants, electron metallography, and electroplating and electroless plating. It was also during this period that she received a patent for a process of preparing corrosion-resistant gold-plated needles for use in surgery.

In 1956 Pellier accepted a position as research metallurgist with the Sigmund Cohn Corporation, where she studied the design and processing of metal alloys for use in fine instruments. In 1958, she joined International Nickel Company as senior scientist. There she explored electron metallography of high temperature alloys, traveling to Europe in 1960 to attend meetings on metallurgy at various places, including Cambridge, England, Delft, Holland, and in Paris. She returned to the United States in 1962 and formed her private consulting firm.

In addition to receiving the SWE Achievement Award, Pellier was awarded the Micrography Prize by the American Society for Metals in 1949 and the Micrography Prize by the American Society for Testing and Materials. Her affiliations include membership in the American Institute of Mining and Metallurgical Engineers, the French Society of Metallurgy, the Electron Microscope Society of America, French Engineers in the U.S.A., New York Electron Microscopists, and the New York Microscopical Society.

SELECTED WRITINGS BY PELLIER:

Periodicals

Fifth International Congress for Electron Microscopy, Direct Examination by Electron Transfer of Inconel-X, Academic Press, 1962.

Sketch by Karen Withem

Mary Engle Pennington
1872–1952
American chemist

Mary Engle Pennington was a bacteriological chemist who revolutionized methods of storing and transporting perishable foods. Denied a B.S. degree in 1895 because she was a woman, Pennington went on to head the U.S. Department of Agriculture's food research lab. As persuasive as she was resourceful, Pennington was able to convince farmers, manufacturers, and vendors to adopt her techniques. She developed methods of slaughtering poultry that kept them fresh longer, discovered ways to keep milk products from spoiling, and determined how best to freeze fruits and vegetables. Pennington was the first female member of the American Society of Refrigerating Engi-

neers. She eventually went into business for herself as a consultant and investigator in the area of perishable foods.

Pennington was born October 8, 1872, in Nashville, Tennessee. She was the first of two daughters born to Henry and Sarah B. Molony Pennington. Pennington spent most of her early life in Philadelphia, where her family moved to be closer to their Quaker relatives. With her father, a successful label manufacturer, she shared a love of gardening.

Pennington found her way to the field of chemistry through a library book on that subject. Her interest prompted her to enter the Towne Scientific School of the University of Pennsylvania, an uncommon occurrence for a woman at that time. In 1895 she received a certificate of proficiency, having been denied a B.S. because of her gender. Not to be deterred, Pennington continued academic work, earning her Ph.D. at age twenty-two from the University of Pennsylvania with a major in chemistry and minors in zoology and botany. This degree was conferred under an old statute that made exceptions for female students in "extraordinary cases." Pennington then accepted a two-year fellowship at the university in chemical botany, followed by a one-year fellowship in physical chemistry at Yale.

From 1898 to 1906 Pennington served as instructor in physiological chemistry at Women's Medical College. During this same period, she started and operated a clinical laboratory performing analyses for physicians, and was a consultant to Philadelphia regarding the storage of perishable foods during the marketing process. Her reputation for quality work led to an appointment as head of the Philadelphia Department of Health and Charities Bacteriological Laboratory. One of her first goals here was the improvement of the quality of milk and milk products. Her natural gift of persuasion aided her in convincing ice-cream manufacturers and vendors to adopt simple steps to help avoid bacterial contamination of their foods.

The Pure Food and Drug Act was passed in 1906, and the U.S. Department of Agriculture planned to establish a research laboratory to help provide scientific information for prosecutions under the act. Specifically, this lab would be concerned with the quality of eggs, dressed poultry, and fish. With the encouragement of Harvey W. Wiley, chief of the chemistry section of the USDA and a longtime family friend, Pennington took and passed the civil service exam in 1907 under the name M. E. Pennington. Unaware that Pennington was a woman, the government gave her a post as bacteriological chemist. Wiley promoted her to head the food research lab in 1908. That same year she delivered an address for Wiley to a startled all-male audience at the First International Congress of Refrigeration.

During Pennington's tenure the laboratory affected alterations in the warehousing of food, its packaging, and use of refrigeration in transport. Pennington eventually developed techniques that were commonly used for the slaughter of poultry, ensuring safe transport and high quality long after the butchering occurred. In the area of eggs, a highly perishable item especially in warm weather, she again used her powers of persuasion. She worked to convince farmers to collect and transport eggs more frequently during warmer weather. She is also credited with developing the egg cartons that prevent excessive breakage during transport.

During World War I, Pennington consulted with the War Shipping Administration. The United States had forty thousand refrigerated cars available for food transport at the start of the war. Pennington determined only three thousand of these were truly fit for use, with proper air circulation. Following the war she was recognized for her efforts with a Notable Service Award given by Herbert Hoover.

Pennington made another career change in 1919 when she accepted a position as manager of research and development for New York's American Balsa Company, a manufacturer of insulating material. In 1922 she made her final career move, starting her own business in New York as a consultant and investigator in the area of perishable foods. She was particularly interested in frozen foods, helping to determine the best strains of fruits and vegetables for freezing, and the best method for freezing them.

Pennington was the author of books, articles, pamphlets, and several government bulletins. She gave many addresses and was the recipient of several awards, including the American Chemical Society's 1940 Garvan Medal to honor a woman chemist of distinction. Pennington, in fact, was one of the first dozen female members of the society. She was the first female member of the American Society of Refrigerating Engineers, and the first woman elected to the Poultry Historical Society's Hall of Fame. She served as director of the Household Refrigeration Bureau of the National Association of Ice Industries from 1923 to 1931.

Pennington earned herself the reputation for always producing quality work. She was accepted in industry even while she was working for the government in enforcing the Pure Food and Drug Act. She maintained her interest in gardening and botany, growing flowers in her apartment. She was a lifelong member of the Quaker Society of Friends. Pennington, who never married, was still working as a consultant and as vice president of the American Institute of Refrigeration when she died on December 27, 1952, in New York City.

SELECTED WRITINGS BY PENNINGTON:

Books

How to Kill and Bleed Market Poultry, Government Printing Office, 1915.
Eggs, Progress Publications, 1933.

FURTHER READING:

Books

American Chemists and Chemical Engineers, edited by Wyndham Miles, American Chemical Society, 1976.

Notable American Women: The Modern Period, edited by Barbara Sicherman and Carol Green, Belknap Press, 1980.

Periodicals

Chemical and Engineering News, Mary E. Pennington, January 5, 1953.

Sketch by Kimberlyn McGrail

Roger Penrose
1931–
English mathematical physicist

Roger Penrose explored a range of topics in mathematical theory and physics, including relativity theory, quantum mechanics, astrophysics, cosmology, possible and impossible geometric shapes, and how the human brain works. With theoretical physicist and professor **Stephen Hawking**, he extended our understanding of black holes and the "big bang" theory of the origin of the universe, and his work with geometric puzzles shed light on the nature of quasi-crystals.

Penrose was born August 8, 1931, in Colchester, England. His father, Lionel S. Penrose, was a geneticist, and his mother, Margaret Newman, a doctor; his uncle, Sir Roland Penrose, was a surrealist painter and a biographer of Picasso. Penrose's older brother Oliver became a mathematics professor, while his younger brother Jonathan, a professor of psychology, was British chess champion ten times. As a boy, Penrose shared his father's interest in nature and geometrical puzzles. In school, he showed an aptitude for mathematics, devising geometry problems that challenged his teachers.

As a mathematics student at University College, London, Penrose discovered a theorem concerning eight conics in a plane, for which three well-known theorems turned out to be special cases. He received a Bachelor of Science degree in 1952 and a Ph.D. from Cambridge in 1957, writing his dissertation on algebraic geometry. As a student, Penrose rediscovered and developed mathematician E. H. Moore's generalized inverse matrix, a method of solving equations that involves rectangular arrays of numbers. At St. John's College, Cambridge, Penrose heard lectures by Paul Dirac on quantum mechanics and by Hermann Bondi on the theory of relativity, and became interested in relating quantum mechanics and space-time structure.

Beginning as a research fellow at St. John's College from 1957 to 1960, Penrose pursued a career of research and teaching at major universities in England and the United States. He was a North Atlantic Treaty Organization (NATO) research fellow at Princeton, Syracuse, and Cornell universities from 1959 to 1961. In the 1960s he had visiting appointments at the University of Chicago, Yeshiva University in New York, the University of Texas in Austin, the University of California at Berkeley, and King's College and Bedford College in London. In 1973 Penrose was named the Rouse Ball professor at Oxford University, and in the 1980s he was the Edgar Odell Lovett Professor of Mathematics at Rice University. Penrose's early honors include the 1966 Adams Prize from Cambridge University and the Dannie Heineman Prize for Physics from the American Physical Society and the American Institute of Physics in 1971. He was elected to the Royal Society in 1972.

Developed Mathematics for Study of Black Holes

In 1965 Penrose showed that, as a consequence of Einstein's theory of general relativity, there must inevitably be points in space that are infinitely dense and hot. At such points—called singularities—the laws of classical physics do not apply; the gravitational field becomes infinite, or other pathological behavior occurs. Penrose's theorem proved that if a star of sufficient mass collapsed, a singularity—the core of what later became known as a black hole—would result. Penrose's work first convinced many physicists of the existence of black holes, and inspired the search for them.

A year later, Stephen Hawking of Cambridge University applied Penrose's theorem to cosmology, proving that the universe started in a singularity. In 1970, Penrose and Hawking, working together, succeeded in proving a singularity theorem much more powerful than their earlier efforts. Previous work by others had indicated that our universe did not begin with a "big bang" singularity; Penrose and Hawking's theorem challenged this view, asserting that in any universe with certain fundamental properties, a big bang singularity must occur. The two scientists proved their theorem using mathematical techniques from the theory of differential topology; using the same techniques, Penrose contributed to Hawking's work on black holes, which showed that the surface area of a black hole must increase as mass is added. In 1975, Penrose and Hawking shared the Royal Astronomical Society's Eddington Medal, and in 1988 they were awarded the Wolf Foundation Prize in Physics.

Penrose's efforts were aided by his invention of the "twistor," a mathematical tool for describing physical objects and space, incorporating energy, momentum, and spin—the three properties possessed by all objects moving through space-time. A twistor has either six or eight dimensions, each of which involves either movement or change in size.

Another of Penrose's primary areas of study is tiling, which involves completely covering a flat surface with a regular pattern of tiles. He shares this interest with numerous other mathematicians, including Johannes Kepler in the seventeenth century. Penrose has said that he inherited his love of puzzles from his father, who used models to understand or explain concepts in genetics. Speaking of his father in an interview for *Omni,* Penrose explained, "With him there was no clear line between making puzzles for his children and his serious work in genetics." While a graduate student in 1954, Penrose saw the drawings of Dutch artist M. C. Escher at a mathematics conference in Amsterdam. Escher's work incorporates geometry and perspective to produce drawings of "impossible" objects. Penrose was fascinated with the illustrations of objects which violate the rules of three-dimensional reality. He proceeded to draw his own such construct—a "tribar" of three beams—which he sent to Escher. The artist later used the tribar figure as the basis for a continuous flow of water in his lithograph, *Waterfall.*

The simplest tiling pattern utilizes identical tiles in the shape of squares, equilateral triangles, or regular hexagons. However, regular pentagons—five-sided tiles—will not tile a surface without leaving gaps. Penrose found that a floor, or any plane surface, can be covered with pentagons plus two other shapes—stars and hat-shaped pieces. The resulting pattern has regularities but does not repeat itself exactly. Some tiling patterns repeat themselves in a certain way: if you placed a sheet of thin paper over the design and traced it, and then moved the paper sideways without rotating it, the tracing would match. Such designs are called "periodic." Penrose's pattern was non-periodic. With some tile designs, such as hexagons, you know from the neighboring tiles where to put down the next one; such patterns are called "local." Penrose's pattern appeared to be non-local; it was necessary to look at the position of pieces some distance away in order to position the next tile correctly.

Penrose worked with pieces of various shapes, trying to find the smallest number of shapes that would force a non-periodic tiling. He discovered several combinations, and finally, in 1974, lowered the number of shapes to two. One of Penrose's most interesting designs used two shapes derived from a rhombus: one piece looked like a kite, and the other resembled a dart or a "stealth" airplane. Following rules about which edges could be fitted together, the two shapes forced a non-periodic tiling. In his book, *Penrose Tiles to Trapdoor Ciphers,* Martin Gardner displays some tiling patterns and explains how to make a set of "Penrose tiles."

Similar Pattern Found in Quasi-Crystals

Following Penrose's work, others extended the tiling concept to three dimensions, devising solid polyhedrons to fill space without any gaps; these tilings were also non-periodic. In the 1980s, crystallographers became interested in Penrose's findings. For a century, scientists had thought that the atoms in crystals were arranged periodically, and that crystals with five-fold symmetry were impossible. It was generally assumed that the atoms in solid matter took one of two forms: either a periodic crystal arrangement or a disordered arrangement in materials such as glass. But in studying an alloy of aluminum and manganese, Dan Schechtman at the National Bureau of Standards saw what appeared to be non-periodic crystals with five-fold symmetry. The complicated sequences in the pattern were only "quasi-periodic." Halfway between crystals and glass-like structures, this new form of matter, quasi-crystals, caused considerable excitement among chemists, physicists, and crystallographers. The similarity between the alloy pattern and the Penrose patterns was recognized by University of Pennsylvania physicist Paul Steinhardt and by crystallographer Alan MacKay of London. Soon scientists found similar non-periodic structures in other alloys. Alloys with five-fold symmetry, as well as seven-fold, nine-fold, and eleven-fold symmetry, proved to be possible.

The apparent non-locality of the structures puzzled scientists, because it was not clear how a growing quasi-crystal would attach new atoms, one at a time, in the right location and sequence. Then in 1988 Steinhardt and George Onoda, an IBM ceramics expert, devised rules for building a Penrose tiling, specifying which vacancy to fill first, which piece to use, and which way the tile should be turned. It was not necessary to pay attention to any distant part of the pattern. These results provided possible clues to the growth of three-dimensional quasi-crystals. Researchers proceeded to study the properties of the new alloys. Because of their intricate structure, it was thought that they might turn out to be harder than crystals and usable as substitutes for industrial diamonds, or as materials in electronic devices.

Possible Link Between the Human Mind and Quantum Gravity

Much of Penrose's work, including topics such as theoretical mathematics, cosmological singularities, and quasi-crystals, came together in his 1989 book, *The Emperor's New Mind: Concerning Computers, Minds, and the Laws of Physics.* The book was on the *New York Times* best-seller list for nine weeks, attracting interest from people in a wide range of fields, and was the topic of more than twenty book reviews in periodicals in fields ranging from science and artificial intelligence to philosophy, as well as popular newspapers.

In the book Penrose disagrees with the view, held by some researchers in the field of artificial intelligence, that computers are capable of mimicking the function of human brains. A computer program, Penrose argues, uses an algorithm, a step-by-step mechanical procedure for working toward an answer from the input data. Certain kinds of human thinking are nonalgorithmic—not formalizable—so, Penrose concludes, the human brain must be making use of nonalgorithmic processes.

Penrose considers the nature of the physics that might underlie conscious thought processes. He sees a significant gap between our physical understanding at the small-scale quantum level (which includes the behavior of molecules, atoms and subatomic particles) and at the larger classical level (which includes the behavior of larger objects such as baseballs). Penrose suspects that a greater understanding of the functioning of the human brain may depend on a fundamentally new understanding of physics, to be sought in a radical new theory of quantum gravity. He believes that until we understand the borderline between quantum mechanics and classical mechanics, computers will not be able to work as human brains do.

SELECTED WRITINGS BY PENROSE:

Books

Spinors and Space-time, Volume 1: Two-Spinor Calculus and Relativistic Fields, Volume 2: Spinor and Twistor Methods in Space-Time Geometry, Cambridge University Press, 1986.

M. C. Escher, Art and Science, North Holland, 1986.

The Emperor's New Mind: Concerning Computers, Minds, and the Laws of Physics, Oxford University Press, 1989.

FURTHER READING:

Books

Gardner, Martin, *Penrose Tiles to Trapdoor Ciphers,* W. H. Freeman and Co., 1989.

Gardner, Martin, *McGraw-Hill Modern Scientists and Engineers,* Volume 2, McGraw-Hill, 1980, pp. 407–408.

Periodicals

Horgan, John, *Scientific American,* The Artist, the Physicist and the Waterfall, February, 1993, p. 30.

Horgan, *Scientific American,* Quantum Consciousness: Polymath Roger Penrose Takes on the Ultimate Mystery, November, 1989, pp. 31–33.

Horgan, *Omni,* Interview: Roger Penrose, June, 1986, pp. 67–68, 70, 73, 106–107.

Landauer, Rolf, *Physics Today,* Is the Mind More Than an Analytic Engine?, June, 1990, pp. 73–75.

Landauer, Rolf, *The Economist,* Many-sided Penrose, September 17, 1988, p. 100.

Landauer, Rolf, *Behavioral and Brain Sciences,* Precis of The Emperor's New Mind: Concerning Computers, Minds, and the Laws of Physics, "Open Peer Commentary," and "Author's Response," 1990, no. 13, pp. 643–705.

Siegel, Matthew, *Physics Today,* Wolf Foundation Honors Hawking and Penrose for Work on Relativity, January, 1989, pp. 97–98.

von Baeyer, Hans C., *Discover,* Impossible Crystals, February, 1990, pp. 69–78.

Sketch by C. D. Lord

Deborah L. Penry
1957–
American oceanographer

As only the second female to receive the National Science Foundation's Alan T. Waterman Award since its inception in 1976, Deborah Penry is not only an important figure within her scientific discipline, but she is also an extraordinary role model for women in the sciences. Handed out annually to outstanding scientists under the age of 35, the award was given to her in 1993 for her correlation between chemical reactors and the digestive behavior of benthic (living on the bottom of the ocean) organisms. Her digestive paradigm enhances the understanding of ocean ecology and lends broader meaning to the effects feeding and digestion have on various ecosystems.

Deborah L. Penry was born in Maryland on February 28, 1957. With a childhood spent living near Chesapeake Bay and fishing with her father, Penry's passion for oceanography blossomed early in her life. She liked to fish, but she was more intrigued by the contents of a fish's stomach when it was being gutted. It was that curiosity that led her to the University of Delaware, where she earned her B.A. in Biology in 1979. She continued her educational training at William and Mary College in Williamsburg, Virginia, and finished her master's degree in 1982. It was at this point that Penry's interest in ichthyology (the study of fish) was diverted to the organisms and invertebrates that the fish ate.

Penry chose to complete her doctoral studies under the direction of Dr. Peter A. Jumars, a Professor of Oceanography at the University of Washington. Jumars focused his research on the processes conducted by an ocean community and its individuals in order to understand why certain organisms congregate to form various ecosystems. Penry completed her Ph.D. in oceanography in 1988 and continued her post-doctorate work at the University of Washington.

In collaboration, Penry and Jumars discovered parallels between chemical reactor types and the digestive practices of benthic organisms. Like chemical reactions, the feeding/digestion of an organism consumes a material, reacts to that material, and expels that material once its nutrients are extracted. Using this model as a basis, they applied it to other types of organisms.

Finished with her post-doctoral research, Penry moved to a faculty position at the University of California, Berkeley. The biology department within which she taught and conducted research was a conglomeration of smaller departments, including zoology, paleontology, oceanography, and botany, for example. Such an integrative approach to the study of biology lends itself to a broader perspective and was unique at the time. Berkeley's Integrative Biology Department was the first of its kind in the United States as of the early 1990s.

At the University of California, Berkeley, Penry is able to spend quite a bit of time nurturing the minds of her students. She teaches undergraduate and graduate level courses. She has even personally developed a course on biological oceanography. She is a mentor to budding scientists, allowing students access to her laboratory in order to pursue their own research. In fact, the moneys she received along with the Waterman Award were used to further her students' research as well as purchase laboratory equipment.

SELECTED WRITINGS BY PENRY:

Periodicals

(With Peter A. Jumars) "Modeling Animal Guts as Chemical Reactors." *American Naturalist* 129 (1987): 69-96.

(With Peter A. Jumars) "Digestion Theory Applied to Deposit Feeding." *Lecture Notes on Coastal and Estuarine Studies* 31 (1989): 114-128.

(With Peter A. Jumars) "Gut Architecture, Digestive Constraints and Feeding Ecology in Deposit-Feeding and Carnivorous Polychaetes." *Oecologia* 82 (1990): 1-11.

(With C. A. Miller and P. M. Glibert) "The Impact of Trophic Interactions on Rates of Nitrogen Regeneration and Grazing in Chesapeake Bay." *Limnol. Oceanography* 40 (1995): 1005-1011.

FURTHER READING:

Books

Murphy, Patricia and Leslie O'Brien. "Deborah L. Penry." *Notable Women in the Life Sciences: A Biographical Dictionary.* Benjamin F. Shearer and Barbara S. Shearer, eds. Westport, Connecticut: Greenwood Press, 1996.

Other

University of California, Berkeley Integrative Biology Department directory. http://ib.berkeley.edu/faculty/Penry,DL.html (October 30, 1997).

Sketch by Jacqueline L. Longe

Arno Penzias
1933–
American astrophysicist

Arno Penzias shared the Nobel Prize for physics in 1978 with **Robert Wilson** for a discovery that supported the big bang theory of the universe. The two radio astronomers at what was then American Telephone & Telegraph's (AT&T) Bell Telephone Laboratories were using a 20-foot horn reflector antenna that year to measure the intensity of radio waves emitted by the halo of gas surrounding our galaxy. And they were bothered by a persistent noise which they could not explain. At first they pinned it on two pigeons that were nesting in the antenna throat. But even after they evicted the birds, the noise continued. Eventually the scientists were able to conclude that the noise came from cosmic background, or microwave, radiation. This came to be widely considered as remnant microwave radiation from the "big bang" in which the universe was created billions of years ago. And the Penzias-Wilson discovery came to be considered a major finding in astrophysics.

Arno Allan Penzias was born in Munich, Germany, April 26, 1933, to Jewish parents Karl and Justine (Eisenreich) Penzias. Hitler's campaign to wipe out the Jews of Europe was well underway when the family escaped in 1940. Arriving in New York, Penzias had to acclimate to a new culture and language and suffer through hard times for his family. Naturalized in 1946, he demonstrated scientific acumen at Brooklyn Technical High School and went on to obtain his B.S. at City College in New York in 1954. He married Anne Pearl Barras that same year; the union produced three children. After a two-year stint in the U.S. Army Signal Corps, Penzias obtained both his master's and Ph.D. degrees at Columbia University. He has said he chose to study physics because he asked a professor if he could make a living in the field and was told, "Well, you can do the same things engineers can do and do them better."

Begins Research Career

In 1961 Penzias was hired at Bell Labs in Holmdel, New Jersey. AT&T was a telecommunications monopoly at that time and Bell Labs was its research center, attracting the best and brightest scientific minds. In this context Penzias demonstrated his capabilities early on. Asked to join a committee of older scientists who were trying to devise how to calculate the precise positions of communication satellites by triangulation, young Penzias suggested they use radio stars, which emit characteristic frequencies from fixed positions, as reference points. The distinguished scientists nodded their heads in agreement—and the committee immediately disbanded. For his abilities, Penzias rose through the Bell ranks to become director of the facility's Radio Research Laboratory in 1976, and executive director of the Communications Sciences Research Division in 1979. He also took part in the pioneering Echo and Telstar communications satellite experiments of the 1970s.

Penzias's Cosmic Finding

It was astronomer **George Gamow** who in 1942 first calculated the conditions of temperature and density that would have been required for a fireball explosion or "big bang" origin of the universe 15 billion years ago. Astronomers Ralph Alpher and Robert Herman later concluded that cosmic radiation would have resulted from this event. This theory was confirmed by Penzias and Wilson. According to the theory, the background radiation resulting from the big bang would have lost energy; it would have essentially "cooled." Gamow and Alpher calculated in 1948 that the radiation should now be characteristic of a perfectly emitting body—or black body—with a temperature of about 5 kelvin, or –268 degrees C. The scientists said this radiation should lie in the microwave region of the spectrum; their calculations were verified by physicists **Robert Dicke** and **P. J. E. Peebles**.

Penzias's and Wilson's contribution to the issue began with a 20-foot directional radio antenna, the same kind of radio antenna designed for satellite communication. Investigating an irritating noise emitted by the antenna, the two men realized in May of 1964 that what they heard was not instrumental noise but microwave radiation coming from all directions uniformly. Penzias and Wilson calculated the radiation's temperature as about 3.5 kelvin. Dicke and Peebles, who had made the earlier calculations, got reinvolved from nearby Princeton University with a scientific explanation of the Penzias-Wilson discovery. More experiments followed, confirming that the radiation was unchanging when measured from any direction. Even after the duo received the Nobel Prize in 1978 (also awarded that year to **Pyotr Kapitsa** for unrelated work in physics) they continued to collaborate on research into intergalactic hydrogen, galactic radiation, and interstellar abundances of the isotopes.

Bringing Bell Labs into a New Era

At the time of the federal lawsuit which led to the breakup of AT&T in 1984, Penzias, who had become vice president of research in 1981, predicted that without the operating companies as a base, Bell Labs would become "a sinking ship." That did not happen. Instead, Penzias in September of 1990 presided over the realignment of Bell Labs into a facility whose research is streamlined and oriented towards the activities of its business units. "We adjusted the food chain," Penzias told *Science* magazine in 1991. "If we'd done everything in the old way we probably would have sunk." Picking up on his former marine metaphor, Penzias added: "But we've fixed the hull; we're back to a healthy operation."

While rearranging Bell Labs, Penzias has kept an eye on the outside world, writing *Ideas and Information:*

Managing in a High-Tech World in 1989 and staying involved in the national dialogue regarding the growth of computer technology and competition with the Japanese. "You've got to understand the Japanese are not superhuman," he told *Forbes* magazine in March of 1989. "You go into Sears, the best cordless telephone you can buy is an AT&T phone. It works better. You try it."

In his personal life, Penzias, who is the proud grandfather of three, is also an avid skier, swimmer, and runner with an interest in kinetic sculpture and writing limericks. Penzias is a member of the National Academy of Sciences and the National Academy of Engineering, as well as the vice chairman of the Committee of Concerned Scientists, devoted to political freedom for scientists internationally. He has written over 100 articles and collected 19 honorary degrees. In all this Penzias argues that technology can be liberating. As he wrote in *Fortune* magazine in March of 1990: "Everybody is overstressed. . . . We've got to stop going to meetings and have them electronically instead. . . . How far away are we from realizing this dream? My guess is that by the time *Fortune* marks its 100th anniversary, a lot of this will have happened. In fact, long before I retire in 1998, I hope to have at least a multimedia terminal in my office so that I can integrate voice, data, high-definition video, conference video, document access, and shared software . . . who's going to do all this? I hope it's AT&T. But it could be IBM, Apple—it could be anybody."

SELECTED WRITINGS BY PENZIAS:

Books

Ideas and Information: Managing in a High-Tech World, Norton, 1989.

Periodicals

Telephone Engineer and Management, The World Beyond Digital Switching: An Integrated Transport and Switching System Will Be Required In Order To Provide the Services of the Future, May 1, 1986.
Discover, The World According To Penzias, Nov. 1988, p. 88.
Computerworld, Present Shock: How Information Technology Transforms Organizations, Management and the Way Things Are Done, Oct. 23, 1989, p. 89.
Telephone Engineer & Management, Networking in the Nineties: A Preview of Telecommunications in the 21st Century, Jan. 15, 1990, p. 511.

FURTHER READING:

Books

Weber, Robert L., *Pioneers of Science: Nobel Prize Winners in Physics,* Institute of Physics, 1980, p. 257.

Periodicals

Weber, Robert L., *Science,* Bell Labs: Shakeout Follows Breakup, June 14, 1991, p. 1480.
Weber, Robert L., *Forbes,* The Japanese Are Not Superhuman, March 20, 1989, p. 122.
Weber, Robert L., *Fortune,* The New Look at America's Top Lab: How Has Bell Labs Weathered the Breakup of AT&T? Feb. 1, 1988, p. 60.
Weber, Robert L., *Science,* We Simply Can't Afford Telephone Tag, March 26, 1990, p. 72.

Other

Weber, Robert L., *Science,* We Simply Can't Afford Telephone Tag, Biographical Information Supplied by Bell Labs' Media Relations.

Sketch by Joan Oleck

Marguerite Perey
1909–1975
French physicist

Marguerite Perey is best known for her discovery of francium, the 87th element in the periodic table. Francium, a rare, highly unstable, radioactive element, is the heaviest chemical of the alkali metal group. Perey's work on francium and on such scientific occurrences as the actinium radioactive decay series led to her admission to the French Academy of Sciences. Perey was the first woman to be admitted to the two-hundred-year-old Academy—even **Marie Curie** had been unable to break the sex barrier.

Marguerite Catherine Perey was born in Villemomble, France, in 1909. As a child, she showed an interest in science and wanted to become a doctor. Her father's early death, however, left her family without the resources for such an education. Nonetheless, Perey was able to study physics and showed a talent for scientific endeavors. Because of her technical prowess, she was able to secure a position as a lab assistant (initially for a three-month stint) in Marie Curie's laboratory at the Radium Institute in Paris. Curie, for all her influence, made an unpretentious first impression, so much so that Perey, upon first meeting her at the Institute, thought she was the lab's secretary. This incident, combined with Curie's tendency to be aloof with strangers, might have portended a short career at the Curie lab for Perey. In fact, after the initial meeting, Perey thought she would only stay at the Radium Institute for her three months and leave. But Curie saw that Perey was both talented and dedicated, and she encouraged the younger woman, thus building a working relationship that extended beyond Perey's initial intentions.

Discovers Francium

Perey worked with Curie until the latter's death in 1934; thereafter she continued her mentor's research. Perey discovered the sequence of events that lead to the process known as the actinium radioactive decay series. This research inadvertently led to her most important discovery. She was aware of the existence of actinouranium, actinium-B, actinium-C, and actinium-D as part of the decay series she was trying to interpret. During this time, scientists were still trying to discover what they then believed to be the only three elements missing in the periodic table (which at the time contained 92 elements). One of these was Element 87. As Perey attempted to confirm her results of actinium radioactive decay, she found that other elements kept cropping up, disrupting the procedure. One of the elements was Element 87, with an atomic weight of 223. The element was highly charged—in fact, the most electropositive of all the elements. Because of this property, she considered naming it catium (from cation, which is a term for positively charged ions). But the word sounded too much like "cat" to her colleagues. As a result, she decided on francium, in honor of her homeland (and the place where the element had been discovered).

The following year, Perey took a position at France's National Center for Scientific Research. She remained there until 1949, when she became a professor of nuclear physics at the University of Strassbourg. She later became director of Strassbourg's Nuclear Research Center, holding that post for the rest of her life. By the time of her admission into the French Academy, Perey had already been diagnosed with the cancer that would slowly kill her. (She was undergoing treatment at the time of her appointment and was unable to attend the ceremonies.) She remained at the Nuclear Research Center and continued to conduct research. Eventually, the battle against the cancer grew more fierce, and, after a fifteen-year struggle, she succumbed in Louveciennes, France, on May 14, 1975.

FURTHER READING:

Books

Brock, William H., *The Norton History of Chemistry,* Norton, 1992.

Heiserman, David L., *Exploring Chemical Elements and Their Compounds,* TAB Books, 1992.

Reid, Robert, *Marie Curie,* Saturday Review Press/Dutton, 1974.

Vare, Ethlie Ann and Greg Ptacek, *Mothers of Invention,* Morrow, 1988.

Periodicals

Vare, Ethlie Ann and Greg Ptacek, *Times,* (London), May 15, 1975, p. 20.

Sketch by George A. Milite

Martin L. Perl
1927–
American physicist

Martin L. Perl is known for his discovery of the tau lepton, a massive particle related to the electron. For this discovery he was awarded the 1995 Nobel Prize in Physics, along with **Frederick Reines**, discoverer of the neutrino. The tau lepton is an unstable particle that decays into other particles in less than a trillionth of a second. It weighs 3,500 times more than the electron (which is also a lepton, although a stable one). It is one of the 12 subatomic particles from which all matter is formed, the others being the muon, the electron, the three neutrinos (electron neutrino, muon neutrino, and tau neutrino), and the six quarks (up, down, charm, strange, top, and bottom).

Martin Lewis Perl was born in New York City on June 24, 1927, the son of Oscar Perl, a printer and advertiser, and Fay Rosenthal, a secretary and later a bookkeeper for a firm of wool merchants. Both parents came to the United States from Russia at the beginning of the century to escape poverty and anti-Semitism. America was in the midst of the Great Depression when the Perls were raising their family, but chiefly because of the family printing business, they were able to live in the better neighborhoods of Brooklyn, and the children, Martin and his sister Lila, attended better schools. Lila later became a professional writer in the United States.

Studies Chemical Engineering

Although Perl won a physics medal when he graduated from high school in 1943, he never considered a career in science. The Perls thought a career in engineering would be more profitable than a career in pure science. This was still an unusual career choice for a Jewish boy at the time because there were feelings of anti-Semitism in the engineering field, but it was an area that combined Perl's interest in mechanics, mathematics, and science. He enrolled at the Polytechnic Institute of Brooklyn. He has attributed his early interest in chemical engineering to the exciting nature of the chemical field at the time. Chemistry had captured the public imagination by introducing such popular synthetic materials as nylon.

A future in physics was still unrealized by Perl during college. A general course in physics that he took dealt only with classical mechanical physics, making the science seem dull in comparison to chemistry. Perl continued in his study of engineering and chemistry.

Perl wanted to put his education on hold and enter the United States Army at the beginning of World War II, but as a result of his accelerated graduation from high school he wasn't yet 18, and his parents refused permission for him to enlist. He was, however, allowed to enter the Kings Point

Martin L. Perl

Merchant Marine Academy as an engineering cadet. He served six months at sea as part of the training. The war ended in 1945, but the draft was still in effect, and Perl was drafted into the army. He spent a year in Washington, D.C., before returning to college and receiving a bachelor's degree in chemical engineering, *summa cum laude*, in 1948. That same year he married Teri Hoch.

Discovers Interest in Physics

After college, Perl worked for the General Electric Company in Schenectady, New York, as a chemical engineer in the electron tube division. He was involved in trouble-shooting and designing production improvements for television picture tubes. It was necessary for him to learn something about the workings of electron vacuum tubes, so he took courses at Union College in Schenectady. One day a professor he had come to know, Vladimir Rojansky, told him, "Martin, what you are interested in is called physics not chemistry!"

Perl entered the physics doctoral program at Columbia University in 1950. His background in physics amounted to only one year of elementary physics and a half year in atomic physics, nowhere near the educational preparation of his fellow students. He has said that he was "arrogant" about his ability to learn anything fast, and that by the time he realized the difficulty of the curriculum, it was too late to back out because he had a wife and child and needed the degree.

Upon graduation in 1955, Perl received job offers from the physics departments at the University of Illinois, Yale University, and the University of Michigan. He said he chose Michigan, despite the better reputations of the other two departments, because he wanted the greater freedom and opportunity for recognition that came with working in a smaller, less-established research group.

Discovers the Tau Lepton

Perl's earliest research was conducted prior to the early 1960s, while he was with the University of Michigan. While affiliated with the University he performed experiments at the Brookhaven Cosmotron in New York state, and the Berkeley Bevatron in California. These experiments were in strong interaction physics, but by 1962 his interests were moving toward lepton physics, a field he considered "simpler." In "The Discovery of the Tau Lepton," Perl states that he had always liked simple theory "and it was clear that strong interaction theory was not becoming simpler . . . [T]he physics of leptons seemed a simpler world."

Perl accepted a position at the Stanford Linear Accelerator Center (SLAC), at Stanford University in California, in 1963. The facility was the site of the SPEAR Positron-Electron storage ring which Perl would use in his positron-electron colliding beam search for heavy leptons. A 1971 proposal for an experiment, the first to involve a search for a heavy lepton, devoted just three pages to the tau lepton search, because "to most others it seemed a remote dream."

Despite the tau lepton's lifespan of less than a trillionth of a second, Perl and his colleagues were able to prove its existence by showing that events in the experiment could not be explained away by the decay or production of any other known particles. The discovery paved the way for other physicists to find the bottom and top quarks, thereby completing the standard model of fundamental particles that explains all of the forces and interactions in matter and energy. The discovery was a total surprise to the physics community in 1975. Stanley Wojcicki, a colleague at SLAC, has called it "the best kind of discovery," and says that Perl "caught people completely out of the blue. No one anticipated it." Perl's hope is that his 1995 Nobel Prize for discovering the tau will help convince people that his current efforts to discover free quarks are "not a waste of time." Perl is still at Stanford.

SELECTED WRITINGS BY PERL:

Books

High Energy Hadron Physics. Wiley, 1974.
The Search for New Elementary Particles. World Scientific Publishing Co., 1992.
The Tau-Charm Factory. Editions Frontiéres, 1994.

Sketch by Paul Lewon

Jean Baptiste Perrin
1870–1942
French physicist

Jean Baptiste Perrin

The contribution made by French physicist Jean Baptiste Perrin to the study of atomic physics was of the most fundamental kind: he helped to prove that atoms and molecules exist. This achievement, which quantitatively extended the original observations of botanist Robert Brown on the movement of pollen grains in water, and put scientific substance into **Albert Einstein**'s exquisite mathematical equations describing the distribution of those particles in solution, won for Perrin the 1926 Nobel Prize in chemistry.

Perrin was born in Lille, France, on September 30, 1870, and raised, along with two sisters, by his widowed mother. His father, an army officer, died of wounds he received during the Franco-Prussian War. The young Perrin attended local schools and graduated from the Lycée Janson-de-Sailly in Paris. After serving a year of compulsory military service, he entered the Ecole Normale Supérieure in 1891, where his interest in physics flowered and he made his first major discovery.

Between 1894 and 1897 Perrin was an assistant in physics at the Ecole Normale, during which time he studied cathode rays and x rays, the basis of his doctoral dissertation. At this time, scientists disagreed over the nature of cathode rays emitted by the negative electrode (cathode) in a vacuum tube during an electric discharge. Physicists disagreed among themselves over whether cathode rays were particles—a logical assumption, since they carried a charge—or whether they took the form of waves.

Confirms Nature of Cathode Rays

In 1895 Perrin settled the debate simply and decisively using a cathode-ray discharge tube attached to a larger, empty vessel. When the discharge tube generated cathode rays, the rays passed through a narrow opening into the vessel, and produced fluorescence on the opposite wall. Nearby, an electrometer, which measures voltage, detected a small negative charge. But when Perrin deflected the cathode rays with a magnetic field so they fell on the nearby electrometer, the electrometer recorded a much larger negative charge. This demonstration was enough to prove conclusively that cathode rays carried negative charges and were particles, rather than waves. This work laid the basis of later work by physicist **J. J. Thomson**, who used Perrin's apparatus to characterize the negatively charged particles, called electrons, which were later theorized to be parts of atoms.

In 1897 Perrin married Henriette Duportal, with whom he had a son and a daughter. He received his doctorate the same year, and began teaching a new course in physical chemistry at the University of Paris (the Sorbonne). He was given a chair in physical chemistry in 1910 and remained at the school until 1940. During his early years at the University of Paris, Perrin continued his study of the atomic theory, which held that elements are made up of particles called atoms, and that chemical compounds are made up of molecules, larger particles consisting of two or more atoms. Although the atomic theory was widely accepted by scientists by the end of the nineteenth century, some physicists insisted that atoms and molecules did not actually exist as physical entities, but rather represented mathematical concepts useful for calculating the results of chemical reactions. To them, matter was continuous, not made up of discrete particles. Thus, at the dawn of the twentieth century, proving that matter was discontinuous (atomic in nature) was one of the great challenges left in physics. Perrin stood on the side of the "atomists," who believed that these tiny entities existed. In 1901 he even ventured (with no proof) that atoms resembled miniature solar systems. His interest in atomic theory led him to study a variety of related topics, such as osmosis, ion transport, and crystallization. However, it was colloids that led him to study Brownian motion, the basis of his Nobel Prize-winning discovery of the atomic nature of matter.

Verifies Einstein's Calculations of Brownian Motion

In 1827 the English botanist Robert Brown reported that pollen grains suspended in water were in violent and irregular motion, a phenomenon at first ascribed to differences in temperature within the fluid. Before the end of the century, however, scientists generally accepted the notion that the motion might be caused by bombardment of the pollen grains by molecules of the liquid—an apparent triumph for atomic theory. Yet some scientists remained skeptical.

In 1905 Albert Einstein calculated the mathematical basis of Brownian motion, basing his work on the assumption that the motion was due to the action of water molecules bombarding the grains. But Einstein's work, though elegant, lacked laboratory experiments needed to demonstrate the reality of his conclusions. It fell to Perrin to bolster Einstein's calculations with observations. From 1908 to 1913, Perrin, at first unaware of Einstein's published paper on the subject, devoted himself to the extremely tedious but necessary experiments—experiments now considered classics of their kind. He hypothesized that if Brownian movement did result from molecular collisions, the average movements of particles in suspension were related to their size, density, and the conditions of the fluid (e.g., pressure and density), in accordance with the gas laws. Perrin began by assuming that both pollen grains and the molecules of the liquid in which they were suspended behave like gas molecules, despite the much greater size of the grains.

According to Einstein's equations governing Brownian motion, the way the particles maintained their position in suspension against the force of gravity depended partly on the size of the water molecules. In 1908 Perrin began his painstaking observations of suspensions to determine the approximate size of the water molecules by observing suspensions of particles. He spent several months isolating nearly uniform, 0.1-gram pieces of gamboge—tiny, dense extracts of gum resin, which he suspended in liquid. According to Einstein's molecular theory, not all particles will sink to the bottom of a suspension. The upward momentum that some particles achieve by being bombarded by molecules of the fluid will oppose the downward force of gravity. At equilibrium, the point at which the reactions balance each other out, the concentrations of particles at different heights will remain unchanged.

Perrin devised an ingenious system to make thousands of observations of just such a system. He counted gamboge particles at various depths in a single drop of liquid only one twelve-hundredth of a millimeter deep. The particle concentration decreased exponentially with height in such close agreement with the mathematical predictions of Einstein's theory that his observations helped to prove that molecules existed.

In essence, his system behaved like the Earth's atmosphere, which becomes increasingly rarified with height, until, at the top of a very tall mountain, people may find it difficult to breathe. Furthermore, it was already known that a change in altitude of five kilometers is required to halve the concentration of oxygen molecules in the atmosphere, and that the oxygen atom has a mass of sixteen. Based on his knowledge of the gas laws, Perrin

realized that if, in his tiny system, the height required to halve the concentration of particles was a billion times less than the height it took to halve the concentration of oxygen in the atmosphere, he could, by simple proportion, calculate the mass of a gamboge particle relative to the oxygen molecule.

Einstein had linked to Brownian motion the concept of Avogadro's number, the number of molecules in any gas at normal temperature and pressure, now known to be 6.023×10^{23}. According to Avogadro's hypothesis, equal volumes of all gases at the same temperature and pressure contain equal numbers of molecules. Furthermore, the total mass of a specific volume of gas is equal to the mass of all the individual molecules multiplied by the total number of these individual molecules. So a gram-molecule of all gases at the same temperature and pressure should contain the same number of molecules. (A gram-molecule, or mole, is a quantity whose mass in grams equals the molecular weight of the substance; for example, one gram-molecule of oxygen equals sixteen grams of oxygen.) Only if this were true would the concept that each individual molecule contributes a minute bit of pressure to the overall pressure hold true, and individual entities called molecules could be said to exist.

Perrin calculated the gram-molecular weight of the 0.1-gram particles in the equilibrium system and therefore knew the number of grams in a gram-molecule of the particles. Then he divided the gram-molecular weight by the mass in grams of a single particle. The result, 6.8×10^{23}, was extremely close to Avogadro's number. Thus, Perrin had demonstrated that uniform particles in suspension behave like gas molecules, and calculations based on their mass can even be used to calculate Avogadro's number. This demonstrated that Brownian motion is indeed due to bombardment of particles by molecules, and came as close as was possible at the time to detecting atoms without actually seeing them. "In brief," Perrin said during his Nobel Prize acceptance speech, "if molecules and atoms do exist, their relative weights are known to us, and their absolute weights would be known as soon as Avogadro's number is known."

Perrin's work ranged farther afield than equilibrium distribution of particles and Avogadro's number, however. As an officer in the engineering corps of the French army during World War I, he contributed his expertise to the development of acoustic detection of submarines. His commitment to science, however, did not inhibit his social graces. He was a popular figure who took a genuine interest in young people, and held weekly parties for discussion groups in his laboratory. Following the war, Perrin's reputation continued to grow. In 1925, he became one of the first scientists to use an electric generator capable of producing a continuous current of 500,000 volts. At the time, he predicted that someday much larger machines of this type would let physicists bombard atoms, and thus make important discoveries about the structure of these particles.

In 1929 after being appointed director of the newly founded Rothschild Institute for Research in Biophysics, he was invited to the United States as a distinguished guest at the opening of Princeton University's new chemical laboratory. In 1936 Perrin replaced Nobel laureate Irene Joliot-Curie as French undersecretary of state for scientific research in the government of Premier Léon Blum. The following year, as president of the French Academy of Science, he assumed the chair of the scientific section of an exhibit in the Grand Palais at the 1937 Paris exposition. The project enabled him to help the average person, including children, to appreciate the wonders of science, from astronomy to zoology.

His flourishing reputation was further enhanced in 1938 when he informed the French Academy of Science, of which he had been a member since 1923, and was then president, that his collaborators had discovered the ninety-third chemical element, neptunium, a substance heavier than uranium. Four years earlier, **Enrico Fermi** (who was awarded the 1938 Nobel Prize in physics and directed the first controlled nuclear chain reaction) had artificially created Neptunium, a so-called transuranium element, by bombarding uranium (element 92) with neutrons. Perrin's announcement that Neptunium existed in nature excited speculation among physicists that there also might exist even more undiscovered elements, which turned out to be the case.

Condemns Totalitarianism and Warns of Impending War

His blossoming career did not shield the French physicist from concerns over what he considered to be a steady encroachment by totalitarian governments around the world on the freedom of science to express itself. A socialist and outspoken opponent of fascism, Perrin expressed his concerns during a speech delivered at the Royal Opera House in London before the International Peace Conference, reported in the *New York Times.* He asserted that world science stands or falls with democracy, and decried the fact that scientists seemed unable to understand "how financiers and capitalists as a whole cannot see that it is to their interest not to support those powers which, if they are successful, will ruin them." Perrin also criticized what he called "an irrational world that made it difficult to extend higher education or grant more aid to science but relatively easy to raise money for costly armaments." He voiced concern over what he believed was the coming war—World War II—which he feared would cost millions of lives, as well as threaten "the democracy that is the spirit of science." Perrin also warned that the victory of totalitarianism would mean "perhaps a thousand years of ruthless subjugation and standardization of thought, which will destroy the freedom of scientific research and theorizing."

Perrin's fears were realized in September of 1939, when France joined Great Britain in entering World War II against Germany following that country's invasion of Poland. By the end of September, the French government

appointed Perrin president of a committee for scientific research to help the war effort. The situation became particularly grim in the summer of 1940, when German troops swept into Paris. Perrin fled the city and took up residence in Lyon as a refugee. In December 1941 he moved to the United States, where he lived with his son, Francis Perrin, a visiting professor of physics and mathematics at Columbia University. While in the United States, Perrin sought American support for the French war effort and helped to establish the French University of New York.

Perrin spoke out against the German occupation and French collaboration with the enemy. He was particularly disturbed when the Germans began operating an armaments industry in the suburbs of Paris using forced labor. Following Allied aerial bombardment of the factories, the *New York Times* reported that Perrin defended the action as "one of the sad necessities" of the war. Speaking before five hundred guests at the first dinner of the French American Club in New York City, in March 1942, Perrin asked, "Who does not understand that it was imperative to put an end to this?" A few weeks later, Perrin took ill, and ten days later he died at the age of seventy-one at Mount Sinai Hospital in New York.

Three years after the defeat of Germany and the end of the war, diplomats and scientists in New York paid homage to Jean Perrin at ceremonies held at the Universal Funeral Chapel. Afterwards, Perrin's ashes were placed aboard the training cruiser Jean d'Arc at Montreal, on which they were transported to France for burial at the Pantheon, a magnificent former eighteenth-century church converted to civic use. Among his many honors in addition to the Nobel Prize, Perrin received the Joule Prize of the Royal Society of London in 1896 and the La Caze Prize of the French Academy of Sciences in 1914. In addition, he held honorary degrees from the universities of Brussels, Liège, Ghent, Calcutta, and Manchester and from New York, Princeton, and Oxford universities. Perrin was also a member of the Royal Society of London and scientific academies in Italy, Czechoslovakia, Belgium, Sweden, Romania, and China.

SELECTED WRITINGS BY PERRIN:

Books

Brownian Movement and Molecular Reality, translated from the Annales de chimie et de physique, 8th series, September, 1909, by F. Soddy, Taylor and Francis, 1910.
Les éléments de la physique, A. Michel, 1929.
Oeuvres scientifiques, Centre National de la Recherche Scientifique, 1950.

FURTHER READING:

Periodicals

New York Times, March 27, 1938, p. 7; August 3, 1938, p. 21; March 10, 1942, p. 7; April 18, 1942, p. 15.

Sketch by Marc Kusinitz

Candace B. Pert
1946–
American neuroscientist and biochemist

Candace B. Pert is a leading researcher in the field of chemical receptors, places in the body where molecules of a drug or natural chemical fit like a key into a lock, thus stimulating or inhibiting various physiological or emotional effects. As a graduate student, Pert codiscovered the brain's opiate receptors, areas that fit painkilling substances such as morphine. Her work led to the discovery of endorphins, the naturally occurring substances manufactured in the brain that relieve pain and produce sensations of pleasure.

Candace Dorinda Bebe Pert was born in New York City on June 26, 1946, to Mildred and Robert Pert. She went to General Douglas MacArthur High School in Levittown, New York. She attended Hofstra University but dropped out in 1966. That year she married Agu Pert and the couple moved to Philadelphia so that her husband could get a doctorate at Bryn Mawr College. In 1966, Candace Pert gave birth to the first of the couple's three children.

In 1967, to help support the family, Pert took a job as a cocktail waitress. On one occasion she chatted with a customer who turned out be an assistant dean at Bryn Mawr. The dean encouraged Pert to finish her B.A. at Bryn Mawr, and helped her through the admissions process. In 1970, Pert got her B.A. in biology and that year entered the doctoral pharmacology program at Johns Hopkins University in Baltimore.

Her first research assignment, working under Dr. Solomon Snyder, was to explore the mechanisms that regulate the production of acetylcholine, the body's most important neurotransmitter. Neurotransmitters are chemicals that stimulate or inhibit other neurons throughout the body, which in turn regulate the heart and other organs. Then in the summer of 1972, again working with Dr. Snyder, she embarked on her next project, the search for an opiate receptor. Opiate receptors were believed to exist, but finding them was another matter. Although techniques for locating receptors of hormones had been put into practice, many scientists thought it would be difficult, if not impossible, to transfer the technique to an opiate receptor.

Makes Surprising Discovery of Opiate Receptors

Receptors evolve from a chain of amino-acid molecules; these molecules are shaped by electrical forces into a three-dimensional shape with an electrically active indentation which recognizes correspondingly shaped molecules. These indentations are the points at which a receptor binds with a chemical substance or neurotransmitter. Using technology borrowed from identifying insulin receptors, Pert used radioactive drugs to identify receptor molecules that bonded with morphine and other opiate drugs in animal brain cells. The first report on her finding was published in *Science* in March 1973. Pert went on to investigate whether opiate receptors developed before birth. She used pregnant rats to evaluate the brains of the fetuses and found that during fetal development opiate receptors were present.

Pert and her colleagues mulled over why opiate receptors existed. It was certainly not that animals had evolved opiate receptors to interact with poppy plants, the natural source of opium. The scientist speculated that there might be an unknown neurotransmitter, naturally produced in the body, that fulfilled a similar function. Other experiments had already shown that stimulating the brainstem of rats caused pain relief, and that the best pain relief was obtained when a specific part of the brain was stimulated. After initial investigations proved inconclusive Pert turned to other areas of research. Eventually two Scottish scientists, John Hughes and Hans Kosterlitz, found the transmitters, which they called endorphins.

The discovery of endorphins led to the discovery of other types of receptors and corresponding chemicals in the brain. Uncovering the intricate system of chemicals changed the scientific conception of the brain as an organ that signals the rest of the body using just a few chemicals. Now it is understood that the nervous system uses many substances to signal pain, pleasure and emotions as well as sensory data. Many had mistakenly hoped that the discoveries would immediately result in a cure for drug addictions or a non-addicting pain killer for cancer patients, especially since the media had sensationalized these possibilities. Although these hopes proved overoptimistic, in 1978 Snyder, Hughes and Kosterlitz received the prestigious Lasker Award for their discoveries; Pert did not. The fact that the biochemist, who had received her Ph.D. in 1974, had not been recognized for her part in the discovery caused a controversy that even erupted on the editorial pages of the prominent journal *Science*.

Pert refused to become involved in any controversy, however, and continued on at Hopkins as a National Institutes of Health fellow from 1974 to 1975, as a staff fellow from 1975 to 1977, a senior staff fellow from 1977 to 1978, and then as research pharmacologist from 1978 to 1982. In 1982, she became chief of the section on brain chemistry at the National Institutes of Mental Health (NIMH). There, the neuroscientist turned her attention to Valium receptors in the brain and the receptors where the street drug PCP, or "angel dust," takes hold. In 1986, Pert led the NIMH team that discovered peptide T. Peptides are substances that are synthesized from amino acids and are intermediate in molecular weight and chemical properties between amino acids and proteins, and have been linked to the manifestation of emotions.

Pert left NIMH in 1987 and worked for laboratories in the private sector. She also started her own company, Peptide Design, to encourage research on peptides. The company was in existence from 1987 to 1990. Since then, Pert has become an adjunct professor in the department of physiology at Georgetown University. Among her other areas of research have been investigations into the immune system and the nature of the human immunodeficiency virus (HIV) that causes AIDS. Pert won the Arthur S. Fleming Award in 1979. She is a member of the American Society of Pharmacologists and Experimental Therapeutics; the American Society of Biological Chemists; the Society of Neuroscientists; and the International Narcotics Research Conference.

Since her first discovery of an opiate receptor, Pert has located endorphin receptors throughout the body, even in the pituitary gland. She suspects that the location of receptors in sites where there is no clear connection with conscious pain serves the function of signalling the central nervous system when there is a problem with an organ. She believes, as she told an *Omni* interviewer, that scientists will eventually be able to chart the various receptors of the brain and the reactions they produce. "There's no doubt in my mind that one day—and I don't think that day is all that far away—we'll be able to make a color-coded map of the brain. A color-coded wiring diagram, with blue for one neurochemical, red for another, and so on—that's the neuroscientist's ambition."

SELECTED WRITINGS BY PERT:

Periodicals

Science, The Opiate Receptor: Demonstration in Nervous Tissue, March 2, 1973.
Academy of Science USA, Octapeptides Deduced From the Neuropeptide Receptor-like Pattern of Antigen T4 in Brain Potently Inhibit Human Immuno-deficiency Virus Receptor Binding and T-Cell Infectivity, Volume 83, 1986, pp. 9254–9258.

FURTHER READING:

Books

Snyder, Solomon, *Brainstorming: The Science and Politics of Opiate Research,* Harvard University Press, 1989.
Weintraub, Pamela, editor, *The Omni Interviews,* Omni Press, 1984, pp. 118–131.

Periodicals

Weintraub, Pamela, editor, *Fortune,* The Body Telling the Mind, Sept. 8, 1980, p. 97.

Sketch by Margo Nash

Max Perutz
1914–
English crystallographer and biochemist

Max Perutz pioneered the use of x-ray crystallography to determine the atomic structure of proteins by combining two lines of scientific investigation—the physiology of hemoglobin and the physics of x-ray crystallography. His efforts resulted in his sharing the 1962 Nobel Prize in chemistry with his colleague, biochemist **John Kendrew**. Perutz's work in deciphering the diffraction patterns of protein crystals opened the door for molecular biologists to study the structure and function of enzymes—specific proteins that are the catalysts for biochemical reactions in cells. Known for his impeccable laboratory skills, Perutz produced the best early pictures of protein crystals and used this ability to determine the structure of hemoglobin and the molecular mechanism by which it transports oxygen from the lungs to tissue. A passionate mountaineer and skier, Perutz also applied his expertise in x-ray crystallography to the study of glacier structure and flow.

Perutz was born in Vienna, Austria, on May 19, 1914. His parents were Hugo Perutz, a textile manufacturer, and Adele Goldschmidt Perutz. In 1932, Perutz entered the University of Vienna, where he studied organic chemistry. However, he found the university's adherence to classical organic chemistry outdated and backward. By 1926 scientists had determined that enzymes were proteins and had begun to focus on the catalytic effects of enzymes on the chemistry of cells, but Perutz's professors paid scant attention to this new realm of research. In 1934, while searching for a subject for his dissertation, Perutz attended a lecture on organic compounds, including vitamins, under investigation at Cambridge University in England. Anxious to continue his studies in an environment more attuned to recent advances in biochemical research, Perutz decided he wanted to study at Cambridge. His wish to leave Austria and study elsewhere was relatively unique in that day and age, when graduate students seldom had the financial means to study abroad. But Hugo Perutz's textile business provided his son with the initial funds he would need to survive in England on a meager student stipend.

In 1936, Perutz landed a position as research student in the Cambridge laboratory of Desmond Bernal, who was pioneering the use of x-ray crystallography in the field of biology. Perutz, however, was disappointed again when he was assigned to research minerals while Bernal closely guarded his crystallography work, discussing it only with a few colleagues and never with students. Despite Perutz's disenchantment with his research assignments and the old, ill-lit, and dingy laboratories he worked in, he received excellent training in the promising field of x-ray crystallography, albeit in the classical mode of mineral crystallography. "Within a few weeks of arriving," Perutz states in

Max Perutz

Horace Freeland Judson's *Eighth Day of Creation: Makers of the Revolution in Biology,* "I realized that Cambridge was where I wanted to spend the rest of my life."

Begins Work with Hemoglobin

During his summer vacation in Vienna in 1937, Perutz met with Felix Haurowitz, a protein specialist married to Perutz's cousin, to seek advice on the future direction of his studies. Haurowitz, who had been studying hemoglobin since the 1920s, convinced Perutz that this was an important protein whose structure needed to be solved because of the integral role it played in physiology. In addition to making blood red, hemoglobin red corpuscles greatly increase the amount of oxygen that blood can transport through the body. Hemoglobin also transports carbon dioxide back to the lungs for disposal.

Although new to the physical chemistry and crystallography of hemoglobin, Perutz returned to Cambridge and soon obtained crystals of horse hemoglobin from Gilbert Adair, a leading authority on hemoglobin. Since the main goal of x-ray crystallography at that time was to determine the structure of any protein, regardless of its relative importance in biological activity, Perutz also began to study crystals of the digestive enzyme chymotrypsin. But chymotrypsin crystals proved to be unsuitable for study by x ray, and Perutz turned his full attention to hemoglobin, which has large crystal structures uniquely suited to x-ray crystallography. At that time, microscopic protein crystal structures were "grown" primarily through placing the proteins in a solution which was then evaporated or cooled below the saturation point. The crystal structures, in effect, are repetitive groups of cells that fit together to fill each space, with the cells representing characteristic groups of the molecules and atoms of the compound crystallized.

In the early 1930s, crystallography had been successfully used only in determining the structures of simple crystals of metals, minerals, and salts. However, proteins such as hemoglobin are thousands of times more complex in atomic structure. Physicists **William Bragg** and **Lawrence Bragg**, the only father and son to share a Nobel Prize, were pioneers of x-ray crystallography. Focusing on minerals, the Braggs found that as x rays pass through crystals, they are buffeted by atoms and emerge as groups of weaker beams which, when photographed, produce a discernible pattern of spots. The Braggs discovered that these spots were a manifestation of Fourier synthesis, a method developed in the nineteenth century by French physicist Jean Baptiste Fourier to represent regular signals as a series of sine waves. These waves reflect the distribution of atoms in the crystal.

The Braggs successfully determined the amplitude of the waves but were unable to determine their phases, which would provide more detailed information about crystal structure. Although amplitude was sufficient to guide scientists through a series of trial and error experiments for studying simple crystals, proteins were much too complex to be studied with such a haphazard and time-consuming approach.

Initial attempts at applying x-ray crystallography to the study of proteins failed, and scientists soon began to wonder whether proteins in fact produce x-ray diffraction patterns. However, in 1934, Desmond Bernal and chemist **Dorothy Crowfoot Hodgkin** at the Cavendish laboratory in Cambridge discovered that by keeping protein crystals wet, specifically with the liquid from which they precipitated, they could be made to give sharply defined x-ray diffraction patterns. Still, it would take twenty-three years before scientists could construct the first model of a protein molecule.

Research Interrupted by War and Internment

Perutz and his family, like many other Europeans in the 1930s, tended to underestimate the seriousness of the growing Nazi regime in Germany. While Perutz himself was safe in England as Germany began to invade its neighboring countries, his parents fled from Vienna to Prague in 1938. That same summer, they again fled to Switzerland from Czechoslovakia, which would soon face the onslaught of the approaching German army. Perutz was shaken by his new classification as a refugee and the clear indication by some people that he might not be welcome in England any longer. He also realized that his father's financial support would certainly dwindle and die out.

As a result, in order to vacation in Switzerland in the summer of 1938, Perutz sought a travel grant to apply his expertise in crystallography to the study of glacier structures and flow. His research on glaciers involved crystallographic studies of snow transforming into ice, and he eventually became the first to measure the velocity distributions of a glacier, proving that glaciers flow faster at the surface and slower at the glacier's bed.

Finally, in 1940, the same year Perutz received his Ph.D., his work was put to an abrupt halt by the German invasions of Holland and Belgium. Growing increasingly wary of foreigners, the British government arrested all "enemy" aliens, including Perutz. "It was a very nice, very sunny day—a nasty day to be arrested," Perutz recalls in *The Eighth Day of Creation.* Transported from camp to camp, Perutz ended up near Quebec, Canada, where many other scientists and intellectuals were imprisoned, including physicists Herman Bondi and Tom Gold. Always active, Perutz began a camp university, employing the resident academicians to teach courses in their specialties. It didn't take the British government long, however, to realize that they were wasting valuable intellectual resources and, by 1941, Perutz followed many of his colleagues back to his home in England and resumed his work with crystals.

Perutz, however, wanted to contribute to the war effort. After repeated requests, he was assigned to work on the mysterious and improbable task of developing an aircraft carrier made of ice. The goal of this project was to tow the carrier to the middle of the Atlantic Ocean, where it would serve as a stopping post for aircrafts flying from the United States to Great Britain. Although supported both by then British Prime Minister Winston Churchill and the chief of the British Royal Navy, Lord Louis Mountbatten, the ill-fated project was terminated upon the discovery that the amount of steel needed to construct and support the ice carrier would cost more than constructing it entirely of steel.

Embarks on Nobel Prize-Winning Research

Perutz married Gisela Clara Peiser on March 28, 1942; the couple later had a son, Robin, and a daughter, Vivian. After the war, in 1945, Perutz was finally able to devote himself entirely to pondering the smeared spots that appeared on the x-ray film of hemoglobin crystals. He returned to Cambridge, and was soon joined by John Kendrew, then a doctoral student, who began to study myoglobin, an enzyme which stores oxygen in muscles. In 1946 Perutz and Kendrew founded the Medical Research Council Unit for Molecular Biology, and Perutz became its director. Many advances in molecular biology would take place there, including the discovery of the structure of deoxyribonucleic acid (DNA).

Over the next years, Perutz refined the x-ray crystallography technology and, in 1953, finally solved the difficult phase dilemma with a method known as isomorphous replacement. By adding atoms of mercury—which, like any heavy metal, is an excellent x-ray reflector—to each individual protein molecule, Perutz was able to change the light diffraction pattern. By comparing hemoglobin proteins with mercury attached at different places to hemoglobin without mercury, he found that he had reference

points to measure phases of other hemoglobin spots. Although this discovery still required long and assiduous mathematical calculations, the development of computers hastened the process tremendously.

By 1957, Kendrew had delineated the first protein structure through crystallography, again working with myoglobin. Perutz followed two years later with a model of hemoglobin. Continuing to work on the model, Perutz and Hilary Muirhead showed that hemoglobin's reaction with oxygen involves a structural change among four subunits of the hemoglobin molecule. Specifically, the four polypeptide chains that form a tetrahedral structure of hemoglobin are rearranged in oxygenated hemoglobin. In addition to its importance to later research on the molecular mechanisms of respiratory transport by hemoglobin, this discovery led scientists to begin research on the structural changes enzymes may undergo in their interactions with various biological processes. In 1962, Perutz and Kendrew were awarded the Nobel Prize in chemistry for their codiscoveries in x-ray crystallography and the structures of hemoglobin and myoglobin, respectively. The same year, Perutz left his post as director of the Unit for Molecular Biology and became chair of its laboratory.

The work of Perutz and Kendrew was the basis for growing understanding over the following decades of the mechanism of action of enzymes and other proteins. Specifically, Perutz's discovery of hemoglobin's structure led to a better understanding of hemoglobin's vital attribute of absorbing oxygen where it is plentiful and releasing it where it is scarce. Perutz also conducted research on hemoglobin from the blood of people with sickle-cell anemia and found that a change in the molecule's shape initiates the distortion of venous red cells into a sickle shape that reduces the cells' oxygen-carrying capacity.

In *The Eighth Day of Creation,* Judson remarks that Perutz was known to have a "glass thumb" for the difficult task of growing good crystals, and it was widely acknowledged that for many years Perutz produced the best images of crystal structures. In the book, published in 1979, Perutz's long-time colleague Kendrew remarks that little changed over the years, explaining, "If I had come into the lab thirty years ago, on a Saturday evening, Max would have been in a white coat mounting a crystal—just the same." Perutz retired in 1979.

SELECTED WRITINGS BY PERUTZ:

Books

Proteins and Nucleic Acids: Structure and Function, Elsevier Publishing Company, 1962.

FURTHER READING:

Books

Judson, Horace Freeland, *The Eighth Day of Creation: Makers of the Revolution in Biology,* Simon & Schuster, 1979.

Periodicals

Judson, Horace Freeland, *The Economist,* X-rays Mark the Spots, November 21, 1992, pp. 100–101.

Sketch by David Petechuk

Rózsa Péter
1905–1977
Hungarian mathematician

Rózsa Péter was one of the early investigators in the field of recursive functions, a branch of mathematical logic. Recursive functions are those mathematical functions whose values can be established at every point, for whole numbers one and above. These functions are used to study the structure of number classes or functions in terms of the complexity of the calculations required to determine them, and have useful applications to computers and other automatic systems. Péter wrote two books and numerous papers on recursive functions, which are related to **Alan Turing**'s theory of algorithms and machines and to **Kurt Gödel**'s undecidability theorem of self-referential equations. Péter also wrote a popular treatment of mathematics, *Playing with Infinity,* which was translated into fourteen languages. A teacher and teacher-training instructor before her appointment to a university post, Péter won national awards for her contributions to mathematics education and to mathematics.

Péter was born in Budapest on February 17, 1905. She received her high school diploma from Mária Terézia Girls' School in 1922, then entered the university in Budapest to study chemistry. Although her father, an attorney, wanted her to stay in that field, Péter changed to the study of mathematics. One of her classmates was László Kalmár, her future teacher and colleague. Péter graduated from the university in 1927, and for two years after graduation she had no permanent job, but tutored privately and took temporary teaching assignments.

In 1932, Péter attended the International Mathematics Conference in Zurich, where she presented a lecture on mathematical logic. She published papers on recursive functions in the period 1934 to 1936, and received her Ph.D. *summa cum laude* in 1935. In 1937, Péter became a contributing editor of the *Journal of Symbolic Logic.* Péter lost her teaching position in 1939 due to the Fascist laws of that year; Hungary was an ally of Nazi Germany and held similar purges of academics. Nevertheless, she published papers in Hungarian journals in 1940 and 1941.

In 1943, Péter published her book, *Playing with Infinity,* which described ideas in number theory, geometry, calculus and logic, including Gödel's undecidability theory, for the layman. The book, many copies of which were destroyed by bombing during World War II, could not be distributed until 1945. The war claimed the life of Péter's brother, Dr. Nicholas Politzer, in 1945, as well as the lives of her friend and fellow mathematician, Pál Csillag, and her young pupil, Káto Fuchs, who had assisted Péter with *Playing with Infinity.*

In the late 1940s, Péter taught high school and then became Head of the Mathematics Department of the Pedological College in Budapest. She also wrote textbooks for high school mathematics. In the fifties, Péter published further studies of recursive functions; her 1951 book, *Recursive Functions,* was the first treatment of the subject in book form and reinforced her status as "the leading contributor to the special theory of recursive functions," as S. C. Kleene observed in the *Bulletin of the American Mathematical Society.*

Péter was appointed Professor of Mathematics at Eötvös Loránd University in Budapest in 1955, where she taught mathematical logic and set theory. The official publication of *Playing with Infinity* occurred in 1957. In this book, she wrote in the preface, she tried "to present concepts with complete clarity and purity so that some new light may have been thrown on the subject even for mathematicians and certainly for teachers."

In the sixties and seventies, Péter studied the relationship between recursive functions and computer programming, in particular, the relationship of recursive functions to the programming languages Algol and Lisp. Péter retired in 1975. She continued her research, however, publishing *Recursive Functions in Computer Theory* in 1976.

Péter's awards included the Kossuth Prize in 1951 for her scientific and pedological work, and the State Award, Silver Degree in 1970 and Gold Degree in 1973. Péter was a member of the Hungarian Academy of Sciences and was made honorary President of the János Bolyai Mathematical Association in 1975. Interested in literature, film and art as well as mathematics, Péter translated poetry from German and corresponded with the literary critic Marcel Benedek. She noted in *Playing with Infinity* that her mathematical studies were not so different from the arts: "I love mathematics not only for its technical applications, but principally because it is beautiful; because man has breathed his spirit of play into it, and because it has given him his greatest game—the encompassing of the infinite." Péter died on February 17, 1977.

SELECTED WRITINGS BY PÉTER:

Books

Playing with Infinity: Mathematics for Everyman, translated by Z. P. Dienes, Simon & Schuster, 1962.
Recursive Functions, 3rd revised edition, translated by István Földes, Academic Press, 1967.

Recursive Functions in Computer Theory, translated by I. Juhász, Wiley, 1981.

FURTHER READING:

Books

Mathematics at a Glance, Algorithms and Recursive Functions, 2nd edition, Van Nostrand Reinhold, 1989, pp. 340–342.

Periodicals

Császár, Akos, *Matematikai Lapok,* Rózsa Péter: February 17, 1905-February 16, 1977, (Hungarian), Volume 25, 1974, pp. 257–258.

Dömölki, Bálint, et al, *Matematikai Lapok,* The Scientific Work of Rózsa Péter, (Hungarian), Volume 16, 1965, pp. 171–184.

Kleene, S.C., *Bulletin of the American Mathematical Society,* Rekursive Funktionen, March, 1952, pp. 270–272.

Nelson, D., *Mathematical Reviews,* Rózsa Péter, Rekursive Funktionen, 1952, pp. 421–422.

Nelson, D., *American Mathematical Monthly,* Playing with Infinity, Telegraphic Reviews Volume 84, February, 1977, p. 147.

Robinson, Raphael M., *Journal of Symbolic Logic,* Rózsa Péter. Rekursive Funktionen, Volume 16, 1951, pp. 280–282.

Ruzsa, Imre Z. and János Urbán, *Matematikai Lapok,* In Memoriam Rózsa Péter, (Hungarian), Volume 26, 1975, pp. 125–137.

Sudborough, I. Hal, *Mathematical Reviews,* Rózsa Péter, Rekursive Funktionen in der Komputer-Theorie, Volume 55, #6926.

Turán, Pál, *Matematikai Lapok,* To the Memory of Mathematician Victims of Fascism, (Hungarian), Volume 26, 1975, pp. 259–263.

Other

Turán, Pál, *Matematikai Lapok,* To the Memory of Mathematician Victims of Fascism, Kocsor, Klára, notes on articles in Hungarian, January, 1994.

Sketch by Sally M. Moite

Mary Locke Petermann
1908–1975
American biochemist

Mary Locke Petermann isolated and worked out the structure of animal ribosomes, organelles that are now known as the sites of protein synthesis in cells. She began her original investigation of the particles (for a time they were known as "Petermann's particles") because they were interfering with her studies of DNA and RNA. Her work was fundamental and pioneering; her continued work established the importance of ions in stabilizing ribosomes and elucidated ribosomal transformations.

Peterman was born in Laurium, Michigan, on February 25, 1908, one of three children and the only daughter of Albert Edward and Anna Mae Grierson Petermann. Her mother was a graduate of Ypsilanti State Teachers' College. Her father, a graduate of Cornell University, became a lawyer for Calumet and Hecla Consolidated Copper Company in Calumet, Michigan, after World War I; he later was president and general manager. The Petermann family lived in a large company house and enjoyed high status in the community.

After graduating from Calumet High School in 1924, Petermann spent a year at a Massachusetts preparatory school before entering Smith College. In 1929, she graduated from Smith with high honors in chemistry and membership in Phi Beta Kappa. After a year at Yale University as a technician, she spent four years working at the Boston Psychopathic Hospital, investigating the acid-base balance of mental patients. In 1936 she entered the University of Wisconsin; she received a Ph.D. degree in physiological chemistry in 1939, with a thesis project on the role of the adrenal cortex in ion regulation.

In 1939 Petermann became the first woman chemist on the staff of the Department of Physical Chemistry at the University of Wisconsin. She remained at Wisconsin as a postdoctoral researcher until 1945. During these six years she and Alwin M. Pappenheimer began to investigate the physical chemisty of proteins. Petermann discovered what were at first called "Petermann's particles" but were named ribosomes at a meeting of the Biophysical Society in 1958. (It was at this meeting that **George Palade**, a research scientist who had independently played a pivotal role in discovering ribosomes, called Petermann "the mother of the particles.") Ribosomes are where protein synthesis occurs in a cell. Petermann's research isolated several types of ribosomes and clarified their properties. She also pioneered the study of antibodies. This research later led to **Rodney Porter** winning a Nobel Prize in 1972 for his work on the structure of immunoglobulins.

After leaving the University of Wisconsin in 1945, Petermann accepted the position of research chemist at Memorial Hospital in New York City to explore the role of plasma proteins in cancer. (According to Mary L. Moller, Petermann had been recommended to the director, Cornelius Rhoads, as "the girl out in Wisconsin.") In 1946 she was appointed Finney-Howell Foundation fellow at the newly founded Sloan-Kettering Institute, where she explored the role of nucleoproteins in cancer. She became an associate member of the institute in 1960, the first woman member in 1963, and member emeritus in 1973 when she retired. Concurrent with her work at Sloan-Kettering, she also taught biochemistry in the Sloan-Kettering Division, Graduate School of Medical Sciences, Cornell University. In 1966, she became the first woman appointed a full professor at Cornell. She authored or co-authored almost 100 scientific papers.

As the Sloan Award recipient in 1963, Petermann was honored for what the accompanying citation explained was her "many basic and distinguished contributions to the knowledge of the relevance of proteins and nucleoproteins in abnormal growth. An even greater contribution has been her fundamental work on the nature of the cell ribosome." Petermann used her award money to work for a year in the Swedish laboratory of Nobel laureate **Arne Tiselius**. She also lectured in several European countries, including England and France. In 1966 she received the Garvan Medal of the American Chemical Society, which honors contributions made by women scientists, an honorary doctorate from Smith College, and the Distinguished Service Award from the American Academy of Achievement.

Petermann never married. In 1974, the year before her death, she organized the Memorial Sloan-Kettering Cancer Center Association for Professional Women and served as its first president. She died in Philadelphia on December 13, 1975, of intestinal cancer, which had been misdiagnosed as a "nervous stomach" earlier that year. In 1976 the Educational Foundation of the Association for Women in Science named one of its graduate scholarships in her honor.

SELECTED WRITINGS BY PETERMANN:

Books

The Physical and Chemical Properties of Ribosomes, Elsevier Publishing Company, 1964.

FURTHER READING:

Books

Moller, Mary L., *Women in Chemistry and Physics,* Mary Locke Petermann (1908–1975) Grinstein, Louise S., Rose K. Rose, and Miriam H. Rafailovich, editorsGreenwood Press, 1993, pp. 476–487.

O'Neill, Lois Decker, editor, *The Women's Book of World Records and Achievements,* Doubleday, 1979, p. 168.

Sketch by Jill Carpenter

Edith R. Peterson
1914–1992
American medical researcher

A medical researcher specializing in cell cultures, Edith R. Peterson was the first scientist to grow myelin, the outer covering of nerve cells, in a test tube. Her discovery aided research into multiple sclerosis, muscular dystrophy, and other diseases of the nervous system.

Peterson was born Edith Elizabeth Runne on June 24, 1914, in Brooklyn, New York, to Hermann and Else Helmke Runne. Peterson's father, co-owner of a restaurant and catering establishment, died suddenly in 1920, shortly before he was to take a trip to Germany to join his wife and two daughters, who were visiting relatives. After staying in Germany for the next six years, the family returned to the United States, where Peterson's mother obtained employment designing custom dresses. In 1937 Peterson received a B.S. degree from Barnard College; two years later she earned a master's degree in zoology from Columbia University. In September of 1941 she married Charles Peterson, a commercial artist. The couple had a son, Wesley, in 1952 and a daughter, Rhonda Lea, in 1954.

In the early 1940s Peterson went to work in the laboratory of Margaret Murray at Columbia University. While working there, she was able to grow functional nerve cells using cultures containing chicken embryos. She utilized organotype culture which, unlike other methods of growing cells, involves having cells simulate the actual structure and functions of the organs from which they have been taken. Peterson succeeded in growing the actual nerve cells, brain, and spinal cord of chickens. In doing so she was also able to grow myelin, the insulating sheath surrounding nerve cells—the first time this had been done. This discovery aided research on multiple sclerosis, a disease that involves the degeneration of the myelin in the brain and spinal cord.

In 1966 Peterson left Columbia to work with Dr. Murray Bornstein at the Albert Einstein College of Medicine of Yeshiva University in the Bronx, New York. There she concentrated her studies on muscular dystrophy, a wasting disease affecting skeletal muscles. In addition to her research, she taught her techniques for organotype culture to students from the United States, Asia, and Europe.

Peterson retired in 1990 following a stroke that hindered her ability to use her right hand. Shortly afterward, she and her husband moved to Middletown, New York. Peterson died of a stroke on August 15, 1992.

FURTHER READING:

Books

Edelson, Edward, *The Nervous System,* Chelsea House, 1991.

Rosner, Louis, and Shelley Ross, *Multiple Sclerosis,*
    Prentice-Hall, 1987.

Periodicals

Rosner, Louis, and Shelley Ross, *New York Times,*
    Edith Peterson, 78; Studied Cell Cultures (obituary)
    p. D14.

Other

Rosner, Louis, and Shelley Ross, *New York Times,*
    Edith Peterson, 78; Studied Cell Cultures Peterson,
    Wesley, personal communication with Francis Rog-
    ers, January 14, 1994.

Sketch by Francis Rogers

Hans Pettersson
1888–1966
Swedish oceanographer

Hans Pettersson was born in Marstrand, on an island off the Swedish coast, on August 26, 1888, the son of Otto and Agnes (Irgens) Pettersson. His father was a scientist who was well-known in Sweden for his studies of the swift tides that run in the Skagerrak, an arm of the North Sea between Norway and Denmark. These tides flowed vigorously just outside the door of Kälhuvudet, the Petters-son's house built on a large, cabbage-shaped rock. Although Hans was to become famous for commanding a trip around the world, he seldom left the Swedish coast for long. From the start of World War I almost up to the start of the Space Age, Pettersson made his main base at the University of Göteborg, a few miles down the Skagerrak from Kälhuvudet and at the top of the Kattegat, another North Sea arm.

Before finally settling at Göteborg, however, Petters-son had bounced between physics and oceanography for a few years. His studies at the Universities of Uppsala and Stockholm and at University College in London culminated in a Doctor of Science in physics from Stockholm in 1914. During this time, he became interested in problems con-nected with radioactivity, which became one of his ongoing interests. Even while he was a physics student, he began to work on oceanography, publishing papers on the tides and currents of the Kattegat. One of his main concerns at this time remains a compelling topic to modern oceanographers, how the currents of the North Atlantic affect the climate of Europe. Another area of study around this time was the amount of radioactivity in sea water and in undersea sediments. Until 1930 Pettersson varied his activities greatly, lecturing regularly on oceanography at Göteborg while also

leading a team at the Institute of Radium Treatment in Vienna. In 1930, however, he accepted a professorship at Göteborg, where he remained until 1956.

While Pettersson was at Göteborg in the 1930s, he worked hard on making oceanography a prime concern for other Swedes. He wrote books and articles, spoke on the radio, and made many personal contacts and appeals to wealthy businessmen in Sweden. Eventually he obtained the financial backing needed to start an oceanographic laborato-ry at Göteborg, the Oceanografiska Institutet, of which Pettersson became the first director. By the time the laboratory was in operation, in 1939, Europe was at war. During the war, Pettersson was able to continue his promotion of oceanography in neutral Sweden. Borja Kullenberg, working for Pettersson in Sweden during World War II, developed new designs for a corer to sample the sediments on the ocean floor, and Pettersson did not neglect his wealthy patrons. As soon as hostilities ended, the Brostrom Shipping Company provided the Oceanografiska Institutet with an ocean-going ship (on loan) to be used for a round-the-world scientific expedition. Other firms, organi-zations, and individuals supplied the money or equipment needed for the trip, which was to last more than a year.

Round-the-World Voyage Provides Invaluable Research on Ocean Floor

The ship, the *Albatross,* could operate as a sailing ship or as a steamship, an important option for a round-the-world voyage. After a trial run in the Mediterranean, the *Albatross* embarked on July 4, 1947, aiming at a 40,000 mile (64,000 km) voyage that would be primarily in the tropics. Along the way, the crew would sample the ocean floor in many ways, not only by obtaining as many sediment cores as they could, but also by studying the ocean floor for pollen, radioactive elements, volcanic ash, and any other materials that could be dredged from the bottom of the sea, including dust from meteorites. The workers on the *Albatross* even measured the clarity of the seawater in various oceans. Furthermore, many parts of the sea floor were mapped for the first time. The Swedish Deep-Sea Expedition in the *Albatross* was among the first scientific expeditions whose main intent was to study the ocean.

At about the same time as the Swedish Deep-Sea Expedition was getting under way, similar research projects were being started in the Atlantic Ocean by the Lamont Geological Observatory under **William Maurice Ewing**. Many of the discoveries of both institutions complemented each other. Both Borja Kullenberg at Göteborg University, who sailed on the *Albatross,* and Maurice Ewing in the United States had developed new devices that could bring back cores of ocean floor, some as long as 60 ft (18 m), although 20 ft (6 m) was the average for the *Albatross* expedition. In 1948 the Swedish Deep-Sea Expedition under Pettersson's leadership discovered a deep abyssal plain south of the Bay of Bengal in the Indian Ocean. This was just a year after a similar deep plain, both of them extremely flat (depth variations of less than 6 ft [1.8 m] in a mile), had been found by Ewing in the North Atlantic.

We have today become so used to the understanding of the oceans based on the theory of plate tectonics that it is surprising to realize how different the concept was in 1948, when Pettersson led the crew of the *Albatross* around the world. Pettersson himself had many ideas that seemed plausible at the time, but which subsequent research has shown to be invalid. He thought that volcanic activity accounted for the great plains, such as the one he discovered in the Indian Ocean, but we now think they are the result of sediment that has slid across the ocean floor and settled. Pettersson was interested in meteorites, and so he thought that the iron nodules and nickel-rich sediments he dredged up showed large bombardments of Earth by meteoroids. Today, these are explained by chemical precipitation from sea water. He tried to use radium to date the sediments on the ocean floor, which was not unlike modern methods of dating, but more difficult because of the small amount of radium present.

After the plate tectonics revolution of the 1950s and 1960s, the findings of the *Albatross* expedition were reinterpreted and provided useful data on many aspects of the sea and the sea floor.

SELECTED WRITINGS BY PETTERSSON:

Books

Westward Ho with the Albatross. New York: Dutton, 1953. (Swedish edition *Med Albatross over havsdjupen,* published in 1950.)
The Ocean Floor. New Haven: Yale University Press, 1954.

FURTHER READING:

Books

Ericson, David B. and Goesta Wollin. *The Ever-Changing Sea.* New York: Alfred A. Knopf, 1967.

Sketch by Bryan Bunch

Michael E. Phelps
1939–

American biophysicist

The biophysicist Michael E. Phelps was born in Cleveland, Ohio, in 1939. After earning his B.S. degree in chemistry and mathematics from Western Washington State University in 1965, he went on to complete graduate studies at Washington University in St. Louis, earning a Ph.D. in chemistry in 1970.

Phelps is best known for his invention of Positron Emission Tomography (PET), an imaging technique that lets doctors view biological processes in the organ systems of live patients. (Positrons are subatomic particles whose mass and spin are the same as those of an electron, but whose electric charge is positive.) Phelps has actually developed four generations of PET scanners, including the prototypes for all of the commercial PET scanning systems that exist today.

First introduced in 1973, PET has been used in medical applications ranging from studies of the brain and heart, to gene expression in the context of molecular medicine. PET images of glucose metabolism have helped scientist study the metabolic function of the brain and heart muscle, and the altered metabolic states that accompany diseases such as Alzheimer's disease and cancer. (PET has been used to make early diagnoses and monitor therapeutic responses in lung, colorectal, breast, ovarian, lymphoma, melanoma, and prostate cancers.) Images of neurotransmitters obtained by PET provide information about abnormal communication between neuronal systems in the brain that occur in diseases such as Parkinson's disease and in drug abuse.

In the course of developing PET, Phelps brought insights from nuclear physics, chemistry, and mathematics to the field of biomedical imaging. Noting that positron decay provided the opportunity for using opposing detectors, he was able to come up with a detection system that permitted unparalleled spatial resolution. Based on a design using a circumferential array of detectors, he developed the electronics and mathematical algorithm that produced three-dimensional tomographic images of the living human body. He also recognized that positron-emitting forms of oxygen, nitrogen, carbon and fluorine provide the tools for labeling biochemical molecules that can be used as probes to produce non-invasive images of biological processes in living persons non-invasively.

Phelps later developed an assortment of biological assay techniques for PET-based measurements of hemodynamic, biochemical, and biological processes in the brain, heart, and tumors. With the success of these techniques, he made further refinements related to PET scanners and biological assay methods. Phelps also worked on the miniaturization, automation, and integration of cyclotron technology and biochemical synthesizers to permit positron-labeled probes to be integrated into a single, PC-controlled device capable of producing positron-labeled compounds for research and clinical use.

Phelps set up and directed the first clinical PET service dedicated solely to patient care. PET-based diagnoses were made at this clinic for such diseases as Alzheimer's disease, multi-infarct dementia, Huntington's disease, depression, Parkinson's disease, epilepsy, cardiovascular disease, and cancer. He also established a large training program to give scientists and physicians the expertise they need to use PET scanning. Many of his students went on to take positions at

PET research and clinical at the over-800 PET centers around the world.

From 1970 to 1975, Phelps was a member of the faculty at Washington University School of Medicine. He then joined the faculty at the University of Pennsylvania in Philadelphia (1975 to 1976). In 1976, he moved to the University of California at Los Angeles School of Medicine, where he has been Professor of Radiological Sciences (1976 to 1992); Professor of Biomathematics (1980 to present); Chief, Division of Biophysics (1981 to 1984); Jennifer Jones Simon Professor (1983 to 1996); Norton Simon Professor (1996 to present); Chief, Division of Nuclear Medicine (1984 to 1992); Associate Director, UCLA/DOE Laboratory of Structural Biology & Molecular Medicine, and Chief, Division of Nuclear Medicine (1984 to present); Director, Crump Institute for Biological Imaging (1989 to present); Chairman, Department of Molecular & Medical Pharmacology (1992 to present); and Chief, Division of Nuclear Medicine, Department of Molecular & Medical Pharmacology (1992 to present). Phelps is a member of the Institute of Medicine of the National Academy of Sciences, and the Institute of Medicine.

Phelps has been awarded many professional honors, including the George von Hevesy Foundation Prize (1978, 1982); Certificate of Excellence, Society of Cerebral Blood Flow and Metabolism (1979); Oldendorf Award, Society for Computerized Tomography and Neurological Imaging (1981); S. Weir Mitchell Award, American Academy of Neurology (1981); Paul Aebersold Award, Society of Nuclear Medicine (1983); Ernest O. Lawrence Award, U.S. Department of Energy (1984); Special Award for Individual Distinction, American Nuclear Society (1984); Sarah L. Poiley Memorial Award, New York Academy of Sciences, 1984; Richard and Hinda Rosenthal Foundation Award, American College of Physicians (1987); Landauer Memorial Award, American Association for Physicists in Medicine (1988); Ted Block Memorial Award, Society of Nuclear Medicine (1989); Robert J. and Claire Pasarow Foundation Award (1992); Distinguished Scientists Award, Institute for Clinical PET (1995); and the Fermi Award, in honor of Enrico Fermi (1999). He was made a member of the National Academy of Sciences in 1999.

In 1999, when Phelps was awarded the Enrico Fermi Award, the U.S. government's oldest science and technology prize, he was specifically commended for "his invention of Positron Emission Tomography, and his seminal contributions to its use in research and patient care in neurological disorders, cardiovascular disease and cancer; and for the breadth of his accomplishments that combine physics, mathematics, chemistry, biology, and medical applications."

Sketch by Randall Frost

William D. Phillips
1948–
American physicist

William D. Phillips has spent his entire professional career at the National Institute of Standards and Technology (NIST), formerly the National Bureau of Standards, of the U.S. Department of Commerce. He has focused much of his research on the development of techniques for cooling atoms to very low temperatures and then studying the properties of these atoms. In 1988 he discovered that atoms could be cooled to a temperature of only $40\mu K$, or 40 millionths of a degree Kelvin. This temperature was about six times lower than the temperature that had been predicted as the lowest possible temperature to which matter can be cooled. As a result of this discovery, he was able to study the interaction of sodium atoms in a form that had never been observed before. For his work with the cooling of matter, Phillips was awarded a share of the 1997 Nobel Prize in Physics along with **Steven Chu** and **Claude Cohen-Tannoudji**.

William Daniel Phillips was born on November 5, 1948, in Wilkes-Barre, Pennsylvania. He grew up in Camp Hill, outside Harrisburg, and attended Juniata College. He was remembered as a very good student who asked a lot of questions to get more information. Phillips was also active in extracurricular activities, participating in the Forensic Club and the Honors Society, and was a member of the tennis team.

Phillips was awarded his B.S. degree from Juniata in 1970. He then continued his studies at the Massachusetts Institute of Technology (MIT), from which he earned a Ph.D. in physics in 1976. He then spent two years as a postdoctoral Chaim Weizmann Fellow at MIT. In 1978, Phillips accepted an appointment as a physicist at NIST, a post he retained for the next two decades.

Studies Low Temperature Phenomena

Phillips has been interested in the problem of cooling and trapping atoms since his years at MIT. This line is of growing interest among physicists because it provides a way of studying the structure and properties of individual molecules and atoms. Traditionally, scientists have been able to study only the bulk properties of matter, that is, the average properties of, at best, trillions and trillions of atoms and molecules. Yet, it is known that these average properties mask the properties of individual particles that make up a sample. The study of atoms and molecules is of interest not only for theoretical reasons, but also because of its potential practical applications on a macroscopic scale. Engineers are beginning to learn how to construct particles that consist of a relatively small number of particles, called nanostructures, with potentially revolutionary applications.

William D. Phillips

In order to advance in this field of research, it has become necessary to understand how individual atoms and molecules behave.

The key to these studies is to find ways to cool atoms and molecules, that is, to reduce the speed at which they travel. At room temperature, the particles in a gas are typically traveling at speeds of a few thousand miles (kilometers) per hour. At these speeds, particles escape from a field of view so quickly that no meaningful measurements can be made. In order to keep the particles within a field of view, their velocity must be reduced. Simply cooling a gas by conventional methods (such as putting it in a refrigerator) does not solve this problem. Under those conditions, the gas particles do lose speed, but they eventually condense to form a liquid or solid. In both liquids and solids, particles are so close to each other that individual properties cannot be determined. The objective, then, is to cool down a gas without permitting it to condense.

Theoreticians were proposing methods for solving this problem since the 1950s. One of the most popular approaches was to bombard a moving particle with a photon of energy moving towards that particle. Imagine, for example, a stream of ping pong balls fired from a gun. Those ping pong balls might be compared to the particles in a gas. Then imagine that short puffs of air are directed at the stream of ping pong balls. The puffs of air correspond to photons of energy. As each puff of air strikes a ping pong ball, it transfers energy to the ball and reduces the speed with which the ball is moving in the forward direction. If this process is repeated over and over again with any given ping pong ball, the ball eventually slows down and comes to a stop.

This analogy is greatly oversimplified, however. Real particles that are struck by a photon quickly give off the energy they have absorbed and recoil in a direction that cannot be predicted. Another photon aimed at the same particle will miss contact because the particle has changed its line of flight.

Another factor to be considered is that atoms and molecules absorb only certain quantized levels of energy. A photon with the wrong energy will have no effect on any particle that it strikes. Furthermore, the energy needed to excite a particle changes as the particle moves toward or away from the source of energy. This effect is known as the Doppler effect and is familiar to anyone who has heard the pitch of a train whistle increase or decrease as it moves toward or away from an observer.

Still, given all these conditions, an experimenter should be able to design an apparatus by which bursts of energy can be used to slow down the movement of atoms and molecules. In the mid-1980s, Steven Chu and his co-workers at the Bell Laboratories in Holmdel, New Jersey, designed an "atom trap" in which particles are bombarded by three pairs of laser guns arranged at right angles to each other. This arrangement was able to slow atoms down to a speed of about 12 in per second (30 cm per second), equivalent to a temperature of about 240 microkelvin. Theoretical calculations had shown that this temperature was probably the lowest that could be reached by the methods described above.

Unexpected Results

In 1988, Phillips attained a remarkable breakthrough by repeating the kinds of experiments carried out earlier by Chu and his colleagues. Phillips's group found that they were able to attain a minimum temperature of 40 microkelvin, six times lower than that predicted by theory and observed by Chu. Phillips later wrote that his results were "at first difficult to believe, especially considering the attractive simplicity of the Doppler cooling theory (and the generally held belief that experiments never work better than one expects)." This turn of events, he went on, "was both welcome and unsettling." The theoretical explanation for these observations was later provided by Claude Cohen-Tannoudji at the École Normale Supérieure in Paris, an accomplishment for which he was awarded a share of the 1997 Nobel Prize in Physics.

Phillips produced other breakthroughs in the study of low temperature behavior. In 1985, for example, he found a way to trap atoms in a maze of laser beams. The beams were arranged so as to produce constructive and destructive interference patterns. When placed into this kind of maze, gaseous atoms at very low temperatures fell into low-energy pockets in somewhat the manner that eggs fall into the depressions of the cartons in which they are sold.

Using devices such as these, Phillips has been able to create entirely new forms of matter that exist only under low temperature conditions and only for very brief periods of time. For example, in one experiment, he brought together a collection of sodium atoms that formed a molecular-like substance but that was much larger than an ordinary molecule. The collection of atoms broke apart after about 10 nanoseconds.

In addition to his position at NIST, Phillips has been Visiting Professor of Atomic Physics at the College de France (1987), Visiting Scientist at the École Normale Supérieure in Paris (1989-1990), and Adjunct Professor of Physics at the University of Maryland (1992-). He was elected to the National Academy of Sciences in 1997. He married the former Jane Van Wynen in 1970, and they have two daughters, Catherine and Christine.

SELECTED WRITINGS BY PHILLIPS:

Periodicals

(With H. J. Metcalf) "Cooling and Trapping Atoms." *Scientific American* (March 1987): 36-44.
(With Claude N. Cohen-Tannoudji) "New Mechanisms for Laser Cooling." *Physics Today* (October 1990): 33-40.

FURTHER READING:

Other

"1997 Nobel Prize in Physics Awarded to Juniata College Graduate." http://www.juniata.edu/news/latest.htm.
"NIST Fellow William D. Phillips Elected to National Academy of Science." http://physics.nist.gov/News/Releases/tn6136.html.
"Physicists Get Hot New Results with Cold Atoms." http://physics.nist.gov/News/Releases/n96-02.html.
"Press Release: The Nobel Prize in Physics 1997." http://www.nobel.se/announcement-97/physics97.html.

Sketch by David E. Newton

Frank Piasecki
1919–
American helicopter engineer

Frank Piasecki, an aviation pioneer who helped develop the concept of vertical take-off/landing (VTOL), introduced many innovations to the design of helicopters. Among his accomplishments was the engineering of helicopters which could achieve heavier load-carrying capacities, an improvement that rendered them more efficient, thus more economical. Piasecki also engineered improvements in the helicopter's handling and stability.

Frank Nicholas Piasecki was born in Philadelphia, Pennsylvania, on October 24, 1919, to Nikodem (a tailor who had emigrated from Poland) and Emilia Piasecki. While growing up in Philadelphia, he worked as a teenager for the Kellet Autogyro Company and the Aero Service Corporation. Piasecki's early exposure to autogyros laid the foundation for his later work, since the autogyro, while not a true helicopter, was a fixed-wing craft with a rotor.

Piasecki received his degree in mechanical engineering from the University of Pennsylvania's Towne School, then soon afterwards earned a bachelor's of science degree in aeronautical engineering from the Guggenheim School of Aeronautics of New York University in 1940. After college, Piasecki became a designer for Platte-LePage Aircraft Company, then worked for the Edward G. Budd Manufacturing Company as an aerodynamicist in its aircraft division.

Piasecki also founded a research group, the PV-Engineering Forum, which was composed of University of Pennsylvania engineering students. Their first helicopter was the PV–2, a single-seat, single-rotor helicopter built for the purpose of proving what were at the time advanced concepts of VTOL. The PV–2, which had the first dynamically balanced rotor blades, a tension-torsion pitch-change system, and overhead stick and a rigid, anti-torque tail rotor, was the second helicopter to fly successfully in the United States. Its maiden flight took place on April 11, 1943, with Piasecki at the controls. Up to that point, Piasecki had only fourteen hours of flying time, all of it in fixed-wing aircraft; nevertheless, he successfully taught himself to fly the PV–2. The following October, Piasecki demonstrated the PV–2 to military commanders and commercial operators in Washington, D.C., and impressed those present with the PV–2's precision finger-tip control.

Develops Choppers for Military Use

Due to his critical skills as an aeronautical engineer, Piasecki was exempted from military service during World War II, although he contributed in other ways to the war effort. In January, 1944, the U.S. Coast Guard signed a contract with Piasecki, who would produce for them a large helicopter capable of rescuing people from torpedoed ships along the coast; this aircraft would be known as the HRP–1. First flown by Piasecki in March, 1945, the HRP–1 was revolutionary as it featured—for the first time—tandem rotors mounted on a helicopter. Far from interfering with each other, the rotors allowed the machine to carry heavy loads without great concern for load balance. The U.S. Navy bought twenty of this model, soon to be dubbed the "Flying Banana," so-called because the ends of the elongated craft were bent up slightly so that the rotors did not interfere with each other.

The Flying Banana proved most useful for a number of military applications such as mine-sweeping, amphibious assault, search and rescue tasks, and heavy load transport. Another model, the HRP–2, was built for the Marine Corps' assault mission and was notable for its vertical landing capability; the craft also featured a thinner shell and stiffer sections which enhanced its strength while keeping its weight to a minimum (to produce the metal Piasecki developed a stretch-milling process now found throughout helicopter manufacturing).

In 1946, the PV Forum was transformed into the Piasecki Helicopter Corporation; Piasecki served as both president and chairman of the board of the new company. The next significant improvement to arrive in helicopter design was the development of the HUP models. Conceived for the U.S. Navy, the HUP–1 featured over-lapping rotors, a necessity when it came to swiftly storing the craft on a lower deck of a ship. The HUP–2 model was the first helicopter to have an autopilot. This permitted IFR (instrument flight rules) flying, as well as hands-off flying, even when the helicopter was hovering. So useful was the HUP–2 that it was not only flown by the military services of the United States, but by those of Canada and France.

While the HUP was the naval version of these helicopters, the army version was designated the H-series. Among them, the H–21 attained an altitude over 22,000 feet and featured a fixed tricycle-type landing gear. Doughnut-shaped floaters around the wheels allowed for landings on any type of terrains. Ideal for rescue operations—especially those where injuries were present, since it could carry up to twelve stretchers—the H–21 also had the distinction of being the first helicopter to make a non-stop transcontinental flight across the United States (the journey lasted thirty-seven hours and involved in-flight refueling). Other countries, such as West Germany, Sweden, Japan, and Canada, employed the H–21 for many years.

The U.S. Air Force commissioned the development of a long range rescue helicopter for picking up stranded bomber crews in 1946. The ensuing helicopter, the YH–16, was the largest in the world, with a length of 134 feet, and was also the first helicopter with twin engines. An improved version, the H–16, was produced for the U.S. Army; it could hold three jeeps and carried various pods for specialized functions, such as an electronics center, a field operating room, and a mobile repair center.

Forms New Company for Further VTOL Advancement

In the mid–1950s, the Piasecki Helicopter Corporation was purchased by Boeing Airplane Company, and Piasecki formed a new company called Piasecki Aircraft Corporation. He became committed to further research and development of VTOL, especially where higher speed and heavier lift capability were concerned. However, Piasecki still maintained his role in developing helicopters for the military. For instance, the deployment of nuclear submarines prompted the navy to seek a good weapons delivery system that could be ship-based; Piasecki not only developed the PA–4 for this need, but made it a drone and installed a system for maintaining a constant azimuth heading no matter which direction the helicopter flew. Known as the "Sea-Bat," this model was followed by the "Mud-Bat" and the "Ice-Bat."

Piasecki's next innovation, the PA–59 "AirGeep," was a terrain-following craft invisible to radar. Its maiden flight was in September, 1958. Unlike conventional helicopters, the AirGeep was unique because its rotors did not stir up clouds of sand, dust or snow as it skimmed the surface of the earth. This aircraft was followed by the PA–59N "SeaGeep" which could land on the water or easily land aboard ship; it first flew in November, 1961.

The army desired the capability to carry its biggest tank, weighing at sixty-two tons, by helicopter (a feat no helicopter could accomplish). One of the solutions Piasecki engineered was that of developing configurations wherein multiple helicopters were joined to provide the needed lift and fly as one unit. This system was known as the PA–39 and led later to a hybrid system where blimps were used connected to helicopters for maximum lift.

The PA–97, developed in the early 1980s, continued the hybrid lift concept, eventually being able to lift from sixty to two hundred tons. Piasecki believed that higher speeds and greater load capacity were the concerns of future helicopter development, along with such considerations as reduced noise and vibrations.

Piasecki, the recipient of twenty-three patents on helicopter development, was the first person the Civil Aeronautics Administration recognized as a helicopter pilot before being a fixed-wing pilot. The United States Coast Guard made him an honorary helicopter pilot on April 23, 1945, at Fort Bennett Field, and in 1955, he was awarded an honorary doctorate in aeronautical engineering from New York University. In addition, Piasecki received a doctor of science degree in 1970 from Alliance College in Cambridge Springs, Pennsylvania. In 1974, he was inducted into the Army Aviation Hall of Fame and also received the Leonardo da Vinci Award from the Navy Helicopter Association.

In December, 1958, Piasecki married the former Vivian O'Gara Weyerhaeuser with whom he had five sons and two daughters. The annual donator of the Dr. Alexander Klemin Award—presented by the American Helicopter Society—Piasecki has also served as both president and fellow of that organization. In addition, he is a founding member and fellow of what is now known as the American Institute of Aeronautics and Astronautics. A frequent lecturer to technological associations in the United States and abroad, Piasecki has testified before Congress on the concept of heavy vertical air lift.

SELECTED WRITINGS BY PIASECKI:

Periodicals

Flight Magazine, Helicopter Air Travel, October 10, 1952.

Aero Digest, International Cooperation, September 4, 1955.

FURTHER READING:

Books

Boyne, Walter J., and Donald S. Lopez, editors, *Vertical Flight,* Smithsonian Institution Press, 1984.

Carey, Keith, *The Helicopter,* Tab Books, 1986.

Lightbody, Andy, and Joe Poyer, *The Illustrated History of Helicopters,* Publications International, 1990.

Young, Warren R., *The Helicopters,* Time-Life, 1982.

Periodicals

Anderton, D. A., *Aviation Week,* Piasecki Tests Ring-Wing VTOL Design Concept, September 26, 1960, p. 54.

Deigan, E., *Flying,* Flying Bananas and How They Grew, July, 1949, p. 24.

Holt, W. J., Jr., *Saturday Evening Post,* He Likes to Fly Straight Up, August 11, 1951, p. 32.

Holt, W. J., Jr., *Business Week,* Piasecki: Getting Set for Mass Transportation, September 26, 1953, p. 144.

Other

Holt, W. J., Jr., *Business Week,* Piasecki: Getting Set for Mass Transportation, Biography provided by Frank Piasecki, 1992.

Holt, W. J., Jr., *The Piasecki Story of Vertical Lift,* Piasecki Aircraft Corporation, Essington, PA.

Sketch by Susan E. Kolmer

Auguste Piccard
1884–1962
Swiss physicist

Auguste Piccard earned his fame by exploring higher into the Earth's atmosphere and deeper into its oceans than had any person before him. Son of the chair of the department of chemistry at the University of Basel, he and his twin brother both earned doctorates in engineering, became professors themselves, and collaborated in a variety of research projects. In 1931, Piccard and a colleague traveled in a balloon to an altitude of about ten miles, more than three miles higher than any human had ever gone before. Shortly after this feat, Piccard became interested in the exploration of the ocean depths and designed a new

vehicle—the bathyscaphe—by which they could be explored.

Auguste Piccard and his twin brother Jean Félix were born in Basel, Switzerland, on January 28, 1884. The Piccard family had a long and notable history in the area. Auguste and Jean Félix's grandfather had been chief commissioner of the region in which the family lived, and their uncle owned the Piccard-Pictet Company in Geneva, manufacturers of hydroelectric turbines. The twins' mother was Hélène Haltenhoff Piccard, and their father Jules Piccard was chairman of the department of chemistry at the University of Basel.

After graduation from the local high school, the twins entered the Federal Institute of Technology in Zürich where Auguste majored in mechanical engineering and Jean Félix majored in chemical engineering. They both received their bachelor of science degrees and then went on to complete doctorates in their respective fields. Between 1907 and 1920, Auguste taught in Zürich. He then accepted an appointment as professor of physics at the Brussels Polytechnic Institute, a post he held until his retirement in 1954.

Uses New Technology to Explore Upper Atmosphere

One of Piccard's earliest interests was the Earth's upper atmosphere and the cosmic rays to be detected there. He was not alone, of course, in this interest. As early as 1783, scientists had been using lighter-than-air balloons to carry themselves and their instruments into the atmosphere to study its properties. In 1804, for example, the French physicist Joseph Louis Gay-Lussac had ridden a balloon 23,000 feet into the atmosphere where he collected samples of air for later analysis. Auguste and Jean Félix made their own first balloon ascension from Zürich in 1913, after which, in 1915, they both joined the balloon section of the Swiss army for a period of service.

The use of balloons to study the atmosphere involved an inherent risk and limitation, however. At a certain altitude, the air becomes so thin that humans can no longer function. In 1862, the English meteorologist James Glashier lost consciousness as his balloon reached an altitude of 29,000 feet. He survived only because his companion was able to maneuver the balloon back to earth. Such occurrences made it clear to scientists that open-air balloons could be used only below certain altitudes.

One solution to this limitation was developed by the French meteorologist Léon Philippe Teisserenc de Bort. Teisserenc de Bort decided that unmanned balloons carrying instruments could more safely record the data that humans had been collecting previously. Between 1899 and 1902, he launched dozens of automated balloons that brought back information about the atmosphere. One discovery he made was the existence of layers in the atmosphere, the first evidence for the presence of the stratosphere. Piccard's view was that unmanned ascents could never provide the quality of data that could be obtained from balloons in which humans could travel. He resolved, therefore, to design a pressurized gondola in which observers could travel well beyond the 29,000 foot level that had marked the previous barrier to manned flight.

By 1930, his first design was ready for testing. The gondola was made of an air-tight aluminum shell that could be pressurized to sea-level pressures and was then suspended from a hydrogen-filled balloon. On May 27, 1931, Piccard and a colleague, Paul Kipfer, took off in their airship from Augsburg, Germany. They eventually reached an altitude of 51,775 feet, by far the highest altitude so far attained by human researchers. About 15 months later, on August 18, 1932, Piccard made another record-breaking ascent, this time to a height of 53,139 feet after departing from Zürich. His companion on this flight was Max Cosyns.

Piccard made more than two dozen balloon ascensions before he retired from the activity in 1937. During that time, he collected valuable new information on atmospheric electricity and radioactivity, as well as cosmic radiation. Probably more important, he continued to improve on the design of his aircraft, making the kinds of improvements that would eventually allow other scientists to reach altitudes of more than 100,000 feet. In recognition of his many accomplishments in balloon flight, Piccard was awarded the Gold Medal of the Belgian Aero Club.

Descends to Record Depths

In the late 1930s, Piccard shifted his attention to a new challenge: the ocean depths. He became convinced that the same techniques used to study the thin upper atmosphere could be used in the high-pressure depths of the oceans. He began work on the design of a *bathyscaphe,* or "ship of the deep." The bathyscaphe consisted of two parts. The lower portion of the vessel was an air-tight steel sphere, built to withstand pressures of 12,000 pounds per square inch, where researchers rode. The upper part of the bathyscaphe consisted of a 5,200 cubic foot metal tank containing heptane that provided the vessel with buoyancy. The bathyscaphe operated under its own power and could rise or sink by having seawater pumped into the flotation chamber or iron pellets dumped from the same chamber.

The first test of the bathyscaphe took place in 1948, but the vessel was able to dive no deeper than about a mile below sea level, far less than Piccard had hoped. He continued to modify the design of his vessel, however, and a second test five years later was more successful. In 1953, he and his son Jacques traveled to a depth of 10,335 feet off the coast of Capri, a depth three times as great as the previous record set by William Beebe in his bathysphere in 1934. The Piccards also built another bathyscaphe, the *Trieste,* which was sold to the U.S. Navy for research use. The *Trieste* was used in a 1960 expedition that took Jacques Piccard and U.S. Navy lieutenant Don Walsh to a depth of 35,802 feet in the Mariana Trench off the coast of Guam. Piccard and his son Jacques were working on yet another modification of the bathyscaphe design—to be called a mesoscaphe—when Piccard died on March 25, 1962, in Lausanne, Switzerland.

SELECTED WRITINGS BY PICCARD:

Books

Audessus des nuages, B. Grasset (Paris), 1933.

Entre terre et ciel, Editions d'Ouchy (Lausanne), 1946, translation by Claude Apcher published as Between Earth and Sky, Falcon Press, 1950.

Au fond des mers en bathyscaphe, Arthaud (Paris), 1954, translation by Christina Stead published as In Balloon and Bathyscaphe, Cassell, 1956, and as Earth, Sky, and Sea, Oxford University Press, 1956.

FURTHER READING:

Books

Field, Adelaide, *Auguste Piccard, Captain of Space, Admiral of the Abyss,* Houghton Mifflin, 1969.

Honour, Alan, *Ten Miles High, Two Miles Deep: The Adventures of the Piccards,* Whitlesey House, 1957.

Malkus, Alida, *Exploring the Sky and Sea: Auguste and Jacques Piccard,* Kingston, 1961.

Stehling, Kurt R., and William Beller, *Skyhooks,* The First Space-Gondola Flight, Doubleday, 1962.

Sketch by David E. Newton

George Edward Pierce
1947–
American microbiologist

George Edward Pierce is noted primarily for his application of microbiological principles to industrial pollution problems. He has linked scientific research to the corporate world in an effort to prevent pollution, produce environmentally friendly products, and to neutralize hazardous waste.

Born in Meriden, Connecticut, on June 6, 1947, Pierce completed his undergraduate degree in biology in 1969 and earned his doctorate in microbiology in 1976 at Rensselaer Polytechnic Institute, Troy, New York. He remained at the institute until 1977, working as a teaching and research assistant and postdoctoral associate in the biology department. In this early part of his career, Pierce focused on the use of microbes to aid the breakdown of petroleum and petroleum-based products.

In 1977, Pierce moved from academia to industry. He accepted a post as a biomedical researcher at Battelle Columbus Division in Columbus, Ohio. He remained with

Battelle until 1988, serving as a senior researcher and associate section manager. It was during this period that Pierce firmly linked microbiology to industry. He studied the effectiveness of activated carbon and silver-impregnated filters in relationship to microbes in water systems; he investigated levels of and resistance to dichlorodiphenyltrichloroethane (DDT) in microorganisms present in soil heavily laden with the pesticide. He looked for commercially feasible methods to manufacture the more environmentally acceptable fuel ethanol and studied herbicide-degrading bacteria. Pierce left Battelle to accept a position as director of bioremediation technology with Celgene Corporation in Warren, New Jersey. Here, he continued his research in the identification and development of microorganisms that could be used to neutralize waste.

Pierce's work emphasizes the elimination of environmental toxins through environmentally friendly methods. Genetic manipulation of microorganisms poses its own potential dangers; Pierce, through his work in the laboratory, his service with regulatory agencies, and his scientific presentations, promotes long-term analysis and scientific responsibility in this area.

Promoting Optimism and Caution

In 1991, Pierce joined American Cynamid, Linden, New Jersey, as manager of technology development in the Environmental Services Group. He became more visible as a spokesman for those in the scientific community who demanded responsible use of microbiological technologies. He addressed in more depth the barriers and issues, as well as the technological advances, surrounding the use of enzymatic and microbiological treatment of industrially produced hazardous waste.

Pierce stepped up his activities in the regulatory community—a key element in developing, applying, and controlling technologies that were advancing faster than their long-term effects could be understood. In 1991, he joined the Environmental Protection Agency's Subcommittee on Pollution Prevention as co-chair, and chaired the committee in 1992. He serves as a member of the U.S. Department of Commerce Committee on Biotechnology, which he joined in 1991, and has served since 1992 as a consultant to the EPA Science Advisory Board and since 1990 as a member of the EPA's Bioremediation Action Committee.

Pierce also feels a commitment to the next generation of scientists. He held an appointment as adjunct professor with Ohio State University from 1983 to 1995 and is currently an adjunct professor at Rensselaer Polytechnic Institute.

Recognition and Professional Affiliations

Pierce is active in the American Society for Microbiology and the Society for Industrial Microbiology. He served as editor-in-chief of *The Journal of Industrial Microbiology* from 1985 to 1993 and co-chaired the 1995 annual meeting of the Society for Industrial Microbiology. Since 1985, he has served as the U.S. national delegate to the International Union of Microbiological Societies and, since 1991, has been a member of the steering committee of the American Academy of Environmental Engineers. He also served as director of the Society for Industrial Microbiology from 1982 to 1985.

Pierce currently holds seven patents in the United States, Europe, Canada, and Japan. He has been awarded patents for the microbial production of hydroxy- and keto-fatty acids; development of recombinant DNA plasmid used to degrade organic compounds; production of new bacteria lipase enzymes; biofilters; aerobic degradation; fluid phase biodegradation; and microorganisms for compound degrading. In 1993, the Society for Industrial Microbiology recognized Pierce's work with the Charles Porter Award. Pierce has also published dozens of scholarly articles and made numerous professional presentations.

Pierce is currently manager of Technology Development and Engineering in the Environmental Services Group of Cytec Industries, a company created by a series of mergers and divestitures involving American Cynamid.

SELECTED WRITINGS BY PIERCE:

Periodicals

"Potential of Genetic Engineering in Microbial Degradation." *Battelle Memorial Institute Proceedings*, 1981, Volume 4, pp. 204-210.

(With J. B. Robinson, G. E. Garrett, D. K. Terman, and S. A. Sojka) "Improved Cloning and Transfer of Pseudomonas Plasmid DNA," *Developments in Industrial Microbiology*, 1985, Volume 26, pp. 793-801.

(With A. H. Lipkkus, K. K. Chitur, S. J. Vesper, and J. B. Robinson) "Evaluation of Infrared Spectroscopy as a Bacterial Identification Method," *Journal of Industrial Microbiology*, 1990, Volume 6, pp. 63-70.

(With C. B. Wick) "Integrated Approach to the Development of Biodegradation Systems to Treat Hazardous Organic Chemicals," *Developments in Industrial Microbiology*, 1990, Volume 31, pp. 81-98.

FURTHER READING:

Books

American Men and Women of Science, 19th edition. R. R. Bowker Co., 1994, p. 1242.

Who's Who of Emerging Leaders in America, 1st edition. Marquis Who's Who, 1987.

Who's Who in Engineering and Science, 1st edition. Marquis Who's Who, 1991.

Sketch by Angie Mullig

Naomi E. Pierce
1954–
American entymologist and molecular biologist

Naomi E. Pierce is best known for her studies of the interactions between butterflies and other species of insects. Her field and laboratory investigations, particularly of the relationship between the Lycaenid "mistletoe butterfly" and the farmer ants that "herd" it, have helped reveal the environmental and behavioral forces that maintain cooperation between insect species. In addition, her recent efforts to use molecular science have helped improve upon the body-structure-based methods previously used to understand the evolutionary relationships between these butterflies.

Pierce is also known for her active efforts to help women scientists train and become established in the scientific community. A MacArthur fellow and the first woman to be tenured in her department at Harvard University, Pierce is a vocal proponent of mentoring in scientific education. She says that her early, positive experiences with mentor relationships have encouraged her to take on a growing number of graduate students and other teaching responsibilities.

Hooked on Butterflies

Pierce was born on October 19, 1954, into an erudite Denver, Colorado, family. Her father was a geophysicist; her grandfather was a novelist in Japan. The latter especially influenced her, leading to a lifelong interest in novels and contemporary fiction. She did not originally want to become a scientist; for the first three years of her college education at Yale University, she majored in history, arts, and letters.

Pierce was also hedging her bets, taking science courses in case she wanted to go to medical school. A course on evolution taught by Charles Remington, which she took in her third year of college, was to trigger a profound change in her life. Intrigued by Remington's lectures touching on his work with butterflies at the Rocky Mountain Biological Laboratory in Colorado, Pierce visited his office one day to find out more about his work. She found his enthusiasm for butterflies to be infectious, and registered for summer courses at the Rocky Mountain laboratory. In her senior year of college, she changed her major to biology, graduating in 1976.

In 1976 Pierce won a John Courtney Murray Fellowship that allowed her to travel to Southeast Asia to study butterflies. There she became acquainted with the Lycaenids, especially the "mistletoe butterfly" of Australia. Half of a unique cooperative arrangement between butterfly and ant, the mistletoe butterfly's larvae are tended, protected, and herded by farmer ants, in exchange secreting a sugary liquid that the ants eat. She was so intrigued by the

relationship that she made it the topic of her doctoral dissertation at Harvard University, where she worked with famous ant expert **Edward O. Wilson** as well as doctoral advisors Bert Hilldobler and R. E. Silberglied. She received her Ph.D. from Harvard in 1983.

Pierce returned to Southeast Asia in that same year, as a Fullbright Postdoctoral Research Fellow at Griffith University in Queensland. There she studied another family of Lycaenid butterflies that are carnivorous, feeding on aphids. Following her year in Australia, she continued her studies of the carnivorous Lycanidae, first as a NATO Postdoctoral Fellowship and a research lecturer at Oxford University from 1984 to 1986, then as an assistant professor at Princeton University from 1986 to 1990.

Pierce's postdoctoral work led her to study larger questions of evolution and species relationships. Dissatisfied with the depth of knowledge of the Lycaenid butterflies' relationships and life histories, Pierce determined to improve the previous phylogenetic "family trees," built mostly by comparing relationships between body structures. As one of only 31 MacArthur fellows named in 1988, Pierce had five years to conduct unrestricted research. She retrained as a molecular biologist, learning how to use genetic technologies to refine and improve upon the maps of evolutionary relationship between the Lycaenidae. In 1991 Pierce was named the first Hessel Professor of Biology at Harvard, becoming the first tenured woman in that university's Department of Organismal and Evolutionary Biology as well as the curator of the world-renowned butterfly collection at Harvard's Museum of Comparative Zoology.

Pierce's willingness and ability to branch out into new specialties and interact with scientists in different fields has characterized her work. In particular, her studies of the chemical signals by which butterflies and ants communicate have brought together field biologists, entymologists, and molecular scientists. Today, her research spans a number of disciplines having to do with the ecological, behavioral, and biochemical mechanisms underlying butterfly/ant interactions. Her work concentrates particularly with the goal of understanding how the Lycaenid butterflies evolved to fill diverse ecological niches in which they can be carnivorous or herbivorous, and cooperative or parasitic on other insect species.

Mentoring Women in Science

While earning a reputation for multidisciplinary flexibility, Pierce has also taken an active role in encouraging other women to rise in the scientific establishment. She credits her relationship with mentor Remington with helping her achieve a strong start in what can sometimes be a challenging career choice for women.

An active teacher with a preference for individual and small-group teaching, Pierce leads a laboratory that she says follows a cooperative rather than a hierarchical model. As well as helping her to add molecular techniques to her laboratory's investigatory armamentarium, her MacArthur fellowship also allowed several of her graduate students to travel and study in Australia. Pierce and her students spend three months out of each year doing field work.

Pierce's most recent "research interest," according to her web page, are her and her husband Andrew Berry's twin daughters, Kate and Megan, born in 1997.

SELECTED WRITINGS BY PIERCE:

Books

"Amplified Species Diversity: A Case Study of an Australian Lycaenid Butterfly and its Attendant Ants." *Biology of Butterflies. XI Symp R Entomol Soc (Lond).* R.I. Vane Wright and P.R. Ackery, editors. London: Academic Press, 1984, pp.197-200.

(With J.T. Costa) "Social Evolution in the Lepidoptera: Ecological Context and Communication in Larval Societies." *Social Competition and Cooperation in Insects and Arachnids, Volume II: Evolution of Sociality.* B.J. Crespi and J.C. Choe, editors. 1996.

Periodicals

"Costs and Benefits of Cooperation Between the Australian Lycaenid Butterfly, Jalmenus evagoras and its Attendant Ants." *Behav Ecol Sociobiol* (1987): 237-248.

(With B.S.W. Chang, et al.) "Cloning of the Gene Encoding Honeybee Long-Wavelength Rhodopsin: A new Class of Insect Long-Wavelength Visual Pigments." *Gene* (1996): 215-219.

FURTHER READING:

Periodicals

Cromie, William J. "Naomi Pierce: Butterfly Behavior Leads to Insights on Evolution." *Harvard Gazette* (November 8, 1991): 9.

Other

"Pierce Laboratory: Harvard University." October 4, 1996. http://www.oeb.harvard.edu/faculty/pierce/lab (November 25, 1997).

"Prof. Naomi Pierce." April 22, 1997. http://www.oeb.harvard.edu/faculty/pierce/npierce/npierce.html (25 November 25, 1997).

Sketch by Kenneth Chiacchia

David R. Pilbeam
1940–
English-born American paleoanthropologist

In the field of physical anthropology, David R. Pilbeam stands out as a scientist whom all recognize as an authority. Pilbeam enjoys the respect of his peers in part because he has not flinched at changing his views when new evidence surfaces.

David Roger Pilbeam was born on November 21, 1940, in the seaside resort of Brighton in Sussex, England. He is the son of Ernest and Edith (Clack) Pilbeam, and was the first member of his family to attend a university. Upon completing his B.A. at Cambridge University in England in 1963, he came to the United States to study at Yale University in New Haven, Connecticut. He returned to Cambridge in 1965 to teach. After receiving his Ph.D. from Yale in 1967, Pilbeam joined the faculty at Yale, where he became Professor of Anthropology in 1974. In 1981 he moved to Harvard University in Cambridge, Massachusetts, where he now is Henry Ford II Professor of the Social Sciences, head of the Paleoanthropology research center, and an Academic Dean. He also was Director of the Peabody Museum from 1990-96. At Harvard he met his wife, Maryellen Ruvolo, who is a molecular geneticist/anthropologist and a Professor in the Anthropology Department.

Pilbeam's research has primarily been focused on interpreting the role of Miocene-period apes in the evolution of humans. During the 1960s, he identified three species of an African and European ape or hominoid genus dating back 20 million years that appeared to be ancestral to the great apes. He also concurred with a Yale colleague that a 15-million-year-old ape discovered in India, known as *Ramapithecus*, possessed teeth more like those of the human line, the hominids. At that time, this classification scheme seemed plausible, since the separation of apes and humans was thought to have occurred early in the Miocene epoch, which spans roughly from 30 million years ago to five million years ago. Pilbeam put the separation of humans from apes at about 20 to 15 million years ago. However, deoxyribonucleic acid (DNA) dating indicated that the common ancestor lived only about five million years ago, at the end of the Miocene. Pilbeam defended *Ramapithecus* and its close relatives as early hominids for a decade after the first DNA evidence appeared. Later in 1981, Pilbeam examined a partial skull from Pakistan that, along with other recently discovered evidence, changed his mind completely. This ape, known as *Sivapithecus*, dated back to approximately 10 million years ago and was clearly similar to the modern orangutan and also related to *Ramapithecus*. Consequently, Pilbeam modified his original theory, leading other anthropologists to accept a more recent date for the divergence of great apes and human ancestors.

David R. Pilbeam

Pilbeam's expeditions to Asia and Africa continue to produce more evidence concerning both Miocene apes and the early line leading to humans. His studies in Pakistan cover a period from early in the Miocene—about 18 million years ago—to the time of early species of *Homo,* about two million years ago, and deal not only with the apes and hominids but also with evolution of animals and their interaction with the environment. At Harvard, he has become a great synthesizer of ideas related to the evolution of hominids and hominoids. When any major new discovery concerning early human ancestry is announced, Pilbeam's phone begins to ring with queries from science writers everywhere who want to know what the new fossil might mean.

SELECTED WRITINGS BY PILBEAM:

Books

The Evolution of Man. London: Thames and Hudson, 1970.
Ascent of Man: An Introduction to Human Evolution. New York: Macmillan Publishing Company, 1972.
(with G.A. Harrison, J.M. Tanner, and P.T. Barker) *Human Biology.* New York: Oxford University Press, 1988.
(Ed. with Stephen Jones and Robert D. Martin) *The Cambridge Encyclopedia of Human Evolution.* New York: Cambridge University Press, 1993.

FURTHER READING:

Books

Lewin, Roger. *The Origin of Modern Humans.* New York: Scientific American Books, 1993.

Sketch by Bryan Bunch

David Pimentel
1925–
American entomologist and ecologist

David Pimentel is professor of insect ecology and agricultural sciences at Cornell University in Ithaca, New York. A widely recognized authority on ecologically sound methods of pest control, sustainable agriculture, and the relationship between human populations and environmental impacts, Pimentel has played a central role in national and international environmental policies.

Pimentel was born on May 24, 1925, in Fresno, California. His parents, Frank Freitas and Marion Silva Pimentel, were farmers raising vegetables and grapes. At age six, Pimentel moved with his family to a farm in Middleborough, Massachusetts. After completing high school, Pimentel left Massachusetts for Saint John's University in Collegeville, Minnesota, where in 1943 he received pilot and officer training as a member of the U.S. Air Force. Pimentel remained in the Air Force for two years before returning to the East Coast to attend the University of Massachusetts at Amherst beginning in 1945. He received his bachelor of science degree in 1948. Also during this period, he spent the summer semester of 1946 at Clark University in Worcester, Massachusetts. Pimentel's scientific career gained an auspicious start when his undergraduate research was published in 1949.

Pimentel earned his Ph.D. from Cornell University in 1951 following just three years of graduate school. Still a member of the Air Force Reserve, Pimentel was called back into active duty after receiving his Ph.D. Pimentel no longer desired a flying career and obtained a transfer into the U.S. Public Health Service (USPHS). He served as chief of the Tropical Research Laboratory in San Juan, Puerto Rico, from 1951 to 1955. Research there primarily focused on mongooses—important in the transmission of rabies—and snails, which contributed to the spread of other major diseases. From 1954 to 1955 Pimentel spent spring and summer in Savannah, Georgia, as project leader at the USPHS Technical Development Laboratory. During winters, Pimentel engaged in postdoctoral insect ecology research at the University of Chicago, Illinois.

Pimentel joined the faculty of Cornell University in 1955 as assistant professor of insect ecology. He has remained there for the duration of his career, becoming a full professor and chairman of the department of entomology and limnology in 1963. Pimentel's research broadened over the course of his career. He explained in an interview with Peter H. Taylor, "I began in entomology and pest control, and then became interested in environmental implications of pesticides. Studying this made me more broadly interested in issues surrounding water resources, soil resources, deforestation, and energy. Ultimately, I became interested in the whole question of human populations and their impact on the environment."

Pimentel has authored over four hundred publications, including seventeen books. One of the most important is a 1973 paper that reported the first-ever measurements of energy use in food production. It appeared at the height of the energy crisis in the 1970s. Other landmark publications include several articles related to reduction of pesticide use and a 1963 paper that led to new methods of selecting pest control agents.

Pimentel's expertise in environmental research led to his participation in numerous national and international committees. Among the most notable was the President's Science Advisory Council of 1964–66. The council assembled basic research information on a wide range of environmental pollution issues into a major report used in policy development. Also significant was a 1969 commission on pesticides that recommended the banning of DDT and that led to the formation of the Environmental Protection Agency. Serving more than sixteen years as an elected member of the Ithaca, New York, mayor's council, Pimentel has been active in the administration of local affairs, such as road repairs and the town budget. He lives in Ithaca with his wife Maria Hutchins, a nutritionist also on the Cornell faculty, whom he married in 1949. They have two daughters and a son.

Pimentel's former students have become major players in research and environmental policy making throughout the world. His accomplishments have attracted many honors, including the 1992 Award for Distinguished Service to Rural Life. Anne H. Ehrlich, a researcher at Stanford University recognized for her expertise in related research areas, said of Pimentel in an interview with Peter H. Taylor, "He has had a substantial impact . . . on the recognition of how agricultural systems fit into the larger ecological picture, and how people altering those systems end up damaging them. Beyond this, David Pimentel has played an important role in influencing public policy related to environmental issues."

SELECTED WRITINGS BY PIMENTEL:

Books

Food, Energy, and Society, Edward Arnold, 1979.

The Pesticide Question: Environment, Economics, and Ethics, Chapman & Hall, 1993.
World Soil Erosion and Conservation, Cambridge University Press, 1993.

Periodicals

Science, Food Production and the Energy Crisis, Volume 182, 1979, pp. 443–449.

Other

Interview with Peter H. Taylor, conducted on January 25, 1994.
Interview with Peter H. Taylor, conducted on January 28, 1994.

Sketch by Peter H. Taylor

Gifford Pinchot
1865–1946
American forester and conservationist

Gifford Pinchot was a pioneer of the forestry movement in the United States. He was the first American to receive formal training in forestry and practice systematic forest management, beginning with his work in the Biltmore Forest of North Carolina in 1892. Eventually serving under Presidents William McKinley, Theodore Roosevelt, and William Howard Taft as the chief of the Forest Service, Pinchot was a major force on the national scene. He was also an early conservationist in the United States and a two-term governor of Pennsylvania.

Born August 11, 1865, in Simsbury, Connecticut, Pinchot was the first of four children by James Wallace Pinchot, a wealthy New York merchant, and Mary Jane (Eno) Pinchot. The children were raised in an atmosphere rich with French culture and—because of their parents' place in society—were exposed to important personalities in the arts and politics. As a boy, Pinchot attended private schools in New York and Paris, as well as the Phillips Exeter Academy.

Upon entering Yale University in 1885, Pinchot had accepted the advice of his father and made up his mind to become a professional forester. Yale, like other American universities, did not offer courses in forestry at the time, so Pinchot took courses in botany, meteorology, and other sciences. After graduating in 1889 with a B.A. degree, he traveled to London to study the British government's forestry program in India. He also attended the National Forestry School in Nancy, France, where he studied silviculture (tree-growing) and forest economics. His examination of forest management in countries like France, Germany, and Switzerland convinced him that the right approach would be to treat forests as a public resource. When Pinchot returned home in 1890, he was determined to introduce the concept of public forestry in the United States.

In 1892 Pinchot was hired to manage the much-neglected Biltmore Forest, located in the North Carolina estate of the railroad magnate George Vanderbilt. This was Pinchot's opportunity to apply the principles of scientific forestry as employed in Europe, and in a year, he was able to show a profit. Pinchot left North Carolina in 1894 to set up his own consultancy service in New York City. His work took him all over the United States and acquainted him with the nation's forest reserves. An advocate of regulating commercial use of public and private forests, he nevertheless favored selective harvesting and other measures to promote the well-being and regrowth of forests.

Pinchot was appointed in 1896 to the newly created National Forest Commission of the National Academy of Sciences. The commission's study of the national forest reserves in the western states culminated in the passage of the Forest Management Act of 1897, which was the legal framework for the commercial use of these reserves.

Enters Government Service

Offered a post in the United States Division of Forestry in 1897, Pinchot was chosen the following year to succeed Dr. Bernhard E. Fernow as the chief of the small agency, which was part of the federal Department of Agriculture. Pinchot then began a campaign for the transfer of all the United States forest reserves—which were then being controlled by the Interior Department—to the Department of Agriculture. He succeeded in 1905 and the division was renamed the Forest Service; in 1907, the transferred reserves became known as national forests. The success of Pinchot's mission largely depended on the support he received from President Theodore Roosevelt, with whom Pinchot developed a close association and friendship. Pinchot's administration of the nation's forests resulted in their increase from fifty-one million acres in area in 1901 to 175 million by 1910.

Pinchot also joined with Roosevelt in bringing conservation ideas to the forefront and helped formulate the conservation policies of the president's administration. He worked to ensure a systematic classification of the nation's natural resources by the United States Geographical Survey and, in 1908, influenced the Inland Waterways Commission (of which he was a member) to set forth proposals aimed at regional development of the nation's river systems. Also in 1908, Pinchot organized the White House Conference on the Conservation of Natural Resources, then served as chairman of the subsequent National Conservation Commission, which inventoried the country's natural resources.

Pinchot's fortunes, however, began to reverse when Taft succeeded Roosevelt at the White House. Losing his favored position as a close presidential advisor, Pinchot faced hostility from Richard A. Ballinger, the Secretary of the Interior and a close associate of Taft, who opposed many of Pinchot's conservation policies and attempted to undermine the smooth functioning of the Forest Service. In the power struggle that ensued between the two, Pinchot was dismissed from government service for publicly criticizing the president.

Begins a Career in Politics

Pinchot increasingly turned his attention to politics, prompted by the belief that public service should include a political career. He campaigned against Taft's reelection, helped found the National Progressive Republican League in 1911, and worked for Roosevelt's renomination in 1912 by the new Progressive Party. On August, 14, 1914, Pinchot married Cornelia Elizabeth Bryce, with whom he would have one son, Gifford Bryce. A suffragist and champion of women's rights, Cornelia took on an important role as Pinchot's closest political advisor, helping to guide her husband's career.

Pinchot was known for his strong views. During his unsuccessful run for the Senate against Pennsylvania's Boies Penrose in 1914, he favored some extreme views such as government ownership of railroads, public utilities, and the coal, copper, and lumber industries (later he softened his stand on these issues). He made an unsuccessful attempt at a senate nomination in 1920, then—the same year—became forestry commissioner of Pennsylvania under Governor William C. Sproul. Still determined to secure a political office, Pinchot was finally elected governor of Pennsylvania in 1922.

The high point of Pinchot's first term was the reform of government operations and state finances. In 1930, he was elected to a second term, but his conflicts with the public utilities prevented him from enacting any major accomplishments. He did succeed, however, in creating jobs during an era hard hit by the Great Depression. Pinchot's ambitions of a presidential or vice presidential nomination were never realized. He ran again—in vain—for a senate seat in 1932 and sought the nomination for governor in the state primary in 1938. Pinchot died of leukemia on October 4, 1946, at Columbia Presbyterian Medical Center in New York and was buried in Milford, Pennsylvania.

Through the years, Pinchot's interest in conservation did not wane. He played a key role in the passage of laws favoring conservation, such as the Weeks Act in 1911 and the Water Power Act of 1920. He became a nonresident lecturer and professor at the Yale School of Forestry, which had been established in 1900 by a grant from his family. He also founded and became president of the Society of American Foresters. His memo on forests for president Franklin D. Roosevelt resulted in the creation of the Civilian Conservation Corps, which recruited young men for reforestation projects.

In his belief that forests should be used, not just preserved, Pinchot ran into opposition from many conservationists of his day. His autobiography, *Breaking New Ground* (which was published posthumously in 1947), is "one of the central documents of the American conservation movement," according to T. H. Watkins in *American Heritage.*

SELECTED WRITINGS BY PINCHOT:

Books

A Primer of Forestry, Government Printing Office, 1899.
The Fight for Conservation, Doubleday, 1910.
The Training of a Forester, Lippincott, 1914.
Breaking New Ground, Harcourt, 1947.

FURTHER READING:

Books

Faber, Doris and Harold Faber, *Great Lives . . . Nature and the Environment,* Charles Scribner's Sons, 1991.
Fausold, Martin, L., *Gifford Pinchot: Bull Moose Progressive,* Syracuse University Press, 1961.
McGeary, M. Nelson, *Gifford Pinchot: Forester-Politician,* Princeton University Press, 1960.
Pinkett, Harold, T., *Gifford Pinchot: Private and Public Forester,* University of Illinois Press, 1970.
Squire, C. B., *Heroes of Conservation,* Fleet Press, 1974.
Wister, Owen, *Roosevelt: The Story of a Friendship, 1880–1919,* Macmillan, 1930.

Periodicals

Watkins, T. H., *American Heritage,* Father of the Forests, February/March 1991, pp. 86–98.
Wister, Owen, *Journal of Forestry,* 9 (Gifford Pinchot Commemorative Issue), Volume 63, No. 8, August, 1965.

Sketch by Kala Dwarakanath

Gregory Goodwin Pincus
1903–1967
American biologist

Gregory Goodwin Pincus's research in endocrinology resulted in pathbreaking work on hormones and animal physiology. However, he is best known for developing the oral contraceptive pill. As his friend and colleague

Hudson Hoagland remarked in *Perspectives in Biology and Medicine:* "[Pincus's] highly important development of a pill . . . to control human fertility in a world rushing on to pathological overpopulation is an example of practical humanism at its very best." In addition, Pincus also participated in the founding of the Worcester Foundation for Experimental Biology and the annual Laurentian Hormone Conference.

Pincus was born in Woodbine, New Jersey, on April 9, 1903, the eldest son of Joseph and Elizabeth Lipman Pincus. His father, a graduate of Storrs Agricultural College in Connecticut, was a teacher and the editor of a farm journal. His mother's family came from Latvia and settled in New Jersey. Pincus's uncle on his mother's side, Jacob Goodale Lipman, was dean of the New Jersey State College of Agriculture at Rutgers University, director of the New Jersey State Agricultural Experiment Station, and the founding editor of *Soil Science* magazine.

After attending a public grade school in New York City, Pincus became an honor student at Morris High School where he was president of the debating and literary societies. As an undergraduate at Cornell University, he founded and edited the *Cornell Literary Review.* After receiving his B.S. degree in 1924, he was accepted into graduate school at Harvard. He concentrated on genetics under W. E. Castle but also did work on physiology with animal physiologist W. J. Crozier. Pincus credited the two scientists with influencing him to eventually study reproductive physiology. He received both his Master of Science and Doctor of Science degrees in 1927 at the age of twenty-four. Pincus married Elizabeth Notkin on December 2, 1924, the same year he completed his undergraduate degree. They had three children—Alexis, John, and Laura Jane.

Pursues Research in Reproductive Biology

In 1927 Pincus won a three-year fellowship from the National Research Council. During this time, he travelled to Cambridge University in England where he worked with F. H. A. Marshall and John Hammond, who were pioneers in reproductive biology. He also studied at the Kaiser Wilhelm Institute with the geneticist **Richard Goldschmidt**. He returned to Harvard in 1930, first as an instructor in biology and then as assistant professor.

Much of the research Pincus did during the early part of his career concentrated on the inheritance of physiological traits. Later research focused on reproductive physiology, particularly sex hormones and gonadotrophic hormones (those which stimulate the reproductive glands). Other research interests included geotropism, the inheritance of diabetes, relationships between hormones and stress, and endocrine function in patients with mental disorders. He also contributed to the development of the first successful extensive partial pancreatectomy in rats.

The development of the oral contraceptive pill began in the early 1930s with Pincus's work on ovarian hormones. He published many studies of living ova (eggs) and their fertilization. While still at Harvard he perfected some of the earliest methods of transplanting animal eggs from one female to another who would carry them to term. He also developed techniques to produce multiple ovulation in laboratory animals. As a consequence of this work, he learned that some phases of development of an animal's ovum were regulated by particular ovarian hormones. Next, he analyzed the effects of ovarian hormones on the function of the uterus, the travel of the egg, and the maintenance of the blastocyst (the first embryonic stage) and later the embryo itself. By 1939 he had published the results of his research on breeding rabbits without males by artificially activating the eggs in the females. This manipulation was called "Pincogenesis," and it was widely reported in the press, but it was not able to be widely replicated by other researchers.

After returning from a year at Cambridge University in 1938, Pincus became a visiting professor of experimental zoology at Clark University in Worcester, Massachusetts, where he stayed until 1945. It was at Clark that Pincus began to work with Hoagland, though they had known each other as graduate students. Together they began to research the relationship between stress and hormones for the United States Navy and Air Force. Specifically, they examined the relationship between steroid excretion, adrenal cortex function, and the stress of flying. While at Clark University, Pincus was named a Guggenheim fellow and elected to the American Academy of Arts and Sciences.

Participates in the Founding of Scientific Organizations

In the spring of 1943, the first conference on hormones sponsored by the American Association for the Advancement of Science was held near Baltimore. Since the conference was held at a private club, African American scientist **Percy Julian** was excluded. Pincus protested to the management, and Julian was eventually allowed to join the conference. Although not an organizer the first year, Pincus was involved in reshaping the conference the following year, along with biochemist Samuel Gurin and physiological chemist Robert W. Bates. They held the conference in the Laurentian mountains of Quebec, Canada, and from then on the conference was known as the Laurentian Conference, and Pincus was its permanent chairperson. In addition to his administrative duties, he edited the twenty-three volumes of *Recent Progress in Hormone Research,* a compendium of papers presented at the annual conferences.

With Hoagland, Pincus also co-founded the Worcester Foundation for Experimental Biology (WFEB) in 1944. Hoagland served as executive director of the WFEB; Pincus served as director of laboratories for twelve years and then as research director. The WFEB served as a research center on steroid hormones and provided training for young biochemists in the methods of steroid biochemistry. From 1946 to 1950 Pincus was on the faculty of Tufts Medical School in Medford, Massachusetts, and then from 1950 until his death he was research professor in biology at Boston

University Graduate School. Many of his doctoral students at these universities completed research at the WFEB.

Uses Hormone Research to Develop Oral Contraceptive

Pincus had been conducting research on sterility and hormones since the 1930s, but it was not until the 1950s that he applied his theoretical knowledge to the idea of creating a solution to the problem of overpopulation. In 1951 he was exposed to the work of Margaret Sanger, who had described the inadequacy of existing birth control methods and the looming problem of overpopulation, particularly in underdeveloped areas. By 1953, Pincus was working with Min-Chueh Chang at the WFEB, studying the effects of steroids on the fertility of laboratory animals.

Science had made it possible to produce steroid hormones in bulk, and Chang discovered a group of compounds called progestins which worked as ovulation inhibitors. Pincus took these findings to the G. D. Searle Company, where he had been a consultant, and shifted his emphasis to human beings instead of laboratory animals. Pincus also brought human reproduction specialists John Rock and Celso Garcia into the project. They conducted clinical tests of the contraceptive pill in Brookline, Massachusetts, to confirm the laboratory data. Pincus then travelled to Haiti and Puerto Rico, where he oversaw large-scale clinical field trials.

Oscar Hechter, who met Pincus in 1944 while at the WFEB, wrote in *Perspectives in Biology and Medicine* that "Gregory Pincus belongs to history because he was a man of action who showed the world that the population crisis is not an 'impossible' problem. He and his associates demonstrated that there is *a* way to control birth rates on a large scale, suitable alike for developed and underdeveloped societies. The antifertility steroids which came to be known as the 'Pill' were shown to be effective, simple, contraceptive agents, relatively safe, and eminently practical to employ on a large scale." Pincus spent much of the last fifteen years of his life travelling to explain the results of research. This is reflected in his membership in biological and endocrinological societies in Portugal, France, Great Britain, Chile, Haiti, and Mexico. His work on oral contraceptives was also recognized by awards such as the Albert D. Lasker Award in Planned Parenthood in 1960 and the Cameron Prize in Practical Therapeutics from the University of Edinburgh in 1966. He was elected to the National Academy of Sciences in 1965.

Pincus died before the issue of *Perspectives in Biology and Medicine* commemorating his sixty-fifth birthday was published. Although ill for the last three years of his life, he had continued to work and travel. He died in Boston on August 22, 1967, of myeloid metaplasia, a bone-marrow disease which some speculate was caused by his work with organic solvents.

SELECTED WRITINGS BY PINCUS:

Books

The Eggs of Mammals, Macmillan, 1936.
The Control of Fertility, New York Academic Press,
    1965.

Periodicals

American Journal of Physiology, On the Interaction of
    Oestrin and the Ovary-Stimulating Principles of Ex-
    tracts of the Urine of Pregnancy, Volume 102,
    1932, pp. 241–248.
Journal of the American Medical Association, The In-
    heritance of Diabetes, Volume 103, 1934, pp.
    105–106.
Journal of Aviation Medicine, Steroid Excretion and the
    Stress of Flying, Volume 14, 1943, pp. 173–193.
Advances in Chemistry Series, Chemical Control of
    Fertility, Volume 44, 1964, pp. 177–189.

FURTHER READING:

Books

Dictionary of Scientific Biography, Volume 10, Scrib-
    ner, 1970, pp. 610–611.
Ingle, Dwight J., *Biographical Memoirs,* Gregory Good-
    win Pincus, Volume 42, Columbia University Press,
    1971, pp. 228–270.

Periodicals

Hechter, Oscar, *Perspectives in Biology and Medicine,*
    Homage to Gregory Pincus, spring, 1968, pp.
    358–370.
Hoagland, Hudson, *Perspectives in Biology and Medi-
    cine,* Creativity—Genetic and Psychosocial, spring,
    1968, pp. 339–349.

Sketch by Marianne P. Fedunkiw

Max Planck

Max Planck
1858–1947
German physicist

Max Planck is best known as one of the founders of
the quantum theory of physics. As a result of his
research on heat radiation he was led to conclude that
energy can sometimes be described as consisting of discrete
units, later given the name *quanta.* This discovery was
important because it made possible, for the first time, the
use of matter-related concepts in an analysis of phenomena
involving energy. Planck also made important contributions
in the fields of thermodynamics, relativity, and the philosophy of science. He was awarded the 1918 Nobel Prize in
physics for his discovery of the quantum effect.

Max Karl Ernst Ludwig Planck was born on April 23,
1858, in Kiel, Germany. His parents were Johann Julius
Wilhelm von Planck, originally of Göttingen, and Emma
Patzig, of Griefswald. Johann had previously been married
to Mathilde Voigt, of Jena, with whom he had two children.
Max was the fourth child of his father's marriage to Emma.

Johann von Planck was descended from a long line of
lawyers, clergyman, and public servants and was himself
Professor of Civil Law at the University of Kiel. Young
Max began school in Kiel, but moved at the age of nine with
his family to Münich. There he attended the Königliche
Maximillian Gymnasium until his graduation in 1874.

As a child, Planck demonstrated both talent in and
enthusiasm for a variety of fields, ranging from mathematics
and science to music. He was accomplished at both piano
and organ and gave some thought to a career in music. He
apparently abandoned that idea, however, when a professional musician told him that he did not seem to have the
commitment needed for that field. Planck did, however,
maintain a life-long interest in music and its mathematical
foundations. Later in life, he held private concerts in his
home which featured eminent musicians, such as Joseph
Joachim and Maria Scherer, as well as fellow scientists,
including **Albert Einstein**, often with Planck at the piano.

Begins His Career at Münich and Berlin

Planck entered the University of Münich in 1874 with plans to major in mathematics. He soon changed his mind, however, when he realized that he was more interested in practical problems of the natural world than in the abstract concepts of pure mathematics. Although his course work at Münich emphasized the practical and experimental aspects of physics, Planck eventually found himself drawn to the investigation of theoretical problems. It was, biographer Hans Kango points out in *Dictionary of Scientific Biography,* "the only time in [his] life when he carried out experiments."

Planck's tenure at Münich was interrupted by illness in 1875. After a long period of recovery, he transferred to the University of Berlin for two semesters in 1877 and 1878. At Berlin, he studied under a number of notable physicists, including Hermann Helmholtz and Gustav Kirchhoff. By the fall of 1878, Planck was healthy enough to return to Münich and his studies. In October of that year, he passed the state examination for higher level teaching in math and physics. He taught briefly at his alma mater, the Maximillian Gymnasium, before devoting his efforts full time to preparing for his doctoral dissertation. He presented that dissertation on the second law of thermodynamics in early 1879 and was granted a Ph.D. by the University of Münich in July of that year.

Planck's earliest field of research involved thermodynamics, an area of physics dealing with heat energy. He was very much influenced by the work of Rudolf Clausius, whose work he studied by himself while in Berlin. He discussed and analyzed some of Clausius's concepts in his own doctoral dissertation. Between 1880 and 1892, Planck carried out a systematic study of thermodynamic principles, especially as they related to chemical phenomena such as osmotic pressure, boiling and freezing points of solutions, and the dissociation of gases. He brought together the papers published during this period in his first major book, *Vorlesungen über Thermodynamik,* published in 1897.

During the early part of this period, Planck held the position of Privat-Dozent at the University of Münich. In 1885, he received his first university appointment as extraordinary professor at the University of Kiel. His annual salary of 2,000 marks was enough to allow him to live comfortably and to marry a childhood sweetheart from Münich, Marie Merck. Marie was eventually to bear Planck three children.

Planck's personal life was beset with tragedy. Both of his twin daughters died while giving birth: Margarete in 1917, and Emma in 1919. His son, Karl, also met an untimely death when he was killed during World War I. Marie had predeceased all her children when she died on October 17, 1909. Planck later married Marga von Hoessli, with whom he had one son.

Nobel Prize Awarded for Discovery of the Quantum

Planck's research on thermodynamics at Kiel soon earned him recognition within the scientific field. Thus, when Kirchhoff died in 1887, Planck was considered a worthy successor to his former teacher at the University of Berlin. Planck was appointed to the position of assistant professor at Berlin in 1888 and assumed his new post the following spring. In addition to his regular appointment at the university, Planck was also chosen to head the Institute for Theoretical Physics, a facility that had been created especially for him. In 1892, Planck was promoted to the highest professorial rank, ordinary professor, a post he held until 1926.

Once installed at Berlin, Planck turned his attention to an issue that had long interested his predecessor, the problem of black body radiation. A black body is defined as any object that absorbs all frequencies of radiation when heated and then gives off all frequencies as it cools. For more than a decade, physicists had been trying to find a mathematical law that would describe the way in which a black body radiates heat.

The problem was unusually challenging because black bodies do not give off heat in the way that scientists had predicted that they would. Among the many theories that had been proposed to explain this inconsistency was one by the German physicist **Wilhelm Wien** and one by the English physicist John Rayleigh. Wien's explanation worked reasonably well for high frequency black body radiation, and Rayleigh's appeared to be satisfactory for low frequency radiation. But no one theory was able to describe black body radiation across the whole spectrum of frequencies. Planck began working on the problem of black body radiation in 1896 and by 1900 had found a solution to the problem. That solution depended on a revolutionary assumption, namely that the energy radiated by a black body is carried away in discrete "packages" that were later given the name *quanta* (from the Latin, *quantum,* for "how much"). The concept was revolutionary because physicists had long believed that energy is always transmitted in some continuous form, such as a wave. The wave, like a line in geometry, was thought to be infinitely divisible.

Planck's suggestion was that the heat energy radiated by a black body be thought of as a stream of "energy bundles," the magnitude of which is a function of the wavelength of the radiation. His mathematical expression of that concept is relatively simple: $E = h\upsilon$, where E is the energy of the quantum, υ is the wavelength of the radiation, and h is a constant of proportionality, now known as *Planck's constant.* Planck found that by making this assumption about the nature of radiated energy, he could accurately describe the experimentally observed relationship between wavelength and energy radiated from a black body. The problem had been solved.

The numerical value of Planck's constant, h, can be expressed as 6.62×10^{-27} erg second, an expression that is engraved on Planck's headstone in his final resting place at the Stadtfriedhof Cemetery in Göttingen. Today, Planck's constant is considered to be a fundamental constant of nature, much like the speed of light and the gravitational constant. Although Planck was himself a modest man, he recognized the significance of his discovery. Robert L. Weber in *Pioneers of Science: Nobel Prize Winners in Physics* writes that Planck remarked to his son Erwin during a walk shortly after the discovery of the quantum concept, "Today I have made a discovery which is as important as Newton's discovery." That boast has surely been confirmed. The science of physics today can be subdivided into two great eras, classical physics, involving concepts worked out before Planck's discovery of the quantum, and modern physics, ideas that have been developed since 1900, often as a result of that discovery. In recognition of this accomplishment, Planck was awarded the 1918 Nobel Prize in physics.

Research on Relativity and Philosophical Speculations

After completing his study of black body radiation, Planck turned his attention to another new and important field of physics: relativity. Albert Einstein's famous paper on the theory of general relativity, published in 1905, stimulated Planck to look for ways on incorporating his quantum concept into the new concepts proposed by Einstein. He was somewhat successful, especially in extending Einstein's arguments from the field of electromagnetism to that of mechanics. Planck's work in this respect is somewhat ironic in that it had been Einstein who, in another 1905 paper, had made the first productive use of the quantum concept in his solution of the photoelectric problem.

Throughout his life, Planck was interested in general philosophical issues that extended beyond specific research questions. As early as 1891, he had written about the importance of finding large, general themes in physics that could be used to integrate specific phenomena. His book *Philosophy of Physics,* published in 1959, addressed some of these issues. He also looked beyond science itself to ask how his own discipline might relate to philosophy, religion, and society as a whole. Some of his thoughts on the correlation of science, art, and religion are presented in his 1935 book, *Die Physik im Kampf um die Weltanschauung.*

Planck remained a devout Christian throughout his life, often attempting to integrate his scientific and religious views. Like Einstein, he was never able to accept some of the fundamental concepts of the modern physics that he had helped to create. For example, he clung to the notion of causality in physical phenomena, rejecting the principles of uncertainty proposed by Heisenberg and others. He maintained his belief in God, although his descriptions of the Deity were not anthropomorphic but more akin to natural law itself.

Tragedy Fills Final Days

By the time Planck retired from his position at Berlin in 1926, he had become probably the most highly respected scientific figure in Europe, if not the world, except for Einstein. Four years after retirement, he was invited to become president of the Kaiser Wilhelm Society in Berlin, an institution that was then renamed the Max Planck Society in his honor. Planck's own prestige allowed him to speak out against the rise of Nazism in Germany in the 1930s, but his enemies eventually managed to have him removed from his position at the Max Planck Society in 1937. The last years of his life were filled with additional personal tragedies. His son by his second marriage, Erwin, was found guilty of plotting against Hitler and executed in 1944. During an air raid on Berlin in 1945, Planck's home was destroyed with all of his books and papers. During the last two and a half years of his life, Planck lived with his grandniece in Göttingen, where he died on October 4, 1947.

SELECTED WRITINGS BY PLANCK:

Books

Vorlesungen über Thermodynamik, Leipzig, 1897.
Vorlesungen über die Theorie der Wärmestrahlung, Leipzig, 1906.
Acht Vorlesungen über Theoretische Physik, Leipzig, 1910.
Einführung in die Theoretische Physic, 5 volumes, Leipzing, 1916–30.
Die Physik im Kampf um die Weltanschauung, Leipzig, 1935.
Abhandlungen and Vorträge, 3 volumes, Brunswick, 1958.
The New Science, (Contains the works Where Is Science Going?, The Universe in the Light of Modern Physics, and The Philosophy of Physics), Meridian Books, 1959.
Scientific Autobiography and Other Papers, New York, 1968.

FURTHER READING:

Books

Hermann, A., *Max Planck,* Hamburg, 1973.
Weber, Robert L., *Pioneers of Science: Nobel Prize Winners in Physics,* American Institute of Physics, 1980, pp. 58–59.

Periodicals

Klein, M. J., *Physics Today,* Thermodynamics and Quanta in Planck's Work, November 1966, pp. 23–27.

Sketch by David E. Newton

Vera Pless
1931–
American mathematician

Vera Pless took her early interest in the pure algebra of ring theory and applied it to the combinatorics of error—correcting computer codes in the developing field of computer science. This line of inquiry cuts to the quick of a computer's weakness—faulty data transmission. As one of the first lay people to recognize this challenge, Pless naturally became a leader in what is now being called discrete mathematics. As projects with computers demand more fidelity (as in compact discs) and greater scale (as with the Sojourner Mars mission), coding theory becomes more central to all technologies.

Vera Pless was born Vera Stepen in Chicago on March 5, 1931. Her parents were Russian immigrants who settled in the predominantly Jewish west side of the city. A friend of the family, who was a graduate student at the University of Chicago, taught Pless calculus when she was 12 years old. He saw a bright kid with a future in math, but may not have realized that she would not welcome a scholarship to the College at the University of Chicago. The fifteen–year–old Pless wanted to play the cello, but acceded to her father's wish that she study a practical subject.

Pless took some inspiration from the woman some call the founder of modern algebra, **Emmy Noether**. "I passed my master's exam two weeks after I got married," in 1952, she states plainly enough in her autobiographical essay. Although her husband was pursuing a Ph.D. in physics, Pless accepted a research associateship at Northwestern University to pursue her own Ph.D. They both relocated to Boston while she was completing her thesis on ring theory and defended her thesis two weeks before giving birth in 1957.

Unfortunately, at that time Boston academia did not welcome a female Ph.D. with two children and a working husband. "I heard people say outright, 'I would never hire a woman'," Pless remembers. However, the nearby Air Force Research Labs in Cambridge were very much in need of her algebraic skills. Error correcting codes were of most immediate use to the military's intelligence and security programs. Pless welcomed the chance to work as part of a group and found the workshops with Andrew Gleason of Harvard University beneficial as well. Later on, she was allowed maternity leave for her third child. Pless's work there included designing programs to compare tracks left behind in experimental bubble chambers.

After the U.S. Congress passed the Mansfield Amendment banning basic research within the defense sector of the government, Pless returned to the possibility of an academic career. It was a struggle to get back into the mode of papers and lecturing. Nonetheless, three years as a research associate at M.I.T., working on such subjects as encryption, led her in 1975 to a position at the University of Illinois, back in her hometown.

Greedy Codes

Pless has worked as a visiting professor, researcher, and scientist at The Technion in Haifa, the Argonne, and a number of American universities including M.I.T. The National Science Foundation (NSF) funded her stay at Caltech during 1985–86 with its visiting professorship for women grant, only the most recent example of NSF aid to Pless's career. There, she organized bimonthly coding seminars over the academic year. Over the years Pless has sat on several thesis committees and personally directed 15 graduate and postdoctoral students, sometimes three at once.

Such a busy schedule has not prevented Pless from figuring out new ways her students can use technology and innovative means of studying computer programs, as Laura Monroe attests. As Monroe's thesis advisor in 1995, Pless encouraged her to apply her ideas about "greedy codes" in computer science to some of the most powerful computers available, including a CRAY–C90 (UNICOS). "As an advisor," Monroe concluded, "she was always interested in her students' new ideas and enthusiastic about their progress."

The dual responsibilities of teaching and research have called for innovation on Pless's part. She started the CAMAC computer system at M.I.T. and brought it out west with her when she relocated in 1975, where she continues to extend and develop it with associate Thom Grace. The system has gained a measure of prominence because of its use in countless projects and being mentioned in over 20 publications. CAMAC I proved so popular that CAMAC II was started by another colleague, Jeff Leon, with Pless's aid.

The All–Professor Team

Pless writes, reviews, referees, and edits extensively, having held concurrent editorships in several publications during the 1980s and 1990s. Some of this is borne of necessity, as her field is still very new. With Joel Berman, she designed the first college course in discrete mathematics based on their lecture notes. Pless's *Introduction to The Theory of Error–Correcting Codes* carries the highest rating in the Mathematical Association of America's Library Recommendations for Undergraduate Mathematics. From 1993 to 1994, the U.S. Department of Education retained her for a paid position as part of their Algebra Initiative.

Pless's professional service includes advisory and elected positions with a variety of mathematics and science groups, helping to oversee projects of the National Science Foundation, the National Research Council, and to review the funding of Fulbright scholars and National Security Agency proposals. As a member of the American Mathematical Society, Pless has served on committees concerning the human rights of mathematicians, academic freedom, and employment security. She is often invited and fully funded to speak at various professional meetings, seminars, and colloquia. Not all of Pless's honors are so formal. In 1993, the *Chicago Tribune* included her in their "All–Professor Team of Academic Champions."

By the middle of 1997, Pless's list of publications on aspects of information theory and code design numbered over 100, written either singly or with such illustrious figures as John H. Conway and **John Thompson.**

SELECTED WRITINGS BY PLESS:

Books

An Introduction to The Theory of Error–Correcting Codes, 1983; revised edition 1990.
(Editor) *Handbook on Coding* (in publication).

Periodicals

"Continuous Transformation Ring of Biorthogonal Bases Spaces." *Duke Mathematics Journal* 25, MR 20, No. 2630 (1958).
"Power Moment Identities on Weight Distributions in Error Correcting Codes." *Information and Control*, MR 41, No. 6614 (1963).
"Attitudes About and of Professional Women: Now and Then," in *Career Guidance for Women Entering Engineering: Proceedings of an Engineering Foundation Conference*. Edited by Nancy Fitzroy. August 1973.

Other

"Short Autobiography of Vera Pless." *Pless Papers*. University of Illinois at Chicago, January 1997.

FURTHER READING:

Periodicals

Birman, Haimo, Landau, Srinivasan, Pless, and Taylor. "In Her Own Words: Six Mathematicians Reflect on Their Lives and Careers." *Notices of the American Mathematical Society* 38 No. 7 (1991): pp. 702–706.

Other

"F. Jessie MacWilliams." *A Survey of Coding Theory.* http://www.math.neu.edu/awm/noetherbrochure/MacWilliams80.html
"MAA Prizes Presented in Orlando." *Notices of the AMS* (April, 1996): http://e–math.ams.org/notices/199604/comm–maa.html
Monroe, Laura, email interview with Jennifer Kramer conducted July 10–18, 1997.

Sketch by Jennifer Kramer

Mark Plotkin
1955–
American ethnobotanist

One of the world's leading ethnobotanists, Mark Plotkin is an impassioned spokesman for the preservation of rain forest environments. His chosen specialty is finding the medically beneficial plant life that grows in a rain forest and cataloging its native people's medicinal uses. Since both the rain forests and their native inhabitants are threatened with annihilation, his goal is the preservation of this knowledge before it disappears. Plotkin's science is inextricably bound with such issues as conservation and the rights of indigenous peoples, and rather than shying away from such topics, he combines his research with his role of being a highly active public advocate of conservation.

Mark Plotkin was born on May 21, 1955, in New Orleans, Louisiana. One of two sons of George Plotkin, a shoe store owner, and Helene Tatar, a teacher, he attended Newman High School in New Orleans and graduated in 1973. One of his earliest formative experiences was recounted in a *Life* magazine profile which describes a very young Plotkin so enjoying his toy *Tyrannosaurus rex* that he asked his parents for a pet dinosaur, only to then learn what the word "extinct" really meant. However, growing up in New Orleans offered him the opportunity of investigating the wildlife of its fertile swamps, and often Plotkin would arrive home covered with mud and carrying a pillowcase full of rat snakes. This was the type of biological investigation Plotkin had in mind when he entered the University of Pennsylvania in 1973. Instead, he found college biology to be mostly cellular and molecular, far removed from the vivid, living reality to which he was accustomed.

Drops Out of School and Discovers a Life's Passion

After dropping out of the University of Pennsylvania in 1974, Plotkin moved to Cambridge, Massachusetts, where he talked his way into an assistant's position working with the herpetology collection at Harvard's Museum of Comparative Zoology. Since his new job allowed him to take low-tuition night courses at Harvard, he joined a class with an intriguing title, "The Botany and Chemistry of Hallucinogenic Plants," taught by ethnobotanist **Richard Evans Schultes**. In the very first class, Schultes showed a slide of three men in grass skirts and bark-cloth masks dancing under the effect of a hallucinogenic potion made from the bark of the tropical vine *Banisteriopsis*. As Plotkin recalled in a 1993 interview with *People* magazine, when Dr. Schultes described them as Yukuna Indians doing the sacred kai-yah-ree dance and added dryly that the one on the left had a Harvard degree, Plotkin was hooked. "People talk about summer jobs that led to their careers. For me it was that one slide. I knew I would become an ethnobotanist."

Mark Plotkin

Working toward that goal, Plotkin entered Harvard's extension school and received his A.B. in 1979. Following his M.A. in 1981 from Yale University's School of Forestry, he was awarded his Ph.D. from Tufts University in 1989.

During these student years, Plotkin traveled to the remote jungles of Suriname (formerly Dutch Guiana, on the north central coast of South America) and other Amazonian countries between semesters to study the natives' use of plant-based medicinals, which was the topic of his dissertation. It was also during that time that he met his wife, Liliana Madrigal, a conservationist from Costa Rica, at a rain forest conference. The couple have two daughters, Gabrielle and Ann Lauren. In 1989, Plotkin joined the Washington-based World Wildlife Fund to become its director of plant conservation, and remained there for four years. In 1993 he joined the non-profit environmental organization Conservation International as vice-president for plant conservation, and also became a research associate at Harvard's Botanical Museum the same year.

Writes Highly Successful Book and Becomes Ethnobotany Spokesman

After the 1991 publication of the scholarly text *Sustainable Harvest and Marketing of Rain Forest Products*, Plotkin published in 1993 his very popular *Tales of a Shaman's Apprentice: An Ethnobotanist Searches for New Medicines in the Amazon Rain Forest.* Into its 14th edition by 1997, this crossover book is well on its way to accomplishing his goal of enlisting a new generation of

students into the study of ethnobotany. The success of his book made Plotkin and his unusual subject matter more visible, allowing him to more fully use his considerable talents as a speaker. In a short time, he became the premier spokesman for the preservation of rain forest environments as well as of the native cultures that used to flourish there. Described by Conservation International colleague Russell A. Mittermeier as "the single best speaker in the conservation business," and "the one who put plant conservation on the map," Plotkin has been hammering his dual theme and achieving results. The notion that native knowledge as well as the environment must be preserved is finally beginning to resonate with his audience. With each visit to the rain forest, Plotkin witnesses the devastating results of acculturation, and stresses the urgency of preserving as much knowledge of native plant use as possible since. As he told *The New York Times* in 1991, "Each time a medicine man dies, it is as if a library has burned down." It is phrases like that, and the lasting effect they have, that underscore Plotkin's high talent for communication.

Co-Founds New Conservation Effort

In 1995, Plotkin co-founded The Ethnobiology and Conservation Team with his wife, Liliana Madrigal, and prominent Canadian environmentalist Adrian Forsyth. Plotkin is executive director of this Virginia-based organization formed to help indigenous people gain control of their environmental and cultural destinies. Plotkin also hopes to persuade drug companies to regard rain forests as he does, as libraries and store houses of future drugs and medicines. It is in this aspect of what might becalled the bioprospecting aspects of his work that he remains adamant about the rights of indigenous peoples. Sensitive to the steady exploitation of these people, Plotkin was able to encourage a partnership between Suriname natives and a major pharmaceutical company to screen plants for drugs that might work on such diseases as cancer and AIDS. Through his efforts and those of companies like Shaman Pharmaceuticals, a native tribe finally will receive financial compensation for its intellectual property.

Always searching for a broader and larger audience, Plotkin has written a children's book, *The Shaman's Apprentice*, with Lynne Cherry, and will publish *Healer's Quest: New Medicines From Mother Nature* in 1999. In late 1997, the IMAX film *Amazon* opened in Los Angeles and Stockholm. Directed by award-winning Keith Merrill, this film depicts the search for new medicines from Amazonian plants. In only the first decade of his professional career, Mark Plotkin has achieved a great deal in a highly impressive manner, attesting to the effectiveness of combining science with integrity and passion.

SELECTED WRITINGS BY PLOTKIN:

Books

(With Lisa Famolare) *Sustainable Harvest and Marketing of Rain Forest Products.* Washington, DC: Island Press, 1991.

Tales of a Shaman's Apprentice: An Ethnobotanist Searches for New Medicines in the Amazon Rain Forest. New York: Viking, 1993.

(With Lynne Cherry) *The Shaman's Apprentice: A Tale of the Amazon Rain Forest.* San Diego, CA: Harcourt Brace & Co., 1998.

FURTHER READING:

Books

Collins, Louise Mooney. *Newsmakers: The People Behind Today's Headlines.* Detroit: Gale Research Inc., 1994, pp.96-97.

Katz, Linda Sobel, Sarah Orrick, and Robert Honig. *Environmental Profiles: A Global Guide to Projects and People.* New York: Garland Publishing, Inc., 1993, pp. 648-649.

Periodicals

Allen, Karen. "Mark Plotkin: Conservation Medalist." *ZooNooz*, The Zoological Society of San Diego (January 1995).

Jackson, Donald Dale. "Searching for Medicinal Wealth in Amazonia." *Smithsonian* (February 1989): 94-103.

Reed, Susan. "Sorcerers' Apprentice." *People* (December 6, 1993): 143-146.

Sketch by Leonard C. Bruno

William Reid Pogue
1930–
American pilot and astronaut

William Reid Pogue achieved prominence as the pilot of the third and final Skylab mission, launched November 16, 1973. By the time they had returned to Earth on February 8, 1974, Pogue and his crew had set a record of eighty-four days in space, the longest spaceflight ever. This record stood until 1978, when it was broken by Soviet cosmonauts Yuri Romanenko and Georgi Grechko on space station Salyut 6.

Pogue was born in Okemah, Oklahoma, on January 23, 1930 to Alex W. and Margaret McDow Pogue. His early education took place at Oklahoma Baptist University, where he earned a Bachelor of Science degree in education in 1951. That same year he enlisted in the Air Force, finishing his B.S. and receiving a commission as a second lieutenant in 1952. In 1953 Pogue logged forty-three combat missions while serving with the Fifth Air Force in Korea. The next year, after returning to the United States, Pogue served as a gunnery instructor at Luke Air Force Base near Phoenix, Arizona. His experience as a combat fighter pilot and his exemplary service won him a place on the Air Force's air acrobatic team, the Thunderbirds.

Pogue returned to school in 1960 to earn his master's degree in mathematics at Oklahoma State University, after which he taught as an assistant professor of math at the Air Force Academy until 1963. Pogue then became an exchange test pilot with the British Royal Aircraft Establishment in Farnborough, England, graduating from the Empire Test Pilots' School in 1966. He also served for a year as an instructor at the USAF Aerospace Research Pilots School at Edwards Air Force Base, California.

Joins NASA

Probably the most interesting part of Pogue's career came with his assignment in 1966 as one of nineteen astronauts with NASA's Manned Spacecraft Center in Houston, Texas, for it was there that Pogue became the pilot for the final Skylab mission. This mission was in some respects unique: Pogue related how he and his crew felt the need for more time to reflect and contemplate on the human aspects of their mission than had previous Skylab crews. While still in space, Pogue explained to a *Science News* interviewer: "I think [the flight has] had a really great impact on me. I feel much more inclined toward humanistic feeling toward other people, other crewmen. . . . I think that I see myself in a much more realistic fashion, and when I see other people, I try to see them as operating human entities and to put myself into the human situation, instead of trying to operate like a machine."

While in space, Pogue was called upon to make a number of repairs to Skylab's equipment, including a potentially mission-ending coolant line leak, a malfunctioning radar antenna, and a misaligned x-ray telescope. Most of these repairs were made from the outside of the spacecraft, forcing Pogue to don a spacesuit and "spacewalk" for a then-record seven straight hours. For successfully enacting these repairs, Pogue was awarded 1974's General Thomas D. White USAF Space Trophy.

According to Henry S. F. Cooper, Jr., who wrote about the third Skylab mission in his *House in Space*, Pogue was "the earthiest of all the astronauts." When asked back on Earth why the final crew of Skylab complained so much more than previous crews, Pogue replied: "The purpose of these debriefings was to be hypercritical!" "If you try to be nice," he continued, "it's a crummy debriefing." For all their complaining, however, the third and longest Skylab mission was regarded by many as having revealed more data about living in prolonged periods of weightlessness than had any prior mission.

After taking an extended leave from NASA and the Air Force, Pogue toured the lecture circuit; this tour resulted in the book *How Do You Go to the Bathroom in Space?*, which sought to answer the types of questions most asked by audiences at his lectures. He retired from the Air Force as a full colonel in 1975, and now serves as a private consultant to aerospace and energy firms. He and his wife, Jean Ann Pogue, have three children: William Richard, Layna Sue, and Thomas Reid. In his leisure hours, Pogue enjoys running and playing handball, gardening, and biblical history. Pogue's many awards include an honorary Doctor of Science degree from Oklahoma Baptist University in 1974, the Air Medal with an oak leaf cluster, and the Robert H. Goddard Medal from the National Space Club. In view of Pogue's accomplishments and his Choctaw descent, he also won a place in the Five Civilized Tribes Hall of Fame.

SELECTED WRITINGS BY POGUE:

Books

How Do You Go to the Bathroom in Space?, Tom Doherty Associates, 1985.

FURTHER READING:

Books

Cooper, Henry S. F., Jr., *A House in Space,* Holt, 1976.

Periodicals

Cooper, Henry S. F., Jr., *Science Digest,* What It's Really Like up There, March, 1985, p. 20.

Other

Cooper, Henry S. F., Jr., *Grolier's Academic American Encyclopedia,* (online service), Grolier Electronic Publishing, 1993.

Cooper, Henry S. F., Jr., *Grolier's Academic American Encyclopedia,* Interview with Alumni Office, Oklahoma Baptist University, February 28, 1994.

Cooper, Henry S. F., Jr., *Grolier's Academic American Encyclopedia,* NASA Historical Archives, Biographical Data on William Reid Pogue.

Cooper, Henry S. F., Jr., *Grolier's Academic American Encyclopedia,* NASA News Release, September 12, 1975.

Sketch by Karl Preuss

Jules Henri Poincaré
1854–1912
French mathematician

Jules Henri Poincaré has been described as the last great universalist—"the last man," E. T. Bell wrote in *Men of Mathematics,* "to take practically all mathematics, pure and applied, as his province." He made contributions to number theory, theory of functions, differential equations, topology, and the foundations of mathematics. In addition, Poincaré was very much interested in astronomy, and some of his best known research is his work on the three-body problem, which concerns the way planets act on each other in space. He worked in the area of mathematical physics and anticipated some fundamental ideas in the theory of relativity. He also participated in the debate about the nature of mathematical thought, and he wrote popular books on the general principles of his field.

Poincaré was born in Nancy, France, on April 29, 1854. The Poincaré family had made Nancy their home for many generations, and they included a number of illustrious scholars. His father was Léon Poincaré, a physician and professor of medicine at the University of Nancy. Poincaré's cousin Raymond Poincaré was later to serve as prime minister of France and as president of the republic during World War I. Poincaré was a frail child with poor coordination; his larynx was temporarily paralyzed when he was five, as a result of a bout of diphtheria. He was also very bright as a child, not necessarily an advantage in dealing with one's peers. All in all he was, according to James Newman in the *World of Mathematics,* "a suitable victim of the brutalities of children his own age."

Poincaré received his early education at home from his mother and then entered the lycée in Nancy. There he began to demonstrate his remarkable mathematical talent and earned a first prize in a national student competition. In 1873, he was admitted to the École Polytechnique, although he scored a zero on the drawing section of the entrance examination. His work was so clearly superior in every other respect that examiners were willing to forgive his perennial inability to produce legible diagrams. He continued to impress his teachers at the École, and he is reputed to have passed all his math courses without reading the textbooks or taking notes in his classes.

After completing his work at the École, Poincaré went on to the École des Mines with the intention of becoming an engineer. He continued his theoretical work in mathematics, however, and three years later he submitted a doctoral thesis. He was awarded his doctorate in 1879 and was then appointed to the faculty at the University of Caen. Two years later, he was offered a post as lecturer in mathematical analysis at the University of Paris, and in 1886 he was promoted to full professor, a post he would hold until his death in 1912.

Jules Henri Poincaré

Discovers Automorphic Functions

One of Poincaré's earliest works dealt with a set of functions to which he gave the name Fuchsian functions, in honor of the German mathematician Lazarus Fuchs. The functions are more commonly known today as automorphic functions, or functions involving sets that correspond to themselves. In this work Poincaré demonstrated that the phenomenon of periodicity, or recurrence, is only a special case of a more general property; in this property, a particular function is restored when its variable is replaced by a number of transformations of itself. As a result of this work in automorphic functions, Poincaré was elected to the French Academy of Sciences in 1887 at the age of thirty-two.

For all his natural brilliance and formal training, Poincaré was apparently ignorant of much of the literature on mathematics. One consequence of this fact was that each new subject Poincaré heard about drove his interests in yet another new direction. When he learned about the work of Georg Bernhard Riemann and Karl Weierstrass on Abelian functions, for example, he threw himself into that work and stayed with the subject until his death.

Two other fields of mathematics to which Poincaré contributed were topology and probability. With topology, or the geometry of functions, he was working with a subject which had only been treated in bare outlines, and from this he constructed the foundations of modern algebraic topology. In the case of probability, Poincaré not only contributed to the mathematical development of the subject, but he also

wrote popular essays about probability which were widely read by the general public. Indeed, he was elected to membership in the literary section of the French Institut in 1908 for the literary quality of these essays.

Contributes to Three-Body Problem

In the field of celestial mechanics, Poincaré was especially concerned with two problems, the shape of rotating bodies (such as stars) and the three-body problem. In the first of these, Poincaré was able to show that a rotating fluid goes through a series of stages, first taking a spheroidal and then an ellipsoidal shape, before assuming a pear-like form that eventually develops a bulge in it and finally breaks apart into two pieces. The three-body problem involves an analysis of the way in which three bodies, such as three planets, act on each other. The problem is very difficult, but Poincaré made some useful inroads into its solution and also developed methods for the later resolution of the problem. In 1889, his work on this problem won a competition sponsored by King Oscar II of Sweden.

The work Poincaré did in celestial mechanics was part of his interest in the application of mathematics to physical phenomena; his title at the University of Paris was actually professor of mathematical physics. Of the roughly 500 papers Poincaré wrote, about seventy deal with topics such as light, electricity, capillarity, thermodynamics, heat, elasticity, and telegraphy. He also made contributions to the development of relativity theory. As early as 1899 he suggested that absolute motion did not exist. A year later he also proposed the concept that nothing could travel faster than the speed of light. These two propositions are, of course, important parts of **Albert Einstein**'s theory of special relativity, first announced in 1905.

As he grew older, Poincaré devoted more attention to fundamental questions about the nature of mathematics. He wrote a number of papers criticizing the logical and rational philosophies of **Bertrand Russell**, **David Hilbert**, and **Giuseppe Peano**, and to some extent his work presaged some of the intuitionist arguments of **L. E. J. Brouwer**. As E. T. Bell wrote: "Poincaré was a vigorous opponent of the theory that all mathematics can be rewritten in terms of the most elementary notions of classical logic; something more than logic, he believed, makes mathematics what it is."

Poincaré died on July 17, 1912, of complications arising from prostate surgery. He was fifty-eight years old. During his lifetime he had received many of the honors then available to a scientist, including election to the Royal Society as a foreign member in 1894. Poincaré was married to Jeanne Louise Marie Poulain D'Andecy, with whom he had four children, one son and three daughters.

SELECTED WRITINGS BY POINCARÉ:

Books

Electricité et Optique, G. Carré (Paris), second edition, 1901. La science et l'hypothèse, [Paris], 1906.

The Value of Science, Science Press (New York), 1907.
Science et méthode, E. Flammarion (Paris), 1908.

FURTHER READING:

Books

Bell, E. T., *Men of Mathematics,* Simon & Schuster, 1937, pp. 526–554.

Gillispie, C. C., editor, *Dictionary of Scientific Biography,* Volume 1, Scribner, 1975, pp. 51–61.

Jones, Bessie Zaban, editor, *The Golden Age of Science,* Simon & Schuster, 1966, pp. 615–637.

Newman, James R., *The World of Mathematics,* Volume 2, Simon & Schuster, 1956, pp. 1374–1379.

Williams, Trevor, editor, *A Biographical Dictionary of Scientists,* Wiley, 1974, pp. 422–423.

Sketch by David E. Newton

Hildrus A. Poindexter
1901–1987
American physician and bacteriologist

Hildrus A. Poindexter had a distinguished career as a medical school professor and a physician in the United States Army and Public Health Service. His careful scientific observations in many countries, including Africa, Asia, Europe, and South America, provided the basis for much medical research and discovery by others. In the preface to his autobiography, *My World of Reality,* Poindexter wrote: "My major interest in life is the physical world, the physical aspects of man and the effects of environment on a human life."

Hildrus Augustus Poindexter, the sixth of eleven children, was born on May 10, 1901, on a farm near Memphis, Tennessee, the son of Fred Poindexter, a tenant farmer, and Luvenia Gilberta Clarke. Poindexter worked on the farm at a very early age and later recalled that he had announced his intention of becoming a physician at about the age of five. He attended the local segregated elementary school from age seven to fifteen, which was considered normal at the time. Poindexter furthered his own education, however, by learning Latin, Greek, and algebra. In 1916, he sold the horse and chickens his parents had given him to start in farm life and went off to Swift Memorial Academy, a secondary school located in eastern Tennessee. He worked his way through school, graduated in 1920, and then enrolled at Lincoln University. He graduated with honors in 1924, the same year he married Ruth Viola Grier, with whom he had one daughter, Patchechole Barbara.

After teaching for a year in a private secondary school in Oxford, North Carolina, and working as a Pullman porter to earn additional money, Poindexter entered the two-year program of the Dartmouth College Medical School in Hanover, New Hampshire. He did well enough there to be accepted for the third-year class at Harvard University Medical School in 1927, from which he received his M.D. in 1929. It was while at Dartmouth and Harvard that he decided to specialize in tropical medicine, the study and treatment of diseases and public health problems found in tropical lands. In late 1929, he entered Columbia University to do graduate work in bacteriology and parasitology; he received his Ph.D. in microbiology and immunology in 1932. Poindexter taught bacteriology, preventive medicine, and public health at the Howard University College of Medicine in Washington, D.C., from 1931 to 1943.

It was during this period that he did much of his scientific research, though he soon found himself preoccupied with administrative duties. From 1943 to 1946 he served as a physician in the U.S. Army in the South Pacific, New Guinea, the Philippines, and later in occupied Japan. In 1947, he became a physician in the U.S. Public Health Service. He served tours of duty in Liberia, Vietnam, Surinam, Iraq, Libya, Somali, Jamaica, and Sierra Leone. In all of these assignments, he used his knowledge of tropical medicine in efforts to improve the poor health situation of the citizens of these countries. In 1977, Poindexter retired from the Public Health Service as medical director and returned to the Howard University College of Medicine as a professor of community health practice.

Poindexter's importance as a medical researcher lies in his careful scientific observations of the many tropical diseases he encountered in his foreign duty posts and the very extensive reports he wrote concerning his findings. He often suggested possible medications to eliminate or alleviate the diseases, which were sometimes based upon his own field experiments. These reports served as valuable raw data upon which other scientists and public health physicians could base their own research. Poindexter received honorary doctorates from Lincoln University, Dartmouth College, and Howard University, and also was awarded the National Civil Service League Career Award in 1963 and the U.S. Public Health Service Meritorious Award in 1965. After a heart attack, Poindexter died in a Maryland suburb of Washington, D.C., on April 21, 1987.

SELECTED WRITINGS BY POINDEXTER:

Books

My World of Reality: An Autobiography, Balamp Publishing, 1973.

Sketch by John E. Little

John C. Polanyi
1929–

Canadian chemist

John C. Polanyi, a pioneer in the field of reaction dynamics, made major contributions toward scientists' knowledge of the molecular mechanisms of chemical reactions. His work on the use of infrared chemiluminescence paved the way for the development of powerful chemical lasers. In recognition of his achievement, he was awarded the Nobel Prize in chemistry in 1986.

Polanyi was born on January 23, 1929, in Berlin, Germany, to Michael Polanyi, a chemistry professor, and Magda Elizabeth Kemeny Polanyi, both of Hungarian descent. Polanyi's family moved to Manchester, England, when he was four years old. There, his father took a position as professor of chemistry at Manchester University. Polanyi attended Manchester Grammar School as a child, and enrolled at Manchester University in 1946. That same year, his father stopped teaching chemistry and joined the university's philosophy department.

Polanyi's father had focused his research on the molecular basis of chemical reactions. Polanyi, who had taken his father's last chemistry classes, began to conduct his own chemistry research under the supervision of Ernest Warhurst, one of his father's former students. Where Warhurst, the senior Polanyi and their colleagues investigated the probability that a chemical reaction would result from a collision between molecules, the young Polanyi began to investigate the motions of the newly created reaction products.

Initially, Polanyi had been only marginally interested in science. As a student, he was more enthusiastic about politics, writing poetry, and newspaper editing. Eventually, however, he developed an interest in chemistry, especially "reaction dynamics," as the study of molecular motions in chemical reactions would eventually be called. He went on to earn a Ph.D. in chemistry in 1952, and then moved to Ottawa to conduct his postdoctoral work at Canada's National Research Council. There he attempted to determine whether the transition state theory of reaction rates, which his father had helped to develop, could predict the rates at which reactions would occur. He concluded that scientists had insufficient understanding of the forces in the transition state to accomplish this.

After two years in Ottawa, Polanyi worked for several months in the laboratory of **Gerhard Herzberg**, studying vibrational and rotational motions in molecular iodine. In 1954, he was invited by the chemist Hugh Stott Taylor to a postdoctoral fellowship at Princeton University. There, the research of Taylor's colleagues, Michael Boudart and David Garvin, impressed Polanyi. In their study of the vibrations produced when atomic hydrogen chemically reacted with ozone, the reaction emitted a visible glow. From this,

Polanyi concluded that it should be possible to determine the vibrational and rotational excitation in newly formed reaction products from the wavelengths of the infrared radiation arising from chemical reactions.

In 1956, Polanyi returned to Canada to take a position as lecturer in the chemistry department at the University of Toronto. He advanced to assistant professor in 1957, and to full professor in 1974. At the University of Toronto, Polanyi and graduate student Kenneth Cashion conducted experiments on the reaction of atomic hydrogen and molecular chlorine. The reaction emitted a faint infrared light "chemiluminescence." The study was significant because it suggested a way to obtain quantitative information, for the first time, concerning the vibrational and rotational energy released in chemical reactions. Polanyi's subsequent report, "An Infrared Maser Dependent on Vibrational Excitation," followed up on **Arthur L. Schawlow**'s and **Charles Townes**'s 1958 proposal that light could be amplified by passing it through a medium containing highly excited atoms and molecules, a proposal that led to the development of the laser (*l*ight *a*mplification by *s*timulated *e*mission of *r*adiation). Polanyi realized that products of the hydrogen-chlorine reaction—and similar chemical reactions—would provide a medium suitable for a laser—a chemical laser. His report, published in the *Journal of Chemical Physics* in September 1960, after its initial rejection by *Physical Review Letters,* paved the way for the University of California, Berkeley's George Pimentel to develop the chemical laser, one of the most powerful lasers that exist.

Awarded Nobel Prize for Chemistry

In 1986, Polanyi and two other scientists, **Dudley R. Herschbach** and **Yuan T. Lee**, shared the Nobel Prize in chemistry for their contributions to "the development of a new field of research in chemistry—reaction dynamics." Polanyi was cited for his work on "the method of infrared chemiluminescence, in which the extremely weak infrared emission from a newly formed molecule is measured and analyzed." He was also recognized for his use of "this method to elucidate the detailed energy disposal during chemical reactions."

Speaks Out on Arms Control Issues

Polanyi's interests extended far beyond the laboratory. Beginning in the late 1950s, he became active in the arms control debate. In an article he'd written for the *Bulletin of the Atomic Scientists* after attending an arms control meeting in Moscow, he was struck by the "symmetry of fears" between the Soviets and Western powers that prompted the arms buildup as a precaution against surprise attacks. His concern as a scientist over "the mounting spiral of precaution, fear, increased precaution, increasing fear" led him to become the founding chairman of the Canadian Pugwash Group. He was also an active member of the American National Academy of Sciences' Committee on International Security Studies and the Canadian Center for

Arms Control and Disarmament. In addition, he has given many lectures on the subject of arms control and has written approximately sixty articles on this topic.

Polanyi's contributions have been officially recognized by various quarters. His many honors and awards, in addition to the Nobel Prize, include the Marlow Medal of the Faraday Society, the Steacie Prize for the Natural Sciences, the Centennial Medal of the Chemical Society, the Remsen Award, and the Royal Medal of the Royal Society of London. He has been awarded more than two dozen honorary degrees from universities in Canada and the United States, including Harvard University and Rensselaer Polytechnic Institute. In recognition of his accomplishments, the Canadian government appointed him an officer and, later, a companion of the Order of Canada and a member of the Privy Council. A fellow of the Royal Society of Canada and the Royal Society of London, he is a foreign member of the American Academy of Arts and Sciences, the American National Academy of Sciences, and belongs to the Pontifical Academy of Rome.

Polanyi married musician Anne Ferrar Davidson in 1958. The couple has two children. Although Polanyi is more knowledgeable about art, literature and poetry than music, he and his wife have collaborated in writing professionally performed skits, for which she wrote the music and he wrote the words. For relaxation, he enjoys skiing and walking; he no longer engages in the white water canoeing and aerobatics he enjoyed when he was younger.

SELECTED WRITINGS BY POLANYI:

Periodicals

Journal of Chemical Physics, An Infrared Maser Dependent on Vibrational Excitation, September, 1960.
Bulletin of the Atomic Scientists, Armaments Policies for the Sixties, December, 1961, p. 403.

FURTHER READING:

Books

Wasson, Tyler, editor, *Nobel Prize Winners,* H.W. Wilson Company, 1987, pp. 824–26.

Periodicals

Wasson, Tyler, editor, *Science,* The 1986 Nobel Prize in Chemistry, November 7, 1986, p. 673.
Wasson, Tyler, editor, *Time,* October 27, 1986, p. 67.

Sketch by Donna Olshansky

Pelageya Yakovlevna Polubarinova-Kochina
1899–
Russian mathematician and hydrologist

In a remarkable career that spanned over seventy years, Pelageya Yakovlevna Polubarinova-Kochina played a major role in the worldwide development of the theory of hydrodynamics. "Kochina's research activity is characterized by a deep and well-organized link with practice, a subtle attention to the physical essence of the phenomena being considered, an exact mathematical formulation of the relevant physical problems, and by a brilliant mastery of the mathematical apparatus," once wrote the respected mathematician **P. S. Aleksandrov**, in an article later printed in the *Association for Women in Mathematics Newsletter.*

Kochina was born in the Russian city of Astrakhan on May 13, 1899. Her mother was Anisiya Panteleimonovna, and her father, an accountant named Yakov Stepanovich Polubarinov. Kochina had an older brother and a younger sister and brother. During her school years, Polubarinov moved the family to St. Petersburg to get the best possible education for his children. After Kochina graduated from the Pokrovskii Women's Gymnasium in 1916, she began taking courses in the Bestudzevskii women's program, which was incorporated into the University of Petrograd following the October Revolution of 1917.

After her father died in 1918, Kochina began working at the main physics laboratory to support her mother and younger siblings while also pursuing her education. Her sister, however, contracted tuberculosis and died; and though Kochina also developed the disease, she managed to graduate in 1921 with a degree in pure mathematics from Petrograd University. She continued to work in the main physics laboratory (now known as the geophysics laboratory) in the division of theoretical meteorology under the direction of A. A. Fridman, whose interest in hydrodynamics greatly influenced Kochina's later work.

Russia's experience in World War I had exposed the country's deficiencies in industrial capacity, and the new Soviet government expanded research efforts in order to apply mathematics to technological and industrial problems. Kochina excelled in this endeavor, as did Nikolai Evgrafovich Kochin, a colleague who attended night classes at Petrograd University. The two young people shared more than a professional interest; after three years of working together, they married in 1925. The couple embraced their country's post-revolutionary attitudes completely, and their wedding was a simple affair at a Leningrad office, followed by tea at a restaurant for their witnesses.

Begins Research on Filteration and Hydrodynamics

Although Kochina remained professionally active, she quit her job at the laboratory to raise her daughters, Ira and Nina. During these years, she taught at a worker's high school and at the Institute of Transportation and the Institute of Civil Aviation. She also served as a deputy in the Leningrad city soviet (legislature). In 1934 Kochina was appointed a professor at Leningrad University. However, the following year, her husband became head of the mechanics division of the Steklov Mathematics Institute, and the family moved to Moscow. Kochina now turned her attention from teaching to research, becoming a senior researcher in Kochin's division; she also served in the Moscow soviet, eventually becoming a deputy in the Supreme Soviet of the Russian Republic. While working at the institute, Kochina began to concentrate on problems in filtration, and in 1940, after completing her dissertation on theoretical aspects of filtration, she was awarded a Ph.D. in physical and mathematical sciences. When her husband died in 1944, Kochina finished delivering his course of lectures on the theory of interrupted currents.

In addition to working at the Academy of Sciences, Kochina lectured on her research activities, teaching at the Hydrometeorological and Aircraft Building Institute and at the University of Moscow's Aviation Industry Academy. In 1946 she was named a corresponding member of the Academy of Sciences and awarded the State Prize of the Soviet Union. Two years later, she became director of the Institute of Mechanics' division of hydromechanics, which focused on filtration problems. In 1958, Kochina was named an academician of the Academy of Sciences, the highest ranking in that organization, and was asked to help create a Siberian branch of that institution. The following year, at age sixty, she left Moscow for a decade of work in Siberia. During this time she was a department director at the Hydrodynamics Institute as well as head of the department of theoretical mechanics at the University of Novosibirsk. She returned to Moscow in 1970 to direct the section for mathematical methods of mechanics at the Academy of Sciences' Institute for Problems in Mechanics.

Although Kochina's training was in pure mathematics, her professional life was dedicated to finding solutions for practical problems in hydrodynamics. In 1952, relatively early in her career, she wrote *Theory of Ground Water Movement;* J. M. Roger De Wiest's English translation of that work notes that "In this book, reference is made to over thirty of her original and significant contributions on the hydromechanics of porous media (groundwater and oil flow)." One of Kochina's major accomplishments was the development of a general method for solving two-dimensional problems of the steady seepage of subsurface water in homogeneous subsoils. This process has important applications in the design of dam foundations. She obtained significant results in the theory of tides and free-flowing currents, and she resolved problems relating to soil drainage and salt accumulation during her work on irrigation and hydroelectric projects. Her solution to the problem of describing the location of the boundary between an oil-bearing domain and surrounding water as the oil is removed by wells was a well-received innovation. Since Kochina's pioneering work, the topic has been widely researched by others.

In addition to technical topics in mathematics and hydrology, Kochina was also fascinated with the history of mathematics and mechanics. She wrote the first extensive studies of mathematician Sofia Kovalevskaia's life and work, published descriptions of the scientific legacy of Karl Weierstrass and A. A. Fridman, and wrote two biographies of her husband, one during the Stalin era and one in the post-Stalinist period beginning in 1970. On her seventieth birthday, Kochina was named a Hero of Socialist Labor. She has actively participated in women's movements for peace, and on her eightieth birthday she was awarded the order of the Friendship of Nations.

SELECTED WRITINGS BY POLUBARINOVA-KOCHINA:

Books

Theory of Ground Water Movement, translated by J. M. De Wiest, Princeton University Press, 1962.

FURTHER READING:

Books

Grinstein, Louise S., and Paul J. Campbell, editors, *Women of Mathematics,* Greenwood Press, 1987, pp. 95–102.

Periodicals

Aleksandrov, P. S., G. I. Barenblum, A. I. Ishlinskii, and O. A. Oleinik, *Association for Women in Mathematics Newsletter,* Pelageya Yakovlevna Kochina: On Her 80th Birthday, January-February, 1982, pp. 9–12.

Sketch by Loretta Hall

George Pólya
1887–1985
Hungarian-born American mathematician

The career of George Pólya was distinguished by the discovery of mathematical solutions to a number of problems originating in the physical sciences. He made contributions to probability theory, number theory, the theory of functions, and the calculus of variations. He also cared about the art of teaching mathematics; he worked with educators, advocating the importance of problem solving, for which the United States gave him a distinguished service award. Pólya continued to do innovative research well into his nineties, but he is probably best known for his book on methods of problem solving, called *How to Solve It,* which has been translated into many languages and has sold more than one million copies.

Pólya was born in Budapest, Austria-Hungary (now Hungary), on December 13, 1887, the son of Jakob and Anna Deutsch Pólya. As a boy, he preferred geography, Latin, and Hungarian to mathematics. He liked the verse of German poet Heinrich Heine and translated some into Hungarian. His mother urged him to become a lawyer like his father, and he began to study law at the University of Budapest, but soon turned to languages and literature. He earned teaching certificates in Latin, Hungarian, mathematics, physics, and philosophy, and for a year he was a practice teacher in a high school. Though physics and philosophy interested Pólya, he decided to study mathematics on the advice of a philosophy professor. In an interview published in *Mathematical People: Profiles and Interviews,* Pólya explained how he chose a career in mathematics: "I came to mathematics indirectly. . . . It is a little shortened but not quite wrong to say: I thought I am not good enough for physics and I am too good for philosophy. Mathematics is in between."

Pólya received his doctorate in mathematics from the University of Budapest in 1912 at the age of twenty-four with a dissertation on the calculus of probability. Traveling to Germany and France, he was influenced by the work of eminent mathematicians at the University of Göttingen and the University of Paris. In 1914, he took his first teaching position, at the Eidgenössische Technische Hochschule in Zurich, Switzerland; he taught there for twenty-six years, becoming a full professor in 1928.

During World War I, Pólya was initially rejected by the Hungarian Army because of an old soccer injury. When the need for soldiers increased later in the war, however, he was asked to report for military service, but by this time he had been influenced by the pacifist views of British mathematician and philosopher **Bertrand Russell** and refused to serve. As a result, Pólya was unable to return to Hungary for several years, and he became a Swiss citizen. He married Stella Vera Weber, the daughter of a physics professor, in 1918.

Pólya proved an important theorem in probability theory in a paper published in 1921, using the term "random walk" for the first time. Many years later, a display demonstrating the concept of a random walk was featured in the IBM pavilion at the 1964 World's Fair in New York; it recognized the work of Pólya and other distinguished scholars. Pólya's work with Gabor Szegö, also a Hungarian, resulted in *Problems and Theorems in Analysis,* published in 1925. The problems in the book were grouped not according to the topic but according to the methods that could be used to solve them. Pólya and Szegö continued to work together and they published another book, *Isoperimetric Inequalities in Mathematical Physics,* in 1951.

Pólya was awarded the first international Rockefeller Grant in 1924 and spent a year in England at Oxford and Cambridge, where he worked with English mathematician **Godfrey Harold Hardy** on *Inequalities,* which was published in 1934. During the 1930s, Pólya frequently visited Paris to collaborate on papers with Gaston Julia. He received another Rockefeller Grant in 1933, this time to visit the United States, where he worked at both Princeton and Stanford universities. In 1940, after World War II had begun in Europe, Pólya left Switzerland with his wife and emigrated to the United States. He taught for two years at Brown University and for a short time at Smith College before joining Szegö at Stanford University in 1942, where he would remain until his retirement in 1953 at age sixty-six. Pólya became a U.S. citizen in 1947.

Before leaving Europe, Pólya had begun writing a book on problem solving. Observing that Americans liked "how-to" books, Hardy suggested the title *How to Solve It.* The book, Pólya's most popular, was published in 1945; it examined discovery and invention and discussed the processes of creation and analysis. Although he officially retired in 1953, Pólya continued to write and teach. Another book on heuristic principles for problem solving, at a more advanced level of mathematics, was published in 1954, entitled *Mathematics and Plausible Reasoning.* A third book on problem solving, *Mathematical Discovery,* was published in 1962. In 1963, Pólya was the recipient of the distinguished service award from the Mathematical Association of America. The citation, as quoted in the *Los Angeles Times,* read: "He has given a new dimension to problem-solving by emphasizing the organic building up of elementary steps into a complex proof, and conversely, the decomposition of mathematical invention into smaller steps. Problem solving *a la Polya* serves not only to develop mathematical skill but also teaches constructive reasoning in general."

Pólya also became interested in the teaching of mathematics teachers, and he taught in a series of teacher institutes at Stanford University supported by the National Science Foundation, General Electric, and Shell. His film, "Let Us Teach Guessing," won the Blue Ribbon from the Educational Film Library Association in 1968. In 1978, the National Council of Teachers of Mathematics held problem-solving competitions in *The Mathematics Student;* they named the awards the Pólya Prizes.

Pólya made significant contributions in many areas, including probability, geometry, real and complex analysis, combinatorics, number theory, and mathematical physics. Perhaps one indication of the breadth of his accomplishments is the range of fields that now contain concepts bearing his name. For example, the "Pólya criterion" and the "Pólya distribution" in probability theory; and "Pólya peaks," the "Pólya representation," and the "Pólya gap theorem" in complex function theory. Pólya's writings have been praised for their clarity and elegance; his papers were called a joy to read. The Mathematical Association of America established the Pólya Prize for Expository Writing in the *College Mathematics Journal.* Pólya's papers were collected and published by MIT Press in 1984.

Pólya received honorary degrees from the University of Wisconsin at Milwaukee, the University of Alberta, the University of Waterloo, and the Swiss Federal Institute of Technology. He was a member of the American Academy of Arts and Sciences, the National Academy of Sciences of the United States, the Hungarian Academy of Sciences, the Academie Internationale de Philosophie des Sciences in Brussels, and a corresponding member of the Academie des Sciences in Paris. The Society for Industrial and Applied Mathematics named an honorary award after him, the Pólya Prize in Combinatorial Theory and Its Applications.

Among his colleagues, Pólya was known as a kind and gentle man, full of curiosity and enthusiasm. In honoring him, Frank Harary praised his depth, his versatility, and his speed and power as a mathematician. The mathematician N. G. de Bruijn wrote of Pólya in *The Pólya Picture Album: Encounters of a Mathematician:* "All his work radiates the cheerfulness of his personality. Wonderful taste, crystal clear methodology, simple means, powerful results. If I would be asked whether I could name just one mathematician who I would have liked to be myself, I have my answer ready at once: Pólya." Pólya suffered a stroke at age ninety-seven and died in Palo Alto, California, on September 7, 1985.

SELECTED WRITINGS BY PÓLYA:

Books

Problems and Theorems in Analysis, Springer-Verlag, 1925.
Inequalities, Cambridge University Press, 1934.
How to Solve It, Princeton University Press, 1945.
Isoperimetric Inequalities in Mathematical Physics, Princeton University Press, 1951.

FURTHER READING:

Books

Albers, Donald J., and G. L. Alexanderson, editors, *Mathematical People: Profiles and Interviews,* Birkhauser Boston, 1985.
Alexanderson, editor, *The Pólya Picture Album: Encounters of a Mathematician,* Birkhauser Boston, 1987.
Szegö, Gabor, editor, *Studies in Mathematical Analysis and Related Topics: Essays in Honor of George Pólya,* Stanford University Press, 1962.

Periodicals

Dembart, Lee, *Los Angeles Times,* George Pólya, 97, Dean of Mathematicians, Dies, September 8, 1985, pp. 3, 29.

Sketch by C. D. Lord

Cyril Ponnamperuma
1923–1994
Sri Lankan-born American chemist

Cyril Ponnamperuma, an eminent researcher in the field of chemical evolution, rose through several National Aeronautics and Space Administration (NASA) divisions as a research chemist to head the Laboratory of Chemical Evolution at the University of Maryland, College Park. His career focused on explorations into the origin of life and the "primordial soup" that contained the precursors of life. In this search, Ponnamperuma took advantage of discoveries in such diverse fields as molecular biology and astrophysics.

Born in Galle, Ceylon (now Sri Lanka) on October 16, 1923, Cyril Andres Ponnamperuma was educated at the University of Madras (where he received a B.A. in Philosophy, 1948), the University of London (B.Sc., 1959), and the University of California at Berkeley (Ph.D., 1962). His interest in the origin of life began to take clear shape at the Birkbeck College of the University of London, where he studied with J. D. Bernal, a well-known crystallographer. In addition to his studies, Ponnamperuma also worked in London as a research chemist and radiochemist. He became a research associate at the Lawrence Radiation Laboratory at Berkeley, where he studied with **Melvin Calvin,** a Nobel laureate and experimenter in chemical evolution.

Chemical Evolution—Searching for Life from Primordial Soup

After receiving his Ph.D. in 1962, Ponnamperuma was awarded a fellowship from the National Academy of Sciences, and he spent one year in residence at NASA's Ames Research Center in Moffet Field, California. After the end of his associate year, he was hired as a research scientist at the center and became head of the chemical evolution branch in 1965.

During these years, Ponnamperuma began to develop his ideas about chemical evolution, which he explained in an article published in *Nature.* Chemical evolution, he explained, is a logical outgrowth of centuries of studies both in chemistry and biology, culminating in the groundbreaking 1953 discovery of the structure of deoxyribonucleic acid (DNA) by **James Watson** and **Francis Crick.** Evolutionist

Cyril Ponnamperuma

Charles Darwin's studies affirming the idea of the "unity of all life" for biology could be extended, logically, to a similar notion for chemistry: protein and nucleic acid, the essential elements of biological life, were, after all, chemical.

In the same year that Watson and Crick discovered DNA, two researchers from the University of Chicago, **Stanley Lloyd Miller** and **Harold Urey,** experimented with a primordial soup concocted of the elements thought to have made up earth's early atmosphere—methane, ammonia, hydrogen, and water. They sent electrical sparks through the mixture, simulating a lightening storm, and discovered trace amounts of amino acids.

During the early 1960s, Ponnamperuma began to delve into this primordial soup and set up variations of Miller and Urey's original experiment. Having changed the proportions of the elements from the original Miller-Urey specifications slightly, Ponnamperuma and his team sent first high-energy electrons, then ultraviolet light through the mixture, attempting to recreate the original conditions of the earth before life. They succeeded in creating large amounts of adenosine triphosphate (ATP), an amino acid that fuels cells. In later experiments with the same concoction of primordial soup, the team was able to create the nucleotides that make up nucleic acid—the building blocks of DNA and ribonucleic acid (RNA).

Search for Life's Origins Extends to Space

In addition to his work in prebiotic chemistry, Ponnamperuma became active in another growing field: exo-

biology, or the study of extraterrestrial life. Supported in this effort by NASA's interest in all matters related to outer space, he was able to conduct research on the possiblity of the evolution of life on other planets. Theorizing that life evolved from the interactions of chemicals present elsewhere in the universe, he saw the research possibilities of spaceflight. He experimented with lunar soil taken by the *Apollo 12* space mission in 1969. As a NASA investigator, he also studied information sent back from Mars by the unmanned Viking, Pioneer, and Voyager probes in the 1970s. These studies suggested to Ponnamperuma, as he stated in an 1985 interview with *Spaceworld,* that "earth is the only place in the solar system where there is life."

In 1969, a meteorite fell to earth in Muchison, Australia. It was retrieved still warm, providing scientists with fresh, uncontaminated material from space for study. Ponnamperuma and other scientists examined pieces of the meteorite for its chemical make-up, discovering numerous amino acids. Most important, among those discovered were the five chemical bases that make up the nucleic acid found in living organisms. Further interesting findings provided tantalizing but puzzling clues about chemical evolution, including the observation that light reflects both to the left and to the right when beamed through a solution of the meteorite's amino acids, whereas light reflects only to the left when beamed through the amino acids of living matter on earth. "Who knows? God may be left-handed," Ponnamperuma speculated in a 1982 *New York Times* interview.

Ponnamperuma's association with NASA continued as he entered academia. In 1979, he became a professor of chemistry at the University of Maryland and director of the Laboratory of Chemical Evolution—established and supported in part by the National Science Foundation and by NASA. He continued active research and experimentation on meteorite material. In 1983, an article in the science section of the *New York Times* explained Ponnamperuma's chemical evolution theory and his findings from the Muchison meteorite experiments. He reported the creation of all five chemical bases of living matter in a single experiment that consisted of bombarding a primordial soup mixture with electricity.

Ponnamperuma's contributions to scholarship include hundreds of articles. He wrote or edited numerous books, some in collaboration with other chemists or exobiologists, including annual collections of papers delivered at the College Park Colloquium on Chemical Evolution. He edited two journals, *Molecular Evolution* (from 1970 to 1972) and *Origins of Life* (from 1973 to 1983). In addition to traditional texts in the field of chemical evolution, he also co-authored a software program entitled "Origin of Life," a simulation model intended to introduce biology students to basic concepts of chemical evolution.

Although Ponnamperuma became an American citizen in 1967, he maintained close ties to his native Sri Lanka, even becoming an official governmental science advisor. His professional life has included several international appointments. He was a visiting professor of the Indian

Atomic Energy Commission (1967); a member of the science faculty at the Sorbonne (1969); and director of the UNESCO Institute for Early Evolution in Ceylon (1970). His international work included the directorship of the Arthur C. Clarke center, founded by the science fiction writer, a Sri Lankan resident. The center has as one of its goals a Manhattan Project for food synthesis.

Ponnamperuma was a member of the Indian National Science Academy, the American Association for the Advancement of Science, the American Chemical Society, the Royal Society of Chemists, and the International Society for the Study of the Origin of Life, which awarded him the A. I. Oparin Gold Medal in 1980. In 1991, Ponnamperuma received a high French honor—he was made a Chevalier des Arts et des Lettres. Two years later, the Russian Academy of Creative Arts awarded him the first Harold Urey Prize. In October 1994, he was appointed to the Pontifical Academy of Sciences in Rome. He married Valli Pal in 1955; they had one child. Ponnamperuma died on December 20, 1994, at Washington Adventist Hospital.

SELECTED WRITINGS BY PONNAMPERUMA:

Books

The Origins of Life. Dutton, 1972.
Cosmic Evolution. Houghton, 1978.
Limits of Life. Kluwer, 1980.
Comets and the Origin of Life. Kluwer, 1981.

Periodicals

Nature (25 January 1964).

FURTHER READING:

Periodicals

Boffey, Philip. "Precursors of Life Found in Meteorite." *New York Times* (30 August 1993).
Boffey, Phillip. "E. T. May Look Like Us." *USA Today Magazine* (June, 1987).
Boffey, Phillip. "Interview: Cyril Ponnamperuma." *Space World* (February 1985).
Boffey, Phillip. "Is There a Cosmic Chemistry of Life?" *Science News* (20 September 1986).
Sullivan Walter. "Cyril Ponnamperuma, Scholar of Life's Origins, Is Dead at 71" (obituary). *New York Times* (24 December 1994): A10.

Sketch by Katherine Williams

John A. Pople
1925–
British chemist

Nobel Laureate John A. Pople was born in 1925 at Burnham-on-Sea in Somerset, U.K. Although Pople has achieved wide recognition as a chemist, his academic training was actually in mathematics. After earning his masters and doctorate degrees at Cambridge University in 1951, Pople spent additional time at Cambridge as a research fellow and a lecturer in mathematics before accepting an appointment as superintendent of the Basic Physics Division of the National Physics Laboratory in Teddington, England.

Pople moved to the United States in 1964, where he joined the faculty of Carnegie-Mellon University in Pittsburgh, Pennsylvania, as Professor of Chemical Physics. His departure from England sparked a furor among British politicians who were outraged that so many (approximately 10 percent) British scientists with doctorates were leaving the country in response to the low salaries and poor opportunities there. But Pople has since said that the main reason he left England was to take advantage of the large number of people in his field at Carnegie-Mellon. In 1986, he moved to Northwestern University, where he became Professor of Chemistry. Although Pople continued to live and work in the United States, he nevertheless retained his British citizenship.

Pople's Nobel Prize came in recognition of his development of computational methods in quantum chemistry that made possible the theoretical study of molecules, their properties and how they act together in chemical reactions. (Quantum chemists attempt to describe molecular systems based on the laws of quantum mechanics, a branch of physics formulated in the early part of the twentieth century that has been concerned with how the interactions of electrons and atomic nuclei interact and lead to the build-up of matter. Today quantum chemistry is used to obtain quantitative information about molecules and their interactions, and to understand molecular processes that cannot be explained by experiments alone.)

By the 1960s, chemists had begun to recognize the potential of computers to perform theoretical calculations. (The quantum physicist P.A.M. Dirac recognized this problem as early as 1929 when he stated that although the fundamental laws required to treat chemistry mathematically were by that time completely known, the equations that had to be solved were in fact too complex to solve.) John Pople was one the leading figures in the development of new theoretical methods for computer-based computation.

By the end of that decade, Pople had developed a computer program, known as GAUSSIAN-70, for analyzing complex molecules. Pople continued to refine this program, which acquired widespread acceptance among theoretical

John A. Pople

chemists, through the 1970s and 1980s, and into the 1990s so that it would handle increasingly complex molecules. The first version of Pople's computer program was published in 1970. Today it is used by thousands of academic and industrial chemists around the world.

In practice, the quantum chemist might use the program in the following manner. Seated in front of a computer, the investigator would start the program and input key information about the molecule of interest, for example, the molecular constituents, to the computer. The program would respond by drawing a rough picture of the molecule on the computer screen. The geometry of the molecule would then be computed to the degree of fineness desired based on quantum-chemical calculations. The program could then calculate various properties for the system, which would be used to predict how the molecule might interact with other molecules. A typical application would be to study how proteins, which consist of amino acids, behave in pharmaceuticals.

These types of calculations have also had applications to the study of interstellar matter in the universe. Although the radiation that many interstellar molecules emit can be studied in the laboratory, it is very difficult to use such data to determine the composition and appearance of these molecules. With the methods of quantum chemistry, however, chemists can perform calculations on tentative structures to obtain information about radiation characteristics that can be directly compared with experimental data obtained using a radio telescope.

Besides the 1998 Nobel Prize in Chemistry, Pole has received the following awards and professional recognitions: Fellow, Royal Society, U.K.; Fellow, American Physical Society; Fellow, American Academy of Arts and Sciences; Foreign Associate, National Academy of Sciences; Corresponding Member, Australian Academy of Science; Marlow Medal, Faraday Society; Langmuir Award; Harrison Howe Award; G. N. Lewis Award; Morley Award; Pauling Award; Award for Computers in Chemistry, American Chemical Society; U.S. Senior Scientist Award, Humboldt Foundation; Wheland Award, University of Chicago; Evans Award, Ohio State University; Oesper Award, University of Cincinnati; Davy Medal, Royal Society, U.K.; and the Wolf Prize. Pople has been a member of the editorial and advisory boards of Molecular Physics, Chemical Physics, and Computers in Chemistry.

Sketch by Randall Frost

George Porter
1920–
English chemist

Sir George Porter shared the Nobel Prize in chemistry in 1967 with his former teacher, **Ronald G. W. Norrish**, and **Manfred Eigen** for their contributions to the study of rapid chemical reactions. Porter's efforts included research on flash photolysis, which has been used widely in the fields of organic chemistry, biochemistry, and photobiology. Porter, who is praised for having an outgoing personality and being a great promotor of science education, has also contributed to the scientific education of non-specialists and children, especially through his role in helping prepare television programs in Great Britain.

Porter was born on December 6, 1920, to John Smith Porter and Alice Ann (Roebuck) Porter in Stainforth, West Yorkshire, where he received his early education at Thorne Grammar School. With the award of an Ackroyd Scholarship, he entered Leeds University in 1938 to study chemistry and received his bachelor of science degree in 1941. While at Leeds he also studied radio physics and electronics, and he drew upon this background while serving in the Royal Navy Volunteer Reserve as a radar specialist during World War II. At the end of the war, Porter entered Emmanuel College at Cambridge University to do graduate work. There he met and studied under Norrish, who had pioneered research in the area of photochemical reactions in molecules. Porter received his doctorate degree from Cambridge in 1949.

Flash Photolysis Successfully Implemented

Using very short pulses of energy that disturbed the equilibrium of molecules, Porter and Norrish developed a method to study extremely fast chemical reactions lasting for only one-billionth of a second. The technique is known as flash photolysis. First, a flash of short-wavelength light breaks a chemical that is photosensitive into reactive parts. Next, a weaker light flash illuminates the reaction zone, making it possible to measure short-lived free radicals, which are especially reactive atoms that have at least one unpaired electron. Flash photolysis made it possible to observe and measure free radicals for the first time and also to study the sequence of the processes of reactants as they are converted into products. When Porter won the Nobel Prize in 1967, he was praised, along with Norrish and Eigen, for making it possible for scientists around the world to use their techniques in a wide range of applications, opening many passageways to scientific investigation in physical chemistry. In his own work, Porter was able to apply his methods from his early work with gases to later work with solutions. He also developed a method to stabilize free radicals, which is called matrix isolation. It can trap free radicals in a structure of a supercooled liquid (a glass). Porter also made important contributions in the application of laser beams to photochemical studies for the purpose of investigating biochemical problems. Some practical applications of photochemical techniques include the production of fuel and chemical feedstocks.

In 1949, Porter became a demonstrator in chemistry at Cambridge University and an assistant director of research in the Department of Physical Chemistry in 1952. While he was at the British Rayon Research Association as assistant director of research in 1954, Porter used his method of flash photolysis to record organic free radicals with a lifetime as short as one millisecond. Also at the Rayon Association, he worked on problems of light and the fading of dye on fabric.

Porter was appointed professor of physical chemistry at Sheffield University in 1955, and in 1963 he became the head of the chemistry department and was honored as Firth Professor. During his years at Sheffield, Porter used his flash photolysis techniques to study the complex chemical interactions of oxygen with hemoglobin in animals. He also investigated the properties of chlorophyll in plants with the use of his high-speed flash techniques. He was able to improve his techniques to the degree that he could examine chemical reactions that were more than a thousand times faster than with the use of flash tubes. Porter also studied chloroplasts and the primary processes of photosynthesis.

In 1966, Porter also became Fullerian Professor of Chemistry at the Royal Institution in London and the Director of the Davy Faraday Research Laboratory. He left there to take the position of chair for the Center for Photomolecular Sciences at Imperial College in London in 1990. During his career, Porter received many other honors and awards in addition to the Nobel Prize. He was knighted in 1972, and he has been granted numerous honorary doctorate degrees and awarded prizes from British and American scientific societies, including the Robertson Prize of the American National Academy of Sciences and the Rumford Medal of the Royal Society, both in 1978.

Promotes Science among Young People

Porter has been active outside scientific circles in the promotion of science to the general public. His concern about communication between scientists and the rest of society induced him to participate as an adviser on film and television productions. He has been praised for his activities in educating young people and people in non-scientific fields about the value of science. He was an active participant during his service with the Royal Institution in a science program series for British Broadcasting Company television (BBC-TV) called *Young Scientist of the Year*. Another BBC-TV program in which he participated was called *The Laws of Disorder* and *Time Machines*. Porter has also served on many policy and institutional committees that are involved in promoting science and education in Europe, England, and America.

Porter married Stella Brooke in 1949 and they have two sons, John Brooke Porter and Christopher Porter. His outgoing personality is considered an asset in promoting scientific knowledge. He has been an active contributor to scientific journals and has also played the role of advisor to industry. Besides sailing, Porter spends some leisure time vacationing on the coast of Kent with his family.

SELECTED WRITINGS BY PORTER:

Books

Progress in Reaction Kinetics, Pergamon Press, 1961.
Chemistry for the Modern World, Barnes and Noble, 1962.

Periodicals

Nature, Chemical Reactions Produced by Very High Light Intensities, Volume 164, 1949, p. 658.
Discussions of the Faraday Society, The Application of Flash Techniques to the Study of Fast Reactions, Volume 17, 1954, pp. 40–46.

FURTHER READING:

Periodicals

New York Times, October 31, 1967.
Science, November 1967, p. 748.

Sketch by Vita Richman

Rodney Porter
1917–1985
English biochemist

R odney Porter was a biochemist who spent most of his professional life investigating the chemical structure and functioning of antibodies, a class of proteins which are also called immunoglobulins. Since 1890 scientists had known that antibodies are found in the blood serum and provide immunity to certain illnesses. However, when Porter began his research in the 1940s, little was known about their chemical structure, or how antigens (substances that cause the body to produce antibodies) interacted with them. Using the results of his own research as well as that of **Gerald M. Edelman**, Porter proposed the first satisfactory model of the immunoglobulin molecule in 1962. The model allowed the development of more detailed biochemical studies by Porter and others that led to a better understanding of the way in which antibodies worked chemically. Such understanding was key to research on the prevention and cure of a number of diseases and the solution to problems related to organ transplant rejection. For his work, Porter shared the 1972 Nobel Prize in physiology or medicine with Edelman.

Rodney Robert Porter was born October 8, 1917, in Newton-le-Willows, near Liverpool in Lancashire, England. His mother was Isobel Reese Porter and his father, Joseph L. Porter, was a railroad clerk. "I don't know why I became interested in [science]," Porter once told the *New York Times.* "It didn't run in my family." He attended Liverpool University, where he earned a B.S. in biochemistry in 1939. During World War II he served in the Royal Artillery, the Royal Engineers, and the Royal Army Service Corps, and participated in the invasions of Algeria, Sicily, and Italy. After his discharge in 1946, he resumed his biochemistry studies at Cambridge University under the direction of **Frederick Sanger**.

Investigates the Nature of Antibodies

Porter's doctoral research at Cambridge was influenced by Nobel laureate **Karl Landsteiner**'s book, *The Specificity of Serological Reactions,* which described the nature of antibodies and techniques for preparing some of them. Antibodies, at the time, were thought to be proteins that belonged to a class of blood-serum proteins called gamma globulins. From Sanger, who had succeeded in determining the chemical structure of insulin (a protein that metabolizes carbohydrates), Porter learned the techniques of protein chemistry. Sanger had also demonstrated tenacity in studying problems in protein chemistry involving amino acid sequencing that most believed impossible to solve, and he was a model for the persistence Porter would show in his later work on antibodies.

Fortunately, Porter chose rabbits to experiment on for his research. Although this was not known at the time, the antibody system is not as complex in this animal as it is in some. The most important antibody, or immunoglobulin, in the blood is called IgG, which contains more than 1,300 amino acids. The problem of discovering the active site of the antibody—the part that combines with the antigen—could be solved only by working with smaller pieces of the molecule. Porter discovered that an enzyme from papaya juice, called papain, could break up IgG into fragments that still contained the active sites but were small enough to work with. He received his Ph.D. for this work in 1948.

Porter remained at Cambridge for another year, then in 1949 he moved to the National Institute for Medical Research at Mill Hill, London. There, he improved methods for purifying protein mixtures and used some of these methods to show that there are variations in IgG molecules. He obtained a purer form of papaya enzyme than had been available at Cambridge and repeated his earlier experiments. This time the IgG molecules broke into thirds, and one of these thirds was obtained in a crystalline form which Porter called fragment crystallizable (Fc).

Obtaining the Fc crystal was a breakthrough; Porter now was able to show that this part of the antibody was the same in all IgG molecules, since a mixture of the different molecules would not have formed a crystal. He also discovered that the active site of the molecule (the part that binds the antigen) was in the other two-thirds of the antibody. These he called fragment antigen-binding (or FAB) pieces. After Porter's research was published in 1959, another research group, led by Gerald M. Edelman at Rockefeller University in New York, split the IgG in another way—by separating amino acid chains rather than breaking the proteins at right angles between the amino acids as Porter's papain had done.

In 1960 Porter was appointed professor of immunology at St. Mary's Hospital Medical School in London. There he repeated Edelman's experiments under different conditions. After two years, having combined his own results with those of Edelman, he proposed the first satisfactory structure of the IgG molecule. The model, which predicted that the FAB fragment consisted of two different amino acid chains, provided the basis for far-ranging biochemical research. Porter's continuing work contributed numerous studies of the structures of individual IgG molecules. In 1967 Porter was appointed Whitley Professor of Biochemistry and chairman of the biochemistry department at Oxford University. In his new position, Porter continued his work on the immune response, but his interest shifted from the structure of antibodies to their role as receptors on the surface of cells. To further this research, he developed ways of tagging and tracing receptors. He also became an authority on the structure and genetics of a group of blood proteins called the complement system, which binds the Fc region of the immunoglobulin and is involved in many important immunological reactions.

Porter married Julia Frances New in 1948. They had five children and lived in a farmhouse in a small town just outside of Oxford. Porter was killed in an automobile accident a few weeks before he was to retire from the Whitley Chair of Biochemistry. He had been planning to continue as director of the Medical Research Council's Immunochemistry Unit for another four years; he had also intended to continue his laboratory work, attempting to crystallize one of the proteins of the complement system. Porter's awards in addition to the Nobel Prize include the Gairdner Foundation Award of Merit in 1966 and the Ciba Medal of the Biochemical Society in 1967.

SELECTED WRITINGS BY PORTER:

Books

Chemical Aspects of Immunology, Carolina Biological Supply Co., 1976.
Defense and Recognition IIB: Structural Aspects, Complement, edited by E. S. Lennox, University Park Press, 1979, pp. 177–212.

FURTHER READING:

Periodicals

Cebra, John J., *Science,* The 1972 Nobel Prize for Physiology or Medicine, October 27, 1972, pp. 384–386.
Chedd, Graham, *New Scientist,* Nobel Prizes for Antibody Structure, October 19, 1972, pp. 142–143.
Steiner, L. A., *Nature,* Rodney Robert Porter (1917–1985), October 3, 1985, p. 383.
Weinraub, Bernard, *New York Times,* Pioneers in Immunology Research: Rodney Robert Porter, October 13, 1972, p. A24.

Sketch by Pamela O. Long

Valdemar Poulsen
1869–1942
Danish inventor

Valdemar Poulsen is known for his work in the development of magnetic recording and radio broadcasting, both of which involved converting sound waves into electrical energy. He invented the first recording device that was entirely electrical, called the telegraphone, as well as a device known as the Poulsen arc transmitter, which greatly extended the range of wireless communication.

Poulsen was born in Copenhagen, Denmark, on November 23, 1869, the son of a high-ranking judge. He studied natural sciences at the University of Copenhagen, but he left the university before graduating to take a position as assistant engineer with the Copenhagen Telephone Company. In 1898, while working for the telephone company, Poulsen developed a method for recording telephone conversations electromagnetically.

Patents the Telegraphone

Poulsen was the first to demonstrate that a generated electromagnetic field could be used to record sound. To do this, he connected a carbon telephone transmitter to an electromagnet. The telephone transmitter, when activated by sound waves, converted the sound waves into an electric current that varied in accordance with the amplitude and frequency of the waves. This current activated an electromagnet that contacted a moving steel wire or ribbon. As the wire moved past the electromagnet it became magnetized in a way that corresponded to the fluctuations in the electric impulses applied to it. These impulses reflected the fluctuations of the original sound waves. The original sound was then reproduced by reversing the process—that is, by moving the magnetized steel wire across the electromagnet connected to the telephone transmitter and earphones. Listening was accomplished by means of earphones. This invention, which Poulsen called the telegraphone, and for which he applied for a patent on December 1, 1898, was demonstrated at the Paris exposition of 1900 and was awarded a Grand Prix. The principle was identical to that of the modern tape recorder, which uses a ribbon of acetate covered with a coating of iron oxide or other magnetizable metal particles.

Poulsen's initial apparatus employed a steel wire moving at a rate of eighty-four inches per second; it could record continuously for thirty minutes. In 1900 Poulsen's telegraphone was used to record the voice of Emperor Franz-Joseph of Austria-Hungary. Over the following decade, Poulsen experimented with recording on four-and-a-half inch steel discs. These had a raised spiral that could be traced by the magnetic recording and playback head. He also designed a brass cylinder with an embedded steel wire to be used as the recording surface.

Poulsen's telegraphone had several advantages over the mechanical recording process used at that time, which employed wax cylinders and rubber discs. Because the playback apparatus was sensitive only to the magnetic energy in the wire and not to the wire's surface imperfections, the background noise of the recording was relatively low; in contrast, the mechanical playback method then in use by the phonograph could not differentiate between the vibrations incised or etched into the playing surface and the irregular surface of the playback medium. Nor was Poulsen's system limited to four minutes, the length of contemporary mechanical recordings. The wire also had another advantage: it could be erased and recorded over.

There were, however, some factors that kept the telegraphone from commercial success. The wire often became entangled, and rewinding took as much time as playback. But it was the lack of sufficient electrical amplification provided by the telephone transmitters through earphones that prevented the telegraphone from supplanting the phonograph. Electrical amplifiers and loud-speakers had not yet been developed, and this fact severely limited playback volume as compared to the phonograph, where large horns and weighted playback styli gave adequate volume despite the fact that the device depended solely on the unamplified mechanical energy of the original sound.

Probably because of the inadequate volume on the telegraphone and the perception that the practical uses of the apparatus were limited, Poulsen was not able to secure financial backing for the development of his invention in Europe. He travelled to the United States and founded the American Telegraphone Company in 1903 with the intention of manufacturing and selling an improved model of the device. With the exception of ten machines purchased by the DuPont Company, however, the machine was never successfully marketed. The telegraphone was relegated to being used as a dictating instrument in offices, and even this use lasted only a short time. It was not until the late 1920s and 1930s, with the development of electrical amplification and magnetic loudspeakers, that a practical magnetic recording instrument became feasible. The same developments, however, also had raised the quality of the phonograph and solidified the position of the 78 rpm record as the primary medium for recording and playback of sound.

Develops the Poulsen Arc

In 1903 Poulsen was awarded a patent for a device that generated continuous radio waves. Previous wireless stations employed spark transmitters based on a device developed by Reginald Fessenden, a chemist for Westinghouse. Poulsen's generator was an adaptation of W. Duddell's "singing arc," developed in 1900, which generated waves within the audio spectrum. Poulsen was able to increase the frequency limit of Duddell's arc from ten kHz to one-hundred kHz—that is, from an audible frequency to a radio frequency. Connecting the output of this arc to a transmitting antenna allowed the transmission of a continuous wave over a distance of 150 miles.

Poulsen's apparatus was manufactured by the Federal Telegraph Company, a chief rival of the American Marconi Company, and the company installed a Poulsen arc transmitter in the Arlington Radio Station, which had begun operations in February 1913. Since a Fessenden spark transmitter had already been in use in the station, it was possible to run comparisons between the two systems. Poulsen's apparatus proved to have a greater transmission range and a greater freedom from static interference. Poulsen's experiments led eventually to the development of a practical system for long-wave radio broadcasts. By the early 1920s Poulsen arc transmitters as powerful as 1,000 kilowatts, with ranges of up to 25,000 miles, had been constructed.

Among the awards bestowed on Poulsen were the gold medal of the Royal Danish Society for Science in 1907, an honorary doctorate of philosophy from the University of Leipzig in 1909, and the Danish Government's Medal of Merit. He was a fellow of the Danish Academy of Technical Science and the Swedish Institute for Engineering Research. He died in Denmark in 1942.

SELECTED WRITINGS BY POULSEN:

Periodicals

Scientific American, Telegraphone, August 25, 1900, p. 20616; January 19, 1901, p. 29044.
Popular Science, Telegraphone, Description, August, 1901, p. 413.

FURTHER READING:

Books

Archer, Gleason L., *History of Radio to 1926,* Arno Press, 1938.
Gelatt, Roland, *The Fabulous Phonograph, 1877–1977,* Collier Books, 1977, pp. 284–286.
Koenigsberg, Allen, *Patent History of the Phonograph, 1877–1912,* revised edition, A.P.M. Press, 1991.
Lewis, Tom, *Empire of the Air: The Men Who Made Radio,* Harper Perennial, 1993.
Read, Oliver, and Walter L. Welch, *From Tin Foil to Stereo: Evolution of the Phonograph,* Howard Sams, 1976.

Periodicals

Read, Oliver, and Walter L. Welch, *Scientific American,* Poulsen's Telegraphone, September 22, 1900.

Sketch by Michael Sims

Robert Pound
1919–
American physicist

During his early career as a Harvard professor, Robert Pound worked closely with Nobel Prize-winning physicist **Edward Mills Purcell** on the study of nuclear magnetic resonance (NMR) and established it as one of physics' most valuable analytical techniques. In the late

1950s, Pound became interested in the use of high-precision gamma rays produced by the Mössbauer process to study a variety of phenomena. In 1960, Pound and a colleague used the Mössbauer effect to measure the gravitational effects of electromagnetic radiation, and in the process they were able to confirm certain predictions of **Albert Einstein**'s theory of relativity.

Robert Vivian Pound was born in Ridgeway, Ontario, May 16, 1919, the son of Vivian Ellsworth and Gertrude C. (Prout) Pound. The Pounds moved to the United States when Robert was four years old and he became a naturalized citizen in 1932 at the age of thirteen. He attended the University of Buffalo where he earned his bachelor's degree in physics in 1941. On June 20, 1941, Pound married Betty Yde Andersen with whom he later had a son, John Andrew.

During the first year of World War II, Pound worked as a research physicist at the Submarine Signal Company before joining the staff of Massachusetts Institute of Technology's (MIT's) radiation laboratory, where he stayed until 1946. Pound's wartime research was related to the development of radar and microwave technology. A year before leaving MIT, Pound was appointed a junior fellow of Harvard University's Society of Fellows. He was a professor at Harvard from 1948 until his retirement in 1989. He also served as chair of the physics department (1968–1972), and as director of the physics laboratory (1975–1983).

While he was a junior fellow at Harvard, Pound worked with Purcell on the development of nuclear magnetic resonance techniques. These techniques make use of the fact that atomic nuclei can be identified on the basis of their behavior in the presence of a magnetic field. Nuclear magnetic resonance (NMR) has become a widely used analytical technique in chemical research, medical diagnosis, and a number of other fields. For his contribution to the development of these techniques, Purcell shared the 1952 Nobel Prize in physics.

Mössbauer Effect Leads to Red Shift Discovery

Pound began the research for which he is best known in 1959. The previous year, German physicist **Rudolf Mössbauer** had made an interesting discovery regarding the emission of gamma rays, the high-energy photons which are emitted by radioactive nuclei. Gamma rays often occur during radioactive decay where they carry away energy released in the nuclear transformation. However, the decay of any specific nucleus typically results in gamma rays with varying energies. The variability of gamma ray energies is the result of other changes taking place within the nucleus besides decay, most notably the recoil of the emitting nucleus.

Mössbauer found, however, that these gamma ray energy variations could be eliminated by binding decaying nuclei tightly within a crystal lattice. Within the lattice, the nuclei undergo little or no recoil and the gamma rays emitted are uniform in frequency. This discovery, called the Mössbauer effect, provided a powerful tool for detecting minute changes in electromagnetic waves, including gamma rays.

Pound realized that the Mössbauer effect would be useful in testing the assumptions of relativity theory. According to Einstein, an electromagnetic wave should be deflected from its path by a strong gravitational field. Scientists had attempted to test this hypothesis by measuring the apparent position of stars at various times. The assumption was that light from a distant star passing close to a massive astronomical body would be displaced and would, therefore, seem to be located in slightly different positions at various times.

These experimental efforts failed, however, because of the number of intervening factors, and the differences that were observed could not be specifically ascribed to the effect predicted by Einstein. Pound saw that monochromatic gamma rays produced by the Mössbauer effect (with their uniform frequencies) might be used to test the theory. The apparatus required was conceptually simple: a gamma ray emitter that produced a precise wave and a detector tuned to absorb the wave of that emitter's frequency. Any signal sent by the emitter and distorted by gravity would be detected by a drop of signal in the receiver. In actuality, the effect of gravity changed the frequency of the transmitted wave, resulting in a shift of the wavelength to the receiver—a change known as the "red shift." Pound carried out the necessary experiments with his associate Glen A. Rebka, Jr. between November 1959 and March 1960, and continued for four more years with the assistance of J. L. Snider. The final results confirmed with little uncertainty the existence and magnitude of the predicted red shift phenomenon.

In addition to his Harvard affiliation, Pound held a number of other appointments as visiting professor, including terms at the Clarendon Laboratory at Oxford in 1951, the College of France in 1973, the Joint Institute Laboratory of Astrophysics at the University of Colorado in 1979 and 1980, the University of Groningen in 1982, the Brookhaven National Laboratory in 1986 and 1987, and the University of Florida in 1987. Among his many honors and awards have been the Thompson Memorial Award of the Institute of Radio Engineers in 1948, the Eddington Medal of the Royal Astronomical Society in 1965, and the National Medal of Science in 1990. Pound became a professor emeritus of physics at Harvard in 1989 and retired from academic life.

SELECTED WRITINGS BY POUND:

Books

Microwave Mixers, 1948.

Sketch by David E. Newton

Cecil Frank Powell
1903–1969
English physicist

Cecil Frank Powell's research into cloud chambers and the detection of subatomic particles led to his development of photographic emulsion systems to detect and identify fast-moving particles, especially those found in cosmic rays. This enabled him to discover the pi-meson, a particle formed from nuclear reactions within cosmic rays. Powell was awarded the 1950 Nobel Prize in physics for his work in this area. He also was a member of the British Atomic Energy Project during World War II, though in his later years he became an advocate for nuclear disarmament.

Powell was born on November 5, 1903, at Tonbridge, Kent, England. His father, Frank Powell, was a gunsmith, and his mother, Elizabeth Caroline Bisacre, came from a family of skilled technicians. Powell developed an interest in science at an early age after becoming captivated by a chemistry book he saw in a store. Inspired by the book to conduct his own chemistry experiments, he eventually convinced his family to let him purchase the makings of a home chemistry set.

Studies at Cambridge under Rutherford and Wilson

In 1914 Powell won a scholarship to the Judd School in Tonbridge. Upon graduation from Judd, he earned two more scholarships that allowed him to attend Sidney Sussex College at Cambridge University. He graduated in 1925 with a degree in physics but turned down a teaching job to continue his graduate work at Cambridge.

At the time **Ernest Rutherford**, the Nobel Prize-winning physicist who had determined the structure of the atom, was the director of the Cavendish Laboratories at Cambridge. It was under **C. T. R. Wilson**, the inventor of the cloud chamber, that Powell conducted his doctoral research, a study of condensation phenomena in cloud chambers, for which he was awarded his Ph.D. in 1927. Cloud chambers are devices that reveal ionized particles by producing a trail of water droplets from air saturated with water. Powell accepted an appointment as research assistant to A. M. Tyndall at Bristol College. In succession he became lecturer in physics, a reader in physics, the Melville Wills Professor of Physics (1948), the Henry Overton Wills Professor of Physics and director of the H. H. Wills Physics Laboratory (1964), and vice-chancellor of the University at Bristol (1964).

Develops Photographic Detection Devices

Powell's initial work at Bristol involved the study of ion mobility in gases—the way electrically charged atoms behave in gases. By 1938, however, Powell became interested in particle detection devices. That interest, which first developed while he was studying cloud chambers, was rekindled when he learned that photographic emulsions could be used to detect particles in the atmosphere. For a number of years, Wilson's cloud chamber had been the instrument of choice for detecting subatomic particles, such as those produced in radioactive reactions and cosmic rays. However, the cloud chamber possessed one serious disadvantage—it required a brief resting phase each time it was used. In contrast, photographic emulsions were ready at all times to record events.

Like other scientists, Powell had been aware of the potential of photographic emulsions for this purpose, but no one had yet used them successfully. The main problem was that emulsions were not sensitive enough to be used for detection purposes, so Powell decided to find a way to overcome this limitation. His first year of research proved disappointing; he found that neither the emulsions nor the microscopes available were of sufficient quality to obtain the results he wanted. His research was interrupted by World War II, and he became involved with the British Atomic Energy Project for its duration. After the war, he again tackled the technical challenges of using photographic emulsions for detection purposes, this time with much greater success.

In 1946 at Powell's request, Ilford Ltd., a photographic company, developed a new emulsion that could more clearly record particle tracks. Powell and his colleagues used this new detection system to study cosmic radiation at altitudes of up to 9,000 feet. These studies resulted in the discovery of a new particle, the pion (or pi-meson), that had been predicted by the Japanese physicist **Hideki Yukawa** in 1935. The pion proved to be a cohesive force within the atomic nucleus, as was the K-meson, another particle discovered by Powell shortly thereafter. It was partly for these discoveries that Powell was awarded the 1950 Nobel Prize in physics. Over the next decade Powell continued his studies of cosmic radiation. As balloon technology improved, he launched his detectors higher into the atmosphere, in some cases reaching and maintaining altitudes of 90,000 feet for many hours. A key element in the success of this research program was the collaborative effort among scientists, technicians, and laypersons throughout Europe who collected and monitored his equipment. That experience proved to be especially helpful in the early 1960s, when Powell became involved in organizing the European Center for Nuclear Research (CERN) in Geneva, Switzerland. Powell served as chairman of CERN's Science Policy Committee from 1961 to 1963.

During the 1950s Powell became increasingly concerned about social problems related to scientific and technological development. He served as president of the Association of Scientific Workers from 1952 to 1954, and as president of the World Federation of Scientific Workers from 1956 until his death. A founding member of the Pugwash Movement for Science and World Affairs, he lent his signature to Bertrand Russell's 1955 petition calling for nuclear disarmament.

Powell was married in 1932 to Isobel Therese Artner, with whom he had two daughters. He died on August 9, 1969, at Bellano, Lake Como, Italy, while on vacation to celebrate his retirement from Bristol a few months earlier. Powell's awards in addition to the Nobel Prize included the Hughes Medal in 1949 and the Royal Medal of the Royal Society in 1961, the Rutherford Medal and Prize in 1961, the Lomonosov Gold Medal of the Soviet Academy of Sciences in 1967, and the Guthrie Prize and Medal of the Institute of Physics and Physical Society in 1969.

SELECTED WRITINGS BY POWELL:

Books

Nuclear Physics in Photographs, Oxford University Press, 1947.
The Study of Elementary Particles by the Photographic Method, Pergamon, 1959.
Selected Papers of Cecil Frank Powell, edited by E. H. S. Burhop, W. O. Lock, and M. G. K. Menon, North-Holland, 1972.*The Study of Elementary Particles by the Photographic Method,* Pergamon, 1959.

FURTHER READING:

Books

Biographical Memoirs of Fellows of the Royal Society, Volume 17, Royal Society (London), 1971, pp. 541–63.
McGraw-Hill Modern Scientists and Engineers, Volume 2, McGraw-Hill, 1980, pp. 436–37.

Sketch by David E. Newton

David Powless
1943–
American environmental scientist

David Powless received the first National Science Foundation grant awarded to an individual Native American in 1977. This research funding allowed Powless to develop a successful method of recycling hazardous iron oxide wastes from steel mills. A member of the Oneida tribe, an Iroquoian-speaking group, Powless was named 1980 American Indian Business Owner of the Year by the United Indian Development Association. The following year, he was presented with the Small Business Administration's National Innovation Advocate of the Year Award by

then Vice President George Bush at a ceremony in the White House Rose Garden.

David Allen Powless was born on May 29, 1943, in Ottawa, Illinois, the fifth of six children born to Merville and Adeline (Tucktenhagen) Powless. His father was a government employee who worked at various times for the Bureau of Indian Affairs, the Department of Navy, and the Department of Army. He was also a staunch believer in the value of education. As Powless recalled in an interview with Linda Wasmer Smith, "My father motivated us all. . . . When I was being raised, we were told that as Oneidas, we had a special obligation to our tribe to act well, because whatever we did, that was the way people would think all Oneida Indians acted. But we were also told that we had been given special skills and abilities with which to fulfill that duty. . . . We were Indian people, first. We were Indian people who were going to get a good education, second."

Powless lived up to his father's high expectations by winning a football scholarship to the University of Oklahoma. He stayed for one year before transferring to the University of Illinois, where he continued to pursue football while studying marketing and economics. After playing on a team that won the 1963 Rose Bowl, Powless graduated with a B.S. in 1966. He was drafted to play professional football for the New York Giants in 1965. He spent a season with them before being traded to the Washington Redskins, but a back injury brought an early end to his sports career.

Recycles Hazardous Wastes from Steel Mills

In 1967, Powless began nine years as a marketing representative for the Foseco company. His job, which involved selling chemical additives and insulation materials to steel mills, gave him a close-up view of how that industry worked. In 1976, he started his own company, convinced that the hazardous wastes generated by the steel mills represented a problem for which he could supply a practical solution. As he told Linda Wasmer Smith, "This is when I started seeking my identity as a Native person. All of our traditions are focused on care and concern for the Earth." Powless developed his recycling method with the aid of scientists at the Colorado School of Mines in Golden. They helped him write an unsolicited proposal to the National Science Foundation, and after almost half a year of negotiations he was awarded the grant. He then established a pilot plant at Kaiser Steel in California.

In Powless's recycling method, various contaminants are first removed from iron oxide wastes using an indirect fired rotary kiln—a constantly set furnace with an external flame hitting the shell. As materials enter the kiln, they become hot enough to ignite. But as the materials move farther into the furnace, there is less oxygen available to support the fire. In this high-temperature, low-oxygen environment, contaminants such as oil, zinc, lead, and cadmium wholly or partly come off the wastes. Then the cleaned-up materials are agglomerated, or collected, into briquettes, which can later be reintroduced into the steel-making process. According to Powless: "This was a spiritual experience for me, because it involved the use of fire and flame for purification."

Powless's company marketed this technology until 1986, when the search for his roots took Powless to the Oneida reservation in Wisconsin. There he soon became involved in the start-up of a tribally owned and managed environmental analytical testing laboratory called ORTEK. This profitable enterprise included an operating group that conducted organic and inorganic testing of soil, water, and air for contaminants. In 1992, Powless left his position as president of ORTEK and accepted a new one as vice president of marketing for the Arctic Slope Regional Corporation. There, Powless has assumed a key role in the Eskimo-owned firm's expansion outside Alaska.

Powless has served on the board of directors of the American Indian Science and Engineering Society. He is also a popular speaker on the relationship between traditional teachings, spiritual growth, and science. Powless was married in 1968 to Carol Monson, with whom he has a son. That marriage ended in divorce, and on November 6, 1983, Powless wed Anna Kormos in Los Angeles. The couple and their daughter make their home in Corrales, New Mexico.

SELECTED WRITINGS BY POWLESS:

Periodicals

Winds of Change, A Successful Economic Development Venture of the Oneida Tribe, spring, 1989, pp. 27–28.

FURTHER READING:

Periodicals

Vogel, Mike, *Buffalo News,* Native American Parley Fuses Culture, Technology. 900 Expected at Conference, November 9, 1990, p. B15.
Weidlein, Jim, *Winds of Change,* People of the Whale, summer, 1993, pp. 10–15.
Weidlein, Jim, *Winds of Change,* Sharing a Piece of the Whale, autumn, 1993, pp. 140–147.

Other

Weidlein, Jim, *Winds of Change,* Sharing a Piece of the Whale, Powless, David Allen, interviews with Linda Wasmer Smith conducted February 14 and 22, 1994.

Sketch by Linda Wasmer Smith

Ludwig Prandtl
1875–1953
German physicist and aerodynamicist

Generally considered the father of aerodynamics, Ludwig Prandtl taught for many years at Germany's Göttingen University and made important contributions to the fields of fluid mechanics, hydraulics, hydrodynamics, and aerodynamics. Prandtl also conducted original research in solid mechanics, heat transfer, elasticity, and even meteorology. He and his many students at Göttingen fundamentally shaped the new field of aerodynamics and its application in airplane design, permitting "aeronautical engineers to move from hit-and-miss methods into scientific design," as Hungarian-American aerodynamicist **Theodore Kármán** wrote in *The Wind and Beyond.* "In my opinion," von Kármán noted, "Prandtl unraveled the puzzle of some natural phenomena of tremendous basic importance and was deserving of a Nobel Prize."

Prandtl was born in Freising, Bavaria, Germany, on February 4, 1875, to Alexander and Magdalene Ostermann Prandtl. Because his mother suffered from a long illness, Prandtl was especially close to his father, who taught surveying and engineering at the Weihenstephen agricultural college near Freising and inspired in his son an early interest in natural phenomenon. Following a humanistic secondary education in Freising and Munich, Germany, Prandtl earned an engineering degree from the Technical Institute at Munich in 1898 and a Ph.D. in solid mechanics from the University of Munich in 1900. His major professor, August Föppl, was a noted authority in engineering mechanics and helped Prandtl obtain a job as an engineer in the Augsburg-Nürnberg Machine Factory. At the factory, Prandtl was assigned to improve a vacuum device that removed wood shavings. He was so successful that the firm rebuilt the piece of equipment according to his design and began to market a new line of shavings conveyors. This work led Prandtl to recognize some basic gaps in the knowledge of fluid mechanics.

Develops Boundary Layer Concept

In 1901, Prandtl became a professor of mechanics at the Technical Institute of Hannover, Germany, where he continued to investigate fluid motion. Existing fluid motion theories failed to explain why the flow of thin (inviscid) liquids in a pipe did not fill the pipe but separated from its wall. Prandtl observed that a thin layer of the fluid always formed between the pipe and the rest of the flowing liquid. In the next three years, he developed an explanation of this phenomenon, set forth in what became a famous paper delivered at the Third International Congress of Mathematics at Heidelberg, Germany, in 1904. Only eight pages long, the paper delineated the concept of a boundary layer in fluid flow that subsequently proved to be of critical importance in understanding such central aviation concepts as lift, the force that causes aircraft to fly, and drag, or air resistance. Subsequent innovations, such as streamlined aircraft designs, resulted from these findings.

Even before Prandtl presented this groundbreaking paper, the famous mathematician Felix Klein had brought him to Göttingen University in 1904 as an extraordinary (junior) professor of applied physics. Although this was a step down from his full professorship in Hannover, at Göttingen Prandtl received a higher salary and the promise of a research laboratory. Klein was attempting to bring together the disciplines of science and engineering that tended to be taught in separate institutions of higher learning throughout Germany; he was also interested in promoting the study of aerodynamics at Göttingen. Both goals fit well with Prandtl's own concerns and he had both a laboratory and a full professorship by 1907. He also played a key role in bringing about the construction of a thirty-five-horsepower wind tunnel, built in 1908 and 1909, which was later joined by several other wind tunnels at Göttingen. In 1909, Prandtl married Gertrude Föppl, the eldest daughter of his former professor, who gave birth to the couple's two daughters in 1914 and 1917.

Prandtl's studies led him to advocate the initially controversial single-winged aircraft at a time when designers favored bi- and tri-wings. His theoretical discoveries also led to improvements in the design of dirigibles, lighter-than-air carriers used by both civilians and the military. In the 1910s, Prandtl was also at work on one of his most important discoveries, induced drag. Induced drag is caused when air races over wing surfaces; though this motion produces lift, the air flowing over the wing from leading to trailing edge also results in two trailing vortices that extend back from the airplane and impede its flight. After struggling to comprehend this little understood phenomenon, Prandtl developed a mathematical explanation and went on to show how to reduce drag through wing design and streamlining, techniques that dramatically influenced the aircraft industry.

Studies Turbulent Air Flow

A problem remaining to be solved in the years between World Wars I and II was turbulent (irregular) air flow. Prandtl worked in friendly competition with von Kármán, who was teaching at the Technical Institute of Aachen. Following some preliminary findings by von Kármán in 1924, Prandtl presented his "mixing length concept" in 1926, which analyzed turbulent air flow in terms of elements colliding and producing molecular friction. Prandtl mathematically demonstrated the distances each fluid element has to travel before collision with other elements reduces its momentum. Thereafter, experimental work by Prandtl and his students, together with important experimental and theoretical findings by von Kármán and his collaborators, led to a summary paper delivered by Prandtl in 1933 that laid the foundation for subsequent knowledge about chaotic motion. The method and concepts von Kármán and Prandtl developed had important applications for avoiding drag in aircraft, describing liquid flow through pipes, and designing rockets.

These discoveries represented only some of the more important contributions Prandtl and his students made to aerodynamics—not to mention hydrodynamics and solid mechanics. Prandtl was instrumental in setting up aerodynamics and hydrodynamics institutes at Göttingen, including the famous Kaiser Wilhelm Institute for Fluid Mechanics, which was founded in 1925 and renamed the Max Planck Institute after World War II.

Prandtl's usual methodology in achieving his discoveries involved a painstaking comparison of theory with experimental data. He also abstracted the basic components from complex processes and described them in a simplified, mathematical way that allowed him to understand the fundamental principles involved. Beyond applying this methodology himself, he was also highly effective in teaching it to his students. Many of them then went on to make their own contributions to fluid and solid mechanics. Described by von Kármán as a "tedious lecturer" whose classroom presentations suffered from excessive precision, Prandtl impressed Adolf Busemann by displaying "amazing clarity in dissecting and composing mechanical phenomena and finding ways to reduce their complexity," as Busemann wrote in *Biographical Memoirs of the Fellows of the Royal Society*. According to Busemann, Prandtl "never [tried] to circumvent difficulties by omitting them," resulting in lectures that were "a rich source of information for all his pupils."

Besides being an accomplished scientist, Prandtl played piano, enjoyed hiking in the hills and mountains, gave annual parties for his laboratory staff, and took a childlike delight in toys and magic tricks. He resisted the Nazis on several occasions after 1933 and even signed a petition opposing the dismissal of Jewish professors from Göttingen. Prandtl's son-in-law was killed during World War II, and he lost his wife immediately afterwards, perhaps occasioning a physical decline that was arrested for a while but resumed in the year before his death in Göttingen on August 15, 1953.

SELECTED WRITINGS BY PRANDTL:

Books

Essentials of Fluid Dynamics, Hafner, 1952.
Gesammelte Adhandlungen zur angewandten Mechanik, Hydro- und Aerodynamik, (title means "Collected Essays on Applied Mechanics, Hydro- and Aerodynamics"), three volumes, Springer-Verlag, 1961.

FURTHER READING:

Books

Biographical Memoirs of Fellows of the Royal Society, Volume 5, Royal Society (London), 1960, pp. 193–205.

The Daniel Guggenheim Medal for Achievement in Aeronautics, [New York], 1936, pp. 11–17.

Dictionary of Scientific Biography, Volume XI, Scribner, 1975, pp. 123–125.

The Great Scientists, edited Frank M. Magill, Volume 10, Grolier Educational Corporation, 1989, pp. 20–25.

von Kármán, Theodore with Lee Edson, *The Wind and Beyond,* Little, Brown, 1967.

Sketch by J. D. Hunley

Fritz Pregl
1869–1930
Austrian analytical chemist

The work of Fritz Pregl is an example of the maxim that every difficulty is an opportunity. It was the problems inherent in analyzing organic matter that motivated Pregl to take microanalysis into new realms of exactitude, developing new instrumentation for the precise measurement of such substances. Such microanalytic tools paved the way for later biochemical research on pigments, hormones, and vitamins. Pregl's innovations in the field earned him the 1923 Nobel Prize in chemistry.

Pregl was born on September 3, 1869, in Laibach, Austria (now Ljubljana, Republic of Slovenia), the only son of Friderike Schlacker and Raimund Pregl, the treasurer of a bank in nearby Krain (now Kranj). Though his father died when he was quite young, Pregl finished Gymnasium or high school in Laibach before he and his mother moved in 1887 to Graz, where he studied medicine at the University of Graz. Early in his academic career, Pregl demonstrated the intelligence and skill that would become more evident in his subsequent work as an analytical chemist. While still a student, his physiology professor, Alexander Rollett, made him an assistant in his laboratory. Upon gaining his medical degree in 1893, Pregl began to practice medicine with a specialty in ophthalmology but also stayed on part-time at Rollett's laboratory.

Turns Attention to Chemistry

Becoming an assistant lecturer in physiology and histology at the University of Graz, and working in Rollett's laboratory, Pregl increasingly turned his attention to biological and physiological chemistry, focusing on organic matter. His early research centered on human physiology and, in particular, the properties of bile and urine. His research on the reaction of cholic acid, which is found in bile, and the causality of the high ratio of carbon to nitrogen in human urine, won him a university lectureship at Graz in 1899. In 1904, Pregl went to Germany to study chemistry with **Friedrich Wilhelm Ostwald** in Leipzig and **Emil Fischer** in Berlin. Fischer was a 1902 Nobel laureate in organic chemistry for his sugar and purine research, and Ostwald, a physical chemist, would win the Nobel in 1909 for his work in catalysis.

Returning to Graz in 1905, Pregl renewed his bile research and began protein investigations, having been intrigued by Fischer's recent work on the structure of proteins. He also became an assistant at the medical and chemical laboratory of the University of Graz, a position which provided him with valuable research space. In 1907 he was appointed as the forensic chemist for central Styria, the province of which Graz is the capital. In the course of his chemical investigations, Pregl continually came up against one problem: the methods of analysis employed by organic chemistry were much too cumbersome, lengthy, and overly complex for the new discipline of biochemistry in which he was becoming increasingly involved. In particular, Pregl found that he would have to prepare large amounts of test samples if he used traditional analytical methods in his studies on bile acids. Because these acids are complicated proteins, only small quantities can be isolated from liver bile, a process that is both time-consuming and costly: Pregl's research in bile acid alone would require processing several tons of raw bile in order to refine enough of the acid for traditional analysis. It was to overcome such difficulties that he set to improve the methods of microanalysis, thereby altering the direction of his research from biochemistry to analytical chemistry.

By the time Pregl entered the field, microanalysis was already over seventy years old, pioneered by Justus von Liebig, who had developed the combustion method. In Liebig's technique, proportionate amounts of elements in an organic substance could be determined by burning the substance in a glass tube under conditions that would convert the carbon to carbon dioxide (CO_2) and all the hydrogen into water. The water and CO_2 would in turn be absorbed by other materials such as potassium hydroxide or a lime and soda mixture, and the change of weight in the respective absorbing materials would thus give the relative amounts of carbon and hydrogen in the combusted substance. Additionally, a contemporary of Pregl's, Friedrich Emich, at the Technical University of Graz had shown the reliability of working with small quantities of substances in an inorganic framework. Pregl set out to achieve Emich's measurement techniques with organic material.

Microanalysis Improvements Lead to Nobel Prize

It was Pregl's achievement to build upon Liebig and Emich's developments, and to refine and improve them to the point where substantially less of the organic substances were required for analysis. In 1910 he left Graz for Innsbruck, where he took the position of professor of medical chemistry at the University of Innsbruck. With this position, Pregl could devote more time to his research. His first priority was to find or create a balance that would accurately weigh much smaller amounts of substances than those currently available. He turned to W. H. Kuhlman, a German chemist who had recently developed a microbalance accurate to between 0.01 and 0.02 milligrams; Pregl found that with careful adjustments he could accurately utilize Kuhlman's balance to within 0.001 milligrams.

Pregl also took on the combustion analysis of carbon and hydrogen, improving that process by scaling down the size of the analytic equipment and adding a universal filling for the combustion tube that consisted of a mixture of lead chromate and copper oxide set in between two pieces of silver. This adaptation improved the absorption of the carbon dioxide and water. With such refinements, Pregl was able to obtain accurate analyses with between 2–4 milligrams of an organic substance—and fairly accurate readings with only 1 milligram—a significant reduction compared to the .2 to 1 grams needed for Liebig's method. With the new materials employed, Pregl was also able to reduce the time needed for such analysis from three hours to an hour. Pregl and his team also went on to devise new microanalytic techniques for boiling substances to determine their molecular weight by creating apparatus that impeded the substances' contamination with air. This allowed determinations to be made with greatly reduced amounts of such substances. Pregl made these advances known in two public presentations: in 1911 at the German Chemical Society in Berlin, and in 1913 at a scientific congress in Vienna.

Although improved techniques since Pregl's time now allow scientists to work with organic samples of only a few tenths of a milligram, his microanalytic improvements were revolutionary in their day and opened the way to new vistas of biochemical research in both science and industry. World renowned, Pregl returned to the University of Graz in 1913 as a full professor at the Medicochemical Institute, and here he perfected the methods he had pioneered, remaining in Graz—despite other tantalizing offers—until his death. In 1916, in the midst of the First World War, he was made dean of the medical school, and in 1920 became vice chancellor of the university. His major publication on his findings, *Die quantitative organische Mikroanalyse,* was published in 1917 and has since gone through numerous editions and translations. He subsequently won the Lieben Prize and membership in the Vienna Academy of Sciences. Pregl continued his research into a wide range of organic substances, employing his own methods of microanalysis on bile acids, enzymes, and sera. He also employed microanalysis in forensics, determining poisonous alkaloids from minute amounts of substance.

In 1923 Pregl was awarded the Nobel Prize in chemistry for his advances in microanalysis of organic substances. Though his work was an improvement rather than an invention, it was a well deserved honor for a man who tirelessly devoted his life to the cause of science. A life-long bachelor, Pregl's only pleasures aside from his research were mountain climbing and bicycling. He was also devoted to his students, lending both money and support when needed. In 1929 he endowed an award for chemistry through the Vienna Academy of Sciences, the

Fritz Pregl Prize, which continues to provide yearly stipends to promising students. Pregl died following an illness in 1930 at the age of sixty-one.

SELECTED WRITINGS BY PREGL:

Books

Die quantitative organische Mikroanalyse, J. Springer, 1917.

FURTHER READING:

Books

A Biographical Dictionary of Scientists, Adam & Charles, 1982, pp. 425–26.
Dictionary of Scientific Biography, Volume 11, Scribner's, 1978, pp. 128–29.
Farber, Eduard, editor, *Great Chemists,* Interscience, 1961, pp. 1327–31.
Farber, Eduard, editor, *Hinduja Foundation Encyclopedia of Nobel Laureates 1901–1987,* Konark, 1988, pp. 145–46.
Farber, Eduard, editor, *Nobel Prize Winners,* H. W. Wilson, 1987, pp. 834–35.

Periodicals

Farber, Eduard, editor, *Journal of Chemical Education,* Fritz Pregl (1869–1930), December, 1958, p. 609.
Lieb, H., *Berichte der Deutschen chemischen Gesellschaft,* Fritz Pregl, Volume 64A, 1931, p. 113.

Sketch by J. Sydney Jones

Vladimir Prelog
1906–
Swiss organic chemist

Vladimir Prelog spent most of his working life investigating the chemistry of natural products. He made major contributions to the synthesis and structure determination of hundreds of natural organic compounds. Additionally, he and his colleagues Robert Cahn and Sir Christopher Ingold formulated a set of rules (abbreviated CIP) for communicating the specific shape and configuration of highly complex organic compounds. Much of Prelog's work was characterized by an unusual cooperative spirit. Almost all of his major discoveries were made in conjunction with accomplished chemists in other laboratories. He shared the 1975 Nobel Prize in chemistry with Sir **John Cornforth**, who said about their work in his acceptance speech, as quoted in Prelog's autobiography (*My 132 Semesters of Chemistry Studies*): "Our backgrounds, and the experience that has shaped us as scientists, are very different. . . . What we have in common is a lifelong curiosity about the shapes, and changes in shape, of entities that we shall never see; and a lifelong conviction that this curiosity will lead us closer to the truth of chemical processes, including the processes of life."

Prelog was born on July 23, 1906, to Milan and Mara (Cettolo) Prelog in Sarajevo, in what was then the Austro-Hungarian monarchy. His father was a historian and teacher at both the high school and university level. Prelog's early life in general was surrounded by the political upheaval and war endemic to that part of the world—as a small child giving out flowers at a procession, he was within 200 yards of the assassination of Archduke Ferdinand, which touched off World War I. He wrote in his autobiography " . . . since then, I have been allergic to all violent mass demonstrations, even when held for just causes." Prelog's parents separated when he was nine, and he was raised for the next four years in Zagreb by a unmarried aunt who encouraged his interest in chemical experiments. At a science high school in Osijek he met a chemistry teacher, Ivan Kuria, who strongly encouraged his interests and helped him, at age 15, to publish his first chemistry paper in the journal *Chemiker Zeitung*. He completed high school in Zagreb in 1924 and moved to Prague to study chemistry at the Czech Institute of Technology.

Initially, Prelog was disillusioned with his university experience; chemistry seemed to consist entirely of disconnected facts, with nothing to hold them together. He eventually apprenticed himself to Rudolf Lukes, an older student in the laboratories of the sugar chemist Emil Votoček. Lukes introduced him to the organizing principles of organic chemistry and rekindled Prelog's interest in the subject. He had to work and learn very quickly because he was short of money, and in 1929 he received his doctorate under the supervision of Votocek. The topic of his dissertation was the structure determination of a natural product called rhamnoconvolvulinoic acid, a sugar derivative.

In the severely depressed economy of the time, and particularly since he was not a citizen of Czechoslovakia, it was impossible to obtain a job with any research organization. Thus, between 1929 and 1934, Prelog worked unofficially with Gothard J. Driza, an entrepreneur who set up a home laboratory to supply specialty chemicals to business, government, and the military. Among these chemicals were chloroacetophenone, which the police used for tear gas ammunition, and ammonium sulfite, which hairdressers used in their work. At the same time, he began trying to synthesize quinine (a principle anti-malarial drug), then available only from the bark of the *Cinchona* tree. He became even more interested in quinine and similar drugs when he himself contracted malaria serving in the Royal

Yugoslav Navy in 1932, and that interest continued for many years.

A teaching position at the University of Zagreb materialized in 1935, but it proved to be a disappointment because the salary was so low and research funding so minimal. Prelog accepted the position anyway, and to make ends meet took a second job with a local pharmaceutical company, Kastel, Ltd. Among other chemicals, they made the sulfa drug called sulfanilamide.

Sanctuary and Research at the Swiss Federal Institute of Technology

The company and university connections proved fruitful, and Prelog finally made sufficient money to support himself for a few months in 1937 working with the chemist **Leopold Ružička** at the Swiss Federal Institute of Technology (Eidgenossische Technische Hochschule, or ETH) in Zurich, Switzerland. His friendship with Ruzicka may have saved his life; later, with World War II raging, Ruzicka obtained Swiss entry visas for Prelog and his wife. Officials who thought Prelog was going to Germany to give a scientific talk permitted him to leave the city, and the Prelogs were thus able to legally escape German-occupied Zagreb and settle in Zurich in late 1941. Prelog became a Swiss citizen in 1959 and spent the rest of his career at the ETH, financially supported for much of that time by the giant Swiss pharmaceutical company CIBA.

At ETH, Prelog initially worked on several natural products from various animal glands, but eventually he switched to research on alkaloids (natural nitrogen-containing compounds), his principle interest. In 1942, he received a promotion, and in 1945 received the title of Professor. During the war, there was no possibility of travel to other countries, or even contact with other scientists by mail, so Prelog and his colleagues caught up on their literature-reading and worked with readily available materials. During this time, he made important contributions to the structure determination and synthesis of both solanine (a chemical extractable from potatoes) and strychnine, among many others.

After the war, Prelog began traveling, meeting other chemists, and conducting joint projects with them. He traveled and lectured extensively in the United States in 1950 and 1951. He seriously considered moving to America when Harvard University and later the Hoffmann-LaRoche Company offered him attractive positions, but ETH created a special chaired professorship for him, so he retained his residence in Switzerland. For a few more years, he worked with naturally occurring alkaloid compounds, collaborating with fellow chemists Sir **Derek Barton** and **Robert B. Woodward**, among others. He then switched his interest to elaborate ring structures, enzymes, and antibiotics, particularly the metabolic products of bacteria and other microbes. Most of these discoveries fall under the title of "basic" research, which develops the science of organic chemistry itself; the most commercially successful outcome was the eventual development of rifampicin, used to treat tuberculosis and leprosy.

In 1957, Prelog was named Ruzicka's successor at ETH and eventually found that he did not care for administrative work. He instituted a policy of rotating the administrative duties among a group of professors, which worked well and allowed him more time for research. In 1960, he joined the board of directors of CIBA (later CIBA-Geigy) and served until 1978. While a member, he helped set up the Woodward Institute in Basel, a research facility where the Nobel Laureate Woodward, also an organic chemist, could conduct research as he liked. The two became lifelong friends. Prelog also continued his world travels, lecturing and accepting guest professorships in many countries, including India, Israel, Australia, England, and South Africa.

Stereochemical Studies Lead to the 1975 Nobel Prize in Chemistry

Beginning in the 1950s, the electronic instrumentation applicable to chemical structure determination improved markedly. A process that once required slow, highly skilled, creative observation and analysis became routine, as various types of spectrometers and other analytical instruments gave almost instantaneous information on the layout of atoms in large molecules. In this environment, the identification and synthesis of new organic compounds grew exponentially.

It became apparent to Prelog, beginning with his work on alkaloids, that the naming of these new millions of organic compounds could be greatly improved. Natural products are not only extremely complex, they are also extremely specific in their three dimensional shapes. Small differences in the way atoms are oriented in space may change the biochemistry of a compound completely. Thus, new synthetic techniques are required to obtain exactly the desired configuration of a molecule. The entire branch of organic chemistry devoted to the shapes and configurations of molecules is called stereochemistry, and the individual configurations of a molecule are called its stereoisomers. Prelog spoke about the requirements in an oral history for the Chemical Heritage Foundation: "If, for example, you have sixty-four stereoisomers [of the same molecule] and only one is a natural compound that is biologically active, you have to be able first to assign to this molecule a model or a stereo formula. Secondly, you have to have a certain language, symbols, descriptors, to speak about it. Finally, you need to be able to [synthesize] this specific stereoisomer [uncontaminated with the others]. . . . We needed symbols to talk about our results."

Together with Robert Cahn and Sir Christopher Ingold, Prelog developed the CIP system of stereochemical nomenclature, which includes single letter symbols to designate specific characteristics of large molecules. The CIP system is now widely used as a standard in reference books and journals. Later, he developed new methods of synthesizing specific stereoisomers. For his body of work, specifically that related to stereochemical nomenclature and stereosyn-

thesis, Prelog won the 1975 Nobel Prize (shared with Sir John Cornforth). He thus became the fifth director of ETH to win a Nobel. Additionally, he was the recipient of numerous honorary degrees throughout his life, as well as the Werner medal in 1945, and the Marcel Benoist award in 1965.

Prelog married Kamila Vitek in 1933, and their only child, a son named Jan, was born in 1949. Jan followed in his grandfather's rather than his father's footsteps and became an historian. Over the course of his life, Prelog learned to speak or read at least four languages fluently—among them English, Czech, Croatian, and German—although he was characteristically modest about the achievement and said that he spoke none of them, including his mother tongue, without an accent. During his career he supervised more than 100 doctoral students and published approximately 400 papers. He also wrote biographical material on the scientists he had worked with, particularly Ruzicka. After his official retirement in 1976, he maintained his attachment to ETH by signing on as a postdoctoral student and working on the separation of complex chemical mixtures by the technique of chromatography. Becoming a student again (at least in name) inspired the title of his autobiography, *My 132 Semesters of Chemistry Studies,* published in 1991 by the American Chemical Society.

SELECTED WRITINGS BY PRELOG:

Books

My 132 Semesters of Chemistry Studies, translated by Otto Theodor Benfey and David Ginsburg, in the series Profiles, Pathways, and Dreams: Autobiographies of Eminent Chemists, series edited by Jeffrey I. Seeman, American Chemical Society, 1991.

FURTHER READING:

Books

Prelog, Vladimir, *Interview with Tonja Koeppel,* Zurich, 1984, tapes and transcript archived at the Chemical Heritage Foundation, Philadelphia, PA.

Sketch by Gail B.C. Marsella

Frank Press
1924–
American geophysicist

One of the most accomplished geophysicists of his generation, Frank Press is best known as a pioneer in the use of seismic waves to explore subsurface geological structures and for his pioneering use of waves to explore

Frank Press

Earth's deep interior. His election to the National Academy of Sciences at the age of 33 made him one of the youngest ever to gain admission to that highly selective and prestigious body. In 1977, he was chosen by President Jimmy Carter to serve as his science advisor, after which Press became the first ever to move from the White House to the presidency of the National Academy of Sciences.

Frank Press was born in Brooklyn, New York, on December 4, 1924. The youngest of three sons of immigrant parents—Solomon Press and Dora Steinholtz—he was raised in the predominantly Jewish neighborhood of Crown Heights and attended Samuel J. Tilden High School in East Flatbush. It was in that neighborhood that he became friends with Leonard Garment, who would later become President Richard Nixon's lawyer. In his book, *Crazy Rhythm*, Garment recalls that, as youngsters, he and his "skinny, shy, hugely intelligent schoolmate" believed that the world was theirs to conquer. "Wide-eyed with excitement, we set out to do just that. Frank and I ran ahead of the pack. Weighing a future in science, history, and journalism, he led his classes in all three."

Publishes Landmark Paper with Ocean-Floor Pioneer

After graduating from Tilden High, Press attended the City College of New York and received his B. S. in 1944. He earned his master's degree from Columbia University in 1946, the same year he married Billie Kallick. They would have two children, William Henry and Paula Evelyn. After receiving his master's, Press remained at Columbia and was

awarded a Ph.D. in geophysics in 1949. It was at Columbia that he studied with **William Maurice Ewing**, a major innovator in modern geology, and with whom he invented in 1950 an improved seismograph. That same year, they published a landmark paper that is recognized as beginning a new era in structural seismology.

Upon receiving his Ph.D. in 1949, Press became an instructor at Columbia. He left there in 1955 as an associate professor of geophysics to serve as professor of geophysics at the California Institute of Technology. Two years later, he became director of the Seismological Laboratory at Caltech, where he remained until 1965. That year he joined Massachusetts Institute of Technology to become chairman of its department of Earth and Planetary Sciences. His quiet leadership is credited with invigorating that program and with guiding its research and teaching units to scholarly preeminence.

Leaves Academe for Position of National Significance

While at Caltech and later MIT, Press became known in public policy circles for his work on seismic detection of underground nuclear tests and for his advocacy of a national program to develop earthquake prediction capabilities. During those years, he served as a consultant or advisor to seven federal departments or agencies, as well as U.S. Delegate to the Nuclear Test Ban Conference in Geneva from 1959 to1961 and Moscow in 1963. As a member of the President's Science Advisory Committee (PSAC) from 1961 to 1964, he also served as U.S. Delegate to the United Nations Conference on Science and Technology in Under-developed Nations in 1963. A week after President Kennedy's assassination, Press resigned from PSAC, later telling *Science* magazine that, "I felt so down I didn't want to continue."

In 1977, however, Press was recalled to the national stage when newly elected President Jimmy Carter chose him to serve as Science Advisor to the President as well as director of the Office of Science and Technology Policy. Press's four-year tenure at the White House was characterized by his judicious, low-key approach. With the Carter administration on record as having a pro-science policy, Press can take credit for the signing of United States-China scientific cooperation agreements, as well as for increased federal support for basic research. Under his direction, measures were initiated that spurred industrial innovation and joint ventures between industry, universities, and government.

Moves from White House to National Academy of Sciences

After leaving government in 1980 and returning for a short time to MIT as Chairman of its Earth and Planetary Sciences department, Press became in July 1981 the first White House science advisor to move into the presidency of the National Academy of Sciences (NAS). As a scientist, Press brought impeccable scientific credentials to that position. As a former member of the White House, he also brought a demonstrated commitment and ability to understand and influence science policy at the highest levels. Press remained NAS President for two six-year terms during which he revamped and reinvigorated its National Research Council, the branch of the Academy that responds to government requests for scientific advice. The Academy also published several landmark studies on such subjects as biology education in the nation's schools, global warming, biodiversity, and science and creationism. Overall, Press left the Academy a more effective and smoother functioning complex, with a goal for monitoring how the nation is doing in educating its young people in science and mathematics.

In 1993, when his two-term presidency was over, Press became the Cecil and Ida Green Senior Fellow at the Carnegie Institution of Washington. He remained in residence at that institution's Geophysics Laboratory and Department of Terrestrial Magnetism until 1997, having joined the Washington Advisory Group as a partner in 1996. The recipient of 30 honorary degrees and a member of 14 major scientific societies worldwide, Press has also received numerous awards and medals. Among these is the Royal Society's Gold Medal, France's Legion of Honor, Germany's Cross of Merit, and the Japan Prize. In October 1994, he was given the United States' highest scientific honor when President Clinton awarded him the National Medal of Science. Authorized by Congress in 1959 and only periodically bestowed, it was given to Press for his contributions to understanding the nature of Earth's deepest interior and the mitigation of natural disasters, as well as in recognition of his service in academia, as a government official, and at the National Academy of Sciences.

In light of his varied career, Press may best be remembered for his efforts as a successful educator. In addition to his own contributions to geophysics and the large number of students that he sent into the world as accomplished earth scientists, he co-authored, in 1974 with Raymond Siever, the classic undergraduate textbook titled *Earth*. As one of the most influential earth science texts for several generations of students worldwide, it was redone and issued in 1994 as *Understanding Earth*. It seems fitting that Press even has a mountain in Antarctica named after him in tribute to his use of seismic waves to ascertain the structure of the Antarctic ice cap and its underlying terrain.

SELECTED WRITINGS BY PRESS:

Books

Thompson, Kenneth W., ed. *The Presidency and Science Advising*. New York: University Press of America, 1988, pp.133-143.
(With Raymond Siever) *Understanding Earth*. New York: W. H. Freeman, 1994.

FURTHER READING:

Periodicals

Boffey, Philip M. "Frank Press, Long-Shot Candidate, May Become Science Advisor." *Science* (February 25, 1977): 763-766.
Culliton, Barbara J. "Frank Press to Be Nominated for NAS." *Science* (October 24, 1980): 405-406.

Other

"Frank Press Wins National Medal of Science." Press Release. National Science Foundation. September 8, 1994.

Sketch by Leonard C. Bruno

Ada I. Pressman
1927–
American control systems engineer

Ada I. Pressman is a recognized authority in power plant controls and process instrumentation. She specialized in the area of shutdown systems for nuclear power plants, working to find ways to ensure that a nuclear power plant's turbine, steam engine, and reactor work together properly and safely to generate electrical power. Pressman's contributions to the technology of emergency systems for nuclear power plants include the development of a secondary cooling system that operates from a diesel generator in the event of a primary power source loss. These measures safeguard people working on site against the danger of radiation as well as protect plant machinery against physical damage if malfunctions occur. She received the Society of Women Engineers (SWE) Annual Achievement Award in 1976 "in recognition of her significant contributions in the field of power control systems engineering."

Ada Irene Pressman was born on March 3, 1927, in Shelby County, Ohio. She graduated from Ohio State University with a bachelor of science degree in mechanical engineering in 1950 and then began her professional career as a project engineer with Bailey Meter Company in Cleveland. Five years later, she accepted a post as project engineer with Bechtel Corporation in Los Angeles. During the next two decades, she was promoted to instrument group leader, control systems engineering group supervisor, and assistant chief control systems engineer. In these capacities, Pressman managed eighteen design teams for more than twenty power generating plants throughout the world. Pressman returned to college to earn her master's degree in business administration, which she obtained from Golden

Gate University in 1974, the same year she was named chief control systems engineer at Bechtel. In 1979, she became engineering manager; she retired in 1987.

In addition to her career at Bechtel, Pressman was noted for her involvement in science and women's organizations. She was president of the Society of Women Engineers in 1979–80, vice president of the Instrument Society of America from 1973 to 1978, and a member of the American Nuclear Society. She is a member of the Institute for Advancement of Engineering's College of Fellows. In the 1970s Pressman successfully campaigned to have control systems engineering classified as a separate field with the state engineering board of California and became the first person to be registered in the new discipline.

Honors awarded to Pressman include the Distinguished Alumna Award from Ohio State University, the E. G. Bailey Award from the Instrument Society of America, the Outstanding Engineer Merit Award, and the YWCA TWIN award. In an interview with contributor Karen Withem, Pressman said that her career in engineering was "a challenge and an opportunity to do a good job, to gain the feeling of accomplishment when something is done well." She believes that being one of a very few women in leadership in engineering caused her to develop resourcefulness. "I was never given the easiest jobs," she said. 'Some of those jobs that no one else wanted were opportunities in disguise. They gave me the chance to do things I wouldn't otherwise have had the opportunity to do." Her hobbies include traveling, bowling, and photography.

FURTHER READING:

Other

Pressman, Ada I., *Interview with Karen Withem,* conducted March 28, 1994.

Sketch by Karen Withem

Diana García Prichard
1949–
American chemical physicist

Diana García Prichard is a research scientist who conducts fundamental photographic materials research for the Eastman Kodak company. Her graduate work on the behavior of gas phases that she completed at the University of Rochester was lauded for its inventiveness and received unusual attention and recognition by the scientific community. She is also an active leader in the Hispanic

community and has garnered numerous awards for her work.

Prichard was born in San Francisco, California, on October 27, 1949. Her mother, Matilde (Robleto) Dominguez García, was originally from Granada, Nicaragua. Her father, Juan García, was from Aransas Pass, Texas, and was of Mexican and Native American descent. He worked as a warehouse foreman at Ray-O-Vac. Although both of her parents received little education, they knew well the value of schooling and saw that Prichard appreciated the worth and the joys of learning. After graduating from El Camino High School in South San Francisco, Prichard entered the College of San Mateo and received her LVN degree (nursing) in 1969.

After taking some years to care for her two children, Erik and Andrea, Prichard chose a dramatic career shift and reentered academia in 1979. Interested in things scientific ever since she was young, and always intrigued and attracted by the thinking process and creativity required to do real scientific research, she enrolled at California State University at Hayward and earned her B.S. degree in chemistry/physics in 1983. She then continued her postgraduate education at the University of Rochester in New York, obtaining her M.S. degree in physical chemistry in 1985. Continuing at Rochester, she entered the doctoral program and earned her Ph.D. in chemical physics in 1988.

Her graduate studies at Rochester emphasized optics, electronics, automation, vacuum technology, and signal processing with data acquisition and analysis. During this graduate work on the high resolution infrared absorption spectrum (which basically involves telling how much or what type of atoms or molecules are present), she was able to construct the first instrument ever to be able to measure van der Waals clusters. Named after Dutch Nobel prize-winning physicist **Johannes Diderick Waals**, the van der Waals equation accounts for the non-ideal behavior of gases at the molecular level. An ideal or perfect gas is one which always obeys the known gas laws. The van der Waals equation allows scientists to predict the behavior of gases that do not strictly follow these laws by factoring in specific corrections. Van der Waals clusters are weakly bound complexes that exist in a natural state but are low in number. Prichard's work allowed other scientists to produce these rare clusters by experimental methods and thus be able to study them. Her graduate publications on this subject were themselves cited in more than one hundred subsequent publications.

Upon graduation, Prichard accepted a position with Eastman Kodak of Rochester, New York. A research scientist in the firm's PhotoScience Research Division, she conducts basic studies in silver halide materials for photographic systems. A member of Sigma Xi and Sigma Pi Sigma honor societies as well as a national board member of the Society for Hispanic Professional Engineers (SHPE) and a charter member of the Hispanic Democratic Women's Network of Washington, D.C., she also served on the

Clinton/Gore Transition Cluster for Space, Science and Technology in 1992.

Prichard founded a program in Rochester called "Partnership in Education" that provides Hispanic role models in the classroom to teach science and math to limited English proficient students. She has also co-founded, within Eastman Kodak, the Hispanic Organization for Leadership and Advancement (HOLA). She is married to Mark S. Prichard, also a research scientist at Eastman Kodak. As to what she is most proud of in her career, she says that it is the fact that although her parents had little schooling, she was nevertheless able to come to love learning, obtain an advanced degree, and work in a professional field that she truly loves.

SELECTED WRITINGS BY PRICHARD:

Periodicals

Journal of Chemical Physics, Microwave and Infrared Studies of Acetylene Dimer in a T-Shaped Configuration, July 1, 1988, pp. 115–123.
Journal of Chemical Physics, Vibration-Rotation Spectrum of the Carbon Dioxide-Acetylene van der Waals Complex in the 3 u Region, August 1, 1988, pp. 1245–1250.

Sketch by Leonard C. Bruno

Ilya Prigogine
1917–
Belgian chemist

Ilya Prigogine was awarded the 1977 Nobel Prize in chemistry for his pioneering work on nonequilibrium thermodynamics. He revolutionized chemistry by introducing the concepts of irreversible time and probability in his approach to unstable chemical states and providing mathematical models of dissipative structures and their self-organization, the processes by which disorder progresses to order. Taking a highly philosophical approach to science, Prigogine has redefined the framework of the laws of nature, insisting on a less deterministic understanding of the natural world.

Prigogine was born in Moscow, Russia, on January 25, 1917, two months before the collapse of the czarist regime and nine months before the Bolshevik revolution. His father, Roman, was a chemical engineer and a factory owner, and his mother, Julia (Wichman) Prigogine, had studied music at the Moscow conservatory of music. Prigogine's brother,

Ilya Prigogine

Alexandre, who was four years older, also became a chemist.

Four years after he was born, Prigogine's father decided to leave Russia because of the restrictions placed on private ownership and enterprise by the new Soviet government. After a year in Lithuania, the family moved to Berlin where they remained until 1929. Their stay in Berlin coincided with the terrible inflation of the early twenties and the beginnings of Nazism in the latter half of the decade. After two of his business attempts failed, and with growing Nazi strength boding ill for Jewish émigrés, Prigogine's father took the family to Brussels, Belgium, where Prigogine, then twelve, was enrolled in the Latin-Greek section of the Athénée d'Ixelles, a secondary school with a strict classical curriculum.

Early Education

At this stage in his life, Prigogine was interested not in science but in history, archeology, art, and music; his mother claimed he could understand musical notes before he could understand words. Taught to play the piano by his mother, he even considered a career as a concert pianist, later regretting that he did not have as much time to devote to his music as he would have liked. He also read widely in the classics and philosophy during his teen years, and was particularly impressed by Henri Bergson's *L'évolution créatrice* and the Bergsonian view of the nature of time. He became a chemist as the result of a chance occurrence after his family had decided, and Prigogine concurred, that he should become a lawyer. Feeling that a first step to that end would be to learn about the criminal mind, he sought information about criminal psychology. In so doing, he came across a book dealing with the chemical composition of the brain, and he was so intrigued that he abandoned the law and took up chemistry.

Prigogine enrolled in the Free University of Brussels in 1935 to study chemistry, as had his brother before him. In 1939 he received his master's degree; he also won a prize for his performance of some Schumann pieces in a piano competition. Under the direction of Théophile De Donder, Prigogine received his Ph.D. in 1941 with the thesis, "The Thermodynamic Study of Irreversible Phenomena." De Donder was the founder of the Brussels school of thermodynamics (the branch of physics that deals with the behavior of heat and related phenomena) and one of the first scientists to attempt to deal with the thermodynamics of systems not at equilibrium, that is, not in balance. Prigogine has credited De Donder with developing the mathematical apparatus needed for studying nonequilibrium states, and these tools would prove important to Prigogine's own work. Another professor who had an influence on the course of Prigogine's career was Jean Timmermans, a chemist and experimentalist interested in applying classical thermodynamics to the study of solutions and other complex systems. In 1957, Prigogine co-wrote *The Molecular Theory of Solutions,* which explained that at a low temperature, liquid helium would spontaneously separate into two phases, one of helium–3 and the other of helium–4. This was later confirmed experimentally. The book also develops methods for dealing with polymer solutions, some of which are still in use.

Incorporates Time and Entropy into Chemistry

With his early interest in the nature of time, it was natural that Prigogine should be attracted to a study of the second law of thermodynamics that states that any spontaneous change in a closed system (one where neither matter nor energy flows into or out of the system) occurs in the direction that increases entropy, the measure of unavailable energy in a system or the measure of its disorder. This law indicates that as time passes in a closed system, disorder always increases, leading Sir **Arthur Stanley Eddington** to refer to the second law as supplying "the arrow of time." The move toward entropy described in the second law is irreversible, which contrasts with all other physical laws in which processes are reversible in time. This contrast begged the question of how the reversible, random workings of molecular and atomic motions could lead to processes that have a preferred direction in time. Furthermore, the second law, when extended to the largest known systems, suggests that the universe is moving toward eventual decay, a point when all energy and matter will reach a uniform state of equilibrium known as heat death.

Intrigued by these issues, Prigogine moved his focus away from the ideal "closed" system described in the second law and instead studied open systems that exchange matter and energy with an outside environment. Prigogine's first success in dealing with irreversible processes and open systems not at equilibrium came in 1945. In his doctoral research, he showed that for systems not too far from equilibrium, changes take place so as to achieve a steady state in which the production of entropy is at a minimum. This is true near equilibrium where the flux (or flow) of energy or matter through the system is directly proportional to the force creating that flux; that is, the flux and the force are linearly related. But such a steady state, once established, is stable and continues unchanged; it cannot evolve into a new state. Prigogine's work in this area led to his book *Thermodynamics of Irreversible Processes.*

In 1947 Prigogine succeeded De Donder to become full professor at the Free University of Brussels, where he assembled an interdisciplinary group to study irreversible processes. He went on to show that far from equilibrium, where fluxes and forces are no longer linearly related, a system can become unstable and evolve new, organized structures spontaneously. Prigogine called these organizations dissipative structures and developed the mathematical means of describing them. Prigogine theorized that such structures can be maintained as long as the energy and material fluxes are kept up. The process by which a new order evolves is labeled self-organization. In a nonlinear system there exist points—Prigogine referred to these as moments of choice or bifurcation points—at which the system is unstable, and small fluctuations can grow to a macroscopic or large size, creating a new structure. Randomness enters at the bifurcation points, so that predictions with respect to outcomes can only be expressed as probabilities. Common examples, although complicated and difficult to analyze, include the development of conduction cells in liquids heated from below (known as the Bénard instability), or the abrupt change from smooth flow to turbulent flow as the velocity of a liquid passing through a pipe is increased.

Empirical Confirmation

Prigogine's findings, while important, remained largely theoretical into the 1960s. Attempting to confirm his ideas, Prigogine worked with G. Nicolis and Réné Lefever to devise a simple mathematical model now called the Brusselator to better test his theories. Then in 1965 the Belousov-Zhabotinskii reaction, discovered in 1951 in the Soviet Union, became widely known abroad. One version of the reaction, in which the dissipative structures can be seen and do not have to be revealed by elaborate measurements, is a solution of malonic acid and bromate ion in sulfuric acid and ferrous phenanthroline (ferroin). Depending on the temperature and concentrations of the various species, the color of the solution may change back and forth from red to blue, or a pattern of red and blue may be formed that is either stationary or moves through the solution in a regular manner. These patterns gave striking visual proof of the existence of Prigogine's dissipative structures. In 1968 Richard Noyes at the University of Oregon was able to establish the mechanism of the reaction and, using Prigogine's work, to describe the phenomenon exactly.

The various processes that take place in cells involve complicated cycles of reactions catalyzed by special proteins called enzymes. Many of these enzymatic cycles meet the requirements for the formation of dissipative structures. For example, the breakdown of sugar in a cell has been shown to occur on a regular, periodic basis. Consequently, Prigogine's work is of great interest to biologists and biochemists. In fact, it was suggested by **Alan Mathison Turing** in 1952 that instabilities in chemical reaction systems could explain the patterns of stripes on a zebra or spots on a leopard. On a still larger scale, the thermodynamics of irreversible systems may explain how evolution, a process that gives rise to ever more specialized forms, is compatible with a physical picture of the world in which systems inevitably move from an ordered to a disordered state.

Prigogine and others have also applied the principles of irreversible thermodynamics to such disparate systems as the development of traffic patterns on a highway in response to driving conditions, the aggregation of slime molds in response to the depletion of nutrients in their environment, and the buildup of giant termite mounds in which a large number of independent termites behave in an orderly, seemingly purposeful, and intelligent fashion. On a larger scale, Prigogine's research allows a somewhat different and brighter view of the universe's ultimate fate. As explained in *Omni,* the theory of dissipative structures "offers a guardedly optimistic alternative to the pessimistic view of mankind's future—that winding down of nature toward a kind of heat death."

In 1949 Prigogine became a Belgian citizen, so that his Nobel Prize in 1977 was the first given to a Belgian. He was named director of the Instituts Internationaux de Physique et de Chimie (the Solvay Institute) in 1959, a post in which he continued after his retirement from the Free University in 1985. From 1961 to 1966 he spent time at the University of Chicago, and since 1967 spends three months of each year as director of the Ilya Prigogine Center for Statistical Mechanics and Thermodynamics at the University of Texas. He and his wife, Marina Prokopowicz, an engineer whom he married in 1961, live in Brussels.

Prigogine has attempted to explain the implications of his work for the general public in two books: *From Being to Becoming: Time and Complexity in the Physical Sciences* in 1980 and, with Isabelle Stengers, *Order out of Chaos: Man's New Dialog with Nature* in 1984. For the latter work, Prigogine was made *commandeur* of the Ordre des Arts et des Lettres by the French government, an honor he especially prized because it is usually given to recognize achievement in the arts. Among the many honors conferred on him are the honorary foreign memberships in the U.S. National Academy of Sciences and the Academy of Sciences of the U.S.S.R. (now Russia).

SELECTED WRITINGS BY PRIGOGINE:

Books

The Molecular Theory of Solutions, North-Holland, 1957.

Thermodynamics of Irreversible Processes, 3rd edition, Interscience, 1967.

Thermodynamic Theory of Structure, Stability and Fluctuations, Interscience, 1971.

Self-Organization in Non-Equilibrium Systems: From Dissipative Structures to Order through Fluctuations, Wiley, 1977.

From Being to Becoming: Time and Complexity in the Physical Sciences, (first appeared in French as La nouvelle alliance), Freeman, 1980.

Order out of Chaos, Bantam, 1984.

Periodicals

Physics Today, Thermodynamics of Evolution, Volume 25, Number 11, 1972, pp. 23–28; Volume 25, Number 12, 1972, pp. 38–44.

Science, Time, Structure, and Fluctuations, Volume 201, September 1, 1978, pp. 777–785.

FURTHER READING:

Books

Current Biography Yearbook, H. W. Wilson, 1987, pp. 447–450.

McGraw-Hill Modern Scientists and Engineers, Volume 2, McGraw-Hill, 1980, pp. 440–441.

Periodicals

Lepkowski, Will, *Chemical and Engineering News,* The Social Thermodynamics of Ilya Prigogine, April 16, 1979, pp. 30–33.

Procaccia, I., and J. Ross, *Science,* The 1977 Nobel Prize in Chemistry, Volume 198, November 18, 1977, pp. 716–717.

Snell, M. B., *New Perspectives Quarterly,* Beyond Being and Becoming, Volume 9, spring, 1992, pp. 22–28.

Tucker, R. B., *Omni,* Ilya Prigogine, Volume 5, Number 8, 1983, pp. 84–92, 120–121.

Sketch by R. F. Trimble

Margie Profet
1958–
American biomedical researcher

As a self-made scientist, Margie Profet's approach to scientific the discipline is relatively unique. She told Terry McDermott in the *Seattle Times*, "I'm very opportunistic and if I think of a neat idea, I work on it." Profet conducts biomedical research from a Darwinian perspective, one that believes that the human body is an adaptation to its environment. In this evolutionary medical theory, bodily defense mechanisms happen for a reason, there are few accidents, and there is a balance between costs and benefits. Her theories concern everyday questions and bodily functions such as menstruation, allergies, and morning sickness in pregnancy. Because Profet lacks advanced degrees, her theories are controversial with scientists and physicians. However, Profet has been lauded for her work, and in 1993 she was awarded a MacArthur Foundation "genius" grant.

Profet was born August 7, 1958, in Berkeley, California, to Bob (a physicist) and Karen (an engineer) Profet. With her three siblings, Profet grew up in Manhattan Beach, California, where her parents worked in the aerospace industry. Profet received her first undergraduate degree from Harvard University in 1980. She majored in political philosophy, and it was while writing her senior thesis that she decided she wanted to devote her intellectual life to original thought. After graduation, Profet went to Europe, where she worked for a year as a computer programmer in Munich, Germany, from 1980 to 1981. After returning to the United States, Profet decided to pursue her lifelong interest in biology. She entered the University of California, Berkeley, and earned another B.A. in 1985, this time in physics. Profet was unhappy with the structures, limitations, and regimentations of academia, and decided to pursue her interests on her own time. She has never taken a college-level biology class.

Living in San Francisco, Profet supported herself with a series of part-time jobs while she pursued her own research. Beginning in 1986, Profet derived what became her first published theory, which concerned morning sickness and pregnancy. It was inspired by conversations she had with pregnant friends and relatives. Profet concluded, after much research and reflection, that morning sickness happens for a reason. She believes that certain foods contain toxins that could harm a developing embryo in the first trimester, when the fetus is most vulnerable and when most significant birth defects can develop.

Profet believes that the nausea caused by certain foods and scents is a defense mechanism to protect the vulnerable embryo when it needs it the most. After the first trimester, when the embryo is less susceptible because it has begun to develop its own defenses, there is usually little to no morning sickness. In 1995, Profet published a book, *Protecting Your Baby-to-Be*, explaining this idea for women in their first trimester of pregnancy. In it, she outlines specific foods to avoid.

While working through her morning sickness theory for publication, Profet had her second insight, inspired by her own experiences with allergies. Beginning with the observation that certain allergic reactions are often immediate—scratching, sneezing, vomiting, etc.—Profet formulated a hypothesis that argues allergies are reactions to toxins. She believes that the human body's immune system battles these environmental toxins—plant-borne compounds—that are potentially harmful to cells. The toxins themselves can cause allergies, or a toxin and allergen can be linked. The toxins must be immediately expelled by the body, hence the immediacy of a sneeze or a scratch. Additionally, Profet theorizes that allergic reactions do not happen to everybody because they are a last ditch defense method against toxins. Because other, first-line defenses work in some people, they do not need to have allergic reactions. Profet published these findings in 1991 in the *Quarterly Review of Biology*.

During this period, Profet was hired by Professor **Bruce Ames**, a toxologist at the University of California at Berkeley, to be a biology research associate in his laboratory. In June 1993, she was awarded a five-year $225,000 grant by the John D. & Katherine T. MacArthur Foundation. Soon after receiving the grant, Profet moved to Seattle, Washington, and became affiliated with the University of Washington and its molecular biotechnology department.

In the fall of 1993, Profet published her seminal theory on why women menstruate in the September issue of the *Quarterly Review of Biology*. This was a subject that had intrigued her since the age of seven when she first learned what it was. Profet wondered why women's bodies cast off so much blood and tissue, including the nutrients therein, and concluded that it is an evolutionary adaptation. She believes the process of menstruation defends the uterus, fallopian tubes, and related organs from pathogens and other potentially damaging microbes that append themselves to sperm. By menstruating, the body sheds the uterus's outer lining where these pathogens persist. The blood that douses the area is full of immune cells that can neutralize any remaining microbes.

Profet's approach to science has been called visionary, because she questions phenomenons for which there are already accepted answers. Still, Profet has many critics to her ideas, methodology, and lack of graduate education. She explained to Terry McDermott that her view is "No matter what aspect of physiology you look at the core question is: What's it there for? Maybe it is just a fluke or a by-product. But maybe it has a function. You have to know that. Otherwise, you're doing blind medical intervention."

SELECTED WRITINGS BY PROFET:

Book

Protecting Your Baby-to-Be. New York: Addison-Wesley Publishing, 1995.

Periodicals

"The Function of Allergy: Immunological Defense Against Toxins." *Quarterly Review of Biology* (March 1991): 23.

"Menstruation as a Defense against Pathogens Transported by Sperm." *Quarterly Review of Biology* (September 1993): 335.

FURTHER READING:

Periodicals

Angier, Natalie. "Biologists Advise Doctors to Think like Darwin." *The New York Times* (December 24, 1991): C1.

Bloch, Hannah. "School Isn't My Kind of Thing." *Time* (October 4, 1993): 72.

McDermott, Terry. "Darwinian Medicine—It's a War Out There and Margie Profet, A Leading Theorist in a New Science, Thinks the Human Body Does Some Pretty Weird Things to Survive." *The Seattle Times* (July 31, 1994): 10.

McNichol, Tom. "Bleach Blanket Biologist." *USA Weekend* (October 8, 1995): 14.

Oliwenstein, Lori. "Dr. Darwin: Darwinian Medicine Studies the Evolutionary Purpose of Disease." *Discover* (October 1995): 110.

"Radical New View of Role of Menstruation." *The New York Times* (September 21, 1993): C1.

Rudavsky, Shari. "Margie Profet. (Researcher of Evolutionary Physiology)." *Omni* (May 1994): 69.

Williams, Emily. "Allergies First Attracted Notice in Modern Times." *The Dallas Morning News* (October 11, 1993): 6F.

Sketch by Annette Petrusso

Aleksandr Prokhorov
1916–
Russian physicist

Aleksandr Prokhorov, a pioneer in the field of quantum electronics, began his scientific career by studying radio wave propagation. His application of these studies to the theoretical design of a molecular generator and amplifier in 1952 formed the basis for the invention of both masers and lasers. For his work in quantum electronics Prokhorov shared the 1964 Nobel Prize in physics with his colleague, **Nikolai G. Basov**, and the American physicist **Charles H. Townes**.

Aleksandr Mikhailovich Prokhorov was born on July 11, 1916, in Atherton, Australia. His parents, Mikhail Ivanovich and Mariya Ivanovna Prokhorov, had fled from Siberia to Australia in 1911 because of Mikhail's involvement in revolutionary activities. The family returned to the Soviet Union in 1923, and Prokhorov received his undergraduate education at the Leningrad State University, receiving his baccalaureate degree in 1939.

Prokhorov embarked on his graduate studies at the P. N. Lebedev Institute of Physics of the Soviet Academy of Sciences in Moscow. His research dealt with the propagation of radio waves and their use in studying the upper atmosphere of Earth. In June 1941 the German invasion of Russia interrupted his studies and he was called to military service. Prokhorov was wounded in battle twice before being discharged in 1944. He then completed his research for the candidate's degree (comparable to a master's degree) with a thesis on nonlinear oscillators. In 1951 he was awarded a Ph.D. in physical and mathematical sciences for his research on the radiation produced by electrons in the high-energy orbits of the synchrotron, a circular particle accelerator that uses electrical and magnetic fields to propel the components of atoms to extremely high speeds. Prior to receiving his degree, Prokhorov had been appointed assistant director of the Oscillation Laboratory at the Lebedev Institute. He continued his research on the uses of radar and radio waves and applied them to the study of molecular structure and properties. In connection with this work, he came into contact with Nikolai G. Basov, with whom he was to collaborate on some of his most important work.

Prokhorov and Basov Develop the Molecular Generator

Prokhorov and Basov soon became involved in the stimulated emission of radiation from gas molecules. Three decades earlier in 1917, **Albert Einstein** had studied the effects of radiation on atoms. Using quantum mechanics, Einstein confirmed earlier hypotheses that electrons in an atom tend to absorb small amounts of energy and jump to higher energy levels in the atom. They then re-emit the absorbed radiation and return to lower, less energetic orbitals. But Einstein also discovered that in some instances an electron in a higher energy level can, simply by virtue of being exposed to radiation, jump to a lower energy level and emit a photon of a wavelength identical to that of the external radiation. This process became known as stimulated emission.

Prokhorov and Basov saw in Einstein's analysis a way of using molecules to amplify the energy of a given beam of radiation. Radiation could be used to stimulate the emission of more photons of the same wavelength within an atom, creating a domino effect among other atoms, thus stimulating the emission of more photons. This cascade of energy emission could result in a mechanism for generating more and more intense beams of radiation with a very narrow range of wavelengths. Later researchers used these findings to develop masers (microwave amplification by stimulated emission of radiation) and lasers (light amplification by stimulated emissions of radiation).

Prokhorov and Basov announced the discovery of their molecular generator in a paper read before the All-Union Conference on Radio Spectroscopy in May 1952. However, they did not publish their results for more than two years, by which time the American physicist Charles H. Townes had built a working maser and published his conclusions in *Physical Review*. In awarding the 1964 Nobel Prize in physics, the Nobel committee recognized the contributions of all three physicists. The discovery of the molecular generator provided the theoretical basis for the development of both masers and lasers, on which Prokhorov has concentrated his research efforts since the mid–1950s.

In 1941 Prokhorov married the former Galina Alekseyevna Shelepina, with whom he had one son, Kiril. He was appointed professor at Moscow State University in 1959 and eventually returned to the Lebedev Institute, where he was appointed deputy director in 1972. He has also been editor-in-chief of the *Great Soviet Encyclopedia* since 1969 and was made a corresponding (associate) member of the Soviet Academy of Sciences in 1960 and an academician (full member) in 1966. Prokhorov was awarded the Lenin Prize in 1959 and the Lomonosov Gold Medal of the Soviet Academy of Sciences in 1988.

SELECTED WRITINGS BY PROKHOROV:

Books

Problems in Solid-State Physics, 1984.

Periodicals

Zhur. Eksptl'. i Teoret. Fiz., Application of Molecular Beams to Radio Spectroscopic Study of the Rotation Spectra of Molecules, Volume 27, 1954, pp. 431–438.

Zhur. Eksptl'. i Teoret. Fiz., Theory of the Molecular Generator and the Molecular Power Amplifier, Volume 30, 1956, pp. 560–563.

FURTHER READING:

Books

Nobel Prize Winners, H. W. Wilson, 1987, pp. 839–841.

Weber, Robert L., *Pioneers of Science: Nobel Prize Winners in Physics,* American Institute of Physics, 1980, pp. 199–200.

Periodicals

Gordon, J. P., *Science,* Research on Maser-Laser Principle Wins Nobel Prize in Physics, November 13, 1964, pp. 897–899.

Gordon, J. P., *Science News,* Nobel Prize Winners, November 7, 1964, p. 295.

Sketch by David E. Newton

Stanley B. Prusiner
1942–
American neurologist

In many ways, it was the classic case of the underdog overcoming adversity, of the lone voice vindicated. A brash young "maverick scientist," according to Lawrence K. Altman in the *New York Times,* flew in the face of conventional medical wisdom to propose a radical new form of infective agent. If proven to exist, such an agent would be the "most remarkable form of life on the planet" and one that "would require a dramatic rewriting of the dogma of molecular biology, a redefinition of the meaning of life itself," as Gary Taubes wrote in *Discover.* For a quarter of a century this scientist stuck to his guns in the face of criticism and sometimes ridicule to be honored for his work in 1997 by the Nobel Prize. For Stanley B. Prusiner, the prize was an indication that his life's work had been validated. However, as he told the *Washington Post* after receiving the award, he still felt that "science should be reticent to accept new ideas. Ninety-nine percent of new ideas are wrong. We have to be very tough on our colleagues."

The furor over Prusiner's work was caused by his novel theory of an infective agent which was neither bacterial, nor viral, nor fungal. Building on the work of British scientists, Prusiner hypothesized in 1981 that a type of protein particle, which he dubbed the prion (pronounced *pree-on*), was responsible for a host of fatal neurodegenerative disorders, including Creutzfeldt-Jakob disease (CJD) as well as diseases of animals such as scrapie and mad cow disease. Prusiner's hypothesis and subsequent research was revolutionary in that it posited the ability of a protein—which lacks genetic material and thus the ability to reproduce—to function as a pathogenic agent and to spread infectious disease. Prusiner's ground-breaking work won him the 1997 Nobel Prize in Physiology or Medicine because it "provides important insights that may furnish the basis to understand the biological mechanisms underlying other types of dementia-related diseases, for example Alzheimer's disease," noted the Karolinska Institute in its announcement of the prize. The Nobel committee went on to say that Prusiner's work also "establishes a foundation for drug development and new types of medical treatment strategies."

Stanley B. Prusiner

Death of Patient Spurs Early Research

Prusiner was born on May 28, 1942, in Des Moines, Iowa. He earned his B.A., *cum laude*, at the University of Pennsylvania, in 1964, and then went on to receive an M.D. in 1968 from the same university. Already during his medical studies, he was interested in biochemical research. Prusiner then served his internship and residency at the prestigious University of California at San Francisco (UCSF) from 1968 to 1969, where he later served a residency in neurology, "the last great frontier of medicine," as he was quoted as saying in *Discover*. Married and the father of two children, Prusiner soon became interested in neurodegenerative diseases. This interest was in part developed after one of his patients died of CJD, a disease of the cerebral cortex which leads to dementia and eventual death.

As a result of this experience, Prusiner learned that an entire category of diseases was yet to be elucidated. At the time, researchers thought many neurodegenerative diseases were caused by so-called slow viruses, which would take years and sometimes decades to incubate in the host. As early as 1967, a British team working at Hammersmith Hospital had proposed the existence of an infective agent that lacked nucleic acid in the sheep disease known as scrapie. Their hypothesis grew out of the fact that when the genetic substance was destroyed in known infected material, extracts from the infected material were still able to spread the disease. This led to the conclusion that perhaps the infective agents in such animal diseases as scrapie (so called because infected sheep tend to scrape the wool off their

bodies) and kuru (a disease of the cannibalistic Fore people of New Guinea which had been traced to the ritual eating of the brains of departed relatives) were non-viral.

Prusiner combined a zeal for research with a disarming political sense to win grants for the study of such diseases, including CJD, scrapie, kuru, fatal familial insomnia, and bovine spongiform encephalopathy (BSE), or mad cow disease. Over three decades, he managed to gain funding totaling 56 million dollars from the National Institutes of Health (NIH).

Three Decades of Research Leads to Prion

Expanding on work by British researchers as well as the NIH's Rocky Mountain Laboratories, which had shown similarities between kuru and scrapie, Prusiner set up a research team at UCSF employing ultimately a quarter million mice infected with diseased brain matter in an attempt to isolate the infective agent in neurodegenerative diseases. Such research was laborious and time-consuming, for the incubation period in mice took upwards of 200 days. Early breakthroughs occurred when Prusiner switched from mice to hamsters, as the onset of illness in those animals would occur twice as fast. By 1981, Prusiner was able to conclude that a protein was the causative agent in these brain diseases, and he dubbed this agent the prion. Such proteins were resistant to any modification of nucleic acids. When he and his team added enzymes that destroy nucleic acids in genes, they discovered that there was no reduction in the infective power of prions.

This early pronouncement caused a stir in the scientific community, with critics finding it implausible that infectious diseases could be transmitted by a substance incapable of reproducing itself. Prusiner answered this criticism with his theory that prions existed in the white blood cells and on the surface cells in the brains of all mammals and were, in their normal state, non-infectious. Such normal particles he called the prion protein, PrP; so-called "rogue" prions which spontaneously altered their form to cause scrapie, he called scrapie PrP, or PrPSc. PrP's consist primarily of alpha helices, that is, as Prusiner described it in *Scientific American*, "regions in which the protein backbone twists into a specific kind of spiral."

Research showed, however, that PrPSc, or the scrapie form of prion, contains beta strands in which the backbone seems to be fully extended. Such PrPScs accumulate in beta sheets. Prusiner concluded that prion-induced diseases spread when such a rogue prion attaches itself to healthy prions and causes a sort of chain reaction in healthy proteins, cascading them into malignant clusters that cause dementia, loss of muscular control, and insomnia, depending upon which part of the brain these renegade prions attack. Smaller than viruses and resistant to the body's immune system because they have been present since birth, these disease-causing prions ultimately destroy parts of the brain by killing brain cells and forming a porous or spongy area. Thus the class of neurodegenerative disorders they cause is called spongiform encephalopathies. Prusiner was also able to demonstrate that such diseases may be inherited, may be transmitted within species and possibly between species, and may also occur in as-yet unknown ways spontaneously.

In 1992, Prusiner's research more clearly demonstrated the nature of the interaction between prion proteins. Prusiner showed that when the gene encoding for the prion protein in mice was destroyed, such mice (called prion knock-out mice) proved resistant to the diseases when injected with preparations of disease-causing prion protein. Later, when the prion gene was re-activated and the same mice were injected with diseased matter, they again became susceptible to infection. Though the role of prion proteins is unclear, what has become clear is the close causative effect of rogue prions in a variety of neural diseases.

The diseases which Prusiner studied are life-threatening to only a tiny fraction of the world's population—the annual death toll of CJD in the United States annually, for example, is about 225, less than the number of traffic fatalities in two days. However, as the Nobel committee noted, Prusiner's researches could lead to new therapies for a larger array of neurological disorders such as Alzheimer's and Parkinson's disease, which may or may not be caused by protein-based infective agents. In the case of prion-based diseases, Prusiner has suggested gene therapy to curtail the production of prion proteins and thus eliminate the spread of such diseases, as was done with his prion knock-out mice.

Critics Remain Unconvinced

Prusiner still has his critics. Some say that there is still no conclusive proof that a viral agent is not involved in neurodegenerative diseases, claiming that Prusiner's work does not rule out the possibility of viral particles working in tandem with prions. Also, only a week before the awarding of the Nobel, *Nature* magazine, in its October 2, 1997 issue, ran an article that suggested a viral cause for transmission of CJD to humans from BSE, or mad cow disease. Prusiner had attributed a cross-species infection from a wild prion for the 21 cases of a new variant of CJD. Other critics note that the variety of strains of each of these neural diseases points to the existence of an agent that is able to adapt and change its reproductive coding. For example, 15 different strains are recognized for scrapie and at least one variant for CJD. Prusiner answers such critics with the explanation that prion folding or the shape-changing of rogue prions could be responsible for such a variety of disease strains; different alpha helix mutations could also explain the phenomena of disease strain variety for prion-based infections. Still other critics complain that Prusiner has extrapolated his findings past credibility, and that he has simply incorporated the work of others into his own, changing terminology so as to make him appear the lone pioneer in the field. Some also assert that his findings are often published in journals without adequate peer review.

When awarding Prusiner with the Nobel, the Karolinska Institute deviated from its norms in two ways. Usually the award is shared by several researchers in one field.

Prusiner is the first individual winner since 1987. Also, the committee usually withholds the Nobel until all controversies have been resolved. But as Dr. Lars Edstrom, a member of the Nobel award committee, noted in Altman's *New York Times* article, "There are still people who don't believe that a protein can cause these diseases, but we believe it. . . . From our point of view, there is no doubt." Other award committees have felt the same. Prusiner has won, among other prominent scientific awards, the Gairdner Foundation Award for Outstanding Achievement in Medical Science in 1993, the Albert Lasker Award for Basic Medical Research in 1994, and the Wolf Prize in Medicine in 1996. But only time will demonstrate if Prusiner or his critics are right. As Prusiner himself said in an interview reported in Altman's *New York Times* article, "No prize, not even a Nobel Prize, can make something true that is not."

SELECTED WRITINGS BY PRUSINER:

Books

Prions, Prions, Prions. Springer, 1995.

Periodicals

(With others) "Evidence for Isolate Specified Allotypic Interactions between the Cellular and Scrapie Prion Proteins in Congenic and Transgenic Mice." *Proceedings of the National Academy of Science U.S.A.* 91 (1994): 5690-5694.

(With others) "Degeneration of Skeletal Muscle, Peripheral Nerves, and the Central Nervous System in Transgenic Mice Overexpressing Wild-Type Prion Proteins." *Cell* 76 (1994): 117-129.

(With others) "Structural Clues to Prion Replication." *Science* 264 (1994): 530-531.

(With others) "Transmission of Creutzfeldt-Jakob Disease from Humans to Transgenic Mice Expressing Chimeric Human-Mouse Prion Protein." *Proceedings of the National Academy of Science U.S.A.* 91 (1994): 9936-9940.

"The Prion Diseases." *Scientific American* 272 (1995): 70-77.

FURTHER READING:

Periodicals

Altman, Lawrence K. "U.S. Scientist Wins Nobel Prize for Controversial Work." *New York Times* (October 7, 1997): A1, A12.

Taubes, Gary. "The Game of the Name Is Fame. But Is It Science?" *Discover* (December 1986): 44-56.

Weiss, Rick. "Nobel Prize Vindicates U.S. Scientist." *Washington Post* (October 7, 1997): A1.

Other

The Nobel Assembly at the Karolinska Institute. "Press Release: The 1997 Nobel Prize in Physiology or Medicine." October 6, 1997. http://www.nobel.se/laureates/medicine-1997.html (October 2, 1997). This web site provides hyperlinks to a vast array of material on Prusiner, his research, and writings.

Sketch by J. Sydney Jones

Theodore T. Puck

Theodore T. Puck
1916–
American biologist

Theodore Puck helped lay the foundations of cytogenetics with his ground-breaking technique of culturing mammalian cells and his subsequent research into the genetic basis of human cell development, differentiation, and mutation. His work has led to modern methods of radiation therapy and genetic screening, as well as helped pave the way toward recent advances in genetic engineering and cancer research.

Theodore Thomas Puck was born September 24, 1916, in Chicago, Illinois, to Joseph and Bessie (Shapiro) Puckowitz. He attended Chicago Public Schools and graduated with a bachelor's degree in chemistry from the University of Chicago in 1937. In 1940, he earned his Ph.D. in physical chemistry from the university.

Launches a Career

After receiving his doctorate, he became a research fellow in the university's department of medicine. Working there from 1941 to 1945, Puck focused on aerosol dynamics and the prevention of infections caused by airborne viruses and bacteria. During his investigations, he discovered that particular aerosols could kill contagions by condensing onto their surfaces to quickly create a sterilizing concentration. Puck applied his findings to his work as a member of the U.S. Army's Commission on Airborne Infections during World War II. In 1945, he joined the faculty of the University of Chicago's departments of medicine and biochemistry as an assistant professor. While at the university he married Mary Hill on April 17, 1946, in Santa Fe, New Mexico.

In 1947, Puck left the Midwest for a senior fellowship at the California Institute of Technology. After a year, he joined the University of Colorado Medical Center as professor and chairman of its new department of biophysics. He remained there from 1948 to 1967, when he joined the medical center's department of biophysics and genetics.

Builds on Single-Cell Plating Techniques

In the years before Puck conducted his research, biologists discovered that if they isolated an individual cell from certain plants or animals and placed it in a specific artificial medium, it could thrive and ultimately be encouraged to asexually replicate, or clone, itself. Using this method, known as single-cell plating, scientists could bypass the time-consuming process of sexual reproduction and grow large colonies of cells in a short time. However, while the cells of many complex species had been replicated, no one had yet devised a way to grow mammalian cells in this manner. Puck made this a research priority and, with his students at the University of Colorado Medical Center, devised a simple and effective means to asexually reproduce mammalian cells in petri dish cultures.

This achievement opened the way to a wide range of investigations into the qualities of mammalian—and ultimately human—cells. Puck and other researchers could measure genetic processes as well as isolate and create reserves of various mutated cells for use in experiments. Puck was also able to observe how a wide range of chemical, biological, and physical conditions could possibly affect the cells and their genetic material. Among his most important discoveries in this regard was his determination of the mean dose of radiation that would kill a mammalian cell. His experiments demonstrated that it took only 100 rads of radiation to kill a cell—a fraction of what had previously been thought of as the lethal dose. This work held important implications for cancer patients undergoing radiation therapy, for they would not have to be subjected to such high doses as had been believed necessary.

Investigates Genes

Another significant finding made by Puck and his laboratory involved the number of chromosomes in a human cell. Able to sample and maintain the cells of a wide range of individuals, Puck eventually concluded that the standard number of chromosomes in a human cell is 46, not 47 or 48 as had previously been believed. The first complete analysis of human chromosomes, Puck's research helped pave the way for the later study of chromosomal and genetic abnormalities.

While these accomplishments may have been sufficient for another scientist, they inspired Puck to continue his work. He turned his attention to studying cell biochemistry and the factors that caused cell differentiation. He and his laboratory also produced the first single-gene mutants in mammalian cells and created a hybrid cell that contained both human and hamster chromosomes. In addition, he also investigated the effect of cyclic adenosine monophosphate (cyclic AMP) on cancer cells, work that has since formed the basis of new theories regarding the disease.

Is Honored for His Work

Theodore Puck has received many honors in recognition of his work. Many universities have invited him to speak, and professional organizations have honored him often. Among his many awards are the Albert Lasker Award in Medical Research (1958), the Borden Award in Medical Research (1959), the General Rose Memorial Hospital Award (1960), the American Clinical and Climatological Association's Gordon Wilson Medal (1977), the Ann Award from the Environmental Mutagen Society (1984), and the E. B. Wilson Medal from the American Society of Cellular Biologists, also in 1984. In 1969, his alma mater presented him with its distinguished alumni award.

Among his many memberships are the National Academy of Science, the Institute of Medicine, the Commission on Physicians for the Future, and the American Academy of Arts and Sciences (1972, fellow). In 1966, the American Cancer Society named him its distinguished research professor.

Currently, Puck is director of the Eleanor Roosevelt Cancer Center in Colorado. He has also been a visiting fellow at Los Alamos National Laboratories in New Mexico since 1987 and a member of the National Institutes of Health's Advisory Committee on Radiologic Health.

FURTHER READING:

Books

National Cyclopedia of American Biography. New York: James T. White & Company, 1930. Volume N-63, pages 79-80.

Sketch by Francis Hodgkins

R. C. Punnett
1875–1967
English morphologist and geneticist

Noted morphologist and geneticist R. C. Punnett was instrumental in introducing the field of genetics to lay audiences, especially to commercial breeders of livestock. His contributions significantly advanced knowledge of the genetics of fowl, ducks, rabbits, sweet pea plants, and humans; his research served as the foundation for poultry genetics for decades. Punnett was among the pioneering investigators who helped revolutionize scientific thought in the field of genetics after the rediscovery of Gregor Mendel's work with genetics and heredity.

Reginald Crundall Punnett, the eldest of three children, was born on June 20, 1875, at Tonbridge in Kent, England, to George Punnett, the head of a Tonbridge building firm, and Emily Crundall. He suffered from appendicitis as a child. During the treatment, which consisted of applying leeches to the lower stomach, and the daily bedrest required afterwards, he spent his time reading Jardine's *Naturalist's Library* and discovered a strong liking for natural history. He recovered and later was accepted to Cambridge University, where he developed an interest in human anatomy, human physiology, and zoology, and decided to pursue a career in zoology, not medicine as he originally had intended. As part of his zoological studies, Punnett observed sharks at the Zoological Station in Naples, Italy, for six months before graduating with first class honors from Cambridge's Caius College in 1898. He received his master's degree in 1902.

Studies Zoology of Worms

In 1899, Punnett was offered the position of demonstrator and part-time lecturer in the Natural History Department of St. Andrews University, where he stayed for three years. In 1901, he was elected a fellow of Caius College. During this time, his appendix had been troubling him sporadically and he decided to have it removed. As the scientific thought at the time was that worms caused appendicitis, he dissected the organ after the surgery, but found no worms. After he recovered from the operation, Punnett became unhappy with his teaching accommodations at St. Andrews and began a search for a new job. In 1902, he returned to Cambridge as a demonstrator in morphology in the Department of Zoology and remained in this position until 1904. While a demonstrator, Punnett had plenty of time to perform research and publish a number of papers on nemertines, a type of worm.

Discovers Several Mendelian Genetic Principles

Punnett then turned from the study of nemertines to genetics, working with **William Bateson**, an investigator also researching Mendelian principles, during a six-year period in which the pair produced noteworthy and lasting advances in Mendelian genetics. Gregor Mendel, an Augustinian monk, had used pea plants to demonstrate how genetic traits are inherited. Using the sweet-pea plant or fowl for their studies, Punnett and Bateson determined several basic classical Mendelian genetic principles, including the Mendelian explanations of sex-determination, sex-linkage, complementary factors and factor interaction, and the first example of autosomal linkage. It was early in his relationship with Bateson that Punnett was awarded the Balfour Studentship in the Department of Zoology, and he resigned as demonstrator. He held the Balfour Studentship position until 1908. Also, during this year he was awarded the Thurston medal of Gonville and Caius College. Punnett wrote *Mendelism,* the first published textbook on the subject of genetics, in 1905. As a reflection on his research, he was appointed superintendent of the Museum of Zoology in 1909. A year later, Punnett became professor of biology at the University of Cambridge. Punnett and Bateson started the *Journal of Genetics* in 1911 and edited it jointly until Bateson died in 1926. Punnett continued to edit the journal, credited with drawing numerous new students to the field of genetics, for twenty more years.

In 1912, the University of Cambridge changed the name of the chair of biology to the chair of zoology, and offered the position to Punnett, making him the first Arthur Balfour Professor of Genetics, a position that was the first of its kind in Great Britain. He held this prestigious position until his retirement at the age of sixty-five. Also in 1912, Punnett was elected a fellow of the Royal Society, and in 1922 he was awarded its Darwin Medal. Punnett's interests in genetics led him to a founding membership in the British Genetical Society; he served as one of the group's secretaries from 1919 to 1930, when he then became president.

During World War I, Punnett bought his expertise in poultry breeding to a position with the Food Production Department of the Board of Agriculture. He suggested that hens' plumage color could be used to determine the sex of the birds much earlier than previously was possible. This enabled the breeders to destroy most of the unwanted males, which were not used for food, and save precious resources for raising females for consumption. After the war ended, Punnett produced the first breed of poultry in which a trait is demonstrated uniquely in one sex or the other. This first auto-sexing breed, the Cambar, was followed a decade later by a second breed, the Legbar. Punnett's work laid the foundation for poultry breeding research for several more decades.

Punnett was married to Eveline Maude Froude, widow of Sidney Nutcombe-Quicke, at age forty-one; they had no children. In his leisure time, he enjoyed playing bridge, participated in many sports including cricket and tennis, and collected Japanese color prints, Chinese porcelain and old and rare biological and medical texts. Upon his death, his collection of Japanese prints was acquired by the Bristol Corporation for the city art gallery. Punnett died suddenly during a game of bridge in Bilbrook, Somerset, England, on January 3, 1967.

SELECTED WRITINGS BY PUNNETT:

Books

Mendelism, Macmillan & Bowes, 1905, sixth edition, 1922.
Embryogeny: An Account of Laws Governing the Development of the Animal Egg as Ascertained through Experiment, (revision of Embryogeny by Hans Przibram, translated by R. Sollas), Cambridge University Press, 1908.
Mimicry in Butterflies, Cambridge University Press, 1915.
Heredity in Poultry, Macmillan, 1923.

Periodicals

Science, The Heredity of Sex, Volume 27, 1908, pp. 785–787.
Harper's, Applied Heredity, December, 1908, pp. 115–122.

FURTHER READING:

Books

Biographical Memoirs of Fellows of the Royal Society, Volume 13, Royal Society (London), 1967, pp. 309–326.

Sketch by Barbara J. Proujan

Edward Mills Purcell
1912–1997
American physicist

Edward Mills Purcell spent much of his lifetime studying the basic particles of matter. Ultimately focusing on the frequencies of atomic particles spinning in magnetic fields, he developed a method of measuring their magnetic moments and investigating their atomic structures. For his simultaneous but independent development of this method, known as nuclear resonance absorption, he shared the 1952 Nobel Prize in physics with physicist **Felix Bloch.** The principle of nuclear magnetic resonance itself has been applied to a wide range of applications, from studying space through radio astronomy to measuring magnetic fields with magnetometers.

Edward Mills Purcell

Purcell was born on August 30, 1912, in Taylorville, Illinois, to Edward A. and Mary (Mills) Purcell. His mother was a high school teacher, and his father was a former country school teacher, who, during Purcell's boyhood, was the general manager of an independent telephone company. Purcell read the Bell System technical magazine that his father received and decided to become an electrical engineer. In addition, he inherited his parents' interest in teaching.

Purcell received a bachelor's degree in electrical engineering from Purdue University in 1933. During his undergraduate days, Purcell's interest in physics was encouraged and strengthened by Karl Lark-Horowitz, a professor from Vienna, who was building Purdue's physics department. After graduation, Purcell spent a year at the Technische Hochschule in Karlsruhe, Germany, as an international exchange student. He received a master's degree from Harvard in 1935 and a Ph.D. in physics in 1938. He remained at Harvard as a physics instructor until 1941, when he became leader of the Fundamental Developments Group at the Massachusetts Institute of Technology's Radiation Laboratory, contributing to the World War II effort by working on advanced radar for night fighting. At MIT, he worked with **I. I. Rabi** and some of Rabi's Columbia University colleagues, who were developing the field of nuclear moments and resonance. The work Purcell and his group did with higher frequencies and shorter wavelengths also played a role in Purcell's later research. He returned to Harvard as an associate professor in 1946, advancing to professor of physics in 1949. He served as

Donner professor of science from 1958 to 1960, and Gerhard Gade University professor from 1960 until his retirement in 1977.

Shares Nobel Prize for Nuclear Measurement Method

During the 1930s, Rabi had experimented with a method of determining nuclear magnetic moments, the rotating force exerted on nuclei when placed in a magnetic field. Purcell pursued a similar methodology by placing atoms in the field of a strong electromagnet and a second magnet activated by radio waves. He aligned the atoms in the magnetic field and then introduced varying frequencies of radio waves to change their orientation, allowing him to determine the one signature frequency at which the atoms absorbed energy, showing nuclear magnetic resonance. As Purcell wrote in his Nobel lecture, "Commonplace as such experiments have become in our laboratories, I have not yet lost a feeling of wonder, and of delight, that this delicate motion should reside in all the ordinary things around us, revealing itself only to him who looks for it. . . . To see the world for a moment as something rich and strange is the private reward of many a discovery."

Discovery Leads to Invention

Purcell put his discovery to work, when, with Harold Ewen, he built a radio telescope. In 1951, they detected for the first time radiation emitted by hydrogen clouds in space, noting a signature wavelength of 21 cm (8.3 in). Thus, they were able to exact a frequency by which radio astronomers could use to track hydrogen clouds. Purcell also found that the nuclear magnetic resonance signatures could change in substances like crystals or liquids because of the influence of their surroundings, a change known as a chemical shift. This phenomenon provided a means of studying molecular structures. Later in his career, Purcell ventured into biophysics to study bacterial behavior and locomotion, particularly the physics of swimming microscopic organisms.

In 1937, Purcell married Beth C. Busser, with whom he had two sons, Frank and Dennis. In addition to his work at Harvard, Purcell served on the scientific advisory board to the U.S. Air Force in 1947 and 1948, and from 1953 to 1957. A member of the President's Science Advisory Committee from 1957 to 1960 and 1962 to 1966, he was elected to the National Academy of Science in 1951 and received an honorary doctorate in engineering from Purdue in 1953. Purcell was a member of a number of scientific organizations and received the National Medal of Science from the National Science Foundation in 1978. Purcell died on March 7, 1997, in Cambridge, Massachusetts.

SELECTED WRITINGS BY PURCELL:

Books

Electricity and Magnetism. New York: McGraw-Hill, 1965.

Periodicals

"Nuclear Magnetism in Relation to Problems of the Liquid and Solid States." *Science* (30 April 1948): 433-40.

"Research in Nuclear Magnetism." *Science* (16 October 1953): 431-36.

FURTHER READING:

Books

McGraw-Hill Encyclopedia of Science and Technology. New York: McGraw-Hill, 1993, pp. 157–66.

Modern Scientists and Engineers. New York: McGraw-Hill, 1980, pp. 445-46.

Pioneers of Science: Nobel Prize Winners in Physics. Philadelphia: The Institute of Physics, 1980, pp. 145-46.

Wasson, Tyler, ed. *Nobel Prize Winners.* New York: H. W. Wilson, 1987.

Periodicals

Calnan, Patrick. "Edward M. Purcell, Won Nobel for Work on Atomic Nuclei" (obituary). *Boston Globe* (9 March 1997): D24.

"Dr. Edward Purcell, 84, Dies; Shared Nobel Prize in Physics" (obituary). *New York Times* (10 March 1997): B9.

Science News Letter (15 November 1952): 307.

Torrey, Volta. "Changing Partners in the Atom Dance." *Saturday Review* (6 May 1961): 68-69.

Weil, Martin. "Nobel-Winning Pysicist Edward Purcell Dies" (obituary). *Washington Post* (9 March 1997): B8.

Sketch by Julie Anderson

Alfred H. Qöyawayma
1938–
American engineer

Alfred H. Qöyawayma (ko-YAH-wy-ma), a Hopi Indian, co-founded and served as the first chairman of the American Indian Science and Engineering Society (AISES). He is a registered professional engineer in Arizona and California, and holds patents for his early work on aircraft guidance systems. In 1990, after a twenty-year career in environmental management, Qöyawayma turned his full attention to the art work he had begun to pursue in 1976. As a potter, he is known for his exceptionally thin-walled and perfectly symmetrical "flying saucer" vessels, fashioned with wooden tools and without the aid of a potter's wheel. His pieces appear in the permanent collections of several museums; they reflect years of research into the Hopi ceramic tradition. His work has been the subject of several videos and documentaries. Qöyawayma is also an investigator for a Smithsonian Institute project to identify clay sources for ancient Hopi ceramics.

Qöyawayma was born February 26, 1938, in Los Angeles, California, the only child of Alfred and Mamie (Colton) Cooyama. About 1980, Qöyawayma adopted his father's original Hopi name, which means "Grey Fox Walking at Dawn." His father worked in watercolors and oils, and at one time painted for Walt Disney. Of notable influence was Qöyawayma's aunt, Polingaysi Qöyawayma (Elizabeth White), who died in 1990. A noted Hopi potter, educator and writer, she taught him to work in clay.

Qöyawayma received a B.S. degree in mechanical engineering from California State Polytechnic University in 1961, and an M.S. in mechanical/control systems engineering from the University of Southern California in 1966. From 1961 through 1971, he worked as a project engineer for Litton Guidance and Control Systems in Woodland Hills, California, where his work in the development of inertial guidance systems and star trackers impelled Litton to open a new corporate division. He left Litton in 1971 to join the Salt River Project in Phoenix, Arizona, serving as a manager and planner in the power and water utility's environmental division. In 1977, he co-founded the American Indian Science and Engineering Society (AISES) to develop leaders and increase Native American participation in science and engineering. From its original seven members, it has expanded into an organization with more than 100 student chapters in the United States, Canada and

Puerto Rico. Qöyawayma continues to work with AISES and its expansion into Mexico and Central America. In 1986, he received the society's Ely S. Parker Award for Engineering Achievement and Service to the American Indian Community.

Qöyawayma joined a Smithsonian Institute research team in 1982 as one of four principal investigators involved in the use of neutron activation and factor analysis techniques to identify the original clay sources used in making ancient Hopi pottery. In 1990, he started the Electric Power Research Institute's study on the removal of carbon dioxide from the atmosphere through halophytes, plants grown in sodium-rich soil that, like trees, can absorb and store carbon dioxide.

Qöyawayma's pottery has been exhibited at the Kennedy Center and the Smithsonian and appears in the permanent collections of several museums. Qöyawayma, who has served on the board of directors of the National Action Committee on Minorities and on the Arizona Commission on the Arts, is a consultant to the Hopi Tribe on environmental and economic issues. In 1986, he received an honorary doctorate of humane letters from the University of Colorado, Boulder. He was named 1989 Alumnus of the Year by California State Polytechnic Institute, and received a Fulbright Fellowship in 1991 to work with Maori Indians in New Zealand, helping to re-establish an ancient tradition in ceramics. Qöyawayma and his wife, Leslie (Thompson), live in Phoenix. They have two children, Kathleen and John.

SELECTED WRITINGS BY QÖYAWAYMA:

Books

Qöyawayma, the Potter, Santa Fe East Gallery, 1984.

Periodicals

Journal of Field Archaeology, The Formation of Ceramic Analytical Groups: Hopi Pottery Production and Exchange, A. D. 1300–1600, Volume 15, 1988, pp. 317–37.
Santa Fe, Going Places with the Arts, Between Two Worlds, summer, 1991, pp. 8–13.
IEEE Spectrum, Diversity at Work, June, 1992, pp. 28–29.

FURTHER READING:

Periodicals

Americana, March/April, 1984, pp. 52–55.

Native Peoples, winter, 1994, pp. 34–43, 48.
Southwest Profile, August, 1993, pp. 22–25.

Sketch by Jill Carpenter

Lloyd Albert Quarterman
1918–1982
American chemist

Lloyd Albert Quarterman was one of only a handful of African Americans to work on the "Manhattan Project," the team that developed the first atom bomb in the 1940s. He was also noted as a research chemist who specialized in fluoride chemistry, producing some of the first compounds using inert gases and developing the "diamond window" for the study of compounds using corrosive hydrogen fluoride gas. In addition, later in his career, Quarterman initiated work on synthetic blood.

Quarterman was born May 31, 1918, in Philadelphia. He attended St. Augustine's College in Raleigh, North Carolina, where he continued the interest in chemistry he had demonstrated from an early age. Just after he completed his bachelor's degree in 1943 he was hired by the U.S. War Department to work on the production of the atomic bomb, an assignment code-named the Manhattan Project. Originally hired as a junior chemist, he worked at both the secret underground facility at the University of Chicago and at the Columbia University laboratory in New York City; the project was spread across the country in various locations. It was the team of scientists at Columbia which first split the atom. To do this, scientists participated in trying to isolate an isotope of uranium necessary for nuclear fission; this was Quarterman's main task during his time in New York.

Quarterman was one of only six African American scientists who worked on the development of atomic bomb. At the secret Chicago facility, where the unused football stadium had been converted into an enormous, hidden laboratory for the "plutonium program," Quarterman studied quantum mechanics under renowned Italian physicist **Enrico Fermi**. When the Manhattan Project ended in 1946, the Chicago facilities were converted to become Argonne National Laboratories, and Quarterman was one of the scientists who stayed on. Although his contributions included work on the first nuclear power plant, he was predominantly a fluoride and nuclear chemist, creating new chemical compounds and new molecules from fluoride solutions. Dr. Larry Stein, who worked at Argonne at the same time as Quarterman, told interviewer Marianne Fedunkiw that Quarterman was very good at purifying hydrogen fluoride. "He helped build a still to purify it, which he ran." This was part of the research which led to the production of the compound xenon tetrafluoride at Argonne. Xenon is one of the "inert" gases and was thought to be unable to react with other molecules, so Quarterman's work in producing a xenon compound was a pioneering effort.

After a number of years at Argonne National Laboratories, Quarterman returned to school and received his master's of science from Northwestern University in 1952. In addition to his fluoride chemistry work, Quarterman was a spectroscopist researching interactions between radiation and matter. He developed a corrosion resistant "window" of diamonds with which to view hydrogen fluoride. He described this to Ivan Van Sertima, who interviewed him in 1979: "It was a very small window—one-eighth of an inch. The reason why they were one-eighth of an inch was because I couldn't get the money to buy bigger windows. These small diamonds cost one thousand dollars apiece and I needed two for a window." Diamonds were necessary because hydrogen fluoride was so corrosive it would eat up glass or any other known container material. Quarterman was able to study the x-ray, ultraviolet, and Raman spectra of a given compound by dissolving it in hydrogen fluoride, making a cell, and shining an electromagnetic beam through the solution to see the vibrations of the molecules. His first successful trial was run in 1967.

Quarterman also began research into "synthetic blood" late in his career but he was thwarted by what he described as "socio-political problems" and later fell ill and died before he could complete it. Besides holding memberships in the American Chemical Society, American Association for the Advancement of Science, and Scientific Research Society of America, Quarterman was an officer of the Society of Applied Spectroscopy. He also encouraged African American students interested in science by visiting public schools in Chicago, and was a member of the National Association for the Advancement of Colored People. In recognition for his contributions to science, Quarterman's alma mater, St. Augustine's College, departed from 102 years of tradition to award him an honorary Ph.D. in chemistry in 1971 for a lifetime of achievement. He was also cited for his research on the Manhattan project in a certificate, dated August 6, 1945, by the Secretary of War for "work essential to the production of the Atomic Bomb thereby contributing to the successful conclusion of World War II."

Quarterman was also a renowned athlete. During his university days at St. Augustine's College he was an avid football player. Van Sertima, who interviewed Quarterman three years before his death, later wrote, "As he spoke, the shock of his voice and his occasional laughter seemed to contradict his illness and I began to see before me, not an aging scientist, but the champion footballer." Quarterman died at the Billings Hospital in Chicago in the late summer of 1982. He donated his body to science.

FURTHER READING:

Books

Le Blanc, Ondine E., *Contemporary Black Biography,* Lloyd Albert Quarterman, Volume 4, Gale, 1993, pp. 199–201.

Sammons, Vivian O., editor, *Blacks in Science and Medicine,* Hemisphere Publishing, 1990, p. 196.

Van Sertima, Ivan, editor, *Blacks in Science: Ancient and Modern,* Transaction Books, 1983, pp. 266–272.

Periodicals

Van Sertima, Ivan, editor, *Ebony,* September, 1949, p. 28.

Van Sertima, Ivan, editor, *Jet,* August 9, 1982.

Other

Stein, Larry, *Interview with Marianne Fedunkiw,* conducted April 7, 1994.

Sketch by Marianne Fedunkiw

Calvin F. Quate
1923–

American engineer

Calvin Quate owns at least part of 42 different patents; he has published or co-published more than 160 articles. Quate is known for developing two important microscopes, the scanning acoustic microscope and an atomic force microscope. The latter has numerous applications and is used throughout many industries. Atomic force microscopy has become an industry unto itself. In addition to microscopy, Quate has also made innovations in physical acoustics, digital information and its storage, as well as solid state devices and microwave electronics.

Quate had relatively humble beginnings. He was born Calvin Forrest Quate on December 7, 1923, in Baker, Nevada, to Graham Shepard Quate and Margie Lake. Quate began his education in a one-room school. He received his undergraduate education at the University of Utah, earning his B.S. in electrical engineering in 1944. The following year he married Dorothy Marshall on June 28th. The couple eventually had four children together, Robin, Claudia, Holly, and Rhodalee. From 1944 to 1946 Quate served as a lieutenant in Navy Reserves. Afterwards he completed his graduate work at Stanford University, where he earned his Ph.D. in electrical engineering in 1950.

After graduation, Quate did not immediately enter academia. He spent approximately ten years working for industrial companies. From 1949 to 1958, he was a member of the technical staff at Bell Telephone Laboratories, in Murray Hill, New Jersey, then at the Sandia Corporation in Albuquerque, New Mexico. He spent two years at Sandia, first as director of research, from 1959 to 1960, then as vice president of research from 1960 to 1961. Quate spent a great deal time at Bell and Sandia's laboratories scrutinizing electronics. This proved productive as it had a profound effect on his long-term research methodology.

It was during this work at Bell and Sandia that Quate became intrigued by a phenomenon he observed when investigating acoustics and microwaves. Quate saw that in optical microscopes the light waves were at a wavelength equal to that of acoustical waves. He continued this research into microscopes when he became a professor.

Wins Guggenheim and Fulbright Awards

In 1961, Quate returned to Stanford University, where he was appointed to a professorship in the applied physics and engineering department. He served as chair of this department from 1969 to 1972, and again from 1978 to 1981. He also held administrative positions at Stanford, serving as the associate dean of the School of Humanities and Sciences twice, from 1972 to 1974, then again from 1982 to 1983. Quate won a Guggenheim fellowship and a Fulbright Scholarship to work as a member of the Faculty of Science in Montpellier, France, from 1968 to 1969.

Part of his first 12 years at Stanford involved continuing his research into acoustics and microscopes. Together with scientist Ross Lemons, Quate announced the creation in 1973 of a scanning acoustic microscope that could see through opaque items. The microscope worked by emitting sound waves which, after passing through a sapphire crystal and spherical lens, traveled through a liquid cell containing the object to be analyzed. The microscope did not merely peer through things like silicon chips; it also gave a sense of the object's other characteristics like softness or hardness.

Throughout the 1980s, Quate received numerous accolades. In 1981, he was awarded the Morris N. Liebmann Award from the Institute of Electrical and Electronic Engineers (IEEE), of which he is a member. He has also won several additional honors from the IEEE, the Rank Prize for Opto-electronics in 1982, the Achievement Award in 1986, and the Medal of Honor in 1988.

Quate continued to build up professional positions in the 1980s as well. While maintaining his relationship with Stanford, he began working at the Xerox Palo Alto Research Center as a senior research fellow in 1984. In 1986, he was appointed to a concurrent position at Stanford as the Leland T. Edwards Professor of Engineering in 1986.

Develops Groundbreaking Microscope

It was during the mid-1980s that Quate began research into what came to be known as the atomic force microscope. After reading about the new scanning tunneling microscope, developed in Switzerland, Quate got the idea for a similar instrument that could work on an atomic level. After much work and conversation, some of it with the scientists who developed the scanning tunneling microscope, Quate built his microscope, using it to scale boron nitrade's atomic structure. As he and his team experimented with the atomic force microscope, they discovered it had an anomaly concerning its cantilever. This finding expanded the microscope's application possibilities, and made it a multi-million dollar industry unto itself. The atomic force microscope has practical applications in such far-ranging fields as electrochemistry and biology. Ironically, when Quate first sent his paper on the microscope to a professional journal, it was rejected because the concept behind the microscope was considered too improbable.

Quate's groundbreaking work continued to be lauded in the 1990s. In 1992, he was awarded the National Medal of Science, the highest honor a scientist can receive from the United States government. In 1995, Quate was voted into the Royal Society of London as well as named *R & D* magazine's scientist of the year. Quate is described as a shy and soft-spoken man, well regarded by his colleagues. In a story published in the July 1995 issue of *R & D* magazine in conjunction with the award, a colleague in the scientific instrument business, Sang-il Park, said, "Cal is a major force in microscopy—I've been watching him in action for 13 years. Whenever I hear his ideas, they're always hard to believe. But he makes them work. He has real insight. He's taken microscopy beyond optics and electricity to a third generation."

SELECTED WRITINGS BY QUATE:

Periodicals

"Atomic Force Microscopy of an Organic Monolayer." *Science* (1988).
"Electrons that Make Waves." *Nature* (1988).
"Variations on an Original Theme." *Nature* (1989).
"Switch to Atom Control." *Nature* (1991).

FURTHER READING:

Periodicals

Koprowski, Gene. "AR & D Magazine's Scientist of the Year." *R & D* (July 1995): 22-25.
"National Medals of Science Given to 1992's Honorees." *Physics Today* (August 1992): 79.

Sketch by Annette Petrusso

Edith H. Quimby
1891–1982
American biophysicist

A pioneer in the field of radiology, Edith H. Quimby helped develop diagnostic and therapeutic applications for x rays, radium, and radioactive isotopes when the science of radiology was still in its infancy. Her research in measuring the penetration of radiation enabled physicians to determine the exact dose needed with the fewest side effects. Quimby also worked to protect those handling radioactive material from its harmful effects. While a radiology professor at Columbia University, she established a research laboratory to study the medical uses of radioactive isotopes, including their application in cancer diagnosis and treatments. In recognition of her contributions to the field, the Radiological Society of North America awarded her a gold medal for work which "placed every radiologist in her debt."

Quimby was born on July 10, 1891, in Rockford, Illinois, to Arthur S. Hinkley, an architect and farmer, and Harriet Hinkley (whose maiden name was also Hinkley). The family—Quimby was one of three children—moved to several different states during Quimby's childhood. She graduated from high school in Boise, Idaho, and went on a full tuition scholarship to Whitman College in Walla Walla, Washington, where she majored in physics and mathematics. Two of her teachers at Whitman, B. H. Brown and Walter Bratton, were major influences in directing her toward a career in scientific research. After graduating in 1912, Quimby taught high school science in Nyssa, Oregon, and then went to the University of California in 1914 to accept a fellowship in physics. While in the graduate program there, she married fellow physics student Shirley L. Quimby. She earned her M.A. in 1915 and returned to teaching high school science, this time in Antioch, California. In 1919, when her husband moved to New York to teach physics at Columbia University, she went with him. The move to New York was a pivotal point in Quimby's career, as she began working under Dr. Gioacchino Failla, chief physicist at the newly created New York City Memorial Hospital for Cancer and Allied Diseases. This began a scientific association that was to last forty years.

Quimby began studying the medical uses of x rays and radium, especially in treating tumors. At that time, physicians and researchers knew extremely little about this area; before Quimby's research, each doctor had to determine on a case-by-case basis how much radiation each patient needed for treatment. Quimby focused her attention on measuring the penetration of radiation so that radiotherapy doses could be more exact and side effects minimized. After several years of research, she successfully determined the number of roentgens (a now obsolete unit of radiation dosage) per minute emitted in the air, on the skin, and in the body. Her research on the effects of radiation on the skin was especially noteworthy to the scientific community, and her study was frequently quoted in the professional literature for many years.

From 1920 to 1940, Quimby conducted numerous experiments to examine various properties of radium and x rays. During this period she wrote dozens of articles for scientific journals, describing the results of her research and listing standards of measurement. In 1940 Quimby was the first woman to receive the Janeway Medal of the American Radium Society in recognition of her achievements in the field.

Becomes Professor and Establishes Isotope Laboratory

From 1941 to 1942, Quimby taught radiology courses at Cornell University Medical College. The following year she became associate professor of radiology at Columbia University College of Physicians and Surgeons, where she taught radiologic physics. While at Columbia, she and Failla founded the Radiological Research Laboratory. There they studied the medical uses of radioactive isotopes in cooperation with members of Columbia's medical departments. They focused their research on the application of radioactive isotopes (different forms of the same element whose unstable nuclei emit alpha, beta, or gamma rays) in treating thyroid disease, and for circulation studies and diagnosis of brain tumors. These inquiries made Quimby a pioneer in the field of nuclear medicine.

Quimby participated in other aspects of radiology research as well. She researched the use of synthetically produced radioactive sodium in medical research, and devoted considerable efforts to investigating ways to protect those handling radioactive substances from the harmful effects of exposure. Very early on, Quimby foresaw the potential for increased diagnostic and therapeutic use of atomic energy in medicine through radioactive isotopes.

In addition to her research and lecturing, Quimby worked on the Manhattan Project (which developed the atom bomb). She also worked for the Atomic Energy Commission, acted as a consultant on radiation therapy to the United States Veterans Administration, served as an examiner for the American Board of Radiology, and headed a scientific committee of the National Council on Radiation Protection and Measurements. A prolific writer, Quimby published a considerable amount of literature on various aspects of the medical uses of x rays, radium, and radioactive isotopes. She also coauthored a widely respected book entitled *Physical Foundations of Radiology*.

After her official retirement in 1960 as professor emeritus of radiology, Quimby continued to write, lecture, and consult well into the 1970s. She was a member of several radiology societies, including the American Radium Society, for which she served as vice president. In her nonprofessional life, Quimby was a member of the League of Women Voters.

On Quimby's death on October 11, 1982, at the age of ninety-one, Harald Rossi of Columbia University wrote in *Physics Today* that "all too often the creative achievements of scientific pioneers are overshadowed by further developments made by others or simply become anonymous components of accepted practice. Fortunately, Quimby's exceptional service to radiological physics was widely recognized."

SELECTED WRITINGS BY QUIMBY:

Books

Radioactive Isotopes in Clinical Practice, Lea & Febiger, 1958.
Safe Handling of Radioactive Isotopes in Medical Practice, Macmillan, 1960.
Physical Foundations of Radiology, Harper, 1970.

FURTHER READING:

Books

Current Biography, H. W. Wilson, 1949, pp. 492–493.

Periodicals

New York Times, October 13, 1982, p. 28.
Physics Today, December, 1982, pp. 71–72.

Sketch by Donna Olshansky

William Samuel Quinland
1885–1953
American pathologist

Willliam Samuel Quinland was a distinguished pathologist and educator who contributed twenty-eight studies to medical journals, including pioneering research on pathology in African Americans. His medical career spanned from Panama, to Brazil, to several regions of the United States, including Alaska. He was the first black member to be elected to the American Association of Pathologists and Bacteriologists, an appointment he received in 1920; the American Board of Pathology in 1937; and the College of American Pathologists in 1947.

Quinland was born on October 12, 1885, in All Saints, Antigua, in what was then the British West Indies, the son of William Thomas and Floretta Victoria (Williams) Quinland. After completing his secondary education in the West Indies, Quinland taught in public schools. He then embarked on his medical career, working for three years as a laboratory assistant in the Ancon Hospital in the Canal Zone, Panama, followed by four years as a laboratory worker at the Candelaria Hospital in Brazil.

After making his way to the United States, Quinland attended Howard University in Washington, D.C., from 1914 to 1915 and earned his B.S. degree from Oskaloosa College in Iowa in 1918. In 1919, he earned his medical degree, with an outstanding record, from Meharry Medical College in Nashville, Tennessee. Quinland was then awarded the first Rosenwald fellowship in pathology and bacteriology for study at Harvard Medical School, which he held from 1919 to 1922. In 1921, Quinland earned his certificate in pathology and bacteriology from Harvard, and also published his first professional article, a study of carcinoma, or malignant, tumors. In 1922, Quinland's final year under the Rosenwald fellowship, he worked as an assistant in pathology at the Peter Bent Brigham Hospital in Boston.

Returns to Meharry Medical College

Although Harvard offered him a professorship in its Medical College, Quinland felt that Meharry, a groundbreaking institution for African-American medical practitioners, needed him more. In 1922, he accepted a post at Meharry as professor and head of the pathology department, a position he held until 1947. In 1923, he married Sadie Lee Watson; they had two children. In addition to his professorship at Meharry Medical College, Quinland worked as a pathologist at Meharry's George W. Hubbard Hospital, where he served as associate medical director from 1931 to 1937, and at the Millie E. Hale Hospital. In 1941 and 1942, he undertook post-graduate studies as a fellow of the University of Chicago.

During these years, Quinland published studies on tuberculosis, syphilis, heart disease, and carcinoma, among other subjects. Much of this research was particularly valuable for its focus on black patients; Quinland noted in his study on "Primary Carcinoma in the Negro," for example, that "while social differences in cancer have long been recognized," little research had been conducted on its occurrence among African Americans. That study looked at three hundred cases of carcinoma and documented which types of cancers were found in samples from African American men and women of various ages. In addition, Quinland served on the editorial board of the *Journal of the National Medical Association* and of the *Punjab Medical Journal*, held a post as a reserve surgeon for the United

State Public Health Service, and directed public health clinics in Virginia, South Carolina, and Georgia.

In 1947, Quinland left Meharry Medical College for a post as pathologist and chief of laboratory service at the Veterans Administration Hospital in Tuskegee, Alaska. His publications in this final phase of his career included a study of tumors. Quinland served at the Veterans Administration Hospital until his death on April 6, 1953.

SELECTED WRITINGS BY QUINLAND:

Periodicals

Journal of the National Medical Association, Tuberculosis from the Standpoint of Pathology, Volume 15, 1923, pp. 1–5.

Meharry News, Primary Carcinoma of Prostrate, 1928.

Journal of the National Medical Association, Syphilis in Combination with Certain Diseases, Volume 31, 1939, pp. 199–205.

Archives of Pathology, Primary Carcinoma in the Negro: Anatomic Distribution of Three Hundred Cases, Volume 30, 1940, pp. 393–402.

Southern Medical Journal, Bronchogenic Carcinoma— Report of Three Cases in Negroes, Volume 35, 1942, pp. 729–732.

Journal of Urology, Cancer of the Prostrate: A Clinicopathologic Study of 34 Cases in Negroes, Volume 50, Number 2, 1943.

Journal of the National Medical Association, Histologic and Clinical Response of Human Cancer to Irradiation, Volume 38, 1946, pp. 171–178.

FURTHER READING:

Books

Blacks in Science and Medicine, Hemisphere, 1990, pp. 196–197.

Dictionary of American Medical Biography, Greenwood, 1984, pp. 618–619.

Periodicals

The Crisis, December, 1919, pp. 64–65.

Journal of the American Medical Association, July, 1953, pp. 298–300.

Sketch by Miyoko Chu

I. I. Rabi
1898–1988
American physicist

Born in Austria, I. I. Rabi came to the United States with his parents at an early age. He attended Cornell and Columbia Universities, receiving his Ph.D. in physics from the latter in 1927. During a post-doctoral year in Germany Rabi worked with **Otto Stern** and learned about Stern's experiments (conducted with Walther Gerlach) on the analysis of atomic and molecular structure by means of atomic and molecular beams. Upon his return to the United States in 1929, Rabi worked on methods for extending and refining the Stern-Gerlach techniques. He eventually made a number of important discoveries regarding the magnetic properties of the nucleus and of subatomic particles— discoveries that later found application in a number of fields, including nuclear magnetic resonance, masers and lasers, and time measurement by means of atomic clocks. During World War II, Rabi worked on the development of radar devices and nuclear weapons. At the war's conclusion, he devoted most of his time and energy to the political aspects of scientific and technological development, serving as chairman of the U.S. Atomic Energy Commission from 1952 to 1956. Rabi died in 1988 at the age of 91.

Isidor Isaac Rabi was born on July 29, 1898, in Rymanow (also given as Raymanou or Rymanov), Galicia, then a part of the Austro-Hungarian empire. Rabi's parents were David Rabi and the former Janet (also given as Jennie or Scheindel) Teig. The senior Rabi emigrated to the United States shortly after his son's birth and, in 1899, sent for his family to join him in New York City. David Rabi has been described by various biographers as an unskilled worker, a tailor, and an owner of a grocery store; Rabi himself said that his father started out by doing odd jobs, such as delivering ice, and then "graduated into work in the sweatshop, making women's blouses." Yiddish was the only language spoken in the Rabi household, and young Isidor learned his English on the streets. He was a quick learner, however, and did well in the public schools of New York City. After graduating from Brooklyn's Manual Training High School in 1916, he entered Cornell University with plans to major in electrical engineering. He eventually changed his major to chemistry, though, graduating with a bachelor of science degree in 1919. He then spent three years working as a chemist before returning to Cornell for graduate work. Rabi soon discovered that his real interest was physics, and in 1923 enrolled in a doctoral program in this field at Columbia University. In order to support himself at Columbia, Rabi took a job teaching physics at the City College (now City University) of New York, a post he held until he received his Ph.D. in 1927.

Pursues Postgraduate Studies in Europe

For his postdoctoral studies, Rabi planned a two-year tour of the most important scientific institutions in Europe, including Münich, Copenhagen, Hamburg, Leipzig, and Zürich. While on tour he studied with such leading figures as **Arnold Sommerfeld**, **Niels Bohr**, **Wolfgang Pauli**, **Werner Heisenberg**, and Otto Stern. The visit with Stern may have been the most significant stop on the tour, because Stern's work at Hamburg closely corresponded to Rabi's own field of interest and the subject of his doctoral thesis, the effects of magnetic fields on matter. In 1922, Stern and Walther Gerlach had developed methods for creating beams of atoms or molecules that could be used to study the magnetic properties of the atomic nuclei in these beams. For his discoveries in this field, Stern would go on to win the 1943 Nobel Prize in physics.

In 1929, when Rabi returned to the United States, he began his own research on the use of atomic and molecular beams to study nuclear properties. This work took place at Columbia, where he had been appointed lecturer in physics; over the next decade, he worked his way up the professional ladder, being promoted to assistant professor in 1930, associate professor in 1932, and then full professor of physics in 1937. Throughout this period, Rabi refined his methods of atomic and molecular beam analysis, eventually making a number of important discoveries.

Discovers Atomic Spin Properties

The Stern-Gerlach experiment of 1922 had showed that a molecular beam passing through a magnetic field splits into two parts. The discovery of electron spin by **George Uhlenbeck** and **Samuel Goudsmit** in 1927 explained this phenomenon: they demonstrated that electrons in an atom can spin in only one of two directions; hence, electrons spinning in one direction split into one beam, while those spinning in the opposite direction split into another.

As Rabi studied this effect in more detail, he realized that the magnetic properties of an atom are more complex than first suggested by the Stern-Gerlach experiment. In the first place, the nucleus itself spins, creating its own magnetic field. Thus, there will be interactions among the magnetic field of the nucleus, the magnetic fields of the orbital electrons, and any external magnetic field that is applied to the atom.

In his research, Rabi was able to sort out and quantify many of these discrete properties. His most important accomplishment was to determine the magnetic moment of the nucleus, an important piece of information essential to the construction of an accurate model of the atom. By 1937, Rabi had made yet another discovery, namely that he could reverse the spin of a nucleus by imposing an external radio-frequency signal on an atomic or molecular beam. That discovery has been used in a number of important applications; one of these, nuclear magnetic resonance (NMR), is now among the most powerful analytical tools available to scientific investigators and medical diagnosticians. Rabi was awarded the 1944 Nobel Prize in physics for his work on "the resonance method for recording the magnetic properties of the atomic nucleus."

During World War II, Rabi took a leave of absence from Columbia to worked on the development of micro-wave radar devices at the Massachusetts Institute of Technology. Though most of his colleagues in the scientific community were devoting their wartime efforts to the development of atomic weapons, Rabi believed that, of the two projects, radar would be more immediately useful to the U.S. war effort—though he did consult on nuclear weapons projects as part of the Manhattan Project. At the war's conclusion, Rabi returned to Columbia as chairman of the physics department. He devoted his time primarily to administrative responsibilities and to the effort by scientists to restrict military control of nuclear technology. "Speaking for the group of men who created these weapons," Rabi once said in *Atlantic Monthly*, "I would say that we are frankly pleased, terrified, and to an even greater degree embarrassed when we contemplate the results of our wartime efforts." In order to monitor the use of atomic energy and weapons, Rabi became a member of the General Advisory Committee of the Atomic Energy Commission in 1945 and then served as chairman of the committee from 1952 to 1956 (after the retirement of J. Robert Oppenheimer). He was an advisor to NATO and the United Nations, and served as a member of the American delegation to UNESCO, overlooking the European Center for Nuclear Research (CERN) in Geneva.

Rabi was married to Helen Newmark in 1926. They had two daughters, Nancy Elizabeth and Margaret Joella. In addition to the Nobel Prize, Rabi won a host of other awards, including the Elliott Cresson Medal of the Franklin Institute in 1942, the U.S. Medal for Merit (the country's highest civilian service award) in 1948, the Niels Bohr International Gold Medal in 1967, the Atoms for Peace Award in 1967, the Franklin Delano Roosevelt Freedom Medal in 1985, and the Public Welfare Medal of the National Academy of Sciences in 1985. Rabi died in New York City on January 11, 1988.

SELECTED WRITINGS BY RABI:

Books

My Life and Times As a Physicist, Claremont College, 1960.
Science: The Center of Culture, World Publishing, 1970.

Periodicals

Physical Review, A New Method of Measuring Nuclear Magnetic Moment, Volume 53, 1938, p. 318.
Physical Review, The Magnetic Moments of 3-Li–6, 3-Li–7, and 9-F–19, Volume 55, 1939, pp. 526–535.

FURTHER READING:

Books

Current Biography Yearbook 1948, H. W. Wilson, 1949, pp. 509–510.
Heathcote, Niels H. de V., *Nobel Prize Winners in Physics, 1901–1950,* Henry Schuman, 1953, pp. 398–410.
Heathcote, Niels H. de V., *McGraw-Hill Modern Scientists and Engineers,* McGraw-Hill, 1980, pp. 1–2.
Heathcote, Niels H. de V., *Nobel Prize Winners,* H. W. Wilson, 1987, pp. 847–849.
Weber, Robert L., *Pioneers of Science: Nobel Prize Winners in Physics,* American Institute of Physics, 1980, pp. 122–124.

Sketch by David E. Newton

James Rainwater
1917–1986
American physicist

J ames Rainwater, an American nuclear physicist who had a lifelong association with Columbia University, conducted some pioneering research in the study of the atomic nucleus, proving that its structure was not the symmetrical sphere many had believed it to be. For his role in formulating a new model of the nucleus, Rainwater, along with fellow physicists **Aage Bohr** and **Ben R. Mottelson**, was awarded the 1975 Nobel Prize in physics.

Leo James Rainwater was born in Council, Idaho, to Edna Eliza Teague and Leo Jasper Rainwater, a civil engineer and general store manager. The elder Rainwater died of influenza a year after his son was born, and the family moved to Hanford, California, where Rainwater's mother remarried. In high school, Rainwater entered a chemistry competition sponsored by the California Institute of Technology (Caltech). He got an outstanding score and after graduation enrolled at Caltech as a chemistry major. Later he switched to physics. After receiving a B.A. in physics from Caltech in 1939, Rainwater went to Columbia University and received a master's degree in physics in 1941. As a doctoral student at Columbia, Rainwater studied under such notable physicists as **Enrico Fermi** and **Edward Teller**.

In 1942 Rainwater was appointed a scientist in the Manhattan Project, thus delaying his thesis research in order to participate in the development of the atom bomb. Rainwater used the Columbia cyclotron particle accelerator to study the behavior of neutrons (uncharged elementary particles with a mass nearly equal to that of protons). In 1946 he received his Ph.D. and became a physics instructor at Columbia; in 1947 he was made assistant professor.

After the Second World War, Columbia University started building an improved particle accelerator, the so-called synchrocyclotron, at the Nevis Laboratory. Rainwater helped build this new accelerator at Nevis, marking the beginning of his own long-standing connection with this lab. His research at Nevis lasted for more than thirty years, during which Rainwater served as director from 1951 to 1953 and then again from 1956 to 1961. When the synchrocyclotron became operational in 1950, it enabled scientists to study other particles besides neutrons. Muons, rapidly decaying particles 200 times larger than electrons, and pi-mesons, other short-lived particles that carry a force binding nuclei together, were of particular interest to Rainwater.

Formulates New Model of Atomic Nucleus

During 1949 and 1950 Rainwater shared an office with Danish physicist Aage Bohr. Their conversations during this period led to the development of a new conception of the atomic nucleus. At the time, physicists were trying to construct a model of the nucleus that would account for the forces acting between the protons and neutrons. Bohr's father, the noted physicist **Niels Bohr**, had earlier suggested the analogy of a drop of liquid as one possible model. Bohr proposed that the nucleus vibrated and changed shape like a drop of liquid. Other possible explanations were suggested by scientists Maria Goeppert Mayer and **J. Hans D. Jensen**, who conceived of the nucleus as a series of onion-like layers or shells. According to this theory, the nucleons move independently in their own concentric orbits in shells. The forces are equal throughout the nucleus, creating a nucleus with a uniform spherical force field. The shell theory succeeded in describing the motion of the nucleons, but its assumption that the nucleus was a symmetrical sphere was proven wrong by later research showing that the electrical charge around the nuclei was not spherical. Rainwater would explain why. After attending a lecture by **Charles H. Townes** in 1949 on the inconsistencies of the two nuclear models, Rainwater came up with the idea that centrifugal

forces within the nucleus might make the spherical shape around the nucleus more like an ellipsoid or football. In 1950, he published his hypothesis in a paper titled "Nuclear Energy Level Argument for a Spheroidal Nuclear Model."

Rainwater convinced Aage Bohr that his hypothesis was correct. After Bohr returned to Copenhagen, he and fellow Danish physicist Ben Mottelson developed a comprehensive theory of nuclear behavior, publishing their findings in 1952. The scientists used Rainwater's hypothesis to combine aspects of the liquid-drop model with the shell model, proposing that the collective action of the protons and neutrons made the surface of the nucleus act a like a drop of liquid, which could be deformed into a football-like shape if the outer shell of the nucleus was not filled with all the nucleons it could hold. It would then appear to oscillate and change its size. But if the outer shell of the nucleus had its complete number of nucleons, it appeared spherical.

While Bohr and Mottelson were publishing their theory, Rainwater was at work in the Nevis laboratory with a colleague, Val L. Fitch, observing x rays emanating from muons. His work revealed that the size of protons was being overestimated at the time. Other research by Rainwater focused on the properties of muons and their interactions with nuclei and advanced insight into the behavior of neutrons.

Receives International Recognition

In 1975, Bohr, Mottelson and Rainwater received the Nobel Prize for their discovery of the connection between collective motion and particle motion in atomic nuclei and for the development of the theory of the structure of the atomic nucleus based on this connection. The U.S. Atomic Energy Commission gave Rainwater the E. O. Lawrence Memorial Award in 1963, and the National Academy of Sciences elected him a member in 1968. He would also become a member of the Institute of Electrical and Electronic Engineers, the New York Academy of Sciences, the American Association for the Advancement of Science and the American Physical Society. In 1983, Rainwater was named Michael I. Pupin Professor of Physics.

In 1942, Rainwater married Emma Louise Smith. They had three sons and a daughter, who died in infancy. Rainwater's interests included geology, astronomy, and classical music. On May 31, 1986, shortly after retiring, Rainwater died in Yonkers, New York.

Sketch by Margo Nash

Vulimiri Ramalingaswami
1921–
Indian medical scientist

A medical researcher for several decades, Vulimiri Ramalingaswami pioneered studies in nutritional disorders in India and other developing countries. His discovery of a syndrome known as protein-energy malnutrition in children has led to treatments that have greatly alleviated suffering around the world. His researches in liver pathology also led to the discovery of a syndrome that produces a fatal form of cirrhosis. A teacher of international repute, Ramalingaswami's later career has been devoted to the application of his and others' discoveries in nutrition and health care.

Vulimiri Ramalingaswami was born August 8, 1921, at Srikakulam, Andhra Pradesh, India. His father, V. Gumpaswami Ramalingaswami, was a government official, and his mother, V. Sundaramma, was a housewife. As a youth, Ramalingaswami attended a school funded by his grandfather, who was also its first headmaster. Ramalingaswami told contributor J. Sydney Jones that his grandfather, whose many interests ranged from English language studies to ancient Indian literature, classical Indian music, and the science of human health, was an influential figure in Ramalingaswami's early life, especially in his choice to become a doctor. Ramalingaswami earned an M.B.B.S. in 1944 from Andhra Medical College, and his M.D. degree two years later from the same institution. In 1947 he married Surya Prabha, a training psychologist, and then attended Magdalen College at Oxford University, where he received his Ph.D. in 1951.

Research Accomplished at All India Institute

Returning to India, Ramalingaswami worked as a pathologist at the Indian Council of Medical Research until 1954 and then served as its deputy director until 1957, when he accepted a position at the All India Institute of Medical Sciences in New Delhi. For the next twenty-two years, he would help to develop an outstanding school of pathology at that institution, both in teaching and research. It was during his tenure at the All India Institute that he focused on some of the major health problems of developing countries, especially nutritional problems and liver disease. His work on protein-energy malnutrition; liver conditions such as non-cirrhotic portal hypertension; and goiter, a hormonal deficiency causing the enlargement of the thyroid gland that is prevalent in India, has done much to relieve suffering in his homeland and throughout the world. He has also worked to adapt European health care and medical education to the culture and structures of developing countries. In 1979, he left his position as director of the All India Institute of Medical Sciences to become director general of the Indian Council of Medical Research. Until his retirement seven years later, Ramalingaswami was responsible for coordinating and promoting biomedical research throughout India and for playing a principal role in establishing a government program called "Health for All by the Year 2000."

Honored worldwide for his research and organizational work, Ramalingaswami is one of the few scientists in the world to have been elected a foreign member of the major scientific academies of the United States, the United Kingdom, and the former Soviet Union. He was also chairman of the Global Advisory Committee on Medical Research for the World Health Organization (WHO) for several years, and was awarded an honorary doctorate from the Karolinska Institute in Sweden in 1974. An emeritus professor at the All India Institute of Medical Sciences since 1990, he is currently president of India's National Institute of Immunology in New Delhi. He has two children, Vulimiri Jagdish and Lakshmi V. Ramanathan. In his free time he enjoys music, literature, and sports.

SELECTED WRITINGS BY RAMALINGASWAMI:

Periodicals

Nature, Perspectives in Protein Malnutrition, Volume 201, 1964, pp. 546–551.

Archives of Pathology, Experimental Protein Deficiency—Pathological Features in the Rhesus Monkey, Volume 80, 1965, pp. 14–23.

Gastroenterology, Reaction of the Small Intestine to Induced Protein Malnutrition in Rhesus Monkeys, Volume 49, 1965, pp. 150–157.

Annals of International Medicine, Endemic Goiter in South-East Asia—New Clothes on an Old Body, Volume 78, 1973, pp. 277–283.

WHO Bulletin, Prevention of Endemic Goiter with Iodized Salt, Volume 49, 1973, pp. 307–312.

Quarterly Journal of Medicine New Series, WHO Sponsored Collaboration Studies on Nutritional Anaemia in India, Volume 44, 1975, 241–258.

Annals of the New York Academy of Science, Under the Volcano—Biomedical Science and the Third World, Volume 569, 1989, pp. 25–35.

FURTHER READING:

Periodicals

Ramalingaswami, Vulimiri, *Interview with J. Sydney Jones conducted April 12,* 1994.

Sketch by J. Sydney Jones

C. V. Raman
1888–1970
Indian physicist

Physicist C. V. Raman helped to usher India into the world of twentieth-century science. Raman overcame obstacles of geographical isolation and political oppression to establish himself, and thus India, as a serious contributor to modern Western science. His primary research interests were acoustics, musical instruments, and wave optics. He was best known for his discovery of the Raman effect (first announced in 1928), a process by which a beam of light passing through a solid, liquid, or gas was diffracted and its frequencies (and so its colors) were changed. In recognition of this discovery Raman was knighted in 1929 and awarded the Nobel Prize in physics in 1930.

Prior to Raman's time, India's development had proceeded along the lines of literature, art, and architecture. After the British colonized this land and set up trade, science was imported only to assist in furthering commerce. The British kept native Indians on the periphery of this activity and did not allow them training in modern scientific methods. It was only after the British introduced Western education that native Indians came in direct contact with twentieth-century European science. Raman, then, had to struggle against his country's delayed interest in science, its geographical isolation, and its oppression by the ruling British. By the end of the nineteenth century when European science had already become mature, science in India was a mere fledgling.

Childhood Education and Early Achievements

Chandrasekhara Venkata Raman, the second of eight children, was born on November 7, 1888, near Trichinopoly on the banks of the Kaveri. His father, Ramanathan Chandrasekaran Iyer, was a lecturer in physics, mathematics, and physical geography. Iyer read avidly, collected books, and played the violin. These pastimes came to have a great influence on his son. Raman's mother, S. Parvati Ammal, was the daughter of Saptarshi Sastri, a great Sanskrit scholar.

As a child, Raman was not strong or athletic, but he excelled at intellectual pursuits. He won many scholarships and prizes at school, and in 1903 at the age of 16 he won a scholarship and entered the prestigious Presidency College as one of its youngest undergraduates. At college Raman pursued his boyhood interest, physics, and also developed a fondness for English. Raman graduated first in his class and won gold medals in physics and English.

After Raman passed his B.A. examination, his teachers encouraged him to go to England to continue his studies. But because of his frail health he was counseled against subjecting himself to the unhealthy English climate. As a

C. V. Raman

result, Raman decided to enroll in the Presidency College's M.A. program in physics. Raman's teacher at this time made few demands on him and let him explore on his own. Raman, guided by his own interests and goaded by his own motivation, conducted his own experiments in the diffraction of light passing through rectangular slits. When he had accumulated a number of findings, he wrote them up and sent a manuscript to the *Philosophical Magazine* in London, which published it as "Unsymmetrical Diffraction Bands Due to a Rectangular Aperture." This accomplishment was remarkable because Raman sent the manuscript on his own, his was the first paper to come out of the Presidency College, and he had done this at the age of eighteen.

After earning his M.A. in 1907, Raman found that there were no opportunities for a career in research open to Indians in India. So he secured through fierce competition a coveted position in the Indian Civil Service as an accountant. He pursued his scientific research in his spare time at home until 1917 when Calcutta University offered him the Palit Chair for Physics at about half the salary he was receiving from the government. Raman accepted the position without hesitation.

Promoting Indian Science

Because of India's great size and diversity, its centers of research often suffered from their isolation. Raman felt a need for some way of consolidating and promoting his country's interests in science. To that end he worked at inciting interest among Indian scientists in establishing an academy of science. His initial attempts were stymied in Bombay by intramural disputes among various scientific factions, so he independently founded his own academy in Bangalore.

The inaugural meeting of the Indian Academy of Sciences was held in August of 1934 in Bangalore. Raman became its first president, and he retained the office until his death. For this reason some called the organization Raman's Academy. Its stated objectives were to provide a forum for discussing the results of scientific research and to publish the achievements of Indian science. G. Venkataraman, in his *Journey into Light: Life and Science of C. V. Raman,* called the Academy "one of Raman's gifts to India."

The Academy's journal, the *Proceedings of the Indian Academy of Sciences,* appeared in 1934 and featured as its opening paper Raman's work entitled "The Origin of the Colours of the Plumage of Birds." By 1935 the amount of publishable material had grown to such an extent that Raman divided the journal into two parts: physical and mathematical sciences, and biological sciences. Eventually the *Proceedings* was divided into six separate specialty journals in 1977.

Fascination with Light and Sound

Raman's fascination with the phenomenal world seemed to be behind most of his research interests. Raman once admitted to letting his attention wander from his English professor at the Presidency College because the glittering waves of the blue sea, which were visible from his lecture hall, caught his eye. Later, color was to become an ever-present aspect of his research on light and optics, which included studies on the color effects of shells, gems, minerals, flowers, and plumage.

Music also influenced Raman's research. His father inspired in his son a love for music, particularly the violin. Raman himself became a competent violinist, and later he approached musical instruments as a physicist. Raman was recognized as the first in this century to rekindle the research into the physics of the violin and other musical instruments. His research in this area included studies on the behavior of bowed strings, the influence of the violin's bridge, and the frequency response of the violin (known as the Raman curve). Raman also investigated the sound-producing mechanisms of the piano and of some traditional Indian instruments like the tabla and the tambura.

At one point, Raman was able to combine his interests in sound and light in the same research project. The fruit of this project was the Raman-Nath theory, perhaps his greatest achievement during his stay at the Indian Institute of Science. The Raman-Nath theory explained what happens to a beam of light as it passes through a liquid that is agitated by a sound wave. This theory became important later to the research on the propagation of starlight through the atmosphere and the propagation of laser emissions through plasma.

As a student, Raman had learned science in a setting where laboratory resources were modest. As a result he became adept at improvising the equipment he needed for his experiments. In a 1905 experiment on the surface tension of liquids, he devised a spark generator that illuminated a suspended drop so its shadow could be photographed. In 1927 while studying the scattering of light, Raman needed to keep the sensitivity of an observer's eye at a maximum, so he fashioned a light-tight wooden enclosure for the observer, which came to be called the "black hole of Calcutta." During his research on the physics of the violin, Raman needed a way to study and control the force of the bow, so he contrived his experimental apparatus from materials he had on hand including parts from an optical bench and the chain and hubs from a cycle. The result was a mechanical violin player where the violin moved while the bow remained stationary.

Soon after discovering the Raman effect (frequency and color changes with respect to light diffraction), Raman became interested in the diamond. Captivated by its beauty and physical properties, he referred to it as the "prince of solids." He began collecting them at his own expense, and by 1944 he had over 300. Raman even admitted that he had used part of his Nobel Prize money to buy diamonds. When he couldn't afford to buy them, he borrowed diamond rings from wealthy friends. Venkataraman reported that Raman once saw his brother sporting a diamond ring and said to him, "I say, why don't you put that thing on your finger to some use?" So strong was his scientific curiosity for diamonds that at one point every one of his students was studying some aspect of diamonds. Raman studied many optical phenomena in diamonds including light absorption, light scattering, and x-ray diffraction.

Later Interests

Raman did not want to become idle once he retired, so he began planning a new research institute two years before his retirement from the Indian Institute of Science. He conducted his own fund raising, and, by 1948, although he had not raised enough money, he had acquired a building. During the first year of its existence, the new Raman Research Institute had no electricity, but that did not prevent Raman from conducting some important optical experiments using sunlight. Eventually Raman had the financial support to complete his new facility, which included gardens for the trees and flowers that he loved and a museum for his collections of crystals, gems, minerals, shells, birds, and butterflies. Raman continued his work on optics at the Institute, which included, in conjunction with his nephew, the development of a theory to explain mirages.

Raman was known to be proud and at times even arrogant. Venkataraman reported that in 1924 at the age of 36, Raman was elected Fellow of the Royal Society. When he was congratulated and asked what was next, he replied, "the Nobel Prize, of course." When he actually did receive the prize six years later, it was discovered that he had booked passage to Stockholm, the site of the awards ceremony, four months before he received the official announcement of the award.

In the course of his 66 years as a physicist, Raman published over 450 research papers and inspired almost three times that number of papers among his students. In promoting Indian science, Raman was hailed as one of India's heroes along with Mohandas Gandhi and Motilal Nehru. Raman died at his research institute in Bangalore on November 20, 1970, and his ashes were scattered there among the trees.

SELECTED WRITINGS BY RAMAN:

Books

Scientific Papers of C. V. Raman, 6 volumes, Indian Academy of Sciences, 1988.

FURTHER READING:

Books

Venkataraman, G., *Journey into Light: Life and Science of C. V. Raman,* Indian Academy of Sciences, 1988.

Sketch by Lawrence Souder

S. I. Ramanujan

S. I. Ramanujan
1887–1920
Indian mathematician

Mathematician S. I. Ramanujan was a self-taught prodigy from India. His introduction to the world of formal mathematics and subsequent fame arose from his correspondence and collaboration with the renowned British mathematician **Godfrey Harold Hardy**. In his short but prolific career Ramanujan made several important contributions to the field of number theory, an area of pure mathematics that deals with the properties of and patterns among ordinary numbers. Three quarters of a century after his death, mathematicians still work on his papers, attempting to provide logical proofs for results he apparently arrived at intuitively. Many of his theorems are now finding practical applications in areas as diverse as polymer chemistry and computer science, subjects virtually unknown during his own times.

Srinivasa Iyengar Ramanujan, born on December 22, 1887, was the eldest son of K. Srinivasa Iyengar and Komalatammal. He was born in his mother's parental home

of Erode and raised in the city of Kumbakonam in southern India, where his father worked as a clerk in a clothing store. They were a poor family, and his mother often sang devotional songs with a group at a local temple to supplement the family income. Ramanujan received all his early education in Kumbakonam, where he studied English while still in primary school and then attended the town's English-language school. His mathematical talents became evident early on; at eleven he was already challenging his mathematics teachers with questions they could not always answer. Seeing his interest in the subject, some college students lent him books from their library. By the time he was thirteen, Ramanujan had mastered S. L. Loney's *Trigonometry,* a popular textbook used by students much older than him who were studying in Indian colleges and British preparatory schools. In 1904, at the age of 17, Ramanujan graduated from high school, winning a special prize in mathematics and a scholarship to attend college.

Pursues Mathematics Independently

Shortly before he completed high school, Ramanujan came across a book called *A Synopsis of Elementary Results in Pure and Applied Mathematics.* This book, written by British tutor G. S. Carr in the 1880s, was a compilation of approximately five thousand mathematical results, formulae, and equations. The *Synopsis* did not explain these equations or provide proofs for all the results; it merely laid down various mathematical generalizations as fact. In Ramanujan, the book unleashed a passion for mathematics so great that he studied it to the exclusion of all other subjects. Because of this, although Ramanujan enrolled in the Fine Arts (F.A.) course at the local Government College, he never completed the course. He began to spend all his time on mathematics, manipulating the formulae and equations in Carr's book, and neglected all the other subjects that were part of his course work at the college. His scholarship was revoked when he failed his English composition examination. In all, he attempted the F.A. examinations four times from 1904 to 1907. Each time he failed, doing poorly in all subjects except mathematics.

During these four years, and for several more, Ramanujan pursued his passion with single-minded devotion. He continued to work independently of his teachers, filling up sheets of paper with his ideas and results which were later compiled in his famous *Notebooks*. Carr's book had merely been a springboard to launch Ramanujan's journey into mathematics. While it gave him a direction, the book did not provide him with the methods and tools to pursue his course. These he fashioned for himself, and using them he quickly meandered from established theorems into the realms of originality. He experimented with numbers to see how they behaved, and he drew generalizations and theorems based on these observations. Some of these results and conclusions had already been proved and published in the Western world, though Ramanujan, sequestered in India, could not know that. But most of his work was original.

Meanwhile, his circumstances changed. Without a degree, it was very difficult to find a job, and for many of these years Ramanujan was desperately poor, often relying on the good graces of friends and family for support. Occasionally he would tutor students in mathematics, but most of these attempts were unsuccessful because he did not stick to the rules or syllabus. He habitually compressed multiple steps of a solution, leaving his students baffled by his leaps of logic. In July 1909 he married Janaki, a girl some ten years his junior. Keeping with local customs and traditions, the marriage had been arranged by Ramanujan and Janaki's parents. Soon afterwards, he traveled to Madras, the largest city in South India, in search of a job. Because he did not have a degree, Ramanujan presented his notebooks as evidence of his work and the research he had been conducting in past years. Most people were bewildered after reading a few pages of his books, and the few who recognized them as the work of a genius did not know what to do with them. Finally, Ramachandra Rao, a professor of mathematics at the prestigious Presidency College in Madras, reviewed the books and supported him for a while. In 1912 Ramanujan secured a position as an accounts clerk at the Madras Port Trust, giving him a meager though independent salary.

During this time, Ramanujan's work caught the attention of other scholars who recognized his abilities and encouraged him to continue his research. His first contribution to mathematical literature was a paper titled "Some Properties of Bernoulli's Numbers," and it was published in the *Journal of the Indian Mathematical Society* c. 1910. However, Ramanujan realized that the caliber of his work

was far beyond any research being conducted in India at the time, and he began writing to leading mathematicians in England asking for their help.

Sends Letter to Hardy

The first two mathematicians he approached were eminent professors at Cambridge University, and they turned him down. On January 16, 1913, Ramanujan wrote to **Godfrey Harold Hardy**, who agreed to help him. Hardy was a fellow of Trinity College, Cambridge, and he specialized in number theory and analysis. Although he was initially inclined to dismiss Ramanujan's letter, which seemed full of wild claims and strange theorems with no supporting proofs, the very bizarreness of the theorems nagged at Hardy, and he decided to take a closer look. Along with J. E. Littlewood, he examined the theorems more thoroughly, and three hours after they began reading, they both decided the work was that of a genius. "They must be true because, if they were not true, no one would have had the imagination to invent them," Hardy is quoted as saying in Robert Kanigel's book *The Man Who Knew Infinity*.

Hardy now set about the task of bringing Ramanujan to England. In the beginning, Ramanujan resisted the idea due to religious restrictions on traveling abroad, but he was eventually persuaded to go. Ramanujan spent five years in England, from 1914 to 1919, during which time he enjoyed a productive collaboration with Hardy, who personally trained him in modern analysis. Hardy described this as the most singular experience of his life, says Kanigel in *The Man Who Knew Infinity:* "What did modern mathematics look like to one who had the deepest insight, but who had literally never heard of most of it?" Ramanujan was to receive several laurels during this period, including a B.A. degree from Cambridge, and appointments as Fellow of the Royal Society (at 30 he was one of the youngest ever to be honored thus) and Trinity College. But the English weather affected Ramanujan's health, and he contracted tuberculosis. In 1919 he returned to India, where he succumbed to the disease, dying on April 26, 1920.

Until the very end, Ramanujan remained passionately involved in mathematics, and he produced some original work even after his return to India. His great love for the subject and his genius are perhaps best exemplified in an incident described by Hardy in his book *A Mathematician's Apology*. He related that while visiting Ramanujan at a hospital outside London, where he lay ill with tuberculosis, Hardy mentioned the number of his taxicab, 1729. Hardy thought it a rather dull number. "No, Hardy! No, Hardy!" Ramanujan replied. "It is a very interesting number. It is the smallest number expressible as the sum of two cubes in two different ways." Kanigel reported another comment Hardy made later. He said that had Ramanujan been better educated, "he would have been less of a Ramanujan and more of a European professor and the loss might have been greater." Ramanujan himself attributed his mathematical gifts to his family deity, the goddess Namagiri. A deeply religious man, he combined his passion with his faith, and he once told a friend that "an equation for me has no meaning unless it expresses a thought of God."

SELECTED WRITINGS BY RAMANUJAN:

Books

Notebooks, 2 volumes, Tata Institute of Fundamental Research, 1957.

The Lost Notebook and Other Unpublished Papers, Narosa Publishing House, 1988.

FURTHER READING:

Books

Hardy, G. H., *A Mathematician's Apology,* Cambridge University Press, 1940.

Hardy, G. H., *Ramanujan: Twelve Lectures on Subjects Suggested by His Life and Work,* Cambridge University Press, 1940.

Kanigel, Robert, *The Man Who Knew Infinity: A Life of the Genius Ramanujan,* Macmillan, 1991.

Periodicals

Hardy, G. H., *Nature,* Obituary, S. Ramanujan, June 17, 1920, pp 494–95.

Seshu Iyer, P. V., and Ramachandra Rao, R., *Journal of the Indian Mathematical Society,* The Late Mr. S. Ramanujan, B.A., F.R.S. June, 1920, pp 81–86.

Other

Sykes, Christopher, *Letters from an Indian Clerk,* (documentary), BBC.

Sketch by Neeraja Sankaran

Pauline Ramart-Lucas
1880–1953
French organic chemist

Pauline Ramart-Lucas was the second woman (after French physicist **Marie Curie**) to become a full professor at the University of Paris. An organic chemist whose interests ranged widely, Ramart-Lucas studied the structure, chemical reactivity, and ultraviolet absorption spectrum of organic compounds. Through her efforts, she discovered a new type of isomerism that revised the electronic structure of carbon in a large class of organic molecules. In addition, she was a prominent educator and science administrator in the French university system. Born on November 22, 1880, Ramart-Lucas grew up in modest circumstances in Paris. Upon finishing elementary school, she worked as an arranger of artificial flowers in the shadow of the Sorbonne, France's premier university. She vowed then to attend the university, and with this goal in mind she took evening courses to obtain a secondary-school diploma. A pharmacist instructed her in English and kindled her passion for chemistry. At age 29 she completed the *licence* in physical sciences—corresponding roughly to an American bachelor of sciences degree—despite encountering prejudice because she was female.

Ramart-Lucas gravitated to the organic chemistry laboratory of Albin Haller, who himself had been apprenticed as a woodworker before finding an academic vocation. There she completed a doctorate in 1913. After a short time working in radiology during World War I, she returned to chemistry when Haller called her back to his laboratory. With the exception of the years between 1941 and 1944, when she was relieved of her post, she worked at the Sorbonne for the rest of her life, rising from laboratory manager to lecturer in 1925, and then to professor in 1930.

In the first part of her career, from 1908 to 1924, Ramart-Lucas concentrated on the molecular changes that occur when various alcohols—organic compounds that include the oxygen-hydrogen radical OH—are dehydrated. During the latter part of her career she studied the structure, chemical reactivity, and ultraviolet absorption spectrum of organic compounds. She cast her net wide, specializing in analyzing diverse dyes. Her research identified a new type of isomerism, or structural difference, that revised the electronic structure of carbon in a large class of organic molecules.

The recipient of many prizes before World War II—including the 1928 Ellen H. Richards Research Prize of the American Association of University Women—Ramart-Lucas emerged as one of France's senior science administrators after 1944, when she became vice-president of the educational section in the Consultative Assembly. She also sat on the councils of the Palais de la découverte, France's national science museum, and the École de physique et de chimie, Paris's famous municipal science school. Admitted as a Knight in the French Legion of Honor in 1928, she was promoted to Officer in 1938; she received the exceptional distinction of Commander in 1953.

Ramart-Lucas preferred original research over synthetic summary, although in 1936 she did contribute a long chapter on molecular structure and absorption spectra to **Victor Grignard**'s multi-volume handbook on organic chemistry. Over nearly half a century, she published more than two hundred scientific articles and directed fifty doctoral theses and graduate memoirs, a large number of these by women students. Her work was her life, and her students and colleagues became her family. She died on March 13, 1953.

FURTHER READING:

Periodicals

Denis, Paul, *Bulletin de la Société chimique de France: Mémoires et documentation,* Madame Pauline Ramart-Lucas, Volume 21, 1954, pp. 269–271.

Martynoff, Modeste, *Bulletin de la Société chimique de France: Mémoires et documentation,* L'oeuvre scientifique de Pauline Ramart-Lucas (bibliography)Volume 21, 1954, pp. 272–280.

Sketch by Lewis Pyenson

Estelle R. Ramey

Estelle R. Ramey
1917–
American physiologist and educator

Estelle Ramey is known for her research in the endocrine aspects of stress, including the relationship between sex hormones and longevity, as well as for her activism in the feminist movement. In 1989 she was named by *Newsweek* magazine as "one of twenty-five Americans who have made a difference."

Ramey was born in Detroit, Michigan, on August 23, 1917, to Henry, a businessman, and Sarah L. White. She graduated from Brooklyn College at the age of nineteen and took a job as a teaching fellow in the department of chemistry at Queens College, New York City. "Dr. Whittaker, my old teacher, was appointed chairman of the department at Queens College," Ramey recalled in correspondence with Jill Carpenter, "and he was a unique man for his times. He did not equate gender with ability."

Ramey completed her M.S. degree in chemistry at Columbia University in 1940 and was working toward a Ph.D. degree when she married law student James T. Ramey (they have two children, James and Drucilla). When her husband's career took them to Knoxville, Tennessee, Ramey applied for a job in the department of chemistry at the University of Tennessee. Ramey told Carpenter: "I was brusquely informed by the chairman that he had never hired a woman, would never hire a woman, and I ought to go home and take care of my husband. A few months later, Pearl Harbor was bombed and the war started. The chemistry department began to lose its male faculty and a chastened chairman called to offer me a job teaching thermodynamics to Air Cadets and biochemistry to Nurse Cadets." Ramey taught at the University of Tennessee from 1942 through 1947.

When her husband joined the newly created Atomic Energy Commission in Chicago, Ramey entered the University of Chicago. She was a Mergler Scholar in 1949, and earned a Ph.D. from the university's School of Medicine in 1950. Also in 1950, she received a U. S. Public Health Service postdoctoral fellowship in endocrinology and became an assistant professor of physiology at the medical school, the first woman faculty member in that department. In 1956 she joined the faculty of Georgetown University Medical School in Washington, D.C. Her tenure at Georgetown was punctuated by stints as visiting professor at Stanford University, Harvard University, and Yale University. In 1977 she was awarded an honorary doctorate by Georgetown, and in 1987 the university named her professor emerita of biophysics.

Advisory boards, boards of directors, and committees on which Ramey has served include Educational Telecommunications, Planned Parenthood, Big Sisters of Washington, the National Institutes of Health, the National Academy of Science, the Veteran's Administration for Women Veterans, the Chief of Naval Operations, the Admiral H. G. Rickover Foundation, the MacDonald Hospital for Women, and President Carter's Committee on the Status of Women. She is a member of the nominating committee of the MacArthur Foundation, and her honors include the Outstanding Alumna Award from the University of Chicago, 1973; the Public Broadcasting Company Woman of Achievement Award, 1984; and the National Women's Democratic Club Woman of Achievement Award, 1993. Ramey is a past president of the Association for Women in Science (AWIS) and founder of the AWIS Educational Foundation. She holds 17 honorary doctorates, has lectured at dozens of colleges and government agencies, and has published more than 150 articles in the scientific and popular press.

SELECTED WRITINGS BY RAMEY:

Periodicals

Harper's, Boredom: The Most Prevalent American Disease, November, 1974, pp. 12–22.

FURTHER READING:

Other

Ramey, Estelle R., correspondence with Jill Carpenter, January, 1994.

Sketch by Jill Carpenter

Santiago Ramón y Cajal
1852–1934
Spanish neurohistologist

The anatomical research of the Spanish neurohistologist Santiago Ramón y Cajal is central to the modern understanding of the nervous system. By adopting and improving the nervous-tissue staining process developed by the Italian scientist **Camillo Golgi**, Ramón y Cajal established that individual nerve cells, or neurons, are the basic structural unit of the nervous system. He also made important discoveries relating to the transmission of nerve impulses and the cellular structures of the brain. For his work in histology, the branch of anatomy concerned with minute tissue structures and processes, Ramón y Cajal shared with Golgi the 1906 Nobel Prize for physiology or medicine.

Ramón y Cajal was born on May 1, 1852, in the remote country village of Petilla de Aragon, Spain. He was the son of Justo Ramón y Casasús, a poor and self-educated barber-surgeon, and Antonia Cajal. The family subsequently moved to the university city of Zaragoza, where against considerable odds Ramón y Cajal's father earned a medical degree and became a professor of anatomy. As a young man, Ramón y Cajal was rebellious and independent-minded. He preferred drawing to studying, and although this passion for drawing would ultimately serve him well, it was vigorously opposed by his iron-willed father, who had determined that his son should become a doctor. As a disciplinary measure, his father apprenticed him to a barber

and later to a shoemaker. During these apprenticeships, Ramón y Cajal also studied anatomy with his father—investigations which partially relied on bone specimens taken from a local churchyard.

When he was sixteen years old, Ramón y Cajal began medical studies at the University of Zaragoza, earning a degree in medicine in 1873. He then joined the army medical service and served as an infantry surgeon in Cuba for one year. He contracted malaria, however, which led to his discharge, and he returned to Spain. In 1879, still convalescent, he passed his examinations at Zaragoza and Madrid for his doctorate in medicine.

Ramón y Cajal was almost exclusively interested in anatomical research, and he embarked on an academic career. Beginning in 1879, Ramón y Cajal turned himself into a skilled histologist, initially working with an old, abandoned microscope he had found at the University of Zaragoza. He studied various anatomical tissues and began to publish articles on cell biology—complete with beautifully rendered ink drawings. His work was not immediately recognized in other countries, but the increasing prestige of his posts attests to his success in Spain. From 1879 to 1883, he directed the anatomical museum at the University of Zaragoza. In 1883, he assumed a professorship of descriptive anatomy at the University of Valencia, and in 1887 he became professor of histology at the University of Barcelona. In 1892, Ramón y Cajal assumed the chair of histology and pathologic anatomy at the University of Madrid, a post he retained until 1922.

Research Provides Evidence for Neuron Theory

Ramón y Cajal eventually turned to the most complex tissues, those of the nervous system. His research method now drew on Camillo Golgi's method of staining tissue samples to reveal their minute components. Under Golgi's method, a potassium dichromate-silver nitrate solution stained the nerve cells and fibers black, while the neuroglia, or supporting tissues, remained much lighter. By refining this staining technique and applying it to embryonic tissue samples, Ramón y Cajal was able to isolate the neuron as the basic component of the nervous system; he also differentiated the neuron from the ordinary cells of the body. His work supported the neuron theory, which held that the nervous system consists of a network of discrete nerve fibers that end in terminal "buttons," which never actually touch the surrounding nerve cells. Up until that time, the majority of scientists were "reticularists," who held that the nervous system formed a continuous and interconnected system. Golgi was among these, and the rivalry between the two scientists was intense. Ramón y Cajal published fierce and relentless attacks both on this theory and on the scientists who held it.

Based on his studies, Ramón y Cajal became convinced that the conduction of nerve impulses occurs in one direction only—a postulate since formalized as the law of dynamic polarization. He also conducted important research on the tissues of the inner ear and the eye, as well as the tissues of the grey matter of the brain, establishing a cellular basis for the localization of different functions within the brain. This research has formed the physiological basis for the understanding of human psychology, intelligence, and memory.

Ramón y Cajal was a prolific writer and he published many articles, textbooks, and research monographs. In 1896, he established a journal of microbiology and published his *Manual de Anatomia Pathologica General* ("Manual of General Pathologic Anatomy"). His major neurohistological work, *Textura del Systema Nervioso del Hombre y de los Vertebrados* ("Texture of the Nervous System of Man and Vertebrates"), was published from 1899 to 1904. These publications were generally printed in Spanish, often at his own expense, and they were largely ignored by the international scientific community.

His struggle for due recognition of the importance of his work came to an end in 1906, when he shared the Nobel Prize in physiology or medicine with his rival Golgi for their work on the structure of the nervous system. In an apparent effort to emphasize what the two scientists had in common, rather than their area of disagreement, they were described by the prize committee as "the principal representatives and standard-bearers of the modern science of neurology." But the tension between them over the reticular doctrine was still evident on the awards platform.

Later Research and Writing

In the same year he received the prize, Ramón y Cajal turned to the problem of the degeneration of tissue in the nervous system and the regeneration of nerve fibers that had been severed. The result of these studies, the two-volume *Estudios Sobre la Degeneracion y Regeneracion del Sistema Nervioso* ("Studies on the Degeneration and Regeneration of the Nervous System"), was published in 1913 and 1914. In 1913, Ramón y Cajal also developed a gold-based method of staining neuroglia; he was able to use this to classify cell types in these tissues. This research provided the basis for the medical treatment of tumors and pathological tissues in the nervous system. A tireless researcher, Ramón y Cajal also studied the eyes and vision processes of insects.

Ramón y Cajal, a patriot, was always sensitive to the international and scientific reputation of Spain and the Spanish language—issues that had a significant impact on the dissemination of his research. It was thus fitting that in 1920 King Alfonso XIII commissioned the construction of the Instituto Cajal, which secured Madrid's position as an international histological research center. Ramón y Cajal worked at this institute named in his honor from 1922 until his death. In addition to sharing the Nobel Prize, Ramón y Cajal received numerous awards and honors, including the Fauvelle Prize of the Society of Biology in Paris in 1896; the Rubio Prize in 1897; the Moscow Prize in 1900; the Martinez y Molina Prize in 1902; the Helmholtz Gold Medal of the Royal Academy of Berlin in 1905; and the Echegaray Medial in 1922. He also received honorary degrees from various foreign universities and held memberships in scientific societies worldwide. The Spanish government bestowed an impressive series of posthumous honors on him, including the republication of his works.

Ramón y Cajal married Silveria Fananas Garcia in 1880. They had three daughters and three sons. In addition to drawing, his hobbies included chess and photography, which he pursued as single-mindedly as his research. In a merging of his work and recreational interests, Ramón y Cajal developed his own photographic process for the reproduction of his delicate histological drawings.

Between 1901 and 1917, Ramón y Cajal published the installments of his autobiographical *Recuerdos de mi Vida* ("Recollections of My Life"). His other published works include the anecdotal *Charlas de Cafe* ("Conversations at the Cafe") and *El Mundo Visto a los Ochenta Años* ("The World as Seen at Eighty"). Ramón y Cajal died in Madrid on October 18, 1934.

SELECTED WRITINGS BY RAMÓN Y CAJAL:

Books

Manual de Anatomia Pathologica General, (title means "Manual of General Pathologic Anatomy"), Moya (Madrid), 1896.

Textura del Systema Nervioso del Hombre y de los Vertebrados, (title means "Texture of the Nervous System of Man and Vertebrates"), Moya (Madrid), 1899–1904.

Estudios Sobre la Degeneracion y Regeneracion del Sistema Nervioso, 1913–14, translated by Raoul M. Day as Degeneration and Regeneration of the Nervous System, Oxford University Press (London), 1928.

Recollections of My Life, two volumes, 1937, Massachusetts Institute of Technology (Cambridge, MA), 1966.

FURTHER READING:

Books

Cannon, Dorothy F., *Explorer of the Human Brain: The Life of Santiago Ramón y Cajal,* H. Schuman, 1949.

Cannon, Dorothy F., *Dictionary of Scientific Biography,* Scribner's, 1975, pp. 273–76.

Shepherd, Gordon M., *Foundations of the Neuron Doctrine,* Oxford University Press, 1992.

Shepherd, Gordon M., *Nobel Prize Winners,* H. W. Wilson, 1987, pp. 852–55.

Periodicals

Knudtson, Peter, *Science,* Painter of Neurons, September 1985, pp. 66–72.

Sketch by David Sprinkle

William Ramsay
1852–1916
English chemist

The first two decades of William Ramsay's career were spent on a variety of comparatively insignificant studies, including work on the alkaloids, water loss in salts, the solubility of gases in solids, and a class of organic compounds known as the diketones. It was not until 1892 that he became engaged in the line of research for which he was eventually to win a Nobel Prize, the study of the inert gases. Those studies were to occupy Ramsay for most of the next decade and to win him worldwide fame for his participation in the discovery of five new chemical elements.

Ramsay was born on October 2, 1852, at Queen's Crescent, Glasgow, Scotland. He was the only child of William Ramsay, a civil engineer, and the former Catharine Robertson, who came from a family of physicians. In spite of this scientific background, young William showed no particular interest in the sciences and had a classical liberal education at Glasgow Academy.

When he entered the University of Glasgow at the age of fourteen in 1866, Ramsay chose to remain in a classical curriculum that included literature, logic, and mathematics, thinking that he might join the clergy. Over a period of time, however, his interests shifted toward the sciences and, from 1869 to 1870, he worked as an apprentice to a local chemist, Robert Tatlock. At the end of this period, Ramsay was ready to make a commitment to a career in chemistry, and in 1871 he enrolled in a doctoral program at the University of Tübingen under the noted organic chemist Rudolf Fittig. Ramsay received his Ph.D. from Tübingen only a year later at the early age of nineteen for a study of toluic and nitrotoluic acids.

After receiving his degree, Ramsay returned to Glasgow and became a research assistant at Anderson's College (later the Royal Technical College). At Anderson's, Ramsay's work dealt primarily with organic chemistry, especially with compounds related to quinine and cinchonine. Six years later, in 1880, he was appointed professor of chemistry at University College, Bristol (later, Bristol University). During his seven years at Bristol, Ramsay worked with an assistant, Sydney Young, on the relationships between the physical properties of a liquid and the liquid's molecular weight.

Resolves the Puzzle of Nitrogen's Atomic Weight

Ramsay's appointment in 1887 as professor of chemistry at University College, London, marked a turning point in his career. For a few years he continued to work on a variety of problems, such as surface tension, the metallic compounds of ethylene, and the atomic weight of boron. But

then, in late 1892, Ramsay was confronted with a puzzle that was to captivate him. That puzzle went back to a discovery made by Henry Cavendish in 1785. Cavendish had found that the compete removal of oxygen and nitrogen from a sample of air still left a small bubble of some additional unknown gas. The puzzle was confounded by the work of **Robert Strutt** (Lord Rayleigh) in the late 1880s that showed the density of nitrogen to be slightly different depending on whether the gas came from air or from a compound of nitrogen.

Ramsay decided to resolve this dilemma. He began by removing all of the nitrogen and oxygen from a sample of air by burning magnesium metal (which reacts with both) in the air. He found a small bubble of gas, similar to that reported by Cavendish a century earlier. But then Ramsay took an additional step that Cavendish could not have taken: he did a spectroscopic analysis of the gas bubble. The result of that analysis was a set of spectral lines that had never been seen before—the gas bubble was clearly a new element. Because of the inertness of the element, Ramsay suggested the name argon for the element, from the Greek *argos*, for "lazy."

Begins the Search for Other Inert Gases

The discovery of argon immediately posed new research possibilities. Determination of the element's atomic weight placed it between chlorine and potassium in the periodic table. Clearly the element was located in a new column in the table, a column that Dmitri Ivanovich Mendeleev could never have imagined when he proposed the periodic law in 1869. The challenge that Ramsay recognized was to locate other members of this new chemical family, those that made up column "0" (or column 18) in the periodic table.

Shortly after announcing the discovery of argon, Ramsay heard about another inert gas that had been discovered by the American chemist William Hillebrand. To see if Hillebrand's gas might also be argon, Ramsay heated a sample of the mineral clevite in sulfuric acid and had the gas produced tested by spectroscopic analysis. The results of that analysis showed that the gas was *not* argon, but it did have the same spectral lines as those of an element discovered in the Sun in 1868 by Pierre Janssen and Joseph Lockyer, an element they had named helium. Ramsay's research showed that helium also existed on the Earth.

Over the next few years, Ramsay looked for the remaining missing inert gases in various minerals, always without success. Then in 1898 he decided on another approach. He and a colleague, Morris Travers, prepared fifteen liters of liquid argon, which they then allowed to evaporate very slowly. Eventually they identified three more new gases, krypton, neon, and xenon, which they announced to the world on June 6, June 16, and September 8, 1898, respectively.

Ramsay remained at London until his retirement in 1912. During the last decade of his tenure there, he became increasingly interested in radioactivity. Among his discoveries in this field was one made with **Frederick Soddy** in 1903, namely that helium is always a product of the radioactive decay of radium. This discovery was later explained when it was found that the alpha particles emitted by a radioactive substance are actually positively charged helium ions. In conjunction with Robert Whytlaw-Gray, Ramsay also determined the atomic weight of the one inert gas in whose discovery he was not involved, radon.

Ramsay was married to Margaret Buchanan in August, 1881; they had two children. After the outbreak of World War I, Ramsay attempted to carry on chemical research for military applications, but his health failed rapidly and he died on July 23, 1916, at his home in Hazlemere, Buckinghamshire, England. In addition to the 1904 Nobel Prize in chemistry for his discovery of the rare gases, Ramsay was awarded the 1895 Davy Medal of the Royal Society and the 1903 August Wilhelm von Hofmann Medal of the German Chemical Society. He was made a fellow of the Royal Society in 1888 and was knighted in 1902.

SELECTED WRITINGS BY RAMSAY:

Books

Modern Chemistry, J. M. Dent, 1900.
Modern Chemistry, Theoretical and Systematic, Macmillan, 1907.
The Electron as an Element, Rice Institute, 1915.
Elements and Electrons, Harper and Brothers, 1912.

Periodicals

Proceedings of the Royal Society, Argon, a New Constituent of the Atmosphere, Volume 57, 1895, pp. 265–287.
Proceedings of the Royal Society, On the Companions of Argon, Volume 63, 1898, pp. 437–440.
Proceedings of the Royal Society, Further Experiments on the Production of Helium from Radium, Volume 73, 1904, pp. 346–358.

FURTHER READING:

Books

Davis, H. W. C., and J. R. H. Weaver, *Dictionary of National Biography, 1912–1921,* Oxford, 1923, pp. 444–446.
Davis, H. W. C., and J. R. H. Weaver, *Dictionary of Scientific Biography,* Volume 11, Scribner, 1975, pp. 277–284.
Hunter, Norman W., and Kimberly Zeigler, *Nobel Laureates in Chemistry: 1901–1992,* William Ramsay, Laylin K. James, editorAmerican Chemical Society and the Chemical Heritage Foundation, 1993, pp. 23–29.

Tilden, W. A., *Sir William Ramsay, K.C.B., F.R.S.,* Macmillan, 1918.
Travers, M. W., *A Life of Sir William Ramsay,* E. Arnold, 1956.
Wasson, Tyler, editor, *Nobel Prize Winners,* H. W. Wilson, 1987, pp. 855–856.
Williams, Trevor, editor, *A Biographical Dictionary of Scientists: Chemists,* Wiley, 1974, pp. 120–121.

Sketch by David E. Newton

Frank Plumpton Ramsey
1903–1930
English mathematician

During his short life, Frank Plumpton Ramsey made important contributions to three fields: mathematics (in particular, mathematical logic), philosophy, and economics. He is perhaps best known for his efforts to deal with some fundamental issues in logic raised by **Alfred North Whitehead** and **Bertrand Russell** in their monumental work *Principia Mathematica.* Those issues involved Whitehead and Russell's theory of types and their axiom of reducibility. Ramsey's work in the field of economics was limited to two published papers on taxation and savings that drew high praise from the eminent economist John Maynard Keynes.

Ramsey was born in Cambridge, England, on February 22, 1903. He was the older son of A. S. Ramsey, a mathematician who later became president of Magdalene College at Cambridge University. Ramsey's mother is described by Nils-Eric Sahlin in *The Philosophy of F. P. Ramsey,* as "active in politics" and a person of "very profound social awareness." Ramsey's younger brother later became Archbishop of Canterbury and his two sisters both graduated from universities.

Ramsey showed an aptitude for mathematics at an early age. He demonstrated special skills in dealing with abstract problems, a promising beginning for one who was to make his mark in logic and philosophy. Ramsey was educated first at home by his mother and then at the Winchester Public School. At Winchester, Ramsey's intellectual prowess quickly became obvious to his teachers and colleagues. In a reminiscence reported by Sahlin, a friend named I. A. Richards recalled how Ramsey learned German; he announced he wanted to do so, went home with a German grammar and a dictionary, and a week or two later he was able to critique Austrian physicist and philosopher Ernst Mach's *Analysis of Sensations* in the author's native language.

After completing his studies at Winchester, Ramsey enrolled at Trinity College, Cambridge. He earned his bachelor's degree in mathematics with first class honors in 1923. He then traveled briefly to Vienna, and upon his return in 1924 he was appointed a fellow at King's College, Cambridge. Although he never earned a Ph.D., Ramsey was soon promoted to lecturer in mathematics at Cambridge (1926) and was then made director of studies in mathematics at King's College. He held these posts until his untimely death.

Contributes to Logic, Philosophy, and Economics

Ramsey's contributions in the field of mathematics rest largely on two papers that he published in 1925 and 1928. The first of these dealt with the efforts of Alfred North Whitehead and Bertrand Russell in *Principia Mathematica* to outline a comprehensive and logical foundation for all of mathematics. Ramsey reinterpreted some of the fundamental premises of the Whitehead-Russell work, and he was able do away with the axiom of reducibility, which Whitehead and Russell had been forced to use to deal with some basic contradictions arising out of their theory of types, which concludes that if classes belong to a particular type, and if they consist of homogenous members, then a class cannot be a member of itself. Contemporaries such as R. B. Braithwaite considered Ramsey's work in this area to be "almost the last word in the treatment of mathematics by this 'logical' school."

In 1928, Ramsey published a paper addressing what was then the most important question facing mathematical logicians, the so-called *Entscheidungs* problem. The focus of this problem was to find a method for determining the consistency of a logical formula. In his paper, Ramsey was able to solve this problem for a certain specified set of conditions: when the axioms, or generally accepted theories, consist of general laws.

John Maynard Keynes has illuminated Ramsey's early powers in economics. Keynes describes how economists at Cambridge were accustomed to bringing their ideas to Ramsey for testing while the young man was still only sixteen years old. Keynes wrote that Ramsey possessed the ability to handle "the technical apparatus of our science with the easy grasp of one accustomed to something far more difficult." Ramsey's actual contributions to economics were also limited to only two published papers, but they were of extraordinary quality. Keynes described the second of these two papers, "A Mathematical Theory of Saving," as "one of the most remarkable contributions to mathematical economics ever made, both in respect of the intrinsic importance and difficulty of the subject, the power and elegance of the technical methods employed, and the clear purity of illumination with which the writer's mind is felt by the reader to play about its subject."

Ramsey's published work on philosophy was even slimmer than that in logic and economics, consisting of a single important paper on universals in the journal *Mind.* But his unpublished works were significant enough to cause Braithwaite to claim that Ramsey's death had "deprived the world of one of its most promising philosophers."

Ramsey was an intriguing and complex individual. He weighed nearly 240 pounds at the time of his death and claimed to take no displeasure in his size. His lectures were popular among undergraduates not only because of his brilliance and clarity of presentation but also because of his subtle humor and booming laugh. He died of a chronic liver disorder on January 19, 1930, at the age of twenty-six. He left behind his wife, the former Lettice C. Baker, whom he had married in 1925, and two young daughters.

SELECTED WRITINGS BY RAMSEY:

Books

The Foundations of Mathematics, edited by R. B. Braithwaite, Routledge & Kegan Paul, 1931.

Periodicals

Proceedings of the London Mathematical Society, The Foundations of Mathematics, Volume 25, 1926, pp. 338–384.

Mathematical Gazette, Mathematical Logic, Volume 13, 1926, pp. 185–194.

Economic Journal, A Contribution to the Theory of Taxation, March, 1927.

Economic Journal, A Mathematical Theory of Saving, December, 1928.

Proceedings of the London Mathematical Society, On the Problem of Formal Logic, Volume 30, 1930, pp. 264–286.

FURTHER READING:

Books

Gillispie, C. C., editor, *Dictionary of Scientific Biography,* Volume 11, Scribner, 1975, pp. 285–286.

Keynes, John Maynard, *Essays in Biography,* Harcourt, 1933, pp. 294–311.

Sahlin, Nils-Eric, *The Philosophy of F. P. Ramsey,* Cambridge University Press, 1990.

Periodicals

Braithwaite, R. B., *Journal of the London Mathematical Society,* Frank Plumpton Ramsey, Volume 6, 1931, pp. 75–78.

Sketch by David E. Newton

Norman Foster Ramsey
1915–
American physicist

Norman Foster Ramsey is a preeminent physicist whose research has focussed on the properties of molecules, atoms, nuclei, and elementary particles. The numerous awards and honors he won throughout his career culminated in the 1989 Nobel Prize in physics. Although the prize seemed to recognize a lifetime of achievements in the field, the Nobel committee specifically cited his work in developing a method of measuring the differences between atomic energy levels. His findings were key to the development of the cesium atomic clock, which measures time with an accuracy previously unknown.

Ramsey was born in Washington, D.C., on August 27, 1915. He was named after his father, a graduate of the United States Military Academy who was then a general serving as assistant to the Chief of Ordnance. His mother was Minnie Bauer Ramsey. After several years in Washington, his father was transferred to the Command and General Staff School in Fort Leavenworth, Kansas. There, Norman Jr. attended high school, distinguishing himself as president of his class. He graduated in 1931. Ramsey studied physics at Columbia University in New York City, where he won the Van Aminge and Van Buren prizes in mathematics. He graduated Phi Beta Kappa from Columbia in 1935 and entered the doctoral program there.

As a graduate student, Ramsey studied at Cambridge University, receiving a B.A. in 1937 and an M.A. in 1941. From 1939 to 1940, he was also a Carnegie Fellow at the Carnegie Institution in Washington. In 1940 he received his Ph.D. from Columbia. His thesis, written on research he had performed with the Nobel laureate I. I. Rabi, focused on the rotational magnetic moments of hydrogen molecules. Ramsey and Rabi had found that magnetic moments were dependent on the weight of the nuclei, which led to the discovery of a new force, called the tensor force, between the neutron and the proton.

From 1940 to 1942 Ramsey continued his research as an associate at the University of Illinois. As the United States became involved in World War II, he also worked at the Massachusetts Institute of Technology Radiation Laboratory as the head of a group developing the magnetron transmitter for radar. The result of this work was the three-centimeter-wavelength radar system, the first of its kind, which was widely used during the war. From 1942 to 1945, Ramsey served as consultant to the Secretary of War, at first advising the Air Force on the use of radar and later consulting with the National Defense Research Committee. In this capacity, he was sent to Los Alamos to study the possibilities of building an atomic bomb, and from 1943 to 1945 he was group leader and associate division chief of the Laboratory of the Atomic Energy Project. In 1945 he went with his group to the Tinian Island bomber base to oversee the first atom bombing missions.

During the war, Ramsey remained active in academics. From 1942 to 1945 he was an assistant professor of physics at Columbia, and in 1945 he was promoted to associate professor. After the war he served as executive secretary of the group that founded the Brookhaven National Laboratory in Long Island, New York. He was named head of the physics department there in 1946. In 1947 he took a job as associate professor at Harvard University, becoming a full professor in 1950.

In 1948, Ramsey was named chair of the Harvard Nuclear Physics Committee and director of the Harvard Nuclear Laboratory. In this capacity he was involved with the development of Harvard's first postwar cyclotron, built in 1949. The 125,000,000-electron-volt cyclotron was designed to smash atoms in order to study the particles that constitute atomic nuclei and the forces that keep the particles together. By 1956, Harvard and MIT had joined forces to build another cyclotron, the world's best at the time, producing the fastest artificially accelerated particles. Ramsey chaired the committee that oversaw its construction.

Ramsey's research during these years led to several important discoveries. One was that some atoms which were thought to exist near a temperature of absolute zero, a value based on the Kelvin temperature scale, could actually have temperatures that were below absolute zero. It had previously been thought that temperatures of matter could never have negative values. Parts of the second law of thermodynamics had to be rephrased in order to accomodate this finding.

Discovers Separate Oscillating Fields

Ramsey also challenged the prevailing practice of measuring atomic energy spectra. Beams of atoms had been measured by passing them through an electromagnetic field tuned to the difference between the atom's two energy levels. The resulting pattern of interference was studied to deduce information regarding the structure and behavior of atoms. However, the accuracy of this technique was limited by the need to maintain a constant magnetic field throughout the process. Ramsey attempted to expose atoms to two separate electromagnetic fields—one as the atoms entered the field and another as they departed. The pattern of interference was much more accurate than the one previously produced by using a homogenous magnetic field. His experiments led to the development of the hydrogen maser (for Microwave Amplification by Stimulated Emission of Radiation).

Improving the techniques of studying atoms led Ramsey to the development of his Nobel-winning achievement: the cesium atomic clock. Announced by Ramsey in 1960, the atomic clock is believed to be a hundred-thousand times more accurate than previous atomic clocks, which used gaseous ammonia molecules. Ramsey's clock uses high-energy atomic hydrogen, which could be measured for the first time due to the method of using separate oscillating fields. It is now the time standard used throughout the world, in which the second is defined as the time in which it takes a cesium atom to make 9,192,631,770 oscillations.

Ramsey was awarded half the 1989 Nobel Prize in physics, the other half being divided between Wolfgang Paul and Hans Dehmelt. Ramsey was cited for his work on the hydrogen maser, as well as the atomic clock. Daniel Kleppner, with whom Ramsey often collaborated, told *Science* magazine: "His work was seminal in the theory of chemical shifts, which underlies the use of the magnetic resonance imaging units in hospitals."

Kleppner also called Ramsey a "statesman of science," and World War II was not the end of his government service. In 1958, Ramsey was named Scientific Advisor to the North Atlantic Treaty Organization. He took a leave from Harvard to head an advisory committee which oversaw all NATO activities in research and applied science. In the late 1970s he was again asked to be a government adviser, and he became the co-chairman of a federal committee to study the possible practical uses of cold nuclear fusion.

In addition to the Nobel Prize, Ramsey also received the Lawrence Award in 1960, and the Davisson-Germer Prize from the American Physical Society in 1974. He was awarded the Karl Compton Prize from the American Institute of Physics, the Rumford Prize, and the National Medal of Science, all in 1985. He was elected to the National Academy of Sciences in 1952.

Ramsey married Elinor Stedman Jameson in 1940; she died in 1983. They had four daughters. In 1985, Ramsey married again, this time to Ellie Welch. He is now Higgins Professor of Physics, Emeritus, at Harvard University.

SELECTED WRITINGS BY RAMSEY:

Books

Nuclear Moments, Wiley, 1953.
Molecular Beams, Oxford University Press, 1955.

Periodicals

Physical Review, A New Molecular-Beam Resonance Method, Volume 76, 1949, p. 996.
Physical Review, A Molecular-Beam Resonance Method with Separated Oscillating Fields, Volume 78, 1950, pp. 695–699.

FURTHER READING:

Books

Current Biography, H. W. Wilson, 1993, pp. 351–353.
McGraw-Hill Modern Men of Science, McGraw-Hill, 1966, pp. 387–388.

Periodicals

New York Times, February 6, 1958, pp. 1, 8.
New York Times, October 13, 1989, p. 10.
Science, Volume 246, October 20, 1989, pp. 327–328.

Sketch by Dorothy Barnhouse

Lucie Randoin
1888–1960
French physiologist

Lucie Randoin is best known for work which demonstrates the role of vitamins in the human diet. She did much of her ground-breaking research on vitamins during the 1920s, when scientists were beginning to understand their relationship to nutrition. Randoin spent years examining both vitamins and blood sugars, and her findings paved the way for a better understanding of how different substances affect human physiology.

Lucie Fandard was born in 1888 in Boeurs-en-Othe, France. She attended schools in Paris and distinguished herself in science, particularly physiology, botany, and chemistry. Receiving a degree in physiology, she became the first woman to compete for a Natural Sciences fellowship, which was awarded to her in 1911 (another individual who received a fellowship was Arthur Randoin, Lucie's future husband). She went on to the University of Clermont-Ferrand, studying general physiology and the physiology of nutrition under Dr. A. Dastre. During World War I Randoin served as Dastre's assistant and, around 1917, began research on the still-vague substances known as vitamins. The work of such scientists as Dutch physician **Christian Eijkman**, British biochemist **Sir Frederick Gowland Hopkins**, and American biochemists **Elmer Mc Collum** and **Marguerite Davis** established the existence of vitamins, which are essential for adequate nutrition. Randoin was intrigued by how vitamins affect the human metabolism, and her curiosity sparked a lifelong interest in the topic.

Randoin received her doctorate in science in 1918. As World War I was drawing to a close, Dastre disappeared and the loss to Randoin was personal as well as professional— Dastre had enthusiastically encouraged and supported her work. She then went on to the laboratory of the Oceanographic Institute in Paris, where she continued her work on vitamins. In 1920 Randoin started working at the Physiology Laboratory of the Research Center of the Ministry of Agriculture, and became its director in 1924. During the 1920s she demonstrated how vitamins B and C affect the body's use of sugars and other chemicals. In addition, Randoin studied the composition of vitamins, producing research which further assisted scientists in understanding how the substances function.

Randoin remained at the Agricultural Research Center until 1953 (in 1942, however, she had also become director of the Institute of Nutritional Science, a position she held until her death). Over the four decades of Randoin's career, her work helped illustrate the roles of specific vitamins, the proper amount required for good health, the role of vitamins as a form of preventive medicine, and how such factors as age and illness affect the body's use of nutrients.

Besides helping to found a national school for dietary studies which trained students to become dieticians in hospitals and cafeterias, Randoin created a set of quality standards for vitamins used in foods and formed a nutritional information service. In 1931 and 1934 she was the official French representative to international conferences on vitamin standardization. She was a member of the French Biological Society and served as president of the French Society of Biological Chemistry as well as general secretary of the Institute of Nutritional Hygiene. She was also named a commander of the Legion d'Honneur (at a time when few women where so honored). Randoin died on September 13, 1960, after a lengthy illness.

SELECTED WRITINGS BY RANDOIN:

Books

Les Données et les Inconnus du Problème Alimentaire, (title means "Facts and Unknowns About Nutrition Problems"), Les Presses Universitaires, 1927.
Les Vitamines, A. Colin, 1932.

FURTHER READING:

Periodicals

Fabre, René, *La Presse Medicale,* Nécrologie: Lucie Randoin, Gale Research
Fabre, René, *La Presse Medicale,* Nécrologie: Lucie Randoin, Volume 68, Number 54, December 3, 1960, pp. 2109–2110.

Sketch by George A. Milite

C. N. R. Rao
1934–
Indian chemist

An Indian professor of chemistry, C. N. R. Rao has been instrumental in the worldwide research into superconductivity. Superconductivity occurs when certain metals experience a total loss of electrical resistance, turning them into superconductors capable of carrying currents without any loss of energy. Electrical transmission through wires normally involves a substantial loss of energy; with superconductivity, this transmission could be vastly improved, saving costs. So far, superconductivity has occurred only at extremely cold temperatures, barring its use in commercial applications. Scientists have for years been working to create the phenomenon at normal temperatures.

Chintamani Nagesa Ramachandra Rao was born on June 30, 1934, in Bangalore, India, the son of Hanumantha Nagesa and Nagamma Nagesa Rao. In 1953 he earned a master's degree from Banares Hundu University; in 1958, a doctor of philosophy degree from Purdue University. In 1958 he became a research chemist at the University of California at Berkeley, returning to India in 1959 to work as a lecturer at the Indian Institute of Science in Bangalore. In 1960 he married Indumati. They have two children, Suchitra and Sanjay.

From 1963–76, Rao was a professor of chemistry at the Indian Institute of Technology in Kanpur. He served as head of the chemistry department from 1964 to 1968, and was dean of research for three years. He was chairman of the Solid State and Structural Chemistry Unit and Materials Research Laboratory at the Indian Institute of Science in Bangalore between 1976–84. Since 1984, Rao has been the director of the Institute of Science. Concurrent with his academic positions in India, Rao was a visiting professor at Purdue University in 1967–68, at Oxford University in 1974–75, and he held a fellowship at King's College of Cambridge University in 1983.

Conducts Superconductivity Research

Since its discovery in 1911 by **Heike Kamerlingh-Onnes**, scientists had considered superconductivity to be a laboratory curiosity, able to be produced only at temperatures approaching absolute zero. In 1986, however, physicists **J. George Bednorz** and **K. Alex Müller** discovered an alloy that was superconductive at 30°K, a much higher temperature than previously known. This discovery led a number of scientists to examine the question. In 1987, **Paul Ching-Wu Chu** found an alloy that was superconductive at an even higher temperature, 95°K.

In 1989 three researchers at Purdue University—Jurgen Honig, Zbigniew Ka polish lc h kol and Józef Spa polish lc l ek—discovered a superconductive material that did not contain copper as part of the alloy. All previous materials were copper-oxide based; the Princeton researchers used nickel oxide, the first time such a compound had been successfully utilized as a superconductor. While initial results of the experiments were still being analyzed, and the crystalline structure of the compound was still a mystery, Rao conducted similar tests with nickel oxide compounds at the Indian Institute of Science and confirmed their superconductivity. His research on the chemical properties of superconductive materials resulted in the publication of three books, *Chemical and Structural Aspects of High Temperature Superconductors,* 1988, *Bismuth and Thalium*

Cuprate Superconductors, 1989, and *Chemistry of High Temperature Superconductors,* 1991. During his career Rao has published more than 25 books and 700 research papers.

Contributions Are Well Rewarded

Rao has received numerous awards for his contributions to chemistry, including the Marlow Medal of the Faraday Society of London in 1967, the Jawaharlal Nehru fellowship in 1973, the American Chemical Society Centennial foreign fellow in 1976, the Indian Chamber of Commerce and Industry Award for Physical Sciences in 1977, the Royal Society of Chemistry (London) Medal in 1981, the Padma Vibhushan Award from the President of India in 1985, the General Motors Modi Award in 1989, and the Hevrosky gold medal from the Czechoslovak Academy of Sciences in 1989.

In addition, Rao has received honorary degrees from many universities, including Purdue University in 1982, the University of Bordeaux in 1983, and the University of Wroclaw (Poland) in 1989. For two years, 1985–87, he served as president of the International Union of Pure and Applied Chemistry (IUPAC), a board of chemists who decide such issues as rules for naming new chemical compounds. Rao is an elected foreign member of the Slovenian Academy of Sciences, the Serbian Academy of Sciences, the American Academy of Arts and Sciences, the Russian Academy of Sciences, the Czechoslovak Academy of Sciences, and the Polish Academy of Sciences. He was a founding member of the Third World Academy of Sciences.

SELECTED WRITINGS BY RAO:

Books

Chemical and Structural Aspects of High Temperature Superconductors, World Scientific Publishing, 1988.
Bismuth and Thalium Cuprate Superconductors, Gordon & Breach, 1989.
Chemistry of High Temperature Superconductors, World Scientific Publishing, 1991.

FURTHER READING:

Periodicals

Science, February 10, 1989, p. 741.

Sketch by M. C. Nagel

Sarah Ratner
1903–
American biochemist

Sarah Ratner is a biochemist whose research has focused on amino acids, the subunits of protein molecules. Her use of nitrogen isotopes to study metabolism—the chemical processes by which energy is provided for the body—resulted in the discovery of argininosuccinic acid, a substance formed by a sequence of reactions that take place in the liver. Ratner's awards for her work include the Carl Neuberg Medal from the American Society of European Chemists in 1959.

Ratner was born in New York City on June 9, 1903, the daughter of Aaron and Hannah (Selzer) Ratner. She received her bachelor of arts degree from Cornell University before proceeding to Columbia University for graduate studies, where she received an M.A. in 1927. Ratner worked as an assistant in biochemistry in the College of Physicians and Surgeons of Columbia University until she received her Ph.D. in biochemistry from the university in 1937. Following her graduation she was appointed a resident fellow at the College of Physicians and Surgeons and rose to the position of assistant professor. In 1946 she became an assistant professor of pharmacology at the New York University College of Medicine in New York City. Later, she became associated with the New York City Public Health Research Institute as an associate member of the division of nutrition and physiology and became a member of the department of biochemistry in 1957.

In her research Ratner used an isotope of nitrogen to study chemical reactions involving amino acids, particularly arginine. Isotopes are atoms of an element that have a different atomic mass than other atoms of the same element. Through her studies she discovered an intermediate molecule, called argininosuccinic acid, which forms when the amino acid citrulline is converted to arginine. Ratner determined that argininosuccinic acid plays an important role in the series of chemical reactions that occurs in the liver and leads to the formation of urine. This sequence of reactions is known as the urea cycle. Urea, a product of protein metabolism, has a high nitrogen content and is excreted by mammals.

The American Chemical Society honored Ratner with the Garvan Medal in 1961, and in 1974 she was elected to the National Academy of Sciences. In addition, she received research grants from the National Institutes of Health (NIH) for over twenty years, and from 1978 to 1979 she was the institutes' Fogarty Scholar-in-Residence and served as a member of the advisory council. She has received honorary doctorates from the University of North Carolina-Chapel Hill, Northwestern University, and State University of New York at Stony Brook.

Sketch by M. C. Nagel

concentrated. The Garden's researchers are cataloging as many of the world's remaining tropical plants as possible. Each year, they gather more than 100,000 specimens, which they store in the Garden's herbarium. This botanical library houses more than four million specimens.

A Prolific Researcher

Dr. Raven's primary research interest is the systematics, evolution, and biogeography of the Onagraceae plant family. He developed Onagraceas as a model used to understand patterns and processes of plant evolution in general. His work showed that, over millions of years, some plants develop a variety of chemical defenses to fight off the animals and insects that live with them, and that these animals or insects have developed an immunity to, or have developed other ways to deal with, the plants' defenses. Raven and Stanford University colleague Paul Ehrlich called his phenomenon "coevolution," a term that is now in widespread use. Dr. Raven is also studying the molecular structure of the members of the Onagraceas family, and plant biogeography. Plant biogeography is the evolutionary history of entire biota and the individual taxa found in certain regions, and the ways in which these organisms have been influenced by movements of the continents. Dr. Raven's research has taken him to Columbia, Mexico, and Costa Rica.

Dr. Raven is the co-author of the best-selling botany textbook in the United States: *Biology of Plants*, as well as a number of other books. His work has also been published in many scientific journals, including the *Quarterly Review of Biology*, *Evolution*, *BioScience*, *Science*, and *American Journal of Botany*.

Dr. Raven has received many awards and honors. In 1985, he received a John D. and Catherine T. MacArthur Foundation Fellowship for his life's work, followed the next year by the International Prize for Biology from the government of Japan. In 1992, he was awarded the Volvo Environment Prize (with Normal Myers). He also received a National Wildlife Federation National Conservation Achievement Award.

Dr. Raven serves as or has served as the home secretary of the National Academy of Sciences, chairman of the Report Review Committee of the National Research Council, a member of the National Science board, and a director of the World Wildlife Fund-US. He is a member of many professional organizations, including: the National Science Board, the Committee of Research and Exploration of the National Geographic Society, the National Academy of Sciences, the American Academy of Arts and Sciences, the Pontifical Academy of Sciences, and the national academies of science in more than 10 other countries.

Peter Hamilton Raven
1936–
American botanist

Dr. Peter H. Raven is an authority on plant classification, the plant lore and agricultural customs of Mexico in the time of the Mayans, coevolution of plants and animals, and population ecology. His work has contributed greatly to the understanding of plant evolution. An advocate of conserving the rainforests, he devotes much of his work to preserving biodiversity, conserving natural resources, and protecting the world's ecosystems. Dr. Raven is the Engelmann Profesor of botany at Washington University, St. Louis, and director of The Missouri Botanical Garden, the world's leading research center studying tropical rain forests.

Dr. Raven was born on June 13, 1936, in Shanghai, China, where his family ran a bank. Shortly after his birth, Peter's parents, Walter and Isabelle Breen Raven, decided to move back to the United States. Peter grew up in San Francisco, California. Even as a toddler, he was interested in nature. By the age of 14, he had published his first scientific paper and made two important botanical discoveries: a kind of manzanita plant that was believed to be extinct and an evening primrose plant called Clarkia franciscana.

Dr. Raven earned an A.B. degree in botany from the University of California at Berkeley and then went on to graduate school, earning his Ph.D. in botany from the University of California at Los Angeles. He spent a year as a National Science post-doctoral fellow at the British Museum of Natural History, and then joined the Rancho Santa Ana Botanic Garden in Claremont, California, as a taxonomist and curator. In 1961, he joined Stanford University in Stanford, California, as an assistant professor, rising to associate professor by the time he left the university 10 years later. In 1971, he joined the faculty of Washington University, St. Louis, Missouri, as the Engelmann Profesor of botany and director of The Missouri Botanical Garden.

The Missouri Botanical Garden is the oldest public garden in the United States. Its mission is to discover and share knowledge about plants and their environment in order to preserve and enrich life. Located on 79 acres in St. Louis, the Missouri Botanical Garden contains more than 30 gardens, a world famous Botanical Research Center, and education division, and more. The Missouri Botanical Garden's major research emphasis is in studying plants in the tropics, where much of the biotic diversity of the earth is

SELECTED WRITINGS BY RAVEN:

Books

Raven, P. H. and Johnson, G.B., *Biology*. 4th edition. Dubuque, IA: Wm. C. Brown Publishers, 1996.

Committee on the Formation of the National Biological Survey, National Research Council, Peter H. Raven, Chairman. *A Biological Survey for the Nation.* Washington, DC: National Academy Press, 1993.

Raven, P. H., Evert, R., Eichhorn, S. E., *Biology of Plants*, 1969.

Periodicals

Chen, C. J., Hock, P. C., Raven, P. H. "Systematics of *Epilobium* in China." *Sayst Bot Monogr*, 34, 1992, p. 1–209.

Tobe, H. Stuessy, T.F., Oginuma, K. "Embryology and karyomorphology of *Lactoridaceae*." *Am J Bot*, 80, 1993, p. 933–46.

FURTHER READING:

Periodicals

Tim Beardsley, "Defender of the Plant Kingdom," *Scientific American*, September 1999, Vol. 281, Issue 3, p. 30.

Other

"Missouri Botanical Garden," Missouri Botanical Garden Web site, http://www.mobot.org.

"Raven, Peter H.," Wilson Web, http://www.wilsonweb.com.

Sketch by Lori De Milto

Dixy Lee Ray
1914–1994
American marine biologist and government official

Through her career as a marine biologist, Dixy Lee Ray developed a concern about both threats to the environment and the need for greater public understanding of science. Her increasing scientific activities in the public sphere brought her to national attention with her appointment by President Richard Nixon to the Atomic Energy Commission (AEC) in 1972. Within a year she was designated to head the AEC as its first woman chair. Later, in 1977, putting into practice her conviction that scientists need to be more active in public affairs, she was elected governor of her home state of Washington.

Ray was born to Alvis Marion Ray, a commercial printer and Frances (Adams) Ray on September 3, 1914, and was one of five girls. Early on, she developed a love of the outdoors and a fascination with marine biology, when the Ray family spent their summers on Fox Island in Puget Sound. She went on to major in zoology at Mills College and graduated Phi Beta Kappa in 1937. One year later, she received her M.A. there and proceeded to teach science in the public schools of Oakland, California, until 1942. She then left to do graduate work on a John Switzer fellowship at Stanford University. Continuing there as a Van Sicklen fellow, she received her Ph.D. degree in biological science in 1945. That year, she started a twenty-seven-year career at the University of Washington, first as an instructor in zoology, then rising to the rank of assistant professor in 1947, and finally to associate professor in 1957. While affiliated with the university, from 1952 to 1953, she was awarded a Guggenheim fellowship.

Conducts Research in Marine Biology

Ray's particular field of marine biology research dealt largely with invertebrates, especially crustacea. She studied the effects of the isopod Limnoria and fungi in damaging submerged wood, and, as an executive committee member of the Friday Harbor Laboratories in Washington in 1957, she was director of a symposium on the damage caused by marine organisms to boats, drydocks, and wharf filings. She also found time to serve as a special consultant in biological oceanography to the National Science Foundation from 1960 to 1962. Ray sailed with the crew of the Stanford University research ship, *Te Vega*, in 1964, as chief scientist and visiting professor in the International Indian Ocean Expedition, which was a multinational exploration of the little-studied environment of the Indian Ocean.

A year earlier, she had accepted the position of director of the Pacific Science Center in Seattle and converted a collection of six imposing buildings left over from the 1962 World's Fair in that city into an active science center. The complex featured a science museum and a meeting place for scientific symposia. The Pacific Science Center also began to sponsor the prestigious Arches of Science Award, which honors scientists for contributing to the understanding of the discipline by the general public.

When she was first appointed to the Atomic Energy Commission, she admitted that she had to learn a great deal more about the potential and problems of atomic energy. Because of the long-term limitations of the fossil fuel supply, she was convinced that atomic power plants could serve as an invaluable source of energy. She proposed a multibillion-dollar program to develop new sources of nuclear power and to generate new ways of converting coal to gaseous and liquid fuels. She also campaigned to eliminate defects in atomic power plants. Her own interest in protecting the environment often led her into disagreement with environmental groups, which she considered "too strident." She expressed outspoken views on the subject in two books, *Trashing the Planet* (1990), and *Environmental Overkill* (1993), as well as in magazine articles and television interviews.

Ray received honorary degrees from her alma mater, Mills College, as well as from a number of other colleges and universities. Among the many other honors she received was the Clapp Award in Marine Biology in 1958, the Seattle Maritime Award in 1967, the Frances K. Hutchinson Medal for Service in Conservation in 1973, the United Nations Peace Medal in 1973, the Francis Boyer Science Award in 1974, and the American Exemplar Medal of the Freedom Foundation at Valley Forge in 1978. She was a member of many scientific societies and was elected a foreign member of the Swedish Academy of Science and the Danish Royal Society for Natural History. Among her hobbies was the study of American Indians, which resulted in a collection of artifacts from the Kwikseutanik tribe. The tribe welcomed her as an honorary member with the name Oo'ma, signifying Great Lady. On the occasion of her death from bronchial complications at the age of seventy-nine, the *New York Times* obituary of January 3, 1994, which ran the day after her death, acknowledged that she showed her mettle early at the age of twelve, when she became the youngest girl to climb Washington's highest peak, Mount Rainier.

SELECTED WRITINGS BY RAY:

Books

Marine Boring and Fouling Organisms, University of Washington Press, 1959.
Trashing the Planet, Regnery Gateway (Washington, D.C.), 1990.
Environmental Overkill, Regnery Gateway (Washington, D.C.), 1993.

Periodicals

Science, Possible Relation between Marine Fungi and Limnoria Attack on Submerged Wood, January 9, 1959.
Marine Biology, An Integrated Approach to Some Problems of Marine Biological Deterioration and Destruction of Wood in Sea Water, Oregon State College Biology Colloquium, 1959.

FURTHER READING:

Books

Current Biography, H. W. Wilson (New York), 1973, pp. 345–348.

Periodicals

Gillette, Robert, *Science,* Ray Nominated to AEC, July 21, 1972, p. 246.

Sketch by Maurice Bleifeld

Grote Reber
1911–
American radio astronomer, engineer, and inventor

Grote Reber is an American engineer and pioneer radio astronomer who built the world's first radio telescope and so spawned the twentieth-century science of radio astronomy. Radio telescopes are antennas that pick up cosmic radio waves—invisible signals from stars, galaxies, nebulae, and other bodies in outer space. Scientists study cosmic radio waves to better understand the nature and origins of the universe and its energy. Reber built his radio telescope in his back yard, at a time when he was only an amateur in the emerging science. Inspired by the work of **Karl Jansky**, who identified the presence of radio waves in outer space, Reber became one of the first scientists to devote his career to the study of radio astronomy and was responsible for much of its early development.

Reber was born on December 22, 1911, in Wheaton, Illinois. As a boy, he exhibited a keen interest in amateur (ham) radio. He attended the Illinois Institute of Technology, graduating as a radio engineer. He went to work as an electronics engineer for a Chicago radio manufacturer, all the while pursing his hobby during the evenings. His hobby became a passion, however, after the discovery in 1932 of short wave radio emissions from outer space by Jansky, a young American engineer working in the Bell Laboratories assigned to determine the cause of static interference with long-distance communications. Jansky observed that the strong steady hissing noise interfering with communication—unattributable to any source on Earth—seemed to be coming from the direction of the constellation Sagittarius. He proposed that stars and other bodies in the universe emit energy not only in the form of light, but also in the form of radio waves. When Jansky's findings were published in the *Proceedings of the Institute of Radio Engineers* journal, Reber immediately recognized their significance. In this he was almost alone. Jansky's paper marked the beginning of radio astronomy, and for many years, Reber was the only person working in the field.

Builds Radio Telescope in Back Yard

Determined to investigate Jansky's findings further, Reber built his own paraboloidal radio telescope in his back garden at a cost of $1,300. It was a dish-shaped structure, constructed of two-by-fours and sheet metal and rotated using power generated by a Model-T engine. (The original telescope is now exhibited at the gate of the National Radio Astronomy Observatory in Greenback, West Virginia.) At first, Reber's efforts were confounded, as the dish was designed to receive radio waves of a shorter wavelength than those studied by Jansky. In 1938, he tried receiving waves of a longer length (up to six feet) and at last met with some success. He was able to confirm the presence of what Jansky had termed the "cosmic static" emanating from the Milky Way. While Reber carried out this early work, he continued to work full time at the radio factory. After the Second World War, Reber's work began to receive fairly widespread recognition as more scientists entered the field, and he was able to devote himself completely to radio astronomy.

After confirming Jansky's findings, Reber began to draw up a chart that mapped the source of the radio waves he was receiving. The pattern of radio wave sources on the chart seemed to coincide with the general positions of stars in the sky. He detected strong signals, for instance, from the areas of the constellations Cygnus, Taurus, and Cassiopeia. From bright individual stars, which he expected would send out strong signals, however, he could detect no activity. It became clear to him that luminosity bore no relation to the strength or location of radio waves. Reber concluded that some radio waves originated in the invisible gas clouds of neutral hydrogen between the stars. Others, of shorter wavelength, came from places near stars where ionized hydrogen atoms are found. Still others, of longer wavelength, emanated from the center of the Milky Way galaxy. In 1940, Reber decided to publish his findings. He sent his article "Cosmic Static" to the *Astrophysical Journal,* but the periodical's board of referees voted against publication. However, Otto Struve, the journal's editor, recognized the importance of Reber's findings and decided to accept the article, against the board's wishes.

In 1951, Reber moved to Hawaii, where his work was less affected by interference from man-made radio signals. He used a radio telescope operating at 5.5–14 meters to locate new sources of radio waves. In 1954, he moved even further afield to Tasmania, where, on a remote 300-acre site, Reber continued to work with a larger version of his satellite dish that could pick up radio waves from distant galaxies. It consisted of eight-story poles, arranged in a giant circle linked by fifty-seven miles of remote controlled wire. With it he was able to design a radio map of the universe from the perspective of the Southern hemisphere. Reber has been described as a pioneer for his work in radio astronomy, particularly for his ingenuity and dogged persistence at a time when he lacked the support of the scientific community. George Seielstad, director of the National Observatory in West Virginia, said of Reber in the *Chicago Tribune,* "[Reber] didn't discover radio astronomy. But he was the only person in the world who pursued it. He did it on his own, with no support, in his own back yard. He did truly admirable work."

FURTHER READING:

Books

Knight, David C., *Eavesdropping on Space: The Quest for Radio Astronomy,* William Morrow, 1975.

Roger, Piper, *The Big Dish: The Fascinating Story of Radio Telescopes,* Harcourt, 1963.
Verschuur, Gerrit L., *The Invisible Universe Revealed: The Story of Radio Astronomy,* Springer-Verlag, 1987.
Wallace, Tucker, and Karen Wallace, *The Cosmic Inquirers: Modern Telescopes and Their Makers,* Harvard University Press, 1986.

Periodicals

Bagnato, Andrew, *Chicago Tribune,* Honoring a Hometown Star: Wheaton Hails Builder of First Radio Telescope, October 23, 1985, p. C1.
Sullivan, Walter, *New York Times,* Radio Astronomy, 50 Years Old, Moves toward a New Frontier, November 17, 1981, p. C1.

Sketch by Avril McDonald

Raj Reddy
1937–
American computer scientist

Raj Reddy is one of the world's leading experts on robotics and artificial intelligence. The director from 1979 to 1992 of the Robotics Institute at Carnegie Mellon University in Pittsburgh, Pennsylvania, Reddy was responsible for the operation of thirteen laboratories and three program centers, and oversaw the research performed at the institute on numerous topics related to computer-integrated manufacturing and robotics design. He is currently the dean of computer science at Carnegie Mellon University.

Dabblal Rajagopal Reddy was born on June 13, 1937, in Katoor, India, near Madras. His father, Srdenivasulu Reddy, was an agricultural landlord and his mother, Pitchamma, was a homemaker. His interest in civil engineering led him to study at the University of Madras College of Engineering, where he received his bachelor's degree in 1958. Soon after finishing his undergraduate work in India, Reddy moved to Australia, calling it home for a number of years. While in Australia, Reddy worked as an applied science representative for the International Business Machines Corporation (IBM) in Sydney. His primary job used computers for structural analysis. Although his formal education was in civil engineering, his first employment and early practical experience were with computers, which prepared him for future work in the computer field. Reddy studied for and received a master's degree in computer science from the University of New South Wales in 1961. During his post-baccalaureate education his interest and course of study changed from the civil to the computer engineering disciplines.

Reddy moved to the United States in 1966 and received his doctorate from Stanford in the same year. He became a naturalized citizen and joined the faculty of Stanford University as an assistant professor of computer science. His time at Stanford only lasted three years; in 1969 he moved to Pittsburgh and joined the faculty of Carnegie Mellon University as a professor. It was here that Reddy began his study of the rapidly expanding fields of robotics and artificial intelligence. He was named director of the Robotics Institute in 1979.

Reddy has focused on two areas within the field of robotics: automatons capable of performing manufacturing and assembly-line tasks, and fully functional robots that can perform, understand, and use more complex functions like speech, hearing, and sight. Although the later part of the twentieth century has seen a tremendous growth in the use of robots for assembly-line manufacturing chores, Reddy feels that researchers are still thirty to one hundred years away from creating machines capable of speech and sight. Aiming to make this goal a reality, Reddy developed an interdisciplinary program at the Institute that trains students in mechanical engineering, computer science, and management in order to give them the background they need to design the complex robotics manufacturing systems of the future.

Reddy remains at the forefront of studies in human-computer interaction. His research projects include building robots capable of speech recognition and comprehension systems, and the Automated Machine Shop, a full manufacturing facility using robotics technology. Reddy is also exploring an area he calls "white-collar robotics," that is, robots programmed to perform such white-collar tasks as production scheduling and other management functions. Reddy and his colleagues at Carnegie Mellon also investigate the possibilities for programming robots to make subjective decisions (artificial intelligence), for building robots that can learn from observation, and for designing robots that can work in environments that are hazardous for humans, such as waste disposal sites and nuclear reactors.

A lecturer in his field and contributor to scholarly journals, Reddy was presented the Legion of Honor by President Mitterrand of France in 1984 for his service at the World Center for Personal Computation and Human Resources in Paris. He was awarded the IBM Research Ralph Gomory Visiting Scholar Award in 1991. He is a member of the National Academy of Engineering, and a fellow of the Institute of Electrical and Electronics Engineers, the Acoustical Society of America, and the American Association for Artificial Intelligence, which he also served as president from 1987 to 1989. Reddy married his wife Anu in 1966 and has two children, Shyamala and Geetha. He looks forward to the day when advances in computer and communication technology will allow every person to use computers in their daily lives.

FURTHER READING:

Periodicals

Dworetzky, Tom, *Omni,* Reddy's Machine Dreams, August, 1990, p. 80.
Goldstein, Gina, *Mechanical Engineering,* Shaping the Next Generation of Robots, June, 1990, pp. 38–42.

Other

Reddy, Raj, *Interview with Roger Jaffe,* conducted March 25, 1994.

Sketch by Roger Jaffe

Walter Reed
1851–1902
American physician and bacteriologist

Walter Reed, an Army surgeon and medical researcher, helped discover that mosquitoes transmitted yellow fever, an infectious, sometimes fatal, disease. During his career, Reed also made contributions toward the control of malaria and typhoid. Although some questioned his practice of using humans as test subjects for his yellow fever work, his findings saved thousands of lives. In honor of his efforts to control epidemics, the Army General Hospital in Washington D.C. was named after Reed.

The youngest of five children, Reed was born on September 13, 1851, in Belroi, Virginia, to Lemuel Sutton Reed, a Methodist minister, and Pharaba White. His father's ministry took the family to different parishes every few years and, as a result, Reed's early education was somewhat sporadic. In 1865, however, Reed began two years of study under William R. Abbot. He entered the University of Virginia at age fifteen and, a year later, took a medical course. Reed received a medical degree in 1869.

Reed subsequently traveled to New York to pursue additional medical studies at Bellevue Hospital. He earned a second medical degree in 1870, but it was not official until 1872, when he turned twenty-one. In the meantime, Reed secured the position of assistant physician at New York Infants' Hospital, undertook residency at Kings County Hospital of Brooklyn and at Brooklyn City Hospital, and acted as district physician for the New York Department of Public Charities. For a year beginning in June of 1873, he served as sanitary inspector for the Brooklyn Board of Health.

In June of 1874, Reed received a commission as assistant surgeon, first lieutenant, with the U.S. Army Medical Corps and moved to Arizona. Before he left, he

Walter Reed

married Emilie Lawrence, a woman he had met while visiting his father in Murfreesboro, North Carolina. For the next eleven years Reed worked variously at bases in Arizona, Nebraska, Minnesota, and Alabama. During this time, Reed and his wife had two children, Lawrence and Blossom.

In the 1890s, Reed wished to pursue his interest in pathology. Because army bases did not offer appropriate facilities, he applied for a leave of absence to conduct advanced work in the field. His request was not granted; instead he was transferred to Baltimore to act as attending surgeon. There he took a brief clinical course at Johns Hopkins Hospital and met William Henry Welch, a pathologist who opened the first pathology laboratory in the United States. Under Welch's tutelage, Reed delved into pathology, performing autopsies, conducting experiments, and refining medical techniques. Reed specifically worked on the bacteriology of erysipelas (an acute fibroid disease accompanied by severe skin inflammation) and diphtheria. This work halted when Reed was sent to an army outpost at Fort Snelling, Minnesota, where he was promoted to major and made a full surgeon.

However, when George Sternberg became the nation's surgeon general, Reed returned to Washington as curator of the Army Medical Museum and also taught bacteriology and clinical microscopy at the Army Medical College. At this time, Reed began to make an impact in his field. When a malaria epidemic broke out at Fort Myer, Virginia, in 1896, Reed proved that contaminated drinking water—as

commonly believed—was not the cause. He noted that many areas of Washington, including the infected section, drew water from the Potomac. Reed also realized that malaria was striking the base's enlisted men, not officers. He traced this to the fact that the enlisted men often traveled to the city via a swamp trail. Reed postulated that "bad air" caused the disease (although it was later determined that mosquitoes spread malaria).

When the Spanish-American War erupted in 1898, Reed volunteered to serve in Cuba. To take advantage of his qualifications, he was instead appointed to chair a board investigating typhoid outbreaks in army camps. Hundreds of new cases—many of which proved fatal—were reported each day. In fact, the epidemic that killed more than fifty times as many soldiers as did combat. The bacillus, or rod-shaped bacterium, was believed to be transmitted by contaminated water, but the typhoid board found that it was passed by flies and contact with infected feces. The board further discovered that the infectious organisms were harbored by carriers—people who showed no signs of the disease. The typhoid board's two-volume report on its investigation is considered a model for epidemiologists.

Confronts Yellow Fever Epidemic

In 1900 Reed was selected to head an army board trying to discover the cause of yellow fever. This disease had spread among army troops in Cuba. In addition, annual outbreaks occurred along the East Coast and in the southern United States, killing thousands of people. Referred to colloquially as yellow jack, the disease was most prevalent in urban areas and was characterized by jaundice, hemorrhaging, fever, bloodshot eyes, hiccups, and dark-colored vomit. Yellow fever regularly hit the same cities during warm weather. By late autumn it was gone.

Alabama physician Josiah Nott postulated that mosquitoes caused the disease, but his evidence was scanty. In 1881 Carlos Finlay, a Cuban physician and epidemiologist who worked with the U.S. yellow fever commission in Havana, suggested that yellow fever was transmitted by *Culex fasciatus* (a mosquito now classified as *Aëdes aegypti*), but he was not taken seriously. Despite these suggestions, Italian physician Giuseppe Sanarelli maintained that *Bacillus icteroides* was the cause. Reed and American army physician James Carroll were assigned to investigate Sanarelli's claim, and they disproved it. A rash of yellow fever subsequently broke out in Havana, killing thousands of soldiers. Reed traveled to Cuba to head a board including Carroll, Jesse W. Lazear and Aristides Agramonte —all physicians with the army medical corps. The board decided to test its theory that mosquitoes transmitted yellow fever.

Finlay secured mosquitoes and mosquito eggs to allow the group to raise the insects. Because animals were not affected by the disease, the board decided to use human test subjects. Participants in the study gave their consent and were paid $100, plus an additional $100 if they contracted the disease. Reed designed and conducted experiments that proved the *Aëdes aegypti* mosquito was a carrier, and not an originator, of the disease. The yellow fever board concluded that the female *Aëdes aegypti* mosquito could only become a carrier of yellow fever if it bit a victim during the first three days of the disease. The mosquito was unable to transmit the disease for two weeks, but could remain infectious for up to two months in a warm climate. The board also discovered that having had the disease provided immunity against further attacks.

During the course of the board's experiments, Lazear was accidentally bitten by an infected mosquito and died twelve days later. He left notes, however, to assist Reed and the others in their experiments. The board induced twenty-two other cases of yellow fever—none of which proved fatal. (Carroll became ill with the first experimental case but recovered.) Although a vaccination against the disease was not developed until the 1920s, yellow fever was virtually eradicated by 1902 in Cuba through mosquito control.

The board's accomplishment not only saved lives, but also paved the way for U.S. ventures in tropical regions of the world. (For instance, the U.S. government insisted that a way to control yellow fever was necessary before construction began on the Panama Canal.) Reed earned special recognition for heading the investigation. Harvard University awarded him an honorary masters degree for his work with the yellow fever board. Reed died November 23, 1902, in Washington following surgery for a ruptured appendix.

SELECTED WRITINGS BY REED:

Periodicals

Medical News, The Specific Cause of Yellow Fever: A Reply to Dr. G. Sanarelli, Volume 75, 1899.
Philadelphia Medical Journal, The Etiology of Yellow Fever, Volume 6, 1900, pp. 790–96.

Other

Yellow Fever: A Compilation of Various Publications. Results of the Work of Major Walter Reed, Medical Corps., United States Army, and the Yellow Fever Commission, (Senate document 822 from the Third Session of the 61st Congress), Washington, D.C., 1911.

FURTHER READING:

Books

De Kruif, Paul, *Microbe Hunters,* Harcourt, Brace & World, 1926, 1953, pp. 286–307.
Kelly, Howard A., *Walter Reed and Yellow Fever,* 3rd ed., The Norman Remington Company, 1923.
Truby, Albert E., *Memoir of Walter Reed, The Yellow Fever Episode,* P. B. Hoeber, 1943.

Wood, Laura N., *Walter Reed, Doctor in Uniform,* J. Messner, 1943.

Periodicals

Wood, Laura N., *Archives of Internal Medicine,* Walter Reed: 'He Gave Man Control of That Dreadful Scourge—Yellow Fever', Volume 89, pp. 171–187.

Sketch by Janet Kieffer Kelley

Mina S. Rees
1902–1997
American mathematician

Mina S. Rees was the founding president of the Graduate Center of the City University of New York, and the first woman elected to the presidency of the American Association for the Advancement of Science. She was recognized by both the United States and Great Britain for organizing mathematicians to work on problems of interest to the military during World War II. After the war she headed the mathematics branch of the Office of Naval Research, where she built a program of government support for mathematical research and for the development of computers.

Rees was born in Cleveland, Ohio, on August 2, 1902, to Moses and Alice Louise (Stackhouse) Rees. Educated in New York public schools, Rees received her A.B. *summa cum laude* from Hunter College in New York City in 1923, and taught at Hunter College High School from 1923 to 1926. She completed an M.A. at the Teacher's College of Columbia University in 1925, and became an instructor at the Mathematics Department of Hunter College the following year. She continued her training in mathematics at the University of Chicago, where she received a fellowship for 1931 to 1932, and earned a Ph.D. in mathematics in 1931 with a dissertation on abstract algebra. Returning to Hunter, Rees was promoted to assistant professor in 1932 and associate professor in 1940.

In 1943, in the midst of World War II, Rees joined the government as a civil servant, working as executive assistant and a technical aide to Warren Weaver, the chief of the Applied Mathematics Panel (AMP) of the National Research Committee in the Office of Scientific Research and Development. The AMP, located in New York City, established contracts with mathematics departments at New York University, Brown, Harvard, Columbia, and other universities. Under these contracts, mathematicians and statisticians studied military applications such as shock waves, jet engine design, underwater ballistics, air-to-air gunnery, the probability of damage under anti-aircraft fire,

Mina S. Rees

supply and munitions inspection methods, and computers. In 1948, in recognition for her wartime service, Rees received a Certificate of Merit from President Truman, as well as the Medal for Service in the Cause of Freedom from King George VI.

Joins Office of Naval Research

From 1946 to 1953, Rees worked for the Office of Naval Research (ONR), first as head of the mathematics branch and then, from 1950, as director of the mathematics division. Under Rees, the ONR supported programs for research on hydrofoils, logistics, computers, and numerical methods. Rees emphasized the study and development of mathematical algorithms for computing. The ONR supported the development of linear programming and the establishment in 1947 of an Institute for Numerical Analysis at the University of California at Los Angeles, and also worked with other military and civilian government agencies on the acquisition of early computers. In addition, the ONR funded university research programs to build computers, such as Project Whirlwind at MIT, lead by **Jay Forrester**, and the Institute for Advanced Study project under **John Neumann**. The ONR also awarded grants to support applied and basic mathematical research.

In 1953, Rees returned to Hunter College as Dean of Faculty and Professor of Mathematics. She was married in 1955, to Dr. Leopold Brahdy, a physician. In 1961, she was appointed dean of graduate studies for the City University of New York (CUNY), which established graduate pro-

grams by pooling distinguished faculty from the City Colleges, including Hunter. The following year, Rees became the first recipient of the Award for Distinguished Service to Mathematics established by the Mathematical Association of America. Rees was appointed provost of the Graduate Division in 1968 and the first president of the Graduate School and University Center in 1969. By the time Rees retired as emeritus president in 1972, CUNY's graduate school had created twenty-six doctoral programs and enrolled over two thousand students. During her postwar years at Hunter and CUNY, Rees served on government, scientific, and educational advisory boards and held offices in mathematical, scientific, and educational organizations. She became the first female president of the American Association for the Advancement of Science in 1971. In 1983 Rees received the Public Welfare Medal of the National Academy of Sciences, an award that confers honorary membership in that organization. She died on October 25, 1997, at the Mary Manning Walsh Home in Manhattan.

SELECTED WRITINGS BY REES:

Periodicals

"The Nature of Mathematics." *Science* (5 October 1962): 9-12.

"The Mathematical Sciences and World War II." *American Mathematical Monthly* (October 1980): 607-21.

"The Computing Program of the Office of Naval Research, 1946-1953." *Annals of the History of Computing* 4, no. 2 (April 1982): 102-20.

FURTHER READING:

Books

Dana, Rosamond, and Peter J. H. Hilton. "Interview with Mina Rees." In *Mathematical People,* edited by Donald J. Albers and G. L. Alexanderson. Cambridge, MA: Birkhauser, 1985, pp. 256-65.

Periodicals

Dana, Rosamond, and Peter J. H. Hilton. "Award for Distinguished Service to Mathematics." *American Mathematical Monthly* (February 1962): 185-87.

Saxon, Wolfgang. "Mina S. Rees, Mathematician and CUNY Leader, Dies at 95" (obituary). *New York Times* (28 October 1997): B10.

Sketch by Sally M. Moite

Elsa Reichmanis
1953–
American chemist

E lsa Reichmanis is a chemist and engineer who has worked to develop sophisticated chemical processes and materials that are used in the manufacture of integrated circuits, or computer chips. She has served as supervisor of the Radiation Sensitive and Applications Group at AT&T Bell Laboratories in Murray Hill, New Jersey, since 1984. As of 1994 she holds eleven patents, and she received the R & D 100 Award for one of the one hundred most significant inventions of 1992. She received the 1993 Society of Women Engineers (SWE) Annual Achievement Award for her contributions in the field of integrated circuitry.

Several of Reichmanis's patents are for the design and development of organic polymers—known as resists—that are used in microlithography. Microlithography is the principal process by which circuits, or electrical pathways, are imprinted upon the tiny silicon chips that drive computers. During the multi-stage process of chip manufacture, layers of resist material are applied to a silicon base and exposed to patterns of ultraviolet light. Portions of the resists harden, becoming templates for the application of subsequent layers of positively and negatively charged semiconductors that serve as the channels through which electric current travels. Reichmanis received the 1992 award for the development of a resist material called Camp–6, which will be used in the late 1990s to make the next generation of integrated circuits smaller and more powerful than ever before.

Reichmanis was born December 9, 1953, in Melbourne, Australia. She completed her undergraduate studies in chemistry at Syracuse University in 1972. She then performed her doctoral studies in organic chemistry, also at Syracuse, as a university research fellow. She earned her Ph.D. in 1975 at age twenty-two with a perfect grade point average. She was a postdoctoral fellow for scientific research at Syracuse from 1976 to 1978, when she left academia for the private sector. In 1978, Reichmanis accepted a position as a member of the technical staff of the organic chemistry research and development department at AT&T Bell Laboratories in New Jersey. In 1984, she was promoted to her current position as supervisor of the Radiation Sensitive and Applications Group at AT&T.

Reichmanis's awards and appointments are numerous. In 1986, she was a member of a National Science Foundation panel to survey Japanese technology in advanced materials. She also served as a member of a National Research Council committee to survey materials research opportunities and needs for the electronics industry. Reichmanis served on the American Chemical Society (ACS) advisory board from 1987 to 1990, and was chair-elect of the ACS Division of Polymeric Materials in 1994. She has authored nearly one hundred publications, and co-edited three books that were presented at American Chemical Society symposia. She was plenary lecturer at the 1989 International Symposium of Polymers for Microelectronics.

An American citizen, Reichmanis is a member of the American Association for the Advancement of Science, and the Society of Photographic Instrumentation Engineering. As the mother of four children, Reichmanis encourages women to embrace both career and family. "If something interests you and you like doing it, then go for it," she told contributor Karen Withem in an interview. "If you ask yourself, 'How can I manage having both a career and children?'—you'll never do it. If you just do it, things will fall into place."

SELECTED WRITINGS BY REICHMANIS:

Books

Polymers for Electronic and Photonic Application, Chemistry of Polymers for Microlithographic Applications, edited by C. P. Wong, Academic Press, 1992, pp. 67–117.

Periodicals

Annual Review of Materials Science, Polymer Materials for Microlithography, Volume 17, 1987, pp. 235–271.

FURTHER READING:

Periodicals

Reichmanis, Elsa, *Interview with Karen Withem,* conducted March 27, 1994.

Sketch by Karen Withem

Tadeus Reichstein
1897–1996
Swiss organic chemist

I t is now known that the hormones of the adrenal gland are essential to controlling many challenges to the human body, from maintaining a proper balance between water and salt to responding to stress. Tadeus Reichstein is one of those responsible for this knowledge; **Edward Kendall** and **Philip Hench** also played an important role in these efforts, and the three men shared the 1950 Nobel Prize in physiology or medicine. Reichstein's work has had effects throughout medicine—in the treatments of Addison's disease and rheumatoid arthritis, for example, and in the understanding of the fundamental biochemical processes of steroid hormone metabolism.

The eldest son of engineer Gustava Reichstein and his wife, Isidor, Reichstein was born on July 20, 1897, near Warsaw in Poland. After moving first to Kiev in the Ukraine and then to Berlin, the family settled in Zürich and became Swiss citizens. Tadeus attended the Eidgenössiche Technische Hochshule and graduated in 1920 with a chemical engineering degree. He worked briefly in a factory, then returned to the Eidgenössiche Technische Hochshule where he earned his doctorate in organic chemistry in 1922.

For several years thereafter Reichstein continued to work with his doctoral advisor, **Hermann Staudinger**, who would later win the 1953 Nobel Prize in chemistry. Reichstein's early work focused on identifying and isolating the chemical species in coffee that give it its flavor and aroma. This interest in plant products was to remain with Reichstein throughout his career. He had an early success when he discovered how to synthesize the newly discovered compound ascorbic acid (vitamin C). He published this method in 1933, and later that year Reichstein developed a second method of synthesis which is still widely used in the commercial production of this dietary supplement.

Isolates and Identifies Adrenal Cortical Hormones

In 1934, Reichstein began work on what he originally believed to be a single hormone produced by the cortex or outer layers of the adrenal glands. He soon realized, however, that the adrenals were producing a milieu of active substances. His work began with 1,000 kilograms (more than a ton) of adrenal glands that had been surgically removed from cattle. His first stage of purification resulted in one kilogram (about 2.2 pounds) of biologically active extract. He established that the extract was biologically active by injecting it into animals whose adrenal cortices had been removed; if the compound was active it replaced what was missing as a result of the operation and allowed the animal to survive. The next stage of purification reduced the kilogram of extract to 25 grams (less than one ounce), only about one-third of which proved to be the critical hormone mixture. Instead of one hormone, this sample contained no fewer than twenty-nine distinct chemical species.

Reichstein isolated the twenty-nine species and then individually examined them. He identified the first four which were found to be biologically active, and later synthesized one of them. It was also Reichstein who demonstrated that these compounds were all steroids. Steroids are a group of chemicals which share a particular structure of four linked carbon-based rings; other important compounds having steroid structure include the sex hormones, cholesterol, and vitamin D.

Synthesizes Steroid Hormones

Reichstein built on his earlier work with plant extracts to synthesize the steroid hormones. He and his colleagues developed several different methods to this end, though a process that used an animal waste product (ox bile) proved to be the most economical. One of the most important syntheses that Reichstein accomplished was that of aldosterone, which controls both water balance and sodium-potassium balance in the body. Aldosterone has been widely used in medical practice. Reichstein's work was also critical to the eventual syntheses of desoxycorticosterone, which for many years was the preferred treatment for Addison's disease, and cortisone, which is used for treating rheumatoid arthritis. It was principally for this latter accomplishment that Reichstein shared the 1950 Nobel Prize in chemistry.

Reichstein moved to the University of Basel in 1938 where he was appointed director of the Pharmaceutical Institute; in 1946 he became head of the organic chemistry division. Here he turned his attention to plant glycosides, a group of compounds with wide-ranging biological effects. They are the basis for a number of widely used drugs, and one of these, digitalis, has proven useful in controlling the heart rate. Reichstein was able to identify both the plants and the parts of the plants that contained glycosides, and his contributions were critical for initiating many botanical studies. He was one of the first researchers to realize the value of the tropical rain forests to the pharmaceutical industry. His work has also been pivotal in the field of chemical taxonomy, where the identities of plants are determined through their chemical composition—a method which has a higher degree of certainty than identification through visible characteristics. This technique has had broad applications in the development of both natural insecticides and drugs.

Reichstein was presented with an honorary doctorate from the Sorbonne in 1947. He received the Marcel Benoist Award in 1947, the Cameron Award in 1951, and a medal from the Royal Society of London in 1968. He is a foreign member of both the Royal Society and the National Academy of Sciences.

Reichstein married Henriette Louise Quarles van Ufford in 1927, while still at the Eidgenössiche Technische Hochshule. They had one daughter. He retired from his academic posts in 1967, but continued to work in the laboratory until 1987. He died on August 1, 1996, in Basel, Switzerland, at the age of 99.

SELECTED WRITINGS BY REICHSTEIN:

Books

Vitamins and Hormones, The Hormones of the Adrenal Cortex, edited by R. S. Harris and K. Volume Thiman, 1943.
Nobel Lectures: Physiology or Medicine, 1942–1962, Chemistry of the Adrenal Cortex Hormones, 1966.

Periodicals

Nature, Synthesis of *d-* and *l-* Ascorbic Acid (Vitamin-C), Volume 132, 1933, p. 280.

Festschrift Emil C. Barell, Synopsis of the Chemical and Biological Effect of the Ascorbic Acid Group, (special issue of Helvetica Chimica Acta), 1936, pp. 107–138.

Perfumery and Essential Oil Record, The Aroma of Coffee, Volume 46, 1955, pp. 86–88.

Nature, Cardenolides (Heart-Poisons) in a Grasshopper Feeding on Milkweeds, Volume 214, 1967, pp. 35–39.

FURTHER READING:

Books

Magill, F. N., editor, *The Nobel Prize Winners: Physiology or Medicine,* Volume 2, Salem Press, 1991, pp. 615–623.

Sketch by Ethan E. Allen

Lonnie Reid
1935–
American engineer

D r. Lonnie Reid became a nationally known expert in fluid dynamics through his work at the National Aeronautics and Space Administration's (NASA) Lewis Research Center in Cleveland, Ohio. For his pioneering work in integrating theoretical and experimental methods in fluid dynamics, Reid was inducted into the Ohio Science, Technology, and Industry (OSTI) Hall of Fame, becoming the first NASA researcher to attain this honor.

Reid was born September 5, 1935, in Gastonia, North Carolina, to Lonnie and Willie Reid. The youngest of seven children, Reid attended elementary and high school in Gastonia. After high school, Reid served in the U.S. Army and was stationed in Korea from February, 1955 until June, 1956. Following his honorable discharge in July, 1957, Reid attended Tennessee State University, where he studied engineering. During the spring of his freshmen year he married Christine Smith and the first of their four sons was born the following year. In June, 1961 Reid received his B.S. in mechanical engineering, and in July of that same year, he joined the Research Staff of NASA's Lewis Research Center.

Reid's early work at Lewis included research into improving efficiency and operating ranges for fans and compressors of "airbreathing" engines, and research on cryogenic fluid pumps for rocket engine applications. Reid did not concentrate solely on research, however; he also found time to continue his education, attaining his M.S. Degree in mechanical engineering from the University of Toledo, Ohio, in June, 1974. In 1978 Reid moved on to Lewis' Compressor Branch, serving first as Head of the Small Compressor Section and then as Head of the Multistage Compressor Section. He left the Compressor Branch to join the Altitude Wind Tunnel Research Office in 1984, where he spent two years as Head of the Aerodynamic Section.

Earns Rapid Promotions

The next few years were very active for Reid; in the span of three years he was promoted three times, with his responsibilities increasing with each change. In 1986 he became Chief of the Computational Applications Branch, where he was responsible for coordinating and directing work on computational fluid dynamics (CFD) codes. CFD codes are a means of modeling or simulating fluid flow. These codes enable computer analyses of propulsion system components to be performed. The work conducted under Reid involved verifying the accuracy of the CFD codes, then applying these codes to the analysis and design of aeropropulsion system components.

Reid became Chief of the Turbomachinery Technology Branch in 1987, directing research focused on flow physics in turbomachinery for gas turbine engines. Results of this research were applied to a wide variety of aircraft, including supersonic cruise and general aviation aircraft. A year later Reid became Chief of the Internal Fluid Mechanics Division. In this position he was responsible for research designed to advance the state-of-technology concerning the fluid mechanics in advanced aerospace propulsion system components. The program's goal was to transfer the developed technologies to the civilian U.S. propulsion industry. Even with the rigors of adjusting to new responsibilities, Reid still found time to continue his education—in December, 1989, Reid received his Ph.D. in Engineering Science from the University of Toledo. Besides being honored by the OSTI Hall of Fame in February, 1993, Reid received the NASA Exceptional Service Medal in 1989, and was named Tennessee State University's Outstanding Mechanical Engineering Alumnus in 1985. He has authored more than twenty-five technical papers on transonic compressors for advanced gas turbine engines. In November, 1993, after thirty-two years of service, Reid left Lewis Research Center and joined NYMA Inc., where he continues to pursue research in fluid dynamics.

SELECTED WRITINGS BY REID:

Periodicals

Transactions of the ASME: Journal of Engineering for Power, Experimental Evaluation of the Effects of a Blunt Leading Edge on the Performance of a Transonic Rotor, July, 1973, p. 199.

Transactions of the ASME: Journal of Engineering for Power, Experimental Study of Low Aspect Ratio Compressor Blading, October, 1980, p. 875.

NASA Technical Memorandum 86919, Analytical and Physical Modeling Program for the NASA Lewis Research Center's Altitude Wind Tunnel, with J. M. Abbott, J. H. Diedrich, J. F. Groenewig, L. A. Povinelli, J. J. Reimnann, and J. R. Szuch; 1985.

FURTHER READING:

Periodicals

Akron Reporter, February 20, 1993.
National Technical News, April 26, 1993, p. 1.

Other

National Technical News, NASA Biographical Data, Dr. Lonnie Reid, February 1993.
National Technical News, Reid, Lonnie, Resume, 1993.

Sketch by George A. Ferrance

Frederick Reines
1918–
American physicist

Frederick Reines is best known for his discovery of the neutrino, a particle that is created during a nuclear reaction. Since that discovery, he has continued to concentrate on the search for neutrinos and study their characteristics and behaviors. In later years, Reines studied the possibility of proton decay, an experiment whose negative results have had important significance for elementary particle theory.

Reines was born in Paterson, New Jersey, on March 16, 1918. His father was Israel Reines and his mother was Gussie Cohen Reines. After graduation from high school in 1935, Reines enrolled at the Stevens Institute of Technology, from which he earned a B.S. in mechanical engineering in 1939 and an M.A. in science in 1941. He then went to New York University, where he was awarded his Ph.D. in theoretical physics in 1944. His first job was at the Los Alamos Scientific Laboratory, where he was first a staff member and later a group leader responsible for studying the blast effects of nuclear weapons. In 1951, he was director of Operation Greenhouse, a group of experiments related to the testing of nuclear weapons at Eniwetok Atoll in the South Pacific.

Discovers the Neutrino

It was during his association with Los Alamos that Reines made the discovery for which he has become most famous, the detection of the neutrino. The neutrino had been predicted by **Wolfgang Pauli** in 1931 as a way of solving a puzzling nuclear phenomenon. When a beta particle is emitted from an unstable nucleus during beta decay (a radioactive nuclear interaction), the energy it carries away is insufficient to account for the energy lost within the nucleus itself. In order to account for this discrepancy, Pauli suggested that a second particle was formed that appropriated the energy discrepancy. **Enrico Fermi** later named this particle the neutrino. The name neutrino ("little neutron") arises from the properties postulated for the particle by Pauli. From the physics of beta decay, it was clear that the particle could have no charge, like the neutron, and no or very small mass; thus it was dubbed a "little neutron."

These properties guaranteed, however, that finding the neutrino would be very difficult. With no charge and perhaps no mass, it would be able to pass through matter (including detection instruments) without undergoing any type of interactions. In the early 1950s, Reines and a colleague, Clyde Cowan, undertook a search for the neutrino. The basis for their research was the assumption that although the chance of a neutrino's interacting with matter was very low, it was not zero. The key to success, they hypothesized, was to focus their detectors on a situation in which very large number of neutrinos would be expected to form, thus greatly increasing the chance of observing at least one reaction.

The best source for observing a flood of neutrinos, Reines and Cowan concluded, was a nuclear reactor. Their first experiments were carried out, therefore, at the Atomic Energy Commission's Hanford Nuclear Laboratory in Washington state. To search for the elusive neutrino, they decided to select one of the many reactions that physicists had hypothesized for it, one in which gamma rays of characteristic energy are generated. They then built a large eighty-gallon liquid scintillator with a bank of ninety photomultiplier tubes (a form of vacuum tube used for detecting very low levels of light) which they placed next to the Hanford reactor. The first evidence for neutrinos began to appear in 1953, but it was not entirely conclusive. Cowan and Reines decided to expand and improve their detection system and to move their experiment to the Savannah River National Laboratory in South Carolina. In 1956, they repeated their experiment there and obtained conclusive evidence for the existence of neutrinos.

In 1959, Reines left Los Alamos and accepted a position as professor of physics and head of the department at Case Institute of Technology (now Case Western Reserve University) in Cleveland. At the same time, he became chair of the Joint Case-Western Reserve High Energy Physics Program. Reines held these positions until 1966, during which time he continued to serve as a consultant at Los Alamos and was also a consultant to the Institute for

Defense Analysis (1965–1969) and trustee of the Argonne National Laboratory.

Reines left Case-Western Reserve in 1966 to accept an appointment as professor of physics and the first dean of physical sciences at the University of California at Irvine. Four years later, he was also appointed professor of radiological sciences at Irvine's Medical School. He retired in 1988 and was named Distinguished Professor of Physics, Emeritus at Irvine.

Searches for Neutrinos in Varied Environments

Following his discovery of the neutrino, Reines continued his research on these elusive particles. He later built huge tanks containing the colorless liquid perchloroethylene in a search for atmospheric neutrinos, that is, neutrinos produced by solar cosmic rays in the Earth's atmosphere. That search achieved success, although the number of neutrinos detected was significantly less than the number predicted by current theories. The detectors constructed for the search for atmospheric neutrinos were also used to find neutrinos produced by the dramatic eruption of Supernova 1987A in 1987. (A supernova is an exploding star that, at the height of its luminosity, can be brighter than the Sun.)

Reines's research has also involved a search for the possible decay of the proton in nuclear interactions. Although the proton has long been considered a stable particle, some current theories of elementary particles suggest that they may have a very long, but not infinite, half-life. Reines's research sought to prove that these half-lives could be many billions of years long. Using detection devices that had been successful with neutrino research, Reines has shown that the minimum proton half-life predicted so far is not possible, although still longer half-lives may be.

Reines married Sylvia Samuels on August 30, 1940. They have two children, Robert and Alisa. Among his numerous honors and awards are the 1981 J. Robert Oppenheimer Memorial Prize, the 1985 National Medal of Science, the Bruno Rossi Prize of the American Astronomical Society in 1989, and the Michelson-Morley Award in 1990. Reines also received the W. K. H. Panofsky Prize and the Franklin Medal of the Benjamin Franklin Institute, both in 1992.

FURTHER READING:

Periodicals

Physics Today, July, 1992, p. 77.

Sketch by David E. Newton

Roger Revelle
1909–1991
American geologist, oceanographer, and environmental scientist

Roger Revelle was a scientist who for more than fifty-five years was associated with the Scripps Institution of Oceanography. In association with the Institution, Revelle and his colleagues laid the foundations for the theory ofplate tectonics, which maintains that the Earth's surface is composed of relatively thin plates bordered by earthquake and volcanic zones. He was also one of the first scientists to predict that continual accumulation of atmospheric carbon dioxide would lead to global warming. In addition, Revelle was a leading advocate of science's social responsibility and was influential in urging government leaders to utilize modern science and technology to assist poorer nations in improving their standards of living. Revelle was also highly instrumental in founding the University of California's San Diego campus (UCSD). An outspoken advocate of educational quality, Revelle told *Scientific American,* "We built from the roof first," appointing senior professors before establishing an undergraduate curriculum. "It is by far the most important thing I've ever been involved with," he added. For Revelle's life-long work as a scientist of international repute, President George Bush presented him with the National Medal of Science in 1990.

Roger Randall Dougan Revelle was born in Seattle, Washington, on March 7, 1909, the son of William Roger and Ella Robena (Dougan) Revelle. He grew up in southern California, his family having left the Northwest for Claremont, California, when Roger was still a boy. He attended schools in Claremont, receiving his B.A. in geology from Pomona College (now Claremont College) in 1929. He remained at Pomona, doing graduate work in geology and serving as a teaching assistant. Then, in 1931, while pursuing a graduate program at the University of California, Berkeley, Revelle was recruited to study deep-sea mud at California's Scripps Institution of Oceanography, in La Jolla, near San Diego. At the time, Scripps was a remote research station, but the assignment appealed to Revelle. That same year Revelle married Ellen V. Clark, grandniece of Ellen Browning Scripps and Edward Willis Scripps, the major benefactors of the institution that bears their name.

Revelle served as a research assistant at Scripps until he received his Ph.D. in oceanography in 1936. He was then named to the faculty as an instructor. He was associated with the institution the remainder of his life. He was named an assistant professor in 1941, but before he could become immersed in university life, World War II intervened. Revelle was commissioned a commander in the U.S. Naval Reserves and, in 1942, was attached to the Hydrographic Office in Washington and put in charge of the oceanographic section of the Bureau of Ships. Following the war he returned to Scripps as a full professor but remained active in Navy oceanographic work. As chief of the geophysics section of the U.S. Office of Naval Research from 1946 to 1947, he supervised scientific measurement of the government'satom bomb tests off Bikini Atoll in the Pacific.

In 1951 Revelle was named director of Scripps, a position he held for thirteen years. Under his leadership the Institution was involved in numerous oceanographic expeditions that laid the foundations for much of modern oceanography. Among his scientific achievements was his innovative work on the upward flow of heat through the ocean floor. Working with other scientists, he built a device to measure amounts of heat being radiated from the bottom of the ocean. His discovery that more heat was being radiated than originally expected led scientists to believe hot material was flowing under the oceans. This discovery was the prelude to the revolutionary theory of plate tectonics, which posits that the earth's crust is made of relatively thin plates that float atop a layer of lava. As new material erupts along ocean ridges, undersea mountain ranges and volcanoes can be created, causing large sections of the ocean floor to shift. This shifting moves the earth's plates, resulting in continental movement, a phenomenon known as continental drift. To further this line of investigation, Revelle became involved in the Deep Sea Drilling Project, which probed the ocean floors. According to the *New York Times,* "Some scientists regard this program as the most productive scientific enterprise ever conducted at sea."

Calls Attention to Global Warming

In 1957, Revelle became one of the first scientists to introduce the concept of global warming. He and a colleague, oceanographer Hans E. Suess, wrote a paper suggesting that the oceans could not absorb most of the carbon dioxide that is poured into the atmosphere when fossil fuels such as coal and gasoline are burned to supply power for industry and automobiles. Predicting a twenty to forty percent increase in atmospheric carbon dioxide levels in future decades, the scientists theorized that long-range climate changes, including a rise in average temperatures on Earth, would be the result—a phenomenon now known as the "greenhouse effect." Increased temperatures could in turn lead to the partial melting of glaciers and a consequent rise in sea levels, coastal flooding, and inland drought. They called the burning of fossil fuels "a large-scale geophysical experiment" and argued for worldwide cooperation in studying global changes in the environment.

Also in 1957, Revelle helped organize the International Geophysical Year of 1957–58, which inaugurated the Space Age and was one of the most ambitious programs of global research ever undertaken. As the result of some of this research, Revelle successfully advocated the institution of yearly global carbon dioxide level measurements from a station on the volcano of Mauna Loa in Hawaii. These measurements are still taken today and are viewed as an authoritative indication of global carbon dioxide levels in the atmosphere.

In 1956, Revelle had begun lobbying the regents of the University of California system for a new campus at San Diego, which would be closely affiliated with the Scripps Institution. Although there was much initial opposition by the regents, with the aid of great local support Revelle's efforts were successful. When the San Diego campus of the University of California was finally established in 1959, Revelle became dean of the School of Science and Engineering, while retaining his directorship of Scripps. As an educator, Revelle held strong views on the state of American education and was determined to make changes. As reported in *Scientific American,* he bemoaned "the god-awful public education too many of our students get in public schools." His educational goal was to separate the San Diego campus into individual colleges so that students and faculty could work more closely in smaller units. Unfortunately, the plan failed. "The faculty didn't give a damn," Revelle said. "Professors are journeyman-scholars with very little loyalty to their institutions. What you have now is a dozen little empires."

Revelle was science advisor to Interior Secretary Stewart L. Udall from 1961 to 1963, an experience that would alter his life. As head of a presidential panel to study the problems of water use in the Indus River basin of Pakistan, he was able to closely observe the problems of Third-World people. Seeing the desperation of millions firsthand left an indelible impression. In 1964 Revelle took leave from UCSD to found the Harvard University Center for Population Studies. His work in Pakistan revealed to him the importance of environmental resources in the study of population growth and improvement of life for those living in poverty in the Third World. "Much to everyone's disapproval," he recalled in *Scientific American,* Revelle and his colleagues concentrated on making resources "a real university subject." As it turned out, he noted, "we were right." Revelle had put into practice his belief that scientists must have a social conscience. He resumed his post at UCSD in 1975. When he led a scientific party to Africa in 1988 to study hunger, he returned with a sense of frustration. "Agriculture is going backward rather than forward," he stated. "It's very, very discouraging." Reversing the trend, he remarked, will require "a whole new green revolution."

Revelle died of complications following a cardiac arrest at the age of 82, on July 15, 1991, in San Diego. He was survived by his wife, Ellen, a son, William Roger, and three daughters, Anne Elizabeth Shumway, Mary Ellen Paci, and Carolyn Hufbauer. When asked how he managed to do so many things in his career, he responded, "Do them in sequence."

SELECTED WRITINGS BY REVELLE:

Books

America's Changing Environment, Houghton, 1970.

The Survival Equation: Man, Resources, and His Environment, Houghton, 1971.
Consequences of Rapid Population Growth, 1972.
Population and Social Change, Crane, 1972.
Population and Environment, Harvard University Press, 1974.

FURTHER READING:

Periodicals

Beardsley, Tim, *Scientific American,* Profile: Dr. Greenhouse, December, 1990, pp. 33–36.
Maranto, Gina, and Allen Chen, *Discover,* Are We Close to the Road's End?, January, 1986, p. 28.
Sullivan, Walter, *New York Times,* Roger Revelle, 82, Early Theorist in Global Warming and Geology, July 17, 1991.

Sketch by Benedict A. Leerburger

Stuart Alan Rice

Stuart Alan Rice
1932–
American chemist

The American physical chemist Stuart Alan Rice has achieved wide recognition for his research on elementary photophysical and photochemical processes, quantum chaos, selectivity in chemical reactions, reaction rate theory, liquid surfaces, monolayers, phase transitions in interfaces, and the properties of quasi-two dimensional systems.

Rice was born on January 6, 1932, in New York City, NY. He attended school in the New York City public school system, before entering Brooklyn College, where he obtained the BS degree in 1952. He subsequently completed studies at Harvard University, obtaining a master's degree in 1954 and a doctorate in 1955. From 1955 to 1957, he was a Junior Fellow, Society of Fellows, at Harvard.

In 1957 Rice became an assistant professor in the Department of Chemistry and the Institute for the Study of Metals (later renamed the James Franck Institute) at the University of Chicago. In 1959 he was promoted to associate professor, and in 1960 to full professor. Since that time, he has held a number of academic appointments, including director of the James Franck Institute (1961-1967) and chairman of the Department of Chemistry (1971-1976). Since 1977, Rice has been Frank P. Hixon Distinguished Service Professor in the James Franck Institute and the Department of Chemistry.

Professor Rice's research interests generally fall in two broad areas: the active control of quantum dynamical processes, and the properties of interfaces. In the former, Rice has studied methods for achieving control of the selectivity of products formed in chemical reactions based on theoretical calculations. Currently, his research is aimed at developing a way to control quantum dynamical systems, understanding the limitations of using time-dependent fields to control the evolution of a molecule, extending control theory to reactions in condensed media, and developing a general theory that can be applied to large molecules.

In research related to the properties of interfaces, Rice has attempted to understand the properties of the interfaces between liquid and vapor and between liquid and solid. Questions in this area that he has sought answers to include: How does the structure of the non-uniform interface of a metallic alloy depend on electronic structure? What determines the concentration of a component that segregates at an interface involving a liquid? How do the properties associated with a change of phase in these systems depend on intermolecular potential? To answer these and related questions, Rice has developed theoretical models; used computer simulations; and employed grazing-incidence x-ray diffraction to study layer structures, x-ray reflection to study non-uniform systems, evanescent-wave dynamical light scattering to study motion in interfaces, and video-microscope studies of phase transitions and diffusion in colloid suspensions.

Among the professional awards and recognitions that have been bestowed upon Rice are the Cressy Morrison

Prize in Natural Sciences, New York Academy of Sciences (1955); Alfred P. Sloan Fellow (1958-1962); Guggenheim Fellow (1960-1961); American Chemical Society Award in Pure Chemistry (1962); Marlow Medal of the Faraday Society (1963); National Science Foundation Senior Postdoctoral Fellow, and Visiting Professor, Universite Libre de Bruxelles (1965-1966); Medal of the Universite Libre de Bruxelles (1966); Elected Fellow, American Academy of Arts and Sciences (1967); Elected Fellow, National Academy of Sciences (1968); National Institutes of Health Special Research Fellow and Visiting Professor, H.C. Orsted Institute, University of Copenhagen (1970-1971); Leo Hendrik Baekeland Award, American Chemical Society (1971); Elected Foreign Member of Royal Danish Academy of Science and Letters (1976); Honorary Doctorate of Science Degree, Notre Dame University (1982); Peter Debye Award, American Chemical Society (1985); Elected Fellow, American Philosophical Society (1986); Joel Henry Hildebrand Award, American Chemical Society (1987); and the Centennial Medal, Harvard University, Graduate School of Arts and Sciences (1997).

Rice serves on a number of advisory and editorial boards for scientific publications, including *Advances in Chemical Physics*, *Encyclopaedia Britannica*, *Chemical Physics Letters*, and the *Encyclopedia of Physical Science and Technology*.

Sketch by Randall Frost

Alexander Rich

Alexander Rich
1924–
American biophysicist

In any account of the history of molecular biology, Alexander Rich must occupy a prominent place as one of the prime architects who shaped the discipline to its modern form. Entering the field in its infancy, Rich made fundamental discoveries about nucleic acids—deoxyribonucleic acid (DNA) and ribonucleic acid (RNA)—molecules that encode the specific information needed by all organisms for performing the various functions of living. His findings have helped answer questions about the basic functions of DNA and RNA molecules.

Rich was born in Hartford, Connecticut, on November 15, 1924, to Max Rich and Bella Shub Rich. His parents had both immigrated to the United States from Russia in the first decade of the twentieth century and his father worked in the dry cleaning industry. Rich grew up in Hartford and served in the U.S. Navy from 1943 to 1945, before going to Harvard Suniversity for a bachelor's degree in biochemical sciences. He went on to receive a Doctor of Medicine

degree from Harvard Medical School in 1949, but never practiced medicine. Instead, upon completing his degree, he undertook a four-year postdoctoral fellowship in physical chemistry in the laboratory of **Linus Pauling** at the California Institute of Technology in Pasadena. He got married in 1952 to Jane Erving King, a nursery school teacher from Cambridge, Massachusetts.

It was in Pauling's laboratory that Rich first began to work on nucleic acid chemistry. During that time, **James Watson** and **Francis Crick** were just formulating their proposal for the double helix structure of DNA, which they published in 1953. Rich, who moved to Bethesda in 1954 as chief of the section of physical chemistry at the National Institute of Mental Health, provided some of the earliest experimental evidence to back up Watson and Crick's structural model.

When Two Strands Meet

As we now know, a DNA molecule is made up of two complementary chains wound around each other to form a double helix. Each chain is a polymer comprised of molecular units called nucleotides made up of a deoxyribose sugar, phosphate groups, and either a purine or pyrimidine side chain. The sugar and phosphate molecules make up the backbone of each strand, while side chains form the basis of DNA specificity and complementarity. A total of four possible side chains—adenine, guanosine, thymine and cytosine (A, G, T, C)—are arranged in specific sequences to make up different genes. An A in one strand binds to a T in the complement while G bind to C, via hydrogen bonds. In contrast to DNA, RNA molecules contain a ribose sugar in the backbone, and have uracil (U) residues instead of T. While they exist, for most part, as single-stranded polymers, they can, and often do, form double helical structures as well.

Working with artificially synthesized single polynucleotide chains—in this case one string each of A and U residues on ribose phosphate backbones—Rich found that when mixed together in solution, these strands wound around each other to form a double helix. The experiment showed that not only was the base pairing possible in nature, but that in fact, it was the configuration that nucleic acids assumed by default if the strands were complementary. Clearly the molecules did not require the help of an enzyme to form a helix, a fact which, Rich recounted later, greatly surprised his colleagues. Furthermore, these experiments showed that contrary to Watson's predictions, RNA molecules too, could form double helices. The reaction, which is known as hybridization, is the basis for many modern molecular biological techniques. For example, using a sequence from a gene in one organism, scientists can probe the DNA from other species or organisms to see if they contain similar sequences.

While experimenting with hybridization, Rich found that when one type of strand was present in excess over the other rather than in equal quantities, the nucleic acids were capable of adopting a triple-stranded configuration. The implications of this finding went largely ignored for many years, and it is only recently that biotechnologists have begun to investigate the therapeutic value of DNA triple helices by attempting to use them to prevent the expression of specific, disease-inducing genes.

Milestones at MIT

Moving to the Massachusetts Institute of Technology (MIT) in 1958, Rich continued to work on the structure and behavior of nucleic acids. In 1960 he discovered that hybridization was also possible between DNA and RNA strands, a finding that had fundamental theoretical implications far beyond its obvious practical applications. "It suggested how DNA might transfer its information to RNA," Rich recounted in an interview in 1995. Yet again, Rich's experiments provided experimental support for a very important biological principle, in this case the "Central Dogma" of biology, which was formulated during the late 1950s to describe the flow of information in living organisms—from DNA to RNA to proteins.

Still more details about this information path came to light from Rich's lab throughout the 1960s. His group isolated and characterized polysomes—clusters of ribosomes and messenger RNA (m-RNA) and transfer RNAs (t-RNAs)—which gave scientists a dynamic picture of how protein synthesis proceeded inside the cell. They went on to solve the crystal structure of a yeast t-RNA specific for the amino acid phenylalanine. This was the first time anyone had elucidated the three-dimensional structure of any

nucleic acid. During this time they also crystallized a single base-pair unit of DNA, which Rich described as "the first crystal structure in which the atomic details of double helical nucleic acid can be visualized."

In 1979 Rich's laboratory announced the discovery of a new configuration of DNA, in which the helix is wound in a left-handed orientation, opposite to the conventional helix proposed by Watson and Crick. While the exact role of Z-DNA is as yet unknown, evidence from different labs indicate it is involved in a wide variety of fundamental biological activities, including transcription and cell division. His attention then turned to different compounds that interacted with DNA, and was responsible for solving the structure of several DNA binding drugs during the 1980s.

His achievements in basic sciences aside, Rich also involved himself in arenas that touched people's lives more directly. Beginning in the late 1960s, Rich worked with the National Aeronautics and Space Administration (NASA) in various capacities. He was a member of the Lunar and Planetary Missions Board from 1968 to 1970, in the Life Sciences Committee from 1970 to 1975, and a member of the biology team for the Viking Mars Mission since 1969. In recognition of his service, NASA awarded him with their Skylab Achievement Award in 1974.

As befits a long productive career marked by many firsts, Rich received scientific honors and awards too numerous to name. He was elected as a member of the National Academy of Science—the highest honor for an American scientist—in 1970, and in 1995 received the National Medal of Science from the President. Probably the best summary of his career came from Northwestern University chemist Irving Klotz at a symposium celebrating 40 years of DNA in 1995, "The young Alexander Rich, a freshly hatched M.D., arrived in Pasadena in 1949, just at the onset of the 'giant leaps forward' in protein and nucleic acid structure, and has been at the very center of the field ever since."

SELECTED WRITINGS BY RICH:

Periodicals

"The Nucleic Acids, A Backward Glance." *DNA: The Double Helix. Perspective and Prospective at Forty Years.* Vol. 758 of *Annals of the New York Academy of Sciences.* Edited by Donald A. Chambers, 1995.

FURTHER READING:

Periodicals

Sankaran, Neeraja. "National Medal of Science Winners Contributed to Birth of Their Fields." *The Scientist* (October 30, 1995): 3.

Sketch by Neeraja Sankaran

Dickinson Woodruff Richards, Jr.
1895–1973
American physician

In refining the technique of cardiac catheterization, Dickinson Woodruff Richards made significant contributions to the study of cardiopulmonary function in human patients. In collaboration with his colleague **André F. Cournand**, Richards elaborated upon earlier research by German physician **Werner Forssmann**, leading ultimately to the discovery of how pulmonary efficiency could be measured. For their work, Richards, Cournand, and Forssmann shared the 1956 Nobel Prize.

Richards was born October 30, 1895, in Orange, New Jersey, to Sally (Lambert) and Dickinson Woodruff Richards. The legacy of the medical profession was established by his maternal forebears, the Lamberts. Richards' grandfather practiced general medicine in New York City, as did three of Richards' uncles; all either received their training or were otherwise affiliated with Bellevue Hospital or Columbia University's College of Physicians and Surgeons, where Richards himself would eventually study.

Richards received his A.B. from Yale University in 1917, and three months later enlisted in the United States Army, serving in France with the American Expeditionary Force. Upon his return to the United States, he entered the College of Physicians and Surgeons at Columbia; there he completed his M.A. in physiology in 1922 and his M.D. in 1923. Richards immediately received his license to practice medicine and interned for two years at Presbyterian Hospital in New York, spending two additional years there as a resident physician once his internship had expired. In 1927, Columbia University granted him a research fellowship to train at London's National Institute for Medical Research. From 1927 to 1928 he studied experimental physiology, working closely with Dr. **Henry Hallett Dale**, who Richards would later refer to as one of his greatest influences. He then returned to Columbia University's Presbyterian Hospital to study pulmonary and circulatory physiology. In 1930 he became engaged to Constance Riley, a Wellesley College graduate who worked as a technician in his research lab at Presbyterian Hospital. They married in September 1931.

Teams with Cournand to Refine Catheterization Technique

Richards' collaboration with André Cournand began in 1931 at Bellevue Hospital. Basing their research on Richards' concept "that lungs, heart, and circulation should be thought of as one single apparatus for the transfer of respiratory gases between outside atmosphere and working tissues," these two physicians began a long and fruitful partnership. Their initial research involved the study of the physiological performance of the lungs and, in particular, a disorder known as chronic pulmonary insufficiency. Characterized by a malfunction in the heart's tricuspid and pulmonic valves, this defect causes blood to flow backward into the heart. Richards concluded, as had others before him, that it was necessary to be able to measure the amount of air in the lungs during different stages of pulmonary activity. Thus, he and Cournand unearthed studies done in 1929 by the German physician Werner Forssmann, wherein Forssmann had attempted to measure gases in the blood as it passed from the heart to the lungs.

Forssmann's technique was proven viable when he successfully inserted a narrow rubber catheter through a vein in his own arm and into the right atrium of his heart. This method gave access to blood as it entered the heart— blood that could then be examined in specific stages of pulmonary and cardiac activity and evaluated in terms of rate of flow, pressure relations, and gas contents. Catheterization would allow physicians to measure oxygen and carbon monoxide in blood returning from the right atrium, allowing for accurate measurement of blood flow through the lungs. Richards and Cournand sought to advance Forssmann's technique and to develop a safe procedure by first experimenting on animals. They began their research in 1936, and by 1941 they had successfully catheterized the right atrium of the human heart.

The measurements made possible through cardiac catheterization led Richards to other important assessments about functions of the heart and circulatory system. In 1941 he developed methods to measure the volume of blood pumped out of either ventricle (lower chamber) of the heart, and to measure blood pressure in the right atrium, the right ventricle, and the pulmonary artery, as well as total blood volume. More recent research has employed catheterization to diagnose abnormal exchange between the right and left sides of the heart, such as is present in some congenital cardiac defects. It has also contributed to the development of more sophisticated techniques such as angiocardiography (the x-ray examination of the heart after injection of dyes), which is used to determine whether normal circulation has resumed following a surgical procedure.

Richards and his colleagues also relied on their revolutionary research technique to study the effects of traumatic shock in heart failure and to identify congenital heart lesions. During World War II Richards and his colleagues were asked by the government to study the circulatory forces involved in shock, with Richards serving as chair of the National Research Council's subcommittee. The goal was to measure the effects of hemorrhage and trauma on the heart and cardiac circulation, and to evaluate various procedures for treatment. The most important result of this project was the discovery that whole blood, rather than just blood plasma, should be used in the treatment of shock to the cardiac system.

Richards was passionate about health issues in the social arena as well as in the laboratory: in 1957 he testified before the Joint Legislative Committee on Narcotics Study to suggest the construction of hospital clinics to legally distribute narcotics to recovering addicts; he lobbied for the building of a new hospital to replace the aging Bellevue; he spoke often about the need for constant reform within medical academia; and he supported the crusade to improve health care benefits for the elderly.

In 1945 Richards became the head of Columbia University's First Medical Division at Bellevue Hospital, and at the same time was promoted to the full-time Lambert Professorship of Medicine at the College of Physicians and Surgeons. He served as associate editor of *Medicine, Circulation, The Journal of the American Heart Association,* and of the *American Review of Tuberculosis.* His articles have appeared in many publications, including *Physiological Review, Journal of Clinical Investigation,* and *Journal of Chronic Diseases.*

Richards was elected to the National Academy of Sciences in 1958, and retired from practice in 1961, though he continued to lecture and publish frequent articles for several years. He died at his home in Lakeville, Connecticut, on February 23, 1973, after suffering a heart attack.

Research Discoveries Rewarded with Nobel Prize and Other Honors

For their refinement of the catheterization procedure and the discoveries that followed, Richards, Cournand and Forssmann were awarded the Nobel Prize in physiology or medicine in 1956. In addition, Richards also received many individual honors and awards, including the John Phillips Memorial Award of the American College of Physicians (1960) and the Kober Medal of the Association of American Physicians (1970). He was made a chevalier of the Legion of Honor of France (1963), and was a fellow of the American College of Physicians, the American Medical Association, and the American Clinical and Climatological Association. He was offered numerous honorary degrees but accepted only two—Yale University, his alma mater, and Columbia University, where he did most of his work.

SELECTED WRITINGS BY RICHARDS, JR.:

Books

Circulation of the Blood: Men and Ideas, Oxford University Press, 1964.
Medical Priesthoods and Other Essays, Connecticut Printers, 1970.

FURTHER READING:

Books

Biographical Memoirs, Volume 58, National Academy Press, 1989, pp. 459–487.

Current Biography Yearbook, 1957, H.W. Wilson, 1957, pp. 457–459.
Nobel Prize Winners, H. W. Wilson, 1987, pp. 862–863.

Sketch by Kelly Otter Cooper

Ellen Swallow Richards
1842–1911
American chemist

Ellen Swallow Richards was an applied scientist, sanitary chemist, and the founder of home economics. For twenty-seven years she was employed by the Massachusetts Institute of Technology (MIT), where she taught chemistry and developed methods for the analysis of air, water, and consumer products. Her work as a scientist and educator led to improvements in the home and opened the door to scientific professions for women.

Swallow was born on December 3, 1842, in Dunstable, Massachusetts. She was the only child of Peter Swallow, a teacher, farmer, and store keeper, and Fanny Gould Taylor, a teacher. She was educated at home by her parents until the family moved to Westford, Massachusetts, in 1859. There she attended Westford Massachusetts Academy, where she enrolled in mathematics, French, and Latin. In 1863 she graduated from the academy, and the family relocated to Littleton, Massachusetts.

Swallow worked at an assortment of jobs—storekeeping, tutoring, housecleaning, cooking, and nursing—to earn enough money to continue her education. Because of her mother's ill health, she struggled with exhaustion and mental depression for a period of several years.

By 1868 Swallow had saved enough money to attend Vassar college, where she excelled in astronomy and chemistry. Her chemistry professor, convinced that science should be applied to practical problems, contributed to Swallow's developing interest in consumer and environmental science. Receiving a bachelor of arts degree in 1870, Swallow decided to apply to MIT to further her study of chemistry and became one of the first women students at that institution. She received a bachelor of science degree from MIT in 1873. In that same year, after submitting a thesis on the estimation of vanadium in iron ore, she received her masters of arts degree from Vassar. Although she continued her studies at MIT an additional two years, she was never awarded a doctorate.

Swallow married Robert Hallowell Richards, a professor of mining engineering, on June 4, 1875. The couple had no children and were able to devote their full support to each other's professional career. In her leisure time Richards enjoyed gardening, entertaining, and traveling. She also took an active interest in improving her own home. At one time she boasted of having year-round hot water and a telephone.

A Successful Career at MIT

Richards helped establish a laboratory at MIT for women. While still an undergraduate, she had taught chemistry at the girls high school in Boston through a project funded by the Woman's Education Association. With the help of this association, Richards convinced MIT of the need for a women's lab, and in 1876, armed with the title of assistant, she began teaching chemical analysis, industrial chemistry, mineralogy, and biology to a handful of women students. In addition to their traditional studies, the students assisted in testing a variety of consumer products for composition and adulterations. After seven years, in which four students graduated and the rest were accepted as regular MIT students, the laboratory closed.

In 1884 MIT opened a new laboratory for the study of sanitation, and Richards was appointed assistant and instructor in sanitary chemistry. Her teaching duties included instruction in air, water, and sewage analysis. In addition, she was responsible for completing a two-year survey of Massachusetts inland waters (begun in 1887 for the state board of health). Her success in analyzing nearly forty thousand water samples was attributed to her knowledge of methodology, apparatus, and her excellent supervisory and record-keeping skills. The water survey work and her involvement with environmental chemistry were significant contributions to the new science of ecology.

Founder of Home Economics

Richards was a pioneer in the effort to increase educational opportunities for women. She was one of the founders of the Association of Collegiate Alumnae, which later changed its title to the American Association of University Women. She organized the science section for the Society to Encourage Studies at Home, a correspondence school founded in 1887 by Anna Tickenor. Her correspondence with students provided insight into the daily life and problems faced by women in the home. Richards learned that women were seeking help with a wide range of problems, not all of which were scientific in nature, including manners of dress, food preparation, and exercise.

In 1890 Richards opened the New England Kitchen in Boston as a means of demonstrating how wholesome foods could be selected and prepared. In 1899 she organized and chaired a summer conference at Lake Placid, New York, that established the profession of home economics. Conference participants explored new ways of applying sociology and economics to the home and developed courses of study for schools and colleges. Later she helped found the American Home Economics Association and provided financial support for its publication, the *Journal of Home Economics*.

In addition to her work at the sanitation laboratory, Richards consulted, lectured, authored ten books, and published numerous papers, including bulletins on nutrition for the United States Department of Agriculture. In 1910, in recognition of her commitment to education, she was appointed to supervise the teaching of home economics in public schools by the council of the National Education Association. In that same year she was awarded an honorary doctorate from Smith College. Richards died of heart disease in 1911 at the age of sixty-eight.

SELECTED WRITINGS BY RICHARDS:

Books

The Chemistry of Cooking and Cleaning: A Manual for House-keepers, Estes and Lauriat, 1882.

FURTHER READING:

Books

Ogilvie, Marilyn, *Women in Science,* Massachusetts Institute of Technology Press, 1986, pp. 149–52.

Sketch by Mike McClure

Theodore William Richards
1868–1928
American chemist

Theodore William Richards, a professor of chemistry at Harvard University, was the first American chemist to receive a Nobel Prize. The prize was awarded to Richards in 1914 in chemistry for his accurate determination of the atomic weights of twenty-five chemical elements. He was renowned for his unsurpassed laboratory skill in chemical analysis. His work provided essential fundamental data for practical and theoretical chemists and physicists, and his graduate program at Harvard produced many eminent educators and research scientists.

Richards, the fifth of six children, was born on January 31, 1868, in Germantown, Pennsylvania, to William Trist Richards, a painter of seascapes, and Anna Matlack Richards, a writer and poet. Until he was fourteen, Richards received all his education from his mother, who had little regard for the public schools of Germantown. His interest in chemical experiments began when he was ten; when he was thirteen, he attended lectures in chemistry at the University of Pennsylvania. At the age of fourteen, Richards enrolled in Haverford College as a sophomore and graduated at the head of his class with a specialty in chemistry in 1885. Upon graduation, Richards enrolled at Harvard to study chemistry with Josiah Cooke, a professor whom he had met on summer vacation when he was six years old. Richards received his second baccalaureate, with *summa cum laude* distinction, at Harvard in 1886, and remained to study for the Ph.D. under Cooke's supervision. He received his doctorate in 1888, when he was twenty.

Richards's dissertation research marked the beginning of his study of atomic weights, which formed the major field of investigation in his long career. Richards published over 150 papers on atomic weights, beginning with his doctoral research on the atomic weight of hydrogen. At the time, chemists theorized that all elements were made from hydrogen and that there should be an integral ratio between the atomic weight of hydrogen and other elements. Although the theory called for the ratio of oxygen to hydrogen in water to be exactly 16, Richards's careful laboratory work, which involved difficult manipulations of gases, showed the ratio was actually 15.869 and strongly suggested that the theory was erroneous.

In the 1888–89 academic year, Richards received a fellowship and visited analytical laboratories in Europe. He returned to Harvard to become an assistant in the analytical chemistry course. He was promoted to instructor in 1891, assistant professor in 1894, and full professor in 1901 (after rejecting an offer from the University of Göttingen). He taught analytical chemistry until 1902 and physical chemistry from 1895, after the death of Josiah Cooke. He was chairman of the chemistry department from 1903 to 1911 and director of the Wolcott Gibbs Laboratory from 1912 until his death in 1928.

Measurement of Atomic Weights Recognized with Nobel Prize

The measurement of atomic weights coincides with the beginning of modern chemistry, with Antoine-Laurent Lavoisier's conception of chemical elements and with John Dalton's atomic theory, which established that atoms are the building blocks of matter. The chemists of the nineteenth century had determined the atomic weights of all the known elements, and Dmitry Mendeleyev based his periodic table of the elements on these values. However, all values of the atomic weights at the time were relative values, where ratios of atomic weights were actually determined in chemical compounds, and an error in a crucial ratio meant that the atomic weights of several elements would be inaccurate. For example, if the silver to chlorine ratio in silver chloride was inaccurate, then the atomic weight of sodium from sodium chloride or potassium from potassium chloride would consequently be erroneous.

Richards found that the long-accepted atomic weight values of the French chemist Jean-Servais Stas were incorrect because of several experimental errors which had been previously overlooked. The crucial part of the analysis of atomic weight involves the complete collection of a pure precipitate; Richards showed that Stas's compounds were impure and that Stas had not accounted for all of the chemical product. Richards and his students were able to redetermine accurately the atomic weights of twenty-five elements, and other chemists who had studied with Richards added thirty more elements. In his studies, Richards showed that the geographical origins of the elements does not affect their atomic weights (he determined that terrestrial and meteoric iron have identical values). Richards's determination of physical constants, which were used by all chemists, won the admiration of the chemistry community and led to his Nobel Prize.

Richards's work was also important to the dramatic new discoveries of early twentieth-century scientists in radioactivity and the structure of the atomic nucleus. Richards determined that the atomic weight of ordinary lead was different from that of lead which came from the radioactive decay of uranium. This critical evidence corroborated theories of radioactivity, and because of Richards's reputation for accuracy, the experimental result was readily accepted by many scientists.

In addition to his work on atomic weights, Richards also directed research in physical chemistry. Before he began to teach physical chemistry at Harvard, he was sent to Germany to study with two leaders in the field, Nobel Prize winners **Friedrich Wilhelm Ostwald** and **Walther Nernst**. Richards invented an improved calorimeter for measuring heat in chemical reactions and published sixty papers in thermochemistry. He also contributed to the field of electrochemistry. His sixty graduate students became distinguished professors at other universities and continued the research studies they began at Harvard. Richards's influence on American chemical research in analytical and physical chemistry was exceptional.

In addition to the Nobel Prize, Richards won scientific awards from many nations. He also served as president of the American Chemical Society (1914), the American Association for the Advancement of Science (1917), and the American Academy of Arts and Sciences (1920–1921). Outside of his scientific interests, he enjoyed sketching, sailing, and golf.

In 1896, Richards married Miriam Stuart Thayer, daughter of Professor Joseph H. Thayer of the Harvard divinity school. Their son William studied chemistry with his father at Harvard and went on to teach at Princeton. Another son, Greenough, became an architect, and their daughter, Grace, married James B. Conant, one of Richards's graduate students. Conant became professor of organic chemistry and president of Harvard University. Richards died in Cambridge, Massachusetts, on April 2, 1928.

SELECTED WRITINGS BY RICHARDS:

Books

Nobelstiftelsen: Nobel Lectures: Chemistry, 1901–1921, Atomic Weights, Elsevier, 1966.

Periodicals

Chemical Reviews, Atomic Weights and Isotopes, 1924, pp. 1–40.

FURTHER READING:

Books

Burke, Helen M., *The Nobel Prize Winners: Chemistry,* Theodore William Richards, edited by F. N. Magill, Salem, 1990, Volume 1, pp. 197–206.

Fleck, George, *Nobel Laureates in Chemistry, 1901–1992,* Theodore William Richards, edited by L. K. James, American Chemical Society, 1993, pp. 100–107.

Ihde, Aaron, *Great Chemists,* Richards—Corrector of Atomic Weights, edited by E. Farber, Interscience, 1961, pp. 822–829.

Kopperl, Sheldon J., *American Chemists and Chemical Engineers,* Theodore William Richards, edited by W. Miles, American Chemical Society, 1976, pp. 407–408.

Sketch by Martin R. Feldman

Lewis Fry Richardson
1881–1953
English physicist and meteorologist

Lewis Fry Richardson was an English physicist with a penchant for trying to solve a wide range of scientific problems using mathematics. During his career as a scientist and educator, Richardson explored mathematical solutions to predict weather, to explain the flow of water through peat, and to identify the origins of war.

Richardson was the youngest of seven children born to David Richardson, a tanner, and his wife, Catherine Fry, who came from a family of corn merchants. Richardson was born on October 11, 1881, in Newcastle upon Tyne. After completing his high school education in 1898, Richardson studied science at Durham College in Newcastle for two years before entering King's College at Cambridge, where he ultimately earned a doctorate in physics and then later returned to study and receive a degree in psychology. After graduating from King's College, Richardson held a number of positions in the years leading up to World War I. These included working as a scientist for a tungsten lamp factory, the National Peat Industries, Ltd., and serving four years as superintendent of the Eskdalemuir Observatory operated by the National Meteorological Office.

Richardson, who was born into a Quaker family, served with the French army as a member of the Friends' Ambulance Unit during the war from 1916 to 1919. Following the end of hostilities, Richardson returned to England, where he combined his scientific inquiry with teaching. In 1920 he accepted a position as director of the physics department at Westminster Training College. This was followed by an appointment as principal of Paisley Technical College in 1929, a post that he held until his retirement in 1940. Retirement allowed Richardson continue his primary love, research.

Attempts to Predict Weather Mathematically

Richardson began his research looking at practical problems, such as examining the flow of water through peat while he worked for the National Peat Industries, Ltd. Using differential equations, Richardson came up with ways to determine water flow that were far more accurate than other methods. His work eventually led to attempts at developing a system of weather prediction based on newly understood knowledge of the upper atmosphere and the roles played by radiation and eddies, or atmospheric currents which move contrary to main air flow. Richardson's work led to the publication of his book, *Weather Prediction by Numerical Process,* in 1922. Richardson's experiences in France during the First World War also inspired him to probe the causes of human conflict using mathematics, and he published a paper in 1919 on the mathematical psychology of war. Eventually, he enlarged upon this early work in the book *Arms and Insecurity* and went on to complete a mathematical study of the world's wars. This work, which resulted in *Statistics of Deadly Quarrels,* examined the causes and magnitude of these conflicts. In his research, Richardson tried to define the relations between countries with mathematical equations.

Richardson's pioneering use of mathematics resulted in him being elected a fellow in the Royal Society in 1926. Richardson married Dorothy Garnett in 1909. The couple adopted a son and two daughters. He died on September 30, 1953.

SELECTED WRITINGS BY RICHARDSON:

Books

Weather Prediction by Numerical Process, Cambridge University Press, 1922.

Arms and Insecurity: A Mathematical Study of the Causes and Origins of War, edited by Nicolas Rashevsky and Ernesto Trucco, Boxwood Press, 1960.

Statistics of Deadly Quarrels, edited by Quincy Wright and C. C. Lienau, Boxwood Press, 1960.

FURTHER READING:

Books

Dictionary of National Biography, Oxford University Press, 1971.

Sketch by Joel Schwarz

Owen W. Richardson
1879–1959
English physicist

Owen W. Richardson is best known for his work in thermionics, the emission of electrons from a heated surface, and specifically for the law that describes that phenomenon, now called Richardson's law. For his work on thermionics, Richardson was awarded the 1928 Nobel Prize in physics. In addition, Richardson's investigations into gyromagnetics led to his theory that a body's magnetism is caused by the movement of its electrons, a phenomenon known as the Richardson-Einstein-de Haas effect.

Owen Willans Richardson was born in Dewsbury, Yorkshire, England, on April 26, 1879. He was the eldest of three children born to Joshua Henry and Charlotte Maria Willans Richardson. Young Owen was a precocious boy and, according to William Wilson in *Biographical Memoirs of Fellows of the Royal Society,* "gained so many scholarships and exhibitions that his education cost his parents nothing at all." That education began at the St. John's Church Day School in Dewsbury, continued at Batley Grammar School in 1841, and then at Trinity College, Cambridge, in 1897. Richardson earned first-class honors in 1900 at Trinity in botany, chemistry, and physics, and was awarded his B.A. degree. He then stayed on at Trinity for his graduate studies in chemistry and physics and, in 1902, was appointed a fellow at the college. Two years later he was chosen for a Clerk Maxwell scholarship and was awarded his D.Sc. by University College, London.

Begins Thermionic Research at Cavendish

Richardson's earliest research dealt with the properties of the electron. As early as 1901 he began the studies for which he was to become most famous, thermionics, a term that Richardson himself coined. The term refers to the emission of electrons from a heated metal. In his first studies, Richardson used platinum metal since it had the highest melting point of any readily available metal, allowing him to heat the material to very high temperatures and observe the emission of electrons. When ductile tungsten (which can be drawn out or hammered down, and

whose melting point is much higher than that of platinum) became available in 1913, Richardson was then able to extend his work to even higher temperatures.

The emission of electrons from heated metals was first described as early as 1603 by Sir William Gilbert, but was not studied systematically until the late nineteenth century. Then, a number of scientists, including Thomas Edison, described a number of phenomena associated with thermionics. In his own studies with platinum metal, Richardson found that the heating of the metal resulted in the loss of a certain number of electrons for each unit area of surface. In addition, the number of electrons lost from the metal increases exponentially with the temperature. He was able to devise a mathematical formula describing these results, a formula now known as Richardson's law. According to that formula, the current released by a metal is a function of certain characteristics of the metal and the temperature. Richardson explained the thermionic phenomenon by assuming that heating a metal provides some electrons on the metal surface with enough energy to overcome the attraction of ions in the metal. These electrons then "evaporate" from the metal surface in much the way that liquid molecules escape from the surface of a liquid.

Becomes Professor of Physics at Princeton

In 1906 Richardson was offered an appointment as professor of physics at Princeton University. Before leaving England, however, he was married to Lilian Maude Wilson, daughter of a goods manager at the North Eastern Railway Company and sister of Richardson's fellow student at the Cavendish, H. A. Wilson. The couple's three children, two sons and a daughter, were all born during Richardson's tenure at Princeton.

Richardson continued his work on thermionic emission during his Princeton years, but also studied other phenomena, including the photoelectric effect, thermodynamics, x rays, and gyromagnetics. The latter term refers to attempts to explain various gravitational effects in terms of electromagnetic theory. Although this effort failed in its broadest goals, one phenomenon he did discover was eventually called the Richardson-Einstein-de Haas effect. This effect relates an object's magnetism to the movement of the object's electrons.

Richardson was just about to become a naturalized citizen of the United States when, in 1913, he was offered the Wheatstone Professorship of Physics at King's College at the University of London. He accepted the offer and returned to England just before the outbreak of World War I. During the war, Richardson worked on the development of more efficient vacuum tubes to be used in military communication systems. At the war's conclusion, Richardson returned to his teaching and research at King's College until 1924, when he was appointed Yarrow Research Professor of the Royal Society. This position relieved him of all teaching responsibilities, and he dedicated the next two decades of his life to research. One of the main foci of this research was an attempt to delineate the connections between chemistry and physics. Even after his retirement from the Royal Society post in 1944, Richardson continued his research activities, publishing his last paper in 1953.

Richardson was awarded the 1928 Nobel Prize in physics for his work on thermionics and was knighted in 1939. He served as president of the Physical Society from 1926 to 1928. After his first wife Lilian died in 1945, Richardson married Henrietta M. G. Rupp, a noted physicist who specialized in electron diffraction and luminescence in solids. Richardson died in Alton, Hampshire, on February 15, 1959.

SELECTED WRITINGS BY RICHARDSON:

Books

The Electron Theory of Matter, Cambridge University Press, 1914.
The Emission of Electricity from Hot Bodies, Longmans Green, 1916.
Molecular Hydrogen and Its Spectrum, Yale University Press, 1934.

Periodicals

Proceedings of the Cambridge Philosophical Society, On the Negative Radiation from Hot Platinum, Volume 11, 1901, pp. 286–295.
Philosophical Transactions A, The Ionisation Produced by Hot Platinum in Different Gases, Volume 207, 1906, pp. 1–64.
Philosophical Magazine, Note on Gravitation; Experimental Test, Volume 43, 1922, pp. 138–145.

FURTHER READING:

Books

Biographical Memoirs of Fellows of the Royal Society, Volume 5, Royal Society (London), 1959, pp. 207–215.
Heathcote, Niels H. de V., *Nobel Prize Winners in Physics, 1901–1950,* Henry Schuman, 1953, pp. 278–286.
Wasson, Tyler, editor, *Nobel Prize Winners,* H. W. Wilson, 1987, pp. 865–867.
Weber, Robert L., *Pioneers of Science: Nobel Prize Winners in Physics,* American Institute of Physics, 1980, pp. 79–81.

Sketch by David E. Newton

Robert C. Richardson
1937–
American physicist

A pioneer in low-temperature physics, Robert C. Richardson received part of the 1996 Nobel Prize in Physics for his role in the work that led to the discovery of superfluidity in helium-3, a rare isotope of helium. He shared the prize with **David M. Lee** and **Douglas D. Osheroff**; their collaboration at Cornell University culminated in their condensation, reported in 1972, of helium-3 to a superfluid state. Superfluidity, an unusual state of matter occurring at extremely low temperatures, close to absolute zero (the lowest possible temperature according to theoretical physics), is a strange phenomenon by everyday standards. For example, a substance in the state of superfluidity will not stay in a cup-like container; it will spontaneously overflow. This behavior, which does not contradict the principles of quantum mechanics, results from the rigid organization of a substance's normally randomly moving atoms, which enables the liquid in superfluid form to flow without any inner resistance. Richardson's important discovery not only shattered the widely held belief that helium-3 could not reach a superfluid state, but also opened new fields of research, both in low-temperature physics and cosmology. Working with Lee, Richardson is currently studying the behavior of metals and other materials at low temperatures.

Richardson was born in Washington, D.C., on June 26, 1937, to Robert Franklin and Lois (Price) Richardson. He married Betty Marilyn McCarthy in 1962; they have two daughters. Having completed his undergraduate studies at Virginia Polytechnic Institute, Richardson earned his B.S. in 1958; two years later, he completed his M.S. After receiving a Ph.D. in physics from Duke University in 1966, he joined the physics department at Cornell University as a research associate. He was named assistant professor of physics in 1969, associate professor in 1972, and full professor in 1975. He became Floyd R. Newman Professor of Physics in 1987, and assumed the directorship of Cornell's Laboratory of Atomic and Solid State Physics three years later. In addition, Richardson has served as a member of the editorial board of the *Journal of Low Temperature Physics* since 1984.

Participates in Historic Discovery

At Cornell, Richardson and Lee conducted experiments in an effort to investigate the behavior of substances at the lowest possible temperatures, just thousandths of a degree above absolute zero. As senior researchers, the scientists included Douglas Osheroff, a graduate student, in their team. In the late 1960s, Richardson and his colleagues, who had constructed their own cooling apparatus, experimented with frozen helium-3, hoping to identify a phase transition to a magnetic order. The outcome, however, was quite different. The team discovered helium-3 in a superfluid state, a discovery which not only significantly enhanced research in condensed-matter physics, but also suggested new ideas to cosmologists, who, using the behavior of superfluid helium-3 as a model, proposed new theories about the genesis of the universe, and suggested possible parallels between the hypothetical behavior of helium-3 a fraction of a second after the Big Bang and particular processes obtained in a laboratory.

A recipient of the John Simon Guggenheim Fellowship in 1975 and 1982, Richardson is a member of the National Academy of Sciences. In 1981, he was elected Fellow of the American Association for the Advancement of Science; two years later, Richardson became a Fellow of the American Physical Society. In 1976, Richardson and his two colleagues shared the Sir Francis Simon Memorial Prize, given by Britain's Institute of Physics. The three scientists also received the 1980 Oliver E. Buckley Solid State Physics Prize from the American Physical Society for their successful research in superfluidity.

SELECTED WRITINGS BY RICHARDSON:

Books

(With Eric N. Smith, et al.) *Experimental Techniques in Condensed Matter Physics at Low Temperature.* Addison-Wesley, 1988.

Periodicals

"Low Temperature Science–What Remains for the Physicist?" *Physics Today* (August 1981): 46.

FURTHER READING:

Books

Leggett, A. J. *The Problems of Physics.* Oxford: Oxford University Press, 1987.

Periodicals

Browne, Malcolm W. "Discoveries of Superfluid Helium, and 'Buckyballs,' Earn Nobels for 6 Scientists." *New York Times* (10 October 1996): D21.

Lounasmaa, O. V., and G. R. Pickett. "The ^{3}He Superfluids." *Scientific American* (June 1990): 104-11.

Peterson, Ivars. "Superfluidity Finding Earn Physics Nobel." *Science News* 150, no. 16 (19 October 1996): 247.

Special Issue: He3 and He4. *Physics Today* (February 1987).

Other

Nobel Foundation WWW Server Posting (9 October 1996). http://www.nobel.ki.se

Sketch by Jane Stewart Cook and Zoran Minderovic

Charles Robert Richet
1850–1935
French physiologist

The French physiologist Charles Robert Richet won the 1913 Nobel Prize for his discovery of a nonprotective, toxic immune system process which he called anaphylaxis, a process related to the shock and allergic reactions which occur when foreign substances are injected into the body. Richet also tried to develop treatments for tuberculosis and to discover a serum to prevent tuberculosis. He was noted for his varied interests in scientific as well as non-scientific activities. He wrote poetry, novels, and plays, and for thirty years he studied and wrote about hypnotism, parapsychology, telepathy, and extrasensory perception. In 1890, he participated in an early attempt to design an airplane. He was a pacifist who was outspoken on social and political issues, and he wrote on the subject of vivisection.

Richet was born August 26, 1850, in Paris. His father, Alfred Richet, taught surgery at the University of Paris. His mother was Eugénie Rouard. After secondary school, Richet decided he wanted to practice medicine. He enrolled in the University of Paris medical school, but he soon found that he was more interested in research than in applied medicine. He also weighed the possibilities of a career in the humanities, and although he chose science instead, he maintained an active interest in literary, philosophical, and political subjects throughout his life.

In 1877 he received his medical degree. As a medical student he did research on hypnotism, digestive tract fluids, and the function of the nerves and muscles in the presence of pain. He quickly went on to obtain his degree as a doctor of science in 1878. In his doctoral thesis Richet showed that various forms of animal and marine life contain stomach hydrochloric acid. He also found the presence of a form of lactic acid in the human stomach. In that same year, he was appointed to the medical faculty of the University of Paris. With this appointment Richet focused his attention on the different ways the muscles contract.

After doing research in 1883 on heat maintenance in warm-blooded animals and the distribution of bacteria in the body fluids (an outgrowth of his work on the digestive system), in 1887 Richet began to work on the problem of creating a serum that could protect an animal against specific diseases. He followed the work of Louis Pasteur, who in 1880 found a way of protecting chickens from coming down with fowl cholera by injecting them with a weak form of the cholera microbe. The injection of the serum containing the weakened forms of the microbes created an antidote in the body that could then later fight off an invasion from a stronger force of the microbes. The injected serum contained the antigen, and the body receiving the injection produced the antibody.

Richet did extensive work in the development of techniques for immunization with his collaborator, Jules Hericourt. Over a ten-year period, Richet and Hericourt tried to develop a serum for tuberculosis, without any success. They were frustrated by the fact that **Emil Behring** had shown positive results for the development of an immunization serum for diphtheria during the same period of time.

Develops Concept of Anaphylaxis

In 1902 Richet was drawn to the problem of shock or allergic reactions in people after they received inoculations of disease-fighting serum. He noticed that some animals who had received a dosage of immunization serum would go into fatal shock when a second shot was administered. He found that the antibody produced by the first shot did not protect the animals against the second shot. The animal was now in a state of hypersensitivity caused by the production of too many antibodies against the foreign intruder. Richet called this condition anaphylaxis, a Greek word that means overprotection.

By 1906 the word allergy had been introduced to describe a wide range of adverse reactions to the use of antiserums and later antibiotics. The term also came into use to describe reactions to plants, animals, foods, chemicals, and many other substances. These substances fall into the category of antigens, meaning foreign substances that cause the immune system to produce antibodies, and they could therefore be understood in terms of Richet's concept of anaphylaxis. Richet was, therefore, a pioneer in the field of medicine dealing with the prevention and treatment of allergies.

For his development of the concept of anaphylaxis, Richet won the 1913 Nobel Prize. In his acceptance speech for the Nobel Prize, Richet acknowledged the difficulties anaphylaxis causes individuals, but he emphasized its biological significance in insuring the chemical integrity of the species. Such an argument was rooted in his philosophy of biological teleology, a view that maintains that there is a purpose in every biological process for the species concerned.

Richet married Amélie Aubry in 1877. The Richets had five sons and two daughters. In 1926 Richet received the Cross of the Legion of Honor from France for his work during World War I studying the problems of blood plasma transfusion. He died in Paris on December 3, 1935.

SELECTED WRITINGS BY RICHET:

Books

Des circonvolutions cérébrales, 1878, translation by E. Fowler, W. Wood, 1879.
Peace and War, 1906.
The Pros and Cons of Vivisection, 1908.
L'anaphylaxic, 1911.
Idiot Man, 1925
The Natural History of a Savant, G. H. Doran, 1927, translation by Oliver Lodge, Arno Press, 1975.
The Importance of Man, 1928.
Our Sixth Sense, 1929.
The Story of Civilization Through the Ages, 1930.

Periodicals

Archives de physiologie normale et pathologique, Contribution à la physiologie des centres nerveux et des muscles de l'écrevisse, second series, Volume 6, 1879, pp. 262–84, 522–76.
Annales de l'Institut Pasteur, De l'anaphylaxie en général et de l'anaphylaxie par le mytilo-congestine en particulier, Volume 21, 1907, pp. 497–534.

FURTHER READING:

Books

Berger, Arthur S., and Joyce Berger, *Encyclopedia of Parapsychology and Psychical Research,* Paragon, 1991.
Berger, Arthur S., and Joyce Berger, *Nobel Prize Winners,* Wilson, 1987, pp. 867–69.
Berger, Arthur S., and Joyce Berger, *A Biographical Dictionary of Scientists,* Wiley, 1982, p. 443.
Wolf, Stewart, *Brain, Mind, and Medicine: Charles Richet and the Origins of Physiological Psychology,* Transaction, 1993.

Sketch by Jordan P. Richman

Burton Richter
1931–
American physicist

Burton Richter is a physicist at Stanford University who was largely responsible for the design of the eight-billion electron-volt accelerator called the Stanford Positron-Electron Accelerating Ring (SPEAR). Designed to cause collisions between electrons and positrons at almost unprecedented energy levels, SPEAR allowed scientists to perform experiments in 1974 that resulted in the discovery of an entirely new and unexpected particle, which Richter named psi (ψ). The discovery had revolutionary implications for particle physics; the lifetime of the psi-particle was many thousands of times longer than other particles, which indicated that it possessed a previously undiscovered property of matter. At almost the same time Richter made his discovery, **Samuel C. C. Ting**, working at the Massachusetts Institute of Technology (MIT), discovered the same particle using a different method. The two men were jointly awarded the Nobel Prize in physics in 1976.

Richter was born in Brooklyn, New York, on March 22, 1931. He was the oldest child and only son of Abraham Richter, a textile worker, and Fannie (Pollack) Richter. Burton attended Far Rockaway High School in Queens and Mercersburg Academy in Mercersburg, Pennsylvania. In 1948, he entered MIT, where he hesitated between studying chemistry and physics. His choice was determined by one of his professors, Francis Friedman, who "opened my eyes to the beauty of physics," as Richter is quoted as saying in *Current Biography*. At MIT, Richter worked with both Francis Bitter and Martin Deutsch, writing his senior thesis on the effect of external magnetic fields on the hydrogen spectrum.

After receiving his B.S. in 1952, Richter stayed on at Bitter's laboratory as a research assistant and doctoral student. His first assignment there was to find a way of producing a short-lived isotope of mercury, mercury–197, which he accomplished by bombarding gold foil with deuterons from the MIT cyclotron. The task accomplished, Richter found that he was interested in further work with particle accelerators. Physicist David Frisch provided him with the opportunity to work with one of the world's most powerful accelerators, the cosmotron at the Brookhaven National Laboratory. In 1953, Richter spent six months pursuing his interest in accelerators. After returning to MIT, Richter began his doctoral research on the production of pi-mesons in MIT's own synchrotron accelerator. He received his Ph.D. in 1956.

Richter accepted an appointment as a research assistant at Stanford University in 1956. This decision was based on his interest in pursuing research on quantum electrodynamics (QED), the modern version of electromagnetic theory. In particular, he wanted to find out if QED was valid at very small distances, such as those corresponding to the dimensions of the atomic nucleus. The 700-million-electron-volt linear accelerator at Stanford was, Richter later wrote in an edition of the University's *Stanford Linear Accelerator Beam Line,* "the perfect device with which to do an experiment on electron-electron scattering which I had been considering." He carried out these studies over the next decade, discovering that QED is indeed valid to distances of at least the diameter of an atomic nucleus, about 10^{-14} centimeter.

Uses Colliding Beams to Discover the Psi-Particle

Even before the QED experiments had been completed, Richter began thinking about another approach to accelerator design. In all accelerators built at that time, particles were accelerated and caused to collide with a stationary target. There was, however, a major limitation to this approach: a large fraction of the energy of the incident beam was lost in the kinetic energy of particles produced in the collision. Richter realized that a more efficient way to study particle collisions would be to have two particle beams collide with each other while travelling in opposite directions. In 1970, Richter obtained funding for the machine he had in mind, the Stanford Positron-Electron Accelerating Ring (SPEAR). Three years later, SPEAR was in operation; with it, Richter was able to make what is considered one of the most important discoveries concerning elementary particles.

In this experiment, two concentric beams of particles, one of electrons and one of positrons, traveled around the circumference of the SPEAR accelerator. At a particular moment, the paths of the two beams were diverted and the particles allowed to collide. A fraction of the enormous energy released in this collision was converted into particles that do not exist at lower energy levels. One of these particles had never been observed before and had dramatically unexpected properties. It was about three times as massive as a proton with a lifetime about 5,000 times greater than would have been predicted for such a particle. Richter named the particle psi. Coincidentally, an identical discovery using a totally different approach was made at almost the same time on the other side of the continent. At the Brookhaven National Laboratory, a research team led by Ting discovered the same particle and gave it the name *J*. Richter and Ting made a joint announcement of their discoveries on November 11, 1974, at Stanford. Two years later, the two were awarded the Nobel Prize in physics for the discovery of the particle, now generally called the J/psi.

The primary significance of the J/psi discovery was the questions it raised. Traditional physical theory, which postulated the existence of three kinds of fundamental particles called quarks, was unable to explain the J/psi particle's peculiar properties. However, the discovery was consistent with a prediction made by American physicist **Sheldon Lee Glashow** in 1964; he had theorized that a previously unknown property, which he called charm, was needed to describe fully the properties of at least some elementary particles. The application of Glashow's theory to the J/psi particle was confirmed, and it is now widely accepted that the particle consists of a fourth quark.

Richter has remained at Stanford throughout his academic career. He was promoted to assistant professor in 1959, associate professor in 1963, and full professor in 1967. Since 1980, he has been Paul Pigott Professor of Physical Sciences. In 1975, he received the E. O. Lawrence Memorial Award from the U.S. Energy Research and Development Agency. In addition to his many awards and honors, Richter was Loeb Lecturer at Harvard University in

1974, De Sholit Lecturer at the Weizmann Institute in Israel in 1975, and visiting researcher at the European Center for Nuclear Research in Geneva from 1975 to 1976. Richter married Laurose Becker, an administrative assistant at Stanford, on July 1, 1960; the Richters have a daughter and a son.

SELECTED WRITINGS BY RICHTER:

Books

Instabilities in Stored Particle Beams, CFSTI, 1965.

Periodicals

U.S. Atomic Energy Commission SLAC-PUB–501, Two-body Photoproduction, 1968, pp. 1–57.
Proceedings of the 17th International Conference on High Energy Physics, Plenary Report on e (+) e (-) Hadrons, 1974, pp. 20–35.
Stanford Linear Accelerator Beam Line, A Scientific Autobiography, November, 1976.

FURTHER READING:

Books

Current Biography 1977, H. W. Wilson, 1977, pp. 359–362.
Nobel Prize Winners, H. W. Wilson, 1987, pp. 869–871.
Weber, Robert L., *Pioneers of Science: Nobel Prize Winners in Physics,* American Institute of Physics, 1980, pp. 245–246.

Periodicals

Bjorken, J. D., *Science,* The 1976 Nobel Prize in Physics, November 19, 1976, pp. 825–826, 865–866.
Bjorken, J. D., *Physics Today,* Nobel Prize to Richter and Ting for Discovery of J/psi, December, 1976, p. 17.

Sketch by David E. Newton

Charles F. Richter

Charles F. Richter
1900–1985
American seismologist

Charles F. Richter is remembered every time an earthquake happens. With German-born seismologist **Beno Gutenberg**, Richter developed the scale that bears his name and measures the magnitude of earthquakes. Richter was a pioneer in seismological research at a time when data on the size and location of earthquakes were scarce. He authored two textbooks that are still used as references in the field and are regarded by many scientists as his greatest contribution, exceeding the more popular Richter scale. Devoted to his work all his life, Richter at one time had a seismograph installed in his living room, and he welcomed queries about earthquakes at all hours. Charles Francis Richter was born on April 26, 1900, on a farm near Hamilton, Ohio, north of Cincinnati. His parents were divorced when he was very young. He grew up with his maternal grandfather, who moved the family to Los Angeles in 1909. Richter went to a preparatory school associated with the University of Southern California, where he spent his freshman year in college. He then transferred to Stanford University, where he earned an A.B. degree in physics in 1920.

Richter received his Ph.D. in theoretical physics from the California Institute of Technology (Caltech) in 1928. That same year he married Lillian Brand of Los Angeles, a creative writing teacher. **Robert A. Millikan**, a Nobel Prize-winning physicist and president of Caltech, had already offered Richter a job at the newly established Seismological Laboratory in Pasadena, then managed by the Carnegie Institution of Washington. Thus Richter started applying his physics background to the study of the earth.

Develops the Richter-Gutenberg Scale

As a young research assistant, Richter made his name early when he began a decades-long collaboration with Beno Gutenberg, who was then the director of the laboratory. In the early 1930s the pair were one of several groups of scientists around the world who were trying to establish a standard way to measure and compare earthquakes. The seismological laboratory at Caltech was planning to issue regular reports on southern California earthquakes, so the Gutenberg-Richter study was especially important. They needed to be able to catalog several hundred quakes a year with an objective and reliable scale.

At the time, the only way to rate shocks was a scale developed in 1902 by the Italian priest and geologist Giuseppe Mercalli. The Mercalli scale classified earthquakes from 1 to 12, depending on how buildings and people responded to the tremor. A shock that set chandeliers swinging might rate as a 1 or 2 on this scale, while one that destroyed huge buildings and created panic in a crowded city might count as a 10. The obvious problem with the Mercalli scale was that it relied on subjective measures of how well a building had been constructed and how used to these sorts of crises the population was. The Mercalli scale also made it difficult to rate earthquakes that happened in remote, sparsely populated areas.

The scale developed by Richter and Gutenberg, which became known by Richter's name only, was instead an absolute measure of an earthquake's intensity. Richter used a seismograph—an instrument generally consisting of a constantly unwinding roll of paper, anchored to a fixed place, and a pendulum or magnet suspended with a marking device above the roll—to record actual earth motion during an earthquake. The scale takes into account the instrument's distance from the epicenter, or the point on the ground that is directly above the earthquake's origin. Richter chose to use the term "magnitude" to describe an earthquake's strength because of his early interest in astronomy; stargazers use the word to describe the brightness of stars. Gutenberg suggested that the scale be logarithmic, so that a quake of magnitude 7 would be ten times stronger than a 6, a hundred times stronger than a 5, and a thousand times stronger than a 4. (The 1989 Loma Prieta earthquake that shook San Francisco was magnitude 7.1.)

The Richter scale was published in 1935 and immediately became the standard measure of earthquake intensity. Richter did not seem concerned that Gutenberg's name was not included at first; but in later years, after Gutenberg was already dead, Richter began to insist that his colleague be recognized for expanding the scale to apply to earthquakes all over the globe, not just in southern California. Since 1935, several other magnitude scales have been developed. Depending on what data is available, different ones are used, but all are popularly known by Richter's name.

A Storehouse of Seismological Knowledge

For several decades Richter and Gutenberg worked together to monitor seismic activity around the world. In the late 1930s they applied their scale to deep earthquakes, ones that originate more than 185 miles below the ground, which rank particularly high on the Richter scale—8 or greater. In 1941 they published a textbook, *Seismicity of the Earth,* which in its revised edition became a standard reference book in the field. They worked on locating the epicenters of all the major earthquakes and classifying them into geographical groups. All his life, however, Richter warned that seismological records only reflect what people have measured in populated areas and are not a true representative sample of what shocks have actually occurred. He long remained skeptical of some scientists' claims that they could predict earthquakes.

Richter remained at Caltech for his entire career, except for a visit to the University of Tokyo from 1959 to 1960 as a Fulbright scholar. He became involved in promoting good earthquake building codes, while at the same time discouraging the overestimation of the dangers of an earthquake in a populated area like Los Angeles. He pointed out that statistics reveal freeway driving to be much more dangerous than living in an earthquake zone. He often lectured on how loss of life and property damage were largely avoidable during an earthquake, with proper training and building codes—he opposed building anything higher than thirty stories, for example. In the early 1960s, the city of Los Angeles listened to Richter and began to remove extraneous, but potentially dangerous, ornaments and cornices from its buildings. Los Angeles suffered a major quake in February of 1971, and city officials credited Richter with saving many lives. Richter was also instrumental in establishing the Southern California Seismic Array, a network of instruments that has helped scientists track the origin and intensity of earthquakes, as well as map their frequency much more accurately. His diligent study resulted in what has been called one of the most accurate and complete catalogs of earthquake activity, the Caltech catalog of California earthquakes.

Later in his career, Richter would recall several major earthquakes. The 1933 Long Beach earthquake was one, which he felt while working late at Caltech one night. That quake caused the death of 120 people in the then sparsely populated southern California town; it cost the Depression-era equivalent of $150 million in damages. Nobel Prize-winning physicist Albert Einstein was in town for a seminar when the earthquake struck, according to a March 8, 1981, story in the *San Francisco Chronicle.* Einstein and a colleague of Richter's were crossing the campus at the time of the quake, so engrossed in discussion that they were oblivious to the swaying trees. Richter also remembered the three great quakes that struck in 1906, when he was a six-year-old on the Ohio farm. That year, San Francisco suffered an 8.3 quake, Colombia and Ecuador had an 8.9, and Chile had an 8.6.

In 1958 Richter published his text *Elementary Seismology,* which was derived from the lectures he faithfully taught to Caltech undergraduates as well as decades of earthquake study. Many scientists consider this textbook to be Richter's greatest contribution, since he never published many scientific papers in professional journals. *Elementary Seismology* contained descriptions of major historical earthquakes, tables and charts, and subjects ranging from the nature of earthquake motion to earthquake insurance and building construction. Richter's colleagues maintained that he put everything he knew into it. The book was used in many countries.

Earthquakes in His Living Room

In the 1960s, Richter had a seismograph installed in his living room so that he could monitor quakes at any time. He draped the seismographic records—long rolls of paper covered with squiggly lines—over the backs of the living room chairs. (His wife, Richter maintained, considered the seismograph a conversation piece.) He would answer press queries at any hour of the night and never seemed tired of talking about his work. Sometimes he grew obsessive about speaking to the press; when a tremor happened during Caltech working hours, Richter made sure he would be the one answering calls—he put the lab's phone in his lap.

Richter devoted his entire life to seismology. He even learned Russian, Italian, French, Spanish, and German, as well as a little Japanese, in order to read scientific papers in their original languages. His dedication to his work was complete; in fact, he became enraged at any slight on it. For instance, at his retirement party from Caltech in 1970, some laboratory researchers sang a clever parody about the Richter scale. Richter was furious at the implication that his work could be considered a joke. During his lifetime he enjoyed a good deal of public and professional recognition, including membership in the American Academy of Arts and Sciences and a stint as president of the Seismological Society of America, but he was never elected to the National Academy of Sciences. After his retirement Richter helped start a seismic consulting firm that evaluated buildings for the government, for public utilities such as the Los Angeles Department of Water and Power, and for private businesses.

Richter enjoyed listening to classical music, reading science fiction, and watching the television series *Star Trek.* One of his great pleasures, ever since he grew up walking in the southern California mountains, was taking long solitary hikes. He preferred to camp by himself, far away from other people. But being alone had its drawbacks; once, he encountered a curious brown bear, which he chased away by loudly singing a raunchy song. After his marriage Richter continued his solo hikes, particularly at Christmas, when he and his wife would go their separate ways for a while. At these times Lillian indulged in her interest in foreign travel. The couple had no children. A little-known fact about them, according to Richter's obituary in the *Los Angeles Times,* is that they were nudists. Lillian died in 1972. Richter died in Pasadena on September 30, 1985, of congestive heart failure.

SELECTED WRITINGS BY RICHTER:

Books

Seismicity of the Earth, The Society, 1941, revised edition, Princeton University Press, 1954.

Elementary Seismology, Freeman, 1958.

FURTHER READING:

Books

Current Biography, H. W. Wilson, 1975, November, 1985.

Periodicals

Los Angeles Times, October 1, 1985.
Los Angeles Times Home Magazine, May 11, 1980.
Pasadena Star-News, May 13, 1991.
San Francisco Chronicle, March 8, 1981.

Sketch by Alexandra Witze

Hyman G. Rickover
1900–1986
American nuclear engineer

Hyman G. Rickover was a charismatic and visionary United States naval officer who gained international fame as the principal architect of the nuclear navy. Although Rickover had an unusual early naval career—his ascension to senior service leadership did not follow the more conventional path from a sea command—he emerged during World War II as the head of the electrical section of the Bureau of Ships. This post allowed Navy Department leaders to view Rickover's effective maneuvering in the complex political environment of military bureaucracy. It also provided Rickover a jumping-off point for pursuing what became a lifelong ambition, the development of larger and more dominant naval vessels powered by nuclear reactors.

For more than thirty years Rickover headed the Navy's nuclear program. From this position he transformed the Navy from one propelled by coal and diesel to one in which nuclear reactors were used as power plants for most of the major warships, including the increasingly significant submarine fleet. At the same time, he worked to reorient the skills of naval officers along more technological lines. In the process, Rickover was largely responsible for creating one of the key weapons employed by the United States during its Cold War with the former Soviet Union.

Early Life, Entrance to Annapolis, and Early Naval Career

Hyman George Rickover was born on January 27, 1900, in Russian-occupied Poland, the son of Abraham and

Hyman G. Rickover

Rachel Unger Rickover. During the Russian anti-Jewish pogroms in the first decade of the century, the Rickovers traveled along with thousands of other immigrants to the United States. The family settled initially in New York City and set up a tailor shop. In 1910 they moved to Chicago, a city with a substantial Polish population, and it was there that young Rickover grew to maturity. As a boy in the public schools he was a good student—graduating with honors from John Marshall High School—but the family did not have the money to send him to college, and it appeared for a time that he would have to follow his father into the tailoring trade.

To help his son attend college, Abraham Rickover obtained the sponsorship of the local congressman for his son's appointment to the U.S. Naval Academy at Annapolis. Although he was once again a good student, Rickover was not well liked by his fellow midshipmen. He believed in later years that his Jewish, immigrant, and impoverished background aroused the prejudices of his classmates, and that nothing he could have done would have brought acceptance. Rickover's classmates, on the other hand, thought him too introverted and bookish and a difficult person to like. Rickover soon gave up trying to fit in and concentrated on mastering technical disciplines at Annapolis. His unpopularity among the midshipmen awakened a strong compensation impulse, and Rickover commented in later years on how committed he was to success in the Navy because of his treatment. On the strength of his academic abilities he graduated 107th out of a class of 540 in 1922.

After accepting his commission, Rickover was assigned to the destroyer *La Vallette,* but within a short time he transferred to the battleship *Nevada.* In both assignments he refrained from social activities, kept to himself, and rigorously studied engineering and mathematics; on the *Nevada,* Rickover earned honors for excelling at his work.

In the late 1920s, Rickover applied for shore duty so he could continue formal studies. Having persuaded the Navy to send him to Columbia University to complete a master of science degree in electrical engineering, he graduated in 1929 and immediately went to submarine school at New London, Connecticut, where he became a convert to the merits of the "silent service." For three years after completing this school Rickover served aboard the submarines S–9 and S–48. This experience reinforced his impression that submarines represented an important change in naval combat and deserved a greater role in the overall order of battle.

In 1933 Rickover returned to shore duty, where he was assigned to the Office of the Inspector of Naval Material in Philadelphia, Pennsylvania. Two years later he was sent as an engineering officer to the USS *New Mexico,* then, in 1937, he was reassigned as commander of the *Finch,* an old minesweeper used to tow gunnery targets. Rickover was so dissatisfied with this assignment that he requested shore duty as an electrical engineer. As punishment for this request, in the fall of 1937 the Navy sent him as an "EDO" (engineering duty only) to the Cavite Navy Yard in the Philippine Islands. At the same time that most of his Annapolis classmates were entering command positions, Rickover seemed to be mired in staff and technical positions with little hope of receiving a major command.

Events began to change in 1939, however, when Rickover returned to the United States for assignment to the Bureau of Ships at the Navy Department in Washington, D.C. This proved to be a significant move for Rickover, as—throughout most of World War II—he headed the bureau's electrical section, directing improvements in the design and implementation of electrical systems. In this capacity he led efforts to maintain "shock-proof" electrical equipment on ships, reduce noise on submarines, and develop underwater detectors and infrared signaling devices. After a three-month stint on temporary duty with the staff of the Commander Service Force of the U.S. Pacific Fleet, Rickover was assigned in 1945 as industrial manager and commanding officer of the Naval Repair Base at Okinawa. He held these positions until the end of the year, when he was assigned as inspector general of the Nineteenth Fleet headquartered at San Francisco, California.

Builds First Nuclear Submarine

Rickover's work with the Bureau of Ships during World War II led directly to his assignment in 1946 to a team which explored the use of nuclear energy for use on ships (work done as part of the Manhattan Project at its Oak Ridge, Tennessee, facility). The team's report recommended the construction of a nuclear submarine, and although this report was tabled by the Navy Department, the effort set the stage for the rest of Rickover's career. On his return to Washington, D.C., in 1947 Rickover resumed his campaign, and by the end of the year he had convinced the chief of naval operations, Admiral Chester A. Nimitz, of the viability of the atomic submarine. Support from the Atomic Energy Commission (AEC) and subsequent appointments as head of the Naval Reactors Branch at the AEC and the Nuclear Power Branch at the Bureau of Ships enabled him to bring his plans to fruition. Throughout the rest of the 1940s the AEC worked on the design and construction of a suitable reactor while Rickover and his staff evolved a scheme for the rest of the vessel.

A breakthrough for Rickover's efforts came in 1950 when he persuaded President Harry S. Truman to formally approve the construction of the first nuclear-powered submarine, the *Nautilus;* thereafter, Rickover presided over an impressive crash program to build the vessel. Pulling together some of the best personnel from the military, the government, industry, and academia, he worked toward the delivery of the new submarine by 1954 on a modest budget of forty million dollars. In 1952 the Navy laid the keel for the *Nautilus,* with Truman giving the keynote address. When the *Nautilus* was launched on January 21, 1954, it confirmed Truman's expectations. Much larger than ordinary submarines, the *Nautilus* was 319 feet long and displaced 3,180 tons. It could also remain underwater for prolonged periods and travel at a speed in excess of twenty knots or nautical miles. This craft set a baseline for the performance of all future submarines built by the U.S. Navy with its impressive submerged mission of August 1–5, 1958, under the polar cap between Alaska and Greenland.

While work on the *Nautilus* was underway, Rickover established an atomic submarine school at the Massachusetts Institute of Technology. Recruiting officers from the regular submarine fleet, he trained them over a three-year course for their new duties aboard nuclear submarines. This training effort reinforced for Rickover a long-held perception that naval officers were inadequately prepared by the academy for service in highly technical fields like nuclear energy. He began a crusade to revamp the Naval Academy's curriculum, expanding it essentially on his own to emphasize the skills necessary to serve in the nuclear navy. He followed this with a similar effort at other service schools and with the overall educational system. Three books he wrote in the late 1950s and early 1960s—*Education and Freedom, Swiss Schools and Ours: Why Theirs Are Better,* and *American Education: A National Failure*—each dealt with the necessity of expanding the educational base in the United States and emphasizing science and technology in the curriculum.

In the following years Rickover continued to expand his base of power within the Navy from his position as head of the Navy's nuclear program. He designed a nuclear aircraft carrier and other seagoing vessels that could be powered by reactors, and also championed and built land-based nuclear power stations. As time progressed Rickover—who had never served in combat or commanded any

ship more important than a target towing barge—assumed power within the Navy to the extent that he personally chose commanders of nuclear vessels. Reaching mandatory retirement age in the early 1960s, Rickover was retained on active duty and remained in uniform for another twenty years as the director of the Division of Nuclear Reactors. In 1982, Secretary of the Navy John Lehman forced Rickover into retirement after a career which almost single-handedly brought the Navy into the nuclear age. Rickover died on July 8, 1986, in Washington, D.C., leaving a wife, Ruth Dorothy Masters, and a son.

SELECTED WRITINGS BY RICKOVER:

Books

Education and Freedom, E. P. Dutton, 1959.
Swiss Schools and Ours: Why Theirs Are Better, Little, Brown, 1962.
American Education: A National Failure, E. P. Dutton, 1963.
Liberty, Science, and Law, Newcomen Society in North America, 1969.
Eminent Americans: Namesakes of the Polaris Submarine Fleet, Government Printing Office, 1972.
How the Battleship Maine Was Destroyed, Government Printing Office, 1976.
No Holds Barred: The Final Congressional Testimony of Admiral Hyman Rickover, Center for the Study of Responsive Law, 1982.

FURTHER READING:

Books

Blair, Clay, *The Atomic Submarine and Admiral Rickover,* Holt, 1954.
David, Heather M., *Admiral Rickover and the Nuclear Navy,* Putnam, 1970.
Duncan, Francis, *Rickover and the Nuclear Navy: The Discipline of Technology,* Naval Institute Press, 1990.
Lewis, Eugene, *Leadership and Innovation: A Biographical Perspective on Entrepreneurs in Government,* Hyman G. Rickover, edited by Jameson W. Doig and Erwin C. Hargrove, Johns Hopkins University Press, 1987.
Lewis, Eugene, *Public Entrepreneurship: Toward a Theory of Bureaucratic Political Power: The Organizational Lives of Hyman Rickover, J. Edgar Hoover, and Robert Moses,* Indiana University Press, 1980.
Polmar, Norman, and Thomas B. Allen, *Rickover,* Simon & Schuster, 1982.
Tyler, Patrick, *Running Critical: The Silent War: Rickover and General Dynamics,* Harper, 1986.

Sketch by Roger D. Launius

Sally Ride
1951–
American astronaut and physicist

Sally Ride is best known as the first American woman sent into outer space. She also served the National Aeronautics and Space Administration (NASA) in an advisory capacity, being the only astronaut chosen for President Ronald Reagan's Rogers Commission investigating the mid-launch explosion of the space shuttle *Challenger* in January, 1986, writing official recommendation reports, and creating NASA's Office of Exploration. Both scientist and professor, she has served as a fellow at the Stanford University Center for International Security and Arms Control, a member of the board of directors at Apple Computer Inc., and a space institute director and physics professor at the University of California at San Diego. Ride has chosen to write primarily for children about space travel and exploration. Her commitment to educating the young earned her the Jefferson Award for Public Service from the American Institute for Public Service in 1984, in addition to her National Spaceflight Medals recognizing her two groundbreaking shuttle missions in 1983 and 1984. Newly elected president Bill Clinton chose her as a member of his transition team during the fall of 1992.

Sally Kristen Ride is the older daughter of Dale Burdell and Carol Joyce (Anderson) Ride of Encino, California, and was born May 26, 1951. As author Karen O'Connor describes tomboy Ride in her young reader's book, *Sally Ride and the New Astronauts,* Sally would race her dad for the sports section of the newspaper when she was only five years old. An active, adventurous, yet also scholarly family, the Rides traveled throughout Europe for a year when Sally was nine and her sister Karen was seven, after Dale took a sabbatical from his political science professorship at Santa Monica Community College. While Karen was inspired to become a minister, in the spirit of her parents, who were elders in their Presbyterian church, Ride's own developing taste for exploration would eventually lead her to apply to the space program almost on a whim. "I don't know why I wanted to do it," she confessed to *Newsweek* prior to embarking on her first spaceflight.

The opportunity was serendipitous, since the year she began job-hunting marked the first time NASA had opened its space program to applicants since the late 1960s, and the very first time women would not be excluded from consideration. NASA needed to cast a wider net than ever before, as *Current Biography* disclosed in 1983. The program paid less than private sector counterparts and offered no particular research specialties, unlike most job opportunities in academia. All it took was a return reply postcard, and Ride was in the mood to take those risks. This was, after all, a young lady who could patch up a disabled Toyota with Scotch tape without breaking stride, as one of

Sally Ride

her friends once discovered. Besides, she had always forged her own way before with the full support of her open-minded family.

Student Sets Own Agenda

From her earliest years in school, Ride was so proficient and efficient at once, she proved to be an outright annoyance to some of her teachers. Though she was a straight-A student, she was easily bored, and her brilliance only came to the fore in high school, when she was introduced to the world of science by her physiology teacher. The impact of this mentor, Dr. Elizabeth Mommaerts, was so profound that Ride would later dedicate her first book primarily to her, as well as the fallen crew of the *Challenger.* While she was adaptable to all forms of sport, playing tennis was Ride's most outstanding talent, which she had developed since the age of ten. Under the tutelage of a four-time U.S. Open champion, Ride eventually ranked eighteenth nationally on the junior circuit. Her ability won her a partial scholarship to Westlake School for Girls, a prep school in Los Angeles. After graduating from there in 1968, Ride preferred to work on her game full time instead of the physics program at Swarthmore College, Pennsylvania, where she had originally enrolled. It was only after Ride had fully tested her dedication to the game that she decided against a professional career, even though tennis pro Billie Jean King had once told her it was within her grasp. Back in California as an undergraduate student at Stanford University, Ride followed her burgeoning love for Shakespeare to a double major, receiving B.S. and B.A. degrees in tandem by 1973. She narrowed her focus to physics for her masters, also from Stanford, awarded in 1975. Work toward her dissertation continued at Stanford; she submitted "The Interaction of X-Rays with the Interstellar Medium" in 1978.

Ride was just finishing her Ph.D. candidacy in physics, astronomy, and astrophysics at Stanford, working as a research assistant, when she got the call from NASA. She became one of thirty-five chosen from an original field of applicants numbering eight thousand for the spaceflight training of 1978. "Why I was selected remains a complete mystery," she later admitted to John Grossmann in a 1985 interview in *Health*. "None of us has ever been told." Even after three years of studying x-ray astrophysics, Ride had to go back to the classroom to gain skills to be part of a team of astronauts. The program included basic science and math, meteorology, guidance, navigation, and computers as well as flight training on a T–38 jet trainer and other operational simulations. Ride was selected as part of the ground-support crew for the second (November, 1981) and third (March, 1982) shuttle flights, her duties including the role of "capcom," or capsule communicator, relaying commands from the ground to the shuttle crew. These experiences prepared her to be an astronaut.

A Series of NASA Firsts

Ride would subsequently become, at thirty-one, the youngest person sent into orbit as well as the first American woman in space, the first American woman to make two spaceflights, and, coincidentally, the first astronaut to marry another astronaut in active duty. She and Steven Alan Hawley were married at the groom's family home in Kansas on July 26, 1982. Hawley, a Ph.D. from the University of California, had joined NASA with a background in astronomy and astrophysics. When asked during a hearing by Congressman Larry Winn, Jr., of the House Committee on Science and Technology, how she would feel when Hawley was in space while she remained earthbound, Ride replied, "I am going to be a very interested observer." The pair were eventually divorced.

Ride points to her fellow female astronauts Anna Fisher, Shannon Lucid, Judith Resnik, Margaret Seddon, and Kathryn Sullivan with pride. Since these women were chosen for training, Ride's own experience could not be dismissed as tokenism, which had been the unfortunate fate of the first woman in orbit, the Soviet Union's **Valentina Tereshkova**, a textile worker. Ride expressed her concern to *Newsweek* reporter Pamela Abramson in the week before her initial shuttle trip. "It's important to me that people don't think I was picked for the flight because I am a woman and it's time for NASA to send one."

From June 18 to June 24, 1983, flight STS–7 of the space shuttle *Challenger* launched from Kennedy Space Center in Florida, orbited the Earth for six days, returned to Earth, and landed at Edwards Air Force Base in California. Among the shuttle team's missions were the deployment of international satellites and numerous research experiments supplied by a range of groups, from a naval research lab to various high school students. With Ride operating the shuttle's robot arm in cooperation with Colonel John M. Fabian of the U.S. Air Force, the first satellite deployment and retrieval using such an arm was successfully performed in space during the flight.

Ride was also chosen for *Challenger* flight STS–41G, which transpired between October 5 and October 13, 1984. This time, the robot arm was put to some unusual applications, including "ice-busting" on the shuttle's exterior and readjusting a radar antenna. According to Henry S. F. Cooper, Jr., in his book *Before Lift-off,* fellow team member Ted Browder felt that because Ride was so resourceful and willing to take the initiative, less experienced astronauts on the flight might come to depend upon her rather than develop their own skills, but this mission also met with great success. Objectives during this longer period in orbit covered scientific observations of the Earth, demonstrations of potential satellite refueling techniques, and deployment of a satellite. As STS–7 had been, STS–41G was led by Captain Robert L. Crippen of the U.S. Navy to a smooth landing, this time in Florida.

Ride had been chosen for a third scheduled flight, but training was cut short in January, 1986, when the space shuttle *Challenger* exploded in midair shortly after takeoff. The twelve-foot rubber O-rings that serve as washers between steel segments of the rocket boosters, already considered problematic, failed under stress, killing the entire crew. Judy Resnik, one of the victims, had flown as a rookie astronaut on STS–41G. Ride remembered her in *Ms.* magazine as empathetic, sharing "the same feelings that there was good news and bad news in being accepted to be the first one." As revealed a few months later in the *Chicago Tribune*, program members at NASA began to feel that their safety had been willfully compromised without their knowledge. "I think that we may have been misleading people into thinking that this is a routine operation," Ride was quoted as saying.

Responds to *Challenger* Tragedy

Ride herself tried to remedy that misconception with her subsequent work on the Rogers Commission and as special assistant for long-range and strategic planning to NASA Administrator James C. Fletcher in Washington, D.C., during 1986 and 1987. In keeping with the Rogers Commission recommendations, which Ride helped to shape, especially regarding the inclusion of astronauts at management levels, Robert Crippen was eventually made Deputy Director for Space Shuttle Operations in Washington, D.C., as well.

As leader of a task force on the future of the space program, Ride wrote *Leadership and America's Future in Space*. According to *Aviation Week and Space Technology,* this status report initiated a proposal to redefine NASA goals as a means to prevent the "space race" mentality that might pressure management and personnel into taking untoward risks. "A single goal is not a panacea," the work stated in its preface. "The problems facing the space program must be met head-on, not oversimplified." The overall thrust of NASA's agenda, Ride suggested, should take environmental and international research goals into consideration. A pledge to inform the public and capture the interest of youngsters should be taken as a given. Ride cited a 1986 work decrying the lack of math and science proficiency among American high school graduates, a mere six percent of whom are fluent in these fields, compared to up to ninety percent in other nations.

Top Priority: Educating Children

While with NASA, Ride traveled with fellow corps members to speak to high school and college students on a monthly basis. As former English tutor Joyce Ride once told a *Boston Globe* reporter, her daughter had developed scientific interests she herself harbored in younger days, before encountering a wall of silence in a college physics class as a coed at the University of California in Los Angeles. As Joyce remarked, she and the only other young woman in the class were "nonpersons." Speaking at Smith College in 1985, Sally Ride announced that encouraging women to enter math and science disciplines was her "personal crusade." Ride noted in *Publishers Weekly* the next year that her ambition to write children's books had been met with some dismay by publishing houses more in the mood to read an autobiography targeted for an adult audience. Her youth-oriented books were both written with childhood friends. Susan Okie, coauthor of *To Space and Back,* eventually became a journalist with the *Washington Post. Voyager* coauthor Tam O'Shaughnessy, once a fellow competition tennis player, grew up to develop workshops on scientific teaching skills.

Ride left NASA in 1987 for Stanford's Center for International Security and Arms Control, and two years later she became director of the California Space Institute and physics professor at the University of California at San Diego. She has flown Grumman Tiger aircraft in her spare time since getting her pilot's license. The former astronaut keeps in shape, when not teaching or fulfilling the duties of her various professional posts, by running and engaging in other sports, although she once told *Health* magazine she winds up eating junk food a lot. Ride admitted not liking to run but added, "I like being in shape."

SELECTED WRITINGS BY RIDE:

Books

To Space and Back, Lothrop, 1986.
Leadership and America's Future in Space: A Report to the Administrator by Dr. Sally K. Ride, August 1987, NASA, August, 1987.
Voyager: An Adventure to the Edge of the Solar System, Crown, 1992.

FURTHER READING:

Books

Astronauts and Cosmonauts Biographical and Statistical Data, U.S. Government Printing Office, 1989.
Cooper, Henry S. F., Jr., *Before Lift-off,* Johns Hopkins University Press, 1987.
Cooper, Henry S. F., Jr., *Current Biography,* H. W. Wilson, 1983, pp. 318–21.
Cooper, Henry S. F., Jr., *Hearing before the Committee on Science and Technology,* U.S. House of Representatives, Ninety-eighth Congress, First Session, July 19, 1983, U.S. Government Printing Office, 1983.
O'Connor, Karen, *Sally Ride and the New Astronauts: Scientists in Space,* F. Watts, 1983.

Periodicals

Adler, Jerry, and Pamela Abramson, *Newsweek,* Sally Ride: Ready for Liftoff, June 13, 1983, pp. 36–40, 45, 49, 51.
Caldwell, Jean, *Boston Globe,* Astronaut Ride Urges Women to Study Math, June 30, 1985, pp. B90, B92.
Covault, Craig, *Aviation Week and Space Technology,* Ride Panel Calls for Aggressive Action to Assert U.S. Leadership in Space, August 24, 1987, pp. 26–27.
Goodwin, Irwin, *Physics Today,* Sally Ride to Leave NASA Orbit; Exodus at NSF, July, 1987, p. 45.
Grossmann, John, *Health,* Sally Ride, Ph.D., August, 1985, pp. 73–74, 76.
Ingwerson, Marshall, *Christian Science Monitor,* Clinton Transition Team Takes on Pragmatic Cast, November 30, 1992, p. 3.
Lowther, William, *Maclean's,* A High Ride through the Sex Barrier, June 27, 1983, pp. 40–41.
Peterson, Sarah, *U.S. News and World Report,* Just Another Astronaut, November 29, 1982, pp. 50–51.
Roback, Diane, *Publishers Weekly,* Sally Ride: Astronaut and Now Author, November 28, 1986, pp. 42, 44.
Rowley, Storer, and Michael Tackett, *Chicago Tribune,* Internal Memo Charges NASA Compromised Safety, March 9, 1986, section 1, p. 8.
Sherr, Lynn, *Ms.,* Remembering Judy: The Five Women Astronauts Who Trained with Judy Resnik Remember Her . . . and That Day, June, 1986, p. 57.
Sherr, *Ms.,* A Mission to Planet Earth: Astronaut Sally Ride Talks to Lynn Sherr about Peaceful Uses of Space, July/August, 1987, pp. 180–81.

Sketch by Jennifer Kramer

Harriett B. Rigas
1934–1989
American electrical engineer

Harriett B. Rigas was an electrical engineer who specialized in computer technology, automatic patching, control system stability, and logic design. Prior to serving as professor and the chair of the department of electrical engineering at Michigan State University, she established the computer engineering program at Washington State University. Rigas made advances in computer coding theory; her research focused on improving methods for creating the digital (binary) code that allows computers to store and manipulate data. Application of her theories would reduce computer memory requirements and facilitate the discovery of software errors. She received the 1982 Annual Achievement Award from the Society of Women Engineers for her "significant contributions in the fields of electrical engineering and computer technology."

Rigas was born on April 30, 1934, in Winnipeg, Manitoba. She earned her undergraduate degree at Queen's University in Ontario in 1956. She pursued her graduate studies at the University of Kansas in Missouri, earning a master of science degree in 1959 and a Ph.D. in electrical engineering in 1963. She launched her professional career as an engineer at the Mayo Clinic, a post she held from 1956 to 1957. She then accepted a position as an instructor of physics, math, and engineering at Ventura College, remaining there for one year before becoming senior research engineer for Lockheed Missile and Space Company in 1963.

In 1965, Rigas began an association with Washington State University that would last nineteen years. In 1968, she was named manager of the Hybrid Facility, a post she held until 1980. Rigas was appointed professor of electrical engineering in 1976. At Washington University she created the university's computer engineering program, taking the responsibility for developing the curriculum and raising necessary funding. Rigas also held concurrent posts at the Naval Postgraduate School, where she was named chair of the electrical engineering department in 1980. In 1987, Rigas joined Michigan State University as professor and chair of the department of electrical engineering. She served as board member of the Institute for Electrical and Electronic Engineers (IEEE), and as the IEEE representative on the Accreditation Board for Engineering and Technology. Rigas was married in 1959; she died on July 26, 1989.

Sketch by Karen Withem

Joseph Risi
1899–1993
Canadian chemist

Joseph Risi, the principal force behind the rise of university research laboratories in French Canada, was born March 13, 1899, in Ennetbürgen, near Lucerne, Switzerland, to Alois and Marie Rothenfluh Risi. His father was a cabinetmaker. The exacting and slow nature of his father's trade persuaded Joseph Risi to find another path in life. He decided on teaching. After completing his secondary education at the Collège St.-Michel in Zug, in 1918, he enrolled in the Catholic University of Fribourg, which had received university status only in 1909. He first finished the four diplomas (*licences*) then required of Swiss science teachers—in mathematics, physics, chemistry, and biology. He stayed on for a doctorate in organic chemistry, which he completed in 1925 under the direction of A. Bistrzycki.

For the preceding five years, the ecclesiastical hierarchy of Laval University, in Quebec City, had been trying to establish an advanced school of chemistry. They had called in chemists (Paul Cardinaux, Julian J. Gutensperger, and Carl Faessler) and a physicist (Alphonse Cristen) from the University of Fribourg. But in 1925 Cardinaux and Cristen were fired, the former for financial improprieties and the latter for a sexual escapade. Other chemists came and went from both Switzerland and France. Offered a position as lecturer in organic chemistry, Risi immigrated to Canada in 1925. He became a full professor at the university in 1931.

Risi plunged immediately into organizing Laval's chemistry program. He supervised the installation of new laboratories, the funding for which had taken five years to obtain. In addition to teaching organic chemistry, he taught mineralogy and botany, served as librarian of his school, and from 1931 to 1936 was the scientific overseer of the first marine biological station on the St. Lawrence River, at Trois-Pistoles. Most importantly, he began original research with local students.

Research on the Chemistry of Aromatics

The research was inspired by the environment of French Canada. From the time of his arrival at Laval, Risi had tirelessly promoted the economic development of the region through industrial chemistry. By 1930, he was focusing on the aromatics of maple sugar. His interest was stimulated by the discovery of a vegetable product in South Africa that could mimic the distinctive taste of maple sugar—a development that threatened an important local industry. Beginning with the results of an experiment reported in a German publication, Risi and a student discovered that the aromatic could be produced artificially from oak resin, and in the process they identified a way to distinguish the true maple-syrup taste. This work was followed by a study of the chemical properties of Canadian rhubarb. At the same time, Risi explored the new domain of polymer chemistry (polymers are natural or synthetic materials, like rubber and plastics, that have a high molecular weight and are composed of repeating units). He and a student presented an early description of the polymerization of styrene. In all, Risi would publish more than fifty scientific papers during his career. The chemistry of aromatics from the natural world captured the attention of a number of chemists in the 1920s. Musk was the starting point for the Croatian-Swiss chemist **Leopold Ružička**, for example, who then moved on to explore the composition of hormones and who garnered a Nobel prize in 1939 for his work in this field. A measure of Risi's eminence is found in his being invited, in 1937, to propose a candidate for the Nobel Prize in chemistry. Although he was not the first to do so, Risi recommended Ruzicka to the Nobel authorities. By this act, Risi established Laval as the premier research university of French Canada.

Beginning about 1940, Risi became interested in the chemistry of wood products; in 1948 he joined the faculty of Forestry Engineering at Laval, and in 1950 he became director of the Canadian Institute of Forestry Products. Elected a fellow of the Royal Society of Canada in 1954, he directed Laval's graduate school from 1960 until his retirement in 1971.

Risi had married Alice Neuhaus in 1926; they had four children. A Roman Catholic, Risi enjoyed playing chess and fishing in his spare time. He died on July 21, 1993.

FURTHER READING:

Books

Ouellet, Danielle, *L'Emergence de deux disciplines scientifiques à l'Université Laval entre 1920 et 1950: La chimie et la physique,* Ph.D. dissertation, Laval University, 1991.

Sketch by Lewis Pyenson

Dennis Ritchie
1941–
American computer scientist

Dennis Ritchie is a computer scientist most well-known for his work with **Kenneth Thompson** in creating UNIX, a computer operating system. Ritchie also went on to develop the high-level and enormously popular computer programming language *C*. For their work on the UNIX operating system, Ritchie and Thompson were awarded the prestigious Turing Award by the Association for Computer Machinery (ACM) in 1983.

Dennis MacAlistair Ritchie was born in Bronxville, New York, on September 9, 1941, and grew up in New Jersey, where his father, Alistair Ritchie, worked as a switching systems engineer for Bell Laboratories. His mother, Jean McGee Ritchie, was a homemaker. Ritchie went to Harvard University, where he received his B.S. in Physics in 1963. However, a lecture he attended on the operation of Harvard's computer system, a Univac I, led him to develop an interest in computing in the early 1960s. Thereafter, Ritchie spent a considerable amount of time at the nearby Massachusetts Institute of Technology (MIT), where many scientists were developing computer systems and software. In 1967 Ritchie began working for Bell Laboratories. Ritchie's job increased his association with the programming world, and in the late 1960s he began working with the Computer Science Research Department at Bell. It was here that he met Kenneth Thompson. Ritchie's lifestyle at Bell was that of a typical computer guru: he was devoted to his work. He showed up to his cluttered office in Murray Hill, New Jersey, around noon every day, worked until seven in the evening, and then went home to work some more. His computer system at home was connected on a dedicated private line to a system at Bell Labs, and he often worked at home until three in the morning. Even in the early 1990s, after he became a manager at Bell Labs, his work habits did not change substantially. "It still tends to be sort of late, but not quite that late," Ritchie told Patrick Moore in an interview. "It depends on what meetings and so forth I have."

UNIX: The Operating System that Changed Everything

When Ritchie and Thompson began working for Bell Labs, the company was involved in a major initiative with General Electric and MIT to develop a multi-user, time-sharing operating system called Multics. This system would replace the old one, which was based on batch programming. In a system based on batch programming, the programmers had no opportunity to interact with the computer system directly. Instead, they would write the program on a deck or batch of cards, which were then input into a mainframe computer by an operator. In other words, since the system was centered around a mainframe, and cards were manually fed into machines to relate instructions or generate responses, the programmers had no contact with the program once it had been activated. Multics, or the multiplexed information and computing service, would enable several programmers to work on a system simultaneously while the computer itself would be capable of processing multiple sets of information. Although programmers from three institutions were working on Multics, Bell Labs decided that the development costs were too high and the possibility of launching a usable system in the near future too low. Therefore, the company pulled out of the project. Ritchie and Thompson, who had been working on the Multics project, were suddenly thrown back into the batch programming environment. In light of the advanced techniques and expertise they had acquired while working on the Multics project, this was a major setback for them and they found it extremely difficult to adapt.

Thus it was in 1969 that Thompson began working on what would become the UNIX operating system. Ritchie soon joined the project and together they set out to find a useful alternate to Multics. However, working with a more advanced system was not the only motivation in developing UNIX. A major factor in their efforts to develop a multi-user, multi-tasking system was the communication and information-sharing it facilitated between programmers. As Ritchie said in his article titled "The Evolution of the UNIX Time-sharing System," "What we wanted to preserve was not just a good environment in which to do programming, but a system around which a fellowship could form. We knew from experience that the essence of communal computing, as supplied by remote-access, time-shared machines, is not just to type programs into a terminal instead of a keypunch, but to encourage close communication."

In 1969 Thompson found a little-used PDP–7, an old computer manufactured by the Digital Equipment Corporation (DEC). To make the PDP–7 efficiently run the computer programs that they created, Ritchie, Thompson, and others began to develop an operating system. Among other things, an operating system enables a user to copy, delete, edit, and print data files; to move data from a disk to the screen or to a printer; to manage the movement of data from disk storage to memory storage; and so on. Without operating systems, computers are very difficult and time-consuming for experts to run.

It was clear, however, that the PDP–7 was too primitive for what Ritchie and Thompson wanted to do, so they persuaded Bell Labs to purchase a PDP–11, a far more advanced computer at the time. To justify their acquisition of the PDP–11 to the management of Bell Labs, Ritchie and Thompson said that they would use the PDP–11 to develop a word-processing system for the secretaries in the patent department. With the new PDP–11, Ritchie and Thompson could refine their operating system even more. Soon, other departments in Bell Labs began to find UNIX useful. The system was used and refined within the company for some time before it was announced to the outside world in 1973 during a symposium on Operating Systems Principles hosted by International Business Machines (IBM).

One of the most important characteristics of UNIX was its portability. Making UNIX portable meant that it could be run with relatively few modifications on different computer systems. Most operating systems are developed around specific hardware configurations, that is, specific microprocessor chips, memory sizes, and input and output devices (e.g., printers, keyboards, screens, etc.). To transfer an operating system from one hardware environment to another—for example, from a microcomputer to a mainframe computer—required so many internal changes to the pro-

gramming that, in effect, the whole operating system had to be rewritten. Ritchie circumvented this problem by rewriting UNIX in such a way that it was largely machine independent. The resulting portability made UNIX easier to use in a variety of computer and organizational environments, saving time, money, and energy for its users.

Inventing a New Computer Language

To help make UNIX portable, Ritchie created a new programming language, called *C*, in 1972. C used features of low-level languages or machine languages (i.e., languages that allow programmers to move bits of data between the components inside microprocessor chips) and features of high-level languages (i.e., languages that have more complex data manipulating functions such as looping, branching, and subroutines). High-level languages are easier to learn than low-level languages because they are closer to everyday English. However, because C combined functions of both high- and low-level languages and was very flexible, it was not for beginners. C was very portable because, while it used a relatively small syntax and instruction set, it was also highly structured and modular. Therefore, it was easy to adapt it to different computers, and programmers could copy preexisting blocks of C functions into their programs. These blocks, which were stored on disks in various libraries and could be accessed by using C programs, allowed programmers to create their own programs without having to reinvent the wheel. Because C had features of low-level programming languages, it ran very quickly and efficiently compared to other high-level languages, and it took up relatively little computer time.

Interestingly, because of federal antitrust regulations, Bell Labs, which is owned by American Telephone & Telegraph (AT&T), could not copyright C or UNIX after AT&T was broken up into smaller corporations. Thus, C was used at many college and university computing centers, and each year thousands of new college graduates arrived in the marketplace with a lot of experience with C. In the mid and late 1980s, C became one of the most popular programming languages in the world. The speed at which C worked made it a valuable tool for companies that developed software commercially. C was also popular because it was written for UNIX, which, by the early 1990s, was shipped out on over $20 billion of new computer systems a year, making it one of the most commonly used operating systems in the world.

At the end of 1990, Ritchie became the head of the Computing Techniques Research Department at Bell Labs, contributing applications and managing the development of distributed operating systems. He has received several awards for his contributions to computer programming, including the ACM Turing award in 1983, which he shared with Thompson.

SELECTED WRITINGS BY RITCHIE:

Books

The C Programming Language, Prentice Hall, 1988.

Periodicals

Communications of the ACM, The UNIX Time-Sharing System, Volume 17.7, July, 1974, pp. 365–375.

Language Design and Programming Methodology, The Evolution of the UNIX Time-Sharing System, edited by Jeffrey M. Tobias, Springer-Verlag, 1980, pp. 25–35.

Communications of the ACM, Reflections on Software Research, Volume 27.8, August, 1984, pp. 758–760.

FURTHER READING:

Books

Slater, Robert, *Portraits in Silicon,* MIT Press, 1987.

Periodicals

Hafner, Katherine, *Data Communications,* Newsmaker: Dennis Ritchie, November, 1985, pp. 106–107.

Rosenblatt, Alfred, *Electronics,* 1982 Award for Achievement: Dennis M. Ritchie and Ken Thompson, October 20, 1982, pp. 108–111.

Other

Rosenblatt, Alfred, *Electronics,* 1982 Award for Achievement: Dennis M. Ritchie and Ken Thompson.

Ritchie, Dennis M., telephone interviews with Patrick Moore conducted February 9 and February 14, 1994.

Sketch by Patrick Moore

Frederick Robbins
1916–
American microbiologist

Frederick Robbins was co-winner of the Nobel Prize in physiology or medicine in 1954 with **John F. Enders** and **Thomas Weller** for his work on the poliomyelitis virus. They were the first to successfully grow poliomyelitis in non-neural tissue culture. This development provided the technology needed to produce a vaccination for polio, which was done in 1953 by virologist **Jonas Salk**.

Frederick Chapman Robbins was born June 21, 1916, in Auburn, Alabama. He was the eldest of three boys born to Dr. William Jacob Robbins and Christine F. (Chapman) Robbins. His father was a noted plant physiologist and was director of the New York Botanical Garden for a time and later a professor of botany at the University of Missouri. Robbins's mother was a Phi Beta Kappa graduate of Wellesley College who was also a researcher in botany before her marriage.

Robbins received his B.A. in 1936 and his B.S. in premedicine in 1938, both from the University of Missouri. He then went on to Harvard Medical School, where he met and roomed with Weller and studied virology under Enders. After graduating with his M.D. in 1940, Robbins began an internship and residency at Children's Hospital in Boston, as he had decided to specialize in pediatrics.

World War II interrupted his residency program, and Robbins ended up serving from 1942 to 1946 in North Africa and Italy. He worked as chief of the section of the 15th Medical General Laboratory devoted to viruses and certain kinds of bacterial diseases, and his research mainly concerned infectious hepatitis, Q fever, and typhus fever. He won the Bronze Star for his work during the war.

After the war, Robbins returned to Children's Hospital, where he was assistant resident from 1946 to 1947 and chief resident in 1948 when he finished his residency. Also in 1948, Robbins married Alice Havemeyer Northrop, who had been Weller's assistant in the Enders laboratory. She was the daughter of **John Howard Northrop**, co-winner of the 1946 Nobel Prize for chemistry. The Robbins had two daughters, Alice and Louise.

Cracks the Polio Puzzle

At this point, Robbins received a two-year senior fellowship from the National Research Council to study viral diseases and went to work in Enders's lab. Still concentrating on pediatrics, Robbins began work on infant epidemic diarrhea, which he had seen much of as a resident. He was also working with the mumps virus and because of this had a strain of mouse intestine cells in culture. Meanwhile, Weller was also working with the mumps virus, and at the end of one experiment he had a few tubes of human embryonic tissue left over. Weller decided to try to grow poliomyelitis in this. The results were positive enough to spark some interest, and next Weller grew the virus in foreskin cells, followed by some of Robbins's supply of mouse intestine. These experiments did not work as well but did spur the two to try polio in human intestine.

Prior to this time, polio had only been shown to grow in neural and brain tissue of men or monkeys. Vaccinations from this type of growth were potentially deadly because of something present in this tissue which could not be refined out, so there was no vaccine for polio. Growth of viruses in tissue culture, or in vitro, had historically been difficult because of the threat of bacterial invasion into the cell cultures. By the 1950s, however, antibiotics had been developed and introduced into the laboratory, such as penicillin and streptomycin, which enabled scientists to begin to grow tissue cultures of viruses without the threat of a bacterial invasion.

Robbins and Weller, in their polio experiments, were taking advantage of the new antibiotics. The human intestine cultures grew, which proved for the first time that polio could grow outside neural tissue. This made the feasibility of a polio vaccine far greater, both because it provided a non-deadly vaccine source and because the supply could be grown more cheaply in vitro than in a live animal. This work was a major breakthrough for scientific research and led to the awarding of the Nobel Prize to Enders, Weller, and Robbins in 1954. Weller and Robbins had already been given the Mead Johnson Prize in 1953 for their contribution to pediatric research.

While working in Enders's laboratory, Robbins also served as associate professor of pediatrics at Harvard. In 1950 he took on the additional position of associate director of Isolation Service at Children's Hospital. Then in 1952 he moved to Cleveland to become director of the pediatrics and contagious diseases department at Cleveland City Hospital as well as a member of the medical faculty at Case Western Reserve Medical School.

Robbins's career then took a turn from laboratory work to the health policy arena. He served as president of the Society for Pediatric Research in 1961 and 1962 and in 1965 became dean of the school of medicine at Case Western Reserve. Robbins also began an intense involvement in national committees on a wide range of topics including human experimentation, Third World health policies, and public food and safety policy. From 1973 to 1974 he served as president of the American Pediatric Society.

In 1979 Robbins was appointed chairman of the advisory council for the congressional Office of Technology Assessment. He retired from his position at Case in 1980, but only to go on with other projects. Elected president of the Institute of Medicine (IOM) for a five-year term beginning in 1980, he also held a concurrent appointment as distinguished professor of pediatrics at Georgetown University from 1981 to 1985. Robbins's work for the Institute of Medicine began long before 1980 with his participation on many of their studies and reports. He chaired a study on the health effects of legalizing abortion and participated in another on the use of saccharin in food. For all his research work, Robbins's peers considered him more a consultant or negotiator than an innovator. When chosen as IOM president he was credited by Joyce McCann, a member of the minority view on the saccharin report, as having an "ability to deal with groups of people who are at opposite ends of the spectrum," according to a March, 1980, article in *Science.*

Robbins's career covered a great deal of territory, from the laboratory to the classroom to the meeting room. His contribution to science in terms of laboratory research has been memorialized by the receipt of the Nobel Prize. In the end, however, it is possible his greater legacy will be in the area of health policy. Regardless, his importance in the field of science is assured.

SELECTED WRITINGS BY ROBBINS:

Periodicals

Science, Cultivation of the Lansing Strain of Poliomyelitis Virus in Cultures of Various Human Embryonic Tissues, January 28, 1949, pp. 85–87.

FURTHER READING:

Books

Current Biography, H. W. Wilson, 1955, p. 183.

Fox, D., Meldrum, M., and Rezak, I., editors, *Nobel Laureates in Medicine or Physiology: A Biographical Dictionary,* Garland Publishing, 1990, pp. 471–74.

Periodicals

Fox, D., Meldrum, M., and Rezak, I., editors, *Science,* Institute of Medicine Names Robbins President, March 14, 1980, pp. 1184–85.

Sun, Marjorie, *Science,* Institute of Medicine Gets New President, November 7, 1980, pp. 616–17.

Sketch by Kimberlyn McGrail

Lawrence Roberts
1937–
American computer scientist

Lawrence Roberts is best known for implementing ARPANET, the first computer network that moved information using what is called "packet switching," transmitting bursts of information via a shared network connection. The success of ARPANET in the late 1960s, while Roberts was director of the Information Processing Techniques Office of the Advanced Research Projects Agency (ARPA), proved that networks could move information economically and quickly, a crucial step toward the development of such computer networks as the vast Internet system of the late twentieth century and most other distributed computer networks. For his role in establishing the viability of networking, Roberts has been dubbed "the father of computer networks."

Lawrence G. Roberts was born in Norwalk, Connecticut, on December 21, 1937. He received a B.S. degree in 1959 from the Massachusetts Institute of Technology (MIT) and went on to receive an M.S. in 1960 and a doctorate in electrical engineering in 1963 from the same institution. His doctoral dissertation treated machine perception of three-dimensional solids.

Establishes the First Computer Network

Until the late–1960s data was transmitted over interactive communication networks by circuit switching, where a particular bandwidth was preallocated for a particular transmission. This system, requiring a dedicated link between points, left more than 90 percent of the possible communication potential of the network unused. With packet switching, computers dynamically allocate unused portions of the communication network to transmission bursts, or "packets," allowing many users to share the same transmission line previously required for one user. Because of its greater efficiency in utilizing network potential, packet switching offers significant economic savings over circuit switching. Dynamic allocation was actually an idea that had been successfully used by early communications technologies, but what worked with postal service and telegraph traffic—which were controlled manually—was at first not considered possible with the complex communications systems of the mid-twentieth century. Computer professionals trying to improve networking capabilities applied dynamic allocation principles in the 1960s with favorable results, however. The application of packet switching to twentieth-century technologies was the work of a number of people, including Paul Baran of the Rand Corporation, J. C. R. Licklider, then at the Advanced Research Projects Agency, Donald Davies of the National Physical Laboratory in the United Kingdom, and Roberts, then at MIT working on computers. In 1966 Roberts staged an early experiment in computer networking, when he created a network at MIT's Lincoln Labs linking a TX–2 with an SDC Q32.

In October 1967 Roberts proposed the ARPANET at a computer conference in Gatlinburg, Tennessee. His plan to link some of the main academic, commercial, and military computer sites originally encompassed four nodes, or database sites, comprising the network in 1969; that number grew to 111 by 1977. By the 1990s the descendants of ARPANET, including the National Science Foundation's Internet, had literally millions of subscribers and, in effect, all the larger networks had become linked into one vast network, where people from all over the world interact electronically.

Roberts has continued to develop networks through his role as a leader of key institutions involved in the fundamental technologies and processes. He remained with ARPA from 1967 to 1973. He then became the president of Telenet Communications Corporation, where, under Robert's leadership, the first public network utilizing packet switching was introduced in August 1975. It quickly grew from seven nodes to 187. Roberts served as president of GTE Telenet Corporation from 1980 to 1982 and of GTE's Subscriber Network during the same period. In 1982 he became president of DHL Corporation and Chair of the Board of NETEXPRESS Inc. The companies that Roberts

has led have continued to introduce innovations in networking technologies, including integrating satellites into networks and in developing the technologies to transmit voices, images, and other forms of data.

Roberts is a member of the National Academy of Engineers, the Institute of Electrical and Electronics Engineers, and the Association of Computing Machinery. He has received several significant awards for his research, including the L. M. Erickson award in 1981 and the 1990 W. Wallace McDowell award from the IEEE Computer Society for bringing packet switching into practical use.

SELECTED WRITINGS BY ROBERTS:

Periodicals

ACM Symposium on Operating System Principles, Multiple Computer Networks and Intercomputer Communication, October, 1967.
Proceedings of the IEEE, The Evolution of Packet Switching, November, 1978, pp. 1307–13.

FURTHER READING:

Books

A History of ARPANET: The First Decade, Bolt Beranek & Newman, Inc. (BBN), 1981.

Sketch by Chris Hables Gray

Richard J. Roberts
1943–
English biochemist

For decades scientists assumed that genes are continuous segments within deoxyribonucleic acid (DNA), the chemical template of heredity. In 1977, however, Richard. J. Roberts, a thirty-four-year-old British scientist working with adenovirus, the same virus that causes the common cold and pink eye, discovered that genes (the functional units of heredity) can be composed of several separate segments rather than of a single chain along the DNA strand. For his discovery of "split genes," Roberts was awarded the Nobel Prize in 1993.

Richard John Roberts was born on September 6, 1943, in Derby, England, a mid-sized industrial city about forty miles northeast of Birmingham. His father, John Roberts, was a motor mechanic, while his mother, Edna (Allsop) Roberts, took care of the family and served as Richard's first tutor. In 1947, the Roberts family moved to Bath, where Richard spent his formative years. At St. Stephen's junior school, Roberts encountered his first real mentor, the school's headmaster known only to the students as Mr. Broakes. Here he was exposed to a variety of mentally stimulating games, ranging from crossword to logical puzzles. "Most importantly, I learned that logic and mathematics are fun!," Roberts wrote in a brief autobiography for the Nobel Foundation.

At the City of Bath Boys School (now Beechen Cliff School), Roberts became enamored with the life and literature of detectives, as they represented the ultimate puzzle solvers. His young career path changed abruptly, however, when he received a chemistry set from his parents. His ever supportive father had a large chemistry cabinet constructed and, with the aid of a local chemist who supplied the myriad chemicals he needed, Roberts soon discovered how to assemble fireworks and other concoctions not found in a beginner's chemistry manual. "Luckily I survived those years with no serious injuries or burns. I knew I had to be a chemist," he wrote in the Nobel Foundation autobiography.

At the age of seventeen, Roberts entered Sheffield University, where he concentrated in chemistry. His initial introduction to biochemistry was totally negative, he recalled in his autobiography: "I loathed it. The lectures merely required rote learning and the laboratory consisted of the most dull experiments imaginable." After graduating with honors in 1965, Roberts remained at Sheffield to study for his doctoral degree under David Ollis, his undergraduate professor of organic chemistry. But the direction of Roberts's scientific interests were profoundly altered after reading a book by John Kendrew on crystallography and molecular biology. Roberts became hooked on molecular biology and was later invited to conduct his postdoctoral work as part of a research team assembled by his colleague, Jack Strominger, a professor of biochemistry and molecular biology at Harvard University.

In 1969, Roberts left the English countryside and moved to Cambridge, Massachusetts, where he spent the next four years deciphering the sequence of nucleotides in a form of ribonucleic acid known as tRNA. Using a new method devised by English biochemist **Frederick Sanger** at Cambridge, he was able to sequence the RNA molecule, while teaching other scientists Sanger's technique. His creative work with tRNA led to the publication of two papers in *Nature* and an invitation by genetic pioneer and Nobel laureate **James Watson** to join his laboratory in Cold Spring Harbor, Long Island, New York.

In 1972, Roberts moved to Long Island to research ways to sequence DNA. American microbiologists **Daniel Nathans** and **Hamilton Smith** had shown that a restriction enzyme, Endonuclease R, could split DNA into specific segments. Roberts thought that such small segments could be used for DNA sequencing and began looking for other new restriction enzymes to expand the repertoire. (Enzymes are complex proteins that catalyze specific biochemical

reactions.) He noted in his autobiography that his laboratory was responsible for discovering or characterizing three-quarters of the world's first restriction enzymes. In 1977, he developed a series of biological experiments to "map" the location of various genes in adenovirus and found that one end of a messenger ribonucleic acid (mRNA) did not react as expected. With the use of an electron microscope, Roberts and his colleagues observed that genes could be present in several, well-separated DNA segments. As he told the *New York Times,* "Everybody thought that genes were laid out in exactly the same way, and so it came as a tremendous surprise that they were different in higher organisms, such as humans."

In 1986, Roberts married his second wife, Jean. He is the father of four children, Alison, Andrew, Christopher and Amanda. He moved back to Massachusetts in 1992 to join New England Biolabs, a small, private company in Beverly, Massachusetts, involved in making research reagents, particularly restriction enzymes. He serves as joint research director. In 1993, Roberts was awarded the Nobel Prize for his discovery of "split genes." The Nobel Committee stated that, "The discovery of split genes has been of fundamental importance for today's basic research in biology, as well as for more medically oriented research concerning the development of cancer and other diseases."

SELECTED WRITINGS BY ROBERTS:

Books

Adenovirus DNA, The Viral Genome and Its Expression, Structure and Function of the Adenovirus–2 Genome, edited by W. Doerfler, Martinus Nijhoff, 1986, pp. 53–95.
Nucleases, Type II Restriction Endonucleases, edited by S. M. Linn, R. S. Lloyd, and R. J. Roberts, Cold Spring Harbor Press, 1993, pp. 35–88.

Periodicals

CRC Critical Reviews in Biochemistry, Restriction Endonucleases, Volume 4, 1976, pp. 123–64.
Cells, An Amazing Sequence Arrangement at the 5' Ends of Adenovirus–2 Messenger RNA, Volume 12, 1977, pp. 1–8.
Cold Spring Harbor Symposium on Quantitative Biology, Adenovirus–2 Messenger—An Example of Baroque Molecular Structure, Volume 42, 1978, pp. 531–53.

FURTHER READING:

Periodicals

New York Times, October 12, 1993. p. B9.

Other

New York Times, Richard J. Roberts, autobiographical sketch, provided by the Nobel Foundation to Benedict A. Leerburger.

Sketch by Benedict A. Leerburger

Julia Robinson
1919–1985
American mathematician

Excelling in the field of mathematics, Julia Robinson was instrumental in solving Hilbert's tenth problem—to find an effective method for determining whether a given diophantine equation is solvable with integers. Over a period of two decades, she developed the framework on which the solution was constructed. In recognition of her accomplishments, she became the first woman mathematician elected to the National Academy of Sciences, the first female president of the American Mathematical Society, and the first woman mathematician to receive a MacArthur Foundation Fellowship.

Robinson was born Julia Bowman on December 8, 1919, in St. Louis, Missouri. Her mother, Helen Hall Bowman, died two years later; Robinson and her older sister went to live with their grandmother near Phoenix, Arizona. The following year their father, Ralph Bowman, retired and joined them in Arizona after becoming disinterested in his machine tool and equipment business. He expected to support his children and his new wife, Edenia Kridelbaugh Bowman, with his savings. In 1925, her family moved to San Diego; three years later a third daughter was born.

At the age of nine, Robinson contracted scarlet fever, and the family was quarantined for a month. They celebrated the end of isolation by viewing their first talking motion picture. The celebration was premature, however, as Robinson soon developed rheumatic fever and was bedridden for a year. When she was well enough, she worked with a tutor for a year, covering the required curriculum for the fifth through eighth grades. She was fascinated by the tutor's claim that it had been proven that the square root of two could not be calculated to a point where the decimal began to repeat. Her interest in mathematics continued at San Diego High School; when she graduated with honors in mathematics and science, her parents gave her a slide rule that she treasured and named "Slippy."

At the age of sixteen, Robinson entered San Diego State College. She majored in mathematics and prepared for a teaching career, being aware of no other mathematics career choices. At the beginning of Robinson's sophomore year, her father found his savings depleted by the Depression and committed suicide. With help from her older sister and an aunt, Robinson remained in school. She transferred to the University of California, Berkeley, for her senior year and graduated in 1940.

At Berkeley, she found teachers and fellow students who shared her excitement about mathematics. In December of 1941, she married an assistant professor named Raphael Robinson. At that time she was a teaching assistant at Berkeley, having completed her master's degree in 1941. The following year, however, the school's nepotism rule prevented her from teaching in the mathematics department. Instead, she worked in the Berkeley Statistical Laboratory on military projects. She became pregnant but lost her baby; because of damage to Robinson's heart caused by the rheumatic fever, her doctor warned against future pregnancies. Her hopes of motherhood crushed, Robinson endured a period of depression that lasted until her husband rekindled her interest in mathematics.

In 1947 she embarked on a doctoral program under the direction of **Alfred Tarski**. In her dissertation, she proved the algorithmic unsolvability of the theory of the rational number field. Her Ph.D. was conferred in 1948. That same year, Tarski discussed an idea about diophantine equations (polynomial equations of several variables, with integer coefficients, whose solutions are to be integers) with Raphael Robinson, who shared it with his wife. By the time she realized it was directly related to the tenth problem on Hilbert's list, she was too involved in the topic to be intimidated by its stature. For the next twenty-two years she attacked various aspects of the problem, building a foundation on which Yuri Matijasevic proved in 1970 that the desired general method for determining solvability does not exist. While working at the RAND Corporation in 1949 and 1950, Robinson developed an iterative solution for the value of a finite two-person zero-sum game. Her only contribution to game theory is still considered a fundamental theorem in the field.

Robinson's heart damage was surgically repaired in 1961, but her health remained impaired. Her fame from the Hilbert problem solution resulted in her appointment as a full professor at Berkeley in 1976, although she was expected to carry only one-fourth of the normal teaching load. Eight years later she developed leukemia and died on July 30, 1985.

SELECTED WRITINGS BY ROBINSON:

Books

Mathematical Developments Arising from Hilbert's Problems, Hilbert's Tenth Problem. Diophantine Equations: Positive Aspects of a Negative Solution, edited by F. E. Browder, American Mathematical Society, 1976.

Periodicals

Journal of Symbolic Logic, Definability and Decision Problems in Arithmetic, Volume 14, 1949, pp. 98–114.

Transactions of the American Mathematical Society, Existential Definability in Arithmetic, Volume 72, number 3, 1952, pp. 437–449.

Annals of Mathematics, The Decision Problem for Exponential Diophantine Equations, Volume 74, number 3, 1961, pp. 425–436.

FURTHER READING:

Periodicals

Notices of the American Mathematical Society, Julia Bowman Robinson, 1919–1985, November, 1985, pp. 738–742.

Reid, Constance, *The College Mathematics Journal,* The Autobiography of Julia Robinson, January, 1986, pp. 2–21.

Smorynski, C., *The Mathematical Intelligencer,* Julia Robinson, In Memoriam, spring 1986, pp. 77–79.

Sketch by Loretta Hall

Robert Robinson
1886–1975
English chemist

Robert Robinson worked on many types of chemical problems, but he received the 1947 Nobel Prize for his work with the alkaloids, complex nitrogen-containing natural compounds that often exhibit high biological activity. His work in synthesis, identification, and reaction theory make him one of the founders of modern organic chemistry. Robinson summed up his philosophy about basic research when he said in his Nobel address, "In both [chemistry and physics] it is in the course of attack of the most difficult problems, without consideration of eventual applications, that new fundamental knowledge is most certainly garnered. . . . Such contributions as I have been able to make are to the science itself and do not derive their interest from the economic or biological importance of the substances studied."

Robinson was born to the inventor William Bradbury Robinson and Jane (Davenport) Robinson on September 13, 1886, near Chesterfield, England. His very large family included eight half-siblings from his father's first marriage, as well as four younger children. The family moved to New Brampton when Robinson was three years old. He received an excellent private education from the Fulneck School, run by the Moravian Church, and entered Manchester University in 1902. Robinson's family had manufactured bandages and other medical products for nearly a century and he was expected to enter the family business, so his father insisted that he study chemistry instead of mathematics. While at Manchester, Robinson studied under William H. Perkin, Jr., and after graduating with high honors in 1905, he worked in Perkin's private laboratory for five years before finishing his Ph.D. in 1910. In 1912, Robinson moved to Australia to take a teaching position at the University of Sydney. He returned to England in 1915 and held university appointments at Liverpool, St. Andrews, and Manchester, before finally landing at Oxford as Waynflete Professor of Chemistry, succeeding his mentor Perkin. Robinson remained at Oxford until his retirement in 1955. He also spent time as a consultant to the dye and petroleum industries.

Robinson's interests spanned all of organic chemistry (molecular structure elucidation, theoretical considerations, and synthesis), and most of them originated in Perkin's laboratory. He first studied such plant pigments as brazilin, a dyestuff obtainable from brazilwood, and the group of red/blue flower pigments called anthocyanins. He also worked on some of the steroid hormones, and synthesized several artificial estrogens. As did many scientists of the time, during World War II Robinson worked on war-related research efforts—from explosives to anti-malarial drugs to penicillin. Later in his life, Robinson became interested in geochemistry, particularly the origin and composition of petroleum. His work convinced him that plants must synthesize chemicals in certain ways, and he proposed a biosynthesis pathway (later confirmed by radioactive tracers) for some of the plant alkaloids. His contributions to chemical theory also include ideas on the electron distribution (and therefore the chemical reactivity) of aromatic compounds like benzene.

Alkaloid Research Leads to Nobel Prize

Alkaloids, although not the largest natural chemical compounds, are arguably the most complex, since they always contain nitrogen and usually some combination of carbon rings. Alkaloids as a group have profound biochemical effects on living things; cocaine, morphine and opium all belong to this class of natural products, as do many natural poisons. Robinson elucidated the structure of morphine and strychnine, and synthesized the alkaloids papaverine, hydrastine, narcotine, and tropinone.

In addition to receiving the 1947 Nobel Prize in chemistry for his work with the alkaloids, Robinson was knighted in 1939; he was also awarded the Order of Merit in 1949, and the Longstaff, Faraday, Davy, Royal, and Copley medals. In addition, he was an active member of numerous professional organizations around the world: at different times during his career, he served as president of the Royal Society, the British Association for the Advancement of Science, and the Society of the Chemical Industry. With the help of Nobel Laureate **Robert B. Woodward**, Robinson established the organic chemistry journal *Tetrahedron*.

Robinson married Gertrude Maude Walsh in 1912; they had a son and a daughter. Robinson's hobbies included music, literature, gardening, and photography, but his most enthusiastic pursuits outside of science were mountain-climbing (he and his wife explored ranges all over the world) and chess. He won several chess championships, served as president of the British Chess Federation, and collaborated on a book entitled *The Art and Science of Chess*. Three years after his wife's death in 1954, Robinson married Stearn Hillstrom. He retired from Oxford in 1955, and died on February 8, 1975.

SELECTED WRITINGS BY ROBINSON:

Periodicals

Journal of the Chemical Society, A Theory of the Mechanisms of the Phytochemical Synthesis of Certain Alkaloids, Volume 111, 1917, p. 876; portions reprinted in Source Book in Chemistry 1900–1950, edited by H. M. Leicester, Harvard University Press, 1968, p. 279.

FURTHER READING:

Books

Nobel Prize Winners in Chemistry: 1901–1961, revised edition, Abelard Schuman, 1963, p. 198.
Wasson, Tyler, editor, *Nobel Prize Winners,* H. W. Wilson, 1987, p. 873.

Sketch by Gail B. C. Marsella

John Rock
1890–1984
American gynecologist and obstetrician

John Rock was a gynecologist, obstetrician, and medical researcher who played a significant role in developing and promoting the use of oral contraceptives. As a leading authority on the reproductive system and embryology, he contributed to the understanding of infertility and reproductive problems and founded the Rock Reproductive Clinic in Brookline, Massachusetts. A devout Roman Catholic, he also challenged his church's opposition to the use of the birth control pill.

Rock, one of five children, was born March 24, 1890, in Marlborough, Massachusetts, to Frank Sylvester Rock and Ann Jane (Murphy) Rock. His father was an enterprising businessman who owned a liquor store, dealt in real estate, and promoted the local baseball team. The younger Rock graduated from Boston High School of Commerce and worked for a year and a half as an accountant for a fruit company in Guatemala and then with a construction firm in Rhode Island. Rock was fired from both jobs and decided to follow his father's advice to attend college.

Graduating with a baccalaureate degree from Harvard in 1915, he received the M.D. degree from Harvard Medical School in 1918. Rock interned at Massachusetts General Hospital, doing his residency in urology there and also at Boston Lying-in Hospital. After one year as a surgeon at Brookline Free Hospital for Women, he set up his own practice. His long professional relations with Harvard Medical School began in 1922 when he was appointed assistant professor of obstetrics.

Seeks Answers to Reproductive Problems

Rock opened one of the first fertility and endocrine clinics at the Free Hospital for Women in the mid–1920s. At that time his main concern was solving reproductive problems rather than birth control. In 1944, along with Harvard scientist Miriam F. Menkin, Rock fertilized the first human egg in a test tube. He is also credited with the first recorded recovery of human embryos 2 to 17 days after fertilization as well as establishing the fact that ovulation occurs 14 days before menstruation.

In the early 1950s Rock began experimenting with progesterone, the female hormone that suppresses ovulation. Progesterone is secreted by the body during pregnancy so that no eggs are discharged—nature's way of preventing overlapping pregnancies. He surmised that giving the reproductive system a "rest" by injecting childless women with progesterone might increase fertility when the injections were stopped. Though he was aware of the contraceptive possibilities of the hormone, he ignored those aspects for fear of the state's anti-birth control laws. At that time in Massachusetts, each instance of birth control advice would result in a fine of $1000 and a possible five-year prison sentence.

Rock corresponded with scientists **Gregory Pincus**, the world's foremost authority on the mammalian egg, and **M. C. Chang**, a specialist in the biology of sperm, about the possibility of developing a useful progestin, or synthetic progesterone, that could be given orally. With Pincus and Chang intent on investigating the hormones contraceptive properties, Rock's focus began to shift in that direction as well. Many pharmaceutical companies had developed progestins but none had been tried on humans. Chang and Pincus had methodically tested hundreds of variations of progestin and found two that could be safely tested on women. While Rock began the first tests for treatment of sterility on 50 females in 1954, simultaneous investigations into the effectiveness of progestin as a contraceptive were also undertaken. The researchers were amazed to discover that although 15 percent of the women on natural progesterone ovulated, none of those using the oral progestins did.

At this point Rock left the clinic at the Free Hospital for Women, having reached the mandatory retirement age of 65, and opened the Rock Reproductive Clinic. Realizing the need for more extensive tests, but aware of the legal and social complications involved, he chose to do field trials in Puerto Rico, Haiti, and Mexico, with a progestin manufactured by G. D. Searle Company. Of the women who followed directions, none became pregnant. The studies were now ready to present in the United States.

In 1959 Searle applied to license the "Pill"—as the oral progestin became known—as a contraceptive, choosing Rock to present the findings of the experiences of 897 women before the Food and Drug Administration (FDA). The requirement at the time was that a drug must be proven safe and not necessarily effective. However, the young reviewer, who was aware of the implications of the Pill, was thorough in his examination, requiring further lab tests before approval. On May 11, 1960, the FDA approved Searle's Enovid, the first drug approved in order to prevent a medical happening. By 1964 some four million women were on the pill.

Rock Takes on Goliath

Rock was a devout member of the Roman Catholic church, whose traditional position was that no unnatural form of birth control be used. Believing in the right of choice, Rock became an outspoken activist for the use of contraceptives to control population explosion, in direct opposition to the teachings of the church. In 1931 he worked for the repeal of a Massachusetts law against the sale of birth control devices, and in 1945 he began teaching students at Harvard Medical School how to prescribe them. Rock took on the hierarchy of the Catholic church, arguing that the pill was a variant of the rhythm method. Using a strategy of logic, he showed that the pill of natural hormones extended the time when a woman was naturally sterile, hence increasing the rhythm method.

In 1963 he took his case through the mass media in a book, *The Time Has Come: A Catholic Doctor's Proposal to End the Battle Over Birth Control.* The book defended the morality of the pill and urged science and religion to unite on a system of population control. He was strongly criticized by conservative Catholic theologians but was described in the press as David taking on Goliath. As a result Pope Paul IV appointed a papal commission to study the issue. Although the commission recommended the pill, the hierarchy said no. With a clear conscience that he was right and the church leaders had made a mistake, Rock remained a devout Catholic, attending mass daily until his death on December 4, 1984.

Rock was a member of many societies, including Planned Parenthood, and was a founding fellow of the American College of Obstetricians and Gynecologists.

Among the awards he received were the Lasker award from Planned Parenthood in 1940 and the Ortho award from the American Gynecological Society in 1949. He is credited not only with being the "father" of the first birth control pill but also popularizing and selling it to a skeptical world.

SELECTED WRITINGS BY ROCK:

Books

Voluntary Parenthood, Random House, 1949.
The Time Has Come: A Catholic Doctor's Proposal to End the Battle Over Birth Control, Knopf, 1963.

FURTHER READING:

Books

Henden, David, *The Life Givers,* William Morrow, 1976.
McLaughlin, Loretta, *The Pill, John Rock, and the Church: The Biography of a Revolution,* Little, Brown, 1983.

Periodicals

McLaughlin, Loretta, *Yankee,* Dr. Rock and the Birth of the Pill, September, 1990, pp. 72–77, 152–155.

Sketch by Evelyn B. Kelly, Ph.D.

Mabel M. Rockwell
19(??)–1979
American electrical and aeronautical engineer

Mabel M. Rockwell was an electrical and aeronautical engineer whose activities ranged from the development of aircraft manufacturing processes to the design of underwater propulsion systems and submarine guidance instrumentation. Believed to be the first woman aeronautical engineer in the United States, she was one of the designers of the control system for the Polaris missile and for the Atlas guided missile launcher. Rockwell also helped design and install electrical power systems for facilities on the Colorado River.

A native of Philadelphia, Pennsylvania, Mabel MacFerran Rockwell was the daughter of Edgar O. MacFerran and Mabel Alexander. She attended Bryn Mawr College before transferring to the Massachusetts Institute of Technology, where she received a bachelor's degree in science, teaching, and mathematics in 1925. Stanford University awarded her a degree in electrical engineering the next year. Rockwell began her career with the Southern California Edison Company as a technical assistant. In this capacity, she pioneered in the application of the method of symmetrical components to transmission relay problems in power systems. This was crucial to the tracing of system malfunctions and to making multiple-circuit lines more reliable. Rockwell was then named assistant engineer with the Metropolitan Water District in Southern California, where she continued to work in the area of power transmission. During this time Rockwell served on the team who designed the Colorado River Aqueduct's power system and was the only woman to participate in the creation of electrical installations at Boulder Dam.

Contributes to U.S. World War II Effort

Three years later Rockwell joined Lockheed Aircraft Corporation as plant electrical engineer. She was named production research engineer in 1940, overseeing twenty-five engineers and technicians in an effort to enhance the aircraft manufacturing process. Rockwell and her staff converted a small factory to a military aircraft plant during World War II. The innovations of Rockwell and many of her contemporaries were shared with other aerospace firms in order to optimize the design and speed the production of military craft during the war. While at Lockheed, Rockwell conducted research on refining the process of spotwelding and developed techniques for maintaining cleaner surfaces, which are necessary to ensure complete fusion of metals during the welding process. She also investigated electrical and mechanical problems in aircraft manufacture, such as the uniform application of heat pressure in welding, the production of aircraft parts from sheet metal, and methods for supplying the huge amounts of electrical power necessary to produce the high temperatures needed for welding metal pieces into sections of airplanes. One result of Rockwell's research was that riveting was replaced by the more sophisticated process of spotwelding, which reduced the cost and accelerated the rate of aircraft production.

Following her wartime endeavors with Lockheed, Rockwell joined the staff of Westinghouse, where she designed the electrical control system for the Polaris missile launcher. Later, while at Convair, she developed the launching and ground controls for the Atlas guided missile system. For her contributions to these programs, President Dwight D. Eisenhower named her Woman Engineer of the Year in 1958. Rockwell also served as an engineer at McClellan Air Force Base in California, the Mare Island Naval Installation, the U.S. Bureau of Reclamation, and the Naval Ordnance Test Station in Pasadena, California. Rockwell was appointed consulting technical editor at Stanford University's electrical engineering department, where her meticulous editing of scholarly papers became known as "Mabelizing." She continued to edit doctoral dissertations into her seventies, on such subjects as computer science, mathematics, and systems theory. In addition to Eisenhower's award, Rockwell was presented with the

Society of Women Engineer's Achievement Award in 1958, for "her significant contributions to the field of electrical control systems." In 1935, she married engineer Edward W. Rockwell; the couple had one daughter. In her spare time she enjoyed tennis, horseback riding, and skiing. Rockwell died in June, 1979.

FURTHER READING:

Books

Goff, Alice C., *Women Can Be Engineers,* Edwards Brothers, 1946, pp. 94–112.

Periodicals

Goff, Alice C., *M.I.T. Technology Review,* June/July 1980, p. B–7.

Sketch by Karen Withem

Martin Rodbell
1925–
American biochemist

Known for his part in the discovery of G-proteins, Rodbell has done ground-breaking work in cell biology, determining the mechanism whereby cells communicate. For his work in this area, Rodbell shared the Nobel Prize in Medicine with scientist **Alfred Gilman**.

Rodbell was born on December 1, 1925, in Baltimore, Maryland. He attended a special high school in Baltimore that accepted boys from all over the city and prepared students to enter college as sophomores. The school emphasized languages, and Rodbell thought he might continue his language studies when he entered Johns Hopkins University in 1943. However, he was more interested in chemistry.

Rodbell was happy to go into the Navy during World War II. He was bored with classes at Johns Hopkins and being Jewish, was motivated to fight Hitler. Most of the war, however, he spent in the South Pacific. He was a radio operator in the Philippine jungles until he contracted malaria. When he recovered, he stayed on ships, traveling to Korea and China. In his autobiography published on the Nobel Foundation's web site, Rodbell describes his experiences in the war as extremely influential. " . . . My interactions with so many different types of people under trying conditions provided me with a healthy respect for the human condition."

Martin Rodbell

When he came back from the war, he continued his studies at Johns Hopkins and was unsure about what direction he wanted to go. He was interested in French literature and existentialist philosophy, and his father wanted him to go to medical school. He was not interested in medical school because of the competition for grades, but a biology class given by James Ebert turned his attention back toward the sciences. When he was close to graduating he went to Professor Bently Glass for advice, who told him to study biochemistry. He hadn't had any course in chemistry, so he stayed at Johns Hopkins an extra year and took every available chemistry course.

Rodbell received a B.A. from Johns Hopkins University in 1949. That same year he met his future wife, Barbara Lederman, a ballet dancer from Holland who had lost her family in the Auschwitz concentration camp. They married a year later, and Rodbell credits his wife for immersing him the world of the arts. Rodbell and his new wife traveled to Seattle, where Rodbell began his graduate studies in biochemistry at the University of Seattle. He studied the chemistry of lipids (the fatty substances in cells), and his thesis was on the biosynthesis of lecithin (fats found in cell membranes) in the rat liver. Unfortunately, his thesis was disproved by another scientist working on the same subject. This experience taught him not to assume that biological chemicials are pure, something that would help him later in his Nobel Prize-winning work.

Chooses Research Over Teaching

Rodbell finished his Ph.D. in 1954 and then went to the University of Illinois for his post-doctoral fellowship. His research involved the biosynthesis of chloramphenicol, an antibiotic. When his fellowship advisor, Herbert Carter, asked him where he wanted to teach, Rodbell had to answer nowhere. After having taught a lecture course to freshman, only a few of whom passed his exams, Rodbell decided that teaching was not his calling. He accepted a position at the National Heart Institute in Bethesda, Maryland, and continued his research into fats, identifying important proteins that pertained to diseases concerning lipoproteins.

In the 1960s he returned to his original interest in cell biology and was awarded a fellowship to work at the University of Brussels. There he learned new lab techniques and enjoyed European culture with his family. He returned to the United States and accepted a postion at the NIH Institute of Arthritis and Metabolic Diseases in the Nutrition and Endocrinology lab. He developed a simple procedure that would separate and purify fat cells. He was also able to remove the fat from a cell, conserving most of the structure of the cell. He named these cells "ghosts."

Conducts Nobel Prize-Winning Research

In several groundbreaking experiments, Rodbell and his colleagues at the NIH showed that cell communication involves three different working devices: (1) a chemical signal; (2) a "second messenger" like a hormone; and (3) a transducer, something that converts energy from one form to another. Rodbell's major contribution was in discovering that there was a transducer function. He and his colleagues also speculated that guanine nucleotides, components of deoxyribonucleic acid (DNA) and ribonucleic acid (RNA), were somehow involved in cell communication, something that would later be confirmed by Alfred Goodman, the biochemist with whom he would share the Nobel Prize. Gilman searched for the chemicals involved with guanine nucleotides and discovered the G-proteins.

G-proteins are instrumental in the fundamental workings of a cell. They allow us to see and smell by changing light and odors to chemical messages that travel to the brain. Understanding how G-proteins malfunction could lead to a better understanding of serious diseases like cholera or cancer. Scientists have already linked improperly working G-proteins to diseases like alcoholism and diabetes. Pharmaceutical companies are developing drugs that would focus on G-proteins.

Rodbell served as director of the National Institute of Environmental Health Sciences in Chapel Hill, North Carolina, from 1985 until his retirement in 1994. Ironically, only a few months before receiving the Nobel Award, Rodbell opted for early retirement, because there were no funds to support the research he wanted to do. Upon receiving the Nobel Prize, Rodbell was vocal in his criticism of the government because of its unwillingness to provide adequate support for fundamental research. He criticized them for favoring projects that yield obviously tangible and potentially profitable results, like drug treatments. Rodbell's other awards include the NIH Distinguished Service Award in 1973 and the Gairdner Award in 1984.

SELECTED WRITINGS BY RODBELL:

Books

(With Robert S. Adelstein and Claude B. Klee) *Advances in Second Messenger and Phosphoprotein Research.* Raven Press, 1988.

(With Robert S. Adelstein and Claude B. Klee) *Advances in Second Messenger and Phosphoprotein Research/Sixth International Conference/Formerly Advances in Cyclic Nucleotide and Protine Phosphoryl.* Raven Press, June 1988.

Periodicals

"Glucagon-Sensitive Adenyl Cyclase System in Plasma Membranes of Rat Liver. Obligatory Role of of Guanyl Nucleotides in Glucagon Action." *Journal of Biological Chemistry*, 1971.

FURTHER READING:

Periodicals

Begley, Sharon. "The Biological Switchboard." *Newsweek*, (October 24, 1994): 65-66.

Bronstein, Scott. "South Carolinian, Texan Win Nobel for Showing How Cells 'Talk'." *Atlanta Constitution*, (October 11, 1994): A3.

Friend, Tim. "U.S. Duo Receive Nobel Prize for Cell Research." *USA Today*, (October 11, 1994) : 3D.

Marx, Jean. "Medicine: A Signal Award for Discovering G-Proteins." *Science*, (October 21, 1994): 368-69.

Silverman, Edward R.. "Colleagues Laud 1994 Nobelists As Overdue for Coveted Prize." *The Scientist*, (November 28, 1994): 1.

Sketch by Pamela Proffitt

Leon Raymand Roddy
1921–1975
American entomologist and arachnologist

Around Louisiana, Leon Roddy was known simply as "The Spider Man." The transplanted Texan taught entomology—the study of insects—for 20 years at Southern University in Baton Rouge and became known nationally as the man to see when you had a strange spider on your hands. When he finished his Ph.D. in entomology at Ohio State University in 1953, he was probably one of only three African-American insect specialists in the United States.

A systematist who specialized in identifying and categorizing insects, Roddy single-handedly organized and catalogued the Southern University collection of more than 1,000 previously unknown insects. But his real passion became spiders, family *Acracnida*. After cleaning up and identifying Southern's small collection of spiders, Roddy began scouring the bayous and woods of Louisiana, looking for new species, often in difficult conditions. He identified many new species and published several well-received papers on spiders. As his reputation grew, he also consulted with worried homeowners and the U.S. Army. Though his position at Southern was primarily a teaching post, he continued his research energetically, often at his own expense, throughout his life. "In my opinion, research is one of the tools of a good teacher," he told an *Ebony Magazine* interviewer in 1962.

Earns a Chance at Education

Roddy was the second son of Floyd and Mattie Roddy of Whitewith, in western Texas. His father worked in the flour mill in Amarillo and got his son summer work there, in the hopes that Leon would follow in his footsteps. But Leon had other ideas, starting with college. After graduating from Sherman High School in nearby Sherman, Texas, Leon had to scrape together the money he needed to attend Texas College, a Methodist school in Tyler. Thanks to strong grades in biology, English, math, and foreign languages, Roddy also earned a small scholarship for college. He continued to work two jobs while attending college, but still managed to earn good grades.

Just one week shy of graduation from Texas College, Roddy, along with hundreds of thousands of other young Americans incensed by the Japanese attack on Pearl Harbor, enlisted in the armed forces. He was in basic training for the U.S. Army when Texas College granted Roddy a bachelor's degree *in absentia*. The Army shipped him out to Europe, where he fought for 18 months in an artillery unit that saw action in the "Battle of the Bulge."

After an honorable discharge in 1945, Roddy resumed his studies as a graduate student at the University of Michigan, with financial support from the federal government under the GI Bill. An encounter there with a dragonfly researcher changed Roddy's focus and made him pursue insects full time, and he moved to Ohio State University's stronger entomology program for his Ph.D.

However, Roddy was supporting a wife and child at the time, and he had to interrupt his studies in Columbus after only one term to earn some money. He accepted a teaching position in biology at Tillotson College in Texas, and stayed there for two years before returning to Ohio State. His Ph.D. was finished in only a year and a half. Roddy apparently had several job offers to choose from upon graduation, but he settled on Southern, one of three traditionally black colleges in the south that made him an offer. "Somehow, I felt needed back home," he told biographer Edward S. Jenkins in *To Fathom More: African American Scientists and Inventors.*

Roddy had three daughters with his wife Marian Daniel Roddy, who was a nurse, and a son, Leon, by an earlier marriage. He died of cancer on June 22, 1975, at the age of 54.

SELECTED WRITINGS BY RODDY:

Periodicals

"New Species, Records of Clubinoid Spiders." *Transactions of the American Microscopic Society* 85: 399-407.

FURTHER READING:

Books

Jenkins, Edward Sidney. *To Fathom More: African American Scientists and Inventors.* Lantham, Maryland: University Press of America, 1996.

Periodicals

"Man Who Understands Spiders." *Ebony* (March 1962): 65-70.

Sketch by Karl Leif Bates

Wendell L. Roelofs
1938–
American biochemist

Wendell L. Roelofs was instrumental in developing insect sex attractants—substances used to attract insects—for pest control in crops. An organic chemist by training, Roelofs has identified more than 100 attractants of different insect species, using a technique that was hailed as a major breakthrough. Roelofs conducted tests in fields to determine how to use the attractants to lure male insects to traps or to confuse them, thus preventing them from mating.

Wendell Lee Roelofs was born on July 26, 1938, in Orange City, Iowa, to Edward and Edith Beyers Roelofs. His father was a life insurance salesman and former superintendent of schools. Roelofs was the youngest of three boys; his two brothers also became scientists, one of

them a chemist and the other an electrical engineer. As an undergraduate at Central College in Pella, Iowa, Roelofs majored in chemistry. He earned his bachelor's degree in 1960 and subsequently married Marilyn Joyce Kuiken. The couple raised four children: Brenda Jo, Caryn Jean, Jeffrey Lee, and Kevin Jon.

Roelofs attended graduate school at Indiana University in Bloomington and studied organic chemistry. He wrote his doctorate thesis on biologically active compounds with potential use in medicine. For his post-doctoral work, Roelofs moved on to the Massachusetts Institute of Technology (MIT). While looking for a job in 1965, Roelofs heard of an opening in the entomology department at Cornell University's New York State Agricultural Experiment Station. The department chair, Paul Chapman, was looking for an organic chemist to explore insect sex attractants called pheromones.

Rachel Carson's book, *Silent Spring,* published in 1962, had raised consciousness about the overuse of toxic pesticides to control insects and the need for alternatives. Female insects relied on pheromones to attract mates. Instead of poisons, pheromones could be used to prevent insects from mating and multiplying. Roelofs had never even taken a college course in biology, but the job piqued his interest in the subject. He was hired as an assistant professor, and his new research soon led him to the interface of the disciplines of chemistry and biology.

Every insect species used a unique blend of chemicals as a sex attractant; when Roelofs began his work in 1965, no more than a few had been identified. After nearly 30 years of research, one team of German researchers had discovered the composition of one sex attractant. The work required removing the glands from thousands of female insects, extracting the pheromone, and running it through tests to determine its chemical composition. The first task Roelofs faced at the agricultural station was to begin a mass breeding program to raise insects. He decided to study the voracious pest of apple crops, the redbanded leafroller moth. After extracting the pheromone from approximately 50,000 female moths, Roelofs used a new instrument called a gas chromatograph. He identified the pheromone's composition after about two years.

Roelofs then developed an even greater shortcut to identifying the pheromones. German researchers had been studying the response of silkworm antennae to pheromones by using an instrument called an electroantennogram. The antenna of a male moth was hooked up to a machine that recorded each time the moth responded to a pheromone. Roelofs realized that he could use the technique on male moths to identify sex attractants. Using the electroantennogram reduced identification time to a matter of days and, in some cases, hours. Roelofs isolated the sex attractants of more than 100 species, including the grape berry moth, the tobacco budworm moth, and the potato tuberworm.

As an anecdote about how the work became virtually routine, Roelofs recalled that he stopped identifying pheromones after those of the major pests of interest had been described. But upon retiring, a professor from the University of Michigan requested that Roelofs pinpoint one last pheromone. Roelofs offered to spend two days on it and pledged to quit if he could not get results. Within two days, he had found a blend that worked.

Once Roelofs knew the composition of the redbanded leafroller pheromone, he made an artificial blend in the lab. He tested it in the field, confirming that it did indeed attract male moths. From 1969 to 1972 Roelofs and his colleagues explored how to use the redbanded leafroller pheromones in pest control. They laced traps with pheromones to lure males. Moth populations could be suppressed, they found, using as few as one trap per tree. Since males detected pheromones in extremely minute amounts, the researchers also tried releasing enough pheromone to completely confuse and disorient them. In addition to using attractants to disrupt mating, Roelofs used them as a tool to lure insects to traps where their numbers could be monitored. Pesticide applications could then be reduced to times when they were strictly needed and most effective.

Throughout his career, Roelofs's work took him to many parts of the world. He joined delegations to the People's Republic of China in 1976, Japan in 1977, and the Soviet Union in 1978. Roelofs went to New Zealand in 1983 to help research the pheromones of pests attacking kiwi fruit crops. Researchers there had successfully identified the pheromones, yet when the pheromones were used in the field, the insects failed to respond. Roelofs and his colleagues discovered the underlying reason: the populations were actually composed of different species that looked very similar but used different pheromones.

Continuing their work in the United States, Roelofs and his colleague Timothy J. Dennehy, an associate professor of entomology, found a way to use pheromones against grape berry moths, the most serious insect pest for grape crops in North America east of the Rocky Mountains. At the time, more than 100 tons of pesticides were required to control the insects each year in New York state alone. In 1984 Roelofs and Dennehy found a way to seal grape berry moth pheromones inside the hollow plastic and wire ties used to keep the grape plants on their trellises. The ties leaked the pheromones slowly over 100 days, distracting the males from finding the females. Experiments showed that vineyards that had been treated with the pheromone generally had less than one percent damage, compared to approximately twenty-three percent in untreated areas.

As Roelofs advanced in his career, he gained pleasure from exploring different facets of pheromone research, from chemical analysis to the design of traps. He investigated how insects made pheromones in their bodies. Once pheromones were in the air, he studied how males honed in on the source. In the basement of a campus building, Roelofs and his colleagues built a wind tunnel for flying insects. A pheromone was released into the tunnel, where they could watch an insect as it navigated toward the source.

Although Roelofs had not foreseen that his work would lead into insect biochemistry, he was pleased with the outcome and timing of his career. "I got in at the ground floor of pheromone research. The field was wide open," Roelofs told Miyoko Chu in an interview. One of the joys of his work, Roelofs said, was the privilege of being able to work in different sub-fields, including molecular biology, endocrinology, and behavior.

In his spare time, Roelofs coaches a youth league football team of kids aged eleven and twelve. Roelofs likened a cooperative effort in the laboratory to teamwork in football. With a coach's natural ability, he fostered an atmosphere where people could contribute their academic strengths and interests. "With our wide range of interests, we can always follow the most interesting lead whether it's my area of expertise or not," he told Chu. "That's how we stay at the forefront. It's synergistic. There's more creativity among us all."

In 1978 Roelofs was named the Liberty Hyde Bailey Professor of Insect Biochemistry at the New York State Agricultural Experiment Station. He was awarded the 1982 Wolf Prize in Agriculture, considered the most prestigious international award in that field. The following year, former U.S. President Ronald Reagan awarded him the National Medal of Science.

SELECTED WRITINGS BY ROELOFS:

Books

Establishing Efficacy of Sex Attractants and Disruptants for Insect Control, Entomological Society of America, 1979.

FURTHER READING:

Books

Roelofs, Wendell L., *Interview with Miyoko Chu,* conducted September 4, 1993.

Sketch by Miyoko Chu

Marguerite M. Rogers
1916(?)–1989
American physicist

Marguerite M. Rogers was a physicist who played a significant role in the development of air-launched weapons systems for the United States Navy. For many years she led the Naval Air Warfare Center Weapons

Division and was considered an authority on air-launched tactical weapons.

Rogers received her undergraduate degree, M.A. and Ph.D. in physics from Rice University. She served as assistant professor at the University of Houston from 1940 to 1943, before joining the Naval Avionics Facility in Indianapolis as manager of the Optics Section of the Research Department. In 1946, she returned to academia as a research associate at the University of North Carolina, a post she held for two years. In 1948, she joined Oak Ridge National Laboratory as senior physicist. Rogers joined the Naval Ordnance Test Station (NOTS) in 1949, but in 1953 accepted a post as professor of physics and chair of the science division at Columbia College in South Carolina.

In 1957, Rogers renewed her association with NOTS, which later became the Naval Air Warfare Center Weapons Division. She at first was appointed electronics scientist, working on the development of fire-control and navigational systems. She led the Heavy Attack Systems Analysis Branch in 1958, the Air-to-Surface Weapons Division in 1962, and the Weapons Systems Analysis Division in 1966.

During her years with the Naval Air Warfare Center, Rogers contributed to the development of early fire-control systems, weapons effectiveness analyses, aerial rocketry, the "eye" weapon series used in the Vietnam War, and computerized aircraft avionics systems. She rose from project leader to acting laboratory director, and during her career managed a staff of 150 and a $100 million budget.

For her work in Naval weapons development, Rogers received the Naval Weapons Center's highest honor, the L. T. E. Thompson Award, in 1966; the Naval Air Systems Command Superior Civilian Service Award, also in 1966; the Harvey C. Knowles Award of the American Ordnance Association in 1967; the Society of Women Engineers Achievement Award in 1967; the Federal Women's Award in 1976; and the Department of Defense Distinguished Civilian Service Award in 1981. In bestowing one of her many honors, Captain J. I. Hardy said of Rogers: "Her sustained individual performance has demonstrated a high degree of personal integrity, sound judgment, and quality of leadership."

Rogers was married to Dr. Fred Rogers, who passed away in 1956; the couple had five children. Her two sons also became physicists in the defense industry. Rogers organized a 4-H Club in China Lake, California, and served as an officer of her church.

FURTHER READING:

Books

Society of Women Engineers Achievement Awards, Society of Women Engineers, 1993.

Periodicals

China Lake Rocketeer, Rogers Led the Way for Women—Devoted Her Life to Science, March 17, 1989, p. 3.
Society of Women Engineers Newsletter,'67 SWE Award Presented to Dr. Rogers, September, 1967, pp. 1–3.

Sketch by Karen Withem

Heinrich Rohrer
1933–
Swiss physicist

Heinrich Rohrer shared half of the 1986 Nobel Prize in physics with **Gerd Binnig** for their development of an entirely new type of microscope that revealed for the first time the atomic structure of the surface of solids. This scanning tunneling microscope (STM) has such a vast array of applications in such a wide range of fields that the Royal Swedish Academy of Sciences was prompted to award its prestigious prize even though the device had only been successfully tested for the first time in 1981.

Rohrer was born on June 6, 1933, in Buchs, St. Gallen, Switzerland, the son of Hans Heinrich Rohrer, a distributor of manufactured goods, and Katharina Ganpenbein Rohrer. When he was sixteen, Rohrer moved with his family from the country to the large city of Zurich. As a student, Rohrer was interested in both physics and chemistry and classical languages, finally settling on the study of physics when he entered the Federal Institute of Technology in Zurich in 1951. He received his diploma in 1955 and his Ph.D. in 1960, both in physics, from the Institute. His doctoral research involved superconductivity.

From 1960 to 1961 Rohrer was a research assistant at the Institute in Zurich and followed this with two years of postdoctoral research in superconducting at Rutgers University in the United States. On his return to Zurich in 1963, Rohrer joined the staff of the research laboratory of International Business Machines (IBM), eventually becoming manager of the physics department as well as an IBM Fellow. Rohrer has remained at the IBM lab throughout his career, except for an academic year as a visiting scholar at the University of California, Santa Barbara, in 1974–75, when he studied nuclear magnetic resonance. In 1961, Rohrer married Rose-Marie Eggar; the couple had two daughters.

After joining IBM, Rohrer expanded his research in physics beyond superconductivity, investigating magnetic fields and critical phenomena. He became interested in the little-understood and complex atomic structures of the surfaces of materials. While electron microscopes had been developed to probe the internal arrangements of atoms in materials, attempts to uncover the very different characteristics of surface atoms had been decidedly unsuccessful. In 1978 Gerd Binnig, a young German who had just received his Ph.D., joined Rohrer's research team in Zurich. Together, Rohrer and Binnig began to explore oxide layers on metal surfaces. They decided to develop a spectroscopic probe and in the process invented an entirely new type of microscope.

Rohrer and Binnig began with the phenomenon called tunneling. As revealed through quantum mechanics, electrons behave in a wavelike manner that causes them to produce a diffuse cloud as they leak out from the surface of a sample. When electron clouds from two adjacent surfaces overlap, electrons tunnel from one surface or cloud to the other. Tunneling through an insulating layer had been used often to reveal information about the materials on either side of the insulation. Rohrer and Binnig decided to tunnel through a vacuum and then use a sharp, needlelike probe within the vacuum to scan the sample's surface. As the scanning tip closely approached the sample, the electron clouds of each overlapped and a tunneling current began to flow. A feedback mechanism used the tunneling current to keep the tip at a constant height above the sample's surface. In this way, the tip followed the contours of the individual atoms of the scanned surface, and a computer processed the tip's motion to produce a three-dimensional, high-resolution image of that surface.

From the beginning, Rohrer told *Science* magazine, "We were quite confident. Even at the beginning, we knew it would be a significant development. The surprising thing is that it went so fast." One large problem was the sensitivity of the scanning tip to disturbances from vibration and noise. Here Rohrer's background in superconductors was helpful, because transducers too are extremely sensitive to vibration. Rohrer and Binnig solved the problem by shielding their scanner from disturbances with magnets and a heavy stone table set on inflated rubber tires. They successfully tested their new device in 1981 and then worked to refine it technologically. By the mid–1980s the STM could fit in the palm of the hand (except for the vacuum chamber) and could show some details as tiny as 0.1 angstrom (with 1 angstrom being about the diameter of a single atom, or 2.5 billionths of an inch). STMs were also developed that worked in water, air, and cryogenic fluids as well as vacuums. By 1987 Rohrer's group at IBM had developed an STM the size of a fingertip.

Rohrer may not have been surprised when he and Binnig shared half of the Nobel Prize in 1986 for their STM. After he received the honor, Rohrer told *Business Week* that when he explained to colleagues at the IBM lab what he and Binnig planned to try, "They all said, 'You are completely crazy—but if it works, you'll get the Nobel Prize'." In awarding the prize, the Swedish Academy conceded that the STM was completely new and barely yet developed. Nevertheless, the Academy stated, because of the STM, "It

is . . . clear that entirely new fields are opening up for the study of the structure of matter." This study has included living organisms such as viruses, catalysts used to produce chemical reactions in the pharmaceutical and petrochemical industries, and semiconductors and metals. (Interestingly, the other recipient of the 1986 Nobel Prize in physics was **Ernst Ruska**, for his design of the first electron microscope in 1931, fifty years before Rohrer and Binnig developed their scanning microscope.)

Rohrer shared other international awards with Binnig for his work on the STM. He is a member of many important scientific societies and has been awarded honorary doctorates by several universities.

SELECTED WRITINGS BY ROHRER:

Periodicals

Scientific American, The Scanning Tunneling Microscope, August, 1985, pp. 50–56.
Review of Modern Physics, Scanning Tunneling Microscopy: From Birth to Adolescence, Volume 59, No. 3, 1987.

FURTHER READING:

Books

Hansma, Paul K., *Tunneling Spectroscopy: Capabilities, Applications, and New Techniques,* Plenum Press, 1982.
Hansma, Paul K., *Nobel Prize Winners,* H. W. Wilson, 1987.
Hansma, Paul K., *Nobel Prize Winners: Physics,* Volume 3, Salem Press, 1989.
Scanning Tunnelling Microscopy, Springer-Verlag, 1992.

Periodicals

Hansma, Paul K., *Business Week,* November, 3, 1986, pp. 134–36.
Hansma, Paul K., *The Lancet,* September, 5, 1992, pp. 600–01.
Hansma, Paul K., *New York Times,* October 16, 1986, pp. A1 & B18.
Hansma, Paul K., *Physics Today,* January, 1987, pp. 17–21, S–70.
Hansma, Paul K., *Science,* November 14, 1986, pp. 821–22.
Hansma, Paul K., *Science News,* October 25, 1986, pp. 262–63.
Wickramasinghe, H. Kumar, *Scientific American,* Scanned-Probe Microscopes, October, 1989, pp. 98–105.

Sketch by Kathy Sammis

Nancy Grace Roman
1925–
American astronomer

Nancy Grace Roman is famous for developing satellite observatories to explore the universe from a vantage point that is free from atmospheric interference. She also pioneered using satellites for gamma, x ray, and radio observations. In addition, she has conducted observational astronomical research using traditional earth-based telescopes, studying topics such as stellar motions, photoelectric photometry and spectroscopy.

Roman was born in Nashville, Tennessee, on May 16, 1925, to a U.S. Geological Survey geophysicist, Irwin Roman, and his wife, Georgia Frances (Smith) Roman. Educated at Western High School in Baltimore, Maryland, Roman graduated in 1943. She then earned a B.A. in astronomy at Pennsylvania's Swarthmore College, where she was named a Joshua Lippincott Memorial Fellow and worked in the Sproul Observatory. From 1946 to 1948 Roman attended graduate courses at the University of Chicago, assisting at the Yerkes Observatory in Williams Bay, Wisconsin. She earned her Ph.D. in astronomy in 1949; her doctoral research investigated the radial velocities, spectra, and convergent point of the Ursa Major group of stars. Her dissertation appeared in the September 1949 *Astrophysical Journal.*

Also in 1949, Roman worked as a summer research associate at the Case Institute of Technology's Warner and Swasey Observatory, cataloguing high luminosity objects and classifying objective spectra. That fall, she returned to Yerkes, where she served as a research associate between 1949 and 1952, and then as an astronomy instructor from 1952 to 1955. She also made a brief visit in 1953 to Toronto's David Dunlap Observatory to study the radial velocities of certain high-speed faint stars. At Yerkes she researched stellar astronomy and galactic structure, specializing in radial velocity measurements, photoelectric photometry, and spectral classification. She was particularly interested in stellar clusters.

In 1955, Roman moved to the United States Naval Research Observatory (NRO) in Washington, D.C., where she first worked in radio astronomy, soon becoming the head of the microwave spectroscopy lab. Using a 50-foot cast aluminum mirror, Roman researched radio star spectra and the galactic distribution of radio emitters. In addition, she used radar to find the distance between the Earth and the Moon. During this time she attended a 1957 Soviet Academy of Sciences Symposium to dedicate their new Bjuraken Astrophysical Observatory, and the following year she edited the fifth International Astronomical Union Symposium on large-scale galactic structure. In 1958 and 1959 she worked as an NRO consulting astronomer, educating others about radio astronomy and planning the institution's research programs. Roman dramatically expanded her work when in March of 1959 she became the head of the observational astronomy program head at the National Aeronautics and Space Administration (NASA). At NASA Roman developed an ambitious plan to observe objects in space by using rockets and satellite observatories. Charged with developing these efforts, in February, 1960, she was named chief of astronomy and astrophysics at NASA's office of satellites and sounding rockets.

Throughout the 1960s Roman designed instrumentation and made substantial measurements from gamma ray, radio, and visible light satellites, such as the Orbiting Solar Observatories. Her programs gave astronomers the planetary surface knowledge that ultimately led to the successful 1976 *Viking* probes that were designed to collect data from Mars. She became the astronomy program head in 1964 and the chief of the astronomy and relativity program in 1972, remaining in this position until 1979. Her published work from this period generally deals with new satellite data, but she still did Earth-based observation, such as her 1967 Kitt Peak Observatory radial velocity and spectral research. She received a NASA award for Exceptional Scientific Research in 1969, and a medal for Outstanding Leadership in 1978. Roman was also granted honorary doctorates from Russell Sage, Hood, Bates, and Swarthmore Colleges between 1966 and 1976.

Roman improved her orbiting observatories throughout the 1970s and 1980s. She measured x ray and ultraviolet readings from the enormously successful OAO–3 or *Copernicus* satellite, launched in 1972, and recorded stellar spectra from the U.S. space station *Skylab*, which circled the Earth between 1973 and 1979. During 1979 and 1980 she was also NASA program scientist for a projected space telescope; unfortunately, a decade of cost overruns and delays postponed the launch of NASA's Hubble space telescope until April 25, 1990. Meanwhile, as a NASA consulting astronomer, beginning in 1980, and a senior scientist for the Astronomical Data Center from 1981 onwards, Roman worked to prepare computer-readable versions of astronomical catalogues, databases, and other bibliographic tools.

SELECTED WRITINGS BY ROMAN:

Books

Comparison of the Large Scale Structure of the Galactic System with That of Other Systems, Cambridge University Press (Cambridge), 1958.

Periodicals

Astrophysical Journal, The Ursa Major Group, Volume 110, 1949, pp. 205–241.

FURTHER READING:

Books

The Women's Book of World Records and Achievements, edited by Lois Decker O'Neill, Anchor Books, 1979, pp. 88, 153.

Periodicals

Blackburn, Harriet B., interview with Roman, *Christian Science Monitor,* June 13, 1957.

Blackburn, Harriet B., interview with Roman, *New York Times,* Scientist Accepts Soviet Bid September 7, 1956, p. 21.

Blackburn, Harriet B., interview with Roman, *New York Times,* 6 Women Hailed for U.S. Service February 6, 1962, p. 39.

Sketch by Julian A. Smith

Alfred Sherwood Romer
1894–1973
American vertebrate paleontologist and anatomist

Some scientists gain prominence through path-breaking research. Others write landmark publications, control key institutions, or train a generation of devoted and skilled disciples. Alfred Sherwood Romer did each of these and more, becoming one of the century's most important vertebrate paleontologists. His unique approach to vertebrate evolution through comparative anatomy led to his prominence in the field, and he also wrote a series of textbooks based on his work.

Born in White Plains, New York, to Harry Houston Romer and Evalyn (Sherwood) Romer on December 28, 1894, Romer claimed an ancestry of predominately New England Puritan, grounded in the 1628–1640 migration, and "a good dash of Scotch-Irish blood," as he wrote to Hugh L. Dryden. Romer's father was a newspaperman who frequently moved the family between New York State and Connecticut. His parents divorced when Alfred was ten; his father's second marriage also collapsed. During this period, Romer lived in a "somewhat miserable situation," often ill, poor, and on his own, as he noted in his letter to Dryden. The situation improved when he went to live with his paternal grandmother for his high school years. After graduating, Romer spent a year doing small jobs and saving money for college.

Romer entered Amherst University in 1914, majoring in German literature and history. He pledged Phi Kappa Psi fraternity, supported himself through small jobs and fraternity loans, and moved from sports reporter to editor-in-chief for *The Amherst Student.* Searching for an easy class to fulfill science requirements while a sophomore, Romer enrolled in a course on evolution, taught in part by vertebrate paleontologist Frederick Brewster Loomis. Captivated by Loomis's section of fossil vertebrates, Romer had, by year's end, chosen his career path, although completing his originally intended liberal arts degree.

Caught in the nation's patriotic fervor in 1917, Romer volunteered for the American Field Service shortly after graduation. He had hoped to drive ambulances in World War I, instead, he transported ammunition in the Soissons sector. Seeking a military commission after his unit was dissolved, Romer joined the U.S. Air Service, where he eventually commanded a repair facility and rose to the rank of second lieutenant. He returned to New York in 1919. With Loomis's recommendation, he entered Columbia University that fall, eager to study vertebrate paleontology at the graduate level. At the time, Columbia provided superb training from internationally renowned biologists and paleontologists. Romer studied under William King Gregory, well-known for his understanding of the vertebrate skull, and became part of a close circle of students, including **G. Kinsely Noble**, Charles Camp, and James Chopin. His dissertation on the evolution of locomotory muscles in early reptile groups developed from a comparative myology course taught by Gregory.

After receiving his Ph.D. within a remarkably short period of time in 1921, Romer accepted an instructorship at Bellevue Medical College in New York. It was not uncommon for vertebrate paleontologists to support themselves by teaching anatomy in medical schools. For two years Romer taught histology, embryology, and gross anatomy. (He was a quick learner and often taught courses in specialties for which he had no formal training.) In 1923, Romer was scheduled to direct the human anatomy laboratory at Bellevue, but instead accepted an offer from the University of Chicago to succeed Samuel Williston as its vertebrate paleontologist.

A Foothold in the Profession

The Chicago associate professorship was an enormous opportunity for Romer. Williston had studied early reptiles and amphibians and, together with his chief preparator Paul Miller, had built a considerable collection along these lines. Also interested in the early evolution of tetrapods, Romer eagerly expanded both Williston's research and the Chicago collections. His first expedition to the Permian red-beds of Texas—from which the majority of the existing collection originated—came in 1926; over the years, he returned many times to that region. Furthermore in 1929, Romer and Miller spent six months in South Africa collecting in the Karroo formation, returning with an impressive set of discoveries. The result of this sustained campaign was one of the world's finest collections of early land vertebrates. Romer was promoted to full professor in 1931.

In Chicago, Romer was active in many social and academic circles, including the university's Quadrangle Club and the city-wide Chaos Club. At the university, Romer cooperated with innovators of the general biology curriculum, such as zoologist Horatio Hackett Newman. He even contributed a chapter on the history of vertebrates to Newman's coursebook, *The Nature of the World and of Man,* published in 1926. Stimulated in part by his participation in this effort, Romer decided to expand his chapter into books for two different markets. His *Man and the Vertebrates,* published in 1933, was a general-audience survey of comparative vertebrate anatomy and vertebrate evolution that hinted at Romer's political and social philosophy. As a textbook designed for training specialists, *Vertebrate Paleontology,* published in the same year, complemented his popular treatment by covering the same domain in considerable technical detail. Both books filled long-neglected markets, became standard reading, and were extensively reprinted and translated.

Vertebrate paleontology had marginal status at Chicago, largely because it operated within a geology department where most professors were uninterested in such "soft" geology. Romer's approach was biological, and he often found himself at odds with department colleagues on matters of financial and academic support. As the Depression grew and the University's administration lost its creativity, Romer found an increasing number of obstacles impeding his research and teaching interests.

Fed up with his departmental situation, Romer left Chicago in 1934 for Harvard University and the Museum of Comparative Zoology (MCZ). He had been offered the position of professor of zoology along with being named curator of vertebrate paleontology at the museum. The year before, the school's new president, James Conant, had begun a program to transform the antiquated college into a world-class, modern teaching and research institution. At Harvard, Romer pursued a diverse research program on early land vertebrates in an atmosphere extremely sympathetic to his biological approach. His annual courses on comparative vertebrate anatomy and vertebrate paleontology were mainstays within the museum.

Romer became director of the MCZ in 1946, following the death of long-time patriarch Thomas Barbour. Knowing his appointment would mean the sacrifice of vital time for research, Romer still accepted the role. At the time, the museum's management was in a poor situation: its endowment was ridiculously small; staff labored under meager salaries and low budgets; and researchers demonstrated severely uneven talents. Romer immediately negotiated for improvements and increased support both from Conant's administration and from the family of Louis Agassiz, the influential nineteenth-century zoologist who had founded the MCZ. Slowly, the museum situation turned around. After nearly two decades as director, Romer believed he had succeeded in returning the MCZ to "first rate" status. Mandatory administration retirement brought his resignation from the post in 1961. Although he had managed to continue some of his research program while director,

Romer returned to research and exploration in full force following retirement. Nearly half his bibliography was published following his sixty-fifth birthday. Romer continued at the MCZ until his unexpected death on November 5, 1973.

Central to Romer's life and career was his companionship with his wife, Ruth (Hibbard) Romer. They married in 1924, raised three children, and kept many close friends. Ruth Romer accompanied her husband on many of his travels. She also collected fossils with him and helped administer both his research and his social life. As Edwin H. Colbert pointed out in his article for the National Academy of Sciences, however, Ruth Romer was no mere assistant; rather she "complimented [Romer] in a marvelous fashion."

Building a Profession for Bone Hunters

Romer made many important contributions to vertebrate paleontology's professional development. Frustrated by a lack of recognition among geologists and invertebrate paleontologists regarding the biological interests of his "vertebrate" colleagues, Romer helped organize an independent Section of Vertebrate Paleontology within the Paleontological Society in 1934. By providing a meeting place for him and his colleagues, this Section provided a means for building the cadre of vertebrate workers into a cohesive group. In 1940, the Section transformed itself into the Society of Vertebrate Paleontology. Romer sought similar developments for comparative anatomy within the American Society of Zoologists in 1959. Throughout his life, Romer demanded informality and camaraderie within his profession. He firmly believed that everyone present at society meetings be given an opportunity to discuss any subject they wished during open forums.

Two themes unified Romer's research. Foremost was an interest in the functional implications of anatomical structures. Romer strove to reconstruct and understand extinct animals as once-living organisms. This emphasis found expression in his research on muscle evolution in amphibians and reptiles, the origin and evolution of limbs, the embryonic and evolutionary history of cartilage and bone, and the structure and function of the nervous system. Second, Romer focused on major evolutionary transitions, choosing research topics with implications for the transition from fish to amphibians, amphibians to reptiles, and reptiles to mammals.

Romer described himself as primarily a comparative anatomist. A comprehensive knowledge of vertebrate anatomy is clear from his classic descriptive monographs and from *Vertebrate Paleontology.* His skills as a technical anatomist and taxonomist were demonstrated in his many studies of vertebrate skull structures, Permian and Carboniferous reptiles, labyrinthodont amphibians, and mammal-like reptiles. Although a solid neo-Darwinian, Romer avoided theorizing about evolutionary mechanisms, preferring instead to emphasize empirical studies of evolutionary change. A non-geologist by preference, Romer occasionally ventured into stratigraphy. His last expedition to the Texas red-beds involved detailed mapping of the region's geological history. As Ronald Rainger notes in *Perspectives on Science,* Romer also was one of the first vertebrate paleontologists to suggest the plausibility of continental drift. Through his academic efforts, his writings, and devotion to his profession, Romer left a rich legacy. His effect on the direction of professional bodies and research institutions continues.

SELECTED WRITINGS BY ROMER:

Books

Man and the Vertebrates, University of Chicago Press, 1933.
Vertebrate Paleontology, University of Chicago Press, 1933.
The Vertebrate Body, W. B. Saunders, 1949.
Osteology of the Reptiles, University of Chicago Press, 1956.
Bibliography of Fossil Vertebrates Exclusive of North America, 1509–1927, two volumes, Geological Society of America, 1962.

Periodicals

Geological Society of America Special Paper, Review of the Pelycosauria, Volume 26, 1940, pp. i-x, 1–538.
Bulletin of the Museum of Comparative Zoology, Review of the Labyrinthodontia, Volume 99, 1947, pp. 1–368.
Bulletin of the Museum of Comparative Zoology, A Classification of Therapsid Reptiles, Volume 114, 1956, pp. 37–89.
Evolution, Early Reptilian Evolution Reviewed, December, 1967, pp. 821–33.
Science, Cynodont Reptile with Incipient Mammalian Jaw Articulation, November 14, 1969, pp. 881–82.

FURTHER READING:

Periodicals

Anatomical Record, Volume 189, 1977, pp. 314–24.
Biographical Memoirs of Fellows of the Royal Society, Volume 21, Royal Society (London), 1975, pp. 497–516.
Geological Society of America Memorials, Volume 5, 1977, p. 10.
National Academy of Sciences. Biographical Memoirs, 1982, pp. 265–94.
Perspectives on Science, Volume 1, 1993, pp. 478–519.

Other

Perspectives on Science, Alfred Romer's letter to George Simpson, July 16, 1933, American Philosophical Society Library.

Perspectives on Science, Alfred Romer's letter to Hugh L. Dryden, June 5, 1961, National Academy of Sciences Archives.

Sketch by Joseph Cain

Juan Carlos Romero
1937–
Argentinian-born American physiologist

Juan Carlos Romero is a renowned authority on the physiology of the kidney. As director of the Hypertension Research Laboratories at the Mayo Clinic since 1982, he has been a prolific investigator into the relationship of the kidney to the development of hypertension (high blood pressure) and has issued more than 175 research papers on kidney functioning during the past thirty years. Since 1984, he has been awarded grants from the National Institute of Health totaling over three million dollars for research and training programs dealing with kidney function and hypertension.

Romero was born on September 15, 1937, in Mendoza, Argentina, the son of Juan Romero and Graciela Vizcaya. He attended San Jose College in Mendoza and graduated with a B.S. in 1955. The next year, he was admitted to the University of Cuyo School of Medicine, Mendoza. While there, he was awarded a scholarship for being one of the two best qualified students. He left school for military service in the Argentine Army in 1958, and rose to the rank of sergeant. He then returned to medical education, married Silvia Divinetz in 1963, and received his M.D. in 1964. Romero began his career in scientific investigation when he became a research assistant in the Institute of Pathological Physiology in 1962 and then continued on as a Fellow at the Consejo Nacional de Investigaciones, also in Mendoza, in 1966.

After Romero was honored with the competitive award of Fellow in the Eli Lilly International Program for Development of Biological Sciences in 1967, he came to the United States to continue his research at the University of Michigan. There, he rose to the position of research associate in the hypertension section of the Department of Internal Medicine. In 1973, he transferred to the Mayo Foundation in Rochester, Minnesota, and has remained there ever since, becoming professor of physiology at the Mayo Medical School and director of the Hypertension Research Laboratories.

Romero has done considerable research on the renin-angiotensin system. It has been discovered that the kidney plays a key role in the incidence of hypertension. With its million or so microscopic nephrons filtering wastes out of the bloodstream, the kidney is a vital organ of excretion that cleanses the blood and also helps maintain the appropriate balance of water and mineral salts in the body. Under certain conditions, the kidney secretes the enzyme renin which reacts in the blood with a protein secreted by the liver to form angiotensin, a vasoconstrictor which causes the smooth muscles of small blood vessels to contract, resulting in elevated blood pressure. He has also explored the effects of the atrial natriuretic peptide, which is produced by the atria of the heart when the blood pressure and volume of blood entering the atria are too high, stimulating the kidneys to excrete more salt and water into the urine. This results in a lowering of blood volume and blood pressure.

Among other areas of his expertise are renal prostaglandin, renal synthesis of nitric oxide, responses of isolated glomeruli (the glomular filters help purify the blood), and evaluation of renal function with computerized tomography, a form of radiology, or x ray, used to examine an organ and the blood flow to an organ. In connection with the latter investigation, in 1991 he received the Cum Laude Research Award from the American Society of Computed Body Tomography for the best scientific work on cross-sectional imaging.

In addition to the Cum Laude Research award, Romero was elected to Sigma Xi and received a competitive award as Established Investigator of the American Heart Association from 1976–1981. He also won the Teacher of the Year Award of the Mayo School of Medicine in 1984. In 1991, he was elected by the Council for High Blood Pressure Research to give the Lewis K. Dahl Memorial Lecture in the American Heart Association's 464th Scientific Session. He has been a key member and chairman of numerous groups specializing in hypertension. Through the years, Romero has also been affiliated with twenty different scientific journals. He is now a U.S. citizen, and he and his wife have two children, Patricia and Gabriela.

SELECTED WRITINGS BY ROMERO:

Books

Hypertension Physiopathology and Treatment, Production and Characteristics of Experimental Hypertension in Animals, McGraw-Hill, 1977, pp. 485–507.

Renal Function Tests: Clinical Laboratory Procedures and Diagnosis, The Renin-Angiotensin System, Little, Brown, 1979, pp. 119–36.

Periodicals

The Physiologist, The Renin-Angiotensin System, Volume 24, Number 5, 1981, p. 59.

American Journal of Physiology, Renal Effects of ANP without Changes in Glomerular Filtration Rate and Blood Pressure, Volume 251, 1986, pp. F532–36.

Hypertension, Are Renal Hemodynamics a Key Factor in the Development of Arterial

Hypertension in Humans?, Volume 23, 1994, pp. 3–9.

Sketch by Maurice Bleifeld

Wilhelm Conrad Röntgen
1845–1923
German physicist

For the first two decades of his scientific career, Wilhelm Conrad Röntgen studied a fairly diverse variety of topics, including the specific heats of gases, the Faraday effect in gases, magnetic effects associated with dielectric materials, and the compressibility of water. He is most famous, however, for his discovery in 1895 of x rays, which had a revolutionary effect not only on physics but also on a number of other areas, particularly medicine. For this discovery, Röntgen was awarded the first Nobel Prize in physics in 1901.

Röntgen was born in Lennep, Germany, on March 27, 1845. He was the only child of Friedrich Conrad Röntgen and the former Charlotte Frowein. His father was a textile merchant who came from a long line of metal workers and cloth merchants. His mother had been born in Lennep but then moved with her family to Amsterdam, where they had become wealthy as merchants and traders. When Röntgen was three years old, his family moved to Apeldorn, Holland. Otto Glasser speculates in *Dr. W. C. Röntgen* that the revolution of 1848 may have been a factor in this move because the family lost its German citizenship on May 23, 1848, and became Dutch citizens a few months later. In any case, Röntgen received his primary and secondary education in the public schools of Apeldorn and at a private boarding school in Middelann.

In December 1862, Röntgen enrolled at the Utrecht Technical School. His education at Utrecht was interrupted after about two years, however, when a childish prank went awry. He confessed to having drawn a caricature of an unpopular teacher for which another student had been responsible. As punishment, Röntgen was expelled from school, and his education was stalled until January 1865, when he was given permission to attend the University of Utrecht as an irregular student. There he attended classes on analysis, physics, chemistry, zoology, and botany. His future still seemed bleak, however, and, according to Glasser, "both Wilhelm and his parents had become resigned to his seeming inability to adjust to the requirements of the Dutch educational system and to obtain the credentials necessary to become a regular university student."

Wilhelm Conrad Röntgen

A friend of Röntgen's told him about the liberal admission policies at the Swiss Federal Institute of Technology in Zurich. Röntgen applied and was admitted at Zurich, and he arrived there to begin his studies in the mechanical technical branch of the institute on November 16, 1865. Over the next three years, Röntgen pursued a course of study that included classes in mathematics, technical drawing, mechanical technology, engineering, metallurgy, hydrology, and thermodynamics. On August 6, 1868, he was awarded his diploma in mechanical engineering. His degree had come in spite of his rather irregular attendance at classes. He later told Ludwig Zehnder that the lake and mountains surrounding Zurich were "too tempting." As a result, he became a devoted mountain climber and boater but an undistinguished student. Only when one of his professors told Röntgen that he would fail his examinations did he settle down to his studies.

Begins Scientific Career under the Influence of August Kundt

At Zurich, the most important influence on Röntgen was the German physicist August Kundt. Kundt suggested to him that he do his graduate studies in physics rather than engineering, and Röntgen took his advice. On June 22, 1869, he was granted his doctoral degree for a thesis entitled "Studies about Gases." Kundt then asked him to become his assistant, an offer he quickly accepted. A year later, when Kundt was offered the chair of physics at the University of Würzburg in Germany, he brought Röntgen with him as his assistant.

While still in Zurich, Röntgen had met his future wife, Anna Bertha Ludwig, the daughter of a German revolutionary who had emigrated to Switzerland. They were married on January 19, 1872, after his move to Würzburg. The couple never had children of their own, although in 1887 they did adopt his wife's six-year-old niece Josephine Bertha.

After two years at Würzburg, Kundt moved once more, this time to the newly established University of Strasbourg in France. Again, he asked Röntgen to accompany him as his assistant. At Strasbourg, in March 1874, Röntgen finally achieved a long-delayed ambition: He was appointed a privatdozent at the university, his first official academic appointment. The appointment was the result of more liberal policies at Strasbourg; his lack of the necessary credentials had prevented him from receiving a formal appointment in any German university.

In 1875, Röntgen accepted a position as professor of physics at the Hohenheim Agricultural Academy. Missing the superb research facilities to which he had become accustomed in Strasbourg, however, he returned there in 1876 as associate professor of physics. Three years later he was appointed professor of physics at the University of Giessen in Germany, where he remained until 1888. He then returned to the University of Würzburg to take a joint appointment as professor of physics and director of the university's Physical Institute. Röntgen would remain at Würzburg until 1900, serving as rector of the university during his last six years there.

Röntgen wrote forty-eight papers on a diverse range of phenomena including the specific heats of gases, the heat conductivity of crystals, the Faraday and Kerr effects, the compressibility of solids and liquids, and pyroelectricity and piezoelectricity. Probably his most significant contribution during this period was a continuation of research originally suggested by James Clerk Maxwell's theory of electromagnetism. That theory had predicted that the motion of a dielectric material within an electrostatic field would induce a magnetic current within the dielectric material. During his last year at Giessen, Röntgen completed studies that confirmed this effect, a phenomenon for which **Hendrik Lorentz** suggested the name "röntgen current."

Work on Cathode Rays Results in Discovery of X Rays

Yet there is no doubt that the discovery for which Röntgen will always be most famous is that of x rays. In 1894 Röntgen began research on cathode rays, which was then one of the most popular topics in physics. Much of the fundamental research on this topic had been carried out in the 1870s by the English physicist William Crookes. Crookes had found that the discharge of an electrical current within a vacuum tube produces a beam of negatively charged rays that causes a fluorescence on the glass walls of the tube. A number of scientists had followed up on this research, trying to discover more about the nature and characteristics of Crookes's cathode rays.

After repeating some of the earlier experiments on cathode rays, Röntgen's own research took an unexpected turn on November 8, 1895. In order to observe the luminescence caused by cathode rays more clearly, Röntgen darkened his laboratory and enclosed the vacuum tube he was using in black paper. When he turned on the apparatus, he happened to notice that a screen covered with barium platinocyanide crystals about a meter from the vacuum tube began to glow. This observation was startling, because Röntgen knew that cathode rays themselves travel no more than a few centimeters in air. It was not they, therefore, that caused the screen to glow.

Over the next seven weeks, Röntgen attempted to learn as much as he could about this form of energy. He discovered that its effect could be detected at great distances from the vacuum tube, suggesting that the radiation was very strong. He learned that the radiation passed easily through some materials, such as glass and wood, but was obstructed by other materials, such as metals. At one point, he even saw the bones in his hand as he held out a piece of lead before it. He also discovered that the radiation was capable of exposing a photographic plate. Because of the unknown and somewhat mysterious character of this radiation, Röntgen gave it the name *X strahlen,* or x rays.

On December 28, 1895, seven weeks after his first discovery of x rays, Röntgen communicated news of his work to the editors of a scientific journal published by the Physical and Medical Society of Würzburg. Six days earlier, he had made the world's first x-ray photograph, a picture of his wife's hand. Within weeks, news of Röntgen's discovery had reached the popular press, and the general public was captivated by the idea of seeing the skeletons of living people. On January 13, 1896, Röntgen was ordered to demonstrate his discovery before the Prussian court and was awarded the Prussian Order of the Crown, Second Class, by the Kaiser.

Röntgen actually devoted only a modest amount of attention to his momentous discovery. He wrote two more papers in 1896 and 1897, summarizing his findings on x rays, and then published no more on the subject. Instead, he went back to his work on the effects of pressures on solids. Röntgen chose not to ask for a patent on his work and refused the Kaiser's offer of an honorific "von" for his name. He did, however, accept the first Nobel Prize in physics, awarded to him in 1901. Even then, however, he declined to make an official speech and gave the prize money to the University of Würzburg for scientific research. His discovery had generated a surprising number of personal attacks, with many dismissing it as an accident or attributing it to other scientists. Glaser speculates that "Röntgen's reticence, bordering on bitterness with advancing years, was doubtless a defense against these attacks."

Röntgen had declined offers from other universities for many years, but in 1900, at the special request of the Bavarian government, he abandoned his chair at Würzburg in order to accept a similar position at the University of Munich. The decision was not an easy one for Röntgen because, as Zehnder later noted, "the nice quiet laboratory at Würzburg suited him so well." Röntgen remained at Munich until 1920 when he retired, a decision he made at least partly because of his grief over his wife's death a year earlier. She had suffered from a lingering disorder during which she became addicted to morphine. Zehnder was later to write that she was always "Röntgen's most understanding and truest friend."

Germany's defeat in World War I also had its effect on Röntgen: The inflationary period following the war resulted in his bankruptcy. He spent the last few years of his life at his country home at Weilheim, near Munich. He died there on February 10, 1923, after a short illness resulting from intestinal cancer. Among the many awards given to him were the Rumford Medal of the Royal Society (1896), the Royal Order of Merit, Bavarian (1896), the Baumgaertner Prize of the Vienna Academy (1896), the Elliott-Cresson Medal of the Franklin Institute (1897), the Barnard Medal of Columbia University (1900), and the Helmholtz Medal (1919).

SELECTED WRITINGS BY RÖNTGEN:

Periodicals

Annalen der Physik und Chemie, Über eine neue Art von Strahlen, Volume 64, 1898.
Annalen der Physik und Chemie, Eine Neue Art von Strahlen. 2. Mitteilung, Volume 64, 1898.

FURTHER READING:

Books

Daintith, John, et al., *A Biographical Encyclopedia of Scientists,* Facts on File, Volume XX, 1981, p. 686.

Gillispie, C. C., editor, *Dictionary of Scientific Biography,* Volume 1, Scribner, 1975, pp. 529–531.

Glasser, Otto, *W. C. Röntgen and the Early History of Röntgen Rays,* Charles C. Thomas, 1934.

Magill, Frank N., editor, *The Nobel Prize Winners— Physics,* Volume 1, 1901–1937, Salem Press, 1989, pp. 23–32.

Nitske, Robert W., *The Life of W. C. Röntgen, Discoverer of the X-Ray,* University of Arizona Press, 1971.

Wasson, Tyler, editor, *Nobel Prize Winners,* Wilson, 1987, pp. 879–882.

Weber, Robert L., *Pioneers of Science: Nobel Prize Winners in Physics,* American Institute of Physics, 1980, pp. 7–9.

Zehnder, Ludwig, *Wilhelm Conrad Röntgen,* Basle University, 192?.

Sketch by David E. Newton

Marshall N. Rosenbluth
1927–
American physicist

Marshall N. Rosenbluth

The American physicist Marshall N. Rosenbluth is a theoretical plasma physicist best known for his work in the physics of magnetic confinement fusion devices. Besides his research on linear and nonlinear instability theory and the transport and wave properties of plasmas, he has also looked at the physics of accelerators and free electron lasers. He currently is a professor and research physicist at the University of California, San Diego. He also conducts research on the International Thermonuclear Experimental Reactor (ITER), an international collaborative project aimed at demonstrating the scientific and technological feasibility of fusion energy for peaceful purposes.

Because Rosenbluth's work has focused on theories involving very hot ionized gases known as plasmas, he was in a position to realize very early on the potential that computers had for solving enormously complicated problems in theoretical physics. For over 40 years, he has studied the physics of nuclear fusion theoretically.

Rosenbluth was born February 5, 1927, in Albany, NY. He received his bachelors degree (Phi Beta Kappa) from Harvard University in 1946 and his doctorate from the University of Chicago in 1949.

From 1950 to 1956, Rosenbluth was a principal theoretician at Los Alamos Scientific Laboratory (which later became the Los Alamos National Laboratory). At Los Alamos, Rosenbluth performed classified fusion research that led to the development of the hydrogen bomb in 1952. Between 1956 and 1967, he served as senior research advisor at the General Atomic Laboratory, while holding a concurrent faculty appointment at the University of California at San Diego part of that time (1960-1967). From 1967 to 1980, he was a professor at the Institute for Advanced Study at Princeton. In 1975, Rosenbluth pointed out that the excitation of Alfven waves by high energy ions in a Tokamak reactor was a potential source of stability in burning plasmas. The Tokamak, a type of fusion reactor that was originally developed in the former Soviet Union, is currently being looked at as a future source of electricity.

In 1980, Rosenbluth became professor and director of the Institute for Fusion Studies at the University of Texas at Austin, and remained there until 1987. In 1987, he returned to the University of California at San Diego as professor.

After becoming an emeritus professor and research physicist in 1993, he devoted his time to work related to the development of a controlled thermonuclear reactor. In addition to conducting fusion research, Rosenbluth has served as a consultant to the Department of Defense on national security issues, anti-submarine warfare and free electron lasers.

Rosenbluth is a member of the American Academy of Arts, the National Academy of Science, the American Physical Society Council, and the National Research Council. He has been honored with the E.O. Lawrence Memorial Award (1964), the Fermi Award (1985) and the National Medal of Science (1997). In 1997, when Rosenbluth was awarded the National Medal of Science, the commendation specifically noted his "fundamental contributions to plasma physics, his leadership in the quest to develop controlled thermonuclear fusion, and his wide-ranging technical contributions to national security."

Sketch by Randall Frost

John Ross

1926–

American physical chemist

The American physical chemist John Ross was born in Vienna, Austria, on October 2, 1926. When Ross was a student, the chemists that he knew had reputations for spending their time observing and recording changes in chemical systems. Ross's research has helped turn chemistry into a science that employs complex instrumentation and that is based on the underlying principles of mathematics, thermodynamics and quantum mechanics.

In response to religious persecution, Ross fled his native Austria shortly before the outbreak of World War II, later settling in New York with his parents. As an undergraduate at Queens College, he majored in chemistry, but had to interrupt his education from 1944 to 1946 to serve in the Army. Following his graduation in 1948, he took up graduate studies at the Massachusetts Institute of Technology, focusing on the transport properties of gases under physical chemist Isador Amdur. He earned his Ph.D. in 1950. He then went on to pursue studies of gas thermometry and the statistical mechanics of irreversible processes with physical chemist John G. Kirkwood at Yale University. Ross quickly achieved a thorough grounding in both experimental and theoretical research.

In 1953, Ross accepted an appointment as assistant professor in the Chemistry Department at Brown University. There, he set up a program to test the viscosity of liquids under various conditions of temperature and pressure. His measurements, even today, set standards for precision and accuracy.

Starting in 1955 and lasting until 1973, Ross collaborated with the physical chemist Edward F. Greene on research on molecular beams. This work led to a better understanding of the behavior (including motion) of molecules in chemical reactions.

From 1966 to 1971, Ross was the chairman of the Chemistry Department at the Massachusetts Institute of Technology. He remained at MIT until 1979, when he moved to Stanford University. At Stanford, he chaired the Chemistry Department from 1983 to 1989. He is currently the Camille and Henry Dreyfus Professor of Chemistry at Stanford.

During his time at Stanford, Ross has conducted research aimed at unraveling the mechanisms behind complex chemical reactions, including some of the biochemical processes that determine how living systems behave. These reactions tend to be complicated, taking place under conditions far from chemical equilibrium and involving many chemical compounds.

Traditionally, chemists studying complex reactions have attempted to identify the reactants and then isolate individual reactions involving those compounds. Ross, however, has developed new methods for analyzing how complex chemical systems behave. He prefers to study intact systems by correlating the inputs and outputs to a complex reaction. This approach has helped scientists identify the most important chemical species in complicated reactions and the ways they are linked in specific types of chemical reactions.

In 1991, Ross and his students designed the chemical equivalent of the mathematician's Turing machine, i.e., a construct that defines the concept of computability. Four years later, Ross and his colleagues designed a "chemical computer" that was capable of executing many computations simultaneously. Using this tool, Ross was able to perform the first pattern-recognition experiments using chemical reactions rather than electronics. Ross's chemical computer is capable of characterizing chemical kinetics on a macroscopic (i.e., laboratory size) scale rather than at the molecular level.

Ross continues to study chemical reactions under conditions that are far from equilibrium. He conducts experimental and theoretical investigations on chemical instabilities in an attempt to determine complex reaction mechanisms; the thermodynamics and statistical mechanics of non-equilibrium systems; and ways to implement digital and parallel chemical computers. He also pursues investigations in neural network theory, and seeks to apply these studies to biological reactions.

Among the awards that Ross has received in the course of his career are National Science Foundation, Sloan and Guggenheim fellowships; Irving Langmuir Award of the American Chemical Society; Honorary degrees from Queens College, the Weizmann Institute and the University of Bordeaux, and a medal from the Collège de France; and the 1999 National Medal of Science and Technology in recognition of his contributions to physical chemistry, especially molecular studies, statistical mechanics and the chemical kinetics of nonlinear systems, and for opening up new fields in chemical science.

Ross has mentored more than 160 doctoral and postdoctoral students. He has also served as an adviser to government and industry and has been awarded three patents. He is a member of the National Academy of Sciences and the American Academy of Arts and Sciences.

Sketch by Randall Frost

Mary G. Ross
1908–
American aerospace engineer

Mary G. Ross's most notable contribution as an engineer has been her work in aerospace technology, particularly in areas related to space flight and ballistic missiles. She was part of the original engineering team at Lockheed's Missile Systems Division, where she worked on a number of defense systems. She also contributed to space exploration efforts with her work relating to the Apollo program, the Polaris reentry vehicle, and interplanetary space probes.

Born in Oklahoma in 1908, Ross took pride in her heritage as a Cherokee Indian. Her great-great-grandfather, John Ross, was the principal chief of the Cherokee Nation between 1828 and 1866. Mary Ross was later to remark that she had been brought up in the Cherokee tradition of equal education for both boys and girls. She was, however, the only girl in her math class, which did not seem to bother her. Indeed, her early interests were math, physics, and science.

Armed with these interests and a sense of purpose, Ross graduated from high school when she was sixteen. She attended Northeastern State Teacher's College and graduated from there in 1928, when she was twenty. After graduating from college, Ross taught mathematics and science for nine and one-half years in public schools. She also served as a girls' advisor at a Pueblo and Navajo school for boys and girls. Ross returned to school herself, this time to Colorado State Teachers College (now the University of Northern Colorado at Greeley), where she graduated with a master's degree in mathematics in 1938.

With the growth of the aviation industry in the early part of World War II, Ross found a position in 1942 as an assistant to a consulting mathematician with Lockheed Aircraft Corporation in Burbank, California. Her early work at Lockheed involved engineering problems having to do with transport and fighter aircraft. Meanwhile, with the support of Lockheed, Ross continued her education at the University of California, Los Angeles, where she took courses in aeronautical and mechanical engineering.

When Lockheed formed its Missiles Systems Division in 1954, it selected Mary Ross to be one of the first forty employees, and she was the only female engineer among them. As the American missile program matured, Ross found herself researching and evaluating feasibility and performance of ballistic missile and other defense systems. She also studied the distribution of pressure caused by ocean waves and how it affected submarine-launched vehicles.

Her work in 1958 concentrated on satellite orbits and the Agena series of rockets that played so prominent a role in the Apollo moon program during the 1960s. As an advanced systems engineer, Ross worked on the Polaris reentry vehicle and engineering systems for manned space flights. Before her retirement from Lockheed in 1973, Ross undertook research on flyby space probes that would study Mars and Venus. After Ross retired she continued her interests in engineering by delivering lectures to high school and college groups to encourage young women and Native American youths to train for technical careers.

Mary Ross authored a number of classified publications relating to her work in national defense and received several awards during her career. A charter member of the Los Angeles chapter of the Society of Women Engineers since 1952, Ross has received a number of honors. In 1961 she garnered the *San Francisco Examiner*'s award for Woman of Distinction and the Woman of Achievement Award from the California State Federation of Business and Professional Clubs. Ross was elected a fellow and life member of the Society of Women Engineers, whose Santa Clara Valley Section established a scholarship in her name. She has also been the recipient of achievement awards from the American Indian Science and Engineering Society and from the Council of Energy Resource Tribes. In 1992 she was inducted into the Silicon Valley Engineering Hall of Fame.

FURTHER READING:

Books

Ross, Mary G., *Interview with Karl Preuss,* conducted February 14, 1994.

Sketch by Karl Preuss

Ronald Ross
1857–1932
English physician and parasitologist

Ronald Ross is best known for his discovery of the method by which malaria is transmitted, research for which he was awarded the 1902 Nobel Prize in physiology or medicine. However, Ross's true passion was the arts, and he became a doctor only because of his father's insistence. Ross's interest in bacteriology led him to study the causes of malaria, a disease that was widespread in India where he lived. His determination that the affliction was transmitted through a parasite common to mosquitos led to more advanced treatments for the condition and more effective means of preventing it. In addition to his Nobel Prize and other honorary awards, Ross was knighted in 1911. Ross was born in Almora, Nepal, on May 13, 1857. He was the first of ten children to be born to General Sir Campbell Claye Grant Ross, a British officer stationed in India, and the former Matilde Charlotte Elderton. General Ross was described by Paul DeKruif in his book *Microbe Hunters* as "a ferocious looking border-fighting English general with belligerent side-whiskers, who was fond of battles but preferred to paint landscapes."

First Passion Is for the Arts

In 1865 at the age of eight, Ross was sent to England for his schooling. When he returned to his family in India, he declared to his father that he wanted to pursue a career in the arts. General Ross's view was that the arts were a legitimate vocation but not a sensible career for a young man. Instead, he insisted that his son plan for a medical career in the Indian Medical Service. Ross returned to England in 1874 and began his medical education at St. Bartholomew's Hospital in London. He did poorly in his classes because he spent most of his time writing novels and reading. His father became so upset with his grades that he threatened to withdraw his son's financial support. In response, Ross took a job as a ship's doctor on Anchor Line ships plying the London-New York City route. DeKruif reports that Ross spent much of his time aboard ship "observing the emotions and frailties of human nature," which gave him more material for his novels and poems.

In 1879 Ross completed his course at St. Bartholomew's and was awarded his medical degree. He returned to India and held a series of posts in Madras, Bangalore, Burma, and the Andaman Islands. He soon became more interested in research than in the day-to-day responsibilities of medical practice and spent long hours working out new algebraic formulas.

Attacks the Problem of Malaria

An important turning point in Ross's life came with his first leave of absence in 1888. He returned to England and became interested in research on tropical diseases, many of which he had seen during his years in India. Ross took a course in bacteriology offered by E. Emanuel Klein and earned a diploma in public health. During this furlough he also met Rosa Bessie Bloxam, whom he married on April 25, 1889, just prior to returning to India. The Rosses later had four children: Charles Claye, Dorothy, Sylvia, and Ronald.

With his new found knowledge of bacteriology, Ross turned his attention to what was then the most serious health problem in India: malaria. In 1880 the French physician **Alphonse Laveran** had discovered that malaria is caused by a one-celled organism called *Plasmodium*. Two decades of research had produced further data on the organism's characteristics, its means of reproduction, and its correlation with disease symptoms, but no one had determined how the disease was transmitted from one person to another.

Ross's original research led him to question Laveran's discovery, but for five years he made little progress in his studies. Then, on a second leave of absence in England during 1894, he met Patrick Manson, an English physician particularly interested in malaria. During Ross's year in England, he studied with Manson and became convinced that Laveran's theory was correct and that the causative agent for malaria was transmitted by mosquitoes.

When Ross returned to India in March of 1895, he was prepared to take up an aggressive research program on the mosquito-transmission theory. However, he was frustrated by working conditions in India—especially the lack of support from his superiors and the primitive equipment available to him—but with Manson's constant letters of support and encouragement, he eventually succeeded.

The key discovery came on August 20, 1897, when Ross first observed in the stomach of an *Anopheles* mosquito Anopheles a cyst with black granules of the type described by Laveran. Ross worked out the life cycle of the disease-causing agent, including its reproduction within human blood, its transmission to a mosquito during the feeding process, its incubation within the mosquito, and then its transmission to a second human during a second feeding (a "bite") by the mosquito.

Ross's work, however, was complicated by several factors. For example, in the midst of his research he was transferred to Rajputana, a region in which human malaria did not exist. He spent his time there instead working on the transmission of another form of the disease that affects birds. In addition, Ross was continually distracted by his passion for writing, and he produced a number of poems when he could no longer work on his battle against malaria.

Adding to Ross's frustration was the news he received late in 1898 that an Italian research team led by Battista Grassi had published reports on malaria closely paralleling his own work. Although little doubt exists about the originality of the Italian studies, Ross called Grassi's team "cheats and pirates." The dispute was later described by DeKruif as similar to a spat between "two quarrelsome small boys."

To some extent, the dispute was resolved in 1902 when the Nobel Prize committee awarded Ross the year's prize in physiology or medicine. By that time, Ross had retired from the Indian Medical Service and returned to England as lecturer at the new School of Tropical Medicine in Liverpool. There he worked for the eradication of the conditions (such as poor sanitation) that were responsible for the spread of malaria. In 1917, after eighteen years at Liverpool, Ross was appointed physician of tropical diseases at King's College Hospital in London. In 1926 he became director of a new facility founded in his name, the Ross Institute and Hospital for Tropical Diseases near London. He remained in this post until his death on September 16, 1932. Among the honors granted to Ross were the 1895 Parke Gold Medal, the 1901 Cameron Prize, and the 1909 Royal Medal of the Royal Society. He was knighted in 1911.

SELECTED WRITINGS BY ROSS:

Books

Memoirs with a Full Account of the Great Malaria Problem, Keynes Press, 1888.
The Deformed Transformed, Chapman and Hall, 1892.
The Prevention of Malaria, J. Murray, 1910.
The Setting Sun, J. Murray, 1912.
The Revels of Orsera, J. Murray, 1920.
Poems, E. Matthews & Marrot, 1928.
Studies on Malaria, J. Murray, 1928.

Periodicals

British Medical Journal, On Some Peculiar Pigmented Cells Found in Two Mosquitoes Fed on Malarial Blood, Volume 2, 1897, pp. 1786–1788.

FURTHER READING:

Books

DeKruif, Paul, *Microbe Hunters,* Harcourt, Brace, 1926.
Kamm, Jacqueline, *Malaria Ross,* Methuen, 1963.
Mégroz, Rodolphe L., *Ronald Ross: Discoverer and Creator,* Allen & Unwin, 1931.

Periodicals

Gorgas, William C., and Fielding H. Garrison, *Scientific Monthly,* Ronald Ross and the Prevention of Malaria Fever, August, 1916, pp. 132–150.
Yoelli, Meir, *Bulletin of the New York Academy of Medicine,* Sir Ronald Ross and the Evolution of Malaria Research, August, 1973, pp. 722–735.

Sketch by David E. Newton

Carl-Gustaf Rossby
1898–1957
Swiss-born American meteorologist

Carl-Gustaf Rossby has been called one of the most brilliant theoretical meteorologists of this century—a scientist who helped transform meteorology into the modern science it is known as today. Among Rossby's scientific achievements are the discovery of planetary waves—also known as Rossby waves—that play a crucial role in weather patterns; the identification of the jet stream; and the development of equations for predicting the weather. Renowned as well for his organizational skills, Rossby revitalized the U.S. Weather Bureau by eliminating bureau-cratic inefficiency and promoting innovative research. The United States became a leader in meteorology largely as a result of his efforts.

Carl-Gustaf Arvid Rossby was born on December 28, 1898, in Stockholm, Sweden, to Arvid Rossby, a construction engineer, and his wife Alma Charlotta Marelius. Rossby was the first of the four boys and one girl in the family. A good student, Rossby was described by his teachers as an excellent scholar. As a child he contracted rheumatic fever, which subsequently damaged his heart. Perhaps as a result, Rossby was not particularly athletic, preferring instead such interests as music, geology, and botany. According to one biographical account, Rossby enjoyed playing the piano and cultivating orchids.

In 1917 Rossby enrolled at the University of Stockholm. He initially chose to study medicine but quickly switched to mathematical sciences. Less than a year later he received his bachelor's degree ("filosofie kandidat") in mathematics, mechanics, and astronomy. (Most students took at least three years to accomplish the same.) In 1919 Rossby abruptly embarked on his career in meteorology by joining the Geophysical Institute in Bergen, Norway. His career choice proved somewhat of a mystery, considering that he had no knowledge of the subject at the time. However, historians believe that Rossby's interest was piqued after attending a lecture on the atmosphere given by **Vilhem Bjerknes**, a pioneer in meteorology and a professor at the Bergen Institute. Evidence also suggests that Rossby's move was spurred by boredom with Stockholm. Meteorology may have also captivated Rossby because he happened to enter the field at a time when the effect of polar fronts on weather was just being discovered.

According to Tor Bergeron, a meteorologist who also worked at Bergen, the twenty-year-old Rossby had "amazing persuasive and organizing" abilities; though inexperienced, Rossby presented ideas that Bergeron reported "took our breath away." Rossby worked in Bergen until 1921, when he joined the Geophysical Institute of the University of Leipzig. In that institute Rossby began studying hydrodynamics and newly discovered features of the upper atmosphere. To help further these interests, he also worked during part of 1921 at the Prussian Aerological Observatory at Lindenberg, a center for research using kites and balloons.

In 1921 Rossby also returned to the University of Stockholm to study mathematical physics. While he worked toward his "filosofie licentiat" (the equivalent of a PhD), Rossby earned a living as a junior meteorologist at the Swedish Meteorologic-Hydrologic Service. During his tenure there, he went on several scientific expeditions, including a meteorological and oceanographic expedition through pack-ice near Greenland and a meteorological expedition around the British Isles. In 1925, Rossby attained his licentiat degree in mathematical physics.

Initial Hostility at the U.S. Weather Bureau

After receiving a fellowship from the American-Scandinavian Foundation, Rossby came to the U.S. Weather Bureau in Washington, D.C., in 1926. Officially, his scholarship was for the purpose of studying "the application of the polar front theory to American weather." By all accounts, the enthusiastic 27-year-old Rossby did not fare well in the Weather Bureau, which the National Academy of Sciences biography describes as being headed by "unimaginative administrators." As a result, Rossby's attempts to introduce the polar front theory and other meteorological innovations of his day were regularly thwarted.

Despite these obstacles, Rossby published three papers in the *Monthly Weather Review* describing his investigations into atmospheric turbulence. He also received a temporary appointment as junior meteorologist in 1926. Simultaneously, the Daniel Guggenheim Fund for the Promotion of Aeronautics chose Rossby to work on the meteorological aspects of flight plans. Unfortunately, this project escalated tensions between Rossby and the Weather Bureau to the point that in 1927, when Rossby left the Bureau to work for the Guggenheim Fund full-time, the Weather Bureau officially declared him "persona non grata." Administrators also sent letters to all its stations warning them against Rossby.

In 1927 aeronautics had captured the country's attention following Charles Lindbergh's solo flight across the Atlantic. That year the Guggenheim, then at the forefront of aeronautics, proposed a model airway between San Francisco and Los Angeles. Rossby, in his capacity as chairman of the committee on aeronautical meteorology, was given the task of establishing an experimental weather service as part of the airway. Enlisting the help of the Weather Bureau in San Francisco (whose director ignored the letter warning against Rossby), he created a system that would later serve as the prototype for all of the Weather Bureau's airways weather services. Needless to say, this success redeemed Rossby in the eyes of the bureau's administrators.

Collaborations at MIT

Once the experimental service was operational, Rossby and the Guggenheim Fund turned it over to the Weather Bureau, and Rossby began a new era in his career: In 1928 he was appointed associate professor as part of the Daniel Guggenheim Aeronautical Laboratory at the Massachusetts Institute of Technology (MIT). Along with Hurd C. Willett, a colleague from the Weather Bureau whom he had persuaded to join him, Rossby taught a graduate-level class in meteorology, the first such course in the United States. Together, Rossby and Willett formed a team that forever changed American meteorology.

On a personal level, in 1929 Rossby married Harriet Alexander of Boston. Together they eventually had three children. According to friends, Rossby had difficulty mastering any mechanical devices, and except for a few brief experiences with a car, left driving to his wife. His favorite form of entertainment was getting together as many friends and colleagues as possible for dinner and conversation in an expensive restaurant.

Rossby quickly developed a following at MIT. An obituary written for the American Meteorological Society recalled the reverential attitude of his students toward him, and their belief that "they were participating in his great crusade—to bring modern meteorology to America where the science had been existing in a stifling atmosphere for many years." Rossby's research at MIT involved both the atmosphere and oceanography: he was a part-time associate at the Woods Hole Oceanographic Institute. Among the subjects he investigated: the application of the principles of thermodynamics to the analyses of air masses; turbulence and the air-ocean boundary; forces at work in the generation and maintenance of ocean currents; and the general circulation of the atmosphere.

Forecasting the Future

From a scientific standpoint, Rossby conducted some of his most significant work in 1938 and 1939: In two of his most important papers, he developed equations for what are now called Rossby waves. At the time, scientists knew that the circulation of the atmosphere controlled both weather and climate. They also knew that storms at the Earth's surface caused waves in the westerly winds above the Northern Hemisphere. According to Patrick Hughes in *A Century of Weather Service,* in 1937 meteorologist Jacob Bjerknes "showed that these waves were hemispheric in scale and circled the globe." Rossby added to this theory by determining that the waves extended vertically through the atmosphere and that they moved the warm and cold air masses that cause local weather. Rossby developed a mathematical equation to predict the motion of the waves.

Rossby waves exist in both the ocean and the atmosphere. They are the reason that weather in the tropics can affect weather in higher latitudes. Partly as a result of Rossby's work, scientists can now make long-range weather forecasts, including the five-day forecast that has become a common part of our lives. In 1939 Rossby became an American citizen. That same year he left MIT to become Assistant Chief for Research and Development at the U.S. Weather Bureau. It was in this position that Rossby helped Weather Bureau chief F. W. Reichelderfer modernize the agency. Rossby established a training program for Weather Bureau personnel and even arranged for some staffers to enroll in the meteorological schools at MIT and New York University.

Rossby stayed only two years at the Weather Bureau, moving on in 1941 to become chairman of the meteorology department at the University of Chicago. He continued his studies of Rossby waves, but with the onset of World War II, he began commuting between Chicago and Washington to promote a training program for military meteorologists. As a result of his efforts, an intense, year-long training program in meteorology was established at the University of Chicago and other institutions. Rossby also assisted in solving the meteorological problems faced by Allied strategists, traveling to Africa, Italy and the South Pacific when necessary. To aid in the understanding of meteorological problems in the tropics, Rossby helped establish the Institute of Tropical Meteorology at the University of Puerto Rico. According to the National Academy of Sciences, *Biographical Memoirs*, Rossby enjoyed making these decisions with "a Hollywoodian flair for dramatic executive action."

Throughout the war Rossby continued to work, publishing two other significant papers dealing with Rossby waves in 1942. In addition, after the war, Rossby and colleagues helped reorganize the American Meteorological Society and founded the *Journal of Meteorology*. During his ten years at the University of Chicago—a period known as the great days of the Chicago School in meteorology—Rossby gathered leading European meteorologists as well as talented graduate students. Under Rossby's leadership, this group identified the jet stream and explored theories to explain it.

In 1948 the Swedish government solicited Rossby's help in developing research and educational programs in meteorology. As part of a commitment that occupied him until his death, Rossby founded and directed the Institute of Meteorology at the University of Stockholm and established *Tellus,* a geophysical research journal. Despite these new administrative duties, Rossby continued his research and in 1950 formulated an equation for predicting the weather—the Rossby equation. In addition, Rossby's new interest in atmospheric chemistry helped motivate others to investigate this field. In a paper published after he died, Rossby described the atmosphere as a carrier of particles and chemicals that continually interacted with the earth and the oceans.

Rossby died in Stockholm on August 19, 1957. He received many awards during his lifetime, including the Symons Medal of the Royal Meteorological Society in 1953 and the American Meteorological Society Service Award in 1956.

SELECTED WRITINGS BY ROSSBY:

Periodicals

Journal of Marine Research, Relation Between Variations in the Intensity of the Zonal Circulation of the Atmosphere and the Displacements of the Semi-Permanent Centers of Action, Volume 2, 1939, pp. 38–55.

Quarterly Journal of the Royal Meteorological Society, Planetary Flow Patterns in the Atmosphere, Volume 66, 1940, pp. 68–87.

FURTHER READING:

Books

Bergeron, Tor, *The Atmosphere and the Sea in Motion,* The Young Carl-Gustaf Rossby, The Rockefeller Institute, 1959, pp. 51–55.

Byers, Horace R., *Biographical Memoirs, The National Academy of Sciences,* Carl-Gustaf Arvid Rossby, Columbia University Press, 1960, pp. 248–263.

Byars, Horace R., *The Atmosphere and the Sea in Motion,* Carl-Gustaf Rossby, the Organizer, The Rockefeller Institute, 1959, pp. 56–59.

Byars, Horace R., *Dictionary of Scientific Biography,* Charles Scribners' Sons, 1975, pp. 557–559.

Hughes, Patrick, *A Century of Weather Service,* Gordon and Breach, 1970, pp. 69–71, 131.

Sketch by Devera Pine

Miriam Rothschild
1908–
English naturalist

Miriam Rothschild's best known work has been in the fields of entomology and parasitology, and she is considered the world's foremost authority on fleas. Although she has made numerous scientific contributions in such fields as marine biology, chemistry, horticulture, and zoology, her scientific background is unorthodox. Rothschild, though widely respected for her work and extensive knowledge of fleas, was never formally educated in these fields. In fact, her scientific endeavors are wholly a result of a natural curiosity about the physical world and the encouraging atmosphere of learning she grew up in.

Miriam Louisa Rothschild was born into the famed Rothschild banking family on August 5, 1908, at Ashton Wold, her parents' estate near Peterborough, England. The oldest of four children of Nathaniel Charles and Rozsika von Wertheimstein Rothschild, her own grandfather was the first Baron Rothschild. Although Nathaniel Charles Rothschild, her father, was a banker by profession, he was a zoologist by avocation; he founded the Society for the Promotion of Nature Preserves, and he studied moths, butterflies, and fleas for years. Rozsika Rothschild, her mother, was Hungarian by birth, and in addition to being astute in business, a champion in women's lawn tennis.

As a child, Rothschild spent six months of every year with her grandparents and uncle Walter at their estate outside London. Although all the Rothschilds expressed an interest in nature, it was Walter Rothschild who most sparked Miriam's interest in science. Walter Rothschild was a prolific collector of natural specimens, and his collection included more than two million butterflies, 300,000 bird skins, 200,000 bird eggs, and numerous other animals. And so, even as a young child of four, Rothschild began her own collection of ladybugs and caterpillars.

Rothschild had no formal education while growing up; her father believed formal education stifled creativity and natural curiosity. She read avidly and was tutored by her governess. When her father committed suicide after several years of chronic illness and depression, she lost interest in natural history, but her enthusiasm eventually returned, and at seventeen years of age, Rothschild enrolled herself in several evening classes at a local polytechnic institute.

A naturalist at the British Natural History Museum recommended her to the University of London in the late 1920s, and Rothschild became a researcher at the University's Biological Station located in Naples, Italy, where she studied marine life. She continued her studies when she went to the Marine Biological Station in Plymouth in 1932. It was at this time that she became interested in the study of parasites after finding out that some of the mollusks were infested with flatworms. She worked tirelessly, studying parasites, hosts, and other related marine animals, and collected numerous specimens and cultures. In 1939, however, the Germans bombed the research station during the Second World War, destroying Rothschild's laboratory completely. Rothschild now returned to Ashton Wold, which had been converted to a military hospital and air field during the war. At this time she was actively involved in the resistance movement, and she worked with mathematician **Alan Turing** on the top-secret British *Enigma* project, trying to crack the German code. She and her family also opened their home to European refugees.

Rothschild continued her scientific pursuits even while helping relocate many refugees after the war. Like her father, she had become interested in fleas. She studied many specimens and worked to catalog her father's collection—her findings were eventually amalgamated into six volumes and took twenty years to compile. She showed through her extensive research how fleas reproduce, how and why they choose their hosts, and the mechanics of how fleas can leap enormous distances. She also showed through research with Nobel laureate **Tadeus Reichstein** how the monarch caterpillar's diet of milkweed plants protects it (the glycosides in the milkweed are distasteful and possibly harmful to birds and other animals, who bypass monarchs for safer, tastier fare).

Rothschild was married to George Lane, a British soldier who had emigrated from Hungary, in 1943. The couple had four children and adopted two more. They divorced in 1957. In addition to science, Rothschild's other interests include travel, reading, and philanthropy. She has written and contributed to numerous articles about nature, and continues her research at Ashton Wold. Her 1983 book, *Dear Lord Rothschild,* honors her family and in particular her uncle Walter, who eventually became the second Baron Rothschild. Her interest in science has a mechanical side as well; she claims to be the first person to put seat belts in an automobile, in 1940.

SELECTED WRITINGS BY ROTHSCHILD:

Books

Dear Lord Rothschild: Birds, Butterflies, and History, American Institute of Physics, 1983.

FURTHER READING:

Periodicals

Gibson, Helen, *International Wildlife,* Britain's Quirky Samaritans, July-August 1993, pp. 38–43.
Gibson, Helen, *Scientific American,* August 1990, p. 116.
Sullivan, Walter, *New York Times,* Miriam Rothschild Talks of Fleas, February 10, 1984, p. C2.

Sketch by George A. Milite

Peyton Rous
1879–1970
American physician and pathologist

Peyton Rous was a physician-scientist at the Rockefeller Institute for Medical Research (later the Rockefeller University) for over sixty years. In 1966, Rous won the Nobel Prize for his 1910 discovery that a virus can cause cancer tumors. His other contributions to scientific medicine include creating the first blood bank, determining major functions of the liver and gall bladder, and identifying factors that initiate and promote malignancy in normal cells.

Francis Peyton Rous was born on October 5, 1879, in Baltimore, Maryland, to Charles Rous, a grain exporter, and Frances Wood, the daughter of a Texas judge. His father died when Rous was eleven, and his mother chose to stay in Baltimore to ensure that her three children would have the best possible education. His sisters were professionally successful, one a musician, the other a painter.

Rous, whose interest in natural science was apparent at an early age, wrote a "flower of the month" column for the *Baltimore Sun* when he was twenty. He pursued his biological interests at Johns Hopkins University, receiving a B.A. in 1900 and an M.D. in 1905. After a medical internship at Johns Hopkins, however, he decided (as recorded in *Les Prix Nobel en 1966*) that he was "unfit to be a real doctor" and chose instead to concentrate on research and the natural history of disease. This led to a full year of studying lymphocytes with Aldred Warthin at the University of Michigan and a summer in Germany learning morbid anatomy at a Dresden hospital. After Rous returned

Peyton Rous

to the United States, he developed pulmonary tuberculosis and spent a year recovering in an Adirondacks sanatorium. In 1909, **Simon Flexner**, director of the newly founded Rockefeller Institute in New York City, asked Rous to take over cancer research in his laboratory. A few months later, a poultry breeder brought a Plymouth Rock chicken with a large breast tumor to the Institute and Rous, after conducting numerous experiments, determined that the tumor was a spindle-cell sarcoma. When he transferred a cell-free filtrate from the tumor into healthy chickens of the same flock, they developed identical tumors. Moreover, after injecting a filtrate from the new tumors into other chickens, a malignancy exactly like the original formed. Further studies revealed that this filterable agent was a virus, although Rous carefully avoided this word. Now called the Rous sarcoma virus (RSV) and classed as an RNA retrovirus, it remains a prototype of animal tumor viruses and a favorite laboratory model for studying the role of genes in cancer.

Rous's discovery was received with considerable disbelief, both in the United States and in the rest of the world. His viral theory of cancer challenged all assumptions, going back to Hippocrates, that cancer was not infectious but rather a spontaneous, uncontrolled growth of cells and many scientists dismissed his finding as a disease peculiar to chickens. Discouraged by his failed attempts to cultivate viruses from mammal cancers, Rous abandoned work on the sarcoma in 1915. Nearly two decades passed before he returned to cancer research.

Enters New Phase of Research on Urgent Medical Problems

After the onset of World War I, Rous, J. R. Turner, and O. H. Robertson began a search for emergency blood transfusion fluids. Nothing could be found that worked without red blood corpuscles so they developed a citrate-sugar solution that preserved blood for weeks as well as a method to transfuse the suspended cells. Later, behind the front lines in Belgium and France, they created the world's first blood bank from donations by army personnel. This solution was used again in World War II, when half a million Rous-Turner blood units were shipped by air to London during the Blitz.

During the 1920s, Rous made several contributions to physiology. With P. D. McMaster, he demonstrated the concentrating activity of bile in the gall bladder, the acid-alkaline balance in living tissues, the increasing permeability along capillaries in muscle and skin, and the nature of gallstone formation. In conducting these studies, Rous devised culture techniques that have become standard for studying living tissues in the laboratory. He originated the method for growing viruses on chicken embryos, now used on a mass scale for producing viral vaccines, and found a way to isolate single cells from solid tissues by using the enzyme trypsin. Moreover, Rous developed an ingenious method for obtaining pure cultures of Kupffer cells by taking advantage of their phagocytic ability; he injected iron particles in animals and then used a magnet to separate these iron-laden liver cells from suspensions.

Returns to Cancer Tumor Research

In 1933, a Rockefeller colleague's report stimulated Rous to renew his work on cancer. Richard Shope discovered a virus that caused warts on the skin of wild rabbits. Within a year, Rous established that this papilloma had characteristics of a true tumor. His work on mammalian cancer kept his viral theory of cancer alive. However, another twenty years passed before scientists identified viruses that cause human cancers and learned that viruses act by invading genes of normal cells. These findings finally advanced Rous's 1910 discovery to a dominant place in cancer research.

Meanwhile, Rous and his colleagues spent three decades studying the Shope papilloma to understand the role of viruses in causing cancer in mammals. Careful observations, over long periods of time, of the changing shapes, colors, and sizes of cells revealed that normal cells become malignant in progressive steps. Cell changes in tumors were observed as always evolving in a single direction toward malignancy.

The researchers demonstrated how viruses collaborate with carcinogens such as tar, radiation, or chemicals to elicit and enhance tumors. In a report co-authored by W. F. Friedewald, Rous proposed a two-stage mechanism of carcinogenesis, or the causilng of cancer, called initiation and promotion. He further explained that a virus can be induced by carcinogens or it can hasten the growth and transform benign tumors into cancerous ones. For tumors having no apparent trace of virus, Rous cautiously postulated that these "spontaneous" growths might contain a virus that persists in a "masked" or latent state, causing no harm until its cellular environment is disturbed.

Rous eventually ceased his research on this project due to the technical complexities involved with pursuing the interaction of viral and environmental factors. He then analyzed different types of cells and their nature in an attempt to understand why tumors go from bad to worse.

In 1915, Rous married Marion de Kay, daughter of a scholarly commentator on the arts, and they had three daughters: Marion, Ellen, and Phoebe. He spent two months every summer in the country near New York City with his family, first on Long Island and later in Connecticut, savoring outdoor life, rambling in the countryside, collecting objects that caught his eye, growing flowers, and fishing.

This carefree time greatly contrasts with Rous's rigorous workday schedule at Rockefeller. His meticulous editing and writing, both scientific and literary, took place during several hours of solitude at the beginning and end of each day. At midday, he spent two intense hours discussing science with colleagues in the Institute's dining room. Rous then returned to work in his laboratory on experiments that lasted into the early evening.

Rous was appointed a full member of the Rockefeller Institute in 1920 and member emeritus in 1945. Though officially retired, he remained active at his lab bench until the age of ninety, adding sixty papers to the nearly three hundred he published. He was elected to the National Academy of Sciences in 1927, the American Philosophical Society in 1939, and the Royal Society in 1940. In addition to the 1966 Nobel Prize for medicine, Rous received many honorary degrees and awards for his work in viral oncology, including the 1956 Kovalenko Medal of the National Academy of Sciences, the 1958 Lasker Award of the American Public Health Association, and the 1966 National Medal of Science.

As editor of the *Journal of Experimental Medicine,* a periodical renowned for its precise language and scientific excellence, Rous dominated the recording of forty-eight years of American medical research. He died of abdominal cancer on February 16, 1970, in New York City, just six weeks after he retired as editor.

SELECTED WRITINGS BY ROUS:

Periodicals

Journal of Experimental Medicine, A Transmissible Avian Neoplasm (Sarcoma of the Common Fowl), Volume 12, 1910, pp. 696–705.

Journal of Experimental Medicine, A Sarcoma of the Fowl Transmissible by an Agent Separable from the Tumor Cells, Volume 13, 1911, pp. 397–411.

Journal of Experimental Medicine, The Preservation of Living Red Blood Cells in vitro. I. Methods of Preservation. II. The Transfusion of Kept Cells, Volume 23, 1916, pp. 219–248.

Journal of Experimental Medicine, A Virus-induced Mammalian Growth with the Characters of a Tumor (the Shope Rabbit Papilloma), Volume 60, 1934, pp. 701–766.

Journal of Experimental Medicine, The Initiating and Promoting Elements in Tumor Production. An Analysis of the Effects of Tar, Benzpyrene, and Methylcholanthrene on Rabbit Skin, Volume 80, 1944, pp. 101–126.

Les Prix Nobel en 1966, The Challenge to Man of the Neoplastic Cell, 1967, P.A. Norstedt & Soner, pp. 162–171.

McGraw-Hill Modern Scientists and Engineers, Francis Peyton Rous, Volume 3, 1980, McGraw-Hill, pp. 48–49.

FURTHER READING:

Books

A Notable Career in Finding Out: Peyton Rous, 1879–1970, The Rockefeller University Press, 1971.

Periodicals

Biographical Memoirs of Fellows of the Royal Society, Volume 17, Royal Society (London), 1971, pp. 643–662.

Dulbecco, Renato, *Biographical Memoirs, National Academy of Sciences,* Francis Peyton Rous, Volume 48, 1976, pp. 275–306.

Henderson, James Stuart, *American Philosophical Society Yearbook,* Peyton Rous, 1971, pp. 168–179.

Henderson, James Stuart, *Roche Medical Image & Commentary,* The Long Road to Stockholm, Volume 12, May 1970, pp. 14–15; June 1970, pp. 18–21.

Moberg, Carol L., *Search,* Peyton Rous, Inquiring Naturalist: Cancer and the Sarcoma Virus, Volume 1, 1991, p. 9.

Other

Moberg, Carol L., *Search,* Peyton Rous, Inquiring Naturalist: Cancer and the Sarcoma Virus, Letter from Peyton Rous to T. Mitchell Prudden, October 14, 1922, The Rockefeller University Archives.

Sketch by Carol L. Moberg

F. Sherwood Rowland
1927–
American atmospheric chemist

In 1974 F. Sherwood Rowland and his research associate, **Mario Molina**, first sounded the alarm about the harmful effects of chlorofluorocarbons, or CFCs, on the Earth's ozone layer. CFCs, which have been used in air conditioners, refrigerators, and aerosol sprays, release chlorine atoms into the upper atmosphere when the Sun's ultraviolet light hits them; chlorine then breaks down atmospheric ozone molecules, destroying a shield that protects the Earth from damaging ultraviolet rays. In the mid–1980s a National Aeronautics and Space Administration (NASA) satellite actually confirmed the existence of a continent-sized hole in the ozone layer over Antarctica. By the early 1990s NASA and National Oceanographic and Atmospheric Administration scientists were warning that yet another ozone hole, this one over the Arctic, could imperil Canada, Russia, Europe, and, in the United States, New England. This news might have been gratifying affirmation for Rowland, a professor of chemistry at the University of California at Irvine, but rather than rest on his laurels he continued to steadfastly—and soberly—warn the world of the ozone danger. His efforts have won him worldwide renown and prestigious awards, including the Charles A. Dana Award for Pioneering Achievement in Health in 1987, the Peter Debye Award of the American Chemical Society in 1993, the Roger Revelle Medal from the American Geophysical Union for 1994, and the Japan Prize in Environmental Science and Technology, presented to Rowland by the Japanese emperor in 1989.

Frank Sherwood Rowland always seemed destined to do something in science. Born June 28, 1927, in Delaware, Ohio, the son of a math professor, Sidney A. Rowland, and his wife, Latin teacher Margaret (Drake), Rowland said in an interview with Joan Oleck that math always came easy for him. "I always liked solving puzzles and problems," he said. "I think the rule we had in our family that applied even to my own children was you had your choice in school as to *what order* you took biology, chemistry, and physics, but not *whether*."

Sidetracked by World War II, Rowland was still in boot camp when peace arrived. In 1948 he received his bachelor of arts degree from Ohio Wesleyan University; after three years—the summers of which he spent playing semiprofessional baseball—he obtained his master's from the University of Chicago. His Ph.D. came a year later, in 1952. That same year he married the former Joan E. Lundberg; the couple would eventually have a son and daughter.

The year 1952 was a banner one in Rowland's life; along with marriage and his doctorate he got his first academic job, an instructorship in chemistry at Princeton University, where he would remain four years. In 1956

Rowland moved his family west to the University of Kansas, where he was a professor for eight years, and then farther west still, to Irvine, California, where he took over as chemistry department chairman at the University of California in Irvine in 1964. He has stayed at Irvine ever since, enjoying stints as Daniel G. Aldrich, Jr., Professor of Chemistry from 1985 to 1989 and as Donald Bren Professor of Chemistry since 1989.

Discovers CFCs

At Chicago, Rowland's mentor had been **Willard F. Libby**, winner of the Nobel Prize for his invention of carbon–14 dating, a way to determine the age of an object by measuring how much of a radioactive form of carbon it contains. The radioactivity research Rowland conducted with Libby led the young scientist eventually to atmospheric chemistry. Realizing, as he told Oleck, that "if you're going to be a professional scientist one of the things you're going to do is stay out ahead of the pack," Rowland looked for new avenues to explore. In the 1970s Rowland was inspired by his daughter's dedication to the then-fledgling environmental movement and by the tenor of the times: 1970 was the year of the first Earth Day. In 1971 the chemist helped allay fears about high levels of mercury in swordfish and tuna by showing that preserved museum fish from a hundred years earlier contained about the same amount of the element as modern fish.

Later events pushed him further in the direction of environmental concerns. At a meeting in Salzburg, Austria, Rowland met an Atomic Energy Commission (AEC) staffer who was trying to get chemists and meteorologists into closer partnerships. Sharing a train compartment with the AEC man to Vienna, Rowland was invited to another professional meeting. And it was there, in 1972, that he first began to think about chlorofluorocarbons in the atmosphere.

In those days, production of CFCs for household and industrial propellants was doubling every five years. A million tons of CFCs were being produced each year alone, but scientists were not particularly alarmed; it was believed they were inert in the atmosphere. Rowland, however, wanted to know more about their ultimate fate. Ozone, a form of oxygen, helps make up the stratosphere, the atmospheric layer located between eight and thirty miles above the Earth. Ozone screens out dangerous ultraviolet rays, which have been linked to skin cancer, malfunctions in the immune system, and eye problems such as cataracts. Performing lab experiments with Molina, Rowland reported in 1974 that the same chemical stability that makes CFCs useful also allows them to drift up to the stratosphere intact. Once they rise thorough the ozone shield, Rowland and Molina warned, they pose a significant threat to ozone: each chlorine atom released when CFCs meet ultraviolet light can destroy up to one hundred thousand ozone molecules.

Sounding the alarm in the journal *Nature* in June of 1974 and in a subsequent presentation to the American Chemical Society that September, Rowland attracted attention: A federal task force found reason for serious concern;

the National Academy of Sciences (NAS) confirmed the scientists' findings; and by 1978 the Environmental Protection Agency (EPA) had banned nearly all uses of CFC propellants. There were setbacks: In the 1980s President Ronald Reagan's EPA administrator, Anne Gorsuch, dismissed ozone depletion as a scare tactic. And Rowland himself discovered that the whole matter was more complex than originally thought, that another chemical reaction in the air was affecting calculations of ozone loss. The NAS's assessment of the problem was similarly vague, generalizing future global ozone losses as somewhere between 2 and 20 percent.

The Hole in the Sky

Then came a startling revelation. In the mid–1980s a hole in the ozone shield over Antarctica the size of a continent was discovered; NASA satellite photos confirmed it in 1985. The fall in ozone levels in the area was drastic—as high as 67 percent. These events led to increased concern by the international community. In 1987 the United States and other CFC producers signed the Montreal Protocol, pledging to cut production by 50 percent by the end of the millennium. Later, in the United States, President George Bush announced a U.S. plan to speed up the timetable to 1995.

There were more accelerations to come: Du Pont, a major producer, announced plans to end its CFC production by late 1994, and the European Community set a 1996 deadline. And producers of automobile air conditioning and seat cushions—two industries still using CFCs—began looking for alternatives. These goals only became more urgent in the face of the 1992 discovery of another potential ozone hole, this one over the Arctic. Scientists have attributed the extreme depletion of ozone over the poles to weather patterns and seasonal sun that promote an unusually rapid cycle of chlorine-ozone chain reactions.

In addition to the development of holes in the ozone layer, the atmosphere is further threatened because of the time delay before CFCs reach the stratosphere. Even after a complete ban on CFC production is achieved, CFCs will continue to rise through the atmosphere, reaching peak concentrations in the late 1990s. Some remained skeptical of the dangers, however. In the early 1990s a kind of "ozone backlash" occurred, with a scientist as prominent as Nobel Prize-winning chemist **Derek Barton** joining those who called for a repeal of the CFC phaseout pact.

Meanwhile Rowland continued his examination of the atmosphere. Every three months, his assistants have fanned out around the Pacific Ocean to collect air samples from New Zealand to Alaska. The news from his research has been sobering, turning up airborne compounds that originated from the burning of rain forests in Brazil and the aerial pollution of oil fields in the Caucasus mountains. "The major atmospheric problems readily cross all national boundaries and therefore can affect everyone's security," Rowland said in his President's Lecture before the American Association for the Advancement of Science (AAAS) in 1993. "You can no longer depend upon the 12-mile offshore limit when the problem is being carried by the winds." An instructive reminder of the international nature of such insecurity was given by the arrival only 2 weeks later in Irvine, California, of trace amounts of the radioactive fission products released by the 1986 Chernobyl nuclear reactor accident in the former Soviet Union.

Rowland has said in interviews that he's pleased with the progress he's helped set in motion. "One of the messages is that it is possible for mankind to influence his environment negatively," Rowland told Oleck. "On the other side there's the recognition on an international basis that we can act in unison. We have the [Montreal] agreement, people are following it, and it's not only that they have said they will do these things but they *are* doing them because the measurements in the atmosphere show it. People have worked together to solve the problem."

SELECTED WRITINGS BY ROWLAND:

Periodicals

Nature, Stratospheric Sink for Chlorofluoromethanes: Chlorine Atom-Catalysed Destruction of Ozone, June 28, 1974, pp. 810–12.

Reviews of Geophysics and Space Physics, Chlorofluoromethanes in the Environment, February, 1975.

Nature, On the Depletion of Antarctic Ozone, June 19, 1986, pp. 755–58.

Technology Review, Can We Close the Ozone Hole?, August-September, 1987, pp. 51–58.

American Scientist, Chlorofluorocarbons and the Depletion of Stratospheric Ozone, January-February, 1989, pp. 36–45.

Science, President's Lecture: The Need for Scientific Communication with the Public, June 11, 1993, pp. 1571–76.

FURTHER READING:

Books

Cagin, Seth, and Dray, Philip, *Between Earth and Sky: How CFCs Changed Our World and Endangered the Ozone Layer,* Pantheon, 1993.

Dotto, Lydia, and Schiff, Harold, *The Ozone War,* Doubleday, 1978.

Roan, Sharon, *Ozone Crisis: The 15-Year Evolution of a Sudden Global Emergency,* Wiley, 1989.

Periodicals

Roan, Sharon, *New Yorker,* Annals of Chemistry: Inert, April 7, 1975, pp. 47–51.

Roan, Sharon, *New Yorker,* Annals of Chemistry: In the Face of Doubt, June 9, 1986, pp. 70–83.

Roan, Sharon, *Consumer Reports,* Can We Repair the Sky? May, 1989, pp. 322–26.

Roan, Sharon, *Newsweek,* Is the Ozone Hole in Our Heads? October 11, 1993, p. 71.

Roan, Sharon, *Popular Science,* The Man Who Knew Too Much, January, 1989, pp. 60–65 and 102.

Roan, Sharon, *People,* Northern Exposure, April 20, 1992, p. 121.

Roan, Sharon, *Time,* The Ozone Vanishes, February 17, 1992, pp. 60–68.

Roan, Sharon, *Register,* Pondering the Mysteries of a Growing Hole in the Ozone: Antarctic Expedition to Explore UCI Researchers' Theory that Man-Made Chemicals Are at Fault, (Santa Ana), August 27, 1986.

Other

Rowland, F. Sherwood, *Interview with Joan Oleck,* conducted on September 17, 1993.

Sketch by Joan Oleck

Janet D. Rowley
1925–
American cytogeneticist

Janet D. Rowley's research on chromosome abnormalities in a form of leukemia have introduced new diagnostic tools for oncologists—those doctors specializing in cancer—and have also opened new avenues of inquiry in possible gene therapies for cancer. A specialist in cytogenetics (the investigation of the role of cells in evolution and heredity), Rowley has helped to pinpoint cancer gene locations and correlate them to chromosome aberrations.

Janet Davison Rowley was born on April 5, 1925, in New York City, the daughter of Hurford Henry and Ethel Mary (Ballantyne) Davison. She attended the University of Chicago where she earned a B.S. degree in 1946 and her M.D. in 1948. During the latter year she married Donald A. Rowley. The couple eventually had four sons: David, Donald, Robert, and Roger. Rowley's professional career took her from a research assistant job at the University of Chicago in 1949 and 1950 to an internship at Marine Hospital in Chicago, a residency at Cook County Hospital, and a clinical instructor position in neurology at the University of Illinois Medical School before returning to the University of Chicago Medical School in 1962. From 1962 to 1969 she was a research associate both in the department of medicine and at Argonne Cancer Research Hospital. Then from 1969 to 1977, she became an associate professor, and in 1977 was made a full professor at the medical school and at Franklin McLean Memorial Research Institute. In 1984 Rowley became the Blum-Riese Distinguished Service professor in the department of medicine and in the department of molecular genetics and cell biology at Franklin McLean Memorial Research Institute.

Pioneering Research in Oncogenes

During her work at the University of Chicago, Rowley has committed her research to understanding the cytogenetic causes of cancer. She developed the use of quinacrine and Giemsa staining to identify chromosomes in cloned cells. Once the chromosomes were easily identifiable, she could then study abnormalities that occur in some chromosomes in certain cancers. With the discovery of oncogenes, or cancer-inducing genes, Rowley focused on chromosome rearrangements which occur in a form of blood cancer known as chronic myeloid leukemia (CML). Studying the so-called Philadelphia chromosome, Rowley was able in 1972 to show a consistent chromosome translocation or shifting of genetic material in CML cells. This was the first recurring translocation to be discovered in any species. Since that time more than seventy such translocations have been detected in human malignant cells. In general, Rowley's research indicates that both translocations and deletions of genetic material occur in malignancy, and that cancer is caused by a complex series of events within a single cell, making some genes overactive (tumor producing) and eliminating other genes that would normally suppress growth. Any cell, according to Rowley's research, is therefore potentially cancerous. What is needed to activate malignant growth is this complex series of events, including translocation and deletion.

Co-founder and co-editor of the journal *Genes, Chromosomes and Cancer,* Rowley has received numerous honors and awards, including the Esther Langer Award in 1983; the Kuwait Cancer Prize in 1984; the A. Cressy Morrison Award from the New York Academy of Sciences in 1985; the Judd Memorial Award from the Sloan-Kettering Cancer Center, the Charles S. Mott Prize from the General Motors Research Foundation, and the G. H. A. Clowes Memorial Award from the American Association for Cancer Research, all in 1989; and the Robert de Villiers award from the Leukemia Society of America in 1993.

SELECTED WRITINGS BY ROWLEY:

Books

Chromosome Changes in Leukaemia, Leukaemia Research Fund, 1978.

Chromosomes and Cancer: From Molecules to Man, Academic Press, 1983.

Genes and Cancer, Liss, 1984.

Consistent Chromosomal Aberrations and Oncogenes in Human Tumors, Oxford University Press, 1984.

Advances in Understanding Genetic Changes in Cancer, National Academy Press, 1992.

Periodicals

Journal of the American Medical Association, Cytogenetics in Clinical Medicine, February 3, 1969, pp. 914–919.

Annales de Genetique, Identification of a Translocation with Quinacrine Fluorescence in a Patient with Acute Leukemia, June, 1973, pp. 109–112.

Lancet, Acquired Trisomy 9, August 18, 1973, p. 390.

Lancet, 15/17 Translocation, a Consistent Chromosomal Change in Acute Promyelocytic Leukemia, March 5, 1977, pp. 549–550.

Nature, Comparable Complex Rearrangements Involving 8;21 and 9;22 Translocations in Leukemia, April 21, 1977, pp. 744–745.

Proceedings of the National Academy of Sciences of the United States of America, Mapping of Human Chromosomal Regions Related to Neoplasia: Evidence from Chromosomes 1 and 17, December, 1977, pp. 5729–5733.

Virchows Archive. B. Cell Pathology, Cytogenetic Patterns in Acute Nonlymphocytic Leukemia, with J. R. TestaNovember 17, 1978, pp. 65–72.

Nature, Human Oncogene Locations and Chromosome Aberrations, January 27, 1983, pp. 290–291.

Nature, Heritable Fragile Sites in Cancer, with M. M. Le BeauApril 12, 1984, pp. 607–608.

Journal of Clinical Oncology, Chromosome Abnormalities in Leukemia, February, 1988, pp. 194–202.

Cancer, The Philadelphia Chromosome Translocation, May 15, 1990, pp. 2178–2184.

Cancer Research, Molecular Cytogenetics: Rosetta Stone for Understanding Cancer, July 1, 1990.

Sketch by J. Sydney Jones

Carlo Rubbia
1934–
Italian physicist

Carlo Rubbia was born in Italy and carried out his first serious scientific experiments as a young boy, using communication equipment abandoned at the end of World War II. Since his postdoctoral year at Columbia University in 1958 and 1959, Rubbia has been particularly interested in the study of elementary particles, and through his affiliations with the European Center for Nuclear Research (CERN) he has had some of the most powerful particle accelerators in the world available for his research. Since the late 1960s, Rubbia's primary research has involved the search for a trio of particles known as the W+, W-, and Z0 bosons, which were postulated in the 1960s as the force particles through which the electroweak force exerts its influence. By 1982, Rubbia and his colleagues at CERN had designed the equipment needed to carry out this search and had successfully located the first W particles. For this accomplishment, he and co-worker **Simon Meer** were awarded the 1984 Nobel Prize in physics.

Rubbia was born on March 31, 1934, in the small town of Gorizia, in northern Italy. His father was Silvio R. Rubbia, a telephone worker; his mother, Bice Liceni Rubbia, was a school teacher. When World War II ended in 1945, eleven-year-old Carlo "scaveng[ed] radio equipment that had been abandoned as various armies marched through on their various advances and retreats," according to Gary Taubes in his book *Nobel Dreams.* He used this equipment to learn everything about radios, becoming something of an "electronics freak," Taubes wrote.

Studies Elementary Particles in Italy and the United States

In 1945, Silvio Rubbia's job brought the family to Pisa, where Rubbia was enrolled at the prestigious Scuola Normale Superiore, a rigorous secondary school affiliated with the University of Pisa. After graduating from the Scuola, Rubbia went on to the university, earning a Ph.D. in physics in 1958 for his dissertation on cosmic radiation and particle detection devices. During the academic year 1958–59, Rubbia continued his studies at Columbia University in the United States, where he worked with some of the world's outstanding physicists, including **Tsung-Dao Lee**, **Chen Ning Yang**, **Chien-Shiung Wu**, **Charles H. Townes**, **Melvin Schwartz**, Leon Ledeberg, and **Steven Weinberg**, acquiring from them an interest in weak-interaction physics.

Rubbia returned to Italy in 1960 to continue his postdoctoral studies at the University of Rome. A year later, he accepted an appointment at CERN in Geneva. A consortium of more than a dozen European nations, CERN is one of the world's most important centers for the study of elementary particles. Rubbia quickly moved up the hierarchy at CERN and was appointed to the prestigious position of team leader before he was thirty years old.

Rubbia's goal during his first years at CERN was the discovery of three "intermediate vector bosons" known as the W+, W-, and Z0 particles. The existence of these particles had been predicted in the 1960s, when **Sheldon Glashow**, **Abdus Salam** and Steven Weinberg had independently developed an electroweak theory proposing that two fundamental forces, the electromagnetic and weak forces, are manifestations of a more fundamental natural force, and predicting the existence of W and Z particles. In 1971, Salam and Weinberg suggested that the neutral Z particle could be detected in "neutral currents" that would be produced by the collision of neutrinos and matter. Rubbia's objective was to design and conduct the experiment that would, for the first time, produce this particle.

Improved Accelerator Design Leads to Discovery of W and Z Particles

In 1969, Rubbia joined a project at the Fermi National Accelerator Laboratory (Fermilab) near Chicago to search for the W particles. In 1971, however, the team switched their efforts to the attempt to prove the existence of neutral weak currents, thus putting them in direct competition with Rubbia's former colleagues at CERN. In 1973, the CERN team published nearly conclusive evidence that neutral weak currents existed. The Fermilab team immediately rushed to publish their own as yet incomplete results, which also supported the existence of the currents. At about the same time, Rubbia's visa expired and he returned to Europe. Soon thereafter, the Fermi team reconducted their experiments and announced that their original findings had been in error. They then realized, however, that this second set of experiments was flawed, and they retracted their earlier retraction. The confusion temporarily tarnished Rubbia's reputation.

Both teams now turned their attention to the search for the W and Z particles. However, no existing particle accelerator could generate the energy needed to produce them. Rubbia proposed a revolutionary new technique in which two particle beams, one composed of protons and one of antiprotons, would be set in motion in opposite directions and caused to collide with each other. The amount of energy released in such a collision, Rubbia said, should be sufficient to result in the formation of W and Z particles. Rubbia's idea was ridiculed by a number of physicists, including the director of Fermilab. Managers at CERN were more open-minded, however, and provided the $100 million needed to redesign the center's super proton synchrotron to Rubbia's specifications.

By 1982, that work had been completed and the search for the W+, W-, and Z bosons began. Within a month's time, the first W particles had been identified and, less than a year later, the first Z's were also discovered. For this accomplishment, Rubbia shared the 1984 Nobel Prize in physics with the Dutch scientist Simon van der Meer, who had devised a means of storing and regulating the erratic antiprotons.

Rubbia has been affiliated with Harvard University since 1970 (1972 according to some biographers), teaching one semester there each year. He has also continued an active program of research at CERN. Rubbia married Marissa Romé, a high school physics teacher, on June 27, 1960. They have two daughters, Laura and Andrea. Rubbia has been described as one of the most controversial figures in modern particle physics, a man driven by his love for science and, according to some, his own ego. His reputation at CERN, for example, has been described by Taubes as "very, very good and very, very bad," and an article in the October 25, 1984, issue of *New Scientist* called him "an ebullient yet irascible Italian whom fellow physicists love to hate."

SELECTED WRITINGS BY RUBBIA:

Periodicals

Proceedings HEP83 of the International Europhysics Conference on High Energy Physics, The Physics of the Proton-Antiproton Collider, 1983, pp. 860–79.

FURTHER READING:

Books

Current Biography 1985, H. W. Wilson, 1985, pp. 347–51.
Taubes, Gary, *Nobel Dreams,* Random House, 1986, pp. 3–9 and passim.
Wasson, Tyler, editor, *Nobel Prize Winners,* H. W. Wilson, 1987, pp. 891–93.

Periodicals

Lederman, Leon M., and Roy F. Schwitters, *Science,* The 1984 Nobel Prize in Physics, January 11, 1985, pp. 131–34.
Sutton, Christine, *New Scientist,* CERN Scoops Up the Nobel Physics Prize, October 25, 1984, pp. 10–11.
Walgate, Robert, *Nature,* CERN's First Nobel Prize, October 25, 1984, p. 701.

Sketch by David E. Newton

Vera Cooper Rubin
1928–
American astronomer

Vera Cooper Rubin, one of America's foremost women astronomers, has spent her life observing galactic structure, rotation and dynamics. Her pioneering spectroscopic research of the 1970s demonstrated the possible existence of a large percentage of dark matter in the universe, matter that is invisible to the naked eye. Scientists now speculate that up to 90 percent of the universe may be composed of dark matter. Rubin was born on July 23, 1928, in Philadelphia, the daughter of electrical engineer Philip Cooper and Rose Applebaum, and was educated at Vassar College, receiving her B.A. in 1948. Rubin earned her M.A. at Cornell in 1951; her thesis studied the evidence for bulk rotation in the universe, and later influenced Gérard de Vaucouleurs' work on the "local supercluster" of galaxies. She received her Ph.D. in astronomy under Russian-American physicist **George Gamow** (1904–1968) three years later

Vera Cooper Rubin

at Georgetown University. Rubin's pioneering dissertation studied galactic distribution, and demonstrated a "clumpiness" in the spread of galaxies; virtually ignored in 1954, this effect was not seriously studied until the 1970s.

Rubin spent a year as an instructor in math and physics at Montgomery County Junior College before moving back to Georgetown University as research associate (1955–65), lecturer (1959–62), and then assistant professor (1962–65). She also did observational work at Kitt Peak Observatory in Arizona, and became the first official female observer at Palomar Observatory in California in 1965 (Margaret Burbidge had previously observed there unofficially). Also in 1965, Rubin joined the Department of Terrestrial Magnetism (DTM) at Washington's Carnegie Institute. For the rest of the 1960s, Rubin studied spectroscopy and galactic rotations, structure and dynamics.

Dark Matter Discovered

In particular, Rubin studied the rotation of spiral galaxies. She and DTM physicist W. Kent Ford used a spectrograph to study the rate of rotation within galaxies. They found that the stars closest to the center of a galaxy and those farthest out were traveling at the same rate of speed. Mathematical research had suggested the stars farthest from a galaxy's center would travel at a slower pace. In addition, the amount of mass in both the darker and brighter parts of a galaxy was constant, suggesting that some form of unseen matter was present. Earlier astronomers, including Fritz Zwicky, had speculated that a previ-

ously unknown "dark matter" might exist. Rubin and Ford's observations of galactic rotation speed seemed to verify that hypothesis. Continuing investigation of dark matter has been a major research effort among astronomers since the 1980s.

Rubin has contributed numerous papers to *Astrophysical Journal, Astronomical Journal,* and *Bulletin of the American Astronomical Society.* She also served as associate editor of the *Astronomical Journal* from 1972 to 1977, of *Astrophysical Journal Letters* from 1977 to 1982, and joined the editorial board of *Science Magazine* from 1979 to 1987. Rubin has sat on numerous astronomical committees, including those of Harvard University, the National Academy of Sciences (to which she was elected in 1981), and the American Astronomical Society. She has also received honorary degrees from Creighton University in 1978, Harvard University in 1988, and Yale University in 1990.

To promote women in astronomy, Rubin joined the council of American Women in Science in 1984, and in 1987 became a president's distinguished visitor at Vassar College. In 1988 she became the Beatrice Tinsley visiting professor at the University of Texas. Meanwhile, to encourage young girls to study science, she wrote a children's book on astronomy. In recent years Rubin has sat on the board of directors of the Astronomical Society of the Pacific, and has been a member of several other scientific societies. She was also on the visiting committee of the Space Telescope Scientific Institute between 1990 and 1992. In 1948 Rubin married physicist Robert J. Rubin. The couple have four children: David, Allan, Judith, and Karl. All four have become scientists as well.

"Observing is spectacularly lovely," Rubin said in *Mercury.* "I enjoy analyzing the observations, trying to see what you have, trying to understand what you're learning. It's a challenge, but a great deal of fun. It's not only fun, but a lot of it is just plain curiosity—this incredible hope that somehow we can learn how the universe works. What keeps me going is this hope and curiosity."

SELECTED WRITINGS BY RUBIN:

Books

Large Scale Motions in the Universe, Princeton University Press, 1988.

Periodicals

"Rotation of the Andromeda Nebula from a Spectroscopic Survey of Emission Regions", *Astrophysical Journal,* Number 159, 1970, p. 379.
"Motion of the Galaxy and the Local Group Determined from the Velocity Anisotropy of Distant Sc I Galaxies. I. The Data. II. The Analysis for the Motion", *Astrophysical Journal,* Number 81, 1976, pp. 681, 719.

"Women's Work", *Science '86,* July-August, 1986, pp. 58–65.

FURTHER READING:

Books

"American Women in Science," *A Hand Up: Mentoring Women in Science,* 1993, pp. 75–78.

Lightman, Alan and Brawer, Roberta, *Origins: The Lives and Worlds of Modern Cosmologists,* Vera Rubin, Harvard University Press, 1990, pp. 285–305.

"First Woman Permitted to Observe the Universe at Palomar," Tufty, Barbara, *The Women's Book of World Records and Achievements,* O'Neill, Lois Decker, editor, Anchor, 1979, p. 151.

Periodicals

Bartusiak, Marcia, "The Woman Who Spins the Stars," *Discover,* October, 1990, pp. 88–94.

Stephens, Sally, "Vera Rubin: An Unconventional Career," *Mercury: The Journal of the Astronomical Society of the Pacific,* January-February, 1992, pp. 38–45.

Sketch by Julian A. Smith

Mary Ellen Rudin
1924–
American mathematician

Mary Ellen Rudin's mathematical specialty is set theoretic topology, a modern, abstract geometry that deals with the construction, classification, and description of the properties of mathematical spaces. Rudin's approach is often to construct examples to disprove a conjecture. As an incoming freshman at the University of Texas, Rudin was chosen by the topologist R. L. Moore and trained almost exclusively by the unorthodox "Moore method" of active and competitive mathematical problem solving. Rudin credits Moore with building her confidence that given the axioms, she should be able to solve any problem, even if it involves building a complicated structure.

Rudin was born December 7, 1924, in Hillsboro, Texas, to Irene Shook and Joe Jefferson Estill. Her father was a civil engineer and her mother, before she married, was a teacher. Rudin's parents were from Winchester, Tennessee, and both of her grandmothers were graduates of Mary Sharp College in Winchester. Advanced education was valued in both families, and her parents expected that she would go to the university to "do something interesting."

Rudin grew up in Leakey, Texas, a small isolated town in the hills of southwest Texas, where her father worked on road building projects. Her childhood surroundings were simple and primitive, and as a child she had lots of time to think and to play elaborate, complicated, and imaginative games, something she says contributed to her later success as a mathematician. Rudin's performance was generally in the middle of her class of five students, and she expected she would make Cs at the university; she made As.

Is Trained by the R. L. Moore "Method"

Rudin had no special course of study in mind when she went to the University of Texas at Austin. On her first day, Moore helped her register for classes, asked about her mathematical background, and enrolled her in his mathematics class. Although she took courses in other fields and was good at them, she continued to study with Moore through her B.S. degree in 1944 and her Ph.D. degree in 1949, and had a class from him every single semester. Rudin has said, "I am a mathematician because Moore caught me and demanded that I become a mathematician."

Moore, known for his unorthodox Socratic teaching style, preferred his students to be naive; he required that they be unspoiled by mathematical terminology, notation, methods, results, or ideas of others. He also required his students to actively think, rather than passively read. Moore forbade them to read the work of others and sometimes removed books from the library so that his students would not see them. He never referred to the work of others; rather, he gave definitions and required his students to prove theorems, some that had been solved, some that had not. Students were required to think about problems just as research mathematicians do. In the classroom, Moore called on the weakest students first, then proceeded through the class to the top students. Rudin was generally at the top of the class.

Rudin solved one of the unsolved problems as her thesis research, finding a counterexample to a well-known conjecture. At the time she wrote her thesis, she had never seen a mathematics paper. While the Moore method produced students who were independent, confident and creative, there were lacunae in their knowledge of mathematics and deficient in their mathematical language. Rudin has used a more traditional approach in her own teaching, requiring her students to learn as much as possible about what has been done by others, but she acknowledges that her students are not always as confident as she was.

Research at Duke, Rochester, and Wisconsin

After Rudin received her Ph.D. in 1949, Moore told her she would be going to Duke University. At Duke, she worked on a problem related to Souslin's conjecture and began to be known for her work. She also met mathematician Walter Rudin at the university and married him in 1953. Together, they went to the University of Rochester where Walter had a position, and Rudin taught part-time and researched mostly as she pleased until 1958, when they moved to Madison, Wisconsin. Rudin held a similar position at the University of Wisconsin; she was a lecturer from 1959 to 1971, when she was appointed full professor.

Rudin has likened facility in research in mathematics to a career in music. "It must be done every day," she says. "If you don't play for three years, you're not likely to be of concert pianist quality when you start playing again, if ever again." She also notes that mathematical research requires a high tolerance for failure; successes are much less frequent than failures; in fact, she may have three exciting break-throughs in a year. Rudin prefers to work on topological problems while lying on the couch in her Frank Lloyd Wright-designed home, surrounded by the activities of her family. Rudin's productivity has been strong and consistent; she has almost 90 scientific papers and book chapters to her credit.

Rudin's counterexamples, she says, are "very messy" topological spaces that show that some ideas you thought were true, are not. She compares her many-dimensional examples, which are difficult for some people to imagine, to a business problem that has 20 aspects. The aspects are the dimensions of the problem, the number of factors taken into account.

Rudin has been at the University of Wisconsin since 1959, where she assembled a strong research group in topology. She is the first to hold the **Grace Chisholm Young** Professorship, which she assumed in 1981. Her visiting professorships include stints in New Zealand, Mexico, and China. Moore imbued Rudin with a sense of responsibility for publication and responsibility to the mathematical community, and she has held offices and worked on numerous committees of the American Mathematical Society, the Mathematical Association of America, the Association for Women in Mathematics, and the Association for Symbolic Logic. Over the years she has received several research grants from the National Science Foundation, and has served on mathematical advisory boards for the National Academy of Sciences, the National Science Foundation, and the United Nations.

Rudin and her husband have four children, and she notes that they are all skilled in pattern recognition. Now professor emerita, Rudin continues to lecture widely, produce vital papers in her field, and to promote and speak about women in mathematics. She is a fellow of the American Academy of Arts and Sciences, has received the Prize of Niewe Archief voor Wiskunk from the Mathematical Society of the Netherlands, and has been awarded four honorary doctorates. In 1995 Rudin was elected to the Hungarian Academy of Sciences.

FURTHER READING:

Books

Albers, Donald J., Gerald L. Alexanderson and Constance Reid, *More Mathematical People: Contemporary Conversations,* Harcourt Brace Jovanovich, 1990, pp. 282–303.

Periodicals

Ford, Jeff, "Geometry with a Twist," *Research Sampler* (Spring 1987): 20–23.

Other

Carr, Shannon. "Mary Ellen Rudin." *Biographies of Women Mathematicians.* June 1997. http://www.scottlan.edu/lriddle/women/chronol.htm (July 21, 1997).

Sketch by Jill Carpenter

S. K. Runcorn
1922–1995
English geophysicist

Geophysicist S. K. Runcorn made significant contributions to the understanding of several areas within his field, including the earth's magnetic field and the theory of continental drift. During the 1950s, he helped establish the discipline called paleomagnetism—the study of the intensity and direction of residual magnetization found in ancient rocks. More recently, his research has encompassed lunar magnetism. In a prolific career marked by the publication of more than one-hundred-and-eighty papers and the editing of over two dozen books, Runcorn exerted a wide-ranging impact on his field.

Stanley Keith Runcorn was born on November 19, 1922 in Southport, England. He was the eldest of two children born to William Henry Runcorn, a businessman, and Lily Idina Roberts Runcorn. As Runcorn related to contributor Linda Wasmer Smith in a letter, "My interest in science as a child was certainly stimulated . . . by excellent maths and physics teaching in my grammar school." In 1941, Runcorn began studies at Gonville and Caius College of Cambridge University. He passed the tripos, or final honors examination, in mechanical sciences two years later. Runcorn earned a B.A. degree from Cambridge in 1944 and an M.A. in 1948, before transferring to Manchester University to obtain a Ph.D. in 1949. Later, he returned to Cambridge, where he received an Sc.D. degree in 1963.

Advances the Theory of Continental Drift

Runcorn's early years at college coincided with World War II. From 1943 through 1946, he worked on radar research for the ministry of supply at Malvern. For three years afterward, he was a lecturer in physics at Manchester University. His department head there was **Patrick Maynard Stuart Blackett,** who won the 1948 Nobel Prize in physics. Under Blackett's leadership, Runcorn first began a long line of investigations into geomagnetism, which extended well past his move back to Cambridge as assistant director of geophysics research in 1950.

At the time, the idea was rapidly gaining currency in England that many rocks contain within them a fossilized record of the magnetic conditions under which they were formed. This is the basic assumption behind paleomagnetic research. Runcorn compared the results of tests done on rocks from Great Britain and the United States. His analyses seemed to support the hypothesis that over hundreds of millions of years the earth's magnetic poles had undergone large-scale movement, or polar wandering. However, the polar migration routes were different depending on whether the tested rocks came from Europe or North America. This suggested that the continents themselves had actually moved. Thus Runcorn became a proponent of the theory called continental drift. Although this idea had first been put forth in 1912, it had not up to that point won widespread acceptance. It was not until the mid-1950s that Runcorn and his colleagues published convincing evidence for its existence.

Advocates of continental drift argued that the direction of magnetization within rocks from different continents would align if only the land masses were oriented differently. However, this suggestion was not immediately embraced by most scientists, partly because a physical mechanism to explain continental drift had yet to be found. By the early 1960s, though, Runcorn had proposed that, under very high temperature and pressure, rocks beneath the earth's cold, outer shell—the lithosphere—might gradually "creep," or flow. The resulting upward transfer of heat by convection currents could be the force that moved continents. This idea contributed to the modern theory of plate tectonics, which posits that the earth's shell is divided into a number of rigid plates floating on a viscous underlayer.

In 1956, Runcorn accepted a post as professor and head of the physics department at King's College, part of the University of Durham. Seven years later, King's College became the University of Newcastle upon Tyne, and Runcorn was appointed head of the school of physics there, a position which he held until 1988. During this period, Runcorn was also a visiting scientist or professor at several institutions around the world, including the University of California, at both Los Angeles and Berkeley; Dominion Observatory, Ottawa; the California Institute of Technology; the University of Miami; the Lunar Science Institute, Houston; the University of Texas, Galveston; and the University of Queensland, Australia.

Proposes New Ideas on Lunar Magnetism

By the late 1960s, Runcorn's attention had turned toward the moon. At the time, the moon was generally presumed to be a dead body. As early as 1962, though, Runcorn had suggested that the moon, too, might be subject to the forces of convection—an idea that was initially rejected by most scientists. However, examination of lunar samples brought back by the Apollo missions showed that some of them were magnetized, which implied that they had been exposed to magnetic fields while they were forming. Runcorn and his colleagues concluded that the moon had probably once possessed its own strong magnetic field, generated within an iron core.

Not only that, but this magnetic field seemed to have pointed in different directions at different times in lunar history. When Runcorn and his coworkers calculated the strengths and directions of this ancient magnetism, they found evidence of polar wandering. Runcorn subsequently proposed that the wandering could have been caused by the same impacts that created large basins near the moon's equator. According to this hypothesis, the force of the impacts could have shifted the moon's entire surface, so that regions once near the poles might have been relocated closer to the equator. However, attempts to confirm this notion have so far proved inconclusive.

Runcorn's remarkable skill as a theorist was widely recognized. In 1989, he assumed an endowed chair in the natural sciences at the University of Alaska in Fairbanks, a position he held until his death. He also received honorary degrees from universities in Utrecht, Netherlands; Ghent, Belgium; Paris; and Bergen, Norway. Among the many prestigious awards he received are the Napier Shaw Prize of Britain's Royal Meteorological Society in 1959, the John Adams Fleming Medal of the American Geophysical Union in 1983, the Gold Medal of Britain's Royal Astronomical Society in 1984, and the Wegener Medal of the European Union of Geosciences in 1987.

In addition, Runcorn was elected a fellow or member of such respected associations as the British Royal Society, the American Physical Society, the European Geophysical Society, the Royal Netherlands Academy of Science, the Indian National Science Academy, the Royal Norwegian Academy of Science and Letters, the Pontifical Academy of Science, and Academia Europaea.

Runcorn, who never married, was an aficionado of sports and the arts. Among his favorite pastimes was rugby, which he enjoyed as a participant until he was past fifty and as a spectator thereafter. In a letter to Wasmer Smith, Runcorn described himself also as an avid fan of "squash rackets and swimming, . . . visiting art galleries, seeing opera and ballet, reading history and politics, hiking in the country, and seeing architecture in my travels." He was murdered in San Diego, on December 5, 1995.

SELECTED WRITINGS BY RUNCORN:

Books

Methods and Techniques in Geophysics. Vols. 1 and 2. Interscience, 1960 and 1966.
Continental Drift. Academic Press, 1962.
Mantle of the Earth and Terrestrial Planets. Interscience, 1967.
Magnetism and the Cosmos. Oliver & Boyd, 1967.

Periodicals

"The Moon's Deceptive Tranquility." *New Scientist* (21 October 1982): 174-80.
"The Moon's Ancient Magnetism." *Scientific American* 257 (1987): 60-68.

FURTHER READING:

Books

A Biographical Encyclopedia of Scientists. Vol. 2. Facts on File, 1981, p. 693.
McGraw-Hill Modern Scientists and Engineers. Vol. 3. McGraw-Hill 1980, pp. 50-51.

Periodicals

Creer, Kenneth M. "Stanley Keith Runcorn" (obituary). *Nature* 379 (11 January 1996): 119.
Dalton, Rex. "UK Geophysicist Killed in San Diego" (obituary). *Nature* 378 (14 December 1995): 657.
Sullivan, Walter. "Leading Expert in Geophysics is Found Slain in Hotel Room" (obituary). *New York Times* (7 December 1995): B17.

Sketch by Linda Wasmer Smith

Ernst Ruska
1906–1988
German physicist

The inventor of the electron microscope, Ernst Ruska, combined an academic career in physics and electrical engineering with work in private industry at several of Germany's top electrical corporations. He was associated with the Siemens Company from 1937 to 1955, where he helped mass produce the electron microscope, the invention for which he was awarded the 1986 Nobel Prize in physics. The Nobel Prize Committee called Ruska's electron microscope one of the most important inventions of the twentieth century. The benefits of electron microscopy to the field of biology and medicine allow scientists to study such structures as viruses and protein molecules. Technical fields such as electronics have also found new uses for Ruska's invention: improved versions of the electron microscope became instrumental in the fabrication of computer chips.

Ruska was born in Heidelberg, Germany, on December 25, 1906. He was the fifth child of Julius Ferdinand Ruska, an Asian studies professor, and Elisabeth (Merx) Ruska. After receiving his undergraduate education in the physical sciences from the Technical University of Munich and the Technical University of Berlin, he was certified as an electrical engineer in 1931. He then went on to study under Max Knoll at Berlin, and received his doctorate in electrical engineering in 1933. During this period he and Knoll created an early version of the electron microscope, and Ruska concurrently was employed by the Fernseh Corporation in Berlin, where he worked to develop television tube technology. He left Fernseh to join Siemens as an electrical engineer, and at the same time accepted a position as a lecturer at the Technical University of Berlin. His ability to work in both academic and corporate milieus continued through his time at Siemens, and expanded when in 1954 he became a member of the Max Planck Society. In 1957 he was appointed director of the Society's Institute of Electron Microscopy, and in 1959, he accepted the Technical University of Berlin's invitation to become professor of electron optics and electron microscopy. He remained an active contributor to his field until his retirement in 1972.

Inventing a Better Way to See

Prior to Ruska's invention of the electron microscope in 1931, the field of microscopy was limited by the inability of existing microscopes to see features smaller than the wavelength of visible light. Because the wavelength of light is about two thousand times larger than an atom, the mysteries of the atomic world were virtually closed to scientists until Ruska's breakthrough using electron wavelengths as the resolution medium. When the electron microscope was perfected, microscope magnification increased from approximately two thousand to one million times.

The French physicist, **Louis Victor de Broglie**, was the first to propose that subatomic particles, such as electrons, had wavelike characteristics, and that the greater the energy exhibited by the particle, the shorter its wavelength would be. De Broglie's theory was confirmed in 1927 by Bell Laboratory researchers. The conception that it was possible to construct a microscope that used electrons instead of light was realized in the late 1920s when Ruska was able to build a short-focus magnetic lens using a magnetic coil. A prototype of the electron microscope was then developed in 1931 by Ruska and Max Knoll at the Technical University in Berlin. Although it was less powerful than contemporary optical microscopes, the prototype laid the groundwork for a more powerful version, which Ruska developed in 1933. That version was ten times stronger than existing light microscopes. Ruska subsequently worked with the Siemens Company to produce for the commercial market an electron microscope with a resolution to one hundred angstroms (by contrast, modern electron microscopes have a resolution to one angstrom, or one ten-billionth of a meter).

Ruska's microscope—called a transmission microscope—captures on a fluorescent screen an image made by a focused beam of electrons passing through a thin slice of metalized material. The image can be photographed. In 1981 **Gerd Binnig** and **Heinrich Rohrer** took Ruska's concept further by using a beam of electrons to scan the surface of a specimen (rather than to penetrate it). A recording of the current generated by the intermingling of electrons emitted from both the beam and specimen is used to build a contour map of the surface. The function of this "scanning electron microscope" complements, rather than competes against, the transmission microscope, and its inventors shared the 1986 Nobel Prize in physics with Ruska.

In 1937 Ruska married Irmela Ruth Geigis, and the couple had two sons and a daughter. In addition to the Nobel Prize, Ruska's work was honored with the Senckenberg Prize of the University of Frankfurt am Main in 1939, the Lasker Award in 1960, and the Duddell Medal and Prize of the Institute of Physics in London in 1975, among other awards. He also held honorary doctorates from the University of Kiev, the University of Modena, the Free University of Berlin, and the University of Toronto. Ruska died in West Berlin on May 30, 1988.

SELECTED WRITINGS BY RUSKA:

Books

The Early Development of Electron Lenses and Electron Microscopy, translated by Thomas Mulvey, S. Hirzel, 1980.

FURTHER READING:

Periodicals

Browne, Malcolm W., *New York Times,* Ernst Ruska, a German Nobel Winner, Dies at 81, May 31, 1988, p. D14.

Lemonick, Michael D., *Time,* Lives of Spirit and Dedication, October 27, 1986, pp. 67–68.

Monastersky, R., *Science News,* Physics: Tiny World Garners Grand Laurels, Volume 130, October 25, 1986, pp. 262–263.

Sullivan, Walter, *New York Times,* Microscope Designs Bring the Nobel Prize to Three Europeans, October 16, 1986, pp. A1; B18.

Sullivan, Walter, *Time,* June 13, 1988, p. 45.

Sketch by Jane Stewart Cook

Bertrand Russell
1872–1970
English mathematician and philosopher

A seminal figure in twentieth-century mathematical logic and philosophy, Bertrand Russell produced more than seventy books and pamphlets on topics ranging from mathematics and logic to philosophy, religion, and politics. He valued reason, clarity, fearlessness, and independence of judgment, and held the conviction that it was the duty of the educated and privileged classes to lead. Having protested against Britain's participation in World War I and against the development of nuclear weapons, Russell was imprisoned twice for his convictions. In writing his own obituary, he described himself as a man of unusual principles, who was always prepared to live up to them.

Bertrand Arthur William Russell was born on May 18, 1872, in Ravenscroft, Trelleck, Monmouthshire, England. His family tree can be traced back to John Russell, a favorite courtier of Henry VIII. His grandfather, Lord John Russell, served as prime minister under Queen Victoria. Bertrand Russell's father, Lord Amberley, served in Parliament briefly, but was defeated because of his rejection of Christianity and his advocacy of voting rights for women and birth control. His mother was Kate Stanley, the daughter of a Liberal politician. Orphaned before the age of five, Russell was raised by his paternal grandmother, a Scotch Presbyterian with strong moral standards who gave duty and virtue greater priority than love and affection. His grandmother did not have confidence in the moral and religious environment at boarding schools, so, after briefly attending a local kindergarten, he was taught by a series of governesses and tutors. Later he wrote in his *Autobiography* that he had been influenced by his grandmother's fearlessness, her public spirit, her contempt for convention, and her indifference to the opinion of the majority. On his twelfth birthday she gave him a Bible in which she had written her favorite texts, including "Thou shalt not follow a multitude to do evil." It was due to her influence, he felt, that in later life he was not afraid to champion unpopular causes.

Intrigued by Euclid

When Russell was eleven, his brother Frank began to teach him Euclidean geometry. As he recounts in his *Autobiography,* "This was one of the great events of my life, as dazzling as first love. I had not imagined that there was anything so delicious in the world." Russell was greatly disappointed, however, to find out that Euclid started with axioms which were not proved but were simply accepted. Russell refused to accept the axioms unless his brother could give a good reason for them. When his brother told him that they couldn't continue unless he accepted the axioms, Russell relented, but with reluctance and doubt

Bertrand Russell

about the foundations of mathematics. That doubt remained with him and determined the course of much of his later work in mathematics.

At fifteen, Bertrand left home to take a training course to prepare for the scholarship examination at Trinity College, Cambridge. Lonely and miserable, he considered suicide but rejected the idea because, as he later said, he wanted to learn more mathematics. He kept a secret diary, written using letters from the Greek alphabet, in which he questioned the religious ideas he had been taught. After a year and a half, he took the Trinity College examination and won a scholarship. One of the scholarship examiners was **Alfred North Whitehead**. Apparently impressed with Russell's ability, Whitehead arranged for him to meet several students who soon became his close friends. He was invited to join a group, "The Apostles," which met weekly for intense discussions of philosophy and history. His chief interest and chief source of happiness, he said, was mathematics; he received a first class degree in mathematics in 1893. He found, however, that his work in preparing for the exams had led him to think of mathematics as a set of tricks and ingenious devices, too much like a crossword puzzle; this disillusioned him. Hoping to find some reason for supposing mathematics to be true, he turned to philosophy. He studied the philosophy of idealism, which was popular in Cambridge at the time, concluding that time, space and matter are all illusions and the world resides in the mind of the beholder. He took the Moral Science examination in 1894 and received an honors degree.

At seventeen, Russell had fallen in love with Alys Pearsall Smith, an American from a wealthy Philadelphia Quaker family, and after graduation they became engaged. His grandmother did not approve. Hoping he would become interested in politics and lose interest in Alys, she arranged for him to become an attaché at the British Embassy in Paris. He found his work at the embassy boring, and upon his return three months later, he and Alys were married.

In 1895, Russell wrote a dissertation on the foundations of geometry, which won him a fellowship at Trinity College and enabled him to travel and study for six years. He and Alys went to Berlin to study the German Socialist movement and the writings of Karl Marx. During his travels, he formulated a plan to write a series of books on the philosophy of the sciences, starting with mathematics and ending with biology, growing gradually more concrete, and a second series of books on social and political questions, working to more abstract issues. During his long life, he managed to fulfill much of this plan. As a result, according to biographer Ronald Clark, no other Englishman of the twentieth century was to gain such high regard in both academic and nonacademic worlds.

Russell returned to London in 1896 and lectured on his experiences to students of the London School of Economics and the Fabian Society, publishing his studies as *German Social Democracy,* the first of his numerous books and pamphlets. In this publication he demonstrated his ability to investigate a subject quickly and then present it in clear and convincing language. He and Alys traveled to the United States, where they visited Alys's friend, the poet Walt Whitman. Russell lectured on non-euclidean geometry at Bryn Mawr College, where Alys had been a student, and at Johns Hopkins University. In 1900 he was asked to lecture on German mathematician Gottfried Wilhelm Leibniz at Cambridge. He wanted to show that mathematical truths did not depend on the mathematician's point of view. He re-examined the philosophy of idealism and abandoned it, concluding that matter, space and time really did exist. He published his views in *A Critical Exposition of the Philosophy of Leibniz.*

Seeks Basic Principles of Mathematics and Logic

Russell then started work on an ambitious task—devising a structure that would allow both the simplest laws of logic and the most complex mathematical theorems to be developed from a small number of basic ideas. If this could be done, then the axioms which mathematicians accepted would no longer be needed, and both logic and mathematics would be part of a single system. At a conference in Paris in 1900, he met **Giuseppe Peano**, whose book on symbolic logic held that mathematics was merely a highly developed form of logic. Russell became interested in the possibility of analyzing the fundamental notions of mathematics, such as order and cardinal numbers, using Peano's approach. He published *The Principles of Mathematics* in 1903; its fundamental thesis was that mathematics and logic are identical.

Applying logic to basic mathematical concepts and working with **Georg Cantor**'s proof that a class of all classes cannot exist, Russell formulated his famous paradox concerning classes that are members of themselves—such as the class of classes. According to Russell's paradox, it is impossible to answer the question of whether the class containing all classes that are not members of themselves is a member of itself—for if it is a member of itself, then it does not meet the terms of the class; and if it is not, then it does. (This is the same kind of paradox as is found in the statement "Everything I say is a lie.") In developing this "Theory of Types", however, Russell realized the absurdity of asking whether a class can be a member of itself. He concluded that if classes belong to a particular type, and if they consist of homogenous members, then a class cannot be a member of itself. In planning *The Principles of Mathematics,* an exposition of his ideas on mathematics and logic, Russell decided on two volumes: the first containing explanations of his claims and the second containing mathematical proofs. His former teacher, Alfred Whitehead, had been working on similar problems. Consequently, the two scholars decided to collaborate on the second part of the task. For nearly a decade they worked together, often sharing the same house, sending each other drafts and revising each other's work. The result, *Principia Mathematica,* was a separate work published in three volumes, the last in 1913. Before it was completed, Russell was elected to the Royal Society, of which Whitehead was already a member.

Russell was persuaded to run for Parliament in 1907 as a supporter of voting rights for women; he lost the election. Appointed a lecturer in logic and the principles of mathematics at Trinity College in 1910, he published a short introduction to philosophy, *The Problems of Philosophy,* in 1912, and *Our Knowledge of the External World* in 1914. Invited to Cambridge, Massachusetts, to give the Lowell Lectures and a course at Harvard University in 1914, he also lectured in New York, Chicago, and Ann Arbor, Michigan.

Imprisoned for Opposing World War I

Russell was an outspoken critic of England's participation in World War I. He worked with the No-Conscription Fellowship to protest the drafting of young men into the army. In 1916 he gave a series of lectures in London that were published as *Principles of Social Reconstruction.* They were also published in the United States as *Why Men Fight: A Method of Abolishing the International Duel.* He was invited to give a lecture series at Harvard based on the book, but he was denied a passport because he had been convicted of writing a leaflet criticizing the imprisonment of a young conscientious objector. As a result of his conviction, he was dismissed from his lectureship at Trinity College. He wrote an open letter to Woodrow Wilson, the President of the United States, urging him to seek a negotiated peace rather than go to war. Since Russell's mail was being intercepted by the British government, he sent the letter with a young

American woman. The story made the headlines in the *New York Times.*

Russell wrote articles for *The Tribunal,* published by the No-Conscription Fellowship. In one article, he predicted that the consequences of the war would include widespread famine and the presence of American soldiers capable of intimidating striking workers. He was charged with making statements likely to prejudice Britain's relations with the United States and was sentenced to six months in prison. Before his imprisonment, he wrote *Roads to Freedom: Socialism, Anarchism and Syndicalism.* While in prison he wrote *Introduction to Mathematical Philosophy,* which explained the ideas of *The Principles of Mathematics* and *Principia Mathematica* in relatively simple terms.

In 1920, Russell visited Russia, where he was disappointed with the results of the 1917 revolution, and China, where he lectured at the National University of Peking. The following year, Russell divorced his wife Alys and married Dora Black. His son John Conrad was born, and in 1922 his daughter Katharine Jane was born. In 1927 he and Dora established Beacon Hill School for their children and others. He traveled to the United States for lecture tours in 1924, 1927, 1929 and 1931, speaking on political and social issues. He divorced Dora in 1935 and married Patricia Spence the following year. A son, Conrad Sebastian Robert, was born in 1937.

Russell lived in the United States during World War II, lecturing at the University of Chicago, the University of California at Los Angeles, Bryn Mawr, Princeton, and the Barnes Foundation at Merion, Pennsylvania. He was invited to teach at New York City College, but the invitation was revoked due to objections to his atheism and unconventional personal morality. He continued to publish works on philosophy, logic, politics, economics, religion, morality and education. In 1944, he returned to Trinity College, where he had been offered a fellowship. He published *A History of Western Philosophy,* participated in radio broadcasts in England, and lectured in Norway and Australia. He was awarded the Order of Merit by the King in 1949 and the Nobel Prize for Literature in 1950. At the age of 80, he divorced Patricia Spence and married Edith Finch.

Acutely aware of the dangers of nuclear war, Russell served as the first president of the Campaign for Nuclear Disarmament in 1958, and as president of the Committee of 100 in 1960. As a member of the Committee of 100, he encouraged demonstrations against the British government's nuclear arms policies; for this he was sentenced to two months in prison, which was reduced to one week for health reasons. In his ninth decade, Russell established the Bertrand Russell Peace Foundation, published his *Autobiography,* appealed on behalf of political prisoners in several countries, protested nuclear weapons testing, criticized the war in Vietnam, and established the War Crimes Tribunal. He died on February 2, 1970, at the age of 98.

SELECTED WRITINGS BY RUSSELL:

Books

German Social Democracy, Longmans, Green, 1896.

An Essay on the Foundations of Geometry, Cambridge University Press, 1897.

A Critical Exposition of the Philosophy of Leibniz, Cambridge University Press, 1900.

The Principles of Mathematics, Cambridge University Press, 1903.

Principia Mathematica, 3 volumes, Cambridge University Press, 1910, 1912, 1913.

Our Knowledge of the External World as a Field for Scientific Method in Philosophy, Allen & Unwin, 1914.

Principles of Social Reconstruction, Allen & Unwin, 1916.

Roads to Freedom: Socialism, Anarchism and Syndicalism, Allen & Unwin, 1918.

Introduction to Mathematical Philosophy, Allen & Unwin, 1919.

A History of Western Philosophy, Simon & Schuster, 1945.

The Autobiography of Bertrand Russell, three volumes, Little, Brown, 1967, 1968, 1969.

FURTHER READING:

Books

Ayer, A. J., *Bertrand Russell,* Viking, 1972.

Clark, Ronald, *Bertrand Russell and His World,* Thames & Hudson, 1981.

Gottschalk, Herbert, *Bertrand Russell,* translated by Edward Fitzgerald, Roy Publishers, 1965.

Schilpp, Paul Arthur, editor, *The Philosophy of Bertrand Russell,* The Library of Living Philosophers, 1946.

Sketch by C. D. Lord

Elizabeth Shull Russell
1913–
American geneticist

Elizabeth Shull Russell

The Roscoe B. Jackson Laboratory in scenic Bar Harbor, Maine, has been the professional home of geneticist Elizabeth Shull Russell since the late 1930s. For the last five decades it has also been the birthplace of millions of laboratory mice which have been meticulously bred and characterized by Russell and the center's staff. Through her efforts, laboratory mice populations—which include dozens of strains exhibiting particular characteristics that make them desirable for research—are available to scientists worldwide. Russell has also used the mice for her own ongoing research in mammalian genetics and the study of such conditions as hereditary anemias, muscular dystrophy, cancer, and aging.

Russell was born on May 1, 1913, in Ann Arbor, Michigan. Her mother, Margaret Jeffrey Buckley, held a master's degree in zoology and was a teacher at Grinnell College in Iowa during an era when few women even attended college. Her father, Aaron Franklin Shull, was a zoologist and geneticist who taught at the University of Michigan. Both the Buckleys and the Shulls had scientists in their families. Elizabeth's uncle on her mother's side was a physicist, and on her father's side there was a geneticist, a plant physiologist and a botanical artist. Her parents met in 1908 when both attended a summer course at the laboratory in Cold Spring Harbor on Long Island, New York. It seemed quite natural that Russell became interested in the plants and animals in her surroundings; as a girl she carefully catalogued every flowering plant near their summer home.

Entering The University of Michigan at the age of sixteen, Russell graduated in 1933 with a degree in zoology. This was during the midst of the Great Depression, however, and few jobs were available teaching science. Upon hearing of a scholarship program at Columbia University, her father convinced her to participate in it. Russell's coursework at Columbia included genetics, which was to prove her greatest interest. She became influenced by a paper written by **Sewall Wright** of the University of Chicago, entitled "Physiological and Evolutionary Theories of Dominance." He proposed that the specific way in which characteristics are inherited must be from either the nucleic acids or proteins on the chromosomes (geneticists now know that inheritance is controlled by the nucleic acid DNA). Upon receiving her master's degree, Russell went to the University of Chicago where she obtained an assistantship and did further graduate work under Wright. Her doctoral thesis explored the effect of genes in the pigmentation of guinea pigs.

Russell received her Ph.D. at Chicago in 1937 and married a fellow graduate student, William L. Russell. They moved to Bar Harbor, Maine, when he was appointed to a position at the Roscoe B. Jackson Memorial Laboratory. As was the general practice of most institutions at the time, only one member of a family could be employed by the laboratory, so Elizabeth Russell was invited to work as an independent investigator, which she did from 1937 to 1946.

Works with Mice at the Jackson Laboratory

While pursuing her research, Russell spent much of her time at the laboratory working with precollege, college and graduate students that came to Jackson each summer. That first summer of 1937 she had twelve summer students. As several other members of the Jackson family were also named Elizabeth, she soon became known as Tibby, a name that stuck. Over the next several years, the Russells started a family. They would eventually have three sons and a daughter together.

Although Russell had begun her investigations into how a gene controls characteristics by using fruit flies, during the 1940s she helped build up a population of laboratory mice that could be used in researching many more genetic questions. She characterized each strain, whether it be by coat color or the presence of a hereditary disease. With great precision Russell managed the genetically controlled inbred populations, and in 1946 she officially became a member of the research staff. The following year, she and her husband divorced. Russell—with four young children—now pursued her career in earnest even as the lab was starting to appreciate her great potential as a researcher.

In October, 1947, a devastating fire spread across Bar Harbor, destroying the Jackson Laboratory. Almost one hundred thousand laboratory mice perished—animals that had been carefully bred by Russell and others. In the years following, however, the team helped to once again build up the mouse population.

One day in 1951, while studying the source of mouse skin pigmentation, Russell looked in a cage and observed a most unusual mouse, a female that was dragging its feet in a peculiar way. The mouse was not injured. It appeared that it was born with some kind of muscular defect and Russell named it "Funnyfoot." By breeding Funnyfoot's brothers and sisters, the same trait cropped up in subsequent generations, leading the team to conclude that Funnyfoot and her related offspring had a genetic disease similar in some ways to muscular dystrophy in humans. This particular fact became of great interest to other researchers working

on muscular dystrophy. At once, scientists flooded the lab with requests for mice with the funnyfoot trait. There was a big problem, however—the funnyfoot females were unable to reproduce and the mice died young.

Russell devised a plan for breeding more funnyfoot mice, transplanting the ovaries of funnyfoot females into those of normal females without the characteristic. The ovaries contained egg cells (ova) in which the chromosomes carried the faulty gene. When the normal females mated, many funnyfoot offspring were produced, which were then sent to researchers. Alongside the cages of funnyfoot mice were many other strains that were meticulously bred by Russell and her team. Each group of mice and its ancestry were clearly labeled and recorded. Some strains, for instance, had hereditary diseases like anemia, while others had characteristics that made them sterile or prone to tumors. Other mice were to be used for research on blood disease, the immune system, the endocrine system, diabetes, nutrition, or aging.

Assumes the Directorship of the Jackson Laboratory

By 1953, Russell was named staff scientific director at the Jackson Laboratory. The following year she organized a conference at the laboratory where—for the first time—scientists from around the globe were invited to contribute what they were studying about mammalian genetics and its relationship to cancer. The conference was a success and in 1957 Russell became senior staff scientist. The following year Russell was awarded a Guggenheim Fellowship to review what was currently known about mammalian physiological genetics; the grant provided time and money to compile all the current research in one place, resulting in reference material useful to scientists the world over.

During her directorship, Russell's responsibilities were twofold—to provide the research mice that helped support the lab financially and to work on her areas of interest. One very important area of research at the lab under Russell involved studying blood cells of mice, especially the cells which provide the immune response (the ability to fight off invading foreign substances). This research became very important in an era in which there were a growing number of organ transplants. These mice were used in experiments that determined when tissue is accepted or rejected by an organism.

Russell also took an avid interest in blood hemoglobin —a substance which carries oxygen to all parts of a mammal's body—and was especially curious about how the hemoglobins develop. A mammal fetus inside its mother (including humans) has hemoglobin from a very early stage; after birth, however, that hemoglobin changes both its structure and the site of its production. Some of Russell's work concerned the processes of these developmental changes.

Other research topics Russell investigated include different kinds of cancers, blood diseases, and the process of aging. She has written or collaborated on over a hundred scientific papers and several books. Since 1978, Russell has been senior staff scientist emeritus. Throughout her long active career, Russell's role has also been one of mentor to many of the students that have come through the Jackson Laboratory, either as permanent staff working together on biochemistry and microbiology or the many summer graduate students that come from all over the world.

Russell has been made a member of the American Academy of Arts and Sciences and the National Academy of Sciences. During the 1970s she was an active member of the Academy's council, acting to edit and evaluate scientific papers. She was also a member of the Genetics Society of America, becoming its vice president in 1974 and president from 1975 to 1976. In 1983 she was made a member of the American Philosophical Society. Russell holds an honorary degree from Ricker College and was a trustee of the University of Maine and the College of the Atlantic. Because of her work on the aging of mice she was asked to be a member of the advisory council to the National Institute of Aging. By attending discussion groups at the laboratory, she continues to closely monitor trends in genetics research.

SELECTED WRITINGS BY RUSSELL:

Periodicals

Genetics, A Quantitative Study of Genetic Effects on Guinea Pig Coat Colors, Volume 24, 1939, pp. 332–53.
Journal of Experimental Zoology, A Comparison of Benign and Malignant Tumors in Drosophila Melanogaster, Volume 34, 1940, pp. 363–85.
Acta Haematologica, The Bone Marrow in Inherited Macrocytic Anemia in the House Mouse, Volume 12, 1953, pp. 247–59.
Journal of the National Cancer Institute, Symposium of Twenty-Five Years of Progress in Mammalian Genetics and Cancer, Roscoe B. Jackson Memorial Laboratory, June 27–30, 1954, Volume 15, 1954, pp. 551–851.
Blood, Characterization and Genetic Studies of Microcytic Anemia in House Mouse, Volume 35, 1970, pp. 838–50.
Science, Fetal Liver Erythropoiesis and Yolk Sac Cells, Volume 177, 1972, p. 187.
Proceedings of the National Academy of Sciences USA, Linkage of Genes for Adult Alpha-Globin and Embryonic Alpha-Like Globin Chains, Volume 77, 1980, pp. 1087–090.
Annual Review of Genetics, A History of Mouse Genetics, Volume 19, 1985, pp. 1–28.

Other

A complete bibliography is on file at the Joan Staats Library at the Roscoe B. Jackson Laboratory in Bar Harbor, Maine.

FURTHER READING:

Books

Noble, Iris, *Contemporary Women Scientists of America,* Messner, 1979, pp. 123–37.

Other

Russell, Elizabeth Shull, *Telephone Interview with Barbara A. Branca,* conducted February 18, 1994.

Sketch by Barbara A. Branca

Frederick Stratten Russell
1897–1984
English marine biologist

Marine biologist Frederick Stratten Russell linked the distribution of planktonic organisms to water masses and the intensity of light in the seas off the British Isles. His work helped explain the long-term changes in the ecosystem of the English Channel. Russell was fascinated by the larval stages of fishes and the life histories of certain types of jellyfish, which he studied in great detail. He wrote and illustrated several books on his findings. Colleagues J. H. S. Baxter, A. J. Southward, and C. Maurice Yonge characterized Russell as possessing "an old world courtesy" as well as "great personal charm and friendliness."

The youngest son of William and Lucy Binfield Russell, he was born on November 3, 1897, in Bridgport, England, on the coast of the English Channel. Russell attended university at Cambridge and planned to study medicine at Gonville and Caius College. But after World War I broke out, he left school to serve in the Royal Naval Air Service in France from 1916 to 1918. He served with distinction, earning the Distinguished Service Cross, the Distinguished Flying Cross, and the Croix de Guerre. After the war he returned to school, earning his degree in 1922.

That year, Russell was assigned to the Egyptian government to study the eggs and larvae of marine fishes. Before embarking on his trip to Egypt, Russell went to the laboratory of the Marine Biological Association in Plymouth, where he studied the early stages in the life histories of fish with R. S. Clark and E. Ford. There, Russell's lifelong interest in marine biology was sparked. When Russell returned from Egypt in 1924 he joined the Plymouth laboratory as a staff member. He continued to study fish larvae and other plankton. Using a special net that allowed him to filter large columns of water, Russell collected plankton, noting their vertical distributions. He built on this initial data over the next fifty years, observing how the composition of the species changed seasonally and over the long term.

Detailed Studies of Plankton and Jellyfish

Russell's work gained international attention when he showed that the depth at which fish plankton were found was related to the intensity of light in the water. He used photoelectric cells to measure the light, finding that the plankton moved up and down the water column in a daily cycle. Seasonal variations in light intensity also affected the migrations. In 1928, C. Maurice Yonge, with whom Russell had coauthored the book *The Seas,* led the Great Barrier Reef Expedition to Australia. Russell and his wife, Gweneth, joined the one-year expedition. Russell compared the distribution of plankton in tropical waters there with that of more temperate regions.

After returning to Plymouth, Russell studied in detail the biology of the torpedo-shaped marine worm, *Sagitta.* Finding that the abundance of different species of *Sagitta* varied from year to year, he traced the cause to the movement of water masses in the English Channel and the North Sea. For example, one species preferred the warmer Atlantic water masses to the Arctic water masses. Russell was able to use *Sagitta* as an indicator species, since other planktonic organisms associated with them. His work helped explain long-term changes in the English Channel ecosystem, including the varying abundance of herring. With a colleague, W. J. Rees, Russell began to study another indicator species, a type of jellyfish, *medusae.* Little was known about its early life stages. Russell and Rees raised *medusae* in captivity, studying the early hydroid stages. In 1938, he was elected a fellow of the Royal Society of London.

The outbreak of World War II interrupted Russell's work on a massive text on the *medusae* that was to contain nearly a thousand illustrations. Russell left Plymouth in 1940 to serve as an intelligence officer for the Royal Air Force. Returning to the Marine Biological Laboratory as director in 1945, he supervised the growth of the laboratory after the war. He also completed his text on the *medusae,* struggling to remember the finer details of his research before it had been interrupted by the war. The first volume of the book, called *The Medusae of the British Isles,* was finally published in 1953. Russell then devoted more time to different types of jellyfish, including the large *Scyphomedusae.* He also studied a red jellyfish from the Bay of Biscay that gave birth to live young. Russell named it *Stygiomedusa fabulosa.* Russell's studies led to his being honored with the Gold Medal of the Linnean Society in 1961. He was knighted in 1965, the same year he retired.

Continuing his studies even in retirement, at age 78 Russell published a definitive work, *The Eggs and Planktonic Stages of British Marine Fishes,* in which he described in detail the development of fish eggs and larvae. In his later years, after his wife Gweneth passed away in 1978, Russell moved from Plymouth to live near his son in Reading. Frederick Stratten Russell died on June 5, 1984. He had left

his influence on the *Journal of the Marine Biological Association,* which he had edited for twenty years, from 1945 to 1965. He had also been the founding editor of the journal *Advances in Marine Biology,* and had participated in its editing and publishing until shortly before his death.

SELECTED WRITINGS BY RUSSELL:

Books

The Seas: Our Knowledge of Life in the Sea and How It Is Gained, Frederick Warne, 1928.
The Medusae of the British Isles, 2 volumes, Cambridge University Press, 1953, 1970.
The Eggs and Planktonic Stages of British Marine Fishes, Academic Press, 1976.

FURTHER READING:

Periodicals

Blaxter, J. H. S., A. J. Southward and C. M. Yonge, *Advances in Marine Biology,* Sir Frederick Russell, 1897–1984, Volume 21, 1984, pp. vii-ix.
——— *Times,* (London), June 6, 1984.

Sketch by Miyoko Chu

Henry Norris Russell
1877–1957
American astronomer and astrophysicist

Henry Norris Russell was an American astronomer and astrophysicist remembered primarily for his work on the origin and evolution of stars and for his publication in 1913 of what would come to be known as the Hertzsprung-Russell diagram, which plots stars' absolute magnitude, or intrinsic brightness, against their spectral type. During his long career Russell published hundreds of scientific papers covering a wide range of subjects. He made significant contributions to the study of eclipsing binary stars (two stars that revolve around a common center of gravity), inventing ways to measure their size and orbits. He was also involved with the study of stellar and solar composition, the origins of the planets and comets, and the characteristics of planetary atmospheres.

Russell was born on October 25, 1877, in Oyster Bay, New York, where his father, the Reverend Alexander G. Russell, was a Presbyterian minister of Scots-Canadian stock. His mother, Eliza Norris, was born in Brazil where her father served as United States consul. Russell was educated at home until the age of twelve. He was in competent hands: his mother and maternal grandmother were both talented mathematicians, the latter having won a mathematical prize on her graduation in 1840 from Rutgers Female Institute in New York, and the former having come first in a "ladies class" in mathematics given by professors of the University of Edinburgh. Russell took a precocious interest in astronomy at age five after being shown the transit of Venus by his parents. The family moved to his mother's hometown of Princeton, New Jersey, in 1889. Russell was enrolled in the Princeton Preparatory School, and in due course, Princeton University, from which he graduated in 1897 *insigne cum laude*—the highest honor ever obtained by a Princeton graduate. He was awarded his Ph.D. in 1899 for research into methods of discovering the orbits of binary stars. By the time of his graduation, he had produced several other papers on a variety of topics.

Works as Research Student at Cambridge

Shortly after he completed his thesis, Russell's health faltered and he spent most of 1900 recuperating. By late 1901, he was well enough to return to Princeton. The following year he left the United States for England, where he had been accepted into King's College, Cambridge, as an advanced student for three years. He worked first at the Cavendish Laboratory, and later with Arthur R. Hinks as a research assistant at the Cambridge Observatory on a grant from the Carnegie Institute. They developed a means of measuring stellar parallax, which allows astronomers to determine the distance of the stars using photography. Their work was interrupted in September, 1904, when Russell once again was stricken with serious illness. It was left to Hinks to complete the observations and later send the results to Russell at Princeton for measurement. There Russell became an instructor in astronomy and continued making his own observations of the stellar magnitudes and the color indices of the sun, moon, planets, satellites, and a few asteroids.

Russell married Lucy May Cole on November 24, 1908, and they had four children: Lucy May, Elizabeth Hoxie, Henry Norris, and Emma Margaret. Russell was made assistant professor of astronomy at Princeton in 1908, a full professor in 1911, and director of the Princeton University Observatory in 1912, a post he held until 1947. In 1912 Russell published the first recorded analysis of the variation of the light received from eclipsing binary stars; later he would provide important insights into the importance of the periastron, or the point of a star's orbit nearest to the center around which it revolves, in understanding the internal structure of eclipsing binary stars. He also began working with astronomers from Harvard and Yale on a project to determine the positions of the moon.

Work Provides New Insights into Stellar Evolution

In 1913 Russell made observations of stars' color, brightness, and spectral class that called into question the prevailing theory of stellar evolution, which posited consecutive stages of stellar development from hot (blue) through cool (red). He noted that there seemed to be two types of red stars of greatly differing magnitudes. (Danish astronomer **Ejnar Hertzsprung** had published similar findings almost ten years earlier, but his work did not receive recognition at the time; Russell adopted Hertzsprung's terms "dwarf" and "giant" for the two types of red stars.) To produce what became known as the Hertzsprung-Russell diagram, Russell gathered data for hundreds of stars and plotted their absolute visual magnitude (which measures stars' intrinsic luminosity or brightness, as opposed to their apparent brightness) against their spectral class (which is dependent on temperature). Most of the stars thus plotted fell into a section of the diagram known as the "main sequence," which ran from the top left to the bottom right of the chart. Some very bright but cool stars, however, fell above the main-sequence red stars; Russell reasoned that the two types of red stars represented the first and last stages of the life of stars. The configuration of the diagram prompted Russell to propose a new theory of stellar evolution, in which stars move along the main sequence, either contracting as they heat up or expanding as they cool down, Although this theory was eventually found inadequate to explain the great complexity of stellar development, it was an influential starting point for much research to follow.

From June 1918 until the beginning of 1919, Russell worked as a consulting and experimental engineer at the Bureau of Aircraft Production of the Army Aviation Service. He was involved in studying problems associated with aircraft navigation. In carrying out his research, he often had to travel in open airplanes at heights of up to 16,000 feet. Afterward, Russell returned to Princeton University to continue his research into the solar spectrum. Soon he was in a position to identify and measure the various chemical elements in the solar atmosphere.

In 1921 Russell made an analysis of radioactive data that led him to make a determination of the age of the earth's crust as between two and eight thousand million years old. Later the same year, he made his first visit to the Mount Wilson Observatory in California. Soon afterward he became one of its research associates, and he worked there for about two months a year for the next twenty years. His work at Mount Wilson centered on radiation and spectrum analysis and yielded important insights into the solar and stellar spectra. Between 1925 and 1930 he produced twenty papers on line spectra of the elements. In 1927, Russell was appointed to the C. A. Young Research Professorship.

Jointly Publishes Astronomy Textbook

Between 1928 and 1931, Russell continued working apace. He was jointly responsible for the Russell-Dugan-Stewart two-volume textbook on astronomy, which redefined the discipline and revolutionized its teaching. He also published a series of papers, contributed an article to *Encyclopedia Britannica* on stellar evolution, and delivered the Terry Lectures on religion at Yale, which he published as *Fate and Freedom.* During the 1930s he devoted himself to spectroscopic research. In 1933 he delivered the Halley Lecture at Oxford, in which he laid out his theories concerning the composition of the stars. He also explained the rules governing the changes of intensity of different elements along the main sequence, and of atoms of the same element at different stages of ionization. Russell's classic book, *The Solar System and Its Origin,* was published to wide acclaim in 1935, and has become a standard authority on the subject.

Much of Russell's enormous body of scientific work was produced in collaboration with other astronomers and astrophysicists. Among over twenty scientists with whom he worked, his closest colleague was **Dr. Charlotte E. Moore Sitterly**. Russell was also associated with many distinguished scientific academies during his career, including the American Astronomical Society, of which he was president from 1934 to 1937; the National Academy of Sciences; the American Association for the Advancement of Science, of which he was president in 1933; the Royal Society, of which he was a foreign member; and the Academies of Rome, Brussels, and Paris, of which he was a correspondent. He also served as president of the commissions of the International Astronomical Union on stellar spectroscopy and on the constitution of stars. Russell received numerous awards and distinctions, including honorary degrees from the following universities: Dartmouth, Louvain, Harvard, Chicago, and Michoacan (Mexico). He was presented with the Draper, Bruce, Rumford, Franklin, Janssen, and Royal Astronomer Society gold medals, and with the Lalande Prize. In 1946, the American Astronomical Society established the annual Henry Norris Russell lectureship in his honor. In 1946, he delivered the first Henry Norris Russell lecture at Radcliffe College, sponsored by the American Astronomy Society. His discussion centered on the difficulty of determining the orbits of eclipsing binary stars.

After he retired, Russell worked at the Harvard and Lick observatories. He also devoted time to his other interests: poetry, geology, archeology, botany, and travel. He continued to pursue scientific work and published the results of his research almost until the day he died. After Russell's death on February 18, 1957, in Princeton, Colonel F. J. M. Stratton, writing in *Biographical Memoirs of Fellows of the Royal Society,* described him thus: "A man of overflowing energy, never sparing himself in his own work or in assisting the researches of others, he was the most eminent and versatile theoretical astrophysicist in the United States if not in the world." **Harlow Shapley** wrote in *Biographical Memoirs of the National Academy of Sciences,* "the word *genius* more rightly applies to him than to any other American astronomer of these or earlier times."

SELECTED WRITINGS BY RUSSELL:

Books

Fate and Freedom, Yale University Press, 1927.

The Solar System and Its Origin, Macmillan, 1935.
The Masses of the Stars, with a General Catalog of Dynamical Parallaxes, Astrophysical Journal Monograph, 1940.

Periodicals

Astrophysical Journal, The Density of the Variable Stars of the Algol Type, Volume 10, 1899, pp. 315–18.
Astronomical Journal, The General Perturbations of the Major Axis of Eros, by the Action of Mars, Volume 21, 1900, pp. 25–8.
Astrophysical Journal, On the Origin of Binary Stars, Volume 31, 1910, pp. 185–207.
Astrophysical Journal, On the Determination of the Orbital Elements of Eclipsing Variable Stars, Volume 35, 1912, pp. 315–40.
Proceedings of the Royal Society, A Superior Limit to the Age of the Earth's Crust, Volume 99A, 1921, pp. 84–6.
Astrophysical Journal, On the Composition of the Sun's Atmosphere, Volume 70, 1929, pp. 11–82.
Monthly Notices of the Royal Astronomical Society, Notes on the Constitution of the Stars, Volume 91, 1931, pp. 951–66.

FURTHER READING:

Books

Biographical Memoirs of Fellows of the Royal Society, Volume 3, Royal Society (London), 1957, pp. 173–91.
Biographical Memoirs of the National Academy of Sciences, Volume 32, 1958, pp. 354–78.
Kaler, James B., *Stars,* Scientific American Library, 1992.
Williams, Henry Smith, *Great Astronomers,* Simon & Schuster, 1930, p. 444.

Sketch by Avril McDonald

Loris Shano Russell
1904–
Canadian paleontologist

In addition to extensive teaching experience and museum administration, Loris Shano Russell has published more than one hundred papers based on extensive fieldwork in the western United States and Canada. During his long career, he proposed several novel theories in geology as well as in dinosaur and early mammalian studies. More importantly for paleontology, Russell developed a methodology that combines findings in stratigraphy—the study of the composition of rock layers and how they form—with fossil records to produce a much broader picture of ancient ecologies than had been previously attempted. After World War II, Russell's interest in museum work led him to accept leading positions at the National Museum of Canada and the Royal Ontario Museum.

Russell was born in Brooklyn, New York, on April 21, 1904, to Milan Winslow, a noted calligrapher, and Matilda Shano Russell, who later became involved in mission work for the Salvation Army. The family moved to Alberta, Canada, and as a boy Russell went to public schools in Calgary, in the foothills of the Canadian Rockies. Russell's interest in zoology and geology began early, and the Calgary area—rich in fossils of early mammals—gave him plenty of opportunities to indulge his interests. Calgary was only one hundred miles from Red Deer, which contained some of the richest Cretaceous fossil beds in the world. (The Cretaceous period is known as the age in which dinosaurs became extinct, about 120 million years ago). Before he went to the University of Alberta in Edmonton in the early 1920s as an undergraduate, Russell had already collected numerous specimens of invertebrate and vertebrate fossils, carefully labeled with locations and largely accurate identifications.

At the University of Alberta, Russell wrote a series of papers based on this collection that correctly demonstrated the similarity of groups of fossils in Alberta and Montana. In 1927 he went on to Princeton University, where he received his master's degree in paleontology in 1929 and his doctoral degree in 1930. The subject of Russell's thesis dealt with the actual boundary between the Cretaceous period and the Tertiary (the dawn of the age of mammals, which began seventy million years ago) in the rock formations of Alberta. Combining the fossil evidence with geologic data, Russell upset some widely held notions about the dating of several key geologic events of that period. He showed that one in particular, the Laramide revolution—which saw the major uplift of the Rockies—occurred much later than was previously assumed.

In 1930 Russell joined the Geological Survey of Canada. During seven years of field work with the Geological Survey, he was able to get very detailed mappings of rock formations and layers to amplify the subject of his thesis. Parts of North America had been covered by sea during the Cretaceous period, and Russell found that the sea had spread quickly and had withdrawn in fits and starts, contradicting the standard model that the sea had spread slowly and subsided evenly. In southwestern Saskatchewan, he found and described the most recent marine animal life on the Canadian plains. Before anyone else, Russell tried to reconcile fossil records of Cretaceous and Tertiary mussels with the classifications assigned to contemporary specimens.

Russell joined the University of Toronto in 1937 as assistant professor in paleontology and assistant director of the Royal Ontario Museum of Paleontology, although his tenure there was interrupted during World War II for three years of military service. In 1950 he became the chief zoologist of the National Museum of Canada at Ottawa. Russell decided in 1956 to accept the directorship of the museum's Natural History branch, permitting him oversight of the fossils available there. Later that year, he found himself heading the entire National Museum. In that role, Russell saw fit to enlarge the biological and anthropological research performed by the museum. In 1963, running into opposition to his plans for the Canadian centenary, he left the National Museum and returned to the University of Toronto to stay, this time taking the positions of professor in the geology department and chief biologist at the Royal Ontario Museum.

Proposes Revolutionary Theory on Dinosaur Anatomy

During Russell's involvement with the Royal Ontario and National museums, he continued his fieldwork and wrote many articles on dinosaur anatomy. Russell was among the first vertebrate paleontologists to notice that the bone structure of dinosaurs resembles more closely that of birds than of reptiles. These and other observations led Russell to publish a paper in 1965 in the *Journal of Paleontology* speculating that dinosaurs were warm-blooded but not insulated by fur or feathers, which might account in part for their extinction. At the time the paper did not garner much attention in academic circles. However, paleontologist Robert Bakker took many of Russell's theories on dinosaurs and combined them with his own in the book *The Dinosaur Heresies*, which kindled considerable debate.

The heart of Russell's work exists in his analysis of the evolution of mammals at the beginning of the Tertiary period. He discovered new mammals from that time in British Columbia and Saskatchewan while greatly expanding on what was already known about early Tertiary mammals in western Canada. Russell considered the fossil-bearing rock formations of the central mountain states of the United States and the Canadian provinces of Alberta and Saskatchewan to be vital resources not only for the richness of the fossils but for the clarity of the rock layers' sequence. He found that this clarity greatly helped to put the fossils in their proper time frames.

Russell married Grace Evelyn Le Feuvre on June 11, 1938. They had no children. Throughout his life, Russell enjoyed working in the field and clearly gathered his inspiration there. Yet he was a gifted administrator, as his numerous museum appointments attest. Russell helped the Canadian museum system take a commanding lead in the field of vertebrate paleontology. He received many awards, among them the Willett G. Miller medal in 1959 from the Royal Society of Canada, to which he was elected a fellow in 1936. He was president of the Society of Vertebrate

Paleontology from 1958 to 1959 and also president of the Canadian Museums Association from 1961 to 1963.

SELECTED WRITINGS BY RUSSELL:

Books

The Cretaceous Reptile Champsosaurus natator, National Museum of Canada, 1956.

Mammal Teeth from the St. Mary River Formation (Upper Cretaceous) at Scabby Butte, Alberta, National Museum of Canada, 1962.

Fauna and Correlation of the Ravenscrag Formation (Paleocene) of Southwestern Saskatchewan, Royal Ontario Museum, 1974.

Periodicals

Journal of Paleontology, Body Temperature of Dinosaurs and Its Relationships to Their Extinction, May, 1965, pp. 497–501.

FURTHER READING:

Books

McGraw-Hill Modern Men of Science, Volume 2, McGraw, 1968, pp. 465–66.

Periodicals

Dolphin, Ric, *Maclean's,* Bones of Contention, December 5, 1988, pp. 57–8.

Other

Russell, Loris Shano, *Telephone Interview with Hovey Brock* conducted September 29, 1993.

Sketch by Hovey Brock

Ernest Rutherford
1871–1937
English physicist

E rnest Rutherford's explanation of radioactivity earned him the 1908 Nobel Prize in chemistry, but his most renowned achievement was his classic demonstration that the atom consists of a small, dense nucleus surrounded by orbiting electrons. He also demonstrated the transmutation of one element into another by splitting the atom. His direction of laboratories in Canada and Great Britain led to

Ernest Rutherford

such triumphs as the discovery of the neutron and helped to launch high-energy, or particle, physics, which concentrates on the constitution, properties, and interactions of elementary particles of matter.

Rutherford was born the fourth of twelve children on August 30, 1871, to James and Martha Thompson Rutherford on the South Island of New Zealand near the village of Spring Grove. Both parents had arrived in New Zealand as children, not long after Great Britain annexed the territory into the Commonwealth in 1840. Rutherford's father, of Scottish descent, logged, cultivated flax, worked in construction, and pursued other endeavors with a mechanical inventiveness inherited from his wheelwright father, George. Martha Rutherford was a schoolteacher of English descent.

Rutherford's early success in school earned him a scholarship to Nelson College, a secondary school in a village on the north end of New Zealand's South Island. He then received a scholarship to Canterbury College at Christchurch, New Zealand, where he earned his bachelor of arts degree in 1892. He continued studying at Canterbury, earning a master of arts degree with honors in mathematics and mathematical physics in 1893 and a bachelor of science degree in 1894. In New Zealand, Rutherford met Mary Newton, the woman who would become his wife in 1900. She was the daughter of the woman who provided Rutherford with lodging while he studied at Canterbury. Rutherford and his wife had one daughter, Eileen (1901–1930), who married Ralph Fowler, a laboratory assistant of Rutherford's in the 1920s and 1930s.

While working toward his bachelor of science degree, Rutherford researched the effects of electromagnetic waves, produced by rapidly alternating electrical currents, on the magnetization of iron. He observed that, contrary to contemporary expectations, iron did magnetize in high-frequency electromagnetic fields. Conversely, he also showed that electromagnetic waves could demagnetize magnetized iron needles. On the basis of this observation, Rutherford devised a device for picking up electromagnetic waves produced at a distance. Italian physicist **Guglielmo Marconi** would later parlay the same principles into the development of wireless telegraphy, or radio.

These experiments earned Rutherford a scholarship in 1895, which was derived from profits from London's Great Exhibition of 1851. Rutherford attended Trinity College at Cambridge University to work under the direction of English physicist **J. J. Thomson** at the Cavendish Laboratory as the university's first research student. The laboratory had been established in 1871 for research in experimental physics and was first led by electromagnetism pioneer James Clerk Maxwell. Rutherford's demonstration of his electromagnetic detector greatly impressed Thomson and other scientists at the Cavendish almost immediately.

Thomson invited Rutherford in 1896 to assist him in studies of the effects of X rays, which had been discovered in 1895 by **Wilhelm Conrad Röntgen**, on the electrical properties of gases. Thomson and Rutherford demonstrated that X rays broke gas molecules into electrically and positively charged ions, making the gas electrically conductive. This work brought Rutherford widespread recognition in the British scientific community for the first time.

Forges Understanding of Radioactivity

In 1897, Rutherford took up the study of radioactivity, the phenomenon discovered almost accidentally by French physicist **Henri Becquerel** in 1896. He began by studying the radioactive emissions of uranium, systematically wrapping uranium in successive layers of aluminum foil to observe the penetrating ability of these emissions. He concluded that uranium emitted two distinct types of radiation: a less penetrating type, which he called "alpha," and a more penetrating type, "beta." He also later observed what was described by French physicist Paul Villard as "gamma" radiation, the most penetrating type of all.

Not assured of a professorship at Cambridge, Rutherford applied for and was appointed Second MacDonald Professor of Physics at McGill University in Montreal, Canada, in 1898. McGill University appealed to Rutherford especially because it had perhaps the best-equipped laboratory in North America, if not the world, at the time. At McGill, Rutherford turned from studying uranium to thorium, another radioactive element. Although thorium emits alpha and beta radiation as does uranium, emission patterns for thorium substances seemed erratic. Rutherford determined in 1899 that an emanation, or new radioactive substance, was being produced. He also observed that the radioactivity of the emanation gradually decreased geomet-

rically with time, an occurrence now known as the half-life of a radioactive substance, which is a measurement of the time it takes for half of a substance to decay. In 1901, Rutherford forged a partnership with **Frederick Soddy**, an Oxford chemistry demonstrator based at McGill who first encountered Rutherford in a debate on the existence of subatomic particles. Rutherford wanted Soddy to help him study the thorium emanations and to explain curious observations of radioactive substances noticed in Europe by Becquerel and by Sir William Crookes, who discovered thallium. Both had isolated the active parts of uranium from an apparently inert part. However, Becquerel also observed that the active part soon lost its activity, while the inert remainder regained its activity.

Rutherford and Soddy isolated the active part of radioactive thorium, which they named thorium-X, from the apparently inert parent, thorium. They charted how thorium-X gradually lost its radioactivity while the original thorium regained its activity, illustrating that thorium-X had its own distinctive half-life, which was much shorter than the half-life of thorium. Soddy tried to get thorium-X to interact chemically with other reagents without success. From these observations, Rutherford and Soddy put together the modern understanding of radioactivity in 1903. Thorium-X was a product of the disintegration or decay of thorium. In nature, radioactive elements and their products decay simultaneously. However, when the product is separated out, it continues to decay but is not replenished by decaying thorium atoms, so its radioactivity falls off. Meanwhile, the inert parent thorium eventually regains its radioactivity as it generates new radioactive products. Rutherford's explanation of radioactivity at the atomic level is what caused a sensation in scientific circles. He explained that radioactivity—alpha, beta, and gamma radiation—was the physical manifestation of this disintegration, the pieces of the thorium atom that were released as it decayed. In other words, thorium was steadily being transformed, or transmuted, into a new element that was lower in atomic number. It was this work that earned Rutherford the 1908 Nobel Prize in chemistry.

Rutherford received, and turned down, offers to teach at Yale and Columbia universities in the United States. He became a Fellow of the Royal Society in 1903 and received the Rumford Medal in 1904. His books on radioactivity became standard textbooks on the subject for years and he was a popular speaker. He attracted a number of talented associates at McGill, the most famous of whom was **Otto Hahn**, a German physicist who would, with Austrian physicist **Lise Meitner**, demonstrate the fissioning of uranium in 1939.

In 1904 Rutherford was the first to suggest that radioactive elements with extremely long half-lives might provide a source of energy for sustaining the heat of the earth's interior. This would supply a means for estimating the age of the earth in the billions of years, allowing plenty of time for evolution by natural selection to proceed along lines outlined by the naturalist Charles Darwin in 1859.

Determines Atomic Structure and Splits Atom

In 1906 Sir Arthur Schuster offered Rutherford his chair as professor of physics at Manchester University in Great Britain. Eager to return to what was then the center of the scientific world, Rutherford accepted the position in 1907. Rutherford was again blessed at Manchester with a well-equipped laboratory and talented associates from around the world, such as **Hans Geiger**, who would develop the radioactivity counter; Charles Darwin, grandson of the famous naturalist; and physicists **Niels Bohr**, Ernest Marsden, and **H. G. J. Moseley**.

Rutherford proceeded with his study of radioactive emissions, particularly the high-energy alpha particles. His research was slowed at first when a sample of radium, his favorite alpha source, was sent by the Radium Institute of the Austrian Academy of Sciences in Vienna to a rival, **William Ramsay**, discoverer of the noble gases. Rutherford had to request and await another sample from the Institute before he could proceed in earnest with his work.

Rutherford wanted to determine precisely the nature of the alpha particles. In 1903, at McGill, he had succeeded in deflecting alpha particles in electric and magnetic fields, proving they had a positive charge. He was certain that the relatively massive particle must be equivalent to helium nuclei, which consist of two protons. At Manchester in 1908, Rutherford and his colleagues proved experimentally through spectroscopic means that the alpha particles were indeed nuclei of helium atoms.

In 1908 Rutherford and Geiger devised a method for counting alpha particles precisely. Alpha particles were fired into a nearly evacuated tube with a strong electric field. The resulting ionizing effect in the gas could be detected by an electrometer, a device that measures electric charge in a gas. The alpha particles could then be detected visually as well as they struck a zinc sulfide screen to cause an identifiable flash or scintillation. Geiger would build upon this technique in developing the electric radiation counter that bears his name.

In 1909 Rutherford had instructed Marsden to study the scattering of alpha particles at large angles. Marsden observed that when alpha particles were fired at gold foil, a significant number of particles were deflected at unusually large angles; some particles were even reflected backward. Metals with a larger atomic number (such as lead) reflected back even more particles. It was not until late in 1910 that Rutherford postulated from this evidence the modern concept of the atom, which he announced early in 1911. He surmised that the atom did not resemble a "plum pudding" of positively charged nuclear particles with electrons embedded within like raisins, as suggested by Thomson. Instead, Rutherford suggested that the atom consisted of a very small, dense nucleus surrounded by orbiting electrons. Geiger and Marsden provided the mathematics to support the theory and Bohr linked this concept with quantum theory to produce the model of the atom employed today. After World War I broke out in 1914, Rutherford was called upon to serve in the British Navy's Board of Invention and Research. His main area of research for the Board was in devising a method for detecting German U-boats at sea. His work established principles applied later in the development of sonar.

The work on alpha particle scattering continued during the war. Marsden observed in 1914 that alpha particles fired into hydrogen gas produced anomalous numbers of scintillations. Rutherford first concluded that the scintillations were being caused by hydrogen nuclei. However, Rutherford later observed the same effect when alpha particles were fired into nitrogen. After a long series of experiments to exclude all possible explanations, in 1919 Rutherford determined that the alpha particles were splitting the nitrogen atoms and that the extraneous hydrogen atoms were remnants of that split. Nitrogen was thus transmuted into another element. In 1925, English physicist **Paul Maynard Stewart Blackett** used the cloud chamber apparatus devised by Scottish physicist **C. T. R. Wilson** to verify Rutherford's observation and to show that the atom split after it had absorbed the alpha particle.

Directs the Cavendish Laboratory

In 1919, Rutherford was persuaded to succeed Thomson as director of the Cavendish Laboratory at Cambridge, a post he would hold until his death. Rutherford directed the Cavendish during its most fruitful research period in its history. English atomic physicist **John D. Cockcroft** and Irish experimental physicist **Ernest Walton** constructed the world's first particle accelerator in 1932 and demonstrated the transmutation of elements by artificial means. Also in the early 1930s, English physicist **James Chadwick** confirmed the existence of the neutron, which Rutherford had predicted at least a decade earlier. Rutherford, with Chadwick, continued to bombard and split light elements with alpha particles. With Marcus Oliphant and Paul Harteck, Rutherford, in 1934, bombarded deuterium with deuterons (deuterium nuclei), achieving the first fusion reaction and production of tritium.

Rutherford was involved significantly in national and international politics during this period, albeit not for himself but for the sake of science. He worked with the civilian Department of Scientific and Industrial Research (DSIR) to obtain grants for his scientific team and served as president of the British Association for the Advancement of Science from 1925 to 1930. Beginning in 1933, Rutherford served as president of the Academic Assistance Council, established to assist refugee Jewish scientists fleeing the advance of Nazi Germany. When the Soviet Union prevented Russian physicist **Pyotr Kapitsa**, a promising Cavendish scientist, from returning to Great Britain from the Soviet Union in 1934, Rutherford launched an ultimately futile effort to convince the Soviets to release him. Rutherford maintained close relations through correspondence with leading scientists in Europe, North America, Australia, and New Zealand. Despite his preference for experimentation, Rutherford corresponded with Bohr, German physicist **Max Planck**, American physicist **Albert Einstein** and other theoretical physicists transforming physics with relativity and quantum mechanics. He also remained close to his mother in New Zealand, exchanging letters with her frequently until her death in 1935.

In his long and distinguished career, Rutherford's most prestigious award, aside from his Nobel Prize, may have been the Order of Merit that he received from King George V in 1925. The Order of Merit is Britain's highest civilian honor. Rutherford was knighted in 1914 and made a peer (Baron Rutherford of Nelson or Lord Rutherford) in 1931. He died from complications after surgery on a strangulated hernia on October 19, 1937, in Cambridge. His cremated remains were buried near the graves of Isaac Newton and Charles Darwin at Westminster Abbey in London.

SELECTED WRITINGS BY RUTHERFORD:

Books

Radio-Activity, Cambridge University Press, 1904, second edition, 1905.
Radioactive Transformations, Scribner, 1906.
Radioactive Substances and Their Radiations, Cambridge University Press, 1913.
Radiations from Radioactive Substances, G. P. Putnam, 1930.
Collected Papers of Lord Rutherford of Nelson, three volumes, 1962–65.
Rutherford and Boltwood: Letters on Radioactivity, 1969.

FURTHER READING:

Books

Dictionary of Scientific Biography, Volume 12, Scribner, 1975.
Eve, Arthur Stewart, *Rutherford,* Macmillan, 1939.
Wilson, David, *Rutherford: Simple Genius,* MIT Press, 1983.
Wilson, David, *World of Scientific Discovery,* Gale, 1994.

Sketch by Michael Boersma

Leopold Ružička
1887–1976
Swiss chemist

Leopold Ružička worked in what he referred to as the "borderland" between bio-organic chemistry and biochemistry. His studies of odorous natural products led to his discovery of carbon rings with many more carbon atoms

than had been originally thought possible. His research also contributed important information on how living things biosynthesize some steroids and sex hormones. For this work he shared the 1939 Nobel Prize in chemistry.

Leopold Stephen Ružička was born on September 13, 1887, to Stjepan and Amalija (Sever) Ružička. He was the first of two boys. They lived at first in Vukovar in Eastern Croatia (later part of Yugoslavia). His father, a cooper, died when Ružička was about four years old, and the family then moved to Osijek to live with relatives. Ružička attended elementary and high school in Osijek, where he received a classical education (Latin and Greek), and was initially determined to enter the Catholic priesthood. As a teenager, he changed his interests to chemistry, and upon graduation began to look for graduate schools in Germany and Switzerland. He eventually settled on the *Technische Hochschule* in Karlsruhe, Germany, choosing it over the Swiss Federal Institute of Technology (Eidgenossische Technische Hochschule, or ETH) in Zurich, because it provided more flexibility in courses and did not require an entrance examination in descriptive geometry.

Ružička obtained his doctorate in only four years, under the direction of **Hermann Staudinger** at Karlsruhe. He then assisted Staudinger in research on the natural products in the *Chrysanthemum* species; these chemicals, called pyrethrins, were of particular interest as insecticides. In September of 1912, they both moved to ETH, where Ružička had originally considered studying, when Staudinger replaced **Richard Willstätter** as professor of organic and inorganic chemistry. Reflecting on these events later in his life, Ružička wrote, in *Annual Review of Biochemistry,* "The fact that I went to Karlsruhe for my training was a very important factor in my life. If I had taken my doctorate degree with Willstätter I should have gone to Germany with him in 1912, and two years later Germany was at war. . . . That war ended in 1918 with the destruction of the Habsburg empire and the beginning of bad times in Germany." Instead, he had established sufficient residency in Zurich by 1917 to obtain Swiss citizenship, and avoided the devastation caused during World War I.

In 1916, Ružička started his own research program, supported financially by a Geneva perfume company. (His position at ETH carried no salary until 1925, two years after he was named a professor.) The University of Utrecht, in the Netherlands, offered him a job as an organic chemistry professor in 1926. After three years there, he went back to Zurich to take on the job of directing ETH. During much of his career he was also supported financially by the Rockefeller Foundation.

Ružička studied various organic compounds early in his career, but in 1921 his most fruitful work began—on the structure and synthesis of several natural compounds important to the fragrance industry. (His collaborations with the Swiss pharmaceutical and perfume industries was to continue throughout his working life.) Before Ružička's discoveries, chemists thought that ring structures containing more than eight carbons would be unstable, because no one had been able to synthesize large rings. Ružička's research on muscone (obtained from the male musk deer) and civetone (from both male and female civet cats), however, indicated rings with as many as seventeen carbons—a huge number. He was able to synthesize some of these very large rings with new procedures developed by his research group.

Another line of research dealt with isoprene. Biochemists are interested in how living things biosynthesize large molecules; they had known for some time that isoprene is one of nature's favorite building blocks. Ružička found many more large biochemicals that were constructed from isoprene units, and he formulated a rule of thumb called the "isoprene rule" for predicting biosynthesis based on this starting material. Ružička also synthesized testosterone and androsterone, the male sex hormones. In recognition of these successes he was awarded the Nobel Prize in chemistry in 1939, which he shared with **Adolf Butenandt**.

Ružička conducted research in an era when instrumentation was primitive by contemporary standards. The elucidation of molecular structure, therefore, depended entirely upon the observation of chemical reactions and the purification of reaction products. In this process an unknown compound would be exposed to various well-characterized reagents; if it reacted to give certain products, the chemist knew that the original molecule contained particular arrangements of atoms. (Ružička, for example, frequently used dehydrogenation—the removal of hydrogen atoms—to gain information about molecular structure.) Once these arrangements had been identified, the chemist would attempt to synthesize the original compound, and then compare the original and the synthetic. If they matched, that was taken as good evidence that the perceived structure was at least partly correct. This time-consuming, "wet" chemistry often gave ambiguous results, and polite arguments frequently occurred in scientific literature as the chemistry community debated the structure of a complicated new molecule. Often old rules had to give way when new discoveries were made. In his Nobel lecture, Ružička said, "Experience has shown that there is no rule governing the architecture of natural compounds which is valid without exception, and which would enable us to dispense with the need to test its validity accurately for every new compound to be examined."

Ružička married Anna Housmann in 1912; they were divorced in 1950. In 1951 he married Gertrud Acklin. He was an avid gardener and collector of paintings, so much so that he once said his chemistry had suffered as a result of his hobbies. He established an important collection of Dutch and Flemish masters of the seventeenth century, as well as an art library on that general period, which he later gave to the Zurich art museum. During World War II, he worked to secure the escape of several Jewish scientists from the Nazis, and founded the Swiss-Yugoslav Relief Society. He was instrumental in providing refuge in Switzerland to the future Nobel Laureate **Vladimir Prelog**, who succeeded Ružička as the director of ETH when the latter retired in 1957. Ružička died on September 26, 1976.

SELECTED WRITINGS BY RUŽIČKA:

Books

Annual Review of Biochemistry, In the Borderland between Bioorganic Chemistry and Biochemistry, Volume 42, 1973, pp. 1–20.

FURTHER READING:

Books

Nobel Prize Winners, H. W. Wilson, 1987.
Nobel Prize Winners in Chemistry: 1901–1961, revised edition, Abelard-Schuman, 1963, p. 171.

Sketch by Gail B.C. Marsella

Martin Ryle
1918–1984
English radio astronomer

The 1974 Nobel Prize for physics, awarded to Martin Ryle and **Antony Hewish**, was the first to be given to astronomers. The award was granted in recognition of their pioneering research in radio astrophysics. Ryle in particular was recognized for his development of the aperture synthesis technique, a method by which computer technology is used to overcome some fundamental problems in the construction of radio telescopes. By using this technique Ryle was able to make a number of important discoveries, including the nature of radio stars and the origins of radio scintillation.

Ryle was born in Brighton, England, on September 27, 1918. The Ryle name was well-known and highly respected in England: Martin Ryles's father, John A. Ryle, was a physician, director of Oxford University's Institute of Social Medicine, and the first professor of social medicine at the university; and an uncle, Gilbert Ryle, was a philosopher. Martin's mother was the former Miriam Scully. Ryle attended Bradfield College and Christ Church at Oxford University, eventually earning first-class honors in the latter's school of natural sciences.

War Research Leads to a Career in Radio Astronomy

Ryle's graduation from Oxford in 1939 coincided with the beginning of World War II in Europe; instead of heading for graduate school, he was assigned to work in the government's Telecommunications Research Establishment (later renamed the Royal Radar Establishment). His primary assignment there was the development of countermeasures for enemy radar. Ryle also made contact with his future colleague, Antony Hewish, during his war-related research. At the war's conclusion Ryle returned to Cambridge, where he had worked briefly before being assigned to the Telecommunications Research Establishment. Like many of his colleagues, Ryle was convinced that the new science of radar could be applied to observational astronomy. Early working conditions were primitive, to be sure, with Ryle's earliest instrument being a captured German radar dish, but progress was made rapidly.

Develops Basic Techniques of Radio Astronomy

The science of radio astronomy had been established largely through the efforts of American engineer **Karl Guthe Jansky** in the early 1930s. Jansky had detected the presence of very short radio waves coming from distant parts of the universe, and had recognized the possibility that such radio waves might carry information about astronomical bodies in much the same way that light waves do. Jansky's hopes for a new field of radio astronomy were disputed by many astronomers who doubted the importance of his discoveries. However, as research continued—especially with the improved instruments and techniques available from war research—those doubts began to fade. By the late 1940s, Ryle and his colleagues were ready to attack the fundamental questions of radio astronomy.

The first challenge was simply to construct a map of the radio-emitting sources in the sky. In his first survey of the heavens, completed in 1950, Ryle identified fifty radio sources; a second survey, conducted five years later, found almost 2,000 sources. During these surveys, Ryle and his colleagues made another important discovery: they located a radio source in the constellation Cygnus, 500 million light years away. The ability to detect an object that distant meant that radio telescopes had the ability to see very far back into the history of the universe. They were, therefore, valuable tools in the science of cosmology, the study of the universe's creation.

As Ryle extended his search for radio sources, he was forced to deal with a difficult technical problem. The resolving power of any telescope (its ability to separate two nearby objects in the sky) depends on the wavelength of the radiation detected. Since the wavelength of radio waves is much longer than that of light waves, a radio telescope must be many times larger than a light telescope of comparable resolving power. In fact, the telescopes Ryle and other radio astronomers needed for their work could easily have been hundreds or thousands of meters in diameter.

Ryle's solution for this problem was conceptually simple and elegant. He designed a number of telescope parts that could be moved from place to place. He located these sections first in one region of his phantom giant telescope, aimed that at the sky, and took pictures. He then moved the sections to another region of the giant phantom telescope

and took more pictures. He continued this process until the sections had been placed over a very large total area, one comparable in size to the desired, if unbuildable, giant telescope. Finally, in order to place the sections in precisely the right places and properly correlate all the individual pictures, Ryle tied the sections into a master computer. The computer then generated the kind of radio picture of the sky that would have been obtained by a single very large radio telescope. It was primarily for the design of this aperture synthesis telescope that Ryle was awarded a share of the 1974 Nobel Prize in physics.

Ryle held a variety of teaching, research, and administrative positions at Cambridge until his retirement in 1982. During that time he accumulated a number of honors and awards, including the Hughes Medal of the Royal Society in 1954, the Gold Medal of the Royal Astronomical Society in 1964, the Henry Draper Medal of the United States National Academy of Sciences in 1965, and the Royal Medal of the Royal Society in 1973. He was knighted in 1966.

Ryle was married in 1947 to Ella Rowena Palmer, a nurse and physiotherapist. During the last decade of his life he became particularly interested in the role of renewable energy in the world's future and argued strongly for the development of wind power in Great Britain. He died of lung cancer in Cambridge on October 16, 1984.

SELECTED WRITINGS BY RYLE:

Periodicals

Nature, The New Cambridge Radio Telescope, May 12, 1962, pp. 517–18.
Nature, High Resolution Observations of the Radio Sources in Cygnus and Cassiopeia, March 27, 1965, pp. 1259–262.

FURTHER READING:

Books

A Biographical Encyclopedia of Scientists, Facts on File, 1981, p. 700.
McGraw-Hill Modern Scientists and Engineers, McGraw, 1980, pp. 57–9.
Nobel Prize Winners, H. W. Wilson, 1987, pp. 902–04.
Weber, Robert L., *Pioneers of Science: Nobel Prize Winners in Physics,* American Institute of Physics, 1980, pp. 237–38.

Periodicals

Findlay, John W., *Science,* The 1974 Nobel Prize in Physics, November 15, 1974, pp. 620–21.
Findlay, John W., *Physics Today,* Radioastronomers Ryle and Hewish Win Nobel Physics Prize, December, 1974, p. 77.

Sketch by David E. Newton

S

Paul Sabatier
1854–1941
French chemist

Paul Sabatier, who shared the 1912 Nobel Prize in chemistry with his countryman **Victor Grignard**, spent thirty-two years of a fifty-year career studying heterogeneous catalysis, especially the catalytic hydrogenation of organic compounds over finely divided metals.

Born on November 5, 1854, in Carcassone, France, Sabatier attended school in Carcassone, where his uncle was a teacher. An older sister helped tutor him, taking Latin and mathematics for that purpose. When his uncle transferred to the Toulouse Lycée, Sabatier followed. While at Toulouse, he used his free time to attend a public course in physics and chemistry that gave him a taste for science.

Accepted at both the École Polytechnique and the École Normale Supérieure in 1874, he entered the latter and graduated at the head of his class in 1877. He worked as an instructor in Nîmes for a year, but teaching secondary school physics was not what he wanted, and he returned to Paris as an assistant to Marcellin Berthelot at the Collège de France. There, in 1880, he earned his doctoral degree with a thesis on metallic sulfides.

After a year of teaching physics at the Faculté des Sciences at Bordeaux, he returned to Toulouse in 1882 to teach physics at the Faculté des Sciences there. In 1883, his duties expanded to include chemistry, and in 1884, at the age of thirty, he was appointed Professor of Chemistry. He remained in that post for the rest of his career, refusing offers from the Sorbonne to succeed **Henri Moissan** and from the Collège de France to succeed Berthelot. He was chosen Dean of the Faculty of Science in 1905, an office which he held for over twenty-five years. In addition to his research and teaching during this period, he was instrumental in the creation of schools of chemistry, agriculture, and electrical engineering at Toulouse. Even after his official retirement in 1929, he continued, by special permission, to lecture until failing health forced him to stop in 1939. Sabatier died on August 14, 1941.

Sabatier was a man of great reserve, and there is little information available about his private life. His marriage to Mlle. Herail was ended by her death in 1898. He never remarried, and their four daughters were raised with the help of his older sisters.

After receiving the Nobel Prize in 1912, Sabatier was elected a year later to be the first member of the Academy of Sciences who did not reside in Paris. He had been a corresponding member since 1901, but the residency requirement kept him from full membership until a special class of six nonresident members was created, in part so that he could become a full member without having to move to Paris. He was made a Chevalier of the Légion d'Honneur in 1907 and named Commander in 1922. Among the many other honors bestowed on him by various organizations in different countries were the Davy Medal from the Royal Society in 1915 and the Franklin Medal from the Franklin Institute in Philadelphia in 1933. He received honorary doctoral degrees from the universities of Pennsylvania (in 1926, in conjunction with the Philadelphia Sesquicentennial celebration), Louvain, and Saragossa.

Switches from Inorganic to Organic Chemistry

For his doctoral research and during his first fifteen years at Toulouse, Sabatier worked in the area of inorganic chemistry. His early work on the sulfides, hydrogen sulfides, and polysulfides of alkali and alkaline earth metals helped to clarify a complicated area of chemistry. He prepared the first pure sample of dihydrogen disulfide and was the first to make silicon monosulfide and tetraboron monosulfide as well as boron and silicon selenides. He carried out a number of thermochemical studies of the hydration (addition of H_2O) of metal chlorides and chromates and various copper compounds and was a pioneer in the use of absorption spectroscopy to study chemical reactions. Absorption spectroscopy exploits the unique patterns of light absorption characteristic of chemical substances to identify them. Spectroscopes scatter the light with a prism so that the dark absorption lines become visible in the spectrum.

In the 1890s it occurred to Sabatier to see if nitric oxide would produce a compound with nickel analogous to the recently discovered compound of nickel and carbon monoxide. These experiments, conducted with the chemist Jean-Baptiste Senderens, were not very fruitful, though some nitrogen compounds of copper, cobalt, nickel, and iron were obtained by the reaction of nitrogen dioxide with the metal. Sabatier then thought to use acetylene, an organic compound, but learned that Moissan and François Moreau had passed acetylene over powdered nickel made by heating nickel oxide with hydrogen and reported the formation of only carbon, some liquid hydrocarbons, and a gas they thought to be hydrogen.

In 1897, after being assured that Moissan and Moreau had no plans to continue their acetylene studies further, Sabatier and Senderens tried the reaction using the gas ethylene, another hydrocarbon. The experiment was successful and thus solidified Sabatier's switch to organic (carbon-based) chemistry. The result was again the formation of carbon, liquid hydrocarbons, and a gas, but on analyzing the gas, they found it to be mostly ethane and only a little hydrogen. Appreciating that the ethane could only have arisen through the addition of hydrogen to the ethylene (hydrogenation), they tried passing a mixture of ethylene and hydrogen over finely divided nickel and found that the smooth hydrogenation of ethylene took place at only a little above room temperature (30–40°C). For the next thirty-two years, Sabatier and his students investigated the heterogeneous catalysis (a process in which a third substance, or catalyst, influences the rate of a chemical reaction) of a variety of organic reactions by metals and metal oxides.

On the basis of his studies, Sabatier explained the catalytic action by the formation of unstable intermediate compounds between the catalyst and the reactant(s). This view, opposed to an earlier theory that the effect was due only to local extremes of pressure and temperature in small pores of the catalyst, proved to be correct and revolutionized organic chemistry.

In 1912 Sabatier's work was recognized by the shared award of the Nobel Prize in chemistry. The following year, he summed up his fifteen years of work on catalysis and reviewed the accumulating literature in the field in the book *La Catalyse en chimie organique.* Although his pioneer work was basic to the development of important industrial processes such as the catalytic cracking of petroleum to increase the yield of gasoline and the hydrogenation of vegetable oils to make shortening, Sabatier did not interest himself in such practical applications, nor did he profit from them.

SELECTED WRITINGS BY SABATIER:

Books

La Catalyse en chimie organique, 2nd edition, 1920, translation by Emmet Reid published with revisions in Reid's Catalysis Then and Now, Franklin, 1965.

Periodicals

Industrial and Engineering Chemistry, How I Have Been Led to the Direct Hydrogenation Method by Metallic Catalysts, Volume 18, number 10, 1926, pp. 1005–008.

FURTHER READING:

Books

Nobel Lectures Including Presentation Speeches and Laureate's Biographies-Chemistry, 1901–1921, Elsevier, 1966, pp. 217–33.

Obituary Notices of Fellows of the Royal Society, Volume 4, Morrison & Gibb, 1942, pp. 62–6.
Partington, J. R., *A History of Chemistry,* Volume 4, Macmillan, 1964, pp. 858–59.

Periodicals

Camichel, Charles, Georges Champetier, and Gabriel Bertrand, *Bulletin de la Société Chimique,* Commémoration du Centenaire de la Naissance de Paul Sabatier, 1955, pp. 465–75.
Taylor, Hugh S., *Journal of the American Chemical Society,* Paul Sabatier, Volume 66, number 10, 1944, pp. 1615–617.

Sketch by R. F. Trimble

Albert Sabin
1906–1993
American virologist

Albert Sabin, a noted virologist, developed an oral vaccine for polio that led to the once-dreaded disease's virtual extinction in the Western Hemisphere. Sabin's long and distinguished research career included many major contributions to virology, including work that led to the development of attenuated live-virus vaccines. During World War II, he developed effective vaccines against dengue fever and Japanese B encephalitis. The development of a live polio vaccine, however, was Sabin's crowning achievement.

Although Sabin's polio vaccine was not the first, it eventually proved to be the most effective and became the predominant mode of protection against polio throughout the Western world. In South America, "Sabin Sundays" were held twice a year to eradicate the disease. The race to produce the first effective vaccine against polio was marked by intense and often acrimonious competition between scientists and their supporters; in addition to the primary goal of saving children, fame and fortune were at stake. Sabin, however, allowed his vaccine to be used free of charge by any reputable organizations as long as they met his strict standards in developing the appropriate strains.

Albert Bruce Sabin was born in Bialystok, Russia (now Poland), on August 26, 1906. His parents, Jacob and Tillie Sabin, immigrated to the United States in 1921 to escape the extreme poverty suffered under the czarist regime. They settled in Paterson, New Jersey, and Sabin's father became involved in the silk and textile business. After Albert Sabin graduated from Paterson High School in 1923, one of his uncles offered to finance his college education if Sabin would agree to study dentistry. But during his dental education, Sabin read the *Microbe Hunters* by Paul deKruif and was drawn to the science of virology, as well as to the romantic and heroic vision of conquering epidemic diseases.

After two years in the New York University (NYU) dental school, Sabin switched to medicine and promptly lost his uncle's financial support. He paid for school by working at odd jobs—primarily as a lab technician—and through scholarships. He received his B.S. degree in 1928 and enrolled in NYU's College of Medicine. In medical school Sabin showed early promise as a researcher by developing a rapid and accurate system for typing (identifying) pneumococci, or the pneumonia viruses. After receiving his M.D. degree in 1931, he went on to complete his residency at Bellevue Hospital in New York City, where he gained training in pathology, surgery, and internal medicine. In 1932, during his internship, Sabin isolated the B virus from a colleague who had died after being bitten by a monkey. Within two years, Sabin showed that the B virus's natural habitat is the monkey and that it is related to the human herpes simplex virus. In 1934 Sabin completed his internship and then conducted research at the Lister Institute of Preventive Medicine in London.

Begins Polio Research

In 1935 Sabin returned to the United States and accepted a fellowship at the Rockefeller Institute for Medical Research. There, he resumed in earnest his research of poliomyelitis (or polio), a paralytic disease that had reached epidemic proportions in the United States at the time of Sabin's graduation from medical school. By the early 1950s, polio afflicted 13,500 out of every 100 million Americans. In 1950 alone, more than 33,000 people contracted polio. The majority of them were children.

Ironically, polio was once an endemic disease (or one usually confined to a community, group, or region) propagated by poor sanitation. As a result, most children who lived in households without indoor plumbing were exposed early to the virus; the vast majority of them did not develop symptoms and eventually became immune to later exposures. But after the public health movement at the turn of the century began to improve sanitation and more and more families had indoor toilets, children were not exposed at an early age to the virus and thus did not develop a natural immunity. As a result, polio became an epidemic disease and spread quickly through communities to other children without immunity, regardless of race, creed, or social status. What made the disease so terrifying was that it caused partial or full paralysis by lodging in the brain stem and spinal cord and attacking the central nervous system. Often victims of polio would lose complete control of their muscles and had to be kept on a respirator, or what became known as an iron lung, to help them breathe.

In 1936, Sabin and Peter K. Olitsky used a test tube to grow some polio virus in the central nervous tissue of human embryos. Not a practical approach for developing the huge amounts of virus needed to produce a vaccine, this research nonetheless opened new avenues of investigation

for other scientists. However, their discovery did reinforce the mistaken assumption that polio only affected nerve cells.

Although primarily interested in polio, Sabin was "never able to be a one-virus virologist," as he told Donald Robinson in an interview for Robinson's book *The Miracle Finders*. Sabin also studied how the immune system battled viruses and conducted basic research on how viruses affect the central nervous system. Other interests included investigations of toxoplasmosis, a usually benign viral disease that sometimes caused death or severe brain and eye damage in prenatal infections. These studies resulted in the development of rapid and sensitive serologic diagnostic tests for the virus.

During World War II Sabin served in the United States Army Medical Corps. He was stationed in the Pacific theater where he began his investigations into insect-borne encephalitis, sandfly fever, and dengue. He successfully developed a vaccine for dengue fever and conducted an intensive vaccination program on Okinawa using a vaccine he had developed at Children's Hospital of Cincinnati that protected more than 65,000 military personnel against Japanese encephalitis. Sabin eventually identified a number of antigenic (or immune response-promoting) types of sandfly fever and dengue viruses that led to the development of several attenuated (avirulent) live-virus vaccines.

After the war, Sabin returned to the University of Cincinnati College of Medicine, where he had previously accepted an appointment in 1937. With his new appointments as professor of research pediatrics and fellow of the Children's Hospital Research Foundation, Sabin plunged back into polio research. He and his colleagues began performing autopsies on everyone who had died from polio within a four-hundred-mile radius of Cincinnati, Ohio. At the same time, Sabin performed autopsies on monkeys. From these observations he found that the polio virus was present in humans in both the intestinal tract and the central nervous system. Sabin disproved the widely held belief that polio entered humans through the nose to the respiratory tract, showing that it first invaded the digestive tract before attacking nerve tissue. Sabin was also among the investigators who identified the three different strains of polio.

Sabin's discovery of polio in the digestive tract indicated that perhaps the polio virus could be grown in a test tube in nonnervous tissue as opposed to costly and difficult-to-work-with nerve tissue. In 1949 **John Franklin Enders**, Frederick Chapman Robbins, and Thomas Huckle Sweller grew the first polio virus in human and monkey nonnervous tissue cultures, a feat that would earn them a Nobel Prize. With the newfound ability to produce enough virus to conduct large-scale research efforts, the race to develop an effective vaccine heated up.

Competes with Salk to Develop Vaccine

At the same time that Sabin began his work to develop a polio vaccine, a young scientist at the University of Pittsburgh—**Jonas Salk** —entered the race. Both men were enormously ambitious and committed to their own theory about which type of vaccine would work best against polio. While Salk committed his efforts to a killed polio virus, Sabin openly expressed his doubts about the safety of such a vaccine as well as its effectiveness in providing lasting protection. Sabin was convinced that an attenuated live-virus vaccine would provide the safe, long-term protection needed. Such a vaccine is made of living virus which is diluted, or weakened, so that it spurs the immune system to fight off the disease without actually causing the disease itself.

In 1953 Salk seemed to have won the battle when he announced the development of a dead virus vaccine made from cultured polio virus inactivated, or killed, with formaldehyde. While many clamored for immediate mass field trials, Sabin, Enders, and others cautioned against mass inoculation until further efficacy and safety studies were conducted. But Salk had won the entire moral and financial support of the National Foundation for Infantile Paralysis, and in 1954 a massive field trial of the vaccine was held. In 1955, to worldwide fanfare, the vaccine was pronounced effective and safe.

Church and town hall bells rang throughout the country, hailing the new vaccine and Salk. However, on April 26, just fourteen days after the announcement, five children in California contracted polio after taking the Salk vaccine. More cases began to occur, with eleven out of 204 people stricken eventually dying. The United States Public Health Service (PHS) ordered a halt to the vaccinations, and a virulent live virus was found to be in certain batches of the manufactured vaccine. After the installation of better safeguards in manufacturing, the Salk vaccine was again given to the public and greatly reduced the incidence of polio in the United States. But Sabin and Enders had been right about the dangers associated with a dead-virus vaccine; and Sabin continued to work toward a vaccine that he believed would be safe, long lasting, and orally administered without the need for injection like Salk's vaccine.

By orally administering the vaccine, Sabin wanted it to multiply in the intestinal tract. Sabin used Enders's technique to obtain the virus and tested individual virus particles on the central nervous system of monkeys to see whether the virus did any damage. According to various estimates, Sabin's meticulous experiments were performed on anywhere from nine to fifteen thousand monkeys and hundreds of chimpanzees. Eventually he diluted three mutant strains of polio that seemed to stimulate antibody production in chimpanzees. Sabin immediately tested the three strains on himself and his family, as well as research associates and volunteer prisoners from Chillicothe Penitentiary in Ohio.

Results of these tests showed that the viruses produced an immunity to polio with no harmful side effects. But by now the public and much of the scientific community were committed to the Salk vaccine. Two scientists working for Lederle Laboratories had also developed a live-virus vaccine. However, the Lederle vaccine was tested in Northern Ireland in 1956 and proved dangerous, as it sometimes reverted to a virulent state.

Although Sabin could not get backing for a large-scale clinical trial in the United States, he remained undaunted. He was able to convince the Health Ministry in the Soviet Union to try his vaccine in massive trials. At the time, the Soviets were mired in a polio epidemic that was claiming eighteen to twenty thousand victims a year. By this time Sabin was receiving the political backing of the World Health Organization in Geneva, Switzerland, which had previously been using Salk's vaccine to control the outbreak of polio around the world; they now believed that Sabin's approach would one day eradicate the disease. Sabin began giving his vaccine to Russian children in 1957, inoculating millions over the next several years. Not to be outdone by Salk's public relations expertise, Sabin began to travel extensively, promoting his vaccine through newspaper articles, issued statements, and scientific meetings. In 1960 the U.S. Public Health Service, finally convinced of Sabin's approach, approved his vaccine for manufacture in the United States. Still, the PHS would not order its use and the Salk vaccine remained the vaccine of choice until a pediatrician in Phoenix, Arizona, Richard Johns, organized a Sabin vaccine drive. The vaccine was supplied for free, and many physicians provided their services without a fee on a chosen Sunday. The success of this effort spread, and Sabin's vaccine soon became "the vaccine" to ward off polio.

The battle between Sabin and Salk persisted well into the 1970s, with Salk writing an op-ed piece for the *New York Times* in 1973 denouncing Sabin's vaccine as unsafe and urging people to use his vaccine once more. But, for the most part, Salk was ignored, and by 1993, health organizations began to report that polio was close to extinction in the Western Hemisphere.

Sabin's drive and commitment (some called it stubbornness) to his work served him well during the scientific turmoil and infighting of the 1950s that surrounded the development of a polio vaccine. Described socially as mild-mannered, quiet, and unassuming, Sabin was known by his colleagues to be egotistical and possessive about his own work. Sabin often insisted that his vaccine was totally safe, despite the evidence that in very rare cases it could cause paralytic poliomyelitis. He continued his virology research focusing on the role of viruses in cancer.

Sabin's personal life largely remained behind the scenes. He married his first wife, Sylvia Tregillus, in 1935, and they had two daughters. After Sylvia Sabin died in 1966, Sabin married Jane Warner; the two later divorced. In 1972, he married Heloisa Dunshee De Abranches, a newspaperwoman.

Sabin continued to work vigorously and tirelessly into his seventies, traveling to Brazil in 1980 to help with a new outbreak of polio. He antagonized Brazilian officials, however, by accusing the government bureaucracy of falsifying data concerning the serious threat that polio still presented in that country. He officially retired from the

National Institute of Health in 1986. Despite his retirement, Sabin continued to be outspoken, saying in 1992 that he doubted whether a vaccine against the human immunodeficiency virus, or HIV, was feasible. Sabin died from congestive heart failure at the Georgetown University Medical Center on March 3, 1993. In an obituary in the *Lancet,* Sabin was noted as the "architect" behind the eradication of polio from North and South America. Salk issued a statement praising Sabin's work to vanquish polio.

SELECTED WRITINGS BY SABIN:

Books

Viruses and Cancer: A Public Lecture in Conversational Style, University of Newcastle upon Tyne, 1965.

Periodicals

American Journal of the Medical Sciences, Behavior of Chimpanzee-Avirulent Poliomyelitis Viruses in Experimentally Infected Human Volunteers, 1955, pp. 1–8.
American Journal of Tropical Medicine and Hygiene, Recent Advances in Our Knowledge of Dengue and Sand Fly Fever, 1955, pp. 198–207.

FURTHER READING:

Books

Great Events from History II, Salem Press, 1991, pp. 1522–526.
McGraw-Hill Modern Men of Science, McGraw-Hill, 1966, pp. 411–12.
Robinson, Donald, *The Miracle Finders,* David McKay, 1976, pp. 42–7.
Shorter, Edward, *The Health Century,* Doubleday, 1987, pp. 60–70.

Periodicals

Beale, John, *Lancet,* March 13, 1993, p. 685.
Schmeck, Harold M., Jr., *New York Times,* Albert Sabin, Polio Researcher, 86, Dies, March 4, 1993, p. B8.

Sketch by David Petechuk

Florence Rena Sabin
1871–1953
American anatomist

Florence Rena Sabin's studies of the central nervous system of newborn infants, the origin of the lymphatic system, and the immune system's responses to infections—especially by the bacterium that causes tuberculosis—carved an important niche for her in the annals of science. In addition to her research at Johns Hopkins School of Medicine and Rockefeller University, she taught new generations of scientists and thus extended her intellectual reach far beyond her own life. Moreover, Sabin's later work as a public health administrator left a permanent imprint upon the communities in which she served. Some of the firsts achieved by Sabin include becoming the first woman faculty member at Johns Hopkins School of Medicine, as well as its first female full professor, and the first woman to be elected president of the American Association of Anatomists.

Sabin was born on November 9, 1871, in Central City, Colorado, to George Kimball Sabin, a mining engineer and son of a country doctor, and Serena Miner, a teacher. Her early life, like that of many in that era, was spare: the house where she lived with her parents and older sister, Mary, had no plumbing, no gas and no electricity. When Sabin was four, the family moved to Denver; three years later her mother died.

After attending Wolfe Hall boarding school for a year, the Sabin daughters moved with their father to Lake Forest, Illinois, where they lived with their father's brother, Albert Sabin. There the girls attended a private school for two years and spent their summer vacations at their grandfather Sabin's farm near Saxtons River, Vermont.

Sabin graduated from Vermont Academy boarding school in Saxtons River and joined her older sister at Smith College in Massachusetts, where they lived in a private house near the school. As a college student, Sabin was particularly interested in mathematics and science, and earned a bachelor of science in 1893. During her college years she tutored other students in mathematics, thus beginning her long career in teaching.

A course in zoology during her junior year at Smith ignited a passion for biology, which she made her specialty. Determined to demonstrate that—despite widespread opinion to the contrary—an educated woman was as competent as an educated man, Sabin chose medicine as her career. This decision may have been influenced by events occurring in Baltimore at the time.

The opening of Johns Hopkins Medical School in Baltimore was delayed for lack of funds until a group of prominent local women raised enough money to support the institution. In return for their efforts, they insisted that

Florence Rena Sabin

women be admitted to the school—a radical idea at a time when women who wanted to be physicians generally had to attend women's medical colleges.

Begins Medical Career at Johns Hopkins

In 1893 the Johns Hopkins School of Medicine welcomed its first class of medical students; but Sabin, lacking tuition for four years of medical school, moved to Denver to teach mathematics at Wolfe Hall, her old school. Two years later she became an assistant in the biology department at Smith College, and in the summer of 1896 she worked in the Marine Biological Laboratories at Woods Hole. In October of 1896 she was finally able to begin her first year at Johns Hopkins.

While at Johns Hopkins, Sabin began a long professional relationship with Dr. Franklin P. Mall, the school's professor of anatomy. During the four years she was a student there and the fifteen years she was on his staff, Mall exerted an enormous influence over her intellectual growth and development into prominent scientist and teacher. Years after Mall's death, Sabin paid tribute to her mentor by writing his biography, *Franklin Paine Mall: The Story of a Mind.*

Sabin thrived under Mall's tutelage, and while still a student she constructed models of the medulla and midbrain from serial microscopic sections of a newborn baby's nervous system. For many years, several medical schools used reproductions of these models to instruct their students.

A year after her graduation from medical school in 1900, Sabin published her first book based on this work, *An Atlas of the Medulla and Midbrain,* which became one of her major contributions to medical literature, according to many of her colleagues.

After medical school, Sabin was accepted as an intern at Johns Hopkins Hospital, a rare occurrence for a woman at that time. Nevertheless, she concluded during her internship that she preferred research and teaching to practicing medicine. However, her teaching ambitions were nearly foiled by the lack of available staff positions for women at Johns Hopkins. Fortunately, with the help of Mall and the women of Baltimore who had raised money to open the school, a fellowship was created in the department of anatomy for her. Thus began a long fruitful period of work in a new field of research, the embryologic development of the human lymphatic system.

Sabin began her studies of the lymphatic system to settle controversy over how it developed. Some researchers believed the vessels that made up the lymphatics formed independently from the vessels of the circulatory system, specifically the veins. However, a minority of scientists believed that the lymphatic vessels arose from the veins themselves, budding outward as continuous channels. The studies that supported this latter view were done on pig embryos that were already so large (about 90mm in length) that many researchers—Sabin included—pointed out that the embryos were already old enough to be considered an adult form, thus the results were inconclusive.

Embryo Research Yields Important Findings

The young Johns Hopkins researcher set out to settle the lymphatic argument by studying pig embryos as small as 23mm in length. Combining the painstaking techniques of injecting the microscopic vessels with dye or ink and reconstructing the three-dimensional system from two-dimensional cross sections, Sabin demonstrated that lymphatics did in fact arise from veins by sprouts of endothelium (the layer of cells lining the vessels). Furthermore, these sprouts connected with each other as they grew outward, so the lymphatic system eventually developed entirely from existing vessels. In addition, she demonstrated that the peripheral ends (those ends furthest away from the center of the body) of the lymphatic vessels were closed and, contrary to the prevailing opinion, were neither open to tissue spaces nor derived from them. Even after her results were confirmed by others they remained controversial. Nevertheless, Sabin firmly defended her work in her book *The Origin and Development of the Lymphatic System.*

Sabin's first papers on the lymphatics won the 1903 prize of the Naples Table Association, an organization that maintained a research position for women at the Zoological Station in Naples, Italy. The prize was awarded to women who produced the best scientific thesis based on independent laboratory research.

Back at Hopkins from her year abroad, she continued her work in anatomy and became an associate professor of anatomy in 1905. Her work on lymphatics led her to studies of the development of blood vessels and blood cells. In 1917 she was appointed professor of histology, the first woman to be awarded full professorship at the medical school. During this period of her life, she enjoyed frequent trips to Europe to conduct research in major German university laboratories.

After returning to the United States from one of her trips abroad, she developed methods of staining living cells, enabling her to differentiate between various cells that had previously been indistinguishable. She also used the newly devised "hanging drop" technique to observe living cells in liquid preparations under the microscope. With these techniques she studied the development of blood vessels and blood cells in developing organisms—once she stayed up all night to watch the "birth" of the bloodstream in a developing chick embryo. Her diligent observation enabled her to witness the formation of blood vessels as well as the formation of stem cells from which all other red and white blood cells arose. During these observations, she also witnessed the heart make its first beat.

Sabin's technical expertise in the laboratory permitted her to distinguish between various blood cell types. She was particularly interested in white blood cells called monocytes, which attacked infectious bacteria, such as *Mycobacterium tuberculosis,* the organism that causes tuberculosis. Although this organism was discovered by the German microbiologist **Robert Koch** during the previous century, the disease was still a dreaded health menace in the early twentieth century. The National Tuberculosis Association acknowledged the importance of Sabin's research of the body's immune response to the tuberculosis organism by awarding her a grant to support her work in 1924.

In that same year, she was elected president of the American Association of Anatomists, and the following year Sabin became the first woman elected to membership in the National Academy of Sciences. These honors followed her 1921 speech to American women scientists at Carnegie Hall during a reception for Nobel Prize-winning physicist **Marie Curie**, an event that signified Sabin's recognized importance in the world of science.

Although her research garnered many honors, Sabin continued to relish her role as a professor at Johns Hopkins. The classes she taught in the department of anatomy enabled her to influence many first-year students—a significant number of whom participated in her research over the years. She also encouraged close teacher-student relationships and frequently hosted gatherings at her home for them.

One of her most cherished causes was the advancement of equal rights for women in education, employment, and society in general. Sabin considered herself equal to her male colleagues and frequently voiced her support for educational opportunities for women in the speeches she made upon receiving awards and honorary degrees. Her civic-mindedness extended to the political arena where she was an active suffragist and contributor to the Maryland *Suffrage News* in the 1920s.

Immune System Research Continues at Rockefeller Institute

Sabin's career at Johns Hopkins drew to a close in 1925, eight years after the death of her close friend and mentor Franklin Mall. She had been passed over for the position of professor of anatomy and head of the department, which was given to one of her former students. Thus, she stepped down from her position as professor of histology and left Baltimore.

In her next position, Sabin continued her study of the role of monocytes in the body's defense against the tubercle bacterium that causes tuberculosis. In the fall of 1925, Sabin assumed a position as full member of the scientific staff at the Rockefeller Institute for Medical Research (now Rockefeller University) in New York City at the invitation of the institute's director, **Simon Flexner**. At Rockefeller, Sabin continued to study the role of monocytes and other white blood cells in the body's immune response to infections. She became a member of the Research Committee of the National Tuberculosis Association and aspired to popularize tuberculosis research throughout Rockefeller, various pharmaceutical companies, and other universities and research institutes. The discoveries that she and her colleagues made concerning the ways in which the immune system responded to tuberculosis led her to her final research project: the study of antibody formation.

During her years in New York, Sabin participated in the cultural life of the city, devoting her leisure time to the theater, the symphony, and chamber music concerts she sometimes presented in her home. She enjoyed reading nonfiction and philosophy, in which she found intellectual stimulation that complemented her enthusiasm for research. Indeed, one of her coworkers was quoted in *Biographical Memoirs* as saying that Sabin possessed a "great joy and pleasure which she derived from her work ... like a contagion among those around her so that all were stimulated in much the same manner that she was. ... She was nearly always the first one at the laboratory, and greeted every one with a *joie de vivre* which started the day pleasantly for all of us."

Meanwhile, she continued to accrue honors. She received fourteen honorary doctorates of science from various universities, as well as a doctor of laws. *Good Housekeeping* magazine announced in 1931 that Sabin had been selected in their nationwide poll as one of the twelve most eminent women in the country. In 1935 she received the M. Carey Thomas prize in science, an award of $5,000 presented at the fiftieth anniversary of Bryn Mawr College. Among her many other awards was the Trudeau Medal of the National Tuberculosis Association (1945), the Lasker Award of the American Public Health Association (1951), and the dedication of the Florence R. Sabin Building for Research in Cellular Biology at the University of Colorado Medical Center.

Plays Prominent Role in Denver's Public Health

In 1938 Sabin retired from Rockefeller and moved to Denver to live with her older sister, Mary, a retired high school mathematics teacher. She returned to New York at least once a year to fulfill her duties as a member of both the advisory board of the John Simon Guggenheim Memorial Foundation and the advisory committee of United China Relief.

Sabin quickly became active in public health issues in Denver and was appointed to the board of directors of the Children's Hospital in 1942, where she later served as vice president. During this time she became aware of the lack of proper enforcement of Colorado's primitive public health laws and began advocating for improved conditions. Governor John Vivian appointed her to his Post-War Planning Committee in 1945, and she assumed the chair of a subcommittee on public health called the Sabin Committee. In this capacity she fought for improved public health laws and construction of more healthcare facilities.

Two years later she was appointed manager of the Denver Department of Health and Welfare, donating her salary of $4,000 to the University of Colorado Medical School for Research. She became chair of Denver's newly-formed Board of Health and Hospitals in 1951 and served for two years in that position. Her unflagging enthusiasm for public health issues bore significant fruit. A *Rocky Mountain News* reporter stated that "Dr. Sabin . . . was the force and spirit behind the Tri-County chest X-ray campaign" that contributed to cutting the death rate from tuberculosis by 50 percent in Denver in just two years.

But Sabin's enormous reserve of energy flagged under the strain of caring for her ailing sister. While recovering from her own illness, Sabin sat down to watch a World Series game on October 3, 1953, in which her favorite team, the Brooklyn Dodgers, were playing. She died of a heart attack before the game was over.

The state of Colorado gave Sabin a final posthumous honor by installing a bronze statue of her in the National Statuary Hall in the Capitol in Washington, D.C., where each state is permitted to honor two of its most revered citizens. Upon her death, as quoted in *Biographical Memoirs,* the Denver *Post* called her the "First Lady of American Science." Sabin's philosophy of life and work might be best summed up by words attributed to Leonardo da Vinci, with which she chose to represent herself on bookplates: "Thou, O God, dost sell unto us all good things at the price of labour."

SELECTED WRITINGS BY SABIN:

Books

An Atlas of the Medulla and Midbrain: A Laboratory Manual, Friedenwald Company, 1901.
The Origin and Development of the Lymphatic System, Johns Hopkins Press, 1916.

Franklin Paine Mall: The Story of a Mind, Johns Hopkins Press, 1934.

FURTHER READING:

Books

Bluemel, Elinor, *Florence Sabin: Colorado Woman of the Century,* University of Colorado Press, 1959.
Kronstadt, Janet, *Florence Sabin,* Chelsea House, 1990.
McMaster, Philip D. and Michael Heidelberger, *Biographical Memoirs,* Florence Rena Sabin, Columbia University Press, 1960.
Yost, Edna, *American Women of Science,* Frederick A. Stokes, 1943.

Periodicals

Yost, Edna, *Rocky Mountain News,* (Denver, CO), March 1, 1951.

Sketch by Marc Kusinitz

Carl Sagan
1934–1996
American astronomer and exobiologist

One of the first scientists to take an active interest in the possibility that life exists elsewhere in the universe, and an astronomer who was both a best-selling author and a popular television figure, Carl Sagan was one of the best-known scientists in the world. He made important contributions to studies of Venus and Mars, and he was extensively involved in planning NASA's Mariner missions. Regular appearances on the *Tonight Show* with Johnny Carson began a television career that culminated in the series Sagan hosted on public television called *Cosmos,* seen in sixty countries by over 400,000,000 people. He was also one of the authors of a paper that predicted drastic global cooling after a nuclear war; the concept of "nuclear winter" affected not only the scientific community but also national and international policy, as well as public opinion about nuclear weapons and the arms race. Although some scientists considered Sagan too speculative and insufficiently committed to detailed scientific inquiry, many recognized his talent for explaining science, and acknowledged the importance of the publicity generated by Sagan's enthusiasm.

Sagan was born in Brooklyn, New York, on November 9, 1934, the son of Samuel Sagan, a Russian immigrant and a cutter in a clothing factory, and Rachel Gruber Sagan. He

Carl Sagan

became fascinated with the stars as a young child, and was an avid reader of science fiction, particularly the novels of Edgar Rice Burroughs about the exploration of Mars. By the age of five he was sure he wanted to be an astronomer, but, as he told Henry S. F. Cooper, Jr., of the *New Yorker,* he sadly assumed it was not a paying job; he expected he would have to work at "some job I was temperamentally unsuited for, like door-to-door salesman." When he found out a few years later that astronomers actually got paid, he was ecstatic. "That was a splendid day," he told Cooper.

Sagan's degrees, all of which he earned at the University of Chicago, include an A.B. in 1954, a B.S. in 1955, an M.S. in physics in 1956, and a doctorate in astronomy and astrophysics in 1960. As a graduate student, Sagan was deeply interested in the possibility of life on other planets, a discipline known as exobiology. Although this interest was then considered beyond the realm of responsible scientific investigation, he received important early support from scientists, such as Nobel laureates **Hermann Joseph Muller** and **Joshua Lederberg.** He also worked with **Harold C. Urey**, who had won the 1934 Nobel Prize in chemistry and had been **Stanley Lloyd Miller**'s thesis adviser when he conducted his famous experiment on the origin of life. Sagan wrote his doctoral dissertation, "Physical Studies of the Planets," under **Gerard Peter Kuiper,** one of the few astronomers who was a planetologist at that time. It was during his graduate student days that Sagan met Lynn Margulis, a biologist, who became his wife on June 16, 1957. She and Sagan had two sons; they divorced in 1963.

From graduate school, Sagan moved to the University of California at Berkeley, where he was the Miller residential fellow in astronomy from 1960 to 1962. He then accepted a position at Harvard as an assistant professor from 1962 to 1968. On April 6, he married the painter Linda Salzman; this second marriage, which ended in a divorce, produced a son. From Harvard, Sagan went to Cornell University, where he was first an associate professor of astronomy at the Center for Radiophysics and Space Research. He was then promoted to professor and associate director at the center, serving in that capacity until 1977 when he became the David Duncan Professor of Astronomy and Space Science.

Suggestions about Mars and Venus Confirmed by Spacecrafts

Sagan's first important contributions to the understanding of Mars and Venus began as insights while he was still a graduate student. Color variations had long been observed on the planet Mars, and some believed these variations indicated the seasonal changes of some form of Martian plant life. Sagan, working at times with James Pollack, postulated that the changing colors were instead caused by Martian dust, shifting through the action of wind storms; this interpretation was confirmed by *Mariner 9* in the early 1970s. Sagan also suggested that the surface of Venus was incredibly hot, since the Venusian atmosphere of carbon dioxide and water vapor held in the sun's heat, thus creating a version of the "greenhouse effect." This theory was also confirmed by an exploring spacecraft, the Soviet probe *Venera IV*, which transmitted data about the atmosphere of Venus back to Earth in 1967. Sagan also performed experiments based on the work of Stanley Lloyd Miller, studying the production of organic molecules in an artificial atmosphere meant to simulate that of a primitive Earth or contemporary Jupiter. This work eventually earned him a patent for a technique that used gaseous mixtures to produce amino acids.

Sagan first became involved with spaceflight in 1959, when Lederberg suggested he join a committee on the Space Science Board of the National Academy of Sciences. He became increasingly involved with NASA (National Aeronautics and Space Administration) during the 1960s and participated in many of their most important robotic missions. He developed experiments for the Mariner Venus mission and worked as a designer on the *Mariner 9* and the *Viking* missions to Mars, as well as on the *Pioneer 10*, the *Pioneer 11*, and the *Voyager* spacecrafts. Both the *Pioneer* and the *Voyager* spacecrafts have left our solar system carrying plaques which Sagan designed with Frank Drake as messages to any extraterrestrials that find them; they have pictures of two humans, a man and a woman, as well as various astronomical information. The nude man and woman were drawn by Sagan's second wife, Linda Salzman, and they provoked many letters to Sagan denouncing him for sending "smut" into space. During this project Sagan met the writer Ann Druyan, the project's creative director, who eventually became his third wife. Sagan and Druyan had two children.

Sagan continued his involvement in space exploration in the 1980s and 1990s. The expertise he developed in biology and genetics while working with Muller, Lederberg, Urey, and others, was unusual for an astronomer, and he extensively researched the possibility that Jupiter's moon, Titan, which has an atmosphere, might also have some form of life. Sagan was also involved in less direct searches for life beyond Earth. He was one of the prime movers behind NASA's establishment of a radio astronomy search program that Sagan called CETI, for Communication with Extra-Terrestrial Intelligence.

One of Sagan's colleagues explained to Cooper of the *New Yorker* that this desire to find extraterrestrial life was the focus of all of Sagan's various scientific works. "Sagan desperately wants to find life someplace, anyplace—on Mars, on Titan, in the solar system or outside it. I don't know why, but if you read his papers or listen to his speeches, even though they are on a wide variety of seemingly unrelated topics, there is always the question 'Is this or that phenomenon related to life?' People say, 'What a varied career he has had,' but everything he has done has had this one underlying purpose." When Cooper asked Sagan why this was so, the scientist had a ready answer. "I think it's because human beings love to be alive, and we have an emotional resonance with something else alive, rather than with a molybdenum atom."

During the early 1970s Sagan began to make a number of brief appearances on television talk shows and news programs; Johnny Carson invited him on the *Tonight Show* for the first time in 1972, and Sagan soon was almost a regular there, returning to discuss science two or three times a year. However, it was *Cosmos,* which Public Television began broadcasting in 1980, that made him into a media sensation. Sagan narrated the series, which he wrote with Ann Druyan and Steven Soter, and they used special effects to illustrate a wide range of astronomical phenomena such as black holes. In addition to being extremely popular, the series was widely praised both for its showmanship and its content, although some reviewers had reservations about Sagan's speculations as well as his tendency to claim as fact what most scientists considered only hypotheses.

Warns about the Possibility of Nuclear Winter

Sagan was actively involved in politics; as a graduate student, he was arrested in Wisconsin for soliciting funds for the Democratic Party, and he was also involved in protests against the Vietnam War. In December 1983, he published—with Richard Turco, Brian Toon, Thomas Ackerman, and James Pollack—an article discussing the possible consequences of nuclear war. They proposed that even a limited number of nuclear explosions could drastically change the world's climate by starting thousands of intense fires that would throw hundreds of thousands of tons of smoke and ash into the atmosphere, lowering the average temperature ten to twenty degrees, and bringing on what

they called a "nuclear winter." The authors happened upon this insight accidentally a few years earlier, while they were observing how dust storms on the planet Mars cooled the Martian surface and heated up the atmosphere. Their warning provoked a storm of controversy at first; their article was then followed by a number of studies on the effects of war and other human interventions on the world's climate. Sagan and his colleagues stressed that their predictions were only preliminary and based on certain assumptions about nuclear weapons and large-scale fires, and that their computations had been done on complex computer models of the imperfectly understood atmospheric system. However, despite numerous attempts to minimize the concept of a nuclear winter, the possibility that even a limited nuclear war might well lead to catastrophic environmental changes was confirmed by later research.

The idea of nuclear winter not only led to the reconsideration of the implications of nuclear war by many countries, institutions, and individuals, but it also produced great advances in research on Earth's atmosphere. In 1991, when the oil fields in Kuwait were burning after the Persian Gulf War, Sagan and others made a similar prediction about the effect the smoke from these fires would have on the climate. Based on the nuclear winter hypothesis and the recorded effects of certain volcanic eruptions, these predictions turned out to be inaccurate, although the smoke from the oil fires represented about 1% of the volume of smoke that would be created by a full-scale nuclear war.

In 1994, Sagan was diagnosed with myelodysplasia, a serious bone-marrow disease. Despite his illness, Sagan kept working on his numerous projects. His last book, *The Demon-Haunted World: Science as a Candle in the Dark,* was published in 1995. At the time of his death, Sagan was coproducing a film version of his novel *Contact.* His partner in this project was his wife, Ann Druyan, who had coauthored *Comet.* Released in 1997, the film received popular and critical acclaim as a testimony to Sagan's enthusiasm for the search for extraterrestrial life. Sagan, who lived in Ithaca, New York, died at the Fred Hutchinson Cancer Research Center in Seattle on December 20, 1996.

Carl Sagan won a Pulitzer Prize in 1978 for his book on evolution called *The Dragons of Eden.* He also won the A. Calvert Smith Prize (1964), NASA's Apollo Achievement Award (1969), NASA's Exceptional Scientific Achievement Medal (1972), NASA's Medal for Distinguished Public Service (twice), the International Astronaut Prize (1973), the John W. Campbell Memorial Award (1974), the Joseph Priestly Award (1975), the Newcomb Cleveland Prize (1977), the Rittenhouse Medal (1980), the Ralph Coats Roe Medal from the American Society of Mechanical Engineers (1981), the Tsiolkovsky Medal of the Soviet Cosmonautics Federation (1987), the Kennan Peace Award from SANE/Freeze (1988), the Oersted Medal of the American Association of Physics Teachers (1990), the UCLA Medal (1991), and the Mazursky Award from the American Astronomical Association (1991). Sagan was a fellow of the American Association for the Advancement of Science, the American Academy of Arts and Sciences, the

American Institute for Aeronautics and Astronautics, and the American Geophysical Union. Sagan was also the chairman of the Division for Planetary Sciences of the American Astronomical Society (from 1975 to 1976) and for twelve years was editor-in-chief of *Icarus,* a journal of planetary studies.

SELECTED WRITINGS BY SAGAN:

Books

The Cosmic Connection: An Extraterrestrial Perspective. New York: Doubleday, 1973.

Other Worlds. New York: Bantam, 1975.

The Dragons of Eden: Speculations on the Evolution of Human Intelligence. New York: Random House, 1977.

Broca's Brain: Reflection on the Romance of Science. New York: Random House, 1979.

Cosmos. New York: Random House, 1980.

Comet. New York: Random House, 1985.

Contact: A Novel. New York: Simon and Schuster, 1985.

A Path Where No Man Thought: Nuclear Winter and the End of the Arms Race. New York: Random House, 1990.

Shadows of Forgotten Ancestors: A Search for Who We Are. New York: Random House, 1992.

Pale Blue Dot. New York: Random House, 1994.

The Demon-Haunted World: Science as a Candle in the Dark. New York: Random House, 1995.

Periodicals

"The Radiation Balance of Venus." *California Institute of Technology Laboratory Technical Report* 32–34 (1960).

"Comets and the Origin of Life." *Astronomy* 20 (February 1992).

FURTHER READING:

Books

Contemporary Authors: New Revision Series. Vol. 11, Detroit: Gale, 1984.

Goodell, Rae. *The Visible Scientists.* New York: Little, Brown, 1975.

Periodicals

Barnes, Bart. "Carl Sagan, the Man Who Reached for the Stars" (obituary). *Washington Post* (21 December 1996): A12.

Baur, Stuart. "Kneedeep in the Cosmic Overwhelm with Carl Sagan." *New York* (1 September 1975): 28.

Cooper, Henry S. F. "A Resonance with Something Alive." *New Yorker* (21 June 1976): 39–80; (28 June 1976): 29–57.

Dicke, William. "Carl Sagan, an Astronomer Who Excelled at Popularizing Science, Is Dead at 62" (obituary). *New York Times* (21 December 1996): A26.

Friend, Tim. "Carrying on without Carl Sagan." *USA Today* (30 June 1997): 1D.

Heise, Kenan. "Carl Sagan, 62; Took Mystery out of Cosmos" (obituary). *Chicago Tribune* (21 December 1996): A21.

Hernbest, Nigel. "Organic Molecules from Space Rained Down on Early Earth." *New Scientist* (25 January 1992): 27.

Hogan, A. R. "Carl Edward Sagan: Astronomer and Popularizer of Science." *Ad Astra* 3 (1991): 30.

Lewin, Roger. "Shadows of Forgotten Ancestors." *New Scientist* 137 (16 January 1993): 40.

Myrna, Oliver. "Astronomer Sagan Dies; Helped Popularize Science" (obituary). *Los Angeles Times* (21 December 1996): A1.

Ridpath, Rian. "A Man Whose Time Has Come." *New Scientist* 63 (4 July 1974): 36.

Ruina, Jack. "A Path Where No Man Thought." *Nature* 352 (29 August 1991): 765.

Zimmer, Carl. "Ecowar." *Discover* 13 (January 1992): 37.

Sketch by Chris Hables Gray

Ruth Sager
1918–1997
American biologist and geneticist

R uth Sager devoted her career to the study and teaching of genetics. She conducted groundbreaking research in chromosomal theory, disproving nineteenth-century Austrian botanist Gregor Johann Mendel's once-prevalent law of inheritance—a principle stating that chromosomal genes found in a cell's nucleus control the transmission of all inherited characteristics. Through her research beginning in the 1950s, Sager revealed that a second set of genes (nonchrosomomal in nature) also play a role in one's genetic composition. In addition to advancing the science of nonchromosomal genetics, she worked to uncover various genetic mechanisms associated with cancer.

Born on February 7, 1918, in Chicago, Illinois, Ruth Sager was one of three girls in her family. Her father worked as an advertising executive, while her mother maintained an interest in academics and intellectual discourse. As a child, Sager did not display any particular

Ruth Sager

interest in science. At the age of sixteen, she entered the University of Chicago, which required its students to take a diverse schedule of liberal arts classes. Sager happened into an undergraduate survey course on biology, sparking her interest in the field. In 1938, she graduated with a B.S. degree. After a brief vacation from education, Sager enrolled at Rutgers University and studied plant physiology, receiving an M.S. in 1944. Sager then continued her graduate work in genetics at Columbia University and in 1946 was awarded a fellowship to study with botanist Marcus Rhoades. In 1948 she received her Ph.D. from Columbia, and in 1949 she was named a Merck Fellow at the National Research Council.

Two years later, Sager joined the research staff at the Rockefeller Institute's biochemistry division as an assistant, working at first in conjunction with Yoshihiro Tsubo. There she began her work challenging the prevailing scientific idea that only the chromosomal genes played a significant role in genetics. Unlike many of her colleagues of the time, Sager speculated that genes that lay outside the chromosomes behave in a manner akin to that of chromosomal genes. In 1953 Sager uncovered hard data to support this theory. She had been studying heredity in *Chlamydomonas*, an alga found in muddy ponds, when she noted that a gene outside the chromosomes was necessary for the alga to survive in water containing streptomycin, an antimicrobial drug. Although the plant—which Sager nicknamed "Clammy"—normally reproduced asexually, Sager discovered that she could force it to reproduce sexually by withholding nitrogen from its environment. Using this tactic, Sager

managed to cross male and females via sexual fertilization. If either of the parents had the streptomycin-resistant gene, Sager showed, the offspring exhibited it as well, providing definitive proof that this nonchromosomal trait was transmitted genetically.

During the time she studied "Clammy," Sager switched institutional affiliations, taking a post as a research associate in Columbia University's zoology department in 1955. The Public Health Service and National Science Foundations supported her work. In 1960 Sager publicized the results of her nonchromosomal genetics research in the first Gilbert Morgan Smith Memorial Lecture at Stanford University and a few months later in Philadelphia at the Society of American Bacteriologists. Toward the end of the year, her observations were published in *Science* magazine. As she continued her studies, she expanded her knowledge of the workings of nonchromosomal genes. Sager's further work showed that when the streptomycin-resistant alga mutated, these mutations occurred only in the nonchromosomal genes. She also theorized that nonchromosomal genes differed greatly from their chromosomal counterparts in the way they imparted hereditary information between generations. Her research has led her to speculate that nonchromosomal genes may evolve before the more common deoxyribonucleic acid (DNA) chromosomes and that they may represent more closely early cellular life.

Sager continued announcing the results of her research at national and international gatherings of scientists. In the early 1960s, Columbia University promoted her to the position of senior research associate, and she coauthored, along with Francis J. Ryan, a scientific textbook titled *Cell Heredity*. In 1963 she travelled to the Hague to talk about her work, and the following year she lectured in Edinburgh on nonchromosomal genes. In 1966 she accepted an offer to become a professor at Hunter College of the City University of New York. She remained in New York for nine years, spending the academic year of 1972 to 1973 abroad at the Imperial Cancer Research Fund Laboratory in London. The following year she married Dr. Arthur B. Pardee. Harvard University's Dana Farber Cancer Institute lured her away from Hunter in 1975 with an offer to become professor of cellular genetics and head the Institute's Division of Cancer Genetics.

In the past twenty years, Sager's work centered on a variety of issues relating to cancer, such as tumor suppressor genes, breast cancer, and the genetic means by which cancer multiplies. Along with her colleagues at the Dana Farber Institute, Sager researched the means by which cancer multiplies and grows in an attempt to understand and halt the mechanism of the deadly disease. She likened the growth of cancer to Darwinian evolution in that cancer cells lose growth control and display chromosome instability. In 1983 she told reporter Anna Christensen that if researchers discover a way to prevent the chromosomal rearrangements, "we would have a potent weapon against cancer." She speculated that tumor suppressor genes may be the secret to halting cancer growth.

Sager continued to publish and serve on numerous scientific panels until her death. In 1992 she offered scientific testimony at hearings of the Breast Cancer Coalition. A member of the Genetics Society of America, the American Society of Bacteriologists, and the New York Academy of Sciences, Sager was appointed to the National Academy of Sciences in 1977. An avid collector of modern art, she was also a member of the American Academy of Arts and Sciences. Sager died of bladder cancer on March 29, 1997, at her home in Brookline, Massachusetts.

SELECTED WRITINGS BY SAGER:

Books

Cell Heredity. New York: Wiley, 1961.

Periodicals

"Tumor Suppressor Genes: The Puzzle and the Promise." *Science* (15 December 1989): 1406–012.

FURTHER READING:

Periodicals

Christensen, Anna. "Potential Weapon in War on Cancer." *United Press International* (7 February 1983).
Pace, Eric. "Dr. Ruth Sager, 79, Researcher on Location of Genetic Material" (obituary). *New York Times* (4 April 1997).

Sketch by Shari Rudavsky

Andrei Sakharov
1921–1989
Russian theoretical physicist

Russian nuclear physicist Andrei Sakharov was as well known as a Soviet dissident and human rights advocate as he was for his role in the development of the hydrogen bomb. The so-called "father of the H-Bomb" won the 1975 Nobel Peace Prize for his calls for détente between the U.S.S.R. and the United States and for an end to the arms race. Once fully committed to the Soviet Union's development of a hydrogen bomb in the belief that nuclear parity between the superpowers would prevent a nuclear war, Sakharov had a change of heart and became active in the fight for nuclear disarmament. He was exiled to the city of Gorky in 1980 as a punishment for his outspokenness. With the rise to power of Mikhail Gorbachev and the

Andrei Sakharov

introduction of *perestroika* (a policy of moderate political and economic "restructuring"), Sakharov and his wife Yelena Bonner were permitted to return to Moscow in 1986.

Andrei Dmitrievich Sakharov was born in Moscow on May 21, 1921, into a family of intellectuals. His father, Dmitri Sakharov, a physicist who wrote popular physics textbooks and taught at the Lenin Pedagogical Institute, was also a talented pianist. Andrei's mother, Ekaterina Sofiano, a teacher of gymnastics before her marriage, was the daughter of a professional soldier. Sakharov had one brother, Georgy, known to the family as Yura. The Sakharovs shared a communal apartment with five other families, including four sets of relatives. The immediate family shared two rooms, equal to 300 square feet, among its four members. Despite these straitened circumstances, by Soviet standards Sakharov's family was reasonably well off—they were able to rent rooms in a country house during the summer—thanks to the extra income generated by Dmitri's writing.

Sakharov taught himself to read when he was about four. His childhood favorites among the mostly prerevolutionary books that filled his parents' and relatives' libraries were the works of Hans Christian Andersen, Jules Verne, Charles Dickens, Mark Twain, H. G. Wells, Jack London, Leo Tolstoy, Jonathan Swift, Aleksander Pushkin, and Nikolai Gogol. He was educated primarily at home until he was about thirteen: in math and physics by his father, and in geography, history, biology, chemistry, and Russian language and literature by private tutors. Late in 1934, he entered the Third Model School. At home, in the meantime, he carried out simple physics experiments in electrostatics and optics. He also became interested in photography, and built a crystal radio based on his father's design. His reading progressed to include science fiction and science books, including those of Yakov Perelman, Sir James Jean's *The Universe Around Us,* and Max Valier's *Space Travel as a Technical Possibility.*

Sakharov graduated from high school as one of only two honors students in his class. In 1938 he enrolled in Moscow State University's physics program. During his third year, Germany invaded the Soviet Union, and Sakharov's work focused on the war effort. He repaired radio equipment for the army and invented a magnetic device for locating shrapnel in injured horses. During his fourth year, the faculty was moved to Ashkhabad, capital of the Turkmen Republic in Central Asia. He graduated in 1942.

Joins War Effort after College

After finishing college, Sakharov was invited to remain on as a graduate student of theoretical physics. He refused the offer, preferring to join in the war effort. He was assigned to work at a cartridge factory in Ulyanovsk, a city on the Volga. Before long, he transferred to the central laboratory's metallurgical department, where he devised a novel method of testing the armor-piercing steel cores of 14.5mm bullets for antitank guns.

November 10, 1942, the day he started work at the laboratory, was also the day he met his first wife, Klavdia (Klava) Vikhireva, a laboratory assistant in the chemical department. They were married on July 10 of the following year. They had three children: Tanya, Lyuba, and Dmitri.

In 1945 Sakharov was invited to join the staff of the P. N. Lebedev Institute of Physics of the Soviet Academy of Science. There, he worked closely with the Russian physicist **Igor Tamm**, who went on to win the 1958 Nobel Prize for physics jointly with **Il'ya Frank** and **Pavel Cherenkov** for their work on Cherenkov radiation. Sakharov produced papers on the generation of a hard component of cosmic rays, on the interaction of electrons and positrons, and on the temperature of excitation in plasma of a gaseous discharge. He also lectured in nuclear physics, relativity theory, and electricity at the Moscow Energetics Institute for three semesters, and for half a year at the Kurchatov Institute's workers night school. In his *Memoirs,* Sakharov described the hardships of these years. He and his family were forced to move house every two months; "at one point, we found ourselves without money even to buy milk," he says. Even more frustrating were the restrictions on his professional freedom: his scientific and technical articles were censored, as was all published material. In 1947, at age twenty-six, he was awarded a Candidate of Doctor of Science degree—equivalent to an American doctorate—for his research into cosmic ray theory.

Disappears to Work on Hydrogen Bomb Project

Despite his straitened circumstances, Sakharov turned down an offer to work for the government and continued working with Tamm. In 1948, they jointly published a paper outlining a principle for the magnetic isolation of high temperature plasma, which was to change the entire course of Soviet thermonuclear physics. That was the last the mainstream scientific establishment heard from either of them for the next twenty years, as the pair went underground to work on the hydrogen bomb project. Although Sakharov had no real choice in the matter, he later admitted that he had welcomed the opportunity to work on what he described as "superb physics" and that he had believed his work to be "essential." He firmly believed that strategic parity in the great powers' nuclear arsenals would prevent a war.

In June 1948, Sakharov and the rest of the H-bomb team were transferred to the "Installation," a secret city where he spent the next eighteen years of his life. By 1950, he and Tamm had come up with a theoretical basis for controlled thermonuclear fusion; that is, a method of using thermonuclear power for peaceful means, such as the generation of electricity. But their work was also geared toward more belligerent ends. By 1953, they were in a position to carry out the first test explosion of a Soviet hydrogen bomb. Although the United States had tested an H-bomb the previous November, the Soviets were the first to explode a compact device deliverable by plane or rocket. Sakharov was credited with developing an essential triggering device that used a fission explosion to set off the process of hydrogen fusion that released the bomb's destructive energy.

Sakharov was richly rewarded for these services. He received the Stalin Prize and three orders of Socialist Labor, all in top secret. In 1953, he became the youngest man to be elected a full member of the Soviet Academy of Sciences. He was given the relatively enormous salary of 2,000 rubles a month (equivalent to about $27,000 a year at current exchange rates), privileged housing, a chauffeured car, access to black-market consumer goods, a bodyguard, and other perks.

Begins Speaking Out against Soviet Policies

By the end of the 1950s, however, Sakharov began to question the morality of some of his scientific work. He first publicly aired his opposition to the Soviet government in 1958, in an article published in *Pravda* jointly with **Yakov B. Zeldovich** on the subject of education. In it, he decried the Soviet educational system and called for reform. Some of his recommendations were adopted by the government. Soon afterwards, he unsuccessfully opposed the government's plan to resume nuclear testing, which it had briefly suspended. This experience changed him profoundly. He also joined with two agricultural scientists, V. P. Efroimson and F. D. Schhepotyev, to denounce the attacks being made on Mendelian genetics.

Sakharov's scientific interests shifted in the 1960s, from thermonuclear energy to the structure of the universe. He published a paper on the appearance of nonuniformity in the distribution of matter in 1965, and one on quarks in 1966. He continued to write on nonscientific subjects, including nuclear disarmament, intellectual freedom, and the need to establish civil liberties in the Soviet Union. His manifesto, *Reflections on Progress, Coexistence, and Intellectual Freedom,* self-published in 1968 in the form of a *samizdat* (an illegal, typewritten book), brought Sakharov a wider audience. In it, he discussed various threats facing humankind, including widespread famine, wars, environmental catastrophe, and the danger of nuclear annihilation, and laid out his vision of a less frightening and threatening world based on convergence between socialism and capitalism and rapprochement between the U.S.S.R. and the United States. He called for disarmament, condemned repression in the Soviet Union, and castigated Stalin. The essay was widely circulated both in the U.S.S.R. and abroad; reportedly 18 million copies in all were published.

Sakharov's complete break with the military-industrial complex came in 1968 with the Soviet invasion of Czechoslovakia. Sakharov and some of his friends had seen the Czechoslovakia of the "Prague Spring" as a model of democratic socialism. Sakharov appealed directly to Soviet President Yuri Andropov to exercise leniency towards the people who had been arrested for demonstrating against the invasion in Red Square. Soon after, he was released from his official duties at the Installation. That year, his wife became seriously ill with gastric hemorrhages. In October, they both moved to the Council of Ministers' sanitarium in Zheleznovodsk. Doctors examining Sakharov found a cardiovascular disorder. In December, his wife was diagnosed with terminal stomach cancer. She died on March 8, 1969.

In 1970 Sakharov came further into conflict with the authorities when he joined other Soviet scientists in forming the Committee for Human Rights to promote the principles espoused in the Universal Declaration of Human Rights. His "Manifesto II" was also published that year in the form of an open address to President Leonid Brezhnev. Written with physicist Valentin F. Turchin and historian Roy A. Medvedev, it accused the government of having failed the people and of having failed to meet the challenges of the modern world. It urged the government to embark on an urgent course of democratization. As the 1970s advanced, Sakharov continued to publish controversial works on these themes, including *Sakharov Speaks* in 1974, *My Country and the World* in 1975, and *Alarm and Hope* in 1979. These writings won him universal acclaim. He was elected a foreign member of the American Academy of Arts and Sciences in 1969, and of the National Academy of Sciences in 1972. He received the Eleanor Roosevelt Peace Award from SANE (Committee for a Sane Nuclear Policy) in 1973; Chicago University's Cino del Duca Prize and Rheinhold Niebuhr Prize in 1974; and the Fritt Ord Prize in 1980. He became a foreign associate of the French Academy of Science in 1981.

In the meantime, Sakharov had remarried. He wed Yelena Bonner, an Armenian-Siberian Jewish dissident, on January 7, 1972. His bride's mother had spent sixteen years in Stalinist gulags. Bonner herself had served as a nurse's aide during World War II, being promoted to lieutenant in the medical corps. Afterwards, she had become a doctor and an activist. She was divorced, with two children.

Prevented from Accepting Nobel Peace Prize

Sakharov's outspokenness on a range of issues—from the exile of the Tartar people of the Crimea to the government's use of punitive psychiatry—brought him into increasing conflict with the government throughout the 1970s, and he was prevented from traveling to Norway to accept the 1975 Nobel Peace Prize. Sakharov was especially vocal in his opposition to the 1979 Soviet invasion of Afghanistan. In consequence, in January 1980, he was stripped of his titles and honors and exiled to Gorky, a town of one million people that is closed to foreigners. He was forbidden contact with foreigners and most other visitors and kept under constant surveillance. In addition, he was continually harassed. His apartment was repeatedly ransacked by the KGB, and twice he had important manuscripts and documents stolen. He eked out a precarious living on a pension provided by the Academy of Sciences. Sakharov's family also suffered: his stepdaughter was dismissed from Moscow University's journalism school, her husband lost his job, and Sakharov's stepson was denied admission to Moscow University.

On November 21, 1981, Sakharov and Bonner began a seventeen-day hunger strike to protest the Soviet government's refusal to issue an exit visa for Liza Alexeyeva, who wanted to join her fiancé, Bonner's son Alexi Semyonov, in the United States. Their protest attracted worldwide attention, and the Soviet government eventually capitulated. In 1984, Sakharov again staged a hunger strike when Bonner was convicted of "slandering the Soviet system," sentenced to internal exile, and prevented from traveling to Moscow. He was detained against his will in Gorky's Semashko Hospital and force-fed. He went on hunger strike again on July 25, 1985, to protest the government's refusal to allow Bonner an exit visa so that she could go to the United States for medical treatment and to visit her children. Once again he was taken to hospital and force-fed. He ended his strike only when his wife was finally given permission to leave in late October.

In February 1986, Sakharov wrote to Gorbachev, calling for the release of prisoners of conscience. In October, he wrote yet again, asking that he and Bonner be released from Gorky. He told the General Secretary that he had been exiled illegally, and promised to cease speaking out on public affairs, except when "he could not remain silent." On December 16, 1986, the phone rang in the Sakharov apartment. Mikhail Gorbachev was on the line. He told Sakharov that he and Bonner were at last free to return to Moscow.

On November 6, 1988, Sakharov traveled abroad for the first time in his life. In the United States he met with President George Bush and British Prime Minister Margaret Thatcher. In France for the fortieth anniversary of the Universal Declaration of Human Rights, he met President François Mitterrand, Polish president Lech Walesa, and Javier Pérez de Cuéllar, the United Nations' secretary general. In February, he and Yelena Bonner traveled to Italy, where they met with Bettino Craxi, the president of the Italian Socialist Party; Alessandro Pertini, the former president of Italy; and the Pope. Afterwards, they visited Canada. In the summer of 1989, shortly after addressing the first Congress of People's Deputies, Sakharov and Bonner traveled to the United States to visit Bonner's children. Sakharov died of a heart attack on December 14, 1989, in Moscow.

SELECTED WRITINGS BY SAKHAROV:

Books

Reflections on Progress, Peaceful Coexistence, and Intellectual Freedom, Self–published, 1968, published as Progress, Peaceful Coexistence, and Intellectual Freedom, Norton, 1968.
Sakharov Speaks, Knopf, 1974.
My Country and the World, Knopf, 1975.
Alarm and Hope, Knopf, 1979.
Collected Scientific Works, Dekker, 1982.
Memoirs, Knopf, 1990.
Moscow and Beyond, 1986 to 1989, Vintage Book, 1992.

FURTHER READING:

Books

Babyonyshev, Alexander, editor, *On Sakharov,* Knopf, 1982.
Bonner, Yelena, *Alone Together,* Knopf, 1986.
———— , *Contemporary Authors,* Volume 128, Gale, 1990, pp. 355–58.
Medvedev, Zhores A., *Soviet Science,* Norton, 1978.
Parry, Albert, *The Russian Scientist,* Macmillan, 1973, p. 172.

Periodicals

Parry, Albert, *Chicago Tribune,* December 17, 1989.
———— , *Los Angeles Times,* December 15, 1989.
———— , *New York Times,* December 16, 1989; December 18, 1989; December 19, 1989.
———— , *Washington Post,* December 16, 1989; December 18, 1989; December 19, 1989.

Sketch by Avril McDonald

Bert Sakmann
1942–
German physician and cell physiologist

Bert Sakmann, along with physicist **Erwin Neher**, was awarded the 1991 Nobel Prize in physiology or medicine for inventing the patch clamp technique. The technique made it possible to realize a goal that had eluded scientists since the 1950s: to be able to examine individual ion channels—pore-forming proteins found in the outer membranes of virtually all cells that serve as conduits for electrical signals. Introduced in 1976, the patch clamp technique opened new paths in the study of membrane physiology. Since then, researchers throughout the world have adapted and refined patch clamping, contributing significantly to research on problems in medicine and neuroscience. The Nobel Committee credited Sakmann and Neher with having revolutionized modern biology.

Sakmann was born in Stuttgart, Germany, on June 12, 1942. His later education involved much time around the laboratory. From 1969 to 1970, he was a research assistant in the department of neurophysiology at the Max Planck Institute for Psychiatry in Munich. Between 1971 and 1973, Sakmann studied biophysics with Nobel Laureate **Bernard Katz** at University College in London as a British Council scholar. In 1974 he received his medical degree from the University of Göttingen. From that year until 1979 he was a research associate in the department of neurobiology at the Max Planck Institute for Biophysical Chemistry in Göttingen.

In the 1950s and 1960s, the existence of ion channels that allow for the transmission of electrical charges from one cell to another was inferred from research since no one had been able to actually locate the sites of these channels. Cell physiologists were being drawn to the question of how electrically charged ions control such biological functions as the transmission of nerve impulses, the contraction of muscles, vision, and the process of conception. Sakmann's early interest in ion channels was stimulated by two papers published in 1969 and 1970 that gave strong evidence for the existence of ion channels. As stronger evidence began to accumulate for their existence, it became clear to Sakmann and Neher, who were sharing laboratory space at the Max Planck Institute, that they would have to develop a fine instrument to be able to locate the actual sites of the ion channels on the cell membrane.

Innovation of Patch Clamp Wins Nobel Prize

Bedeviling efforts of researchers to that point was the electrical "noise" generated by the cell's membrane, which made it impossible to detect signals coming from individual channels. Sakmann and Neher set about to reduce the noise by shutting out most of the membrane. They applied a glass micropipette one micron wide and fitted with a recording electrode to a cell membrane and were able to measure the flow of current through a single channel. "It worked the first time," Sakmann recalled in *Science* magazine. The biophysical community was exultant.

Over the next few years, Sakmann and Neher refined their "patch clamp" technique, solving a residual noise problem caused by leaks in the seals between pipette and cell by applying suction with freshly made and fire-polished pipettes. The refinements made it possible to measure even very small currents, and established the patch clamp as a tremendously versatile tool in the field of cell biology. Patch clamping has been instrumental in studies of cystic fibrosis, hormone regulation, and insulin production in diabetes. The technique has also made possible the development of new drugs in the treatment of heart disease, epilepsy, and disorders affecting the nervous and muscle systems. In 1991 Sakmann and Neher won the 1991 Nobel Prize in physiology or medicine for their work on ion channels. The Nobel Awards citation congratulated the researchers for conclusively establishing the existence and function of the channels, and contributing immeasurably to the understanding of disease mechanisms.

Sakmann has continued to work with other research teams, altering the genes for identified ion channels in order to trace the molecules in the channel responsible for opening and closing the ion pore. Even though Sakmann expressed surprise at receiving the Noble Prize, given all the other important work going on in cell physiology, the opinion of many of his colleagues was that the award was long overdue. Sakmann is married to Christianne, an ophthalmologist; they have three children. He is described by friends as someone who enjoys playing tennis and soccer, having a good sense of humor, and someone who enjoys spending time with his family. In 1989 he moved from the Max Planck Institute in Göttingen to the University of Heidelberg as a professor on the medical faculty. Among his other awards are the Spencer and Louisa Gross-Horwitz Awards from Columbia University in 1983 and 1986, respectively.

SELECTED WRITINGS BY SAKMANN:

Periodicals

Pfluegers Archiv: European Journal of Physiology, Improved Patch-Clamp Techniques for High-Resolution Current Recording from Cells and Cell-Free Membrane Patches, August, 1981, pp. 85–100.

Pfluegers Archiv: European Journal of Physiology, A Thin Slice Preparation for Patch Clamp Recordings from Neurons of the Mammalian Central Nervous System, September, 1989, pp. 600–12.

Scientific American, The Patch Clamp Technique, March, 1992, pp. 44–51.

Science, Elementary Steps in Synaptic Transmission Revealed by Currents through Single Ion Channels, April 24, 1992, pp. 503–12.

FURTHER READING:

Periodicals

New York Times, October 13, 1991, pp. C1, C3.
Physics Today, January, 1992, pp. 17–18.
Science, Volume 254, 1991, p. 380.

Sketch by Jordan Richman

Abdus Salam
1926–1996
Pakistani physicist

A bdus Salam's major field of interest in the 1950s and 1960s was the relationship between two of the four basic forces governing nature then known to scientists: electromagnetic and weak forces. In 1968, Salam published a theory showing how these two forces may be considered as separate and distinct manifestations of a single more fundamental force, the electroweak force. Experiments conducted at the European Center for Nuclear Research (CERN) in 1973 provided the empirical evidence needed to substantiate Salam's theory. For this work, Salam shared the 1979 Nobel Prize in physics with physicists **Sheldon Glashow** and **Steven Weinberg**, who had each independently developed similar theories between 1960 and 1967. Salam's longtime concern for the status of science in Third World nations prompted him in 1964 to push for the establishment of the International Center for Theoretical Physics (ICTP) in Trieste, Italy. The Center provides the kind of instruction for Third World physicists that is generally not available in their own homelands.

Salam was born on January 29, 1926, in the small rural town of Jhang, Pakistan, to Hajira and Muhammed Hussain. Salam's father worked for the local department of education. At the age of sixteen, Abdus Salam entered the Government College at Punjab University in Lahore, and, in 1946, he was awarded his master's degree in mathematics. Salam then received a scholarship that allowed him to enroll at St. John's College at Cambridge University, where he was awarded a bachelor's degree in mathematics and physics, with highest honors, in 1949.

Attempts to Return to Pakistan

Salam remained at Cambridge as a graduate student for two years, but felt an obligation to return to Pakistan.

Abdus Salam

Accepting a joint appointment as professor of mathematics at the Government College of Lahore and head of the department of mathematics at Punjab University, Salam soon discovered that he had no opportunity to conduct research. "To my dismay," he told Nina Hall for an article in the *New Scientist,* "I learnt that I was the only practicing theoretical physicist in the entire nation. No one cared whether I did any research. Worse, I was expected to look after the college soccer team as my major duty besides teaching undergraduates."

As a result, Salam decided to return to Cambridge, from which he had received a Ph.D. in theoretical physics in 1952. He taught mathematics for two years at Cambridge and, in 1957, was appointed professor of theoretical physics at the Imperial College of Science and Technology in London. He held that post for most of his life.

Attacks the Problem of Force Unification

Beginning in the mid–1950s, Salam turned his attention to one of the fundamental questions of modern physics, the unification of forces. Scientists recognize that there are four fundamental forces governing nature—the gravitational, electromagnetic, strong, and weak forces—and that all four may be manifestations of a single basic force. The unity of forces would not actually be observable, they believe, except at energy levels much greater than those that exist in the everyday world, energy levels that currently exist only in cosmic radiation and in the most powerful of particle accelerators.

Attempts to prove unification theories are, to some extent, theoretical exercises involving esoteric mathematical formulations. In the 1960s, three physicists, Salam, Steven Weinberg, and Sheldon Glashow, independently derived a mathematical theory that unifies two of the four basic forces, the electromagnetic and weak forces. A powerful point of confirmation in this work was the fact that essentially the same theory was produced starting from two very different beginning points and following two different lines of reasoning.

One of the predictions arising from the new electroweak theory was the existence of previously unknown weak "neutral currents," as anticipated by Salam and Weinberg. These currents were first observed in 1973 during experiments conducted at the CERN in Geneva, and later at the Fermi National Accelerator Laboratory in Batavia, Illinois. A second prediction, the existence of force-carrying particles designated as W^+, W^-, and Z^0 bosons was verified in a later series of experiments also carried out at CERN in 1983. By that time, Salam, Glashow, and Weinberg had been honored for their contributions to the electroweak theory with the 1979 Nobel Prize in physics. Salam was the first Muslim to win the Nobel Prize.

Theoretical physics was only one of Salam's two great passions in life. The other was an ongoing concern for the status of theoretical physicists in Third World nations. His own experience in Pakistan was a lifelong reminder of the need for encouragement, instruction, and assistance for others like himself growing up in developing nations. His concern drove Salam to recommend the establishment of a training center for such individuals. That dream was realized in 1964 with the formation of the ICTP in Trieste, Italy, which invites outstanding theoretical physicists to teach and lecture aspiring students on their own areas of expertise. In addition, the center acts, according to Nina Hall, as a "sort of lonely scientist's club for Brazilians, Nigerians, Sri Lankans, or whoever feels the isolation resulting from lack of resources in their own country." Salam also served as a member of Pakistan's Atomic Energy Commission (1958–1974) and its Science Council (1963–1975), as Chief Scientific Advisor to Pakistan's President (1961–1974) and as chairman of the country's Space and Upper Atmosphere Committee (1962–1963).

Salam, director of ICTP since its founding, was involved in a host of other international activities linking scientists to each other and to a variety of governmental agencies. He was a member (1964–1975) and chairman (1971–1972) of the United Nations Advisory Committee on Science and Technology, vice president of the International Union of Pure and Applied Physics (1972–1978), and a member of the Scientific Council of the Stockholm International Peace Research Institute (1970–). Salam was awarded more than two dozen honorary doctorates and received more than a dozen major awards, including the Atoms for Peace Award for 1968, the Royal Medal of the Royal Society in 1978, the John Torrence Tate Medal of the American Institute of Physics in 1978, and the Lomonosov Gold Medal of the U.S.S.R. Academy of Sciences in 1983. He was also awarded an honorary knighthood by Queen Elizabeth.

Salam died on November 21, 1996, at his home in Oxford, England. He had been suffering from a neurological disorder for some years before his death at the age of 70.

SELECTED WRITINGS BY SALAM:

Books

Aspect of Quantum Mechanics. Cambridge: Cambridge University Press, 1972.
Ideas and Realities: Selected Essays of Abdus Salam. World Scientific, 1987.

Periodicals

"The Electroweak Force, Grand Unification, and Super-unification." *Physical Sciences* 20 (1979): 227–34.

FURTHER READING:

Books

Wasson, Tyler, ed. *Nobel Prize Winners.* New York: H. W. Wilson, 1987, pp. 914–16.
Weber, Robert L. *Pioneers of Science: Nobel Prize Winners in Physics.* American Institute of Physics, 1980, pp. 263–64.
———— . *The Way of the Scientist.* New York: Simon & Schuster, 1962, pp. 67–76.

Periodicals

Browne, Malcolm W. "Abdus Salam is Dead at 70: Physicist Shared Nobel Prize" (obituary). *New York Times* (23 November 1996).
Coleman, Sidney. "The 1979 Nobel Prize in Physics." *Science* (14 December 1979): 1290–291.
Hall, Nina. "A Unifying Force for Third World Science." *New Scientist* (27 January 1990): 31.
———— . "Nobel Prizes: To Glashow, Salam and Weinberg for Physics . . . " *Physics Today* (December 1979): 17–19.
———— . "Nobels for Getting It Together in Physics." *New Scientist* (18 October 1979): 163–64.

Sketch by David E. Newton

Jonas Salk
1914–1995
American microbiologist

Jonas Salk was one of the United States's best-known microbiologists, chiefly celebrated for his discovery of the polio vaccine. His greatest contribution to immunology was the insight that a "killed virus" is capable of serving as an antigen, prompting the body's immune system to produce antibodies that will attack invading organisms. This realization enabled Salk to develop a polio vaccine composed of killed polio viruses, producing the necessary antibodies to help the body to ward off the disease without itself inducing polio.

The eldest son of Orthodox Jewish-Polish immigrants, Jonas Edward Salk was born in East Harlem, New York, on October 28, 1914. His father, Daniel B. Salk, was a garment worker, who designed lace collars and cuffs and enjoyed sketching in his spare time. He and his wife, Dora Press, encouraged their son's academic talents, sending him to Townsend Harris High School for the gifted. There, young Salk was both highly motivated and high achieving, graduating at the age of fifteen and enrolling in the legal faculty of the City College of New York. Ever curious, however, he attended some science courses and quickly decided to switch fields. Salk graduated with a bachelor's degree in science in 1933, at the age of nineteen, and went on to New York University's School of Medicine. Initially he scraped by on money his parents had borrowed for him; after the first year, however, scholarships and fellowships paid his way. In his senior year, Salk met the man with whom he would collaborate on some of the most important work of his career, Dr. Thomas Francis, Jr.

On June 7, 1939, Salk was awarded his M.D. The next day, he married Donna Lindsay, a Phi Beta Kappa psychology major who was employed as a social worker. The marriage would produce three sons: Peter, Darrell, and Jonathan. After graduation, Salk continued working with Francis, and concurrently began a two-year internship at Mount Sinai Hospital in New York. Upon completing his internship, Salk accepted a National Research Council fellowship and moved to The University of Michigan to join Dr. Francis, who had been heading up Michigan's department of epidemiology since the previous year. Working on behalf of the U.S. Army, the team strove to develop a flu vaccine. Their goal was a "killed-virus" vaccine—able to kill the live flu viruses in the body, while simultaneously producing antibodies that could fight off future invaders of the same type, thus producing immunity. By 1943, Salk and Francis had developed a formalin-killed-virus vaccine, effective against both type A and B influenza viruses, and were in a position to begin clinical trials.

Jonas Salk

Gets Backing of National Foundation For Infantile Paralysis

In 1946, Salk was appointed assistant professor of epidemiology at Michigan. Around this time he extended his research to cover not only viruses and the body's reaction to them but also their epidemic effects in populations. The following year he accepted an invitation to move to the University of Pittsburgh School of Medicine's Virus Research Laboratory as an associate research professor of bacteriology. When Salk arrived at the Pittsburgh laboratory, what he encountered was not encouraging. The laboratory had no experience with the kind of basic research he was accustomed to, and it took considerable effort on his part to bring the lab up to par. However, Salk was not shy about seeking financial support for the laboratory from outside benefactors, and soon his laboratory represented the cutting edge of viral research.

In addition to building a respectable laboratory, Salk also devoted a considerable amount of his energies to writing scientific papers on a number of topics, including the polio virus. Some of these came to the attention of Daniel Basil O'Connor, the director of the National Foundation for Infantile Paralysis—an organization that had long been involved with the treatment and rehabilitation of polio victims. O'Connor eyed Salk as a possible recruit for the polio vaccine research his organization sponsored. When the two finally met, O'Connor was much taken by Salk—so much so, in fact, that he put almost all of the National Foundation's money behind Salk's vaccine research efforts.

Poliomyelitis, traceable back to ancient Egypt, causes permanent paralysis in those it strikes, or chronic shortness of breath often leading to death. Children, in particular, are especially vulnerable to the polio virus. The University of Pittsburgh was one of four universities engaged in trying to sort and classify the more than one hundred known varieties of polio virus. By 1951, Salk was able to assert with certainty that all polio viruses fell into one of three types, each having various strains; some of these were highly infectious, others barely so. Once he had established this, Salk was in a position to start work on developing a vaccine.

Salk's first challenge was to obtain enough of the virus to be able to develop a vaccine in doses large enough to have an impact; this was particularly difficult since viruses, unlike culture-grown bacteria, need living cells to grow. The breakthrough came when the team of **John F. Enders**, **Thomas Weller**, and **Frederick Robbins** found that the polio virus could be grown in embryonic tissue—a discovery that earned them a Nobel Prize in 1954.

Salk subsequently grew samples of all three varieties of polio virus in cultures of monkey kidney tissue, then killed the virus with formaldehyde. Salk believed that it was essential to use a killed polio virus (rather than a live virus) in the vaccine, as the live-virus vaccine would have a much higher chance of accidentally inducing polio in inoculated children. He therefore exposed the viruses to formaldehyde for nearly 13 days. Though after only three days he could detect no virulence in the sample, Salk wanted to establish a wide safety margin; after an additional ten days of exposure to the formaldehyde, he reckoned that there was only a one-in-a-trillion chance of there being a live virus particle in a single dose of his vaccine. Salk tested it on monkeys with positive results before proceeding to human clinical trials.

Despite Salk's confidence, many of his colleagues were skeptical, believing that a killed-virus vaccine could not possibly be effective. His dubious standing was further compounded by the fact that he was relatively new to polio vaccine research; some of his chief competitors in the race to develop the vaccine—most notably **Albert Sabin**, the chief proponent for a live-virus vaccine—had been at it for years and were somewhat irked by the presence of this upstart with his unorthodox ideas.

As the field narrowed, the division between the killed-virus and the live-virus camps widened, and what had once been a polite difference of opinion became a serious ideological conflict. Salk and his chief backer, the National Foundation for Infantile Paralysis, were fairly lonely in their corner. But Salk failed to let his position in the scientific wilderness dissuade him and he continued, undeterred, with his research. To test his vaccine's strength, in early 1952 Salk administered a type I vaccine to children who had already been infected with the polio virus. Afterwards, he measured their antibody levels. His results clearly indicated that the vaccine produced large amounts of antibodies. Buoyed by this success, the clinical trial was then extended to include children who had never had polio.

In May 1952, Salk initiated preparations for a massive field trial in which over four hundred thousand children would be vaccinated. The largest medical experiment that had ever been carried out in the United States, the test finally got underway in April 1954, under the direction of Dr. Francis and sponsored by the National Foundation for Infantile Paralysis. More than one million children between the ages of six and nine took part in the trial, each receiving a button that proclaimed them a "Polio Pioneer." A third of the children were given doses of the vaccine consisting of three injections—one for each of the types of polio virus—plus a booster shot. A control group of the same number of children was given a placebo, and a third group was given nothing.

At the beginning of 1953, while the trial was still at an early stage, Salk's encouraging results were made public in the *Journal of the American Medical Association.* Predictably, media and public interest were intense. Anxious to avoid sensationalized versions of his work, Salk agreed to comment on the results thus far during a scheduled radio and press appearance. However, this appearance did not mesh with accepted scientific protocol for making such announcements, and some of his fellow scientists accused him of being little more than a publicity hound. Salk, who claimed that he had been motivated only by the highest principles, was deeply hurt.

Despite the doomsayers, on April 12, 1955, the vaccine was officially pronounced effective, potent, and safe in almost 90 % of cases. The meeting at which the announcement was made was attended by five hundred of the world's top scientists and doctors, 150 journalists, and sixteen television and movie crews.

Instant Celebrity

The success of the trial catapulted Salk to instant stardom. He was inundated with offers from Hollywood and with pleas from top manufacturers for him to endorse their products. He received a citation from President Eisenhower and addressed the nation from the White House Rose Garden. He was awarded a congressional medal for great achievement in the field of medicine and was nominated for a Nobel Prize but, contrary to popular expectation, did not receive it. He was also turned down for membership in the National Academy of Sciences, most likely a reflection of the discomfort the scientific community still felt about the level of publicity he attracted and of continued disagreement with peers over his methods.

Wishing to escape from the glare of the limelight, Salk turned down the countless offers and tried to retreat into his laboratory. Unfortunately, a tragic mishap served to keep the attention of the world's media focused on him. Just two weeks after the announcement of the vaccine's discovery, eleven of the children who had received it developed polio; more cases soon followed. Altogether, about 200 children developed paralytic polio, eleven fatally. For a while, it appeared that the vaccination campaign would be railroaded. However, it was soon discovered that all of the rogue

vaccines had originated from the same source, Cutter Laboratories in California. On May 7, the vaccination campaign was called to a halt by the Surgeon General. Following a thorough investigation, it was found that Cutter had used faulty batches of virus culture, which were resistant to the formaldehyde. After furious debate and the adoption of standards that would prevent such a reoccurrence, the inoculation resumed. By the end of 1955, seven million children had received their shots, and over the course of the next two years more than 200 million doses of Salk's polio vaccine were administered, without a single instance of vaccine-induced paralysis. By the summer of 1961 there had been a 96% reduction in the number of cases of polio in the United States, compared to the five-year period prior to the vaccination campaign.

After the initial inoculation period ended in 1958, Salk's killed-virus vaccine was replaced by a live-virus vaccine developed by Sabin; use of this new vaccine was advantageous because it could be administered orally rather than intravenously, and because it required fewer "booster" inoculations. To this day, though, Salk remains known as the man who defeated polio.

Founds Institute for Biological Studies

In 1954, Salk took up a new position as professor of preventative medicine at Pittsburgh, and in 1957 he became professor of experimental medicine. The following year he began work on a vaccine to immunize against all viral diseases of the central nervous system. As part of this research, Salk performed studies of normal and malignant cells, studies that had some bearing on the problems encountered in cancer research. In 1960, he founded the Salk Institute for Biological Studies in La Jolla, California; heavily funded by the National Foundation for Infantile Paralysis (by then known as the March of Dimes), the institute attracted some of the brightest scientists in the world, all drawn by Salk's promise of full-time, uninterrupted biological research.

When his new institute finally opened in 1963, Salk became its director and devoted himself to the study of multiple sclerosis and cancer. He remained a driven man, thinking nothing of working sixteen to eighteen hours a day, six days a week. In 1968, his marriage ended in divorce, and he made the headlines again in 1970 when he remarried, this time to Françoise Gilot, Pablo Picasso's first wife and mother of two of the artist's children. During the 1970s Salk turned to writing, producing books about the philosophy of science and its social role. In 1977, he received the Presidential Medal of Freedom.

Despite the sense of expectancy that he seemed to encourage, Jonas Salk took his successes and failures in stride. In the early 1990s, many people looked to him as the one would might finally develop a vaccine against the HIV virus. But Salk, though continuing to strive toward scientific breakthroughs, seems content simply to work at his chosen craft. "I don't want to go from one crest to another," he once said, as quoted by Sarah K. Bolton in *Famous Men of*

Science. "To a scientist, fame is neither an end nor even a means to an end. Do you recall what Emerson said?—'The reward of a thing well done is the opportunity to do more.'"

Salk died on 23 June 1995, at a San Diego area hospital. His death, at the age of 80, was caused by heart failure.

SELECTED WRITINGS BY SALK:

Books

Man Unfolding. Harper, 1972.
Anatomy of Reality. Columbia University Press, 1973.
The Survival of the Wisest. Harper, 1973.
How Like an Angel. David and Charles, 1975.
World Population and Human Values. Harper, 1981.

FURTHER READING:

Books

Berger, Melvin. *Famous Men of Modern Biology.* Crowell, 1968, p. 177.
Bolton, Sarah K. *Famous Men of Science.* Crowell, 1960, p. 267.
Carter, Richard. *Breakthrough: The Saga of Jonas Salk.* Trident Press, 1966.
Curson, Majorie. *Jonas Salk.* Silver Burdett, 1990.
Hargrove, Jim. *The Story of Jonas Salk and the Discovery of the Polio Vaccine.* Children's Press, 1990.
Hendin, David. *The Life Givers.* Morrow, 1976.
———. *McGraw-Hill Modern Men of Science.* McGraw-Hill, 1966, p. 413.
Robinson, Donald. *The Miracle Finders.* David McKay, 1976, p. 39.
Rowland, John. *The Polio Man: The Story of Dr. Jonas Salk.* Roy Publishing, 1961.
Siemens, Pliny. *The Great Scientists.* Grolier, 1989, p. 137.

Periodicals

Schmeck, Harold M. Jr. "Dr. Jonas Salk, Whose Vaccine Turned Tide on Polio, Dies at 80" (obituary). *New York Times* (24 June 1995).

Sketch by Avril McDonald

Bengt Samuelsson
1934–
Swedish biochemist

Bengt Samuelsson shared the 1982 Nobel Prize for physiology or medicine with his compatriot **Sune K. Bergström** and British biochemist **John R. Vane** "for their discoveries concerning prostaglandins and related biologically active substances." Because prostaglandins are involved in a diverse range of biochemical functions and processes, the research of Bergström, Samuelsson, and Vane opened up a new arena of medical research and pharmaceutical applications.

Bengt Ingemar Samuelsson was born on May 21, 1934, in Halmstad, Sweden, to Anders and Kristina Nilsson Samuelsson. Samuelsson entered medical school at the University of Lund, where he came under the mentorship of Sune K. Bergström. Called "the father of prostaglandin chemistry," Bergström was on the university faculty as professor of physiological chemistry. In 1958, Samuelsson followed Bergström to the prestigious Karolinska Institute in Stockholm, which is associated with the Nobel Prize awards. There, Samuelsson received his doctorate in medical science in 1960 and his medical degree in 1961, and he was subsequently appointed as an assistant professor of medical chemistry. In 1961, he served as a research fellow at Harvard University, and then in 1962 he rejoined Bergström at the Karolinska Institute, where he remained until 1966.

At the Karolinska Institute, Samuelsson worked with a group of researchers who were trying to characterize the structures of prostaglandins. Prostaglandins are hormone-like substances found throughout the body, which were so named in the 1930s on the erroneous assumption that they originated in the prostate. They play an important role in the circulatory system, and they help protect the body against sickness, infection, pain, and stress. Expanding on their earlier research, Bergström, Samuelsson, and other researchers discovered the role that arachidonic acid, an unsaturated fatty acid found in meats and vegetable oils, plays in the formation of prostaglandins. By developing synthetic methods of producing prostaglandins in the laboratory, this group made prostaglandins accessible for scientific research worldwide. It was Samuelsson who discovered the process through which arachidonic acid is converted into compounds he named endoperoxides, which are in turn converted into prostaglandins.

Prostaglandins have many veterinary and livestock breeding applications, and Samuelsson joined the faculty of the Royal Veterinary College in Stockholm in 1967. He returned to the Karolinska Institute as professor of medicine and physiological chemistry in 1972. Samuelsson served as the chair of the department of physiological chemistry from 1973 to 1983, and as dean of the medical faculty from 1978 to 1983, combining administrative duties with a rigorous research schedule. During 1976 and 1977, Samuelsson also served as a visiting professor at Harvard University and the Massachusetts Institute of Technology.

During these years, Samuelsson continued his investigation of prostaglandins and related compounds. In 1973, he discovered the prostaglandins that are involved in the clotting of the blood; he called these thromboxanes. Samuelsson subsequently discovered the compounds he called leukotrienes, which are found in white blood cells (or leukocytes). Leukotrienes are involved in asthma and in anaphylaxis, the shock or hypersensitivity that follows exposure to certain foreign substances, such as the toxins in an insect sting.

In the wake of such research, prostaglandins have been used to treat fertility problems, circulatory problems, asthma, arthritis, menstrual cramps, and ulcers. Prostaglandins have also been used medically to induce abortions. As noted by *New Scientist* magazine, the 1982 Nobel Prize shared by Bergström, Samuelsson, and Vane acknowledged that they had "carried prostaglandins from the backwaters of biochemical research to the frontier of medical applications." In 1983, succeeding Bergström, Samuelsson was appointed as president of the Karolinska Institute.

The importance of Samuelsson's research has been recognized by numerous awards and honors in addition to the Nobel Prize. Such acknowledgments include the A. Jahres Award in medicine from Oslo University in 1970; the Louisa Gross Horwitz Prize from Columbia University in 1975; the Albert Lasker Medical Research Award in 1977; the Ciba-Geigy Drew Award for biomedical research in 1980; the Gairdner Foundation Award in 1981; the Bror Holberg Medal of the Swedish Chemical Society in 1982; and the Abraham White Distinguished Scientist Award in 1991. Samuelsson has published widely on the biochemistry of prostaglandins, thromboxanes, and leukotrienes.

Samuelsson married Inga Karin Bergstein on August 19, 1958; they have three children.

SELECTED WRITINGS BY SAMUELSSON:

Books

Prostaglandins, Interscience Publishers, 1967.
Third Conference on Prostaglandins in Fertility Control, Karolinska Institute, 1972.

Periodicals

Science, Leukotrienes: Mediators of Immediate Hypersensitivity Reactions and Inflammation, May 6, 1983, pp. 568–75.

FURTHER READING:

Books

Nobel Prize Winners, H. W. Wilson, 1987, pp. 919–21.

Periodicals

Miller, J. A., *Science News*, Nobel Prize in Medicine for Prostaglandin Discoveries, October 16, 1982, p. 245.
———— , *New York Times*, October 12, 1982.
Oates, John A., *Science*, The 1982 Nobel Prize in Physiology or Medicine, November 19, 1982, pp. 765–68.
Sattaur, Omar, *New Scientist*, On the Trail of Prostaglandins, October 14, 1982, pp. 82–3.
———— , *Time*, Sharing the Nobel Prize, October 25, 1982, p. 84.

Sketch by David Sprinkle

David A. Sanchez
1933–
American mathematician

David A. Sanchez is a mathematics scholar with international teaching experience whose recent positions have led him into science administration and academic research program development. Through his study of calculus during his early career, Sanchez developed a particular interest in using ordinary differential equations to create mathematical models for the study of population growth and competing populations. More recently, he has been actively interested in minority participation in academics, and as the vice chancellor for academic affairs of the Texas A & M University System, he provides leadership and coordination to a system of seven universities with an enrollment of over 75,000 students.

David Alan Sanchez was born in San Francisco, California, on January 13, 1933, to Cecilio and Concepcion Sanchez. After obtaining his bachelor of science degree in mathematics from the University of New Mexico in 1955, Sanchez entered the U.S. Marine Corps in 1956. In 1959 he left the Corps as a lieutenant to attend The University of Michigan, where he earned his M.S. in 1960 and his Ph.D. in 1964. During those graduate school years, he also worked as a research assistant in the Radar Laboratory of the university's Institute of Science and Technology, where he investigated signal processing and battlefield simulations for U.S. Army applications. In 1963 he accepted an instructor's position at the University of Chicago; he remained there until 1965 when he became a visiting professor for a year at Manchester University in Manchester, England. In 1966 he returned to the United States, becoming an assistant professor at the University of California at Los Angeles (UCLA). In 1970 he took another year as visiting assistant professor, this time at Brown University in Providence,

Rhode Island, and then returned to UCLA as associate professor. After spending a school year during 1973 and 1974 as visiting associate professor at the University of Wisconsin's Mathematics Research Center, Sanchez became a full professor at UCLA in 1976. In 1977 he returned to his alma mater, accepting a professorship at the University of New Mexico. He remained there until 1986, serving as chair of the department of mathematics and statistics from 1983 to 1986. He took time during 1982 to teach at the University of Wales in Aberystwyth.

During this period, Sanchez developed an interest in biomathematics—math that can be applied to the study of biology. He began using mathematical models to study population growth and competing populations. In his study on an ordinary game bird—the sand hill crane, for instance—Sanchez used a mathematical model to predict the effect of an external force that reduces a population, in this case by hunting. He wanted to formulate a simple mathematical equation that could predict the point at which the crane population would face extinction because it was being hunted at a rate faster than it could reproduce and grow. In this and other research studies, Sanchez constructed mathematical models that have implications for the study of human populations.

In 1986 Sanchez made a career switch and accepted a position as vice president and provost at Lehigh University in Bethlehem, Pennsylvania. After four years of administrative experience there, he became the assistant director for mathematical and physical sciences for the National Science Foundation in Washington, D.C. In 1992 he changed from administering science funds to helping to run a federal laboratory, joining the Los Alamos National Laboratory in New Mexico as deputy associate director for research and education. On November 1, 1993, he became vice chancellor for academic affairs for the Texas A & M University System. This large state system, which is composed of seven universities and eight agencies, has an enrollment of over 75,000 students, employs more than 19,000 people, and has operations in each of the 254 counties in Texas. In a *Texas A & M Fortnightly* article, university chancellor William Mobley said that Sanchez's extensive experience with academic and research program development both at the university and at the federal level made him capable of providing the long-range academic planning and linkages needed by its vast university system.

Sanchez is a member of the American Mathematical Society, the Mathematical Association of America, the Society of Industrial and Applied Mathematics, and the Society for the Advancement of Chicanos and Native Americans in Science. A specialist in differential equations, he has published more than fifty articles in professional and technical journals and also is the author of three books on mathematics. He has served on several boards of governors, directors, advisory boards, and policy committees. Always interested in minority participation in academics, he served on the American Mathematical Society's Committee on Opportunities in Mathematics for Disadvantaged Groups,

and the Committee on Minority Participation in Mathematics for the Mathematics Association of America.

Sanchez married Joan Patricia Thomas in 1957, and they have two children, Bruce and Christina. Besides mathematics and administration, Sanchez enjoys fishing, bridge, and fiction writing and has published articles in *Flyfishing News* and *The Steamboat Whistle*.

SELECTED WRITINGS BY SANCHEZ:

Books

Ordinary Differential Equations and Stability Theory: An Introduction, W. H. Freeman and Co., 1968.
Topics in Ordinary Differential Equations: A Potpourri, Prindle, Weber & Schmidt, 1970.
Differential Equations: An Introduction, 2nd edition, Addison-Wesley, 1988.

Periodicals

Texas A & M Fortnightly, Vice Chancellor for Academic Affairs Chosen, September 27, 1993.

Other

Interview with Donna Olendorf, April 20, 1994.

Sketch by Leonard C. Bruno

Pedro A. Sanchez
1940–
American soil scientist

Pedro A. Sanchez has spent his career improving the management of tropical soils for sustained food production. He has focused on overcoming tropical deforestation, land depletion, and rural poverty through improved agroforestry. His research interests as a soil scientist also include nutrient cycling. Sanchez has served as director general of the International Centre for Research in Agroforestry in Nairobi, Kenya, since 1991.

Pedro Antonio Sanchez was born October 7, 1940, in Havana, Cuba, the oldest of four children of Georgina (San Martin) and Pedro Antonio Sanchez. His interest in agroforestry and soil science began early—Sanchez told contributor Marianne Fedunkiw in an interview that he travelled throughout Cuba with his father, who managed the family farm and fertilizer business. His mother was a pharmacist and high school teacher. After completing high school at the Colegio de la Salle in Havana, Sanchez travelled to the United States to study at Cornell University. He received his B.S. in agronomy in 1962; two years later he finished his master of science degree in soil science and in 1968 received his Ph.D., also in soil science. While studying for his doctorate, he was a graduate assistant in soil science in the University of the Philippines-Cornell Graduate Education Program in Los Baños, Philippines. He was both a researcher and a teacher of soil fertility courses at the university. Having completed his education, Sanchez joined the faculty of North Carolina State University (NCSU) as an assistant professor of soil science in 1968, followed by a three-year stint as coleader of the university's National Rice Program of Peru, an agricultural mission established by NCSU. In this capacity, he supervised a research and extension program aimed at helping Peruvians achieve self-sufficiency by improving and sustaining their rice production. Sanchez continued his work in South America from 1971 until 1983, first as the leader of the Tropical Soils Program responsible for field soil research projects in the Cerrado of Brazil, the Amazon of Peru, and in Central America (1971–1976); then as coordinator for the Beef-Tropical Pastures Program, Centro International de Agricultural Tropical (CIAT), in Cali, Colombia (1977–1979); and as chief of the North Carolina State University Mission to Lima, Peru (1982–1983). During these years, he was also promoted first to associate professor of soil science at NCSU in 1973, and then to full professor in 1979.

In 1984 Sanchez expanded his work into other parts of the world—for seven years he was coordinator of the Tropical Soils Program at NCSU, supervising activities throughout Bolivia, Indonesia, and Madagascar. Concurrently, from 1990 to 1991 he was also director of the Center for World Environment and Sustainable Development, a joint project sponsored by Duke University, North Carolina State University, and the University of North Carolina at Chapel Hill.

The year 1991 marked a time of change for Sanchez. He became professor emeritus of soil science and forestry at NCSU and moved to Nairobi, Kenya, to become the third director general at the International Centre for Research in Agroforestry. Sanchez married Cheryl Palm in 1990; she is also a soil scientist, and they have coauthored a number of articles. He was married previously in 1965 and has three children: Jennifer Sanchez Goebel, an environmental lawyer; Evan, who studies business administration and works in the music business in New York; and Juliana, a high school senior.

Sanchez, who is fluent in English, Spanish, and Portuguese, is the author of two books and has also edited or coedited eight books and written or contributed to more than 125 articles. In recognition of his work, he received both the International Soil Science Award from the Soil Science Society of America, and the International Service in Agronomy Award from the America Society of Agronomy in 1993. His work has been noted in other countries as well: in 1984 the Peruvian government presented him with the Orden de Merito Agricola, which is seldom given to a non-Peruvian citizen, and in 1979 he received the Diploma de Honor from the Instituto Colombiano Agropecuario. Sanchez is a member of more than ten professional and honorary societies, including the American Society of Agronomy; the International Society of Soil Science; and the Asociación Latinoamericana de Ciencias Agrícolas.

SELECTED WRITINGS BY SANCHEZ:

Books

Properties and Management of Soils in the Tropics, John Wiley and Sons, 1976.

Periodicals

Soil Science Society of America Journal, Soil Fertility Dynamics after Clearing a Tropical Rainforest in Peru, Volume 47, 1983, pp. 1171–178.
Science, Low Input Cropping for Acid Soils of the Humid Tropics, Volume 238, 1987, pp. 1521–527.

FURTHER READING:

Periodicals

Sanchez, Pedro A., *Interview with Marianne Fedunkiw,* conducted March 4, 1994.

Sketch by Marianne Fedunkiw

Allan R. Sandage
1926–
American astronomer

Allan R. Sandage has won international recognition for his telescopic discoveries at the Hale Observatories at Mount Wilson and Palomar Mountain in California. In 1960, Sandage became the first person to identify a quasar, the most luminous object in the universe, by optical means. Sandage's discovery led the way for the identification of other quasars. Radioastronomers, who study celestial and extragalactic objects according to the radio waves they emit, have used quasars to refine estimations of the age and evolution of the universe. Since quasars are considerably more luminous than other cosmological bodies, they are detectable at greater distances and thus make it possible, in effect, to look farther back in time. Sandage has also gained renown for his work in determining the age of stars or globular clusters of stars and the age and size of the universe. The worldwide scientific community recognized Sandage's achievements in 1991 by bestowing upon him the

$260,000 Crafoord Prize, astronomy's equivalent of the Nobel Prize.

Allen Rex Sandage was born in Iowa City, Iowa, on June 18, 1926, the son of Charles Harold Sandage and Dorothy (Briggs) Sandage. He began college studies at Miami University in Ohio, where his father was a professor of advertising, was drafted into the U.S. Navy in 1945, and completed his baccalaureate degree at the University of Illinois in 1948. He pursued graduate studies as a member of the first class of astronomy students at the California Institute of Technology, where he received his Ph.D. in 1953. Sandage wrote his doctoral thesis on the stellar components of the globular cluster M3 (M for Charles Messier, the French astronomer who identified the nebulae or fuzzy clouds of light in our galaxy), a group of stars clustered together thousands of light-years away that appears to form a halo around the Milky Way. In 1952, Sandage had joined the Mount Wilson Observatory overlooking Pasadena, California, as a research assistant to the renowned astronomer **Edwin P. Hubble**. Sandage's outstanding efforts as a young astronomer were recognized with the Helen Warner Prize from the American Astronomical Society in 1958, for a lecture on problems in the extragalactic distance scale.

Although Sandage has maintained a research position at the Mount Wilson and Palomar Observatories (later known collectively as the Hale Observatories) since the early 1950s, visiting lectureships and fellowships have taken him around the world to universities including Cambridge (1957), Harvard (1957), Haverford (1958 and 1966), the University of South Africa (1958), Australian National University (1968–1969), the University of Basel (1985), the University of California at San Diego (1985–1986), the University of Hawaii (1986), and Johns Hopkins (1987–1989).

Observes Mysterious Quasi-Stellar Object

Using the large 200-inch diameter reflecting telescope at the Palomar Observatory, commonly believed to be the world's largest telescope, Sandage built his career by employing the methods of radioastronomers, who survey the traveling electromagnetic disturbances or radio waves whose frequency and wavelengths lie within the radio region of the electromagnetic spectrum. In particular, Sandage examined the spectra of light emitted from stars and star clusters in the radio sky. In late summer 1960, Sandage, together with the young radioastronomer Thomas Matthews, optically identified a distant star-like object in another galaxy as the source of radio waves being emitted from the same sky coordinates. Before this time, no individual star had been identified as a radio source. This mysterious object was soon to be labeled a quasi-stellar radio source or, more commonly, a quasar.

Sandage's identification spurred astronomical observatories around the world to hunt for additional quasars. Astronomers began to think of quasars as what Dennis Overbye, in *Lonely Hearts of the Cosmos*, calls "beacons

from deep time and space." In 1965 Sandage thought he had uncovered a way to identify cosmological objects as quasars by the large quantities of either ultraviolet or blue wavelength radiation they emitted. Although his quickly reported findings proved to be erroneous, he did confirm that, unlike his initial find, most quasars did not emit radio waves. Quasars remain an enigma, as astronomers continue to dispute their nature.

Dating the Age of the Universe

Sandage has also worked toward an answer to one of the greatest questions addressed by science: What is the age and origin of the universe? Early in his career, Sandage attempted to date the age of the universe by studying globular clusters, using as his basis the findings of his mentor, Edwin Hubble, the "father of observational cosmology." Hubble had gathered spectrophotometric data demonstrating that the spectral lines of globular clusters in distant galaxies are diverted towards longer red wavelengths of the electromagnetic spectrum. These spectral patterns, called red-shifts, are indicative of objects which are moving away from us. Quantitatively, the larger the shift, the greater the velocity at which the object is receding. Hubble concluded that a galaxy's distance was proportional to its red-shift displacement (Hubble's law).

Sandage refined measurements of the cosmological constant known as the Hubble Constant or Hubble Parameter, a number that greatly affects determination of the age of the universe and of the speed at which the universe is expanding. Sandage attempted to fit his spectrophotometric analyses of globular clusters and quasars into Hubble's equation. From this work, Sandage depicted the universe in terms of diverse, dynamic galaxies that are receding from our own at velocities proportional to their distances. This pattern, according to Sandage, was most likely put into motion by a primordial "big bang": like Hubble and Einstein, Sandage considered the universe to have originated in a massive explosion, after which it is still expanding. Sandage described the dynamics of this expansion in terms of oscillation. Specifically, the rate of expansion appears to be decreasing; the universe will eventually cease expanding and begin an oscillatory phase of contraction. Sandage estimated that the universe is approximately 15 billion years old, and that the entire period of oscillation will be approximately 80 billion years.

Sandage's contributions have been recognized by professional societies throughout the world. He has received awards from England's Royal Astronomical Society (1963), the Pontifical Academy of Science (1966), the Franklin Institute (1973), the American Astronomical Society (1958 and 1973), the Astronomical Society of the Pacific (1975), and the Swiss Physics Society (1991). The award of greatest professional significance was the Royal Swedish Academy's Crafoord Prize, bestowed upon Sandage in 1991. As astronomy is a science not considered by the Swedish Academy's Nobel Prize committee, the Crafoord award ranks as astronomy's equivalent to a Nobel Prize.

While giving a series of guest lectures at Harvard in 1957, Sandage met Mary Lois Connelly, a University of Indiana and Radcliffe graduate, who was teaching at Mount Holyoke College. They were married on June 8, 1959, and have two children, David Allan and John Howard. Sandage resides in Pasadena, where in his spare time he enjoys gardening and cooking. A passionate opera fan, Sandage listened to operatic music on the countless cold nights he spent galaxy-gazing through Palomar's 200-inch telescope. According to Overbye, Sandage is a dedicated Christian who maintains that "life is not a dreary accident."

SELECTED WRITINGS BY SANDAGE:

Books

The Hubble Atlas of the Galaxies, Carnegie Institute, 1961.
A Revised Shapley-Ames Catalogue of the Bright Galaxies, Carnegie Institute, 1981, 2nd edition, 1987.
Atlas of Galaxies Useful for Measuring the Cosmological Distance Scale, National Aeronautics and Space Administration, 1988.

Periodicals

Scientific American, The Red-Shift, September 1956, pp. 170–82, reprinted in New Frontiers in Astronomy: Readings from Scientific American, edited by Owen Gingerich, W.H. Freeman, 1975, pp. 309–15.
Physics Today, Cosmology: A Search for Two Numbers, February 1970, pp. 34–41.
Endeavour, The Size and Shape of the Universe: the Quest for the Curvature of Space, 1990, pp. 104–11.

FURTHER READING:

Books

Overbye, Dennis, *Lonely Hearts of the Cosmos: The Story of the Scientific Quest for the Secret of the Universe,* HarperCollins, 1991.

Periodicals

Osmer, Patrick S., *Scientific American,* Quasars as Probes of the Distant and Early Universe, February 1982, pp. 126–38.

Sketch by Philip K. Wilson

Katherine Koontz Sanford
1915–
American biologist and medical researcher

Throughout her accomplished career, Katherine Koontz Sanford remained a private person committed to her research in cell biology, genetic predisposition to cancer, andneurodegenerative disease. Described as a gracious colleague who readily shared credit with her coworkers, Sanford demonstrated amazing stamina in a career than spanned more than half a century. Even after she retired from the National Cancer Institute (NCI) at the age of 80, Sanford continued to conduct research at the institute and work on manuscripts.

In the late 1940s, Sanford was a young woman entering what had traditionally been a man's world. However, Sanford's keen and resourceful intellect earned her colleagues' admiration and respect. She went on to become a world leader in research of tissue culture and in vitro carcinogenesis (cancer) and was the first person to clone a mammalian cell. Part of Sanford's success can be attributed to her ability to work well with people and her willingness to listen to their ideas and suggestions. Occasionally, she could be blunt and outspoken. "She never hesitated to tell me when she thought I was wrong," said Dr. Ram Parshad, of Howard University School of Medicine. "Yet, she was always willing to share credit, even with technicians who contributed to her work. Her example caused me to think about my own values."

Sanford was born in Chicago, Illinois, on July 19, 1915, to William James and Alta Rache Koontz. She attended college in Massachusetts, receiving her B.A. from Wellesley College, which she attended along with her two sisters. She earned her M.A. and Ph.D. in zoology from Brown University in 1942 and was one of an elite group of women at that time who graduated from the university's biology graduate program and went on to distinguished scientific careers. After graduation, Sanford spent two years as a biology instructor, first at Western College in Oxford, Ohio, and then at Allegheny College in Meadville, Pennsylvania. From there, she became an assistant director of the science program at the John Hopkins University Nursing School in Baltimore, Maryland.

In 1947 Sanford accepted a position that was to define her career. Joining the tissue culture section of the National Cancer Institute's (NCI) Laboratory of Biology, she began her lifelong focus on cancer research. Working with the section's director Virginia Evans and others, she developed techniques for establishing tissue cultures, with a strong focus on cancerous transformation in cultured cells.

Develops Vital Tool for Studying Cancer-Causing Mechanisms in Cells

Sanford made her mark in cell biology and cancer research early in her career at NCI. As the first person to isolate and clone a single mammalian (rodent) cell *in vitro* (in an artificial environment outside the living body), Sanford paved the way for a new field of research on the *in vitro* malignant transformation of cells. Sanford's isolated single cell could propagate itself to produce a colony of genetically identical cells. Although Sanford's method was cumbersome and hard to duplicate, scientists had a method they could further develop to produce pure cell lines with known metabolic and genetic properties. This "cloning" method would eventually lead to virus cultures, vaccine research, and new approaches for studying metabolic disorders. In 1954 she received the Ross Harrison Fellowship Award for her accomplishment.

Discovers Test for Cancer and Alzheimer's Disease

While most noted for her cloning discovery, Sanford—who married Charles Fleming Richards Mifflin on December 11, 1971—continued to make important contributions in the field of cancer and cell research. In the 1990s, she developed the first laboratory tests to distinguish people with Alzheimer's disease (a neurodegenerative disorder) and those with a predisposition to cancer. The test, or assay, involves exposing a person's skin fibroblasts, or blood lymphocyte cells, in culture to fluorescent light that causes deoxyribonucleic acid (DNA) damage. After treatment with DNA repair inhibitors, the cells are compared for chromatid breaks. Alzheimer's and cancer patients' cells have exhibited many more chromatid breaks under certain conditions. Although somewhat controversial because of other scientists' difficulty in repeating it, the test has correlated well with identifying genetic predispositions to some forms of cancer.

"The cytogenetic assay developed by Dr. Sanford is a great contribution," said Sanford's longtime colleague, Dr. Ram Parshad, in an article in the *NIH Record*. "It has the potential to be used as both a marker of cancer predisposition and for certain neurodegenerative disorders."

As early as 1985, Sanford had developed a cytogenetic test to evaluate DNA repair of mammalian cells in culture. This test showed that people genetically predisposed to cancer have a common defect in the processing of x-ray-induced DNA damage to their tumors and unaffected skin fibroblasts or to blood lymphocytes. In 1995, Sanford and colleagues found that phenolic compounds derived from green tea and a plant phenolic called curcumin can inhibit the DNA-damaging effects of fluorescent light on cultured cells.

Sanford "Officially" Retires

In 1974, Sanford was appointed head of NCI's cell physiology and oncogenesis section, in the Laboratory of Biochemistry. In 1977, she became chief of the *in vitro* carcinogenesis section at the institute's Laboratory of Cellular and Molecular Biology. After a 49-year career at NCI, Sanford announced her retirement in late 1995. However, her energy was far from spent. Committed to

completing her research into the new cytogenetic test, Sanford continued over the next year to work five days a week and sometimes on weekends in an unofficial capacity at the institute. Even after leaving her government laboratory for good in 1996, she continued to work from her home in Delaware with colleagues on manuscripts concerning the test. She also continued to be sought out and consulted by scientists from around the world.

"She is a first-class scientist, leaving behind a good set of experiments still to be done," said Charles W. Boone of NCI's Division of Cancer Prevention and Control in the *NIH Record*. "Her research will endure and will not be lost in the molecular woodlands."

SELECTED WRITINGS BY SANFORD:

Periodicals

"Studies On the Difference in Sarcoma-Producing Capacity of Two Lines of Mouse Cells Derived *in vitro* from One Cell." *Journal of the National Cancer Institute* (1958): 121.

"Fluorescent Light-Induced Chromatid Breaks Distinguish Alzheimer Disease Cells from Normal Cells in Tissue Culture." *Proceedings of the National Academy of Science, USA* (May 1996): 5146-150.

"Familial Clustering of Breast Cancer: Possible Interaction between DNA Repair Proficiency and Radiation Exposure in the Development of Breast Cancer." *International Journal of Cancer* (February 1995): 107-14.

FURTHER READING:

Books

Parry, Melanie, ed. *Biographical Dictionary of Women.* Chambers, 1996.

Kass-Simon, G. and Patricia Farnes, eds. *Women of Science: Righting the Record.* Bloomington: Indiana University Press, 1990.

Sketch by David A. Petechuk

Frederick Sanger
1918–
English biochemist

Frederick Sanger's important work in biochemistry has been recognized by two Nobel Prizes for chemistry. In 1958 he received the award for determining the arrangement of the amino acids that make up insulin, becoming the first

Frederick Sanger

person to thusly identify a protein molecule. In 1980 Sanger shared the award with two other scientists, being cited for his work in determining the sequences of nucleic acids in deoxyribonucleic acid (DNA) molecules. This research has had important implications for genetic research, and taken in conjunction with Sanger's earlier work on the structure of insulin, represent considerable contributions to combatting a number of diseases.

Frederick Sanger was born in Rendcombe, Gloucestershire, England, on August 3, 1918. His father, also named Frederick, was a medical doctor, and his mother, Cicely Crewsdon Sanger, was the daughter of a prosperous cotton manufacturer. Young Frederick attended the Bryanston School in Blandford, Dorset, from 1932 to 1936 and was then accepted at St. John's College, Cambridge. By his own admission, Sanger was not a particularly apt student. Later in life he wrote in *Annual Review of Biochemistry* that "I was not academically brilliant. I never won scholarships and would probably not have been able to attend Cambridge University if my parents had not been fairly rich."

Upon arriving at Cambridge and laying out his schedule of courses, Sanger found that he needed one more half-course in science. In looking through the choices available, Sanger came across a subject of which he had never heard—biochemistry—but that sounded appealing to him. "The idea that biology could be explained in terms of chemistry," he later wrote in *Annual Review of Biochemistry,* "seemed an exciting one." He followed the introductory course with an advanced one and eventually earned a first–class degree in the subject.

Sanger rapidly discovered his strengths and weaknesses in science. Although he was not particularly interested in or skilled at theoretical analysis, he was a superb experimentalist. He found that, as he later observed in *Annual Review of Biochemistry,* he could "hold my own even with the most academically outstanding" in the laboratory. This observation was to be confirmed in the ingenious experiments that he was to complete in the next four decades of his career.

Graduate Studies Lead to Protein Research

After receiving his bachelor's degree from St. John's in 1939, Sanger decided to continue his work in biochemistry. Though World War II had just begun, Sanger avoided service in the English army because his strong Quaker pacifist beliefs qualified him as a conscientious objector. Instead, he began looking for a biochemistry laboratory where he could serve as an apprentice and begin work on his Ph.D. The first position he found was in the laboratory of protein specialist, N. W. Pirie. Pirie assigned Sanger a project involving the extraction of edible protein from grass. That project did not last long because Pirie left Cambridge, and Sanger was reassigned to Albert Neuberger. Neuberger changed Sanger's assignment to the study of lysine, an amino acid. By 1943, Sanger had completed his research and was awarded his Ph.D. for his study on the metabolism of lysine.

After receiving his degree, Sanger decided to stay on at Cambridge, where he was offered an opportunity to work in the laboratory of A. C. Chibnall, the new professor of biochemistry. Chibnall's special field of interest was the analysis of amino acids in protein, a subject in which Sanger also became involved. The structure of proteins had been a topic of considerable dispute among chemists for many years. On the one hand, some chemists were convinced that proteins consisted of some complex, amorphous material that could never be determined chemically. Conversely, other chemists believed that, while protein molecules might be complex, they did have a structure that could eventually be unraveled and understood.

Probably the most influential theory of protein structure at the time of Sanger's research was that of the German chemist **Emil Fischer**. In 1902, Fischer had suggested that proteins consist of long chains of amino acids, joined to each other head to tail. Since it was known that each amino acid has two reactive groups, an amino group and a carboxyl group, it made sense that amino acids might join to each other in a continuous chain. The task facing researchers like Sanger was to first determine what amino acids were present in any particular protein, and then to learn in what sequence those amino acids were arranged. The first of these steps was fairly simple and straight forward, achievable by conventional chemical means. The second was not.

The protein on which Sanger did his research was insulin. The reason for this choice was that insulin—used in the treatment of diabetes—was one of the most readily available of all proteins, and one that could be obtained in very high purity. Sanger's choice of insulin for study was a fortuitous one. As proteins go, insulin has a relatively simple structure. Had he, by chance, started with a more complex protein, his research would almost certainly have stretched far beyond the ten years it required.

New Techniques Yield Structure of Insulin

In 1945 Sanger made an important technological breakthrough that made possible his later sequencing work on amino acids. He discovered that the compound dinitrophenol (DNP) will bond tightly to one end of an amino acid and that this bond is stronger than the one formed by two amino acids bonding with one another. This fact made it possible for Sanger to use DNP to take apart the insulin molecule one amino acid at a time. Each amino acid could then be identified by the newly discovered process of paper chromatography. This was a slow process, requiring Sanger to examine the stains left by the amino acids after they were strained through paper filters, but the technique resulted in the eventual identification of all amino acid groups in the insulin molecule.

Sanger's next objective was to determine the sequence of the amino acids present in insulin, but this work was made more difficult by the fact that the insulin molecule actually consists of two separate chains of amino acids joined to each other at two points by sulfur-sulfur bonds. In addition, a third sulfur-sulfur bond occurs within the shorter of the two strands. Despite these difficulties, Sanger, in 1955, announced the results of his work: he had determined the total structure of insulin molecule, the first protein to be analyzed in this way. Sanger's work in this area was considered important because it involved proteins—"the most important substances in the human body," as Sanger described them in a *New York Times* report on his work. Proteins are integral elements in both the viruses and toxins that cause diseases and in the antibodies that prevent them. Sanger's research, in laying the groundwork for future work on proteins, greatly increased scientists' ability to combat diseases. For his important work on proteins, Sanger was awarded the Nobel Prize in chemistry in 1958.

Writing in *The Annual Review of Biochemistry,* Sanger referred to the decade after completion of the insulin work as the "lean years when there were no major successes." Part of this time was taken up with various research projects aimed at learning more about protein structure. In one series of experiments, for example, he explored the use of radioactive isotopes for sequencing. The work was not particularly productive, however, and Sanger soon undertook a new position and a new area of research.

In 1962 he joined the newly established Medical Research Council (MRC) Laboratory of Molecular Biology at Cambridge, a center for research that included such scientists as **Max Perutz**, **Francis Crick**, and **Sydney Brenner**. This move marked an important turning point in Sanger's career. The presence of his new colleagues—and Crick, in particular—sparked Sanger's interest in the subject of nucleic acids. Prior to joining the MRC lab, Sanger had

had little interest in this subject, but he now became convinced of their importance. His work soon concentrated on the ways in which his protein-sequencing experiences might be used to determine the sequencing of nucleic acids.

The latter task was to be far more difficult than the former, however. While proteins may consist of as few as 50 amino acids, nucleic acids contain hundreds or thousands of basic units, called nucleotides. The first successful sequencing of a nucleic acid, a transfer RNA molecule known as alanine, was announced by **Robert William Holley** in 1965. Sanger had followed Holley's work and decided to try a somewhat different approach. In his method, Sanger broke apart a nucleic acid molecule in smaller parts, sequenced each part, and then determined the way in which the parts were attached to each other. In 1967 Sanger and his colleagues reported on the structure of an RNA molecule known as 5S using this technique.

Work on DNA Earns Second Nobel Prize

When Sanger went on to the even more challenging structures of DNA molecules, he invented yet another new sequencing technique. In this method, a single-stranded DNA molecule is allowed to replicate itself but stopped at various stages of replication. Depending on the chemical used to stop replication, the researcher can then determine the nucleotide present at the end of the molecule. Repeated applications of this process allowed Sanger to reconstruct the sequence of nucleotides present in a DNA molecule.

Successful application of the technique made it possible for Sanger and his colleagues to report on a 12-nucleotide sequence of DNA from bacteriophage λ in 1968. Ten years later, a similar approach was used to sequence a 5,386-nucleotide sequence of another form of bacteriophage. In recognition of his sequencing work on nucleic acids, Sanger was awarded his second Nobel Prize in chemistry in 1980, shares of which also went to **Walter Gilbert** and **Paul Berg**. Their work has been lauded for its application to the research of congenital defects and hereditary diseases and has proved vitally important in producing the artificial genes that go into the manufacture of insulin and interferon, two substances used to treat diseases.

In 1983, at the age of 65, Sanger retired from research. He was beginning to be concerned, he said in the *Annual Review of Biochemistry,* about "occupying space that could have been available to a younger person." He soon found that he very much enjoyed retirement, which allowed him to do many things for which he had never had time before. Among these were gardening and sailing. He also had more time to spend with his wife, the former Margaret Joan Howe, whom he had married in 1940, and his three children, Robin, Peter Frederick, and Sally Joan.

During his career, Sanger received many honors in addition to his two Nobel Prizes. In 1954, he was elected to the Royal Society and in 1963 he was made a Commander of the Order of the British Empire. He has been given the

Corday-Morgan Medal and Prize of the British Chemical Society, the Alfred Benzons Prize, the Copley Medal of the Royal Society, and the Albert Lasker Basic Medical Research Award, among other honors.

SELECTED WRITINGS BY SANGER:

Periodicals

Science, Chemistry of Insulin, May 12, 1959, pp. 1340–345.
Annual Review of Biochemistry, Sequences, Sequences, and Sequences, Volume 57, 1988, pp. 1–28.

FURTHER READING:

Books

Current Biography 1981, H. W. Wilson, 1981, pp. 354–56.
Nobel Prize Winners, H. W. Wilson, 1987, pp. 921–24.
Silverstein, A., *Frederick Sanger: The Man Who Mapped Out a Chemical of Life,* John Day, 1969.

Periodicals

Silverstein, A., *Chemistry and Industry,* December 13, 1958, pp. 1653–1654.
———, *New York Times,* October 29, 1958, p. 10.

Sketch by David E. Newton

David Satcher
1941–
American medical geneticist

David Satcher has devoted his career to ensuring that all members of society receive the benefits of health care. Satcher, himself an educator and administrator, has made sure that minorities, women and children, and the impoverished are not locked out of the system. In addition to his efforts to improve the quality and availability of health care, Satcher has achieved fame in the medical community for his research on sickle-cell anemia and his efforts in revitalizing Meharry Medical College, a historically African American medical school in Tennessee. Satcher's work has won him respect and several honors from the medical community.

Born in Anniston, Alabama, on March 2, 1941, David Satcher was one of nine children born to self-educated farmers. He credits his parents for his lifelong commitment

to providing better health care for minorities. In an interview with Marlene Cimons, published in the *Los Angeles Times,* Satcher said, "I may have come from a poor family economically, but they were not poor in spirit." When he was two years old, Satcher came close to dying from whooping cough, and was saved only by his mother's ministrations and the efforts of a local black doctor—the only one who would come to serve the poor family. The story of his near-death became a family shibboleth, and by age eight, Satcher had determined that he would become a doctor and help those who were traditionally ignored by society: the poor and minorities.

Satcher, whose parents instilled in their children a love of learning and a respect for educators, did well in school. When it came time for college, he won scholarships in addition to working his way through Morehouse College, graduating Phi Beta Kappa in 1963. He went on to Case Western Reserve University in Cleveland, Ohio, where he earned an M.D. and then a Ph.D. in cytogenetics in 1970 with a dissertation on "The Effects of Iodine–131 and X-Radiation on the Chromosomes of Peripheral Blood Leukocytes." While he conducted genetic research, Satcher also became interested in community medicine and administration. In 1972 he was made director of the King-Drew Medical Center in Los Angeles, California, also serving as associate director of its Sickle Cell Center from 1973 to 1975. From 1975 to 1979, he was a professor and chair of the department of family medicine as well as acting dean of the Charles R. Drew Postgraduate Medical School in Los Angeles. At Drew, Satcher created a cooperative program with the University of California, Los Angeles, whereby medical students would study two years at each institution and also provide medical care to the people of Watts. In 1979 Satcher returned to his undergraduate alma mater, Morehouse College, as a professor and chair of the department of community medicine.

Helps Breathe Life into Meharry

Although he successfully continued his efforts in administrating and teaching at Morehouse, it was in 1982 that Satcher took on his most challenging position. Appointed the president of Meharry Medical College in Nashville, Tennessee, Satcher was faced with the unenviable task of reorganizing and revitalizing a university plagued by annual deficits and decreasing enrollment. By all accounts, Meharry was on the brink of collapse when Satcher arrived. Undaunted, Satcher worked with a team of faculty and administrators to turn Meharry around, and by 1986 the institution had hired 40 new faculty members, raised $25 million in gifts and pledges, organized a health maintenance organization (HMO) for Nashville employers, and was running with a balanced budget for the first time in years. Satcher, a popular and energetic administrator, also made it a priority to ensure that black medical students received the same quality education as their white counterparts. He stayed at Meharry until 1993, when President Bill Clinton appointed him director of the Centers for Disease Control and Prevention in Atlanta, Georgia. His priorities for the center included prevention, women's health, education, and creating a sense of community to stop the violence in America. "That's why kids join gangs," Satcher said in his *Los Angeles Times* interview, "to try to have a family, a community."

Satcher's first wife, Calli Herndon, died of breast cancer in 1976. They had four children, Gretchen, David, Daraka, and Daryl. In 1978 he married poet Nola Richardson. A member of the American Academy of Family Physicians and the American Society of Human Genetics, Satcher was a Macy Foundation Faculty fellow in community medicine in 1972 and 1973. He was honored with the Outstanding Morehouse Alumnus Award in 1973, the Award for Medical Education for Sickle Cell Disease in 1973, and the Outstanding Alumnus award from Case Western Reserve University in 1980.

SELECTED WRITINGS BY SATCHER:

Books

Sickle Cell Counseling, National Foundation—March of Dimes, 1973.

Periodicals

Journal of the American Medical Association, Does Race Interfere with the Doctor-Patient Relationship?, March, 26, 1973, pp. 1498–499.

Urban Health, Study in Watts—Family Practice for the Inner City, October, 1976, p. 72.

Urban Health, Future Family Physicians Get Early Community Contact in Morehouse Curriculum, January, 1983, pp. 46–8.

Journal of Medical Education, Introducing Preclinical Students to Primary Care through a Community Preceptorship Program, March, 1983, pp. 179–85.

Journal of Health Care for the Poor and Underserved, Crime—Sin or Disease: Drug Abuse and AIDS in the African-American Community, Fall, 1990, pp. 212–18.

Journal of the American Medical Association, Improving Access to Health Care through Physician Workforce Reform, September 1, 1993, pp. 1074–078.

Health Affairs, Violence as a Public Health Priority, Winter, 1993, pp. 123–25.

FURTHER READING:

Periodicals

Applebome, Peter, *New York Times,* CDC's New Chief Worries as Much about Bullets as about Bacteria, September 26, 1993, p. E7.

Cimons, Marlene, *Los Angeles Times,* To Heal a Nation, March 1, 1994, p. E1.

——— , *Jet,* March 17, 1986, p. 23; June 16, 1986, p. 37.

——— , *Journal of the National Medical Association,* February, 1983, pp. 210, 213.

Martin, Thad, *Ebony,* Turnaround at Meharry, March, 1986, pp. 42–50.

——— , *Washington Post,* Medical School Chief Named CDC Director, August 21, 1993, p. A3.

——— , *New York Times,* Meharry Medical School Finds Its 8th President, February 1, 1982, p. B12.

Sketch by J. Sydney Jones

Alice T. Schafer
1915–
American algebraist and educator

Alice T. Schafer was born in Richmond, Virginia, on June 18, 1915. Her mother died during childbirth and Schafer was sent to the countryside area of Scottsburg, Virginia, to live with family friends. She was raised by Pearl Dickerson, a woman Schafer considered her mother and who was supportive of Schafer's ambitions throughout her life.

As a child, Schafer wanted to write novels, but by the third grade she became intrigued with mathematics after a teacher expressed concern that she would not able to master long division. Schafer not only mastered long division, but took math courses throughout her years of primary education. In her senior year of high school Schafer asked the principal to write a letter of recommendation for a scholarship to study mathematics in college. He was only willing to write the letter if she would promise to major in history instead.

After graduating from high school Schafer enrolled at the University of Richmond, where, at the time, the classes for men and women were held on separate sides of the campus. Mathematics classes were not offered on the female side of the campus, however, and as the only woman majoring in math, Schafer had to walk to the men's area of the campus to receive instruction. Women were also not allowed in the main library at the university. Books had to be sent over to the women's section of the campus upon request. In Schafer's junior year she questioned this policy and was finally allowed to sit in the library to read *Cyrano de Bergerac*, a book that was not available for circulation. After reading the book, Schafer was asked not to make any more requests to visit the library. The following summer she was offered a job in the library alphabetizing books. Schafer later quipped that she took the job because she needed the money.

Also in her junior year at Richmond, Schafer won the mathematical prize competition in Real Analysis but received no congratulatory praise from the chairman of the prize committee. Schafer graduated Phi Beta Kappa in 1936 when she was 21 years old with a degree in mathematics.

A Long and Varied Career

Schafer was offered a position at a high school in Glen Allen, Virginia, where she taught for three years. In 1939 she was awarded a fellowship at the University of Chicago and attained her Ph.D. in 1942. (Her dissertation was titled "Projective Differential Geometry.") While at the university, Schafer studied with Ernest P. Lane and Adrian Alberts.

Schafer's first teaching job as a Ph.D. was at Connecticut College, where she taught such classes as linear algebra, calculus, and abstract algebra for two years before accepting a position with Johns Hopkins University in the Applied Physics Laboratory doing research for the war effort. She was the only woman on the five-member team of scientists.

Schafer married Richard Schafer, a professor of abstract algebra at MIT, in 1942. They have two children, Richard Stone Schafer, born in 1945, and John Dickerson Schafer, born in 1946. Between the years 1945 and 1961 Schafer taught at such institutions as The University of Michigan, the Drexel Institute of Technology, and Swarthmore College, among others. In 1962 she joined the staff at Wellesley College and stayed there until her forced retirement at the age of 65 in 1980. The retirement proved to be short–lived, however, when in that same year Schafer went to Harvard University as a consultant and teacher of mathematics in the management program. She again became a professor of mathematics, this time at Marymount University, in 1989 and retired in 1996.

A Trailblazer for Women

Schafer has been a visiting professor and lecturer at various colleges, including Brown University and Simmons College. Schafer was the first woman to receive a Honorary Doctor of Science degree from the University of Richmond in 1964 and was presented with the Distinguished Alumna Award, Westhampton College, at the University of Richmond in 1977. During her tenure at Wellesley College, Schafer and two other women professors succeeded at implementing the black studies department there. She is also a cofounder of the Association for Women in Mathematics (AWM), along with Mary W. Gray, and others. The organization was established in 1971 to encourage women to study and seek careers in the mathematical sciences; currently, it boasts a membership of 4,500 from the United States and abroad. More than 300 academic institutions are supporting members of AWM in the United States. The AWM is open to both women and men. Schafer served as its president from 1973 to 1975 and remains active on various committees. A prize was established in her name in 1989 and is given annually to an undergraduate woman for excellence in mathematics.

Schafer is the author of eight articles concerning the progress of women in the field of mathematics and affirmative action. Her other articles include research on space curves and theorems on finite groups. A book published by the American Mathematical Society includes talks given by Schafer at their "100 Years of Annual Meetings Celebration." Her fields of specialization are abstract algebra (group theory). Schafer has three times been the leader of the delegation of women mathematicians to China, the last of which was the U.S.–China Joint Conference on Women's Issues held in Beijing between August 24 and September 2, 1995.

Schafer currently lives in Arlington, Virginia, with her husband.

SELECTED WRITINGS BY SCHAFER:

Books

"Women and Mathematics," in *Mathematics Tomorrow*. Edited by Lynn Arthur Steen. New York: Springer–Verlag, 1981.

Periodicals

"The Neighborhood of an Undulation Point of a Space Curve." *American Journal of Mathematics* 70 (1948): 351–63.
"Mathematics and Women: Perspectives and Progress." *American Mathematical Notices* (September 1991).
(With M. W. Gray) "Guidelines for Equality: A Proposal." *Academe* (December 1981).
"Two Singularities of Space Curves." *Duke Mathematical Journal* (November 1994): 655–70.

Other

"Alice T. Schafer." *Biographies of Women Mathematicians.* June 1997. http://www.scottlan.edu/lriddle/women/chronol.htm (July 22, 1997).
Schafer, Alice T., interview with Kelley Reynolds Jacquez conducted May 8, 1997.

Sketch by Kelley Reynolds Jacquez

George Schaller
1933–
American zoologist, naturalist, and conservationist

George Schaller, the widely-respected zoologist and author, has accomplished groundbreaking research on a variety of different animals by studying them in their natural habitats. Associated with the New York Zoological

Society since 1966 (he was named the director of the Society's Animal Research and Conservation Center in 1979, and subsequently its Director for Science), Schaller has sought to inform—through his numerous published works—a public that has frequently misunderstood and exploited wildlife. In the *New York Times Book Review,* Schaller told Lynn Karpen that "there's a moral obligation to do more for conservation. If you only study, you might get to write a beautiful obituary but you're not helping to perpetuate the species."

George Beals Schaller was born on May 26, 1933, in Berlin, Germany, to Georg Ludwig and Bettina Byrd (Beals) Schaller. After World War II, he accompanied his mother to an uncle's home in Missouri, where he developed an interest in animals and the outdoors. This pursuit influenced Schaller's college choice, and he entered the University of Alaska to study wildlife and the wilderness with the idea of making these subjects his life's work. Shortly after his graduation in 1955 (he received a B.S. in zoology and a B.A. in anthropology), Schaller joined his first expedition.

Explores Brooks Range in Northern Alaska

Hired as an assistant to Olaus Murie—president of the Wilderness Society in 1956 and Schaller's lifelong role model—Schaller traveled to the last true wilderness in the United States: the Brooks Range in northeastern Alaska. The New York Zoological Society sponsored the expedition, which was the first biological survey of the region. Approximately thirty-four years later Schaller wrote about the experience in an article for *Wildlife Conservation*: "We traversed many mountains and nameless valleys to collect information. We pressed plants, made bird lists, examined places where grizzlies had turned sod in search of voles, and analyzed wolf and lynx droppings to determine what these predators had eaten. . . . Each of us received, in the words of Margaret Murie, 'the gift of personal satisfaction, the personal well-being purchased by striving.'"

Schaller was doing graduate work in bird behavior in 1957 at the University of Wisconsin when he was offered the opportunity to study gorillas in Africa. "Here is a creature, considered with the chimpanzee the nearest relative of man, and we know almost nothing about its life in the wild," Schaller noted in his introduction to *The Year of the Gorilla.* "Does it live in small family units or in large groups; how many males and females are there in each group; what do groups do when they meet; how far do they travel each day; how long are infants dependent on their mothers?" These questions, which were answered as he studied free-living gorillas in Uganda, formed the basis of all his future field studies of large mammals. (A preceding work, *The Mountain Gorilla,* received the Best Terrestrial Wildlife Publication Award from the Wildlife Society in 1965.)

No-Weapons Policy: Unarmed and Unharmed

In 1962 Schaller earned a Ph.D. from the University of Wisconsin and became a fellow at the Center for Advanced Study in the Behavioral Sciences at Stanford University. Then, under the auspices of Johns Hopkins University (where he was a research associate from 1963 to 1966), Schaller studied the tiger in central India. A year of field research led to the book *The Deer and the Tiger: A Study of Wildlife in India,* published in 1967. Meanwhile, Schaller had became a research associate at the Institute for Research in Animal Behavior at the New York Zoological Society. The institute, along with Rockefeller University, sponsored his study of lions in Tanzania's Serengeti Park. Schaller's findings on predator-prey relations were published in *The Serengeti Lion,* which won the National Book Award in 1973.

Schaller refuses to carry weapons in his field work because he is convinced that the sight of an armed person makes the animals hostile. Despite the dangers commonly associated with working with wild animals, Schaller has remained unharmed; in a *National Geographic* article, he described one close call on the Serengeti Plain: "The breathing of a drugged lioness faltered while I was tagging her. As I administered artificial respiration by pressing on her chest, another lioness charged. I had to dash to the safety of my Land-Rover. Fortunately, the immobilized lioness survived—and so did I."

First Encounter with Pandas in the Wilderness

In all of his wildlife studies, Schaller attempts to enter the world of his subjects by sharing their lifestyle. During a cold January in 1980, Schaller trailed a male panda named Wei-Wei for five-and-a-half days through the snow-covered Wolong Natural Reserve in China's Sichuan province. "I learned that he averaged just over three-quarters of a mile of travel a day, surprisingly little for such a large animal, that he left his scent on forty-five trees, that he had nine lengthy rest periods, that he deposited an average of ninety-seven droppings per day. . . . I developed at least a more perceptive mind by following Wei's tracks and could appreciate even more the uniqueness of his personal world," Schaller wrote in his book *The Last Panda.*

According to Geoffrey C. Ward in the *New York Times Book Review,* "*The Last Panda* is really two books in one: a group portrait of the animals [Schaller] calls 'the most endearing creatures I have ever seen,' and a litany of human errors—of crimes against nature—that may already have insured the panda's disappearance from the wild." Among the various human factors that have impeded on the panda's survival are zoos which "vie for status, publicity and profit through 'rent a panda' deals," Schaller told Sharon Bagley in *Newsweek.* Bagley further explained that "panda rentals disrupt the breeding of a species that reproduces poorly in captivity even without transoceanic sabbaticals. When they take up long-term residence, any cubs they have rarely survive."

A Touch of the Poet

"No one else ever will have the chance to do what Schaller has done," William Conway told contributor Rayma Prince in an interview, referring to the range of his colleague's subjects: lions, tigers, jaguars, giant pandas, snow leopards, and mountain gorillas. Conway, who is general director of the New York Zoological Society/The Wildlife Conservation Society, worked with Schaller for thirty-five years. Conway commented, "George differs from most of the scientists in that he is an exceptionally shy and thoughtful person, with a bit of the poet in his soul and the way he looks at life, and I think this comes through in his writings." In *The Year of the Gorilla* Schaller wrote, "To see African wildlife in all its abundance and variety, living as it has always lived, was one of the most priceless experiences I have ever had."

The list of honors bestowed on Schaller is extensive: besides a 1971 Guggenheim fellowship, a 1971 gold medal from the San Diego Zoological Society, and a 1980 gold medal from the World Wildlife Fund (among other honors), he has received the Order of the Golden Ark from Prince Bernhard of The Netherlands (1978) and, from West Germany, the 1985 Bruno H. Schubert Conservation Award. When Schaller was awarded the Explorers Medal by the Explorers Club in 1990, his name was added to a list of famous people that began with Admiral Peary, the first man to reach the North Pole.

Schaller married Kay Suzanne Morgan in 1957 and the couple has two sons, Eric and Mark. Kay Schaller, a trained anthropologist, went on many expeditions with her husband and often helped him with his books. William Weber, director of conservation operations at the Bronx facility, traced his interest in conservation to Schaller's influence. "When my wife Amy and I were working as Peace Corps volunteers in Zaire, we read his books," Weber told Rayma Prince in an interview. "The goal to save gorillas came from George's original work. He is certainly somebody who's inspired a lot of people to go out and carry on. In our case, it's quite something twenty years later to be working in the same organization with this person." Weber reported that Schaller, after thirty-five years, is probably going back out to do some more surveys on gorillas. "When Amy asked him how far he intended to walk, George said, 'Well, I think I've got a few hundred kilometers left in me.'"

SELECTED WRITINGS BY SCHALLER:

Books

The Mountain Gorilla, University of Chicago Press, 1963.
The Year of the Gorilla, University of Chicago Press, 1964.
The Deer and the Tiger, University of Chicago Press, 1967.
The Serengeti Lion, University of Chicago Press, 1972.
The Last Panda, University of Chicago Press, 1993.

Periodicals

Wildlife Conservation, American Serengeti, November/ December 1990, pp. 54–69.
National Geographic, Life with the King of the Beasts, April, 1969, pp. 494–519.
National Geographic, Pandas in the Wild, December, 1981, pp. 735–49.

FURTHER READING:

Periodicals

Bagley, Sharon, *Newsweek,* Killed by Kindness, April 12, 1993, pp. 50–6.
Karpen, Lynn, *New York Times Book Review,* A Beautiful Obituary Won't Help, March 28, 1993, p. 18.

Other

Conway, William, *Interview with Rayma Prince,* conducted August, 1993.
Weber, William, *Interview with Rayma Prince,* conducted August, 1993.

Sketch by Rayma Prince

Andrew V. Schally
1926–
American biochemist

Andrew V. Schally helped conduct pioneering research concerning hormones, identifying three brain hormones and greatly advancing scientists' understanding of the function and interaction of the brain with the rest of the body. His findings have proved useful in the treatment of diabetes and peptic ulcers, and in the diagnosis and treatment of hormone-deficiency diseases. Schally shared the 1977 Nobel Prize with French-born American endocrinologist **Roger Guillemin** and **Rosalyn Yalow** (an American scientist whose work in the discovery and development of radioimmunoassay, the use of radioactive substances to find and measure minute substances—especially hormones—in blood and tissue, helped Schally and Guillemin isolate and analyze peptide hormones).

Andrew Victor Schally was born on November 30, 1926, in Wilno, Poland, to Casimir Peter Schally and Maria Lacka Schally. His father served in the military on the side of the Allies during World War II, and Schally grew up during Nazi occupation of his homeland. The family later left Poland and immigrated to Scotland, where Schally entered the Bridge Allen School in Scotland. He studied chemistry at the University of London and obtained his first research position at London's highly regarded National Institute for Medical Research. Leaving London for Montreal, Canada, in 1952, Schally attended McGill University, where he studied endocrinology and conducted research on the adrenal and pituitary glands. He obtained his doctorate in biochemistry from McGill in 1957. Also in 1957, Schally became an assistant professor of physiology at Baylor University School of Medicine in Houston, Texas. There he was able to pursue his interest in the hormones produced by the hypothalamus.

Expands on Geoffrey Harris's Discoveries

Scientists had long thought that the hypothalamus, a part of the brain located just above the pituitary gland, regulated the endocrine system, which includes the pituitary, thyroid and adrenal glands, the pancreas, and the ovaries and testicles. They were, however, unsure of the way in which hypothalamic hormonal regulation occurred. In the 1930s British anatomist Geoffrey W. Harris theorized that hypothalamic regulation occurred by means of hormones, chemical substances secreted by glands and transported by the blood. Harris was able to support his hypothesis by conducting experiments that demonstrated altered pituitary function when the blood vessels between the hypothalamus and the pituitary were cut. Harris and others were unable to isolate or identify the hormones from the hypothalamus.

Schally devoted his work to identifying these hormones. He and Roger Guillemin, who also worked at Baylor University's School of Medicine, were engaged in research to unmask the chemical structure of corticotropin-releasing hormone (CRH). Their efforts, however, were unsuccessful—the structure was not determined until 1981. The two then focused their work, independently, on other hormones of the hypothalamus. Schally left Baylor in 1962, when he became director of the Endocrine and Polypeptide Laboratory at the Veterans Administration (VA) Hospital in New Orleans, Louisiana. Also that year, Schally became a U.S. citizen and took on the post of assistant professor of medicine at Tulane University Medical School.

Schally's first breakthrough came in 1966 when he and his research group isolated TRH, or thyrotropin-releasing hormone. In 1969 Schally and his VA team demonstrated that TRH is a peptide containing three amino acids. It was Guillemin, though, who first determined TRH's chemical structure. The success of this research made it possible to decipher the function of a second hormone, called luteinizing-hormone releasing factor (LHRH). Identified in 1971, LHRH is a decapeptide and controls reproductive functions in both males and females. The chemical makeup of the growth-releasing hormone (GRH) was also discovered by Schally's team in 1971. Schally was able to show that GRH, a peptide consisting of ten amino acids, causes the release of gonadotropins from the pituitary gland. These gonadotropins, in turn, cause male and female sex hormones to be released from the testicles and ovaries. In conjunction with

this, Schally was able to identify a factor that inhibits the release of GRH in 1976. Guillemin, however, had determined its structure earlier and named it somatostatin. Subsequent studies by Schally showed that somatostatin serves multiple roles, some of which relate to insulin production and growth disorders. This led to speculation that the hormone could be useful for treating diabetes and acromegaly, a growth-disorder disease.

The hormone research done by Schally and his colleagues was tedious and expensive. Thousands of sheep and pig hypothalami were required to extract the smallest amount of hormone. These organs were solicited from many area slaughterhouses and required immediate dissection to prevent the hormones from degrading. Their accomplishment of isolating the first milligram of pure thyrotropin-releasing hormone, Guillemin stated, cost many times more than the NASA space mission that brought a kilogram of moon rock back to earth.

Schally's intense years of hard work and accomplishment were capped by the Nobel Prize, but he has also received many other awards and honors. In 1974 he was given the Charles Mickle Award of the University of Toronto, and the Gairdner Foundation International Award. He received the Borden Award in the Medical Sciences of the Association of American Medical Colleges in 1975 and, that same year, the Lasker Award and the Laude Award. He has held memberships in the National Academy of Sciences, the American Society of Biological Chemists, the American Physiology Society, the American Association for the Advancement of Science, and the Endocrine Society. In the years prior to receiving the Nobel Prize, Schally and his colleagues published more than 850 papers. Married to Brazilian endocrinologist Ana Maria de Medeiros-Comaru, Schally often lectures in Latin America and Spain. He and his first wife, Margaret Rachel White, have two children.

SELECTED WRITINGS BY SCHALLY:

Books

The Hypothalamus and Pituitary in Health and Disease, Thomas Press, 1972.

Periodicals

Biochemical and Biophysical Research Communications, Isolation of Thyrotropin Releasing Factor (TRF) from Porcine Hypothalamus, Volume 25, 1966, p. 165.

Endocrinology, Purification of Thyrotropic Hormone Releasing Factor from Bovine Hypothalamus, Volume 78, 1966, p. 726.

Journal of Biological Chemistry, The Amino Acid Sequence of a Peptide with Growth Hormone Releasing Activity Isolated from Porcine Hypothalamus, Volume 246, 1971, p. 6647.

FURTHER READING:

Periodicals

Meites, Joseph, *Science,* The 1977 Nobel Prize in Physiology or Medicine, November 11, 1977, pp. 594–96.

——— , *New York Times,* October 14, 1977, pp. A1, A18.

Sketch by Jane Stewart Cook

Berta Scharrer
1906–1995
German-born American biologist

Berta Scharrer, together with her husband Ernst Scharrer, pioneered the field of neuroendocrinology—the interaction of the nervous and endocrine systems. Fighting against the then-accepted belief that nerve cells were only electrical conductors, as well as against the prejudice toward women in the sciences, Berta Scharrer established the concept of neurosecretion through her research with insects and other invertebrates. A highly respected educator, she was also among the founding faculty of the department of anatomy at the Albert Einstein College of Medicine in New York.

Berta Vogel Scharrer was born in Munich, Germany on December 1, 1906, the daughter of Karl Phillip and Johanna (Greis) Vogel. She developed an early interest in science, and attended the University of Munich, earning her Ph.D. in 1930 in biology for research into the correlation between sweetness and nutrition in various sugars. Upon graduation, Scharrer took a position as research associate in the Research Institute of Psychiatry in Munich, and in 1934 she was married to Ernst Albert Scharrer, a biologist. Together they formed an intellectual and domestic partnership that would last until Ernst Scharrer's death in 1965.

In 1928 Ernst Scharrer had discovered what he termed nerve-gland cells in a species of fish and made the rather startling hypothesis that some nerve cells actually were involved in secreting hormonal substances just as cells of the endocrine system do. It was a thesis sure to upset the more conservative members of the scientific community, as the synaptic function between neurons or nerve cells was then thought to be purely electrical. The idea of neurons having a dual function was looked on as something of a heresy: either cells secreted hormones, in which case they were endocrine cells belonging to the endocrine system, or they conducted electrical impulses, making them nerve cells, part of the nervous system. But what Ernst and Berta Scharrer demonstrated was that there existed an entire class of cells which performed both functions. The nerve-gland or neurosecretory cells are actually a channel between the nervous system and the endocrine system—an interface between an organism's environment and its glandular system. Some of the neurohormones secreted by neurosecretory cells actually control the release of other hormones via the anterior pituitary gland. To elucidate such action fully, the Scharrers divided up the animal kingdom between them: Ernst Scharrer took the vertebrates and Berta Scharrer the invertebrates.

Working as a research associate at the Neurological Institute of the University of Frankfurt, where her husband had been named director of the Edinger Institute for Brain Research, Berta Scharrer discovered other nerve-gland cells: in mollusks in 1935, in worms in 1936, and in insects beginning in 1937. But if research into neurosecretion was going well, life in Germany under Hitler was far from positive. The Scharrers decided, in 1937, to emigrate to the United States.

Introduce Neurosecretion to American Neuroscientists

The Scharrers travelled the long way to America via the Pacific, collecting specimens for research along the way. They joined the Department of Anatomy at the University of Chicago for a year, and then moved on to New York, where Ernst Scharrer was visiting investigator at the Rockefeller Institute from 1938 to 1940. Berta Scharrer continued her insect research in New York, and together the Scharrers prepared the results of their research for presentation at the 1940 meeting of the Association for Research in Nervous and Mental Diseases, the first presentation of the concept of neurosecretion in the United States, and one that was warmly received. That same year, Ernst Scharrer took a position as assistant professor in the anatomy department of Western Reserve University School of Medicine in Cleveland, Ohio, a post he would hold until 1946. Berta Scharrer was offered a fellowship assisting in the histology laboratory, which gave her research facilities, but scant professional standing. It was during these years that she accomplished some of her most important research into the localization of neurosecretory cells and their role in animal development, using the South American cockroach *Leucophaea maderae* as her research subject.

After the Second World War, Ernst Scharrer accepted a position at the University of Colorado Medical School in Denver, and Berta Scharrer won a Guggenheim Fellowship to continue her research, becoming an assistant professor in Denver in 1947. The next years were some of the Scharrers' most fruitful, as they loved the mountains, skiing, and horseback riding. Professionally these were also important times, for the theory of neurosecretion was beginning to be accepted around the world, especially after a German scientist was able to successfully stain neurosecretory granules—the packaging for neurohormones that some neurons secrete. Thus it became possible to study the fine structure of such granules and follow their course upon secretion. Neurosecretion became an accepted fact, the cornerstone of the emerging field of neuroendocrinology. By 1950 it had also become an accepted fact that a chemical transmission took place at the synapse along with electrical charge. These advancements not only confirmed the Scharrers' work, but also paved the way for advances in their research. Berta Scharrer applied the new findings to her own work on the maturation of the ovarian systems of her South American cockroaches with results that verified earlier findings in the endocrinology of invertebrates.

Wins Full Professorship at Albert Einstein College

In 1955 the Scharrers were offered joint positions at the new Albert Einstein College of Medicine at Yeshiva University in New York: Ernst as department head of anatomy, and Berta as full professor in the same department. This was the first real professional recognition for Berta Scharrer, and the couple left Denver for New York. Here she taught histology—the microscopic structure of tissues—and continued with research into insect glands. Using the electron microscope, she was able to accomplish some of the earliest detailing of the insect nervous system and especially the neurosecretory system. Together with her husband, she published *Neuroendocrinology* in 1963, one of the basic texts in the new discipline. Tragically, her husband died in a swimming accident in Florida in 1965, but Berta Scharrer carried on with their research, acting as chair of the department for two years until a successor could be found. She also went on to elucidate the fine structure of the neurosecretory cell—composed of a cell body, projecting dendrites, the extending long axon, and synaptic contacts at one end, just as in other neurons or nerve cells. Additionally, neurosecretory cells have special fibers allowing for feedback, as well as neurohemal organs—the point at which the neurohormones pass into the blood stream. Neurosecretory cells, it was shown, can affect targets contiguous with them or distant, through the bloodstream, as with other hormones. Scharrer also investigated the makeup of the secretory material, discovering that it was a peptide or polypeptide—a combination of amino acids. Scharrer's later research deals with the immunoregulatory property of neuropeptides, or the relationship between the immune and nervous systems in invertebrates.

Continuing with her research and instruction, as well as coediting *Cell and Tissue Research,* Scharrer became an emeritus professor of anatomy and neuroscience at Albert Einstein College of Medicine in 1978. She was honored with a National Medal of Science in 1983, for her "pioneering contributions in establishing the concept of neurosecretion and neuropeptides in the integration of animal function and development." She also won the F. C. Koch Award of the Endocrine Society in 1980, the Henry Gray Award of the American Association of Anatomists in 1982, and was honored by her former country with the Kraepelin Gold Medal from the Max Planck Institute in Munich in 1978 and the Schleiden Medal in 1983. She was a member of the National Academy of Sciences and held honorary degrees from colleges and universities around the world, including Harvard and Northwestern. Reading and music were among Berta Scharrer's free-time activities, and she continued scientific research virtually till her death. Scharrer died on July 23, 1995, at her home in Bronx, New York. She was 88.

SELECTED WRITINGS BY SCHARRER:

Books

Neuroendocrinology. New York: Columbia University Press, 1963.
An Evolutionary Interpretation of the Phenomenon of Neurosecretion. New York: American Museum of Natural History, 1978.

Periodicals

"Comparative Physiology of Invertebrate Endocrines." *Annual Review of Physiology* 25 (1953): 456-72.
"The Fine Structure of the Neurosecretory System of the Insect Leucophaea Maderae." *Memoirs of the Society of Endocrinology* 12 (1962): 89-97.
"Insects as Models of Neuroendocrine Research." *Annual Review of Entomology.* 32 (1987): 1-16.
"Neurosecretion: Beginnings and New Directions in Neuropeptide Research." *Annual Review of Neuroscience* 10 (1987): 1-17.
"Peptidergic Neurons: Facts and Trends." *General and Comparative Endocrinology* (January 1978): 50-62.
"Recent Progress in Comparative Neuroimmunology." *Zoological Science* (December 1992): 1097-010.

FURTHER READING:

Periodicals

"Honorary Degrees Given By Harvard." *New York Times* (16 October 1982): 9.
"Medal of Science to Berta Scharrer." *Einstein* (Spring 1985): 2.
Saxon, Wolfgang. "Berta Scharrer, 88, Research Scientist and Roach Expert" (obituary). *New York Times* (25 July 1995).

Other

Palay, Sanford L. "Presentation of the Henry Gray Award to Professor Berta Scharrer at the Ninety-Fifth Meeting of the American Association of Anatomists" (speech). 5 April 1982.

Sketch by J. Sydney Jones

Arthur Leonard Schawlow
1921–1999
American physicist

Arthur L. Schawlow, a coinventor of the laser, winner of the Nobel Prize in Physics in 1981 for work in laser spectroscopy, and recipient of the National Medal of Science in 1991, made fundamental contributions to the fields of laser and maser spectroscopy. In this field of spectroscopy, spectra that have been amplified by either a laser or a maser are examined in order to discover properties of a targeted material. Schawlow is also remembered as an important professor, lecturer, and highly visible member of the scientific community.

Schawlow was born on May 5, 1921, in Mount Vernon, New York. His father, Arthur Schawlow, was an insurance agent who had come to the United States from Latvia circa 1910, and his mother, the former Helen Mason, was a citizen of Canada. After the Schawlow family moved to Toronto, Canada, in 1924, young Arthur was educated at the Winchester Elementary School, the Normal Model School, and the Vaughan Road Collegiate Institute, all in Toronto.

After graduating from high school at the age of sixteen in 1937, Schawlow entered the University of Toronto. He originally planned to major in radio engineering, but the only scholarship he was able to find was one in physics and mathematics. Thus, it was in these fields that he studied for his bachelor's degree, which he received in 1941. Schawlow also found time during his student days to pursue his favorite hobby, jazz music. A biographer, Boris P. Stoicheff, reports in *Science* that Schawlow "distinguished himself in certain Toronto circles as a clarinetist playing Dixieland jazz at a time when his idols were Benny Goodman and 'Jelly Roll' Morton."

Shortly after Schawlow received his bachelor's degree, Canada and the United States became involved in World War II. His assignment for the next three years was to teach physics to military personnel at the University of Toronto. At the same time, he was able to complete the work necessary for his M.A. degree, which he received in 1942. At the war's conclusion, Schawlow returned to his graduate studies full time. In 1949 he was awarded his Ph.D. in physics for research completed under the supervision of Malcolm F. Crawford.

Begins Collaboration with Charles H. Townes

In 1941 Schawlow was awarded a Carbide and Carbon Chemicals scholarship that allowed him to spend two years as a postdoctoral researcher at Columbia University. While there, Schawlow met **Charles H. Townes**, who was later to win the 1964 Nobel Prize in physics for his work on the development of the maser. A maser (microwave amplifica-

tion by stimulated emission of radiation) is a device for amplifying microwave signals. Schawlow and Townes began a long and productive collaboration on the subjects of masers, lasers, and laser spectroscopy. One product of that collaboration was a book, *Microwave Spectroscopy,* published in 1955. Also, towards the end of his postdoctoral work at Columbia, on May 19, 1951, Schawlow married Townes's sister, Aurelia. The couple later had three children: two daughters, Helen Aurelia and Edith Ellen, and a son, Arthur Keith. With the birth of their son, who was autistic, the Schawlows became active in efforts to help people with autism, and succeeded in developing techniques for communicating with individuals with this disease. Professor Schawlow donated a hall to the group home where his son resided, and this home now bears his name.

In 1951 Schawlow accepted a job as a research physicist at the Bell Telephone Laboratories in Murray Hill, New Jersey. He worked on a variety of topics there, including superconductivity and optical and microwave spectroscopy. But he also remained interested in a problem he and Townes had been investigating, an optical maser.

Building a Laser

The first maser had been designed and built in the mid-1950s by Townes and two Russian physicists, **Nikolai Gennadiyenich Basov** and **Aleksandr Prokhorov**. Following that achievement, a number of physicists had explored the possibility of extending the maser principle to the optical region of the electromagnetic spectrum. After much discussion, Schawlow and Townes developed a proposal for building such an instrument, one that was later given the name laser (for light amplification by stimulated emission of radiation). They published their ideas in the December, 1958, issue of *Physical Review.*

Their next step was to attempt the actual construction of a laser. Unfortunately for Schawlow and Townes, they took a somewhat more difficult approach than was necessary and were to see their concept brought to reality by a fellow physicist, **Theodore Maiman**, who built the first successful laser in 1960. Schawlow and Townes were not far behind in constructing their own laser, however, and they put the new device to use in a number of ways.

One of the most productive uses of laser technology has been in the area of laser spectroscopy, a field in which Schawlow became one of the world's authorities. In laser spectroscopy, a laser beam is directed at a material to be studied. The wavelengths absorbed and then re-emitted by the sample are determined by the electron energy levels and chemical bonds present in the material. By studying the spectra produced by laser analysis, a researcher can determine a number of fundamental properties of a material as well as the changes that take place within the material. For his contributions to the design of the laser and to its applications in laser spectroscopy, Schawlow (along with **Nicolaas Bloembergen** and **Kai M. Siegbahn**) was awarded a share of the 1981 Nobel Prize in physics.

In 1961 Schawlow left Bell Laboratories to accept a post as professor of physics at Stanford University. He served as chair of the department from 1966 to 1970 and in 1978 became J. G. Jackson-C.J. Wood Professor of Physics. Schawlow was honored not only for his accomplishments as a researcher, but also for his skills as a teacher. Boris Stoicheff's report on the 1981 Nobel Prize in *Science* referred to Schawlow and fellow Nobel laureate Bloembergen as "celebrated teachers, possessed of a characteristic flair and combination of talents that have marked them as outstanding scientists and gifted lecturers."

Schawlow was a highly visible scientist. He appeared on Walter Cronkite's television series *The 21st Century*, Don Herbert's *Experiment* series, and on a variety of other U.S. and British educational programs. Among his many awards were the Ballantine Medal of the Franklin Institute (1962), the Thomas Young Medal and Prize of London's Physical Society and Institute of Physics (1963), the Morris Liebmann Memorial Award of the Institute of Electricians and Electrical Engineers, and the Frederick Ives Medal of the Optical Society of America (1976).

Schawlow died in 1999 at the age of 77. In the course of his career, he trained a generation of graduate and postdoctoral students who went on to shape the fields of coherent optics and quantum electronics.

SELECTED WRITINGS BY SCHAWLOW:

Books

Microwave Spectroscopy, McGraw-Hill, 1955.

Periodicals

Physical Review, Infrared and Optical Masers, Volume 112, December, 1958, pp. 1940–949.
Physical Review Letters, Simultaneous Optical Maser Action in Two Ruby Satellite Lines, Volume 6, 1961, pp. 605–07.

FURTHER READING:

Books

Weber, Robert L., *Pioneers of Science: Nobel Prize Winners in Physics,* American Institute of Physics, 1980, pp. 275–76.
Yen, William M., and Marc D. Levenson, *Lasers, Spectroscopy, and New Ideas: A Tribute to Arthur L. Schawlow,* Springer-Verlag, 1987.

Periodicals

Yen, William M., and Marc D. Levenson, *Physics Today,* Nobel Physics Prize to Bloembergen, Schawlow and Siegbahn, December, 1981, pp. 17–20.

Stoicheff, Boris P., *Science,* The 1981 Nobel Prize in Physics, November 6, 1981, pp. 629–33.

Sketch by David E. Newton

Bela Schick
1877–1967
Hungarian-born American pediatrician

Bela Schick was a pioneer in the field of child care; not only did he invent the diphtheria test, which helped wipe out this disease in children, but he also formulated and publicized child care theories that were advanced for his day. Schick also defined the allergic reaction, was considered the leading pediatrician of his time, and made contributions to knowledge about scarlet fever, tuberculosis, and infant nutrition. Schick received many honors for his work, including the Medal of the New York Academy of Medicine and the Addingham Gold Medal, a British award. Schick was also the founder of the American Academy of Pediatrics.

Schick was born on July 16, 1877 in Boglar, Hungary, the child of Jacob Schick, a grain merchant, and Johanna Pichler Schick. He attended the Staats Gymnasium in Graz, Austria, graduating in 1894. He then received his M.D. degree at Karl Franz University, also in Graz. After a stint with the medical corps in the Austro-Hungarian army, Schick started his own medical practice in Vienna in 1902. From then on he devoted his ample energies to teaching, research, and medical practice at the University of Vienna, where he served from 1902 to 1923—first as an intern, then as an assistant in the pediatrics clinic, and finally as lecturer and professor of pediatrics.

It was in 1905 that Schick made one of his most significant contributions. While working with collaborator Clemens von Pirquet, Schick wrote his first research study describing the phenomenon of allergy, which was then called "serum sickness." The study not only described the concept of allergy, but also the best ways to treat it.

Develops Diphtheria Test

At age 36, Schick moved on to make one of the most important discoveries of the twentieth century—the test for diphtheria. The test, announced in 1913, was a remarkably simple one that could tell whether a person was vulnerable to the disease. It showed whether a patient had already been exposed to the diphtheria toxin, which would make him immune from getting it again. A tiny amount of the diluted toxin was injected into the patient's arm. If the spot turned red and swollen, the doctors would know whether or not the

Bela Schick

patient been exposed to the disease. The treatment was then injection with an antitoxin.

Diphtheria was a common disease in the early twentieth century and afflicted thousands of children in every city throughout the world. It was especially common in Europe, where the close quarters of many cities made infection more likely. At the time Schick embarked on his research, scientists had already isolated the microbe or toxin that caused diphtheria. A horse serum had also been developed that could prevent or even cure the disease. But the serum had so many side effects that doctors were unwilling to prescribe it unless they knew a patient was seriously in danger of catching diphtheria. Thus, Schick's discovery made it easier for them to treat those who were the most vulnerable.

In 1923, an antitoxin without side effects was developed and was then given to babies during their first year of life. Later on, the Schick test would show whether the baby's immunity lasted. Schick's test technique was also used years later to treat people with allergies, using the same technique of injecting small doses of an antitoxin.

Schick left Vienna in 1923 to become pediatrician-in-chief at Mt. Sinai Hospital in New York City. Schick became an American citizen that same year and two years later married his wife, Catherine C. Fries. He held his post at Mt. Sinai Hospital until his retirement in May 1943, when he became a consulting pediatrician. During his career, he also worked simultaneously at other hospitals, acting as director of pediatrics at Sea View Hospital in Staten Island,

New York and consulting pediatrician at the Willard Parker Hospital, the New York Infirmary for Women and Children, and Beth Israel Hospital. He also taught as a professor of the diseases of children at Columbia University's College of Physicians and Surgeons, starting in 1936.

Schick directed a private practice in New York City as well. His office held a collection of dolls and animals that he had acquired in travels throughout the world. He would often play the piano in his office, or take out one of his doll or animal figures to calm a child. He never displayed a stethoscope until he made sure a child was relaxed. At one time, he estimated that he had treated over a million children. Often visitors would be surprised to see him on the floor with his small charges, making faces at them. "To be a good pediatrician, it helps to be a little childish yourself," he often said.

Childless himself, he had a great fondness for children and in 1932 authored a popular book containing his firm beliefs about how children should be raised, *Child Care Today*. Many of his ideas were advanced for his time. He advocated little punishment for children and no corporal punishment. He also said that trauma in a child's early life often had a lasting effect.

Schick and his wife lived in a large apartment in New York City and were frequent travelers around the world. On a cruise to South America with his wife during his later years, Schick fell ill with pleurisy. Eventually brought back to the United States to Mt. Sinai Hospital, he died on Dec. 6, 1967. He was 90 years old.

SELECTED WRITINGS BY SCHICK:

Books

Child Care Today. Greenberg, 1932.
(With C. F. Von Pirquet) *Serum Sickness.* Williams and Wilkins, 1951.

FURTHER READING:

Books

Gronowicz, Antoni. *Bela Schick and the World of Children.* New York: Abelard-Shuman, 1954.

Periodicals

Whitman, Alden. "Schick, Who Devised Diphtheria Test, Dies." *New York Times* (Dec. 7, 1967): 1, 47.

Sketch by Barbara Boughton

Stephen H. Schneider
1945–
American climatologist

Stephen H. Schneider, formerly a longtime senior scientist at the National Center for Atmospheric Research and later a professor in the department of biological sciences at the Institute for International Studies at Stanford University in California, is among the most respected scientists in the field of climatology. He has conducted research in many areas, including such publicized topics as nuclear winter and global warming, participated in numerous conferences, and published widely. Schneider is known outside the scientific community for his books and television appearances, in which he explains often difficult scientific concepts in a fashion understandable to the nonscientist.

Stephen Henry Schneider was born on February 11, 1945, in New York City to Samuel and Doris C. Swarte Schneider, both educators. He earned his undergraduate and graduate degrees in mechanical engineering from Columbia University, culminating his studies there with a doctorate in mechanical engineering and plasma physics in 1971. For the next year Schneider held a postdoctoral research associateship at the Goddard Institute for Space Studies in New York City. He followed this position with a year-long fellowship at the National Center for Atmospheric Research in Boulder, Colorado, where he remained for the next twenty years, heading various research groups. During this time, Schneider married Cheryl Kay Hatter. Their wedding was on August 19, 1978, and they have two children, Rebecca Eden and Adam William. In 1992 Schneider joined the faculty at Stanford University.

Conducts Vital Research

A tireless researcher, Schneider has received numerous grants to study the earth's climate. His work has touched on climate modeling, the climatic effects of a nuclear war (known as nuclear winter), climatic impact on society, and ecological implications of climate change, particularly of the phenomenon described as the greenhouse effect. Carbon dioxide and water in the earth's atmosphere help keep heat from escaping into space and enable life to flourish; deforestation and atmospheric pollution—in particular, high levels of carbon dioxide—are thought to increase the natural "greenhouse effect" of the atmosphere and thus increase global temperatures.

With grant support from the federal government in the 1980s, Schneider worked extensively on the theory of nuclear winter. This theory deals with the possible cooling of the atmosphere should the detonations of nuclear weapons spew tons of dust and debris into the atmosphere, blocking the sun's rays and adversely affecting plant growth. Schneider's later work involves history and climate models. Very interested in policy issues, Schneider deals not only with science but also with politics. He has been called many times to testify before congressional committees and was a member of the Defense Science Board Task Force on Atmospheric Obscuration, and he also served as a consultant to the administrations of presidents Richard Nixon and Jimmy Carter.

Adopts Activist Stance

Schneider's experiences in Washington led him to believe that many scientists' concerns about possible climate-related crises were being ignored by shortsighted government officials. To bring climatological issues directly to the public, Schneider embarked on the additional career of scientific activist. He has, like most scientists, made the results of his research known in numerous scientific publications. Yet he has gone a step further and written several books geared to the layperson, among them *The Coevolution of Climate and Life,* written with Randi Londer, and *Global Warming: Are We Entering the Greenhouse Century?*

In the preface to *Global Warming,* which he dedicated to his children, Schneider explained the rationale behind his forays from the ivory towers of scientific research: "I believe that scientists have the obligation to explain to those who pay our salaries what we have learned about complex issues: what we think we know well, what we don't know, what we might be able to learn, when we might learn it, how much it might cost to learn, and, most importantly, what it might mean for civilization." Schneider continued, "This means explaining issues in plain language, using appropriate but familiar metaphors, and holding back nothing—that is, letting the public decide whether a certain amount of uncertainty or knowledge is sufficient for action." Although Schneider has been the object of criticism from academic colleagues for his efforts to popularize complicated and uncertain scientific concepts, he believes that his activist efforts are necessary. He has appeared on network nightly news programs, talk shows, and programs created by the Corporation for Public Broadcasting. He also acted as scientific adviser and script consultant for several episodes of the television series *Nova.* In addition, he has spread his message by editing the journal *Climatic Change* since 1975. As Schneider told *Contemporary Authors, New Revision Series,* "I intend to continue to study, write and speak on the urgent need for society to anticipate potential long-term consequences of its short-term policies with emphasis on issues with a technological component."

SELECTED WRITINGS BY SCHNEIDER:

Books

The Genesis Strategy: Climate and Global Survival, Plenum, 1976.

The Primordial Bond: Exploring Connections between Man and Nature through the Humanities and Sciences, Plenum, 1981.

The Coevolution of Climate and Life, Sierra Club, 1984.

Global Warming: Are We Entering the Greenhouse Century?, Sierra Club, 1989.

FURTHER READING:

Books

Contemporary Authors New Revision Series, Volume 12, Gale, 1984.

Schneider, Stephen H., *Global Warming: Are We Entering the Greenhouse Century?,* Sierra Club, 1989.

Periodicals

Schneider, Stephen H., *Earth Science,* spring, 1990, pp. 33–4.

———— , *New York Times,* September 1, 1981.

Smil, Vaclav, *Bulletin of the Atomic Scientists,* Heat, Little Light, June, 1990, p. 39.

———— , *Washington Post,* July 18, 1981.

Sketch by Jeanne M. Lesinski

Mogens Schou
1918–

Danish physician, psychiatrist, and psychopharmacologist

Mogens Schou is today's foremost exponent of lithium therapy in the treatment of manic-depressive disorder. Although the drug had been used to treat the manic, or "up" side of manic-depressive patients, it was Schou who insisted that the drug prevented recurrences of the depressive side as well, making it an optimum therapeutic solution for victims of the disease.

Mogens Abelin Schou, the second son of Dr. Hans Jacob Schou and Margrethe Brodersen, was born in Copenhagen on November 24, 1918. His father was medical superintendent of a large hospital for mental disorders and epilepsy in Dianalund. His mother was a pianist. After graduating from high school, Schou attended a Danish folk high school where he met his wife, Agnete Henriette Jessen. They married in 1943 and soon after began studies in their respective fields—medicine and teaching. Schou graduated from Copenhagen University Medical School in 1944 and undertook clinical training in psychiatry at Danish, Swedish,

and Norwegian hospitals. He received further training at the Institute of Cytophysiology in Copenhagen and the Department of Psychiatry at Columbia University, New York, and was a research fellow at the New York State Psychiatric Institute. He also studied at the Institute of Physiology at Aarhus University in Denmark. From 1956 to 1988 he headed the Psychopharmacology Research Unit at the Aarhus Institute of Psychiatry at the Psychiatric Hospital in Risskov. From 1965 to 1988 he served as professor (from 1971 full professor) of pharmacology at Aarhus University. Schou and his wife have four children.

Joins Aarhus Department of Psychiatry

In 1953 Schou joined the Department of Psychiatry at Aarhus University Psychiatric Hospital as a research associate specializing in biological psychiatry. Soon after his arrival, Schou's superior, Professor Erik Strömgen, brought to his attention the claims of Australian doctor John Cade that the drug lithium could be used to treat manic symptoms. During the mid-nineteenth century, lithium salts had been used to treat mood disorders in Denmark, but the drug was considered dangerous and in need of further study. Strömgen urged Schou to pursue the anti-manic claims for lithium as a research topic, an investigation which would spark a renaissance of lithium therapy in Denmark.

Conducts Clinical Trial to Test Lithium Claim

To test lithium's possible anti-manic properties, Schou set up a clinical trial in collaboration with Strömgen and N. Juel-Nielsen and H. Voldby, who were psychiatrists at the hospital. Published in 1954, their report verified the findings from Australia. Lithium had beneficial effects against mania in a high number of cases, and a switch from lithium to a placebo, or dummy tablet, had clinical consequences which verified these findings. This was done through the use of what is believed to be the first double-blind trial in psychopharmacology, in which neither the psychiatrists nor the manic patients knew who was to receive lithium and who was to receive the placebo. "I sat in the laboratory and flipped a coin to decide whether lithium or placebo should be used for the next patient for the next period, but I did not see the patients or participate in the clinical assessment, so the trial remained fully blind throughout," writes Schou in *The Neurosciences: Paths of Discovery II.*

The study also gave Schou an idea of lithium concentrations in the blood, as he took pains during the trials to keep accurate measurements. Finally Schou paid especially close attention to matters of side effects and toxic reactions during the trial. Taking the findings into consideration, Schou concluded that lithium therapy was of value in some cases of mania, but that it was a treatment to be dealt with cautiously, requiring careful clinical and biochemical monitoring.

Schou and his associates increased their data on lithium therapy over the next few years, and by 1955 they were able to report that of forty-eight patients treated with lithium alone, eighty-one percent showed significant clinical improvement. In 1959 he added an additional 119 patients to the total, of whom seventy-six percent had improved. Other research centers in France, Australia, England, Italy and Denmark were showing similar results. The combined improvement rate of these studies taken together was sixty-four percent, and although this was less than the result first presented by Schou, it indicated to him that lithium certainly had potential concerning anti-mania therapy. Working in a mental hospital, the Aarhus group, led by Mogens Schou, instituted a clinical approach with supporting animal work in the further study of lithium, particularly in lithium physiology.

Work in Anti-Manic Study Leads to Discovery Regarding Depression

Manic-depressive patients experience extreme mood swings, from mania to depression. Mania is characterized by easily aroused anger, increased mental speed, feelings of elation and sometimes violence, feelings of self-confidence and a lack of self-criticism. Patients often lack discrimination regarding their actions and may destroy their marriages and reputations and ruin themselves financially. The depressive side of the disease is marked by inhibition, extreme sadness, slow mental speed and a lack of self-confidence in which a patient may harbor such feelings of guilt and self-reproach that he or she considers or even commits suicide. This bipolar nature of the disease, together with an important factor of regular recurrence, is essential concerning its diagnosis.

Schou had verified that lithium therapy provided clinical improvement concerning the mania side of the disorder. At this point he took another look at the records of those treated with lithium over a two-year period and discovered that one of his patients had responded with not only a reduction in manic episodes, but with some dissipation of depressive episodes as well. He considered the possibility that although the symptoms of mania and depression were different, they often occurred together in the same patient and might have some factor in common regarding their control mechanisms. If, by acting on one of these mechanisms, lithium produced its therapeutic effect, then it was possible that the depression occurring in association with mania might also respond to lithium therapy. Schou then initiated another double-blind trial, but he later abandoned the study when, due to how it had been set up, it failed to show any clear evidence that depression responded to lithium.

Schou's interest in the treatment of manic-depression was due in large part to the fact that his younger brother suffered from the disorder on a regular basis, and from the age of twenty had experienced depressions every year. Electroconvulsive or "shock" therapy and anti-depressant drugs provided some temporary relief from current episodes, but did not stop the attacks, which came year after year, putting him out of work and devastating his family. Lithium therapy, started in the mid-sixties, freed Schou's brother from depressive episodes, in effect curing him of the disease.

Work with Lithium as Antidepressant Sparks Other Studies

Although Schou's test had failed to produce satisfactory results, two independent studies begun in 1957—one conducted by Poul Baastrup of Vordingborg, Denmark, the other by G. P. Hartigan of Canterbury, England—demonstrated that lithium had the potential to limit psychosis and block depression. When these results were brought to Schou's attention, he actively encouraged both scientists to bring these results to the attention of the public, as he had suspected that in some cases depressive states, as well as manic ones, might respond to lithium therapy. He began to work with Baastrup, who collected the clinical data and cooperated with Schou in interpreting it. This constituted a systematic, substantial study on lithium prophylaxis in which eighty-eight manic-depressive patients were observed for one to two years without lithium treatment and then given lithium continuously for one to five years. Baastrup and Schou found that the lithium treatment lessened the frequency and duration of both manic and depressive recurrences. The action of lithium blocked relapse in both states of the disease, and was called relapse-preventive, or prophylactic. Furthermore, they found lithium's prophylactic action effective also in patients who experienced depression only, without signs of mania.

The study, however, met with some criticism. A few psychiatrists felt that the study should have been conducted on a double-blind basis, in which Baastrup and Schou randomly administered a placebo to patients to find out if the lithium really worked, to eliminate the factors of chance or bias from the study. Yet the two scientists knew that this would mean the deliberate subjection of some patients to relapse, and, with a disease which often renders patients suicidal, the two were faced with a major ethical dilemma when contemplating a second study. This was especially difficult for Schou, whom the disease affected so personally. However, the two eventually decided to proceed with the double-blind study, but took extreme care in monitoring it. It showed conclusively that lithium, under strictly controlled circumstances, exerted a prophylactic action in patients with depression and with manic-depression.

In 1967 Baastrup and Schou drew on these findings as part of a detailed and thorough review of lithium usage that extended the use of lithium worldwide. Other clinical reports were published that confirmed Baastrup and Schou's findings. In 1987 Schou received the Albert Lasker Clinical Medical Research Award for his work on lithium treatment of manic-depressive illness, especially pertaining to the discovery of its relapse-preventive action. He has received innumerable other scientific awards and honors and has served in many honorary offices. He also has published numerous books and articles in many languages on the subject of lithium.

SELECTED WRITINGS BY SCHOU:

Books

The Neurosciences: Paths of Discovery II, Phases in the Development of Lithium Treatment in Psychiatry, edited by Fred Samson and George Adelman, Birkhauser, 1992, pp. 149-66.

Lithium Treatment of Manic-Depressive Illness: A Practical Guide, Karger, 5th ed., 1993.

Periodicals

Journal of Neurological Neurosurgical Psychiatry, The Treatment of Manic Psychoses by the Administration of Lithium Salts, Volume 17, 1954, pp. 250–60.

British Journal of Psychiatry, Normothymotics, 'Mood Normalizers': Are Lithium and the Imipramine Drugs Specific for Affective Disorders?, Volume 109, 1963, pp. 803–09.

Archives of General Psychiatry, Lithium as Prophylactic Agent: Its Effect Against Recurrent Depressions and Manic-Depressive Psychosis, Volume 16, 1967, pp. 162–72.

Lancet, Prophylactic Lithium: Double-Blind Discontinuation in Manic-Depressive and Recurrent Depressive Disorders, Volume 2, 1970, pp. 326–30.

Journal of Psychiatric Resources, Effects of Long-Term Lithium Treatment on Kidney Function: An Overview, Volume 22, 1988, pp. 287–96.

FURTHER READING:

Books

Johnson, F. Neil, *The History of Lithium Therapy,* Macmillan, 1984.

Periodicals

Baastrup, P. C., *Comprehensive Psychiatry,* The Use of Lithium in Manic-Depressive Psychosis, Volume 5, 1964, pp. 396-408.

Blackwell, B., *Medical Counterpoint,* Lithium: Prophylactic or Panacea?, November 1969, pp. 52–9.

Cade, J. F. J., *Medical Journal of Australia,* Lithium Salts in the Treatment of Psychotic Excitement, Volume 36, 1949, pp. 349–52.

Hartigan, G. P., *British Journal of Psychiatry,* The Use of Lithium Salts in Affective Disorder, Volume 109, 1963, pp. 810–14.

Sketch by Janet Kieffer Kelley

J. Robert Schrieffer
1931–
American physicist

As a young doctoral student, J. Robert Schrieffer was working under Nobel laureate **John Bardeen** at the University of Illinois when, together with **Leon Cooper**, the three men developed a theory of the superconductivity of metals. Known as the BCS theory (the initials of their last names), it explains how certain metals and alloys lose all resistance to electrical current when chilled to extremely low temperatures. This means that once a superconducting magnet is set in motion, it will flow forever with no loss of power. This proved to be one of the major discoveries of twentieth-century physics, and the three shared the 1972 Nobel Prize in physics.

Known as an "unassuming man with a quip for any occasion," according to a *New York Times* profile written on the occasion of his winning the Nobel Prize, John Robert Schrieffer was born in Oak Park, Illinois, on May 31, 1931, to John and Louise Anderson Schrieffer. He received his B.S. in 1953 from the Massachusetts Institute of Technology and then went on to the University of Illinois, where he began his work with Bardeen and Cooper. He received his M.S. in 1954 and his Ph.D. in 1957.

The practical implications of the theoretical work Schrieffer did on superconductivity are numerous. "Superconductivity is a most accurate determinant of the measure of electrical potential, voltage," said Dr. Erik Rudberg, secretary of the Swedish Royal Academy of Sciences, when he announced the Nobel Prize. "The application of superconductivity is important not only for scientific instruments, but also for accelerators and motors." As a result of this theory, certain alloys have been developed that are superconductors at less extreme temperatures. These alloys can be used, for example, in underground cables to store and transmit electricity without the loss of power characteristic of overhead electrical wires.

Authors Work on Superconductivity Theory

Schrieffer began his teaching career as an assistant professor at the University of Chicago in 1957, returned to the University of Illinois as an associate professor from 1960 to 1962, and then moved to a position as full professor at the University of Pennsylvania. After publication in 1964 of his book, *Theory of Superconductivity,* he was named the Amanda Wood Professor of Physics at the University of Pennsylvania, a position he held until 1979. In 1980 Schrieffer took a position at the University of California in Santa Barbara, where he was named Essan Khashoggi Professor of Physics in 1985. He also was director of the Institute of Theoretical Physics there from 1984 to 1989. In 1992, he became a professor at Florida State University in

Tallahassee and chief scientist at the National High Magnetic Field Laboratory.

Throughout these years he continued to focus his research on particle physics, metal impurities, spin fluctuations, and chemisorption. He has been honored with numerous awards besides the Nobel Prize, among them the Comstock Award from the National Academy of Sciences, which he received in 1968, and the National Medal of Science, which he received in 1984. He has been known to speak out on social and political issues. At the time he won the Nobel, he was critical of science's focus on the arms and space race. "The crying needs of society and of science itself can use the manpower and the money," he told the *New York Times.*

Schrieffer was married in 1960 to Anne Grete Thomsen. They have two daughters and a son.

SELECTED WRITINGS BY SCHRIEFFER:

Books

Theory of Superconductivity, W. A. Benjamin, 1964, revised edition, 1983.

Periodicals

Physical Review, Microscopic Theory of Superconductivity, Volume 106, 1957, pp. 162–64.
Physica, Recent Advances in the Theory of Superconductivity, Volume 26, 1960, pp. S1-S16.

FURTHER READING:

Periodicals

New York Times, October 21, 1972, pp. 1, 14.

Sketch by Dorothy Barnhouse

Erwin Schrödinger
1887–1961
Austrian physicist

Erwin Schrödinger shared the 1933 Nobel Prize for physics with English physicist **Paul Dirac** in recognition of his development of a wave equation describing the behavior of an electron in an atom. His theory was a consequence of French theoretical physicist **Louis Victor de Broglie**'s hypothesis that particles of matter might have properties that can be described by using wave functions.

Erwin Schrödinger

Schrödinger's wave equation provided a sound theoretical basis for the existence of electron orbitals (energy levels), which had been postulated on empirical grounds by Danish physicist **Niels Bohr** in 1913.

Schrödinger was born in Vienna, Austria, on August 12, 1887. His father, Rudolf Schrödinger, enjoyed a wide range of interests, including painting and botany, and owned a successful oil cloth factory. Schrödinger's mother was the daughter of Alexander Bauer, a professor at the Technische Hochschule. For the first eleven years of his life, Schrödinger was taught at home. Though a tutor came on a regular basis, Schrödinger's most important instructor was his father, whom he described as a "friend, teacher, and tireless partner in conversation," as Armin Hermann quoted in *Dictionary of Scientific Biography.* From his father he also developed a wide range of academic interests, including not only mathematics and science but also grammar and poetry. In 1898 he entered the Akademische Gymnasium in Vienna to complete his precollege studies.

Hasenöhrl Inspires Early Interest in Physics

Having graduated from the Gymnasium in 1906, Schrödinger entered the University of Vienna. By all accounts, the most powerful influence on him there was Friedrich Hasenöhrl, a brilliant young physicist who was killed in World War I a decade later. Schrödinger was an avid student of Hasenöhrl's for the full five years he was enrolled at Vienna. He held his teacher in such high esteem that he was later to remark at the 1933 Nobel Prize ceremonies that, if Hasenöhrl had not been killed in the war, it would have been Hasenöhrl, not Schrödinger, being honored in Stockholm.

Schrödinger was awarded his Ph.D. in physics in 1910 and was immediately offered a position at the university's Second Physics Institute, where he carried out research on a number of problems involving, among other topics, magnetism and dielectrics. He held this post until the outbreak of World War I, at which time he became an artillery officer assigned to the Italian front. As the war drew to a close, Schrödinger looked forward to an appointment as professor of theoretical physics at the University of Czernowitz, located in modern-day Ukraine. However, those plans were foiled with the disintegration of the Austro-Hungarian Empire, and Schrödinger was forced to return to the Second Physics Institute.

During his second tenure at the institute, on April 6, 1920, Schrödinger married Annemarie Bertel, whom he had met prior to the war. Not long after his marriage, Schrödinger accepted an appointment as assistant to Max Wien in Jena, but remained there only four months. He then moved on to the Technische Hochschule in Stuttgart. Once again, he stayed only briefly—a single semester—before resigning his post and going on to the University of Breslau. He received yet another opportunity to move after being at the university for only a short time: he was offered the chair in theoretical physics at the University of Zürich in late 1921.

Work at Zürich Results in Wave Equation

The six years that Schrödinger spent at Zürich were probably the most productive of his scientific career. At first, his work dealt with fairly traditional topics; one paper of particular practical interest reported his studies on the relationship between red-green and blue-yellow color blindness. Schrödinger's first interest in the problem of wave mechanics did not arise until 1925. A year earlier, de Broglie had announced his hypothesis of the existence of matter waves, a concept that few physicists were ready to accept. Schrödinger read about de Broglie's hypothesis in a footnote to a paper by American physicist **Albert Einstein**, one of the few scientists who did believe in de Broglie's ideas.

Schrödinger began to consider the possibility of expressing the movement of an electron in an atom in terms of a wave. He adopted the premise that an electron can travel around the nucleus only in a standing wave (that is, in a pattern described by a whole number of wavelengths). He looked for a mathematical equation that would describe the position of such "permitted" orbits. By January of 1926, he was ready to publish the first of four papers describing the results of this research. He had found a second order partial differential equation that met the conditions of his initial assumptions. The equation specified certain orbitals (energy levels) outside the nucleus where an electron wave with a whole number of wavelengths could be found. These orbitals corresponded precisely to the orbitals that Bohr had

proposed on purely empirical grounds thirteen years earlier. The wave equation provided a sound theoretical basis for an atomic model that had originally been derived purely on the basis of experimental observations. In addition, the wave equation allowed the theoretical calculation of energy changes that occur when an electron moves from one permitted orbital to a higher or lower one. These energy changes conformed to those actually observed in spectroscopic measurements. The equation also explained why electrons cannot exist in regions between Bohr orbitals since only nonwhole number wavelengths (and, therefore, nonpermitted waves) can exist there.

After producing unsatisfactory results using relativistic corrections in his computations, Schrödinger decided to work with nonrelativistic electron waves in his derivations. The results he obtained in this way agreed with experimental observations and he announced them in his early 1926 papers. The equation he published in these papers became known as "the Schrödinger wave equation" or simply "the wave equation." The wave equation was the second theoretical mechanism proposed for describing electrons in an atom, the first being German physicist **Werner Karl Heisenberg**'s matrix mechanics. For most physicists, Schrödinger's approach was preferable since it lent itself to a physical, rather than strictly mathematical, interpretation. As it turned out, Schrödinger was soon able to show that wave mechanics and matrix mechanics are mathematically identical.

Rise of Nazis Forces Schrödinger to Oxford and Dublin

In 1927 Schrödinger was presented with a difficult career choice. He was offered the prestigious chair of theoretical physics at the University of Berlin left open by German physicist **Max Planck**'s retirement. The position was arguably the most desirable in all of theoretical physics, at least in the German-speaking world; Berlin was the center of the newest and most exciting research in the field. Though Schrödinger disliked the hurried environment of a large city, preferring the peacefulness of his native Austrian Alps, he did accept the position.

Hermann quoted Schrödinger as calling the next six years a "very beautiful teaching and learning period." That period came to an ugly conclusion, however, with the rise of National Socialism in Germany. Having witnessed the dismissal of outstanding colleagues by the new regime, Schrödinger decided to leave Germany and accept an appointment at Magdalene College, Oxford, in England. In the same week he took up his new post he was notified that he had been awarded the 1933 Nobel Prize for physics with Dirac.

Schrödinger's stay at Oxford lasted only three years; then, he decided to take an opportunity to return to his native Austria and accept a position at the University of Graz. Unfortunately, he was dismissed from the university shortly after German leader Adolf Hitler's invasion of Austria in 1938, but Eamon de Valera, the prime minister and a mathematician, was able to have the University of Dublin establish a new Institute for Advanced Studies and secure an appointment for Schrödinger there.

In September 1939, Schrödinger left Austria with few belongings and no money and emigrated to Ireland. He remained in Dublin for the next seventeen years, during which time he turned to philosophical questions such as the theoretical foundations of physics and the relationship between the physical and biological sciences. During this period, he wrote one of the most influential books in twentieth-century science, *What Is Life?* In this book, Schrödinger argued that the fundamental nature of living organisms could probably be studied and understood in terms of physical principles, particularly those of quantum mechanics. The book was later to be read by and become a powerful influence on the thought of the founders of modern molecular biology.

After World War II, Austria attempted to lure Schrödinger home. As long as the nation was under Soviet occupation, however, he resisted offers to return. Finally, in 1956, he accepted a special chair position at the University of Vienna and returned to the city of his birth. He became ill about a year after he settled in Vienna, however, and never fully recovered his health. He died on January 4, 1961, in the Alpine town of Alpbach, Austria, where he is buried.

Schrödinger received a number of honors and awards during his lifetime, including election into the Royal Society, the Prussian Academy of Sciences, the Austrian Academy of Sciences, and the Pontifical Academy of Sciences. He also retained his love for the arts throughout his life, becoming proficient in four modern languages in addition to Greek and Latin. He published a book of poetry and became skilled as a sculptor.

SELECTED WRITINGS BY SCHRÖDINGER:

Books

Abhandlungen zür Wellenmechanik, [Leipzig], 1927, second edition, 1928.

What Is Life?, Cambridge University Press, 1945.

Space-time Structure, Cambridge University Press, 1950.

Science and Humanism, Cambridge University Press, 1952.

Statistical Thermodynamics, Cambridge University Press, 1952.

Nature and the Greeks, Cambridge University Press, 1954.

Expanding Universes, Cambridge University Press, 1956.

Mind and Matter, Cambridge University Press, 1958.

Einstein, Lorentz, Briefe zur Wellenmechanik, [Vienna], 1963.

FURTHER READING:

Books

Biographical Memoirs of Fellows of the Royal Society, Volume 7, Royal Society (London), 1961, pp. 221–28.

Dictionary of Scientific Biography, Volume 12, Scribner, 1975, pp. 217–23.

Weber, Robert L., *Pioneers of Science: Nobel Prize Winners in Physics,* American Institute of Physics, 1980, pp. 99–100.

Sketch by David E. Newton

Richard Evans Schultes
1915–
American ethnobotanist

R ichard Evans Schultes is a pioneer in ethnobotany, the study of the relationship between people and their plant environment. He also contributed extensively to existing knowledge about the use of plants by humans, especially in the fields of medicine and narcotics, by combining a traditional background in botanical taxonomy with the growing field of economic botany.

Schultes was born January 12, 1915, in Boston, Massachusetts, to Otto Richard and Maude Beatrice (Bagley) Schultes. He attended Harvard University, receiving a bachelor of arts in 1937 with Phi Beta Kappa honors, a master's degree the next year, and a doctorate in 1941. On March 26, 1959, Schultes married Dorothy Crawford McNeil; together they had three children, Richard Evans II, and twins, Neil Parker and Alexandra Ames.

Upon receiving his doctorate, Schultes joined the staff of the Harvard Botanical Museum and would later become its director, a position he held from 1967 to 1985. At the museum, Schultes wrote and edited numerous leaflets on botanical subjects. While curator of the Orchid Herbarium of Oakes Ames at Harvard, he wrote *Generic Names of Orchids,* a book giving the etymological history of some 1,250 generic names of Orchidaceae, with morphological characteristics of each plant, along with its geographic distribution. Meanwhile, he served as a Harvard University professor from 1968 until his retirement in 1985. He has also worked in the taxonomy of rubber plants.

Investigation of Jungle Plants Leads to Discoveries

Schultes explored jungles of the northwest Amazon from 1941 to 1954 and acquired firsthand knowledge of the indigenous flora there. During this pivotal time in his career, he collected and taxonomically catalogued about 24,000 specimens. By enlisting the aid of the Makunas, Puinave, and Tanimuka Indians of the region, he investigated tropical rainforest areas in search of plants used by the natives as medicines, narcotics, and poisons. He gained the Indians' confidence by his serious devotion to plant collecting and by participating in dances and rituals. He even sampled their botanical preparations personally, and later wrote in *Lloydia* that on one occasion, after sampling a narcotic snuff prepared in the Amazon, he was "ill in [his] hammock for several days, so strong was the snuff."

Another time, despite serious leg ulcers resulting from exposure to flooded tropical forests, he forsook the clean accommodations of a Columbian river gun-boat to accompany a native on a three-day journey upstream and through flooded swamp forest to search out an undescribed species known to the Indians as yoco, which was later shown to be rich in caffeine. In another incident, his respect for Indian customs enabled him to do what he called "fascinating detective work" in uncovering a plant source of curare, used by the natives in preparing their poison arrows.

During the 1960s, when drug use proliferated in American society, Schultes drew on his interest and experience in ethnobotany to make detailed studies of hallucinogens. He explained that his research in the Amazon showed that primitive societies used some plant species to induce visual, auditory and other hallucinations, which were considered to have religious significance. On the basis of their unearthly effects, these plants were considered sacred by the natives, who included them in their rituals. By contrast, as he read about the use, misuse, and abuse of drugs in modern civilized society, he felt the time had come to consolidate existing knowledge about hallucinogens. Also, Schultes expected that scientific interest in these substances might lead to the discovery of drugs which could be useful in psychiatry and as possible tools in explaining some types of mental abnormalities. In 1969 the government of Colombia recognized Schultes's scientific contributions by bestowing upon him the Orden de la Victoria Regia.

Campaigns for Preservation of Rain Forests

In his analysis of psychoactive plant species, Schultes found they were concentrated mostly among fungi and angiosperms. He classified these species, mentioned their location, identified the biochemical nature of their compounds, and explained their physiological and psychological effects. He described two broad groups of organic substances having hallucinogenic properties, nitrogenous and nonnitrogenous. Nitrogenous species include fungi, such as psychedelic mushrooms and plants, which are used to produce mescaline and cocaine. As an example of one of the most important nonnitrogenous hallucinogens, he described in detail the *Cannabis* species (the source of marijuana) and other narcotic products. He wrote that of the total number of existing plant species, estimated as ranging from 400,000 to 800,000, only sixty are known to be sources of hallucino-

gens—twenty of which can be considered important—with most occurring in the New World. He stated that the destruction of tropical rainforests and the disappearance of primitive cultures were disturbing threats to our knowledge of yet-unknown hallucinogenic species. For his efforts in promoting tropical rain forest conservation by demonstrating, through ethnobotany, the value of tropical species to industry and medicine, he was awarded the Tyler Prize for Environmental Achievement from the University of Southern California in 1987.

Throughout his career, Schultes has pursued many fields of professional activity in addition to his positions at Harvard. Respected as an authority in economic botany, at various times he has served as a visiting professor and consultant in universities, symposia, and pharmaceutical companies with international itineraries. He has written a number of books expounding his knowledge of hallucinogenic drugs, economic botany, taxonomy of rubber plants, orchids, the Amazon tropical rain forest, and the Harvard Botanical Museum's collection of the famous Blaschka glass flowers. A contributor of four-hundred-and-fifty articles and reviews to various books and science journals, Schultes also served as editor of *Chronica Botanica* from 1947 to 1952 and *Economic Botany* from 1962 to 1979. He has also served as an editorial board member of *Lloydia, Journal of Psychedelic Drugs, Journal of Latin American Folklore, Altered States of Consciousness,* and other journals. In addition, Schultes was called upon to contribute to *Encyclopedia Britannica, Encyclopedia of Biological Sciences, Encyclopedia of Biochemistry, International Encyclopedia of Veterinary Medicine,* and the *McGraw-Hill Yearbook of Science and Technology.* He has been elected a member of scientific and academic societies throughout the world, and his travels have taken him to Brazil, Colombia, Switzerland, Hawaii, Berlin, Stockholm, Canada, India, Peru, England, Sri Lanka, Ecuador, Omen, Italy, and Malaysia.

In addition to his other recognitions, Schultes was named Distinguished Economic Botanist by the Society for Economic Botany in 1979. He has also received various honorary degrees, as well as the Lindbergh Award, 1981; the Cross of Boyaca from the Republic of Colombia, 1983; the Gold Medal of the World Wide Fund for Nature, 1984; the Gold Medal of Sigma Xi, 1985; the Botanical Society of America Merit Award, 1988; the Linnean Medal, 1992; and the Harvard University Medal, 1992.

SELECTED WRITINGS BY SCHULTES:

Books

Economic Botany of the Kiowa Indians, Harvard University Botanical Museum, 1941, AMS Press, 1981.
Native Orchids of Trinidad and Tobago, Pergamon, 1960.
Generic Names of Orchids—Their Origin and Meaning, Academic Press, 1963.

The Botany and Chemistry of Hallucinogens, Thomas, 1973, revised edition, 1980.
Hallucinogenic Plants, Western Publishing, 1976.
Plants of the Gods: Origins of Hallucinogenic Use, McGraw-Hill, 1979.
The Glass Flowers at Harvard, Dutton, 1982.

Periodicals

Lloydia, The Role of the Ethnobotanist in the Search for New Medicinal Plants, December, 1962, pp. 257–66.
Lloydia, The Search for New Natural Hallucinogens, Volume 29, 1966, pp. 293–308.
Science, Hallucinogens of Plant Origin, January, 1969, pp. 245–54.
Annual Review of Plant Physiology, The Botanical and Chemical Distribution of Hallucinogens, 1970, pp. 571–98.

FURTHER READING:

Books

Contemporary Authors, New Revisions Series, Volume 25, Gale, 1989, pp. 397–99.

Sketch by Maurice Bleifeld

Melvin Schwartz
1932–
American physicist

Melvin Schwartz's research and experimentation in the weak force of the four fundamental forces of nature resulted in the proof of the existence of the neutrino (a particle of zero-rest mass), and the Nobel Prize-winning discovery and definition of the two existing types of neutrinos: the electron neutrino, and the muon neutrino.

Schwartz was born in New York City on November 2, 1932, to Harry and Hannah Shulman Schwartz. Desperately poor as a result of the Great Depression, his parents "worked extraordinarily hard," Schwartz was later to say, as quoted in *Nobel Prize Winners Supplement,* to provide some level of "economic stability" in their lives. He entered the world-famous Bronx High School of Science in 1944 at the age of twelve, and graduated five years later. By that time, he had made up his mind to become a theoretical physicist. That decision having been made, his choice for a college education was easy. At the time New York City's own Columbia University had, as Schwartz later characterized it,

a physics department that was "unmatched by any in the world."

Attacks the Problem of the Weak Force

Schwartz earned his bachelor's degree in mathematics and physics in 1953. That same year, Schwartz was married to Marilyn Fenster, with whom he later had two daughters, Diane and Betty Lynne, and a son, David. He began his doctoral studies under the direction of **Jack Steinberger**, whom Schwartz has called "the best experimental physicist I have ever been associated with, and the best teacher," as quoted by Bertram Schwarzschild in *Physics Today.* It was from Steinberger that Schwartz gained his special interest in particle physics, an interest that was to dominate much of his research over the next four decades.

Schwartz was awarded his Ph.D. in physics in 1959 and then joined the faculty at Columbia. Within a year, an event was to take place that would dramatically alter Schwartz's future. During an afternoon coffee hour in November 1959, at Columbia's Pupin Laboratory, a group of physicists discussed the problems of studying the weak force, one of the four fundamental forces of nature (the others being gravitation, electromagnetism and the strong force). **Tsung-Dao Lee**, a theoretical physicist, challenged his colleagues to find a way to obtain additional empirical evidence on the weak force. The challenge at first seemed an enormous one, since at atomic dimensions, the weak force is much weaker—and therefore much harder to observe—than are the electromagnetic and strong forces. According to Schwarzschild, Schwartz later described his feeling about Lee's challenge as one of "hopelessness. There seemed to be no decent way," he said, "of exploring the terribly small cross-sections characteristic of weak interactions." This feeling lasted less than twenty-four hours, as that evening, Schwartz suddenly had the answer. "It was incredibly simple," he decided. "All you had to do was use neutrinos."

Neutrinos turned out to be the perfect tool with which to study the weak force. Because these tiny particles are uncharged and have very small mass, they are essentially unaffected by electromagnetic or strong forces. When a beam of neutrinos passes through matter, the only interactions it undergoes are those involving the weak force.

Confirms the Existence of Two Kinds of Neutrinos

To work out the details of the neutrino/weak force experiment, Schwartz met with his former doctoral advisor, Steinberger, and Columbia colleague Leon Max Lederman. The three devised a method for generating an intense beam of neutrinos using the Brookhaven National Laboratory's new 30-billion-electron-volt alternating gradient synchrotron (AGS). Proton beams from the AGS would be directed at a target of beryllium metal. The collision between beam and target would tear apart beryllium atoms and release an avalanche of subatomic particles, neutrinos among them. The neutrinos thus produced would then be directed through a block of steel where at least some would interact with atoms by means of the weak force.

One issue involved in the experiment was the nature of the neutrinos to be used, as relatively little was known about these particles. When the neutrino was discovered, physicists assumed that it existed in only one form, the form now known as the electron neutrino. For various theoretical reasons, however, Columbia theoretical physicist Gerald Feinberg posed the possibility in 1958 that a second neutrino, associated with mu mesons (muons), which are particles of a different weight, might also exist. The Schwartz-Steinberger-Lederman experiment was designed to determine also the validity of Feinberg's hypothesis.

By September 1961, the experiment was under way. Eight months later, an estimated 10^{14} neutrinos had been produced, of which fifty-one interactions with matter were observed. In every one of these cases, the interaction was such that it confirmed the existence of a muon neutrino distinct from the electron neutrino. Feinberg's hypothesis had been confirmed. The 1988 Nobel Prize awarded to Schwartz, Steinberger, and Lederman recognized not only the discovery of the muon neutrino, but also the development of a technique that, the Nobel committee said, promised to provide "entirely new opportunities for research into the innermost structure and dynamics of matter."

Schwartz resigned his post at Columbia in 1966 in order to take a position as professor of physics at Stanford University, where the new 2-mile long linear accelerator was available for his research. He remained at Stanford until 1979 when he decided to establish his own software development business, Digital Pathways, Inc. After dividing his time between Stanford and Digital for four years, he resigned the former post and became a full-time business man. In 1991 Schwartz returned to the academic world by accepting the post of associate director of high energy and nuclear physics at the Brookhaven National Laboratory. Schwartz is a member of the National Academy of Sciences and is a fellow of the American Physical Society, which awarded him the Hughes Prize in 1964.

SELECTED WRITINGS BY SCHWARTZ:

Books

Principles of Electrodynamics, McGraw-Hill, 1972.

Periodicals

Physical Review Letters, Observation of High-Energy Neutrino Reactions and the Existence of Two Kinds of Neutrinos, Volume 9, 1961, p. 36.
Physical Review Letters, Search for Intermediate Bosons, Volume 15, 1965, p. 42.

FURTHER READING:

Books

Nobel Prize Winners Supplement 1987–1991, H. W. Wilson, 1992, pp. 124–26.

Periodicals

Schwarzschild, Bertram, *Physics Today,* Physics Nobel Prize to Lederman, Schwartz and Steinberger, January 1989, pp. 17–20.
Sutton, Christine, Ian Anderson, and Christopher Joyce, *New Scientist,* When Particle Physics Was Still Fun, October 29, 1988, p. 30.
Waldrop, M. Mitchell, *Science,* A Nobel Prize for the Two-Neutrino Experiment, November 4, 1988, pp. 669–70.

Sketch by David E. Newton

John Henry Schwarz
1941–
American theoretical physicist

Murray Gell-Mann, the Nobel-Prize winning theorist who described and named quarks, said in 1985 of superstring theory—the main work of John H. Schwarz—that a version of it would someday be understood as the theory underlying the whole universe. "It's *the* candidate," he said.

The story of superstrings begins with string theory, an attempt to construct a theory of nuclear forces. While trying to overcome some of the difficulties of this approach, Pierre Ramond, André Neveu, and Schwarz combined string theory and another idea, known as supersymmetry, in 1971. Even in this modified form there remained an another apparent difficulty for the theory; it predicted a kind of zero-mass particle that was not possible for nuclear forces. In 1974, however, Schwarz and coworker Joël Scherk showed that the zero-mass particle had the right properties to be the particle that transmits the gravitational force, known as the graviton. This particle, although not yet observed, is thought to exist. At that point, string theory graduated from being a theory of strong nuclear forces only to being a theory candidate for a unified theory of all fundamental particles and gravity. Schwarz introduced the term *superstring* in 1982 to describe theories that combine strings and supersymmetry.

One problem with early superstring theories was that the most likely versions showed mathematical inconsistencies, called *anomalies,* when applied to quantum theory. Superstring unification did not become popular until Schwarz and another collaborator, Michael Green, showed in 1984 that there was a subtle mechanism that causes the anomalies to cancel. This mechanism only worked for two choices of symmetry structures. Schwarz and Green also showed that one of these structures seemed promising as a basis for a realistic model of particle interactions. Almost immediately, superstring theory became a part of mainstream theoretical physics.

Since 1994 there has been another period of dramatic progress. What once appeared to be five different superstring theories are actually different realizations of a unique underlying concept, which has been named M theory. Spinoffs of M theory have brought about deeper understanding of black holes and of supersymmetric versions of quantum theory. Schwarz and many other physicists believe that M theory is a conceptual revolution as profound as those associated with relativity and quantum theory.

John Henry Schwarz was born on November 22, 1941, in a hospital in North Adams, Massachusetts, near to his parent's home in Williamstown, where his father managed a branch of the company now known as Agfa-Gevaert. John's parents were both Hungarians from a Jewish background. His father, George Schwarz, was a research chemist specializing in photographic processes, and his mother, Madeline "Magda" (Haberfeld) Schwarz, was trained as a physicist. Both parents received Ph.D.s from the University of Vienna, where they met. They and John's elder sister Mimi had been living in Antwerp, Belgium, when the Germans invaded in May, 1940. After some narrow escapes, the Schwarz family reached the United States a year before John was born.

Schwarz's family moved to Glen Head, Long Island, New York in 1951, where Schwarz graduated in the first class of North Shore High School. Schwarz entered Harvard University in Cambridge, Massachusetts, where he got his A.B. in mathematics in 1962. A National Science Foundation fellowship helped Schwarz obtain a Ph.D. in physics at the University of California, Berkeley, in 1966, from which he returned east to teach physics and continue his research at Princeton University in New Jersey. He began working on string theory in 1969 while at Princeton.

In 1972 Schwarz headed back west to the California Institute of Technology, which has been his base ever since. Currently Schwarz is the Harold Brown Professor of Theoretical Physics at Caltech. One of his main retreats from Caltech has been a summer program at the Aspen Center for Physics in Colorado. His breakthrough with Green came at Aspen; it was in Aspen on July 11, 1986, that Schwarz married Patricia Moyle, whom he had met a year and a half before at a physics conference that they both attended in Jerusalem.

The theory of superstrings is still being developed by the continuing work of Schwarz and other theoreticians, but its goals are already reasonably clear: to explain the origin of the forces and subatomic particles observed in nature, including their masses and other properties. They also hope to understand the structure of space and time and to explain the origin of the universe. Their theoretical structures so far resemble reality in many ways, making scientists optimistic that superstring theory will eventually succeed in these goals. Because of this broad program, superstring theory is sometimes labeled a "theory of everything," although Schwarz does not like this label.

The underlying nature of superstring theory can only be understood through its mathematics, but the superstring description of reality can be described roughly as follows. The fundamental entities from which everything is built are very short curves, or strings, with one dimension-length-instead of pointlike particles. The strings are typically as short compared to an atom as an atom is compared to the solar system. Some strings have ends while others form loops. The strings exist in ten dimensions, including the three familiar space dimensions of length, width, and height, a time dimension, and six other space dimensions that must be wound up so tightly that we do not observe them. Strings interact by joining or splitting. This can be described by a two-dimensional surface in spacetime called the *worldsheet* of the string. Such surfaces are classified and studied by known mathematical techniques. The view of superstrings just described is the one technically called *perturbative* superstring theory. M theory and other newer versions also employ additional methods, and sometimes even an eleventh dimension.

Schwarz's work has been recognized by the MacArthur Foundation with one of its "genius grants" for the period 1987-1992, which are awarded to encourage the brightest and most creative young people by giving them a large measure of financial freedom. In 1989 Schwarz received the Dirac Medal, and in 1997 he was elected to the U.S. National Academy of Sciences.

SELECTED WRITINGS BY SCHWARZ:

Books

(With Edward Witten and Michael B. Green) *Superstring Theory*. 2 volumes. New York: Cambridge University Press, 1988.

Periodicals

(With A. Neveu) "Factorizable Dual Models of Pions." *Nuclear Physics* B31 (1971): 86-112.
(With J. Scherk) "Dual Models for Nonhadrons." *Nuclear Physics* B81 (1974): 118-44.
(With M. B. Green) "Anomaly Cancellations in Supersymmetric D=10 Gauge Theory and Superstring Theory." *Physics Letters* 149B (1984): 117-22.
"Lectures on Superstring and M Theory Dualities." *Nuclear Physics B (Proceeding Supplement)* 55B (1997): 1-32.

FURTHER READING:

Books

Crease, Robert, and Charles C. Mann. *The Second Creation*. New York: Macmillan, 1986.

Weinberg, Steven. *Dreams of a Final Theory.* New York: Vintage Books, 1994.

Sketch by Bryan Bunch

Julian Schwinger
1918–1994
American physicist

Julian Schwinger

American physicist Julian Schwinger worked primarily to develop a quantum theory of radiation. As a theorist, he produced mathematical frameworks that showed the relationships between charged particles and electromagnetic fields, and his equations eventually united relativity and quantum theory. In recognition of this work, Schwinger received the National Medal of Science in 1964 and the Nobel Prize for physics in 1965, which he shared with American theoretical physicist **Richard P. Feynman** and Japanese physicist **Sin-Itiro Tomonaga**.

Julian Seymour Schwinger was born on February 12, 1918, in the Jewish Harlem section of New York City. His father was Benjamin Schwinger, a garment manufacturer, and his mother was Belle (Rosenfeld) Schwinger. Julian was the younger of two brothers. As a child, Schwinger had an insatiable appetite for science. He became interested by reading popular scientific magazines. When he entered high school, he had already decided to study physics. He had read all that the *Encyclopedia Britannica* offered in physics, and he scoured the New York Public libraries for all the books he could find on mathematics and physics, starting at the uptown branches and methodically working his way down to the main branch. He also combed used bookstores for texts in mathematics and physics.

Schwinger was known to be very shy, but he became a member of the world of adults at a very young age. He skipped three grades in high school and graduated at the age of 14. While he was still in high school, Schwinger studied scientific papers about quantum mechanics by the English physicist **Paul Dirac** as they appeared in the *Proceedings of the Royal Society of London*. Schwinger would later base his mathematical work in quantum electrodynamics on Dirac's theories.

Schwinger started his undergraduate studies at the College of the City of New York, where he began writing papers on theoretical physics. One of these papers was on quantum mechanics and was published in the *Physical Review*. It so impressed Isador Issac Rabi, a physicist at Columbia University, that he helped Schwinger to get a scholarship at Columbia. While at Columbia, Schwinger was interested almost solely in science to the neglect of his other classes, particularly English composition. Were it not for Rabi's intervention, Schwinger would have been expelled from Columbia. He excelled in physics, however, and often served as a substitute lecturer in quantum mechanics. Schwinger graduated from Columbia in 1936 at the age of 17. Three years later at Columbia he earned his Ph.D. degree.

Works on Atomic Bomb and Radar

After Columbia, Schwinger continued his research at the University of California under **J. Robert Oppenheimer**. In 1941 he joined Purdue University as an instructor and left there in 1943 as an assistant professor. In 1943 he went to the Metallurgical Laboratory at the University of Chicago to assist in developing the atomic bomb. In the same year he joined the radiation laboratory at the Massachusetts Institute of Technology, where he worked on microwave problems and helped to improve radar systems.

During these early years of moving from one position to another, his reputation for maintaining nocturnal working habits and sleeping until the afternoons preceded him. But it was rarely an issue. In 1945 he became an associate professor at Harvard University, and in 1947 he was made one of the youngest full professors in the university's history. In addition to his research in theoretical physics, Schwinger also distinguished himself in his presentations in scientific journals and in lecture halls. His published papers were considered exemplars for the scientific community.

In the lecture hall Schwinger's presentations often drew applause, a rare response from a scientific audience. He gave his lectures extemporaneously, with little preparation, and without the use of notes. Jeremy Bernstein, in an article for the *American Scholar,* said of Schwinger's lecture, "It's like poetry." Schwinger was known for speaking with long measured periods delivered without pause. He took equal care in his accompanying board work; he rarely made mistakes with formulas. In addition, James Gleick in his biography of Richard Feynman, *Genius,* reports that Schwinger was ambidextrous and able to list on the board the steps for two equations simultaneously.

Since his high school days Julian Schwinger had shown a great respect for and faith in the work of Paul Dirac. Dirac's work was a mathematical account of the interaction between electric and magnetic forces inside the atom. It was a useful description of these forces, but physicists who studied radiation through observation began to find discrepancies between calculations based on the theory and their measurements in the laboratory. In particular, the theory required the electron to behave as though it were a particle with infinite mass. The unreal nature of this notion led William Laurence in a 1948 *New York Times* article to call it the "cosmic ghost."

Adjusts Dirac's "Cosmic Ghost" Theory

Because of this discrepancy, quantum physicists were anxious to discard Dirac's theory. But Schwinger believed that with some corrections this theory could still be an accurate account of observable phenomena. At a 1948 meeting of the American Physical Society, Schwinger showed his colleagues how Dirac's theory could be corrected. Schwinger had found the terms in Dirac's work that produced the ghost of infinite mass and showed how to account for them in a way that both preserved Dirac's theory and kept it congruent with reality. With this work, Schwinger routed the cosmic ghost and eventually earned the Nobel Prize in 1965.

Almost all of Schwinger's writings are abstract and directed to a highly specialized audience of theoretical physicists. One of Schwinger's more recent books, however, *Einstein's Legacy: The Unity of Space and Time,* attempts to reach a general audience. In it, Schwinger explains in lay terms how **Albert Einstein**'s theories of special and general relativity are unified and what consequences they have for experiments.

Julian Schwinger and Clarice Carrol were married in 1947 and had no children. Outside of the lecture hall Schwinger was known for his reserved manner but firm convictions. He was one of the few scientists of his stature open to the possibility of achieving cold fusion. He died of cancer in Los Angeles on July 16, 1994.

SELECTED WRITINGS BY SCHWINGER:

Books

Discontinuities in Waveguides, Gordon & Breach, 1968.

Particles and Sources, Gordon & Breach, 1969.
Quantum Kinematics and Dynamics, W. A. Benjamin, 1970.
Einstein's Legacy: The Unity of Space and Time, Scientific American Library, 1986.

FURTHER READING:

Books

Current Biography, H. W. Wilson, 1967, pp. 379–81.
Gleick, James, *Genius: The Life and Science of Richard Feynman,* Pantheon, 1992.

Periodicals

Bernstein, Jeremy, *American Scholar,* A Scientific Education, Volume 50, 1981, pp. 237–93.
Laurence, William L., *New York Times,* Schwinger States His Cosmic Theory, June 25, 1948.

Sketch by Lawrence Souder

Charlotte Angas Scott
1858–1931
English mathematician

Charlotte Angas Scott was the first mathematics department head at Bryn Mawr College and a member of its founding faculty. She developed the curriculum for graduate and undergraduate math majors and upgraded the minimum mathematics requirements for entry and retention at Bryn Mawr. Scott also initiated the formulation of the College Entrance Examination Board in order to standardize such requirements nationwide. At one time, she was the only woman featured in the first printing of *American Men of Science,* and the only mathematician in another venerable reference book, *Notable American Women 1607–1950.* Scott was one of the main organizers of the American Mathematical Society and the only female to leave such an extensive mark on its first 50 years of existence.

Breaking "The Iron Mould"

Scott was born in Lincoln, England, on June 8, 1958, to Caleb and Eliza Exley Scott. As the daughter of the president of Lancashire College, she was provided with mathematics tutors as early as age seven. Her father and grandfather, Walter, were both social reformers as well as educators, and encouraged her to "break the iron mould" and seek a university education. At the age of 18, Scott won

Charlotte Angas Scott

a scholarship to Hitchin College, now known as Girton College, the women's division of Cambridge University.

As the nineteenth century drew to a close, Girton was still an anomaly. Scott and her classmates numbered 11. The young women had to walk three miles to Cambridge to attend classes with those lecturers who allowed them in their classroom, but they had to sit behind a screen where they could not see the blackboard. At that time, a woman caught unescorted on Cambridge campus grounds could be sent to The Spinning House, a prison for prostitutes both active and suspected. A hint of the future could be seen in the changing attitudes of male undergraduates and graduate students, however. Tutors offered to prepare female undergraduates for the "Tripos," a grueling oral examination that lasted over a week's time. The first female student took the mathematics Tripos in 1872, and thereafter more women applied for permission to take the tests along with their male counterparts. Scott took the examination in January 1880, placing eighth. Although university policy kept her accomplishment a secret, the news spread throughtout the campus. The awards ceremony was disrupted by a crowd of young men shouting "Scott of Girton!" over the name of the man honored in her place. Scott was later "crowned with laurels" in a private ceremony. In February 1881, Cambridge reversed its policy and women were allowed to take examinations with the male students.

Double Duty

Scott remained at Girton as a lecturer for four years while finishing her graduate studies at the University of London. The algebraist Arthur Cayley, a leader in coeducational reform, became Scott's mentor and recommended her for jobs as well as guiding her graduate research. Her doctorate was the first of its kind to be earned by a British female. In the nascent specialty of analysis within algebraic geometry, Scott focused on analyzing singularities in algebraic curves. Both of Scott's degrees at London were of the highest rank.

In 1885 Scott emigrated to the United States, where she joined the faculty of Bryn Mawr College in Pennsylvania. Founded that same year by the Society of Friends, Bryn Mawr was the first women's college to offer graduate degrees. Between 1885 and 1901 Scott successfully lobbied for a series of reforms to the admissions policies and entrance procedures at Bryn Mawr. Once the College Entrance Examination Board was instituted with her help, she served as chief examiner from 1902 to 1903. Scott's dedication was finally rewarded in 1909 with Bryn Mawr's first endowed chair and a formal citation.

Helps Organize the AMS

In 1891 Scott was one of the first women to join the New York Mathematical Society, which later evolved into the American Mathematical Society (AMS) in 1895. Scott served on the council that oversaw this transition and received an "acclaimed review" from the group. She would serve on the AMS council again (between 1899 and 1901), and as vice president in 1905.

Also, in 1899 Scott became the coeditor of the *American Journal of Mathematics*. She would continue to edit and peer review for this publication until two years after her official retirement from Bryn Mawr. Her influence spread internationally with her proof of **Emmy Noether**'s "fundamental theorem," an accomplishment that helped place Bryn Mawr and American mathematics on the world map.

"Auntie Charley"

During her long sojourn in America, Scott was visited regularly by her father and younger brother, Walter, while her sisters remained in England. "Auntie Charley," as Scott was called, would travel to Europe during spring and summer breaks to visit with her expanding circle of relatives and with mathematicians in major European cities. Scott's own personal life was more circumspect, clouded further by the fact that all her personal correspondence was apparently disposed of or lost. She traveled often to Baltimore to visit her close friend Frank Morley, but she never married.

As Scott aged, the deafness that had plagued her since her student days became a stumbling block. However, even rheumatoid arthritis could not dampen her ambitions although it disrupted her publications' schedule for many years. On the advice of a physician Scott took up gardening, only to breed a new species of a chrysanthemum.

Scott retired at age 67, after a 40–year career as one of the many European women who could only find work as scientists and mathematicians in the United States. She stayed on voluntarily at Bryn Mawr until the following year, however, when her last doctoral student graduated. Scott continued mentoring younger mathematicians and inspired another generation of women to follow in her footsteps. She died in November 1931 in Cambridge, England, and was buried next to her cousin Eliza Nevins in St. Giles's Churchyard. Her textbook on analytical geometry, having gone through a second edition in 1924, would be reissued in a third edition 30 years after her death.

SELECTED WRITINGS BY SCOTT:

Books

An Introductory Account of Certain Modern Ideas and Methods in Plane Analytical Geometry. First Edition, 1894 (republished as *Projective Methods in Plane Analytical Geometry* in 1961).
Cartesian Plane Geometry, Part I: Analytical Conics, 1907.

Periodicals

"A Proof of Noether's Fundamental Theorem." *Mathematische Annalen* 52 (1899): 592–97.

FURTHER READING:

Books

Eves, Howard. *An Introduction to the History of Mathematics.* Sixth Edition. Philadelphia, PA: Saunders College Publishing, 1990.
Green, Judy and Jeanne LaDuke. "Contributors to American Mathematics: An Overview and Selection," in *Women of Science: Righting the Record.* Edited by G. Kass–Simon and Patricia Farnes. Bloomington and Indianapolis: Indiana University Press, 1990.
——— . "Women in American Mathematics: A Century of Contributions," in *A Century of Mathematics in America.* Volume 2. Providence, RI: American Mathematical Society, 1989, pp. 379–89.
Kenschaft, Patricia Clark. "Charlotte Angas Scott," *Women of Mathematics.* Edited by Louise S. Grinstein and Paul J. Campbell. New York: Greenwood Press, 1987, pp. 193–203.
Lehr, Marguerite. "Charlotte Angas Scott." *Notable American Women, 1607–1950.* Volume 3. Cambridge, MA.: Belknap Press of Harvard University, 1971, pp. 249–50.
Ogilvie, Marilyn Bailey. "Charlotte Angas Scott," *Women in Science.* Cambridge, MA.: MIT Press, 1986, pp. 158–59.

Rossiter, Margaret W. *Women Scientists in America: Struggles and Strategies to 1940.* Baltimore, MD: Johns Hopkins University Press, 1982.

Periodicals

Katz, Kaila and Patricia Kenschaft. "Sylvester and Scott." *The Mathematics Teacher* 75 (1982): 490–94.
Kenschaft, Patricia C. "The Students of Charlotte Angas Scott." *Mathematics in College* (Fall 1982): 16–20.
——— . "Why Did Charlotte Angas Scott Succeed?" *Association for Women in Mathematics Newsletter* 17, no. 2 (1988): 9–11.
——— . "Charlotte Angas Scott 1858–1931." *College Mathematics Journal* 18 (March 1987): 98–110.
Maddison, Isabel and Marguerite Lehr. "Charlotte Angas Scott: An Appreciation." *Bryn Mawr Alumni Bulletin* 12 (1932): 9–12.

Other

Chaplin, Stephanie. "Charlotte Angas Scott." http://www.agnesscott.edu/lriddle/women/chronol.htm (July 1997).
"Charlotte Angas Scott." http://www–groups.dcs.st–and.ac.uk/~history /Mathematicians/Scott.html (July 1997).

Sketch by Jennifer Kramer

Glenn T. Seaborg
1912–1999
American nuclear chemist

Glenn T. Seaborg was a pioneering nuclear chemist whose work with isotopes and transuranium elements contributed to the development of nuclear technology in medicine, power, and weapons. His early research was on the identification of radioisotopes, advanced radiological imaging techniques, and radiotherapy; he was the codiscoverer of technetium–99m, one of the most widely used radioisotopes in nuclear medicine. Seaborg's most significant accomplishments resulted from his discovery of a number of transuranic elements, including plutonium, which is used to build atomic bombs. His contributions to the "atomic age" began during World War II with his work on the Manhattan Project to develop nuclear weapons. His impeccable reputation as a scientist and administrator earned him an appointment as chairman of the Atomic Energy Commission, where he was influential in the

Glenn T. Seaborg

development and testing of nuclear energy and weapons and in the establishment of nuclear arms control agreements.

Glenn Theodore Seaborg was born in Ishpeming, Michigan, on April 19, 1912, to Swedish immigrants Herman Theodore Seaborg, a machinist, and Selma O. (Erickson). Both had come to the United States in 1904, entering through the historic landmark Ellis Island in New York City, and then traveling to Ishpeming, Michigan. As a child Seaborg learned how to speak Swedish before English, and his early upbringing included the cultural traditions of his mother's homeland. His parents moved to southern California when he was ten, in part to seek better educational opportunities for him and his sister. He was educated in the multicultural Watts district of Los Angeles, where he gained the ability to deal effectively with people of different backgrounds, a skill that was useful to him in later life. Although his parents urged the young Seaborg to focus on commercial studies in high school, a dynamic chemistry teacher inspired his interest in science. After graduating as valedictorian of his class in 1929, Seaborg enrolled at the University of California, Los Angeles (UCLA), earning his tuition through a series of odd jobs, including stevedore and farm laborer. After graduating from UCLA in 1934 with a degree in chemistry, Seaborg pursued his graduate work at the University of California, Berkeley, which had renowned chemistry and physics departments. There he studied under chemist **Gilbert Newton Lewis** and physicist **Ernest Orlando Lawrence**, who had a twenty-seven-inch cyclotron (a circular device that serves as an accelerator in which charged particles are propelled by an alternating electric field in a constant magnetic field). Seaborg often worked all night, conducting research with the cyclotron when it was not being used by Lawrence and his colleagues. He earned a Ph.D. in 1937 for his thesis concerning the interaction of "fast" neutrons with lead and was appointed to the faculty at Berkeley, where he worked as an assistant in Lewis's laboratory. Shortly thereafter, Seaborg met Lawrence's secretary, Helen L. Griggs, whom he married in 1942.

While still working on his Ph.D., Seaborg began to collaborate with physicist Jack Livingood on the chemical separations that occurred in the cyclotron to produce radioactive isotopes (different forms of the same element having the same atomic number but a different number of protons). Radioisotopes have vital applications in the field of radiology, both in radiotherapy and diagnosing disease with radiological imaging techniques. Seaborg, Livingood, and colleagues discovered iodine–131, iron–59, cobalt–60, and technetium–99m, one of the most widely used radioisotopes in nuclear medicine.

Embarks on Nobel Prize-Winning Research

In 1934 physicist **Enrico Fermi** attempted to create new elements by irradiating uranium with neutrons. Uranium was the element with the "heaviest" nuclei on the periodic table, a chart that systematically groups together the elements with similar properties in order of increasing atomic number. In 1939 the German scientists **Otto Hahn** and **Fritz Strassmann** were able to split a uranium nucleus by bombarding it with neutrons, and this fission reaction produced a powerful release of energy. **Edwin M. McMillan** and **Philip Hauge Abelson**, working with the cyclotron at the Lawrence Radiation Laboratory at Berkeley, discovered the first transuranium element (elements with atomic number higher than 92), element 93. Although they also created nuclear fission with their experiments, McMillan and Abelson noticed that some of the nuclei bombarded by neutrons did not undergo fission but had decayed through electron emission, creating the new element. Since uranium was named after Uranus, the seventh planet in our solar system, they named their new element neptunium, after Neptune, the eighth planet.

Seaborg soon took over the work of searching for element 94 when McMillan left Berkeley to conduct war research on the East Coast. Working with Joseph W. Kennedy and graduate student Arthur C. Wahl, Seaborg discovered the chemically unstable element 94 in 1941 by bombarding neptunium with deuterons, the nuclei of the hydrogen isotope deuterium, and named the new element plutonium–238, after the ninth planet, Pluto. During the course of these experiments, Seaborg and colleagues isolated the isotope plutonium–239, which was a fissionable isotope with potential for use in the development of nuclear weapons and nuclear power. The following year, Seaborg, John W. Gofman, and Raymond W. Stoughton identified the isotope uranium–233, which would lead to the use of thorium, an abundant element, as a source of nuclear fuel.

On April 19, 1942, Seaborg left Berkeley to work on the Manhattan Project in Chicago, a large–scale scientific effort supported by the government with the goal of creating an atomic bomb. He led a group of scientists, including B. B. Cunningham and L. B. Werner, in the difficult task of developing methods for chemically extracting plutonium–239 from uranium in amounts that could be used to produce nuclear energy. Seaborg later reflected on this work as being the most exciting efforts of his career as he and his colleagues worked feverishly to develop an atomic weapon before Germany.

Because of their nearly identical chemical makeup, separating plutonium from uranium was a difficult task. In the course of their work, Seaborg and colleagues pioneered ultramicrochemical analysis, a technique used in working with minute amounts of radioactive material, and discovered that minuscule amounts of plutonium existed in pitchblende and carnotite ores. Seaborg was a primary influence in the decision to use plutonium instead of uranium for the first atomic-bomb experiments. By 1944 Seaborg's group had achieved success in isolating large amounts of plutonium, which enabled the Manhattan Project scientists to construct two nuclear weapons.

After Seaborg met his primary responsibility of developing enough plutonium to construct atomic weapons, he returned his attention to the transuranium elements. In 1944 Seaborg postulated that the element actinium and the 14 elements heavier than it were similar in nature and should be placed in a separate group on the periodic table. Known as the actinide concept, this theory helped scientists to accurately predict the chemical properties of heavier elements in the periodic table, and was the most significant alteration to the table since it was devised by Dmitry Mendeleev in 1869. Interestingly, **Niels Bohr** had predicted this alteration to the table many years earlier. Using his new actinide concept, Seaborg and colleagues began to predict the chemical makeup of other possible transuranics and, as a result, discovered two new elements: element 95, americium; and element 96, curium. Seaborg applied for and received patents for these elements, the only person ever to do so for a chemical element.

When Seaborg returned to Berkeley in 1946, he began to assemble a premiere group of scientists (many of whom were colleagues on the Manhattan Project) to search for transuranium elements. From 1948 to 1959, under Seaborg's guidance as associate director of the university's Lawrence Radiation Laboratory, this group isolated and identified the transuranic elements berkelium (element 97), californium (element 98), einsteinium (element 99), fermium (element 100), mendelevium (element 101), and nobelium (element 102). In 1951 Seaborg shared the Nobel Prize for chemistry with McMillan for their groundbreaking work in discovering transuranic elements. In 1974 scientists working under Seaborg discovered element 106 (unnilhexium).

Becomes Involved in Politics and Policy

Patriotism required Seaborg and his colleagues on the Manhattan Project to contribute to the war effort, but once they achieved success in creating atomic weapons, they urged the government not to use this new-found means of mass destruction on the Japanese, who doggedly refused to surrender despite the fall of Germany. Seaborg and six others signed the Franck Report, which recommended that the government merely demonstrate the bomb's terrible power by inviting the Japanese to watch a detonation. Yet the bomb was used twice, and the enormous loss of human life that resulted from it inspired Seaborg and other scientists to crusade actively for the control of nuclear weapons. They realized that the creators of such weapons were morally obligated to contribute to the outcome of a debate that might determine the survival of life on earth.

Seaborg's accomplishments as an administrator at the University of California, Berkeley, were nearly as impressive as his scientific discoveries. In 1958 he became the second vice-chancellor at the university and helped guide the institution during a period of dynamic growth. There was an ambitious building program at Berkeley, and the College of Environmental Design and the Space Sciences Laboratory were established at this time. He was also the faculty representative from Berkeley to the panel that oversaw the development of the Pac Ten athletic conference, which aimed at resolving abuses and corruption in California's collegiate athletic system. During this period, Seaborg also contributed to national educational reform by chairing the steering committee that created a new chemistry curriculum to help improve science education in schools. This curriculum was, in part, a response to the Soviet's first manned space flight, *Sputnik*, in 1957, which seemed to demonstrate the Soviet Union's superior scientific talent. Seaborg also served on the National Commission on Excellence in Education, which published *A Nation at Risk* (1983), a book that delineated the failings of the U.S. educational system.

Seaborg's knack for handling difficult issues was tested during his tenure as chairman of the Atomic Energy Commission (AEC) in the turbulent decade that stretched from 1961 to 1971. He entered the debate raging over society's concerns about nuclear power and its potential to harm the environment and produce mass destruction. Seaborg received this appointment during a conversation with President Kennedy in what he described in his book *Kennedy, Khrushchev and the Test Ban* as "the telephone call that changed my life." He continued, "Within a few days I accepted, and soon I was plunged into a new kind of chemistry, that of national and international events."

In 1961, Seaborg was a member of the American delegation that signed the Limited Nuclear Test Ban Treaty, outlawing nuclear testing in the atmosphere, water, and space. He also contributed to the ratification of the Non-Proliferation Treaty of 1970 by developing safeguards for handling nuclear materials, and by ensuring that those products meant for industrial and medical technology would not be illegally diverted to weapons' manufacture. In spite of these victories, Seaborg was disappointed by the failure to develop a "*comprehensive* treaty to prohibit *any* nuclear weapons testing. . . . [D]espite some near misses," he wrote, "this glittering prize, which carried with it the opportunity to arrest the viciously spiraling arms race, eluded our grasp."

In 1971 he returned to the University of California at Berkeley as University Professor of Chemistry. He continued to foster international cooperation in science and arms control. He was one of the founders, and in 1981 he became president of the International Organization for Chemical Sciences in Development (IOCD), an organization that seeks solutions to Third World problems through scientific collaboration. In the 1980s he also published two influential books, the first of which was *Kennedy, Khrushchev and the Test Ban* (1981). Based on his scrupulous memoirs, this book was an attempt "to contribute some facts and insights not previously published" about nuclear testing. Seaborg hoped that it might aid future negotiations by providing "a wider understanding of what is involved in the achievement of an important arms control agreement." He also wrote *Stemming the Tide: Arms Control in the Johnson Years,* which was published in 1987.

During the course of his career, Seaborg acquired many honors and appointments, including election to the American Association for the Advancement of Science and ten foreign national academies of science. Many of the younger scientists, however, disapproved of Seaborg, and suspicious of nuclear power, they opposed his appointment to the National Academy of Sciences. Outside of the political and scientific arenas, Seaborg was devoted to his family of four sons and two daughters. An outdoor enthusiast, he spent his rare free time playing golf, gardening, and hiking. He was also a passionate conservationist, who helped to establish the "Golden State Trail" in California and served as vice president of the American Hiking Society.

Seaborg died in 1999 at the age of 86 from complications from a stroke he had suffered the previous year. During his career he served as science adviser to 10 U.S. presidents. He was the only scientist to have an element (seaborgium) named after him while still alive.

His passing was noted by Chancellor Robert M. Berdahl of the University of California at Berkeley with the following remarks: "The world . . . . has lost a great man of science. He came here in 1934 as a graduate student enchanted by the possibilities of science, and he leaves us . . . . a legend in his own right. He advanced the frontiers of scientific discovery in a way that few have, but this son of a machinist never forgot the opportunities the University of California and the citizens of this state provided him, and he never stopped returning the favor. His service to this campus is equaled only by his service to this country."

SELECTED WRITINGS BY SEABORG:

Books

The Transuranium Elements, Yale University Press, 1958.

Education and the Atom, McGraw-Hill, 1964.
Man and Atom, W. R. Corliss, 1971.
Kennedy, Khrushchev and the Test Ban, University of California Press, 1981.
Stemming the Tide: Arms Control in the Johnson Years, Lexington Books, 1987.

FURTHER READING:

Books

Frank N. Magill, The Great Scientists, Grolier Educational Corporation, 1989.
McGraw-Hill Modern Men of Science, McGraw-Hill, 1966, p. 423.
The New Illustrated Science and Invention Encyclopedia, Stuttman, 1987, pp. 864–65.
Nobel Prize Winners, H. W. Wilson, 1987, pp. 945–48.

Sketch by David Petechuk

Emilio Segrè
1905–1989
American physicist

E milio Segrè is credited as the codiscoverer of three chemical elements: technetium in 1937, astatine in 1940, and plutonium in 1941. In addition, he was codiscoverer, with his former student **Owen Chamberlain**, of the antiproton in 1955, an achievement for which he shared the 1959 Nobel Prize in physics. Segrè's early academic career is closely intertwined with that of nuclear physicist **Enrico Fermi**, under whom he received his doctorate at the University of Rome in 1928. Segrè then continued his affiliation with that university for most of the next eight years. In 1936, he was appointed professor of physics at the University of Palermo, but was discharged two years later by the Fascist government of Benito Mussolini. Already in the United States at the time of his dismissal, Segrè accepted an appointment at the University of California at Berkeley, where he remained until his retirement in 1972. He returned to the University of Rome, where a special chair in physics had been created for him by the Italian government.

Emilio Gino Segrè was born on February 1, 1905 in Tivoli, Italy, one of three sons born to Giuseppe Segrè, a manufacturer, and the former Amelia Treves. Segrè attended the local elementary school in Tivoli and graduated in 1922 from the Liceo Mamiani in Rome. He subsequently entered the University of Rome, where he majored in engineering. Segrè eventually switched to physics, however, and completed his Ph.D. in that field in 1928. Biographers have conjectured that Segrè's decision to change majors was strongly influenced by his mentor, Enrico Fermi, on the Rome faculty. In any case, Segrè was Fermi's first doctoral student at Rome.

Discovers Technetium

After receiving his degree, Segrè spent a year in the Italian army and then returned to the University of Rome as an instructor in physics. From 1930 to 1932, he studied in Hamburg under Otto Stern and in Amsterdam under Pieter Zeeman. He returned to Rome as associate professor of physics, where he again collaborated with Fermi. At Fermi's suggestion, Segrè's early research into atomic spectroscopy, molecular beams, and X rays soon gave way to neutron physics, Fermi's own field of specialization. As part of Fermi's research team, Segrè was involved in the discovery that showed that slow neutrons are more effective in bringing about nuclear fission than are fast neutrons.

In 1936 Segrè was invited to become chairman of the department of physics at the University of Palermo. Shortly after accepting that position, he traveled to the United States to visit **Ernest Orlando Lawrence** and observe Lawrence's cyclotron at the University of California. During his visit, Segrè talked with Lawrence about a possible search for element number forty-three, one of the two elements known to exist that had not yet been discovered. The discovery of the element had been announced in the 1920s by German chemists Walter Noddack, Ida Tacke, and Otto Berg, but had not been confirmed. Only its missing space in the periodic table was evidence that it existed.

Based on his earlier work with Fermi, Segrè reasoned that the bombardment of molybdenum (element forty-two) with neutrons should result in the production of an element with an atomic number one greater than that of molybdenum—the missing forty-three. When he left Berkeley to return to Italy, therefore, Segrè obtained from Lawrence a sample of molybdenum that had been bombarded with deuterons (in this case, the equivalent of neutrons). In the following year, in collaboration with a colleague, C. Perrier, Segrè was able to confirm chemically the presence of the anticipated element forty-three in the molybdenum sample. This was the first artificially produced new element in scientific history. Segrè and Perrier suggested the name technetium for the element from the Greek word teknetos, for "artificial."

Assists in the Discovery of Astatine and Plutonium 239

Segrè returned to the United States again in 1938 to work with Lawrence at Berkeley. While there, he designed an experiment by which he was convinced the last remaining missing element, number eighty-five, could be prepared. Working with Dale R. Corson and K. R. MacKenzie, Segrè bombarded a small sample of polonium (element eighty-four) with deuterons and obtained evidence

for the existence of element eighty-five. The team suggested the name astatine, from the Greek *astatos,* for "unstable," since the element is a radioactive element without stable isotopes.

Segrè's planned return to Italy in the summer of 1938 was interrupted by an unexpected development. The Fascist government of Italy had instituted a purge of Jews similar to that which was carried out by the Nazis in Germany. Segrè, a Jew, was consequently expelled from his post at Palermo. Segrè's response to this snub, according to Isaac Asimov in *Asimov's Biographical Encyclopedia of Science and Technology,* was that he "shrugged and remained in the United States, becoming a citizen in 1944." Offered a research post at Berkeley, Segrè continued his work on neutron physics and artificial radioactivity. Two years later, he was involved in the discovery of yet another new element—plutonium—element number ninety-four. This line of research, along with Segrè's previous work on neutron physics, made him an invaluable asset during work on the development of the atomic bomb and, in 1943, he was appointed a group leader at the Los Alamos Scientific Laboratory of the Manhattan Project.

Discovers the Antiproton with Chamberlain

After the war, Segrè returned to Berkeley as professor of physics and began his collaboration with Owen Chamberlain on the search for the antiproton. In 1928 the English physicist **Paul Dirac** had predicted the existence of a particle identical to the electron in all respects except for its having a positive rather than a negative electrical charge. The discovery of the positron in 1932 by **Carl David Anderson** confirmed Dirac's prediction.

An extension of Dirac's original hypothesis suggested that all subatomic particles, not just the electron, should have their "anti-" counterparts. The search for the next antiparticle, a negatively-charged proton, was hampered by the fact that the particle was known to exist only at very high energies, such as the energy of cosmic radiation.

The construction of the 6.2 billion-electron-volt bevatron in the early 1950s provided another possible source of antiprotons. The accelerator had the potential to produce levels of energy at which the antiproton might be generated. Working with the bevatron, Segrè and Chamberlain finally discovered the hypothesized particle in 1955. For that discovery and the further confirmation it provided for Dirac's antimatter theory, Segrè and Chamberlain were awarded the 1959 Nobel Prize in physics.

Segrè was married to Elfriede Spiro on February 2, 1936. After she died in 1970, he married Rosa Mines. Segrè had three children, Claudio, Amelia, and Fausta, by his first wife. In addition to his Nobel Prize, Segrè was awarded the Hofmann Medal of the German Chemical Society in 1954, the Cannizzaro Medal of the Accademia Nazionale de Lincei in 1956, and honorary doctorates from the University of Palermo, Gustavus Adolphus College, and Tel Aviv

University. Segrè died in Lafayette, California, on April 22, 1989, of a heart attack.

SELECTED WRITINGS BY SEGRÈ:

Books

Experimental Nuclear Physics, Wylie, 1953.
Nuclei and Particles, Benjamin Company, 1953.
Enrico Fermi, Physicist, University of Chicago Press, 1970.
From X-Rays to Quarks: Modern Physicists and Their Discoveries, W. H. Freeman, 1980.
From Falling Bodies to Radio Waves: Classical Physicists and Their Discoveries, W. H. Freeman, 1984.

Periodicals

Physical Review, Observations of Antiprotons, Volume 100, 1955, pp. 947–50.
Nature, Antiprotons, Volume 177, 1956, pp. 11–12.

FURTHER READING:

Books

Weber, Robert L., *Pioneers of Science: Nobel Prize Winners in Physics,* American Institute of Physics, 1980, pp. 177–78.

Sketch by David E. Newton

Florence B. Seibert
1897–1991
American biochemist

A biochemist who received her Ph.D. from Yale University in 1923, Florence B. Seibert is best known for her research in the biochemistry of tuberculosis. She developed the protein substance used for the tuberculosis skin test. The substance was adopted as the standard in 1941 by the United States and a year later by the World Health Organization. In addition, in the early 1920s, Seibert discovered that the sudden fevers that sometimes occurred during intravenous injections were caused by bacteria in the distilled water that was used to make the protein solutions. She invented a distillation apparatus that prevented contamination. This research had great practical significance later when intravenous blood transfusions became widely used in surgery. Seibert authored or coauthored more than a hundred scientific papers. Her later research involved the

Florence B. Seibert

study of bacteria associated with certain cancers. Her many honors include five honorary degrees, induction into the National Women's Hall of Fame in Seneca Falls, New York (1990), the Garvan Gold Medal of the American Chemical Society (1942), and the John Elliot Memorial Award of the American Association of Blood Banks (1962).

Florence Barbara Seibert was born on October 6, 1897, in Easton, Pennsylvania, the second of three children. She was the daughter of George Peter Seibert, a rug manufacturer and merchant, and Barbara (Memmert) Seibert. At the age of three she contracted polio. Despite her resultant handicaps, she completed high school with the help of her highly supportive parents, and entered Goucher College in Baltimore, where she studied chemistry and zoology. She graduated in 1918, then worked under the direction of one of her chemistry teachers, Jessie E. Minor, at the chemistry laboratory of the Hammersley Paper Mill in Garfield, New Jersey. She and her professor, having responded to the call for women to fill positions vacated by men fighting in World War I, coauthored scientific papers on the chemistry of cellulose and wood pulps.

Although Seibert initially wanted to pursue a career in medicine, she was advised against it as it was "too rigorous" in view of her physical disabilities. She decided on biochemistry instead and began graduate studies at Yale University under Lafayette B. Mendel, one of the discoverers of Vitamin A. Her Ph.D. research involved an inquiry into the causes of "protein fevers"—fevers that developed in patients after they had been injected with protein solutions that contained distilled water. Seibert's assignment was to discover which proteins caused the fevers and why. What she discovered, however, was that the distilled water itself was contaminated—with bacteria. Consequently, Seibert invented a distilling apparatus that prevented the bacterial contamination.

Seibert earned her Ph.D. in 1923, then moved to Chicago to work as a postgraduate fellow under H. Gideon Wells at the University of Chicago. She continued her research on pyrogenic (fever causing) distilled water, and her work in this area acquired practical significance when intravenous blood transfusions became a standard part of many surgical procedures.

After her fellowship ended, she was employed part-time at the Otho S. A. Sprague Memorial Institute in Chicago, where Wells was the director. At the same time, she worked with Esmond R. Long, whom she had met through Wells's seminars at the University of Chicago. Supported by a grant from the National Tuberculosis Association, Long and Seibert would eventually spend thirty-one years collaborating on tuberculosis research. Another of Seibert's long-time associates was her younger sister, Mabel Seibert, who moved to Chicago to be with her in 1927. For the rest of their lives, with the exception of a year in Sweden, the sisters resided together, with Mabel providing assistance both in the research institutes (where she found employment as secretary and later research assistant) and at home. In 1932, when Long moved to the Henry Phipps Institute—a tuberculosis clinic and research facility associated with the University of Pennsylvania in Philadelphia—Seibert (and her sister) transferred as well. There, Seibert rose from assistant professor (1932–1937), to associate professor (1937–1955) to full professor of bio-chemistry (1955–1959). In 1959 she retired with emeritus status. Between 1937 and 1938 she was a Guggenheim fellow in the laboratory of **Theodor Svedberg** at the University of Upsala in Sweden. In 1926 Svedberg had received the Nobel Prize for his protein research.

Works on Unknown Aspects of Tuberculosis

Seibert's tuberculosis research involved questions that had emerged from the late-nineteenth-century work of German bacteriologist **Robert Koch**. In 1882 Koch had discovered that the tubercle bacillus was the primary cause of tuberculosis. He also discovered that if the liquid on which the bacilli grew was injected under the skin, a small bite-like reaction would occur in people who had been infected with the disease. (Calling the liquid "old tubercu-lin," Kock produced it by cooking a culture and draining off the dead bacilli.) Although he had believed the active substance in the liquid was protein, it had not been proven.

Using precipitation and other methods of separation and testing, Seibert discovered that the active ingredient of the liquid was indeed protein. The next task was to isolate it, so that it could be used in pure form as a diagnostic tool for tuberculosis. Because proteins are highly complex organic molecules that are difficult to purify, this was a daunting task. Seibert finally succeeded by means of crystallization.

The tiny amounts of crystal that she obtained, however, made them impractical for use in widespread skin tests. Thus, she changed the direction of her research and began working on larger amounts of active, but less pure protein. Her methods included precipitation through ultrafiltration (a method of filtering molecules). The result, after further purification procedures, was a dry powder called TPT (Tuberculin Protein Trichloracetic acid precipitated). This was the first substance that was able to be produced in sufficient quantities for widespread use as a tuberculosis skin test. For her work, Seibert received the 1938 Trudeau Medal from the National Tuberculosis Association.

At the Henry Phipps Institute in Philadelphia, Seibert continued her study of tuberculin protein molecules and their use in the diagnosis of tuberculosis. Seibert began working on the "old tuberculin" that had been created by Koch and used by doctors for skin testing. As Seibert described it in her autobiography *Pebbles on the Hill of a Scientist,* old tuberculin "was really like a soup made by cooking up the live tubercle bacilli and extracting the protein substance from their bodies while they were being killed." Further purification of the substance led to the creation of PPD (Purified Protein Derivative). Soon large quantities of this substance were being made for tuberculo-sis testing. Seibert continued to study ways of further purifying and understanding the nature of the protein. Her study in Sweden with Svedberg aided this research. There she learned new techniques for the separation and identifica-tion of proteins in solution.

Upon her return from Sweden, Seibert brought the new techniques with her. She began work on the creation of a large batch of PPD to serve as the basis for a standard dosage. The creation of such a standard was critical for measuring the degree of sensitivity of individuals to the skin test. Degree of sensitivity constituted significant diagnostic information if it was based upon individual reaction, rather than upon differences in the testing substance itself. A large amount of substance was necessary to develop a standard that ideally would be used worldwide, so that the tuberculo-sis test would be comparable wherever it was given. Developing new methods of purification as she proceeded, Seibert and her colleagues created 107 grams of material, known as PPD-S (the S signifying "standard"). A portion was used in 1941 as the government standard for purified tuberculins. Eventually it was used as the standard all over the world.

In 1958 the Phipps Institute was moved to a new building at the University of Pennsylvania. In her memoirs, Seibert wrote that she did not believe that the conditions necessary for her continued work would be available. Consequently, she and Mabel, her longtime assistant and companion, retired to St. Petersburg, Florida. Florence Seibert continued her research, however, using for a time a small laboratory in the nearby Mound Park Hospital and another in her own home. In her retirement years she devoted herself to the study of bacteria that were associated with certain types of cancers. Her declining health in her last two years was attributed to complications from childhood polio. She died in St. Petersburg on August 23, 1991.

In 1968 Seibert published her memoirs, which reveal her many friendships, especially among others engaged in scientific research. She particularly enjoyed international travel as well as driving her car, which was especially equipped to compensate for her handicaps. She loved music and played the violin (privately, she was careful to note).

SELECTED WRITINGS BY SEIBERT:

Books

Pebbles on the Hill of a Scientist, self-published (printed by St. Petersburg Printing Co.), 1968.

FURTHER READING:

Periodicals

New York Times, August 31, 1991.

Sketch by Pamela O. Long

Frederick Seitz
1911–
American physicist

F rederick Seitz, a physicist and science administrator, has made fundamental contributions to the theory of solids, nuclear physics, fluorescence, and crystals. He has also been a leader in the post-World War II scientific establishment in the United States. The honors presented to Seitz for his scientific contributions include the National Medal of Science in 1973, the NASA Distinguished Service Award in 1979, and the Department of Energy Award for Public Service in 1993. The University of Illinois dedicated the Frederick Seitz Materials Research Laboratory in 1993.

Seitz was born on July 4, 1911, in San Francisco, California, to Frederick and Elizabeth Hofman Seitz. His mother was a native of San Francisco while his father had emigrated as a child from Heidelberg, Germany. Seitz credits his father—a baker who had a deep interest in science—for the implicit assurance from childhood that he would go to college and become a scientist. In his youth Seitz was an avid reader of popular science and engineering magazines as well as science fiction. He attended Lick-Wilmerding high school in San Francisco because it had a level of science preparation acceptable to most colleges. Graduating at the end of 1928, Seitz entered Stanford

University in January, 1929, starting out as a biochemistry major on the advice of his father. Soon, however, he focused on mathematics and physics.

At Stanford (and at the California Institute of Technology, which he attended for the Fall 1930 semester), Seitz was able to meet and hear presentations by the world's leading mathematicians and physicists. He graduated from Stanford in three years with a degree in mathematics, then started doctoral studies in physics at Princeton University in 1932.

Develops Wigner-Seitz Method for Solid-State Wave Functions

Seitz's mentors at Princeton were professors Edward Uhler Condon and **Eugene Pauk Wigner**. Condon was among the new generation of American physicists whose contributions to the field first achieved parity with the accomplishments of physicists in Europe; he already had a reputation for leadership in wave theory by the time Seitz arrived at Princeton. Wigner, a student of physicist **Max Born**, was a German theoretician with a particular interest in the properties of metals. A few months after Seitz arrived at Princeton, Condon suggested to Seitz that he become Wigner's first doctoral student. Working in Wigner's laboratory late in 1932, Seitz developed the cellular method of deriving solid-state wave functions that became known as the Wigner-Seitz method. They illustrated its application in two studies of the energy bands of metallic sodium published in *Physical Review,* 1933–34. The widespread application of the Wigner-Seitz method to the understanding of metals usually is regarded as the catalyst for the formation of the field of solid-state physics in the United States.

Completing his doctorate in 1934, Seitz remained at Princeton for a year as a Proctor fellow. In 1935 he was appointed as an instructor at the University of Rochester, where he stayed for two years before working as a research physicist for the General Electric laboratories at Schenectady, New York, from 1937 to 1939.

Publishes Important Text on Physics

Seitz's partner in these moves was Elizabeth (Betty) K. Marshall, a graduate student in physics at Cornell University; he had met her in the fall of 1934 while she was teaching at Bryn Mawr College. They married in May 1935, and in that same year teamed up to begin work on the publication *The Modern Theory of Solids.* Based on lectures Frederick presented at Rochester, Betty created a consistent and well-documented text that was finally published in 1940. Seitz later said that although the book was attributed to him alone, it should have appeared under joint authorship.

At General Electric, Seitz worked on fluorescent crystals and dyes both for illumination purposes and for coatings on cathode-ray tubes. At the same time he was publishing papers on the related topics of the constitution and magnetic properties of lithium and sodium. In 1939

Seitz moved to the University of Pennsylvania, first as assistant professor, then as an associate professor in the Morgan Laboratory of Physics. While there, he was a consultant at the U.S. Army's Frankford Arsenal in Philadelphia, Pennsylvania, where he studied metallurgical problems associated with armor-piercing bullets and cartridge casings. This was the first in a series of defense-related activities that stretched over the next thirty years.

Contributes to Military Application

The Carnegie Institute of Technology convinced Seitz to join its staff as professor of physics in 1942. His service there, however, was interrupted frequently by the demands of wartime. Wigner (working on reactor designs at the University of Chicago as part of the atomic bomb program), asked **Arthur Compton**, the head of the laboratory, to invite Seitz to assist with problems related to both the uranium fuel and the graphite moderator. Seitz worked at the facility from 1943 to 1945, regularly traveling back to Pittsburgh where his wife held a teaching appointment.

At the end of the war in Europe, Seitz served several months in the army's field intelligence agency as an interviewer of German scientists thought to have knowledge of nuclear physics. In 1946 Wigner persuaded Seitz to go to the atomic energy laboratory at Oak Ridge, Tennessee, to assist in establishing the Monsanto Company's "reactor school," a year-long series of lectures on atomic energy for civilian purposes.

At Chicago and Oak Ridge, Seitz came to know the key scientists in the postwar nuclear physics community, including **Robert Oppenheimer**, **Leo Szilard**, and **Edward Teller**. Seitz took a middle road in the debate regarding the public responsibilities of those physicists whose knowledge had created the atomic bomb that ended World War II and began the pursuit of more powerful and deadlier weapons. Seitz participated in the early Pugwash conferences intended to create international dialogue at the height of the Cold War, but he also spoke out supporting development of the hydrogen bomb as a countervailing force against what he saw as an expansionary Soviet Union. Later, during the Kennedy administration, he supported the resumption of nuclear tests in the atmosphere after the Soviet Union broke the voluntary moratorium on testing.

Seitz moved to the University of Illinois in 1949 to take an appointment as a professor of physics. While at Illinois he also served as the director and technical director of the Control Systems Laboratory from 1951 to 1957, head of the physics department from 1957 to 1964, and dean of the graduate college and vice president for research from 1964 to 1965. During the 1940s and 1950s Seitz's research focused on the theory and properties of crystals. His published work included studies of dislocations and imperfections in crystal structures, the effect of irradiation on crystals, and the process of diffusion (the movement of atoms or particles caused by random collision) in crystalline materials.

Moves into Administrative Role

Seitz's major scientific contributions ended in the late 1950s as administrative tasks fully claimed his time. Among his responsibilities were the chairmanship of the governing board of the American Institute of Physics, a year in Paris serving as science advisor to the secretary-general of the North Atlantic Treaty Organization, chairmanship of the Naval Research Advisory Committee, presidency of the American Physical Society, and membership on the President's Science Advisory Committee.

In 1962 Seitz was elected president of the National Academy of Sciences in Washington, D.C., a part-time role that nonetheless involved a considerable commitment. Seitz helped to restructure the presidency into a full-time role with a six-year term, and beginning in 1965 he was selected to be the first incumbent. During his years in Washington, he was an advocate for government support of basic science and was an ex officio member of several government councils. In 1964 Seitz was elected a trustee of Rockefeller University in New York City, and in 1968 he succeeded **Detlev Bronk** (who had been the president of the National Academy of Sciences prior to Seitz) as president of the university. Bronk had transformed Rockefeller—originally a biomedical research institution dependent wholly on the endowment created by philanthropist John D. Rockefeller—into a learning center that brought in federal research money; he persuaded the university's trustees to establish a Ph.D. program, and also expanded the faculty and constructed several new buildings.

From the beginning of Seitz's presidency it was clear that Bronk's expansionary program could not be sustained. The federal government was ending two decades of increased spending on the basic sciences, and many at Rockefeller believed that some of Bronk's innovations needed to be rolled back. These pressures set the tone for much of the Seitz administration, which was characterized by limits on faculty growth. The university's options also were shaped by the poor investment climate of the 1970s, which had a particularly negative effect on institutions such as Rockefeller that depended heavily on endowment income. Faced with a series of deficit budgets, Seitz nonetheless was able to see through a modest building program, which included a new animal research facility and a new faculty residence. He negotiated for the acquisition of air rights over the adjacent FDR Drive, which gave the university future opportunities for expansion, and he welcomed the opportunity to have the Rockefeller Archive Center, an institution housing the records of numerous Rockefeller family philanthropies, become a division of the university.

Retiring from the presidency of Rockefeller University in 1978, Seitz was subsequently appointed to a variety of consulting roles and directorships, including the chair of the Scientific and Technology Advisory Group to the premier of Taiwan, the chair of the Strategic Defense Initiative ("Star Wars") Organization Advisory Committee, and the boards of several corporations.

SELECTED WRITINGS BY SEITZ:

Books

The Modern Theory of Solids, McGraw, 1940.
The Physics of Metals, McGraw, 1943.
Research and Development and the Prospects for International Security, Crane, 1973.
The Science Matrix: Past, Present, and Future, Springer-Verlag, 1991.

Periodicals

Physics Today, Solid, Volume 2, 1949, pp. 18–22.
Physics Today, The Government Science Administrator, Volume 14, 1961, pp. 36–8.
Physics Today, Science and the Government, Volume 16, 1963, pp. 28–30, 32.
Science, Space Science and the Universities, 1963, pp. 614–18.

FURTHER READING:

Books

Current Biography, H. W. Wilson, 1956, pp. 563–64.

Periodicals

New York Times, April 25, 1962.

Other

New York Times, Frederick Seitz, oral history transcript, 1981–82, American Institute of Physics, College Park, Maryland.
———— , Frederick Seitz's personal papers are at the Rockefeller Archive Center, North Tarrytown, New York, and the University of Illinois archives at Urbana.

Sketch by Darwin H. Stapleton

Atle Selberg
1917–
Norwegian number theorist

Atle Selberg's most newsworthy achievement came in 1950, when he won the Fields Medal for an elementary proof of the eighteenth-century conjecture known as the Prime Number Theorem. Since this achievement, Selberg has been affiliated with the Institute for Advanced Studies (IAS) at Princeton, New Jersey. However, he continues to venture out to visit with children in their early teens, and to take part in special math-oriented programs held around the country.

Selberg was born in Langeslund, Norway, on June 14, 1917, to Ole Michael and Anna Kristina (nee Skeie) Selberg. He received all his early schooling there and earned a Ph.D. from the University of Oslo in 1943. Selberg was resident fellow at the university for a total of five years. However, he would soon become part of that wave of European emigres who enriched American mathematics after World War II.

Selberg married Hedvig Liebermann on August 13, 1947, the year he relocated to the United States. They would eventually have two children, Ingrid Maria and Lars Atle. Aside from a year-long stint at Syracuse University in New York, Selberg did not teach full-time in America. He was granted membership to the IAS and by 1951 was a member of the faculty there. Selberg was one of the three top European number theorists working in America, including Hungarian mathematician **Paul Erdös**, with whom he discovered the proof for the Prime Number Theorem.

Originally, Selberg and Erdös agreed to publish back-to-back papers in the same journal, but Selberg jumped ahead at the last minute. The fact that he published first led to his being awarded the Fields Medal by the International Mathematics Union. Selberg received more awards, including the Wolf Prize in 1986 and an honorary commission of Knight Commander with Star from the Royal Norwegian Order of St. Olav in 1987. He also holds an honorary doctorate from the University of Trondheim in his home country.

Math Camp

As Selberg approached age 80, he traveled widely, taking part in commemorative and experimental events. For example, Selberg was invited to give the keynote address at the 1996 Seattle Mathfest celebrating the 100th anniversary of the Prime Number Theorem. That same month, he visited the "Math Camp" at the University of Washington. The Math Camp is an annual summer workshop designed to bring together and inspire bright youngsters from the Americas, Europe, and Asia. Selberg was one of many distinguished speakers invited who had made significant strides in their particular areas of mathematics.

Selberg's specialty is in generalizing the works of others, an important step towards solidifying the foundations of number theory. He arrived at generalizations of Viggo Brun's sieve methods, and also summarized the Prime Number Theorem to include all prime numbers in an arbitrary arithmetic progression. His investigations also hinge on group theory and analysis. Not all of Selberg's work follows others, though; his conjecture that Lie groups are arithmetical was eventually proven in 1968 by Russian mathematicians Gregori Aleksandrovitch Margulis and D. A. Kazhdan.

SELECTED WRITINGS BY SELBERG:

Books

"The General Sieve–Method and Its Place in Prime–Number Theory," in *Proceedings of the International Congress of Mathematicians, Cambridge, MA, 1950, Volume 1,* 1952, pp. 286–92.

"Recent Developments in the Theory of Discontinuous Groups of Motions of Symmetric Spaces," in *Proceedings of the 15th Scandinavian Congress, Oslo, 1968.* Lecture Notes in Mathematics, Volume 118, 1970, pp. 99–120.

Periodicals

"On the Zeros of Riemann's Zeta–Function." *Skrifter utgitt av Det Norske Videnskaps–Akademi i Oslo I. Mat.–Natruv. Klasse* no. 10 (1942): 1–59.

"An Elementary Proof of the Prime Number Theorem." *Annals of Mathematics* 50, no. 2 (1949): 305–15.

FURTHER READING:

Books

Albers, Alexanderson, and Reid. *International Mathematical Congresses: An Illustrated History 1893–1986.* Revised edition. New York: Springer–Verlag, 1986.

Sands, Karen. "Gregori Aleksandrovitch Margulis," in *Notable Twentieth Century Scientists.* Volume 3. Edited by Emily J. McMurray. Detroit, MI: Gale Research, Inc., 1995, p. 1318.

Tarwater, Dalton, editor. *The Bicentennial Tribute to American Mathematics: 1776–1976.* Mathematical Association of America, Inc. 1977.

World Who's Who in Science. First Edition. Edited by Allen G. Debus. Chicago: Marquis, 1968, p. 1519.

Other

Peterson, Ivars. "Math Camp." *Ivars Peterson's Math-Land* (August 26, 1996). http://www.maa.org/mathland/mathland_8_26.html

"Atle Selberg." *MacTutor History of Mathematics Archive.* http://www–groups.dcs.st–and.ac.uk/˜history/Mathematicians/Erdös.html (July 1997).

Sketch by Jennifer Kramer

Nikolai N. Semenov
1896–1986
Russian physical chemist and physicist

Nikolai N. Semenov was a physical chemist and physicist who was the first Soviet citizen living in Russia to win the Nobel Prize. His scientific work focused on chain reactions and their characteristic "explosiveness" during chemical transformations. This influenced the development of greater efficiency in automobile engines and other industrial applications where controlled combustion was involved, such as jet and rocket engines. Enjoying important academic success, he also played a significant role as a spokesperson for the Soviet scientific community. He was instrumental in establishing institutions where physical chemistry could be studied, and he collaborated in creating a journal dedicated to the field. In addition, he actively participated in scientific conferences dealing with physical chemistry.

Nikolai Nikolaevich Semenov was born on April 16, 1896, in Saratov, Russia, to Nikolai Alex and Elena (Dmitrieva) Semenov. He graduated from Petrograd University (later renamed Leningrad; now called St. Petersburg, its original name) in 1917, the year of revolution that led to the establishment of communism in Russia. Semenov had shown an interest in science from the time he entered Petrograd University at age sixteen in 1913 to study physics and mathematics. He published his first paper at the age of twenty on the subject of the collision of molecules and electrons. After graduation from Petrograd, Semenov accepted a post in physics at the Siberian University of Tomsk, but in 1920, he returned to Petrograd where he was associated with the Leningrad Institute of Physics and Technology for eleven years. In 1928, Semenov organized the mathematics and physics departments at the Leningrad Polytechnical Institute. He became the head of the Institute of Physical Chemistry of the Soviet Academy of Sciences in 1931, where he remained for more than thirty years. In 1944, Semenov became the head of the department of chemical kinematics at the University of Moscow.

Kinetics Critical to Semenov's Research

The branch of physical chemistry concerned with the rates and conditions of chemical processes, called chemical kinetics, dominated Semenov's research from his earliest studies. His work led to the understanding of the sequence of chemical reactions and provided insight into the conversion of substances into products. Along with some of his colleagues, Semenov felt that physics held the key to understanding chemical transformations. The branch of science referred to as chemical balances was a consequence of their work.

Semenov was awarded the Nobel Prize in chemistry in 1956 with English chemist **Cyril Hinshelwood** for their researches into the mechanism of chemical reactions. Both scientists had worked independently for twenty-five years on chemical chain reactions and their importance in explosions. There is wide agreement in the scientific community that Semenov and Hinshelwood were responsible for the development of plastics and the improvement of the automobile engine. There remains some controversy over whether their work on chain reactions contributed to atomic research.

Other experiments by Semenov had culminated in his theory of thermal explosions of mixtures of gases. As a result of this research, he increased the understanding of free radicals—highly unstable atoms that contain a single, unpaired electron. Semenov demonstrated that when molecules disintegrate, energy-rich free radicals are formed. His extensive works on this subject were published first in Russian in the 1930s and later in English.

Chain Reaction Theory Holds Important Applications

In subsequent research, Semenov found that the walls of an exploding chamber can influence a chain reaction as well as the substances within the chamber. This concept was particularly beneficial in the development of the combustion engine in automobiles. Semenov's chemical chain reaction theory and his observations on the inflammable nature of gases informed the study of how flames spread, and had practical applications in the oil and chemical industries, in the process of combustion in jet and diesel engines, and in controlling explosions in mines. This work was based on Semenov's earlier investigations of condensation of steam on hard surfaces and its reaction under electric shock.

Semenov made substantial contributions to the development of Soviet scientific institutions and journals. He was active in the training of Soviet scientists and the organizing of important institutions for scientific research in physical chemistry. His long association with the Academy of Sciences of the U.S.S.R. earned him an appointment as a full member in 1932. When the Academy moved to Moscow in 1944, Semenov began teaching at Moscow University. Semenov's theories of combustion, explosion, and problems of chemical kinetics, along with a bibliography of his work by the Academy, were published during the 1940s and 1950s and helped secure his role in his field.

Semenov was not immune to the politics of his country. He became a member of the Communist Party in 1947, and he was the person who answered criticism of the Soviet Union from the *Bulletin of the Atomic Scientists,* a publication of the United States. The *Bulletin* challenged Soviet scientists to protest against Soviet restrictions on release of scientific publications from the country. Semenov replied that there were no such restrictions and accused the American scientists of ignoring their own government restrictions. It was discovered later that some Soviet publications had been arriving regularly at the Library of Congress in Washington, D.C.

In his own country, Semenov was highly regarded. He had received the Stalin Prize, the Order of the Red Banner of Labor, and the Order of Lenin, the latter seven times. He served his country in the political capacity of deputy in the Supreme Soviet in the years 1958, 1962, and 1966, and he was made an alternate to the Central Committee of the Communist Party in 1961. While he was a loyal Soviet citizen, he did work diligently for freedom in scientific experimentation.

On September 15, 1924, he married Natalia Nikolaevna Burtseva, who taught voice, and they had a son, Yurii Nikolaevich, and a daughter, Ludmilla Nikolaevna. Semenov enjoyed hunting, gardening, and architecture in his leisure time. He died in 1986.

SELECTED WRITINGS BY SEMENOV:

Books

Chain Reactions, Clarendon Press, 1935.
Chemical Kinetics and Chain Reactions, Clarendon Press, 1935.
Problems of Chemical Kinetics and Reactivity, Princeton University Press, 1958–1959.

Periodicals

Bulletin of the Atomic Scientists, February, 1953.

FURTHER READING:

Books

Prado and Seymour, *McGraw-Hill Encyclopedia of World Biography,* Jack Heraty & Associates, 1973, pp. 504–05.
——— , *Current Biography,* H. W. Wilson, 1947, pp. 498–500.

Sketch by Jordan Richman

Jean-Pierre Serre
1926–
French mathematician

Educated at the École Normale Supérieure in Paris, Jean-Pierre Serre received a Fields Medal for his work in topology, the study of geometric figures whose properties are unaffected by physical manipulation. The award, which was given to him in 1954, when he was only twenty-eight years old, is the equivalent in mathematics to the Nobel Prize in other fields of study. He has been professor of algebra and geometry at the Collège de France since 1956.

Serre was born in Bages, France, on September 15, 1926, to Jean and Adèle Serre. Both pharmacists, they instilled in their son an early interest in chemistry. That interest eventually gave way to mathematics, however, when Serre began reading his mother's calculus books. In a short time, he was teaching himself the fundamentals of derivatives, integrals, series, and other topics. During high school at the Lycée de Nîmes, Serre found a practical use for his mathematical talents. He told C. T. Chong and Y. K. Leong in *Mathematical Intelligencer* that some of the older students at the school had a tendency to bully him. "So to pacify them," he said, "I used to do their math homework. It was as good a training as any."

In 1945 Serre passed the entrance examination for the prestigious École Normale Supérieure in Paris. Soon after he enrolled at the institution, he decided to abandon his plans to become a high-school math teacher and to concentrate instead on research in mathematics. It was not until then, he later told Chong and Leong, that he realized he could earn a living as a research mathematician. Serre's earliest research at the École was in the field of topology. He was awarded his doctorate in this subject in 1952 for a dissertation on homotopy groups. For his work in this area, he was also awarded a 1954 Fields Medal from the International Congress of Mathematics.

Since receiving the Fields Medal, Serre has gone on to other topics in mathematics, including complex variables, cohomology and sheaves, algebraic geometry, and number fields. He explained to Chong and Leong that he finds it easy to move gradually from one topic to another, as he perceives their relationships to each other. In 1956 Serre was appointed professor of algebra and geometry at the Collège de France, a post he continues to hold.

Serre was married in 1948 to Josiane Heulot, a chemist. The couple has one daughter. Serre is a member of the French, Dutch, Swedish, and U.S. academies of science and has been made an honorary fellow of the Royal Society in London. In addition to the Fields Medal, he has been awarded the Prix Balzan in 1985 and the Médaille d'Or of the Centre National de la Recherche Scientifique.

SELECTED WRITINGS BY SERRE:

Books

Faiseaux algébriques cohérents, 1955.
Groupes algébriques et corps de classes, 1959.
Corps Locaux, 1962.
Cohomologie galoisienne, 1964.
Abelian l-adic representations, 1968.
Cours d'arithmétique, 1970.
Représentations linéaires des groupes finis, 1971.

FURTHER READING:

Periodicals

Chong, C. T., and Y. K. Leong, *Mathematical Intelligencer,* An Interview with Jean-Pierre Serre, Volume 8, 1986, pp. 8–12.

Sketch by David E. Newton

Claude Shannon
1916–
American mathematician and information theorist

Claude Shannon is considered by many to be the father of the information sciences. At the Massachusetts Institute of Technology (MIT) in 1940, Shannon first applied Boolean algebra to electrical systems, laying the groundwork for both the computer industry and telecommunications. Later that same decade, while working at Bell Laboratories, he formulated a sweeping theory explaining the communication of information. By distinguishing between meaning and information and reconceptualizing information as all of the possible messages in a communication, he was able to quantify information for the first time. This made it possible to analyze mathematically various communication technologies. His general theory of information, however, is not restricted to the analysis of specific technologies; it has broad philosophical implications as well, and Shannon has also made major contributions to research on artificial intelligence.

Claude Elwood Shannon was born in Gaylord, Michigan, on April 30, 1916, to Claude Elwood and Mabel Wolf Shannon. He earned his B.S. degree from The University of Michigan in 1936; he then went on to MIT, where he studied both electrical engineering and mathematics, receiving a master's degree in the former and a doctorate in the latter. For his master's degree in electrical engineering, he applied George Boole's logical algebra to the problem of electrical switching. Boole's system for logically manipulating 0s and 1s was little known at the time, but it is now the nervous system of every computer in the world. For his Ph.D. dissertation, Shannon applied mathematics to genetics. He received both his master's degree and his doctorate in 1940. He was named a National Research Fellow and spent a year at Princeton's Institute for Advanced Study.

In 1941, Shannon joined Bell Laboratories as a research mathematician, and he spent most of World War II working in a top secret section of the laboratories on cryptanalysis and anti-aircraft gun directors. It was there that he met **Alan Turing**, the leader of the British team that was designing one of the first computers to crack Germany's secret codes. Shannon had been interested in computing since he was a graduate student at MIT, where he was in charge of **Vannevar Bush**'s differential analyzer, an analog computer. Turing was thrilled to meet Shannon, because they had both independently conceived of logical machines. After they had met, Turing—as quoted in *Alan Turing: The Enigma*—exclaimed in joy: "Shannon wants to feed not just *data* to a Brain, but *cultural* things! He wants to play *music* to it!"

Lays the Foundation for Information Science

In the late forties and early fifties, Shannon designed programs for chess playing machines and a maze-running mechanical mouse, and in 1956 he helped **John McCarthy** organize the very first conference on artificial intelligence at Dartmouth College. But his greatest contribution was a series of papers he wrote that established the field of information science—the theoretical and mathematical basis for the mechanical conveyance of information. As Howard Rheingold explains in *Tools for Thought,* Shannon "presented a set of theorems that were directly related to the economical and efficient transmission of messages on noisy media, and indirectly but still fundamentally related to the connection between energy and information." These theorems, endlessly elaborated and refined by engineers making color televisions, running telephone systems, establishing radio networks, and proliferating various types of computers, have had a tremendous impact on the late twentieth century.

Like his friend Alan Turing, Shannon is much more interested in ideas than fame. In fact, he seems to loathe public accolades, and he even went out of his way to criticize the mania about information that swept the sciences in the 1950s, after his work became known. In an article called "Bandwagon," printed in the *IEEE Transactions on Information Theory,* he warned that the mania for information "has perhaps ballooned to an importance beyond its actual accomplishments . . . Seldom do more than a few of nature's secrets give way at one time."

In addition to his work at Bell Laboratories, Shannon has spent many years teaching at MIT. He was a visiting professor of electrical communication in 1956, and then in 1957 he was named professor of communications sciences and mathematics. He was the Donner Professor of Science from 1958 to 1978, when he retired. Shannon has received many honors including the Morris Liebmann Memorial Award in 1949, the Ballantine Medal in 1955, and the Mervin J. Kelly Award of the American Institute of Electrical Engineers in 1962. He was awarded the National Medal of Science in 1966, as well as the Medal of Honor that same year from the Institute of Electrical and Electronics Engineers. He also received the Jaquard award in 1978, the John Fritz Medal in 1983, and the Kyoto Prize in Basic Science in 1985, as well as numerous other prizes and over a dozen honorary degrees. He is a member of the American Academy of Arts and Sciences, the National Academy of Sciences, the National Academy of Engineering, the American Philosophical Society, and the Royal Society of London.

On March 27, 1949, Shannon married Mary Elizabeth Moore; they had three children together. While he has lectured or published only intermittently since the early 1960s, he continues to research information in its many forms, from the stock market to the English language. He currently he lives in Winchester, Massachusetts.

SELECTED WRITINGS BY SHANNON:

Books

The Mathematical Theory of Communication, University of Illinois Press, 1949.
Automata Studies: Annals of Mathematics Studies Number 34, Princeton University Press, 1956.

Periodicals

Bell System Technical Journal, The Mathematical Theory of Communication, Volume 27, 1948, pp. 379–423 and 623–56.
Proceedings of the IRE, Communication in the Presence of Noise, Volume 37, 1949, pp. 10–21.

FURTHER READING:

Books

Hodges, Andrew, *Alan Turing: The Enigma,* Simon and Schuster, 1983, pp. 250–51.
Rheingold, Howard, *Tools for Thought,* Simon and Schuster, 1985.

Periodicals

Aspray, William, *Annals of the History of Computing,* The Scientific Conceptualization of Information: A Survey, Volume 7, April, 1985, pp. 117–40.

Sketch by Chris Hables Gray

Irwin Shapiro
1929–
American radio astronomer and educator

Irwin Shapiro, a noted innovator of techniques in radar and radio astronomy, was appointed director of the Harvard-Smithsonian Center for Astrophysics (CfA) in January 1983. Respected as both teacher and physicist,

Shapiro became the guiding force behind one of the largest astrophysical centers in the world. While continuing his own research, Shapiro found himself controlling a $40 million budget and the work of hundreds of CfA staff members. Besides radio and microwave astronomy, Shapiro has worked on geophysics, planetary physics, and tests of gravitation theories.

Irwin Ira Shapiro was born in New York City on October 10, 1929, to Samuel Shapiro, a civil engineer and teacher who had come to America from Russia at age two, and Esther Feinberg Shapiro, a schoolteacher. Becoming interested in science at six, Shapiro learned math from an uncle and was doing fractions by the second grade. As a teenager he commuted from his home in Far Rockaway, New York, to the elite Brooklyn Technical High School, an experience he found intellectually enriching. At fifteen Shapiro built a telescope in his attic, grinding the mirror himself and making its tube out of wood. Shapiro majored in math at Cornell University, receiving his bachelor's degree in three years.

After receiving a master's degree at Harvard University in 1951, Shapiro was appointed a member of the staff of the Lincoln Laboratory of the Massachusetts Institute of Technology (MIT) in Lexington in 1954; the following year he received a Ph.D. in physics from Harvard. At the Lincoln Laboratory, Shapiro worked on radar applications, writing a book on missile trajectory observations in 1958. On December 20, 1959, he married Marian Helen Kaplun, and the couple eventually had two children, Stephen and Nancy. A few years later Shapiro was involved with a controversial project intended to duplicate the radio-reflective properties of the Earth's ionosphere—a region of electrically-charged particles surrounding the planet—with millions of hairlike, man-made materials scattered through the upper atmosphere. The project, carried out in 1963, drew criticism from various sources; astronomers complained it would ruin their observations, and Soviets called it an imperialist scheme. Shapiro's predictions of the experiment's effectiveness and duration proved correct nonetheless, and the worried radio astronomers could not even locate the objects before they fell out of orbit. In another early experiment, Shapiro used radar and light to verify physicist **Albert Einstein**'s theory of general relativity, which includes the idea that although the speed of light in a vacuum is constant, the pull of gravity can affect it. Shapiro sent a light signal past the sun to reflect off a planet and measured with radar the extra delay in its return caused by the sun's gravitational pull.

Among First to Study Superluminal Motion

Shapiro was appointed professor of geophysics and physics at MIT in 1967, and four years later he headed a team of researchers that observed motion within the quasars 3C 273 and 3C 279. (A joint team led by Marshall Cohen and Kenneth Kellermann was studying these two objects at that time as well.) Quasars are mysterious, compact sources of tremendous amounts of radio emission, and Shapiro's team discovered that both quasars had a double structure.

Four months later, his group noticed that the separation between the two parts of each double structure had widened, doing so at a velocity apparently exceeding that of light. This so-called superluminal motion—motion faster than light—observed by Shapiro in 1971 has been attributed to observing effects and the angle at which the quasars were seen. This apparent faster-than-light motion did not in fact contradict the theory of special relativity (which holds that the speed of light and the laws of physics are constant; therefore nothing can exceed light's speed), since no actual objects were moving that quickly. In order to detect these quasars' motions, Shapiro relied on a technique called very long baseline interferometry (VLBI), a form of radio astronomy using widely separated radio telescopes and combining the data from each in a computer.

Thrust into Spotlight as Head of Center for Astrophysics

After a series of academic appointments in the 1970s and 1980s at the California Institute of Technology, Harvard University, and MIT, Shapiro became a senior scientist at the Smithsonian Astrophysical Observatory in 1982. In January of 1983 Shapiro was chosen as director of the Center for Astrophysics. Originally formed by astronomer and Smithsonian Institute secretary Samuel Pierpont Langley in 1890, the CfA boasted about five hundred staff members, including 170 scientists, by the early 1980s. The CfA headquarters are located on Observatory Hill, about one mile from Harvard University, in Cambridge, Massachusetts, and about fifteen minutes away from Shapiro's home in Lexington, Massachusetts. With facilities in Massachusetts, Texas, and Arizona, the CfA sustains research on a wide variety of areas from theoretical astrophysics to the planetary sciences. Shapiro has tried to steer researchers into the most valuable lines of research. "I try to get the very best people I can—that's where the bright new ideas come from—and I attempt to provide researchers with world-unique facilities," Shapiro told *Smithsonian* writer Bruce Fellman in 1990. Discussing the center's ongoing efforts to study a wide range of radio waves, he added, "Every time we've looked at the Universe in a new wavelength band, we've discovered something new."

Over the years, Shapiro has received many awards and honors, including the Benjamin Apthorp Gould prize of the National Academy of Sciences in 1979, a Guggenheim Fellowship in 1982, and the Charles A. Whitten medal of the American Geophysical Union in 1991.

SELECTED WRITINGS BY SHAPIRO:

Books

The Prediction of Ballistic Missile Trajectories from Radar Observations, McGraw-Hill, 1958.

FURTHER READING:

Periodicals

Fellman, Bruce, *Smithsonian,* After 100 Years Discoveries Come Faster and Faster, December, 1990, pp. 125–26, 128–38, 140, 142.

Park, Edwards, *Smithsonian,* Around the Mall and Beyond, December, 1983, pp. 24, 26, 28–9.

Sketch by Sebastian Thaler

Harlow Shapley

Harlow Shapley
1885–1972
American astronomer

American astronomer Harlow Shapley was known for his accomplishments in astronomy, education, and humanitarian causes. Shapley, whose obituary in the *New York Times* described him as the "dean of American astronomers," was chiefly known for discovering that the Milky Way galaxy was much larger than originally thought and that Earth's solar system was not in fact at the center of the galaxy. For this achievement, he was compared to Nicolaus Copernicus, the Polish astronomer who in 1514 proposed that the Earth was not the center of the solar system. As an educator, Shapley helped make the Harvard Observatory the leading center for astronomy in the United States during his time. Finally, through his humanitarian efforts, Shapley helped save Jewish scientists from Nazi Germany; he also founded and supported international causes and organizations such as the United Nations Educational, Scientific and Cultural Organization (UNESCO).

Shapley was born on November 2, 1885—along with his twin brother, Horace—in Nashville, Missouri. The twins were later followed by a younger brother, John. Shapley's father was farmer and teacher Willis Shapley, and his mother was Sarah Stowell, whose ancestors were early settlers in Massachusetts. Shapley's youth was marked by the death of his father and by limited schooling: a mere five grades' worth of education in a local rural school. Shapley received his high school education from the Presbyterian Carthage Collegiate Institute, from which he graduated in two semesters. In addition, during this time Shapley worked as a reporter for the Chanute *Daily Sun* in Kansas; he was the paper's city editor by age twenty.

Shapley attended college beginning at age twenty, enrolling in the University of Missouri. He originally planned to study journalism but switched to astronomy when he found out that the university's journalism school was still a year away from opening. By his junior year at the

university, Shapley was working as assistant to the director of the Laws Observatory, Frederick H. Seares. Shapley graduated in 1910 with a B.A. in mathematics and physics; the following year he received his M.A.

From the University of Missouri, Shapley went directly to Princeton Observatory as a recipient of the Thaw fellowship in astronomy. Under the guidance of **Henry Norris Russell**, director of the observatory, Shapley completed his graduate work, receiving his Ph.D. in 1913. In his dissertation, Shapley presented information about the properties of stars known as eclipsing binary (or double) stars. He eventually expanded and published his thesis; the resulting work, which analyzed ninety binaries, is considered a significant contribution to the field of astronomy.

In 1913 Shapley interviewed with **George Ellery Hale**, director of the Mount Wilson Observatory in Pasadena, California, about the possibility of obtaining a position there. Shapley got the post, but before moving to California he spent five months touring Europe with his brother John and then returned to Princeton for several months to complete his work there. In addition, on his way to California in 1914, Shapley married Martha Betz, a former classmate from Missouri. Shapley and his wife eventually had five children. Martha Betz Shapley was herself a mathematician and astronomer, and she wrote several scientific papers with her husband.

The Center of the Galaxy

In his seven years at Mount Wilson, Shapley was to make some of his most significant discoveries. Shapley concentrated his efforts on studying stars known as Cepheid variables and on globular clusters—concentrated areas of stars. Shapley found that the Cepheid variables (named for the first star of this type to be discovered, Delta Cephei) were pulsating stars, whose size and brightness fluctuated regularly. Another Harvard astronomer, **Henrietta Leavitt**, had shown that the rate at which a Cepheid pulsed was directly related to its brightness. Using this information, Shapley could then determine the star's absolute brightness (or luminosity) and by comparing this to its observed brightness could calculate how far away the star was.

It was this measuring system that allowed Shapley to determine the placement of Earth's solar system in the Milky Way. Shapley charted the distance and location of the globular clusters and found that they were distributed almost symmetrically above and below the plane of the Milky Way. He then used this information as a guide to the general outline of the Milky Way and estimated that the center of the galaxy was located fifty thousand light-years from the sun, in the constellation Sagittarius. The Shapley Center, as it came to be known, is actually 33,000 light-years from the sun. Shapley also estimated the diameter of the Milky Way to be about 300,000 light-years, later revising that figure to 150,000 light-years.

At the time, Shapley's conclusions were almost revolutionary: his figures increased the then-estimated size of the Milky Way by a factor of ten and as a result, many astronomers believed he overestimated. In fact, Shapley's conclusions weren't fully accepted until he took part in a famous debate at the National Academy of Sciences in Washington in 1920 with Heber D. Curtis of the Lick Observatory. It is generally agreed that at this debate Shapley won his point about the size and structure of the Milky Way.

In addition to his work on the question of the center of the galaxy, Shapley also studied spiral nebulae while at Mount Wilson (in that era, the term "nebula" described anything not positively identified as a star). At the time, astronomers were not sure whether the nebulae were part of the Milky Way or were what was known as "island universes"—in modern terms, galaxies. Several new stars had been discovered in the nebulae, and Shapley, using information about the luminosity of the stars, estimated the distance to the Andromeda nebula (now known as the Andromeda galaxy) to be one million light-years. The theories of other scientists at the time caused Shapley to withdraw this estimate; ironically, his figures turned out to be nearly correct.

Shapley also pursued scientific interests that went beyond astronomy at Mount Wilson. He discovered a relationship between temperature and the speed at which ants run, for instance, and published five scientific papers on ants. According to Shapley biographers, he was especially proud of his work in this area.

Made Harvard Observatory U.S. Leader

Shapley returned to Cambridge, Massachusetts, in 1921 to become director of the Harvard Observatory and Paine Professor of Practical Astronomy. At Harvard he concentrated his research on stars in the Magellanic Clouds (later revealed as two neighboring galaxies), working on a unique round desk that rotated. A few years into his tenure, in 1924, he was elected to the National Academy of Sciences, and he received that organization's Draper Medal in 1926. Among Shapley's scientific achievements in this period was, in the 1930s, the first discovery of two dwarf galaxies in the constellations of Sculptor and Fornax (in the Southern Hemisphere). Interestingly, he used the term "galaxy," while his fellow astronomer and rival of the period, **Edwin Hubble**, used the term "extragalactic nebulae." Shapley maintained that galaxies were distributed irregularly, in contrast to Hubble's view that the universe was more uniform. Shapley's work at Harvard also included overseeing group projects that cataloged tens of thousands of galaxies in both the Northern and Southern hemispheres (the Harvard Observatory had observatories in both hemispheres) and that worked on a catalog of the spectral classifications of stars (the light from a star, broken into its rainbow or spectrum of colors, reveals its chemical make-up).

Perhaps more significantly, Shapley helped make the Harvard Observatory the leading astronomy education center in the United States in the 1920s. He set up a graduate program in astronomy and attracted scientists from the international community as well as from across America. Among the scientists that Shapley brought to Harvard and the United States were refugees from Nazi Germany; in fact, Shapley personally led an effort to bring in Jewish scientists. According to Shapley biographer Bart J. Bok in an article for *Sky and Telescope,* "One of these who came to Harvard was Richard Prager of Berlin Observatory, who told me quietly and seriously that every night at least a thousand Jewish scientists must say a prayer of thanks for Harlow Shapley's humanitarian efforts to help save them and their families." His activities in the early 1940s also included serving as president of the American Academy of Arts and Sciences.

International Efforts

After World War II Shapley continued to focus on international affairs. He helped form the United Nations Educational, Scientific and Cultural Organization, serving as a U.S. representative in writing UNESCO's charter in 1945. Shapley lobbied the U.S. government for the creation of the posts of Secretary of Peace and Welfare, Secretary of Education, and Secretary of Science and Technology after World War II. According to the *New York Times,* Shapley believed that peace should be the first concern of government. Eventually, only the Department of Health, Education, and Welfare was established.

After a visit to the Soviet Union in 1945 as the Harvard representative at the 220th anniversary of the Academy of Sciences in Moscow, Shapley became a supporter of scientific cooperation with the Soviets. He served as chairman of the Independent Citizens Committee of the Arts, Sciences, and Professions, a fund-raising group for liberal congressional candidates. In addition, he was the chairman of several meetings of left-wing groups that dared to invite Russian delegates. Shapley, who believed that the Soviet government's support of science would speed its development, urged the United States to give similar support to research in order to remain competitive. His views were not popular at the time, and in 1946 the House Committee on Un-American Activities subpoenaed Shapley to question him about his views. Shapley's obituary in the *New York Times* reported that Representative John E. Rankin, a Mississippi Democrat who had questioned Shapley as a one-man subcommittee, reported after the meeting, "I have never seen a witness treat a committee with more contempt." The paper reported that in return Shapley charged the committee with "Gestapo methods" and called for its elimination. The same year, Shapley was elected president of the American Association for the Advancement of Science, a move widely regarded as a show of support by the scientific community. Despite his encounter with reactionary politics, Shapley continued with his efforts against the committee, becoming, for example, acting chairman of the Committee of One Thousand, an organization geared toward protecting First Amendment rights. Physicist **Albert Einstein** and author-lecturer Helen Keller were also members. In March of 1950, Senator Joseph McCarthy "charged that Dr. Shapley had belonged to many Communist-front organizations," according to the *New York Times*. Later that year, a Senate subcommittee cleared him of the charges.

Shapley was director of the Harvard Observatory until 1952; he continued to teach courses there until 1956 and then traveled and lectured through his seventies, speaking on astronomy, religion, philosophy, and evolution. His many appearances during his career included one at the 1939 New York World's Fair, at which he gave the speech "Astronomy in the World of Tomorrow." He also wrote extensively, publishing hundreds of scientific papers as well as newspaper and magazine articles and several popular books, including *Through Rugged Ways to the Stars*. At eighty-five Shapley moved to Boulder, Colorado, where one of his four sons lived; he died there in a nursing home at age eighty-six after a long battle with illness.

SELECTED WRITINGS BY SHAPLEY:

Books

Starlight, George H. Doran, 1926.
Flights from Chaos: A Survey of Material Systems from Atoms to Galaxies, McGraw, 1930.
Star Clusters, (monograph), McGraw, 1930.

Of Stars and Men: The Human Response to an Expanding Universe, Beacon Press, 1958, revised edition, 1964.
The View from a Distant Star: Man's Future in the Universe, Basic Books, 1963.
Beyond the Observatory, Scribner, 1967.
Through Rugged Ways to the Stars, Scribner, 1969.

Periodicals

Astrophysical Journal, Sixth Paper: On the Determination of the Distances of Globular Clusters, and "Seventh Paper: The Distances, Distribution in Space, and Dimensions of 69 Globular Clusters," Volume 48, 1918, pp. 89–124, 154–81.
Astrophysical Journal, Twelfth Paper: Remarks on the Sidereal Universe, Volume 49, 1919, pp. 311–36.
Bulletin of the National Research Council, The Scale of the Universe, (article includes material by Heber D. Curtis), Volume 2, number 11, 1921.
Nature, Two Stellar Systems of a New Kind, Volume 142, 1938, pp. 715–16.

FURTHER READING:

Books

Biographical Memoirs, The National Academy of Sciences, Volume 48, Columbia University Press, 1976.
Dictionary of Scientific Biography, Scribner, 1975, pp. 345–52.

Periodicals

Bok, Bart J., *Sky and Telescope,* Harlow Shapley—Cosmographer and Humanitarian, December, 1972, pp. 354–57.
———— , *New York Times,* October 21, 1972, p. 1.

Sketch by Devera Pine

Phillip A. Sharp
1944–
American biologist

Phillip A. Sharp has conducted research into the structure of deoxyribonucleic acid (DNA—the chemical blueprint that synthesizes proteins) which has altered previous views on the mechanism of genetic change. For his work in this area, Sharp was presented with the 1977 Nobel Prize in medicine along with **Richard J. Roberts**. In addition to the Nobel Prize, Sharp has received honors from the American Cancer Society and the National Academy of Science, and is the recipient of the Howard Ricketts Award, the Alfred P. Sloan Jr. Prize, the Albert Lasker Basic Medical Research Award, and the Dickson Prize.

Born in Falmouth, Kentucky, on June 6, 1944, Sharp grew up on a small agricultural farm owned by his parents, Katherin Colvin and Joseph Walter Sharp. Earnings from tobacco land given to him by his parents allowed him to attend Union College in Barbourville, Kentucky, where he received a B.A. degree in chemistry and mathematics in 1966. Sharp earned his Ph.D. degree from the University of Illinois in 1969; he later received an honorary L.H.D. from Union College in 1991.

Sharp and Roberts discovered in 1977 that, in some higher organisms, genes may be comprised of more than one segment, separated by material that apparently plays no part in the creation of the proteins. Previously, most scientists believed that genes were continuous sections of DNA and that the string of coding information that makes up each gene was a single, linear unit. Sharp and Roberts, however, distinguished between the *exons,* the sequences that contain the vital information needed to create the protein, and the *introns,* incoherent biochemical information that interrupts the protein-manufacturing instructions. Each gene is apparently composed of fifteen to twenty exons, in between which introns may be located. During protein synthesis, exons are copied and spliced together, creating complete sequences, while the introns are ignored.

This discovery had not been made earlier largely because scientists had conducted most of their genetic research on prokaryotic organisms, such as bacteria, which do not have their genetic material located in clearly defined nuclei. Studies of bacteria had indicated that gene activity resulted in the transcription of double-stranded DNA into single-stranded messenger ribonucleic acid (mRNA); this is translated to the corresponding protein by ribosomes. Prokaryotic organisms have no introns, however, and therefore could not supply evidence for the existence, or the significance, of noncoding regions of DNA. Roberts and Sharp carried their research out on adenoviruses, the virus responsible for the common cold in humans. Although these are also prokaryotic organisms, Roberts and Sharp were able to take advantage of the fact that viruses reproduce themselves using the mechanisms of eukaryotic cells. Since their genome has some similarities to the genetic material in human cells, their protein synthesis was therefore relevant to the study of the cells of higher organisms.

In their experiments, Sharp's team created hybrid molecules in which they could observe mRNA strands binding to their complementary DNA strands. Electron micrographs allowed the scientists to identify which parts of the viral genomes had produced the mature mRNA molecules. What they discovered was that substantial sections of DNA were ignored in producing the final mRNA. This unexpected result gave evidence of a greater complexity of mRNA synthesis in eukaryotic organisms than in prokaryot-

ic ones. Further research indicated that the mRNAs of eukaryotic organisms are synthesized as large mRNA precursor molecules; the introns are spliced out by means of enzyme activity to produce the mature mRNA that manufactures proteins. They found that a single gene could produce a variety of proteins—some defective—as a result of different splicing patterns.

Further research has indicated that the introns, rather than simply being "junk" DNA, contain some information that is necessary for the production of proteins, but the nature of this information is not yet understood.

It is now believed that many hereditary diseases are caused by imperfect splicing of the genetic material, leading to the creation of faulty proteins. This may occur if the copying and splicing of the exons is not carried out accurately. One such disease is beta-thalassemia, a form of anemia prevalent in some Mediterranean areas that is caused by a faulty protein responsible for the formation of hemoglobin. Because of the insight Sharp and Roberts's research has produced into the mechanisms of cell reproduction, it has important ramifications for research on malignant tumors and the viruses responsible for their development. It has also led to an investigation of methods for stopping the replication of the Human Immunodeficiency Virus type 1 (HIV–1), with potential benefits in the search for a treatment for AIDS.

Sharp and Roberts's work has also led to new theories on the nature of evolutionary change; rather than being the cumulative effect of genetic mutation over time, it is now believed that it may be the result of the shuffling of large segments of DNA into new combinations to produce new proteins.

In 1990, before his earlier work had led to his Nobel Prize, Sharp was offered, and accepted, the presidency of the Massachusetts Institute of Technology. A short time later, he decided not to accept the position in order to devote his time exclusively to research. He has remained active in the field of academic administration, however, and has lobbied for research funding. He has also been active in industry; he was one of the founders of Biogen, a corporation started in Switzerland and now operating in Cambridge, Massachusetts, that has employed techniques developed in genetic engineering to produce the drug interferon.

SELECTED WRITINGS BY SHARP:

Periodicals

Science, Splicing of Messenger RNA Precursors, Volume 235, 1987, pp. 766–71.
Journal of the American Medical Association, Five Easy Pieces, Volume 260, 1988, pp. 3035–041.
Science, Messenger RNA Transport and HIV Rev Regulation, Volume 249, 1990, pp. 614–15.

FURTHER READING:

Periodicals

New York Times, October 12, 1993, p. C3.
Science, Volume 262, October 22, 1993, p. 506.
Science News, October 16, 1993, p. 245.

Sketch by Michael Sims

Robert Phillip Sharp
1911–
American geologist and geomorphologist

Robert Phillip Sharp is primarily known for his investigations into the causes of landscape forms on the surface of the earth and other planets. He has employed techniques derived from the disciplines of geophysics and geochemistry to analyze the problems of landform development, and he isolated and observed the processes producing enough visible changes on a planet within a single human lifetime to allow for adequate research and conclusive results. His research topics have included glaciers and sand dunes, as well as oxygen isotopes in ice and the terrains and landforms on Mars.

Sharp was born on June 24, 1911, in Oxnard, California, to Julian and Alice Darling Sharp. He attended Oxnard Union High School and then earned a B.S. from the California Institute of Technology in 1934, followed by an M.A. in 1935. He completed a Ph.D. in geology at Harvard University in 1938. He taught geology at the University of Illinois from 1938 until he entered military service in 1942 as a captain in the United States Air Force. He taught at the University of Minnesota from 1945 to 1947, and then he returned to the California Institute of Technology, where he taught until 1979, serving as chairman of the geology department from 1952 to 1967. Though he officially retired in 1979, Sharp continues as instructor of the introductory field course in geology at Cal Tech that he has taught for more than thirty years.

Sharp has participated in field explorations and expeditions that have yielded significant discoveries and stimulated further research. In 1937 he accompanied other researchers on an expedition by boat of the Grand Canyon; their findings contributed to the scientific understanding of erosion in the Precambrian era, the earliest geologic era. In 1941 Sharp participated in an expedition to the Ice Field Ranges in the Saint Elias mountains along the border between Alaska and Canada. This project served as the catalyst for comprehensive research on glaciers in Alaska, Canada, and the northwestern United States.

Discovers Causes of Desert Sand Dunes

While employed in the Midwest, Sharp investigated the contrasting characteristics of continental and mountain glaciation, and he identified patterns and formations in the soil created by frozen ground that lay outside of glaciers in Illinois. After moving to southern California, Sharp took the opportunity to study the various processes acting on the earth's surface in desert areas. He studied desert domes and sand dunes, in particular, and among his many findings are his discoveries about sand transport by wind, sandblasting of natural and artificial objects, dune movements, and the causes for the shapes and activities of sand dunes.

Sharp has provided a substantiated theory for how the five-hundred-foot Kelso Dunes of the Mojave Desert were developed; he explained why they were located in the middle of the valley instead of piled up against the mountains, as would be expected given the prevailing wind direction. Because the wind regime in that area is so complex, storm winds are able to cancel out the strong westerly winds. This scenario also explains the asymmetrical shape of sand dunes. His research into dune movement also led Sharp to the important, but as of yet unsubstantiated, projection that the large intradune flats of the Algodones Dunes chain in southeastern California are advancing southeasterly and will eventually jeopardize the All-American Canal. He also studied glacial deposits in the Sierra Nevada of California and distinguished the glacial deposits and features in the earth's surface created by separate episodes of ice advance. His investigations are responsible for expanding the accepted model of Sierra glaciation.

Appointed to Research Landforms on Mars

Sharp's knowledge of terrestrial landforms and processes earned him a position on the team analyzing the results of the various *Mariner* flights to Mars between 1965 and 1971. Sharp and his colleagues interpreted terrains and surface features from photographs of Mars taken from the spacecraft. The team was able to recognize various terrains, and they concluded that although Mars does not now have water, conditions of the planet's surface indicate it did at one time. He theorized that the large chasms in the surface of Mars were due to water trapped underground that froze and melted before it could reach the surface. There were forms on Earth that served as good models for terrestrial features on Mars, but the configuration and scale of these features represent processes that have not occurred here.

Sharp's honors and awards include the Kirk Bryan Award in 1964, the Exceptional Science Achievement Medal from NASA in 1971, and the Penrose Award from the Geology Society of America in 1977. He also received the National Medal of Science in 1989, and the Charles P. Daly Medal from the American Geographical Society in 1991.

In 1938 Sharp married Jean Prescott Todd, whom he met while she was at Radcliffe College. They have two adopted children, a daughter and a son. Sharp now has two grandchildren and he lives in California where he continues his association with the California Institute of Technology; in 1978 an endowed professorship in geology was created there in his name. His research continues to involve those processes that affect land surfaces and that are measurable, as well as forms on the earth's surface such as glaciers and volcanoes.

SELECTED WRITINGS BY SHARP:

Books

Glaciers, University of Oregon Press, 1960.
Geology Field Guide to Southern California, W. C. Brown, 1972.
Geology Field Guide to Coastal Southern California, Kendall Hunt, 1978.
Geology under Foot in Southern California, Mountain Press, 1993.

FURTHER READING:

Books

Sharp, Robert Phillip, *Interview with Kelly Otter Cooper,* conducted October 12, 1993.

Sketch by Kelly Otter Cooper

Mary Shaw
1943–
American computer scientist

Professor of computer science and dean of professional programs at Carnegie-Mellon University in Pittsburgh, Pennsylvania, Mary Shaw has made major contributions to the analysis of computer algorithms, as well as to abstraction techniques for advanced programming methodologies, programming-language architecture, evaluation methods for software performance and reliability, and software engineering. She has also been involved in the development of computer-science education. She was elected to the Institute of Electrical and Electronic Engineers in 1990 and the American Association for the Advancement of Science in 1992; she received the Warnier Prize in 1993.

Mary M. Shaw was born in Washington, D.C., on September 30, 1943, to Eldon and Mary Holman Shaw. Her father was a civil engineer and an economist for the Department of Agriculture, and Shaw attended high school in Bethesda, Maryland, at the height of the Sputnik—the

first artificial satellite—era, when the country was making a concerted effort to bolster science and mathematics education. Her father encouraged her interest in science with books and simple electronic kits when she was in the seventh and eighth grades, and her high school years provided opportunities to delve more deeply into both computers and mathematics.

An International Business Machines (IBM) employee named George Heller from the Washington area participated in an after-school program that taught students about computers; he arranged for the students to visit an IBM facility and run a program on an IBM 709 computer. This was Shaw's introduction to computers. For two summers during high school, as well as during the summer after she graduated, she worked at the Research Analysis Corporation at the Johns Hopkins University Operation Research Office. This was part of a program begun by a woman named Jean Taylor to give advanced students a chance to explore fields outside the normal high school curriculum. "They would give us a system analysis problem and ask us to investigate," Shaw told contributor Rowan Dordick. Among the problems she worked on was a study of the feasibility of using irradiated foods to supply army units.

Shaw entered Rice University with the idea of becoming a topologist, having become enamored with Moebius strips and Klein bottles while in high school. She quickly changed her mind, however, after looking through a textbook on topology. Though there were no courses at that time in computer science, there was something called the Rice Computer Project, a group that had built a computer—the Rice I—under the leadership of an electrical engineering professor named Martin Graham. Shaw wandered into the project area one day and asked a question about the computer. By way of an answer, she was given a machine reference manual and was told to read it first and then come back. She surprised the project members by doing just that. It was a small group, consisting mostly of faculty and graduate students, and Shaw ended up working with the project part-time during her last three years, under the mentorship of Jane Jodeit, the head programmer. Shaw gained valuable experience on the Rice I; she worked on a programming language, wrote subroutines, and helped figure out ways to make the operating system run faster.

After her junior year, Shaw attended summer school at The University of Michigan, where she met Alan Perlis, a professor at Carnegie Mellon University. After receiving her B.A. cum laude in mathematics from Rice in 1965, she entered Carnegie Mellon, where Perlis became one of her advisors. She received her Ph.D. in 1971 in computer science, with a thesis on compilers—programs that translate language a human can easily understand into language that the computer understands. Shaw was invited to join the faculty after receiving her degree. One of her first notable accomplishments, in collaboration with Joseph Traub, was the development of what is known as the Shaw-Traub algorithm, an improved method for evaluating a polynomial that allows computers to compute faster. This effort was part of a general interest Shaw had in finding ways to formalize computations in order to make them more efficient.

Clarifies the Organization of Data in Programs

Shaw's focus on improved software design led her to pursue an approach to the organization of computer programs called abstract-data types. This approach is one of the foundations of object-oriented programming. Large programs are difficult to read or modify unless there is some intrinsic structure, and this is the problem abstract-data-type programming was designed to address. Abstract-data types is a method of organizing the data and computations used by a program so that related information is grouped together. For example, information about electronic details of a telephone-switching network would be grouped in one part of the program, whereas information about people and their telephone numbers would be grouped in another part.

Shaw's work in this area came to fruition in two ways. The first was in the creation of a programming language called Alphard that implemented abstract-data types; she developed this language with William A. Wulf and Ralph L. London between 1974 and 1978. The second, more theoretical result, was the clarification of abstractions in programming. Shaw made it easier to design programs that are more abstract—the word "abstract" in this context means that elements of the program are further removed from the details of how the computer works and closer to the language of the problem that a user is trying to solve. This work can be viewed as a continuation of the trend in programming languages, begun with FORTRAN, to write programs in a higher-order language that reflects the nature of the problem, as opposed to programming in the binary machine language—ones and zeros—that the computer understands.

Charts a Future for Software Engineering

Shaw's concerns with abstraction proved a natural bridge to a more general issue, which she posed to herself as a question: What other ways are there of organizing programs? The answer emerged as Shaw came to realize that what she was really looking for was the organization of software engineering. In "Prospects for an Engineering Discipline of Software," she wrote: "The term 'software engineering' was coined in 1968 as a statement of aspiration—a sort of rallying cry." The problem, as she and others realized, was that the term was not so much the name of a discipline as a reminder that one did not yet exist.

Through historical study of the evolution of civil and chemical engineering, Shaw has developed a three-stage model for the maturation of a field into a complete engineering discipline. She has shown that an engineering discipline begins with a craft stage, characterized by the use of intuition and casually learned techniques by talented amateurs; it then proceeds through a commercial stage, in which large-scale manufacturing relies on skilled craftsmen using established techniques that are refined over time.

Finally, as a scientific basis for the discipline emerges, the third stage evolves, in which educated professionals using analysis and theory create new applications and specialties and embody the knowledge of the discipline in treatises and handbooks. Shaw has concluded that contemporary software engineering lies somewhere between the craft and commercial stages, and this conclusion has led to an effort on her part first to promote an understanding of where software engineering should be headed and second to develop the scientific understanding needed to move the discipline into the third stage.

The transformation of a discipline proceeds through its practitioners, so it is natural that Shaw has devoted much of her career to improving computer-science education. She was a coauthor of the first undergraduate text to incorporate the concept of abstract-data structures, and she led a group that redesigned the undergraduate computer-science curriculum. She was also involved in the execution of an innovative Ph.D. program that has been widely adopted.

Shaw's accomplishments are not limited to computer science. She was the National Women's Canoe Poling Champion from 1975 to 1978, and she placed in the Whitewater Open Canoe National Championships in 1991. Her marriage to Roy R. Weil—a civil engineer, software engineer, and commercial balloon pilot—spurred an interest in aviation. She has become an instrument-rated pilot, a single-engine commercial glider pilot, and a Federal Aviation Administration (FAA) certified ground instructor.

SELECTED WRITINGS BY SHAW:

Books

Fundamental Structures of Computer Science, Addison-Wesley, 1981.

Periodicals

Journal of the ACM, On the Number of Multiplications for the Evaluation of a Polynomial and Some of Its Derivatives, January, 1974, pp. 161–67.
IEEE Transactions on Software Engineering, An Introduction to the Construction and Verification of Alphard Programs, December, 1976, pp. 253–65.
Proceedings of the IEEE, The Impact of Abstraction Concerns on Modern Programming Languages, September, 1980, pp. 1119–130.
IEEE Software, Prospects for an Engineering Discipline of Software, November, 1990, pp. 15–24.

Other

Interview with Rowan Dordick, conducted on February 2, 1994.

Sketch by Rowan L. Dordick

Rupert Sheldrake
1942–
English biochemist

Rupert Sheldrake, a British biochemist, is best known for his controversial hypothesis of "formative causation," or the idea that nature itself has memory. According to Sheldrake's theory, every system in the universe—molecules, cells, crystals, organisms, societies—reacts in similar or established patterns in response to invisible fields of influence. This is known as "morphic resonance." Sheldrake purports that the invisible field, known as a "morphic field," is where established patterns collect to influence a like activity that may be taking place contemporaneously. An example that he often uses to convey this idea more readily is that of crystallization; in his book *The Rebirth of Nature,* Sheldrake explained morphic resonance thus: "The development of crystals is shaped by morphogenetic fields with an inherent memory of previous crystals of the same kind. From this point of view, substances such as penicillin crystallize the way they do not because they are governed by timeless mathematical laws but because they have crystallized that way before; they are following habits established through repetition." Sheldrake further claims that morphic resonance transcends time and space.

Born Alfred Rupert Sheldrake on June 28, 1942, in Newark Notts, England, Sheldrake received his Ph.D. in biochemistry from Cambridge University. He was a research fellow of the Royal Society and a fellow of and director of studies in cell biology and biochemistry at Clare College at Cambridge. He studied philosophy at Harvard from 1963 to 1964 as a Frank Knox Fellow in the special studies program. Beginning in 1974, Sheldrake conducted research on tropical plants at the International Research Institute in India, as well as in Malaysia. He is married to Jill Purce, has two sons, and lives in London. Sheldrake's father was an herbalist and pharmacist. Sheldrake credits his strong interest in plants and animals to both of his parents, who encouraged him in his studies.

Sheldrake developed the necessary emotional detachment required of one pursuing scientific study during his early years at Cambridge. He came to believe—as he was taught—that nature was, in fact, a lifeless mechanistic system without purpose. But a tension persisted between his scientific studies and his personal experiences. He felt the two bore little relationship to each other and were often irreconcilable. He later came to see this conflict as rooted in the mechanistic view of nature—nature as lifeless as opposed to nature as alive and evolving. Sheldrake's hypothesis of formative causation, with its morphic fields creating morphic resonance, subscribes to the latter view.

Sheldrake's books, *A New Science of Life* (1981), *The Presence of the Past* (1988), and *The Rebirth of Nature* (1991) address his theory of formative causation—one not openly embraced by the scientific community at large. Sheldrake's theory that nature has memory and is, therefore, alive challenges the basic foundations of modern science. According to Sheldrake, the conventional scientific approach has been unable to answer the questions relative to morphogenesis—how things come into being or take form—because of their mechanistic outlook.

Sheldrake's hypothesis has elicited much criticism from his contemporaries. Joseph Hannibal, writing for *Library Journal* on *The Rebirth of Nature,* stated, "This new work is even more unorthodox—some might say outrageous—as Sheldrake attempts to combine scientific, religious, and even mystical views." Critic Patrick H. Samway wrote in *America,* "Sheldrake's methodology parallels in many ways that of the Jesuit paleontologist Teilhard de Chardin, who formulated his view that the world in its entirety is developing toward the Omega Point."

Some of Sheldrake's contemporaries who do not subscribe to the theory of formative causation do, nonetheless, believe that science must be open to new possibilities. "Science is not threatened by the imaginative ideas of the Sheldrakes of the world," wrote fellow scientist **James Lovelock** in *Nature,* "but those who would censor them." Lovelock went on to say, "Sheldrake is a threat, but only to the established positions of those who teach and practice an authoritarian science. A healthy scientific community would accept or reject formative causation as the evidence appeared." Critic Theodore Roszak allowed in *New Science,* "If for no better reason than to exercise their wits against a first class polemic, his critics should value this work. Finding answers to his questions will fortify their ideology." And though terms such as "unrealistic," "fanciful," and "off-the-wall" have been used to describe Sheldrake's hypothesis of formative causation, his theory has indeed received significant attention from the scientific community.

SELECTED WRITINGS BY SHELDRAKE:

Books

A New Science of Life: The Hypothesis of Formative Causation, Blonds & Briggs, 1981.
The Presence of the Past: Morphic Resonance and the Habits of Nature, Times Books, 1988.
The Rebirth of Nature: The Greening of Science and God, Bantam, 1991.

Periodicals

Biological Reviews, The Production of Auxin in Higher Plants, Volume 48, 1973, pp. 509–59.
Nature, The Ageing, Growth and Death of Cells, Volume 250, 1974, pp. 381–85.

FURTHER READING:

Periodicals

Hannibal, Joseph, review of *The Rebirth of Nature,* *Library Journal,* December, 1990.

Lovelock, James E., *Nature,* A Danger to Science?, Volume 348, December, 1990, p. 685.

Marbach, William D., *Newsweek,* A New Theory of Causation, July 7, 1986, p. 64.

Raeburn, Paul, *Psychology Today,* Morphic Fancies, July-August, 1988.

——— , *Time,* The Rebirth of Nature: The Greening of Science and God, by Rupert Sheldrake, December 3, 1990.

Roszak, Theodore, *New Science,* The Greening of Rupert Sheldrake, January, 1991, p. 54.

Samway, Patrick H., review of *The Rebirth of Nature, America,* March 2, 1991.

Sketch by Paula M. Morin

Alan B. Shepard, Jr.
1923–
American astronaut

One of the original seven American astronauts, Alan B. Shepard, Jr. became the first American to venture into space in a suborbital flight aboard the Mercury capsule, *Freedom 7*. His achievements—including his landmark *Freedom 7* flight on May 5, 1961—symbolized the beginning of a technological revolution in the 1960s and marked the onset of "new frontiers" in space. A decade later, he commanded the *Apollo 14* lunar mission, becoming the fifth man to step on the moon's surface and the only one of the original astronauts to make a flight to the moon. In addition to his space flight accomplishments, he served as chief of the astronaut office and participated in the overall astronaut training program. He received the National Aeronautics Space Administration (NASA) Distinguished Service Medal from President John F. Kennedy for his Mercury flight. In 1971, appointed by President Nixon, he served as a delegate to the 26th United Nations General Assembly. He was promoted to rear admiral by the Navy in 1971, the first astronaut to achieve flag rank. In 1979 President Jimmy Carter awarded him the Medal of Honor for gallantry in the astronaut corps.

Alan Bartlett Shepard, Jr. was born on November 18, 1923, in East Derry, New Hampshire, and spent most of his formative years in this New England setting. The son of a career military man—his father was an Army colonel—Shepard showed a strong interest at an early age for mechanical things, disassembling motors and engines and building model airplanes. He attended primary school in East Derry and received his secondary education from Pinkerton Academy in Derry in 1940. During high school, he did odd jobs at the local airport hangar in exchange for a chance to take airplane rides. There was little doubt in the family that Shepard would pursue a military career, and after completing a year's study at Admiral Farragut Academy, in New Jersey, he entered the U.S. Naval Academy, graduating in 1944 with a B.S. in science. Shepard married the former Louise Brewer of Kennett Square, Pennsylvania, and has two daughters, Laura and Julie.

Shepard's flying career began in 1947 after he served aboard the destroyer USS *Cogzwell* in the Pacific during the last year of World War II. He received flight training at both Corpus Christi, Texas, and Pensacola, Florida, receiving his wings in 1947. Between the years 1947 and 1950, he served with Fighter Squadron 42 at bases in Virginia and Florida, completing two cruises aboard carriers in the Mediterranean. In 1950 as a lieutenant, junior grade, he was selected to attend U.S. Navy Test Pilot School at Patuxent River in Maryland, serving two years in flight test work at that station. During those tours, he participated in high-altitude tests and experiments in the development of the navy's in–flight refueling system. He was project test pilot on the FSD *Skylancer* and was involved in testing the first angled deck on a U.S. Navy carrier. During his second tour to Patuxent for flight test work, the navy sent him to the Naval War College in Newport, Rhode Island. Upon graduation he became a staff officer at Atlantic Fleet Headquarters in Norfolk, in charge of aircraft readiness for the fleet. Being skipper of an aircraft squadron was a goal of any career pilot in the navy and one that was of interest to Shepard. About this same time, NASA was developing Project Mercury and was seeking astronauts for America's space program.

Making Space History

Knowing that he met the required qualifications of NASA's advertised program, Shepard eagerly applied for a chance to serve his country and meet the challenge of the race to space. On April 27, 1959, NASA announced that Shepard and six other astronauts were selected as the first class of astronauts. A rigorous and intensive training program followed as preparations were being made for the first manned space flight. With the Russian space program forging ahead, it was imperative that a U.S. astronaut follow cosmonaut **Yury Gagarin** into space as soon as possible. Three astronauts, Shepard, Virgil Grissom, and **John Glenn** were selected to make three suborbital "up-and-down" missions to ready Mercury for orbital flight. Interest in the first manned American space flight was keen, forcing NASA to keep Shepard's identity secret until three days before the launch. At 9:45 A.M. on May 5th, 1961, Shepard, enclosed in the tiny bell-shaped Mercury capsule named *Freedom 7,* was thrust into space by a Redstone rocket to a distance of 2300 miles and a height of 113 miles above the surface of the Earth. The flight lasted only 15 minutes and 22 seconds and travelled at a speed of 5,180 mph. According to *Space Almanac,* Shepard, reporting from space that everything was "AOK," was weightless just five minutes before splashdown in the Atlantic Ocean. The USS *Lake Champlain* spotted his orange and white parachute 297 miles downrange from Cape Canaveral. Just before landing, the heat shield was dropped 4 feet, pulling out a rubberized landing bag designed to reduce shock. Shepard exclaimed "Boy what a ride," according to Tim Furniss in *Manned Spaceflight Log,* and with that successful, textbook perfect launch, NASA's space program gained support from the government and from people around the world.

Shepard's performance also showed the world the tradition of engineering excellence, professionalism and dedication that was evident in the subsequent missions. About ten weeks after this historic flight another Mercury-Redstone blasted Virgil Grissom's spacecraft for a similar flight. Shepard continued his training and space preparation and was selected for one of the early Gemini flights, but in early 1964 his career was sharply changed by an inner–ear ailment called Meniere's syndrome, which causes an imbalance and a gradual degradation of hearing. The Navy doctors would not let Shepard fly solo in jet planes, which forced NASA to ground him. The offer of a job as chief of the astronaut office with NASA came along about this time, and it helped allay some of the intense disappointment that Shepard experienced. As chief, Shepard was in charge of all phases of the astronaut training program and played an influential role in the selection of crews for upcoming missions. Periodic checks on his condition during this time showed a continued loss of hearing on the left side, and in May 1968, he submitted to an experimental operation to insert a plastic tube to relieve the pressure in his inner ear. After waiting six months for the final results of the operation, Shepard was declared by NASA officials and doctors fully fit to fly and to resume his role in the space flight program.

A Ride to the Moon

Shepard worked extremely hard and long to ready himself for his next space endeavor, *Apollo 14,* which would last nine days and send a crew of three to the moon. The crew for this flight, Shepard as mission commander, Stuart Roosa as Command module pilot, and Edgar Mitchell as pilot of the lunar excursion module, was chosen in August 1969, just after the successful moon landing by *Apollo 11.* The mission was tentatively scheduled for an October 1970, launch date, but the explosion of the oxygen tank aboard *Apollo 13* called for several alterations in the *Apollo 14* spacecraft. One of the goals of this flight was to explore the Fra Mauro region of the Moon, and Shepard and Mitchell each spent more than 300 hours walking in desert areas and using simulators that resembled the lunar surface. A Saturn V rocket launched the *Apollo 14* capsule at 4:03 p.m. on January 3l, 1971. The astronauts had chosen the name *Kitty Hawk* as a tribute to the first manned powered flight in 1903 and named the lunar lander *Antares* for the star on which it would orient itself just before descending to the Fra Mauro landing site. *Apollo 14* entered lunar orbit on February 4, with touchdown in the uplands of the cone crater scheduled for the next day. Shepard and Mitchell departed from *Kitty Hawk* and *Antares* and descended

smoothly to the surface, coming to rest on an 8 degree slope. Shepard descended the lander's ladder, stepping on the moon at 9:53 A.M., February 5, becoming the fifth man to walk on the moon. With much emotion, he reported to Houston, "I'm on the surface. It's been a long way, and I'm here," as quoted by Anthony J. Cipriano in *America's Journeys into Space.* He and Mitchell then collected 43 pounds of lunar samples and deployed TV, communications, and scientific equipment in their first extra vehicular activity (EVA), which lasted 4 hours, 49 minutes. Their second EVA lasted 4 hours, 35 minutes, and the two astronauts used a Modularized Equipment Transporter for this landing. It was a rickshaw-like device in which they pulled their tools, cameras and samples with them across the moon. Shepard and Mitchell set off the first two moon-quakes to be read by seismic monitors planted by earlier *Apollo* moonwalkers. As they prepared to leave the lunar surface in *Antares,* Shepard, an avid golfer, surprised his audience by making the first golf shot on the Moon, rigging a 6-iron club head to the end of a digging tool and hitting a ball hundreds of yards. On February 6, *Kitty Hawk* rocketed out of lunar orbit and headed for Earth. After nearly three days of coasting flight, *Apollo 14* splashed down in the Pacific Ocean, 4.6 miles from the recovery vessel *New Orleans,* on February 9—216 hours, 42 minutes after launch.

Return to Private Life

At Shepard's retirement from NASA and the U.S. Navy on August 1, 1974, Dr. James C. Fletcher, NASA Administrator, praised the astronaut's dedication and determination in a *NASA News* bulletin. "Al Shepard was the first American to make a space flight and his determination to overcome a physical ailment after his suborbital mission carried him to a highly successful manned lunar landing mission." Shepard joined the private sector as partner and chairman of the Marathon Construction Company of Houston, Texas. He has become an extremely successful businessman in Houston, pursuing interests as a commercial property developer, a venture capital group partner, and director of mutual fund companies. He also chairs the board of the Mercury Seven Foundation, created by the six living Mercury Seven astronauts and Grissom's widow to raise money for science and engineering scholarships. The Mercury capsule *Freedom 7* is on display at the National Air and Space Museum in Washington, D.C., and the *Apollo 14* command module *Kitty Hawk* is displayed at the Los Angeles County Museum in California.

SELECTED WRITINGS BY SHEPARD:

Books

We Seven, Simon and Schuster, 1962.

FURTHER READING:

Books

Bell, Joseph N., *Seven into Space: The Story of the Mercury Astronauts,* University of Chicago Press, 1960.

Caiden, Martin, *The Astronauts: The Story of Project Mercury America's Man-in-Space Program,* Dutton, 1960.

Cipriano, Anthony J., *America's Journeys into Space: The Astronauts of the United States,* Messner, 1979, pp. 136–40.

Furniss, Tim, *Manned Spaceflight Log,* Jane's Publishing, 1983.

Kennedy, Gregory P., *The First Men in Space,* Chelsea House, 1991.

———— , *Research Guide to American Historical Biography,* Volume 5, Beacham Pub., 1991.

Spangenburg, Ray and Diane Moser, *Space Exploration; Space People from A-Z,* Facts-on-File, 1990.

Westman, Paul, *Alan Shepard: The First American in Space,* Dillon Press, 1979.

Wolf, Tom, *The Right Stuff,* Farrar Straus, 1979.

Periodicals

Cole, Dandridge, *Ad Astra,* Alan B. Shepard, Jr., July/August, 1991, p. 60.

Hall, A. J., *National Geographic,* Climb up Cone Crater, Volume 140, July, 1971, p. 136–48.

———— , *NASA News,* (bulletin), NASA, July 19, 1974, p. 2.

Wainwright, Louden, *Life,* The Old Pro Gets His Shot at the Moon, July 3l, 1970.

Sketch by Nancy E. Bard

Roger N. Shepard
1929–

American psychologist

Roger Newland Shepard is a psychologist whose work has advanced our understanding of how the human mind perceives the physical world. Shepard made great progress in studying mental processes that were previously thought to be beyond the scope of rigorous research. In the process, he changed the way scientists and the public alike view mental imagery, and he influenced fields ranging from psychology and neuroscience to philosophy and computer science. His basic research laid the groundwork for a number of practical applications by others. These include the design of better organized cockpit displays, the develop-ment of improved ways to detect breast cancer, and the discovery of more accurate ways to predict the skill of future pilots.

Shepard was born on January 30, 1929, in Palo Alto, California. He was the elder of two children born to Orson Cutler Shepard, an engineering professor at Stanford University, and Grace Newland Shepard, a homemaker. Writing to author Linda Wasmer Smith in 1997, Shepard recalled that as a boy he "was enthralled by science, but less from exposure in school than from early exposure through my father." He also enjoyed drawing, a hobby he traced to his mother, who dabbled in watercolor, weaving, and needlework. These interests endured, as did Shepard's childhood penchant for perceptual pranks. In his 1990 book, *Mind Sights,* Shepard noted that the types of pranks that especially appealed to him "were those whose essential elements were perceptual incongruity and surprise." For example, he once surreptitiously removed the rug, curtains, and all the furniture from his sister's bedroom, so as to shock her when she tried to go to bed.

As an undergraduate at Stanford, Shepard had trouble deciding upon a major course of study. His agile mind was alternately attracted by art, music, philosophy, and physics. He finally settled on psychology, however, and he received a B.A. degree in that field in 1951. One factor shaping his decision was a growing conviction that there were general principles of the mind not unlike the universal laws of physics. Shepard wanted to apply mathematical methods to studying the mind, something that had rarely been done in the past. For graduate school, Shepard moved to Yale University, where he completed a M.S. degree in 1952 and a Ph.D. in 1955. For postdoctoral training, Shepard moved once again, this time to Harvard University, where he served as a research fellow from 1956 to 1958. At both schools, he sought out the guidance of mathematically oriented professors, such as cognitive psychologist George A. Miller at Harvard.

In 1958 Shepard accepted a post with the technical staff at Bell Telephone Laboratories in Murray Hill, New Jersey. There he had access to state-of-the-art computer facilities. Shepard used these facilities to develop a method for converting qualitative data into quantitative representations. This method, which came to be known as nonmetric multidimensional scaling, has since been applied to a wide range of behavioral, social, and medical problems. Also while at Bell Labs, Shepard used the computer to generate an auditory illusion: a repeating series of tones that sound as if they are forever rising in pitch. These "Shepard tones" have since been incorporated into the works of several composers as well as used in studies of human auditory perception.

The Art and Science of Mental Imagery

In 1966 Shepard returned to Harvard as a psychology professor. Then, in 1968, he joined the faculty at Stanford, in the same year that his father retired from that university. Three years later, he published the first of many papers coauthored with graduate students that explored what came to be known as mental rotation. Shepard showed that when people visualize objects, they imagine them moving in much the same way that the physical objects might be rotated. He also showed that these mental movements can be measured. The idea that mental imagery could be analyzed in a rigorous manner was a revolutionary concept at the time. Shepard and graduate student Lynn A. Cooper covered this topic in their 1982 book, *Mental Images and Their Transformations.*

The direction that Shepard's work has taken over the years has been guided by his personal beliefs. In his letter to author Linda Wasmer Smith, he explained his philosophy. "Having evolved in a world governed by general laws, we have internalized a knowledge of these laws, both through natural selection of our genes and through individual learning. This knowledge is deeply built into our perceptual and representational systems at a level that is not accessible to conscious introspection." Yet Shepard says we have some access to this knowledge through "thought experiments," in which we do mental manipulations based upon our inborn but unconscious wisdom about the fundamental nature of the physical world. One thing Shepard believes we have internalized is a principle of generalization. This lets us recognize, for example, that poodles and collies are both dogs. In 1987, he proposed a "universal law of generalization," in which he argued that generalization is the most basic principle of behavioral and cognitive science.

In 1995 Shepard was presented the National Medal of Science by President Bill Clinton. The citation noted, among other things, "his creative theoretical and experimental work elucidating how the human mind perceives and represents the physical world." His other awards include the 1976 Distinguished Scientific Contribution Award from the American Psychological Association. Shepard has been elected to the National Academy of Sciences and the American Academy of Arts and Sciences. He has also been named a Guggenheim fellow as well as a fellow of the Center for Advanced Study in the Behavioral Sciences.

Shepard married Barbaranne Bradley, an early childhood educator, on August 18, 1952, in her hometown of Redfield, South Dakota. The couple have three grown children: Newland, Todd, and Shenna. Shepard is not only a scientist but also a skilled artist, and several of his drawings of visual illusions appear in the book *Mind Sights*. His recreational passions are as varied as his professional ones. He enjoys composing music, writing poetry, taking photographs, hiking, in-line skating, and reading about science.

SELECTED WRITINGS BY SHEPARD:

Books

(With Lynn A. Cooper) *Mental Images and Their Transformations.* Cambridge, MA: MIT Press, 1982.

Mind Sights: Original Visual Illusions, Ambiguities, and Other Anomalies, with a Commentary on the Play of Mind in Perception and Art. New York: W.H. Freeman, 1990.

FURTHER READING:

Periodicals

"Roger N. Shepard." *American Psychologist* (January 1977): 62-5.

Salisbury, David. "For Roger Shepard, It's All in the Mind." *Stanford Report* (September 27, 1995): 5-6.

Salisbury, David F. "Visualization: The Secret Key to Progress." *Stanford Observer* (March-April 1994): 13.

Stites, Janet. "Roger Shepard." *The Bulletin of the Santa Fe Institute* (Summer 1994): 13-15.

Other

National Medal of Science, citation dated September 11, 1995.

"Psychologist Receives National Medal of Science." http://www.apa.org/psa/novdec95/shep.html (October 22, 1997).

"The Mind's Eye: Finding Truth in Illusion." *Frontiers Newsletter* (June 1996). http://www.nsf.gov/od/lpa/news/publicat/frontier/6-96/6illusio.htm (October 22, 1997).

Sketch by Linda Wasmer Smith

Charles Scott Sherrington
1857–1952
English neurophysiologist

Charles Scott Sherrington helped to found the discipline of neurophysiology by his research on how nerve impulses are transmitted between the central nervous system and muscles. Sherrington focused much of his career on understanding the structure and the function of the nervous system. Drawing on the research of Spanish neuroanatomist **Santiago Ramón Cajal**, Sherrington proposed viewing nervous activity as part of an integrated and complex system. For his work on how the central nervous system elicits motor activity from muscles, Sherrington shared the 1932 Nobel Prize in physiology or medicine with **Edgar Douglas Adrian**.

Born November 27, 1857, in London, England, Sherrington was the son of James Norton and Anne (Brookes)

Charles Scott Sherrington

Sherrington. James Sherrington died while his son was still very young, and later Sherrington's mother married Caleb Rose, Jr., a physician in Ipswich, England. Rose was broadly and classically educated, and his home served as a gathering place for artists, writers, and scholars. Exposure to these diverse arts influenced Sherrington and was reflected in his own broad interests in the humanities and the sciences. After attending Ipswich Grammar School, Sherrington began medical training in 1875 at St. Thomas's Hospital in London. In 1879 he enrolled in Caius College at Cambridge University. Two years later, Sherrington began work in the laboratory of Michael Foster, England's foremost physiologist. In Foster's laboratory, Sherrington also met John Newport Langley, Newell Martin, Walter Gaskell, and Sheridan Lea, individuals who would become important physiologists in their own right.

Proposes an Integrated Nervous System

After earning a bachelor's degree in medicine in 1884, Sherrington left Cambridge to pursue graduate studies in German laboratories. He remained abroad for three years, receiving training and conducting research in physiology, histology, and pathology, and working in the laboratories of Rudolf Virchow, **Robert Koch**, and Friedrich Goltz, with whom he studied the central nervous system. Upon returning to England, Sherrington assumed a post teaching systematic physiology to medical students at his training site, St. Thomas's Hospital in London. He left this position in 1891 to become professor and superintendent of the

Brown Institute for Advanced Physiological and Pathological Research. A year later, Sherrington married Ethel Mary Wright; their only child, Charles E. R. Sherrington, was born in 1897.

Sherrington accepted the physiology chair at the University of Liverpool in 1895. Seeking to understand the structures and the mechanisms that operated the nervous system, Sherrington began to draw on the work of Ramón y Cajal. Prior to the latter scientist's work in the late 1880s, neurophysiologists believed that nerve fibers formed a continuous network or system through the body. This proposition was known as the reticular theory. Ramón y Cajal refuted the reticular theory by using a silver-based dye developed by the Italian anatomist **Camillo Golgi**. Golgi's preparation stained individual nerve cells a black color and demonstrated to neuroanatomists that nerve cells were discrete entities and not part of a nexus as was previously thought. The new theory that saw nerve cells as independent units was called the neuron theory, or popularly, the neuron doctrine. Although nerve cells were discrete units, neurons in a series could form pathways through which information can be transmitted. Nerves—consisting of a bundle of fibers—relay sensations (like touch and smell) and instructions on motor activity (like moving an arm or a leg) by electrical impulses. Sherrington became interested in understanding how nerves formed integrative pathways between the central nervous system and muscles. He considered some simple reflexive behavior, such as the knee-jerk, and attempted to explain the neurophysiology of the phenomena. Finding that he had an insufficient knowledge of neural anatomy to conduct the research, Sherrington stoically devoted the next decade to mapping the pathways between the central nervous system and muscle groups and to identifying the sensory nerves that innervated muscle tissue.

Sherrington's commitment to understanding the neural pathways proved to have an important impact. He came to realize that a particular reflexive behavior was not controlled by a single pathway or an isolated response to a single stimulus. Rather, a simple reflex was the product of a complex process that involved the inhibition and excitation of many nerve cells in many different pathways. Sherrington concluded that the central nervous system was an integrated whole that coordinated multiple pathways to produce any single action. His contributions on this point were not only theoretical but experimental. He introduced seminal research strategies for studying questions of the central nervous system. For example, the spinal animal, an animal with a transected spinal cord, and the decerebrate rigid animal, an animal partially paralyzed by the excision of the cerebral cortex, were introduced as important approaches to exploring the activity of the nervous system. Sherrington's analysis of the hind limb scratch of a dog helped to elucidate neuronal action.

Continues Explorations of the Central Nervous System

Sherrington's study of the scratch reflex in dogs elucidated other important principles of how the central nervous system is organized. He concluded that reflexes can have "reciprocal innervation" so that inhibitory and excitatory reflexes are coordinated simultaneously. Sherrington also concluded that there are two levels on which actions are controlled—higher level control by the brain and lower level control by the muscle nerves. His most important idea perhaps reflected in the integrative scheme is that there is a break between one nerve cell and another, between brain and muscles, between inhibitory and excitatory processes. To describe this break, Sherrington coined the term "synapse." The idea of a synapse became important for two reasons. First, it acknowledged that nerve cells were not organized in the reticular fashion as it was previously argued. Second, understanding how synapses were transcended became the next challenge for twentieth-century neurophysiologists. Sherrington lucidly offered these ideas about the nervous system in his seminal work, *The Integrative Action of the Nervous System,* published in 1906.

In 1913 Sherrington left the University of Liverpool after eighteen years of service to assume the Waynflete Professorship of Physiology at Oxford University. The post offered Sherrington the opportunity to continue his research on the central nervous system, but the entry of Great Britain into World War I in August 1914 meant Sherrington had to postpone his studies for some time. He joined the war effort, serving as chair of the Industrial Fatigue Board. Not satisfied with merely reading about the conditions of wartime industrial workers, in 1915 Sherrington worked incognito in a shell factory to experience first hand the hardships and long shifts faced by workers. Although he managed to complete a textbook of physiology during the war period, Sherrington did not return to his normal research work until the mid–1920s. He successfully recruited a number of promising assistants, including E. G. T. Liddell and **John Carew Eccles**. Eccles would go on to win the 1963 Nobel Prize in physiology or medicine for research that had its roots in his stint in Sherrington's Oxford laboratory. Eccles, Liddell, and Sherrington's other students grew in reputation as the "Sherrington school," and their assistance allowed Sherrington to complete a minimum of an experiment a week.

Sherrington's research at Oxford after the 1920s differed from the work that he had been doing prior to World War I. Rather than studying the nervous system as a whole, Sherrington focused his attention on specific mechanisms in the central nervous system. He developed with Eccles the idea of a "motor unit"—a nerve cell that coordinates many muscle fibers. He also concluded that neuronal excitation and inhibition were separate and distinct processes; one was not merely the absence of the other.

Leads an Active Life during Retirement

Although Sherrington retired in 1936, four years after being named a Nobel Prize-winner, he maintained an active life after his formal retirement. He cultivated many of the interests that he had as child in the eclectic home of his stepfather, including poetry, history, and philosophy. In 1925 Sherrington wrote and published a book of poems titled *The Assaying of Brabantius.* His deep interests in philosophy and history were reflected in two post-retirement publications, *Man on His Nature* (1941) and *The Endeavor of Jean Fernel* (1946). In addition to being a popular and sought-after speaker, Sherrington was a trustee of the British Museum in London and served as governor of the Ipswich School from which he had graduated.

In addition to the Nobel Prize, Sherrington garnered virtually every honor that could be given to a British scientist. At the time of his death in 1952, he held memberships in more than forty scholarly societies and had been given honorary degrees from twenty-two universities. Most notably, Sherrington was a past president of the Royal Society of London (1920–1925), and recipient of the Knight Grand Cross of the British Empire in 1922 and the Order of Merit in 1924. He died on March 4, 1952, from heart failure.

SELECTED WRITINGS BY SHERRINGTON:

Books

The Integrative Action of the Nervous System, Yale University Press, 1906.
Reflex Activity of the Spinal Cord, Oxford University Press, 1932.
The Brain and Its Mechanism, Cambridge University Press, 1933.
Man on His Nature, Cambridge University Press, 1941.

FURTHER READING:

Books

Brazier, Mary, *Handbook of Physiology, Section I: Neurophysiology,* The Historical Development of Neurophysiology, edited by John Field, H. W. Magoun, and Volume E. Hall, American Physiological Society, 1959.
Fearing, Franklin, *Reflex Action: A Study in the History of Physiological Psychology,* Johns Hopkins University Press, 1930.
Swazey, Judith P., *Reflexes and Motor Integration: Sherrington's Concept of Integrative Action,* Harvard University Press, 1969.

Periodicals

Denny-Brown, Derek, *Journal of Neurophysiology,* The Sherrington School of Physiology, Volume 20, 1957, pp. 543–48.
Fulton, John F., *Journal of Neurophysiology,* Sir Charles Scott Sherrington, O. M., Volume 15, 1952, pp. 167–90.

Penfield, Wilder, *Brain,* Sir Charles Sherrington, Poet and Philosopher, Volume 80, 1957, pp. 402–10.

Sketch by D. George Joseph

FURTHER READING:

Periodicals

Ebony, A Veteran at Meharry Medical College, August, 1977, p. 116.

Sketch by David E. Newton

Dolores Cooper Shockley
1930–
American pharmacologist

Dolores Cooper Shockley is the first African American woman to earn a Ph.D. from Purdue University and the first African American woman in the United States to receive a Ph.D. in pharmacology. In 1977 she became chair of the department of microbiology at Meharry Medical College.

Shockley was born in Clarksdale, Mississippi, on April 21, 1930. She enrolled at Louisiana State University in 1947, intending to pursue a major in pharmacy with the goal of eventually opening her own drugstore. During her college years, however, Shockley's interests shifted from retail business to research. When she earned her bachelor of science degree in 1951, she decided to continue her education in the field of pharmacology at Purdue University in Lafayette, Indiana. She was awarded her M.S. at Purdue in 1953 and then her Ph.D. in pharmacology two years later. After graduation, Shockley used a Fulbright Fellowship to do postdoctoral research at the University of Copenhagen.

When Shockley returned to the United States, she accepted an appointment as assistant professor of pharmacology at Meharry Medical College in Nashville, Tennessee. She was greeted in her new job with a certain amount of suspicion, she later told an interviewer for *Ebony,* because "some men thought that I was just working temporarily." She soon put those doubts to rest and became a valued and respected member of the faculty. In 1967 Shockley was promoted to associate professor, and ten years later she became head of the college's department of microbiology. She has since served also as Meharry's foreign student advisor and its liaison for international activities to the Association of American Medical Colleges. Shockley's research interests have focused on the consequences of drug action on stress, the effects of hormones on connective tissue, the relationships between drugs and nutrition, and the measurement of non narcotic analgesics (painkillers). She was visiting assistant professor at the Einstein College of Medicine in New York City from 1959 to 1962 and was a recipient of the Lederle Faculty Award from 1963 to 1966. Shockley is married and the mother of four children.

William Shockley
1910–1989
American physicist

William Shockley was a physicist whose work in the development of the transistor led to a Nobel Prize. By the late 1950s, his company, the Shockley Transistor Corporation, was part of a rapidly growing industry created as a direct result of his contributions to the field. Shockley shared the 1956 Nobel Prize in physics with **John Bardeen** and **Walter Brattain**, both of whom collaborated with him on developing the point contact transistor. Later, Shockley became involved in a controversial topic for which he had no special training, but in which he became avidly interested: the genetic basis of intelligence. During the 1960s, he argued, in a series of articles and speeches, that people of African descent have a genetically inferior mental capacity when compared to those with Caucasian ancestry. This hypothesis became the subject of intense and acrimonious debate.

William Bradford Shockley was born in London, England, on February 13, 1910, to William Hillman Shockley, an American mining engineer, and May (Bradford) Shockley, a mineral surveyor. The Shockleys, living in London on a business assignment when William was born, returned to California in 1913. Shockley did not enter elementary school at the usual age, however; as he told *Men of Space* author Shirley Thomas, "My parents had the idea that the general educational process was not as good as would be done at home." As a result, he was not enrolled in public schools until he had reached the age of eight.

Shockley's interest in physics developed early, inspired in part by a neighbor who taught the subject at Stanford and by his own parents' coaching and encouragement. By the time he had completed his secondary education at Palo Alto Military Academy and Hollywood High School at the age of seventeen, Shockley had made his commitment to a career in physics. Shockley and his parents agreed that he should spend a year at the University of California at Los Angeles (UCLA) before attending the California Institute of Technology (Caltech), where he earned a bachelor's degree in physics in 1932. Offered a teaching fellowship at the Massachusetts Institute of Tech-

William Shockley

nology (MIT), Shockley taught while working on his doctoral dissertation, "Calculations of Wave Functions for Electrons in Sodium Chloride Crystals," for which he was awarded his Ph.D. in 1936. Shockley later told Thomas that this research in solid-state physics "led into my subsequent activities in the transistor field."

Begins Research on Semiconductors at Bell Labs

Upon graduation from MIT, Shockley accepted an offer to work at the Bell Telephone Laboratories in Murray Hill, New Jersey. An important factor in that decision was the opportunity it gave him to work with **Clinton Davisson**, who was to win the 1937 Nobel Prize in physics for proving **Louis Victor Broglie**'s theory that electrons assumed the characteristics of waves. Shockley's first assignment at Bell was the development of a new type of vacuum tube that would serve as an amplifier. But, almost as soon as he had arrived at Bell, he began to think of a radically new approach to the transmission of electrical signals using solid-state components rather than conventional vacuum tubes. At that time, vacuum tubes constituted the core of communication devices such as the radio because they have the ability to rectify (create a unidirectional current) and multiply electronic signals. They have a number of serious practical disadvantages, however, as they are relatively fragile and expensive, and have relatively short life spans.

As early as the mid–1930s, Bell scientists had begun to think about alternatives to vacuum tubes in communication systems, and by 1939, Shockley was experimenting with semiconducting materials to achieve that transition. Semiconductors are materials such as silicon and germanium that conduct an electrical current much less efficiently than do conductors like silver and copper, but more effectively than do insulators like glass and most kinds of plastic. Shockley knew that one semiconductor, galena, had been used as a rectifier in early radio sets, and his experience in solid-state physics led him to believe that such materials might have even wider application in new kinds of communication devices.

World War II Interrupts Research

The limited research Shockley was able to complete on this concept of alternative conductors was unsuccessful, largely because the materials available to him at the time were not pure enough. In 1940, war was imminent, and Shockley soon became involved in military research. His first job involved the development of radar equipment at a Bell field station in Whippany, New Jersey. In 1942, he became research director of the U.S. Navy's Anti-Submarine Warfare Operations Research Group at Columbia University, and served as a consultant to the Secretary of War from 1944 to 1945.

In 1945, Shockley returned to Bell Labs as director of its research program on solid-state physics. Together with John Bardeen, a theoretical physicist, and Walter Brattain, an experimental physicist, Shockley returned to his study of semiconductors as a means of amplification. After more than a year of failed trials, Bardeen suggested that the movement of electric current was being hampered by electrons trapped within a semiconductor's surface layer. That suggestion caused Shockley's team to suspend temporarily its efforts to build an amplification device and to concentrate instead on improving their understanding of the nature of semiconductors.

Bardeen and Brattain Bring Shockley's Idea to Fruition

By 1947, Bardeen and Brattain had learned enough about semiconductors to make another attempt at building Shockley's device. This time they were successful. Their device consisted of a piece of germanium with two gold contacts on one side and a tungsten contact on the opposite side. When an electrical current was fed into one of the gold contacts, it appeared in a greatly amplified form on the other side. The device was given the name transistor (for *trans* fer re*sistor*). More specifically, it was referred to as a point contact transistor because of the three metal contacts used in it.

The first announcement of the transistor appeared in a short article in the July 1, 1948 edition of the *New York Times*. Few readers had the vaguest notion of the impact the fingernail-sized device would have on the world. A few months later, Shockley proposed a modification of the point contact transistor. He suggested using a thin layer of P-type semiconductor (in which the charge is carried by holes) sandwiched between two layers of N-type semiconductor (where the charge is carried by electrons). When Brattain built this device, now called the junction transistor, he found that it worked much better than did its point contact predecessor. In 1956 the Nobel Prize for physics was awarded jointly to Shockley, Bardeen, and Brattain for their development of the transistor.

Shockley left Bell Labs in 1954 (some sources say 1955). In the decade that followed, he served as director of research for the Weapons Systems Evaluation Group of the Department of Defense, and as visiting professor at Caltech in 1954–1955. He then founded the Shockley Transistor Corporation to turn his work on the development of the transistor to commercial advantage. Shockley Transistor was later incorporated into Beckman Instruments, Inc., and then into Clevite Transistor in 1960. The company went out of business in 1968.

Studies the Genetic Basis of Intelligence

In 1963 Shockley embarked on a new career, accepting an appointment at Stanford University as its first Alexander M. Poniatoff Professor of Engineering and Applied Science. Here he became interested in genetics and the origins of human intelligence, in particular, the relationship between race and the Intelligence Quotient (IQ). Although he had no background in psychology, genetics, or any related field, Shockley began to read on these topics and formulate his own hypotheses. Using data taken primarily from U.S. Army pre-induction IQ tests, Shockley came to the conclusion that the genetic component of a person's intelligence was based on racial heritage. He proposed that people of African ancestry were inherently less intelligent than those of Caucasian lineage. He also surmised that the more "white genes" a person of African descent carried, the more closely her or his intelligence corresponded to that of the general white population. He ignited further controversy with his suggestion that inferior individuals (those whose IQ numbered below 100) be paid to undergo voluntary sterilization.

The social implications of Shockley's theories were—and still are—profound. Many scholars regarded Shockley's whole analysis as flawed, and they rejected his conclusions. Others were outraged that such views were even expressed publicly. Educators pointed out the significance of these theories for their field, a point pursued by Shockley himself when he argued that compensatory programs for blacks were doomed because of their inherent genetic inferiority. For a number of years, Shockley could count on the fact that his speeches would be interrupted by boos and catcalls, provided that they were allowed to go forward at all.

During his life, Shockley was awarded many honors, including the U.S. Medal of Merit in 1946, the Morris E. Liebmann Award of the Institute of Radio Engineers in 1951, the Comstock Prize of the National Academy of Sciences in 1954, and the Institute of Electrical and Electronics Gold Medal in 1972 and its Medal of Honor in 1980. He was named to the National Inventor's Hall of Fame in 1974. Shockley remained at Stanford until retire-

ment in 1975, when he was appointed Emeritus Professor of Electrical Engineering. In 1933, Shockley had married Jean Alberta Bailey, with whom he had three children, Alison, William, and Richard. After their 1955 divorce, Shockley married Emily I. Lanning. He died in San Francisco on August 11, 1989, of prostate cancer.

SELECTED WRITINGS BY SHOCKLEY:

Books

Electrons and Holes in Semiconductors, with Applications to Transistor Electronics, Van Nostrand, 1950.
Imperfections of Nearly Perfect Crystals, Wiley, 1952.
Mechanics, C. E. Merrill, 1966.

Periodicals

Physical Review, Density of Surface States on Silicon Deduced from Contact Potential Measurements, Volume 72, 1947, p. 345.
Physical Review, Modulation of Conductance of Thin Films of Semiconductors by Surface Charges, Volume 74, 1948, pp. 232–33.

FURTHER READING:

Books

McGraw-Hill Modern Scientists and Engineers, Volume 3, McGraw-Hill, 1980, pp. 111–12.
National Geographic Society, Special Publications Division, *Those Inventive Americans,* National Geographic Society, 1971, pp. 209–16.
Thomas, Shirley, *Men of Space,* Volume 4, Chilton Books, 1962, pp. 170–205.
Thomas, Shirley, *Nobel Prize Winners,* H. W. Wilson, 1987, pp. 962–64.

Sketch by David E. Newton

Eugene M. Shoemaker
1928–
American geologist

Eugene M. Shoemaker is a geologist whose research interests and expertise range far beyond the earth. Shoemaker has studied impact craters (craters created by the collision of an asteroid or comet and a planet) on both the earth and the moon, as well as searched for the comets and asteroids that could have caused the craters. He was a key figure in formulating the scientific exploration of the lunar surface during the 1960s. Intrigued by the study of craters in general, Shoemaker then turned his focus back to the planet Earth and has become a leader in studying the impact history of the planet.

Eugene Merle Shoemaker was born in Los Angeles on April 28, 1928, to George Estel and Muriel May Scott Shoemaker. His mother was a teacher, and his father at different times worked in teaching, business, farming, and for motion picture studios. The family moved to Oregon, New York, Wyoming, and finally back to Los Angeles when Shoemaker was fourteen years old. He has one younger sister. Shoemaker's interest in geology coalesced early in his life. He began collecting rocks, minerals, and fossils when he was seven. He took classes in mineralogy and geology at the science museum in Buffalo, New York, starting when he was nine. By the time he finished high school in Los Angeles he wanted to be a geologist. Shoemaker earned his bachelor's degree in geology from the California Institute of Technology in 1947 and his master's degree the next year.

In July 1948 he moved to Grand Junction, Colorado, to join the United States Geological Survey (U.S.G.S.) as a geologist. For two years he searched for uranium deposits and investigated salt structures in Colorado and Utah. During the early 1950s he concentrated on the geochemistry, volcanology, and structure of the rocks of the Colorado Plateau. He took a leave from the U.S.G.S. to study at Princeton University from 1950 to 1951 and 1953 to 1954, receiving his M.A. from Princeton in 1954. During the late 1950s Shoemaker became interested in craters, both those created by meteorite impacts and by nuclear explosions. His doctoral thesis was to draw the first detailed geological map of the huge Meteor Crater in Arizona, also known as the Barringer Crater. In 1960 Shoemaker and Edward C. T. Chao discovered the presence of the mineral coesite at Meteor Crater. Since coesite is a high-pressure form of silica that forms when quartz is squeezed at intense pressures, Shoemaker and Chao had essentially proven that the Barringer Crater was indeed formed by a meteorite striking the earth, rather than by volcanic action as some scientists had thought. That year Shoemaker received his Ph.D. from Princeton.

From Arizona to the Moon

Shoemaker had begun working on Meteor Crater and other impact-related craters because of his interest in the moon and its pocketed surface. "I got a bug in my ear in 1948, shortly after I went to work for the U.S. Geological Survey, that during my professional career human beings would go to the Moon. I made up my mind then that I was going to be the first scientist to get to the Moon," he told *Astronomy* in 1993. During the 1960s, the decade that astronauts did indeed walk on the moon, Shoemaker became heavily involved with the science of lunar exploration.

In 1960 Shoemaker established a lunar geological time scale and developed improved ways to map the moon's surface. He then organized a U.S.G.S. unit on astrogeology at the survey's office in Menlo Park, California, where he had been working. (The unit later became a full branch and moved to Flagstaff, Arizona, in 1965.) In 1962 and 1963 the U.S.G.S. loaned Shoemaker to the National Aeronautics and Space Administration (NASA) to help develop plans for exploring the moon. For several months Shoemaker was acting director of NASA's Manned Space Sciences Division, which was charged with formulating the scientific objectives for the first astronauts to land on the moon.

While an administrator at NASA and the U.S.G.S., Shoemaker continued to work on terrestrial impact craters in addition to attempting to figure out what the lunar surface was like. He promoted using television systems to investigate the geology of other moons and planets. Shoemaker was in charge of the television experiments on Project Ranger and, later, Project Surveyor. (From 1979 to 1990 he was also coinvestigator for the television setup on the two *Voyager* probes that visited the outer planets of the solar system.) During the mid–1960s Shoemaker studied photographs of the lunar surface sent back by exploratory spacecraft to determine the nature of the surface. With photos from the Ranger 7 probe, Shoemaker used his method of "photoclinometry," which computed the steepness of craters' edges by the amount of shadow they threw onto the ground. He announced that the surface was quite smooth. With later photographs, Shoemaker determined that the moon is predominantly gray and that it is covered with shallow, silty soil. (Before the *Surveyor* spacecraft landed on the surface, there was worry that a thick layer of dust might preclude a probe landing.) Shoemaker became the principal scientist for the geological field studies of the *Apollo* landings from 1965 to 1970.

In 1966 Shoemaker resigned as administrator of the U.S.G.S. astrogeology branch so that he could return to full-time research as chief scientist in Flagstaff. He began an association with the California Institute of Technology (Caltech), as a visiting professor in 1962 and 1987, and a full-time professor of geology from 1969 to 1985. He chaired Caltech's Division of Geological and Planetary Sciences from 1969 to 1972.

By this time Shoemaker's experience with Moon studies prompted him to consider the objects that create impact craters on the earth as well. His research in the late 1960s shifted to Earth-crossing asteroids, those objects that one day might hit the earth and form another Meteor Crater. He decided to try to catalogue the asteroids, a task that would take assiduous sky-searching. At Caltech he hired the young geologist Eleanor Helin to begin an asteroid search program. He and Helin started in 1973 to use the 18-inch Schmidt telescope atop Palomar Mountain in California for the first-ever systematic asteroid search, named the Palomar Planet-Crossing Asteroid Survey. It took them six months to find their first asteroid, and two and a half years for the second one. Eventually they decided to step up their search and spend more nights at the telescope.

Shoemaker has continued to supervise the hunt for near-Earth asteroids. He calculated that about 1,000 to 1,500 asteroids at least half a mile across are on potential collision courses with the earth. When Helin left the search in 1982, Shoemaker's wife Carolyn soon joined the hunt, renamed the Palomar Asteroid and Comet Survey. The two Shoemakers developed a stereoscopic technique for comparing pairs of film: one eye looks at one photograph, the other eye looks at a snapshot taken 45 minutes to an hour later, and any moving asteroid or comet appears to float above the combined image.

Mass Extinctions and Monster Collisions

Shoemaker also continued to work on the impact history of the earth. In 1980, his line of research got a shot of excitement when a group led by the physicist **Luis Alvarez** suggested that a cataclysmic impact had struck the Earth 65 million years ago, triggering the chain of events that led to the death of the dinosaurs and many other species. Scientists had previously blamed the dinosaurs' demise on many other causes, from climate change to constipation. The Berkeley group offered as proof the thin layer of iridium appearing in 65-million-year-old sediments around the world. Iridium is a rare element on Earth, but extraterrestrial sources like meteorites are relatively rich in iridium. Thus, the Alvarez group suggested, a giant meteorite must have struck the earth, kicking up a cloud of dust that covered the earth, blocking the planet from sunlight and causing a massive extinction.

Soon after the Alvarez hypothesis, the hunt began for the giant scar that must have been left by such an impact. Scientists have identified the Chicxulub crater, buried under water and sediments off the coast of the Yucatan, as the most likely candidate for the impact's calling card, since it is at least 120 miles across. However, a smaller crater in Iowa—22 miles across—has been dated at roughly the same age of 65 million years. Shoemaker suggested that it was just too coincidental to have two large craters of the same age. He proposed instead that multiple impacts smashed the earth, one right after another on the scale of geologic time. And since the probability of several huge meteorites coming at the same time is slim, Shoemaker suggested that perhaps a comet had broken up and shed its remains on our planet in a destructive repetition, leaving both the Mexican and the Iowa craters. Most scientists now believe that the Chicxulub crater is the scar of the primary impact that killed off the dinosaurs. The question of multiple impacts has not been resolved.

Shoemaker's career has been recognized with numerous honors, including honorary doctorates of science from Arizona State College, Temple University and the University of Arizona. He is a fellow of the American Academy of Arts and Sciences and a member of the National Academy of Sciences. Among other awards, he has received the NASA Medal for Scientific Achievement, the Kuiper Prize of the American Astronomical Society, and the National Medal of Science.

Shoemaker married Carolyn Jean Spellman in 1951. They have two daughters, Christine and Linda, and one son, Patrick. Carolyn Shoemaker, a former teacher, became involved with the Palomar asteroid search after her three children were grown. She has since discovered more comets than any other person in history except for the nineteenth-century observer Jean-Louis Pons. But only twenty-six comets bear Pons's name; that record was broken in 1992, as Carolyn Shoemaker found her twenty-seventh comet. The Shoemakers work at spotting asteroids for a week at Palomar every month. Gene uses the telescope to take the photographs; Carolyn searches the film for fuzzy objects that might have moved. Together they have discovered more than three-hundred asteroids, some of which are named after the Shoemakers' children and grandchildren.

One of the comets found by Carolyn Shoemaker became a once-in-a-lifetime chance for stargazers to witness a rare event. Comet Shoemaker-Levy 9, discovered in March 1993, collided with Jupiter in July 1994. Gene Shoemaker calculated that this sort of celestial collision happens once in a millennia, or once in a thousand years. "I've been hoping for many decades that I would live long enough to see the impact of a significant object," he told Alexandra Witze in an interview. "I was thinking it might be something small on Earth. I never dreamed we would discover something to impact another planet."

FURTHER READING:

Periodicals

Astronomy, June, 1993, pp. 13–17.
Time, February 1, 1992, p. 58.

Other

Shoemaker, Eugene M., *Interview with Alexandra Witze,* conducted July 22, 1993.

Sketch by Alexandra Witze

Yuly Mikhaylovich Shokalsky
1856–1940
Russian geographer and oceanographer

Yuly Mikhaylovich Shokalsky was a pioneering geographer and oceanographer whose career spanned the transition between Czarist Russia and the Soviet Union. Although the majority of his works have not been translated from Russian, he has influenced the fields of cartography, hydrography, and hydrometeorology. One of his most important accomplishments was the oceanographic exploration of the Black Sea. He also compiled a standard general map of Russia, and there are twelve geographic features in that country named in his honor, including Shokalsky Island in the Kara Sea.

Shokalsky was born in St. Petersburg, Russia, in October 1856. He demonstrated an early interest in geography, and in 1873 he entered the Naval College in St. Petersburg. He graduated in 1877 and served briefly with the Russian fleet in the Baltic Sea. The duties of a naval officer, however, left little time for his scientific interests, and in 1878 he enrolled in the Naval Academy. He graduated in 1880, and in 1881 he was put in charge of the marine meteorology division at the Central Physics Observatory. Shokalsky also worked at the Main Hydrographic Administration, measuring and mapping surface waters for navigation. In 1882, he published his first scientific paper, "On Forecasting Weather and Storms."

Shokalsky began his teaching career at the Naval College in 1883, where he would teach geography and marine description until 1908. During this period, he also served in the Russian navy's department of hydrography. He was named director of the naval library in 1890, and in 1907 he was placed in charge of the hydrometeorological division. Hydrometeorology is the study of the effects of water in the atmosphere, such as hail, rain, or clouds.

In 1900, Shokalsky began designing an oceanographic project in the Arctic Ocean which was to last fifteen years. He played a key role in the preparations for the icebreaker expeditions which discovered Severnaja Zemlya, a group of islands off the northern coast of Russia near the North Pole. In 1908, Shokalsky moved to the Naval Academy, where he became the first professor of oceanography in Russia. He continued to teach physical geography and meteorology, and in 1908 he helped organize the Eleventh International Congress on Navigation in 1908, which was held in St. Petersburg.

Shokalsky published *Okeanografia* ("Oceanography") in 1917; this is his most famous work. Here, he argued that all marine phenomena are interdependent. Shokalsky saw all bodies of saltwater as being interconnected in some fashion, and he later maintained that there was a "worldwide ocean." This book also discussed the methodology and techniques for making scientific observations from a ship. *Okeanografia* was both popular and scientifically well respected, and it earned prizes for its author from the Russian Academy of Sciences in 1919 and the Paris Academy of Sciences in 1923.

Plans and Executes Exploration of the Black Sea

In 1909 the Hydrographic Administration commissioned Shokalsky to lead an oceanographic exploration of the Black Sea. He developed all aspects of the project from planning to methodology, designing the expedition to include the Kerchenskiy Proliv strait, the Bosporus and Dardanelles straits, as well as the Azov and Marmara seas.

His plans, as it turned out, were long delayed; the outbreak of World War I, the collapse of Czarist Russia, and the Bolshevik Revolution made it impossible to conduct the first expedition until 1923. At first Shokalsky was only able to concentrate on the narrowest section of the Black Sea, near the Anatolian coast of Turkey. But by 1925, he had the resources to expand the survey, but it still took fifty-three voyages and twelve years to complete the project.

Shokalsky oversaw the extraction of over 1600 hydrological and 2000 soil and biological samples. Some of the most important accomplishments of this expedition were discoveries relating to the density of seawater. Scientific opinion had previously held that distinct layers of different chemical composition existed in relation to depth, but Shokalsky demonstrated a high level of mobility between the layers and perpetual intermingling. The expedition was also involved in studying the Northern Sea Route in the hope of developing it. The project drew to a close in 1935.

During this period, Shokalsky served in a variety of academic and official posts. He remained on the faculty at the Naval Academy until 1930, and he added teaching responsibilities at Leningrad State University in 1925. He was elected president of the Russian Geographic Society in 1914, and following the Soviet Revolution he served as president of the Geographic Society of the U.S.S.R. from 1917 to 1931. He had his hand in the compilation and editing of a number of geographic maps and atlases. He was responsible for a new topographical map of the North Polar region; he also produced what was to become the standard general map of Russia. Working with A. A. Tillo, he was able to calculate the surface of the asiatic region of Russia and the lengths of the most prominent rivers.

At the age of seventy-six, Shokalsky showed no signs of slackening the pace of his scientific endeavors. He served on a commission to develop programs for the Second International Polar Year (1932–33), and he pressed for oceanographic studies to be included. In 1933 he sat on the organizing committee of the Fourth Hydrologic Conference of Baltic Nations. He was the Soviet delegate to the Fourteenth International Geographical Congress in Warsaw the following year.

Shokalsky continued to teach at Leningrad State University until the time of his death. This distinguished academic and field worker was a member of fifteen foreign geographic societies. A prolific writer, Shokalsky published over 1300 articles during his career. In 1929, the American Geographical Society bestowed on him their Cullum Geographical Medal. Presented to those "who distinguish themselves by geographical discoveries, or in the advancement of geographical science," it was the first awarding of the medal in four years. The Russian Geographic Society bestowed the title of "honored scientist" to his long list of accomplishments. Shokalsky died in Leningrad on March 26, 1940.

SELECTED WRITINGS BY SHOKALSKY:

Books

Okeanografia, [Petrograd], 1917.

Periodicals

Morskoi sbornik, O predskazanii veroyatnoy pogody i
shtormov, (title means "On Forecasting Weather
and Storms") Volume 192, 1882, pp. 87–125.

FURTHER READING:

Books

Gillespie, Charles, editor, *Dictionary of Scientific Biog-
raphy,* Volume 12, Scribner's, 1975.
Prokhorov, A. M., editor, *Great Soviet Encyclopedia,*
Volume 29, Macmillan, 1982.

Periodicals

Prokhorov, A. M., editor, *Science,* The Medal Awards
of the American Geographical Society, March 28,
1930, pp. 333–34.

Sketch by Chris McGrail

Vladimir Borisovich Shtokman
1909–1968
Russian oceanographer

Recognized among Soviet scientists, Vladimir Borisovich Shtokman influenced the development of physical oceanography in the former Soviet Union as well as
around the world. By focusing on the relationship between
the overall wind field and current field—rather than looking
at wind and current velocities at a given point—Shtokman
led the way into a new era in understanding the overall
dynamics of ocean currents. Shtokman also formulated
important equations by which the total transport capability
of ocean currents could be determined. In an article in the
1969 issue of *Oceanography,* fellow scientist A. D.
Dobrovol'skiy called Shtokman "one of the greatest physical oceanologists of our country."

Shtokman was born on March 11, 1909, in Moscow,
where his father was a mechanical and construction
engineer. Shtokman attended the First Moscow University,
where he joined the mathematics department of the physical
mathematics faculty in 1929. There he decided to specialize
in geophysics, finding his niche in oceanography and
quickly gaining recognition for his work. During his tenure
at the First Moscow University, the geophysics curriculum
of the physical mathematics faculty split in two, becoming
the Moscow Geological Exploration Institute and the
Moscow Hydrometeorological Institute. Shtokman connected with the latter because it allowed him to work on the
dynamics of the oceans, as well as to pursue his intense
interest in mathematics and logic.

Rises to Prominence in the Scientific Community

During the early 1930s, Shtokman rose from senior lab
assistant in the hydrological division of the State Oceanographic Institute, located in Yekaterininskaya Gavan', to a
senior scientific position, which he acquired after successfully leading an expedition to Motovskiy Zaliv (Murman
Peninsula). In 1934 he transferred to Baku to establish the
All-Union Institute of Fisheries and Oceanography's physical oceanology laboratory, which he headed for approximately eight years. It was here that Shtokman's career
began in earnest. His first professional journal article was
published during this year, and he continued to write until
his death in 1968, producing more than one hundred
articles. According to Dobrovol'skiy, these publications
became models of well-organized oceanographic research.

In 1938 Shtokman was awarded the degree of candidate of physical and mathematical science. A year later the
USSR Academy of Sciences recognized his achievements in
the field of oceanography by inviting him to join the staff of
the Institute of Theoretical Geophysics. Shtokman accepted
and began work in the sea physics division. Once settled as
a researcher at the institute, he commenced his career as a
teacher when, in addition to his full-time position at the
institute, he began teaching oceanography at the Moscow
Hydrometeorological Institute. His research and teaching
duties, however, were soon interrupted by World War II.

In the early 1940s Shtokman joined the Arctic
Research Institute in Krasnoyarsk because of his background investigations on the mixing of the Atlantic Ocean
in the Arctic Basin. Two years later he transferred to the
oceanology laboratory of the Academy of Sciences, also in
Krasnoyarsk. Later that year he moved back to Moscow,
where he remained for the rest of his life. In 1944 he
received the degree of doctor of physical and mathematical
science and two years later was appointed head of the
physical oceanology division of the Institute of Oceanology
of the Academy of Sciences. In 1947 he rose to the position
of professor of geophysics.

According to Dobrovol'skiy in *Oceanography,* Shtokman dedicated himself to the study of the dynamics of ocean
currents. "His first great achievement in this field," Dobrovol'skiy pointed out, "was his development of the idea of
wind variations affecting these currents. He showed that if
the wind direction is constant, but the speed not constant
(transverse nonuniformity, as he called it), countercurrents
will be created transversely on the sea surface, i.e., there
will be currents flowing in the direction opposite to that of
the wind. . . . The development of this idea subsequently led
Shtokman to formulate the theory of oceanic equatorial
countercurrents and then to interpret the features of current
systems in straits and around islands."

A scientist, educator, writer, and participant in over fifteen ocean expeditions, Shtokman also made time for other pursuits. A naturalist, he especially enjoyed hiking through the woodlands around Moscow with his dog by his side. He loved dogs, and enjoyed a huge collection of pictures and statuettes of his favorite animal, as well as monographs on dog breeding and some rare dog magazines. In addition, he collected paintings, about which he was knowledgeable. He was married to Galina Vasil'yevna.

Shtokman had been diagnosed with heart disease when he was forty-eight, but he had been well and productive during most of the following eleven years. He passed away suddenly during a trip to the country on June 14, 1968. Upon his death, his colleagues named a research vessel in his honor. The *RV Shtokman* has completed more than twenty major expeditions—primarily in the Atlantic, Arctic, and Indian Oceans; the Baltic and Black Seas; and the Bering Strait—continuing the work of a scientist who influenced the development of physical oceanography for four decades.

SELECTED WRITINGS BY SHTOKMAN:

Periodicals

Meteorologiya i Gidrologiya, Are Countercurrents Possible in an Unbounded Sea Due to Local Variations of Wind?, Number 5, 1947.

Meteorologiya i Gidrologiya, On the Magnitude of the Deflection of Sea Currents Caused by Bottom Relief, Number 8, 1952.

Okeanologiya, A Scientific Conference on Sea Currents, Volume 4, 1964.

Okeanologiya, A Development of the Theory of Sea and Ocean Circulation over 50 Years in the USSR, Volume 7, 1967.

FURTHER READING:

Periodicals

Dobrovol'skiy, A. D., *Oceanography,* Vladimir Borisovich Shtokman, Volume 9, 1969, pp. 1–8.

Sketch by Patricia M. McAdams

Clifford Glenwood Shull
1915–
American physicist

Shull won a share of the 1994 Nobel Prize in physics for his pioneering development of neutron scattering techniques. Like **Bertram N. Brockhouse,** the Canadian physicist with whom he shared the prize, Shull was recognized belatedly for research conducted more than 40 years earlier. Working at one of the first nuclear reactors in the United States, Shull found that the atomic structure of solid or fluid matter could be determined by directing waves of neutrons at a sample and measuring the angle at which they bounce off, or are scattered by, the atoms in the sample. This discovery has had significant impact on a wide range of scientific fields, since neutron scattering, also known as neutron diffraction, has been used to analyze the atomic structure of such diverse substances as viruses, polymers, and superconductive materials.

The youngest child of David and Daisy Shull, Clifford Glenwood Shull was born on September 23, 1915, in the Glenwood section of Pittsburgh, Pennsylvania. Several years earlier, his parents had moved from rural, central Pennsylvania to the city and opened a small business that eventually became a hardware store and home repair service. Along with his older brother and sister, Shull attended neighborhood schools, then enrolled in Schenley High School, which was 45 minutes away by streetcar. At Schenley, a dynamic instructor sparked Shull's interest in physics, causing him to reconsider his initial ambition to be an aeronautical engineer. After graduating, he won a partial scholarship to the Carnegie Institute of Technology, now Carnegie Mellon University, and immersed himself in his studies. During Shull's freshman year, however, his father died suddenly, precipitating not only an emotional, but a financial crisis for the family. As a result, Shull's older brother, Perry, quit his job as an art teacher and ran their father's business until his younger sibling had graduated from college.

Works with Accelerators

After receiving his B.A. from Carnegie, Shull entered the graduate physics program at New York University. Early on he became associated with the nuclear physics research group and took part in several different experiments using particle accelerators. For his Ph.D. thesis he used the department's newly constructed Van de Graaff accelerator to determine whether or not electrons have a spin or polarization. While at the university, he also met Martha-Nuel Summer, a native of South Carolina and graduate student in early American history. They married in 1941 after completing their studies and eventually had three sons: John, Robert, and William.

A month after receiving his Ph.D. from New York University, Shull accepted a research position at The Texas Company, now Texaco, in Beacon, New York. There, he used gas absorption as well as X-ray diffraction and scattering to analyze catalysts used in the production of high-performance aviation fuel. This research took on great importance following the entry of the United States into World War II. However, Shull, like many other young physicists of the time, was very interested in the Manhattan Project. He had seen several of his former university friends and professors join in the race to produce the first nuclear weapon and longed to take part as well. Yet when an attempt was made to recruit him, The Texas Company blocked his way, eventually convincing a government manpower board that his research for them was more crucial to the wartime effort.

Develops Neutron Scattering Techniques

At the end of the war Shull was free to pursue his interest in nuclear physics, and in 1946 he left The Texas Company for the Clinton Laboratory in Oak Ridge, Tennessee. Eventually renamed the Oak Ridge National Laboratory, it had been one of the top-secret sites of the Manhattan Project, and its nuclear reactor had supplied a significant portion of the plutonium used in the atomic bombs dropped on Hiroshima and Nagasaki. At the time Shull arrived, the laboratory's administrators had begun to shift its focus from military to civilian uses, and he was assigned to work with Ernest Wollan. Wollan, who had been with the laboratory since its inception, had begun to investigate how the neutron beams produced by the reactor could be used to analyze the structure of matter. Over the next decade, the two scientists developed a method of neutron diffraction that eventually became the foundation of an entirely new branch of physics research.

Shull and Wollan discovered that neutrons, upon hitting the atoms within a fluid or solid sample, ricochet in a characteristic fashion. Specifically, the angle at which the neutrons are deflected shows how the atoms are arranged. In other words, neutron scattering effectively determines the atomic structure of a sample. Neutron scattering was a truly revolutionary discovery, opening new avenues of research as it shed new light on important substances, such as the element hydrogen, that had been resistant to earlier methods of analysis. Sadly, by the time that the Nobel committee recognized the significance of their work, Wollan had died. Shull wrote in his autobiography for the Nobel Foundation, "I regret very much that Wollan's death in 1984 precluded his sharing in the Nobel honor . . . since his contributions were certainly deserving of recognition."

Shull left the Oak Ridge National Laboratory in 1955 to become a professor of physics at the Massachusetts Institute of Technology, retiring as emeritus professor in 1986. His other awards include the Buckley Prize, which he received in 1956.

FURTHER READING:

Periodicals

Allen, Scott. "MIT Physicist Shares Nobel for Analysis of Matter with Neutrons." *Boston Globe*, October 13, 1994, p. 261.

Peterson, Ivars. "Physics Nobel for Neutron-Scattering Work." *Science News*, October 22, 1994, p. 261.

Silverman, Edward R. "Colleagues Laud 1994 Nobelists As Overdue for Coveted Prize." *The Scientist*, November 28, 1994.

Suplee, Curt. "Molecular Research Wins Prize, American, Canadian Share Physics Nobel." *Washington Post*, October 13, 1994, p. A3.

Sketch by Bridget Travers

Robert E. Shurney
American aeronautical engineer

Perhaps the most noteworthy of Robert E. Shurney's engineering accomplishments was the development of the wheels for the lunar roving vehicle (LRV) or "moon buggy" used by America's Apollo astronauts in the early 1970s. Shurney has also been active in doing tests under weightless conditions, and has logged over six hundred hours of weightlessness in tests aboard the weightless KC–135 aircraft.

Shurney obtained his physics degree from A & I State University in Nashville, Tennessee, before accepting a position as an aeronautical engineer at Alabama's Marshall Space Flight Center in 1962. Though his appointment came only through he direct urging of Attorney General Robert Kennedy, Shurney soon became something of an expert on microgravity, or weightlessness, spending a great deal of time in the weightless conditions created by the KC–135 Zero 9 aircraft. A converted Air Force tanker, the KC–135 describes a parabolic flight path; during the final 30 seconds of its flight the aircraft approaches free-fall, creating a condition similar to the weightlessness that affects free-falling spacecraft and their passengers. Much of Shurney's work in the KC–135 involved perfecting space toilets (or refuse disposal units) and other devices that had been proposed for use in space. Although Shurney had a hand in designing the toilets for the space shuttle, his most important work as a designer of space commodes went into NASA's Skylab.

Shurney's greatest contribution to the space program, however, was his design for the tires used on the Apollo moon buggy. The moon buggy required wheels that conformed to very strict standards: they had to be compact, yet strong enough to withstand sudden bumps and jolts; they had to be light weight, so as not to add substantially to the payload of the Apollo rocket; and they could not kick up a great deal of the flour-like dust that covered the surface of the moon. Shurney's design, which prevailed over others under consideration, called for tires to be made from a spring-wire mesh; such a construction would be strong, light, have good traction, and would resist abrasion and other kinds of damage as they rolled over rocks and rough surfaces. In addition, wire would withstand the extreme temperatures found on the moon better than rubber. Commenting on the requirements for a moon tire, S. F.

Morea, the LRV project manager at NASA, commented in *Machine Design* magazine that upon hitting a rock on the moon at ten or twelve miles per hour there was no way to know how high the wheel would bounce, hence the need for a tire with considerable resilience.

In addition to the moon tire, Shurney helped construct the Penitromiter, a device used by astronauts to measure the density and depth of the lunar "topsoil" as well as any vibrations present on the moon's surface. He also made improvements to the design of the spacecraft's solar panels, making it possible to retrieve and reuse the panels once they'd been deployed.

Shurney and his wife, the former Susie Flynt, have four children: Darrell, Glyndon, Glenn, and Ronald.

FURTHER READING:

Books

Blacks in Science & Medicine, Hemisphere, 1990, p. 213.
Van Sertima, Ivan, editor, *Blacks in Science: Ancient and Modern,* Transaction Books, 1984, pp. 249–51.

Periodicals

Van Sertima, Ivan, editor, *Machine Design,* March 19, 1970, pp. 40–2.
Van Sertima, Ivan, editor, *Oakwood College Update,* November, 1993, pp. 6–7.

Sketch by Karl Preuss

Kai M. Siegbahn
1918–
Swedish physicist

Kai M. Siegbahn, the son of a Nobel physics laureate, himself won the Nobel Prize in physics for his development of electron spectroscopy for chemical analysis (ESCA). This reliable technique reveals many more details about the atomic and molecular structure of matter than was previously possible to determine. Siegbahn's electron spectroscopy soon became widely used around the world in scientific and industrial research labs.

Siegbahn was born to **Karl M. G. Siegbahn** and Karin Högbom Siegbahn on April 20, 1918, in Lund, Sweden. His father was a lecturer in physics at the University of Lund and the director of the Nobel Institute for Physics of the Royal Swedish Academy of Sciences for nearly thirty years. The elder Siegbahn's discoveries and research in X-ray

spectroscopy won him the 1924 Nobel Prize in physics. About growing up with such a role model, Kai Siegbahn was quoted in *Newsweek* as saying, "It's a decided advantage if you start discussing physics every day at the breakfast table."

The younger Siegbahn pursued his interests in mathematics, physics, and chemistry at the University of Uppsala, from which he earned his bachelor of science degree in 1939 and his master of science degree in 1942. He received his doctorate in 1944 from the University of Stockholm and worked as a researcher from 1942 to 1951 at the Nobel Institute of Physics. After a few years as a physics professor at the Royal Institute of Technology in Stockholm, Siegbahn left in 1954 to become professor and then head of the physics department at the University of Uppsala, where he remained and conducted his important research.

It was while he was pursuing his graduate degree that Siegbahn's interest in spectroscopy developed. Spectroscopy studies the frequencies, or wavelengths, at which particles of matter emit light or radiation. Since the frequencies are specific, or characteristic, of the matter being studied, they can yield valuable information about the atomic and molecular structure of that matter. Heinrich Hertz had discovered the photoelectric effect in 1883: objects struck by ultraviolet light release electrons, called photoelectrons. The nature of the effect was further examined by **Max Planck** and **Albert Einstein**, and researchers, hoping to advance scientific knowledge about the composition of matter, began attempting to use spectroscopy to analyze the photoelectrons. Electrons collide and scatter as they leave matter, losing unknown amounts of energy and creating spectra that are very difficult to read. Existing spectroscopes were inadequate to analyze the particles, but Siegbahn solved this problem.

Adaptations to Instrument Lead to ESCA

When he was in graduate school during the 1940s, Siegbahn studied electrons given off by radioactive nuclei, a process called beta decay. If he could measure the energies of these beta-ray electrons, he could learn much more about the nuclei. Existing instruments were of limited use for this purpose, so Siegbahn developed a mushroom-shaped magnet that allowed focusing in two directions. Siegbahn's high-resolution instrument increased the accuracy of measurements of these photoelectrons ten times. By the 1950s Siegbahn had turned his attention to electron spectroscopy—knocking electrons out of nonradioactive atoms with light or X rays—to determine the energies that bind electrons to atoms. Again, he found the spectroscopes he was using unable to produce accurate measurements. He decided to apply the double-focusing method he had developed for nuclear physics to the energy spectra of photoelectrons. The outcome was a double-focusing spectrometer with a high resolution that revealed previously unseen, narrow, but well-defined electron lines.

Siegbahn and his colleagues completed the first high-resolution, double-focusing spectrometer in 1954, and again it improved measurement accuracy tenfold. In 1957 the team recorded the first extremely sharp lines that allowed precise measurement of binding energies. In the 1960s the usefulness of the device was greatly extended when Siegbahn and two fellow researchers found that their electron spectrometer also revealed the chemical environment of the atoms that released the photoelectrons being studied, yielding details about chemical bonding as atoms combined into molecules. The technique now became known as electron spectroscopy for chemical analysis, or ESCA. Siegbahn and his team also adapted ESCA for the analysis of gases and liquids as well as solids.

Siegbahn's ESCA technique changed electron spectroscopy from a laboratory concept with a very limited application to a widely-used tool. ESCA provides high-resolution analysis of the atomic, molecular, and chemical characteristics of a nearly unlimited range of scientific, commercial, and industrial materials that includes atmospheric pollutants and surface corrosion. To acknowledge his contribution, Siegbahn was awarded the 1981 Nobel Prize in physics for his role in the development of a technique that provided a better understanding of the nature of matter.

SELECTED WRITINGS BY SIEGBAHN:

Books

ESCA-Atomic, Molecular, and Solid State Structure Studied by Means of Electron Spectroscopy, Almqvist & Wicksell (Uppsala, Sweden), 1967.
ESCA Applied to Free Molecules, North-Holland (Amsterdam, the Netherlands), 1969.

Periodicals

Review of Modern Physics, Electron Spectroscopy for Atoms, Molecules, and Condensed Matter, July, 1982, pp. 709–28.

Other

Royal Society Meeting on Studies of the Surfaces of Solids by Electron Spectroscopy: Recent Trends, Photoelectron Spectroscopy: Retrospects and Prospects, 1985.

FURTHER READING:

Books

Nobel Prize Winners, H. W. Wilson, 1987.
Nobel Prize Winners: Physics, Volume 3 (1968–88), Salem Press, 1989.

Periodicals

Begley, Sharon, *Newsweek,* The Physics of Chemistry, November 2, 1981, p. 100.
————, *New York Times,* October 20, 1981, p. C2.
————, *Science,* November 6, 1981, pp. 629–631.
————, *Scientific American,* December, 1981, pp. 83–86.
————, *Time,* November 2, 1981, p. 52.

Sketch by Kathy Sammis

Karl M. G. Siegbahn
1886–1978
Swedish physicist

Noted for modernizing Swedish physics, Karl M. G. Siegbahn contributed significantly to the field of X-ray spectroscopy begun in Germany and England. His design and application of equipment and techniques in this field vastly improved the accuracy of existing methods by which X-ray wavelengths were distinguished, and led to important discoveries about the nature of X rays (electromagnetic radiation invisible to the unaided human eye) and atomic structure. In recognition of his work, Siegbahn was awarded the 1924 Nobel Prize in physics. He became the first director of the Nobel Institute of Experimental Physics in 1937, and remained director of the institute until his retirement in 1964.

Karl Manne Georg Siegbahn was born in Örebro, Sweden, on December 3, 1886. His father was Nils Reinhold Georg Siegbahn, a station master for the Swedish national railway system, and his mother was the former Emma Sofia Mathilda Zetterberg. After his father's retirement, the family moved to Lund, Sweden, where Siegbahn entered the University of Lund in 1906. He studied astronomy, chemistry, mathematics, and physics there, eventually receiving his bachelor's degree in 1908, and his licentiate degree (comparable to a master's degree) in 1910. Studying electromagnetism as a research assistant to Johannes Rydberg, Siegbahn was awarded a doctorate in physics in 1911 for his dissertation on the measurement of magnetic fields. He spent the summer semesters of 1908 and 1909 studying at the universities of Göttingen and Münich respectively, and took up studies in Paris and Berlin during the summer of 1911.

Begins Studies on X rays

Upon receiving his doctorate, Siegbahn remained in his position as assistant to Rydberg, eventually assuming Rydberg's duties as lecturer when the older man was ill for long periods of time. When Rydberg died in 1920, Siegbahn succeeded him as professor of physics. Siegbahn's work under Rydberg had dealt primarily with studies of electrical and magnetic phenomena. By 1914, however, visits to research centers in Paris and Heidelberg turned his attentions toward the study of X-ray spectroscopy, a field to which he would devote the rest of his academic life.

Fundamental research on the properties of X rays had been carried out by the English physicist **Charles Barkla** in the first decade of the twentieth century. Barkla had found that X rays emitted from certain elements were of two types: "hard" or "K" X rays, and "soft" or "L" X rays, based on an element's atomic weight. Barkla's equipment was too primitive, however, to permit more detailed characterization of their wavelengths, or spectrums. In 1912 the German physicist **Max Laue** developed a technique for revealing the spectral lines of X rays based on the diffraction grating technique used for visible light. But, because the wavelengths of X rays are much shorter than wavelengths of visible light, von Laue needed a finer grating or spacing device. He discovered that the regular spacing between atoms in a crystal would serve this purpose, so that X rays passed through an analyzing crystal, such as zinc sulfide, would separate into a series of spectral lines similar to those in an optical spectrum. The father-and-son team of physicists **William Henry Bragg** and **William Lawrence Bragg** refined the process and developed the first X-ray spectrometer shortly thereafter.

Perfects the Techniques of X-ray Spectroscopy

By 1914, Siegbahn had embarked on his research program in X-ray spectroscopy, one aspect of which involved the improvement of equipment used in the field. Over a period of more than three decades, Siegbahn designed improvements in the tubes, vacuum systems, and spectrometers used in X-ray spectroscopy, all with the objective of attaining more precise measurements of X-ray wavelengths. One of his first developments was the vacuum spectrometer, which enclosed the whole analytical system—X-ray tube, target, and spectroscopic and photographic plates—in a high vacuum, thus reducing the possibility of any extraneous interference. Siegbahn also designed more accurate spectrometers capable of reading specific wavelength regions.

Each improvement in technology achieved by Siegbahn was soon followed by new discoveries. He was able not only to confirm the existence of Barkla's K and L series of lines, for example, but also to discover two new series, which he named the M and N. He also found that the two K lines discovered by the English physicist **Henry Moseley** were actually doublets and, where Moseley had found four or five L lines, Siegbahn found as many as twenty-eight.

These discoveries were especially important because of the information they provided about atomic structure. Spectral lines are emitted when electrons move from one energy level to another in an atom. **Niels Bohr**'s 1913 model of the atom had offered a simplistic view of electron

energy levels, one in which electrons were restricted to a small number of orbitals around the nucleus. With the discovery of elliptical orbitals, magnetic effects within the atom, and electron spin, however, this picture became much more complex. The number and type of electron transitions possible within an atom became much greater and Siegbahn's analysis of X-ray spectra provided invaluable keys to learning more about them. For both his discoveries and contributions to the improvement of X-ray spectroscopic technology, Siegbahn was awarded the 1924 Nobel Prize in physics. He also earned a number of other honors and awards throughout his life, including the Hughes (1934) and Rumford (1940) medals of the Royal Society, and the Duddel Medal of the London Physical Society, as well as honorary degrees from a number of universities throughout the world.

In 1923, Siegbahn was offered the position of professor of physics at the University of Uppsala, a post he held until 1937. He then became the first director of the newly created Nobel Institute of Experimental Physics in Stockholm. In addition to his continuing interest in X-ray spectroscopy, Siegbahn established a school of nuclear physics at the institute and, by 1938, had overseen the construction of Sweden's first particle accelerator. Siegbahn also served as president of the International Union of Pure and Applied Physics from 1938 to 1947.

Siegbahn's influence on the history of science goes beyond his own personal accomplishments. For most of his life, he maintained a strong commitment to the expansion and improvement of scientific facilities and programs of science education in Sweden. At both Uppsala and the Nobel Institute, he took facilities with poor or limited equipment and built them into first-class research institutions. Siegbahn was married to Karin Högbom in 1914. They had two sons, Bo Siegbahn and **Kai M. Siegbahn**, the latter a Nobel Laureate in physics himself in 1981. Karl M. G. Siegbahn died in Stockholm on September 26, 1978.

SELECTED WRITINGS BY SIEGBAHN:

Books

The Spectroscopy of X-rays, translation by George A. Lindsay, Oxford University Press, 1925.
On the Methods of Precision Measurements of X-ray Wavelengths, 1929.

FURTHER READING:

Books

Dictionary of Scientific Biography, Volume 12, Scribner, 1975, pp. 821–26.
Heathcote, Niels H. de V., *Nobel Prize Winners in Physics, 1901–1950,* Henry Schuman, 1953, pp. 218–28.

————, *McGraw-Hill Modern Scientists and Engineers,* Volume 10, McGraw-Hill, 1980, pp. 114–16.

————, *Nobel Prize Winners,* H. W. Wilson, 1987, pp. 969–71.

Sketch by David E. Newton

Waclaw Sierpiński
1882–1969
Polish mathematician

Waclaw Sierpiński and his colleagues are credited with revolutionizing Polish mathematics during the first half of the twentieth century. They took a couple of relatively new fields of mathematics and devoted whole journals to them. Although detractors had opined that such an experiment could not succeed, the mathematical heritage of the Polish community between the world wars has left a legacy of results, problems, and personalities—chief among them being Sierpiński.

Sierpiński was born in Warsaw on March 14, 1882. His father was Constantine Sierpiński, a successful physician, and his mother was Louise Lapinska. Sierpiński received his secondary education at the Fifth Grammar School in Warsaw, where he studied under an influential teacher named Wlodarski. From there, he entered the University of Warsaw and began studying number theory under the guidance of G. Voronoi. In 1903 Sierpiński's work in mathematics was recognized by a gold medal from the university, from which he graduated the next year. After graduation, he taught in secondary schools, a standard career path due to the shortage of positions available to Poles under Russian rule. In that capacity, he was involved in the school strike that occurred during the revolution of 1905. Even though the strike was not wholly unsuccessful, Sierpiński resigned his teaching position and moved to Kraków.

In 1906 Sierpiński received his doctorate from the Jagiellonian University in Kraków. Two years later he passed the qualifying examination to earn the right to teach at Jan Kazimierz University in Lwów. There, Sierpiński offered perhaps the first systematic course in set theory, the subject of his investigations for the next 50 years. In 1912 he gathered his lecture notes and published them as *Zarys Teorii Mnogósci* ("Outline of Set Theory"). Sierpiński's texts were recognized by prizes from the Academy of Learning in Kraków.

With the outbreak of World War I in 1914, Sierpiński was interned by the Russians, first at Vyatka, then in Moscow. This internment was not particularly severe, for while he was in Moscow, Sierpiński was accorded a cordial reception by the leading Russian mathematicians of the era. In fact, he was able to conduct some joint research with N. Lusin during this period in the field of set-theoretic topology.

Blends Set Theory with Topology

The area of set–theoretic topology in which Sierpiński worked depended on a few basic notions. One of these is that of a closed set, or a set that includes its boundary. A simple example is the interval of real numbers between 0 and 1, including both endpoints. Related to the notion of a closed set is that of an open set, one which does not include its boundary. An example of an open set is the interval between 0 and 1, not including either 0 or 1. If one takes that interval and includes 0 but not 1, then the set is neither closed nor open. Much time was spent investigating the results of combining open and closed sets in various infinite combinations. The entrance of infinity is what required the use of methods and ideas from set theory.

When the war ended Sierpiński returned to Lwów, but in the fall of that year he was appointed to a position at Warsaw. He devoted a number of papers to the set–theoretic topics of the continuum hypothesis and the axiom of choice. The continuum hypothesis, which had been known to **Georg Cantor**, claimed that there were no infinite numbers between the number of integers and the number of real numbers. If the continuum hypothesis is present, it reduces the complexity of the hierarchy of infinite numbers. The axiom of choice had been a matter for much discussion at the turn of the nineteenth century, allowing for the possibility of making an infinite number of choices simultaneously. Some distinguished French mathematicians like **Émile Borel** questioned the meaningfulness of such a choice, and one of the early consequences of investigation into the axioms of set theory was the discovery that the axiom of choice was equivalent to a number of other propositions of set theory. Sierpiński took an agnostic position with respect to the axiom, using it in proofs and also trying to eliminate it wherever possible.

It was during the period between the world wars that Sierpiński, in conjunction with several Polish colleagues, created what has since become known as the Polish school of mathematics. The subjects that dominated the Polish school were logic and set theory, topology, and the application of these subjects to questions in analysis. To make certain that there would be an audience for the work in these areas, the journal *Fundamenta Mathematicae* was founded in 1919. Although by the end of the twentieth century a profusion of specialized journals within mathematics had sprung up, *Fundamenta* was the first of its kind and was greeted with some suspicion about its likelihood for survival. The quality of its papers was high, the contributors were international, and the problems proposed and solved were substantial. As a permanent record of the Polish mathematical school, *Fundamenta Mathematicae* supplements the reminiscences of those who took part in the work.

Presides over the Polish Mathematical Community

Sierpiński often led the Polish delegations to international congresses and conferences of mathematicians. One of the most ambitious projects in which he was involved was a Congress of Mathematicians of Slavic Countries, whose very existence attests to a political consciousness side–by–side with the mathematical one. The event took place in Warsaw in 1929 and was chaired by Sierpiński.

During World War II Sierpiński was in Warsaw, holding classes in whatever secret settings were available. A good deal of the discussion went on in Sierpiński's home, where his wife did her best to make guests feel as comfortable as possible in such troubled times. In 1944, the Nazis took control of Warsaw and Sierpiński was taken by the Germans to a site near Kraków. After the latter city was liberated by the Allies, he held lectures at the Jagiellonian University there before returning to Warsaw.

The period after the war was marked by further honors to Sierpiński as his students dominated the mathematical landscape. He served as vice president of the Polish Academy of Sciences from its inception and was awarded the Scientific Prize (First Class) in 1949, as well as the Grand Cross of the Order of Polonia Restituta in 1958. There were not many mathematicians in any country who approached his publication records of more than 600 papers in set theory and approximately 100 articles about number theory.

Sierpiński died in Warsaw on October 21, 1969. His mathematical textbooks educated an entire generation, and he helped to lay the foundations of the discipline of set–theoretic topology. Sierpiński's legacy was in establishing a Polish mathematical community, a contribution at the same time to mathematics and to national identity.

SELECTED WRITINGS BY SIERPIŃSKI:

Books

Hypothèse du continu, 1934.
Cardinal and Ordinal Numbers, 1958.
Elementary Theory of Numbers, 1964.

FURTHER READING:

Books

Kuratowski, Kazimierz. *A Half Century of Polish Mathematics*. Warsaw: Polish Scientific Publishers, 1980, pp. 167–73.
Kuzawa, Sister Mary Grace. *Modern Mathematics: The Genesis of a School in Poland*. New Haven, CT: College and University Publishers, 1968.

Sketch by Thomas Drucker

Igor I. Sikorsky
1889–1972
American aeronautical engineer

Igor I. Sikorsky was one of the most significant aeronautical engineers and aircraft designers of the twentieth century. He was a leader in the design of four-engine bombers in World War I and large passenger-carrying seaplanes in the interwar years, but he is best known for designing the first single-rotor helicopters. During and after World War II the Sikorsky Aircraft Division of United Aircraft Corporation became synonymous with a multitude of helicopter designs used for everything from military operations to forest firefighting.

In some respects, Sikorsky's career in the United States was a rags-to-riches story. After gaining a reputation for aeronautical design in Russia, he fled the country following the Bolshevik Revolution and arrived nearly penniless in New York City in 1919. Teaching mathematics to other Russian emigres to make ends meet, he soon obtained financial backers and formed an aeronautical engineering company on Long Island in 1923. Within a decade he had established a central place in the expanding American aviation industry, a place he maintained until his death in 1972.

Perhaps Sikorsky's fascination with helicopters throughout his long life is an appropriate metaphor for his own experience. The search for freedom, whether in flight or in his personal life, motivated much of Sikorsky's career. Sikorsky said he fled Russia for freedom's sake, and he founded his own company and pursued helicopter design for the same reason. According to *Air Force* magazine, in a speech Sikorsky gave in 1967 when he received the Wright Memorial Trophy for his contributions to aeronautics, he summarized his beliefs by emphasizing the importance of "individual initiative, individual work, and total freedom" in the accomplishment of great tasks.

Igor Ivan Sikorsky was born on May 25, 1889, in Kiev, Russia, the youngest of Ivan and Zinaida Temrouk-Tcherkoss Sikorsky's five children. His family was prominent in Tsarist Russia, where his father was a professor of psychology at St. Vladimir University in Kiev and his mother was a medical school graduate. Well educated, the young Sikorsky learned about and was fascinated by fifteenth-century Italian artist Leonardo da Vinci's aeronautical studies, especially his drawings of a helicopter-like flying machine.

At age fourteen Sikorsky entered the Imperial Naval College in St. Petersburg and after graduating in 1906 entered the Mechanical College of the Polytechnic Institute in Kiev. During his two years at the Mechanical College, he concentrated on the new science of aviation. There Sikorsky learned everything he could about early aviators **Wilbur** and **Orville Wright** and their experiments in the United

States. He also studied the work of Count Ferdinand von Zeppelin, who developed lighter-than-air craft in Germany. In 1909 Sikorsky went to Paris, considered the mecca of aeronautics in Europe at the time, to study the latest design efforts.

Even during that early part of his career, Sikorsky was already studying the possibilities of building a helicopter. He purchased in Paris, for instance, a small 25-horsepower engine to power the rotor on his planned helicopter. For almost two years after his return to Russia, Sikorsky concentrated on designing and building helicopters, but the two prototypes he constructed were unable to lift their own weight. While the designs were sound, the engines needed to be more powerful. As a result, Sikorsky turned to more conventional, winged aircraft, on which a larger body of technical knowledge was available. In 1911 he produced the S–5 racer, which set a speed record of 70 miles per hour. The next year Sikorsky's S–6A design earned an award at a military competition and on the basis of these efforts the Russo-Baltic Railroad Car Works hired him to design a bomber for the Imperial Army.

Designs *Ilya Mourometz* Bomber

Sikorsky responded with a huge four-engine aircraft, the *Ilya Mourometz,* which first flew on May 13, 1913. Its four engines each generated from 100 to 220 horsepower, its crew of five had sleeping compartments in the rear fuselage, and it was protected from air attack by either three or four machine guns. The most advanced variant of the *Ilya Mourometz* could remain aloft for five hours at an altitude of approximately 9,000 feet and a speed of eighty-five miles per hour. It could carry a bomb load of between 992 and 1,543 pounds, depending on other operational factors. The aircraft also enjoyed a sixty percent bombs-on-target rating because of precise bombsights and excellent training of bombardiers.

During World War I, Russian Major-General M. V. Shidlovski, commanding the *Eskadra Vozdushnykh Korablei* (Squadron of Flying Ships), equipped his unit with the *Ilya Mourometz.* Formed specifically to exploit the weakness in the air of the Central Powers on the Eastern Front early in the war, Shidlovski made his squadron into a self-contained force with its own test operations, training, and other activities. He first employed it in combat on February 15, 1915, when it left from its base at Jablonna, Poland, and raided a German base in East Prussia. Between this time and November of 1917, Shidlovski's unit made more than 400 bombing raids over Germany and the Baltic states.

Sikorsky's *Ilya Mourometz* was a rugged airplane. Its only casualty from air attack occurred on September 12, 1916, but only after the aircraft's gunners had shot down three German fighters. Two other bombers were lost in crashes, but the force was not crippled until February of 1918, when thirty planes were destroyed by the Russians at Vinnitza to prevent capture by an advancing German army.

Immigrates to the United States

When the Bolshevik Revolution was successful in Russia in 1917, Sikorsky's career as the tsar's bomber designer came to an abrupt end. Not only was Sikorsky targeted as an enemy of Communist revolutionaries because of his family's prominence, but also because of his importance to the tsar as the designer of the *Ilya Mourometz.* Sikorsky abandoned his business and land holdings and went to France, where he was commissioned to build a bomber for the Allied forces still fighting in World War I. The aircraft had not yet progressed beyond the design stage when the Armistice was signed in 1918, and the French cancelled his contract. The next year he came to the United States and lived for a time in New York City, where he lived hand-to-mouth.

Soon after arriving in the United States, Sikorsky tried to obtain a military contract to produce an aircraft, but the War Department declined. It was not until four years later that he found sufficient financial backing to set up the Sikorsky Aero Engineering Corporation on a farm near Roosevelt Field, Long Island.

Builds Passenger Aircraft

Immediately after starting his own company, Sikorsky began work on an all-metal passenger monoplane. It became known as the S–29, a twin-engine, fourteen-passenger aircraft with a top speed of 115 miles per hour. In 1925 he organized the Sikorsky Manufacturing Corporation to build the S–29 and combined the engineering and manufacturing companies into the Sikorsky Aviation Corporation in 1928. A string of successful designs that reestablished Sikorsky as a leading aeronautical designer followed. The most important of his designs was the S–38, a ten-passenger amphibian, sold to Juan Trippe's Pan American Airways. It was in this business arrangement that Sikorsky first met Charles A. Lindbergh, who had gained international fame for making a solo flight nonstop over the Atlantic in 1927. The two eventually became good friends and sometime business associates.

Sikorsky eventually turned out more than 100 S–38 seaplanes, and they were used extensively in opening the airline connections between North and South America. Because of this success, in 1929 Sikorsky was bought out by the United Aircraft Corporation, although he continued to direct his operation as a subsidiary. More advanced variations on the S–29 seaplane appeared throughout the 1930s, among them the S–40, called the *American Clipper,* a four-engine amphibian that became a standard vehicle for international flights in the 1930s.

Returns to the Helicopter Problem

By the mid–1930s Sikorsky had persuaded United Aircraft to allow him to develop a helicopter, and it invested a reported $300,000 in the effort. On September 14, 1939, he flew the first true single-rotor helicopter, the VS–300, a strange configuration of welded pipes and open-air cockpit powered by a seventy-five-horsepower engine that turned a three-bladed rotor by means of an automobile fanbelt. Sikorsky was elated when it flew. He wrote in his autobiography, *Recollections and Thoughts of a Pioneer,* "It is a dream to feel the machine lift you gently up in the air, float smoothly over one spot for indefinite periods, move up or down under good control, as well as move not only forward or backward but in any direction."

Recognizing that this new air vehicle had military potential, the U.S. Army purchased its first helicopter from Sikorsky in 1941. Two years later it ordered the production of the R–4 helicopter, a VS–300 variant. Several years elapsed before the helicopter became a military staple—few of them were used during World War II—but by the time of the Korean War (1950–1953) several different designs were being routinely used for observation, transportation of wounded, and movement of high priority cargo and passengers into areas without airfields. In acknowledgment of this use, American helicopter manufacturers received the 1951 Collier Trophy, given annually to the person or group making the most significant contribution to American aviation. U.S. President Harry S. Truman chose Sikorsky to accept the award on behalf of the industry. Since that time the military has found increasingly sophisticated uses for helicopters, including as gunships, transport vehicles for its "air cavalry" units, and rescue and recovery and commando craft.

Sikorsky was especially delighted with the business and humanitarian uses found for the helicopter during the same era. For instance, in January of 1944 his helicopters were called upon to carry vital blood plasma from New York to Sandy Hook, New Jersey, for the victims of a steamship explosion. Sikorsky recalled in his autobiography, "It was a source of great satisfaction to all the personnel of our organization, including myself, that the helicopter started its practical career by saving a number of lives and by helping man in need rather than by spreading death and destruction." In the late 1940s other uses were found for Sikorsky's helicopter, including as an airmail carrier and as air buses transporting passengers from airports to the hearts of major cities. By the early 1960s they were also being routinely used for traffic observation, forest firefighting, crop dusting, rescue, and a host of other practical jobs.

The Sikorsky Aeronautical Division built a succession of helicopters for various purposes during the 1940s and 1950s. After the VS–300 and the R–4 military production model, Sikorsky's helicopters grew in size and complexity. The S–55 was the first certified transport helicopter in the United States, while the twin-engine S–56 was capable of carrying 50 combat troops. An important breakthrough design was the economical S–58, which could carry twelve passengers and was excellent for moving people short distances. Subsequent incarnations of the helicopter included the S–62, an amphibious helicopter with a flying-boat hull, and the S–61 twin-turbine helicopter, used for antisubmarine warfare. Sikorsky also developed the giant S–64

"Skycrane" helicopter, which could haul cargoes of up to ten tons suspended from its belly.

Sikorsky retired from active involvement in aircraft design and production in 1957 but continued as a consultant to his company. Furthermore, after his retirement, Sikorsky enjoyed the role of aviation sage. He was in the spotlight on numerous public occasions, as when he received the National Medal of Science from U.S. President Lyndon B. Johnson in 1968. He also lectured widely on aeronautical development to government organizations, at universities, and within the industry. In every case, Sikorsky spoke of his quest for freedom and his commitment to both technological and personal excellence.

Sikorsky was a deeply religious man, a member of the Russian Orthodox Church and author of two books on Christianity— *The Message of the Lord's Prayer* and *The Invisible Encounter.* He died of a heart attack on October 26, 1972, at the age of 82 in his home in Easton, Connecticut. His second wife, Russian-born Elizabeth A. Semion, whom he married in 1924, survived him. Additionally, he had four sons and a daughter, some of whom followed him into the aviation business.

SELECTED WRITINGS BY SIKORSKY:

Books

Story of the Winged-S, Dodd, 1938.
The Message of the Lord's Prayer, Scribner, 1942.
The Invisible Encounter, Scribner, 1947.
Recollections and Thoughts of a Pioneer, 1964.

Periodicals

Air Force, Free Men Are the True Pioneers, February, 1968, pp. 100–01.

FURTHER READING:

Books

Finne, K. N., *Igor Sikorsky: The Russian Years,* edited by Carl J. Bobrow and Von Hardesty, Smithsonian Institution Press, 1987.

Periodicals

Hughes, Albert D., *Christian Science Monitor,* Pioneer of Flight Frontiers, September, 1963.
Witze, Claude, *Air Force Magazine,* A Tribute to Igor Sikorsky, December, 1972, pp. 26–7.

Other

Witze, Claude, *The Aviation Careers of Igor Sikorsky,* Exhibit at the National Air and Space Museum, Smithsonian Institution, Washington, DC, 1990.

————, *The Aviation Careers of Igor Sikorsky,* Letter from Thurman H. Bane, Engineering Division, Air Service, to Jerome C. Hunsaker, Navy Department, U.S. War Department document, 1919.

Sketch by Roger D. Launius

Ellen Kovner Silbergeld
1945–
American toxicologist

Ellen Silbergeld is an American environmental toxicologist and public health policy advocate. She has conducted research and advised policy makers on the toxicological effects of such substances as lead, mercury, dioxin, dibenzofurans, manganese, and Agent Orange.

Ellen Kovner Silbergeld was born on July 29, 1945, in Washington D.C., the first girl and second child of Joseph Kovner, a lawyer, and Mary Gion Kovner, a journalist. Joseph Kovner fell victim to the witch hunts of the House Committee on un-American Activities during the early 1950s and was forced to leave his government job, an event that left a lasting impression on Silbergeld. When she was seven years old, her family moved to Concord, New Hampshire, where her father took up private legal practice. In nearby Boston, one of her father's closest childhood friends, civil liberties lawyer Reuben Goodman, became a mentor to the young Silbergeld. His commitment to civil rights, his rigorous intellect, and his zest for life were, according to Silbergeld, a constant source of stimulation. She was also influenced intellectually by her mother's friends, who eventually played a role in her decision to attend a women's college. When Silbergeld was in the eighth grade, her family returned to Washington, D.C. Although as a young student she enjoyed mathematics and puzzle solving, she avoided the study of science as much as possible and believed she had no talent in the subject.

In 1967 Silbergeld began her undergraduate work in history at Vassar College, in Poughkeepsie, New York. Graduating in 1967 with an A.B. degree in modern history, she accepted a Fulbright Fellowship to England and began a doctoral degree program at the London School of Economics. A year later, disenchanted with the field of economics, she returned to Washington D.C. and took a position as a secretary and program officer for the Committee on Geography at the National Academy of Sciences. It was in this post that Silbergeld first began to develop an interest in science. She remained at the National Academy of Sciences until 1970. By then Silbergeld had begun graduate studies in environmental engineering at Johns Hopkins University in Baltimore. In 1972 she received her Ph.D. and assumed a

postdoctoral fellowship in environmental medicine and neurosciences, also at Johns Hopkins University. Her graduate and postgraduate research on the topic of lead neurotoxicity prompted Silbergeld to get involved in public policy regarding lead exposure.

In 1975 Silbergeld became a staff fellow in the Unit on Behavioral Neuropharmacology at the National Institutes of Health (NIH) in Bethesda, Maryland. There, she continued her research on lead and began investigating the toxicology of food dyes. She also conducted research on neurological disorders such as Huntington's disease and Parkinson's disease. In 1979, she became chief of the section on Neurotoxicology at NIH, a post she held until 1981. As section chief, Silbergeld directed research on the mechanisms of neurotoxicagents such as lead and manganese. She also directed research into the effects of estradiol on the central nervous system.

From 1982 until 1991, she served as the chief toxic scientist and director of the Toxic Chemicals Program for the Environmental Defense Fund in Washington, D.C. Simultaneously, she maintained research programs at several institutions. As a guest scientist at the National Institute of Child Health Development from 1982 to 1984, she researched the effects of polycyclic aromatic hydrocarbons (PAHs) on ovarian function.

From 1985 till 1987, as visiting professor at the University of Maryland School of Medicine, she studied the effects of tetrachlorodibenzo-p-dioxin (TCDD) on glucocorticoid receptors, and from 1987 to 1989 she investigated lead toxicity and the genetic effects of TCDD as a visiting professor in the Program for Toxicology at the University of Maryland. In 1987, as an associate faculty member in the Johns Hopkins School of Hygiene and Public Health, she began supervising research into lead toxicity and risk assessment. Her affiliation with Johns Hopkins continued in 1991 as an adjunct professor. Ongoing programs of research on the neural and reproductive effects of lead and on the molecular mechanism of TCDD were begun at the University of Maryland School of Medicine in 1989.

Other appointments at the University of Maryland include an affiliate professorship in the School of Law, begun in 1990, a professorship in the Department of Pathology, begun in 1991, and a professorship in the Department of Epidemiology and Preventive Medicine, begun in 1992. Since 1993, Silbergeld has been a senior consultant toxicologist for the Environmental Defense Fund, and since 1996, the director of the program in Human Health and the Environment at the University of Maryland.

Silbergeld has published over 200 research and policy articles and is a member of the editorial board for more than half a dozen journals related to environmental health and toxicology. She has served as an advisor and consultant for environmental and health causes throughout her career. She has organized a variety of international symposia and workshops on chemically-induced diseases and lead toxicology. Highly commended for both her scientific research and her environmental advocacy, she was designated one of the

Four Outstanding Women of Maryland by the Maryland Education Association in 1987. That same year, she received the Warner-Lambert Award for Distinguished Women in Science. In 1990, she received the Governor's Citation for Excellence, in 1991, the Abel Wolman Award, and in 1992, the Barsky Award. The MacArthur Foundation made her a Fellow in 1993, and that year she also received the Earth Month Award of the Maryland Department of the Environment. In 1994, she was an honoree in the Maryland Women's History Project, and, the following year, Chatham College named her one of the Women Who Make a Difference. That year, Silbergerld was awarded a patent for a lead detection procedure.

In 1969, she married Mark Silbergeld, with whom she has two children. Sophia, their daughter, was born in 1981, and their son Nicholas Reuben, named after Reuben Goodman, was born in 1985.

SELECTED WRITINGS BY SILBERGELD:

Books

"Risk assessment and risk management: an uneasy divorce." In *Acceptable Evidence: Science and Values in Risk Management*, Deborah G. Mayo and Rachelle D. Hollander, eds. New York: Oxford University Press, 1991.

FURTHER READING:

Books

Shearer, Benjamin F., and Barbara S. Shearer. *Notable Women in the Life Sciences*. Westport: Greenwood Press, 1996.

Sketch by Leslie Reinherz

Howard Ensign Simmons, Jr.
1929–1997
American organic chemist

Howard Ensign Simmons Jr. built a fruitful scientific career exploring the relationship between chemical structures and chemical activity, contributing to both organic chemistry practice and theory. Simmons' contributions extended to corporate administration as well. As director and vice president of central research for E. I. du Pont de Nemours and Company, he led a major expansion of the company's research and development program. In

Howard Ensign Simmons, Jr.

addition to his career achievements, Simmons is remembered for his interests in foreign languages, prehistoric Native American cultures, and boating. He held visiting professorships in chemistry at Harvard University in 1968; the University of Chicago in 1978; and the University of Delaware from 1970 until his death.

Simmons was born on June 17, 1929, in Norfolk, Virginia, to a merchant marine captain and a homemaker. He received a B.S. in chemistry from Massachusetts Institute of Technology (MIT) in 1951, followed three years later by an organic chemistry Ph.D. from MIT. In 1954 he joined Du Pont, launching a 37-year career topped by scientific and administrative achievement.

Contributions to Chemical Toolbox and Thinking

Simmons' most significant pre-Du Pont discovery was benzyne, the chemically unstable key to a large family of reactions for adding or removing chemical groups from the benzene molecule. Along with later work at Du Pont that demonstrated the chemical structure of benzyne, this research allowed organic chemists to better understand and control these industrially important reactions. Du Pont colleague R. D. Smith and Simmons also developed the Simmons-Smith reaction—an efficient method of synthesizing the chemical workhorse cyclopropane and its derivatives, in a manner that controls the structure of the final product. In later work, Simmons and collaborator Chung Ho Park synthesized a new class of large cyclic molecules that are today being used to create synthetic enzymes and catalysts.

Simmons also contributed greatly to organic chemical theory. In a 1989 monograph, Simmons and Richard E. Merrifield introduced a new theoretical field to the chemical community: topological chemistry, which predicts chemical activity by computing the exact shapes and surfaces of reactant molecules without resorting to the usual physics necessary for such predictions. Recognition for Simmons' research has come in the form of membership in the American Academy of Arts and Sciences and the National Science Foundation in 1975, Columbia University's Chandler Medal of chemistry in 1991, the National Medal of Science in 1992, and the American Chemical Society Priestley Medal in 1994.

Successful Administrator As Well As Scientist

As Simmons was compiling research achievements, he was also rising in the Du Pont organization. Named a research supervisor in the company's Central Research Department in 1959, he rose to associate director of research in 1970 and then overall director of the department in 1974. Arguably, his greatest administrative contributions to the company came during his tenures as director of the Central Research and Development Department from 1979 to 1983, and vice president of the department from 1983 to 1990. This period saw a dramatic growth in the department, including the strengthening of Du Pont's already world-class programs in organic and physical chemistry and an expansion into the fields of life science, materials science, and electronics. In 1990 he was made vice president and senior science advisor at Du Pont; he retired in 1991.

Simmons also served his country in key administrative positions, including a term on the National Science Board (NSB), a 24-member committee that determines policy for the National Science Foundation. He served on the NSB from 1990 to 1996.

Simmons died on April 26, 1997, of congestive heart failure. He was survived by his wife, the former Elizabeth Warren, as well as sons Howard E., III, and John W., both chemists at du Pont.

SELECTED WRITINGS BY SIMMONS:

Books

Orbital Symmetry Papers. American Chemical Society, 1974.
(With Richard E. Merrifield) *Topological Methods in Chemistry*. John Wiley, 1989.

Periodicals

"Basic Research–A Perspective." *Chemical & Engineering News* (March 14, 1994): 27-31.

FURTHER READING:

Periodicals

Kreeger, Karen Young. "Du Pont Chemist Receives Priestley Medal." *The Scientist* (March 21, 1994): 23.
Milford, Phil. "Award-Winning Du Pont Scientist Dies." *Wilmington News Journal* (April 28, 1997): B1.
"Simmons, Howard." *The New York Times* (May 5, 1997): A30.

Other

"Howard Ensign Simmons, Jr." http://www.dupont.com/corp/r-and-d/lavoisier/simmons (November 20, 1997).
"Five Du Pont Scientists Honored with Lavoisier Medals (Eleuterio, Ibrahim, Kwolek, Shivers, and Simmons)." April 27, 1995. http://www.dupont.com/corp/whats-new/releases/95archive/950427.html (November 22, 1997).
"ACS Awards: List of Awards Administered." September 5, 1997. http://www.acs.org/acsgen/awards/quicklst.htm#53 (November 22, 1997).

Sketch by Kenneth Chiacchia

Dorothy Martin Simon
1919–
American chemist

Dorothy Martin Simon has been responsible for several significant advances in space engineering, particularly in the area of combustion. By relating the fundamental properties of flame to each other through the principles of heat and mass transfer and chemical reaction, she helped establish the present-day theory of flame propagation and quenching. She also contributed to the development of ablative coatings, which protect missiles from heat damage upon reentering the Earth's atmosphere. In recognition of these accomplishments, as well as her success in executive management and public speaking, the Society of Women Engineers presented Simon with their Achievement Award in 1966.

Simon was born Dorothy Martin on September 18, 1919, in Harwood, Missouri. Her parents were Robert William Martin, head of the chemistry department at Southwest Missouri State College, and Laudell Flynn Martin. Simon attended high school at Greenwood Laboratory School in Springfield, where she won the highest sports honor while also earning the highest grade-point average in the school's history. After graduation, she attended the college at which her father taught, where she received a bachelor's degree with honors in 1940. Once again, she was class valedictorian. From there, she went on to the University of Illinois, where her thesis research on active deposits from radon and thoron gas was among the earliest work on radioactive fallout. She obtained a Ph.D. in chemistry in 1945.

Upon completing college, Simon first spent a year as a chemist at the Du Pont Company in Buffalo, New York. During this time, she studied the chemical reactions involved in producing the synthetic fiber now known as Orlon. In 1946 she began working for the Atomic Energy Commission (AEC) at Oak Ridge Laboratory in Tennessee and the Argonne Laboratory in Illinois. Among her accomplishments while with the AEC was the isolation of a new isotope of calcium.

Advances the Understanding of Combustion

In 1949 Simon began six years with the National Advisory Committee for Aeronautics, the agency that evolved into NASA. These proved to be her most fruitful years as a researcher. During this period, her work elucidating the fundamental nature of flames was recognized with a Rockefeller Public Service Award. Simon used the stipend of $10,000 to visit university and technical laboratories in England, France, and the Netherlands. She studied at Cambridge University with **Ronald G. W. Norrish**, who later won the Nobel Prize in chemistry.

In 1955 she spent a year as group leader at the Magnolia Petroleum Company in Dallas. Then, in 1956, Simon began a lengthy association with Avco Corporation, where her early work addressed the design problems of reentry vehicles for intercontinental ballistic missiles. Her research dealt with ablation cooling—a method of protecting the missile body from extreme heat while reentering the Earth's atmosphere by absorbing the heat in a shielding material that is changing phase. This was the topic of a Marie Curie Lecture that Simon delivered at Pennsylvania State University in 1962.

Soon Simon's interests turned toward management within the giant conglomerate. She was appointed the first female corporate officer at Avco in 1968. In her capacity as vice president of research, she was responsible for guiding the company's various high-tech divisions. At that time, she was one of the few women to have scaled such heights on the corporate ladder, a fact that was recognized by Worcester Polytechnic Institute when conferring an honorary doctorate upon Simon in 1971. The institute cited her position as "perhaps the most important woman executive in American industry today." Simon later received a second honorary doctorate, this one from Lehigh University. She is a fellow of the American Institute of Chemists, as well as a member of the American Chemical Society and the American Institute of Aeronautics and Astronautics.

Simon is known as an outstanding speaker, who has frequently lectured and written on the challenges of space, research management, and women in science. She served on President Jimmy Carter's Committee for the National Medal of Science, the National Research Council's National Materials Advisory Board, the Department of Defense's Defense Policy Advisory Committee, and the Department of Commerce's Statutory Committee for the National Bureau of Standards. In her free time, she enjoys traveling, cooking, and gardening. Simon was married on December 6, 1946, to Sidney L. Simon—a leading scientist in his own right who became vice president at Sperry Rand. He died in 1975. Simon currently makes her home in Pittsboro, North Carolina.

SELECTED WRITINGS BY SIMON:

Periodicals

Industrial and Engineering Chemistry, Pressure Limits of Flame Propagation of Propane-Air Mixtures, Volume 46, 1954, p. 1010.
Selected Combustion Problems: Fundamentals and Aeronautical Applications, Diffusion Processes as Rate-Controlling Steps in Laminar Flame Propagation, Butterworths Scientific Publications, 1954, pp. 59–91.

FURTHER READING:

Books

O'Neill, Lois Decker, editor, *The Women's Book of World Records and Achievements,* Doubleday, 1979, pp. 189, 519.

Periodicals

Kelly, Mary, *Christian Science Monitor,* Earthling Eyes Cast on Space, August 2, 1965, p. 12.

Other

Burton, David, *Interview with Linda Wasmer Smith,* conducted February 9, 1994.
Burton, David, *Interview with Linda Wasmer Smith,* Southwest Missouri State University, material including award nominations, biographical sketches, news clippings, and press release.
Burton, David, *Interview with Linda Wasmer Smith,* University of Illinois Archives, material including award nomination and citation, biographical sketch, news clipping, and résumé.

Sketch by Linda Wasmer Smith

Herbert A. Simon
1916–
American computer scientist

Generally considered one of the fathers of artificial intelligence—computer programs capable of complex problem-solving—Herbert A. Simon has made distinguished contributions in a number of fields, including computer science, the psychology of learning, business administration, political science, economics, and philosophy. Recipient of the 1978 Nobel Prize in economics for his work on human decision-making, he also, in 1986, became the first person to receive the National Medal of Science for work in the behavioral sciences. In addition to his varied professional interests, he also paints and plays the piano and enjoys mountain-climbing, traveling, and learning foreign languages.

Simon was born in Milwaukee, Wisconsin, on June 15, 1916. His father, Arthur Simon, was a German-born electrical engineer and his mother, Edna (Merkel) Simon, was an accomplished pianist. After being skipped ahead three semesters in the Milwaukee public school system, Simon was just seventeen when he enrolled in the University of Chicago, where he would earn his B.A. in political science in 1936. As an undergraduate, Simon conducted a study of the administration of the Milwaukee Recreation Department. This study sparked Simon's interest in how administrators make decisions—a topic that would be a focal point of his career. In 1937, Simon married Dorothea Isobel Pye, also a graduate student in political science at the University of Chicago; they would have three children, Katherine, Peter, and Barbara.

After graduating, Simon was hired by the International City Managers' Association (ICMA) in Chicago as an assistant to Clarence Ridley, who had been his instructor in a course on evaluating municipal governments. Ridley and Simon became widely recognized experts on mathematical means of measuring the effectiveness of public services. While at the ICMA, Simon had his first experience with computers. As an assistant editor of the *Municipal Yearbook,* Simon started using IBM keypunch, sorting, and tabulating machines to prepare statistical tables. His consequent fascination with these machines would play a major part in his research and his career.

In 1939 Simon moved to the University of California at Berkeley to head a three-year study of local government funded by a grant from the Rockefeller Foundation. While at Berkeley, Simon completed the requirements for his Ph.D. from the University of Chicago. His dissertation, on decision-making in organizations, later evolved into his first book, *Administrative Behavior.* In 1942, Simon joined the faculty of the political science department at the Illinois Institute of Technology, where he remained for seven years, becoming department chair in 1946. Then, in 1949, he was tapped by the Carnegie Institute of Technology (later known as Carnegie Mellon University) in Pittsburgh, Pennsylvania, to teach in its new graduate school in business administration. Simon would play a major role in shaping the curriculum, which was designed to provide students with the basic tools necessary for independent learning and problem-solving.

Defining the Field of Artificial Intelligence

In his autobiography, *Models of My Life,* Simon describes 1955 and 1956 as the most important years of his scientific career. It was at this time that Simon, along with **Allen Newell** and Clifford Shaw of the RAND Corporation, began using computers to study problem-solving behavior. To do this, they observed individuals as they worked through well-structured problems of logic. Subjects verbalized their reasoning as they worked through the problems. Simon and his colleagues were then able to code this reasoning in the form of a computer program. The program was not subject-matter specific; rather, it focused on the problem-solving process. Together, Simon, Allen, and Shaw developed Logic Theorist and General Problem Solver, the first computer programs to simulate human reasoning in solving problems. This work was at the forefront of the newly developing field of artificial intelligence. Simon and J. R. Hayes later developed the "Understand" program, which was designed to allow computers to solve even poorly structured problems. The program first worked to define the problem, and then focused on the problem's solution. Simon's work in artificial intelligence would lead to his being named Richard King Mellon University Professor of Computer Science and Psychology at Carnegie Mellon University in 1966.

In 1957 Simon released a second edition of *Administrative Behavior.* In the new edition, Simon built on his original contention that because of the complexity of the economy, business decision-makers are unable to obtain all of the information they need in order to maximize profits. As a result, he had argued, most companies try to set goals that are acceptable but less than ideal—a behavior he termed "satisficing." In the second edition, Simon pointed out that his findings undermined a basic assumption of classical economic theory that the decision-maker in an organization has access to all of the information needed to make decisions and will always make rational decisions that maximize profits. Simon's conclusions met with resistance from many economists, although those specializing in business operations were more accepting.

Research In Decision-Making Earns the Nobel Prize

Simon's distinguished career received significant recognition in the 1960s and 1970s. He was elected to the National Academy of Sciences and became chairman of the Division of Behavioral Sciences for the National Research Council in 1967; the following year, he was appointed to the President's Science Advisory Committee. In 1969, Simon received the American Psychological Association's Distinguished Scientific Contributions Award, and in 1975, he shared the Association for Computing Machinery's A. M. Turing Award with his longtime collaborator Allen Newell. This string of awards and honors culminated in 1978 when he was awarded the Nobel Prize in economic science for his research into the decision-making process within organizations.

In the 1980s, Simon continued to be an active researcher, with his work including a study of short-term memory with colleagues from China. He continued his activity with the National Academy of Sciences and published a second volume of *Models of Thought* in 1989. In 1991, he published his autobiography, *Models of My Life.* In the introduction to this book, Simon commented on the varied academic paths he has chosen: "I have been a scientist, but in many sciences. I have explored mazes, but they do not connect into a single maze. My aspirations do not extend to achieving a single consistency in my life. It will be enough if I can play each of my roles creditably, borrowing sometimes from one for another, but striving to represent fairly each character when he has his turn on stage."

SELECTED WRITINGS BY SIMON:

Books

Administrative Behavior: A Study of Decision-making Processes in Administrative Organization, Macmillan, 1947, third edition, 1976.
Models of Man, Wiley, 1958.
Organizations, Wiley, 1958.
The New Science of Management Decision, Harper, 1960, revised edition, Prentice-Hall, 1977.
The Sciences of the Artificial, MIT Press, 1969, second edition, 1981.
Human Problem Solving, Prentice-Hall, 1972.
Models of Discovery, and Other Topics in the Methods of Science, Reidel, 1978.
Models of Thought, Yale University Press, 1979.
Models of My Life, Basic Books, 1991.

FURTHER READING:

Books

Baars, Bernard J., *The Cognitive Revolution in Psychology,* Guilford, 1986.
Lindzey, Gardner, editor, *A History of Psychology in Autobiography,* Volume 7, Freeman, 1980.
McCorduck, Pamela, *Machines Who Think,* W. H. Freeman, 1979.

Periodicals

McCorduck, Pamela, *Business Week,* December 5, 1970.
———— , *Chicago Tribune,* October 27, 1986.

———— , *Newsweek,* October 30, 1978.
———— , *New York Times,* November 26, 1978.
———— , *New York Times Book Review,* March 17, 1991, pp. 1, 28–29.
———— , *People,* January 15, 1979.
———— , *Psychology Today,* October, 1986.
———— , *Saturday Evening Post,* May 4, 1968.
———— , *Time,* October 30, 1978.
———— , *Times Literary Supplement,* August 22, 1980.

Sketch by Daniel Rooney

George Gaylord Simpson
1902–1984
American paleontologist

George Gaylord Simpson was a pioneer in the use of statistical methods in paleontology, the scientific study of prehistoric life as revealed in the fossil record. By analyzing fossil remains, particularly those of mammals, Simpson was able to deduce much about the animals' migration patterns, distribution changes, and evolutionary histories. In addition, he was a major architect of synthetic theory, which applies the principles of modern genetics to the study of evolution. His 1944 book, *Tempo and Mode in Evolution,* is considered a seminal work in the field.

Simpson was born in Chicago, Illinois, on June 16, 1902, the youngest of three children. His parents were Joseph Alexander Simpson, a lawyer, and Helen Julia (Kinney) Simpson. While he was still a baby, the family moved to Denver, Colorado, where his father was first a claims adjuster for the railroad, and later a speculator in irrigation, land, and mining. As Simpson related in *Concession to the Improbable: An Unconventional Autobiography,* "When I was a bit older [my father and I] frequently went for weekends or longer holidays in the Colorado mountains; each with cans of food rolled in a blanket tied at the ends and slung over a shoulder, we would walk all day at a leisurely pace and sleep on the ground whenever night overtook us. . . . I acquired a deep love for nature . . . that was a factor in entering a profession that included camping out during many active years."

Rises to Curatorship at the American Museum

A gifted student, Simpson managed to pass eight grades of grammar school in only six years, despite missing an entire year for illness. He graduated from East Denver High School in 1918, shortly before his sixteenth birthday. The following autumn, he entered the University of Colorado. Financial problems the next year, however, forced him to drop out briefly and take jobs in Chicago,

George Gaylord Simpson

Texas, and the Colorado mountains. By 1920, he was back at college, thanks to a combination of scholarship money and menial jobs. Simpson transferred to Yale for his senior year at the urging of a professor of historical geology, who had himself recently made the same transition. Simpson received a bachelor's degree from Yale in 1923 and a Ph.D. in 1926.

Simpson began a prolific publishing career while still in graduate school. In his autobiography, he recalled, "I went to college thinking vaguely that I might become a writer, but I was soon bothered by the fact that unapplied writing, like unapplied mathematics, isn't *about* anything." Fortunately, he soon discovered his subject matter, as well as a knack for presenting technical information in clear, readable prose. His first papers appeared a year before he completed his doctorate, and by 1926, he already had 25 articles, abstracts, and reviews in print. At the time of his death, he had over 700 publications to his credit, including nearly 50 books.

Early in his graduate studies, Simpson began to concentrate on vertebrate paleontology. In the summer of 1924, he worked as a field assistant for an expedition that collected vertebrate fossils in Texas and New Mexico. Upon his return to Yale, Simpson made good use of the Peabody Museum's rare collection of mammal fossils dating from the Mesozoic Era—the period during which the first mammals appeared. These fossils eventually became the subject of his dissertation. The year following his graduation, Simpson was awarded a fellowship to study European Mesozoic

mammals at the British Museum (Natural History) in London.

Later in 1927, Simpson returned to the United States to assume a post as assistant curator at the American Museum of Natural History in New York. It was the start of a very fruitful association lasting until 1959, during which time Simpson rose to the position of curator of fossil mammals and birds. He also became chairman of the museum's department of geology and paleontology. In addition, from 1945 to 1959, he held a joint teaching appointment at Columbia University. His position at the museum afforded Simpson many opportunities for field work. His early expeditions included trips to such places as the San Juan Basin in New Mexico, the Pleistocene deposits in Florida, and the badlands of Patagonia, a region in southern Argentina and Chile. The latter produced several technical papers, a large monograph, and a popular book, *Attending Marvels: A Patagonian Journal.* Simpson visited South America once again from 1938 to 1939, this time at the invitation of the Venezuelan government. Fossil-hunting there took Simpson to the remote territory of the Kamarako-to tribe, whose customs he recorded in another monograph.

Incorporates Genetics into Evolutionary Theory

On February 2, 1923, while Simpson was still a graduate student, he married Lydia Pedroja. That union produced four daughters—Helen, Gaylord (known as Gay), Joan, and Elizabeth—before ending in divorce in April 1938. On May 27, 1938, Simpson married Anne Roe, a psychologist who had been a childhood friend. The next year, Simpson and his second wife published a textbook, *Quantitative Zoology,* that was itself a wedding of his training in zoology and her knowledge of statistics. This book helped spur changes in zoological methodology.

Next Simpson expanded his use of statistical tools, this time applying them to the difficult task of explaining evolution. The result was *Tempo and Mode in Evolution,* a landmark book in several respects. First, Simpson demonstrated that fossil findings could be not only described, but also quantified. Second, he showed that the fossil record could indeed be reconciled with the emerging synthesis of population genetics and natural history. Synthetic theory gave scientists the means for the first time to demonstrate how natural selection could work. In brief, it stated that genetic variability among individuals in a population of sexually reproducing organisms is produced by mutation and genetic recombination. Such genetic variability is subject to natural selection. Simpson established that the fossil record was consistent with what this theory would predict.

Another major accomplishment dating from this period was the publication of a lengthy monograph titled "The Principles of Classification and a Classification of Mammals." Shortly after joining the American Museum staff, Simpson had begun compiling a catalog to help organize that institution's extensive mammal collection. In 1942, Simpson completed a greatly expanded version of this catalog, in which he classified all the mammals then known, living or extinct. To this, he appended a now-famous essay on taxonomy, the branch of biology dealing with classification. It was the first attempt to set forth the principles of evolutionary taxonomy.

Just at this point, however, World War II intervened in Simpson's career. From 1942 to 1944, he served in the U.S. Army, first as a captain and later promoted to major. His assignments—most in military intelligence—took him to Algeria, Tunisia, Sicily, and mainland Italy. Simpson continued to sport his trademark Vandyke beard, a fact that did not escape the attention of General George S. Patton. This led to an amusing incident relayed back to the States by a reporter. As Simpson told the story in his autobiography, "He sent an aide, a chicken colonel, to tell me that if I did not shave my beard he (Patton) would pluck it out hair by hair. With perfect military courtesy I explained to the colonel that according to army regulations a commissioned officer could wear a neat beard if he had permission from his commanding officer, and that General Patton was not my commanding officer. General Eisenhower was. . . . I received no apology, but I did keep my beard."

Resumes the Search for Vertebrate Fossils

Upon returning from the service, Simpson promptly resumed his field work. Starting in 1946, he made frequent trips to New Mexico and Colorado to search for mammal fossils from the Eocene and Paleocene, epochs beginning 54 and 65 million years ago, respectively. His most celebrated finds were the skulls of eight 15-inch-high creatures called Dawn Horses. In 1947, Simpson and his wife built a second home, dubbed Los Pinavetes, in the mountains above Cuba, New Mexico. Over the next two decades, they spent at least part of every summer and all of one winter there.

In 1949, Simpson published *The Meaning of Evolution,* in which he set about presenting the complex subject of evolution to the general public. It became his best-known work, reissued several times over the years and translated into many languages, including French, Italian, Persian, Danish, Dutch, Spanish, Japanese, Portuguese, and Finnish. Because it was widely adopted as a text for introductory physical anthropology courses, it also influenced a whole new generation of anthropologists.

In 1954 Simpson traveled to Brazil to lecture and consult as a guest of the Brazilian National Research Council. In 1956 he returned to that country to lead an expedition up the Juruá River, a tributary of the Amazon. Unfortunately, this trip ended in a serious mishap for Simpson. While clearing a campsite, an assistant felled a tree that struck Simpson, leaving the 54-year-old man with a concussion, bruised back, dislocated left shoulder and ankle, and shattered right leg. A series of twelve operations ensued, and it was two years before he could walk again with a cane. "That event changed my life quite radically," Simpson reported in his autobiography. "The then director of the American Museum removed me from the chairmanship of the department. . . . When at last I could get to my office without a wheelchair he explained to me that I would no longer be allowed to travel on any museum business and would only have to report for work in New York."

Concentrates on New Travels and Writings

Simpson resigned in 1959 rather than accept what he considered a humiliating situation. Shortly thereafter, he took a position as Alexander Agassiz Professor at Harvard's Museum of Comparative Zoology. During this period, he published his own favorite among his many books, *This View of Life: The World of an Evolutionist,* half the chapters of which were adapted from earlier lectures. He also continued to travel widely. The high point may have been a 1961 expedition to Africa. Simpson was with anthropologist **Louis Leakey** in Kenya when Leakey discovered a skull fragment from a 14-million-year-old apelike creature named Ramapithecus, believed by many to have been an early human ancestor. In the early 1970s, Simpson also made three journeys to Antarctica, where he delighted in observing the many penguin colonies. Four decades earlier, he had collected a large number of penguin fossils in Patagonia, and his attention now turned to these once again. The result, characteristically, was a book: a 1976 volume titled *Penguins: Past and Present, Here and There.*

The failing health of both Simpson and his wife led to yet another move in 1967, this time to Tucson, where Simpson assumed a post as a professor of geosciences at the University of Arizona. The couple also established the Simroe Foundation, a nonprofit foundation dedicated to making their private technical libraries and research facilities more accessible to others. It was housed in a separate building especially constructed for that purpose behind the Simpsons' home. Another of Simpson's lasting preoccupations was the study of languages. In addition to English, he claimed to speak French and Spanish fluently, and German and Italian moderately well. He could also read Portuguese, and he had learned to decipher ancient Egyptian hieroglyphs. Years before, his encounter with the Kamarakoto Indians of South America had prompted him to make the first written record of their language, a phonetic rendering of hundreds of words.

Simpson's preeminence in his discipline was reflected by the many honors bestowed upon him. Honorary degrees were conferred on him by such universities as Yale, Princeton, Oxford, the University of Glasgow, and the University of Paris. In 1976, the Smithsonian Institution presented him with the International Award for distinguished contributions to natural history. Among the numerous other awards he received were the 1942 Lewis Prize of the American Philosophical Society, the 1943 Thompson Medal and the 1944 and 1961 Elliott Medals of the National Academy of Sciences, the 1952 Penrose Medal of the Geological Society of America, the 1962 Darwin Medal of the Royal Society of London, and the 1965 National Medal of Science.

Simpson was active in the founding of two professional associations: the Society of Vertebrate Paleontology and the Society for the Study of Evolution. He became the first president of both groups, and he served a term as president of the American Society of Zoologists and the Society of Systematic Zoology as well. In addition, he was a fellow or member of such select organizations as the American Academy of Arts and Sciences, the National Academy of Sciences, the American Philosophical Society, the Royal Society of London, the two Italian national academies of science, and the national academies of Venezuela, Brazil, and Argentina.

Although Simpson retired from the University of Arizona in 1982, he continued to devote himself tirelessly to his writing. A press release issued by the American Museum the following year noted that he currently had six books in progress. At the time of his death from pneumonia at the age of 82, his reputation as an world-renowned authority on vertebrate paleontology had long been secure, yet he continued to work to the end. He died in a hospital in Tucson on October 6, 1984.

SELECTED WRITINGS BY SIMPSON:

Books

Attending Marvels: A Patagonian Journal, Macmillan, 1934, reprinted, University of Chicago Press, 1982.

Quantitative Zoology: Numerical Concepts and Methods in the Study of Recent and Fossil Animals, McGraw-Hill, 1939, revised edition (with Roe and Richard Lewontin), Harcourt, 1960.

Tempo and Mode in Evolution, Columbia University Press, 1944, reprinted, 1984.

The Meaning of Evolution: A Study of the History of Life and Its Significance for Man, Yale University Press, 1949, revised and abridged edition, New American Library, 1951, revised edition, Yale University Press, 1967.

This View of Life: The World of an Evolutionist, Harcourt, 1964.

Penguins: Past and Present, Here and There, Yale University Press, 1976.

Concession to the Improbable: An Unconventional Autobiography, Yale University Press, 1978.

Simple Curiosity: Letters from George Gaylord Simpson to His Family, 1921–1970, edited by Leo F. Laporte, University of California Press, 1987.

Periodicals

Bulletin of the American Museum of Natural History, The Principles of Classification and a Classification of Mammals, Volume 85, 1945, pp. 1–350.

FURTHER READING:

Books

Gould, Stephen Jay, *The Evolutionary Synthesis: Perspectives on the Unification of Biology,* G. G. Simpson, Paleontology, and the Modern Synthesis, edited by Ernst Mayr and William B. Provine, Harvard University Press, 1980, pp. 153–72.

Hecht, Max K., Bobb Schaeffer, Bryan Patterson, Richard Van Frank, and Florence D. Wood, *Evolutionary Biology,* George Gaylord Simpson: His Life and Works to the Present, edited by Theodosius Dobzhansky, Max K. Hecht, and William C. Steere, Appleton-Century-Crofts, Volume 6, 1972, pp. 1–29.

———— , *McGraw-Hill Modern Scientists and Engineers,* McGraw-Hill, 1980, pp. 118–20.

Periodicals

Hecht, Max K., Bobb Schaeffer, Bryan Patterson, Richard Van Frank, and Florence D. Wood, *American Journal of Physical Anthropology,* Volume 84, 1991, pp. 1–16.

Sketch by Linda Wasmer Smith

Clive Marles Sinclair
1940–
English electronics engineer

A self-taught electronics specialist, Clive Sinclair developed and introduced the first widely available pocket calculator and a host of other innovative products, including watches, miniature televisions, a motor-powered, three-wheeled bicycle, and a line of personal computers.

The son of a mechanical engineer, Sinclair was born in Richmond, Surrey, England on July 30, 1940. Both his father and grandfather, also an engineer, encouraged Sinclair's interest in designing and building. As a youngster, Sinclair planned and built a submarine, using government surplus fuel tanks; in his teens, he discovered electronics. His room at home—"a tangle of wires, radio parts and circuit components"—was viewed with amused tolerance by his family.

In his early teens, Sinclair invented a calculating machine that he programmed with punch cards, using a binary system to perform calculations. Although fascinated by mathematics and electronics, Sinclair had no desire to attend a university. After completing courses at Box Grove Preparatory School, he attended several secondary schools

Clive Marles Sinclair

before completing a course of study at Highgate School, supplemented with advanced course work in physics and mathematics at St. George's College in Weybridge. At the age of 17, Sinclair considered his formal education complete.

Almost immediately, Sinclair landed a job as an editorial assistant with *Practical Wireless*, a magazine dedicated to radio and sound technology. Shortly after Sinclair joined the magazine staff, the editor retired, and Sinclair took over as editor (at the age of 18) of the publication. In addition to his editorial duties, Sinclair churned out technical works and how-to manuals for radio enthusiasts. He published plans for his own circuit designs, which emphasized reduced size and inexpensive components.

Following the Entrepreneurial Urge

Sinclair's duties at the magazine allowed him time to tinker and think. He wanted to manufacture and distribute the items he designed, and in 1961, he officially registered his own business as Sinclair Radionics Ltd. He planned to launch his new company with the introduction of a miniature transistor radio kit, but unable to find an investor for his design and short of funds, he accepted a position as technical editor with *Instrument Practice* in 1962.

Sinclair continued to develop ideas for his fledgling business. He began to advertise products of his own design, such as a micro amplifier, the Sinclair Slimline (the

miniature transistor radio on which he founded his firm), and a host of radio and high-fidelity products.

In 1972 Sinclair introduced the Sinclair Executive, his first pocket calculator, which won a Design Council Ward for Electronics in 1973. That was followed with the Cambridge Scientific Calculator in 1974, which won two Queen's Awards for Industry, and by 1975, Sinclair Radionics was the largest European manufacturer of calculators.

But Sinclair's triumph was short-lived. He introduced a series of commercial disappointments, including a quartz digital watch and a pocket television, and it became clear that his inventive genius did not extend into the realm of marketing. By 1979 Sinclair Radionics was on the brink of financial disaster and the firm was split into various components and sold.

Research Successes, Business Failures

When Sinclair Radionics went under, Sinclair formed his own research firm, called Sinclair Research, and began to explore the personal computer market. In 1980 Sinclair Research introduced the ZX80, followed by the ZX81. By 1982 Sinclair Research was producing 500,000 computers a year, but Sinclair, in the quest for an inexpensive, small, versatile, and reliable home computer, continued to refine the microcomputer design. In 1982 he introduced the ZX Spectrum, his most commercially successful microcomputer and one which developed a cadre of devotees.

Although knighted for his achievements in 1983, the pattern that had plagued his first firm recurred in his second venture. Sinclair failed to negotiate important contracts to supply microcomputers; then, in 1984, he introduced the QL model. Sinclair's firm belief in the QL's merits did not impress the now fiercely competitive consumer marketplace. The QL was a commercial disaster, and in 1986, Sinclair was again forced to preside over the dismemberment and sale of his firm, turning over the computer product line to Amstrad.

In a 1985 interview with the *Observer*, Sinclair said "I am not a management type. I am an inventor. I am awful at managing established businesses." The lack of business acumen has not diminished Sinclair's inventiveness. In 1985 he introduced an environmentally friendly, financially disappointing electric tricycle; the Z88 computer in 1987; miniaturized integrated circuits, satellite TV antennas, inexpensive portable telephones, the LC3 (an inexpensive color computer), and a second electric cycle.

In a 1984 address to the U.S. Congressional Clearinghouse on the Future, Sinclair asserted that "It often seems that each new step in technology brings misery rather than contentment . . . By the end of this decade manufacturing decline will be almost complete . . . and technical change will virtually remove all employment. . . . The future promises a better solution."

Sinclair's vision includes a future in which computer systems and artificial intelligence will perform routine calculating and decision-making tasks "such as navigating a car" and free the human mind to tackle both abstract and concrete challenges that require the kind of intuition that has fueled much of Sinclair's own work.

A retiring man who is happiest in a laboratory, Sinclair avoids public attention. Ironically, the man responsible for popularizing computer technology and focusing the spotlight on the potential of such systems has no electronic mail address. "I don't think I want to have my stuff spewing all over the Internet," he said in an interview with *Cyberia Magazine.*

FURTHER READING:

Books

Jenkins-Jones, S., ed. *Hutchinson Dictionary of Scientists.* Oxford, England: Helicon Publishing Ltd., 1996, p. 441.

Porter, Roy, ed. *Biographical Dictionary of Scientists.* New York: Oxford University Press, 1994, pp. 448-49.

Other

"After the Fall: Sir Clive Looks Back." August 1986. (July 6, 1995) http://www.nvg.unit.no/spectrum/sell-out.html (November 24, 1997).

Dale, Rodney. "The Sinclair Story, Part 1: Early Days." (July 7, 1995). http://www.nvg.unit.no/spectrum/clive1.html (November 24, 1995).

Godlovitch, Ilsa. "Netted–Sir Clive Sinclair." http://www.magazine./cyberiacafe.net/issue4/features/features.3.html (November 24, 1997).

Scolding, Bill. "Riding High: Sir Clive on the Future." 1985. (March 6, 1995) http://ttp.nvg.unit.no/spectrum/intervieww.html (November 24, 1997).

"Sir Clive Addresses Congress." 1984. (July 7, 1995). http://www.nvg.unit.no/spectrum/speech.html (November 24, 1995).

Sketch by A. Mullig

I. M. Singer

1924–

American mathematician

Oone of the eminent research mathematicians of the twentieth century, I. M. Singer has contributed to many areas of modern mathematics, but he is most recognized for the Atiyah-Singer Index Theorem. Combining geometry, topology, and partial differential equations, he and Sir **Michael Atiyah** were, as Singer stated in *Science,* "able to count the number of global solutions to differential equations. Our theorem unified many special cases that looked different." Cited as one of the most important mathematical works since World War II, the Atiyah-Singer Index Theorem has numerous applications in many fields, including elementary particle physics.

Isadore M. Singer was born on May 3, 1924, in Detroit, Michigan. The elder son of Simon, a printer, and Freda (Rose) Singer, he was educated in Detroit public schools. While he was a student at Central High School, his English and chemistry teachers urged him to develop his intellectual abilities. As Singer later recalled in *The Joys of Research,* "When I learned about science and mathematics as a teenager, I discovered that the manipulation of abstract objects, their construction, and their rearrangement, were things I could do very well." Singer attended The University of Michigan, where he majored in physics with a specialty in infrared spectroscopy. He received a B.S. degree in 1944 at the age of nineteen and served in the U.S. Army from 1944 until 1946. In the military, Singer tried to master two important areas in physics—relativity and quantum mechanics—but found that he needed to study more advanced mathematics. He entered the University of Chicago for graduate studies in mathematics, earning an M.S. in 1948 and a Ph.D. two years later.

In 1950 Singer began his teaching career at the Massachusetts Institute of Technology (MIT) and has remained, for the most part, affiliated with that institution; he briefly held positions at the University of California at Los Angeles, Columbia University, the Institute for Advanced Study, and the University of California at Berkeley. Singer was appointed Institute Professor at MIT in 1987. Even though he has had a distinguished career in mathematical research, Singer has been very active in teaching young mathematicians both on the graduate and undergraduate levels.

Singer's major contributions to mathematics have been in several diverse areas. In the 1950s, the primary focus of his work was functional analysis; in the 1960s and 1970s, the major emphasis of his work was on the Atiyah-Singer Index Theorem; and in the 1980s and 1990s his research has been devoted to the interface of geometry and physics. Singer told Cathleen M. Zucco in an interview that he wanted his future accomplishments to involve "important unsolved problems in modern physics where geometry should play an important role."

Collaborates with Sir Michael Atiyah

Singer was awarded a Sloan Fellowship in 1959 and decided to write his research paper on the Isle of Capri, where there would be no distractions to his work. He found, however, that isolation was not conducive to the writing of his mathematical ideas. After three months Singer left Capri and went to Oxford so that he could have the stimulation of books and colleagues to develop his ideas. It was on his first day at Oxford's Mathematics Institute that he and professor Michael Atiyah began a conversation that nine months later evolved into the Atiyah-Singer Index Theorem. This theorem combines different fields of mathematics in a novel way. The great significance of this theorem is that applications of it are still being found in both mathematics and physics.

During the 1970s and 1980s, Singer actively served on committees in Washington that had a direct impact on national science policy. He worked to make the public aware of the important applications of mathematics and to reverse the deterioration of federal funding for mathematical research. Notably, he was chairperson of the National Academy's influential Committee on Science, Engineering, and Public Policy from 1973 to 1978, and he was a member of the White House Science Council during Ronald Reagan's administration. In 1993 Singer was bestowed with the American Mathematical Society Award for Distinguished Public Service in recognition of his efforts to support mathematics in the public sector.

Throughout his career, Singer has earned numerous accolades. He was a Guggenheim fellow twice and received the Bocher Memorial Prize in mathematics in 1969. In 1985 he was awarded the National Medal of Science, a distinct honor for a mathematician. Singer was presented, in 1988, with the Eugene Wigner Medal in physics. In addition to these numerous honors, Singer acquired a wide reputation as an eloquent spokesperson for differential geometry, his area of specialty in geometry, and how it connects to other fields of mathematics and physics.

As a research mathematician, time has been essential in the development of Singer's ideas. His research work has involved highly abstract concepts that require uninterrupted concentration. Throughout the latter part of his career, he has set aside several afternoons a week for his continuing research. Given his demanding academic schedule, Singer has noted his satisfaction in obtaining one good idea a year. When asked what he likes best about his work, Singer told Zucco that it is "the excitement of new ideas and their development."

SELECTED WRITINGS BY SINGER:

Books

The Joys of Research, Mathematics, edited by Walter Shropshire, Jr., Smithsonian Institution Press, 1981, pp. 38–46.

Periodicals

Uspekhi, On Some Problems of Gelfand, Matematicheskikh Nasuk, Volume XIV, number 3 (87), 1959, pp. 99–114.

Bulletin of the American Mathematical Society, The Index of Elliptic Operators on Compact Manifolds, Volume 69, 1963, pp. 422–33.

Journal of Differential Geometry, Curvature and the Eigenvalues of the Laplacian, March, 1967, pp. 43–69.

Advances in Mathematics, Reidemeister Torsion and the Laplacian on Riemannian Manifolds, October, 1971, pp. 145–210.

Bulletin of the London Mathematical Society, Spectral Asymmetry and Riemannian Geometry, Volume 5, 1973, pp. 229–34.

FURTHER READING:

Periodicals

Kolata, Gina Bari, *Science,* Isadore Singer and Differential Geometry, June 1, 1979, pp. 933–34.

————, *Notices of the American Mathematical Society,* June, 1985, pp. 366–67.

————, *Notices of the American Mathematical Society,* March, 1993, pp. 226–28.

Other

Singer, I. M., *Interview with Cathleen M. Zucco,* conducted January 10, 1994.

Sketch by Cathleen M. Zucco

Maxine Singer
1931–
American biochemist and geneticist

Maxine Singer, a leading scientist in the field of human genetics, is also a staunch advocate of responsible use of biochemical genetics research. During the height of the controversy over the use of recombinant deoxyribonucleic acid (DNA) techniques to alter genetic characteristics, she advocated a cautious approach. She helped develop guidelines to balance calls for unfettered genetics research as a means of making medically valuable discoveries with demands for restrictions on research to protect the public from possible harm. After the DNA controversy waned, Singer continued to contribute to the field of genetics, researching cures for cancer, hemophilia, and other diseases related to genetics.

Singer was born on February 15, 1931, in New York City, to Hyman Frank, an attorney, and Henrietta (Perlowitz) Frank, a hospital admissions officer, children's camp director, and model. Singer received her B.A. from Swarthmore College in Pennsylvania in 1952, and earned her Ph.D. in biochemistry from Yale in 1957. From 1956 to 1958 she worked as a U.S. Public Health Service postdoctoral fellow at National Institute for Arthritis, Metabolism and Digestive Diseases (NIAMD), National Institutes of Health (NIH), in Bethesda, Maryland. She then became a research chemist on the staff of the section on enzymes and cellular biochemistry from 1958 to 1974. There she conducted DNA research on tumor-causing viruses as well as on ribonucleic acid (RNA). In the early 1970s, Singer also served as a visiting scientist with the Department of Genetics of the Weizman Institute of Science in Rehovot, Israel.

While Singer was working at NIH, scientists learned how to take DNA fragments from one organism and insert them into the living cells of another. This "recombinant DNA" could direct the production of proteins in the foreign organism as if the DNA was still in its original home. This technique had the potential of creating completely new types of organisms. On one hand, the new research brought unprecedented opportunities to discover cures for serious diseases, to develop new crops, and otherwise to benefit humanity. Yet the prospect of creating as-yet-unknown life forms, some possibly hazardous, was frightening to many.

In 1972, one of Singer's colleagues and personal friends, **Paul Berg** of Stanford University, was the first to create recombinant DNA molecules. He later voluntarily stopped conducting related experiments involving DNA manipulation in the genes of tumor-causing viruses because of some scientists' fears that a virus of unknown properties might escape from the laboratory and spread into the general population.

Warns Public of Gene-Splicing Risks

Although Berg's self-restraint was significant, the catalyst for the debate over gene-splicing was the 1973 Gordon Conference, an annual high-level research meeting. Singer, who was co-chair of the event, was approached by several nucleic acid scientists with the suggestion that the conference include consideration of safety issues. Singer agreed. She opened the discussion with an acknowledgment that DNA manipulation could assist in combatting health problems, yet such experimentation brought to bear a number of moral and ethical concerns.

The scientists present decided, by ballot, to send a public letter about the safety risks of recombinant DNA research to the president of the National Academy of Sciences, and asked *Science* magazine to publish it. Singer and her co-chair, Dieter Söll of Yale University, wrote the letter warning that organisms of an unpredictable nature could result from the new technique, and suggested that the National Academy of Sciences study the problem and recommend guidelines. Concern generated by this letter led to another meeting at the Asilomer Conference Center in Pacific Grove, California, where a debate ensued. Such proceedings—to consider the ethical issues arising from the new DNA research—were unprecedented in the scientific community. Immediately after the Asilomer Conference concluded, a NIH committee began formulating guidelines for recombinant DNA research.

In helping develop the guidelines, Singer advocated a careful analytic approach. In 1976 she presented four principles to the committee to be used in drafting the guidelines. She advised that certain experiments posed such serious hazards that they should be banned altogether; that experiments with lesser or no potential hazards should be permitted if their benefits are unobtainable through conventional methods and if they are properly safeguarded; that the more risk in an experiment, the stricter the safeguards should be; and that the guidelines should be reviewed annually.

Singer provided a calm voice of reason throughout the public debate over gene-splicing that followed. Committees of lay people, such as the Coalition for Responsible Genetic Research, held demonstrations calling for a complete ban on recombinant DNA research. Some members of the media made analogies to the nightmarish vision contained in Aldous Huxley's book *Brave New World,* which described a genetically altered society. When sent to address a public forum on the issue in 1977, for example, Singer responded to accusations that scientists ignore public concerns. As Clifford Grobstein recounted in his book, *A Double Image of the Double Helix: The Recombinant-DNA Debate,* Singer maintained that "scientists recognize their responsibility to the public . . . (but) dispute over the best way to exercise responsibility must not be confused with the negation of it." According to Grobstein, Singer explained that "while freedom of inquiry is a democratic right, it is clearly unacceptable to cause harm in the name of research. But [Singer] warned that levels of anxiety are not necessarily directly related to levels of real risk."

During her career, Singer has also served on the editorial Board of *Science* magazine and has contributed numerous articles. In her writing for that publication about recombinant DNA research, she stressed the benefits to humanity that recombinant DNA techniques could bring, especially in increasing the understanding of serious and incurable disease. After the NIH guidelines were implemented, she told *Science* readers that "under the Guidelines work has proceeded safely and research accomplishments have been spectacular." By 1980, when public near-hysteria had waned, Singer called for a "celebration" of the progress in molecular genetics. In *Science* she wrote: "The manufacture of important biological agents like insulin and interferon by recombinant DNA procedures," as well as the failure of any "novel hazards" to emerge, was evidence of the value of the cautious continuation of DNA research.

Appointed Head of Cancer Research Lab

In 1974 Singer accepted a new position at NIH as chief of the Section of Nucleic Acid Enzymology, Division of Cancer Biology and Diagnosis (DCBD) at the National Cancer Institute in Bethesda, Maryland. In 1980 she became chief of the DCBD's Laboratory of Biochemistry. She held this post until 1988, when she became president of the Carnegie Institution, a highly regarded research organization in Washington, D.C. Singer remains affiliated with the

National Cancer Institute, however, as scientist emeritus, where she continues her research in human genetics.

In addition to her laboratory research, Singer has devoted considerable time and energy to other scientific and professional pursuits. In 1981, she taught in the biochemistry department at the University of California at Berkeley. A skilled and prolific writer, she has issued more than one hundred books, articles, and papers. Most are highly technical, including numerous articles published in scientific journals. Singer also compiled a graduate-level textbook with Paul Berg on molecular genetics called *Genes and Genomes: A Changing Perspective.* Reviewers gave the work high praise for its clear presentation of difficult concepts. Marcelo Bento Soares in *Bioscience* also commented that the book was "superbly written" and "magnificently captures the sense of discovery, understanding, and anticipation that has followed the so-called recombinant DNA breakthrough."

Singer has also written extensively on less technical aspects of science. She and Berg authored a book for laypeople on genetic engineering, and she continued to promote the benefits of recombinant DNA techniques and battle public suspicion and fear long after the controversy peaked in the 1970s. In the early 1990s, for example, Singer issued an article encouraging the public to try the first genetically engineered food to reach American supermarket shelves. In describing the harmlessness of the "Flavr Savr" tomato, she decried public objections that eating it was dangerous, unnatural, or immoral to readers of the *Asbury Park Press.* Pointing out that "almost all the foods we eat are the product of previous genetic engineering by cross-breeding," Singer said that the small amount of extra DNA in the tomato would be destroyed in the digestive tract, and that people already consume the DNA present in the other foods in their diets. Moreover, she said the decision to eat a genetically altered tomato did not reduce her admiration for nature's creations.

In addition to her writing and lecturing, Singer has served on numerous advisory boards in the United States and abroad, including science institutes in Naples, Italy, Bangkok, Thailand, and Rehovot, Israel. She also has served on an advisory board to the Pope and as a consultant to the Committee on Human Values of the National Conference of Catholic Bishops. She worked on a Yale committee that investigated the university's South African investments, and serves on Johnson and Johnson's Board of Directors. Concerned about the quality of science education in the United States, she started First Light, a science program for inner-city children.

Singer travels extensively and maintains long work weeks to accommodate all her activities. She married Daniel Singer in 1952; the couple have four children: Amy Elizabeth, Ellen Ruth, David Byrd, and Stephanie Frank. Singer is the recipient of more than forty honors and awards, including some ten honorary doctor of science degrees and numerous commendations from NIH.

SELECTED WRITINGS BY SINGER:

Books

Genes and Genomes: A Changing Perspective, University Science Books, 1990.
Dealing with Genes: The Language of Heredity, University Science Books, 1992.

Periodicals

Science, In Vitro Synthesis of DNA: A Perspective on Research, December 22, 1967, pp. 1550–551.
Science, Guidelines for DNA Molecules, September 21, 1973, p. 1114.
Science, The Recombinant DNA Debate, April 8, 1977, p. 127.
Science, Spectacular Science and Ponderous Process, January 5, 1979, p. 9.
Science, Recombinant DNA Revisited, September 19, 1980, p. 1317.
Asbury Park Press, Seeing a Red Menace in the New Hot Tomato, August 15, 1993.

FURTHER READING:

Books

Grobstein, Clifford, *A Double Image of the Double Helix: The Recombinant-DNA Debate,* W. H. Freeman and Company, 1979, pp. 18–19, 72–3.
Krimsky, Sheldon, *Genetic Alchemy: The Social History of the Recombinant DNA Controversy,* MIT Press, 1982, pp. 181–83.
Lappé, Marc, *Broken Code: The Exploitation of DNA,* Sierra Club Books, 1984, pp. 19–25.
Lear, John, *Recombinant DNA: The Untold Story,* Crown, 1978, pp. 68–75.
Wade, Nicholas, *The Ultimate Experiment: Man-Made Evolution,* Walker, 1977, pp. 34–6.

Periodicals

Hoffee, Patricia A., *Science,* The New Genetics, December 13, 1991.
—— , *U.S. News and World Report,* The Scientific Method, August 26-September 2, 1991, p. 94.
Soares, Marcelo Bento, *Bioscience,* Precise Genetic Concepts, March, 1992, p. 211.

Other

Singer, Maxine F., *Interview with Donna Olshansky,* conducted August 19, 1993.
Singer, Maxine F., *Interview with Donna Olshansky,* Singer, Maxine F., Curriculum Vitae, current as of August, 1993.

Sketch by Donna Olshansky

Richard H. Sioui
1937–
American chemical engineer

Richard H. Sioui is a chemical engineer of Native American descent who has worked on both liquid fuels and composite materials. He is most noted, however, for his extensive work in the field of abrasives and has over 30 patents in this area. Because of his achievements, the American Indian Science and Engineering Society has asked to use him as a role model to encourage children of Native Indian descent to enter the engineering field.

Richard Henry Sioui, a member of the Huron people, was born in Brooklyn, New York, on September 25, 1937, to Joseph Fernand Sioui, a waiter, and Ellen Anita (Johnson) Sioui. His career began in the United States Air Force, in which he served from 1955 to 1959. When his tour of duty was complete, he entered a cooperative work program at Northeastern University where he studied chemical engineering. Through the coop program, he had a chance to work on a variety of different projects at companies such as DuPont and Monsanto. In addition to studying and working, he also married Mary Ann Kapinos in July of 1962, and started a family with the addition of their first daughter in 1963.

After obtaining his B.S. degree in 1964, he spent the summer at Millers Falls Company in Greenfield, Massachusetts, where he evaluated polymer applications. He then moved to the University of Massachusetts to continue his education, studying under a National Science Foundation Traineeship. He received his M.S. in 1967, and went on to complete his Ph.D. in 1968. His graduate research looked at the combustion of small droplets of liquid fuels, which was research important in the design of various types of engines and rocket motors.

Following completion of his studies, Sioui joined the Norton Company's Superabrasives Division in Worcester, Massachusetts, as a Senior Research Engineer. He remained in this position until promoted to research supervisor in 1971. While research supervisor, he was awarded patents on some of his improvements in the production of abrasive grinding tools. His first patent covered a new way to prepare abrasive surfaces used for the grinding of metals and other materials. Through the addition of silver, copper, and graphite to the resins in which industrial diamond or cubic boron nitride (CBN) abrasive were embedded, he greatly improved the performance of these grinding surfaces. Furthermore, this enhanced the economics and applicability of using CBN in place of diamond abrasives. His invention of metal/polymer composite materials has also earned praise, as well as been awarded a patent. In addition, Sioui has received patents covering the production of resin grinding wheel cores, methods of bonding the abrasive surfaces to the cores, and a new type of magnetic core.

Sioui continued to advance both his education and career. After receiving a diploma from the School of Industrial Management at Worcester Polytechnic Institute in 1976, he was promoted to technical manager in 1979, research manager in 1982, then to research director in 1984. Following completion of his diploma from the Tuck Executive Program at Dartmouth College in 1986, he was promoted to director of technology at Norton in 1987.

In his role as director of technology, Sioui is responsible not only for all of the ongoing research at Norton, but also for control and development of the manufacturing processes. Norton Company is one of the world's largest users of diamond and CBN abrasive, and Sioui is responsible for the quality control of materials which the company purchases. He is also accountable for the quality of the grinding products produced, which are supplied to companies all over the world.

Outside of work, his time has been taken up by his family, which grew with the addition of five more children (two boys and three girls). He has also been involved extensively with the Boy Scouts of America. Sioui has achieved the rank of Eagle Scout himself, and is a member of the National Eagle Scout Association. He has also spent five years as committee chairman of troop 178 in Holden, Massachusetts, from 1981 to 1986.

SELECTED WRITINGS BY SIOUI:

Books

Proceedings: Diamonds in the 80's, The Evolution of Tests for Diamond Wheel Performance in Dry Tool and Cutter Sharpening, Industrial Diamond Association of America, 1980, pp. 131–38.

Periodicals

Combustion and Flame, The Prediction of the Burning Constants of Suspended Hydrocarbon Fuel Droplets, Volume 13, 1969, p. 447.
Cutting Tool Engineering, The Use of Silver in Diamond and CBN Wheels for Dry Grinding Hard Materials, July/August, 1980, pp. 6–8.

Sketch by Jerome P. Ferrance

Folke Karl Skoog
1908–
American botanist

Botanist Folke Karl Skoog is renowned for his pioneering research on auxins and cytokinins (hormones responsible for plant growth) and his development of a plant growth medium. His discovery of cytokinins in 1954 and subsequent studies of them have provided new insight into plant growth and paved the way toward research in biotechnology, or applied biological science, for decades. Cytokinins also prevent the yellowing of plants and are used commercially to keep vegetables green on store shelves.

Skoog was born in Halland, Sweden in 1908, the son of Karl and Sigrid (Person) Skoog. His father worked as an agronomist (a branch of agriculture dealing with field-crop production and soil management), while his mother stayed home to raise her three sons. The young Swede left his homeland to study chemistry at California Institute of Technology, where he earned his bachelor's degree in 1932. Back then, he was better known as a runner and in 1932 represented Sweden in the Olympics.

Skoog continued his graduate studies at Cal Tech, which was then the premier institute for plant hormone research. His professors included **Frits Went**, who discovered a class of plant growth hormones called auxins. Skoog earned his Ph.D. in biology from Cal Tech in 1936, then continued his studies as a postdoctorate fellow at the University of California at Berkeley. Skoog had decided to remain in the United States and in 1935 became a citizen. Skoog accepted a teaching and research position at Harvard University in 1937, where he worked until 1941, when he moved to Johns Hopkins University to serve as an assistant professor until 1944.

Skoog took a hiatus from his plant research for two years during World War II to work as a chemist for the Defense Department in Washington, D.C. In 1946, he resumed his teaching and research career at Washington University in St. Louis, but left after only three months. He was hired in 1947 as an associate professor at the University of Wisconsin in Madison, where over the next thirty-two years he would earn his reputation as one of the world's foremost botanists. The year Skoog arrived in Madison, he married Birgit Anna Lisa Bergner. Birgit had been trained as an engineer, but gave up her career ambitions to raise their only child, Karin (Skoog) Shepard. Skoog thrived at the Wisconsin university and in 1949 was appointed as a full professor.

Discovered New Class of Growth Hormones

In the early 1950s, the only known plant growth hormones were auxins. Skoog, who had in the 1930s performed pioneering research in the field of auxins, was experimenting with tobacco tumor tissue when he realized that he could promote growth even in the absence of auxins. "He had an intuitive feel for what the growing plants were telling him," former colleague Professor Eldon Newcomb of Oregon State University told Cynthia Washam in an interview. "He could sense when the data were telling him something important." Research on the tobacco tumor tissues led to Skoog's discovery in 1954 of a new class of growth hormones, called cytokinins. These hormones are produced in plant roots and travel up the stem to leaves and fruit. Skoog's discovery was initially met with skepticism.

Many botanists thought that auxins were the only hormones responsible for plant growth.

Skoog, however, proved that cytokinins did exist, and he also showed that by manipulating the levels of auxins and cytokinins, he could promote the growth of only roots, only shoots, or both. His finding revolutionized horticulture by enabling scientists to control plant propagation. Cytokinins are also used to prevent green vegetables from yellowing.

Skoog was welcomed as a member of the American Academy of Arts & Sciences in 1954, and the National Academy of Sciences in 1956. In 1954 Skoog also earned the prestigious Stephen Hales Prize from the American Society of Plant Physiologists and his first honorary Ph.D., from Lund University in Sweden.

While building his reputation worldwide as a top researcher, Skoog was building his reputation back home as everyone's favorite professor. "He was warm and patient with his students," Newcomb said. "He formed a close relationship with all of them." Although Skoog taught only graduate students, he took a strong interest in the education of undergraduates. He formed a committee in the mid-1960s to develop what became one of the strongest undergraduate biology programs in the country. Another of Skoog's major scientific contributions came in 1962, when he developed a medium that promoted plant growth faster and more effectively than older media.

Throughout his busy career, the athletic botanist always managed to find time for recreation. Colleagues remember him taking afternoon swims in a campus lake and playing touch football with fellow professors and students. On weekends, he often retreated to the family cottage in rural Door County, Wisconsin, where he enjoyed boating, swimming, fishing, and deer hunting.

Skoog retired in 1979 as a professor emeritus, giving occasional lectures and reviewing scientific papers for several years afterward. In addition to earning many honorary doctorate degrees throughout the years, Skoog was awarded the National Medal of Science, his most prestigious honor, in 1991. In addition, the Cell Culture Association honored him with its Life Membership Award in 1991, and in 1992, the Tissue Culture World Congress gave him the Distinguished Life Achievement Award.

SELECTED WRITINGS BY SKOOG:

Books

Plant Growth Substances, University of Wisconsin Press, 1951.

Periodicals

Science, Cytokinins, Volume 148, 1965, pp. 532–33.

FURTHER READING:

Periodicals

Newcomb, Eldon, *Interview with Cynthia Washam,* conducted March 29, 1994.

Shepard, Karin, *Interview with Cynthia Washam,* conducted March 29, 1994.

Sketch by Cynthia Washam

Jens C. Skou
1918–
Dutch biochemist

J ens C. Skou was one of three men who shared the 1997 Nobel Prize in chemistry. Skou received the award in recognition of discovering the first "molecular pump," Na⁺, K⁺ ATPase, an enzyme that promotes movement through the membrane surrounding a cell and maintains the balance of sodium ions (Na⁺) and potassium ions (K⁺) in a living cell.

Jens Christian Skou was born October 8, 1918, in Lemvig, Denmark, to Magnus Martinus Skou, a timber merchant, and Ane-Margrethe (Jensen Knak) Skou. He received his M.D. degree (cand.med.) from the University of Copenhagen in 1944. Ten years later, he received his Doctor of Medical Sciences degree (dr.med.) from Aarhus University. In 1948 he married Ellen-Margrethe (Nielsen); they have two children, Hanne and Karen.

After receiving his M.D., Skou went for clinical training at the Hospital at Hjørring and Orthopaedic Clinic at Aarhus, Denmark. He remained there until 1947, when he became an assistant professor in the University of Aarhus's Institute of Physiology. In 1954, the same year he received his Doctor of Medical Sciences degree, he became associate professor at the institute. In 1963 Skou became a full professor and was named chairman of the Institute of Physiology. From 1978-1988, he was professor of biophysics at the University of Aarhus.

Skou has devoted his career to both education and research. He has served as an advisor for many Ph.D. and doctor of medical science students and as an examiner at doctoral dissertation presentations. He has published more than 90 papers on his research, which has investigated the actions of local anesthetics and what mechanisms made them work, as well as the work that earned him the 1997 Nobel Prize, the transport of sodium and potassium ions through the cell membranes.

A Delicate Balance

A cell's health depends on maintaining a balance between its inner chemistry and that of the cell's surroundings. This balance is controlled by the presence of the cell membrane, the wall between the cell's inner workings and its environment.

For more than 70 years, scientists have known that one of the delicate balances that are maintained involves ions (electrically charged particles) of the elements sodium (Na) and potassium (K). A cell maintains its inner concentration of sodium ions (Na⁺) at a level lower than that of its surroundings. Similarly, it maintains its inner concentration of potassium ions (K⁺) at a level higher than its surroundings.

This balance is not static, however. In the 1950s, English researchers **Alan Hodgkin** and Richard Keynes found that sodium ions rush into a nerve cell when it is stimulated. After the stimulation, the cell restores its original sodium/potassium levels by transporting the extra sodium out through its membrane. Scientists suspected that this transport involved the compound adenosine triphosphate (ATP). ATP was discovered in 1929 by German chemist Karl Lohmann. Further research by **Franz Lippman** between 1939 and 1941 showed that ATP carries chemical energy in the cell. It has been called the cell's "energy currency." Scientists noticed that, when ATP's presence was inhibited, cells did not rid themselves of the extra sodium that they absorbed during stimulation.

Begins Investigating Problem with Crab Cells

In the 1950s, Skou began his investigations into the workings of ATP. For his experimental material he chose nerve membranes from crabs. He wanted to find out if there was an enzyme in the nerve membranes that degraded ATP, and that could be involved with the transport of ions through the membrane.

He did find such an ATP-degrading enzyme, which needed ions of magnesium. In his experiments, Skou found that he could stimulate the enzyme by adding sodium ions—but there was a limit to the stimulation he could achieve. Adding small amounts of potassium ions, however, stimulated the enzyme even more. In fact, Skou noted that the enzyme—called ATPase—reached its maximum point of stimulation when he added quantities of sodium and potassium ions that were the same as those normally found in nerve cells. This evidence made Skou hypothesize that the enzyme worked with an ion "pump" in the cell membrane.

Skou published his first paper on ATPase in 1957. Years of further experimentation followed. In them, Skou learned more about this remarkable enzyme. He learned that different places on the enzyme attracted and bound ions of sodium and potassium.

When ATP breaks down and releases its energy, it become adenosine diphosphate (ADP) and releases a phosphate compound. Skou's work discovered that this freed phosphate bound to the ATPase as well, a process known as phosphorylation. The presence or absences of this phosphate changed the enzyme's interaction with sodium and potassium ions, Skou discovered. When the ATPase lacked a phosphate group, it became dependent on potassium. Similarly, when it has a phosphate, it became dependent on sodium.

This latter discovery was key to learning just how ATPase moved sodium out of the cell. ATPase molecules are set into the cell membrane, and they consist of two parts, one which stabilizes the enzyme and the other which carries out activity.

Part of the enzyme pokes inside the cell. There, one ATP molecule and three sodium ions can bind to it at a time. A phosphorus group is taken from the ATP to bind to the enzyme, and the remaining ADP is released. The enzyme then changes shape, carrying the attached sodium ions with it to the outside of the cell membrane. There, they are released into the cell's surroundings, as is the attached phosphorus. In place of the three sodium ions, two potassium ions attach themselves to the enzyme, which again changes shape and carries the K^+ into the cell's interior.

This activity uses up about one-third of the ATP that the body produces each day, which can range from about half of a resting person's body weight to almost one ton in a person who is doing strenuous activity.

Thanks to this molecular pump, the cell is able to maintain its balance of potassium ions on the inside and sodium ions on the outside, maintaining the electrical charges that allow cells to pass along or to react to stimulation from nerve cells.

This enzyme is important for other reason as well. For example, the pump's action on the balance of sodium and potassium makes it possible for the cell to take in nutrients and to expel waste products. If the molecular pump were to stop—as it can when a lack of nourishment or oxygen shuts down ATP formation—the cell would swell up, and it would be unable to pass along nerve impulse. If this were to happen in the brain, unconsciousness would rapidly follow.

Since Skou discovered ATPase, scientists have found other molecular pumps hard at work in the cell. They include H^+, K^+-ATPase, which produces stomach acid, and $Ca2^+$-ATPase, which helps control the contraction of muscle cells.

Other Honors and Awards

In addition to the Nobel Prize, Skou has received much recognition for his work. He is a regular participant and organizer of symposia on transmembrane transport. In addition, he has received the Leo Prize, the Novo Prize, the Swedish Medical Association's Anders Retzius gold medal, and the Dr. Eric K. Ferntroms Big Nordic Prize.

He is a member of the Danish Royal Academy, and has served on a number of its committees and science foundation board. He is also a member of the Danish Royal Society, the Deutsche Akademie der Naturfoscher, Leopoldins, and the European Molecular Biology Organization (EMBO). He is a foreign associate of the American National Academy of Sciences. In addition, Skou is an honorary member of the Japanese Biochemical Society and the American Physiological Society. He received and honorary doctorate from the University of Copenhagen. Skou lives in Denmark.

SELECTED WRITINGS BY SKOU:

Books

(With Boyer, P.D.) "The Binding Change Mechanism of ATP Synthesis." *Membrane Bioenergetics.* C. P. Lee, G. Schatz, and L. Ernester, eds. Reading, MA: Addison-Wesley, 1979, p. 461-79.

Periodicals

"The Influence of Some Cations on an Adenosine Triphosphatase from Peripheral Nerves." *Biochimica et Biophysica Acta* 23 (1957): 394-401.
(With M. Esmann). "The Na, K-ATPase." *Journal of Bioenergetics and Biomembranes* 24 (1992): 249-61.

FURTHER READING:

Periodicals

Broad, William. "Six Researchers Awarded Nobel Prizes in Chemistry and Physics." *The New York Times* (October 16, 1997).
Lingrel, J. B. "Na-K-ATPase: Isoform Structure, Function, and Expression." *Journal of Bioenergetics and Biomembranes* 24 (1992): 263-70.
Lutsenko, S. and J. H. Kaplan. "Organization of P-type ATPases: Significance of Structural Diversity." *Biochemistry* 34 (1996): 15607-5613.
Møller, J.V., Juul, B., and le Maire, M. "Structural Organization, Ion Transport, and Energy Transduction of P-type ATPases." *Biochimica et Biophysica Acta* 1286 (1996): 1-51.

Other

1997 Nobel Prize in Chemistry announcement. www.nobel.se/announcment-97/chemistry97.html (January 5, 1998).
Curriculum vitae, Jens C. Skou. Posted on Aarhus University's web site at http://www.au.dk/uk/sun/biofysik/nobel/cv.htm (January 5, 1998).

The Nobel Prize Internet Archive. "Jens C. Skou." URL: http://www.almaz.com/nobel (January 5, 1998).

Sketch by Fran Hodgkins

John Clarke Slater
1900–1976
American theoretical physicist

John Clarke Slater was one of the foremost theoretical physicists in the United States, whose work contributed significantly to the development of atomic, molecular, and solid-state physics. He was one of very few American theoretical physicists to embrace and advance quantum mechanics, which studies the interactions between matter and radiation. Perhaps foremost among his achievements was his idea that light consists of probability waves. Slater is also remembered for his outstanding ability as a teacher and administrator, and for his prodigious output as a writer of physics textbooks and academic papers.

Slater was born on December 22, 1900, in Rochester, New York. His father was head of the English department at the University of Rochester. Slater expressed a precocious interest in all things mechanical and electrical, which eventually blossomed into a love of physics. He enrolled in the University of Rochester in 1917 as an undergraduate student in physics, chemistry, and mathematics. In his sophomore year, he worked in the physics lab. His first brush with quantum theory—which was then still in its infancy and had not yet made it into Rochester's curriculum—came from his reading of **Niels Bohr**'s 1913 paper on the specific-orbits model of atomic structure.

In 1921 Slater moved to Harvard graduate school on an assistantship. There he worked with **P. W. Bridgman** and attended Bridgman's course in fundamental physics. He was more interested, though, in a course in quantum physics offered by E. C. Kemble. Within three years, Slater had completed work on his Ph.D. thesis, an experimental study devoted to an examination of the compressibility of the alkali halides. A Harvard Sheldon fellowship enabled him to continue his studies abroad. Slater first visited Cambridge University, whose Cavendish Laboratory was producing some of the most exciting results in quantum physics, before heading for Copenhagen. His destination was Niels Bohr's center for physical research, a mecca for theoretical physicists.

Publishes Controversial Theory with Bohr

Slater explained to Bohr his theory that classical radiation fields guide light quanta, in other words, photons.

Although Bohr did not accept the idea of a photon, the general principles of the idea intrigued him and his colleague, H. A. Kramers. They agreed to collaborate with Slater on a paper. It appeared in a 1924 issue of *Philosophical Magazine* as "The Quantum Theory of Radiation," under all of their names. This highly controversial paper rejected the prevailing notion of light quanta—that light consists of packages of energy—and instead suggested that light consists of probability waves, that is, mathematical entities that enabled physicists to predict the probability that certain events would or would not occur. Although the mathematics used in the paper were eventually proven wrong, the basic idea Slater and his colleagues advanced was correct. Later, based on a different mathematical model, probability waves became a central tenet of quantum mechanics.

His association with such a luminary as Bohr catapulted Slater to instant celebrity and paved the way for his invitation to join the staff of Harvard's physics department on his return to the United States. In 1925 he published two important papers. The first was on the correlation of the width of a spectral line with the reciprocal lifetime of a stationary state. The second dealt with the interpretation of the spectra of hydrogen and ionized helium. Despite being geographically isolated from the hotbed of the new quantum mechanics in Europe, Slater kept abreast of developments. In 1926 he married Helen Frankenfeld. The match produced three children—Louise Chapin, John Frederick, and Clarke Rothwell—all of whom pursued academic careers.

In 1927 Slater produced his first paper on quantum mechanics proper, entitled "Radiation and Absorption on Schrödinger's Theory." Here, Slater employed the Austrian physicist **Erwin Schrödinger**'s idea of atoms as standing waves.

Heads Department of Physics at MIT

In 1930, on his return from a brief visit to Europe on a Guggenheim fellowship, Slater was appointed chairman of the Massachusetts Institute of Technology's physics department. His ambition as a teacher and administrator was to bring American physics education up to par with that in Europe, so that young American physicists would no longer have to make the pilgrimage abroad to finish their education. He directed a member of his department, N. H. Frank, to rework the undergraduate curriculum, and personally rewrote the senior course in theoretical physics. Slater did not neglect graduate training. He reorganized the available programs and the examination system to allow students more time for research.

The upshot of all of this activity was that Slater became, at the age of thirty-one, one of the National Academy's youngest members. He justified that honor with an interminable output of papers and books. Of the latter, he published fourteen during his lifetime, on subjects ranging from microwaves and chemical physics to quantum theory. His papers examined an assortment of phenomena, including directed valence and the quantum theory of the equation of state (1931); energy bands in metals (1934); ferromagnetism in nickel (1936); the structure of alloys and the superconductive state (1937); and the structure of insulating crystals (1938).

When World War II broke out, Slater joined the staff of the Radiation Laboratory, which had been set up at MIT to develop microwave radar. His resultant book, *Microwave Transmission,* quickly became the authority in the field. Later in the war he worked at the Bell Telephone Laboratories in Manhattan. There he undertook theoretical and experimental work on magnetrons, that is, diode vacuum tubes in which the flow of electrons is controlled by an external magnetic field to generate power at microwave frequencies.

After the war, Slater redirected his attention to reshaping MIT's physics department, particularly reorienting wartime pursuits to peaceful ends. He was determined to maintain the department's unique diversity despite the trend toward specialization. He converted the Radiation Laboratory into a research laboratory of electronics, established a laboratory of nuclear science and engineering, and established an acoustics laboratory. Peacetime also enabled him to redevote himself to his own interests, especially in solid-state and molecular physics. In 1950 he set up a research group called the Solid-State and Molecular Theory Group (SSMTG), a precursor to the Interdepartmental Center for Materials Science and Engineering, which was established ten years later.

The following year, acting on his desire to free himself of his administrative burdens, Slater accepted an invitation to become an institute professor at Brookhaven National Laboratory on Long Island. There, with some members of the SSMTG, he continued his research into the quantum theory of atoms, molecules, and solids using primitive computers. Sixty people were involved with the group during its fifteen-year history. Slater had a hand in almost all of its work. He also produced five books related to the group's work. Slater remarried in 1954, having divorced his first wife. His second wife, Rose Mooney, was also a physicist.

In 1964 Slater had the special pleasure of standing next to his father when both were awarded honorary degrees by the University of Rochester. The following year, having reached the retirement age at MIT, Slater accepted the position of research professor at the University of Florida, where the retirement age was seventy. There, he joined the Quantum Theory Project, which had been set up by one of his colleagues from the SSMTG, Per-Olov Löwdin. With its emphasis on solid-state and statistical physics, Florida represented a welcome change from MIT, which at his leaving had "been literally captured by the nuclear theorists," Slater wrote in his autobiography. He persevered in his research into quantum mechanics, aided by more powerful computers, and studied compressibility and magnetic properties of solids, binding energies and magnetic properties of polyatomic molecules, and X-ray absorption.

Until his death on July 25, 1976, he led an active professional and personal life.

SELECTED WRITINGS BY SLATER:

Books

Introduction to Chemical Physics, McGraw-Hill, 1933.
Microwave Transmission, McGraw-Hill, 1942.
Electromagnetism, McGraw-Hill, 1947.
Mechanics, McGraw-Hill, 1947.
Microwave Electronics, Van Nostrand, 1950.
Quantum Theory of Matter, McGraw-Hill, 1951.
Modern Physics, McGraw-Hill, 1955.
Quantum Theory of Atomic Structure, Volumes 1 and 2, McGraw-Hill, 1960.
Solid-State and Molecular Theory: A Scientific Biography, Wiley-Interscience, 1975.

Periodicals

Philosophical Magazine, The Quantum Theory of Radiation, Volume 47, 1924, pp. 785–802.
Proceedings of the National Academy of Sciences, Radiation and Absorption on Schrödinger's Theory, Volume 13, 1927, pp. 7–12.
Physics Review, Light Quanta and Wave Mechanics, Volume 31, 1928, pp. 895–99.
Physics Review, The Self-Consistent Field and the Structure of Atoms, Volume 32, 1928, pp. 339–48.
Physics Review, Directed Valence in Polyatomic Molecules, Volume 37, 1931, pp. 481–89.
American Journal of Physics, The Electron Theory of Solids, Volume 19, 1951, pp. 368–74.
Review of Modern Physics, Interaction of Waves in Crystals, Volume 30, 1958, pp. 197–222.
Journal of Applied Physics, Energy-Band Theory of Magnetism, Volume 39, 1968, 761–67.
Advanced Quantum Chemistry, Statistical Exchange-Correlation in the Self-Consistent Field, Volume 6, 1972, pp. 1–91.

FURTHER READING:

Periodicals

Biographical Memoirs of the National Academy of Sciences, Volume 53, National Academy Press, 1982.

Sketch by Avril McDonald

Vesto M. Slipher
1875–1969
American astronomer

Vesto M. Slipher discovered that most spiral galaxies are racing outward into space, providing key evidence (for **Edwin Hubble** and other researchers) that the universe is expanding. For more than 50 years the director of the Lowell Observatory in Flagstaff, Arizona, Slipher directed the search leading to astronomer **Clyde Tombaugh**'s 1930 discovery of Pluto and was one of the first to provide evidence that gas and dust exists between stars. Slipher also discovered that spiral galaxies are rotating, and he was the first to measure the velocities of star clusters. Slipher is generally recognized as the one of the greatest spectroscopists in astronomy in the first half of the twentieth century, for both his innovations and specific discoveries.

Vesto Melvin Slipher was born on a farm in Mulberry, Indiana, on November 11, 1875. His parents, David Clarke Slipher and Hannah (App) Slipher, were both farmers. Nicknamed "V.M.", Slipher attended high school in Frankfurt, Indiana, and taught at a small rural school until 1897, when he entered Indiana University at age 21. Under the tutelage of Wilbur Cogshall, who had worked at the Lowell Observatory in 1896–1897, Slipher received a B.A. in celestial mechanics and astronomy in 1901. Cogshall persuaded Percival Lowell, an influential astronomer, to hire Slipher as a temporary assistant. Lowell asked Slipher to come to his observatory on Mars Hill in western Flagstaff, and Slipher arrived on August 10, 1901. The position proved more than temporary, as Slipher remained there for the rest of his working life.

He worked as an assistant from 1901 until 1915, making the bulk of his discoveries with a 24-inch refracting telescope made by Alvan Clark. Slipher worked with this instrument only because a more powerful 40-inch telescope at the Lowell Observatory was being used to look at Mars and search for a ninth planet. Besides carrying out astronomical observations, Slipher's duties also included taking care of Lowell's cow, Venus, and its calves, as well as tending to the observatory vegetable garden when Lowell was away.

Slipher's first task as Lowell's assistant was to install and test a spectrograph—an instrument capable of breaking starlight into its component colors for analysis—which Lowell intended to use for the study of planetary rotation. Built for the observatory by John A. Brashear of the Allegheny Observatory near Pittsburgh, Pennsylvania, the device may have been the best of its kind in the world; it was especially resistant to changes in temperature and vibrations. Slipher got the spectrograph in running order by the spring of 1902, the year before he received his M.A. from Indiana University, using it first to search for the presence of water vapor and oxygen on Mars and to make a measurement of the rotation period of Venus.

In 1904, Slipher married Emma Rosalie Munger at Frankfurt, Indiana. They set up house at the observatory, raising two children there, Marcia Frances and David Clark. Lowell was especially intrigued by the possibility that biological life existed on Mars, and Slipher made an unsuccessful search for the spectrum of chlorophyll on Mars in 1905–1907 (and again in 1924). By 1909, Slipher had already built a reputation as a skilled astronomer, and Indiana University, waiving its residence requirement as well as any need for separate graduate study, granted him a Ph.D. on the basis of a single published paper.

Discovers Recession of Galaxies

The same year, Lowell asked him to begin a spectral study of spiral nebulae. At the time, some astronomers believed that these nebulae rested within the Milky Way, while some speculated that they were actually "island universes" or "galaxies" at vast distances from the Milky Way. Lowell thought that spiral nebulae might be solar systems in formation, and assigned Slipher the task of comparing nebular spectra with those found within the solar system. Other work came first, however. In 1912, working with Lowell, Slipher carried out a study of planetary rotation. He found that Uranus' spectrum exhibited a pattern suggesting that it rotated on its axis once every 10.8 hours. Using similar spectral analysis, he was able to determine the rotation rates of Venus, Mars, Jupiter, and Saturn.

Concentrating at last on spiral nebulae, Slipher had obtained by 1913 four images of the Andromeda nebula's spectrum. Slipher noticed a peculiarity in the images; the entire wave band of this great spiral object was shifted toward the blue end of the spectrum. Interpreting this phenomenon as a Doppler shift, Slipher deduced that the object was racing toward the earth at a high rate of speed. A *Doppler shift* is a change in the apparent frequency of a wave emitted by a moving body. This change is proportionate to the relative motion of the wave source and the wave's observer. For example, the horn of a passing car sounds higher as the car approaches an observer and lower when the car is moving away from the observer. In the same way, the spectrum of an approaching luminous object has a higher frequency (shifted toward the blue end of the spectrum), while a receding object's light has a lower frequency (shifted toward the red end of the spectrum). In February 1913, Slipher determined from the magnitude of shift that the Andromeda nebula's speed was roughly 300 km/s. This was, at the time, the highest velocity ever recorded for any object in space.

In the 18 months following this measurement, Slipher obtained the speeds of 14 other spirals. (To obtain the spectrum of a faint nebula, Slipher sometimes had to leave the spectrograph shutter open for 60 hours or more.) A number of astronomers initially questioned Slipher's results, as the nebular speeds he obtained seemed impossibly high; even Slipher remained skeptical for a time. But before long it became clear that the speed data supported the notion that spiral nebulae were not within our own Milky Way galaxy, but were in fact separate galaxies at extreme distances from our own. At an August 1914 meeting of the American Astronomical Society in Evanston, Illinois, Slipher formally announced that most of the 15 spirals for which he had obtained spectra were receding, some in excess of 1,000 km/s. For over ten years after, Slipher was the only observer obtaining such spectra. By 1917, 21 of the 25 nebular spectra recorded by Slipher showed red shifts indicating recession.

Slipher determined that spiral nebulae were rotating as well as receding. Using a spectroscopic technique, he detected the rotation of galaxy NGC 4594 in the constellation Virgo in 1914. Measurements made by Slipher in the following years indicated that spiral galaxies rotated in a fashion similar to the winding of a spring, which contradicted a widely-held view that spirals were actually spinning as if unwinding. During this period, Slipher was promoted to assistant director of the Lowell Observatory, and when Lowell died in 1916, Slipher became acting director. In the following years, Slipher led solar eclipse expeditions to Syracuse, Kansas and Ensenada, Mexico, made spectroscopic studies of the chemical components of the night sky (including a study of the aurora phenomenon), and received several important honors: the Lalande prize and the gold medal of the Paris Academy of Sciences in 1918, and an honorary Sc.D. from the University of Arizona in 1923. Slipher also continued his studies of the chemical composition of planets, helping to identify the existence of iron and copper in the spectrum of Jupiter. His observations led to the 1934 discovery (by Ruppert Wildt) of methane and ammonia in planetary atmospheres.

Slipher made additional measurements of the spectra of spiral nebulae through the mid–1920s, at which time the work was taken up by astronomers **Milton Humason** and Edwin Hubble. Hubble, a supporter of the "island universe" theory who attended Slipher's 1914 address as a graduate student, seized upon Slipher's data, working out a method to determine the distances to spiral nebulae. With Humason's help, Hubble eventually demonstrated beyond a doubt that spiral nebulae are indeed immensely distant galaxies. Moreover, the work of Slipher and Hubble, integrated with the theories of astronomers **Willem Sitter** and **Georges Lemaître**, provided the foundation for the "big bang" theory, an explanation of the origin and large-scale behavior of the universe which is widely accepted today.

Discovers Interstellar Gas and Dust

During the period in which he studied nebulae, Slipher also made significant contributions to the search for interstellar gas and dust. Analyzing the fuzzy haze of light surrounding the Pleiades star cluster in the 1910s, he detected a spectrum resembling that of the stars within it; he concluded that the diffuse light was a cloud of dust grains reflecting starlight, and detected similar clouds in other regions of space. Following up on the work of astronomer

Johannes Hartmann, Slipher also detected interstellar sodium around the star Beta Scorpii as well as a number of other stars, but it took nearly 20 years before his study of interstellar gas was validated by Hertzsprung, Eddington, and others.

Slipher was named permanent director of the Lowell Observatory in 1926. After this appointment, he primarily busied himself with administrative duties. He paved the way for Tombaugh's discovery of Pluto by procuring a 13-inch telescope, and preparing the lab equipment needed to analyze its photographs. During this phase of his career, Slipher's pioneering work was recognized with several awards: Slipher won both the Henry Draper gold medal of the National Academy of Sciences and the gold medal of the Royal Astronomical Society in 1933, as well as the Catherine Wolf Bruce gold medal of the Astronomical Society of the Pacific in 1935. Slipher retired from the Lowell Observatory in 1954 at the age of 79.

Active in the International Astronomical Union and the American Academy of Arts and Sciences, Slipher was "deliberate, fastidious, patient, and showed a high order of technical knowledge," according to the Lowell Observatory's John S. Hall in the February 1970 issue of *Sky & Telescope.* Slipher mostly kept to himself and rarely attended scientific meetings; when thrust into the limelight by the presentation of an award, Slipher humbly downplayed his accomplishments, emphasizing instead his simple joy in exploration. Though he spent less time performing research in his later years, Slipher remained very active. Even at age 60 he could climb, with ease, the 12,661-foot San Francisco Peaks north of Flagstaff, said colleague Henry Giclas in the National Academy of Science's *Biographical Memoirs.* When asked for advice on a career in astronomy, Slipher would often emphasize the need for robust health.

Beyond his astronomical studies, Slipher involved himself in a wide range of activities. He bought ranch property around Flagstaff, operated a retail furniture store, and managed rental properties. He also helped found a community hotel for which he was board chairman for many years. Slipher helped found the Northern Arizona Society for Science and Art, and the Museum of Northern Arizona. He became a member and chairman of the Flagstaff school board and helped establish Flagstaff's first high school.

Slipher died of natural causes on November 8, 1969 in Flagstaff, just three days shy of his 94th birthday. In his will, he funded an annual grant and scholarship for science students and programs on behalf of the National Academy of Sciences and the Northern Arizona University Foundation in Flagstaff.

SELECTED WRITINGS BY SLIPHER:

Periodicals

Lowell Observatory Bulletin, A Spectrographic Investigation on the Rotational Velocity of Venus, no. 3 (1903), pp. 9–18.

Lowell Observatory Bulletin, On the Efficiency of the Spectrograph for Investigating Planetary Rotations and on the Accuracy of the Inclination Method of Measurement: Tests on the Rotation of the Planet Mars, no. 4 (1903), pp. 19–33.

Lowell Observatory Bulletin, The Radial Velocity of the Andromeda Nebula, no. 58 (1913), pp. 56–7.

FURTHER READING:

Books

The American Philosophical Society Year Book 1970, The American Philosophical Society, 1971, pp. 161–66.

Dictionary of Scientific Biography, Charles Scribner's Sons, 1975, pp. 454–56.

National Academy of Sciences Biographical Memoirs, Volume 52, National Academy Press, 1980, pp. 411–41.

Periodicals

New York Times, November 10, 1969, p. 47.

Parker, Barry, *Sky & Telescope,* Discovery of the Expanding Universe, September, 1986, pp. 227–30.

Sketch by Sebastian Thaler

Maud Slye
1879–1954
American pathologist

M aud Slye devoted her life to cancer research by investigating the inheritability of the disease in mice. Performing extensive breeding studies on the hereditary transmission of cancer, she kept meticulous pedigree records and autopsied thousands of mice during her lifetime. Her work was controversial, however; advocating the archiving of complete medical records for individuals, she believed that human beings could eradicate cancer by choosing mates with the appropriate genotype. Sometimes referred to as "America's Curie," Slye received wide publicity for her work and was honored by many organizations.

Slye was born in Minneapolis, Minnesota, on February 8, 1879, the daughter of James Alvin and Florence Alden Wheeler Slye. Her family, though poor, traced their ancestry back to John Alden of the Plymouth colony. At age seventeen, Slye entered the University of Chicago with savings of forty dollars and the desire to become a scientist.

Attending the university for three years, she supported herself by working as a secretary for university president William Harper. After a nervous breakdown, Slye convalesced in Woods Hole, Massachusetts, then completed her B.A. degree at Brown University in 1899. Hired as a teacher at the Rhode Island State Normal School, she stayed at the institution until 1905.

In 1908 Slye received a grant to do postgraduate work at the University of Chicago. Interested in the hereditary basis of disease, she began her work with six Japanese "waltzing" mice that were afflicted with a hereditary neurological disorder. Slye became intrigued by the inheritability of cancer when she heard of several heads of cattle at the Chicago stock yards—all with cancer of the eye—that had come from the same ranch. Inspired by this and other data, Slye went forward with her studies, breeding cancerous mice with one another as well as healthy mice with other healthy mice.

In 1911 Slye became a member of the university's newly created Sprague Memorial Institute, and in 1913 she presented her first paper on cancer before the American Society for Cancer Research. Becoming director of the Cancer Laboratory at the University of Chicago in 1919, she was promoted to assistant professor in 1922, then to associate professor in 1926. In 1936 Slye left her mice in the care of an assistant and took her first vacation in twenty-six years (earlier, when she had visited her ailing mother in California, she rented a boxcar and took her mice with her).

Although Slye discredited a prevailing theory that cancer was contagious, it became clear as her work proceeded that the appearance of cancer in an individual was not as simple as the presence of one gene. In later years, Slye posited that two conditions were necessary to produce cancer: inherited susceptibility, and prolonged irritation of the cancer-susceptible tissues. Nonetheless, further studies by other scientists have confirmed that while heredity can be a factor in certain types of cancer, it is much more complex than Slye had perceived.

Slye's work was recognized with several awards and honors, including the gold medal of the American Medical Association in 1914, and the Ricketts Prize in 1915. She also received the gold medal of the American Radiological Society in 1922. A member of the Association for Cancer Research, the American Medical Association, and the American Association for the Advancement of Science, Slye was the author of forty-two brochures on cancer and two volumes of poetry, *Songs and Solaces* and *I in the Wind.* At the time of her retirement in 1945 Slye was made professor emeritus of pathology, and she spent her retirement years analyzing data accumulated during her years of research. Slye never married. She died September 17, 1954, and was buried in Chicago's Oak Woods Cemetery.

FURTHER READING:

Books

Current Biography, H. W. Wilson, 1940, pp. 743–45.

Kass-Simon, G., and Patricia Farnes, editors, *Women of Science: Righting the Record,* Indiana University Press, 1990, pp. 278–79.

O'Neill, Lois Decker, editor, *The Women's Book of World Records and Achievements,* Doubleday, 1979, p. 217.

Periodicals

O'Neill, Lois Decker, editor, *Reader's Digest,* March 1936, pp. 77–80.

———— , *Newsweek,* April 10, 1937, pp. 26–28.

———— , *New York Times,* September 18, 1954, p. 15.

Sketch by Jill Carpenter

Stephen Smale

Stephen Smale
1930–
American mathematician

Stephen Smale has worked in a number of mathematical fields, including topology and dynamical systems. In the 1970s he became especially interested in the application of mathematical theory to economics. More recently, his research has focused on computer science and its relevance to fundamental principles of mathematics. In recognition of his work in these fields, Smale has been honored with the Veblen Prize, the Fields Medal, and the Chauvenet Prize.

Smale was born in Flint, Michigan, on July 15, 1930. His parents were Lawrence and Helen Smale. Smale has described his father as an "armchair revolutionary" who was once expelled from Albion College in Michigan for publishing a newsletter whose political and social views were offensive to college administrators. The elder Smale never returned to college and eventually became an assistant in the ceramics laboratory at the AC Sparkplug factory in Flint.

Becomes Politically Active at an Early Age

In 1935 when Smale was five years old, his family moved to a small farm outside of Flint and he began school in a one-room schoolhouse. In high school, Smale's primary interest was chemistry, and for a while he planned on a career in that field. He also became politically active during his high-school years, organizing a protest against the omission of evolution from his biology class curriculum. The protest was not very successful, as he told Donald J. Albers and Constance Reid in *More Mathematical People,* "I am not sure I succeeded in getting even one other person to sign the petition."

In 1948 Smale enrolled at The University of Michigan planning to major in physics rather than chemistry. He did poorly in physics, however, and gradually drifted into mathematics because it was a subject in which he had always excelled. Still, until his second year in graduate school, he did not make a firm decision to pursue a career in mathematics. In 1953 he added an M.S. to the B.S. he had received the year before and, three years later, he received his Ph.D., also from The University of Michigan.

During his college career Smale was involved in number of activities beyond his academic studies. As he told Albers and Reid, he "play[ed] a lot of chess and . . . a lot of Go [a Japanese game similar to chess or checkers]." Smale was also a member of the Communist party and was very active in opposition to the Korean War. His primary motivation for staying in college, he later admitted, was to avoid being drafted into fighting a war to which he was strongly opposed.

Begins Work in Topology

The mathematical topic that first attracted Smale's attention was topology, the mathematical study of the properties of figures that are not affected by changes in shape or size. For a period of about seven years beginning in graduate school, Smale worked on topological questions, a field that he later described as "very fashionable" at the time. He chose to pursue research in topology, he told Albers and Reid, because it was "just there." Despite this attitude, his work proved valuable, and he was awarded the prestigious Fields Medal of the International Mathematical Union in 1966 for his research in the field.

Smale accepted an appointment as professor of mathematics at Columbia University in 1961, the same year he made a surprising decision: he chose to abandon his work in topology and begin research in a new field, that of dynamical systems. Dynamical systems refers to mathematical methods for dealing with changes that take place in some real or abstract system over time. For the next five years Smale vacillated among a number of mathematical fields, including the calculus of variations and infinite dimensional manifolds. He also decided to leave Columbia University and accepted a position as professor of mathematics at the University of California in Berkeley in 1964 where he began to concentrate once again on dynamical systems. In 1970 Smale experienced yet another career transformation that was prompted by a series of conversations he had with Gerard Debreu, a Nobel laureate in economics. From these conversations, Smale began to work on the applications of mathematical theory to economic systems.

Smale remained politically active during his years at Columbia and Berkeley. He was outspoken in his opposition to the war in Vietnam and helped organize, along with Jerry Rubin and others, the "days of protest" held against the war. However, his political attitudes have undergone an evolution over the past two decades. After a series of trips to Russia in the 1960s, Smale became disillusioned with communism and eventually found himself in agreement with at least some principles of conservative political philosophy. He recently described himself to Albers and Reid as being "consistently . . . against the military" and having beliefs that are "more radical than those of most liberals," but "conservative part of the time."

In recent years, Smale has become interested in computer sciences. He has expressed an interest in bringing the mathematics used in this field into closer relationship with mainstream mathematics. Although his objective is not yet defined, Smale feels that establishing such a relationship may result in some revolutionary changes in the nature of mathematics itself.

Smale married Clara Davis, a classmate at The University of Michigan, in 1955. The couple has two children, Laura, a biological psychologist, and Nat, a mathematician. Smale has a number of leisure interests including a large mineral collection and a forty-three-foot, ocean-going ketch. In addition to his Fields Medal, Smale has been given the 1966 Veblen Prize of the American Mathematical Society and the 1988 Chauvenet Prize of the Mathematical Association of America.

SELECTED WRITINGS BY SMALE:

Books

Differential Equations, Dynamical Systems and Linear Algebra, Academic Press, 1974.

The Mathematics of Time: Essays on Dynamical Systems, Economic Processes, and Related Topics, Springer-Verlag, 1980.

FURTHER READING:

Books

Albers, Donald J., Gerald L. Alexanderson, and Constance Reid, editors, *More Mathematical People,* Harcourt, 1991, pp. 305–23.

Sketch by David E. Newton

Richard Errett Smalley
1943–
American chemist and physicist

American scientist Richard E. Smalley is best known as one of the winners of the 1996 Nobel Prize for chemistry, along with fellow Rice University professor **Robert F. Curl, Jr.**, and Briton **Harold W. Kroto** from the University of Sussex, for the discovery of a new carbon molecule, the buckminsterfullerene. It was given that name, or more simply "fullerene," in honor of architect Buckminster Fuller, whose geodesic dome the carbon molecule resembles. A pioneer of supersonic beam laser spectroscopy, Smalley is also renowned for his elaborate supersonic beam experiments, which use lasers to produce and study clusters, aggregates of atoms that occur for a short time under specific conditions. The discovery of fullerenes promises to be the basis for not only a new area of carbon chemistry, but also a way to produce remarkably strong and lightweight materials, new drug delivery systems, computer semiconductors, solar cells, and superconductors.

Smalley was born in Akron, Ohio, on June 6, 1943. Smalley's mother, Esther Virginia Rhoads, was from a furniture manufacturing family. Smalley credits his mother with sparking his interest in science. He spent many hours with her collecting samples from a local pond and looking at them under the microscope. His mother taught him to love literature and nature and the practical skill of mechanical drawing. His father, Frank Dudley Smalley, Jr., was the CEO of a trade journal for farm implements, *Implement and Tractor.* His father taught him machinery repair as well as woodworking. In his autobiography published online through Rice University's web site, Smalley believes that these childhood activities were the perfect preparation for a scientific career.

Several more events inspired Smalley to become a scientist. One was the launching of Sputnik in 1957.

Another was his aunt, Dr. Sara Jane Rhoads, who was one of the first women in the United States to achieve a full professorship in chemistry. Smalley used to refer to this bright, active woman as "the Colossus of Rhoads." She encouraged Smalley to study chemistry and one of Smalley's best memories is of working in her organic chemistry laboratory at the University of Wyoming.

Learns Real-World Applications of Chemistry

Smalley's aunt also encouraged him to attend Hope College in Holland, Michigan, which was known for its undergraduate programs in chemistry. Smalley spent two years at Hope College but decided to transfer to The University of Michigan after one favorite professor died and another retired. When Smalley graduated in 1965, he decided to take a job rather than go directly to graduate school. He worked for three years at Shell Chemical Company's polypropylene manufacturing plant and at their Plastics Technical Center in Woodbury, New Jersey. There Smalley learned what he called in his autobiography "real-world applications of chemistry." It was also there that Smalley met his wife, Judith Grace Sampieri, a secretary for Shell. They were married on May 4, 1968.

Smalley enjoyed his work at Shell but he knew it was time to begin graduate school. His graduate school prospects became entangled with several near misses in the Vietnam War draft. He was close to accepting an offer from the University of Wisconsin when he discovered that graduate students were no longer automatically deferred from the draft. His industrial deferment was still valid, so he decided to stay at Shell. However, that deferment eventually expired, so he decided to reapply to graduate school anyway and take his chances. He applied to Princeton University because his wife's family lived there. In the fall of 1968 he was in fact drafted, but within a week of that event, his wife became pregnant and he was reclassified. The Smalley's son Chad Richard was born on June 9, 1969.

That fall the Smalleys moved to Princeton, New Jersey, and Smalley began his Ph.D. work. Here Smalley learned a concentrated style of research as well as chemical physics and molecular systems. In 1973 Smalley began his postdoctoral research with Professor Don Levy at the University of Chicago. Part of his oral exam was three original research proposals; in researching topics, Smalley became interested in the work of Nobel Prize winner **Yuan Lee** and Stuart Rice. Yuan Lee had built a universal molecular beam apparatus and had used it to slow down molecules. This was the germ of Smalley's future Nobel Prize-winning work. His collaboration with Don Levy on supercooled molecules led to supersonic beam laser spectroscopy. This technology allowed scientists to examine molecules with the kind of detail only achieved before on atoms.

Smalley became an assistant professor in the chemistry department of Rice University in Houston, Texas, in 1976. He was aware of Rice University professor Robert Curl's work with laser spectroscopy and had wanted to collaborate with him. Smalley's first work was building a supersonic beam apparatus similar to one he had used at the University of Chicago. His first proposal to the National Science Foundation was for a larger apparatus that would allow him to increase the beam's intensity and be able to study a larger variety of molecules.

Interruption Leads to Discovery of "Buckyballs"

At the same time Smalley was using his laser apparatus to examine molecules, a professor at Sussex University in England, Harold Kroto, was researching chains of carbons in space. Kroto thought these chains might be the products of red-giant stars, but was not sure how the chains actually formed. In 1984 Kroto traveled to the United States to use Smalley's beam apparatus. He thought that he could use the machine to simulate the temperatures in space needed to form the carbon chains. Smalley and Curl had had no reason to look at simple carbon in their complex laser apparatus. It was something of a favor as well as a break in their research when Kroto asked them to look at carbon in order to verify his research. So in September 1984, the scientists turned the laser beam on a piece of graphite and found something they were not looking for, a molecule that had 60 carbon atoms. Carbon had previously been known to have only two molecular forms, diamond and graphite. They surmised correctly that this was a third form of carbon and that it had a cage-like structure resembling a soccer ball, or a geodesic dome. They named the structure buckminsterfullerene, which later became known as fullerene, and also by the nickname "buckyball."

Evidence for the existence of large carbon clusters had existed before, but Smalley, Curl, and Kroto were the first scientists to fully identify and stabilize carbon-60. In October of 1996, all three were recognized for this remarkable discovery with the Nobel Prize in chemistry.

Fullerene research took off quickly, and today scientists can manufacture pounds of buckyballs in a day. Extraordinarily stable because of their molecular structure and resistant to radiation and chemical destruction, fullerenes have many potential uses.

Smalley's research group is now looking at the tubular versions of fullerenes. In his autobiography, Smalley writes that he is "convinced that major new technologies will be developed over the coming decades from fullerene tubes, fibers, and cables, and we are moving as fast as possible to bring this all to life."

SELECTED WRITINGS BY SMALLEY:

Periodicals

"Lasers, Supersonic Beams, NO_2, and New Possibilities for Molecular Spectroscopy," National Meeting of the Division of Electron and Atomic Physics of the American Physical Society (invited paper), 1974.

(With T. Guo and C. Jin) "Doping Bucky: Formation and Properties of Boron-Doped Buckminsterfullerene," *Journal of Physical Chemistry*, 1991.

(With D. M. Poirier, T. R. Ohno, G. H. Kroll, Y. Chen, P. J. Benning, J. H. Weaver, and L. P. F. Chibante) "Formation of Fullerides and Fullerene-Based Heterostructure," *Science*, 1991.

(With A. P. Ramirez, R. C. Haddon, O. Zhou, R. M. Fleming, J. Zhang, and S. M. McClure) "Magnetic Susceptibility of Molecular Carbon: Nanotubes and Fullerite," *Science*, 1994.

"Solar Generation of the Fullerenes." *Journal of Physical Chemistry* 97, 1994.

"Discovering the Fullerenes," Nobel Lecture, *Reviews of Modern Physics*, 1997.

(With J. Liu, H. J. Dai, J. H. Hafner, D. T. Colbert, S. J. Tans, and C. Dekker) "Fullerene Crop Circles," *Nature*, 1997.

FURTHER READING:

Periodicals

Nash, Madeleine. "SCIENCE: Great Balls of Carbon." *Time* (May, 6 1991).

Wu, Corinna. "Buckyballs Bounce into Nobel History." *Science News*, Vol. 150 (October 19, 1996): 247.

Zimmer, Carl. "Buckyballs From Space." *Discover Magazine* (August 1, 1996).

Other

"Chemistry, Physics Nobel Winners Announced." *CNN Interactive.* 1996. http://cnn.com/WORLD/9610/09/nobel.physics/index.html (December 17, 1997).

"Richard E. Smalley." Rice Chemistry Department. http://pchem1.rice.edu/FacultyStaff/Smalley.html (December 17, 1997).

Sketch by Pamela Proffitt

Hamilton O. Smith

Hamilton O. Smith
1931–
American molecular biologist

Hamilton O. Smith shared the 1978 Nobel Prize in physiology or medicine with fellow biologists **Werner Arber** and **Daniel Nathans** for the set of linked discoveries that started off the boom in biotechnology. Because of these discoveries, researchers can more easily elucidate the structure and coding of deoxyribonucleic acid (DNA) molecules (the basic genetic map of an organism), and they hope to correct many genetic illnesses in the future. It is also possible to design new organisms, a controversial but potentially beneficial technology. Smith purified and explained the activity of the first restriction enzyme, which became the principal tool used by genetic engineers to selectively cut up DNA. (Arber had linked restriction and modification to DNA, and predicted the existence of restriction enzymes. Nathans, under Smith's encouragement at Johns Hopkins, developed techniques that enabled their practical use.)

Hamilton Othanel Smith was born on August 23, 1931, in New York City, to Bunnie (Othanel) Smith and Tommie Harkey Smith. His father, an assistant professor of education at the University of Florida, finished his Ph.D. at Columbia University in 1937 and took a new teaching job at the University of Illinois. The family then moved to Urbana, where Smith and his brother attended public school. It was here that Smith's interest in science began. He and his brother even equipped a laboratory in their basement with money from their paper routes. Smith graduated from University High School in three years, enrolling at a local university in 1948.

Smith came to the study of genetics by way of medicine. Initially a mathematics major at the University of Illinois, he transferred to the University of California at Berkeley in 1950 to study biology and graduated with a bachelor's degree in 1952. He obtained a medical degree from the Johns Hopkins School of Medicine in 1956. The following year, Smith married Elizabeth Anne Bolton, a nurse. They eventually had four sons and a daughter. During the years 1956 to 1962, he held various posts, including an internship at Washington University in St. Louis, Missouri, a two-year navy stint in San Diego, California, and a residency at Henry Ford Hospital in Detroit, Michigan. He gradually taught himself genetics and molecular biology in his spare time. In 1962 he began a research career at The University of Michigan on a postdoctoral fellowship from the National Institutes of Health, before finally returning to Johns Hopkins in 1965 as a research associate in the microbiology department. He was named a full professor of microbiology in 1973, and professor of molecular biology and genetics in 1981. In 1975 Smith was awarded a Guggenheim Fellowship for a year of study at the University of Zurich in Switzerland.

Restriction Enzyme Discovery Leads to Nobel Prize

DNA, the genetic material in all cells, is a long, chain-like molecule encoded along its structure for individual genes and thereby individual proteins. Each link in the chain is one of four possible nucleotides (adenine, guanine, cytosine, and thymine) arranged in varying sequences. An individual gene's function is coded by the order of the links, as a word's meaning is coded by the order of the letters. Much of the fundamental research in biotechnology was accomplished by studying DNA from both bacteria and the viruses—also called bacteriophages—that can infect bacteria. If a bacterium can break up invading viral DNA without harming its own DNA, it destroys the virus and thus resists infection. Bacteria that resist infection chemically modify parts of their DNA, usually with a methylating enzyme called a methylase, so it cannot be cut. Then they damage the viral DNA with a specific restriction enzyme (also called a restriction endonuclease). The bacterial DNA remains undamaged because of its chemical alteration, while the viral DNA is cut apart by the endonuclease.

Restriction enzymes are classified as Class I or Class II. Class I enzymes recognize specific DNA sequences, but they do not cut DNA only at those locations. Each Class II endonuclease, however, cuts only between two specific sequences of nucleotides, and no others. The mechanism of this type of bacterial resistance is called restriction-modification and involves the matched set of Class II endonuclease—methylase enzymes. "Restriction" means cutting DNA at a specific location, and "modification" means the enzyme-driven chemical change in the DNA that prevents such cutting. (Of course, viruses eventually can evolve modifications of their own that prevent their destruction by restriction enzymes; an appropriately modified virus can thus infect a formerly resistant strain of bacteria.)

Smith had been interested in bacterial genetics for many years, and spent 1966 working in Geneva, Switzerland with Werner Arber. After his return to the U.S., Smith purified the first Type II restriction endonuclease, which he obtained from the bacterium *Hemophilus influenzae,* and identified the nucleotide sequence which the enzyme would cut. He gave a supply of the enzyme to Daniel Nathans, who used it in his own work. The three men eventually won the

1978 Nobel Prize. The presenter of the prize noted that Smith proved Arbor's hypothesis about restriction enzymes, pointing the way for future research.

The exacting specificity of Class II restriction enzymes makes them useful because biotechnologists can now cut DNA apart selectively. Then they can add and subtract specific nucleotides, and reproducibly weld (recombine) the links back together in a new order. This new piece of DNA now codes for a different protein. The current and potential uses of these procedures are enormous. Biotechnologists can genetically engineer bacteria that produce a particular chemical; human insulin for the treatment of diabetes is now made by such "recombinant" bacteria. Other bacteria have been designed to chew up oil slicks. One of the tasks that biotechnologists would like to accomplish is the eradication of genetic illness by correcting the mistaken DNA codes that cause it. Sickle-cell anemia, for example, is a life-threatening and incurable disease resulting from a mistake in two of the genes that code for the blood protein hemoglobin. Gene therapies are still highly experimental and controversial, but tests are beginning on them.

SELECTED WRITINGS BY SMITH:

Periodicals

Journal of Molecular Biology, A Restriction Enzyme from Hemophilus Influenzae: I. Purification and General Properties, Volume 51, 1970, p. 379.

Journal of Molecular Biology, A Restriction Enzyme from Hemophilus Influenzae: II. Base Sequence of the Recognition Site, Volume 51, 1970, p. 393.

Annual Review of Biochemistry, Restriction Endonucleases in the Analysis and Restructuring of DNA Molecules, Volume 44, 1975, pp. 273–293.

FURTHER READING:

Books

Nobel Prize Winners: An H. W. Wilson Biographical Dictionary, Wilson, 1987, pp. 983–85.

Periodicals

Science, December 8, 1978, pp. 1068, 1069.

Sketch by Gail B.C. Marsella

Michael Smith
1932–
Canadian biochemist

Michael Smith began his professional research career in salmon physiology and endocrinology, but returned to the chemical synthesis that had been his first interest, including the chemical synthesis of deoxyribonucleic acid (DNA). Smith experimented with isolating genes and invented site-directed mutagenesis, a technique for deliberately altering gene sequences. Smith's work was hailed as having tremendous implications for genetic studies and the understanding of how individual genes function, and already has been applied in the study of disease-producing viruses. In 1993 Smith shared the Nobel Prize in chemistry independently with **Kary Mullis**. The Royal Swedish Academy of Sciences credited Smith and Mullis with having revolutionized basic research and saluted the possibilities offered by their research toward the cure of hereditary diseases.

Smith was born in Blackpool, England, on April 26, 1932. His parents were Rowland Smith, a market gardener, and Mary Agnes Armstead Smith, a bookkeeper who also helped with the market gardening. Smith was admitted to Arnold School, the local private secondary school, with a scholarship he earned based on his examination results (this examination was taken, at the time, by all English children when they finished their primary education). Without this scholarship, Smith would have had little opportunity for advanced education, as his parents did not have the money to pay for it. While at Arnold School, Smith became involved in scouting, which eventually led to a lifelong interest in camping and other outdoor activities.

After graduating from Arnold School in 1950, Smith enrolled at the University of Manchester in order to study chemistry, realizing a natural inclination toward the "hard" sciences. He moved rapidly through school, receiving a B.Sc. in 1953, and a Ph.D. in chemistry in 1956, both sponsored by scholarship. Smith's desire following completion of his Ph.D. was to earn a fellowship on the West Coast of the United States. This did not work out, but he was accepted into biochemist **Har Gobind Khorana**'s laboratory in Vancouver, Canada. Smith's original plan in migrating to Canada was to work for a year, then return to England and work for a chemical company. However, his experience working with Khorana, who would win the Nobel Prize in 1968 for his contributions to genetics, changed his plans. Smith decided university research was the path he wanted to take and that British Columbia, with its natural beauty, would be his home. Smith is now a Canadian citizen.

Smith stayed with the Khorana group and moved with it in 1960 to the Institute for Enzyme Research at the University of Wisconsin. (Smith had recently married Helen Christie. The couple later separated, but they had three children, Tom, Ian, and Wendy.) Until then, Smith's work in Canada had been in several different areas of chemical synthesis. In 1961 he decided it was time for a change and decided to relocate to the West Coast. Smith accepted a position as head of the chemistry section of the Vancouver Laboratory of the Fisheries Research Board of Canada. His work there was mainly in salmon physiology and endocrinology, but he also continued to work in chemical synthesis.

Move to Academia Culminates in Nobel Prize

In 1966 Smith entered the academic field, taking an appointment as associate professor of biochemistry and molecular biology at the University of British Columbia (UBC), and bringing with him an interest in chemically synthesized DNA (the molecule of heredity). Also beginning in 1966 Smith held a concurrent position as medical research associate of the Medical Research Council of Canada. He was made full professor in 1970, and has continued his teaching duties ever since. In 1986 he was asked to establish a biotechnology laboratory on the campus of UBC, which he has headed since that time.

Smith has taken three sabbaticals from his duties at the University of British Columbia, spending three months in 1971 at Rockefeller University in New York, one year during 1975 and 1976 at the Medical Research Council laboratory in Cambridge, and eight months in 1982 at Yale University. The middle excursion was spent in English biochemist **Frederick Sanger**'s laboratory learning about DNA sequence determination, essential to Smith's later research.

Smith was first able to isolate genes using chemical synthesis in 1974. Slowly he developed what became known as site-directed mutagenesis, a technique that allows gene sequences to be altered deliberately. More specifically, it involves separating one strand of a piece of DNA and producing a mirror image of it. This mirror image can then be used as a probe into a gene. It can also be used with chemical enzymes—proteins that act as catalysts in biochemical reactions—that are able to cut and splice DNA in living cells. Jeffrey Fox, editor of *Bioscience,* called this process the "intellectual bombshell that triggered protein engineering," as quoted in the Toronto *Globe and Mail.* Smith's findings were published in 1978 in *Journal of Biological Chemistry.* This paper lays the foundation of the research Smith has done since. The paper concludes, "This new method of mutagenesis has considerable potential in genetic studies. Thus, it will be possible to change and define the role of regions of DNA sequence whose function is as yet incompletely understood."

Smith, in demonstrating that biological systems are chemical, has allowed scientists to tinker systematically with genes, altering properties one at a time to see what effect each alteration may have on the gene's functioning. Genes are the building blocks for countless proteins that make up skin, muscles, bone, and hormones. Changes in the expression of these proteins reveal to the scientist how his or her tinkering has altered the gene function. This process has been used specifically to study disease-producing viruses, such as those that cause cancer. The eventual goal is to uncover the functioning of the genes, so drugs to combat the viruses can be developed.

After being a nominee several times, Smith was awarded the Nobel Prize in chemistry in 1993 jointly with Kary Mullis from California. Their work was not collaborative, though both dealt with biotechnology. Announcing the award, the Royal Swedish Academy of Sciences credited Smith for having "revolutionized basic research and entirely changed researchers' way of performing their experiments," as quoted in the Toronto *Globe and Mail.* The academy further asserted Smith's work holds great promise for the future with the "possibilities of gene therapy, curing hereditary diseases by specifically correcting mutated code words in the genetic material."

The award money from the Nobel Prize amounted to close to $500,000 Cdn for Smith. With it he established an endowment fund, half of which will be earmarked to aid research on molecular genetics of the central nervous system, specifically in relation to schizophrenia research. The other half is to be divided between general science awareness projects and the Society for Canadian Women in Science and Technology in an effort to induce more women to pursue careers in science. He also convinced both the provincial and federal governments to contribute to his funds.

In addition to his receipt of the Nobel Prize, Smith has garnered numerous other honors in the course of his career, including the Gairdner Foundation International Award in 1986, and the Genetics Society of Canada's Award of Excellence in 1988. He has assumed several administrative responsibilities, including becoming acting director of the Biomedical Research Center, a privately funded research institute, in 1991, and is a member of the Canadian Biochemical Society, the Genetics Society of America, and the American Association for the Advancement of Science. He is a fellow of the Chemical Society of London, the Royal Society of Canada, and the Royal Society of London, and has served on several medical committees, such as the advisory committee on research for the National Cancer Institute of Canada. He is a popular speaker, and has delivered over 150 addresses throughout the world during the course of his career. His scientific research articles number more than two hundred.

SELECTED WRITINGS BY SMITH:

Books

Genetic Engineering: Principles and Methods, Constructed Mutants Using Synthetic Oligodeoxyribonucleotides as Site-Specific Mutagens, edited by J. K. Setlow and A. Hollaender, Volume 3, Plenum, 1981, pp. 1–52.

Periodicals

Journal of the American Chemical Society, The Synthesis and Properties of Ribonucleoside–3',5' Cyclic Phosphates, Volume 83, 1961, pp. 698–706.
Journal of Biological Chemistry, Mutagenesis at a Specific Position in a DNA Sequence, September 25, 1978, pp. 6551–560.
Annual Review of Genetics, In Vitro Mutagenesis, Volume 19, 1985, pp. 423–62.

FURTHER READING:

Periodicals

Boei, William, *Vancouver Sun,* Nobelist to Give Prize Money Away, November 27, 1993, p. A3.
Matas, Robert, *Globe and Mail,* B.C. Scientist Awarded Nobel, (Toronto), October 14, 1993, pp. A1, A4.
Surtees, Lawrence, *Globe and Mail,* Genetics Society Prize Won by UBC Scientist, (Toronto), August 24, 1988, p. A8.

Other

Smith, Michael, *Interview with Kimberlyn McGrail,* conducted January 4, 1994.

Sketch by Kimberlyn McGrail

George Davis Snell
1903–1996
American immunogeneticist

Geneticist George David Snell's pioneering research on the immune system in the 1930s and 1940s enabled medical science to develop the process of organ transplantation. Through skin grafts performed on mice at the Jackson Hole Laboratory, he discovered the factor (known as histocompatibility) that enables doctors to determine whether organs and tissues can be successfully transplanted from one body to another. Snell's research earned him the 1980 Nobel Prize for medicine or physiology.

One of three children, Snell was born on December 19, 1903, in Bradford, Massachusetts, to Cullen Snell and the former Kathleen Davis. Snell's father developed and manufactured many inventions, including a mechanism for starting motorboat engines. In Snell's fifth year the family moved to Brookline. Snell's interests while growing up were varied, and included science, math, sports, and music.

After enrolling at New Hampshire's Dartmouth College in 1922, Snell was influenced to major in biology after taking a genetics course taught by Professor John Gerould. He obtained a B.S. degree in that subject in 1926 and enrolled at Harvard that same year so he could study genetics under the renowned biologist William Castle, who was among the first American scientists to delve into the biological laws of inheritance regarding mammals. Snell received a Ph.D. in 1930 after completing his dissertation on linkage, the means by which two or more genes on a chromosome are interrelated. That same year he became an instructor of zoology at Rhode Island's Brown University, only to leave in 1931 to work at the University of Texas at Austin following receipt of a National Research Council Fellowship.

Snell's decision to accept the fellowship turned out to be a momentous one, as he began work for the famed geneticist **Hermann Joseph Muller**, whose research with fruit flies led to the discovery that X rays could produce mutations in genes. At the university, Snell experimented with mice, showing that X rays could produce mutations in rodents as well. Although Snell left the University of Texas in 1933 to serve as assistant professor at the University of Washington, he ventured to the Jackson Laboratory in Bar Harbor, Maine, in 1935 to return to research work. The laboratory, specializing in mammalian genetics, was well-known for its work in spite of its small size.

After continuing his work with X rays and mice, Snell decided to embark on a new study. Snell's project was concerned with the notion of transplants. Earlier scientific research had indicated that certain genes are responsible for whether a body would accept or reject a transplant. The precise genes responsible had not then been identified, however.

Snell began his experiments by performing transplants between mice with certain physical characteristics. He quickly discovered those mice with certain identical characteristics—in particular a twisted tail—tended to accept each other's skin grafts. In 1948 Peter Gorer came to Jackson Laboratory from London, England. Gorer, who had also conducted experiments on mice, developed an antiserum. He had discovered the existence of a certain antigen (foreign protein) in the blood of mice that induced an immune reaction when injected into other mice. Gorer had called this type of substance "Antigen II."

Partnership Leads to Key Discovery

In collaboration, Snell and Gorer proved that Antigen II was present in mice with twisted tails, indicating that the genetics code for Gorer's antigen and the code found by Snell to be vital for tissue acceptance were identical. They called their discovery of this factor "H–2," for "Histocompatibility Two" (a term invented by Snell to describe whether a transplant would be accepted or rejected).

Later research revealed that instead of only a single gene being responsible for this factor, a number of closely related genes controlled histocompatibility. As a result, this was subsequently designated as the Major Histocompatibility Complex (MHC). The discovery of the MHC, and subsequent research by other scientists in the 1950s that proved it also existed in humans, made widespread organ transplantation possible. Donors and recipients could be matched (as had been done with blood types) to see if they were compatible.

Eventually Snell was able to produce what he called "congenic mice"—animals that are genetically identical except for one particular genetic characteristic. Unfortunately, the first strains of these mice were destroyed in a 1947 forest fire which burned down the laboratory. However, Snell's tenacity and dedication enabled him to rebound from this setback. Within three years he had created three strains of mice that differed genetically only in their ability to accept tissue grafts. The development of congenic strains of mice opened up a new field for experimental research, with Jackson Laboratory eventually being able to supply annually tens of thousands of these mice to other laboratories.

In 1952 Snell became staff scientific director and, in 1957, staff scientist at Jackson Laboratories. In those capacities he continued his research, particularly on the role that MHC plays in relation to cancer. Experiments he conducted with congenic mice found that on some occasions the mice rejected tumors that had been transplanted from their genetic twins. This "hybrid resistance" indicated that some tumors provoke an immune response, causing the body to produce antibodies to fight the tumor. This discovery could eventually be of great importance in developing weapons to fight cancer.

Although he retired in 1968, Snell continued to visit the lab, discuss scientific and medical matters with colleagues, and write articles and books. Elected to the American Academy of Arts and Sciences in 1952 and to the National Academy of Science in 1970, he was also a member of international scientific societies, including the French Academy of Science and the British Transplantation Society. Snell won numerous awards during the 1960s and 1970s, such as the Hectoen Silver Medal from the American Medical Association, the Gregor Mendal Award for genetic research, and a career award from the National Cancer Institute. This culminated in his winning the 1980 Nobel Prize in medicine or physiology for his work on histocompatibility. He shared this with two other immunogeneticists, **Jean Dausset** and **Baruj Benacerraf**. After being told of the Nobel committee's decision, Snell said there should have been a fourth recipient—his colleague Peter Gorer who died in 1962 and was thus ineligible to receive the prize.

Married in 1937 to the former Rhoda Carson, Snell and his wife had three sons—Peter, Roy, and Thomas. He died at his home in Bel Harbor, Maine, on June 6, 1996, at the age of 92.

SELECTED WRITINGS BY SNELL:

Books

The Biology of the Laboratory Mouse, Blakiston, 1941.

Cell Surface Antigens: Studies in Mammals Other Than Man, MSS Information Corporation, 1973.
Genetic and Biological Aspects of Histocompatibility Antigens, Munksgaard, 1973.
Histocompatibility, Academic Press, 1976.

FURTHER READING:

Books

Dowie, Mark, *"We Have A Donor": The Brave New World of Medical Transplants,* St. Martin's, 1988.
Kittridge, Mary, *Organ Transplants,* Chelsea House, 1989.

Periodicals

Borders, William, *New York Times,* Three Cell Researchers Win Medicine Nobel, October 11, 1980, p. 1.
Clark, Matt, *Newsweek,* A Nobel Piece of Research, October 20, 1980, p. 66.
Marx, Jean, *Science,* 1980 Noble Prize in Physiology or Medicine, November 7, 1980, pp. 621–23.

Sketch by Francis Rogers

Solomon H. Snyder

Solomon H. Snyder
1938–
American neuroscientist

Solomon H. Snyder is best known for his work in locating opiate receptors in the human brain and isolating opiate-like substances made by the body. It is for this achievement that he shared the 1978 Albert Lasker Medical Research Award for basic research, one of the most prestigious prizes in medicine. However, Snyder's contributions extend to many other areas of neuroscience as well, including the development of techniques to study receptors, the identification of a protein that plays a role in odor detection, the demonstration of adult brain cell reproduction in the lab, and the discovery of what may be a novel class of neurotransmitters. In a *Scientific American* profile, author Marguerite Holloway described Snyder as "one of the country's most prolific and creative neuroscientists."

Solomon Halbert Snyder was the second of five children. He was born on December 26, 1938, in Washington, D.C. His father, Samuel Simon Snyder, was a cryptanalyst for the National Security Agency who helped break enemy codes during World War II. Later his father pioneered the use of computers for code-breaking. His mother, Patricia Yakerson Snyder, was a real estate broker and avid contest participant. When Snyder was just nine years old, his father taught him to program computers. As a teenager, though, he was more interested in reading, writing, and philosophy than science. He was also a serious student of classical guitar, and his parents suggested that he attend a music conservatory after high school. He chose to train for a medical career, however, partly because many of his friends wanted to become doctors, and partly because he was attracted to the writings of Sigmund Freud.

Rises Quickly from Intern to Laboratory Director

In 1955 Snyder enrolled in the premedical program at Georgetown University in Washington, D.C. Three years later, he was admitted to Georgetown Medical School, before he had even completed a bachelor's degree. He received his M.D. degree in 1962, when he was just 23 years old. He spent the next year as an intern at the Kaiser Foundation Hospital in San Francisco. Then, starting in 1963, Snyder worked for two years at the National Institute of Mental Health as a research associate in the laboratory of Nobel Prize-winner **Julius Axelrod**. In the preface to *Biological Aspects of Mental Disorder*, Snyder later recalled that he took this position "largely in an effort to avoid the doctor draft. However, working in the stimulating environment of this Nobel laureate's laboratory addicted me to the basic research enterprise. Research in a laboratory at the forefront was vastly different from the boring science of classes and textbooks." Despite this he was determined to become a psychiatrist, and in 1965, he began a residency in psychiatry at Johns Hopkins Hospital in Baltimore.

Thus began a long and fruitful association with Johns Hopkins University School of Medicine. In 1966, while still a resident, Snyder joined the faculty there as an assistant professor of pharmacology. He quickly rose through the ranks, and since 1980, he has held the position of distinguished service professor in neuroscience, pharmacology, and psychiatry, as well as director of the neuroscience department. Like Axelrod before him, Snyder does not have a permanent staff of researchers in his lab. Instead, he relies on an ever-changing pool of graduate students. Since he gives the training of young scientists high priority, he collaborates on various projects with up to a dozen students at a time. Many ideas for projects come from the students themselves during brainstorming sessions with Snyder. Others come from Snyder's voracious reading habits. As Gina Kolata reported in *The New York Times*, "Snyder says that his secret is to read widely, keeping up with research that seems completely unrelated to studies of the brain, and then to think about ways the findings might apply to the brain."

Collaboration Leads to New Insights into Addiction and Stroke

Snyder's most famous collaboration began in 1972, when he and graduate student Candace Pert embarked on a search for opiate receptors. Scientists at the time assumed that there must be receptors in the brain for heroin and other opiate drugs, but this had never been proven. Such receptors were thought to function as molecular locks, with opiates being the keys that would fit these locks, starting a sequence of events leading up to a feeling of euphoria or a reduction in pain. By devising a technique to study receptors, Snyder and Pert were able to pinpoint the locations of opiate receptors and study the way drugs bind to these sites. In 1973, just nine months after starting their quest, the pair published their findings in *Science*. Their work paved the way for greater understanding of the communication system within the brain, the actions of drugs such as painkillers, and the dynamics of narcotic addiction.

More recently, Snyder and his colleagues launched an investigation into novel neurotransmitters, substances that transmit impulses between nerve cells. They found that a gas called nitric oxide seems to deliver messages from one nerve cell to another, even though it bypasses traditional receptors. Carbon monoxide is another gas that appears to carry messages within the brain, raising the possibility of a whole new class of neurotransmitters. Snyder and his colleagues also showed that nitric oxide may be a critical link in the chain of biochemical events that leads to brain cell death after a stroke.

Snyder has been married to psychotherapist Elaine Borko since June 10, 1962. The couple have two grown daughters, Judith and Deborah. Snyder still plays classical guitar, and he swims every morning before work. He is also actively involved in his synagogue. Writing in *The New York Times*, Kolata described Snyder as "soft-spoken" and "self-effacing." Yet she noted that "in his quarter of a century in science Dr. Snyder has made some breathtaking discoveries about how the brain works."

SELECTED WRITINGS BY SNYDER:

Books

(Editor) *Perspectives in Neuropharmacology: A Tribute to Julius Axelrod.* New York: Oxford University Press, 1972.
Madness and the Brain. New York: McGraw, 1974.
(With Steven Matthysse) *Opiate Receptor Mechanisms: Neurochemical and Neurophysiological Processes in Opiate Drug Action and Addiction.* Cambridge, MA: MIT Press, 1975.
The Troubled Mind: A Guide to Release from Distress. New York: McGraw, 1976.
Biological Aspects of Mental Disorder. New York: Oxford University Press, 1980.

Periodicals

(With Candace B. Pert) "Opiate Receptor: Demonstration in Nervous Tissue." *Science* (March 1973): 1011-014.

Other

"Neurotransmitters, Second Messengers and Drug Action in the Nervous System." http://www.med.jhu.edu/neurosci/webtextneurosci-PRI-MARY-SNYDER.html (October 10, 1997).

FURTHER READING:

Books

Graham, Judith, ed. *Current Biography Yearbook 1996.* New York: H. W. Wilson, 1996, pp. 523-527.

Periodicals

Holloway, Marguerite. "The Reward of Ideas That Are Wrong." *Scientific American* (August 1991): 29-30.
Kolata, Gina. "Brain Researcher Makes It Look Easy." *The New York Times.* 25 May 1993, C: 1, 8.
Stutz, Christine. "Master of Science: Inside the Mind of Sol Snyder." *Baltimore Jewish Times.* December 27, 1996.

Other

"New Discovery May Offer Protection Against Stroke." September 30, 1997. http://hopkins.med.jhu.edu/NewsMedia/news.release.html (October 10, 1997). This Web site includes several press releases and news reports from Johns Hopkins Medicine about Snyder's research.

Sketch by Linda Wasmer Smith

Frederick Soddy
1877–1956
English chemist

Frederick Soddy

Frederick Soddy's major contribution to science was his discovery of the existence of isotopes in 1913, an accomplishment for which he was awarded the 1921 Nobel Prize in chemistry. That discovery came as the result of extensive research on the radioactive elements carried out first with British physicist **Ernest Rutherford** at McGill University and later with British chemist **Sir William Ramsay** at London University. Among Soddy's contributions during this period was his recognition of the relationship between helium gas and alpha particle emanations—the latter being the ejection of a type of nuclear particle during a radioactive transformation—as well as his enunciation of the disintegration law of radioactive elements (which states that when a substance decays, it emits a particle and is transformed into a totally new substance). Soddy's most important work was carried out while he was lecturer in physical chemistry at the University of Glasgow between 1904 and 1919. Later in life, Soddy's interests shifted to politics and economics, although he was able to make relatively little lasting impact in these fields.

Soddy was born on September 2, 1877, in Eastbourne, England. He was the seventh and last child of Benjamin Soddy and Hannah (Green) Soddy. His mother died eighteen months after his birth, and his father was a successful and prosperous corn merchant in London who was already fifty-five years of age when Frederick came into the world. Soddy's interest in science, evident from an early age, was further developed at Eastbourne College by its science master, R. E. Hughes. Hughes and Soddy coauthored a paper on the reaction between dry ammonia and dry carbon dioxide in 1894, when Soddy was only seventeen years old. Hughes encouraged Soddy to continue his education in chemistry at Oxford. Teacher and student agreed, however, that an additional year of preparation would be desirable before going on to the university, so Soddy spent a year at University College, Aberystwyth, in 1895. In that year, he won the Open Science Postmastership Scholarship, offered by Merton College, Oxford; and in 1896, he enrolled at that institution.

During his years at Merton College, Soddy published his first independent paper, on the life and work of German chemist Victor Meyer, which was received as an accomplished paper for a young undergraduate. He stood for his chemistry examination in 1898 and was awarded a First Class in the Honors School of Natural Science. One of his examiners was Sir William Ramsay, with whom he was later to collaborate in London.

Works with Rutherford at McGill and Ramsay at London

Soddy stayed on at Oxford for two years following his graduation. The chemical research he pursued during this period led to no substantial results. By 1900, however, he felt he was ready to move on and applied for a position that opened in the chemistry department at the University of Toronto. Deciding to pursue the post aggressively, Soddy traveled to Canada to make his case in person. When he failed to receive the Toronto appointment, he traveled on to Montreal, where he accepted a position as a junior demonstrator at McGill University. The McGill appointment may have been attractive both because of the superb physical facilities provided by the young institution and because of the presence of a rising young star at the university, Ernest Rutherford. In any case, Soddy's family fortune made it possible for him to accept the modest annual salary without hardship.

By the fall of 1900, Soddy and Rutherford had begun to collaborate on studies of the disintegration of radioactive elements. These studies led to a revolutionary theory of nuclear disintegration. Prior to the Soddy-Rutherford research, scientists were unclear as to what happens during nuclear decay. The most common notion was that radioactive materials give off some form of energy, such as X rays, without undergoing any fundamental change themselves. Rutherford and Soddy were able to demonstrate that the process is more substantial than previously believed and that, in the process of decaying, the composition of a radioactive substance is altered.

In 1903, Soddy returned to London. He wanted to work with Ramsay on a study of the gaseous products of radioactive decay. In his brief stay at London, the two were able to demonstrate that helium is always produced during the disintegration of radium. Five years later, Rutherford was to confirm that connection when he showed that alpha particles are doubly-charged helium nuclei.

Discovery of Isotopes Brings the Nobel Prize

In the spring of 1904, Soddy accepted an appointment as lecturer in physical chemistry at Glasgow University. Before moving to Scotland, however, he also accepted another commission, that from the extension service of London University. In this assignment, Soddy gave a series of lectures on physical chemistry and radioactivity at venues in Western Australia. At the conclusion of the tour in the fall of 1904, Soddy returned to Great Britain by way of New Zealand and the United States, to begin what was to be a ten-year tenure at Glasgow.

Soddy's work at Glasgow was primarily concerned with the chemical identification of the elements involved in the radioactive decay of uranium and radium, which was the subject of intense investigation by a number of scientists. The problem was that the disintegration of uranium and radium appeared to result in the formation of about a dozen new elements, elements that were tentatively given names such as uranium X, radium A, radium B, radium C, radium D, radium E, radium F, ionium, and mesothorium. How all these elements could be fitted into the few remaining spaces in the periodic table was entirely unclear.

By 1907, some clues to the answer to this problem had begun to appear; H. N. McCoy and W. H. Ross at the University of Chicago showed that two of the elements produced during radioactive decay, thorium and radiothorium, were chemically identical to each other. Soon, similar results were being announced for other pairs, such as ionium and radium, mesothorium and thorium K, and radium D and lead. These results were similar to those being obtained by Soddy in his own laboratory. By 1910, he began to formulate a possible explanation for the research findings. In a paper published that year, he first raised the possibility that many of the products of radioactive decay are not different from each other, but are variations of the same element. He began to develop the concept of different forms of a chemical element with identical chemical properties, but different atomic weights.

That idea came to fruition in 1913 when Soddy first proposed the term isotope for these forms of an element. Soddy's paper published in *Chemical News* summarized his views on isotopes. He wrote that "it would not be surprising if the elements . . . were mixtures of several homogeneous elements of similar but not completely identical atomic weights." It was for this hypothesis that Soddy would be awarded the 1921 Nobel Prize for chemistry.

At this time Soddy was also working on an explanation of the patterns observed during radioactive decay. In 1911, he pointed out that each time an element loses an alpha particle, it changes into a new element whose atomic number is two less than that of the original element. This generalization became known as the Displacement Law. Shortly thereafter, A. S. Russell and Kasimir Fajans independently extended that law to include beta decay, in which an element's atomic number increases by one after the loss of a beta particle. In 1914 Soddy left Glasgow to take a chair in chemistry at the University of Aberdeen. His major work there involved the determination of the atomic weight of lead extracted from the radioactive ore Ceylon thorite. He showed for the first time that the atomic weight of an element (lead, in this case) can differ significantly and consistently from its normally accepted value as published in the periodic table.

During World War I, Soddy was involved in military research for the marine subcommittee of the Board of Inventions and Research. The major part of this work involved the development of methods for extracting ethylene from coal gas.

Postwar Interests Shift to Economic and Political Topics

At the conclusion of the war, Soddy was appointed to the Lees Chair in Chemistry at Oxford University. He remained in this post until 1936. Soddy's interest in scientific research had largely dissipated by the time he reached Oxford, and he published no original research in chemistry during his seventeen years there. Instead, he showed interest in social, political, and economic issues, motivated to some extent by a feeling that progress in science had not produced or had not been accompanied by a comparable development of human civilization. He became—and remained—actively involved in a number of social and political causes, including the women's suffrage movement and the controversy over the status of Ireland.

Soddy's academic career ended in 1936 when he took early retirement from Oxford. The occasion for this decision was the unexpected death of his wife Winifred Moller (Beilby) Soddy. The couple had been married in 1908 and, although childless, had been happy together. They enjoyed traveling and spent some of their most pleasant moments in mountain climbing. Winifred's death from a coronary thrombosis was so distressing that Soddy almost immediately left Oxford.

Even after his retirement, Soddy continued to think, write, and speak about current events. He was particularly concerned with his fellow scientists who, he believed, had not demonstrated sufficient social conscience about the difficult issues their own research had brought about. Soddy died in Brighton, England, on September 22, 1956. According to one provision of his will, a trust was to be established to study social problems in various regions of the country.

Sir Alexander Fleck, Soddy's former student, colleague, and biographer, has described Soddy's personality in *Biographical Memoirs of Fellows of the Royal Society* as "complex." On the one hand, he was often kind and generous to friends and fellow workers, and could be "a live and inspiring leader" to those students he worked with in small groups. On the other hand, he seems to have been, more generally, a failure as a teacher. "His mental processes were different from those of the ordinary run of students so that the latter could not easily follow the words with which he clothed his thoughts," Fleck wrote. Soddy held very strong moralistic views on a number of issues and was not hesitant to make those views known and to defend them with vigor and little tact. Fleck observes that "he very frequently found himself in acrimonious discussions" during his tenure at Oxford, although his personal life appears to have been filled with personal happiness and many enjoyable social events.

SELECTED WRITINGS BY SODDY:

Books

Radioactivity: An Elementary Treatise from the Standpoint of the Disintegration Theory, [London], 1904.
The Interpretation of Radium, [London], 1909.
The Interpretation of the Atom, [London], 1932.

Periodicals

Chemical News, The Radio-Elements and the Periodic Law, February, 28, 1913, pp. 97–9.
Management & Human Relation in Industry, The Evil Genius of the Modern World, Volume 1, [New York], 1947.

FURTHER READING:

Books

Biographical Memoirs of Fellows of the Royal Society, Volume 3, Royal Society (London), 1957, pp. 203–16.
Farber, Eduard, editor, *Great Chemists,* Interscience, 1961, pp. 1463–468.
Howorth, Muriel, *Atomic Transmutation: Memoirs of Professor Frederick Soddy,* [London], 1953.
Howorth, Muriel, *Pioneer Research on the Atom,* [London], 1958.
Trenn, T. J., *The Self-Splitting Atom,* [New York], 1977.

Periodicals

Kent, A., *Proceedings of the Chemical Society,* Frederick Soddy, November, 1963, pp. 327–30.
Paneth, F., *Nature,* A Tribute to Frederick Soddy, Volume 180, 1957, pp. 1085–087.
Russell, Alexander S., *Science,* F. Soddy, Interpreter of Atomic Structure, Volume 124, 1956.

Sketch by David E. Newton

Halvor Solberg
1895–1974
Norwegian meteorologist

Halvor Solberg, one of the original members of the pioneering meteorology group formed in Bergen, Norway, during the early twentieth century, made seminal analytical and mathematical contributions to early modern dynamic meteorology research. Solberg's research on cyclonic systems and his discovery of the polar frontal boundary greatly advanced modern meteorology and weather forecasting. For his contributions to this field, Solberg received the Fridtjof Nansen Award from the Norwegian Academy of Science and Medicine in 1937.

Halvor Skappel Solberg was born in the district of Rinsaker, south of Lillehammer, Norway, in 1895. The son of farmer Petter Julius Solberg and Johanne Skappel, Solberg graduated from high school in 1912 and then attended the University of Kristiania (now the University of Oslo). While working for his bachelor's degree, which he received in 1916, Solberg also served as an assistant to the Norwegian mathematician and geophysicist **Fredrik Sto.** That same year, on a trip to Leipzig, Germany, Solberg became acquainted with **Jacob Bjerknes**, son of the Norwegian theoretical physicist and geophysicist **Vilhelm Bjerknes**. In 1912 the elder Bjerknes had been offered the directorship of a new geophysical institute at the University of Leipzig, to validate his theories of dynamic meteorology with surface data analysis. But when Vilhelm Bjerknes lost two young collaborators—Theodor Hesselberg, who went to the Norwegian Meteorological Institute, and Harald Ulrik Sverdrup, who had been offered a chief scientist position with Roald Amundsen's North Pole voyage for 1918—he turned to Norwegian scientists to fill these positions. He hired Johan Holtsmark, Solberg, and later, his own son Jacob. By late 1917, however, conditions at Leipzig had become untenable due to World War I, and Bjerknes accepted the opportunity to start a geophysical institute at the new University of Bergen, taking his assistants with him. Solberg and Jacob Bjerknes had already embarked on the task of promoting the elder Bjerknes' new dynamic meteorological theories and weather forecasting applications, and they carried on this research even after the move back to Norway. Further research was started in February of 1918, and by June 26, 1918, Solberg and the Bjerkneses had inaugurated the first experimental weather service for western Norway at Bergen as part of the new geophysical institute. By July, Solberg was asked by Bjerknes to head an extension office in Kristiania (Oslo) to serve eastern Norway. A year later, in 1919, the Western Norwegian Weather Bureau at Bergen was officially recognized as a division of the Norwegian Meteorological Institute in Kristiania.

Exporting the Bergen meteorological approach to research centers abroad had been planned as essential to sustaining the support of the Norwegian government. Armed with Vilhelm Bjerknes' theory and practical application agenda, Solberg and Jacob began the important task of disseminating the research to meteorologically competitive Sweden, where the Bergen ideas were initially criticized. Nevertheless, Solberg and Jacob recruited young Swedes, for the foresighted Vilhelm Bjerknes looked to younger collaborators and their interest in independent research to provide loyal and enthusiastic support. They enlisted four young scientists to collaborate with them on the research—two of the Swedes, **Carl-Gustaf Rossby** and Tor Bergeron, along with Solberg and Jacob, would become long-term members of the team that further developed Bjerknes' dynamic meteorology.

Discovers the Cyclone Life Cycle and the Polar Front

Beginning in 1919, when Jacob Bjerknes published a paper on the structure of moving cyclones or the extratropical cyclone model, the research at Bergen centered on further defining airmass dynamics. Solberg contributed an acute mathematical insight to the project, as well as a gift for close analysis. In studying weather data plotted on surface maps, he noticed that, as a cyclone's wave-like "squall line" (the convergent cloud boundary which seemed to define major precipitation patterns from north to south) dissipates to the east, it generates a new wave back westward along that boundary. The configuration usually totaled four waves in all, the last leading to an outbreak of cold air southward. Solberg realized that this sequence generation of a "cyclone family," as he called it, refined the understanding of the extratropical cyclone life cycle.

Solberg, Jacob Bjerknes, and their colleagues also further described the polar temperature homogeneity to the north of the boundary line that separates the polar easterly winds from the warmer westerlies and along which the cyclone and its weather develops. They theorized that this polar demarcation delineates the potential sources for wave-like perturbations that become unstable in amplitude as warm air (called a "warm tongue") crosses the boundary and generates the extratropical cyclone phenomenon. They christened this boundary over which periodic cold air and weather invades the mid-latitudes the "polar front" and

conjectured that it generally extends across an entire hemisphere.

Solberg himself took on the task of proving that the polar frontal boundary physically exists. This entailed an exhaustively detailed analysis of surface maps, particularly those plotted for North America and the North Atlantic Ocean. Basing his work on the dense surface maps prepared by another Bergen recruit, Ernst Calwagen, Solberg had finished his basic analysis by early 1920. He defined four prominent polar frontal boundaries or "leaves," rather than the continuous boundary that Vilhelm Bjerknes had originally envisioned. These findings further modified the original extratropical cyclone model. In addition, Solberg and the elder Bjerknes set about a further expansion of the Bergen mathematical formulas used in weather forecasting, to reflect further insight into the polar front.

Though the polar front was not continuously hemispheric, the theory now provided a global basis for the cyclone model, described circulation of the atmosphere in general, and justified international cooperation in a network of stations for weather analysis and forecasting. The Bergen group began to disseminate the polar front theory, sending Rossby to Sweden and Solberg to Paris. Subsequent research was focused on developing a more subtle understanding of conditions contributing to frontal development and local unstable weather. Solberg and Jacob Bjerknes studied shower activity and its migration independent of frontal weather. The research on rain was aimed at perfecting daily forecasting for commercial aviation, and focused on humidity content, instability, and variation in moisture and temperature rather than the larger-scale pressure distribution. These more sophisticated studies of the lower three-dimensional atmosphere led Solberg and Jacob Bjerknes to detailed local airmass dynamics theory. They studied, for example, the cooling processes of air by radiation, induction, mixing, and the expansion and rise of air into the atmosphere. These ideas were published in their joint paper "Meteorological Conditions for the Formation of Rain." The classic paper Solberg coauthored with Jacob Bjerknes on cyclone life cycles, "The Life Cycle of Cyclones and the Polar Front Theory of Atmospheric Circulation," appeared a year later.

Develops Mathematics for Unstable Atmospheric Waves

By concentrating on surface and lower-level atmospheric conditions in regard to frontal analysis, the Bergen meteorologists successfully promoted the practical viability of the polar front theory. In doing so, they ensured the survival of the Geophysical Institute and the Weather Service of Bergen with commercial, government, and international cooperation. Amid his atmospheric research, Solberg continued his studies in mathematics and hydrodynamics, first at the universities of Paris and Göttingen (Germany) between 1921 and 1927. He then returned to the University of Oslo, working as a doctoral assistant to his mentor, Vilhelm Bjerknes. Solberg finished several projects, including a study of photographic techniques to determine upper atmospheric cloud height during the night (1925), but most importantly his 1928 paper on the integration of atmospheric first-order equations with the mathematics of the extratropical cyclone and polar front theories.

The initial conditions of the base model from which Solberg, a brilliant mathematician, derived his equations of this problem consisted of two fluid layers moving zonally (horizontally) on a rotating earth but with different velocities and separated by a sloping surface of discontinuity that is analogous to the frontal surface. He found solutions of integrated velocity equations for all possible waves. Most significantly, two unstable wave solutions were for a short wave (now called the Kelvin-Helmholtz Wave) and a longer period wave (1000 kilometers from crest to crest). The longer wave was indeed the cyclone wave (actually about 1000–2000 km), which Solberg and Jacob Bjerknes had analyzed in their 1922 paper. Though the complexity of Solberg's formulas made them difficult to use for many scientists, his findings were used most importantly by Jacob Bjerknes and Jörgen Holmboe in their 1944 paper on cyclone wave development coupled with an inducive upper level wave.

The publication of Solberg's classic wave equations paper in 1928 coincided with the completion of his Ph.D. Admitted to the Norwegian Science Academy in Oslo, he accepted a professorship in theoretical meteorology at the University of Oslo in 1930. His cooperative research included association with the Rockefeller Foundation in 1931 and chairing the Norwegian Geophysical Research Committee (1937–1938). In 1933 he coauthored, with the Bjerkneses and Bergeron, a book on Vilhelm Bjerknes' physical hydrodynamics with applications to dynamic meteorology. His interest in the further discovery of processes of the developing extratropical cyclone was reflected in his 1936 paper on the inertial and stable states of the atmosphere. Between 1942 and 1945, Solberg was a member of the Faculty of Mathematics and Natural Sciences at Oslo. He served as general secretary of the Norwegian Science Academy from 1946 to 1953, and then as vice president of the International Council of Science Unions from 1949 to 1955. He was also called upon to chair Norwegian national committees on mechanics and geophysics/geodetics research. Solberg remained at the University of Oslo until his retirement in 1964. Solberg had married Ingeborg Germeten in 1931, but they divorced in 1943. They had two daughters. Solberg died of an undisclosed illness at Oslo on January 31, 1974.

SELECTED WRITINGS BY SOLBERG:

Books

Physikalische Hydrodynamik mit Anwendung auf die dynamische Meteorologie, Verlag Springer (Berlin), 1933.

Periodicals

Geofysiske Publikasjoner, Meteorological Conditions for the Formation of Rain, Volume 2, no. 3, 1921.
Geofysiske Publikasjoner, The Life Cycle of Cyclones and the Polar Front Theory of Atmospheric Circulation, Volume 3, no. 1, 1922.
Geofysiske Publikasjoner, Integrationen der Atmosphärischen Störungsgleichungen, Volume 5, no. 9, 1928.

FURTHER READING:

Books

Byers, Horace R., *General Meteorology,* McGraw-Hill, 1959.
Friedman, Robert Marc, *Appropriating the Weather: Vilhelm Bjerknes and the Construction of a Modern Meteorology,* Cornell University Press, 1989.
Wurtele, Morton G., *Selected Papers of Jacob Aall Bonnevie Bjerknes,* Western Periodicals Co., 1975.

Other

Bjerknes, Hedvig Borthen, *Interview with William J. McPeak,* conducted October 30, 1993.

Sketch by William J. McPeak

Susan Solomon
1956–
American atmospheric chemist

Susan Solomon has achieved recognition for her key role in the discovery of the cause of a major threat to the earth—the loss of the protective ozone layer in the upper atmosphere. Ozone protects all life on earth from large amounts of damaging ultraviolet radiation from the sun. Solomon, an atmospheric chemist, was first to propose the theory explaining how chlorofluorocarbons, gases used in refrigerators and to power aerosol spray cans, could in some places on the globe lead to ozone destruction in the presence of stratospheric clouds.

Solomon has said (in an interview with Lee Katterman) that she recalls "exactly what got me first interested in science. It was the airing of **Jacques Cousteau** on American TV when I was nine or ten years old." Solomon said that as a child she was very interested in watching natural history programming on television. This sparked an interest in science, particularly biology. "But I learned that biology was not very quantitative," said Solomon in the

Susan Solomon

interview. By the time she entered the Illinois Institute of Technology, Solomon met her need for quantitative study by choosing chemistry as her major. A project during Solomon's senior year turned her attention toward atmospheric chemistry. The project called for measuring the reaction of ethylene and the hydroxyl radical, a process that occurs in the atmosphere of Jupiter. As a result of this work, Solomon did some extra reading about planetary atmospheres, which led her to focus on atmospheric chemistry.

During the summer of 1977, just before entering graduate school at University of California at Berkeley, Solomon worked at the National Center for Atmospheric Research (NCAR) in Boulder, Colorado. She met research scientist Paul Crutzen at NCAR, who introduced her to the study of ozone in the upper atmosphere. In the fall at Berkeley, Solomon sought out **Harold Johnston**, a chemistry professor who had done pioneering work on the effects of the supersonic transport (SST) on the atmosphere. Solomon credits Crutzen and Johnston for encouraging her interest in atmospheric chemistry. After completing the course work toward her Ph.D. in chemistry at Berkeley, Solomon moved to NCAR to do her thesis research with Crutzen.

Solomon received a Ph.D. in chemistry in 1981 and then accepted a research position at the National Oceanic and Atmospheric Administration (NOAA) Aeronomy Laboratory in Boulder, Colorado. Initially, Solomon's research focused on developing computer models of ozone in the upper atmosphere. Ozone is a highly reactive molecule

composed of three atoms of oxygen. By comparison, the oxygen that is essential to the metabolism of living things is a relatively stable combination of two oxygen atoms. In the upper atmosphere between about 32,000 and 100,000 feet altitude, a layer of ozone exists that absorbs much of the sun's deadly ultraviolet radiation, thereby protecting all life on earth.

Sets New Career Course with Antarctic Trip

In 1985 scientists first reported that the density of the ozone layer over Antarctica had been decreasing rapidly during the months of spring in the Southern Hemisphere (September and October) in recent years. The cause of this "hole" in the ozone layer was unknown and many scientists began to look for its cause. In 1986 the scientific community wanted to send some equipment to Antarctica to measure atmospheric levels of ozone and nitrogen dioxide. Much to the surprise of her scientific colleagues, Solomon volunteered to travel to Antarctica to get the needed measurements; until then, she had concentrated on theoretical studies, but the chance to understand the cause of the ozone hole prompted Solomon to take up experimental work. Solomon led an expedition to Antarctica during August, September, and October of 1986, where she and coworkers measured the amounts of several atmospheric components, including the amount of chlorine dioxide in the upper atmosphere. The level of this atmospheric chemical was much higher than anyone expected and provided an important clue in determining why the ozone hole had appeared. Back at her NOAA lab in Boulder, Solomon wrote a research article that provided a theoretical explanation for the ozone hole. Solomon showed how the high level of chlorine dioxide was consistent with fast chemical destruction of ozone triggered by reactions occurring on stratospheric clouds. The extra chlorine dioxide was derived from chlorofluorocarbons released into the atmosphere from sources such as foams and leaking refrigeration equipment. Solomon returned to Antarctica for more measurements in August of 1987. Her explanation for the cause of the ozone hole is now generally accepted by scientists, and has led many countries of the world to curtail the production and use of chlorofluorocarbons.

Solomon's scientific studies to uncover the likely cause of the ozone hole have led to public recognition and many awards. In 1989 Solomon received the gold medal for exceptional service from the U.S. Department of Commerce (the agency that oversees the NOAA). She has testified several times before congressional committees about ozone depletion and is increasingly sought out as an expert on ozone science and policy (although the latter role is one she does not welcome, Solomon admitted in her interview, since she considers herself a scientist and not a policy expert).

Solomon was born on January 19, 1956, in Chicago, Illinois. Her father, Leonard Solomon, was an insurance agent. Susan's mother, Alice Rutman Solomon, was a fourth-grade teacher in the Chicago public schools. She has one brother, Joel. She married Barry Lane Sidwell on

September 20, 1988, and has a stepson by the marriage. She continues to study the atmospheric chemistry of ozone and has added Arctic ozone levels to her research subjects.

In 1994, an Antarctic glacier was named in her honor in recognition her contributions to explaining the cause of the Antarctic ozone hole. She has also been the recipient of the J.B. MacElwane award of the American Geophysical Union, the Department of Commerce Gold Medal for Exceptional Service, the Ozone Award from the United Nations Environment Programme, and the 1999 Carl-Gustaf Rossby Award from the American Meteorological Society. She is a member of the National Academy of Sciences, a foreign associate of the French Academy of Sciences, and a foreign member of the Academia Europaea.

In 1999 Solomon was awarded the National Medal of Science, the nation's highest scientific honor. In accepting the award, she became the first National Oceanic and Atmospheric Administration scientist to be awarded the prize. In announcing the award, U.S. Secretary of Commerce William M. Daley stated that "Solomon has been one of the most important and influential researchers in atmospheric science during the past 15 years. Her work to unravel the mysteries of the Antarctic ozone hole is an example of the important role played by government scientists in figuring out the answers to the larger picture of global change."

SELECTED WRITINGS BY SOLOMON:

Books

Aeronomy of the Middle Atmosphere: Chemistry and Physics of the Stratosphere and Mesosphere, second edition, Reidel, 1986.

Periodicals

Nature, On Depletion of Antarctic Ozone, June 19, 1986, pp. 755–58.
Nature, Progress towards a Quantitative Understanding of Antarctic Ozone Depletion, September 27, 1990, pp. 347–54.

FURTHER READING:

Periodicals

Bylinsky, Gene, *Fortune,* America's Hot Young Scientists, October 8, 1990, p. 56.
Glanz, James, *R & D,* How Susan Solomon's Research Changed Our View of Earth, September, 1992, p. 46.

Other

Solomon, Susan, *Interview with Lee Katterman,* conducted December 14, 1993.

Sketch by Lee Katterman

Arnold Sommerfeld
1868–1951
German theoretical physicist

Arnold Sommerfeld is remembered for his immense contribution to various aspects of quantum physics; he was one of the first physicists to recognize the genius of **Albert Einstein**'s theory of relativity, which he later worked to refine along with Danish theorist **Niels Bohr**'s theory of atomic structure. Sommerfeld is also celebrated as a great teacher and a firm believer in physics as a collaborative enterprise whose practitioners should work together to further the frontiers of the field rather than work in competition with each other.

Arnold Johannes Wilhelm Sommerfeld was born in Königsberg, East Prussia, on December 5, 1868, the son of a doctor. He was educated at the University of Königsberg, from which he received his doctorate in 1891. In his thesis, Sommerfeld applied the theory of functions of a complex variable to boundary-value problems, initiating a topic of study that would later yield his most valuable work.

From 1895 to 1897, he lectured at the University of Göttingen in Germany, then transferred to the Bergakademie in Clausthal. There, he drew upon his experience with boundary-value problems in studying the movement of electromagnetic waves and the diffraction of X rays. He also began work with fellow German physicist **Felix Klein** on their *Theorie des Kreisels* (*Theory of Crystals*), which was published in a series of volumes between 1897 and 1910. Sommerfeld remained at Clausthal until 1900, teaching and continuing his work in atomic physics; he then moved to the Technische Hochschule of Aachen, where he assumed a teaching position and began collaborative investigations with a number of his colleagues on the hydrodynamics of viscous fluids. Their goal was to explain the onset of turbulence in fluids and to develop a theory of the lubrication of machines. The result was a series of papers on the general dynamics of electrons published in 1904 and 1905 which cemented Sommerfeld's reputation as one of Germany's most important theoretical physicists.

In 1906 Sommerfeld left Aachen for the University of Munich to take up its chair of theoretical physics. He would remain there for the rest of his career. At Munich, his work took a new direction as he immersed himself in the study of X rays and gamma rays. It was also in 1906 that Sommerfeld first heard of Einstein's theory of relativity. He immediately recognized its genius and was one the first physicists to do so. In 1907 he issued a vigorous defense of the theory. He also applied Einstein's theory to his own studies of electron deceleration.

Another instance of Sommerfeld's building upon and improving other physicists' work occurred in 1914. After Bohr published a paper on the constitution of atoms and molecules in 1913, Sommerfeld worked on applying Bohr's model of the atom to the splitting of spectral lines emitted in a magnetic field known as the Zeeman effect. Sommerfeld became one of the great champions of Bohr's atomic theory after overcoming his initial skepticism, to the extent that he devoted a good deal of his energies to promoting it and refining it. He and Bohr developed a close working and personal relationship and were in frequent contact by letter, exchanging ideas and critiquing each other's work.

Reworks Bohr's Atomic Theory

In 1915 Sommerfeld turned his full attention to Bohr's atomic theory, and set about reconfiguring it into a more formal structure. Bohr, in turn, improved Sommerfeld's approach. In 1916 Sommerfeld further modified Bohr's theory by suggesting that the electrons, which Bohr believed to move about an atom's central core or nucleus in circular orbits, actually moved in elliptical orbits. He took note of the relativistic increase in the mass of the electron as it sped about the nucleus, which led him to introduce a second quantum number, the azimuthal quantum number (l), in addition to that introduced by Bohr (n). This breakthrough allowed for an explanation of atomic spectral lines, which Bohr's model alone had been unable to satisfactorily explain and culminated in a quantum theory of the normal Zeeman effect. Sommerfeld's improvements upon Bohr's theory, in addition to his vigorous support for it, contributed to its rapid and widespread acceptance in the international physics community. Bohr was grateful for the support, and the two continued to refine the theory. Their joint efforts finally led to Bohr's second atomic theory (the theory of the periodic tables of the elements), known as the Bohr-Sommerfeld atomic theory.

Takes Reins of German Physical Society

In 1918 Sommerfeld was confronted with a new challenge and one for which he had had no formal training. He was elected presiding officer of the German Physical Society—the first person outside Berlin to be granted such an honor. Although gratified, Sommerfeld quickly realized the enormity of the burden he had undertaken. The group was riven with internecine strife and Sommerfeld's task of reconciliation was complicated by special interests and divided goals. At the society's inception in 1845, membership included scientists of every concentration, but by the turn of the century its bias was toward pure science. Although the task was daunting, Sommerfeld worked hard to restore peace and common purpose to the society and to build bridges between its various members, and was an amiable and much-liked leader.

In 1918 Sommerfeld was also preoccupied with applying the Bohr-Sommerfeld atomic theory to the analysis of X-ray spectra and the splitting of hydrogen spectral lines in the presence of an electric field. In 1919 Sommerfeld published an atomic physics textbook, *Atomic Structure and Spectral Lines,* which quickly established itself as the definitive text. In its preface he betrayed his passion for his subject, writing, "Today, when we listen to the language of spectra, we hear a true atomic music of the spheres." It was Sommerfeld, an amateur pianist of no mean ability, who wryly noted of the spectra of the hydrogen atom [which emits over one hundred different frequencies] that it appeared to be more complicated than a grand piano, which emits only eighty-eight.

For all the insight into atomic structure that the Bohr-Sommerfeld theory provided, it could not explain all the phenomena that confounded physicists grappling with the new quantum physics. For example, it failed to explain the optical and much of the X-ray radiations of atoms with more than one outer electron. Such atoms, when subjected to an external magnetic field, emit complex spectra. Some atomic physicists, including the German theoretician Alfred Lande, explained this as being due to some sort of magnetic coupling of the atoms, although Sommerfeld himself explained it in terms of the theory of relativity.

During Germany's Weimar years, Sommerfeld was one of the country's leading atomic physicists. His work on quantum theory brought him renown, but no less noteworthy was his record as an educator. He had a true vocation as a teacher and attracted Germany's leading young physicists to his school. He turned out a record number of doctorates and no fewer than four Nobel Prize winners. Among his star pupils was **Werner Heisenberg**, who later identified Sommerfeld's unflagging pursuit of explanations for mysterious phenomena as one of three influences from which his quantum mechanics resulted. During the 1920s, Sommerfeld was a frequent visitor to the United States, where he taught at the University of California at Berkeley. During one such visit, he revealed the key to success as a physicist: "If you want to be a physicist, you must do three things—first, study mathematics, second, study more mathematics, and third, do the same."

With the rise to power of the National Socialists in 1933, many Jewish physicists were undermined and forced to leave their posts. Sommerfeld was an ardent defender of the Jews and spoke out against the Nazi regime; his reputation as a teacher was such that his word in academic appointments carried a great deal of weight, and he did not hesitate to recommend his Jewish colleagues for academic appointments or promotions. As a result of his influence, many Jewish physicists were able to maintain their positions, at least in the short-term. Sommerfeld appeared not to be personally threatened by the Nazis. He continued to be staunchly opposed to National Socialism and especially to the movement's leader, Adolf Hitler. By 1940, however, Sommerfeld was finally denounced by the government and forced to retire.

Sommerfeld died on April 26, 1951, after being struck by a car while strolling with his grandchildren one afternoon in Munich. Victor Guillemin, writing in *The Story of Quantum Mechanics,* summarized Sommerfeld's view of the role of the scientist: "Sommerfeld, in common with many other scientists, felt that there is an intolerable arrogance in the thought of 'prescribing' to nature. Rather, scientists in a spirit of humility should hope that through unremitting labors they might achieve some small comprehension of her wonders."

SELECTED WRITINGS BY SOMMERFELD:

Books

Theorie des Kreisels, (Theory of Crystals), 1897–1910.

Atombau und Spektrallinien, (Atomic Structure and Spectral Lines), 1919, 3rd edition, [New York], 1923.

Lectures on Theoretical Physics, Academic Press, 1949–1956.

FURTHER READING:

Books

Beyerchen, Alan D., *Scientists under Hitler: Politics and the Physics Community in the Third Reich,* Yale University Press, 1977.

French, A. P., and P. J. Kennedy, editors, *Niels Bohr: A Centenary Volume,* Harvard University Press, 1985.

Guillemin, Victor, *The Story of Quantum Mechanics,* Scribner, 1968.

Heilbron, John L., *The Dilemmas of an Upright Man: Max Planck as Spokesman for German Science,* University of California Press, 1986.

Kevles, Daniel J., *The Physicists: The History of a Scientific Community in Modern America,* Harvard University Press, 1987.

Periodicals

Haldane, J. B. S., *Forum,* Nationality and Research, May, 1926, p. 720.

Harmon, L. R., *Physics Today,* Physics Ph.D.'s: Whence, Whither, When?, October, 1962, p. 21.

Heilbron, John L., *Isis,* The Kossel-Sommerfeld Theory and the Ring Atom, winter, 1987, pp. 451–85.

Sketch by Avril McDonald

Duncan McLaren Young Sommerville
1879–1934
Scottish mathematician

Duncan McLaren Young Sommerville made important contributions to Euclidean and non-euclidean geometry as a teacher and as a researcher. His research into tesselations, the study of how geometric shapes fit together

to fill a plane, led to new understanding of crystallography. In 1934, H. W. Turnbull called him the leading geometer of Scotland.

Duncan McLaren Young Sommerville was born in Beawar, Rajasthan, India, on November 24, 1879, the son of Reverend James Sommerville. He was educated in Scotland, where he attended Perth Academy and the University of St. Andrews. There he was awarded a Ramsay Scholarship in 1899 and a Bruce Scholarship the following year. His major field of study was geometry but he was interested in other sciences as well, including anatomy and chemistry.

Sommerville's first published research paper, entitled "Networks of the Plane in Absolute Geometry," appeared in 1905 in the *Proceedings of the Royal Society of Edinburgh.* That same year he became a lecturer in the mathematics department at St. Andrews. At the college, according to Turnbull, he won the admiration of his colleagues and pupils for his teaching and for his scholarly and unobtrusive manner. He also investigated branches of geometry other than the Euclidean system, publishing several research papers. In 1911, he published the 400-page *Bibliography of Non-Euclidean Geometry,* which included a bibliography of *n*-dimensional geometry as well. In 1911 and 1912 he served as president of the Edinburgh Mathematical Society. He married Louisa Agnes Beveridge, of Belfast, Ireland, in 1912.

In 1915 Sommerville accepted a position as professor of pure and applied mathematics at Victoria College, Wellington, New Zealand. Students saw him as an outwardly shy person, but they appreciated the time and effort he devoted to his teaching. At one point, the students at the University of Otago in New Zealand were temporarily without a mathematics professor; Sommerville helped to fill the gap through weekly correspondence with the students.

Explored Non-Euclidean Geometries

Sommerville's first book, on non-euclidean geometry, appeared at a time when few people knew about systems other than Euclid's. Euclidean geometry assumes that, given a straight line and a point not on the line, there is only one line that passes through the point and is parallel to the first line. From this basic assumption, many of the concepts in high school geometry books can be shown to follow. However, if this basic assumption (the "parallel postulate") is not made, the conclusions that follow will be quite different. If, for example, it is assumed that there is no parallel line that passes through the point, the resulting system is elliptic geometry. On the other hand, if it is assumed that there is more than one parallel line through the point, the resulting geometry is hyperbolic. Sommerville and others studied these non-euclidean geometries and their relationships to Euclidean geometry.

Tesselations and crystallography also interested Sommerville. He studied how geometric shapes fit together in a mosaic-like pattern to cover a flat surface, such as a bathroom floor covered with tiles. He found that a

Euclidean plane can be covered with a regular pattern of identical tiles in the shape of squares, or equilateral triangles, or regular hexagons; other shapes, such as regular pentagons, will leave gaps. He then investigated the ways that planes could be covered in non-euclidean geometries. Although the Euclidean plane could be successfully covered by only three different mosaics of regular polygons, an elliptic plane could be covered by mosaics of five regular polygons; and for the hyperbolic plane, there was an infinite number of such patterns. He found that, for each type of plane, there were more possibilities if combinations of different kinds of regular polygons were allowed.

Sommerville asked similar questions about how three-dimensional space can be filled with cubes and other polyhedrons, as in honeycombs. He went on to draw generalizations about spaces with four, five, or more dimensions—in both Euclidean and non-euclidean systems. Decades later, other geometers such as **Roger Penrose** continued the study of tiling patterns. The work of Sommerville and his successors influenced the approach taken by scientists to the study of the formation of crystals and the development of new ceramic materials.

Most of Sommerville's more than thirty papers dealt with his study of geometry. In other research, he drew connections between his geometric concepts and group theory, analyzed preferential voting in terms of geometric concepts, and developed an original analysis of the musical scale. Two of his early papers dealt with statistical issues related to research in biometrics by **Karl Pearson**. Sommerville wrote four textbooks. The first, *Elements of Non-Euclidean Geometry,* was published in 1914. It was followed by *Analytical Conics* in 1924, *An Introduction to the Geometry of n Dimensions* in 1929, and *Analytical Geometry of Three Dimensions* in 1934.

At the meeting of the Australasian Association for the Advancement of Science in 1924 in Adelaide, Sommerville presided over the mathematics section. He became interested in astronomy and was one of the founders of the New Zealand Astronomical Society, serving as its first secretary. He was skilled in making models, and he made watercolor paintings of New Zealand outdoor scenes. Sommerville died on January 31, 1934, in Wellington, New Zealand.

SELECTED WRITINGS BY SOMMERVILLE:

Books

Bibliography of Non-Euclidean Geometry, London, 1911.
Elements of Non-Euclidean Geometry, London, 1914 and 1919.
Analytical Conics, London, 1924.
An Introduction to the Geometry of n Dimensions, London, 1929.
Analytical Geometry of Three Dimensions, Cambridge, 1934.

Periodicals

Proceedings of the Royal Society of Edinburgh, Networks of the Plane in Absolute Geometry, 1905, pp. 392–94.

FURTHER READING:

Periodicals

Turnbull, H. W., *Proceedings of the Edinburgh Mathematical Society,* Professor D. M. Y. Sommerville, series 2, Volume 6, part 1, March, 1934, pp. 57–60.

Sketch by C. D. Lord

Charles E. Sorensen
1881–1968
American engineer

Charles E. Sorensen was a founder of the automobile industry in the United States. During his forty years at the Ford Motor Company, he helped develop the Model T and played a central role in the development of mass production. An architect of the world's first moving, fully mechanized assembly line, Sorensen was widely considered a master of production techniques, and he was an innovator in manufacturing methods for airplanes during World War II.

Sorensen was born on September 7, 1881 to Soren and Eva Abrahamsen Sorensen in Copenhagen, Denmark. He was the oldest of four children. His father had descended from a long line of Danish farmers and he worked with wood, fashioning models of household furnishings. When Sorensen was four, he and his mother moved to the United States to join his father, who had arrived a year and a half earlier. Sorensen's formal education ended at age sixteen and at seventeen he became an apprentice in a pattern shop, making wooden molds for metal castings. By the next year, he had become the foreman of a pattern shop. The family then moved to Detroit, where he began his career in the automobile industry.

In 1902 Sorensen was introduced to **Henry Ford**, who was at that time a local race-car driver. Ford and his partner were designing two race cars, for which Sorensen's employer made patterns. They kept in contact with each other during the next few years. When Sorensen quit a job as a traveling salesman, he turned in his accounts to a bookkeeper named Helen Mitchell; he married her in June of 1904. Their son Clifford was born about a year later. In

1905 Sorensen joined Ford Motor Company as a pattern maker. He was soon working closely with Ford, listening to his ideas, creating sketches, and building rough models. Ford soon put him in charge of the pattern-making department and the foundry.

Develops Mass Production for the Model T

Ford had developed a handful of automobiles, but his dream was to create an inexpensive car for the masses. This required him to find methods of keeping his production costs very low. Sorensen was one of the handful of men who helped Ford develop his dream of an affordable car. During the winter of 1906 to 1907, Ford asked him to build a private room that became the birthplace of the Model T. During the years of the Model T's secret development, Sorensen helped create many automotive innovations, such as the use of the new vanadium steel and a new transmission.

By 1908, Sorensen was the assistant plant superintendent in charge of all production development. His responsibilities included coordinating the movement of parts to assembly areas for Ford's Model N cars. He considered handling the numerous parts of a car harder than assembling the car itself. He saw the inefficient methods in use at the time as barriers to increasing production and lowering costs. This pushed him to search for a simpler and faster production technique, and he first tested the idea of a fully synchronized flow of car parts in 1908. After planning the experiment for several weeks, Sorensen and a few helpers pulled a Model N chassis past car parts and subassemblies, which were quickly attached to the moving chassis. Sorensen showed the experiment to Ford who, according to Sorensen, was skeptical of the idea but encouraged Sorensen to continue his experiments.

Sorensen was not able to implement his idea fully for five years, primarily because Ford's Piquette Avenue plant was too small to house a moving assembly line. The enormous success of the Model T, however, helped Sorensen develop mass production; Ford now had the capital to build a larger assembly plant to meet the demand for his affordable car, and Sorensen designed most of the layout of the new Highland Park factory, which opened in 1910. Special tools and machines were designed and built for faster and more efficient parts manufacturing, and he used overhead conveyer systems to improve the movement of car subassemblies within the factory. Sorensen hired Clarence Avery to design the precise flow of parts needed to synchronize the assembly of a car. In 1913, the moving assembly line was added to Sorensen's production facility and the world's first mass production assembly plant was in operation. The result was an orderly flow of parts to subassembly operations and then to final assembly. Sorensen's efforts shortened the time to assemble a car chassis from over twelve hours to less than two. While both Ford and Sorensen later claimed to be the father of mass production, it is clearly the most famous of Sorensen's many contributions to the automotive industry, regardless of who first thought of the concept.

Contributes to War Effort during Both World Wars

Sorensen also helped Ford contribute to the World War I effort. The British government needed to increase their production of tractors, and in 1917 Sorensen and his assistants were "loaned" to them to help. British factories were too busy manufacturing munitions to produce the tractors, and Sorensen agreed to produce 5,000 tractors at fifty dollars over cost with the first shipments in just sixty days. He rushed back to Detroit to prepare facilities to build the tractors. True to his word, the first tractors were delivered on time and the entire order was completed in less than three months.

Sorensen had great loyalty to Ford and was uniquely able to maintain good relations with him, and these factors increased his influence within the company. Ford made him chief of production, manager of his enormous production facilities. Sorensen's temper could be fierce and many considered his methods domineering, even ruthless and tyrannical. But, as the *New York Times* observed in his obituary, "his judgment was unusually sound and he got spectacular results."

Sorensen played a major role in the production of B–24 bombers for World War II. In what he considered to be the greatest challenge of his career, Sorensen designed a plant to produce a B–24 every hour, at a time when they were being produced at a rate of only one plane a day. It was the first application of mass production to aircraft construction. Sorensen had difficulty persuading the designers of the aircraft to use his ideas, but the Ford Willow Run plant opened November 15, 1941. The assembly line was a mile long and the building a quarter-of-a-mile wide. President and Mrs. Roosevelt toured the factory soon after it opened, riding right down the center of the plant on the assembly line, stopping as Sorensen explained the bomber's assembly. One historian later questioned whether the United States could have defended itself in World War II without the mass production techniques that Sorensen helped develop.

In July of 1941, Sorensen was elected executive vice president of Ford Motor Company, but the war and changes within the Ford family made leading the company exceptionally difficult. The aging Ford resisted giving up control of the company despite his reduced leadership abilities, and politicians discussed nationalizing the company for the war effort. Harry Bennett, who had gained great favor in Ford's eyes, sought control of the company for himself. Sorensen was extensively involved in the fight for control of the company, but he was forced to resign in 1944, after Henry Ford II became president of the firm. Sorensen turned down several offers of government assignments to serve for a short time as president of Willys-Overland, a competing automobile company. He retired soon after to his home in Miami Beach, Florida and wrote his autobiography. His wife Helen died in 1959 and Sorensen subsequently married

Edith Montgomery. On August 13, 1968, he died at his summer home in Bethesda, Maryland, after a prolonged illness.

SELECTED WRITINGS BY SORENSEN:

Books

My Forty Years with Ford, Norton, 1956.

FURTHER READING:

Books

Crabb, Richard, *Birth of a Giant,* Chilton, 1969.

Ford, Henry, and Samuel Crowther, *My Life and Work,* Doubleday, 1925.

Herndon, Booton, *Ford: An Unconventional Biography of the Men and their Times,* Weybright and Talley, 1969.

Nevins, Allan, *Ford: The Times, the Man the Company,* Scribner, 1954.

Nevins, Allan, and Frank Ernest Hill, *Ford: Decline and Rebirth, 1933–1962,* Scribner, 1963.

Rae, John B., *American Automobile Manufacturers, The First Forty Years,* Chilton, 1959.

Sward, Keith, *The Legend of Henry Ford,* Rinehart, 1948.

Periodicals

Sward, Keith, *New York Times,* August 14, 1968.

Sketch by David N. Ford

Søren Peter Lauritz Sørensen
1868–1939
Danish chemist

The pH scale, invented by Søren Peter Lauritz Sørensensen, "has become so much a part of scientific literature and its influence so important a factor in considering biological problems that one wonders how theories of acidity and alkalinity were ever formulated without a knowledge of Sørensen's fundamental conceptions," A. J. Curtin Cosbie commented in *Nature.* Potential of hydrogen, or pH, is a simplified measure of the acidity of any given mixture. Though of immense value to scientist and layman alike, the pH scale is only one of Søren Sørensen's many achievements in a career devoted to the application of classical physico-chemical methods to the

new realms of biochemistry and specifically to fermentation problems. His research on enzymes and proteins in particular—for which the invention of the pH scale was merely a methodological improvement—were invaluable, laying the groundwork for precise and thorough studies of these nitrogenous compounds.

Sørensen was born on January 9, 1868, in Havrebjerg, Slagelse, Denmark, the son of a farmer, Hans Sørensen. Sørensen was a high-strung, nervous youth, suffering from epileptic-like attacks and a pronounced stammer. His schoolwork became something of a refuge for him and upon graduation from high school in Sorø in 1886, he entered the University of Copenhagen. Initially Sørensen intended to study medicine, but was diverted from this course after studying chemistry under S. M. Jorgensen, who inspired him with an interest in the structure of inorganic compounds. In 1889 Sørensen was already proving his academic worth, winning a gold medal for an essay on chemical radicals. A second gold medal award came in 1896 for his research into strontium compounds. It was during this period of study that Sørensen's interest was turning toward research in analytical chemistry, a development that would later become very important for the progress of his work, as he would be able to blend his flair for experimentation with a precise attention to detail. After receiving his Master of Science degree in 1891, he worked as an assistant at the chemistry laboratory of the Danish Polytechnic Institute, consulted for the Royal Naval Dock Yard, and also found time to assist on a geological survey of Denmark. In 1899 he received his doctorate in chemistry, writing his dissertation on cobaltic oxalates.

Research Focus Shifts at Carlsberg Laboratory

Throughout the period of study for his doctorate, Sørensen focused on inorganic chemistry and related questions. In 1901, however, this focus changed with an appointment to the directorship of the prestigious Carlsberg Laboratory in Copenhagen. Sørensen, age thirty-three, took over from Johann Kjeldahl, whose work had been primarily in biochemistry; and it was with similar investigations that Sørensen would spend the rest of his scientific career. He became interested in proteins and especially in amino acids, successfully synthesizing ornithine, proline, arginine, and several others. His interest in analytical methods led him to further research into the measurement of nitrogen concentration and improving methods of titration, the process by which the concentration of ingredients in a solution is determined by adding carefully measured amounts of a reagent until a desired chemical reaction occurs.

Develops pH Scale

Much of Sørensen's fame rests in his papers on enzyme study, the first of which was a study of enzyme action utilizing the titration method. But it was in the second paper, published in 1909, where he examined the electromotive force or EMF method for determining hydrogen ion concentration, that Sørensen addressed the topic that would lead to his pH scale. Other investigators had already suggested that hydrogen ion concentrations could be used as valid indicators of the acidity or alkalinity of a solution, and the hydrogen electrode also had become the standard for such measurements. Sørensen sought to simplify the cumbersome analytical apparatus then used to measure acidity and alkalinity, and devised the familiar scale numbered 1 to 14 in which 7 represents a neutral solution, the acids are represented by numbers lower than that, and alkalines or bases by numbers above 7. Other scientists, such as Leonor Michaelis with his book on hydrogen ion concentration, and **Arnold Beckman** with a simplified pH meter, helped to popularize the pH method, which is simple enough to be grasped by laymen, yet accurate enough for scientific use.

From methodological work and studies on enzymes, Sørensen and his laboratory turned to the investigation of proteins, applying many of the classical principles of chemistry to their description and characterization, and by 1917 the laboratory had succeeded in crystallizing egg albumen, a pioneering step in the characterization of proteins. Sørensen was able to determine the molecular weight of the albumen by osmotic measurement and determine its acid and base capacity by pH. He and his assistants—later including his wife, Magrethe Høyrup Sørensen—went on to study serum proteins, lipoproteins, and the complexes of hemoglobin and carbon monoxide.

In addition to his lifelong work at the Carlsberg Laboratory, Sørensen was also involved in the role of science in industry, working with spirits, yeast, and explosives. He also contributed knowledge in the medical field, his first love at university, researching epilepsy and diabetes. Honors and awards attested to his contributions to science: he was president of the Danish Scientific Society and an honorary member of societies in both Europe and the United States. Sørensen died in Copenhagen on February 12, 1939, following a year-long illness. In a memorial address delivered to the Chemical Society, E. K. Rideal remarked, "By his death the world loses a perfect example of a man whose devotion to scientific accuracy and consistency should serve as an example to many who, claiming to be scientific in this ever-accelerating age of speed, serve their science badly by neglecting the solid in their search for the superficial and spectacular."

SELECTED WRITINGS BY SØRENSEN:

Periodicals

Biochemische Zeitschrift, Enzymstudien. II. Über die Messung und die Bedeutung der Wasserstoffionkonzentration bei enzymatischen prozessen, Volume 21, 1909, pp. 131–200.
Comptes rendus du Laboratoire de Carlsberg, On the Composition and Properties of Egg-Albumin Separated in Crystalline Form by Means of Ammonium Sulphate, Volume 12, 1917, pp. 164–212.

FURTHER READING:

Periodicals

Cohn, Edwin J., *Journal of the American Chemical Society,* Søren Peter Lauritz Sørensen, October 9, 1939, pp. 2573–574.
Cosbie, A. J. Curtin, *Nature,* Prof. S. P. L. Sørensen, April 15, 1939, p. 629.
Rideal, E. K., *Journal of the Chemical Society,* Søren Peter Lauritz Sørensen, 1940, pp. 554–61.

Sketch by J. Sydney Jones

Mary Spaeth
1938–
American physicist

Mary Spaeth invented the tunable dye laser, an innovation that rendered lasers far more useful for research in such fields as chemistry, nuclear physics, and medicine.

Born on December 17, 1938, in Houston, Texas, Mary Dietrich Spaeth is the oldest of two children. Her father, Fred, was an insurance salesman who was often assisted in his business by his wife, Louise (Dittman) Dietrich. Intending from an early age to become a doctor, Spaeth became interested in physics as a result of a seventh-grade science lesson. Her curiosity led her into studying science and, eventually, conducting research on eyes and on saturable dyes. She received her bachelor's degree from Valparaiso University in 1960, then earned her master's degree in physics from Wayne State University in 1962; later that year she began working as a member of the technical staff at Hughes Aircraft Company.

While Spaeth was a graduate student, **Theodore Maiman** introduced the first working laser. At the time, lasers could be built to emit different colors, but once the color was chosen it could not be changed, which limited their flexibility in research applications. Research on saturable dyes increased Spaeth's interest as to whether a laser could be made to change color. While at Hughes Aircraft, she had a two-week break in a research project because equipment she needed was not available. She turned her attention to the idea of a dye laser, and within a few days had a working prototype. At the time she built the prototype, she was not aware of the work of Peter Sorokin, who showed how dyes could affect the color of a laser; another scientist at Hughes saw the article in a journal and brought it to her attention. Spaeth at first had some difficulty convincing people that her invention was a true laser because the wavelengths varied and at the time a fixed wavelength was part of the definition of a laser. However, it passed all the experimental tests for a laser.

Spaeth's tunable laser has an array of applications. It allows scientists to separate elemental isotopes, especially of plutonium and uranium. Isotopes (or varieties of the same element) absorb light differently, and the energy alters the size, shape, and electrical charge of the isotope. If the electrical charge of one of a pair of similar isotopes is changed, they can easily be separated, making the preparation of nuclear fuel for reactors far more easy. One of the most promising applications of the tunable dye laser is as part of the guide star project that will allow ground-based stellar observatories to achieve resolution comparable to that received through the Hubble Space Telescope, an orbiting observatory that was launched in 1990.

Spaeth left Hughes for Lawrence Livermore National Laboratory in 1974 in order to work on laser development. During her time there, she was named deputy associate director of the isotope separation project. Divorced in 1988, Spaeth has three daughters and lives in Livermore, California.

SELECTED WRITINGS BY SPAETH:

Periodicals

Applied Physics Letters, Simulated Emission from Polymethine Dyes, Volume 9, 1966.
Laser Focus, Status and Prospects for Lasers in Isotope Separation, September, 1982, pp. 49–54.

FURTHER READING:

Books

World of Invention, Spaeth, Mary, Gale, 1994, pp. 574–75.

Other

World of Invention, interview conducted by F. C. Nicholson, February 19, 1994.

Sketch by F. C. Nicholson

Rebecca H. Sparling
1910–1996
American mechanical engineer

Rebecca H. Sparling worked extensively in the fields of high temperature metallurgy and nondestructive testing of materials. She was also an outspoken advocate for the environment and an enthusiastic promoter of engineer-

ing as a profession for women. She was honored by the Society of Woman Engineers with their Achievement Award in 1957, and by the Institute for the Advancement of Engineering with an Outstanding Engineering Merit Award in 1978.

Rebecca Hall Sparling was born in Memphis, Tennessee, on June 7, 1910, the tenth child of Robert Meredith and Kate (Sampson) Hall. Both of her parents were college graduates; her father completed a law degree although he chose a business career. Sparling began her undergraduate education at Hollins College in Virginia, transferring later to Vanderbilt University, from which she received a B.A. degree in chemistry in 1930 and an M.S. in physical chemistry in 1931.

That same year, Sparling began her career in the metallurgical department of American Cast Iron Pipe Company, but stayed only a year. For the next few years, she worked in a variety of positions including writing and translating metallurgical technical papers for the American Foundrymen's Association and writing promotional materials for International Nickel Co. In 1935 she married Edwin K. Smith, a metallurgist, and continued to publish papers and do consulting work for foundries and other companies. Through 1944 she worked out of her home so that she could take care of her son, Douglas, born in 1938. From 1942 to 1944 she wrote *American Malleable Iron,* a textbook on iron castings that became an industry standard.

Sparling returned to industry in 1944, joining Northrop Aircraft's turbodyne division as chief materials and process engineer. She remained at Northrop through her divorce in 1947 and her second marriage to Joseph Sparling in 1948. In 1951 she accepted a position as design specialist in materials at General Dynamics in Pomona, California. Most of the work Sparling did at both Northrop and General Dynamics was classified, since she worked on selecting and specifying materials for use in aerospace and missile technology. As a pioneer in these new fields, her research included finding ways of using and processing materials. More importantly, it involved development of methods for testing these materials to ensure they would perform as expected. Her advances included the application of nondestructive and high temperature testing methods. This allowed better and faster testing to evaluate the performance of materials under the conditions in which they are used. She continued her pioneering work at General Dynamics until her retirement in 1968.

During her working life and her retirement, Sparling was a prominent speaker and writer, who stressed the importance of communication among engineers, government, and the public. She gave numerous presentations in high schools and colleges, and promoted engineering as a career for women. Additionally she wrote and testified on a variety of energy matters, including nuclear power and energy conservation. Deeply involved in technical and civic organizations, Sparling was elected a fellow of the American Society for Metals, Society of Woman Engineers, and the Institute for the Advancement of Engineering and did work in a number of other societies, including the American Association of University Women. Her civic work included being a founder of the Desert Environment Conservation Association, and president of the Conserve Our Air and Water Committee. Her efforts to use her engineering background for both civil and technical advancements won her an Engineering Merit Award from the Orange County Engineering Council in 1978. She died in 1996.

SELECTED WRITINGS BY SPARLING:

Books

American Malleable Iron, Malleable Founders' Society, 1944.
Proceedings, First International Conference of Women Engineers and Scientists, How I Got into Engineering, 1964.

Periodicals

The Iron Age, High Temperature Materials for Gas Turbines, Volume 161, 1948, p. 56.
Western Metals, Nondestructive Testing of Metals, Volume 7, 1949, p. 32.
Nondestructive Testing, Tools of Inspection, Volume 12, 1954, p. 19.
Western Metalworking, Of Course Women Can Be Engineers, Volume 22, 1964, p. 37.

FURTHER READING:

Periodicals

Sparling, Rebecca H., correspondence with Jerome Ferrance, January, 1994.

Sketch by Jerome P. Ferrance

Frank Harold Spedding
1902–1984
American chemist

Frank Harold Spedding played an important role in the Manhattan Project—the U.S. government's effort to develop an atomic bomb during World War II. With his colleagues, he also devised chemical techniques for isolating rare-earth elements, thus making them available for industry at affordable cost.

Spedding was born in Hamilton, Ontario, Canada, on October 22, 1902, but his photographer father, Howard

Leslie Spedding, and mother, the former Mary Ann Elizabeth Marshall, were American citizens. While at The University of Michigan, he majored in metallurgy, receiving his B.S. degree in 1925. He earned his M.S. degree in analytical chemistry there in 1926, and was awarded his Ph.D. in physical chemistry from the University of California, Berkeley, in 1929. While working on his doctorate at UC, Spedding studied the mathematics underlying the chemical relationships among properties of rare-earth metals, the elements consisting of scandium and yttrium, and the fifteen elements from lanthanum to lutetium. These elements exist in nature only as oxides, and are never found in the pure mineral state.

While at UC he collaborated with noted chemist **Gilbert Newton Lewis** in developing methods for concentrating heavy water, which contains deuterium, the hydrogen isotope with a mass double that of ordinary hydrogen (i.e., 2 instead of 1). The young chemist was a National Research Council fellow at UC from 1930 to 1932 and a chemistry instructor there from 1932 to 1934.

In 1931 he married Ethel Annie MacFarlane; they would eventually have one daughter, Mary Ann Elizabeth. Spedding moved to Cambridge, England, in 1934 to study theoretical chemistry and physics on a Guggenheim Fellowship. The following year, he moved to Cornell University, where he taught from 1935 to 1937. During this time, he collaborated at Cornell with **Hans Bethe**, the noted physicist and one of the developers of the atomic bomb, on studies of the atomic structures of rare-earth elements. He continued his studies of these elements at Iowa State University, where he began to develop methods for separating individual rare-earth elements and their isotopes. He was to stay at Iowa State University for much of the remainder of his career, functioning as professor of physical chemistry from 1937 to 1941, professor of chemistry from 1941 to 1973, professor of physics from 1950 to 1973, and professor of metallurgy from 1962 to 1973. He was named distinguished professor of science and humanities in 1957, and emeritus professor of chemistry, physics, and metallurgy in 1973.

During World War II, Spedding began dividing his time between the University of Chicago, where scientists were trying to evoke a self-sustaining nuclear chain reaction, and Iowa. As director of the Plutonium Project, he directed chemical and metallurgical research to support the chain reaction program from 1942 to 1943. During 1942, Spedding and his colleagues developed processes for producing high-purity uranium using a column of resinous material that attracted metallic ions, a process called ion exchange. Using this technique, the team produced a third of the pure uranium that was used for the first self-sustaining nuclear chain reaction, which occurred at Stagg Field in Chicago on December 2, 1942.

Spedding's lab turned the new uranium purification process over to industry, which scaled up the process. The lab then concentrated its attention on producing pure thorium and cerium. Iowa State University received the

Chemical Engineering Achievement Award for its wartime efforts, and Spedding himself received an honorary LL.D. degree from Drake University. Because the team of experts in pure materials, high-temperature metallurgy, and rare elements that Spedding had assembled was too valuable to disband after the war, the government asked Iowa State to operate a national laboratory, called the Institute for Atomic Research (later renamed the Ames Laboratory), with Spedding as director. He also served as principal scientist of the Ames Laboratory in 1968.

Spedding continued his research on the purification of rare-earth elements and the production of rare-earth alloys and compounds. In the 1950s, Spedding's team developed processes for the large-scale production of yttrium, which the Atomic Energy Commission needed for research.

During his career he was awarded the William H. Nichols Medal of the American Chemical Society's New York Section for his "outstanding contributions in the constitution, properties and chemistry of the rare earth and actinide elements." He also received the James Douglas Medal of the American Institute of Mining, Metallurgical, and Petroleum Engineers in 1961 and the Francis J. Clamer Medal of the Franklin Institute in 1969. The National Academy of Sciences elected him to membership in 1952. In addition to his other honors, Spedding was technical representative for the Atomic Energy Commission at the Geneva Conference on Peaceful Uses of Atomic Energy in 1955, and a U.S. Department of State representative at the Fifth World Power Conference in Vienna in 1956. He was a member of the American Physical Society, the American Association for the Advancement of Science, the Faraday Society, and the American Association of University Professors.

After his retirement, Spedding devoted much of his time to researching and writing papers on the properties of the rare earths. He died on December 15, 1984, in Ames, Iowa.

SELECTED WRITINGS BY SPEDDING:

Books

The Rare Earths and Related Elements, Wiley, 1961.

FURTHER READING:

Books

McGraw-Hill Modern Scientists and Engineers, McGraw-Hill, 1980.

Periodicals

New York Times, October 2, 1951; March 15, 1952; December 17, 1984.

Sketch by Marc Kusinitz

Hans Spemann
1869–1941
German embryologist

Hans Spemann was recognized for his research into the development of embryos, and in particular for his studies into the causes behind the specialization and differentiation of embryonic cells. In the mid-1930s he discovered "organizers"—regions within developing embryos that cause undifferentiated tissue to evolve in a specific way—and for this finding he was awarded the 1935 Nobel Prize for physiology or medicine. In addition to these achievements, Spemann is credited with founding the early techniques of microsurgery, the minute manipulations of tissue or living structure.

The son of a well-known book publisher, Spemann was born on June 27, 1869, in Stuttgart. He was the eldest of four children of Johann Wilhelm Spemann and the former Lisinka Hoffman. The family, which was socially and culturally active, lived in a large home that was well stocked with books, which helped shape the young Spemann's intellect. Upon entering the Eberhard Ludwig Gymnasium, Spemann first wished to study the classics. Although he later turned to embryology—the branch of biology that focuses on embryos and their development—he never relinquished his love of artistic endeavors; throughout his lifetime he organized evening gatherings of friends to discuss art, literature, and philosophy.

Before entering the University of Heidelberg in 1891 to study medicine, Spemann worked at his father's business and served a tour of duty in the Kassel hussars. His strict interest in medicine lasted only until he met German biologist and psychologist Gustav Wolff at the University of Heidelberg. Only a few years older than Spemann, Wolff had begun experiments on the embryological developments of newts and had shown how, if the lens of an embryological newt's eye is removed, it regenerates. Spemann remained interested and intrigued by both Wolff's finding and also in the newt, on which he based much of his future work. But more than the regeneration phenomenon, Spemann was interested in how the eye develops from the start. He devoted his scientific career to the study of how embryological cells become specialized and differentiated in the process of forming a complete organism.

Spemann left Heidelberg in the mid-1890s to continue his studies at the University of Munich; he then transferred to the University of Würzberg's Zoological Institute to study under the well-known embryologist Theodor Boveri. Spemann quickly became Boveri's prize student, and completed his doctorate in botany, zoology, and physics in 1895. Shortly thereafter he married Clara Binder; the couple eventually had two sons. Spemann stayed at Würzburg until 1908, when he accepted a post as professor at the University of Rostock. During World War I, he served as director of the Kaiser Wilhelm Institute of Biology (now the Max Planck Institute) in Berlin-Dahlem, and following the war, in 1919, he took a professorship at the University of Freiburg.

Crafts Precise Experiments

By the time Spemann began research at the Zoological Institute in Würzburg, he had already developed a keen facility and reputation for conducting well-designed experiments that centered on highly focused questions. His early research followed Wolff's closely. The eye of a newt is formed when an outgrowth of the brain, called the optic cup, reaches the surface layer of embryonic tissue (the ectoderm). The cells of the ectoderm then form into an eye. In removing the tissue over where the eye would form and replacing it with tissue from an entirely different region, Spemann found that the embryo still formed a normal eye, leading him to believe that the optic cup exerted an influence on the cells of the ectoderm, inducing them to form into an eye. To complete this experiment, as well as others, Spemann had to develop a precise experimental technique for operating on objects often less than two millimeters in diameter. In doing so, he is credited with founding the techniques of modern microsurgery, which is considered one of his greatest contributions in biology. Some of his methods and instruments are still used by embryologists and neurobiologists today.

In another series of experiments—conducted in the 1920s—Spemann used a method somewhat less technically demanding to make an even more critical discovery.By tying a thin hair around the jelly-like egg of a newt early in embryogenesis (embryo development), he could split the egg entirely, or squeeze it into a dumbbell shape. When the egg halves matured, Spemann found that the split egg would produce either a whole larva and an undifferentiated mass of cells, or two whole larva (although smaller than normal size). The split egg never produced half an embryo. In the case of the egg squeezed into a dumbbell shape, the egg formed into an embryo with a single tail and two heads. Spemann's primary finding in these experiments was that if an egg is split early in embryogenesis, the two halves do not form into two halves of an embryo; they either become two whole embryos, or an embryo and a mass of cells.

This led Spemann to the conclusion that at a certain stage of development, the future roles of the different parts of the embryo have not been fixed, which supported his experiments with the newt's eye. In an experiment conducted on older eggs, however, Spemann found that the future role of some parts of the embryo had been decided, meaning that somewhere in between, a process he called "determination" must have taken place to fix the "developmental fate" of the cells.

Receives Nobel Prize for Organizer Effect

One of Spemann's greatest contributions to embryology—and the one for which he won the 1935 Nobel Prize in physiology or medicine—was his discovery of what he called the "organizer" effect. In experimenting with transplanting tissue, Spemann found that when an area containing an organizer is transplanted into an undifferentiated host embryo, this transplanted area can induce the host embryo to develop in a certain way, or into an entirely new embryo. Spemann called these transplanted cells organizers, and they include the precursors to the central nervous system. In vertebrates, they are the first cells in a long series of differentiations of which the end product is a fully formed fetus.

Spemann remained at the University of Freiburg until his retirement in the mid–1930s. When not busy with his scientific endeavors, he cultivated his love of the liberal arts. He died at his home near Freiburg on September 12, 1941.

SELECTED WRITINGS BY SPEMANN:

Books

Experimentelle Beiträge zu einer Theorie der Entwicklung, [Berlin], 1936, translated into English as *Embryonic Development and Induction*, Yale University Press, 1938.
Forschung und Leben, Errinerungen, (autobiography), [Stuttgart], 1943.

FURTHER READING:

Books

Gillispie, Charles Coulston, editor, *Dictionary of Scientific Biography,* Volume 12, Scribner, 1975.

Sketch by James Klockow

Elmer Sperry
1860–1930
American inventor and engineer

Elmer Sperry was one of the twentieth century's most prolific inventors. A pioneer in the applications of electricity, he held more than four hundred patents. The devices and machines he designed were used in such diverse enterprises as transportation and navigation, the production of metal and chemical products, outdoor lighting, and mining. Among his most famous inventions are an electric car, a high-intensity arc light, and the gyroscopic compass.

The Sperry family in America can be traced back to 1634, the year the first Sperry settled on a farm outside what is now New Haven, Connecticut. Elmer Ambrose Sperry was born on October 12, 1860, in Cortland, New York, to Stephen Decatur and Mary Burst Sperry. His mother died while giving birth to him, her only child, and he was reared by his widowed aunt, Helen Sperry Willett. As a young boy, Sperry demonstrated his abilities in engineering by building a tricycle that could be pedaled on railroad tracks in a game of thrill, just ahead of a pursuing freight train. In his teenage years Sperry attended the Cortland Normal School, one of the first schools in the country to offer courses about electricity. There he developed an interest in electrical devices. After graduation, he enrolled at Cornell University, a short buggy ride from the town of Cortland; he remained at the university for only one year, from 1879 to 1880—the extent of his formal education.

Sperry's work at Cornell University concentrated on generators and arc lights, which produce light by means of an arc made when a current passes through two incandescent electrodes surrounded by gas. His success in building these lights led to his first business endeavor: in December of 1879, Sperry built an assembly of electrical lights that was used to illuminate his hometown Christmas festival. Less than a year later he brought his design to Chicago and set up the Sperry Electric Illuminating and Power Company. Soon he was providing lights for towns across the Midwest, and Sperry-designed lighting equipment was responsible for most of the illumination at the Chicago World's Fair of 1892–1893. Eventually Sperry sold the patents on his generator and arc lights to the General Edison Company of Schenectady, which later merged with other enterprises to become the General Electric Company.

When Sperry had first arrived in Chicago in 1880, he brought a letter of introduction from his Cortland, New York pastor. A Chicago deacon of the Baptist church arranged for him to teach Sunday school; Sperry's classes covered a unique combination of topics, including not only religion but lighting and electricity. Sperry was introduced to the deacon's daughter, Zula Augusta Goodman, whom he married in 1887 and with whom he had four children—Helen, Edward, Lawrence, and Elmer. While on his honeymoon with Zula, he had the occasion to meet a mine operator who convinced Sperry that electricity had the potential to revolutionize the mining industry.

The technical challenge Sperry had to work out was how to prevent corrosion of electrical wires in the damp environment of the mine; he accomplished this by creating small currents that raised the temperature of the copper conducting wires, evaporating the dampness before it could corrode the wires. Within a few years he had developed electrical chain cutters for carving out coal deposits, as well as an electrical locomotive that could haul out one thousand tons of coal a day; this latter device relied on a specially designed wheel-to-motor connection to keep it from toppling off the irregularly turning tracks. Applying the same design principles, Sperry was able to build an electric trolley that would take first prize in the competitive hill-climbing test at the Chicago World's Fair.

In 1890 Sperry organized the Sperry Electric Railway Company in Cleveland, Ohio; four years later, after hundreds of electric rail cars had been manufactured, the General Electric Company bought both the business and Sperry's patents. Before the business was sold, Sperry designed an electric automobile, which was eventually sold as the Waverly Electric and which enjoyed brief popularity, especially in Europe. The automobile's battery, which was the precursor to portable lead storage batteries, was also designed by Sperry. The development of the automobile battery introduced Sperry to the field of electrochemistry, and in 1900 he set up a laboratory in Washington, D.C., for electrochemical research. Over the next decade many chemical manufacturing processes were developed in this laboratory, including the Townsend process which uses salt to produce caustic soda, hydrogen, and chlorine. Sperry also developed methods for purifying lead and for chlorine detinning.

In 1905 Sperry moved his family to Brooklyn, New York, where he was to live for the rest of his life. By 1910 he had formed the Sperry Gyroscope Company to take over work on what had become his new technical interest, gyroscopes. In the 1890s, when he had encountered problems in stabilizing the motion of his electric vehicles, Sperry began studying gyros. He determined that it was possible to use them, coupled with electric motors, as stabilizing devices. Orders for ship stabilizers were filled during the early 1900s for the U.S. Navy and for various international vessels. In 1913 Sperry used his gyro-stabilizer equipment to build an automatic pilot device for airplanes. Sperry also saw the potential of gyroscopes for navigation. The heavy steel composition of ships caused magnetic navigational compasses to shift unpredictably. In 1908 Sperry began modifying his gyroscopic stabilizer so that it could sense the earth's rotation to indicate true north, and by 1911 his invention passed its first sea trial. The gyroscopic compass eventually became part of an automatic steering control system known as Metal Mike. Sperry's gyroscopic navigational instruments were in such high demand by World War I that several new production factories had to be built, both in Europe and the United States. In 1917 Sperry adapted his navigational device for airplane use, producing the gyro turn indicator.

The U.S. Navy called upon Sperry in 1914 for help with searchlights. Sperry developed the high-intensity arc light, a searchlight with one billion candlepower (a candlepower, or candela, has a frequency of 540×10^{12} hertz), capable of matching the newly expanded range of naval turret guns. Sperry's lights were initially used to scan the skies over London and Paris during World War I; they eventually found application as airport beacons and floodlights. His lights also made outdoor drive-in movie viewing possible, illuminating the large-format screen.

Throughout the 1920s Sperry continued to design and develop machines for navigation as well as new types of searchlights, creating sighting and signaling devices for the military. Though in 1928 his health began to fail, he continued nonetheless to work on new ideas, including an automatic car transmission, a supercharged diesel engine, a variable pitch propeller for airplanes, and a rail flaw detector for railroad tracks. Sperry died on June 16, 1930, in Brooklyn, New York.

During his career he received wide recognition and honor for his inventions. He was awarded three honorary doctoral degrees; he was a member and officer of many technical and engineering societies, and he received numerous medals and trophies for his inventions, including decoration from the czar of Russia in 1915 and the emperor of Japan in 1922 and 1929.

SELECTED WRITINGS BY SPERRY:

Periodicals

American Institute of Electrical Engineers Transactions, Electricity in Bituminous Mining, Volume 9, 1892, pp. 374–400.

American Institute of Electrical Engineers Transactions, Electric Automobiles, Volume 16, 1899, pp. 509–25.

Scientific American, Gyroscopic Stabilizers for Ships, Volume 75, 1913, pp. 203–05.

International Air Congress Report, Sperry Gyro Turn Indicator, 1923, pp. 404–05.

FURTHER READING:

Books

Durgin, Russell L., *Dr. Sperry as We Knew Him,* Nichi-Bei Press, 1931.

Hughes, Thomas Parker, *Elmer Ambrose Sperry: Inventor and Engineer,* Johns Hopkins Press, 1971.

Periodicals

Hughes, Thomas Parker, *Smithsonian Studies in History and Technology,* Science and the Instrument-Maker: Michelson, Sperry, and the Speed of Light, 1976, pp. 1–18.

Hunsaker, H. C., *National Academy of Sciences,* Biographical Memoir of Elmer Ambrose Sperry, 1954, pp. 223–260.

Sketch by Leslie Reinherz

Roger W. Sperry
1913–1994
American psychobiologist

R oger W. Sperry, a major contributor to at least three scientific fields—developmental neurobiology, experimental psychobiology, and human split-brain studies—conducted pioneering research in the functions of the left and right hemispheres of the brain. He was awarded the Nobel Prize for physiology or medicine in 1981 for his work. The system of split-brain research that he created has enabled scientists to better understand the workings of the human brain.

Sperry was born on August 20, 1913, in Hartford, Connecticut, to Francis Bushnell Sperry, a banker, and Florence Kramer Sperry. When Sperry was 11 years old, his father died and his mother returned to school and got a job as an assistant to a high school principal. Sperry attended local public schools through high school and then went to Oberlin College in Ohio on a scholarship. There, he competed on the track team and was captain of the basketball squad. Although he majored in English, Sperry was especially interested in his undergraduate psychology courses with R. H. Stetson, an expert on the physiology of speech. Sperry earned his B.A. in English in 1935 and then worked as a graduate assistant to Stetson for two years. In 1937 he received an M.A. in psychology.

Thoroughly committed to research in the field of psychobiology by that time, Sperry went to the University of Chicago to conduct research on the organization of the central nervous system under the renowned biologist Paul Weiss. Before Weiss's research, scientists believed that the connections of the nervous system had to be very exact to work properly. Weiss disproved this theory by surgically crossing a subject's nerve connections. After the surgery was performed, the subject's behavior did not change. From this, Weiss concluded that the connections of the central nervous system were not predetermined, so that a nerve need not connect to any particular location to function correctly.

Challenges Mentor's Theories

Sperry tested Weiss's research by surgically crossing the nerves that controlled the hind leg muscles of a rat. Under Weiss's theory, each nerve should eventually "learn" to control the leg muscle to which it was now connected. This did not happen. When the left hind foot was stimulated, the right foot responded instead. Sperry's experiments disproved Weiss's research and became the basis of his doctoral dissertation, "Functional Results of Crossing Nerves and Transposing Muscles in the Fore and Hind Limbs of the Rat." He received a Ph.D. in zoology from the University of Chicago in 1941.

Roger W. Sperry

Sperry did other related experiments that confirmed his findings and further contradicted Weiss's theory that "function precedes form" (that is, the brain and nervous system learn, through experience, to function properly). In one experiment, Sperry rotated a frog's eyeball and cut its optic nerve. If Weiss's theory was correct, the frog would reeducate itself, adjust to seeing the world upside down, and change its behavior accordingly. This did not happen. In fact, the nerve fibers became tangled in the scar tissue during healing. When the nerve regenerated, it ignored the repositioning of the eyeball and reattached itself correctly, albeit upside down. From this and other experiments, Sperry deduced that genetic mechanisms determine some basic behavioral patterns. According to his theory, nerves have highly specific functions based on genetically predetermined differences in the concentration of chemicals inside the nerve cells.

In 1941 Sperry moved to the laboratory of the renowned psychologist Karl S. Lashley at Harvard to work as a National Research Council postdoctoral fellow. A year later, Lashley became director of the Yerkes Laboratories of Primate Biology in Orange Park, Florida. Sperry joined him there on a Harvard biology research fellowship. While there, he disproved some Gestalt psychology theories about brain mechanisms, as well as some theories of Lashley's.

During World War II, Sperry fulfilled his military service duty by working for three years in an Office of Scientific Research and Development (OSRD) medical research project run by the University of Chicago and the Yerkes laboratory. His work involved research on repairing nerve injuries by surgery. In 1946 Sperry returned to the University of Chicago to accept a position as assistant professor in the school's anatomy department. He became associate professor of psychology during the 1952–1953 school year and also worked during that year as section chief in the Neurological Diseases and Blindness division of the National Institutes of Health.

In 1954 he transferred to the California Institute of Technology (Caltech) to take a position as the Hixon Professor of Psychobiology. At Caltech, Sperry conducted research on split-brain functions that he had first investigated when he worked at the Yerkes Laboratory. It had long been known that the cerebrum of the brain consists of two hemispheres. In most people, the left hemisphere controls the right side of the body, and vice versa. The two halves are connected by a bundle of millions of nerve fibers called the corpus callosum, or the great cerebral commissure.

Neurosurgeons had discovered that this connection could be cut into with little or no noticeable change in the patient's mental abilities. After experiments on animals proved the procedure to be harmless, surgeons began cutting completely through the commissure of epileptic patients in an attempt to prevent the spread of epileptic seizures from one hemisphere to the other. The procedure was generally successful, and beginning in the late 1930s, cutting through the forebrain commissure became an accepted treatment method for severe epilepsy. Observations of the split-brain patients indicated no loss of communication between the two hemispheres of the brain.

From these observations, scientists assumed that the corpus callosum had no function other than as a prop to prevent the two hemispheres from sagging. Scientists also believed that the left hemisphere was dominant and performed higher cognitive functions, such as speech. This theory developed from observations of patients whose left cerebral hemisphere had been injured; these patients suffered impairment of various cognitive functions, including speech. Since these functions were not transferred over to the uninjured right hemisphere, scientists assumed that the right hemisphere was less developed.

Discovers Role of Right Brain

Sperry's work shattered these views. He and his colleagues at Caltech discovered that the corpus callosum is more than a physical prop; it provides a means of communication between the two halves of the brain and integrates the knowledge acquired by each of them. They also learned that in many ways, the right hemisphere is superior to the left. Although the left half of the brain is superior in analytic, logical thought, the right half excels in intuitive processing of information. The right hemisphere also specializes in nonverbal functions, such as understanding music, interpreting visual patterns (such as recognizing faces), and sorting sizes and shapes.

Sperry discovered these different capacities of the two cerebral hemispheres through a series of experiments performed over a period of several decades. In one such experiment, Sperry and a graduate student, Ronald Myers, cut the nerve connections between the two hemispheres of a cat's brain. They discovered that behavioral responses learned by the left side of the brain were not transferred to the right, and vice versa. In an article published in *Scientific American* in 1964, Sperry observed that "it was as though each hemisphere were a separate mental domain operating with complete disregard—indeed, with a complete lack of awareness—of what went on in the other. The split-brain animal behaved in the test situation as if it had two entirely separate brains." It was evident from this experiment that the severed nerves had been responsible for communication between the two halves of the brain.

In another experiment on a human subject, he showed a commissurotomy patient (one whose corpus callosum had been surgically severed) a picture of a pair of scissors. Only the patient's left visual field, which is governed by the nonverbal right hemisphere, could see the scissors. The patient could not verbally describe what he had seen because the left hemisphere, which controls language functions, had not received the necessary information. However, when the patient reached behind a screen, he sorted through a pile of various items and picked out the scissors. When asked how he knew the correct item, the patient insisted it was purely luck.

Sperry published technical papers on his split-brain findings in the late 1960s. The importance of his research was recognized relatively quickly, and in 1979 he was awarded the prestigious Albert Lasker Basic Medical Research Award, which included a $15,000 grant. The award was given in recognition of the potential medical benefits of Sperry's research, including possible treatments for mental or psychosomatic illnesses.

Awarded Nobel Prize for Split-Brain Studies

Two years later, Sperry was honored with the 1981 Nobel Prize in physiology or medicine. He shared it with two other scientists, **Torsten N. Wiesel** and **David H. Hubel**, for research on the central nervous system and the brain. In describing Sperry's work, the Nobel Prize selection committee praised the researcher for demonstrating the difference between the two hemispheres of the brain and for outlining some of the specialized functions of the right brain. The committee, as quoted in the *New York Times,* stated that Sperry's work illuminated the fact that the right brain "is clearly superior to the left in many respects, especially regarding the capacity for concrete thinking, spatial consciousness and comprehension of complex relationships."

In his acceptance speech, as quoted in *Science* in 1982, Sperry talked about the significance of his discovery of the previously unrecognized skills of the nonverbal right half-brain. He commented that an important gain from his work is increased attention to "the important role of the nonverbal

components and forms of the intellect." Because split-brain research increased appreciation of the individuality of each brain and its functions, Sperry believed that his work helped to point out the need for educational policies that took into consideration varying types of intelligence and potential.

Sperry rejected conventional scientific thinking that viewed human consciousness solely as a function of physical and chemical activity within the brain. In his view, which he discussed in his Nobel Prize lecture, "cognitive introspective psychology and related cognitive science can no longer be ignored experimentally.... The whole world of inner experience (the world of the humanities) long rejected by twentieth-century scientific materialism, thus becomes recognized and included within the domain of science."

Known as a private, reserved person, Sperry was, quite characteristically, camping with his wife in a remote area when the news of his Nobel Prize award was announced. He had married Norma Gay Deupree in 1949, and they had two children, Glenn Tad and Janet Hope. In addition to camping, Sperry's avocational interests included sculpture, drawing, ceramics, folk dancing, and fossil hunting. He retired from Caltech in 1984 as Professor Emeritus. In 1989, Sperry was awarded a National Medal of Science. He died in Pasadena.

In addition to the Nobel prize, Sperry received many awards and honorary doctorates. He was member of many scientific societies, including the Pontifical Academy of Sciences and the National Academy of Sciences. Sperry was always held in high regard by his students. One of them, Michael Gazzaniga, described him in *Science* as "exceedingly generous" to many students at Caltech. Gazzaniga also defined Sperry as a teacher "constitutionally only able to be interested in critical issues," who drove his "herd of young scientists to consider nothing but the big questions."

SELECTED WRITINGS BY SPERRY:

Books

Problems Outstanding in the Evolution of Brain Function. New York: American Museum of Natural History, 1964.
Science and Moral Priority: Merging Mind, Brain, and Human Values. New York: Columbia University, 1983.

Periodicals

"The Great Commisure." *Scientific American* (January 1964).
"Mental Unity Following Surgical Disconnection of the Cerebral Hemispheres." *Harvey Lectures* 62 (1968): 293–322.

FURTHER READING:

Books

Wasson, Tyler, ed. *Nobel Prize Winners.* New York: H. W. Wilson, 1987.

Weintraub, Pamela. *The Omni Interviews.* New York: Ticknor & Fields, 1984.

Periodicals

"Brain Mappers Win a Nobel Prize." *Newsweek* (19 October 1981): 110.

Gazzaniga, Michael S. "1981 Nobel Prize for Physiology or Medicine." *Science* (30 October 1981): 517–18.

Gazzaniga, Michael S. "The Nobel Prizes." *Scientific American* (December 1981): 80.

Heise, Kenan. "Roger Sperry, 80; Studied Functions of Human Brain" (obituary). *Chicago Tribune* (23 April 1994): 15.

Oliver, Myrna. "Roger Sperry, Nobel Prize Winner, Dies" (obituary). *Washington Post* (19 April 1994): 22.

Pearson, Richard. "Roger Sperry, Nobel Prize Winner, Dies" (obituary). *Washington Post* (20 April 1994): B4.

Puente, Antonio E. "Roger Sperry" (obituary). *American Psychologist* 50 (1 November 1995): 940–41.

Schmeck, Harold M., Jr. "Three Scientists Share Nobel Prize for Studies on the Brain." *New York Times* (10 October 1981): 1; 50–51.

Sperry, Roger W. "Nobel Prize Lecture." *Science* (24 September 1982).

Wade, Nicholas. "Roger Sperry, A Nobel Winner for Brain Studies, Dies at 80" (obituary). *New York Times* (20 April 1994): D27.

Sketch by Donna Olshansky

Lyman Spitzer, Jr.

Lyman Spitzer, Jr.
1914–1997
American astrophysicist

Lyman Spitzer, Jr., through his research into galactic structure, made important insights into the understanding of star formation. Through continued investigations into the nature of stars, he pioneered theoretical research into the techniques of achieving controlled nuclear fusion in a laboratory setting.

Spitzer was born in Toledo, Ohio, on June 26, 1914. He studied at Phillips Academy in Massachusetts before moving on to Yale University, where he received a B.A. in physics in 1935. He broadened his academic development as a Henry fellow, spending a year in Cambridge, England, studying with Sir **Arthur Stanley Eddington**. After returning to the United States, Spitzer worked with **Henry Norris Russell** at Princeton where he received his Ph.D. in astrophysics in 1938. He immediately obtained a National Research Council fellowship for a year of study at Harvard after which he returned to Yale as an instructor in physics and astronomy. As was the case with many young Americans, Spitzer's fast-rising career was interrupted by World War II. From 1942 to 1946, he supervised projects at Columbia University in underwater warfare research, including the development of sonar. When the war ended, Spitzer continued at Yale for a year or so. In 1947 he moved to Princeton, where he became the chair of the astronomy department. He was later appointed Charles A. Young Professor in 1951 and elected to the National Academy of Sciences in 1952.

By 1950, with the disruptions and distractions of war behind them, astronomers were poised for a new leap forward in knowledge. Helping them was the massive new 200-inch (508-cm) Hale telescope on Mount Palomar, which had just come on line in 1949 and promised to deliver a treasure trove of new data for scientists to ponder. Also, theories concerning the expansion of the universe in the first half of the century and more recent work on the process of stellar evolution both served to help knit the sum of astronomical progress into an emerging, coherent "story." What was missing was an understanding of how stars formed in the first place.

It was apparent from studies of the Milky Way and nearby spiral galaxies that hot, massive stars seemed to be generated almost constantly from within the spiral arms. Calculations verified that the massive stars burned their fuel at so furious a rate that they could only live for a few tens of millions of years, a short time by cosmic standards, before burning themselves out. The fact that astronomers could observe these brilliant stars at all meant that some process was continually at work replacing the burned-out stars with new ones. The arms of spiral galaxies had the most plentiful abundance of such massive stars, so it became obvious that some feature or attribute of the spiral arms was responsible for star formation. The one major feature that characterizes the spiral arms of galaxies is their large concentration of gas and dust. Lyman Spitzer, along with others, attempted to untangle the mystery of how clouds of gas and dust could combine to form stars.

Spitzer analyzed the characteristics of ionized gas clouds that existed near massive, hot stars and compared them with the cooler regions of interstellar molecular clouds. He found that the hot gas, or plasma, regions exerted a strong thermal pressure, created by temperatures of 10,000 degrees Kelvin. The pressure was sufficient to churn the nearby molecular clouds. This explained the high gas velocities observed in such regions. With instability introduced into an otherwise quiescent gas cloud, the stage was set for the cloud's gravitational collapse and the onset of star formation.

Pioneering Work on Nuclear Fusion Begins

Spitzer analyzed the effects of interstellar magnetic fields on plasma clouds and became one of the leading contributors to the burgeoning field of plasma physics. He calculated that it would be possible to contain hydrogen gas plasma at the incredible temperature of 100 million degrees Kelvin by keeping the plasma within magnetic fields. The trapped, super-heated hydrogen would then fuse into helium, releasing a tremendous amount of energy. Indeed, nuclear fusion is the energy source that powers the stars, wherein the tremendous pressure of gravity at the star's core transforms hydrogen into helium at high temperatures. Spitzer's insight was to show how a hydrogen plasma could be fused to produce energy without requiring the presence of a massive star to do it. The implications of this idea, which is nothing less than the creation of energy by controlled thermonuclear fusion, is still being studied in laboratories around the world and stems directly from the work of Spitzer.

Something of the depth of Spitzer's contributions to astronomy and physics can be glimpsed from the numerous awards he received during his long career, including the Rittenhouse Medal of the Franklin Institute in 1957, the Exceptional Science Achievement Medal from NASA in 1972, The Bruce God Medal from the Astronomical Society of the Pacific in 1973, the Henry Draper Medal from the National Academy of Sciences in 1974, the James Clerk Maxwell Prize from the American Physics Society in 1975, the Distinguished Public Service Medal from NASA in 1976, the Gold Medal of the Royal Astronomical Society in 1978, the Jules Janssen Medal from the Société Astrono-

mique de France in 1980, and the Franklin Medal from the Franklin Institute in 1980.

Spitzer also speculated on the possibility of artificial, earth-orbiting satellites and telescopes. As head of the Princeton University Observatory, he was among the first to promote the use of rockets for scientific research. Princeton played a leading part in his endeavor with programs designed to perform studies using high-altitude balloons and rockets. The critical role that orbiting observatories play in current astronomical research is testimony to Spitzer's vision. Lyman Spitzer Jr. died March 31, 1997, at his home in Princeton, New Jersey. The 82-year-old had suffered from heart disease.

SELECTED WRITINGS BY SPITZER:

Books

Physics of Fully Ionized Gases. New York: Interscience Publishers, 1956.
Diffuse Matter in Space. New York: Interscience Publishers, 1968.
Physical Processes in the Interstellar Medium. New York: Wiley, 1978.
Searching between the Stars. New Haven, CT: Yale University Press, 1982.
Dynamical Evolution of Globular Clusters. Princeton, NJ: Princeton University Press, 1987.

FURTHER READING:

Periodicals

Saxon, Wolfgang. "Lyman Spitzer, Jr., Dies at 82; Inspired Hubble Telescope" (obituary). *New York Times* (2 April 1997): A19.

Sketch by Jeffery Bass

Franklin W. Stahl
1929–
American molecular biologist

Franklin W. Stahl, in collaboration with **Matthew Meselson**, discovered direct evidence for the semiconservative nature of deoxyribonucleic acid (DNA) replication in bacteria. In experiments, Stahl and Meselson showed that when a double-stranded DNA molecule is duplicated, the double strands are separated and a new strand is copied from each "parent" strand forming two new double-stranded

DNA molecules. The new double-stranded DNA molecules contain one conserved "parent" strand and one new "daughter" strand. Therefore, the replication of a DNA molecule is semiconservative: it retains some of the original material while creating some new material. The understanding of the semiconservative nature of DNA in replication was a major advancement in the field of molecular biology.

Franklin William Stahl, the youngest of three children, was born on October 6, 1929, in Boston, Massachusetts, to Oscar Stahl, an equipment specialist with New England Telephone and Telegraph, and Eleanor Condon Stahl, a homemaker. He received a baccalaureate degree from Harvard University in 1951 in the area of biological sciences; he continued with graduate studies in the field of biology, earning a Ph.D. degree at the University of Rochester in New York, in 1956. From 1955 to 1958, Stahl was a research fellow at the California Institute of Technology, where he collaborated with Matthew Meselson on the semiconservative replication experiment.

In 1952, having just graduated from Harvard, Stahl attended a course at Cold Spring Harbor Laboratories in New York given by A. H. Doermann. Doermann was well known for research on bacteriophages, microscopic agents that destroy disease-producing bacteria in a living organism. This course gave Stahl his first exposure to the genetics of bacteriophages. The subject so fascinated him that he spent his summers in the laboratory of Dr. Doermann while working on his doctorate at the University of Rochester during the school year. Bacteriophage genetics would later become the major focus of his own laboratory's scientific research. Stahl would also come to teach the same course at Cold Spring Harbor.

After receiving his doctorate in biology, Stahl moved to California to work in the laboratory of **Max Delbrück** at the California Institute of Technology as a postdoctoral fellow. While at Cal Tech, he began a collaboration with graduate student Meselson to design an experiment to describe the nature of DNA replication from parent to offspring using bacteriophages. The idea was to add the substance 5-bromouracil, which would become incorporated into the DNA of a T4 bacteriophage upon its replication during a few rounds of reproduction. Phage samples could then be isolated by a density gradient centrifugation procedure that was originally designed by Stahl, Meselson, and Jerome Vinograd. It was thought that the phage samples containing the incorporated 5-bromouracil would separate in the density gradient centrifugation to a measurable degree based on the length of the new strands of DNA acquired during replication. Several attempts to obtain measurable results were unsuccessful. Despite these first setbacks, Stahl had confidence in the theory of the experiment. After further contemplation, Stahl and Meselson decided to abandon the use of the T4 bacteriophage and the labelling substance 5-bromouracil and turned to the use of a bacteria, *Escherichia coli,* with the heavy nitrogen isotope 15N as the labelling substance. This time, when the same experimental steps were performed using the new substitutions, the analysis of the density gradient centrifugation samples showed three distinct types of bacterial DNA, two from the original parent strands of DNA and one from the new offspring. Analysis of the new offspring showed each strand of DNA came from a different parent. Thus the theory of semiconservative replication of DNA had been proven.

Recognized as Expert in Bacteriophage Genetics

After spending 1958 at the University of Missouri as an associate professor of zoology, Stahl took a position as associate professor of biology and research associate at the Institute of Molecular Biology, located at the University of Oregon in Eugene, Oregon. In 1963 he was awarded status of professor; he was appointed acting director of the Institute from 1973 to 1975. Stahl has held a concurrent position as resident research professor of molecular genetics at the American Cancer Society.

Stahl set up his own laboratory at the institute, contributing further to the scientific research and understanding in the area of bacteriophage genetics, as well as the genetic recombination of bacteriophages and fungi. In the early years at Eugene, he continued to focus his research in the area of genetic recombination and replication in bacteriophages using the techniques of density gradient and equilibrium centrifugations. Through the years, he was able to map the DNA structure of the T4 bacteriophage. The experiments involved T4 bacteriophages inactivated by decay of DNA incorporated radionucleotides or by X-irradiation of the DNA that would cause breaks in the DNA sequence. By performing reactivation-crosses of these bacteriophage, Stahl studied the patterns in which markers on the DNA were "knocked out" or lost. Although the inactivated phages are unable to produce offspring themselves, they can contribute particular markers to their offspring when they are grown in the presence of rescuing phages that supply the functions necessary for phage development. By the pattern of markers seen in the offspring of these reactivation crosses, a map can be constructed. From the map constructed, the correlated knockout markers reflected a linkage relationship in the form of a circle. With this map in hand, particular DNA sequences could be shown to be important for various functions of the bacteriophage.

Much of Stahl's later work focused on the bacteriophage Lambda, which has a more complex structure than bacteriophage T4, and its replication inside of a bacterial cell. He determined particular "hot spots" in the DNA sequence that were susceptible to various mutations or recombinations during the process of replication. These "hot spots" were particular sites in the DNA sequence of the phage that tended to show crossing over between two DNA strands of the chromosome. The resulting mutations (Chi mutations), which occurred at four or five particular sites in the Lambda phage, conferred a particular large plaque-forming character by accelerating the rate of crossing over at these sites. These mutations affected the overall function of the bacteriophage, sometimes causing complete inactivation. Through further studies of genetic recombination in bacteriophages, Stahl became known to the scientific world as an expert on their structure and life cycle.

From 1964–1985, Stahl held several year-long positions as visiting professor or volunteer scientist in various universities throughout the world. He was the volunteer scientist in the Division of Molecular Genetics for the Medical Research Council in Cambridge, England. He took a sabbatical leave from Oregon and conducted research in the Medical Research Council Unit of Molecular Genetics at the University of Edinburgh, Scotland, as well as at the Laboratory of International Genetics and Biophysics in Naples, Italy. He held the position of Lady Davis Visiting Professor in the Genetics Department at Hebrew University in Jerusalem, Israel. Stahl also taught courses on bacterial viruses at Cold Spring Harbor Laboratories and in Naples. He is a member of the National Academy of Sciences, the American Academy of Arts and Sciences, and the Viral Study Section of the National Institutes of Health.

Reflections on a Scientific Career

During a personal interview, when asked what was a leading factor in choosing scientific research in biology as a career, Dr. Stahl responded, "The currency of science is truth and understanding opposed to power and money, leading to contact with people that are fun and exciting." This difference between the world of scientific research and the business world has been a primary factor in influencing the path of Stahl's scientific career. His main goal as a scientist was never fame or fortune, but the opportunity to interact with exciting people and share innovative ideas. According to Dr. Stahl, his greatest contribution to the scientific world has been "the ability to act as mentor to graduate students and scientists by giving encouragement and direction to their research." He has gained great pleasure in passing on his knowledge and experiences to future generations of scientists.

Throughout his career as a scientist, Stahl has written more than one hundred articles published in major scientific journals, received numerous honors including two honorary degrees, and been awarded the prestigious Guggenheim Fellowship award three times. Franklin Stahl married Mary Morgan, also a scientist, in 1955; the couple had three children, Emily, Joshua and Andy. Mary worked alongside Frank in the laboratory, frequently carrying on experiments while Frank took care of administrative responsibilities. He enjoys watching "Monday Night Football" and getting together with family members.

SELECTED WRITINGS BY STAHL:

Books

The Mechanics of Inheritance, 2nd edition, Prentice-Hall, 1969.
Genetic Recombination: Thinking about It in Phage and Fungi, W. H. Freeman, 1979.

Periodicals

Proceedings of the National Academy of Sciences, The Replication of DNA in Escherichia coli, Volume 44, pp. 671–82, 1958.
Genetics, Circularity of the Genetic Map of Bacteriophage T4, Volume 48, pp. 659–1672, 1963.
Journal of Cellular Physiology, Circular Genetic Maps, Volume 70 (Supplement 1), pp. 1–12, 1967.

FURTHER READING:

Books

Daintith, John, Mitchell, Sarah, and Tootill, Elizabeth, *A Biographical Encyclopedia of Scientists,* Facts on File, 1981.

Other

Stahl, Franklin W., *Interview with Karen S. Kelly,* conducted December 2, 1993.

Sketch by Karen S. Kelly

Richard Stanley
1944–
American mathematician

Richard Stanley is a pioneer in the field of combinatorics, a specialty not highly regarded when Stanley was emerging as a mathematician, but one that has gained greater acceptance throughout his career. His *Enumerative Combinatorics,* which is based on concepts presented in commutative algebra, homological algebra and algebraic topology, is one of the seminal texts in this area.

Stanley was born in New York City on June 23, 1944, to Alan Stanley, a chemical engineer, and Shirley Stanley, a homemaker. Stanley did not remain in New York City long, spending his early childhood in Tahawus, New York, a city that was later moved to another location building by building. During his time in Tahawus, he explains in a document on his early years available on his World Wide Web site on the Internet, he dreamed of being a ventriloquist. As an adolescent, then living in Lynchburg, Virginia, he set his sights on astronomy, which triggered his interest in mathematics as well. He credits an elderly resident of Lynchburg—who taught him the standard synthetic algorithm for finding the square root of a positive real number—with getting him started. Around the same time, he also began to read the mathematics section of his father's *Handbook of Chemistry and Physics,* which detailed the

Richard Stanley

cube root algorithm. Just before his family's move to Savannah, Georgia, when the younger Stanley was 13, he shifted his interest from astronomy to nuclear physics until he met a classmate who was working on determining synthetic algorithms for finding roots higher than the cubic. His interest was piqued, and he began to read widely on mathematical topics in addition to his high school mathematics courses. Stanley often worked independently of his classmates since only basic courses were available at his school.

Stanley earned his Bachelor of Science degree in mathematics in 1966 from the California Institute of Technology and went on to receive a Ph.D. in mathematics from Harvard University in 1971, with G. C. Rota, a professor at the Massachusetts Institute of Technology (MIT), as his thesis advisor. He also worked as the C.L.E. Moore Instructor of Mathematics at MIT in the final year of his Ph.D. program. While at Harvard, Stanley met his wife, Doris, who became a French teacher. The Stanleys have two children.

After receiving his Ph.D., Stanley conducted postdoctoral studies through a Miller Research Fellowship at the Berkeley campus of the University of California. In 1973, he returned to MIT as an assistant professor in mathematics and, in 1979, was named a full professor of applied mathematics, eventually serving as chair of the Applied Mathematics Committee. He relinquished that post when he accepted a visiting professor position at Berkeley, where he spent a year as the Chern Visiting Professor in the

Mathematical Sciences Research Institute, over which Stanley served as chair from 1993 to 1997. Stanley also spent a year as a visiting professor at the University of California at San Diego for the 1978–1979 academic year.

Stanley has held other visiting professor positions across the world, including short stints at the University of Stockholm, University of Augsburg, and Tokai University in Japan. In addition, Stanley spent a semester as the Göran Gustafsson Professor at the Royal Institute of Technology and the Institute Mittag–Leffler in Sweden in 1992. He was recruited for this position by Anders Björner, one of Sweden's leading mathematicians, for whom Stanley had served as an advisor when Björner spent time at MIT as a visiting student.

Among his awards and honors, Stanley received a Guggenheim Fellowship in 1983, which he used to fund research on reduced combinatorics. He has published widely on the topic of combinatorics, including authoring the definitive text on the topic, *Enumerative Combinatorics*. As of 1997, he was at work on a second volume of *Enumerative Combinatorics*, which he had spent 11 years researching at that time. In addition to teaching, Stanley works as a consultant for Bell Telephone Laboratories in Murray Hill, New Jersey, and serves on editorial boards for several prestigious mathematical journals, including the *Journal on Algebraic and Discrete Methods*, *Studies in Applied Mathematics*, and *PanAmerican Mathematics*.

In an interview with Kristin Palm, Stanley discussed the qualities that drew him to his profession. "To me it's just a very elegant, beautiful structure. It's been developed for thousands of years. You can go exploring on your own with it and add to it," he explained.

SELECTED WRITINGS BY STANLEY:

Books

Combinatorics and Commutative Algebra, second edition, 1996.
Enumerative Combinatorics, 1986.

FURTHER READING:

Other

Richard Stanley. http://www–math.mit.edu/~rstan (August 26, 1997).
Stanley, Richard, in an interview with Kristin Palm, conducted July 11, 1997.

Sketch by Kristin Palm

Wendell Meredith Stanley
1904–1971
American biochemist

Wendell Meredith Stanley was a biochemist who was the first to isolate, purify, and characterize the crystalline form of a virus. During World War II, he led a team of scientists in developing a vaccine for viral influenza. His efforts have paved the way for understanding the molecular basis of heredity and formed the foundation for the new scientific field of molecular biology. For his work in crystallizing the tobacco mosaic virus, Stanley shared the 1946 Nobel Prize in chemistry with **John Howard Northrop** and **James B. Sumner**.

Stanley was born in the small community of Ridgeville, Indiana, on August 16, 1904. His parents, James and Claire Plessinger Stanley, were publishers of a local newspaper. As a boy, Stanley helped the business by collecting news, setting type, and delivering papers. After graduating from high school he enrolled in Earlham College, a liberal arts school in Richmond, Indiana, where he majored in chemistry and mathematics. He played football as an undergraduate, and in his senior year he became team captain and was chosen to play end on the Indiana All-State team. In June of 1926 Stanley graduated with a bachelor of science degree. His ambition was to become a football coach, but the course of his life was changed forever when an Earlham chemistry professor invited him on a trip to Illinois State University. Here, he was introduced to **Roger Adams**, an organic chemist, who inspired him to seek a career in chemical research. Stanley applied and was accepted as a graduate assistant in the fall of 1926.

In graduate school, Stanley worked under Adams, and his first project involved finding the stereochemical characteristics of biphenyl, a molecule containing carbon and hydrogen atoms. His second assignment was more practical; Adams was interested in finding chemicals to treat leprosy, and Stanley set out to prepare and purify compounds that would destroy the disease-causing pathogen. Stanley received his master's degree in 1927 and two years later was awarded his Ph.D. In the summer of 1930, he was awarded a National Research Council Fellowship to do postdoctoral studies with **Heinrich Wieland** at the University of Munich in Germany. Under Wieland's tutelage, Stanley extended his knowledge of experimental biochemistry by characterizing the properties of some yeast compounds.

Stanley returned to the United States in 1931 to accept the post of research assistant at the Rockefeller Institute in New York City. Stanley was assigned to work with W. J. V. Osterhout, who was studying how living cells absorb potassium ions from seawater. Stanley was asked to find a suitable chemical model that would simulate how a marine plant called *Valonia* functions. He discovered a way of

Wendell Meredith Stanley

using a water-insoluble solution sandwiched between two layers of water to model the way the plant exchanged ions with its environment. The work on *Valonia* served to extend Stanley's knowledge of biophysical systems, and it introduced him to current problems in biological chemistry.

Begins Chemical Studies on Tobacco Mosaic Virus

In 1932 Stanley moved to the Rockefeller Institute's Division of Plant Pathology in Princeton, New Jersey. He was primarily interested in studying viruses. Viruses were known to cause diseases in plants and animals, but little was known about how they functioned. His assignment was to characterize viruses and determine their composition and structure.

He began work on a virus that had long been associated with the field of virology. In 1892, D. Ivanovsky, a Russian scientist, had studied tobacco mosaic disease, in which infected tobacco plants develop a characteristic mosaic pattern of dark and light spots. He found that the tobacco plant juice retained its ability to cause infection even after it was passed through a filter. Six years later M. Beijerinck, a Dutch scientist, realized the significance of Ivanovsky's discovery: the filtration technique used by Ivanovsky would have filtered out all known bacteria, and the fact that the filtered juice remained infectious must have meant that something smaller than a bacterium and invisible to the ordinary light microscope was responsible for the disease. Beijerinck concluded that tobacco mosaic disease was caused by a previously undiscovered type of infective agent—a virus.

Stanley was aware of recent techniques used to precipitate the tobacco mosaic virus (TMV) with common chemicals. These results led him to believe that the virus might be a protein susceptible to the reagents used in protein chemistry. He set out to isolate, purify, and concentrate the tobacco mosaic virus. He planted Turkish tobacco plants, and when the plants were about six inches tall, he rubbed the leaves with a swab of linen dipped in TMV solution. After a few days the heavily infected plants were chopped and frozen. Later, he ground and mashed the frozen plants to obtain a thick, dark liquid. He then subjected the TMV liquid to various enzymes and found that some would inactivate the virus and concluded that TMV must be a protein or something similar. After exposing the liquid to more than 100 different chemicals, Stanley determined that the virus was inactivated by the same chemicals that typically inactivated proteins, and this suggested to him, as well as others, that TMV was protein-like in nature.

Stanley then turned his attention to obtaining a pure sample of the virus. He decanted, filtered, precipitated, and evaporated the tobacco juice many times. With each chemical operation, the juice became more clear and the solution more infectious. The end result of two-and-one-half years of work was a clear concentrated solution of TMV which began to form into crystals when stirred. Stanley filtered and collected the tiny, white crystals and discovered that they retained their ability to produce the characteristic lesions of tobacco mosaic disease.

After successfully crystallizing TMV, Stanley's work turned toward characterizing its properties. In 1936 two English scientists at Cambridge University confirmed Stanley's work by isolating TMV crystals. They discovered that the virus consisted of ninety-four percent protein and six percent nucleic acid, and they concluded that TMV was a nucleoprotein. Stanley was skeptical at first. Later studies, however, showed that the virus became inactivated upon removal of the nucleic acid, and this work convinced him that TMV was indeed a nucleoprotein. In addition to chemical evidence, the first electron microscope pictures of TMV were produced by researchers in Germany. The pictures showed the crystals to have a distinct rod-like shape. For his work in crystallizing the tobacco mosaic virus, Stanley shared the 1946 Nobel prize in chemistry with John Howard Northrop and James Sumner.

Develops Influenza Vaccine

During World War II, Stanley was asked to participate in efforts to prevent viral diseases, and he joined the Office of Scientific Research and Development in Washington, D.C. Here, he worked on the problem of finding a vaccine effective against viral influenza. Such a substance would change the virus so that the body's immune system could build up defenses without causing the disease. Using fertilized hen eggs as a source, he proceeded to grow, isolate, and purify the virus. After many attempts, he

discovered that formaldehyde, the chemical used as a biological preservative, would inactivate the virus but still induce the body to produce antibodies. The first flu vaccine was tested and found to be remarkably effective against viral influenza. For his work in developing large-scale methods of preparing vaccines, he was awarded the Presidential Certificate of Merit in 1948.

In 1948 Stanley moved to the University of California in Berkeley, where he became director of a new virology laboratory and chair of the department of biochemistry. In five years Stanley assembled an impressive team of scientists and technicians who reopened the study of plant viruses and began an intensive effort to characterize large, biologically important molecules. In 1955 **Heinz Fraenkel-Conrat**, a protein chemist, and R. C. Williams, an electron microscopist, took TMV apart and reassembled the viral RNA, thus proving that RNA was the infectious component. In addition, their work indicated that the protein component of TMV served only as a protective cover. Other workers in the virus laboratory succeeded in isolating and crystallizing the virus responsible for polio, and in 1960 Stanley led a group that determined the complete amino acid sequence of TMV protein. In the early 1960s, Stanley became interested in a possible link between viruses and cancer.

Stanley was an advocate of academic freedom. In the 1950s, when his university was embroiled in the politics of McCarthyism, members of the faculty were asked to sign oaths of loyalty to the United States. Although Stanley signed the oath of loyalty, he publicly defended those who chose not to, and his actions led to court decisions which eventually invalidated the requirement.

Stanley received many awards, including the Alder Prize from Harvard University in 1938, the Nichols Medal of the American Chemical Society in 1946, and the Scientific Achievement Award of the American Medical Association in 1966. He held honorary doctorates from many colleges and universities. He was a prolific author of more than 150 publications and he coedited a three volume compendium entitled *The Viruses*. By lecturing, writing, and appearing on television he helped bring important scientific issues before the public. He served on many boards and commissions, including the National Institute of Health, the World Health Organization, and the National Cancer Institute.

Stanley married Marian Staples Jay on June 25, 1929. They had met at the University of Illinois, where they both were graduate students in chemistry. They coauthored a scientific paper together with Adams, which was published the same year they were married. The Stanleys had three daughters and one son. On June 15, 1971, while attending a conference on biochemistry in Spain, Stanley died from a heart attack.

SELECTED WRITINGS BY STANLEY:

Books

The Viruses: Biochemical, Biological, and Biophysical Properties, Academic Press (New York), 1959.

Viruses and the Nature of Life, Dutton (New York), 1961.

Periodicals

Phytopathology, Chemical Studies on the Virus of Tobacco Mosaic, 24, 1934, pp. 1055–085.

Science, Isolation of a Crystalline Protein Possessing the Properties of Tobacco-Mosaic Virus, 81, 1935, pp. 644–45.

Journal of Experimental Medicine, Preparation and Properties of Influenza Virus Vaccines Concentrated and Purified by Differential Centrifugation, 81, 1945, pp. 193–218.

FURTHER READING:

Books

Berger, Melvin, *Famous Men of Modern Biology,* Crowell, 1968, pp. 165–76.

———— , *Dictionary of Scientific Biography,* Scribner's, 1976, pp. 841–48.

———— , *Nobel Prize Winners,* H. W. Wilson, 1987, pp. 1001–003.

Periodicals

Berger, Melvin, *Les prix Nobel en 1946,* The Nobel Prize in Chemistry, 1946, Stockholm, 1948, pp. 29–32.

———— , *Nature,* Wendell Meredith Stanley, 233, 1971, pp. 149–50.

———— , *Chemical and Engineering News,* The William H. Nichols Medalist for 1946, 24, 1946, pp. 750–55.

Sketch by Mike McClure

Johannes Stark
1874–1957
German physicist

Johannes Stark's life can be divided into two fairly distinct and contrasting halves. During the earlier period, he demonstrated unusual skills as an experimentalist and won acclaim as a brilliant physicist, holding posts at universities throughout Germany. Founder and editor of the prestigious *Jahrbuch der Radioaktivität und Elektronik* (*Yearbook of Radioactivity and Electronics*), he is credited with discovering the Doppler effect in canal rays, and the splitting of the spectral lines of hydrogen by means of an external electrical field, a phenomenon now known as the Stark effect. For these discoveries, Stark received the 1919 Nobel Prize in physics. After 1913, however, Stark began to withdraw from the scientific community and to ally himself with Adolf Hitler's program of National Socialism. Along with **Philipp Lenard**, Stark called for a "purification" of German science, an adoption of a non-Jewish "Aryan science." He failed to receive the recognition he sought in the political arena and eventually found himself ostracized by fellow scientists in Germany and throughout the world.

Stark was born on April 15, 1874, in Schickenhof, Bavaria. Raised on a farm, he attended local schools in Bayreuth and Regensburg. In 1894 he entered the University of Münich as a science major, earning his doctorate in 1897 for a dissertation entitled "Investigations on Lampblack." He then accepted a post as assistant to Eugen Lommel at Münich, a position he held for the next three years. In the spring of 1900, Stark moved to the University of Göttingen as assistant to Eduard Riecke, and was appointed privatdozent in 1903.

Stark Discovers the Doppler Effect in Canal Rays

During his tenure at Göttingen, Stark made the first of his important discoveries: the Doppler effect in canal rays. The Doppler effect is the change in frequency that occurs in a wave as its source advances toward or retreats from an observer. Wavelengths shorten as they approach, producing a higher pitch or frequency, and lengthen as they recede, producing a lower pitch. The apparent change in pitch of a train whistle as it passes an observer is a familiar example of the Doppler effect. The Doppler effect had been predicted by Johann Christian Doppler in 1842, and, by 1900, had been observed by the American astronomer **Edwin Hubble** in the red shift of galaxies, though no terrestrial example had yet been described. Stark decided that an appropriate way to observe the Doppler effect in the laboratory was with canal rays, beams of positively-charged particles generated in a vacuum tube. In 1905, Stark used canal rays of hydrogen atoms to conduct the experiment and observed the predicted Doppler effect in hydrogen spectral lines—as they approached they reached higher frequencies, the violet end of the spectrum, and, like Hubble's galaxies, they shifted to the red, or lower, frequencies as they receded.

In 1906 Stark was appointed lecturer in applied physics and photography at the Technical College in Hannover. During his three-year tenure there, Stark was continuously on bad terms with his superior, Julius Brecht. Finally, in 1909, Stark accepted an appointment as professor at the Technical College at Aachen, where he remained for eight years.

Observes the Splitting of Spectral Lines

Since his days at Hannover, Stark had been thinking about a problem originally suggested by the work of the Dutch physicist **Pieter Zeeman**. In 1896 Zeeman had observed that the presence of a magnetic field can cause an element's spectral lines to split. This analogy to an electric field was too obvious for physicists to miss, and while a number of them had tried in the first decade of the twentieth century to produce this effect, none were successful. But in 1913, Stark succeeded in splitting spectral lines in an electric field. He placed a third electrode a few centimeters from the cathode in a vacuum tube and applied a potential difference of 20,000 volts between the two. When canal rays were generated in the tube, Stark was able to observe the splitting of the spectral lines of hydrogen gas, a phenomenon that is now known as the Stark effect. For his work on the Doppler and Stark effects, Stark was awarded the 1919 Nobel Prize in physics. In addition, he received the Baumgartner Prize of the Vienna Academy of Sciences in 1910, the Vahlbruch Prize of the Göttingen Academy of Sciences in 1914, and the Matteuci Gold Medal of the National Academy of Sciences of Italy.

Shifts from Scientific to Political Activities

After 1913, Stark slowly fell out of the mainstream of scientific research. Scholars have suggested a number of reasons for this change. A major factor seems to have been his inability to get along with other scientists and subsequent failure to receive an appropriate academic appointment. In 1917 he accepted a post as professor of physics at the University of Greifswald. He seems to have been happy in the conservative climate of this university, but decided to leave in 1920 to accept a similar post at the University of Würzburg. Stark was much less comfortable there, as his colleagues and superiors found a number of reasons to object to his presence, including his use of Nobel Prize money to finance the construction of a new ceramics factory. Although he devoted an increasing amount of time and attention to the factory, it eventually failed. Stark's colleagues found his attention to nonacademic concerns ethically questionable. In addition, Stark's increasingly conservative political views were not well received in the liberal environment of Würzburg.

By 1922, Stark had become so uncomfortable at Würzburg that he resigned his post. He then became increasingly active politically in opposition to the post-World War I Weimar Republic, and in efforts to establish conservative, anti-governmental scientific organizations. One of these, the Fachgemeinschaft der deutschen Höchschulehrer der Physik (Professional Association of the German Higher Education Teachers of Physics), he established as an attempt to counterbalance the older, more liberal Deutsche Physikalische Gesellschaft (German Physical Society), based in Berlin.

When Stark decided to return to academic life, he found that he had made too many enemies and offended too many colleagues. He was rejected for posts at the universities of Berlin and Tübingen in 1924, Breslau and Marburg in 1926, Heidelberg in 1927, and Münich in 1928. By the early 1930s, Stark had become almost entirely an administrator of science, and then only in posts that his political influence had won for him. During the mid–1930s, he

worked diligently to gain control over the direction of German science policy making, but eventually lost out in that struggle to men who were even more closely allied to Adolf Hitler and the Nazi party.

By the beginning of World War II, Stark had become a self-made loner, having angered and annoyed both his former scientific colleagues and his former political allies. He sat out the war in his estate of Eppenstatt, in Bavaria, where he had constructed a laboratory. Stark had married Louise Uepter and had five children; beyond his professional interests Stark also enjoyed forestry and cultivating fruit trees. In 1947 he was sentenced to four years in a labor camp by a German de-Nazification court; he died in Eppenstatt on June 21, 1957.

SELECTED WRITINGS BY STARK:

Books

Die Elektrizität in Gasen, (title means "Electricity in Gases"), J. A. Barth (Leipzig), 1902.
Die Prinzipien der Atomdynamik, three volumes, [Leipzig], 1910–1915. Die gegenwärtige Krisis in der deutschen Physik (title means "The Present Crisis in German Physics"), [Leipzig], 1922.
Die Axialität der struktur und Atombindung, [Berlin], 1928.
Adolf Hitler und die deutsche Forschung, [Berlin], 1935.
Jüdische und deutsche Physik, [Leipzig], 1941.

Periodicals

Annalen der Physik, Beobachtungen über der Effekt des Elektrischen Feldes auf Spektrallinien, I-VI, 4th series, Volume 43, 1914, pp. 965–1047, and Volume 48, 1915, pp. 193–235.
Physikalische Zeitschrift, Der Doppler Effekt und bei den Kanalstrahlen und die Spektra der Positiven Atomionen, Volume 6, 1905, pp. 892–97.

FURTHER READING:

Books

Beyerchen, Alan D., *Scientists under Hitler: Politics and the Physics Community in the Third Reich,* Yale University Press, 1977, pp. 103–22.

Sketch by David E. Newton

Ernest H. Starling
1866–1927
English physiologist

An experimentalist who discovered a number of significant fundamental facts about the cardiovascular system, Ernest H. Starling is known for his discovery, along with longtime collaborator **William Maddock Bayliss**, of secretin. In 1902 Starling and Bayliss found that the release of digestive juices by the pancreas is caused by a chemical they named "secretin." Starling later suggested the name "hormone" for any chemical, such as secretin, that is released in one part of the body and causes an effect in another part of the body. In the course of his career, Starling also conducted studies into the circulatory system, as well as into the secretion of lymph and other body fluids. For his work, he was awarded the Medal of the Royal Society, the Baly Medal from the Royal College of Physicians, and several honorary degrees from such institutions as Trinity College, Dublin, the University of Strasbourg, and the University of Sheffield.

Ernest Henry Starling was born in London on April 17, 1866. His father was Matthew Henry Starling, a clerk for the British government who served in Bombay and returned to England only once every three years. Rearing of the Starling children was the responsibility, therefore, of Matthew's wife, the former Ellen Mathilda Watkins. In *Dictionary of Scientific Biography,* essayist Carleton B. Chapman described the family as one "of limited financial means and fundamentalist religious beliefs."

Starling began his schooling at the age of six when he was enrolled at the Islington School. He then attended King's College School from 1880 to 1882 and, in the latter year, enrolled at Guy's Hospital Medical College in London. He interrupted his schooling at Guy's briefly in the summer of 1885 when he traveled to Heidelberg to study with German physiologist Wilhelm Kühne, who was known for his research into nerves and muscles. Kühne apparently had a significant impact on Stanley's growing view of the role of basic physiology in the understanding and treatment of medical disorders.

Even before receiving his medical degree in 1889, Starling achieved distinction by being appointed demonstrator in physiology at Guy's. At the time, the hospital had simple and inadequate research facilities, a condition that changed after Starling was promoted to head of the physiology department a few years later. By the time he left Guy's in 1899, Starling had overseen the construction and equipping of a new physiology building that ultimately earned a reputation as one of the best research facilities for physiology in London.

Starling was married in 1891 to Florence Amelia Wooldridge Sieveking, daughter of an eminent London physician and widow of another physiologist, Leonard Charles Wooldridge. The Starlings had four children, three daughters and a son; Florence assisted immensely with her husband's work.

The deplorable working conditions at Guy's prompted Starling to look elsewhere for research facilities even as he was working to improve those conditions at Guy's. Thus, in 1890 he was given a part-time appointment in the physiology laboratories of Edward Albert Schäfer at University College. There he met and began working with fellow physiologist William Maddock Bayliss, an association that was to last throughout Starling's life and, incidentally, resulted in the marriage of Starling's sister to Bayliss.

Starling's first important work resulted from an 1892 visit to the Breslau laboratories of German physiologist Rudolf Heidenhain, an authority on the study of lymph. During his stay in Breslau, Starling repeated many of Heidenhain's experiments (and conducted some of his own) and came to radically different conclusions about their meaning. He was able to demonstrate that a combination of hydrostatic blood pressure and osmotic forces could account for all of the observations made by Heidenhain and himself about the way lymph is formed and transported in the body. In *The Dictionary of National Biography, 1922–1930,* contributor J. Barcroft asserted that Starling's findings "so completely superseded previous work in this field as to put Starling, in his early thirties, into the first rank of experimental physiologists."

Bayliss Collaboration Results in Discovery of Secretin

Probably the discovery for which Starling is most famous occurred shortly after his return to London and his election to the Jodrell Chair of Physiology at University College in 1899. He and Bayliss began a study of the secretion of digestive juices by the pancreas. They eventually found that the process takes place under the control of a substance secreted by the small intestine, a substance they named "secretin." Starling suggested that the name "hormone" be given to any chemical, such as secretin, that transmits a message from one part of the body to another part. Although hormones had actually been known before the discovery of secretin in 1902, it was Starling who first clearly defined the concept and elucidated the role that such substances have in the body.

The year Starling and Bayliss discovered secretin also marked the beginning of the former scientist's research on the heart. In order to carry out this research, Starling used a "heart-lung preparation" consisting of a heart that has been isolated in an anesthetized animal from all other organs except the lungs. Starling focused his research on various factors—such as temperature and blood pressure—that affect the beating of the heart. As a result of his studies, he discovered a number of facts about the heart, including one that has become known as Starling's Law of the heart: the energy of contraction is a function of the length of the muscle fibers in the heart.

Starling's heart research was interrupted by the outbreak of World War I. After his enlistment, he first served as a medical officer at Herbert Hospital, then became a researcher on defensive mechanisms against poison gas. His contributions to the war effort were apparently somewhat limited, however, because of his "outspoken impatience with the obtuseness, where scientific matters were concerned, of his military superiors," as Chapman explained in *Dictionary of Scientific Biography*.

The intensity of Starling's research diminished after the war, but he continued to exert influence in the field of physiology. In 1922 he was appointed to the newly created post of Foulerton Research Professor at the Royal Society. He also became very much interested in the state of education in Great Britain, particularly with regard to the role of the natural sciences in a liberal education. His health began to deteriorate after the war, and he died on May 2, 1927, aboard a cruise ship outside Kingston, Jamaica, where he was buried.

SELECTED WRITINGS BY STARLING:

Books

Principles of Human Physiology, Lea & Febiger, 1912.

Periodicals

Journal of Physiology, The Mechanism of Pancreatic Secretion, September 12, 1902, pp. 325–53.
Journal of Physiology, On the Mechanical Factors which Determine the Output of the Ventricles, September 8, 1914, pp. 357–79.
Science Progress, Science in Education, 1918–1919, Volume 13, pp. 466–75.

FURTHER READING:

Books

Gillispie, Charles Coulson, editor, *Dictionary of Scientific Biography,* Volume 12, Scribner's, 1975. pp. 617–19.
Williams, E. T., and Helen M. Palmer, *The Dictionary of National Biography, 1922–1930,* Oxford, 1971, pp. 807–09.

Sketch by David E. Newton

Chauncey Starr
1912–
American physicist

Chauncey Starr is perhaps best known as the first president of the Electric Power Research Institute. But his many contributions to the field of nuclear power are at least as important as the final episode in his long career. An accomplished researcher on nuclear propulsion systems for space vehicles, Starr foresaw the potential of nuclear energy for space applications. He has earned numerous awards for his work on peaceful uses of atomic power, and received the 1990 National Medal of Technology from the president of the United States for contributions to engineering and the electric industry.

Starr was born on April 14, 1912 in Newark, New Jersey to Rubin, a building contractor, and Rose (Dropkin) Starr. He received an electrical engineering degree in 1932 and a Ph.D. in physics in 1935 from Rensselaer Polytechnic Institute in Troy, New York. He then became a research fellow in physics at Harvard University, working with Nobel prize winner **Percy Williams Bridgman** on the physics of metals at high pressures. From 1938 to 1941, Starr was a research associate in physical chemistry at the Massachusetts Institute of Technology. Starr married Doris Evelyn Diebel in 1938 and has two children, Ross M. and Ariel E.

Space Applications of Nuclear Power

As an engineer with the Manhattan Project in the early to mid-1940s, Starr conducted research on an electromagnetic process for uranium separation, and became technical director of the Oak Ridge, Tennessee, pilot plant where the process was developed and improved. In 1946, as vice president of North American Aviation Inc., (later known as Rockwell International) and president of its Atomics International Division, he was launched into the space program by a study of the technical feasibility of using nuclear rockets for the Air Force.

The team of scientists and engineers that he formed for this study went on to make significant contributions in nuclear propulsion systems. In 1956, the Atomic Energy Commission incorporated Atomic International's design for a lightweight zirconium-hydride reactor (which allowed for the controllable release of nuclear energy) into its Systems for Nuclear Auxiliary Power (SNAP) program. By 1965, the reactor system was functional and was tested in orbit from California's Vandenberg Air Force Base. It operated for forty-three days, signalling the beginning of the space age.

Call for Accountability in the Power Industry

Starr's twenty-year industrial career was followed by a short stay in academe. From 1967 to 1973 he was Dean of the School of Engineering and Applied Science at the University of California at Los Angeles (UCLA). During his time at UCLA, Starr pioneered the concept of risk analysis as a basis for optimal risk management in emerging engineering developments. Risk analysis calls for quantifying societal risks as part of the development process and has been incorporated into risk assessment guidelines that are used by the nuclear power industry and by government agencies.

Passionate about the environmental implications of energy production and usage, Starr has published hundreds of papers on energy-related topics. It was one of these papers ("Energy and Power," published in the September 1971 issue of *Scientific American*) that caught the attention of Shearon Harris, who was then president of the Edison Electric Institute (EEI). The EEI was working with the Electric Research Council on the creation of a comprehensive industry-sponsored research and development program. According to *EPRI Journal,* impressed with Starr's call for "sensible choices of technological alternatives" in meeting ever expanding energy demands, Harris approached Starr with the prospect of heading up the newly formed Electric Power Research Institute (EPRI).

EPRI, as it is known today, has become one of the largest private research organizations in the world. Starr, as founding president, not only ruled over the creation of the organizational structure of EPRI, but also determined the research directions and priorities the power industry would set. Given a free hand, Starr ran EPRI for its first formative five years, giving the industry much more than it expected in the process. EPRI was originally envisioned as a technical research organization, but under Starr's leadership, it took on a conscience as well. He developed a program that included broad technical, environmental, social and economic considerations, and which drew on the expertise of scientists and nonscientists alike in making conclusions. Starr became vice chairman of EPRI in 1978 and retired in 1987. He is now president emeritus and a consultant to EPRI.

In addition to numerous professional memberships, Starr is a member and past vice president of the National Academy of Engineering, and a founder and past president of the American Nuclear Society. He is also a member and past director of the American Association for the Advancement of Science, a Foreign Member of the Royal Swedish Academy of Engineering Science, and Officer of the French Legion of Honor. He has received honorary doctorate degrees from Rensselaer Polytechnic Institute, the Swiss Federal Institute of Technology, and Tulane University. In addition to the 1990 National Medal of Technology, he received the 1974 Atomic Energy Commission Award for meritorious contributions to the national atomic energy program, the 1990 United States Energy Award for long-term contributions to energy and international understanding, and numerous others.

SELECTED WRITINGS BY STARR:

Books

Sodium Graphite Reactors, Addison-Wesley, 1958.
Economic Growth, Employment, and Energy, IPC Science and Technology Press, 1977.
Current Issues in Energy, Pergamon, 1979.
The Growth of Limits, Pergamon, 1979.

Periodicals

Scientific American, Energy, and Power, September 1971, pp. 37–49.
Annual Review of Energy, Philosophical Basis of Risk Analysis, Volume 1, Annual Reviews, 1976.
Proceedings of the Edison Centennial Symposium on Science, Technology and the Human Prospect, The Growth of Limits, Pergamon, 1979.
Science, Energy Sources: A Realistic Outlook, May 15, 1992, pp. 98–105.

Other

Risk Management Commentary, for Dr. A. Allan Bromley, Assistant to the President for Science and Technology, Washington, DC, 1990.

FURTHER READING:

Periodicals

EPRI Journal, The Right Person at the Right Time, (special twentieth anniversary issue), January/February, 1993, pp. 10–14.

Sketch by Olga K. Anderson

Thomas Starzl
1926–
American surgeon

Thomas Starzl is a world-renowned transplant surgeon. He performed the first human liver transplant in 1963 and was a pioneer in kidney transplantation. He has continued his pioneering work by helping to develop better drugs to make human organ transplants safer and more successful. Starzl has also contributed to the fields of general and thoracic surgery and neurophysiology.

Thomas Earl Starzl was born on March 11, 1926, in Le Mars, Iowa, to Roman F. Starzl, the editor and publisher of the *Globe Post,* a local newspaper, and Anna Laura

Fitzgerald Starzl. He was the second son and was followed by two younger sisters. He finished high school during World War II and enlisted in officers' training school at Westminster College in Fulton, Missouri, in 1944. After his discharge from military service, he entered the premedical program at Westminster College, graduating in 1947. After graduation he immediately returned home to care for his mother, who was suffering from breast cancer. She died less than two months later, on June 30.

In September 1947 he entered Northwestern University Medical School in Chicago. After completing three years of medical school, Starzl took a year off to do research with Dr. Horace W. Magoun, a professor of neuroanatomy. While in Magoun's laboratory, Starzl developed a recording technique to track deep brain responses to sensory stimuli. He and his advisor published the work, which continues to be cited, in 1951. His work in Magoun's laboratory earned him a Ph.D. degree in neurophysiology from Northwestern in 1952, the same year in which he received his M.D. Starzl also received an M.A. degree in anatomy from Northwestern.

Starzl enrolled in the prestigious surgical training program at Johns Hopkins University Hospital in Baltimore in 1952. During his time at Johns Hopkins he met and married Barbara J. Brothers of Hartville, Ohio. (The two had three children, Timothy, Rebecca and Thomas. The marriage ended in divorce in 1976, in part, Starzl admits, because of his nonstop work schedule.) Starzl stayed in the Johns Hopkins training program for four years, but left in anger when he learned he would not be offered the coveted position of chief resident. He went to Jackson Memorial Hospital in Miami for his fifth and final year as a resident. During this time he was attracted to the idea of liver transplantation. In an empty garage on the grounds of Jackson Memorial Hospital, Starzl set up a laboratory and began his research on the liver, doing experimental surgeries on dogs he obtained from the city pound. He developed a new technique for removing the liver, the first step in liver transplantation. He published his method, and it quickly became the worldwide standard.

Turns to Academic Medicine

In 1958 Starzl returned to Northwestern, where he had accepted a fellowship in thoracic surgery. He passed the thoracic surgery boards in 1959. More importantly, he received two awards to fund his experimental research. One was a five-year grant from the National Institutes of Health. The other was the prestigious Markle Scholarship, which persuaded him to remain in academic medicine. Starzl was a member of Northwestern's surgical faculty for four years. During that time, he further perfected techniques for liver transplantation.

Starzl accepted a position at the University of Colorado School of Medicine as an associate professor of surgery in 1962, believing it offered better opportunities to develop an active organ transplant program. In the late 1950s, surgeons had begun to experiment with the first immune-suppressive drugs to prevent the body from rejecting a transplanted organ. As a consequence, transplantations became possible for the first time. Despite his interest in liver transplantation, Starzl considered a human liver transplant to be too risky given current knowledge of immunosuppression. On March 27, 1962, Starzl performed his first kidney transplant operation in Denver. Starzl was to achieve considerable success in kidney transplantation, but his real target was the liver, and he soon turned to that challenge.

First Attempted Liver Transplant

On March 1, 1963, five years before the surgeon **Christiaan Neethling Barnard** undertook the first human heart transplant, Starzl attempted the world's first liver transplant. His patient was a three-year-old boy named Bennie Solis born with an incomplete liver. The child did not survive the operation because of uncontrolled bleeding. Starzl was widely criticized because he failed in his attempt, but, undaunted, he tried again in May 1963. This time he gave his patient, a man with cancer of the liver, huge amounts of fibrinogen, a protein that forms blood clots. The operation appeared to be a success, but the patient died three weeks later from complications due to blood clotting.

During the next few years, Starzl worked to solve the problem of uncontrolled bleeding and tissue rejection. In 1964 he directed the first extensive trial of tissue matching ever attempted. In the early 1960s, the physician Paul Terasaki of the University of California at Los Angeles had developed a method for detection of tissue antigens, the agents responsible for organ rejection. This method began the field of human histocompatibility research, the search for compatible tissue types. These efforts made it possible to match organ donors and recipients. In addition, Starzl turned his attention to development of drugs that would block the immune system from rejecting a new organ.

In the late 1960s Starzl was ready to attempt liver transplantation once again. This time all the attempts were on infants and young children with severe liver disease, and a number of them were successful, although some of the patients who survived the operation died from unrelated illnesses not too long afterwards. By the late 1970s the survival rate for liver transplants had risen to 40 percent.

During the 1970s and early 1980s, Starzl's career reputation skyrocketed. He was promoted to professor of surgery at the University of Colorado in 1964 and was made chairman of the department in 1972. During the late 1970s Starzl was wooed by the University of California at Los Angeles to move his transplantation program there. But he finally settled on the University of Pittsburgh and moved there in 1981. The same year he married Joy Conger, who had been a research technician working on a project with Starzl in Denver.

In the early 1980s the availability of cyclosporin, a new, superior drug to prevent organ rejection, was an encouraging sign to Starzl that the survivor rate for liver transplantation could be raised. However, bureaucratic roadblocks were in the way of using cyclosporin and other promising new drugs in organ transplant operations other than kidney transplantations, because they were considered by the federal government to be experimental. Starzl took the problem to the then-acting U.S. Surgeon General C. Everett Koop. Koop suggested Starzl appear before a government committee at the National Institutes of Health that could approve the operation. Starzl assembled a group of children who had survived liver transplants performed in the 1970s and early 1980s. They served as witnesses to the value of the operation, and after much testimony the committee approved liver transplantation as a service to mankind.

What followed was a rush by surgeons to begin performing the operation. All came to learn from Starzl and the physicians he had trained, who were scattered across the country. At the same time it became clear that the country needed a national system of organ procurement and distribution. Starzl worked diligently to get a bill passed by Congress in 1984 that would set up such as system. Starzl designed the system at the University of Pittsburgh, which became the national standard.

Performs Baboon Liver Transplants

Starzl also enhanced his fame by directing a series of multiple-organ transplants in these years. In 1984 a young child received a heart and liver in a single operation, while a young woman received a heart, liver, and kidney in 1986. Starzl's attempts to transplant baboon livers into human patients remained controversial into the late 1980s, however. He had experimented with such transplantations since the early 1960s, performing the first successful one in 1989. The patient was dying from hepatitis B, to which baboon livers do not appear to be susceptible. Although the operation was initially successful, a surgical error caused a fatal infection some three weeks later. Although some people objected to the use of animals for "spare parts," a major controversy arose over the fact that the patient had been HIV positive. Virtually all medical centers take the position that organ transplants, which require a suppression of the immune system, are inappropriate for patients who have been infected with the virus that also attacks the immune system.

In 1990 Starzl underwent coronary bypass surgery himself, and shortly afterwards retired from active surgery. He now concentrates his efforts on research. He claims that the decision was motivated in part by his emotional involvement with patients, which made the surgeries particularly difficult and stressful for him.

Over the years, Starzl has won many awards and honors and has been awarded many honorary degrees, including a merit Award from Northwestern University in 1969, a Distinguished Achievement Award in Modern Medicine in 1969, Colorado Man of Year Award in 1967, David Hume Memorial Award from the National Kidney Foundation in 1978, and Pittsburgh Man of the Year Award

in 1981. Starzl has written hundreds and hundreds of scientific papers, averaging fifty papers a year during the 1980s.

SELECTED WRITINGS BY STARZL:

Books

Experience in Hepatic Transplantation, W. B. Saunders, 1969.
The Puzzle People: Memoirs of a Transplant Surgeon, University of Pittsburgh Press, 1992.

FURTHER READING:

Periodicals

Altman, Lawrence, K., *New York Times,* A Transplant Surgeon Who Fears Surgery, July 7, 1992, pp. C1, C9-C10.
Clark, Matt, and Dan Shapiro, *Newsweek,* The Master Transplanter, January 11, 1982, p. 36.
Gorner, Peter, *Chicago Tribune,* Cutting Edge, September, 27, 1992, pp. 5–6.
Salvatierra, O., *Renal Transplantation,* Renal Transplantation—The Starzl Influence, February, 1988 (supplement 1), pp. 343–49.
Werth, Barry, *New York Times Magazine,* The Drug that Works in Pittsburgh, September 30, 1990, pp. 35, 58–9.

Sketch by Karyn Hede George

Hermann Staudinger
1881–1965
German organic and polymer chemist

Hermann Staudinger's interest in organic chemistry was wide-ranging and he made many important contributions in that field. He is principally known, however, for his concept of the "macromolecule," or polymer, a long chain of repeating chemical units. Although initially this idea was greeted with incredulity and scorn in the chemistry community, Staudinger eventually overcame his critics' objections with patient explanation, careful research, and dogged insistence. Polymers are now known to be extraordinarily useful substances, ubiquitous in natural systems as well as human society. The entire plastics and materials science industry bases itself on polymers, and the science of molecular biology was immeasurably aided by the concept of macromolecules. Staudinger was awarded a

Hermann Staudinger

Nobel Prize in 1953, three years after he had retired from active research.

Staudinger was born on March 23, 1881, in Worms, Germany, to Dr. Franz and Auguste (Wenck) Staudinger. His father was a philosopher and professor at various German institutions of secondary education, and was interested in social reform. Staudinger graduated from the Gymnasium at Worms in 1899 (a German *gymnasium* is roughly the equivalent of an American prep school) and began his university studies at Halle under the guidance of the botanist Professor Klebs. While there, Staudinger began a lifelong detour from his original interest in botany. His family encouraged him to study chemistry to provide a strong background for his biological investigations, and he not only took their advice, but actually stayed in chemistry for most of the rest of his career. He studied in Darmstadt under the direction of professors Kolb and Stadel, and in Munich under the direction of Professor Piloty. In 1901 he returned to the University of Halle and in 1903 finished his doctoral work under the direction of Professor Vorlander. Although Staudinger had begun his studies in the analytical subdivision of chemistry, Vorlander's influence and ideas caused him to develop an intense interest in theoretical organic chemistry. His doctoral thesis was on the malonic esters of unsaturated compounds.

Mainstream Organic Chemistry Research

Initially, Staudinger's organic chemical investigations were relatively routine, although they resulted in the synthesis of some interesting new classes of organic molecules. In 1905, while in his first teaching position (as instructor) with Professor Thiele in Strassburg, he discovered the first ketene (colorless, poisonous gasses). Ketenes as a class are extremely reactive—they even react with traces of water and the oxygen in the air—and Staudinger and other researchers investigated their properties and chemistry for several years. In 1907 he prepared a special dissertation on the ketenes and was awarded the title of assistant professor. Shortly thereafter, he accepted an associate professor position at the Technische Hoshschule in Karlsruhe. Staudinger began many basic organic synthesis projects in Karlsruhe, including a new synthesis of isoprene (a constituent part of rubber), although some of the newer projects slowed when he moved to the Swiss Federal Institute of Technology (Eidgenossische Technische Hochschule) in Zurich in 1912. The Zurich position was a prestigious one, but the teaching load was many hours per week, so he curtailed his research in some areas. He proved to be a dedicated teacher and instilled in his students an appreciation not only for chemistry, but also for the power of technology in society.

During his fourteen years in Switzerland, Staudinger continued investigations on the chemistry of the ketenes, oxalyl chloride, and several materials that are shock-sensitive, that is, they explode when bumped or dropped. He also continued work on pyrethrin insecticides, and when they could not be easily synthesized, drew on his botanical interests and suggested that new strains of chrysanthemum (from which natural pyrethrines are extracted) might yield better quantities than any laboratory. During World War I, much of Staudinger's work was driven by wartime shortages. He investigated the aromas of pepper and coffee to see if synthetic substitutes could be produced for those foods, and attempted to synthesize some important pharmaceuticals. He was successful enough to patent some of the artificial flavors and fragrances, although generally they proved uneconomical if the natural material was available. In 1926, Staudinger accepted a position as director of the chemical laboratories at Freiburg University, where he remained until his retirement in 1951. He continued to be internationally respected in his field, winning the LeBlanc medal given by the French Chemical Society in 1931 and the Cannizzarro Prize in Rome in 1933.

The Beginnings of the Macromolecule Theory

In 1924, Staudinger wrote in *Berichte der Deutschen Chemischen Gesellschaft*, "The molecules of rubber . . . have entirely different sizes . . . and these can be changed, by temperature for example. . . . It is very important here to use the idea of the molecule . . . ; [the] particles are held together by normal chemical bonds and in the structural sense we are dealing with very long carbon chains. The polymerization of isoprene to these long chains . . . goes on until a sufficiently large, little reactive, and thus strongly saturated molecule . . . has been formed. For those . . . particles in which the molecule is identical with the primary particle and in which the individual atoms of the . . . molecule are linked by normal valences, we propose to differentiate the type by the term *macromolecules*."

The move to Freiberg University signaled Staudinger's break with traditional organic chemistry. He had first proposed the idea of macromolecules in 1920 while still in Zurich, but at Freiberg he gave up most of his other chemical research to pursue the study of rubber and synthetic polymers. It was a decision that caused his colleagues some consternation because he was well respected in his field, and they felt he would do damage to his reputation by working on such unpromising materials from such an unorthodox point of view.

When Staudinger began work on his theory of very high molecular weight compounds, several entrenched ideas about molecular weight existed. Chemists believed, for example, that the size of a molecule was governed by its "unit cell," or smallest nonrepeating piece, and that its molecular weight was a fixed number. For low molecular weight compounds, those principles remained true. Many chemical methods had been devised for determining the structure of molecules, and nonrepeating structures with unit cells of up to 5000 atomic mass units had been elucidated. The relatively new science of X-ray crystallography also helped in structure determination. Additionally, researchers knew of compounds, soaps for example, which aggregated (clumped together) in water and other solvents, instead of dissolving in the normal way. These aggregates possessed some of the same unusual physical characteristics as rubber and other known polymers. Many chemists therefore insisted that Staudinger had mistaken aggregates of smaller molecules for single large molecules.

With carefully designed experiments, Staudinger gradually accumulated evidence that a group of extremely large molecules indeed existed. They did not comprise oddly associated clumps of smaller molecules, and were not themselves single unit cells. Instead, these molecules resembled chains of repeating units, strung together and bonded to each other—like pearls on a wire. Additionally, because any number of units might be bonded together during synthesis, these large molecules had differing molecular weights, depending on the length of the chain.

While working in this area, Staudinger developed some new analytical methods and discovered a relationship between the viscosity of a polymer solution and its molecular weight. He had developed the method in desperation when he could not get funding for more sophisticated equipment, but it was soon widely used in industry because it was inexpensive, fast, and accurate. The equation, now called Staudinger's Law, allows a fairly simple estimation of molecular weight by measuring the "drag" or "stickiness" of a liquid flowing through a small tube (viscosity).

During World War II, the Freiburg University chemistry facilities were virtually destroyed in an Allied air bombardment in November 1944, and it was several years before they were fully operational again. Staudinger's work slowed after the enormous stresses of the war, although he still found the energy to start and edit two new journals, one on macromolecular chemistry. He gave many talks and wrote prolifically on the subject of macromolecules until the end of his career.

Achievements Finally Recognized with Nobel Prize in 1953

In spite of the evidence, however, chemists had difficulty in accepting his conclusions. Spirited discussions bordering on uproar often greeted him when he gave scientific lectures; his persistence and patience in the face of such hostility became legendary. Historians have noted such resistance before on the part of the scientific community whenever a truly revolutionary idea is advanced. Some have speculated that chemists simply found the idea of huge molecules too messy; they preferred the neat, tidy unit cell with its fixed structure and weight, for which they had developed many good analytical procedures.

As time went on, however, evidence from other areas of scientific study built unequivocal support for macromolecules. X-ray crystallographers had refined their techniques to the point where they could obtain structural information on polymeric materials. Various microscope and optical techniques also lent important evidence, particularly for biological molecules. Staudinger had speculated for years that living systems must require macromolecules to function, and the new science of molecular biology began to lend vigorous support to that idea.

So controversial were Staudinger's macromolecular theories, that it was not until 1953, when he was seventy-two years of age, that he was finally rewarded with the Nobel Prize for his efforts. The presenter of the prize, Professor Fredga, noted in his speech, "In the world of high polymers, almost everything was new and untested. Long standing, established concepts had to be revised or new ones created. The development of macromolecular science does not present a picture of peaceful idylls."

After his retirement, Staudinger once again took up his original interest in botany, although his biological bent had always been apparent even in his chemical work. His wife, the former Magda Woit, was a Latvian plant physiologist who often participated in his research, collaborated in writing many of his papers, and made some important connections of her own between his macromolecular theories and the molecules of biology. Staudinger listed some of her considerable contributions in his Nobel Prize address, and dedicated his autobiography to her. They married in 1927, and she survived him upon his death on September 8, 1965.

SELECTED WRITINGS BY STAUDINGER:

Books

From Organic Chemistry to Macromolecules, translated by J. Fock and M. Fried, Interscience, 1970.

Periodicals

Source Book in Chemistry, 1900–1950, On Polymerization, portions translated and reprinted in Leicester, Henry M., editor, Harvard University Press, 1968, p. 260, from original in Berichte der Deutschen Chemischen Gesellschaft, Volume 53, 1920, pp. 1073–085.

Source Book in Chemistry, 1900–1950, On the Constitution of Rubber (Sixth Paper), portions translated and reprinted in Leicester, Henry M., editor, Harvard University Press, 1968, p. 264, from original in Berichte der Deutschen Chemischen Gesellschaft, Volume 57, 1924, pp. 1203–208.

FURTHER READING:

Periodicals

Flory, P. J., *Journal of Chemical Education,* Macromolecules Vis-a-Vis the Traditions of Chemistry, Volume 50, 1973, p. 732.

Mark, H., *Journal of Chemical Education,* The Early Days of Polymer Science, Volume 50, 1973, p. 757. Russell, C. A., editor, Recent Developments in the History of Chemistry, 1985, p. 128.

Olby, R., *Journal of Chemical Education,* The Macromolecular Concept and the Origins of Molecular Biology, Volume 47, 1970, p. 168.

Sketch by Gail B. C. Marsella

Milan Ratislav Stefanik
1880–1919
Czechoslovakian astronomer

Milan Ratislav Stefanik's importance to the scientific community consisted primarily in his efforts to establish astronomical observatories and meteorological research stations in many parts of the world. However, his scientific career came to an end when he enlisted in the French army at the outbreak of World War I. He died in a plane crash shortly after accepting the position of minister of war of the newly-created state of Czechoslovakia.

Son of a Protestant pastor in Hungarian Slovakia, Stefanik studied mathematics and physics in Prague, at Charles University and at the Institute of Technology. He also studied in Zurich. Upon receiving a doctorate from the Charles University in 1904, he traveled to Paris for postdoctoral work where he became an assistant at the Meudon astrophysical observatory, then under the direction of the observatory's founder, the aged patriarch of astrophysics, Pierre Jules Cesar Janssen. An invalid, Janssen had given effective control of the observatory to his wife and daughter, whom Stefanik charmed. Under Janssen's patronage, Stefanik traveled widely to make astrophysical measurements. He visited the new international observatory atop Mt. Blanc and went to Central Asia to witness an eclipse.

Further Astronomical Travels

Janssen died in 1907, and directorship of Meudon went to Henri Alexandre Deslandres. Following this change, Stefanik's association with the observatory ceased, but he now began a career as an astronomical traveler, supported by short-term grants from French authorities. He investigated setting up an observatory in the Sahara Desert in Africa, and then he landed a mission to establish an observatory on the island of Tahiti. In 1910 he brought several large telescopes to Tahiti and installed them in an observatory building with an 8-meter cupola overlooking the administrative center in Papeete, the largest island in French Polynesia. He also set up a meteorological network for French Oceania and then returned to Paris in anticipation of being named director of a permanently funded Tahitian observatory. While awaiting his appointment, he journeyed to Brazil in order to observe the eclipse of 1912 at Passa Quatro.

In 1913 French political interests finally decided to fund the Tahiti observatory. This was accomplished through a complex web of international politics. The observatory would be fitted with a radio mast capable of communicating with France through a relay station. This relay station was to be erected on the Galapagos Islands, which are an island province of Ecuador, situated in the Pacific Ocean. The Ecuadoran government was asked to erect the Galapagos relay in exchange for help in renovating the Quito astronomical observatory. The real reason for the Galapagos station, however, was to have it serve as a French-controlled coaling station for ships using the new Panama Canal. Stefanik, who had become a French citizen in 1912, spent a number of months in Ecuador making arrangements to set up the radio relay-station until the outbreak of World War I scuttled French plans for the Galapagos. Upon returning to France, Stefanik traveled to Morocco as a scientific adviser to the French army which had recently conquered that kingdom.

At the beginning of the First World War, Stefanik joined the French air corps. He was most effective, not as a meteorologist (his first posting), but as an organizer of the Czech and Slovak legions that France supported. He was wounded in Serbia and rose up the ranks to become brigadier general in 1918. As a French general, he traveled to Siberia to deal with the repatriation of the Czech-Slovak legion that had been marooned there following the Russian revolution. A spokesman for the independence of his people, Stefanik became the first minister of war of the new state of Czechoslovakia. He died in 1919 when the plane that was returning him to Czechoslovakia crashed at the Bratislava airport.

SELECTED WRITINGS BY STEFANIK:

Books

Zapisnik Dr. M. R. Stefanika z Ecuadoru z r. 1913,
  Banska Bystrica, Czechoslovakia, 1933.
Zapisniky M. R. Stefanika, edited by Josef Bartusek
  and Jaroslav Bohac, [Prague], 1935.
*Stefanik, knihadruha: Vzpominky, dokumenty a jine
  prtsprvky,* edited by Josef Bartušek, [Prague], 1938.

FURTHER READING:

Books

Ihnat, Joseph, and others, editors, *General Milan R.
  Stefanik, 1880–1980: Historical Profile,* [New
  York], 1981.
Pyenson, Lewis, *Civilizing Mission: Exact Sciences and
  French Overseas Expansion, 1830–1940,* Johns
  Hopkins University Press, 1993, pp. 318–29.

Sketch by Lewis Pyenson

William Howard Stein
1911–1980
American biochemist

William Howard Stein, in partnership with **Stanford Moore**, was a pioneer in the field of protein chemistry. Although other scientists had previously established that proteins could play such roles as that of enzymes, antibodies, hormones, and oxygen carriers, almost nothing was known of their chemical makeup. Stein and Moore, during some forty years of collaboration, were not only able to provide information about the inner workings of protein molecules, but also invented the mechanical means by which that information could be extracted. Their discovery of how protein amino acids function was accomplished through a study of ribonuclease (RNase), a pancreatic enzyme that assists in the digestion of food by catalyzing the breakdown of nucleic acids. But their work could not have been accomplished without the development of a technology to assist them in collecting and separating the amino acids contained in ribonuclease. Their invention of the fraction collector and an automated system for analyzing amino acids was of great importance in furthering protein research, and these devices have become standard laboratory equipment.

Stein and Moore began their collective work in the late 1930s under Max Bergmann at the Rockefeller Institute (now Rockefeller University). After Bergmann's death in 1944, the pair developed the protein chemistry program at the institute and began their research into enzyme analysis. Except for a brief period during World War II when Moore served with the Office of Scientific Research and Development in Washington, D.C., and the two years when Stein taught at the University of Chicago and Harvard University, the partnership continued uninterrupted until Stein's death in 1980. Their joint inventions and coauthorship of most of their scientific papers were said to make it impossible to separate their individual accomplishments. Their combined efforts were acknowledged in 1972 with the Nobel Prize in chemistry. According to Moore, writing about Stein in the *Journal of Biological Chemistry* in 1980, they received the award "for contributions to the knowledge of the chemical structure and catalytic function of bovine pancreatic ribonuclease." **Christian Anfinsen** shared the Nobel Prize with Stein and Moore for related research.

The son of community-minded parents, Stein was born in New York City on June 25, 1911. He was the second of three children. His father, Fred M. Stein, was involved in business and retired at an early age to lend his services to various health care associations in the community. The scientist's mother, Beatrice Borg Stein, worked to improve recreational and educational conditions for underprivileged children. From an early age, Stein was encouraged by his parents to develop an interest in science. He received a progressive education from grade school on, attending the Lincoln School of the Teacher's College of Columbia University, transferring at sixteen years of age to Phillips Exeter Academy for his college preparatory studies. He graduated from Harvard University in 1933, then took a year of graduate study in organic chemistry there. Finding that his real interest was biochemistry, he completed his graduate studies at the College of Physicians and Surgeons of Columbia University, receiving his Ph.D. in 1938. His dissertation concerned the amino acid composition of elastin, a protein found in the walls of veins and arteries. This work marks the beginning of his long search to understand the chemical function of proteins.

Improved Methodology Solves Amino Acid Puzzle

The successful research being done at the Rockefeller Institute under the direction of Max Bergmann caught Stein's attention. He pursued postgraduate studies there in 1938, spending his time improving analytical techniques for purifying amino acids. Moore joined Bergmann's group in 1939. There, he and Stein began work in developing the methodology for analyzing the amino acids glycine and leucine. Their work was interrupted when the United States entered World War II. Then, Bergmann's laboratory was given over to the study of the physiological effects of mustard gases, in the hope of finding a counteractant.

The group's efforts to find accurate tools and methods for the study of amino acid structure increased in importance when they assumed the responsibility of establishing the institute's first program in protein chemistry. Looking for ways to improve the separation process of amino acids, they turned to partition chromatography, a filtering technique developed during the war by the English biochemists **A. J. P. Martin** and **Richard Synge**. Building on this technology, as well as that of English biochemist **Frederick Sanger**'s column chromatography and the ion-exchange technique of Werner Hirs, Stein and Moore went on to invent the automatic fraction collector and develop the automated system by which amino acids could be quickly analyzed. This automated system replaced the tedious two-week sequence that was previously required to differentiate and separate each amino acid.

From then on, the isolation and study of amino acid structure was advanced through these new analytical tools. Ribonuclease was the first enzyme for which the biochemical function was determined. The discovery that the amino acid sequence was a three-dimensional, chain-like structure that folds and bends to cause a catalytic reaction was a beginning for understanding the complex nature of enzyme catalysis. Stein and Moore were certain that this understanding would result in crucial medical advances. By 1972, the year Stein and Moore shared the Nobel Prize, other enzymes had been analyzed using their methods.

Editorial Work Complements Research

Because he was extremely eager to see that research done in laboratories all over the country be disseminated as widely and as quickly as possible, Stein devoted many years in various editorial positions to the *Journal of Biological Chemistry*. Under his leadership, the journal became a leading biochemistry publication. He had joined the editorial board in 1962 and became editor in 1968. He only held the latter post for one year, however. While attending an international meeting in Denmark, he contracted Guillain-Barré Syndrome, a rare disease often causing temporary paralysis. In grave danger of dying, he managed to recover somewhat. The illness left him a quadriplegic, confined to a wheelchair for the rest of his life. Although he remained involved with the work of his colleagues both in the laboratory and at the *Journal*, he was unable to participate actively.

In addition to the Nobel Prize, Stein shared with Moore the 1964 Award in Chromatography and Electrophoresis and the 1972 Theodore Richard Williams Medal of the American Chemical Society. He served as chairperson of the U.S. National Committee for Biochemistry from 1968 to 1969, as trustee of Montefiore Hospital, and as board member of the Hebrew University medical school. He married Phoebe L. Hockstader on June 22, 1936. They had three sons: William Howard, Jr., David, and Robert. Stein died in Manhattan on February 2, 1980.

SELECTED WRITINGS BY STEIN:

Periodicals

Journal of Biological Chemistry, A Chromatographic Investigation of Pancreatic Ribonuclease, Volume 200, 1953.

Journal of Biological Chemistry, The Amino Acid Composition of Ribonuclease, Volume 211, 1954.
Scientific American, The Structure of Proteins, Volume 204, 1961.
Science, Chemical Structures of Pancreatic Ribonuclease and Deoxyribonuclease, Volume 180, 1973.

FURTHER READING:

Books

Fruton, Joseph S., *Molecules and Life: Historical Essays on the Interplay of Chemistry, and Biology,* Wiley, 1972.

Periodicals

Moore, Stanford, *Journal of Biological Chemistry,* William H. Stein, Volume 255, 1980, pp. 9517–518.
Moore, Stanford, and William H. Stein, *Science,* Chemical Structures of Pancreatic Ribonuclease and Deoxyribonuclease, Volume 180, 1973, pp. 458–64.
——— , *New York Times,* October 21, 1972.
——— , *New York Times,* February 3, 1980.
Richards, Frederic M., *Science,* The 1972 Nobel Prize for Chemistry, Volume 178, 1972, pp. 492–93.

Sketch by Jane Stewart Cook

Jack Steinberger
1921–
American physicist

Jack Steinberger is an experimentalist in high-energy physics who discovered a new type of neutrino with the physicists **Leon Max Lederman** and **Melvin Schwartz**. In a groundbreaking experiment, the three scientists were able to create the first laboratory-made beam of neutrinos. Their discovery led to the development of the so-called "standard theory" of matter. In recognition of these contributions, Steinberger and his coinvestigators were awarded the 1988 Nobel Prize in physics.

Steinberger was born on May 25, 1921, in Bad Kissingen, Germany. His father was Ludwig Lazarus Steinberger, a cantor and leader of the local Jewish community, and his mother was Berta May Steinberger. Jack Steinberger and his brother left Germany in 1934 and immigrated to Chicago, Illinois. There, they lived with the family of Barnard Faroll, a grain broker. Later, Faroll was instrumental in bringing the rest of Steinberger's family to the United States.

Steinberger studied chemical engineering at the Illinois Institute of Technology, but left to enlist in the U.S. Army following the attack on Pearl Harbor. The army sent him to the Radiation Laboratory at the Massachusetts Institute of Technology, where he made radar bomb sights and studied physics. After the war, he enrolled at the University of Chicago, earning a bachelor of science degree in 1942, and a doctorate in physics in 1948. During his doctoral studies at Chicago, Steinberger had studied muons (semi-stable electrical particles) and showed that, when they decay, they yield two neutrons (nuclear particles with the mass of protons but not the charge) and an electron (a negatively charged atomic particle). He proposed at the time that muons could be broken down into muon-neutrinos and electron-neutrinos. (The neutrino is an elusive electrically uncharged basic particle of matter that lacks mass). The neutrino was important because Steinberger and other nuclear physicists believed neutrinos could be harnessed to study the weak nuclear force, which is responsible for certain types of radioactivity. The weak force, like electromagnetism, is one of the fundamental interactions between elementary particles.

Creates Neutrino Beam

Steinberger's professional career began at the University of California at Berkeley, with his appointment as professor of physics in 1949. He remained there for a year, and then moved on to Columbia University, also as a professor of physics. It was during a coffee break at the Pupin Physics Building of Columbia University that Melvin Schwartz, then Steinberger's graduate student, broached the idea to Leon Max Lederman and Steinberger of making beams of high-energy neutrinos for use in research. They decided to use the Brookhaven accelerator in Upton, Long Island, New York, to make the beam. They set up the accelerator to produce masses of protons at 15 billion electron volts and shoot them at a beryllium metal target. The protons (elementary positively charged particles) smashed the beryllium atomic nuclei into their component protons and neutrons. The impact also created pions, elusive short-lived particles that decay into muons and neutrinos. Seeking to filter out the neutrinos, the researchers constructed a forty-foot barrier of steel built from the scrap of the Battleship Missouri. The massive obstacle filtered out all the particles but the neutrinos, creating the first laboratory made beam of high-intensity neutrinos.

Until then, scientists had only been aware of the existence of neutrinos produced by the type of radioactive decay that also creates an electron. But the neutrinos that came out of the steel filter were accompanied by muons. These were muon-neutrinos. This finding led to the development of the "standard model theory," which posits the existence of three generations of matter: a first generation consisting of seven electrons, electron neutrinos and the up and the down quarks (hypothetical particles from which fundamental particles are built); a second generation of matter—that revealed by the experiments carried out by Steinberger and his colleagues—consisting of muons, muon-neutrinos and varieties of quarks called charmed and strange quarks; and a third generation, which physicists are exploring now and which includes tau particles (particles produced when electrons and anti-electrons are smashed together), tau neutrinos and the top and the bottom quarks. The discovery of the muon-neutrino was a pioneering step in a road that enabled high-energy physicists to use neutrinos in scientific investigations. In astronomy, for instance, neutrino telescopes detect explosions of neutrinos associated with far-off supernovas (stars that blow up with great brilliance).

Steinberger left Columbia University in 1968, moving on to become director, administrator, and researcher of the European Center for Nuclear Research in Geneva. He retired from his administrative duties in 1986, but remained as a staff physicist. He has continued to work on experiments in elementary particles and conduct research using the Large Electron-Positron Collider. In 1988 Steinberger received extensive public recognition for his discovery of the muon-neutrino and for a lifetime of contributions to physics. He was awarded not only the Nobel Prize in that year, but also received the National Medal of Science from the United States. Steinberger married Joan Beauregard in 1943. The marriage ended in divorce. In 1961 he married Cynthia Eve Alff. Steinberger is the father of three sons, Joseph, Richard and John, and a daughter, Julia Karen. Steinberger has become a United States citizen.

SELECTED WRITINGS BY STEINBERGER:

Periodicals

Physical Reviews Letters, Observation of High-Energy Neutrino Reactions and the Existence of Two Kinds of Neutrinos, Volume 9, 1962, p. 36.

Physical Reviews, Resonances in Strange-Particle Production, Volume 128, 1962, p. 1930.

Physical Reviews Letters, Lifetime of the w-Meson, Volume 11, 1963, p. 436.

FURTHER READING:

Books

Nobel Prize Winners: Physics, Salem Press, 1989, Volume 3, pp. 1353–364.

Periodicals

New York Times, October 20, 1988, pp. B11–12.

Sketch by Margo Nash

David B. Steinman
1886–1960
American engineer

David B. Steinman designed more than four hundred bridges worldwide, including the longest cantilever bridge in the United States, the largest bridge in South America, and the bridge with the longest fixed arch in the world. Among his technical achievements were improvements in the design of suspension bridges, a new loading system for railway bridges, and simplified techniques for design analysis; he was the first to construct a bridge specifically to withstand earthquakes. He believed that bridges should be visually appealing as well as functional, and eight of his creations were recognized as being among America's most beautiful bridges.

David Barnard Steinman, who was born in New York City on June 11, 1886, and his six brothers were the sons of Eva Scollard Steinman and Louis Kelvin Steinman, an immigrant factory worker. The family lived a sparse existence in a three-room tenement on the lower East Side in view of the Brooklyn Bridge, a landmark that became a childhood inspiration to Steinman.

A talented student, Steinman enrolled at the City College of New York at age thirteen. At that time, the Williamsburg Bridge over the East River was under construction, and Steinman was awarded a pass permitting him to inspect the structure and observe the engineers at work. He received his bachelor of science degree in 1906, then applied to Columbia University, where he was granted two scholarships; in three years, he earned a master's degree and a civil engineering degree. In 1910 he accepted a post at the University of Idaho, where he taught for four years; in the meantime he completed his doctoral work at Columbia, receiving an engineering Ph.D. in 1911. His dissertation, "The Design of the Henry Hudson Memorial Bridge as a Steel Arch," became a standard text. Twenty-five years later, he would be chosen to build that bridge, which contained the world's longest fixed arch, much as he had designed it as a student.

Steinman's dissertation caught the attention of Gustav Lindenthal, the designer in charge of the $20-million Hell Gate Arch project. At Lindenthal's invitation, Steinman returned to New York in 1914 to work on that railway bridge over the East River. The extremely strong tides at the site offered unprecedented challenges, but the project was completed in 1917. Steinman then taught civil and mechanical engineering at the City College of New York until 1920, when he became an independent consultant and design engineer.

A short time later, Manhattan Bridge builder Holton D. Robinson convinced Steinman to join him in a competition to design the Florianópolis Bridge in Brazil. The pair not only won the contest but were awarded the contract to build the bridge. The duo's creation, which was the largest bridge in South America and had the longest eyebar suspension span in the world, used a revolutionary concept that achieved four times the standard rigidity while using one-third less steel. Completed in 1926, the $1.4 million structure was remarkably inexpensive, and it was constructed without a single accident.

The partnership continued until Robinson's death in 1945. During that time, Steinman designed bridges in many countries, including Thailand, England, Italy, Korea, and Iraq. His 1927 design of the Carquinez Strait Bridge, over the entrance of the Sacramento and San Joaquin Rivers into San Francisco Bay, was at the time the longest cantilever bridge in the United States. It was also the first bridge to be constructed specifically to withstand earthquakes. Decades later, a similar structure was built as a twin span next to the original bridge. A transporter bridge (a single-cable suspension span carrying people in baskets) designed by Steinman for the 1933 Chicago World's Fair remained the world's longest until 1960. Steinman's Triborough Bridge, which linked New York City's Manhattan, Queens, and the Bronx with three and one-half miles of linked suspension, truss, and vertical lift spans, was completed in 1936. Two years later, President Franklin D. Roosevelt and Canadian Prime Minister Mackenzie King dedicated Steinman and Robinson's impressive Thousand Islands International Bridge, whose eight and one-half mile length included five inter-island spans.

In 1948 Steinman was asked to repair and modernize the Brooklyn Bridge. Three years earlier, he had published a biography, *The Builders of the Bridge,* about John A. and Washington A. Roebling, the father-and-son team who had built the bridge that had been his childhood inspiration. Under Steinman's careful hand, the sixty-five-year-old structure was transformed from a two-lane roadway into a modern six-lane highway, without altering its appearance.

Connects Michigan's Peninsulas

The Mackinac Straits Bridge in Michigan is regarded as Steinman's crowning achievement. Connecting Michigan's main body with its upper peninsula across four miles of water between Lakes Michigan and Huron, the bridge was completed in 1957. According to an article in the October 1956 issue of *Reader's Digest,* it was the longest suspension bridge in the world, from one anchorage to the other; its 3,800-foot main span was exceeded only by that of the Golden Gate Bridge. Among its technical challenges were the terrific winds common to the strait and the massive annual ice accumulations that would threaten its piers and foundations. Using his design expertise, along with new metallurgical developments and innovative construction techniques, Steinman built an impressive structure fully up to nature's challenges.

Among Steinman's 750 publications are standard engineering textbooks, poetry (much of it relating to bridges), a book about bridges for young readers, and more than six hundred technical papers. In 1934 he helped found the National Society of Professional Engineers and served as its first president. He received eighteen honorary degrees and over 150 honorary awards, including the French Legion d'Honneur. He was particularly pleased in 1947 when Columbia University presented him with its Medal for Excellence.

Professionally, Steinman had a reputation as an individualist; privately, he enjoyed playing chess and working on mechanical inventions—at one point he developed new techniques in stereo photography. He had married Irene Hoffman in 1915; their two sons, John Francis and David, became doctors, and their daughter, Alberta, earned a doctorate in psychology. Steinman died on August 21, 1960, at his home in New York following a three-month illness. At the time of his death, he was working on several projects, including a feasibility study for adding rapid transit to the Golden Gate Bridge.

SELECTED WRITINGS BY STEINMAN:

Books

The Builders of the Bridge: The Story of John Roebling and His Son, Harcourt, 1945.
Famous Bridges of the World, Random House, 1953.
Modes and Natural Frequencies of Suspension-bridge Oscillations, New York Academy of Sciences, 1959.
Songs of a Bridge Builder, Ind-US, 1959.

FURTHER READING:

Books

Ratigan, William, *Highways over Broad Waters; Life and Times of David B. Steinman, Bridgebuilder,* Eerdmans, 1959.

Periodicals

New York Times, August 23, 1960, p. 29.
Wolfert, Ira, *Reader's Digest,* Master Bridge-Builder October 1956, pp. 138–42.

Sketch by Sandra Katzman

Charles P. Steinmetz
1865–1923
American electrical engineer and mathematician

Charles P. Steinmetz was a mathematician and electrical engineer whose theories and research fostered the widespread use of electrical energy. A scientist of prodigious inventiveness, Steinmetz was granted some two hundred patents. His discovery of the phenomenon known as magnetic hysteresis led to the development of energy-efficient motors. He worked out mathematical theories that made practical the use of alternating current in long-distance power transmission. His work in changes in electrical circuits of very short duration was used to develop new cables and improved methods of operating transmission systems. He also built artificial lightning generators that led to the development of lightning arrestors to protect electrical apparatus and transmission lines.

Charles Proteus Steinmetz was born in Breslau, Germany (now Wroclaw, Poland), on April 9, 1865. His mother, Caroline Neubert, died when he was one year old; his father, Karl Heinrich, worked for the government-owned railroad. Steinmetz was the third of three sons and had two step-sisters and one half-sister. He changed his name from Karl August Rudolph when he immigrated to America. He was born with an inherited condition that gave him a hunchback. He never married for fear of passing the trait on to his children.

As a young boy, Steinmetz had a difficult first year at school; however, the slow start and concerns soon evaporated as he quickly ascended to the top of the class. At the University of Breslau he studied mathematics and worked toward a Ph.D. He would have graduated in 1888 were it not for his political activities. While at the university, Steinmetz became a socialist, eventually taking over the publication of a student-run socialist newspaper. The secret police had a warrant for his arrest when he fled Germany for Switzerland on the eve of his graduation. He immigrated to the United States in 1889.

The Law of Hysteresis

Steinmetz's first job in the United States was with the Eikemeyer and Osterheld Manufacturing Company in Yonkers, New York, where he set up a small research lab and worked on alternating current (an electric current that reverses its direction at regularly recurring intervals) motors. While working at Eikemeyer's, he discovered how the influence of a changing magnetic field operates in a motor to consume energy. Characterizing the relationship between the fluctuating strength of a magnetic field in a motor and the amount of energy lost—a phenomenon known as magnetic hysteresis—his discovery showed engineers how they could design motors with a minimal loss of energy. Steinmetz published a 178-page paper on the law of hysteresis in 1892 that brought him instant recognition.

Steinmetz then turned his attention to mathematical theories that could make practical the use of alternating current in long-distance power transmission. Alternating current had no constant value or direction, and its large-scale behavior was at that time impossible to predict. Nevertheless, Steinmetz was able to fit the principles of alternating current into predictable mathematical models.

A Lifetime Career at General Electric

The Eikemeyer plant was bought by General Electric Company (GE) in 1892, when the company was just being organized. Steinmetz was hired by GE and eventually moved to Schenectady, New York, where he lived the rest of his life. It was at GE that he completed his work on the mathematics of alternating current, and published in the late 1890s a three-volume work so complex that most engineers had trouble understanding it at first. For four years, until his theories became well understood, Steinmetz spent much of his time explaining them to engineers throughout the country.

Another of Steinmetz's major achievements was his study of changes in electrical circuits of very short duration, for which he designed a 220,000-volt experimental transformer. His research was used to develop new cables, and new and improved methods of operating transmission systems. He even created artificial lightning by designing generators that could produce electricity at very high potential. This was used to study the effect of lightning on the power lines that were just going up around the country, and led to the development of lightning arrestors, devices that protect electrical apparatus and electric transmission lines from damage by lightning. In all, Steinmetz held about two hundred patents.

A Public Servant

Steinmetz taught electrical engineering at Union College in Schenectady from 1903 to 1913, heading the new department that was formed owing to his presence. He was known as a tough lecturer, but was popular with the students. Faithful to the philosophy of his youth, he continued to espouse socialism. When George R. Lunn was elected Schenectady's Socialist mayor in 1911, Steinmetz volunteered his services to the administration. He was appointed to the board of education and was later elected president of the board. In 1915 he was elected a member of the common council in Schenectady. As president of the council, he established classes for handicapped children. He ran for state engineer in 1922.

Steinmetz, who never married and had no children, adopted Roy Hayden, his associate at General Electric. When Hayden married, he and his family lived in Steinmetz's house on Wendall Avenue in Schenectady. Steinmetz also legally adopted Hayden's three children as his grandchildren. Steinmetz loved animals and at times kept a full range of wild animals in his backyard. His favorite pets were a pair of crows, John and Mary. He was an avid grower of orchids and cacti. Steinmetz died in Schenectady on October 26, 1923, of heart failure.

SELECTED WRITINGS BY STEINMETZ:

Books

Theory and Calculation of Alternating Current Phenomena, [New York], 1897.

Theoretical Elements of Electrical Engineering, [New York], 1901.

Theory and Calculation of Transient Electrical Phenomena and Oscillations, [New York], 1909.

Electrical Discharges, Waves, Impulses, and Other Transients, McGraw-Hill, 1914.

Relativity and Space, McGraw-Hill, 1923.

FURTHER READING:

Books

Caldecott, E., and P. L. Alger, editors, *Steinmetz: The Philosopher,* Gordon & Breach, 1965.

Garlin, Sender, *Three American Radicals: John Swinton, Charles P. Steinmetz, and William Dean Howells,* Westview, 1991.

Hammond, John Winthrop, *Charles Proteus Steinmetz: A Biography,* Century, 1924.

Lavine, Sigmund A., *Steinmetz: Maker of Lightning,* Dodd, Mead, 1959.

Leonard, Jonathan Norton, *Loki: The Life of Charles Proteus Steinmetz,* Doubleday, 1929.

Sketch by Olga K. Anderson

Joan Argetsinger Steitz
1941–
American biochemist and geneticist

Joan Steitz is an American biochemist and geneticist, best known for her discovery of small nuclear ribonucleoproteins or snRNPs, which play an important role in converting the information encoded in mammalian DNA into instructions for building protein molecules. Her work has led to a deeper understanding of the way in which genetic transcription and translation is controlled.

Joan Argetsinger Steitz was born on January 26, 1941, in Minneapolis, Minnesota. Her father, Glenn Davis Argetsinger, a high school guidance counselor, and her mother, Elaine Magnusson Argetsinger, a speech pathologist, encouraged her to pursue her intellectual interests, and she developed an interest in science at an early age. Steitz attended Antioch College, in Yellow Springs, Ohio, and received a bachelor of science degree in chemistry in 1963. In addition to her college chemistry studies, she had taken classes in molecular genetics, a field that was undergoing rapid development as a result of the 1953 discovery of the double helical structure of the deoxyribonucleic (DNA) molecule. **James Watson**, **Francis Crick**, and **Maurice Wilkins** had received the 1962 Nobel Prize in Medicine for this important work. Two of these three laureates were soon to become her mentors.

Under the direction of James Watson at Harvard University, Steitz received a Ph.D. in 1967. Her graduate research centered on the *in vitro* assembly of R17, a ribonucleic acid bacteriophage (a type of virus that attacks bacteria). This research led to a better understanding of how the protein and nucleic-acid components of viruses interact. From 1967 till 1970, Steitz pursued post-doctoral studies under the direction of Francis Crick, at the Medical Research Council Laboratory of Molecular Biology, in Cambridge, England. There, her research focused on the way in which bacterial ribosomes, intracellular organelles that play a role in building proteins within the cell, locate themselves on messenger ribonucleic acid (RNA), the molecule that carries the protein building instructions from a cell's nucleus to its cytoplasm.

In 1970, Steitz returned to the United States, accepting an assistant professorship in the Department of Molecular Biophysics and Biochemistry at Yale University, in New Haven, Connecticut. Her work in molecular genetics yielded, within the decade, a discovery which she considers her most significant, that of small nuclear ribonucleoproteins or snRNPs (pronounced "snurps"). The intricate molecular process by which the double stranded DNA molecule dictates protein synthesis begins with a step known as transcription. During this step, DNA information is transferred to a single stranded heterogeneous nuclear RNA molecule, called hnRNA. Typically, a DNA molecule contains a vast amount of "nonsense," encoded instructions that are not useful during the process of protein synthesis. The snRNPs that Steitz discovered play a significant role in insuring that this nonsense is removed from the hnRNA. They coordinate a process called RNA splicing, in which the hnRNA molecule is snipped into pieces and its useful parts rejoined. The end result of this splicing is that a messenger RNA molecule is formed.

Steitz has identified many different types of snRNPs and helped to determine how they operate within the nucleus. Currently, she is examining snRNPs that are formed when certain herpes viruses infect their host cells. Her research into the structure and function of snRNPs has already seen direct clinical application, especially in the area of diagnosis and treatment of rheumatic disorders.

Steitz was promoted to full professorship at Yale in 1978, and has been a Henry Ford II Professor there since 1988. During the 1976-77 academic year, while on sabbatical as a Josiah Macy Scholar, she conducted research at the Max Planck Institute for Biophysical Chemistry in Göttingen, Germany, and at the Medical Council Center Laboratory of Molecular Biology in Cambridge, England. As a Fairchild Distinguished Fellow she spent the 1984-85 academic year on sabbatical at the California Institute of Technology in Pasadena.

The list of scientific honors that have been bestowed upon Steitz is extensive, beginning in 1975 with the Passano Foundation Young Scientist Award, and followed in 1976 by the Eli Lilly Award in Biological Chemistry. In 1982, Steitz received the U.S. Steel Foundation Award in Molecular Biology, and the following year she shared the Lee Hawley, Sr. Award for Arthritis Research with J. A. Hardin and M. R. Lerner. For her pioneering work on snRNPs, President Ronald Reagan presented her with the National Medal of Science in 1986. She received the Radcliffe Graduate Society Medal for Distinguished Achievement in 1987, and the Dickson Prize for Science from Carnegie Mellon University in 1988. Steitz shared the Warren Triennial Prize with Thomas R. Cech in 1989, and in 1992 she received the Christopher Columbus Discovery Award in Biomedical Research. The Antioch College Alumni Association presented her with the Rebecca Rice Award for Distinguished Achievement in 1993. Steitz considers one of her greatest honors to be the Weizman Women and Science Award, which she received in 1994. In 1996, she received the Distinguished Service Award at the Miami Bio-Technology Winter Symposium, as well as the City of Medicine Award.

Steitz has been granted honorary doctoral degrees from various academic institutions, including Lawrence University, the University of Rochester School of Medicine, Mount Sinai School of Medicine, Trinity College, and Harvard University. She has served on the editorial boards of several of the leading journals in the field of genetics and is a member of the National Academy of Sciences, the American Philosophical Society, and the American Academy of Arts and Sciences. She became the director of the Jane Coffin Childs Memorial Fund for Medical Research, a fund that supports postdoctoral fellows, in 1991. Steitz is married to a fellow scientist, with whom she has one son.

FURTHER READING:

Books

Shearer, Benjamin F., and Barbara S. Shearer. *Notable Women in the Life Sciences*. Westport: Greenwood Press, 1996.

Sketch by Leslie Reinherz

Patrick Steptoe
1913–1988
English gynecologist

Patrick Steptoe, an English gynecologist and medical researcher, helped develop the technique of *in vitro* fertilization. In this process, a mature egg is removed from the female ovary and is fertilized in a test tube. After a short

Patrick Steptoe

Performs Groundbreaking Work in Laparoscopy

While at Oldham General and District Hospital, Steptoe pursued his interest in fertility problems. He developed a method of procuring human eggs from the ovaries by using a laparoscope, a long thin telescope replete with fiber optics light. After inserting the device—through a small incision in the navel—into the inflated abdominal cavity, Steptoe was able to observe the reproductive tract. Eventually the laparoscope would become widely used in various types of surgery, including those associated with sterility. But, at first, Steptoe had trouble convincing others in the medical profession of the merits of laparoscopy; observers from the Royal College of Obstetricians and Gynecologists considered the technique fraught with difficulties. Five years passed before Steptoe published his first paper on laparoscopic surgery.

In 1966 Steptoe teamed with Cambridge University physiologist Robert G. Edwards to propel his work with fertility problems. Utilizing ovaries removed for medical reasons, Edwards had pioneered the fertilization of eggs outside of the body. With his laparoscope, Steptoe added the dimension of being able to secure mature eggs at the appropriate moment in the monthly cycle when fertilization would normally occur. A breakthrough for the duo came in 1968 when Edwards successfully fertilized an egg that Steptoe had extracted. Not until 1970, however, was an egg able to reach the stage of cell division—into about 100 cells—when it generally moves to the uterus. In 1972 the pair attempted the first implantation, but the embryo failed to lodge in the uterus. Indeed, none of the women with implanted embryos carried them for a full trimester.

As their work progressed and word of it leaked out, the researchers faced criticism from scientific and religious circles concerning the ethical and moral issues relating to tampering with the creation of human life. Some opponents considered the duo's work akin to the scenario in Aldous Huxley's 1932 work, *Brave New World,* in which babies were conceived in the laboratory, cloned, and manipulated for society's use. Members of Parliament demanded an investigation and sources of funds were withdrawn. A *Time* reporter quoted Steptoe as saying, "All I am interested in is how to help women who are denied a baby because their tubes are incapable of doing their small part." Undaunted, Steptoe and Edwards continued their work at Kershaw's Cottage Hospital in Oldham, with Steptoe financing the research by performing legal abortions. Disturbed with the criticism, Steptoe and Edwards became more secretive, which made the speculation and criticism more intense.

Efforts Yield Success

In 1976 Steptoe met thirty-year-old Leslie Brown, who experienced problems with her fallopian tubes. Steptoe removed a mature egg from her ovary, and Edwards fertilized the egg using her husband Gilbert's sperm. The fertilized egg—implanted after two days—thrived, and on July 25, 1978, Joy Louise Brown, a healthy five pound

incubation period, the fertilized egg is implanted in the uterus, where it develops as in a typical pregnancy. This procedure gave women whose fallopian tubes were damaged or missing, and were thus unable to become pregnant, the hope that they too could conceive children. Steptoe and his colleague, English physiologist Robert G. Edwards, received international recognition—both positive and negative—when the first so-called test tube baby was born in 1978.

Patrick Christopher Steptoe was born on June 9, 1913 in Oxfordshire, England. His father was a church organist, while his mother served as a social worker. Steptoe studied medicine at the University of London's St. George Hospital Medical School and, after being licensed in 1939, became a member of the Royal College of Surgeons. His medical career, though, was interrupted by World War II. Steptoe volunteered as a naval surgeon, but he and his shipmates were captured by Italian forces in 1941 after their ship sank in the Battle of Crete. Initially granted special privileges in prison because he was a physician, Steptoe was placed in solitary confinement after officials detected his efforts to help fellow prisoners escape. Steptoe left the prison camp via a prisoner exchange in 1943. Following the war, Steptoe completed additional studies in obstetrics and gynecology. In 1948 he became a member of the Royal College of Obstetricians and Gynecologists and moved to Manchester to set up a private practice. In 1951 Steptoe began working at Oldham General and District Hospital in northeast England.

twelve ounce girl, was born in Oldham District and General Hospital. Even before the birth, reporters and cameramen congregated outside of the four-story brick hospital, hoping for a glimpse of the expectant mother. After the birth, according to an article in *Time,* headlines in Britain heralded "OUR MIRACLE" and "BABY OF THE CENTURY."

Steptoe and Edwards were reluctant to discuss the procedures in press conferences and did not immediately publish their findings in a medical journal. In October of 1978, Steptoe was to receive an award from the Barren Foundation, a fertility research organization based in Chicago. The foundation suddenly cancelled the presentation because Steptoe and Edwards had not published an article on the event. As reported in a 1978 issue of *Time,* Steptoe called the foundation's action "the most utterly disgraceful exhibition of bad manners I've come across in the scientific world." In addition, rumors that the pair had sold their story to the tabloid the *National Enquirer* for a six figure amount were rampant. Steptoe declared that he rejected such offers and did not make any money on the highly publicized birth. Despite the furor, the New York Fertility Society subsequently presented Steptoe with an achievement award.

As to the claim of publishing, Steptoe answered that most scientists do not publish until several months after data is in and research complete. The procedures were fully presented at the January 26, 1979 meeting of the Royal College of Obstetricians and Gynecologists and at the conference of the American Fertility Society in San Francisco. Steptoe reported that, with modified techniques, ten percent of the *in vitro* fertilization attempts could succeed. He further predicted that there could one day be a fifty percent success rate for the procedure.

In the aftermath of the first successful test tube baby, Steptoe received thousands of letters from couples seeking help in conception. He retired from the British National Health Service and constructed a new clinic near Cambridge. For their efforts, Steptoe and Edwards were both named Commanders of the British Empire, and in 1987 Steptoe was honored with fellowship in the Royal Society. Steptoe and his wife, a former actress, had one son and one daughter. His interests outside of medicine included piano and organ, cricket, plays, and opera. Steptoe died of cancer on March 21, 1988, in Canterbury. Yet, since the birth of baby Brown and the pioneering techniques of Steptoe, couples with various physiological problems have had children in clinics throughout the world.

SELECTED WRITINGS BY STEPTOE:

Books

A Matter of Life: The Story of a Medical Breakthrough, Morrow, 1980.

FURTHER READING:

Books

Doctors on the New Frontier, McGraw-Hill, 1980.

Periodicals

Time, The First Test Tube Baby, July 31, 1978, pp. 58–69.

Sketch by Evelyn B. Kelly

Otto Stern
1888–1969
American physicist

Otto Stern received the 1943 Nobel Prize in physics for his development of molecular beam methods and the use of these methods to determine a number of important physical constants, especially the magnetic moment of atoms and nuclei. The molecular beam—the introduction of a gas or vapor into a vacuum which results in the formation of a stream of atoms or molecules that is similar to a light beam—had been discovered by French physicist Louis Dunoyer. This molecular or atomic beam can be used to study the properties of the gas or vapor of which it is made.

Stern was born in Sohrau, Upper Silesia, Germany (later Zory, Poland), on February 17, 1888. He was the oldest of five children born to Oskar Stern and the former Eugenie Rosenthal. Both parents had come from prosperous grain merchants and flour millers and eagerly encouraged the intellectual development of their children. When Otto was four years old, his family moved to Breslau (later Wroclaw, Poland), where he attended the local Johannes Gymnasium. Most of Stern's training in science came from his home, where books, conversation and even some simple experimentation were the primary means of instruction.

Earns Doctorate and Joins Einstein

As was common at the time, Stern traveled to a number of universities for his further education after graduating from the gymnasium in 1906. Finally, he undertook a doctoral program in chemistry at Breslau under Otto Sackur. He was awarded his Ph.D. in 1912 for a thesis on the kinetic theory of osmotic pressure in concentrated solutions. Through Sackur's influence, Stern was able to take a position as research assistant to **Albert Einstein** from 1912 to 1914, first in Prague and later in Zürich, at the Federal Institute of Technology. Einstein was to have an important influence on Stern's career. It was from the great man, biographer Emilio Segrè pointed out in the *Biographical Memoirs of the National Academy of Sciences,* that Stern "learned what were the really important problems of contemporary physics: the nature of the quantum of light with its double aspect of particle and wave, the nature of atoms, and relativity."

With the outbreak of World War I in 1914, Stern was drafted into the German army where he served first as a private and later as a noncommissioned officer. He was assigned with the Meteorology Corps on the Russian front. During his four years in the military, Stern had enough spare time to continue his theoretical research, writing two important papers during the war years on the application of quantum theory to statistical thermodynamics.

Begins Molecular Beam Studies at Frankfurt

As the war drew to a close, Stern was finally able to accept an appointment as Privat dozen at the University of Frankfurt-on-the-Main that he had been offered in 1915, but which the war had prevented his accepting. At Frankfurt, Stern became assistant to **Max Born**, who had just moved there from the University of Berlin. The research topic in which Stern became interested was the use of molecular beams to study atomic and molecular properties. Stern had first learned about molecular beams during the war. The techniques for using such beams had been developed in 1911 by the French physicist Louis Dunoyer. By introducing a gas or vapor into a vacuum, a beam of atoms or molecules is formed. This beam allows the researcher to study atomic structure and properties.

Stern spent the greatest part of his professional career developing the molecular beam technology and using it to determine a number of atomic and molecular properties. The first application he studied was the determination of molecular velocities in gases. In the 1850s, James Clerk Maxwell had calculated the theoretical distribution of molecular velocities in a gas. Although there was not much doubt about the accuracy of Maxwell's findings, no empirical data supporting his results had ever been obtained. In 1920, Stern completed an experiment using the molecular beam technique to find the actual distribution of molecular velocities in a gas. His results unequivocally substantiated Maxwell's predictions.

The following year, Stern went on to a more significant application of the molecular beam technique. According to quantum theory, the atom is an electrically charged particle rotating in space. As such, it was thought to have associated with it a magnetic field whose magnetic field could be expressed as its "magnetic moment." Furthermore, the atom's magnetic moment could have only a finite, discrete number of values. This notion was described as the atom's "spatial quantization." (In fact, the same argument applies to the components of an atom, its electrons, nucleus, protons, and neutrons, all of which have their own unique magnetic moments.)

In 1922, Stern used molecular beams to test the theory of spatial quantization. He passed a beam of silver atoms through a nonuniform magnetic field and found that it split into two distinct parts. The now-famous experiment was given the name the Stern-Gerlach experiment for Stern and his associate in the work, Walther Gerlach. The experiment not only confirmed the concept of space quantization, but also allowed Stern to calculate the magnetic moment of the silver atom. His result was in agreement with the theoretical values calculated by means of quantum theory. For this experiment, and others like it carried out later, Stern was awarded the 1943 Nobel Prize in physics.

Stern's tenure at Frankfurt had ended in 1921 in the midst of planning for his famous experiment with Gerlach. The experiment was carried out at the University of Rostock, where he had been appointed associate professor of theoretical physics in 1921. Two years later, Stern moved on to the University of Hamburg as professor of physical chemistry and director of the Institute for Physical Chemistry. At Hamburg, Stern continued to explore the use of molecular and atomic beams. He found experimental proof for **Louis Broglie**'s theory of the wave nature of particles and determined the magnetic moment of the proton and deuteron, subatomic particles. The value he found for the proton was at least twice that predicted by theory, a discrepancy that has yet to be totally explained.

Adolf Hitler's rise to power in Germany convinced Stern that he had to leave his homeland. Although he was probably not in any personal danger, he decided to resign his post at Hamburg in protest of the new government's anti-Semitic policies. He accepted an appointment as research professor in physics at the Carnegie Institute in Pittsburgh and became a naturalized U.S. citizen on March 8, 1939. During World War II Stern served as a consultant to the War Department and then, in 1946, resigned his post at Carnegie to move to Berkeley where he could be near his two sisters. He lived largely in isolation for the rest of his life. He died in a Berkeley movie theater on August 17, 1969. Stern never married and was said by biographer Segrè to have "liked good cuisine, excellent cigars, and in general all the refinements of life."

SELECTED WRITINGS BY STERN:

Periodicals

Zeitschrift für Physik, Ein Weg zür Experimentellen Prüfung der Richtungsquantelung im Magnetfeld, Number 7, 1921, pp. 249–253.
Zeitscrift für Physik, Das Magnetische Moment des Silberatoms, Number 9, 1922, pp. 353–355.

FURTHER READING:

Books

Gillispie, Charles Coulson, editor, *Dictionary of Scientific Biography,* Volume 13, Scribner's, 1975, pp. 40–43.

Heathcote, Niels H. de V., *Nobel Prize Winners in Physics, 1901–1950,* Henry Schuman, 1953, pp. 389–397.

Segrè, Emilio, *Biographical Memoirs,* Otto Stern, Volume 43, National Academy of Sciences, 1973.

Weber, Robert L., *Pioneers of Science: Nobel Prize Winners in Physics,* American Institute of Physics, 1980, pp. 119–121.

Sketch by David E. Newton

Nettie Maria Stevens
1861–1912
American biologist and cytogeneticist

Nettie Maria Stevens was a biologist and cytogeneticist and one of the first American women to be recognized for her contributions to scientific research. "She . . . produced new data and new theories," wrote Marilyn Bailey Ogilvie in *Women in Science,* "yet beyond these accomplishments passed along her expertise to a new generation. . . . illustrat[ing] the importance of the women's colleges in the education of women scientists." Although Stevens started her research career when she was in her thirties, she successfully expanded the fields of embryology and cytogenetics (the branch of biology which focuses on the study of heredity), particularly in the study of histology (a branch of anatomy dealing with plant and animal tissues) and of regenerative processes in invertebrates such as hydras and flatworms. She is best known for her role in genetics—her research contributed greatly to the understanding of chromosomes and heredity. She theorized that the sex of an organism was determined by the inheritance of a specific chromosome—X or Y—and performed experiments to confirm this hypothesis.

Stevens, the third of four children and the first daughter, was born in Cavendish, Vermont, on July 7, 1861, to Ephraim Stevens, a carpenter of English descent, and Julia Adams Stevens. Historians know little about her family or her early life, except that she was educated in the public schools in Westford, Massachusetts, and displayed exceptional scholastic abilities. Upon graduation, Stevens taught Latin, English, mathematics, physiology and zoology at the high school in Lebanon, New Hampshire. As a teacher she had a great zeal for learning that she tried to impart both to her students and her colleagues. Between 1881 and 1883, Stevens attended the Normal School at Westfield, Massachusetts, consistently achieving the highest scores in her class from the time she started until she graduated. She worked as a school teacher, and then as a librarian for a number of years after she graduated; however, there are gaps in her history that are unaccounted for between this time and when she enrolled at Stanford University in 1896.

Furthers Education at Stanford and Bryn Mawr

In 1896, Stevens was attracted by the reputation of Stanford University for providing innovative opportunities for individuals aspiring to pursue their own scholastic interests. At the age of thirty-five she enrolled, studying physiology under professor Oliver Peebles Jenkins. She spent summers studying at the Hopkins Seaside Laboratory, Pacific Grove, California, and pursuing her love of learning and of biology. During this time, Stevens decided to switch careers to focus on research, instead of teaching. While at Hopkins she performed research on the life cycle of *Boveria,* a protozoan parasite of sea cucumbers. Her findings were published in 1901 in the *Proceedings of the California Academy of Sciences.* After obtaining her masters degree—a highly unusual accomplishment for a woman in that era—Stevens returned to the East to study at Bryn Mawr College, Pennsylvania, as a graduate biology student in 1900. She was such an exceptional student that she was awarded a fellowship enabling her to study at the Zoological Station in Naples, Italy, and then at the Zoological Institute of the University of Würzburg, Germany. Back at Bryn Mawr, she obtained her doctorate in 1903. At this time, she was made a research fellow in biology at Bryn Mawr and then was promoted to a reader in experimental morphology in 1904. From 1903 until 1905, her research was funded by a grant from the Carnegie Institution. In 1905, she was promoted again to associate in experimental morphology, a position she held until her death in 1912.

Contributes to the Understanding of Chromosomal Determination of Sex

While Stevens' early research focused on morphology and taxonomy and then later expanded to cytology, her most important research was with chromosomes and their relation to heredity. Because of the pioneering studies performed by the renowned monk Gregor Mendel (showing how pea plant genetic traits are inherited), scientists of the time knew a lot about how chromosomes acted during cell division and maturation of germ cells. However, no inherited trait had been traced from the parents' chromosomes to those of the offspring. In addition, no scientific studies had yet linked one chromosome with a specific characteristic. Stevens, and the well-known biologist **Edmund Beecher Wilson**, who worked independently on this type of research, were the first to demonstrate that the sex of an organism was determined by a particular chromosome; moreover, they proved that gender is inherited in accordance with Mendel's laws of genetics. Together, their research confirmed, and therefore established, a chromosomal basis for heredity. Working with the meal worm, *Tenebrio molitor,* Stevens determined that the male produced two kinds of sperm—one with a large X chromosome, and the other with a small Y chromosome. Unfertilized eggs, however, were all alike and had only X chromosomes. Stevens theorized that sex, in some organisms, may result from chromosomal inheritance. She suggested that eggs fertilized by sperm carrying X chromosomes produced females, and those by sperm carrying the Y chromosome resulted in males. She performed further research to prove this phenomenon, expanding her studies to other species. Although this theory was not accepted by all scientists at the time, it was profoundly important in the evolution of the field of genetics and to an understanding of determination of gender.

Stevens was a prolific author, publishing some thirty-eight papers in eleven years. For her paper, "A Study of the Germ Cells of *Aphis rosae* and *Aphis oenotherae*", Stevens was awarded the Ellen Richards Research Prize in 1905, given to promote scientific research by women. Stevens died of breast cancer on May 4, 1912, before she could occupy the research professorship created for her by the Bryn Mawr trustees. Much later, **Thomas Hunt Morgan**, a 1933 Nobel Prize recipient for his work in genetics, recognized the importance of Stevens' ground-breaking experiments, as quoted by Ogilvie in the *Proceedings of the American Philosophical Society:* "Stevens had a share in a discovery of importance and her name will be remembered for this, when the minutiae of detailed investigations that she carried out have become incorporated in the general body of the subject."

SELECTED WRITINGS BY STEVENS:

Periodicals

Carnegie Institution Publications, Studies in Spermatogenesis with Especial Reference to the 'Accessory Chromosome,' 1905.

Journal of Experimental Zoology, A study of the Germ Cells of *Aphis rosae* and *Aphis Oenotherae,* 1905, pp. 313–333.

Biological Bulletin of the Marine Biological Laboratory, Further Studies on Heterochromosomes in Mosquitoes, 1911, pp. 109–120.

FURTHER READING:

Books

Ogilvie, Marilyn Bailey, *Women in Science: Antiquity through the Nineteenth Century,* Massachusetts Institute of Technology, 1986.

Periodicals

Ogilvie, Marilyn Bailey, *Isis,* June, 1978, pp. 163–72.

Ogilvie, Marilyn Bailey, *Proceedings of the American Philosophical Society, Held at Philadelphia for Promoting Useful Knowledge,* Volume 125, American Philosophical Society, 1981, pp. 292–311.

Sketch by Barbara J. Prouian

H. Guyford Stever
1916–
American aeronautical engineer

One of the most significant science policy makers of the last thirty years, H. Guyford Stever has played an important and generally respected role in the shaping of the nation's scientific and technical policies. He rose to prominence in the scientific and engineering community because of his aeronautical research in the development of guided missiles and spacecraft as well as in flight aerodynamics. He gained a reputation as an able administrator and a thoughtful advocate for applying technical expertise to the problems of the nation. As a result Stever served in several key advisory positions in the 1960s and 1970s, especially as head of the National Science Foundation and science advisor to Presidents Richard M. Nixon and Gerald R. Ford.

Early Professional Experiences

Horton Guyford Stever was born on October 24, 1916, in the glass manufacturing city of Corning, New York. The son of Ralph Raymond, a merchant, and Alma Matt Stever, he was educated in the local public schools. He attended Colgate University and completed his B.A. degree in physics in 1938. From there he journeyed cross-country to work on a Ph.D. in physics at the California Institute of Technology, graduating in 1941. As World War II began, Stever, like so many of his generation and training, went to work in the defense effort as a researcher at the Massachusetts Institute of Technology's (MIT) Radiation Laboratory. There he met director Lee A. DuBridge, who later was Nixon's first science advisor in the late 1960s. Within a short time Stever joined the Office of Scientific Research and Development (OSRD), headed by **Vannevar Bush**, where he saw up close the linkage of science and government on a variety of wartime projects. This experience was critical to Stever's development as a scientific and technical advisor in the postwar era.

In 1942, with World War II underway and going badly for the Allies, Stever was sent to Great Britain as a science liaison officer at the London Mission of the OSRD. Serving there until the end of the war in 1945, he analyzed developments in German and British radar systems as a means of strengthening the defenses against German V–1 and V–2 rocket attacks. After the cross-channel invasion in June, 1944, Stever moved with forward elements of the OSRD to the continent to continue studying enemy technology.

After the war Stever returned to the United States and returned to purely civilian pursuits. He took a position with MIT as an assistant professor in the Department of Aeronautical Engineering, headed by **Jerome C. Hunsaker**. Altogether, he was at MIT almost twenty years, progressing through the academic ranks to full professor in 1956. Between 1961 and 1965 he headed the mechanical engineering and naval architecture and marine engineering departments.

While at MIT Stever was heavily involved in research projects to define and solve a number of problems associated with aerospace flight. Although trained as a physicist, Stever was adept at aeronautical engineering, and he contributed greatly to solving problems of control on guided missiles and of transonic (speeds of five hundred-fifty to nine hundred miles per hour) flight. In early experiments, conducted about 1949, Stever used the MIT wind tunnels to test models of missiles and transonic aircraft for their aerodynamic properties, and he published several important papers on the subject. Of special importance were methods Stever developed of stabilizing aircraft and missiles at transonic speeds, where normal aerodynamic rules did not apply.

At the same time, Stever was always interested in furthering the linkage between science and technology, and government, and he served on several government and military advisory committees. With his help, technology was mobilized to help the United States in its rivalry with the Soviet Union. In 1947 he became a member of the U.S. Air Force Scientific Advisory Board, and in 1955 Stever took a leave of absence from MIT to serve as chief scientist with the air force. He also served on advisory committees with the National Advisory Committee for Aeronautics (NACA), its successor (NASA), the National Science Foundation, and Congress in the 1950s and 1960s. In addition, Stever was a technical advisor to several private corporations such as Goodyear Tire and United Aircraft, helping them mostly with military issues.

Stever left MIT in 1965 to take over the presidency of the Carnegie Institute of Technology in Pittsburgh. He served as president until 1972, and is best known for arranging the merger of Carnegie with the Mellon Institute in 1967. Both organizations had been struggling separately, but the new Carnegie Mellon University became a strong technical institution of higher learning. Under Stever's direction it developed a curriculum that emphasized the integration of science with other disciplines.

Becomes Governmental Advisor

Beginning in 1970 Stever served on two key advisory committees for President Nixon, the Ad Hoc Science Panel and the Task Force on Science Policy. At the same time Nixon, who was impressed with Stever's capabilities, appointed him to the National Science Board, the policy-making arm of the National Science Foundation (NSF). These positions gave him greater visibility inside the Nixon administration, and opened the way for his appointment as director of the NSF in February 1972.

Stever suffered intense pressure in 1973 when Nixon abolished the office of science advisor to the president as being without real value and sent the responsibilities to

Stever at the National Science Foundation. To many, Stever's dual role as head of NSF and science advisor to the president represented a conflict of interest. Moreover, Stever was perceived as lacking access to Nixon—a serious liability for one charged with advocating the nation's scientific and technical programs—and as being less than effective when he did get the president's ear. Well aware of the controversy, Stever nevertheless maintained he could do both jobs and had all the access to the administration he needed.

When Nixon resigned in the aftermath of the Watergate scandal in August, 1974, Stever remained at the NSF and continued to help the Ford administration with science policy. As a result, when Ford reestablished the position of science advisor to the president in August 1976, he asked Stever to take the position; Stever served in that capacity until the change in administrations in January 1977. Although he again weathered criticism for his role in the Nixon administration, Stever found the situation with Ford more conducive to his position and suggested that his role was "to try to be the translator—take ideas welling up in the scientific community and see that the government takes action on them."

When he left government service, Stever continued to be very active as an advisor on several commissions, panels, and other task forces. He began consulting for several corporations, and also became a director of TRW, of Schering Plough, and of Goodyear.

FURTHER READING:

Books

Golden, William, editor, *Science Advice to the President,* Pergamon, 1980.

Herken, Gregg, *Cardinal Choices: Presidential Science Advising from the Atomic Bomb to SDI,* Oxford University Press, 1992.

Katz, James, *Presidential Politics and Science Advice,* Praeger, 1978.

Periodicals

Shapley, Deborah, *Science,* NSF Appointment: Science Elite, White House Reward Favorite Son, March 31, 1972, pp. 1441, 1443.

Sketch by Roger D. Launius

Frederick Campion Steward
1904–1993
American plant physiologist

Frederick Campion Steward was a leading plant physiologist who conducted research in a broad spectrum of botanical fields; he was noted in particular for his 1958 discovery that it was possible to produce an entire plant from one cell, since all the data needed to regenerate a plant is found in a single cell. Steward also made significant contributions to the understanding of how plants absorb mineral salts, carry on respiration, and utilize nitrogen. Throughout his career, Steward wrote more than one hundred papers for scientific journals in which he described his research on these subjects. The importance of his contributions was recognized by his fellow scientists, who honored him with the Merit Award of the Botanical Society of America in 1961 and the Stephen Hales Award of the American Society of Plant Physiologists in 1964. He was also elected a Fellow of the American Academy of Arts and Sciences in 1956, and a year later became a member of the Royal Society of London, where he delivered its Crosnian Lecture in 1969.

Steward was born on June 16, 1904, in London, the son of Frederick Walter and Mary (Daglish) Steward. He received his B.Sc. in chemistry with first-class honors in 1924 from the University of Leeds, and his Ph.D. in botany in 1926. He came to the United States in 1927 to serve as a Rockefeller Foundation fellow, and two years later, on September 7, 1929, he married Anne Temple Gordon, a colleague of his in the botany department at Cornell. The couple had one son, Frederick Gordon. Upon Steward's return to England, he served as an assistant lecturer in botany at Leeds beginning in 1929, and as a reader in botany at Birkbeck College, University of London, where he also received his D.Sc. During World War II, he served as director of aircraft equipment in the British Ministry of Aircraft Production. After the war, he returned to the United States to become a visiting professor of botany—and later chair of the department—at the University of Rochester. In 1950, he became a professor of botany at Cornell University and director of the Laboratory of Cell Physiology, Growth, and Development, a post he held for nearly twenty years.

Delves into Research on Plant Metabolism

Early in his career, Steward applied his background in chemistry to problems in botany. He studied the active transport of ions such as potassium and chlorine in sections of beets and potatoes grown aseptically, and determined that variables such as oxygen supply and temperature regulated the metabolic activity. In active transport, cells utilize energy obtained from aerobic respiration to absorb increasing amounts of ions through the cell membrane against the concentration gradient. This results in a greater concentration of these ions within the cells than in the external environment. By comparison, during passive transport, when ions diffuse into a cell without the input of energy, the process does not result in a greater concentration of the ions within the cell.

After World War II, with the collaboration of a number of other scientists, Steward devoted his research to several objectives. One of his goals was to investigate how plants obtain their nitrogen for protein synthesis. Through the application of paper chromatography Steward opened doors leading to new ideas on nitrogen metabolism. In his various research projects, he studied the nutrition, growth, and metabolism of a number of plant varieties, such as carrot, potato, beet, banana, mint, and artichoke.

It was in the late 1950s, however, that Steward performed the work for which he was best known: Along with collaborators, he was able to develop complete carrot plants from isolated adult cells in nutrient culture solution, a process which required the application of aseptic techniques. This was necessary if the cultures were to be free from bacterial or fungal contamination. Steward first included the plant hormone auxin, then added coconut milk to achieve the complete development of new, entire carrot plants. Coconut milk normally nourishes the coconut embryo and has been found to contain plant hormones called cytokinins. This success illustrated the concept of totipotency, in which a mature cell can achieve the potential of its genes and can give rise to a complete plant. With the correct mixture of mineral nutrients, hormones, sucrose, and vitamins in the tissue culture medium, the genes of a mature cell can be switched on and off to differentiate into the variety of tissues needed to build an entire plant.

Assumes Additional Educational Posts

Steward remained at Cornell until 1973, then transferred to the University of Madras, India, where he served as the institution's C. V. Raman Visiting Professor. In the mid–1970s he received an honorary doctorate from the University of Delhi and also was appointed the Cecil H. and Ida Green Professor at the University of British Columbia. He later was awarded honorary positions at the State University of New York at Stony Brook and at the University of Virginia at Charlottesville, both of which involved active duties. He had been suffering from poor health, though, and died in mid-September, 1993, in Tuscaloosa, Alabama. In Steward's obituary in the *New York Times,* writer Ronald Sullivan, in addition to noting the botanist's significant scientific contributions, also pointed out the scientist's reputation as a skilled educator: Steward "was ... responsible for creating and inspiring a generation of biological scientists from his Cornell lecture halls, classrooms and laboratories," asserted Sullivan. "Former students said his lectures in advanced plant physiology were the high point of their educations. He was a spellbinding lecturer, and his classroom ultimately became a kind of international salon for visiting scientists from all over the world." Many of these students collaborated with him in research described in various scientific journals, such as *Annals of Botany, Journal of Experimental Biology,* and *Plant Physiology.*

SELECTED WRITINGS BY STEWARD:

Books

Plant Physiology: A Treatise, six volumes, Academic Press, 1959–72.
Plants at Work: A Summary of Plant Physiology, Addison-Wesley, 1964.
About Plants: Topics in Plant Biology, Addison-Wesley, 1966.
Growth and Organization of Plants, Addison-Wesley, 1968.
Plants, Chemicals, and Growth, Academic Press, 1971.

Periodicals

Scientific American, The Control of Growth in Plant Cells, October 1963.
Science, Growth and Development of Cultured Plant Cells, Volume 143, 1964, pp. 20–27.

FURTHER READING:

Books

Keeton, W. T., *Biological Science,* Norton, 1972, pp. 272–73.

Periodicals

Sullivan, Ronald, *New York Times,* Frederick C. Steward, 89, Leading Botanist, Dies, September 18, 1993, p. 9.

Sketch by Maurice Bleifeld

Thomas Dale Stewart
1901–1997
American anthropologist

Thomas Dale Stewart was a renowned physical anthropologist whose affiliation with the National Museum of Natural History at the Smithsonian Institution stretched over seven decades. Stewart was an international authority in comparative human osteology (the sciences of bones), human identification, and forensic anthropology. Among his many achievements were numerous studies of pre-Columbian and early post-Columbian man in the Americas including the skeletal remains of Tepexpan man in Mexico and Midland man in Texas, among the oldest human remains found in North America. Stewart's reconstruction of Neanderthal skeletons from Shanidar in Iraq and his interpretations of Neanderthal anatomy from these fossils are considered to be major contributions. Stewart's expertise as a forensic anthropologist led him to do work for the Federal Bureau of Investigation (FBI) and the U.S. Army. He examined human skeletal remains in numerous homicide cases for the FBI and worked with the army in the identification of soldiers killed during the Korean War.

Stewart was born in Delta, Pennsylvania, on June 10, 1901, the son of Thomas Dale Stewart and Susan Price Stewart. He grew up in Delta, graduating from the local high school in 1920. Stewart moved to Washington, D.C. for his education and life's work in anthropology. While a student at George Washington University in 1924, he began his long association with the National Museum of Natural History by working as an aide under the famous Czechoslovakian-born American anthropologist **Aleš Hrdlička**. Stewart earned an A.B. degree from George Washington University and then went on to study medicine at Johns Hopkins University in Baltimore, Maryland, where he completed work on his M.D. in 1931. Stewart then returned to Washington and the Museum of Natural History where he became an assistant curator of physical anthropology in 1931, an associate curator in 1939, curator in 1942, and head curator of the department of anthropology in 1961. The following year he was appointed director of the museum and held that position until 1965. In 1966, the Smithsonian Institution honored Stewart with the rare title of senior scientist. He was given the status of emeritus physical anthropologist in 1971.

Research Carries Him in Many Directions

Stewart also found time to teach, and served as a visiting professor of anatomy at Washington University School of Medicine in St. Louis, Missouri, during World War II and later as a visitor professor of anthropology at the Escuela Nacional de Anthropología in Mexico. Stewart's long career carried him on a number of different, yet sometimes overlapping, research tracks. He was the author of about two hundred scientific papers and books. The breadth of his research was apparent from the very start of his career. His first dozen published papers covered such topics as monkey musculature, dental caries in Peruvians, and age-change sequence differences among Eskimos and Native Americans.

Stewart inevitably became involved in the still unresolved question of when humans first crossed the Bering Sea land-bridge from Asia to the New World. His reexamination of a Florida artifact called the Melbourne Skull in the 1940s led him to contradict Hrdlička's earlier claim that it was similar to recent resident Indians. Stewart went on to study human remains in Mexico and Texas, observing the so-called Tepexpan man and Midland man, and made cases for them being the oldest known humans in North America in papers published in 1949 and 1955. Stewart delved further back on humanity's family tree when he was invited to Iraq in 1957 to help restore two Neanderthal skeletons discovered by Ralph Solecki, a Columbia University anthropologist. He returned in 1960 and 1962 to recover, restore, and study four more skeletons found by Solecki in caves at Shanidar. Stewart's careful reconstructions of the Shanidar fossils provided new anatomical data about the skull, pelvis, and shoulder blades of Neanderthals. As a curator at the National Museum of Natural History, Stewart often worked as a forensic anthropologist for the FBI. The museum and FBI are close to each other and FBI agents started bringing occasional skeletal remains of suspected homicides for analysis in the 1920s. The remains ranged from single bones or a tooth to one or more entire skeletons of unknown age. Stewart handled these cases, as well as ones from state medical examiners. These calls for expert help were infrequent at first, but by the time Stewart retired he was regularly handling a half dozen cases a month. Forensic anthropology was poorly developed when the FBI first requested help, and Stewart found that the standards for estimating such basic data as the age, sex, and stature from human remains, let alone possible ranges for these traits, were primitive. He promoted scientific study to cure these shortcomings.

Learns How Bones Mature

Stewart made significant contributions in the field of osteology, working with the U.S. Army to help identify American casualties in the Korean War. As part of this work, Stewart made detailed observations of growth change on 450 skeletons. Working with fully identified remains, Stewart looked at how bones in the human body matured. He discovered that there were far bigger variations in maturation rates than previously thought. He also developed a method of estimating skeletal age by studying pubic bones. Later on, while working with an Eskimo skeleton, Stewart determined that pits and depressions in the cartilage joint between the pubic bones were tell-tale signs of childbirth and that the remains were of a female.

Stewart married Julia Wright in 1932, and they had one daughter, Cornella. After his first wife died, Stewart remarried in 1952 to Rita Frame Dewey, a former newspaper reporter and editor.

Stewart received numerous awards during his career, including an honorary doctorate from the University of Cuzco, the Wenner-Gren Foundation's Viking Medal in Physical Anthropology (1953), the Smithsonian's Joseph Henry Medal (1976), and the Charles R. Darwin Lifetime Achievement Award from the American Association of Physical Anthropologists (AAPA). He published over 200 articles and books. He was elected to the National Academy of Sciences and was an honorary member of the American Academy of Forensic Sciences. He was president of the Anthropological Society of Washington and of the American Institute of Human Paleontology, vice president of the Washington Academy of Sciences, and a member of the Committee on Research and Exploration of the National Geographic Society. He served as an editor of the American Journal of Physical Anthropology and president and treasurer-secretary of the AAPA. He died in 1997.

SELECTED WRITINGS BY STEWART:

Books

The People of America, Scribner, 1973.

FURTHER READING:

Books

Modern Men of Science, McGraw-Hill, 1968.
Modern Scientists and Engineers, McGraw-Hill, 1980.

Periodicals

Angel, Lawrence J., *Physical Anthropology,* T. Dale Stewart, November 1976, pp. 521–530.

Sketch by Joel Schwarz

George R. Stibitz
1904–1995
American mathematician and computer scientist

George R. Stibitz joined the Bell Telephone Laboratories as a mathematical engineer in 1930. His work at Bell Labs convinced him of the need to develop techniques for handling a large number of complex mathematical operations much more quickly than was currently possible with traditional manual systems. His research eventually led to the development of one of the first binary computers ever built. Stibitz was also the first to transmit computer data long-distance. Later in his life the mathematician became especially interested in the application of mathematics and the computer sciences to biomedical problems.

George Robert Stibitz was born on April 20, 1904, in York, Pennsylvania. His mother was the former Mildred Amelia Murphy, a math teacher before her marriage, and his father was George Stibitz, a professor of theology. Stibitz's childhood was spent in Dayton, Ohio, where his father taught at a local college. Because of the interest in and aptitude for science and engineering that he had exhibited, Stibitz was enrolled at an experimental high school in Dayton established by **Charles Kettering**, inventor of the first automobile ignition system.

For his undergraduate studies, Stibitz enrolled at Denison University in Granville, Ohio. After earning his bachelor of philosophy degree there in 1926, he went on to Union College in Schenectady, New York, where he was awarded his M.S. degree in 1927. After graduating from Union, he worked as a technician at General Electric in Schenectady for one year before returning to Cornell University to begin his doctoral program. Stibitz received his Ph.D. in mathematical physics from Cornell in 1930.

Stibitz's first job after graduation was as a research mathematician at the Bell Telephone Laboratories in New York City. His job there was to work on one of the fundamental problems with which modern telecommunication companies have to deal: How to carry out the endless number of mathematical calculations required to design and operate an increasingly complex system of telephones. At the time, virtually the only tool available to perform these calculations was the desktop mechanical calculator. It was obvious that this device would not long be adequate for the growing demands of the nation's expanding telephone network.

In the fall of 1937 Stibitz made the discovery for which he is now best known, the use of relays for automated computing. A relay is a metallic device that can assume one of two positions—open or closed—when an electrical current passes through it. The relay acts as a kind of gate, therefore, that will control the flow of electrical current, and was a common device used to regulate telephone circuits.

Stibitz Designs the "K-Model" Computing Machine

In November 1937 Stibitz decided to see if relays could be used to perform simple mathematical functions. He borrowed a few of the metal devices from the Bell stockroom, took them home, and assembled a simple computing system on his kitchen table. The system consisted of the relays, a dry cell, flashlight bulbs, and metal strips cut from a tobacco can. He soon had a device in which a lighted bulb represented the binary digit "1" and an unlighted bulb, the binary digit "0." The device was also able to use binary mathematics to add and subtract decimal numbers. Stibitz's colleagues later gave the name "K-Model" to this primitive computer because it was built on his kitchen table.

When Stibitz first demonstrated his K-model computer for company executives, they were not very impressed. "There were no fireworks, no champagne," he was quoted as saying in *The Computer Pioneers*. Less than a year later, however, Bell executives had changed their minds about the Stibitz invention. An important factor in that decision was the increasing pressure on Bell to find a way of solving its increasingly complex mathematical problems. The company agreed to finance construction of a large experimental model of Stibitz's invention. Construction on that machine began in April 1939, and the final product was first put into operation on January 8, 1940. Called the Complex Number Calculator (CNC), the machine had the capacity to add, subtract, multiply, and divide complex numbers—just the

kinds of problems that were particularly troublesome for engineers at Bell.

Nine months later, Stibitz recorded another milestone in the history of computer science. At a meeting of the American Mathematical Society at Dartmouth College, he hooked up the new Complex Number Calculator in New York City with a telegraph system. He then sent problems from Dartmouth to the CNC in New York, which solved the problems and sent the answers back to Dartmouth by means of the telegraph. This type of data transmission has now become commonplace in a modern day society of modems and fax machines.

During World War II, Bell Labs permitted Stibitz to join the National Defense Research Council. There the demands of modern military artillery convinced Stibitz even more of the need for improved computer hardware, and he spent most of the war working on improved versions of the CNC, also known as the Model 1. The Model 2 computer, for instance, used punched tapes to store programs that would give the computer instructions; in this manner the computer could perform the same complex calculations many times on different sets of numbers. This proved useful in calculating weapons trajectories.

At the end of World War II, Stibitz decided not to return to Bell Labs. Instead he moved with his family to Vermont where he became a consultant in applied mathematics. After two decades in this line of work Stibitz was offered a job at Dartmouth's Medical School, where he was asked to show how computers can be used to deal with biomedical problems. He accepted that offer and was appointed professor of physiology at Dartmouth; in that capacity he investigated the motion of oxygen in the lungs and the rate at which drugs and nutrients are spread throughout the body. In 1972 he retired from his position and was made professor emeritus; nevertheless, he continued to contribute his knowledge to the department.

Stibitz was married on September 1, 1930, to Dorothea Lamson, with whom he had two daughters, Mary and Martha. Among the awards he has received are the Harry Goode Award of the American Federation for Information Processing (1965), the Piore Award of the Institute of Electrical and Electronic Engineers (1977), and the Babbage Society Medal (1982). He was also the recipient of honorary degrees from Keene State College and Dartmouth College. The holder of 35 patents, Stibitz was named to the Inventors Hall of Fame in 1983. He died in his Hanover, New Hampshire, home on January 31, 1995. He was 90.

SELECTED WRITINGS BY STIBITZ:

Books

Mathematics and Computers, New York: McGraw-Hill, 1957.

Mathematics in Medicine and the Life Sciences, Year Book Medical Publishers, 1966.

FURTHER READING:

Books

Ceruzzi, Paul E., *Reckoners: The Prehistory of the Digital Computer, from Relays to the Stored Program Concept, 1935–1945,* Westport, CT: Greenwood Press, 1983, pp. 78–79.

Cortada, James W., *Historical Dictionary of Data Processing: Biographies,* Westport, CT: Greenwood Press, 1987, pp. 240-42.

Ritchie, David, *The Computer Pioneers: The Making of the Modern Computer,* New York: Simon & Schuster, 1986, pp. 33–52.

Periodicals

Loveday, Evelyn, "George Stibitz and the Bell Labs Relay Computer," *Datamation* (September 1977): 80–83.

Saxon, Wolfgang, "Dr. George Stibitz, 90, Inventor of First Digital Computer in '40" (obituary), *New York Times* (2 February 1995): p. B11.

Sketch by David E. Newton

Alfred Stock
1876–1946
German chemist

Alfred Stock was an experimentalist who made significant contributions to chemistry and designed several important chemical instruments. He worked on the creation of new boron and silicon compounds and the development of the chemical high-vacuum apparatus, which allowed him to work with volatile materials. The latter part of his life was particularly devoted to the study of mercury and mercury poisoning and, in particular, developing precautionary guidelines for other scientists to follow in order to avoid suffering from it. Stock contracted mercury poisoning while working with the substance in laboratories since his time in school; he was afflicted with the disease the rest of his life.

Stock was born in Danzig, West Prussia (now Gdansk, Poland) on July 16, 1876. His father was a banking executive. As a schoolboy, Stock developed an early interest in science, and he earned scholarships that allowed him to pursue a degree in chemistry at the University of Berlin in 1894. He chose to work at the chemical institute at the university, directed by **Emil Fischer**, but had to wait a year for space in the lab, which was overcrowded. He finally began his doctoral research in 1895 under the auspices of

organic chemist Oscar Piloty. During his summer breaks from school, Stock worked in the private laboratory of the Dutch physical chemist Jacobus van 't Hoff. It was there that Stock performed his first significant research in the areas of magnesium and oceanic salt deposits. After graduating magna cum laude in 1899, he spent a year in Paris assisting the chemist **Henri Moissan** at the Ecole superieure de Pharmacie, with support of the Prussian Ministry of Culture. At Moissan's lab he first investigated compounds of silicon and boron, which were to occupy him throughout his career.

Stock began his professional career in 1900 by working for nine years as a lab assistant with Fischer at the University of Berlin. There he investigated the preparation and characterization of such elements as phosphorus, arsenic, and antimony (a brittle, white metallic element). One result of Stock's investigation was that he could clearly explain their reactions with hydrogen, sulfur, and nitrogen. He also identified an unstable yellow form of antimony, and two new compounds of phosphorus: a polymeric hydride, which is a compound including hydrogen and another element or group, and a nitride, which is a compound including nitrogen and one other element. Stock's research clarified misconceptions in scientific literature and established the existence of three of today's four well-established phosphorus sulfides, which are organic compounds of phosphorous and sulfur.

Unfortunately, it was also during these early years in Berlin that symptoms associated with Stock's mercury poisoning would begin surfacing. Headaches, dizziness, and upper respiratory infections started plaguing Stock while he was pioneering his work with a device known as the vapor-tension thermometer. His success with the apparatus became well known throughout Germany and he later developed it into his tension-thermometer. Many years later, the work with the tension-thermometer was traced as the first of many sources of mercury poisoning to which Stock was exposed during the course of his life.

Develops Pump for Working with Volatile Substances

In July 1909, Stock was named full professor and director of the new Inorganic Chemistry Institute at Breslau. It was here that he surpassed previous chemists' successes with his imaginative work with hydrocarbons, inorganic carbon compounds and the development of a high-vacuum apparatus that allowed Stock to work with volatile and gaseous materials. The apparatus was later referred to as the Stock high-vacuum pump. He also envisioned at this time the possibility of developing the equivalent of organic chemistry's carbon-based system around boron, an element whose unanticipated potential he was just beginning to discover. His work with borohydrides, however, was interrupted with the outbreak of World War I. Stock was then charged with studying carbon subsulfide, an irritant, to determine its effectiveness as a war gas. The gas was never used, however, due to problems with polymerization, which is a chemical reaction in which molecules combine to form larger molecules that contain repeating structural units.

Stock left Breslau in April 1916 to continue his research and take charge of **Richard Willstätter**'s laboratory at the Kaiser Wilhelm Institute near Berlin. It was not long, however, before the military moved in and took over the institute. Since his still undiagnosed physical problems (including, by that time, an acute loss of hearing) kept him from serving in the military, he and his staff moved their equipment to the University of Berlin so that they could continue their work. When the war ended, he returned to the Kaiser Wilhelm Institute and continued to study silicon and boron hydrides. His work yielded a number of halogen and alkyl derivatives which, in turn, led to the discovery of new compounds such as silyl amines and silicones. In the process, Stock developed a chemistry based on silicon; this was similar to his work with boron at Breslau. At the suggestion of Hans Goldschmidt, Stock also collaborated on the production of metallic beryllium. This substance had become a worthwhile element to pursue because it is a metal which had possible applications in industry, so a beryllium study group was formed. By 1940, their new technique for making the material yielded enough beryllium to significantly reduce the market value per kilogram, thus increasing the element's cost-effectiveness in scientific experiments.

Investigates Mercury Poisoning

Stock's unexplained medical problems kept growing worse. Besides headaches, vertigo, respiratory infections, and deafness, he now also suffered frequent numbness. None of these symptoms was alleviated by medical treatment. In 1923, he suffered virtually total hearing and memory loss, and he almost didn't make it through the winter of 1924. At that time, many scientists in addition to Stock were unknowingly being exposed to mercury poisoning. It wasn't until after he saw similar symptoms in a colleague that Stock finally realized the volatility of this odorless substance. He began researching mercury poisoning, often experimenting on himself. As a result of his investigations, Stock published several articles outlining the dangers of mercury and offered up numerous precautionary guidelines for working with the substance.

It was a difficult decision, but the opportunity to establish a new mercury-free laboratory convinced Stock to leave the Kaiser Wilhelm Institute in 1926 to become the director of the Chemical Institute at Karlsruhe. The next ten years of his life were devoted exclusively to the study of mercury poisoning and borohydrides. His concepts and working models of laboratory rooms equipped with extensive safety precautions were sought after by scientists from around the world. Further experiments proved that inhaled mercury vapor was much more dangerous than ingested mercury because the vapor, entering through the nose, moved more quickly into the pituitary gland, where it wreaked havoc on the body. Stock also pioneered a teaching method during his tenure at Karlsruhe which used reflected light to project chemical objects on a large screen. Stock

worked with his lecture assistant, Hans Ramser, and with Carl Zeiss-Jena, to create this apparatus, which was called an epidiascope.

Stock married Clara Venzky in August of 1906 and later had two daughters. He was the president of the Verein Deutscher Chemiker (Association of German Chemists) in Paris in 1927 and later the Deutsche Chemische Gesellschaft (German Chemical Society) from 1936 to 1938. He was a guest professor at Cornell University for several months in 1932 under the George Fisher Baker Nonresident Lectureship in Chemistry. The last ten years of Stock's life were nearly unbearable, both physically and professionally. His mercury poisoning became debilitating and interfered with his work. His political differences with the Nazi government were increasing. In 1936, at the age of 60, he asked for his retirement. He returned with his family to Berlin where he continued to trace and validate the chemical path of mercury poisoning. By 1940, movement became difficult as he developed hardening of the muscles. Stock relinquished his laboratories in 1943 because they were needed for the war effort, and he and his wife moved to Bad Warmbrunn in Silesia to live with his brother-in-law. As the Russians were approaching in 1945, Stock and his wife again moved and sought shelter with an old friend, Ernst Kuss, in Dessau. The Stocks finally found refuge in a barracks in Aken, a small city on the Elbe. Stock died in the early morning of August 12, 1946.

SELECTED WRITINGS BY STOCK:

Books

Hydrides of Boron and Silicon, Cornell University Press, 1957.
The Structure of Atoms, Dutton, 1923.

FURTHER READING:

Books

Farber, Eduard, *Great Chemists,* Interscience Publishers, 1961.

Sketch by Amy M. Punke

George Gabriel Stokes
1819–1903
British mathematical physicist

Sir George Gabriel Stokes made important advances in the fields of hydrodynamics and optics. He also did significant work in wave theory, as well as the elasticity and light diffraction of solids. With his work on viscous fluids,

George Gabriel Stokes

he helped develop the theoretical foundation for the science of hydrodynamics. These equations, known as the Navier–Stokes equations (he shared credit with Claude Navier) describe the motion of viscous fluids. The word "fluorescence" entered the English language when Stokes first used it to explain his conclusions about the blue light emitting from the surface of colorless, transparent solutions. He then applied the phenomena of fluorescence to study light spectra. An important practical use for fluorescence was in the pharmacy, where British chemists used it—instead of relying on the availability of sunlight—to tell the difference among chemicals. Stokes is also considered a pioneer in scientific geodesy (publishing a major work on the variation of gravity at Earth's surface in 1849), and spectrum analysis. In 1849, he assumed the Lucasian chair at Cambridge University, which he held until his death. Stokes was also very active in various scientific and academic societies. He served as president of the Cambridge Philosophical Society from 1859 to 1861, and was president of the Royal Society of London from 1885 to 1890. In 1887, he became a member of Parliament, representing the University of Cambridge, serving until 1891. The Royal Society awarded Stokes the Rumford Medal in 1852 for his work with fluorescence; he was also awarded the Copley Medal in 1893. His scientific contributions were recognized by a knighthood in 1889.

Stokes was born in Skreen, County Sligo, Ireland, on August 13, 1819. His family was of Anglo–Irish extraction, whose forebears included many clergy in the Church of Ireland. His father, Gabriel, was rector in Skreen, and his mother, Elizabeth Haughton Stokes, was the daughter of a rector. Stokes was the youngest of six children. He was educated by his father as a young boy, later attending a Dublin school. He went to Bristol College in England to prepare for university.

Begins Long Tenure at Cambridge

In 1837, he entered Pembroke College, Cambridge, to study mathematics. He graduated in 1841, winning senior Wrangler and 1st Smith's prizeman academic honors. He was given a fellowship at Pembroke and remained at Cambridge the rest of his life. His appointment as Lucasian professor coincided with teaching at the Government School of Mines in London, which he did to increase his income—his Cambridge position being poorly endowed at that time. He married Mary Susanna Robinson in 1857, giving up his fellowship to marry, as was the custom at that time. They became the parents of three children, two sons and a daughter. He was able to regain a fellowship in 1859 when a change in University rules regarding married professors was made.

Introduces Advances in Hydrodynamics

Pure mathematics was never the sole focus of Stokes' inquiry—his experimental work was equally important. For him, theory was placed in the service of answering specific physical questions, and his mathematical papers reflect his interest in developing problem–solving methods or proving out existing formulas. His investigations into hydrodynamics led him to test out and publish his theories on the internal friction of fluids. Although French physicists (Claude Navier in particular) had already done work in this area, Stokes introduced new applications for their mathematical equations. In 1846, he presented a paper on hydrodynamic advances to the British Association for the Advancement of Science, which greatly enhanced his reputation. Later hydrodynamic experiments involved a study of the propagation of oscillatory waves in water, and led to a method of calculating their shape.

In 1850, Stokes published a major paper on hydrodynamics that included Stokes' Law governing the fall of an object through a liquid, using the action of pendulums to test out his fluid theories. Based on his observations, and also using the experiments conducted by others in the field, he was able to explain how clouds formed in the atmosphere. These conclusions, combined with his studies on surface gravity, caused Stokes to be regarded in England as an authority on the emerging science of geodesy. In 1854 he published Stokes' Theorem, a three–dimensional generalization of Green's Theorem invector calculus.

To compilment his study of hydrodynamics, Stokes also delved into the principles of sound. He analyzed how sound was produced and the effect of wind on its intensity. Using this information, he explained why stringed instruments required sounding boards in order to transmit sound.

Stokes also explained how sound is produced through telegraph wires.

Examines Concept of Light Propagation

The wave theory of light also captured Stokes' attention. His early mathematical studies revolved around the nature of ether—then a concept for explaining how light is propagated. Although he attempted to work around conceptual flaws by connecting his work on elastic solids to the properties of ether, its existence was eventually disproved in later experiments by other scientists. However, Stokes' work in light diffraction bore fruit in many other areas. For example, in 1849, he developed instruments which allowed him to measure the amount of astigmatism in the human eye, and in 1851 he invented a device to analyze polarized light. Stokes subsequently published, in 1852, a mathematical formula for the characteristics and behavior of polarized light, known as Stokes' Parameters.

Important Light Experiments Involve Fluorescence

Stokes used the results of his many experiments with fluorescence for further investigation into the properties of light and other elements of nature. One example is his use of fluorescence to study ultraviolet spectra. He eventually was able to determine that the dark spectral lines discovered by Joseph von Fraunhofer were lines of elements which absorbed light from the sun's outer crust. Stokes' last major work was the mathematical study on the dynamical theory of double refraction, which were presented to the British Association for the Advancement of Science in 1862.

Stokes is regarded as having great influence on later Cambridge physicists, not only through his own research, but also through his knowledge of the work physicists outside Britain were doing. His promulgation of French mathematical physics—at a time when Cambridge had little knowledge of it—is one example.

Because of the time–consuming administrative duties Stokes was responsible for in the several scientific societies of which he served as an officer, his scholarly output was curtailed toward the end of his career. Stokes was, however, quick to respond to the many queries he received from other physicists regarding the progress and problems of their work. His voluminous correspondence with his contemporaries, notably George Green, James Challis, and William Thomson, details his influence and guidance. From 1883 to 1885, he delivered a series of lectures on light at the University of Aberdeen, and a series of lectures on theology at Edinburgh from 1891 to 1983. These lectures were later published. Stokes died at Cambridge on February 1, 1903.

SELECTED WRITINGS BY STOKES:

Books

Mathematical and Physical Papers, 5 volumes, 1880–1905.

Burnett Lectures. On Light. In Three Courses Delivered at Aberdeen in November, 1883, December, 1884, and November, 1885.

Natural Theology. The Gifford Lectures Delivered Before the University of Edinburgh in 1891.

FURTHER READING:

Books

Asimov, Isaac, *Asimov's Biographical Encyclopedia of Science and Technology*, Garden City, NY: Doubleday & Company, Inc., 1972.

Daintith, John, editor, *Biographical Encyclopedia of Scientists*, Volume 2. New York: Facts on File, Inc., 1981, pp. 759–760.

Debus, Allen G., editor, *Who's Who In Science*. Chicago: Marquis Who's Who, Inc., 1968, p. 1616.

Parkinson, E. M., "George Gabriel Stokes," in *Dictionary of Scientific Biography*, Edited by Charles Coulston Gillespie, Volume XIII, New York: Charles Scribner's Sons, 1976, pp. 74–79.

Porter, Roy, editor, *The Biographical Dictionary of Scientists*, New York: Oxford University Press, 1994, pp. 647–648.

Wilson, D. B., *Kelvin and Stokes: A Comparative Study in Victorian Physics*, 1987.

Sketch by Jane Stewart Cook

Alice M. Stoll
1917–
American biophysicist

A scientist who worked in the field of medical biophysics, Alice M. Stoll conducted research into the effects of heat and acceleration on the human body, and the rate that heat is given off by burning materials. Her investigations, which permitted evaluation of the thermal protection offered by fire-resistant and fire-retardant fabrics, led to the development of new fabrics for use in fire-hazard protection. Among the honors accorded to Stoll in recognition for her scientific work was the 1969 Society of Women Engineers' Achievement Award.

Stoll, a native of New York City, was born on August 25, 1917. She obtained her undergraduate education at Hunter College, earning a B.A. degree in 1938. Joining the New York Hospital and Medical College at Cornell University, she worked as an assistant in the areas of metabolism, allergies, and spectroscopy. In 1943 Stoll joined the U.S. Navy, remaining in active duty until 1946, then returned to Cornell University where she began research into temperature regulation. She completed a dual M.S. degree in physiology and biophysics in 1948. Remaining at the Medical College until 1953, Stoll worked as a research associate in the area of environmental thermal radiation and as an instructor in the school of nursing. To conduct her research, Stoll had to develop the instrumentation necessary for her work. The instruments she developed—and for which she received patents—measure the heat transferred to the surroundings from flames and other thermal radiation sources. At this time, Stoll also worked as a consultant for various laboratories, including the Arctic Aerospace Medicine Laboratory at Ladd Air Force Base in Alaska during 1952 and 1953. Part of her time was also spent on her duties with the Naval Reserve, which she had joined upon completion of her active duty.

Leaving Cornell in 1953, Stoll joined the Naval Air Development Center (NADC) in Warminster, Pennsylvania, as a physiologist in the medical research department. Advancing to special technical assistant in 1956, she became head of the Thermal Laboratory in 1960, and then chief of the Biophysics & Bioastronautics Division in 1964. Stoll retired from the Naval Reserve in 1966 with the rank of commander, but remained at NADC where she was promoted to head of the Biophysics Laboratory in 1970, a position she held until her retirement in 1980.

Stoll conducted research at NADC into the effects of acceleration on the cardiovascular system. Most of her work, however, centered on the transfer of heat from flames and other thermal radiation sources and how this heat transfer affected the human body. Stoll's studies on tissue damage and pain sensation established a relationship between the amount of heat absorbed and the damage which resulted; she established that the source of the heat was not important, as all heat sources could cause the same damage. Models that Stoll designed based on this research were valuable in determining the amount of thermal protection needed to protect the body from different heat sources.

Stoll also investigated the heat transfer properties of various fabrics which could be used to provide thermal protection. Clothing, however, acts not only to protect the skin from heat but can also be a source of heat if it catches on fire; an accidental burning of a test participant during simulated space capsule clothing fires at NADC prompted Stoll to study the burning properties of fabrics under high oxygen concentrations—conditions which could be found in the aerospace environment. This research resulted in the development of methods for measuring the burn protection provided by clothing and fabrics, as well as the invention of "Nomex" (produced by DuPont), a fire-resistant fabric which is now widely used in apparel for fire fighters and race car drivers.

In addition to being recognized by the Society of Women Engineers, Stoll was honored in 1965 with the Federal Civil Service Award and the Paul Bert Award from the Aerospace Medical Association in 1972. A charter member of the Biophysical Society, she has been elected a fellow of the American Association for the Advancement of Science. Stoll has remained active in the American Society of Mechanical Engineers, particularly in the heat transfer and biotechnology sections.

SELECTED WRITINGS BY STOLL:

Periodicals

Journal of Applied Physiology, Relationship Between Pain and Tissue Damage due to Thermal Radiation, Volume 14, 1959, pp. 373–382.

Journal of Heat Transfer, Flame Contact Studies, Volume 86, 1964, pp. 449–456.

Aerospace Medicine, Mathematical Model of Skin Exposed to Thermal Radiation, Volume 40, 1969, pp. 24–30.

Aerospace Medicine, Method and Rating System for Evaluation of Thermal Protection, Volume 40, 1969, pp. 1232–1237.

Journal of Fire & Flammability, Thermal Analysis of Combustion of Fabric in Oxygen-Enriched Atmospheres, Volume 4, 1973, pp. 309–324.

Aviation, Space, and Environmental Medicine, Facility and a Method for Evaluation of Thermal Protection, November 1976, pp. 1177–1181.

FURTHER READING:

Books

American Men & Women of Science, 14th Edition, R. R. Bowker, 1979, p. 4928.

Engineers of Distinction, 2nd Edition, Engineers Joint Council 1973, p. 297.

O'Neill, Lois Decker, editor, *The Woman's Book of World Records and Achievements,* Anchor Press/Doubleday, 1979, pp. 187–188.

Other

O'Neill, Lois Decker, editor, *The Woman's Book of World Records and Achievements,* Stoll, Alice M., correspondence with Jerome Ferrance, January 1994.

Sketch by Jerome P. Ferrance

Henry Stommel
1920–1992
American oceanographer

Oceanographer Henry Stommel considered a variety of careers: ministry, law, chemistry, and astronomy, before settling on the field of oceanography. He is a pioneer in the theory of ocean currents, a field largely untouched when he began his career in 1944. Stommel is considered the leading authority on Gulf Stream dynamics and his foremost achievement is the development of his Gulf Stream theory in 1947. Stommel also made major contributions to studies of cumulus clouds, ocean salinity and thermal gradients, and plankton distribution.

Stommel was awarded the National Medal of Science for his contributions to oceanography in 1989 and the Craaford Prize of the Royal Swedish Academy (shared with Edward Lorenz) in recognition of his influence on geophysical hydrodynamics and climatology in 1983. He was elected to the National Academy of Sciences in 1959, The Royal Society, London in 1983, the Soviet Academy of Sciences in 1977, and the Académie des Sciences de Paris.

Stommel was born September 27, 1920, in Wilmington, Delaware. Soon after, his family moved to Sweden. Then his mother left his father and moved to Brooklyn, New York, where Stommel grew up. Stommel first studied mathematics at Yale University, receiving his B.S. degree in 1942. He remained at Yale as an instructor in analytic geometry and celestial navigation for two years. In 1944, Stommel met Columbus Iselin, the director of the Woods Hole Oceanographic Institution in Woods Hole, Massachusetts, who offered him a position as research associate there. Stommel accepted the offer and spent much of his career at Woods Hole.

Develops Landmark Gulf Stream Theory

Stommel built his niche in oceanography after observing the near-complete absence of theory in the study of ocean currents. He applied relatively simple mathematical models to the study of the ocean, and devised the landmark theory of the Gulf Stream. The Gulf Stream is an ocean current that runs north along the eastern coast of the United States and Canada and then crosses the Atlantic to northern Europe. Before Stommel did his ground-breaking research, this current was considered a river of warm water that gave northern Europe its temperate climate. Stommel was able to determine that the Gulf Stream in fact forms the boundary between the cold northern waters and the warm, currentless Sargasso Sea at the center of the North Atlantic. An increase in the volume of the Gulf Stream would probably result in a drop in temperature in northern Europe.

The techniques Stommel pioneered in creating this model also proved to be applicable to other ocean currents.

It had always been assumed that ocean currents are surface phenomena, but Stommel discovered that there are patterns of motion all the way down to the ocean floors. Comparing deep currents to patterns of air circulation in the atmosphere, he found that the rotation of the earth creates similar systems of currents in the earth's oceans. The Gulf Stream itself is fed by waters flowing west along the equator, propelled by the motion of the earth. The effects of the earth's rotation are known as Coriolis forces. Stommel's joint research with scientist Friedrich Schott also established a correlation between density and velocity in ocean currents. A comprehensive account of Stommel's work on the Gulf Stream and on ocean currents in general appeared in 1965 in his book *The Gulf Stream.*

Participates in Ocean Study Programs

Stommel recognized that the Gulf Stream wanders about, and this fact led him to instigate numerous programs to gather data on the variability of ocean currents. One of these programs was the Bermuda Biweekly Hydrographic Station PANULIRUS, which he began in 1954. In 1959 Stommel left Woods Hole to take a position at the Massachusetts Institute of Technology (MIT) as a professor of oceanography. The following year he joined the faculty at Harvard University, where he spent three years, and also cofounded the ARIES deep-float experiment with oceanographers John C. Swallow and James Crease. The ARIES experiment was the first systematic attempt to measure deep currents with a float newly designed by Swallow.

In 1963, Stommel returned to MIT, where he remained until 1978. In those years, he headed the MEDOC study in the Mediterranean, to gather information about deep-water formation with the scientists Henri Lacombe and Paul Tchernia. With the oceanographer Allan Robinson, Stommel began the Mid-Ocean Dynamics Experiment, which ran from 1970 to 1978, and the Seychelles Study of Equatorial Currents in the Indian Ocean, carried out with Ants Leetmaa in 1975 and 1976. In 1979, Stommel returned to Woods Hole as a senior scientist and continued his research there until his death.

In 1987, Stommel published a book for lay readers, *A View of the Sea,* which discusses his own research into ocean circulation, focusing specifically on the upper ocean. The complex theory of ocean circulation is made simple in the book, which is set up as a dialogue between the chief engineer and an oceanographer on a research vessel. Stommel speaks to the lay reader through anecdotes, told by the fictional oceanographer, discussing Coriolis forces, density field measurements, wind-driven models, gravity, and the earth's rotation. A review in *Science* describes *A View of the Sea* as "a highly successful attempt to explain important aspects of the ocean circulation to a wide audience."

Stommel did not limit himself to ocean currents, although they undoubtedly form the central focus of his life's work. He also conducted research on cumulus clouds; a study of the diurnal thermocline (a stratum of water separating warm upper layers heated by the sun and lower, colder layers, where temperature does not vary); and a study of the distribution of phytoplankton in the oceans. Stommel expressed gratitude for his career in oceanography and the opportunities it gave him to explore the seas and the boundaries of his own thinking. Stommel died on January 17, 1992.

SELECTED WRITINGS BY STOMMEL:

Books

The Gulf Stream, California University Press, 1965.
A View of the Sea, Princeton University Press, 1987.
Volcano Weather: The Story of 1816, the Year Without a Summer, Seven Seas Press, 1983, with E. Stommel.
Lost Islands: The Story of Islands That Have Vanished From the Nautical Charts, University of British Columbia Press, 1984.

FURTHER READING:

Books

Behrman, Daniel, *The New World of the Oceans: Men and Oceanography,* Little, Brown, 1969.

Periodicals

Hide, Raymond, review of, *A View of the Sea, Science,* October 1987.
Schmitt Jr., Raymond W., "The Ocean's Salt Fingers," *Scientific American,* May 1995.

Other

Wunsch, Carl, *Henry Stommel,* National Academy of Sciences, http://www.nap.edu/readingroom/books/biomems/hstommel.html.

Sketch by Lori De Milto

Fredrik Størmer
1874–1957
Norwegian mathematician and geophysicist

Fredrik Størmer contributed both important photographic observations and mathematical data to the understanding of the polar aurora, of stratospheric and mesospheric clouds, and of the structure of the ionosphere. Besides his many honorary academic memberships in Europe, he was elected a foreign member of the Royal Society of London in 1951.

Fredrik Carl Mülertz Størmer was born at Skien, Norway, on September 3, 1874, to Georg Størmer and Elisabeth Mülertz. The Størmer family moved to Christiania (now Oslo) while he was still a boy. Størmer's ability to excel in mathematics was already apparent in high school, and further encouragement came from a family friend, a professor of mathematics at the University of Christiania in Oslo. In 1892 Størmer published his first mathematical paper while still in secondary school; later that year he enrolled at the university, receiving his master's degree in 1898 and his doctorate in 1903. As soon as he finished his studies, he was appointed professor of pure mathematics at the university and made the acquaintance of the Norwegian physicist Olaf Kristian Birkeland, whose research centered on the earth's magnetic field.

Although Størmer had already begun to publish mature and important mathematical papers (on number and function theory, and on the nontrivial determination of trigonometric function solutions), he became thoroughly intrigued with Birkeland's momentous first laboratory demonstration of the aurora phenomenon. An aurora is the light emitted by energetic protons and electrons at the top of Earth's atmosphere when they come in contact with solar wind particles; this phenomenon occurs regularly at both the North and South Poles. In 1896 Birkeland had succeeded in simulating auroral light by bombarding a magnetized sphere with cathode ray electrons in a vacuum; French theoretical physicist Paul Villard—whose research centered on cathode ray electrons, X rays, and radioactivity—also performed this simulation in 1906. Størmer recalled in his book *The Polar Aurora* that Villard "made some very fine experiments" and "succeeded in producing threadlike currents of cathode rays, which made it possible to follow the trajectories in detail." Those trajectories were immediately significant, for the electrons collided with the sphere only at the top and bottom—analogous to the polar zones of the earth—and observation had long shown that the aurora was a high-latitude phenomenon.

Creates an Upper Atmospheric Photographic Archive

The approximate physical extent of the aurora phenomenon had already been studied for almost two hundred years beginning in 1726, when it was realized to occur at much greater altitudes than had been thought before. Størmer sought to determine the exact altitude of the aurora, as well as to derive the mathematical formulas governing the phenomenon through close observation. With the advent of photography, the possibility of more accurate altitude determination was recognized. Though the earliest photographs, made by Danish meteorologist Sophus Tromholt in 1885, did not in fact demonstrate greater accuracy, Størmer considered the photographic method essential and invaluable to the recording of auroral observations and the evaluation of his theoretical conclusions.

Possessed of an independent experimental disposition, Størmer constructed, among other instruments, a photographic apparatus by which he could take photos of actual auroral displays. Beginning in 1909, he used two cameras at different locations to take simultaneous photographs of the aurora, with the shutters of each camera synchronized by a telephone link; by comparing the parallax, or shift, of the images in the two photographs, Størmer could estimate the aurora's distance from the cameras.

Over forty years, Størmer collected a prodigious file of photographs and compiled them into a library of observational analysis, yielding data on altitudes, extent, shape, and periodicity of the polar aurora. This library was enriched by the first collection of photographs of rare noctilucent clouds (more formally known as polar stratospheric clouds, or PSCs) and the higher mesospheric nacreous, or mother-of-pearl, clouds (polar mesospheric clouds, or PMCs). These photographic observations were so significant that Størmer set up a network of observational stations to collect auroral and higher atmospheric cloud data.

Develops the Mathematics of the Auroras

Alongside his photographic efforts, Størmer developed a mathematical theory of the directional dynamics of the auroral phenomenon as it was observed in simulation experiments. He started with French mathematician **Jules Henri Poincaré**'s equations of motion for electrically charged particles influenced by a single magnetic pole, and then proceeded to the magnetic dipole—the actual case for Earth.

Størmer's work on the mathematical theory continued from 1904 to 1950 and resulted in a configuration of the trajectories of charged particles in a magnetic dipole, rather than a cloud of particles. In order to process this information, the series of differential equations that he had derived had to be numerically integrated. With no high-speed computers to aid him, Størmer called upon a volunteer staff of his students to take on the arduous task of calculation. With their help, Størmer concluded that the electrical particles traced out only certain trajectories, which were distributed in a cone shape (known as Størmer's Cone); all other trajectories were labeled "forbidden directions." Størmer demonstrated that the particular directions traced out by particles allowed them to be bent around Earth and into Earth's dark side, which explains the nighttime occurrence of the aurora.

His further research into electron behavior in the upper atmosphere prompted the hypotheses that there is a circular electric current in the equatorial plane of Earth and that electrons might become trapped in oscillatory trajectories in Earth's magnetic field. In the 1930s, the latitudinal variation in cosmic radiation was discovered and was found to conform to Størmer's calculations of it; furthermore, the discovery of the Van Allen Radiation Belts by **James Van Allen** confirmed with surprising accuracy Størmer's theoretical analysis of solar charged particle trajectories in Earth's magnetic field.

Størmer taught for forty-one years, and both his research and his teaching cast a long shadow in the foundations of the geophysics of aeronomy and of the magnetic field of the Earth. Størmer also had a great gift for communicating the abstractions of his science to the public in general articles, and most of his written work appeared in the Norwegian academic services publication *Norske Videnskabsakademiets Skrifter.* He died of heart failure in Oslo on August 13, 1957.

SELECTED WRITINGS BY STØRMER:

Books

Fra verdensrummets dybder til atomenes indre, [Oslo], 1923.
The Polar Aurora, Oxford University Press, 1955.

FURTHER READING:

Books

Petrie, William, *Keoeeit—The Story of the Aurora Borealis,* Pergamon Press, 1963, pp. 48–50, 122–123.

Sketch by William J. McPeak

Alicia Boole Stott
1860–1940
Irish-born English mathematician

Alicia Boole Stott is considered noteworthy for her famous relatives as much for her own discoveries that translate Platonic and Archimedean solids into higher dimensions. She is more likely described when mentioned in other contexts as the daughter of mathematician and Royal Medal recipient George Boole and Mary Everest Boole.

Stott was born on June 8, 1860, in Cork, Ireland, where her father held a professorship at Queen's College. When George Boole died of a fever in 1864, Stott's sisters were dispersed to live with relatives while their mother struggled to support herself in London. Stott was shuttled between her grandmother in England and a great–uncle in Ireland, and was not reunited with her sisters until she was more than 10 years old.

Cardboard Models

Stott was well into her teens by the time she became seriously interested in mathematics. A family friend named

Howard Hinton, soon to become her brother–in–law, introduced her to the tesseract, or four–dimensional hypercube. He not only offered Stott intellectual stimulation, he got her a job as secretary to an associate, John Falk. At that time, Hinton was working on a book that would eventually see publication in 1904.

In 1900, Stott (with the encouragement of Walter Stott, an actuary whom she later married) published an article on three–dimensional sections of hypersolids. They led an ordinary middle–class existence following their marriage and had two children, Mary and Leonard. Walter took note of his wife's interests and introduced her to the work of Pieter Hendrik Schoute of the University of Groningen. The Stotts took a chance and wrote to him describing Stott's work.

Upon viewing photographs of Stott's cardboard models, Schoute elected to relocate to England from the Netherlands in order to collaborate with her. Over their twenty–year relationship, Schoute arranged for the publication of Stott's own papers and cowrote others. Stott refined her approach towards deriving the Archimedean solids from the Platonic solids to improve upon Johannes Kepler's. She also coined the term "polytope" as a name for a four–dimensional convex solid form.

Schoute's university colleagues were impressed enough to invite Stott to their tercentenary celebration in 1914, to bestow upon her an honorary doctorate. Unfortunately, the 71–year–old Schoute died before the event. At a loss, Stott resumed her role as homemaker for nearly 20 years.

Stott found another collaborator, H.S.M. Coxeter, a writer who specialized in the geometry of kaleidoscopes, in 1930. She was quite taken with these "magic mirrors" and the challenge they would present to more old–fashioned mathematicians. Stott was inspired to devise a four–dimensional analogue to two of the Archimedean solids, which she called the "snub 24–cell." This construction was not original to her, having been discovered earlier by Thorold Gosset. However, her cardboard models of it in its "golden ratio" relationship with the regular 24–cell are still stored at Cambridge University.

Stott was an animal lover who enjoyed bird watching. She became ill around the time England entered World War II and died on December 17, 1940.

SELECTED WRITINGS BY STOTT:

Periodicals

"On Certain Sections of the Regular Four–Dimensional Hypersolids," in *Verhandelingen der Koninklijke Akademie van Wetenschappen* (1. sectie) 7 (3) (1900): pp. 1–21.

"Geometrical Deduction of Semiregular from Regular Polytopes and Space Fillings," in *Verhandelingen der Koninklijke Akademie van Wetenschappen* (1. sectie) 11 (1) (1910): pp. 1–24.

FURTHER READING:

Books

Coxeter, H. S. M., "Alicia Boole Stott," in *Women of Mathematics*, Edited by Louise S. Grinstein and Paul J. Campbell, Westport, CT: Greenwood Press, 1987, pp. 220–24.

Other

Frost, Michelle, "Mary Everest Boole," *Biographies of Women Mathematicians*, http://www.scottlan.edu/lriddle/women/chronol.htm (July 1997).
"Alicia Boole Stott," *MacTutor History of Mathematics Archive*, http://www–groups.dcs.st–and.ac.uk/~history/Mathematicians/Stott.html (July 1997).

Sketch by Jennifer Kramer

Fritz Strassmann
1902–1980
German chemist

Fritz Strassmann's experiments with the bombardment of neutrons on uranium atoms resulted in the discovery of nuclear fission, which has been employed in making the world's first atomic bomb and nuclear energy. He also developed a widely used geological dating method employing radiation techniques, and served as a well-respected teacher of nuclear chemistry.

Friedrich Wilhelm Strassmann, the youngest of nine children, was born on February 22, 1902, in Boppard, Germany, to Richard Strassmann, a court clerk, and Julie Bernsmann. Strassmann attended primary schools in Cologne and Düsseldorf and secondary school at the Düsseldorf Oberrealschule. During this time, he became interested in chemistry. However, the death of his father in 1920 and the desperate economic conditions of post-World War I Germany made it impossible to enroll at a university. Instead, he entered the Technical Institute at Hanover, where he supported himself as a private tutor.

In 1924 Strassmann was awarded his diplomate (comparable to a master's degree) in chemistry at Hanover. He then stayed on to pursue a doctoral program in physical chemistry under Hermann Braune. Strassmann completed that program in 1929 and was awarded his Ph.D. for a thesis on the solubility of iodine in carbon dioxide. In the *Dictionary of Scientific Biography* it is noted that Strassmann's choice of physical chemistry as a major was largely due to the increased likelihood of finding employment in that field during a tight labor market.

Strassmann Begins Collaboration with Otto Hahn

Shortly after receiving his Ph.D., Strassmann was offered a scholarship to the Kaiser Wilhelm Institute for Chemistry in Berlin by its director, **Otto Hahn**. That scholarship was renewed twice and then, in 1932, Strassmann was invited to continue his work at the institute with Hahn, first at no salary and later at a minimal wage.

The 1930s were a difficult time for Strassmann, partly because of his restrictive financial situation and partly because of his views regarding the policies of Adolf Hitler's new regime. Although he was not in any immediate personal or professional danger, Strassmann decided to refuse all offers of employment that would have required his joining the Nazi party. He continued his work, therefore, with Hahn and later, **Lise Meitner** at the Kaiser Wilhelm Institute.

The subject on which Strassmann, Hahn, and Meitner were working during the mid–1930s was the bombardment of uranium by neutrons. The great Italian physicist **Enrico Fermi** had found that the bombardment of an element by neutrons often results in the formation of a new element one place higher in the periodic table. Fermi had successfully applied this technique to a number of elements during the early 1930s.

The one example that most intrigued Fermi—and other scientists familiar with his work—was the bombardment of uranium. Should earlier patterns hold, they realized, such a reaction would result in the formation of an element one place higher than uranium (number 92) in the periodic table, that is, element 93. Since no such element was known to exist naturally, a successful experiment of this design would result in the first artificially produced element.

Strassmann, Hahn, and Meitner Discover Nuclear Fission

Unfortunately, the uranium bombardment yielded results that were not easily interpreted. Original indications seemed to be that the products of the reaction were largely elements close to uranium in the periodic table, thorium, radium, and actinium, for example. Such results would not have been surprising since all nuclear reactions known up to that time involved changes in atomic number between reactants and products of no more than one or two places.

More detailed studies by Strassmann yielded troubling results, however. His chemical analysis consistently showed the presence of barium, whose atomic number is 36 less than that of uranium. The formation of barium seemed so unlikely to Strassmann and Hahn that their reports of their work were hedged with doubts and qualifications. In fact, it was not until Lise Meitner, then a refugee in Sweden, received word of the Hahn-Strassmann experiment that the puzzle was solved. With a fearlessness that Strassmann and Hahn had lacked, Meitner stated forthrightly that barium *had* been formed and that this change had occurred as a result of the splitting apart of the uranium nucleus.

The significance of this discovery can hardly be overestimated. Within a decade, it had been put to use in the development of the world's first atomic bombs and, shortly thereafter, was being touted as one of humankind's great new sources of power for peacetime applications. For his part in this historic event, Strassmann was awarded the 1966 Enrico Fermi Prize of the U.S. Atomic Energy Commission.

A second line of research in which Strassmann's analytical skills resulted in an important discovery was that of geological dating. Beginning in 1934, he and Ernst Walling studied the radioactive decay of rubidium, a process that results in the formation of strontium. Strassmann's careful analysis of the characteristics of this process eventually led to its use in the dating of geological strata, a process that has become a standard tool in geology.

Strassmann remained at the Kaiser Wilhelm Institute during the war, first in Berlin and later in Tailfingen, where the institute was moved to avoid destruction by bombing. After the war, he was appointed professor of inorganic and nuclear chemistry at the University of Mainz. At Mainz he became involved in complex negotiations over the construction of two new institutes. One was a new physical facility for the Max Planck Institute of Chemistry, successor to the former Kaiser Wilhelm Institute in Berlin. The second was a new Institute for Nuclear Chemistry, designed as part of the newly reestablished University of Mainz. Although beset by all manner of political, technical, and economic problems, Strassmann made major contributions to the establishment of both institutions. In addition, he saw through to completion the construction of the TRIGA Mark II nuclear reactor in Mainz.

Strassmann died in Mainz on April 22, 1980. He was remembered not only for his discoveries in nuclear fission and geological dating and for his skills as an administrator of scientific research, but also for his qualities as a teacher. His achievements were recognized in 1969 when the Society of German Chemists established the Fritz Strassmann award, to be given to an outstanding young nuclear chemist each year. Strassmann was married twice, the first time on July 20, 1937, to Maria Heckter, a former pupil. The couple had one son, Martin. Three years after Maria's death in 1956, Strassmann was married a second time, to Irmgard Hartmann, a good friend of his first wife.

SELECTED WRITINGS BY STRASSMANN:

Periodicals

Berichte der Deutschen Chemischen Gesselschaft, Die Abscheidung des Reinen Strontium-Isotops 87 aus einem Alten Rubidium Haltigen Lepidolith und die Halbwertszeit des Rubidiums, Volume 71B, 1938, pp. 1–9.

Die Naturwissenschaften, Über den Nachweis und das Verhalten der bei der Bestrahlung des Urans Mittels Neutronen Entstehenden Erdalkalimetallie, Volume 27, 1939, pp. 89–95.

FURTHER READING:

Books

Dictionary of Scientific Biography, Volume 18, Scribners, 1976, pp. 880–887.
McGraw-Hill Modern Men of Science, Volume 2, McGraw-Hill, 1984, p. 527.

Periodicals

Graetzer, Hans G., *American Journal of Physics,* Discovery of Nuclear Fission, January, 1964, pp. 9–15.
Sparberg, Esther B., *American Journal of Physics,* A Study of the Discovery of Fission, January, 1964, pp. 2–8.

Sketch by David E. Newton

William Levi Straus, Jr.
1900–1981
American anatomist and physical anthropologist

William Levi Straus, Jr. was a major figure in the science of physical anthropology through most of the middle decades of the twentieth century. He began his academic career as an instructor of anatomy and became increasingly interested in the comparative anatomy of the primates. At first he concentrated entirely on living members of that order, but he eventually expanded his research to include fossil primates. For many years Straus was an outspoken advocate of the theory that humans are derived not from humanoid apes, but from some earlier ancestor common to both humans and apes.

Straus was born on October 29, 1900, in Baltimore, Maryland. His parents were William Levi Straus and the former Pauline Gutman. Straus attended public schools in Baltimore and entered Harvard University in 1917. He remained at Harvard for only one year, however, before returning to Baltimore and enrolling at Johns Hopkins University. He earned his bachelor of arts degree in 1920 and his Ph.D. in 1926, both from Johns Hopkins in the field of zoology.

Begins a Long Association with Johns Hopkins

A National Research Council fellowship enabled Straus to spend a postdoctoral year at Western Reserve University (now Case Western Reserve) in Cleveland. There he studied comparative anatomy of the pelvis with T. Wingate Todd before returning to Johns Hopkins to become an instructor of anatomy at the university's medical school. After being promoted to associate professor, Straus left the medical school in 1952 to become professor of physical anthropology in the university. Five years later he returned to the medical school and was given a joint appointment as professor of anatomy and physical anthropology. Upon his retirement in 1966, Straus was made professor emeritus.

Straus was "not much of a traveler," according to his biographer T. D. Stewart in the *American Journal of Physical Anthropology.* He spent a year working with H. H. Woollard and D. H. Barron in London in 1937–38 on a Guggenheim fellowship and a brief period in 1950 as visiting professor of anatomy at Wayne University in Detroit, Michigan. But otherwise he stayed close to the Johns Hopkins campus in Baltimore.

Proposes Theory of Human Origins

Straus is noted for his extensive research on the comparative anatomy of the primates. His studies covered nearly every aspect of the primate body, including the skeleton, muscular system, internal organs, skin, fingers and toes, teeth, and skull. By 1949 Straus had come to the conclusion that humans are less complex and less advanced than are many of their primate cousins.

This notion conflicted with the accepted theory of the day that stated that humans had evolved from and were more advanced than members of the ape family. Straus argued, conversely, that humans, apes, and other primates had all evolved from some earlier common ancestor. As the science of paleoanthropology (the study of the fossilized remains of hominids) developed, increasing evidence for Straus's theory accumulated. By the mid–1950s, he had become convinced that the fossil evidence confirmed his view that Homo sapiens had never passed through a brachiating ("swinging through the trees") phase as did their cousins, the apes.

In addition to his own research career, Straus was active in a variety of professional organizations. He was a founding member of the American Association of Physical Anthropologists, of which he was president from 1953 to 1955. He also served on the editorial board of five journals, the *American Journal of Anatomy* (1946–58), *Human Biology* (1953–81), *Science* and *Scientific Monthly* (1953–64), and *Folia Primatologia* (1961–81).

Straus was married twice, the first time on September 19, 1926, to Henrietta S. Hecht. The couple had one daughter, Pauline. After his first wife's death in 1954, Straus married Bertha L. Nusbaum, on June 15, 1955. Straus was awarded the Viking Fund Medal and Award in physical anthropology of the Wenner-Gren Foundation in

1952. He was elected to the National Academy of Sciences in 1962. Straus died at his home in Baltimore on January 28, 1981.

SELECTED WRITINGS BY STRAUS, JR.:

Books

Anatomy of the Rhesus Monkey, Williams and Wilkins, 1933.

Anthropology Today: An Encyclopedic Inventory, University of Chicago Press, 1952, pp. 77–92.

Forerunners of Darwin, 1754–1859, Johns Hopkins Press, 1959.

Classification and Human Evolution, The Classification of *Oreopithecus,* S. L. Washburn, editor, Viking Fund Publications in Anthropology, 1963, pp. 146–177.

Periodicals

Quarterly Review of Biology, The Riddle of Man's Ancestry, Volume 24, 1949, pp. 200–223.

FURTHER READING:

Periodicals

Stewart, T. D., *American Journal of Physical Anthropology,* William Levi Straus, Jr., 1900–1981, December 1982, pp. 359–360.

Sketch by David E. Newton

John William Strutt
1842–1919
English physicist

In 1873 John William Strutt's father, the second Baron Rayleigh, died and Strutt succeeded to that title. He is, therefore, almost universally referred to in the scientific literature as Lord Rayleigh. While the majority of his work dealt with sound and optics, Rayleigh may be most familiar to the layperson as the discover of the rare gas argon. For this accomplishment he was awarded the 1904 Nobel Prize in physics. Rayleigh served for a period of five years as director of the Cavendish Laboratory at Cambridge University. With that exception, he spent nearly all of his adult life at his home in Terling Place where he constructed a well-equipped scientific laboratory. There he carried out experiments on a remarkable variety of subjects that led to the publication of some 450 papers.

John William Strutt was born at Langford Grove, near Maldon, in Essex, on November 12, 1842. He was the eldest son of John James Strutt, second Baron Rayleigh, and the former Clara Elizabeth Vicars. Strutt's health as a child was not very good, and he was unable to remain at school for very long. He attended Eton and Harrow for about one term each and spent three years at a private school in Wimbledon. Finally, in 1857, his education was entrusted to a private tutor, the Reverend George Townsend Warner, with whom he stayed for four years.

In 1861 Strutt entered Trinity College, Cambridge, where he studied mathematics under the famous teacher E. J. Routh. During his four years at Trinity, Strutt went from being a student of only adequate skills to one who captured major prizes at graduation. One examiner is reported to have said that Strutt's answers were better than those found in books.

Following graduation, Strutt was elected a fellow of Trinity College, a position he held until 1871. In 1868 he took off on the extended "Grand Tour" vacation traditional among upper class Englishmen, except that he chose to visit the post-Civil War United States rather than the continent of Europe. In 1871, at the conclusion of his tenure at Trinity, Strutt was married to Evelyn Balfour, sister of Arthur James Balfour, later to be prime minister of Great Britain in 1902. The Strutts had three sons, Robert John, Arthur Charles, and Julian.

Within a few months of his marriage, Strutt became seriously ill with a bout of rheumatic fever. As his health returned, he decided to make a recuperative visit to Egypt and Greece with his young bride. It was on a trip down the Nile during this vacation that he began the scientific work that was to occupy his attention for most of the rest of his life, a massive work on *The Theory of Sound.*

Succeeds His Father as Lord Rayleigh

Shortly after the Strutts returned to England in the spring of 1873, his father died and Strutt succeeded to the hereditary title of Baron Rayleigh. He also took up residence in the family mansion at Terling Place, Witham, where he was to live for most of the rest of his life. He soon constructed a modest, but well-equipped, laboratory in which he was to carry out experiments for the next forty years. At first he divided his time between the laboratory and the many chores associated with the maintenance of the Rayleigh estate. Gradually he spent less time on the latter, and after 1876 he left the management of his properties to his younger brother Edward.

Rayleigh always seemed to be a man of unlimited interests. The two fields to which he devoted the greatest amount of time, however, were sound and optics. In 1871, for example, he derived a formula expressing the relationship between the wavelength of light and the scattering of that light produced by small particles, a relationship now known as Rayleigh scattering. One of his first projects in his new Terling laboratory was a study of diffraction gratings and their use in spectroscopes (instruments with which scientists may study the electromagnetic spectrum). Rayleigh appeared to be totally satisfied with his life and work at Terling Place. Then, in 1879, James Clerk Maxwell, the first Cavendish Professor of Experimental Physics at Cambridge, died. The post was offered first to Sir William Thomson, who declined, and then to Lord Rayleigh. With considerable reluctance, he accepted the appointment with the understanding that he would remain for only a limited period of time. During his tenure at Cambridge, Rayleigh made a number of changes that placed the young Cavendish Laboratory on a firm footing and prepared it for the period of unmatched excellence that was to follow in succeeding decades. The most important experimental work carried out under his auspices was a reevaluation of three electrical standards, the volt, ampere, and ohm. This work was so carefully done that its results remained valid until relatively recently.

In 1884 Rayleigh resigned his post at Cambridge and returned to his work at Terling Place. Over the next decade he took on an even more diverse set of topics, including studies of electromagnetism, mechanics, capillarity, and thermodynamics. One of his major accomplishments during this period was the development of a law describing radiation from a black body, a law later known as the Rayleigh-Jeans law.

Research Leads to the Discovery of Argon

At the end of the 1880s, Rayleigh began work on the problem for which he is perhaps best known, his discovery of the inert gas argon. That work originated as a by-product of Rayleigh's interest in Prout's hypothesis. In 1815 the English chemist William Prout had argued that all elements are made of some combination of hydrogen atoms. An obvious test of this hypothesis is to find out if the atomic weights of the elements are exact multiples of the atomic weight of hydrogen.

By 1890 most scientists were convinced that Prout's hypothesis was not valid. Still, Rayleigh was interested in examining the problem one more time. In so doing, he made an unexpected discovery, namely that the atomic weight of nitrogen varied significantly depending on the source from which it was obtained. The clue that Rayleigh needed to solve this puzzle was a report that had been written by the English chemist Henry Cavendish in 1795. Cavendish had found that, whenever he removed oxygen and nitrogen from a sample of air, there always remained a small bubble of some unknown gas.

To Rayleigh, Cavendish's results suggested a reason for his own discovery that the atomic weight of nitrogen depends on the source from which it comes. Nitrogen taken from air, he said, may include a small amount of the unknown gas that Cavendish had described, while nitrogen obtained from ammonia would not include that gas. Still, Rayleigh was not entirely sure how to resolve this issue. As

a result, he wrote a short note to *Nature* in 1892 asking for ideas about how to solve the nitrogen puzzle.

The answer to that note came from **William Ramsay**, who was working on the same problem at about the same time. Eventually, the two scientists, working independently, obtained an answer to the problem of the mysterious gas. They discovered that Cavendish's "tiny bubble" was actually a previously unknown element, an inert gas to which they gave the name argon, from the Greek *argos,* for "inert." On January 31, 1895, Rayleigh and Ramsay published a joint paper in the *Philosophical Transactions of the Royal Society* announcing their discovery of argon. A decade later, in 1904, Rayleigh was given the Nobel Prize in physics and Ramsay the Nobel Prize in chemistry for this discovery.

Even after returning to Terling Place in 1884, Rayleigh remained active in a number of professional positions. He was appointed professor of natural philosophy at the Royal Institute in 1887 and gave more than a hundred popular lectures there over the next fifteen years. In 1885 he became secretary of the Royal Society, a post he held until his election as president of the organization in 1905. When he left that post in 1908, he became chancellor of Cambridge University, a position he held until his death at Terling Place on June 30, 1919.

In addition to the 1904 Nobel Prize, Rayleigh received the Royal Medal of the Royal Society in 1882, Italy's Bressa Prize in 1891, the Smithsonian Institution's Hodgkins Prize in 1895, Italy's Matteuci Medal in 1895, the Faraday Medal of the Chemical Society in 1895, the Copley Medal of the Royal Society in 1899, the Rumford Medal of the Royal Society in 1914, and the Elliott Cresson Medal of the Franklin Institute in 1914.

SELECTED WRITINGS BY STRUTT:

Books

The Theory of Sound, 2 volumes, Macmillan, 1877–78.
Scientific Papers, 6 volumes, Cambridge University Press, 1899–1920.

Periodicals

Philosophical Magazine, On the Light from the Sky, Its Polarization and Colour, Volume 41, 1871, pp. 107–120, 274–279.
Philosophical Magazine, On the Manufacture and Theory of Diffraction Gratings, Volume 47, 1874, pp. 81–93, 193–205.
Nature, Density of Nitrogen, Volume 46, 1892, pp. 512–513.
Proceedings of the Royal Institution, Argon, Volume 14, 1895, pp. 524–538.

FURTHER READING:

Books

Davis, H. W. C., and J. R. H. Weaver, *Dictionary of National Biography: 1912–1921*, Oxford University Press, 1923, pp. 514–517.

Davis, H. W. C., and J. R. H. Weaver, *Dictionary of Scientific Biography*, Volume 13, Scribner, 1975, pp. 100–107.

Lindsay, Robert Bruce, *Lord Rayleigh: The Man and His Work*, Pergamon, 1966.

Strutt, Robert John, *Life of William Strutt, Third Baron Rayleigh, O.M., F.R.S.*, second edition, University of Wisconsin Press, 1968.

Wasson, Tyler, editor, *Nobel Prize Winners*, H. W. Wilson, 1987, pp. 1021–1023.

Weber, Robert L., *Pioneers of Science: Nobel Prize Winners in Physics*, American Institute of Physics, 1980, pp. 23–25.

Sketch by David E. Newton

Robert Strutt
1875–1947
English physicist

Best known for his work on radioactivity and atmospheric chemistry, Robert John Strutt was born at Terling Place, Witham, Essex, England, on August 28, 1875. His father was the famous physicist and Nobel Prize winner in physics, **John Wiliiam Strutt**, Third Baron Rayleigh. Robert John's mother, Evelyn Georgiana Mary Balfour, was sister of the first and second earls of Balfour. Strutt attended Eton from 1889 to 1894 and then enrolled at Trinity College. He graduated with first class honors in the natural sciences in 1898, sharing with Henry Dale (later Sir Henry) the Coutts Trotter Award. Strutt then became affiliated with the Cavendish laboratories at Cambridge, working under the direction of **J. J. Thomson**. His first scientific paper was published in 1899 during his first year at the Cavendish.

Follows in Father's Footsteps and Evolves into Prolific Scientist

In 1900, Strutt was appointed fellow at Trinity College, a position he held until 1906. Two years later, he was appointed professor of physics at the Imperial College of Science and Technology in London, where he remained until his father's death in 1919. He then succeeded his father as Fourth Baron Rayleigh and became emeritus professor at the Imperial College in 1920.

A. C. Edgerton, Strutt's biographer in the *Dictionary of National Biography*, described him as one who "worked independently out of pure curiosity, inquiring zealously into the ways of nature." Most of Strutt's research was done in a private laboratory at his home in Terling Place. He worked primarily alone, working with only one assistant for nearly forty years. Strutt's more than three hundred scientific papers testify to his prolific nature. During his lifetime, he pursued a number of fields of study, including research into radioactivity, the nature of "active" nitrogen, and the characteristics of the atmosphere. Some of his earliest works dealt with the nature of alpha radiation—a natural decaying process where the atomic nucleus disintegrates into a lighter nucleus and an alpha particle. He contributed to **Ernest Rutherford's** later discovery that alpha particles are the same as helium nuclei in that both are made of two neutrons and two protons. Strutt also found that the concentration of helium in rocks could be used to estimate the age of those rocks. In 1904, he published one of the first books on radioactivity, *The Becquerel Rays and the Properties of Radium*. He also published two important biographies, one on his father and the other on his mentor, Thomson.

Documents Existence of Ozone

Strutt's most important work involved his studies of the atmosphere. In 1916, Strutt and a colleague, Alfred Fowler, were able to confirm the existence of ozone in the atmosphere and to estimate the upper limit of the stratosphere's ozone layer. Strutt was also very interested in nightglow and airglow—patterns of light surrounding planets which appear when solar radiation triggers atmospheric chemical reactions. In honor of Strutt's work in this field, the unit for measuring the brightness of the sky was named "raleigh" after his aristocratic title.

After taking on his hereditary title in 1919, Strutt became more active in the administrative aspects of science. He was elected foreign secretary of the Royal Society in 1929, a post he held until 1934. Strutt also served as president of the Royal Institution from 1945 and as chair of the governing board of the Imperial College from 1936, both until his death in 1947. Other posts he held include chair of the executive committee of the National Physical Laboratory from 1932 to 1939, president of the Physical Society of London from 1934 to 1936, and president of the British Association for the Advancement of Science in 1938.

Strutt was also active in a number of nonscientific roles. He was a justice of the peace in Essex for many years, served as trustee for the Beit Memorial Fellowships from 1928 to 1946, was a fellow of Eton College from 1935 to 1945, and was chosen as president of the Central Council of Milk Recording Societies in 1939. In recognition of his scientific accomplishments, Strutt was awarded honorary doctorates by the universities of Dublin in 1913, Durham in 1929, and Edinburgh in 1933.

Strutt was married twice, first to Lady Mary Hilda Clements in 1905 and, following her death in 1919, to Kathleen Alice Culbert in 1920. His first marriage brought three sons and two daughters, while the second brought one son. Strutt died in his home in Terling on December 13, 1947.

SELECTED WRITINGS BY STRUTT:

Books

The Life of John William Strutt, Third Baron Rayleigh, Arnold, 1924.

FURTHER READING:

Books

Gillispie, Charles Coulson, editor, *Dictionary of Scientific Biography,* Volume 13, Scribner's, 1975, pp. 107–108.
Gillispie, Charles Coulson, editor, *Obituary Notices of Fellows of the Royal Society,* Volume 18, Royal Society (London), 1949, pp. 503–538.

Sketch by David E. Newton

JoAnne Stubbe
1946–
American chemist

JoAnne Stubbe's research has helped scientists understand the ways in which enzymes catalyze, or cause, chemical reactions. Her major research efforts have focused on the mechanism of nucleotide reductases, the enzymes involved in the biosynthesis of deoxyribonucleic acid (DNA), the molecule of heredity. Her work has led to the design and synthesis of nucleotide analogs—structural derivatives of nucleotides—that have potential antitumor, antivirus, and antiparasite activity. In 1986 the American Chemical Society honored Stubbe with the Pfizer Award which is given annually to scientists under forty for outstanding achievement in enzyme chemistry.

Stubbe was born June 11, 1946. She earned a B.S. in chemistry with high honors from the University of Pennsylvania in 1968 and her Ph.D. in chemistry at University of California at Berkeley under the direction of George Kenyon in 1971. Stubbe's first two publications in scientific journals outlined the mechanism of reactions involving the enzymes enolase, which metabolizes carbohydrates, and pyruvate kinase.

Following completion of her doctorate, Stubbe spent a year at the University of California at Los Angeles doing postdoctoral research in the Department of Chemistry with Julius Rebek. In 1972 she accepted a post as assistant professor of chemistry at Williams College in Massachusetts where she stayed until 1977. In late 1975 she accepted a second postdoctoral fellowship, took a leave of absence from her teaching duties, and spent a year and a half at Brandeis University on a grant from the National Institutes of Health (NIH).

From 1977 to 1980 Stubbe was assistant professor in the Department of Pharmacology at the Yale University School of Medicine. She then began a seven-year association with the University of Wisconsin at Madison, beginning as assistant professor and rising to full professor of biochemistry in 1985. In 1987 the Massachusetts Institute of Technology (MIT) beckoned, and Stubbe accepted a position as professor in the Department of Chemistry. In 1992 she was named John C. Sheehan Professor of Chemistry and Biology.

Stubbe's research focused on the mechanism of enzymes called ribonucleotide reductases, which catalyze the rate-determining step in DNA biosynthesis. This mechanism involves radical (that is, with at least one unpaired electron) intermediates and requires protein-based radicals for catalysis. Ribonucleotide reductases are major targets for the design of antitumor and antiviral agents, because inhibiting these enzymes interferes with the biosynthesis of DNA and cell growth. In collaboration with colleague John Kozarich, Stubbe has also explained the mechanism by which the antitumor antibiotic bleomycin degrades DNA. Bleomycin is used to kill cancer cells, a function that is thought to be related to its ability to bind to and degrade DNA. Other research interests of Stubbe's include the design of so-called suicide inhibitors and mechanisms of DNA repair enzymes.

Stubbe has published over eighty scientific papers and has been recognized frequently for her research achievements. She was the recipient of a NIH career development award, the Pfizer Award in enzyme chemistry in 1986, and the ICI-Stuart Pharmaceutical Award for excellence in chemistry in 1989. She received a teaching award from MIT in 1990 and the Arthur C. Cope Scholar Award in 1993. Stubbe was elected to the American Academy of Arts and Sciences in 1991 and to the National Academy of Sciences in 1992. Stubbe is a member of the American Chemical Society, the American Society for Biological Chemists, and the Protein Society. She has been active on several committees, including review boards for the NIH grants committee and the editorial boards for various scientific journals.

SELECTED WRITINGS BY STUBBE:

Periodicals

Advances in Enzymology, Ribonucleotide Reductases, Volume 63, 1989, p. 349.

Science, Mechanism of Assembly of the Tyrosyl Radical-Dinuclear Iron Cluster Cofactor of Ribonucleotide Reductase, Volume 253, 1991, p. 292.

Biochemistry, N⁵-Carboxyaminoimidazole Ribonucleotide: Evidence for a New Intermediate and Two New Enzymatic Activities in the *de novo* Purine Biosynthetic Pathway of *Escherichia Coli,* Volume 33, 1994, pp. 2269–2278.

FURTHER READING:

Periodicals

Chemical and Engineering News, ACS Division of Biological Chemistry Awards, April 28, 1986, pp. 75–76.

Sketch by Kimberlyn McGrail

A. H. Sturtevant
1891–1970
American geneticist

A H. Sturtevant, an influential geneticist and winner of the National Medal of Science in 1968, is best known for his demonstrations of the principles of gene mapping. This discovery had a profound effect on the field of genetics and led to projects to map both animal and human chromosomes. He is the unacknowledged father of the Human Genome Project, which is attempting to map all of man's 100,000 chromosomes by the year 2000. Sturtevant's later work in the field of genetics led to discovery of the first reparable gene defect as well as the position effect, which showed that the effect of a gene is dependent on its position relative to other genes. He was a member of Columbia University's "Drosophila Group," whose studies of the genetics of fruit flies advanced new theories of genetics and evolution.

Alfred Henry Sturtevant, the youngest of six children, was born in Jacksonville, Illinois, on November 21, 1891, to Alfred and Harriet (Morse) Sturtevant. Five of his early ancestors had come to America aboard the Mayflower. Julian M. Sturtevant, his grandfather, a Yale Divinity School graduate, was the founder and former president of Illinois College. Sturtevant's father taught at Illinois College briefly but later chose farming as a profession. When Alfred Sturtevant was seven, his family moved to a farm in southern Alabama. He attended high school in Mobile, which was 14 miles from his home and accessible only by train.

Sturtevant enrolled in Columbia University in New York City in 1908, boarding with his older brother, Edgar, who taught linguistics at Columbia's Barnard College. Edgar and his wife played a significant role in young Sturtevant's life. They sent him Columbia's entrance examination, pulled strings to get him a scholarship, and welcomed him into their home in Edgewater, New Jersey, for four years. Edgar was also responsible for steering his brother toward a career in the sciences. The young Sturtevant had discovered genetic theory at an early age and often drew pedigrees of his family and of his father's horses. Edgar encouraged him to write a paper on the subject of color heredity in horses and to submit the draft to Columbia University's **Thomas Hunt Morgan**, the future Nobel Laureate geneticist. The paper used the recently rediscovered theories of Gregor Mendel, the 19th-century Austrian monk and founder of genetics, to explain certain coat-color inheritance patterns in horses. Sturtevant somehow mastered this subject in spite of his color-blindness.

Student Work Leads to Major Genetic Breakthrough

As a result of his paper on horses, which was published in 1910, Sturtevant was given a desk in Morgan's famous "fly room," a small laboratory dedicated to genetic research using *Drosophila* Drosophila (fruit flies) as subjects. Fruit flies are ideal subjects for genetic research. They mature in ten days, are less than one-eighth inch long, can live by the hundreds in small vials, require nothing more substantial than yeast for food, and have only four pairs of chromosomes.

Morgan's early work focused on the phenomenon of "crossing-over" in the fruit fly. By 1910, he had already described the sex-limited inheritance of white eye. From this observation, he postulated the idea that genes were linked because they were carried by the same chromosome and that genes in close proximity to one another would be linked more frequently than those that were farther apart. Sometimes, dominant linked traits, such as eye color and wing size, became "unlinked" in offspring. Sturtevant studied the process of crossing-over of sex-linked traits, which are carried on the X chromosome. Female fruit flies have two X chromosomes. In addition to one X chromosome, males have a Y chromosome, which carries very few genes. Sturtevant correctly hypothesized that the exchange between X chromosomes probably occurred early on in the process of egg formation, when the paired chromosomes lie parallel to each other.

Morgan believed that the relative distance between genes could be measured if the crossing-over frequencies could be determined. From this lead, Sturtevant developed a practical method for determining this frequency rate. He began by studying six sex-linked traits and measured the occurrence of this related trait. The more frequently the traits occurred, Sturtevant reasoned, the closer the genes must be. He then calculated the percentages of crossing-over between the various traits. From these percentages, he determined the relative distance between the genes on the chromosome, the first instance of gene mapping. This major discovery, which Sturtevant published in 1913 at the age of 22, eventually enabled scientists to map human and animal genes. It is often considered to be the starting point of modern genetics.

In 1914, Sturtevant received his Ph.D. from Columbia and stayed on in Morgan's lab as an investigator for the Carnegie Institution of Washington, D.C. Along with C. B. Bridges, **Hermann Joseph Muller**, and Morgan, he formed part of an influential research team that made significant contributions to the fields of genetics and entomology. He later described the lab as highly democratic and occasionally argumentative, with ideas being heatedly debated. The 16 x 24-foot lab had no desks, no separate offices, one general telephone, and very few graduate assistants. Sturtevant thrived in this environment. He worked seven days a week, reserving his mornings for *Drosophila* research and his afternoons for reading the scientific literature and consulting with colleagues. He possessed a near photographic memory and wide-ranging interests. His only shortcoming as a researcher was his incessant pipe-smoking, which often left flakes of tobacco ash mixed in with the samples of fruit flies. In spite of this minor flaw, the fly-room group raised research standards and elevated research writing to an art form. They also perfected the practice of chromosome mapping, using Sturtevant's methods to develop a chromosome map of *Drosophila,* detailing the relative positions of fifty genes.

Sturtevant published a paper in 1914 that documented cases of double crossing-over, in which chromosomes that had already crossed-over broke with one another and recrossed again. His next major paper, published in 1915, concerned the sexual behavior of fruit flies and concentrated on six specific mutant genes that altered eye or body color, two factors that played important roles in sexual selection. He then showed that specific genes were responsible for selective intersexuality. In later years, he discovered a gene that caused an almost complete sex change in fruit flies, miraculously transforming females into near males. In subsequent years, researchers identified other sex genes in many animals, as well as in humans. These discoveries led to the development of the uniquely twentieth-century view of sex as a gene-controlled trait which is subject to variability.

During the 1920s, Sturtevant and Morgan examined the unstable bar-eye trait in *Drosophila* Drosophila. Most geneticists at that time believed that bar eye did not follow the rules of Mendelian heredity. In 1925, Sturtevant showed that bar eye involved a recombination of genes rather than a mutation and that the position of the gene on the chromosome had an effect on its action. This discovery, known as the position effect, contributed greatly to the understanding of the action of the gene.

In 1928, Morgan received an offer from the California Institute of Technology to develop a new Division of Biological Sciences. Sturtevant followed his mentor to California, where he became Caltech's first professor of

genetics. The new genetics group set up shop in Caltech's Kerckhoff Laboratory. Sturtevant continued working with fruit flies and conducted genetic investigations of other animals and plants, including snails, rabbits, moths, rats, and the evening primrose, *Oenothera.*

In 1929, Sturtevant discovered a "sex ratio" gene that caused male flies to produce X sperm almost exclusively, instead of X and Y sperm. As a result, these flies' offspring were almost always females. In the early 1930s, giant chromosomes were discovered in the salivary glands of fruit flies. Under magnification, these chromosomes revealed cross patterns which were correlated to specific genes. The so-called "physical" map derived from these giant chromosomes did not exactly match Sturtevant's "relative" location maps. In the physical map, some of the genes tended to cluster toward one end of the chromosome and the distances between genes was not uniform. But the linear order of the genes on the chromosome matched Sturtevant's relative maps gene for gene. This discovery confirmed that Sturtevant had been correct in his assumptions about chromosomal linearity.

In 1932, Sturtevant took a sabbatical leave and spent the year in England and Germany as a visiting professor of the Carnegie Endowment for International Peace. When he returned to America, he collaborated with his Caltech colleague **Theodosius Dobzhansky**, a Russian-born geneticist, on a study of inversions in the third chromosome of *Drosophila pseudoobscura* Drosophila pseudoobscura. In the 1940s, Sturtevant studied all of the known gene mutations in *Drosophila* and their various effects on the development of the species. From 1947 to 1962, he served as the Thomas Hunt Morgan Professor of Biology at Caltech. His most significant scientific contribution during that time occurred in 1951, when he unveiled his chromosome map of the indescribably small fourth chromosome of the fruit fly, a genetic problem that had puzzled scientists for decades.

During the 1950s and 1960s, Sturtevant turned his attention to the iris and authored numerous papers on the subject of evolution. He became concerned with the potential dangers of genetics research and wrote several papers on the social significance of human genetics. In a 1954 speech to the Pacific Division of the American Association for the Advancement of Science, he described the possible genetic consequences of nuclear war and argued that the public should be made aware of these possible cataclysmic hazards before any further bomb testing was performed. One of his last published journal articles, written in 1956, described a mutation in fruit flies that, by itself, was harmless but which proved lethal in combination with another specific mutant gene.

Sturtevant was named professor emeritus at Caltech in 1962. He spent the better part of the early 1960s writing his major work, *A History of Genetics,* which was published in 1965. In 1968, he received the prestigious National Medal of Science for his achievements in genetics. He died on April 5, 1970, at the age of 78. Sturtevant married Phoebe

Curtis Reed in 1923, and the couple honeymooned in Europe, touring England, Norway, Sweden, and Holland. He arranged excursions to every laboratory and museum he could find. The Sturtevants had three children.

SELECTED WRITINGS BY STURTEVANT:

Books

The Mechanism of Mendelian Heredity, Holt, 1915.
An Analysis of the Effects of Selection, Carnegie Institution of Washington, 1918.
A History of Genetics, Harper & Row, 1965.

Periodicals

Journal of Experimental Zoology, The Linear Arrangement of Six Sex-Linked Factors in *Drosophila,* Volume 14, 1913, pp. 43–59.
American Naturalist, The Himalayan Rabbit Case, with Some Considerations on Multiple Allelomorphs, Volume 47, 1913, pp. 234–238.
Drosophila, "Genetic Studies onsimulanus, Genetics", Volume 5, 1920, pp. 488–500.
Biological Bulletin, Autosomal Lethals in Wild Populations of *Drosophila pseudoobscura,* Volume 73, 1937, pp. 742–751.

FURTHER READING:

Books

Carlson, E. A., *The Gene: A Critical History,* Sanders, 1971.

Periodicals

Beadle, G. W., *Yearbook, American Philosophical Society,* A. H. Sturtevant, 1970, pp. 166–171.
Emerson, S., *Annual Review of Genetics,* Alfred Henry Sturtevant, Volume 5, 1970, pp. 1–4.

Sketch by Tom Crawford

James B. Sumner
1887–1955
American biochemist

Biochemist James B. Sumner's natural perseverance was strengthened by his efforts to overcome a handicap suffered in an accident as a youth. He set out to isolate an enzyme in 1917—a task believed to be impossible

at the time. By 1926, he had crystallized an enzyme and proven it was a protein, but spent many years defending the veracity of discovery. Sumner's achievement was finally recognized in 1946, when he shared the Nobel Prize in chemistry for proving that enzymes can be crystallized.

James Batcheller Sumner was born just south of Boston in Canton, Massachusetts, on November 19, 1887, the son of Charles and Elizabeth Kelly Sumner. They were an old New England family, whose ancestors had arrived in 1636 from Bicester, England, and Sumner's relatives included industrialists as well as artists. His own family was wealthy, and his father owned a large country estate. As a boy Sumner was interested in firearms and enjoyed hunting, a hobby that led to tragedy when he lost his left forearm and elbow to an accidental shooting. The handicap was doubly traumatic since Sumner had been left-handed, but he trained himself to use his right arm instead. He continued to participate in sports, including tennis, canoeing, and clay pigeon shooting, and he would learn to perform intricate laboratory procedures with only one arm.

Sumner received his early education at the Eliot Grammar School, and he graduated from the Roxbury Latin School in 1906. He enrolled at Harvard to study electrical engineering, but discovered he was more interested in chemistry and graduated with a degree in that discipline in 1910. He then joined the Sumner Knitted Padding Company, which was managed by an uncle, but stayed only a few months before he was offered the chance to teach chemistry for one term at a college in New Brunswick. This appointment was followed by a position at the Worcester Polytechnic Institute in Worcester, Massachusetts. He remained there for just one term as well before enrolling in the doctoral program at Harvard in 1912.

Sumner conducted his doctoral work under the supervision of Otto Folin, who had originally told him that a one-armed man could not possibly succeed in chemistry. Sumner completed his master's degree in 1913 and his doctorate in 1914. Part of his doctoral thesis was published in 1914 as "The Importance of the Liver in Urea Formation from Amino Acids" in the *Journal of Biological Chemistry.* While on a trip to Europe after completing his graduate studies, Sumner was offered an appointment as assistant professor of biochemistry at the Ithaca Division of the Cornell University Medical College. Initially detained by the beginning of World War I, he finally made it to Ithaca and discovered that he would also be teaching in the College of Arts and Sciences.

Sumner would spend his entire academic career at Cornell. He began as an assistant professor, a position he held for fifteen years, and then spent nine years as professor in the Department of Physiology and Biochemistry at the Medical College. In 1938, Sumner was appointed professor of biochemistry in the Department of Zoology of the College of Arts and Sciences. In 1947 he became the founding director of the Laboratory of Enzyme Chemistry within the Department of Biochemistry.

Embarks on Effort to Isolate Enzyme

Sumner's teaching load at Cornell was always very heavy. He enjoyed teaching and was regarded as an excellent professor, but his schedule did not leave much time for research. His research was also limited by the minimal equipment and laboratory help available at Cornell. In his Nobel lecture Sumner recounted why had chosen to work on enzymes. "At that time I had little time for research, not much apparatus, research money or assistance," he recalled. "I desired to accomplish something of real importance. In other words, I decided to take a 'long shot.' A number of persons advised me that my attempt to isolate an enzyme was foolish, but this advice made me feel all the more certain that if successful the quest would be worthwhile."

He chose to isolate urease, an enzyme that catalyzed the breakdown of urea into ammonia and carbon dioxide. He found that relatively large amounts of urease were present in the jack bean (*Canavalia ensiformis*). Sumner disagreed with the belief, then commonly held, that enzymes were low-molecular-weight substances which were easily adsorbed on proteins but were not in fact proteins themselves. He concentrated on fractionating the proteins of the jack bean, and this effort took him nine years. In 1926, he published a paper in the *Journal of Biological Chemistry* announcing that he had isolated a new crystalline globulin, which he believed to be urease, from the jack bean. Urease was the first enzyme prepared in crystalline form and the first that was proven to be a protein.

His results, and his interpretation of them, were not immediately accepted. On the contrary, he spent years engaged in a controversy with those who believed that enzymes contained no protein. One of his strongest opponents was **Richard Willstätter**, a German chemist who had won the Nobel Prize in 1915 for his work on chlorophyll. Willstätter had tried to produce pure enzymes and failed, and he argued that what Sumner had isolated was merely the carrier of the enzyme and not the enzyme itself. Although Sumner continued to publish additional evidence over the next few years, it was not until 1930 that he received support for his discovery, when **John Howard Northrop** of the Rockefeller Institute announced he had crystallized pepsin. Sumner was jointly awarded the 1946 Nobel Prize in chemistry; his corecipients were Northrop and **Wendell Meredith Stanley**, also at the Rockefeller Institute, honored for their preparation of enzymes and virus proteins in pure form.

After the crystallization of urease and the debates with Willstätter and others, Sumner continued his research on enzymes, among them peroxidases and lipoxidase, doing most of his own laboratory work. In 1937, he and his student Alexander L. Dounce crystallized the enzyme catalase and helped prove it was a protein. Sumner was the first to crystallize haemagglutinin concanavalin A, and he noted that this protein required the presence of a divalent metal to act. He also continued his original research work on new and improved laboratory methods. He was a prolific author, writing or contributing to about 125 research papers and a number of books.

In 1929 Sumner, who spoke Swedish, French, and German, went to the University of Stockholm to work on urease with **Hans Euler-Chelpin** and **Theodor Svedberg**. He returned to Sweden in 1937 to work at the University of Uppsala on a Guggenheim fellowship, and while there he was awarded the Scheele Medal from the Swedish Chemical Society for his work on enzymes. Other professional honors include his election to both the Polish Institute of Arts and Sciences and the American Academy of Arts and Sciences. Sumner was also a member of many associations including the National Academy of Sciences, the American Association for the Advancement of Sciences, the Society for Experimental Biology and Medicine, and the American Society of Biological Chemists.

Sumner was married three times and divorced twice. He married his first wife, Bertha Louise Ricketts on July 20, 1915, the year after he completed his Ph.D. They had five children, and were divorced in 1930. Sumner married Agnes Paulina Lundquist of Sweden in 1931; they had no children. After his second divorce, Sumner married Mary Morrison Beyer in 1943; they had two sons, one of whom died as a child.

In 1955, while preparing for his retirement from Cornell, Sumner was diagnosed with cancer. He had intended to work at the Medical School of the University of Minas Gerais, in Belo Horizonte, Brazil, organizing an enzyme research program and laboratory. However, the day after attending a symposium held partly in his honor, he was hospitalized, and died on August 12, 1955, at the Roswell Park Memorial Institute in Buffalo, New York.

SELECTED WRITINGS BY SUMNER:

Books

Textbook of Biological Chemistry, Macmillan, 1927.
Chemistry and Methods of Enzymes, Academic Press, 1943.
Laboratory Experiments in Biological Chemistry, Academic Press, 1944.

Periodicals

Journal of Biological Chemistry, The Importance of the Liver in Urea Formation from Amino Acids, Volume 18, 1914, pp. 285–295.
Journal of Biological Chemistry, The Isolation and Crystallization of the Enzyme Urease (Preliminary Paper), Volume 69, 1926, pp. 435–441.
Journal of Biological Chemistry, Crystalline Catalase, Volume 121, 1937, pp. 417–424.

FURTHER READING:

Periodicals

Dounce, Alexander L., *Nature,* Prof. James B. Sumner, Volume 176, 1955, p. 859.

Maynard, Leonard A., *Biographical Memoirs,* James Batcheller Sumner, National Academy of Sciences, Volume 31, 1958, pp. 376–396.

Sketch by Marianne P. Fedunkiw

Verner E. Suomi
1915–1995
American meteorologist

Verner E. Suomi

Verner E. Suomi helped pioneer the use of space satellites to study weather on Earth and other planets. A meteorologist with a knack for building gadgets, Suomi invented the spin-scan camera which takes pictures of Earth from a spinning satellite. He also developed a global data system called McIDAS (Man-computer Interactive Data Access System) that gave scientists worldwide access to the satellite data. The images and information gathered in space through his developments have improved forecasting and contributed to a greater understanding of weather systems.

Verner Edward Suomi was born in the small mining town of Eveleth, Minnesota, on December 6, 1915. His father, John E. Suomi, was a carpenter for a mining company. His mother, Anna Emelia Sundquist Suomi, had seven children—five girls and two boys. At the age of 22, Suomi began teaching science and mathematics at a Minnesota high school. The following year, he earned a bachelor's degree at Winona Teachers' College. Suomi married Paula Meyer in 1941, and the couple eventually had three children: Lois, Stephen, and Eric.

As an aviation student, Suomi's interest in meteorology was sparked by student handbook charts that described how the atmosphere and the amount of water in the atmosphere differed according to altitude. But it was World War II that changed the course of Suomi's career. Prompted by a radio message from noted meteorologist **Carl-Gustaf Rossby** for meteorologists to help in the war effort, Suomi returned to school. At the University of Chicago he studied under Rossby himself, an arrangement that Suomi called "a happy accident," in *Omni* magazine in 1989.

Suomi's dissertation, "The Heat Budget of a Cornfield," was a study that gave him a background that would be useful in a more ambitious project in the future: measuring the heat budget of the entire planet. Although Suomi earned his Ph.D. in 1953, he had belonged to the faculty at the University of Wisconsin at Madison since 1948. He co-founded the Space Science and Engineering Center at the University of Wisconsin in 1966 and acted as its director from its inception until his retirement in 1988.

Suomi's activities at the University of Wisconsin extended well beyond the classroom. Before any U.S.

weather satellite had been launched into space, Suomi developed an instrument called a radiometer that measured the amount of heat going into and coming out of the earth's atmosphere. The radiometer was made of four metallic balls with the temperature sensors at the tips of long antennas. From a satellite orbiting the planet, it would measure the heat coming to the earth from the sun, as well as the heat reflected back into space by clouds, snow, and water. Suomi watched as the Vanguard Rocket carrying his invention was launched in 1959. Unfortunately, the rocket crashed. "When . . . my gadget fell into the ocean, it was almost like a death in the family," Suomi told *Omni* magazine. Undeterred, he built another radiometer, but it too exploded along with the Juno rocket that it was aboard.

When the first successful U.S. meteorological satellite was finally launched on the *Explorer VII* in 1959, another of Suomi's radiometers was on board. Suomi set up a radio station in his bedroom to collect data as the satellite orbited the earth. The information he gathered showed that the energy changes in the atmosphere varied much more than scientists previously believed. Although clouds and other materials such as snow reflect sunlight, they also absorb energy. Thus, from the satellite, the earth appeared dark, because it was reflecting much less solar energy back into space than people had come to believe.

One of Suomi's most noted contributions was the spin-scan camera that took pictures of the planet from a rapidly spinning satellite 22,000 miles above the earth. The images displayed dynamic weather patterns and brought about a revolution in forecasting. The satellite, designed to travel at the same speed as the earth, hovered over a given region. With each spin, the satellite viewed a narrow swath of the earth. As the satellite tilted gradually, the camera could take pictures of the entire earth in 2400 revolutions. Previous satellites had been able to take pictures, but the spin-scan camera, introduced in 1963, took sequential photos that showed how the weather was changing. Those first sets of images from the spin-scan camera caught many meteorologists by surprise. They had expected the atmosphere to appear turbulent and chaotic. Instead, the images showed organized weather patterns—"clouds that looked like someone was pulling taffy across the sky," Suomi told *Omni* magazine in 1989. The camera provided images that enabled meteorologists to study patterns of air motion, cloud growth, and atmospheric pollution which resulted in improved forecasting of storms.

In 1959 Suomi and three others founded the Global Atmospheric Research Program which attempted to form a central location for the atmospheric data which was collected by more than sixty nations. To make the best use of the immense amounts of data gathered by weather satellites, Suomi developed the Man-computer Interactive Data Access System (McIDAS) in 1972 to manage the data for research and weather forecasting. The system also made data readily accessible to other nations. In 1978 the Global Atmospheric Research Program sponsored an experiment with the spin-scan camera that doubled the amount of time for which meteorologists could forecast accurately.

In 1971, Suomi proposed an ambitious experiment to study the atmosphere's temperature and water vapor using infrared technology, but the experiment was not launched until nine years later. The results showed how storms developed over a region of several hundred thousand square miles, and the infrared technique became useful for warnings of storms and hurricanes. Looking beyond our own planet, Suomi also used satellite technology to study the atmospheres of Venus, Jupiter, and Saturn. With colleagues at the Space Science and Engineering Center, he designed and built an instrument that entered the atmosphere of Venus and discovered an intense vortex over each pole.

In addition to the directorship of the Space Science and Engineering Center at the University of Wisconsin, Suomi's other positions included a term as president of the American Meteorological Association in 1968 and a year as chief scientist of the United States Weather Bureau in 1964. Though honored for his inventions that revolutionized the way meteorologists forecast the weather, colleagues and students thought of Suomi foremost as an educator. His contributions went beyond developing technology to include fostering an interest in meteorology among several generations of students.

Suomi received the Carl-Gustaf Rossby Award in 1968, the highest honor bestowed on an atmospheric scientist by the American Meteorological Society. He was also presented with the National Medal of Science by President Carter in 1977. Suomi died on July 30, 1995, of congestive heart failure at a Madison, Wisconsin, hospital. He was 79.

FURTHER READING:

Periodicals

Bagne, Paul, "Verner Suomi," *Omni* (July 1989).

Broad, William J., "A 30-Year Feud Divides Experts on Meteorology," *New York Times* (24 October 1989): p. C1.

Stout, David, "Verner E. Suomi, 79, Pioneer in Weather Forecasting, Dies" (obituary), *New York Times* (1 August 1995): p. D20.

Sketch by Miyoko Chu

Earl Sutherland
1915–1974
American biochemist

E arl Sutherland was a biochemist who expounded upon the manner in which hormones regulate body functions. His early work showed how the hormone adrenaline regulates the breakdown of sugar in the liver to release a surge of energy when the body is under stress. Later, Sutherland discovered a chemical within cells called cyclic adenosine 3'5'-monophosphate, or cyclic AMP. This chemical provided a universal link between hormones and the regulation of metabolism within cells. For this work, Sutherland was awarded the Nobel Prize in physiology and medicine in 1971.

Earl Wilbur Sutherland, Jr., the fifth of six children in his family, was born on November 19, 1915, in Burlingame, Kansas, a small farming community. His father, Earl Wilbur Sutherland, a Wisconsin native, had attended Grinnell College for two years and farmed in New Mexico and Oklahoma before settling in Burlingame to run a dry-goods business, where Earl Wilbur, Jr., and his siblings worked. Sutherland's mother, Edith M. Hartshorn, came from Missouri. She had been educated at a "ladies college," and had received some nursing training. She taught Sutherland to swim at the age of five and then allowed him to go fishing by himself, a pastime that became a lifelong passion. While in high school, Sutherland also excelled in sports such as football, basketball, and tennis. In 1933 he entered Washburn College in Topeka, Kansas. Supporting his studies by working as an orderly in a hospital, Sutherland graduated with a B.S. in 1937. He married Mildred Rice the same year. Sutherland then entered Washington University Medical School in St. Louis, Missouri. There he enrolled in a pharmacology class taught by **Carl Ferdinand Cori**, who would share the 1947 Nobel Prize in medicine and physiology with his wife Gerty Cori. Impressed by Sutherland's abilities, Cori offered him a job as a student assistant. This was Sutherland's first experience with research. The research on the sugar glucose that Sutherland undertook in Cori's laboratory started him on a line of inquiry that led to his later groundbreaking studies.

Sutherland received his M.D. in 1942. He then worked for one year as an intern at Barnes Hospital while continuing to do research in Cori's laboratory. Sutherland was called into service during World War II as a battalion surgeon under General George S. Patton. Later in the war he served in Germany as a staff physician in a military hospital.

In 1945, Sutherland returned to Washington University in St. Louis. He was unsure whether to continue practicing medicine or to commit himself to a career in research. Sutherland later attributed his decision to stay in the laboratory to the example of his mentor Carl F. Cori. By 1953, Sutherland had advanced to the rank of associate professor at Washington University. During these years he came into contact with many leading figures in biochemistry, including **Arthur Kornberg**, **Edwin G. Krebs**, T. Z. Posternak, and others now recognized as among the founders of modern molecular biology. But Sutherland preferred, for the most part, to do his research independently. While at Washington University, Sutherland began a project to understand how an enzyme known as phosphorylase breaks down glycogen, a form of the sugar stored in the liver. He also studied the roles of the hormone adrenaline, also known as epinephrine; and glucagon, secreted by the pancreas, in stimulating the release of energy-producing glucose from glycogen.

Discovers A Molecule Basic to Life

Sutherland was offered the chairmanship of the Department of Pharmacology at Western Reserve (now Case Western) University in Cleveland in 1953. It was during the ten years he spent in Cleveland that Sutherland clarified an important mechanism by which hormones produce their effects. Scientists had previously thought that hormones acted on whole organs. Sutherland, however, showed that hormones stimulate individual cells in a process that takes place in two steps. First, a hormone attaches to specific receptors on the outside of the cell membrane. Sutherland called the hormone a "first messenger." The binding of the hormone to the membrane triggers release of a molecule known as cyclic AMP within the cell. Cyclic AMP then goes on to play many roles in the cell's metabolism, and Sutherland referred to the molecule as the "second messenger" in the mechanism of hormone action. In particular, Sutherland studied the effects of the hormone adrenaline, also called epinephrine, on liver cells. When adrenaline binds to liver cells, cyclic AMP is released and directs the conversion of sugar from a stored form into a form the cell can use.

Sutherland made two more important discoveries while at Western Reserve. He found that other hormones also spur the release of cyclic AMP when they bind to cells, in particular, the adrenocorticotropic hormone and the thyroid-stimulating hormone. This implied that cyclic AMP was a sort of universal intermediary in this process, and it explained why different hormones might induce similar effects. In addition, cyclic AMP was found to play an important role in the metabolism of one-celled organisms, such as the amoeba and the bacterium *Escherichia coli,* which do not have hormones. That cyclic AMP is found in both simple and complex organisms implies that it is a very basic and important biological molecule and that it arose early in evolution and has been conserved throughout millennia.

In 1963 Sutherland became professor of physiology at Vanderbilt University in Nashville, Tennessee, a move which relieved him of his teaching duties and enabled him to devote more of his time to research. The previous year he and his first wife had divorced, and in 1963 Sutherland married Dr. Claudia Sebeste Smith, who shared with him, among other interests, a love of fishing. The couple later had two girls and two boys.

At Vanderbilt Sutherland continued his work on cyclic AMP, supported by a Career Investigatorship awarded by the American Heart Association. Sutherland studied the role of cyclic AMP in the contraction of heart muscle. He and other researchers continued to discover physiological processes in different tissues and various animal species that are influenced by cyclic AMP, for example in brain cells and cancer cells. Sutherland also did research on a similar molecule known as cyclic GMP (guanosine 3',5'-cyclic monophosphate). In the meantime, his pioneering studies had opened up a new field of research. By 1971, as many as two thousand scientists were studying cyclic AMP.

For most of his career Sutherland was well-known mainly to his scientific colleagues. In the early 1970s, however, a rush of awards gained him more widespread public recognition. In 1970 he received the prestigious Albert Lasker Basic Medical Research Award. In 1971 he was awarded the Nobel Prize for "his long study of hormones, the chemical substances that regulate virtually every body function," as well as the American Heart Association Research Achievement Award. In 1973 he was bestowed with the National Medal of Science of the United States. During his career Sutherland was also elected to membership in the National Academy of Sciences, and he belonged to the American Society of Biological Chemists, the American Chemical Society, the American Society for Pharmacology and Experimental Therapeutics, and the American Association for the Advancement of Science. He received honorary degrees from Yale University and Washington University. In 1973 Sutherland moved to the University of Miami. Shortly thereafter, he suffered a massive esophageal hemorrhage, and he died on March 9, 1974, after surgery for internal bleeding, at the age of 58.

SELECTED WRITINGS BY SUTHERLAND:

Books

Cyclic AMP, Academic Press, 1971.

Periodicals

Pharmacological Reviews, The Role of Cyclic 3'5'-AMP in Responses to Catechlolamines and Other Hormones, Volume 18, 1966, pp. 145–161.

FURTHER READING:

Books

Cori, Carl F., *Biographical Memoirs of the National Academy of Sciences,* Earl Wilbur Sutherland, Volume 49, National Academy of Sciences, 1978.

Periodicals

Cori, Carl F., *Time,* October 25, 1971, p. 63.

Sketch by Betsy Hanson

Ivan Sutherland
1938–

American computer scientist

Ivan Sutherland is a pioneer in the field of computer graphics. His 1960 "Sketchpad" system contributed to the development of computer graphics, computer simulation, and video games as we know them today.

Ivan Edward Sutherland was born in Hastings, Nebraska, on May 16, 1938. His first experience with computing was in high school, where as a young student he build various relay-driven machines. In the early 1950s, computers were exciting and exotic devices, and many bright students set their sights on that field.

Sutherland received his B.S. from Carnegie Mellon University in 1959, his M.S. from the California Institute of Technology in 1960, and his Ph.D. in electrical engineering from the Massachusetts Institute of Technology (MIT) in 1963. Throughout college Sutherland was always interested in logic and computing; he held a summer job with International Business Machines (IBM) after he got his bachelor's degree, and he switched from Cal Tech to MIT for his doctoral studies because of the latter's superior computer department. His doctoral thesis committee comprised some of the biggest names in computing at the time, including **Claude Shannon**, **Marvin Minsky**, and Steven

Coons. At MIT, Sutherland worked at the Lincoln Laboratory. There he had the use of a large, modern computer called the TX–2, which played a significant role in the research for his doctoral dissertation, entitled "Sketchpad."

"Sketchpad" was arguably Sutherland's greatest work and the basis for much of what he subsequently accomplished. The principle behind "Sketchpad" is that of a pencil moving on paper, but instead it uses a light-sensitive pen moving on the surface of a computer screen. By measuring the vertical and horizontal movements of the pen by means of a grid system, the computer could recreate the lines on the computer screen. Once on the screen, lines could be manipulated (lengthened, shortened, moved to any angle) and connected to represent solid objects, which could then be rotated to display them at any angle, exactly as if they were true three-dimensional artifacts. (Previously existing graphics systems were strictly two-dimensional.) Sutherland documented his dissertation research with a film called "Sketchpad: A Man-Machine Graphical Communication System," and the film became very well known in the computer research community of the time. The concept of "Sketchpad" was revolutionary, and its direct repercussions extend down to this day.

From MIT, Sutherland went into the army, due to a Reserve Officers Training Corps commitment left over from Carnegie Mellon. After brief assignments with the National Security Agency and a radar and infrared tracking project called Project Michigan, he was made director of the Information Processing Techniques Office (IPTO) of the Defense Advanced Research Projects Agency (DARPA), where he stayed for two years. This was a heady assignment for the twenty-six-year-old lieutenant, and it had a profound influence on his later career; virtually every business partner he subsequently had was someone he had met at DARPA.

From DARPA he went to Harvard as an associate professor of engineering and applied physics. He remained at Harvard for almost three years, during which time he developed computer graphics tools that became invaluable to his later work on computer simulation. In 1967, he was recruited by David Evans, a contractor he had worked with at DARPA, to join the computer science program at the University of Utah. Evans, who had recently moved to Utah from Berkeley, also had in mind developing a company that would exploit some of the exciting developments in computer graphics.

At the University of Utah, Sutherland worked with a group of brilliant graduate students, and the computer department became an experimental center for computer graphics. Sutherland and his students refined the animation of their simulated figures; they developed "smooth curves" and lighting and highlight effects that began to replace the original "wireframe" models. One of Sutherland's students, Nolan Bushnell, eventually went on to develop the original video arcade and home video game, Pong.

Cofounds Company to Expand Computer Simulation

In 1968, Evans and Sutherland formed the firm Evans & Sutherland in Salt Lake City. Computers at that time were being used for well-understood routine tasks, such as billing, filing, and information processing. Evans and Sutherland, however, recognized that computers had exciting possibilities as design and training tools, a potential that was not being exploited anywhere. As Evans noted in an Evans & Sutherland newsletter, computers are essentially simulators that can "replace real objects on occasions when a simulation can be built more cheaply than the physical model can be."

Evans & Sutherland's first products were computer-aided design tools, which they sold in small quantities. The company did not begin making a profit until its fifth year of operation, but by the mid–1970s it was beginning to develop a broad range of products for several market niches, principally in flight training and computer-aided design. Evans & Sutherland remains in business today. Although Sutherland left the company's day-to-day operation in 1974, he remains on the board of directors.

From 1976 to 1980, Sutherland headed the department of computer science at the California Institute of Technology. In 1980, he joined forces with Robert Sproull, the son of one of Sutherland's superiors at DARPA, to form Sutherland, Sproull & Associates in Pittsburgh, Pennsylvania, later moving to Palo Alto, California. Sutherland's last written work in computer graphics was a joint paper with Sproull titled, "A Characterization of Ten Hidden Surface Algorithms." Sutherland would say in a 1989 interview that this "seemed to tidy up a loose end," and he counts it as the time at which he stopped being involved with computer graphics for good.

Sutherland remains associated with Sutherland, Sproull & Associates, doing research in computer architecture and logic circuits. Married, with two children, he is a plain-spoken man who avoids publicity and rarely grants interviews. He has, however, been frequently honored by his peers in the computer industry. He has received many honorary degrees and has won many prestigious honors and awards, including the first Zworykin Award from the National Academy of Engineering and the first Steven Anson Coons Award.

FURTHER READING:

Books

Aspray, William, *An Interview with Ivan Sutherland,* Charles Babbage Institute, Center for the History of Information Processing, University of Minnesota, 1989.

Kettelkamp, Larry, *Computer Graphics: How It Works, What It Does,* Morrow, 1989.

Periodicals

Kettelkamp, Larry, *Evans & Sutherland News,* special issue, 1974.

Sketch by Joel Simon

Walter Stanborough Sutton
1877–1916
American geneticist, cytologist, and biologist

Walter Stanborough Sutton was a surgeon and a biologist who advanced the findings and confirmed the genetic theories of Gregor Mendel. A physician in private practice for the last half of his life, Sutton discovered the role of chromosomes in meiosis (sex cell division) and their relationship to Mendel's laws of heredity. From his research with grasshoppers collected at his parent's farm in the summer of 1899, he went on to make a major contribution to the understanding of the workings of chromosomes in sexual reproduction.

The fifth of six sons, Sutton was born in Utica, New York, on April 5, 1877, to William Bell Sutton and Agnes Black Sutton. At age ten, Sutton moved with his family to Russell County, Kansas, where he attended public schools. He studied engineering at the University of Kansas, Lawrence, beginning in 1896. Following his younger brother's death from typhoid in 1897, however, he made a pivotal change in the course of his education that would eventually lead him to the study of medicine and to his discoveries in genetics.

Sutton earned a bachelor's degree from the University of Kansas School of Arts in 1900. He was elected to Phi Beta Kappa and Sigma Xi, the scientific fraternity. While an undergraduate, he met Clarence Erwin McClung, a zoology instructor. Their four-year association would greatly influence Sutton's later work. McClung persuaded Sutton to study histology, which led the young student to other areas of inquiry, including cytological examinations of the lubber (grass) hopper (*Brachystola magna*).

Publishes Significant Papers in Graduate School

Sutton's careful camera lucida drawings of the stages of spermatogenesis in the lubber hopper were described in his first paper, "The Spermatogonial Divisions in Brachystola Magna," which appeared in the *Kansas University Quarterly* in 1900 and served as his master's thesis the following year. Following this work, McClung and other faculty members encouraged Sutton to pursue his doctoral studies under biologist **Edmund Beecher Wilson** at Columbia University. In 1901, Sutton began work there. He continued his cytological studies on chromosomal division in germ cells, and in 1902 detailed his research in "On the Morphology of the Chromosome Group in Brachystola Magna." Earlier that year, based on his readings of work done by British biologist **William Bateson** on the relationship between meiosis in germ cells and body characteristics, Sutton made the connection between cytology and heredity, and thus opened the field of cytogenetics. Sutton's hypotheses and generalizations were later published in what has become a landmark work, "The Chromosomes in Heredity" in the *Biological Bulletin,* 1903.

In these papers, Sutton explained that through his observation of meiosis he found that all chromosomes exist in pairs very similar to each other; that each gamete, or sex cell, contributes one chromosome of each pair, or reduces to one-half its genetic material, in the creation of a new offspring cell during meiosis; that each fertilized egg contains the sum of chromosomes of both parent cells; that these pairs control heredity; and that each particular chromosome's pair is based on independent assortment, that is, the maternal and paternal chromosomes separate independently of each other. The result, Sutton found, was that an individual in a species may posses any number of random combinations of different pairs of maternal and paternal chromosomes. Sutton also hypothesized that each chromosome carries in it groups of genes, each of which represents a biological characteristic—a thought that contradicted the then prevalent theory that ascribed one inherited trait to each chromosome.

At the time Sutton's paper was published, Austrian scientist **Theodor Boveri** claimed he had reached the same conclusions. As a result, the biological generalizations of the association of paternal and maternal chromosomes in pairs and their subsequent separation, which makes up the physical basis of the Mendelian law of heredity, is called the Sutton-Boveri Hypothesis. This 1903 discovery, however, was to be Sutton's last in cytology; due to unknown reasons, he never completed his course of study at Columbia.

Returning to Kansas after his laboratory research, Sutton worked as a foreman in the Chautauqua County oil fields until 1905. While there he used his abilities to solve technical problems. He developed the first technique for starting large gas engines with high pressure gas. In 1907 he patented a device to raise an oil pump mechanism from a well when worn valve components required replacement. Sutton also began a design to use electric motors to run drilling devices, but did not complete it.

Pursues Further Study in the Life Sciences

Still fascinated with the intricacies of the life sciences, and at the request of his father, Sutton returned to the Columbia University College of Physicians and Surgeons. He earned his medical degree in 1907 and for the next two years served as surgical house officer at Roosevelt Hospital in New York City. During that time, Sutton designed and built a device to deliver rectal anesthesia to patients unable to inhale ether. In 1909 he moved back to Kansas to practice

privately in Kansas City, and to teach in the Department of Surgery at the University of Kansas. Six years later, he took a leave of absence from the university to work at the American Ambulance Hospital in Juilly, France, during World War I. His experiences of working on injured soldiers led to a book chapter on wound surgery. In addition, Sutton developed a method of finding and removing foreign bodies in soft tissue involving the use of fluoroscopy and a simple device made from a hooked piece of wire. After the war, Sutton returned to his private practice and his teaching duties in Kansas. He continued his work there until his death from a ruptured appendix on November 10, 1916. He never married. Sutton's manual dexterity—evident in his surgical skills and handling of cells under a microscope—was nurtured by his love and talent for drawing and the mechanical abilities he practiced while working on farm machinery and oil wells. His mechanical repairs and inventions, home-built camera, and laboratory and surgical practice all bore obvious examples of his creativity, skill, and inventiveness.

SELECTED WRITINGS BY SUTTON:

Books

Manual of Operative Surgery, War Surgery, Blakeston, 1916, pp. 1285–1316.

Periodicals

Kansas University Quarterly, The Spermatogonial Divisions of *Brachystola Magna,,* Volume 9, 1900, p. 135.

Biological Bulletin, Morphology of the Chromosome Group *Brachystola Magna,,* Volume 4, 1902, p. 24.

Biological Bulletin, The Chromosomes in Heredity, Volume 4, 1903, pp. 231–251.

Annals of Surgery, Anesthesia by Colonic Absorption of Ether, Volume 51, 1910, p. 457.

Journal of the American Medical Association, A New Incision for Epithelioma of the Upper and Lower Lips of the Same Side, Volume 55, 1910, p. 647.

Annals of Surgery, The Proposed Fistuo-enterostomy of Von Stubenrauch, Volume 52, 1910, p. 380.

FURTHER READING:

Periodicals

Whitehead, Fred, *Family Matters,* Answer to Quiz, March 1992.

Other

Nelson, Stanley, M.D., professor of anatomy, University of Kansas Medical Center, *Interview with Denise Arnold,* conducted October 13, 1993.

Sketch by Denise Adams Arnold

Theodor Svedberg
1884–1971
Swedish chemist

Theodor Svedberg, helped to turn the arcane field of colloid chemistry into a vigorous and productive field of study. In so doing, he developed the ultracentrifuge, one of the most basic and useful tools in the modern biomedical laboratory, and an achievement for which he won the 1926 Nobel Prize in chemistry. Svedberg's work was not only innovative but cross-disciplinary, having valuable applications in a variety of fields, beginning with colloid chemistry. Colloids, of which milk fat and smoke are examples, are substances dispersed (as opposed to being dissolved) in a medium; colloids cannot be observed directly under the microscope, nor do they settle out under the force of gravity. Svedberg's development of the ultracentrifuge to study solutions was of enormous importance to biologists, who believed that gaining an understanding of colloids would help them to create models of biological systems.

Theodor Svedberg—called "The Svedberg" by his colleagues—was born on August 30, 1884, in Fleräng, Sweden, a small town near Gävle on the eastern coast. The only child of Elias Svedberg, a civil engineer employed at the local ironworks, and Augusta Alstermark Svedberg, the young Theodor often accompanied his father on long trips through the countryside, and performed simple experiments in a small laboratory at the ironworks under Elias's guidance.

Theodor attended the Karolinksa School in Örebro and showed a special aptitude for the natural sciences. Botany in particular peaked his interest, but he chose chemistry because of his interest in biological processes. His education progressed rapidly; he entered the University of Uppsala in January 1904, and received his B.S. in September of 1905 and his doctorate in 1907. He wrote his dissertation on colloids.

Until Svedberg's thesis describing his new method for producing colloidal solutions of metals, chemists made these mixtures by passing an electric arc between metal electrodes submerged in a liquid. Svedberg used an alternating current with an induction coil whose spark gap was submerged in a liquid to produce relatively pure colloidal mixtures of metals. The level of purity of these colloids, and the fact that the results were reproducible, permitted researchers to perform quantitative analyses during physicochemical studies. Svedberg's work propelled him quickly in the educational hierarchy at Uppsala, beginning with a lectureship in physical chemistry from 1907 to 1912. In 1912 he was awarded Sweden's first academic chair of physical chemistry, created by the University of Uppsala specifically for Svedberg and retained by him for thirty-six years.

Svedberg continued his work with colloids, using an ultramicroscope (a microscope that uses refracted light for visualizing specimens too small to be seen with direct light) to study the Brownian movement of particles. Brownian motion, the continuous random movement of minute particles suspended in liquid medium caused by collision of the particles with molecules of the medium, was named for the British botanist Robert Brown, who observed the phenomenon among pollen grains in water. Brownian movement was of great interest to a number of other researchers, including two future Nobel Prize winners, **Albert Einstein** and **Jean Perrin**. Perrin's work had provided verification of the theoretical work of Einstein and Marian Smoluchowski, and established definitively the existence of molecules. Perrin determined the size of large colloidal particles by measuring their rate of settling, a time-consuming process.

Using the ultramicroscope, Svedberg showed that the behavior of colloidal solutions obeys classical laws of physics and chemistry. But his method failed to distinguish the smallest particle sizes or determine the distribution of colloidal particles—the constant collisions of particles with water molecules kept the particles from settling out. In 1923 Svedberg and his colleague Herman Rinde began determining particle size distribution by measuring sediment accumulation in colloidal systems suspended on a balance. Although the technique itself was not new, Svedberg and Rinde increased its resolution by controlling air currents and other factors that disturbed the balance scale. While further refining this technique, Svedberg was also contemplating other approaches, especially electrophoresis (separation of particles in an electric field based on size and charge), and centrifugation.

Centrifugation—spinning solutions around a fixed circumference at high speed—mimics the force of gravity. Centrifuges were already being used to separate milk from cream and red blood cells from plasma. But fat globules and red cells are relatively large and heavy, and thus relatively easy to force out of solution. In order to force the much tinier and lighter colloidal particles out of solution, Svedberg needed a stronger centrifuge than was currently available.

In 1923 Svedberg accepted the offer of an eight-month guest professorship at the University of Wisconsin, where he taught and continued his research into centrifugation, electrophoresis, and diffusion of colloidal solutions. Working with J. Burton Nichols, Svedberg constructed the first ultracentrifuge, which could spin at up to thirty thousand revolutions per minute, generating gravitational forces thousands of times greater than Earth's. This early ultracentrifuge was elaborate, equipped with both a camera and illumination for photographing samples during centrifugation. Using this device, Svedberg and Nichols determined particle size distributions and radii for gold, clay, barium sulfate, and arsenious sulfide.

Following his sabbatical in Wisconsin, Svedberg and his students continually increased the speed of successively higher-speed ultracentrifuges, pushing the limit from 100,000 g (gravitational force equivalent to that of Earth's) at forty-five thousand revolutions per minute during the 1920s to 750,000 g by 1935. He used the machine to study proteins, which, although huge molecules, retain their colloidal properties when in solution. Among the proteins whose weight and structure he studied using the ultracentrifuge were hemoglobin, pepsin, insulin, catalase, and albumin. The technique caught on, and Svedberg's invention became an invaluable tool used by most protein chemists. He extended his ultracentrifuge studies of large carbohydrate molecules, combining his interest in biomolecules with his interest in botany by undertaking a pioneering study of the complex sugars of the Lillifloreae family, which includes lilies and irises. His work contributed to the understanding of carbohydrate structure and provided a useful tool for later studies of evolution by biologists.

In 1926 Sweden, like much of Europe, was still recovering from the devastating effects of World War I, and research seemed destined to languish in an era of reduced government support and hopelessly outmoded facilities. Svedberg's Nobel Prize, however, gave Swedish science a boost, and led directly to the establishment in 1930 of Svedberg's proposed Institute of Physical Chemistry at Uppsala. Announced the same year that Perrin received the Nobel Prize for physics for his work with colloids, Svedberg's award greatly enhanced the recognition by science and society of the importance of the field of colloid chemistry to biological and physical processes. Svedberg became director of the new Institute for Physical Chemistry in 1931, allowing him to continue his research for the remainder of his career. During World War II, however, he was forced to switch his laboratory's research efforts to the development of polychloroprene (synthetic rubber), as well as other synthetic polymers. Despite this distraction from his main work, he was still able to devise ways to incorporate the use of the electron microscope and X-ray diffraction to study the properties of cellulose biomolecules. And he developed the so-called osmotic balance, which weighed colloid particles by separating particles through a permeable membrane.

On reaching mandatory retirement age in 1949, the Swedish government honored Svedberg with a promotion to emeritus professor and made a special exception to the retirement rule by appointing him lifelong director of the Gustav Werner Institute for Nuclear Chemistry; there he studied radiochemotherapy and the effects of radiation on macromolecules. Physical chemists also honored Svedberg by naming the so-called centrifugation coefficient unit after him: the svedberg unit, *s,* is equal to 1×10^{-13} seconds and represents the speed at which a particle settles out of solution divided by the force generated by the centrifuge. The coefficient depends on the density and shape of the particles, with specific values of *s* corresponding to specific masses measured in daltons, a unit that expresses relative atomic masses.

Svedberg was married four times, first to Andrea Andreen (1909), then to Jan Frodi Dahlquist (1916), Ingrid

Blomquist Tauson (1938), and Margit Hallen Norback (1948); he had six daughters and six sons. He held memberships in the Royal Society, the American National Academy of Sciences, the Academy of Sciences of the USSR, among many other organizations. Svedberg received honorary doctorates from the universities of Delaware, Groningen, Oxford, Paris, Uppsala, Wisconsin, and Harvard. In addition, he was active in the Swedish Research Council for Technology and the Swedish Atomic Research Council. He died in Örebro, Sweden, on February 25, 1971.

SELECTED WRITINGS BY SVEDBERG:

Books

The Ultracentrifuge, Clarendon, 1940.

Periodicals

Journal of the American Chemical Society, Determination of Size and Distribution of Size of Particles by Centrifugal Methods, Volume 45, 1923.
Journal of the American Chemical Society, A New Method for the Determination of the Molecular Weight of the Proteins, Volume 48, 1926.
Chemical Reviews, Sedimentation of Molecules in Centrifugal Fields, Volume 14, 1934.

FURTHER READING:

Books

Abbott, David, editor, *Biographical Dictionary of Scientists: Chemists,* Peter Bedrick Books, 1984, pp. 133–134.
Magill, Frank N., editor, *The Nobel Prize Winners: Chemistry,* Salem Press, 1990, pp. 279–287.
Magill, Frank N., editor, *Nobel Prize Winners,* H. W. Wilson, 1987, pp. 1030–1033.

Periodicals

Tiselius, Arne, and Stig Claesson, *Annual Review of Physical Chemistry,* The Svedberg and Fifty Years of Physical Chemistry in Sweden, Volume 18, 1967, pp. 1–8.

Sketch by Marc Kusinitz

M. S. Swaminathan
1925–
Indian geneticist and agricultural scientist

As a university student in India, M. S. Swaminathan read of the terrible Bengal famine of 1942 to 1943, in which millions of his countrymen starved to death, and determined that India would make such famines a thing of the past. A genetic researcher, an agricultural administrator, and the first recipient of the World Food Prize—the equivalent of a Nobel Prize for agriculture—Swaminathan has devoted nearly five decades of his life to making this goal a reality. At the award ceremony in Washington, Secretary General of the United Nations Javier Perez de Cuellar asserted that Swaminathan's "contributions to agricultural science have made an indelible mark on food production in India and elsewhere in the developing world."

Monkombu Sambasivan Swaminathan, born on August 7, 1925, in Kumbakonam, India, knew from a young age that much was expected of him. His father, M. K. Sambasivan, was a surgeon who worked closely with Mahatma Gandhi on the freedom movement and who established within his son a deep commitment to individual freedom as well as to national self-reliance. His mother, Shrimati Thangammal, came from an old and influential family. After his father's early death, Swaminathan, his two brothers, and one sister were brought up by other members of an extended family, academics, and government administrators. He attended Travancore and Madras Universities and appeared to have a brilliant future ahead of him in the civil service, but decided to follow a career in plant genetics instead. In 1949 he joined the Department of Genetics at Netherlands Agricultural University in Wageningen as a UNESCO Fellow. He completed his studies at Cambridge University in London, earning a Ph.D. at its School of Agriculture in 1952. His early research involved the origin of the cultivated potato as well as the development of new commercial varieties. This research was continued at the University of Wisconsin, where Swaminathan held a research fellowship from 1952 to 1953. Turning down a job offer from the university, Swaminathan returned to India in 1954.

Leads India's Green Revolution

Back in India, Swaminathan accepted a position as research cytogeneticist at the Central Rice Research Institute, and the following year joined the staff of the Indian Agricultural Research Institute in New Delhi, where he would remain for the next eighteen years, working mainly in the field of wheat improvement. It was during these years that Swaminathan carried out some of his most vital research in raising the yield of wheat production by the introduction of various hybrid strains of wheat—including the dwarf Mexican—into the Indian agricultural system.

Swaminathan and his students also carried out genetic research into rice varieties, transferring the gene for dwarfing into the popular basmati variety of Indian rice. He also adapted strains of rice for both drought and deep water conditions and instituted a gene bank for rice plants now comprising some 75,000 varieties, many of which would otherwise be in danger of extinction. It is via this gene bank that much of the hybridization research at the institute is carried out. Additionally, Swaminathan ensured that India's Green Revolution would be in harmony with the land and that it would stress environmental issues as well as economic ones. Pesticides and inorganic fertilizers were used sparingly, and the latest technologies were passed on to illiterate farmers through his "techniracy" program, which taught advanced agricultural skills through direct work experience.

By the 1970s, the new policies had paid off: India had progressed from having the largest food deficit in the world to producing enough grain to feed all of its people. With further work in disaster preparation, Swaminathan also ensured a safe nutritional future for his country even in times of natural catastrophe. His concern for the welfare of women was also evidenced by his studies of the effects of technological changes on women in rice-based agricultural systems. Such studies have led to greater opportunities for women in the lesser developed countries to earn money and participate more fully in the economy. In 1979, Swaminathan became principal secretary of the Ministry of Agriculture and Irrigation, a position that gave him more freedom to institute agricultural policies, particularly those relating to sustainable rice production.

Swaminathan became internationally known in 1982 when he was named director general of the International Rice Research Institute in the Philippines, a post he filled until 1989, when he founded the Center for Research on Sustainable Agricultural and Rural Development in Madras. His environmental endeavors were acknowledged by an honorary vice-presidential position with the World Wildlife Fund from 1985 to 1987. He was also the president of the International Union for Conservation of Nature and Natural Resources from 1984 to 1990. In 1991 Swaminathan was awarded the Tyler Prize for Environmental Achievement for his accomplishments in preserving biological diversity and ecologically sustainable agricultural policies. That same year he also won the prestigious Honda Award. Swaminathan holds thirty-two honorary degrees and is a member of numerous scientific societies worldwide. A tireless researcher and administrator, he is also an educator, having guided fifty-five Ph.D. students in their thesis work.

Public service is a tradition in the Swaminathan family. Married in 1955, Swaminathan is the father of three daughters. His wife, Mina, also a Cambridge graduate, gave up a government job to teach the children of unskilled laborers. One of his daughters is a pediatrician, another is an economist working with landless families, and the youngest is a rural sociologist. "Helping fellow human beings is our mission in life," Swaminathan said in the *Bangkok Post,* "because it brings the greatest satisfaction, mentally and spiritually. It would be short-sighted to think that we can be happy while millions of people are impoverished."

SELECTED WRITINGS BY SWAMINATHAN:

Books

Building a National Food Security System, Indian Environmental Society, 1981.
Science and Integrated Rural Development, Concept Publishing Company, 1982, reprinted 1991.
Science and the Conquest of Hunger, Concept Publishing Company, 1983.
Biotechnology for Asian Culture: Public Policy Implications, Asian and Pacific Development Center, 1991.

Periodicals

Farming, Wild Relatives in Potato Breeding, Volume 4, 1950, pp. 370–373.
New Biology, Polyploidy and Plant Breeding, Volume 13, 1952, pp. 31–49.
Nature, Disomic and Tetrosomic Inheritance in a *Solanum* Hybrid, Volume 178, 1956, pp. 599–600.
Indian Journal of Agricultural Science, Advances in Plant Genetics and Breeding in India, Volume 31, 1961, pp. 1–7.
Science, Mutation Incidence in *Drosophila Melanogaster* Reared on Irradiated Medium, Volume 41, 1963, pp. 637–638.
Indian Farming, New Varieties Destroy Barriers to High Rice Yields, Volume 17, number 3, 1967, pp. 4–7.
Indian Farming, Dwarf Varieties Open New Yield and Income Possibilities in Wheat, Volume 17, no. 5, 1967, pp. 4–7.
Fertilizer News, Synergistic Effects of Coordinated Use of Fertilizer and Other Inputs, Volume 16, 1971, pp. 45–47.
Current Science, Indian Agriculture at the Crossroads, Volume 51, 1981, pp. 13–24. "Biodiversity and Sustainable Agriculture," Outlook on Agriculture, Volume 20, 1991, pp. 3–4.
Environmental Conservation, Ecotechnology and Global Food Security, Volume 20, 1993, pp. 6–7.

FURTHER READING:

Books

Science and Agriculture: M. S. Swaminathan and the Movement for Self-Reliance, Arid Zone Research Association of India, 1980.

Periodicals

Havener, Robert D., *Science,* Scientists: Their Rewards and Humanity, September 11, 1987, p. 1281.

Thongtham, Normita, *Bangkok Post,* Tribute to a Hero of the Green Revolution, April 28, 1985, p. 31.

Other

Swaminathan, M. S., *Interview with J. Sydney Jones conducted February 28,* 1994.

Sketch by J. Sydney Jones

Richard Synge
1914–1994
English biochemist and physical chemist

Richard Synge made important contributions in the fields of physical chemistry and biochemistry. He is best known for the development of partition chromatography, a collaborative effort undertaken with **A. J. P. Martin** in the late 1930s and early 1940s. As a result of their work, Synge and Martin received the 1952 Nobel Prize in chemistry.

Richard Laurence Millington Synge was born on October 28, 1914, in Liverpool, England, to Laurence Millington Synge, a stockbroker, and Katherine Charlotte (Swan) Synge. He was the oldest of three children and the only son. After growing up in the Cheshire area of England, he attended Winchester College, a private preparatory school, where he won a classics scholarship to attend Trinity College at Cambridge University. After listening to a speech given by the noted biochemist **Frederick Gowland Hopkins,** however, he decided to forego his education in the classics and instead pursue a degree in biochemistry at Trinity.

Synge undertook graduate studies at the Cambridge Biochemical Laboratory in 1936, receiving his Ph.D. in 1941. His doctoral research concerned the separation of acetyl amino acids. It was at this time that Synge first met Archer Martin, who was engaged in building a mechanism for extracting vitamin E. They began to work together on a separation process, which was delayed when Martin left for a position at the Wool Industries Research Laboratories in Leeds, England. Synge was able to join Martin there in 1939, when he received a scholarship from the International Wool Secretariat for his work on amino acids in wool.

The Development of Partition Chromatography

Synge and Martin's work built on the adsorption chromatographytechniques first developed by **Mikhail Tswett**, a Russian botanist, who evolved the procedure in his work on plant colors. Like Tswett, Synge and Martin's goal was to separate the various molecules that make up a

Richard Synge

complex substance so that the constituent molecules could be further studied. In order to achieve this goal, Tswett had filled a glass tube with powder, then placed a sample of the complex material to be studied at the top of the tube. When a solvent was trickled into the tube, it carried the complex material down into the powder. As the solution moved through the tube, the molecules of the different substances would separate and move at different speeds, depending on their chemical attraction to the powder. While Tswett's technique was useful, it did not have universal application; there were a limited number of materials that could be used for the powder filling, and therefore only a limited number of substances could be identified in this manner.

In addition to Tswett's adsorption chromatography, there also existed the process of countercurrent solvent extraction. This technique involves a solution of two liquids that do not mix, such as alcohol and water. When a complex substance is applied to this solution, the molecules separate, depending on whether they are more attracted to the water or the alcohol. Synge and Martin's breakthrough involved the combination of adsorption chromatography and countercurrent solvent extraction. This was achieved by using a solid substance adsorbent such as fine cellulose paper in place of Tswett's powder. In one application of the procedure, a complex mixture of molecules is spotted on one end of the paper, then that end is placed in a solution that might contain alcohol and water or chloroform and water. As the liquids flow through the paper, transporting the complex substance, the molecules in the substance separate, depending both on their rate of adsorption by the

paper and also by their affinity for either of the two liquids. When the process is completed, a series of spots is visible on the strip of paper. Each spot depicts one type of molecule present in the complex substance.

Synge and Martin had made early progress on partition chromatographyduring their time at Cambridge, but the need by industry and medicine for a more reliable technique spurred further research. At Leeds, they built a forty-unit extraction machine and experimented with various solvents and filtering materials. Their collaboration continued after Synge left to become a biochemist at the Lister Institute of Preventive Medicine in London in 1943, and by 1944 the improved cellulose filter method resulted. Later, they developed a two-dimensional chromatography process wherein two solvents flow at right angles to one another. This technique yielded an even sharper degree of molecular separation.

Partition chromatography was readily adopted by researchers for a variety of biochemical separations, especially those involving amino acids and proteins. Using the process in his doctoral research, Synge was able to separate and analyze the twenty amino acids found in protein. The technique was used in studies of enzyme action as well as in analyses of carbohydrates, lipids, and nucleic acids. Partition chromatography also became a useful tool for the food, drug, and chemical industries. Further experimentation with the process allowed proteins to be identified through the use of radioactive markers. The result of this marking was the ability to produce a photograph of the biochemical separation. The marking technique was used extensively by other biochemists, notably **Melvin Calvin** for his work in plant photosynthesis, and **Walter Gilbert** and **Frederick Sanger** for their research into DNA sequencing. All three would later receive the Nobel Prize for discoveries made using partition chromatography.

Later Research Builds on Chromatography Knowledge

Continuing his research of amino acids and peptides, Synge traveled to the Institute of Biochemistry at the University of Uppsala, Sweden, in 1946. There, he and **Arne Tiselius**, the Swedish biochemist, studied other separation methods, especially electrophoresis and adsorption. Back home, Synge applied this knowledge toward the isolation of amino acids in rye grass in order to study their structure, a subject he collaborated on with J. C. Wood. He also used the new techniques to study the molecular makeup of plant juices, examining the juices' role as a stimulator in bacteria growth. Partition chromatography was an important factor in other research carried on by Synge at that time. With D. L. Mould, he separated sugars through electrokinetic ultrafiltration in order to study the metabolic process. With Mary Youngson, he studied rye grass proteins. He and E. P. White were able to isolate a toxin called sporidesmin, which produces eczema in sheep and other cud-chewing animals. Synge's findings in all of these areas benefited efforts by agriculture, industry, and medicine to improve human health and well-being.

In 1948 Synge accepted a position as director of the Department of Protein Chemistry at Rowett Research Institute in Scotland. From 1967 until his retirement in 1976, he was a biochemist with the Food Research Institute in Norwich. He closed out his academic career as an honorary professor in the School of Biological Sciences at the University of East Anglia from 1968 until 1984. In addition to the Nobel Prize, Synge received the John Price Wetherill Medal of the Franklin Institute in 1959. He held memberships in the Royal Society, the Royal Irish Academy, the American Society of Biological Chemists, and the Phytochemical Society of Europe. He married Ann Stephen, a physician and the niece of writer Virginia Woolf, in 1943. They had seven children. Synge died on August 18, 1994, of myelodysplastic syndrome.

SELECTED WRITINGS BY SYNGE:

Periodicals

"A New Form of Chromatography Employing Two Liquid Phases," *Biochemical Journal* 35 (1941): pp. 1358-68.
"Partition Chromatography," *The Analyst* 71 (1946).
"Methods for Isolating Amino-Acids: Aminobutyric Acid from Rye Grass," *Biochemical Journal* 48 (1951).
"Applications of Partition Chromatography," Nobel lecture, 1952.
"Note on the Occurrence of Diaminopimelic Acid in Some Intestinal Micro-organisms from Farm Animals," *Journal of General Microbiology* 9 (1953).
"Experiments on Electrical Migration of Peptides and Proteins Inside Porous Membranes: Influences of Adsorption, Diffusion and Pore Dimensions," *Biochemical Journal*, 65 (1957).
"A Retrospect on Liquid Chromatography," *Biochemical Society Symposium*, no. 30 (1969).

FURTHER READING:

Books

The Nobel Prize Winners, Chemistry. Vol. 2: 1938–1968, edited by Frank N. Magill, Englewood Cliffs, NJ: Salem Press, 1990, pp. 598-607.
Wasson, Tyler, ed. *Nobel Prize Winners,* New York: H. W. Wilson, 1987, pp. 1033-34.

Other

Facts on File World News Digest (8 September 1994).

Sketch by Jane Stewart Cook

Gabor Szegö
1895–1985
Hungarian-born American mathematician

Gabor Szegö was a product of the German–Hungarian mathematical school, something of a child prodigy who, by age 20, had published a seminal paper in an internationally recognized mathematical journal. By the age of 30, he had published some 30 noteworthy papers, and also coauthored with **George Polyá**, a fellow Hungarian, a famous mathematical problem book, *Problems and Theorems in Analysis*. Szegö's most important theoretical work was in orthogonal polynomials and Toeplitz matrices, and he was, according to **Richard Askey** and Paul Nevai writing in *The Mathematical Intelligencer*, "one of the most prominent classical analysts of the twentieth century." Forced to immigrate to the United States to avoid Nazi persecution, Szegö helped build the mathematics department at Stanford University, where he taught from 1938 until his retirement.

Szegö was born on January 20, 1895 in Kunhegyes, then part of Austro–Hungary, to Adolf Szegö and Hermina Neuman. Szegö completed elementary school in the town of Szolnok, some 60 miles southeast of Budapest, and in 1912 enrolled in the Pázmány Péter University in the capital, now known as Eotvos Lorand University. It was in that same year that he won his first mathematic prize, the coveted Eotvos Competition. As Askey and Nevai noted in their article, it was fortunate for Szegö that he won such a prize at the outset of his studies, for, as a Jew, he might not otherwise have secured a university post. He followed this impressive beginning with a further prize the next year, this time for a paper on polynomial approximations of continuous functions.

World War I Interrupts Studies

Szegö's first publication in a notable journal came in 1913 when he published the solution of a problem given by George Polyá in *Archiv der Mathematik und Physik*. His first research paper, on the limit of the determinant of a Toeplitz matrix formed from a positive function, was published in 1915 and again inspired by a conjecture by Polyá. As Askey and Nevai stated, "Szegö spent another 45 years working on sharpening, extending, and finding applications of the results published in this article." It was during this time also that Szegö became a tutor to another mathematical prodigy, **John von Neumann.**

With the onset of World War I, however, this life of research came to a temporary halt. Szegö joined the cavalry, though he was a self–admitted poor horseman. He remained in the army from 1915 to 1919, even after the collapse of the Austro–Hungarian Empire. He was able, while posted in Vienna, to finish his doctorate, and after the war he married

Erzébet Anna Neményi, herself the holder of a Ph.D. in chemistry. The couple had two children, Peter and Veronica. But the effects of the war did not end with the Armistice. The early 1920s were a turbulent time in much of Central Europe, and Hungary was no exception. Szegö worked for a time as an assistant at the Technical University of Budapest, but by 1921 he and his family were forced to move to Germany in search of a more secure living. In Berlin, Szegö secured a post with the university for his work on orthogonal polynomial series, and became friends and worked with Issai Schur and **Richard von Mises**, among others. He continued his research and won the Julius Konig Prize in 1924, yet was only an associate professor without tenure at the University of Berlin.

Writes a Classic Problem Book

Together with his old acquaintance Polyá, Szegö collaborated on "the best–written and most useful problem book in the history of mathematics," according to Askey and Nevai. In 1925, the two published *Aufgaben und Lehrsatze aus der Analysis*, a two–volume work later translated into English as *Problems and Theorems in Analysis*. Students are introduced to mathematical research via a series of problems in analysis, number theory, combinatorics, and geometry, such that the solution to a group of problems prepares the reader for independent research in that area. Publication of this book rightly placed Szegö as not only a noted researcher, but also as an educator with innovative ideas.

The following year, Szegö was invited to assume to position of full professor at the University of Könisgsberg, succeeding Knopp in that position. He remained at Könisgsberg for eight years, but increasingly the situation for Jews in Germany was becoming untenable. It slowly became apparent to Szegö and his wife that they would need to move once again, and this time not simply to a neighboring country.

Emigrates to America

In 1934, Szegö secured, through the intercession of friends, a teaching position at Washington University in St. Louis. The money to pay for his salary was raised by a Rockefeller Grant, and by grants from local Jewish merchants as well as the Emergency Committee in Aid of Displaced Scholars. Szegö remained in St. Louis until 1938, during which time he advised five Ph.D. students, and worked on his seminal book, published in 1939, *Orthogonal Polynomials*. This book has become a standard reference work for both pure and applied mathematicians. Orthogonal polynomials are polynomialsthat first appeared in connection with numerical analysis and approximation theory. It was Szegö's accomplishment to reduce many of these problems to the asymptotic behavior of certain Toeplitz determinants, which come into consideration as a variable reaches a limit, most usually infinity. Applications of Szegö's theory have proved of significance in the fields of numerical methods, differential equations, prediction theory, systems theory, and statistical physics. Also, Szegö's work on Toeplitz matrices led to the concept of the Szegö reproducing kernel and the Szegö limit theorem.

Builds Stanford Mathematics

In 1938, Szegö accepted an offer to lead the Department of Mathematics at Stanford University in Palo Alto, California. He remained Head until 1953, and during those 15 years he succeeded in building the department to one of the most renowned in the world, bringing people such as Polyá, Loewner, Bergman, and Schiffer to the school, and helping to train an entire generation of new mathematicians. It was while he was at Stanford also, in 1940, that Szegö became a naturalized American citizen.

Szegö retired from Stanford in 1960 as professor emeritus. His wife died in 1968, and Szegö remarried in 1972 to Irén Vajda in Budapest. Ten years later, his second wife also died. In 1985, after several years of declining health, Szegö passed away, leaving behind a body of work of some 140 articles and six books authored or coauthored, as well as a generation of trained mathematicians to carry on his research in orthogonal polynomials, a field which he pioneered. In 1995, the centenary of his birth, Szegö was posthumously honored by the dedication of a statue in his hometown of Kunhegyes, replications of which were also installed at Washington University and at Stanford.

SELECTED WRITINGS BY SZEGÖ:

Books

Orthogonal Polynomials, 1939.
(With George Polya) *Problems and Theorems in Analysis*, Volumes 1 and 2, translated by Dorothee Aeppli and C. E. Billingheimer, 1972–76.
Gabor Szegö: Collected Papers, Volumes 1–3, edited by Richard Askey, 1982.

FURTHER READING:

Books

Askey, Richard, "Gabor Szegö: A Short Biography." *Gabor Szegö: Collected Papers*, Volume 1, edited by Richard Askey, Boston, Basel: Birkhauser, 1982, pp. 1–7.

Periodicals

Askey, Richard, and Paul Nevai, "Gabor Szegö: 1895–1985," in *The Mathematical Intelligencer* 18, no. 3 (1996): pp. 10–22.

Sketch by J. Sydney Jones

Albert Szent-Györgyi
1893–1986
American biochemist, molecular biologist, and physiologist

Albert Szent-Györgyi was a controversial, charismatic, and intuitive scientist whose career took many paths in the course of his life: physiologist, pharmacologist, bacteriologist, biochemist, and molecular biologist. In 1937 he was awarded the Nobel Prize in physiology or medicine for his work in isolating vitamin C and his advances in the study of intercellular respiration; in 1954 he received the Albert and Mary Lasker Award from the American Heart Association for his contribution to the understanding of heart disease through his research in muscle physiology. In later years, Szent-Györgyi moved into the electron sphere, where he studied matter smaller than molecules, seeking the substances that would define the basic building blocks of life. In his late seventies, he founded the National Foundation for Cancer Research.

Albert Szent-Györgyi von Nagyrapolt was born in Budapest, Hungary, on September 16, 1893, to Miklos and Josephine Szent-Györgyi von Nagyrapolt. He was the second of three sons. His father, whose family claimed a title and was said to have traced their ancestry back to the seventeenth century, was a prosperous businessman who owned a two-thousand-acre farm located outside Budapest. His mother came from a long line of notable Hungarian scientists.

As a student, Szent-Györgyi did not begin to develop his potential until his last two years in high school, when he decided to become a medical researcher. In 1911 he entered Budapest Medical School. His education was interrupted by World War I, when he was drafted into the Hungarian Army. He was decorated for bravery; but in 1916, disillusioned with the country's leadership and the progress of the war, he deliberately wounded himself in his upper arm. He was released from the army and sent back home, where he resumed his medical studies. He received his medical degree in 1917 and that same year married Cornelia (Nelly) Demeny. Their daughter, Cornelia (Little Nelly), was born in 1918.

Hungary's Political Upheaval Forces Emigration

The political situation in Hungary after the Austrian defeat caused many families to lose all they had. Szent-Györgyi's family was no exception. With Budapest under Communist rule, Szent-Györgyi decided to leave and accepted a research position at Pozony, Hungary, one hundred miles away. It was there, at the Pharmacological Institute of the Hungarian Elizabeth University, that Szent-Györgyi gained experience as a pharmacologist. In 1919 war broke out between Hungary and the Republic of

Albert Szent-Györgyi

Czechoslovakia. The Czechs seized Pozony, renaming it Bratislava. In order to continue his scientific training, Szent-Györgyi joined the millions of intellectuals who left Hungary during this time.

In 1921 he accepted a position at the Pharmaco-Therapeutical Institute of the University of Leiden in the Netherlands. This began a period of intense productivity for Szent-Györgyi: by the time he was twenty-nine years old, he had written nineteen research papers, and his research spanned the disciplines of physiology, pharmacology, bacteriology, and biochemistry. Szent-Györgyi is quoted by Ralph W. Moss, author of his biography, *Free Radical: Albert Szent-Györgyi and the Battle over Vitamin C,* as saying: "My problem was: was the hypothetical Creator an anatomist, physiologist, chemist or mathematician? My conclusion was that he had to be all of these, and so if I wanted to follow his trail, I had to have a grasp on all sides of nature." The scientist added that he "had a rather individual method. I did not try to acquire a theoretical knowledge before starting to work. I went straight to the laboratory, cooked up some senseless theory, and started to disprove it."

It was while in the Netherlands, as assistant to the professor of physiology at Groningen, that he presented the first of a series of papers on cellular respiration (the process by which organic molcules in the cell are converted to carbon dioxide and water, releasing energy), a question whose answer was considered central to biochemistry. Competing theories put forth on this question (one citing the priority of oxygen's role in the process; the other championing hydrogen as having the primary role) had caused biochemists to take one side or the other. Szent-Györgyi's contribution was that both theories were correct: active oxygen oxidized active hydrogen. Szent-Györgyi's research into cellular respiration laid the groundwork for the entire concept of the respiratory cycle. The paper discussing his theory is considered to be a milestone in biochemistry. Here, also, was the beginning of the work for which he was eventually given the Nobel Prize.

Cambridge and Frederick Gowland Hopkins

While still at Groningen, Szent-Györgyi began studying the role of the adrenal glands (responsible for secreting adrenaline and other important hormones), hoping to isolate a reducing agent (electron donor) and explain its role in the onset of Addison's disease. This work was to occupy him for almost a decade, produce unexpected results, and bring him worldwide attention as a scientist. He was sure he had made a breakthrough when silver nitrate added to a preparation of minced adrenal glands turned black. That indicated a reducing agent was present, and he set out to explain its function in oxidative metabolism. He thought the reducing agent might be a hormone equivalent to adrenalin. Frustrated because scientists in Groningen seemed unconvinced of the importance of his discovery, he wrote to **Henry Hallett Dale**, a prominent British physiologist. As a result of their correspondence, Szent-Györgyi was invited to England for three months to continue his work.

Unfortunately, his testing proved a failure—the color change of the silver nitrate turned out to be a reaction of adrenaline with the iron in the mincer in which he ground the adrenal glands. Szent-Györgyi returned to the Netherlands, where he continued his work on cellular respiration in plants, writing a paper on respiration in the potato. But increasing friction with the head of the laboratory caused him to resign his position. Unable to support his wife and daughter, he sent them home to Budapest. In August 1926 he attended a congress of the International Physiological Society in Stockholm, Sweden. It was there that his luck turned. The chairman of the event was Sir **Frederick Gowland Hopkins**, considered to be the greatest living biochemist of his day. Much to Szent-Györgyi's surprise, Hopkins referred to Szent-Györgyi's paper on potato respiration in his address to the congress. After the address, Szent-Györgyi introduced himself to Hopkins, who invited him to Cambridge, where he was to remain until he returned to Hungary in 1932, eventually becoming president of the University of Szeged.

With the assurance of a fellowship from the Rockefeller Foundation (the foundation was to be a source of much financial support throughout his career), Szent-Györgyi sent for his family, rented a house, and set to work. Hopkins became his mentor—and the man Szent-Györgyi regarded as having the most influence on him as a scientist. While at Cambridge, he was awarded a Ph.D. for the isolation of hexuronic acid, the name given to the substance he had isolated from adrenal glands. One of the puzzling things about this substance was its similarity to one also found in citrus fruits and cabbage. Szent-Györgyi set out to analyze the substance, but the main obstacle to doing this was obtaining a sufficient supply of fresh adrenal glands. He finally was able to isolate a small quantity of a similar substance from orange juice and cabbage, learning that it was a carbohydrate and a sugar acid.

In 1929 Szent-Györgyi made his first visit to the United States. It was at this time that he visited the scientific community at Woods Hole, Massachusetts. He then went on to the Mayo Clinic in Rochester, Minnesota, where he had been invited to use the research facilities to continue his work isolating the adrenal substance. He managed to purify an ounce of the substance, and sent ten grams of it back to England for analysis. Nothing came of this, however, as the amount sent was too small. After almost ten years, the research appeared to be at a dead end. Szent-Györgyi took what remained of the purified crystals and returned to Cambridge.

Vitamin C and the Nobel Prize

In 1928 Szent-Györgyi had been offered a top academic post at the University of Szeged in Hungary. He accepted, but did not take up his duties there until 1931 because of delays in completing the Szeged laboratory. At Szeged, in addition to his duties as teacher, Szent-Györgyi continued his research, still trying to solve the puzzle of the adrenal substance, hexuronic acid.

It had been known since the sixteenth century that certain foods, especially citrus fruits, prevented scurvy, a disease characterized by swollen gums and loosened teeth. Although scurvy could be prevented by including citrus fruit in the diet, isolation of the antiscurvy element from citrus eluded researchers. It was not until after World War I that drug companies began a concentrated search for the antiscorbutic element (now called vitamin C). Scientists in Europe and the United States began competing to be the first to isolate this element. Vitamin C was not unfamiliar to Szent-Györgyi, and he had written of its possible connection with hexuronic acid. Now he was able to positively identify hexuronic acid as vitamin C and not an adrenal hormone, as he had previously thought. He suggested the compound be called ascorbic acid, and continued his study of its function in the body, using vitamin C-rich Hungarian paprika as the source material.

Although Charles Glen King had also isolated vitamin C and made the connection between it and hexuronic acid— and announced his findings just two weeks before Szent-Györgyi made his report, in 1937 Szent-Györgyi was given the Nobel Prize. His acceptance speech, "Oxidation, Energy Transfer, and Vitamins," gave details of the extraordinary circumstances under which his discoveries were made.

Work during Nazi Occupation

In 1941 Szent-Györgyi and his wife were divorced. He married Marta Borbiro Miskolczy that same year. Bitterly opposed to Nazi rule in Hungary, he became an active member of the Hungarian underground. It was during the war years that he made some of his most important discoveries. His work during this time still concentrated on cellular respiration. His research in this area proved to be the basis for one of the fundamental breakthroughs in biology: the citric acid cycle. This cycle explains how almost all cells extract energy from food. It was during the war years that he also studied the chemical mechanisms of muscle contraction. His discoveries about how muscles move and function were fundamental to twentieth-century physiology, and made him a pioneer in molecular biology.

By 1944 Szent-Györgyi's outspoken opposition to Hitler's regime had put his life in danger. He and his wife went into hiding for the remainder of the war, surfacing in Budapest when the Russians liberated Hungary from the Nazis in 1945. Disillusioned with Soviet rule, he emigrated to the United States in 1947, and became an American citizen in 1954.

Woods Hole, Cancer Research, and the Vietnam War

Szent-Györgyi and his wife settled in Woods Hole, Massachusetts. Research facilities were provided for him at the Marine Biological Laboratories. He struggled to find backing to continue his work. With the help of five wealthy businessmen, he set up the Szent-Györgyi Foundation (later called the Institute for Muscle Research), whose purpose was to raise money for muscle research and bring a group of Hungarian scientists to America to assist him. This endeavor met with partial success, but its full potential was not realized because of concerns about the legitimacy of the financial backing (and suspicion about the political loyalties of the Hungarians). As a result, Szent-Györgyi had a research team, but was unable to support them. To remedy this, he took a position in 1948 with the National Institutes of Health (NIH). He left there in 1950 for a short assignment at Princeton University's Institute for Advanced Studies. Then grants began to come in for his muscle research. Major funding came from Armour and Company (the Chicago meatpacking company), the American Heart Association, the Association for the Aid of Crippled Children, the Muscular Dystrophy Association, and NIH.

During these years, Szent-Györgyi and his team of researchers continued to make strides in the analysis of muscle protein. He also published three books: *Chemistry of Muscular Contraction, The Nature of Life,* and *Chemical Physiology of Contraction in Body and Heart,* and 120 scientific papers. These writings brought him to the attention of the American scientific community and had great influence on scientists worldwide.

Szent-Györgyi's wife Marta died of cancer in 1963. He married twice after her death. During the sixties and seventies, his opposition to the Vietnam War made him a hero to those connected to the peace movement. He wrote two books during this period that characterized his personal philosophy: *Science, Ethics, and Politics* and *The Crazy Ape* (which included his poem series, "Psalmus Humanus and Six Prayers"). He spoke out against the war on numerous occasions, both in public lectures and through letters to newspapers and periodicals.

Szent-Györgyi was almost eighty years old when he founded the National Foundation for Cancer Research. Funding from the NFCR supported his research until the end of his life. For more than forty years, his research had been concerned with the development of a basic theory about the nature of life. Szent-Györgyi called this new field of endeavor "submolecular biology." It was not just a cure for cancer that he was looking for, but a new way of looking at biology. He was convinced that his study of the structure of life at the level of electrons would not only make possible a cure for cancer but would also provide the knowledge to ensure the human body's optimum health.

Ralph Moss, the author of *Free Radical,* asked Szent-Györgyi for his philosophy of life shortly before the scientist's death of kidney failure on October 22, 1986. He scrawled on a piece of paper: "Think boldly. Don't be afraid of making mistakes. Don't miss small details, keep your eyes open and be modest in everything except your aims."

SELECTED WRITINGS BY SZENT-GYÖRGYI:

Books

On Oxidation, Fermentation, Vitamins, Health, and Disease, The Abraham Flexner Lectures, Williams & Wilkens, 1937.
Chemistry of Muscular Contraction, Academic Press, 1947.
The Nature of Life, Academic Press, 1948.
Chemical Physiology of Contraction in Body and Heart, Academic Press, 1953.
Introduction to a Submolecular Biology, Academic Press, 1960.
Science, Ethics, and Politics, Vantage Press, 1963.
The Crazy Ape: Written by a Biologist for the Young, Philosophical Library, 1970.
Electronic Biology and Cancer: A New Theory of Cancer, Dekker, 1976.

FURTHER READING:

Books

Moss, Ralph W., *Free Radical: Albert Szent-Györgyi and the Battle over Vitamin C,* Paragon House, 1988.

Sketch by Jane Stewart Cook

Leo Szilard
1898–1964
American physicist and biophysicist

A native of Hungary, Leo Szilard was one of the leading contributors to the development of nuclear energy and the first atomic weapons. He was also among the earliest and most active campaigners for nuclear arms control. In 1942, with **Enrico Fermi**, he set up the first nuclear chain reaction. He later became increasingly interested in the fields of molecular energy and biophysics, and helped develop the electron microscope.

Leo Szilard was born in Budapest, Hungary, on February 11, 1898, to Louis Szilard, an architect and engineer, and his wife, the former Thekla Vidor. The eldest of three children, Leo was a sickly child, and for a number of years his mother taught him at home.

Educated in Budapest and Berlin

In the fall of 1916, Szilard entered the Budapest Institute of Technology, intending to major in electrical engineering. At the end of his first year at the institute, he was called to service in the Austro-Hungarian army and assigned to officer training school. He became very ill with influenza, however, and had not fully recovered by the time World War I ended in 1918. He returned to the Budapest Institute of Technology for just over a year before transferring first to the Technische Hochschule at Berlin-Charlottenburg.

At Berlin, Szilard's career outlook underwent a significant change. He came into contact with some of the finest physicists in the world, including **Albert Einstein**, **Max Planck**, and **Max Laue**, the last of whom was to become Szilard's own doctoral advisor. Szilard decided that his real interests lay in the field of physics rather than engineering, and in 1922 he was awarded his Ph.D. in that field. His doctoral thesis, written under the supervision of von Laue, dealt with the statistical implications of the second law of thermodynamics. Szilard's work on this topic continued for a number of years, culminating in a paper published in 1929, "On the Decrease of Entropy in a Thermodynamic System by the Intervention of Intelligent Beings," in which he investigated the application of thermodynamical laws to information theory. That paper is regarded as an important precursor to modern cybernetic theories.

After receiving his degree, Szilard was appointed first a research assistant and then, in 1925, *Privatdozent* at the Institute of Theoretical Physics at the University of Berlin. Director of the institute at the time was von Laue, his former advisor. In addition to his continuing work on thermodynamics during this period, Szilard also originated a series of studies on X-ray crystallography, a field in which von Laue

Leo Szilard

was a world leader. Szilard also worked closely with Albert Einstein on the development of a pump for liquid metals, for which he eventually obtained a patent. In addition, he became interested in the problem of particle accelerators and invented a number of devices that were later to be incorporated into early cyclotrons.

Emigrates from Germany to England and the United States

In 1933, the rise of Adolf Hitler convinced Szilard, who was Jewish, that he should leave Germany. Fearing for both his career and his life, he fled first to Vienna and then, six weeks later, to England. There he joined the physics department at St. Bartholomew's Hospital in London. In 1935 he moved to the Clarendon Laboratory at Oxford.

It was during this period that Szilard received news of **Frédéric** and **Irène Joliot-Curie**'s discovery of artificial radioactivity. He began to think about the possibility of a nuclear chain reaction in which the nuclear decay of one atom, brought about by some type of particle, would result in the production of a new atom with the release of more particles of the kind needed to start the reaction. In such a case, the reaction, once initiated, would be self-sustaining over many, many episodes of decay. The value of such a reaction, Szilard knew, was that energy would be released in each step of the process. After countless repetitions of the reaction, huge amounts of energy—sufficient, for instance, to make a powerful bomb—would be released.

Szilard first explored the possibility of using beryllium in such a chain reaction. He and a colleague, T. A. Chalmers, found that gamma rays directed at a beryllium target would cause the emission of a neutron from the beryllium nucleus. The two hoped that this reaction could act as the first step in a chain reaction in which beryllium atoms would break apart to form helium atoms and more neutrons. The neutrons thus formed would, they hoped, then cause more beryllium atoms to break apart into helium atoms with the release of more neutrons, and so on. More detailed studies showed, however, that such a reaction could not be sustained.

In addition to his research, Szilard continued his efforts to find new jobs for scientists fleeing the Nazi purges on the continent. These efforts were characteristic of Szilard's life-long commitment to helping others. He once said that this humanitarian impulse was largely the result of reading, at the age of ten, Hungarian author Imre Madách's *The Tragedy of Man.*

Toward the end of 1938, Szilard decided to move to the United States. He had no more settled in at his new workplace, Columbia University, than he received startling news from Europe. **Otto Hahn** and **Fritz Strassman** had produced the first fission of an atomic nucleus, an event that was fully understood and explained by **Lise Meitner** in January 1939. Szilard immediately recognized the significance of this discovery. It held the potential for making possible the very kind of nuclear chain reaction on which he had been working in London.

With a colleague, Walter Zinn, Szilard set up a replica of the Hahn-Strassman experiment at Columbia. Their goal was to find out whether the fission of a uranium nucleus would result in the formation of at least one neutron, a condition necessary for the maintenance of a chain reaction. On March 3, the experiment was ready. A few flashes of light on an oscilloscope gave Szilard and Zinn the answer they sought: neutrons were being released during the fission of uranium. A nuclear chain reaction was possible. Szilard would later say he knew immediately that this discovery would cause the world great sorrow.

Leads Effort to Establish Nuclear Bomb Project

News of the discovery of nuclear fission swept through the physics community like wildfire. Few failed to grasp the military potential of the discovery. A group of physicists in the United States who were particularly concerned about this potential became convinced that the U.S. government must take fast and aggressive action to see whether nuclear fission could really be used in the development of weapons. Szilard composed a letter, which Albert Einstein signed, presenting their arguments to President Franklin D. Roosevelt. Roosevelt responded by appointing an Advisory Committee on Uranium to investigate the issue. After some initial hesitation, the committee produced a favorable recommendation, and the Manhattan Engineering District Project was created to pursue the development of the world's first atomic bombs. The first contract let under the Manhattan Project was to a group of scientists at Columbia that included Szilard.

In 1942, Szilard left Columbia to become part of the Manhattan Project's Metallurgical Laboratory at the University of Chicago. Working there with **Enrico Fermi**, he witnessed the first controlled nuclear reaction on December 2, 1942, when the world's first atomic pile (nuclear reactor) was put into operation. The hopes and dreams—as well as the fears—that Szilard had long held for nuclear chain reactions had become a reality.

Shortly thereafter, Szilard began to argue for a cessation of research on nuclear weapons. A number of factors influenced his position. First, he was convinced that the tide of war had turned in favor of the Allies, and he thought the war could soon be ended with conventional weapons. Second, he feared that the successful development of nuclear weapons would lead to an all-out arms race with the Soviet Union after the war. Finally, he recognized the horrible human tragedies that would result from the use of an atomic bomb. His suggestions for a demonstration test of nuclear weapons in an uninhabited area to which the Japanese government would be invited fell on deaf ears, however. Instead, on August 6 and 9, 1945, the first atomic bombs were dropped on Hiroshima and Nagasaki in Japan. The war ended a week later.

Turns to Biological Studies

In the postwar years, Szilard spent a major portion of his time working for the control of the demon he had helped release, atomic energy. He joined a large number of his fellow nuclear scientists in forming the Federation of Atomic Scientists, which worked to keep control of atomic energy out of the hands of the military and within a civilian department. He also made efforts to encourage mutual disarmament and the reduction of tensions between the United States and the Soviet Union. To this end, he was active in the formation and planning of the Pugwash Conferences on Science and World Affairs, a series of conferences on nuclear safety that met in the late 1950s and early 1960s. In 1962, he helped found the Council for a Livable World, a Washington, D.C.-based lobby for nuclear arms control.

In the late 1940s, Szilard once again turned to scientific research, but this time in the field of biology. In 1946, he accepted an appointment as professor of biophysics at the University of Chicago. One of his first accomplishments was the development of the chemostat, an instrument that aids in the study of bacteria and viruses by making it possible to regulate various growth factors. Later he became interested in the biology of aging. Another topic in which Szilard became interested, memory and recall, was the subject of his final scientific paper, published after his death.

Szilard became a U.S. citizen in 1943. In 1951 he married Gertrud Weiss, whom he had first met in 1933 in Vienna, where Weiss was a medical student. The couple had no children. Szilard was awarded the Einstein Gold Medal in 1958 and the Atoms for Peace Award in 1959. He died of a heart attack on May 30, 1964, in La Jolla, California, where he had been a resident fellow at the Salk Institute.

SELECTED WRITINGS BY SZILARD:

Books

The Voice of the Dolphin and Other Stories, (science fiction), Simon & Schuster, 1961.
Collected Words of Leo Szilard, edited by Bernard T. Feld and Gertrud W. Szilard, Massachusetts Institute of Technology, 1972.
Leo Szilard: His Version of the Facts: Selected Recollections and Correspondence, edited by Spencer R. Weart and Gertrud Weiss Szilard, Massachusetts Institute of Technology, 1978.

FURTHER READING:

Books

McGraw-Hill Modern Scientists and Engineers, Volume 10, McGraw-Hill, 1980, pp. 181–182.
Wigner, Eugene, *Biographical Memoirs,* Leo Szilard, 1898–1964, Volume 40, National Academy of Sciences, 1969, pp. 337–341.

Periodicals

Coffin, Tristram, *Holiday,* Leo Szilard: The Conscience of a Scientist, February 1964.
Coffin, Tristram, *New York Times,* May 31, 1964.

Sketch by David E. Newton